1001

1001 RECIPES

THE *Ultimate* COOKERY BOOK

1001 RECIPES

THE *Ultimate* COOKERY BOOK

Edited by
Alexa Stace

PARRAGON

NOTE

Cup measurements in this book are for American cups
Tablespoons are assumed to be 15ml

Unless otherwise stated
Milk is assumed to be full-fat
Eggs are standard size 2
Pepper is freshly ground black pepper

First published in 1997 by Parragon

Unit 13-17, Avonbridge Trading Estate
Atlantic Road, Avonmouth
Bristol BS11 9QD
England

ISBN 0-7525-1918-2

Printed in Great Britain

Produced by Kingfisher Design, London

Acknowledgements
Project Editor: Alexa Stace
Art Director: Pedro Prá-Lopez
Editors: Diana Craig, Alison Stace
Typesetting and layout: Frank Landamore, Frances Prá-Lopez, Alison Stace
Illustrations: Roger Hutchins, Roy Hutchins
Index: Hilary Bird

Recipes in this book have previously been published in the
Parragon *Step-by-Step Cookery* Series, published 1995-1996.

Contents

◆

Introduction

◆

Containing over 1,001 recipes, this
book offers a whole cookery library in
one handy volume. Easy to consult and
simply laid out, it provides a wealth of
imaginative recipes for every occasion,
from simple suppers to grand dinner
parties, from children's parties to
barbecues, summer picnics and the
whole Christmas season.

An exciting bonus is the international
section, which gives you a global
overview of cooking around the world,
with over 200 pages of recipes covering
Caribbean, Cajun and Creole, Mexican,
Italian, Indian, Balti, Chinese
and Thai cuisines.

Never again will you need to ask, what
shall I cook tonight? With this book at
your side, you will never run
out of ideas.

·1·

Soups and Starters

◆

This varied assortment caters for every occasion, whether you are looking for something light and elegant, warm and filling or quick and easy. There is plenty of choice for vegetarians too.

◆

INTRODUCTION

Making soup is one of the most satisfying cookery techniques: it is simple to do yet always produces tasty results. A wide range of ingredients can be used and it is easy to make substitutions when certain ingredients are not available. Soup making is also an excellent way of using up leftovers, whether the bones or carcass of roast meat or poultry, or cooked meat or vegetables.

STOCKS
The secret of a good soup lies in preparing a very good stock to use for the base, and although there are excellent stock cubes of all flavours readily available, it is home-made stock that puts the edge on any soup.

Stocks can be made in a variety of flavours and colours. A light or white stock requires raw, light-coloured bones, preferably veal, but these are not always available, so lamb and beef bones may also be used. For a darker stock it is necessary to use beef bones that have been roasted, so they darken. A poultry stock using chicken or turkey bones and carcasses is also light-coloured, but if you use game carcasses, the stock will be darker and much stronger in flavour. To make fish stock, use fish heads, tails and trimmings.

Bones alone are not sufficient for a good stock; you will also need a couple of chopped or sliced onions and two or three root vegetables, such as carrots, swede (rutabaga) or turnips, but avoid potatoes as they break up and make the stock cloudy. Celery and leeks can also be included. Flavourings such as one or two bay leaves may be added (use fresh ones if they are available as they have a better flavour) or a Bouquet Garni (see right), but do not add any seasoning (it should be added when the soup is made and depends on the other ingredients).

Put all the ingredients in a large saucepan, with the measured amount of water or enough to cover the contents of the pan: usually 1.75–2.25 litres/3–4 pints/1½ –2 quarts. Once the water comes to the boil it is essential to remove the scum that forms on the surface, using a perforated spoon, before covering the pan and simmering for the recommended time. Fish stock should be simmered for only 30 minutes, as overcooking will give it a slightly bitter taste. Vegetable stock needs one hour's cooking, but all other stocks need at least 2 hours, and for beef bones 3–4 hours is best.

General-purpose stock
about 1 kg/2 lb bones from a cooked joint or raw chopped beef, lamb or veal bones
2 onions, chopped coarsely
2 carrots, sliced
1 leek, sliced
1–2 celery sticks, sliced
1 Bouquet Garni
about 2.25 litres/4 pints/2 quarts water

Chop or break up the bones and place in a large saucepan with the other ingredients. Bring to the boil and remove any scum from the surface with a perforated spoon. Cover and simmer gently for 3–4 hours. Strain the stock and leave to cool. Remove any fat from the surface and chill. If stored for more than 24 hours the stock must be boiled every day, cooled quickly and chilled again. The stock may be frozen for up to 2 months; place in a large plastic bag and seal, leaving at least 2.5 cm/1 inch of headspace.

INTRODUCTION

White stock
Make as above but use knuckle of veal, veal bones or raw lamb or beef bones, and add a sliced lemon.

Brown beef stock
Use chopped marrow bones with a few strips of shin of beef if possible. Put in a roasting tin and cook in a preheated oven at 230°C/450°F/Gas Mark 8 for 30–50 minutes until browned. Transfer to a large saucepan, add the vegetables and water and continue as before.

Chicken, turkey or game stock
1 raw or cooked carcass of a chicken, turkey or 1–2 game birds
giblets, if available
2 onions, sliced or chopped
2 carrots, sliced
2–4 celery sticks, sliced
1 Bouquet Garni (see right)

Break up the carcasses and place in a large saucepan with the remaining ingredients. Add enough water to cover. Bring to the boil, remove any scum and simmer for 2–3 hours. It is a good idea to give the bones a good stir and break them up a little during cooking. Strain, cool and store as for general-purpose stock.

Fish stock
1 head of a cod or salmon, etc, plus the trimmings, skin and bones or just the trimmings, skin and bones
1–2 onions, sliced
1 carrot, sliced
1–2 celery sticks, sliced
good squeeze of lemon juice
1 Bouquet Garni or 2 fresh or dried bay leaves

Wash the fish head and trimmings and place in a saucepan. Cover with water and bring to the boil. Remove any scum with a perforated spoon, then add the remaining ingredients. Cover and simmer for about 30 minutes. Strain and cool. Store in the refrigerator and use within 2 days.

Vegetable stock
To make vegetable stock you need a good selection of green and root vegetables, including onion and, if possible, leeks, but not potatoes. Take care when using very strongly flavoured vegetables such as celeriac (celery root) and artichokes as they will overpower the others. Coarsely chop about 500 g/1 lb mixed vegetables, cover generously with water, cover and simmer for about 1 hour. Strain and keep in the refrigerator for up to 24 hours.

BOUQUET GARNI
A bouquet garni is simply a bunch of herbs which is used to give flavour to stocks, soups, stews and sauces. The herbs can be made into a small bunch and tied with string, or they can be tied in muslin (cheesecloth), which is essential if you include dried herbs, cloves or peppercorns, as they should be easy to remove before serving.

Traditional bouquet garni
1 fresh or dried bay leaf
few sprigs of fresh parsley
few sprigs of fresh thyme

Tie the herbs together with a length of string or cotton.

Dried bouquet garni
1 dried bay leaf
good pinch of dried mixed herbs
good pinch of dried parsley
8–10 black peppercorns
2–4 cloves
1 garlic clove (optional)

INTRODUCTION

Put all the ingredients in a small square of muslin (cheesecloth) and secure with string or cotton, leaving a long tail so it can be tied to the handle of the pan for easy removal.

GARNISHES

The appearance of a soup can be greatly enhanced by a suitable garnish. The simplest garnishes are chopped herbs, which can be added to the soup itself and sprinkled on top. The type of herb should complement the flavour of the soup, but parsley and chives blend with almost any type. Whole leaves and small sprigs of herbs such as mint, oregano, fennel and dill can also be used as they will float on the surface.

Vegetables such as carrots, turnips, swede (rutabaga) and celeriac (celery root) can be coarsely grated into a soup just before serving, to add colour and texture. Leeks can be cut into very thin rings and used either raw or blanched. Fried thin onion rings and blanched or lightly fried, thinly sliced mushrooms can also be used as garnishes. Coarsely grated cheese such as Cheddar, Leicester (red), Gruyère (Swiss) and Stilton (blue) are good sprinkled over soups.

Croûtons

These can be served separately to be sprinkled on the soup by your guests or placed on each portion before serving.

Toasted croûtons

Toast slices of bread and cut into cubes, triangles or other shapes while hot. Cocktail cutters or aspic cutters will allow you to cut out a variety of shapes. Allow to cool. They can be stored in an airtight container for two to three days.

Fried croûtons

These are best cut into shapes before cooking. Fry in shallow oil for a few minutes, turning until golden on both sides. The oil must be hot, but take care as the bread will brown very quickly. Drain on paper towels. Croûtons may be dipped in chopped herbs, paprika or chopped hard-boiled (hard-cooked) egg.

Garlic croûtons

Make as for fried croûtons, adding 3–4 crushed garlic cloves to the oil.

Pastry crescents

Crescents or other shapes can be cut from puff or shortcrust pastry, glazed with beaten egg or milk and topped with sesame seeds, poppy seeds or finely chopped nuts. Bake in a preheated oven at 200°C/400°F/Gas Mark 6 for about 10 minutes until golden brown.

Garnishes for consommé

This clear soup is traditionally served with a garnish of freshly cooked tiny pasta shapes, noodles, rice, lightly cooked diced or julienne of vegetables, or thinly sliced mushrooms. Or make a one-egg omelette, drain thoroughly on paper towels, then cut into strips or shapes.

THICKENING SOUPS

A variety of thickening agents can be used, depending on the type of soup.

Cream

To prevent curdling, put the cream in a basin, add a little of the hot soup, then stir into the soup. Reheat gently but don't allow it to boil.

Flour and cornflour (cornstarch)

Blend plain (all-purpose) flour or cornflour (cornstarch) with a little

INTRODUCTION

cold milk or water, add a little of the hot soup, then whisk back into the soup. Simmer until thickened.

Beurre manié
Blend equal quantities of sifted plain (all-purpose) flour and butter or margarine, then whisk small amounts into the soup, until blended. Simmer for 3–4 minutes.

Egg yolks
Blend egg yolks with a little milk or cream, then add a little of the soup. Strain the mixture into the soup, off the heat, whisking thoroughly. Reheat gently but do not boil.

Scones
Warm scones with savoury flavours and toppings make excellent accompaniments to soups, especially when freshly made and served warm.

250 g/8 oz/2 cups self-raising flour
60 g/2 oz/ ¼ cup butter or margarine
1 egg, beaten
good squeeze lemon juice
about 75 ml/3 fl oz/ ⅓ cup milk
salt and pepper

Sift together the flour and seasoning, then rub in the butter or margarine until the mixture resembles fine breadcrumbs. Add the egg and lemon juice and enough milk to bind to a soft dough. Turn onto a floured surface and flatten out with your hands to about 2 cm/ ¾ inch thick. Either shape into a bar or cut into rounds, squares, triangles or fingers and place on a floured baking sheet. Dredge with flour or glaze with beaten egg or milk. Sprinkle with sesame, pumpkin, sunflower or poppy seeds, finely chopped or flaked nuts, grated cheese, crumbled crisp bacon, or oatmeal, if liked.

Bake in a preheated oven at 220°C/425°F/Gas Mark 7 for about 15 minutes for individual scones or 20–25 minutes for a scone bar. Cool slightly on a wire rack.

Variations
Herb scones: Add 2 tbsp chopped fresh herbs (one type or mixed) or 2 teaspoons dried herbs.

Cheese scones: Add 90 g/3 oz/ ⅓ cup grated blue or mature (sharp) Cheddar cheese or 3 tablespoons grated Parmesan cheese.

Anchovy scones: Add a drained and minced can of anchovy fillets

Nut scones: Add 60 g/2 oz/scant ½ cup finely chopped walnuts, pecan nuts, hazelnuts or almonds.

Bacon scones: Add 90 g/3 oz/scant ½ cup minced (ground) lean bacon.

Cheese & anchovy twists
Unroll a packet of thawed, ready-rolled puff pastry and cut in half lengthwise. Spread one piece evenly with Gentleman's Relish or anchovy paste, then cover evenly with about 175 g/6 oz/1½ cups finely grated Gouda or Emmental (Swiss) cheese. A little grated Parmesan cheese may also be sprinkled over. Place the other piece of pastry on top and press together firmly. Using a sharp knife and ruler, cut into strips about 1 cm/½ inch wide. If liked, brush with beaten egg or milk. Give each strip two twists and place on a greased baking sheet. Shape the ends into points and make sure they are evenly shaped all over. Bake in a preheated oven at 200°C/400°F/Gas Mark 6 for about 15 minutes until well puffed up and golden brown.

COLD SOUPS

VICHYSOISSE

SERVES 4-6

3 large leeks
45 g/1½ oz/3 tbsp butter or margarine
1 onion, sliced thinly
500 g/1 lb potatoes, chopped
900 ml/1½ pints/3½ cups Chicken or
    Vegetable Stock (see pages 8-9)
2 tsp lemon juice
pinch of ground nutmeg
¼ tsp ground coriander
1 dried bay leaf
1 egg yolk
150 ml/¼ pint/⅔ cup single (light) cream
salt and white pepper
snipped chives or crisply fried and
    crumbled bacon to garnish

1 Trim the leeks and remove most of the green part (it can be served as a vegetable). Slice the white part of the leeks very finely.

2 Melt the butter or margarine in a saucepan and fry the leeks and onion gently for about 5 minutes without browning, stirring from time to time.

3 Add the potatoes, stock, lemon juice, seasoning, nutmeg, coriander and bay leaf to the pan and bring to the boil. Cover and simmer for about 30 minutes until all the vegetables are very soft.

4 Cool the soup a little, discard the bay leaf and then press through a sieve (strainer) or blend in a food processor or blender until smooth. Pour into a clean pan.

5 Blend the egg yolk into the cream, add a little of the soup to the mixture and then whisk it all back into the soup and reheat gently without boiling. Adjust seasoning to taste. Cool and chill thoroughly.

6 Serve the soup sprinkled with snipped chives or crisply fried and crumbled bacon.

SPICED APPLE & APRICOT SOUP

SERVES 4-6

125 g/4 oz/⅔ cup dried apricots, soaked
    overnight or no-need-to-soak dried
    apricots
500 g/1 lb dessert apples, peeled, cored
    and chopped
1 small onion, chopped
1 tbsp lemon or lime juice
700 ml/1¼ pints/3 cups Chicken Stock (see
    page 9)
150 ml/¼ pint/⅔ cup dry white wine
¼ tsp ground ginger
good pinch of ground allspice
salt and pepper

TO GARNISH:
4-6 tbsp soured cream or natural fromage
    frais
little ground ginger or ground allspice

1 Drain the apricots, if necessary, and chop.

2 Put in a saucepan and add the apples, onion, lemon or lime juice and stock.

3 Bring to the boil, cover and simmer gently for about 20 minutes until all the fruit is soft and broken down.

4 Leave the soup to cool a little, then press through a sieve (strainer) or blend in a food processor or blender until smooth. Pour the soup into a clean pan.

5 Add the wine and spices and season to taste. Bring back to the boil, then leave to cool. If too thick, add a little more stock or water and then chill thoroughly

6 Put a spoonful of soured cream or fromage frais on top of each portion and lightly dust with ginger or allspice.

AVOCADO & MINT SOUP

SERVES 4-6

45 g/1½ oz/3 tbsp butter or margarine
6 spring onions (scallions), sliced
1 garlic clove, crushed
30 g/1 oz/ ¼ cup plain (all-purpose) flour
600 ml/1 pint/2½ cups Chicken Stock (see page 9)
2 ripe avocados
2–3 tsp lemon juice
good pinch of grated lemon rind
150 ml/ ¼ pint/⅔ cup milk
150 ml/ ¼ pint/ ⅔ cup single (light) cream
1–1½ tbsp chopped fresh mint
salt and pepper
sprigs of fresh mint to garnish

MINTED GARLIC BREAD:
125 g/4 oz/ ½ cup butter
1–2 tbsp chopped fresh mint
1–2 garlic cloves, crushed
1 wholemeal (whole wheat) or white French loaf

1 Melt the butter or margarine in a large saucepan, add the spring onions (scallions) and garlic and fry gently for about 3 minutes until soft but not coloured.

2 Stir in the flour and cook for a minute or so. Gradually stir in the stock then bring to the boil. Leave to simmer gently while preparing the avocados.

3 Peel the avocados, discard the stones (pits) and chop coarsely. Add to the soup with the lemon juice and rind and seasoning. Cover and simmer for about 10 minutes until tender.

4 Cool the soup slightly then press through a sieve (strainer) or blend in a food processor or blender until smooth. Pour into a bowl.

5 Stir in the milk and cream, adjust the seasoning, then stir in the mint. Cover and chill thoroughly.

6 To make the minted garlic bread, soften the butter and beat in the mint and garlic. Cut the loaf into slanting slices but leave a hinge on the bottom crust. Spread each slice with the butter and reassemble the loaf. Wrap in foil and place in a preheated oven at 180°C/350°F/Gas Mark 4 for about 15 minutes.

7 Serve the soup garnished with a sprig of mint and accompanied by the minted garlic bread.

GAZPACHO

SERVES 4

½ small cucumber
½ small green (bell) pepper, chopped very
  finely
500 g/1 lb ripe tomatoes, skinned or
  425 g/14 oz can chopped tomatoes
½ onion, chopped coarsely
2–3 garlic cloves, crushed
3 tbsp olive oil
2 tbsp white wine vinegar
1–2 tbsp lemon or lime juice
2 tbsp tomato purée (paste)
450 ml/¾ pint/scant 2 cups tomato juice
salt and pepper

TO SERVE:
chopped green (bell) pepper
thinly sliced onion rings
Garlic Croûtons (see page 10)

1 Coarsely grate the cucumber into a
  bowl and add the chopped green
(bell) pepper.

2 Blend the tomatoes, onion and garlic
  in a food processor or blender, then
add the oil, vinegar, lemon or lime juice
and tomato purée (paste) and blend until
smooth. Alternatively, finely chop the
tomatoes and finely grate the onion, then
mix both with the garlic, oil, vinegar,
lemon or lime juice and tomato purée
(paste).

3 Add the tomato mixture to the
  cucumber and green (bell) pepper
and mix well, then add the tomato juice
and mix again.

4 Season to taste, cover the bowl with
  clingfilm (plastic wrap) and chill
thoroughly – for at least 6 hours and
preferably longer for the flavours to blend
together.

5 Prepare the side dishes and arrange
  in individual bowls.

6 Ladle the soup into bowls,
  preferably from a soup tureen set on
the table with the side dishes around it.
Hand the dishes around to allow the
guests to help themselves.

CURRIED PRAWN (SHRIMP) SOUP

SERVES 4

2 tbsp ground almonds
2 tbsp unsweetened desiccated (shredded)
  coconut
150 ml/ ¼ pint/ ⅔ cup boiling water
60 g/2 oz/ ¼ cup butter or margarine
1 onion, minced or chopped very finely
2 celery sticks, minced (ground) or
  chopped very finely
30 g/1 oz / ¼ cup plain (all-purpose) flour
1½ tsp medium curry powder
600 ml/1 pint/2½ cups Fish or Vegetable
  Stock (see pages 8-9)
2 tsp lemon or lime juice
3–4 drops Tabasco sauce
1 dried bay leaf
90–125 g/3–4 oz/ ½–⅛ cup peeled prawns
  (shrimp), thawed if frozen
300 ml/ ½ pint/ 1¼ cups milk
4–6 tbsp double (heavy) cream
salt and pepper

1 Put the almonds and coconut into a
  bowl. Pour on the water, mix well
and leave until cold. Strain, pushing down
firmly with a potato masher or the back
of a spoon, and reserve the liquor.

2 Melt the butter or margarine in a
  large saucepan. Add the onion and
celery and fry gently for 3–4 minutes until
soft but not coloured.

3 Stir in the flour and curry powder
  and cook gently for 2 minutes, then
add the stock and coconut liquor and
bring to the boil.

4 Add the lemon or lime juice,
  Tabasco, seasoning and bay leaf,
cover and simmer for 10 minutes.
Coarsely chop half the prawns (shrimp),
add to the soup and simmer for a further
10 minutes.

5 Discard the bay leaf, stir in the milk
  and remaining prawns (shrimp) and
bring back to the boil. Simmer for 3–4
minutes. Adjust the seasoning and stir in
the cream. Chill thoroughly.

MINTED PEA & YOGURT SOUP

SERVES 6

2 tbsp vegetable ghee or oil
2 onions, peeled and coarsely chopped
250 g/8 oz potato, peeled and coarsely chopped
2 garlic cloves, peeled
2.5 cm/1 in ginger root, peeled and chopped
1 tsp ground coriander
1 tsp ground cumin
1 tbsp plain flour
900 ml/1½ pints/3½ cups vegetable stock
500 g/1 lb frozen peas
2-3 tbsp chopped fresh mint, to taste
salt and freshly ground black pepper
150 ml/ ½ pint/ ⅔ cup strained Greek yogurt
½ tsp cornflour (cornstarch)
300 ml/ ½ pint/1¼ cups milk
a little extra yogurt, for serving (optional)
mint sprigs, to garnish

1 Heat the ghee or oil in a saucepan, add the onions and potato and cook gently for 3 minutes. Stir in the garlic, ginger, coriander, cumin and flour and cook for 1 minute, stirring.

2 Add the stock, peas and half the mint and bring to the boil, stirring. Reduce the heat, cover and simmer gently for 15 minutes or until the vegetables are tender.

3 Purée the soup, in batches, in a blender or food processor. Return the mixture to the pan and season with salt and pepper to taste. Blend the yogurt with the cornflour (cornstarch) and stir into the soup.

4 Add the milk and bring almost to the boil, stirring all the time. Cook very gently for 2 minutes. Serve hot, sprinkled with the remaining mint and a swirl of extra yogurt, if wished, or serve chilled. Thin the cold soup with a little extra stock, yogurt or milk, if necessary.

COOK'S TIP

The yogurt is mixed with a little cornflour (cornstarch) before being added to the hot soup – this helps to stabilize the yogurt and prevents it separating when heated.

HOT SOUPS

CREAM CHEESE & FRESH HERB SOUP

SERVES 4

30 g/1 oz/2 tbsp butter or margarine
2 onions, chopped
900 ml/1½ pints/3½ cups vegetable stock
30 g/1 oz coarsely chopped mixed fresh
  herbs, such as parsley, chives, thyme,
  basil and oregano
200 g/7 oz/1 cup full-fat soft cheese
1 tbsp cornflour (cornstarch)
1 tbsp milk
chopped fresh chives to garnish

1 Melt the butter or margarine in a
  large saucepan and add the onions.
Fry for 2 minutes, then cover and turn the
heat to low. Allow the onions to cook
gently for 5 minutes, then remove the lid.

2 Add the stock and herbs to the
  saucepan. Bring to the boil, then
turn down the heat. Cover and simmer
gently for 20 minutes.

3 Remove the saucepan from the heat.
  Blend the soup with a hand blender
or in a food processor or blender for
about 15 seconds, until smooth.
Alternatively, press it through a sieve
(strainer). Return the soup to the
saucepan.

4 Reserve a little of the cheese for
  garnish. Spoon the remaining cheese
into the soup and whisk until the cheese
is incorporated.

5 Mix the cornflour (cornstarch) with
  the milk, then stir into the soup and
heat, stirring constantly, until thickened
and smooth.

6 Pour the soup into 4 warmed bowls.
  Spoon some of the reserved cheese
into each bowl and garnish with chives.
Serve at once.

SUMMER SOUP

In summer, this soup is wonderful
when served chilled.

ASPARAGUS SOUP

SERVES 4-6

1 bunch asparagus, about 350 g/12 oz,
  or 2 packs mini asparagus, about
  150 g/5 oz each
700 ml/1¼ pints/3 cups chicken or
  vegetable stock
60 g/2 oz/ ¼ cup butter or margarine
1 onion, chopped
3 tbsp plain (all-purpose) flour
¼ tsp ground coriander
1 tbsp lemon juice
450 ml/ ¾ pint/2 cups milk
4-6 tbsp double (heavy) or single (light)
  cream or fromage frais
salt and pepper

1 Wash and trim the asparagus,
  discarding the woody part of the
stem. Cut the remainder into short
lengths, keeping a few tips for garnish.
Mini asparagus does not need to be
trimmed.

2 Cook the tips in the minimum of
  boiling salted water for 5–10
minutes. Drain and set aside.

3 Put the asparagus in a saucepan with
  the stock, bring to the boil, cover
and simmer for about 20 minutes until
soft. Drain and reserve the stock.

4 Melt the butter or margarine in a
  saucepan and fry the onion very
gently until soft, but only barely coloured.
Stir in the flour and cook for a minute or
so then stir in the reserved stock and
bring to the boil.

5 Simmer the sauce for 2–3 minutes
  until thickened, then stir in the
cooked asparagus, seasoning, coriander
and lemon juice. Simmer for 10 minutes,
then cool a little and either press through
a sieve (strainer), or mix in a blender or
food processor until smooth.

6 Pour into a clean pan, add the milk
  and reserved asparagus tips and
bring to the boil. Adjust the seasoning
and simmer for 2 minutes. Stir in the
cream or fromage frais and reheat gently.
Garnish with reserved tips.

SPINACH & TOFU SOUP

SERVES 4

125-175 g/4-6 oz fresh spinach leaves, or
*   frozen leaf spinach, defrosted*
small bunch of chives
2 tbsp sesame oil
1 garlic clove, crushed
125-175 g/4-6 oz tofu (bean curd), cut
*   into 1 cm/ ½ in cubes*
60 g/2 oz/ ½ cup pine kernels
1 litre/1¼ pints/4 cups good chicken or
*   vegetable stock*
½ tsp turmeric
½ tsp ground coriander
2 tsp cornflour (cornstarch)
salt and pepper

1 Wash the spinach thoroughly and strip off the stalks. Dry on paper towels, then slice into thin strips. If using frozen spinach, drain well, then slice or chop roughly.

2 Take 12 chives and tie 3 at a time into a knot to use for a garnish, if liked. Chop the remainder.

3 Heat the oil in a wok, swirling it around until really hot. Add the garlic and tofu and stir-fry for 2-3 minutes until they are beginning to colour. Add the pine kernels and continue to cook until they turn a light golden brown.

4 Add the stock, turmeric, coriander and seasoning and bring to the boil; simmer for 10 minutes.

5 Blend the cornflour (cornstarch) with a little cold water and stir into the wok. Add the strips of spinach and simmer for a further 2-3 minutes, stirring frequently.

6 Adjust the seasoning, stir in the snipped chives and garnish each serving with a chive knot, if liked.

TOFU (BEAN CURD)

Tofu can be added to many dishes to provide extra protein. It is very bland and almost tasteless, so some extra flavouring is usually required.

CREAMED PARSNIP & TARRAGON

SERVES 4-6

1 carrot
500 g/1 lb parsnips
45 g/1½ oz/3 tbsp butter or margarine
1 large onion, chopped
1 garlic clove, crushed (optional)
900 ml/1½ pints/3½ cups Chicken or
*   Vegetable Stock (see pages 8-9)*
2 tbsp lemon juice
2-3 sprigs fresh tarragon or 2 tsp dried
*   tarragon*
300 ml/½ pint/1¼ cups milk
150 ml/¼ pint/ ⅔ cup natural fromage frais
*   or single (light) cream*
2 tsp chopped fresh tarragon
salt and pepper
Fried Croûtons (see page 10) to serve

1 Peel the carrot and slice. Peel the parsnips and cut into chunks.

2 Melt the butter or margarine in a large saucepan and fry the onion and garlic, if using, until soft but not coloured.

3 Add the parsnips and carrot and continue to fry for a few minutes, tossing the vegetables and stirring frequently. Add the stock and bring to the boil.

4 Add the seasoning, lemon juice and tarragon, cover and simmer for about 30 minutes until the vegetables are very tender.

5 Discard the fresh tarragon sprigs, if using, cool the soup a little, then press through a sieve (strainer) or blend in a food processor or blender until smooth.

6 Pour into a clean saucepan and add the milk. Bring slowly to the boil. Beat the fromage frais, if using, until smooth and add this or the cream to the soup and reheat again gently, but do not allow to boil. Adjust the seasoning and stir in half the chopped tarragon. Serve the soup with the fried croûtons and the remaining tarragon sprinkled on top.

FRENCH ONION SOUP

SERVES 4

30 g/1 oz/2 tbsp butter or margarine
2 tbsp oil
500 g/1 lb onions, sliced thinly
1–2 garlic cloves, crushed
1 litre/1¾ pints/4 cups strong Beef or
    Vegetable Stock (see pages 8-9)
2 bay leaves, preferably fresh
1 tbsp brown sugar
1 tbsp white wine vinegar
good pinch of ground allspice
8 thin slices French bread
60 g/2 oz/½ cup Gruyère, Emmental
    (Swiss) or Cheddar cheese, grated
salt and pepper
chopped fresh parsley to garnish

1 Heat the butter or margarine and oil in a saucepan, add the onions and garlic and fry very gently for 10–15 minutes until soft.

2 Increase the heat a little and continue to fry, stirring frequently, until the onions turn a golden brown and become caramelized.

3 Add the bay leaves, sugar, vinegar, seasoning and allspice. Add the stock and bring to the boil. Cover the pan and simmer gently for about 30 minutes. Discard the bay leaves and adjust the seasoning.

4 Toast 1 side of each slice of French bread under a preheated grill (broiler). Turn the slices over and sprinkle with the cheese. Put under the grill (broiler) until the cheese is bubbling.

5 Reheat the soup. Carefully ladle the soup into warmed soup bowls and float 2 slices of toasted bread on each portion. Sprinkle with chopped parsley. Allow the bread to soak up the soup a little and serve.

CARAMELIZING

Cooking the onions slowly and gently is vital to the success of this soup. It allows the natural sugars in the onions to caramelize, which gives the soup its characteristic rich flavour and colour.

CREAMED CARROT & CUMIN SOUP

SERVES 4-6

45 g/1½ oz/3 tbsp butter or margarine
1 large onion, chopped
1–2 garlic cloves, crushed
350 g/12 oz carrots, sliced
900 ml/1½ pints/3½ cups Chicken or
    Vegetable Stock (see pages 8-9)
¾ tsp ground cumin
2 celery sticks, sliced thinly
125 g/4 oz potato, diced
2 tsp tomato purée (paste)
2 tsp lemon juice
2 fresh or dried bay leaves
about 300 ml/½ pint/1¼ cups milk
salt and pepper
celery leaves to garnish

1 Melt the butter or margarine in a large saucepan. Add the onion and garlic and fry very gently until the onion begins to soften.

2 Add the carrots and continue to fry gently for a further 5 minutes, stirring frequently and taking care they do not brown.

3 Add the stock, cumin, seasoning, celery, potato, tomato purée (paste), lemon juice and bay leaves and bring to the boil. Cover and simmer gently for about 30 minutes until all the vegetables are very tender.

4 Discard the bay leaves, cool the soup a little and then press it through a sieve (strainer) or blend in a food processor or blender until smooth.

5 Pour the soup into a clean pan, add the milk and bring slowly to the boil. Taste and adjust the seasoning.

6 Garnish each serving with a small celery leaf and serve.

FREEZING

This soup can be frozen for up to 3 months. Add the milk when reheating.

BEETROOT SOUP

SERVES 4-6

BORTSCH:
500 g/1 lb raw beetroot, peeled and grated
2 carrots, chopped finely
1 large onion, chopped finely
1 garlic clove, crushed
1 Bouquet Garni (see page 9)
1 litre/1¾ pints /4 cups Chicken or
*   Vegetable Stock (see pages 8-9)*
2-3 tsp lemon juice
salt and pepper
150 ml/¼ pint/⅔ cup soured cream to serve

CREAMED BEETROOT SOUP:
60 g/2 oz/¼ cup butter or margarine
2 large onions, chopped finely
1-2 carrots, chopped
2 celery sticks, chopped
500 g/1 lb cooked beetroot, diced
1-2 tbsp lemon juice
900 ml/1½ pints/3½ cups Chicken, Beef or
*   Vegetable Stock (see pages 10-11)*
300 ml/½ pint/1¼ cups milk
salt and pepper
grated cooked beetroot or 6 tbsp soured or
*   double (heavy) cream, lightly whipped,*
*   to serve*

1 To make bortsch, place the beetroot, carrots, onion, garlic, bouquet garni, stock, lemon juice and seasoning in a saucepan. Bring to the boil, cover and simmer for 45 minutes.

2 Pour the soup through a sieve (strainer) lined with muslin (cheesecloth) or a fine sieve (strainer), then pour into a clean pan. Adjust the seasoning and add extra lemon juice if necessary.

3 Bring to the boil and simmer for 1-2 minutes. Serve with a spoonful of soured cream swirled through.

4 To make creamed beetroot soup, melt the butter or margarine in a saucepan and fry the onions, carrots and celery until just beginning to colour.

5 Add the beetroot, 1 tablespoon of the lemon juice, the stock and seasoning and bring to the boil. Cover and simmer for 30 minutes until tender.

6 Cool slightly, then press through a sieve (strainer) or blend in a food processor or blender. Pour into a clean pan. Add the milk and bring to the boil. Adjust the seasoning, add extra lemon juice if necessary, top with grated beetroot or cream and serve.

CREAM OF ARTICHOKE SOUP

SERVES 4-6

1.25 litres/2¼ pints/5 cups Chicken or
    Vegetable Stock (see pages 8-9)
750 g/1½ lb Jerusalem artichokes
1 lemon, sliced thickly
60 g/2 oz/¼ cup butter or margarine
2 onions, chopped
1 garlic clove, crushed
2 bay leaves, preferably fresh
¼ tsp ground mace or ground nutmeg
1 tbsp lemon juice
150 ml/¼ pint/⅔ cup single (light) cream
    or natural fromage frais
salt and pepper

TO GARNISH:
coarsely grated carrot
chopped fresh parsley or coriander
    (cilantro)

1   Make the stock, if necessary (see
    pages 8-9).

2   Peel and slice the artichokes. Put
    into a bowl of water with the lemon
slices.

3   Melt the butter or margarine in a
    large saucepan. Add the onions and
garlic and fry gently for 3–4 minutes until
soft but not coloured.

4   Drain the artichokes and add to the
    pan. Mix well and cook gently for
2–3 minutes without allowing to colour.

5   Add the stock, seasoning, bay leaves,
    mace or nutmeg and lemon juice
and bring slowly to the boil. Cover and
simmer gently for about 30 minutes until
the vegetables are very tender.

6   Discard the bay leaves, cool slightly
    then press through a sieve (strainer)
or blend the soup in a food processor or
blender until smooth. If liked, a little of
the soup may be only partially puréed
and added to the rest of the puréed soup,
to give extra texture.

7   Pour into a clean pan and bring to
    the boil. Adjust the seasoning and
stir in the cream or fromage frais. Reheat
gently without boiling. Garnish with
grated carrot and chopped parsley or
coriander (cilantro) and serve.

PUMPKIN SOUP

SERVES 4-6

about 1 kg/2 lb pumpkin
45 g/1½ oz/3 tbsp butter or margarine
1 onion, sliced thinly
1 garlic clove, crushed
900 ml/1½ pints/3½ cups Chicken or
    Vegetable Stock (see pages 8-9)
½ tsp ground ginger
1 tbsp lemon juice
3–4 thinly pared strips of orange rind
    (optional)
1–2 fresh or dried bay leaves or 1 Bouquet
    Garni (see page 9)
300 ml/½ pint/1¼ cups milk
salt and pepper

TO GARNISH:
4-6 tablespoons single (light) or double
    (heavy) cream, natural yogurt or
    fromage frais
snipped chives

1   Peel the pumpkin, remove the seeds
    and then cut the flesh into 2.5 cm/1
inch cubes.

2   Melt the butter or margarine in a
    large saucepan, add the onion and
garlic and fry gently until soft but not
coloured.

3   Add the pumpkin and toss with the
    onion for a few minutes.

4   Add the stock and bring to the boil.
    Add the seasoning, ginger, lemon
juice, strips of orange rind, if using, and
bay leaves or bouquet garni, cover and
simmer gently for about 20 minutes until
the pumpkin is very tender.

5   Discard the orange rind, if using,
    and the bay leaves or bouquet garni.
Cool the soup a little and then press
through a sieve (strainer) or blend in a
food processor or blender until smooth.
Pour into a clean saucepan.

6   Add the milk and reheat gently.
    Adjust the seasoning. Garnish with a
swirl of cream, natural yogurt or fromage
frais and snipped chives and serve.

GARDENER'S BROTH

SERVES 4–6

45 g/1½ oz/3 tbsp butter or margarine
1 onion, chopped
1–2 garlic cloves, crushed
1 large leek
250 g/8 oz Brussels sprouts
125 g/4 oz French (green) or runner
    beans
1.25 litres/2¼ pints/5 cups Vegetable or
    Chicken Stock (see pages 8-9)
125 g/4 oz/¾ cup frozen peas
1 tbsp lemon juice
½ tsp ground coriander
4 tbsp double (heavy) cream
salt and pepper

MELBA TOAST:
4–6 slices white bread

1 Melt the butter or margarine in a
saucepan, add the onion and garlic
and fry very gently, stirring occasionally,
until they begin to soften but not colour.

2 Slice the white part of the leek very
thinly and reserve; slice the
remaining leeks. Slice the Brussels sprouts
and thinly slice the beans.

3 Add the green part of the leeks, the
Brussels sprouts and beans to the
saucepan. Add the stock and bring to the
boil. Simmer for 10 minutes. Add the
frozen peas, seasoning, lemon juice and
coriander and continue to simmer for
10–15 minutes until the vegetables are
tender.

4 Cool the soup a little, then press
through a sieve (strainer) or blend in
a food processor or blender until smooth.
Pour into a clean pan.

5 Add the reserved slices of leek to
the soup, bring back to the boil and
simmer for about 5 minutes until the leeks
are tender. Adjust the seasoning, stir in
the cream and reheat gently.

6 Make the melba toast. Toast the
bread on both sides under a
preheated grill (broiler). Cut horizontally
through the slices then toast the
uncooked sides until they curl up. Serve
immediately with the soup.

HARICOT BEAN & PASTA SOUP

SERVES 4

250 g/8 oz/generous 1 cup dried haricot
    beans, soaked, drained and rinsed (see
    below)
4 tbsp olive oil
2 large onions, sliced
3 garlic cloves, chopped
1 x 425 g/15 oz can chopped tomatoes
1 tsp dried oregano
1 tsp tomato purée (paste)
900 ml/1½ pints/3½ cups water
90 g/3 oz small pasta shapes, such as
    fusilli or conchigliette
125 g/4 oz sun-dried tomatoes, drained
    and thinly sliced
1 tbsp chopped coriander, or flat-leaved
    parsley
2 tbsp grated Parmesan
salt and pepper

1 Put the soaked beans into a large
pan, cover with cold water and bring
them to the boil. Boil rapidly for 15
minutes, to remove any harmful toxins.
Drain the beans in a colander.

2 Heat the oil in a pan over a medium
heat and fry the onions until they
are just beginning to change colour. Stir in
the garlic and cook for 1 further minute.
Stir in the chopped tomatoes, oregano
and the tomato purée and pour on the
water. Add the beans, bring to the boil
and cover the pan. Simmer for 45
minutes, or until the beans are almost
tender.

3 Add the pasta, season the soup and
stir in the sun-dried tomatoes. Return
the soup to the boil, partly cover the pan
and continue cooking for 10 minutes, or
until the pasta is nearly tender.

4 Stir in the chopped herb. Taste the
soup and adjust the seasoning if
necessary. Transfer to a warmed soup
tureen to serve, sprinkled with the cheese.
Serve hot.

DRIED BEANS

You can soak the dried beans for
several hours or overnight in a large
bowl of cold water.

CHICK-PEA (GARBANZO BEAN) TOMATO SOUP

••

SERVES 4

2 tbsp olive oil
2 leeks, sliced thinly
2 courgettes (zucchini), chopped
2 garlic cloves, crushed
2 x about 425 g/14 oz cans chopped
  tomatoes
1 tbsp tomato purée (paste)
1 fresh bay leaf
900 ml/1½ pints/3 ¾ cups chicken stock
about 425 g/14 oz can chick-peas
  (garbanzo beans), drained
250 g/8 oz spinach
25 g/1 oz thin shavings of Parmesan
  cheese
salt and pepper
crusty bread to serve

1 Heat the oil in a saucepan, add the
  leeks and courgettes (zucchini) and
cook briskly for 5 minutes, stirring
constantly.

2 Add the garlic , tomatoes, tomato
  purée (paste), bay leaf, stock and
chick-peas (garbanzo beans). Bring to the
boil and simmer for 5 minutes.

3 Shred the spinach finely, add to the
  soup and boil for 2 minutes. Season
to taste.

4 Remove the bay leaf. Pour into a
  soup tureen and sprinkle over the
Parmesan cheese. Serve with crusty bread.

CHICK-PEAS (GARBANZO BEANS)

Chickpeas (garbanzo beans) are used
extensively in North African cuisine
and are also found in Spanish, Middle
Eastern and Indian cookery. They have
a nutty flavour with a firm texture and
are an excellent canned product.

SCOTCH BROTH

••

SERVES 6

750 g–1 kg/1½–2 lb stewing lamb on the
  bone
2 litres/3½ pints/9 cups water
2 fresh or dried bay leaves
250 g/8 oz carrots, chopped finely
1 turnip, chopped
2 onions, chopped finely
2 leeks, sliced very thinly
125–250 g/4–8 oz potatoes, diced finely
60 g/2 oz/¼ cup pearl barley
salt and pepper
3 tbsp chopped fresh parsley to garnish

1 Trim the meat, removing any excess
  fat. Put in a large saucepan with the
water and bring to the boil.

2 Remove any scum from the surface
  then add the bay leaves and plenty
of seasoning. Cover and simmer gently for
1½ hours.

3 Add all the vegetables and the
  barley, stir and bring back to a
gentle simmer. Cover the pan and simmer
for 1 hour until the barley and vegetables
are very soft.

4 Cool slightly then skim the fat from
  the surface. Remove the last of the
fat by placing paper towels on the surface
to absorb the fat.

5 Adjust the seasoning. Remove the
  lamb, strip the meat from the bones
and return to the soup. Alternatively, the
pieces of meat can be served still on the
bone: put a piece of meat in each serving
bowl and ladle over the soup (a fork will
then be required to eat the soup).

6 Sprinkle the parsley over each
  portion and serve.

REMOVING THE FAT

If time allows, leave the soup to cool
after step 3. It will then be easy to lift
the solidified fat from the surface.

SPICY LENTIL SOUP

SERVES 4

125 g/4 oz/½ cup red lentils
2 tsp vegetable oil
1 large onion, chopped finely
2 garlic cloves, crushed
1 tsp ground cumin
1 tsp ground coriander
1 tsp garam masala
2 tbsp tomato purée (paste)
1 litre/1¾ pints/4½ cups Fresh Vegetable
  Stock (see page 9)
about 350 g/12 oz can sweetcorn, drained
salt and pepper

TO SERVE:
low-fat natural yogurt
chopped fresh parsley
warmed pitta (pocket) bread

1 Rinse the lentils in cold water, drain well and set aside.

2 Heat the oil in a large non-stick saucepan and fry the onion and garlic gently until softened but not browned.

3 Stir in the cumin, coriander, garam masala, tomato purée (paste) and 4 tablespoons of the stock. Mix well and simmer gently for 2 minutes.

4 Add the lentils and pour in the remaining stock. Bring to the boil, reduce the heat and simmer, covered, for 1 hour until the lentils are tender and the soup thickened.

5 Stir in the sweetcorn and heat through for 5 minutes. Season well.

6 Ladle into warmed soup bowls and top each with a spoonful of yogurt and a sprinkling of parsley. Serve accompanied with warmed pitta (pocket) bread.

NOTE

Many of the ready-prepared ethnic breads available today either contain fat or are brushed with oil before baking. Always check the ingredients list for fat content.

PLUM TOMATO SOUP

SERVES 4

2 tbsp olive oil
2 red onions, chopped
2 celery sticks, chopped
1 carrot, chopped
500 g/1 lb fresh plum tomatoes, halved
750 ml/1¼ pints/3 cups vegetable stock
1 tbsp chopped fresh oregano, or 1 tsp
  dried oregano
1 tbsp chopped fresh basil, or 1 tsp dried
  basil
150 ml/¼ pint/⅔ cup dry white wine
2 tsp caster (superfine) sugar
125 g/4 oz/1 cup hazelnuts, toasted
125 g/4 oz/1 cup black or green olives
handful of fresh basil leaves
1 tbsp olive oil
1 loaf ciabatta bread (Italian-style loaf)
salt and pepper
sprigs of fresh basil to garnish

1 Heat the olive oil in a large saucepan and fry the chopped onions, celery and carrot gently until softened.

2 Add the tomatoes, stock, chopped herbs, wine and sugar. Bring to the boil, then cover and simmer gently for about 20 minutes.

3 Place the toasted hazelnuts in a blender or food processor with the olives and basil leaves and process until combined, but not too smooth. Alternatively, chop the nuts, olives and basil leaves finely and pound in a mortar and pestle, then turn into a small bowl. Add the olive oil, process or beat thoroughly for a few seconds, and then turn the mixture into a serving bowl.

4 Warm the ciabatta bread in a preheated oven at 190°C/375°F/Gas Mark 5 for 3–4 minutes.

5 Blend the soup in a blender or a food processor, or press through a sieve, until smooth, Check the seasoning, adding salt and pepper according to taste. Ladle into 4 warmed soup bowls. Garnish with sprigs of basil. Slice the warm bread and spread with the olive and hazelnut paste. Serve with the soup.

SPINACH & MASCARPONE SOUP

SERVES 4

60 g/2 oz/¼ cup butter
1 bunch spring onions (scallions),
   trimmed and chopped
2 celery sticks, chopped
350 g/12 oz/3 cups spinach or sorrel, or
   3 bunches watercress
900 ml /1½ pints/3½ cups vegetable stock
250 g/8 oz/1 cup Mascarpone cheese
1 tbsp olive oil
2 slices thick-cut bread, cut into cubes
½ tsp caraway seeds
salt and pepper
sesame bread sticks to serve

1 Melt half the butter in a very large
   saucepan. Add the spring onions
(scallions) and celery, and cook gently for
about 5 minutes, until softened.

2 Pack the spinach, sorrel or
   watercress into the saucepan.
Add the stock and bring to the boil; then
reduce the heat and simmer, covered, for
15–20 minutes.

3 Transfer the soup to a blender or
   food processor and blend until
smooth, or rub through a sieve. Return to
the saucepan.

4 Add the Mascarpone cheese to the
   soup and heat gently, stirring, until
smooth and blended. Taste and season
with salt and pepper.

5 Heat the remaining butter with the
   oil in a frying pan. Add the bread
cubes and fry in the hot fat until golden
brown, adding the caraway seeds towards
the end of cooking, so that they do not
burn.

6 Ladle the soup into 4
   warmed bowls. Sprinkle
with the croûtons and
serve at once,
accompanied by the
sesame bread sticks.

YOGURT & SPINACH SOUP

SERVES 4

600 ml/1 pint/2½ cups chicken stock
60 g/2 oz/4 tbsp long-grain rice, rinsed
   and drained
4 tbsp water
1 tbsp cornflour (cornstarch)
600 ml/1 pint/2½ cups natural yogurt
juice of 1 lemon
3 egg yolks, lightly beaten
350 g/12 oz young spinach leaves, washed
   and drained
salt and pepper

1 Pour the stock into a large pan,
   season and bring to the boil. Add the
rice and simmer for 10 minutes, until
barely cooked. Remove from the heat.

2 Pour the water into a small bowl
   and sift the cornflour (cornstarch)
into it. Stir to make a thin, smooth paste.

3 Pour the yogurt into a second pan
   and stir in the cornflour (cornstarch)
mixture. Set the pan over a low heat and
bring the yogurt slowly to the boil, stirring
with a wooden spoon in one direction
only. This will stabilize the yogurt and
prevent it from separating or curdling on
contact with the hot stock. When the
yogurt has reached boiling point, stand
the pan on a heat diffuser and leave to
simmer slowly for 10 minutes. Remove
the pan from the heat and allow the
mixture to cool slightly before stirring in
the beaten egg yolks.

4 Pour the yogurt mixture into the
   stock, stir in the lemon juice and stir
to blend thoroughly. Keep the soup
warm, but do not allow it to boil.

5 Blanch the spinach leaves in a large
   pan of boiling, salted water for 2-3
minutes until they begin to soften but
have not collapsed. Tip the spinach into a
colander, drain well and stir it into the
soup. Taste the soup and adjust the
seasoning if necesary. Serve in wide,
shallow soup plates, with hot, crusty
bread.

FISH & VEGETABLE SOUP

•••••••••••••••••••••••••••••••••••••••

SERVES 4

*250 g/8 oz white fish fillets (cod, halibut,
   haddock, sole etc)*
½ tsp ground ginger
½ tsp salt
1 small leek, trimmed
*2-4 crab sticks, defrosted if frozen
   (optional)*
1 tbsp sunflower oil
1 large carrot, cut into julienne strips
8 canned water chestnuts, thinly sliced
*1.25 litres/2 pints/5 cups fish or vegetable
   stock*
1 tbsp lemon juice
1 tbsp light soy sauce
*1 large courgette (zucchini), cut into
   julienne strips*
black pepper

1 Remove any skin from the fish and
   cut into cubes, about 2.5 cm/1 in.
Combine the ground ginger and salt and
use to rub into the pieces of fish. Leave to
marinate for at least 30 minutes.

2 Meanwhile, divide the green and
   white parts of the leek. Cut each
part into 2.5 cm/1 in lengths and then
into julienne strips down the length of
each piece, keeping the two parts
separate. Slice the crab sticks into
1 cm/½ in pieces.

3 Heat the oil in the wok, swirling it
   around so it is really hot. Add the
white part of the leek and stir-fry for a
couple of minutes, then add the carrots
and water chestnuts and continue to cook
for 1-2 minutes, stirring thoroughly.

4 Add the stock and bring to the boil,
   then add the lemon juice and soy
sauce and simmer for 2 minutes.

5 Add the fish and continue to cook
   for about 5 minutes until the fish
begins to break up a little, then add the
green part of the leek and the courgettes
(zucchini) and simmer for about 1 minute.
Add the sliced crab sticks, if using, and
season to taste with black pepper. Simmer
for a further minute or so and serve
piping hot.

PARTAN BREE

•••••••••••••••••••••••••••••••••••••••

SERVES 4-6

1 medium-sized boiled crab
90 g/3 oz/scant ½ cup long-grain rice
600 ml/1 pint/2½ cups milk
*600 ml/1 pint/2½ cups Fish Stock (see
   page 9)*
1 tbsp anchovy essence (paste)
2 tsp lime or lemon juice
*1 tbsp chopped fresh parsley or l tsp
   chopped fresh thyme*
3-4 tbsp soured cream (optional)
salt and pepper
snipped chives to garnish

1 Remove and reserve all the brown
   and white meat from the crab, then
crack the claws and remove and chop
that meat; reserve the claw meat.

2 Put the rice and milk into a
   saucepan and bring slowly to the
boil. Cover and simmer gently for about
20 minutes until the rice is very tender.

3 Add the reserved white and brown
   crab meat and seasoning and simmer
for a further 5 minutes.

4 Cool a little, then press through a
   sieve (strainer), or blend in a food
processor or blender until smooth.

5 Pour the soup into a clean saucepan
   and add the fish stock and the
reserved claw meat. Bring slowly to the
boil, then add the anchovy essence
(paste) and lime or lemon juice and adjust
the seasoning.

6 Simmer for a further 2-3 minutes.
   Stir in the parsley or thyme and then
swirl soured cream, if using, through each
serving. Garnish with snipped chives.

CRAB

Cooked crabs are readily available from
fishmongers and larger supermarkets
that have a fish counter. They are also
available frozen from some shops. If
you are unable to buy a whole crab,
use about 175 g/6 oz frozen crab meat,
which must be thoroughly thawed
before use.

SMOKY HADDOCK SOUP

SERVES 4-6

250 g/8 oz smoked haddock fillet
1 onion, chopped finely
1 garlic clove, crushed
600 ml/1 pint/2½ cups water
600 ml/1 pint/2½ cups milk
250–350 g/8–12 oz/1–1½ cups hot mashed
*   potatoes*
30 g/1 oz/2 tbsp butter
about 1 tbsp lemon juice
6 tbsp double (heavy) cream, soured
*   cream or natural fromage frais*
4 tbsp chopped fresh parsley
salt and pepper

1 Put the fish, onion, garlic and water into a saucepan. Bring to the boil, cover and simmer gently for about 15–20 minutes until the fish is tender.

2 Remove the fish from the pan; strip off the skin and remove all the bones. Flake the flesh finely.

3 Return the skin and bones to the cooking liquor and simmer for 10 minutes. Strain, discarding the skin and bones, and pour the liquor into a clean saucepan.

4 Add the milk, flaked fish and seasoning to the pan, bring to the boil and simmer for about 3 minutes.

5 Gradually whisk in sufficient mashed potato to give a fairly thick soup, then stir in the butter and sharpen to taste with lemon juice.

6 Add the cream, soured cream or fromage frais and 3 tablespoons of the chopped parsley. Reheat gently and adjust the seasoning. Sprinkle with the remaining parsley and serve.

SMOKED HADDOCK

Undyed smoked haddock may be used in place of the bright yellow fish; it will give a paler colour but just as much flavour. Alternatively, use smoked cod or smoked whiting.

SALMON BISQUE

SERVES 4-6

1–2 salmon heads (depending on size) or
*   a tail piece of salmon weighing about*
*   500 g/1 lb*
900 ml/1½ pints/3½ cups water
1 fresh or dried bay leaf
1 lemon, sliced
a few black peppercorns
30 g/1 oz/2 tbsp butter or margarine
2 tbsp finely chopped onion or spring
*   onions (scallions)*
30 g/1 oz/ ¼ cup plain (all-purpose) flour
150 ml/ ¼ pint / ⅔ cup dry white wine or
*   Fish Stock (see page 9)*
150 ml/ ¼ pint/⅔ cup single (light) cream
1 tbsp chopped fresh fennel or dill
2–3 tsp lemon or lime juice
salt and pepper

TO GARNISH:
30–45 g/1–1½ oz smoked salmon pieces,
*   chopped (optional)*
sprigs of fresh fennel or dill

1 Put the salmon, water, bay leaf, lemon and peppercorns into a saucepan. Bring to the boil, remove any scum from the surface, then cover the pan and simmer gently for 20 minutes.

2 Remove from the heat, strain the stock and reserve 600 ml/1 pint/2½ cups.

3 Remove and discard all the skin and bones from the salmon and flake the flesh, removing all the pieces from the head, if using.

4 Melt the butter or margarine in a saucepan and fry the onion or spring onions (scallions) gently for about 5 minutes until soft. Stir in the flour and cook for 1 minute then gradually stir in the reserved stock and wine or fish stock. Bring to the boil, stirring.

5 Add the salmon, season well, then simmer gently for about 5 minutes.

6 Add the cream and the chopped fennel or dill and reheat gently, but do not boil. Sharpen to taste with lemon or lime juice and adjust the seasoning. Serve hot or chilled, garnished with smoked salmon, and fennel or dill.

PRAWN (SHRIMP) GUMBO

SERVES 4-6

1 large onion, chopped finely
2 slices lean bacon, chopped finely
   (optional)
1–2 garlic cloves, crushed
2 tbsp olive oil
1 large or 2 small red (bell) peppers,
   chopped finely or minced coarsely
900 ml/1½ pints/3½ cups Fish or Vegetable
   Stock (see pages 8-9)
1 fresh or dried bay leaf
1 blade mace
good pinch of ground allspice
45 g/1½ oz/3 tbsp long-grain rice
1 tbsp white wine vinegar
125–175 g/4–6 oz okra, trimmed and
   sliced very thinly
90–125 g/3–4 oz/ ½–⅔ cup peeled prawns
   (shrimp)
1 tbsp anchovy essence (paste)
2 tsp tomato purée (paste)
1–2 tbsp chopped fresh parsley
salt and pepper
Cheese & Anchovy Twists (see page 11)
   to serve
whole prawns (shrimp), to garnish
sprigs of fresh parsley, to garnish

1 Gently fry the onion, bacon, if using, and garlic in the oil in a large saucepan for 4–5 minutes until soft, but only lightly coloured. Add the (bell) peppers to the pan and continue to fry gently for a couple of minutes.

2 Add the stock, bay leaf, mace, allspice, rice, vinegar and seasoning and bring to the boil. Cover and simmer gently for about 20 minutes, giving an occasional stir, until the rice is just tender.

3 Add the okra, prawns (shrimp), anchovy essence (paste) and tomato purée (paste), cover and simmer gently for about 15 minutes until the okra is tender and the mixture slightly thickened.

4 Meanwhile, make the cheese and anchovy twists (see page 11).

5 Discard the bay leaf and mace from the soup and adjust the seasoning. Stir in the parsley and serve each portion garnished with a whole prawn (shrimp) and parsley sprigs. Serve with warm cheese and anchovy twists.

CHICKEN SOUP WITH ALMONDS

SERVES 4

1 large or 2 small boneless skinned
   chicken breasts
1 tbsp sunflower oil
4 spring onions (scallions), thinly sliced
   diagonally
1 carrot, cut into julienne strips
750 ml/1¼ pints/3 cups chicken stock
finely grated rind of ½ lemon
45 g/1½ oz/ ⅓ cup ground almonds
1 tbsp light soy sauce
1 tbsp lemon juice
30 g/1 oz/ ¼ cup flaked almonds, toasted
salt and pepper

1 Cut each breast into 4 strips lengthways, then slice very thinly across the grain to give shreds of chicken.

2 Heat the oil in the wok, swirling it around until really hot. Add the chicken and toss it for 3-4 minutes until sealed and almost cooked through, then add the carrot and continue to cook for 2-3 minutes, stirring all the time. Add the spring onions (scallions) and stir.

3 Add the stock to the wok and bring to the boil. Add the lemon rind, ground almonds, soy sauce, lemon juice and plenty of seasoning. Bring back to the boil and simmer, uncovered, for 5 minutes, stirring from time to time.

4 Adjust the seasoning, add most of the toasted flaked almonds and continue to cook for a further 1-2 minutes.

5 Serve the soup very hot, in individual bowls, sprinkled with the remaining almonds.

GAME STOCK

To make game stock, break up a pheasant carcass and place in a large pan with 2 litres/3½ pints/8 cups of water. Bring to the boil slowly, skimming off the scum as it rises to the surface. Add 1 bouquet garni, 1 small onion, peeled, and salt and pepper. Cover and simmer gently for about 1½ hours, skimming regularly.

CHICKEN & SWEETCORN SOUP

SERVES 4

1 boneless, skinned chicken breast, about
    175 g/6 oz
2 tbsp sunflower oil
2-3 spring onions (scallions), thinly sliced
    diagonally
1 small or ½ large red (bell) pepper, cored,
    seeded and thinly sliced
1 garlic clove, crushed
125 g/4 oz baby sweetcorn, thinly sliced
1 litre/1¾ pints/4 cups chicken stock
1 x 200 g/7 oz can sweetcorn niblets, well
    drained
2 tbsp sherry
2-3 tsp bottled sweet chilli sauce
2-3 tsp cornflour (cornstarch)
2 tomatoes, peeled, quartered and seeded,
    then sliced
salt and pepper
freshly chopped coriander or parsley, to
    garnish

1 Cut the chicken breast into 4 strips
lengthways, then cut each strip into
narrow slices across the grain.

2 Heat the oil in a wok, swirling it
around until it is really hot. Add the
chicken and stir-fry for 3-4 minutes,
spreading it out over the wok until it is
well sealed all over and almost cooked.

3 Add the spring onions (scallions),
(bell) pepper and garlic and
continue to stir-fry for 2-3 minutes, then
add the baby sweetcorns and stock and
bring to the boil.

4 Add the corn niblets, sherry and
sweet chilli sauce and salt to taste
and simmer for 5 minutes, stirring from
time to time.

5 Blend the cornflour (cornstarch) with
a little cold water, add to the soup
and bring to the boil. Add the strips of
tomato, adjust the seasoning and simmer
for a few minutes. Serve the soup very
hot, sprinkled with finely chopped
coriander or parsley.

THAI-STYLE CHICKEN & COCONUT SOUP

SERVES 4

350 g/12 oz/1¾ cups cooked, skinned
    chicken breast
125 g/4 oz/1⅓ cups unsweetened
    desiccated coconut
500 ml/16 fl oz/2 cups boiling water
500 ml/16 fl oz/2 cups Chicken Stock (see
    page 9)
4 spring onions (scallions), white and
    green parts, sliced thinly
2 stalks lemon grass
1 lime
1 tsp grated ginger root
1 tbsp light soy sauce
2 tsp ground coriander
2 large fresh red chillies
1 tbsp chopped fresh coriander (cilantro)
1 tbsp cornflour (cornstarch) mixed with
    2 tbsp cold water
salt and white pepper
chopped red chilli to garnish

1 Slice the chicken into thin strips.
Place the coconut in a heatproof
bowl and pour the boiling water over.

2 Place a fine sieve over another bowl
and pour in the coconut water. Work
the coconut through the sieve. Pour the
coconut water into a large saucepan and
add the stock.

3 Add the spring onions (scallions) to
the saucepan. Slice the base of each
lemon grass and discard damaged leaves.
Bruise the stalks and add to the saucepan.

4 Peel the rind from the lime, keeping
it in large strips. Slice the lime in
half and extract the juice. Add the lime
strips, juice, ginger, soy sauce and ground
coriander to the saucepan. Bruise the
chillies with a fork then add to the
saucepan. Heat the pan to just below
boiling point.

5 Add the chicken and fresh coriander
to the saucepan, bring to the boil,
then simmer for 10 minutes. Discard the
lemon grass, lime rind and chillies. Pour
the blended cornflour (cornstarch)
mixture into the saucepan and stir until
slightly thickened. Season to taste then
serve, garnished with chopped red chilli.

CHICKEN & CHESTNUT SOUP

SERVES 4-6

2 onions
raw or cooked chicken carcass, chopped,
  plus trimmings
chicken giblets, if available
1.5 litres/2½ pints/6¼ cups water
1 Bouquet Garni (see page 9)
125 g/4 oz/ ½ cup fresh chestnuts, pierced
  and roasted for about 5 minutes or
  boiled for 30–40 minutes, drained, or
  175 g/6 oz/1 cup canned peeled
  chestnuts
45 g/1½ oz/3 tbsp butter or margarine
45 g/1½ oz/ ⅓ cup plain (all-purpose) flour
150 ml/ ¼ pint/ ⅔ cup milk
½ tsp ground coriander
90 g/3 oz/1½ cups carrots, grated coarsely
1 tbsp chopped fresh parsley (optional)
salt and pepper

1 Cut 1 of the onions into quarters. Put the chicken carcass, giblets, if available, water, the quartered onion and bouquet garni into a saucepan. Bring to the boil, cover and simmer for about 1 hour, giving an occasional stir.

2 Strain the stock and reserve 1 litre/1¾ pints/4 cups.

3 Remove 90–125 g/3–4 oz/½–¾ cup of chicken trimmings from the carcass and chop finely. If using fresh chestnuts, peel them; if using canned ones, drain well. Finely chop the chestnuts. Chop the remaining onion.

4 Melt the butter or margarine in a saucepan and fry the onion gently until soft. Stir in the flour and cook for a minute or so. Gradually stir in the reserved stock and bring to the boil, stirring.

5 Simmer for 2 minutes, then add the milk, seasoning, coriander, chopped chicken, carrots and chestnuts.

6 Bring back to the boil and simmer for 10 minutes, then stir in the parsley, if using. Adjust the seasoning and serve.

LENTIL & HAM SOUP

SERVES 4-6

250 g/8 oz/1 cup red lentils
1.5 litres/2½ pints/6¼ cups stock or water
2 onions, chopped
1 garlic clove, crushed
2 large carrots, chopped
1 ham knuckle or 175 g/6 oz lean bacon,
  chopped
4 large tomatoes, skinned and chopped
2 fresh or dried bay leaves
250 g/8 oz potatoes, chopped
1 tbsp white wine vinegar
¼ tsp ground allspice
salt and pepper
chopped spring onions (scallions) or
  chopped fresh parsley to garnish

1 Put the lentils and stock or water in a saucepan and leave to soak for 1–2 hours.

2 Add the onions, garlic, carrots, ham knuckle or bacon, tomatoes, bay leaves and seasoning.

3 Bring to the boil, cover and simmer for about 1 hour until the lentils are tender.

4 Add the potatoes and continue to simmer for about 20 minutes until both the potatoes and ham knuckle are tender.

5 Discard the bay leaves. Remove the knuckle and chop about 125 g/ 4 oz/ ¾ cup of the meat and reserve. If liked, press half the soup through a sieve (strainer) or blend in a food processor or blender until smooth. Return to the pan with the rest of the soup.

6 Adjust the seasoning, add the vinegar and allspice and the reserved chopped ham. Simmer gently for a further 5–10 minutes. Serve sprinkled liberally with spring onions (scallions) or chopped parsley.

OXTAIL SOUP

••

SERVES 6

1 oxtail
2 tbsp vegetable oil
2 onions, sliced
2 carrots, sliced
2 celery sticks, sliced
2 litres/3½ pints/2 quarts brown or beef
*   stock*
2 slices bacon, derinded and chopped
1 fresh bouquet garni
45 g/1½ oz/3 tbsp butter or margarine
45 g/1½ oz/6 tbsp plain (all-purpose) flour
1 tbsp lemon juice
3–4 tbsp port (optional)
salt and pepper

1 Cut the oxtail into slices about 5 cm/2 in thick, or ask the butcher to do it for you.

2 Heat the oil in a large saucepan and fry the oxtail until beginning to brown. Add the vegetables and fry for about 5 minutes until well browned. Pour any excess fat from the pan.

3 Add the stock, bacon and bouquet garni and bring to the boil. Skim off any scum from the surface, cover the pan and simmer very gently for 3–4 hours until the meat is very tender. As oxtail is very fatty, it is necessary to skim the soup occasionally during cooking to remove as much fat from the surface as possible.

4 Strain the soup and, if time allows, cool and chill so a layer of fat solidifies on the surface and can easily be lifted off. Alternatively, skim off excess fat from the surface with kitchen paper.

5 Remove the meat from the bones and chop it neatly. If liked, purée the vegetables in a food processor or blender or pass through a sieve (strainer) and place in a clean pan with the strained soup and chopped meat. Reheat gently.

6 Blend the butter or margarine and flour and gradually whisk small pieces into the soup. Simmer until thickened.

7 Add the lemon juice, then the port, if using. Adjust the seasoning and reheat gently.

SPLIT PEA & HAM SOUP

••

SERVES 6

300 g/10 oz/1¼ cups dried yellow split peas
1.75 litres/3 pints/7½ cups water
2 onions, chopped finely
1 small turnip, chopped finely
2 carrots, chopped finely
2–4 celery sticks, chopped finely
1 ham knuckle
1 Bouquet Garni (see page 9)
½ tsp dried thyme
½ tsp ground ginger
1 tbsp white wine vinegar
salt and pepper

1 Thoroughly wash the dried peas under cold running water, then place in a bowl with half the water and leave to soak overnight.

2 Put the soaked peas and their liquor, the remaining water, the onions, turnip, carrots and celery into a large saucepan, then add the ham knuckle, bouquet garni, dried thyme and ginger. Bring slowly to the boil.

3 Remove any scum from the surface of the soup, cover the pan and simmer gently for 2–2½ hours until the peas are very tender.

4 Remove the ham knuckle and bouquet garni. Strip about 125–175 g/4–6 oz/ ¾–1 cup meat from the knuckle and chop it finely.

5 Add the chopped ham and vinegar to the soup and season to taste.

6 Bring back to the boil and simmer for 3–4 minutes. Serve.

VARIATION

If preferred, this soup can be sieved (strained) or blended in a food processor or blender until smooth. You can add more or less any type of vegetable depending on what is available. Leeks, celeriac (celery root), or chopped or canned tomatoes are particularly good.

MULLIGATAWNY SOUP

SERVES 4-6

45 g/1½ oz/3 tbsp butter or margarine
1 large onion, chopped
2 carrots, chopped
2–3 celery sticks, chopped
1 dessert apple, peeled, cored and chopped
1 tbsp plain (all-purpose) flour
1–2 tsp Madras curry powder
1–2 tsp curry paste
½ tsp ground coriander
1.25 litres/2¼ pints/5 cups Beef, Chicken or
   Vegetable Stock (see pages 8-9)
225 g/7 oz can chopped tomatoes
60 g/2 oz/½ cup cooked long grain rice
   (optional)
60–90 g/2–3 oz/ ⅓–½ cup cooked chicken,
   beef or lamb, chopped very finely
salt and pepper
poppadoms to serve (optional)

1 Melt the butter or margarine in a
   large saucepan and fry the onion,
carrots, celery and apple, stirring
occasionally, until just soft and lightly
browned.

2 Stir in the flour, curry powder, curry
   paste and coriander and cook for a
minute or so, stirring all the time.

3 Gradually add the stock and bring to
   the boil, stirring constantly. Add the
tomatoes and plenty of seasoning, cover
the pan and simmer for about 45 minutes
until the vegetables and apple are very
tender.

4 Cool the soup a little, then press
   through a sieve (strainer) or blend in
a food processor or blender until smooth.
Pour into a clean pan.

5 Add the rice, if using, and the
   chicken or meat, adjust the
seasoning and bring to the boil. Simmer
gently for 5 minutes.

6 Serve the soup in warmed bowls,
   with poppadoms, if liked.

FREEZING

Store for only a month or the spices
may cause the soup to taste musty.

LAMB & BARLEY BROTH

SERVES 4

1 tbsp vegetable oil
500 g/1 lb neck of lamb
1 large onion, sliced
2 carrots, sliced
2 leeks, sliced
1 litre/1¾ pints/4 cups vegetable stock
1 bay leaf
few sprigs of fresh parsley
60 g/2 oz/ ⅓ cup pearl barley

1 Heat the oil in a large, heavy-based
   saucepan and add the pieces of
lamb, turning them to seal and brown on
both sides. Lift the lamb out of the pan
and set aside.

2 Add the onion, carrots and leeks to
   the saucepan and cook gently for
about 3 minutes.

3 Return the lamb to the saucepan and
   add the stock, bay leaf, parsley and
pearl barley to the saucepan. Bring to the
boil, then reduce the heat. Cover and
simmer for 1½ –2 hours until the lamb is
tender.

4 Discard the parsley sprigs. Lift the
   pieces of lamb from the broth and
allow them to cool slightly. Remove the
bones and any fat and chop the meat.
Return the lamb to the broth and reheat
gently. Serve the broth in warmed

TIPS

This broth will taste even better if
made the day before, as this allows
the flavours to develop fully. It also
means that any fat will solidify on the
surface so you can then lift it off. Keep
the broth in the refrigerator until
required.

ONE-POT MEAL

For a more substantial meal make
small dumplings and add them to the
soup 20 minutes before serving.

VEGETARIAN STARTERS

These delicious starters demonstrate how good vegetarian food can be tempting enough to convince even a hardened carnivore. There are recipes here for most occasions, from family meals and informal suppers with friends, to special celebrations and elegant dinner parties. If you are out to impress, try the Artichoke Mousse (below) or Spinach Roulade (page 41). And if you have to cater for both vegetarians and non-vegetarians, the Samosas on page 39 are the answer, giving the choice of a vegetarian or tuna filling.

ARTICHOKE MOUSSE

SERVES 6

1 x 425 g/15 oz can artichoke hearts
150 ml/ ¼ pint/ ⅔ cup condensed
    consommé
juice of ½ orange
large pinch of grated nutmeg
4 tbsp warm water
1 sachet gelatine
2 egg whites
300 ml/ ½ pint/1¼ cups Greek-style yogurt
salt and pepper

SALAD:
3 large (bell) peppers, various colours
3 tbsp olive oil
juice of ½ orange
2 tbsp natural yogurt
2 tbsp chopped parsley

1 Drain the artichoke hearts, reserving the liquid. Place the hearts in a food processor with 3 tablespoons of liquid, the consommé, orange juice and nutmeg. Process until finely chopped. Season, pour into a large bowl and set aside.

2 Pour the water into a small bowl and sprinkle on the gelatine. Place the bowl in a pan of simmering water and stir until the crystals have dissolved, then remove and set aside to cool.

3 Whisk the egg whites until they are stiff but not dry.

4 When the gelatine is syrupy and on the point of setting, blend well into the artichoke mixture. Stir in the yogurt, using an up-and-over movement, until thoroughly blended. Fold in the egg whites, using a metal spoon. Pour into a wetted ring mould or 6 individual moulds, cover and chill for at least 3 hours or until set.

5 Heat the grill (broiler) to high and sear the (bell) peppers close to the heat until evenly blackened all round. Plunge into cold water and as soon as they are cool enough to handle peel off the skins. Core and seed, cut into thick strips and leave to cool.

6 Beat together the olive oil, orange juice and yogurt and season. Pour over the (bell) peppers and stir in the chopped parsley.

7 Run a knife around the inside of the moulds and invert on to serving plates, shaking the mould to release it. Pile the salad into the centre of the mould and serve chilled, with crispy bread rolls or black rye bread.

CHEESE, GARLIC & HERB PÂTÉ

SERVES 4

15 g/ ½ oz butter
1 garlic clove, crushed
3 spring onions (scallions), chopped finely
2 tbsp chopped mixed fresh herbs, such as parsley, chives, marjoram, oregano and basil
125 g/4 oz/ ½ cup cream cheese
175 g/6 oz/1½ cups mature Cheddar cheese, grated finely
pepper
4–6 slices of white bread from a medium-cut sliced loaf
mixed salad leaves and cherry tomatoes, to serve

TO GARNISH:
ground paprika
sprigs of fresh herbs

1 Melt the butter in a small frying pan (skillet) and fry the garlic and spring onions (scallions) together gently for 3–4 minutes, until softened. Allow to cool.

2 Put the cream cheese into a large mixing bowl and beat until soft. Then add the garlic and spring onions (scallions). Stir in the herbs, mixing well.

3 Add the Cheddar cheese and work the mixture together to form a stiff paste. Cover and chill until ready to serve.

4 To make the Melba toast, toast the slices of bread on both sides, and then cut off the crusts. Using a sharp bread knife, cut through the slices horizontally to make very thin slices. Cut into triangles and then grill (broil) the untoasted sides lightly.

5 Arrange the mixed salad leaves on 4 serving plates with the cherry tomatoes. Pile the cheese pâté on top and sprinkle with a little paprika. Garnish with sprigs of fresh herbs and serve with the Melba toast.

LEEK & SUN-DRIED TOMATO TIMBALES

SERVES 4

90 g/3 oz angel-hair pasta (cappellini)
30 g/1 oz/2 tbsp butter
1 tbsp olive oil
1 large leek, sliced finely
60 g/2 oz/ ½ cup sun-dried tomatoes in oil, drained and chopped
1 tbsp chopped fresh oregano or 1 tsp dried oregano
2 eggs, beaten
90 ml/3½ fl oz/generous ⅓ cup single (light) cream
1 tbsp grated Parmesan cheese

SAUCE:
1 small onion, chopped finely
1 small garlic clove, crushed
350 g/12 oz tomatoes, peeled and chopped
1 tsp mixed dried Italian herbs
4 tbsp dry white wine
salt and pepper

1 Cook the pasta in plenty of boiling, lightly salted water for about 3 minutes until al dente (just tender). Drain and rinse with cold water to cool quickly.

2 Meanwhile, heat the butter and oil in a frying pan. Fry the leek gently until softened, about 5–6 minutes. Add the tomatoes and oregano, and cook for a 2 minutes. Remove from the heat.

3 Add the leek mixture to the pasta. Stir in the beaten eggs, cream and Parmesan cheese. Season with salt and pepper. Divide between 4 greased ramekin dishes or dariole moulds.

4 Place the dishes in a roasting tin with enough warm water to come halfway up their sides. Bake in a preheated oven at 180°C/350°F/Gas Mark 4 for about 30 minutes, until set.

5 To make the tomato sauce, fry the onion and garlic in the remaining butter and oil until softened. Add the tomatoes, herbs and wine. Cover and cook gently for 20 minutes until pulpy. Blend in a food processor until smooth.

6 Turn out the timbales on to 4 warmed serving plates. Pour over a little sauce. Garnish with oregano sprigs.

BUTTERED NUT & LENTIL DIP

••

SERVES 4

60 g/2 oz/ ¼ cup butter
1 small onion, chopped
90 g/3 oz/ ⅓ cup red lentils
300 ml / ½ pint/1¼ cups vegetable stock
60 g/2 oz/ ½ cup blanched almonds
60 g/2 oz/ ½ cup pine kernels (nuts)
½ tsp ground coriander
½ tsp ground cumin
½ tsp freshly grated root ginger
1 tsp chopped fresh coriander (cilantro)
salt and pepper
sprigs of fresh coriander (cilantro) to
    garnish

TO SERVE:
fresh vegetable crudités
bread sticks

1 Melt half the butter in a saucepan
and fry the onion gently until golden
brown.

2 Add the lentils and vegetable stock.
Bring to the boil, then reduce the
heat and simmer gently, uncovered, for
about 25–30 minutes until the lentils are
tender. Drain well.

3 Melt the remaining butter in a small
frying pan (skillet). Add the almonds
and pine kernels (nuts) and fry them
gently until golden brown. Remove from
the heat.

4 Put the lentils, almonds and pine
kernels (nuts), with any remaining
butter, into a blender or food processor.
Add the ground coriander, cumin, ginger
and fresh coriander (cilantro). Blend
until smooth, about 15–20 seconds.
Alternatively, push the lentils through a
sieve (strainer) to purée them and mix
with the finely chopped nuts, spices and
herbs.

5 Season the dip with salt and pepper
and garnish with sprigs of fresh
coriander (cilantro). Serve with fresh
vegetable crudités and bread sticks.

BITE-SIZED BAJEES

••

MAKES 20

2 heaped tbsp gram flour (chick-pea
    (garbanzo bean) flour)
½ tsp turmeric
½ tsp cumin seeds, ground
1 tsp garam masala
pinch of cayenne
1 egg
1 large onion, quartered and sliced
1 tbsp chopped fresh coriander (cilantro)
3 tbsp breadcrumbs (optional)
oil for deep-frying
salt

SAUCE:
1 tsp coriander seeds, ground
1½ tsp cumin seeds, ground
250 ml/8 fl oz/1 cup natural yogurt
salt and pepper

1 Put the gram flour into a large bowl
and mix in the spices. Make a well
in the centre and add the egg. Stir to form
a gluey mixture. Add the onion and
sprinkle on a little salt. Add the coriander
(cilantro) and stir. If the mixture is not
stiff enough, add the breadcrumbs.

2 Heat the oil for deep-frying over a
medium heat until fairly hot – it
should just be starting to smoke.

3 Push a teaspoonful of the mixture
into the oil with a second teaspoon
to form fairly round balls. The bajees
should firm up quite quickly. Cook in
batches of 8–10. Keep stirring them so
that they brown evenly. Drain on plenty
of paper towels and keep them warm in
the oven until ready to serve.

4 To make the sauce, roast the spices
in a frying pan (skillet). Remove
from the heat and stir in the yogurt.
Season well.

USING HOT OIL

Make sure that the pan and all the
utensils are properly dried before use.
Do not let any water come into contact
with the hot oil or the oil will spit and
splutter, which could be dangerous.

FRIED TOFU (BEAN CURD) WITH PEANUT SAUCE

SERVES 4

500 g/1 lb tofu (bean curd), marinated or
  plain
2 tbsp rice vinegar
2 tbsp sugar
1 tsp salt
3 tbsp smooth peanut butter
½ tsp chilli flakes
3 tbsp barbecue sauce
1 litre/1¾ pints/4 cups sunflower oil
2 tbsp sesame oil

BATTER:
4 tbsp plain (all-purpose) flour
2 eggs, beaten
4 tbsp milk
½ tsp baking powder
½ tsp chilli powder

1 Cut the tofu (bean curd) into
  2.5 cm/1 in triangles. Set aside.

2 Combine the vinegar, sugar and salt
  in a saucepan. Bring to the boil and
then simmer for 2 minutes. Remove from
the heat and add the peanut butter, chilli
flakes and barbecue sauce.

3 To make the batter, sift the flour into
  a bowl, make a well in the centre
and add the eggs. Draw in the flour,
adding the milk slowly. Stir in the baking
powder and chilli powder.

4 Heat both the oils in a deep-fryer or
  large saucepan until a light haze
appears on top.

5 Dip the tofu (bean curd) triangles
  into the batter and deep-fry until
golden brown. Drain on paper towels.

6 Serve with the peanut sauce.

FRYING TOFU

You may find it easier to pick up the
tofu (bean curd) triangles on a fork or
skewer in order to coat them in batter
before placing them in the hot oil.

AUBERGINE (EGGPLANT) DIPPING SAUCE PLATTER

SERVES 4

1 aubergine (eggplant), peeled and cut
  into 2.5 cm/1 inch cubes
3 tbsp sesame seeds, roasted in a dry pan
  over a low heat
1 tsp sesame oil
grated rind and juice of ½ lime
1 small shallot, diced
½ tsp salt
1 tsp sugar
1 red chilli, seeded and sliced
125 g/4 oz/1¼ cups broccoli florets
2 carrots, cut into matchsticks
125 g/4 oz/8 baby corn, cut in half
  lengthways
2 celery sticks, cut into matchsticks
1 baby red cabbage, cut into 8 wedges, the
  leaves of each wedge held together by
  the core

1 Cook the diced aubergine (eggplant)
  in boiling water for 7–8 minutes.

2 Meanwhile, grind the sesame seeds
  with the oil in a food processor or
pestle and mortar.

3 Add the aubergine (eggplant), lime
  rind and juice, shallot, salt, sugar
and chilli in that order to the sesame.
Process, or chop and mash by hand, until
smooth, Check for seasoning before
spooning into a bowl. Serve surrounded
by the broccoli, carrots, baby corn, celery
and red cabbage.

SALTING AUBERGINES

I never salt the aubergine (eggplant)
unless it is particularly large and likely
to be bitter. The Thais never salt
aubergines (eggplants) as theirs are so
fresh and tender.

BUTTER-CRUST TARTLETS WITH FETA CHEESE

SERVES 4

8 slices of bread from a medium-cut large
    loaf
125 g/4 oz/ ½ cup butter, melted
125 g/4 oz Feta cheese, cut into small
    cubes
4 cherry tomatoes, cut into wedges
8 stoned (pitted) black or green olives,
    halved
8 quail's eggs, hard-boiled
2 tbsp olive oil
1 tbsp wine vinegar
1 tsp wholegrain mustard
pinch of caster (superfine) sugar
salt and pepper
sprigs of parsley to garnish

1 Remove the crusts from the slices of
    bread. Trim the bread into squares
and flatten each piece with a rolling pin.

2 Brush the pieces of bread with
    melted butter, and then arrange them
in bun or muffin tins. Press a piece of
crumpled foil into each bread case to
secure in place. Bake in a preheated oven
at 190°C/375°F/Gas Mark 5 for about 10
minutes, or until crisp and browned.

3 Meanwhile, mix together the Feta
    cheese, tomatoes and olives. Shell
the eggs and quarter them. Mix together
the olive oil, vinegar, mustard and sugar.
Season with salt and pepper.

4 Remove the bread cases from the
    oven and discard the foil. Leave
to cool.

5 Just before serving, fill the cooked
    bread cases with the cheese and
tomato mixture. Arrange the eggs on top
and spoon over the dressing. Garnish
with sprigs of parsley.

BITE-SIZE

To make party canapés and nibbles,
the bread can be cut into smaller
pieces and used to line mini muffin
tins. They can then be filled with
mixtures of your choice.

FIERY SALSA WITH TORTILLA CHIPS

SERVES 6

2 small red chillies
1 tbsp lime or lemon juice
2 large ripe avocados
5 cm/2 in piece of cucumber
2 tomatoes, peeled
1 small garlic clove, crushed
few drops of Tabasco sauce
salt and pepper
lime or lemon slices to garnish
tortilla chips to serve

1 Remove and discard the stem and
    seeds from 1 chilli. Chop very finely
and place in a mixing bowl. To make a
chilli 'flower' for garnish, slice the
remaining chilli from the stem to the tip
several times without removing the stem.
Place in a bowl of cold water, so that the
'petals' open out.

2 Add the lime or lemon juice to the
    mixing bowl. Halve, stone (pit) and
peel the avocados. Add to the mixing
bowl and mash with a fork. (The lime or
lemon juice prevents the avocado from
turning brown.)

3 Chop the cucumber and tomatoes
    finely and add to the avocado
mixture with the crushed garlic.

4 Season the dip to taste with Tabasco
    sauce, salt and pepper.

5 Transfer the dip to a serving bowl.
    Garnish with slices of lime or lemon
and the chilli flower. Put the bowl on a
large plate, surround with tortilla chips
and serve.

CHILLIES

If you're not keen on hot, spicy
flavours, make a milder version by
omitting the chillies and Tabasco
sauce. Take care when handling fresh
chillies, as they can irritate the skin.
Prepare them quickly and wash your
hands afterwards. Be careful to avoid
touching your eyes during preparation.

CRISPY-FRIED VEGETABLES WITH HOT & SWEET DIPPING SAUCE

SERVES 4

vegetable oil, for deep-frying
500 g/1 lb selection of vegetables, such as
cauliflower, broccoli, mushrooms,
courgettes (zucchini), (bell) peppers
and baby corn, cut into even-sized
pieces

BATTER:
125 g/4 oz/1 cup plain (all-purpose) flour
½ tsp salt
1 tsp caster (superfine) sugar
1 tsp baking powder
3 tbsp vegetable oil
200 ml/7 fl oz/scant 1 cup warm water

SAUCE:
6 tbsp light malt vinegar
2 tbsp Thai fish sauce or light soy sauce
2 tbsp water
1 tbsp soft brown sugar
pinch of salt
2 garlic cloves, crushed
2 tsp grated fresh root ginger
2 red chillies, deseeded and chopped finely
2 tbsp chopped fresh coriander (cilantro)

1 To make the batter, sift the flour, salt, sugar and baking powder into a large bowl. Add the oil and most of the water. Whisk together to make a smooth batter, adding extra water to give it the consistency of single cream. Chill for 20–30 minutes.

2 Meanwhile, make the sauce. Heat the vinegar, fish sauce or soy sauce, water, sugar and salt until boiling. Remove from the heat and leave to cool.

3 Mix together the garlic, ginger, chillies and coriander (cilantro) in a small serving bowl. Add the cooled vinegar mixture and stir together.

4 Heat the vegetable oil for deep-frying in a wok or deep-fat fryer. Dip the prepared vegetables in the batter and fry them, a few at a time, until crisp and golden – about 2 minutes. Drain on paper towels.

5 Serve the vegetables accompanied by the dipping sauce.

TOFU & VEGETABLE MINI-KEBABS

SERVES 6

300 g/10 oz smoked tofu, cut into cubes
1 large red and 1 large yellow (bell)
pepper, deseeded and cut into small
squares
175 g/6 oz button mushrooms, wiped
1 small courgette (zucchini), sliced
finely grated rind and juice of 1 lemon
3 tbsp olive oil
1 tbsp chopped parsley
1 tsp caster (superfine) sugar
salt and pepper
sprigs of parsley to garnish

SAUCE:
125 g/4 oz/1 cup cashew nuts
15 g/1/2 oz/1 tbsp butter
1 garlic clove, crushed
1 shallot, chopped finely
1 tsp ground coriander
1 tsp ground cumin
1 tbsp caster (superfine) sugar
1 tbsp desiccated (shredded) coconut
150 ml / ¼ pint/ ⅔ cup natural yogurt

1 Thread the tofu cubes, (bell) peppers, mushrooms and courgettes (zucchini) on to bamboo satay sticks. Arrange them in a shallow dish.

2 Mix together the lemon rind and juice, oil, parsley and sugar. Season well with salt and pepper. Pour over the kebabs, and brush them with the mixture. Leave for 10 minutes.

3 To make the sauce, scatter the cashew nuts on to a baking sheet and toast them until lightly browned.

4 Melt the butter in a saucepan and cook the garlic and shallot gently until softened. Transfer to a blender or food processor and add the nuts, coriander, cumin, sugar, coconut and yogurt. Blend until combined, about 15 seconds. Alternatively, chop the nuts finely and mix with the remaining ingredients.

5 Place the tofu kebabs under a preheated grill (broiler) and cook, turning and basting with the lemon juice mixture, until lightly browned. Garnish with sprigs of parsley, and serve with the cashew nut sauce.

HERB, TOASTED NUT & PAPRIKA CHEESE NIBBLES

SERVES 4

125 g/4 oz Ricotta cheese
125 g/4 oz Double Gloucester (brick)
  cheese, grated finely
2 tsp chopped parsley
60 g/2 oz/ ½ cup chopped mixed nuts
3 tbsp chopped fresh herbs, such as
  parsley, chives, marjoram, lovage and
  chervil
2 tbsp mild paprika
pepper
sprigs of fresh herbs to garnish

1 Mix together the Ricotta and Double
  Gloucester (brick) cheeses. Add the
parsley and pepper, and work together
until combined.

2 Form the mixture into small balls.
  Cover and chill for about 20 minutes
to firm.

3 Scatter the chopped nuts on to a
  baking sheet and place them under
a preheated grill (broiler) until lightly
browned. Take care as they can easily
burn. Leave them to cool.

4 Sprinkle the nuts, herbs and paprika
  into 3 separate small bowls. Divide
the cheese balls into 3 equal piles and
then roll 1 quantity in the nuts, 1 quantity
in the herbs and 1 quantity in the paprika.

5 Arrange on a serving platter. Chill
  until ready to serve, and then
garnish with sprigs of fresh herbs.

CHEESE AND NUTS

You can buy small bags of chopped
mixed nuts at most supermarkets.
Alternatively, buy whole, blanched nuts
and chop them finely in a food
processor or blender.
  To ring the changes, use soft cheese
instead of Ricotta, and mature Cheddar
or Red Leicester instead of the Double
Gloucester (brick) cheese.

GARLICKY MUSHROOM PAKORAS

SERVES 6

175 g/6 oz/1½ cups gram flour
½ tsp salt
¼ tsp baking powder
1 tsp cumin seeds
½-1 tsp chilli powder, to taste
200 ml/7 fl oz/ ¾ cup water
2 garlic cloves, peeled and crushed
1 small onion, peeled and finely chopped
vegetable oil, for deep frying
500 g/1 lb button mushrooms, trimmed
  and wiped
lemon wedges and coriander sprigs, to
  garnish

1 Put the gram flour, salt, baking
  powder, cumin and chilli powder
into a bowl and mix well together. Make
a well in the centre of the mixture and
gradually stir in the water, mixing to form
a batter.

2 Stir the crushed garlic and the
  chopped onion into the batter and
leave the mixture to infuse for 10 minutes.
One-third fill a deep-fat fryer or pan with
vegetable oil and heat to 180°C/350°F or
until hot enough to brown a cube of day-
old bread in 30 seconds. Lower the basket
into the hot oil.

3 Meanwhile, mix the mushrooms into
  the batter, stirring to coat. Remove a
few at a time and place them into the hot
oil. Fry for about 2 minutes or until
golden brown.

4 Remove from the pan with a slotted
  spoon and drain on paper towels
while cooking the remainder in the same
way. Serve hot, sprinkled with coarse salt
and garnished with lemon wedges and
coriander sprigs.

GRAM FLOUR

Gram flour (also known as besan flour)
is a pale yellow flour made from chick
peas. It is now readily available from
larger supermarkets as well as Indian
food shops and some ethnic
delicatessens. Gram flour is also used
to make onion bhajis.

SAMOSAS

MAKES 32

PASTRY:
500 g/1 lb/4 cups plain (all-purpose) flour
½ tsp turmeric
½ tsp salt
100 g/3½ oz/scant ½ cup ghee
about 200 ml/7 fl oz/scant 1 cup milk,
*   mixed with a little lemon juice*

TUNA FILLING:
½ tsp each of turmeric and cayenne
1 tsp ground cumin
1 tsp ground coriander
200 g/7 oz can of tuna, drained
60 g/2 oz/½ cup frozen peas, cooked
60 g/2 oz/½ cup boiled potatoes, diced
salt and pepper

VEGETARIAN FILLING:
250 g/8oz white potatoes, boiled
½x425 g/14 oz can artichoke hearts,
*   drained and puréed*
1 tsp black pepper, ground
2 tsp coriander seeds, ground
1 tsp cumin seeds, ground
½ tsp fenugreek seeds, ground
2 large tomatoes, peeled and deseeded
90g /3 oz/ ½ cup frozen peas, cooked

SAUCE:
6 anchovies
2 tbsp natural yogurt

1 To make the pastry, sift the flour, turmeric and salt into a bowl. Rub in the ghee. Add enough milk to form a fairly soft dough. Cover and set aside.

2 To make the tuna filling, roast the spices in a large frying pan (skillet). Remove from the heat and add the tuna, peas and potatoes. Stir well and season. Continue from step 4.

3 To make the vegetarian filling, mash the potatoes and combine with the artichokes. Roast the spices in a large frying pan (skillet). Remove from the heat and add the potato mixture. Stir well to combine. Chop the tomatoes and carefully fold in with the peas. Season.

4 Roll out the pastry and cut out 16 x 12 cm/5 in circles. Cut each circle in half and put a teaspoonful of filling on each half.

5 Brush the edges with milk and fold each half over to form a triangle. Seal well, and crimp the edges. Bake in a preheated oven at 190°C/375°F/Gas Mark 5.

6 To make the sauce, mash the anchovies, mix with the yogurt and season. Serve with the hot samosas.

COUNTRY CROÛTE

SERVES 4

*4 thin slices of country-style French bread
  (sourdough for example)*
*4 small goat's cheeses or 1 x 125 g/ 4 oz
  chèvre log, sliced into 4 portions*
2–3 tbsp olive or hazelnut oil
1 clove garlic, crushed (optional)
*mixed salad leaves to serve (lamb's lettuce,
  frisée, rocket/arugala, endive and
  radicchio for example)*
*4 tbsp French dressing with herbs (either a
  good quality prepared dressing or your
  own blend)*

1 Heat the oven to 200°C, 400°F, Gas
  Mark 6. Place the slices of bread on
a lightly greased baking sheet and top
each with a whole small goat's cheese or
thick slice of chèvre log.

2 Mix the oil with the crushed garlic, if
  used, then drizzle over the cheese
and bread.

3 Bake in the oven for about 10–15
  minutes or until the cheese bubbles
and browns on top.

4 Meanwhile, toss the salad leaves in
  the dressing and divide between
four individual serving plates.

5 Top each serving of salad with a
  freshly baked croûte and serve while
still warm.

6 A supply of croûtes can be kept in
  reserve in the freezer for later use.
Drain the fried croûtes on absorbent
paper and then pack them, interleaved
with greaseproof or waxed paper, in a
double layer of freezer wrap. Warm
thoroughly when needed.

MARINATED COUNTRY MUSHROOMS

SERVES 4

500 g/1 lb button mushrooms
4 tbsp olive oil
4 tbsp sunflower oil
2 garlic cloves, crushed
1 tbsp wholegrain mustard
good pinch of sugar
2 tbsp white wine vinegar
*1 tbsp chopped fresh tarragon or 1 tsp
  dried tarragon*
2–3 tbsp soured cream
salt and pepper
mixed salad leaves
crisply fried bacon, crumbled (optional)

CROUTONS:
3 slices white bread
about 4 tbsp olive oil
1 garlic clove, crushed

1 Trim the mushrooms, cutting the
  stems off level with the caps. Wipe
the mushrooms and place in a large bowl.
If the mushrooms are large, halve or
quarter them.

2 Whisk together the olive and
  sunflower oils, garlic, mustard, sugar,
seasoning and vinegar until completely
emulsified, then add the tarragon.

3 Pour the dressing over the
  mushrooms, toss them thoroughly in
the dressing and leave to marinate for at
least 30 minutes and up to 2 hours, giving
an occasional stir so they are all well
coated.

4 To make the croûtons, remove the
  crusts from the bread and cut it into
1 cm/ ½ in cubes. Heat the oil with the
garlic in a frying pan (skillet) and fry the
bread cubes for a few minutes until
golden brown. Drain thoroughly on paper
towels.

5 Drain the mushrooms, reserving the
  marinade. Mix 3 tablespoons of the
marinade with the soured cream and
season to taste.

6 Arrange the salad leaves on
  individual serving plates and spoon
the mushrooms on top. Spoon the
dressing over the mushrooms, then
sprinkle with the croûtons and bacon.

SPINACH ROULADE

SERVES 4-6

500 g/1 lb small spinach leaves
2 tbsp water
4 eggs, separated
½ tsp ground nutmeg
salt and pepper
300 ml/ ½ pint/1¼ cups tomato sauce
to serve

FILLING:
175 g/6 oz small broccoli florets
30 g/1 oz/ ¼ cup freshly grated Parmesan
cheese
175 g/6 oz/1½ cups grated Mozzarella
cheese

1 Wash the spinach and pack, still wet, into a large saucepan. Add the water. Cover with a tight-fitting lid and cook over a high heat for 4–5 minutes until reduced and soft. Drain thoroughly, squeezing out excess water. Chop finely and pat dry with paper towels.

2 Mix the spinach with the egg yolks, seasoning and nutmeg. Whisk the egg whites until very frothy but not too stiff, and fold into the spinach mixture.

3 Grease and line a 32 x 23 cm/13 x 9 in Swiss roll tin. Spread the mixture in the tin and smooth the top. Bake in a preheated oven at 220°C/ 425°F/Gas Mark 7 for 12–15 minutes until firm and golden.

4 Meanwhile, cook the broccoli in boiling water for 4–5 minutes until just tender. Drain and keep warm.

5 Sprinkle a sheet of baking parchment with Parmesan. Turn the cooked base on to the paper and peel away the lining paper. Sprinkle the base with Mozzarella and top with broccoli.

6 Hold one end of the paper and carefully roll up the spinach base like a Swiss roll. Heat the tomato sauce and spoon on to 4 warmed serving plates. Slice the roulade and place on top of the sauce.

POTATO GNOCCHI WITH GARLIC & HERB SAUCE

SERVES 4-6

1 kg/2 lb old potatoes, cut into 1 cm/ ½ in
pieces
60 g/2 oz/ ¼ cup butter or margarine
1 egg, beaten
300 g/10 oz/2½ cups plain (all-purpose)
flour
salt

SAUCE:
120 ml/4 fl oz/ ½ cup olive oil
2 garlic cloves, chopped very finely
1 tbsp chopped fresh oregano
1 tbsp chopped fresh basil
salt and pepper

1 Cook the potatoes in boiling salted water for about 10 minutes or until tender. Drain well.

2 Press the hot potatoes through a sieve (strainer) into a large bowl. Add 1 teaspoon of salt, the butter or margarine, egg and 150 g/5 oz/1¼ cups of the flour. Mix well to bind together.

3 Turn on to a lightly floured surface and knead, gradually adding the remaining flour, until a smooth, soft, slightly sticky dough is formed.

4 Flour the hands and roll the dough into 2 cm/ ¾ in thick rolls. Cut into 1 cm/ ½ in pieces. Press the top of each one with the floured prongs of a fork and spread out on a floured tea towel (dish cloth).

5 Bring a large saucepan of salted water to a simmer. Add the gnocchi and cook in batches for 2–3 minutes until they rise to the surface.

6 Remove with a perforated spoon and put in a warmed, greased serving dish. Cover and keep warm.

7 To make the sauce, put the oil, garlic and seasoning in a saucepan and cook gently, stirring, for 3–4 minutes until the garlic is golden. Remove from the heat and stir in the herbs. Pour over the gnocchi and serve immediately.

TEMPURA-STYLE TOFU (BEAN CURD) & VEGETABLES

SERVES 4

125 g/4 oz baby courgettes (zucchini)
125 g/4 oz baby carrots
125 g/4 oz baby sweetcorn
125 g/4 oz baby leeks
2 baby aubergines (eggplant)
250 g/8 oz tofu (bean curd)
vegetable oil for deep-frying
julienne strips of carrot, ginger root and
*   baby leek to garnish*
noodles to serve

BATTER:
2 egg yolks
300 ml/ ½ pint/1¼ cups water
250 g/8 oz/2 cups plain (all-purpose) flour

DIPPING SAUCE:
5 tbsp mirin or dry sherry
5 tbsp Japanese soy sauce
2 tsp clear honey
1 garlic clove, crushed
1 tsp grated ginger root

1 Slice the courgettes (zucchini) and carrots in half lengthways. Trim the sweetcorn. Trim the leeks at both ends. Quarter the aubergines (eggplant).

2 Cut the tofu (bean curd) into 2.5 cm/1 in cubes.

3 To make the batter, mix the egg yolks with the water. Sift in 175 g/ 6 oz/1½ cups of the flour and beat with a balloon whisk to form a thick batter. Don't worry if there are any lumps. Heat the oil for deep-frying to 190°C/375°F or until a cube of bread browns in 30 seconds.

4 Place the remaining flour on a large plate and toss the vegetables and tofu (bean curd) until lightly coated.

5 Dip the tofu (bean curd) in the batter and deep-fry for 2–3 minutes until lightly golden. Drain on paper towels and keep warm.

6 Dip the vegetables in the batter and deep-fry a few at a time for 3–4 minutes until golden. Drain and place on a warmed serving plate.

7 To make the dipping sauce, mix all the ingredients together. Serve with the vegetables and tofu (bean curd), accompanied with noodles and garnished with julienne strips of vegetables.

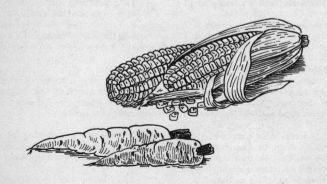

SPICY BITES

•••

SERVES 4

SPICED NUTS:
125 g/4 oz/1 cup mixed nuts, such as
*   peanuts, cashews and blanched*
*   almonds*
1 dried red chilli
1 tsp sunflower oil
1 garlic clove
½ tsp salt
1 tsp garam masala
½ tsp clear honey

1 Cook the nuts in a dry, heavy-based pan over a moderate heat until the oil comes off, about 5 minutes.

2 Add the remaining ingredients except the honey, and cook for a further 3 minutes, stirring frequently. Add the honey and cook for 2 minutes.

3 Remove from the heat, turn into a serving dish and serve.

DEEP-FRIED COURGETTES (ZUCCHINI)
125 g/4 oz/1 cup plain (all-purpose) flour
½ tsp each turmeric and cayenne
150 ml/1/4 pint/ ⅔ cup water
2 eggs
vegetable oil

1 Sift the flour and spices together, Add the water, eggs and 1 tablespoon oil. Whisk until smooth.

2 Heat some oil in a wok. Dip the batons into the batter, and drop into the oil. When evenly cooked, remove and drain on paper towels.

MUSSEL MORSELS:
1 kg/2 lb small mussels, scrubbed
3 tbsp mayonnaise
1 tsp garam masala
½ red chilli, deseeded and chopped finely
2 spring onions (scallions), chopped finely
45 g/1½ oz/ ¾ cup white breadcrumbs
salt

1 Put a little water in the bottom of a large pan. Discard any mussels that are not firmly closed. Add the mussels and cover the pan. Set over a high heat and leave for 5 minutes; do not uncover.

2 Drain the mussels and discard any unopened ones. Remove the shells and reserve.

3 Chop the mussel meat finely. Stir the mayonnaise into the mussel meat. Add the remaining ingredients and season to taste. Spoon the mixture back into the shells, and arrange on a plate.

BRUSCHETTA

•••••••••••••••••••••••••••••••••••

SERVES 4

60 g/2 oz/ ¼ cup dry-pack sun-dried
   tomatoes
300 ml/ ½ pint/1¼ cups boiling water
35 cm/14 in long Granary or wholemeal
   (whole wheat) stick of French bread
1 large garlic clove, halved
30 g/1 oz/ ¼ cup pitted black olives in
   brine, drained and quartered
2 tsp olive oil
2 tbsp chopped fresh basil
45 g/1½ oz/ ⅓ cup grated low fat Italian
   Mozzarella cheese
salt and pepper
fresh basil leaves to garnish

1 Place the sun-dried tomatoes in a heatproof bowl and pour over the boiling water. Set aside for 30 minutes to soften. Drain well and pat dry with paper towels. Slice into thin strips and set aside.

2 Trim and discard the ends from the bread and cut into 12 slices. Arrange on a grill (broiler) rack and place under a preheated hot grill (broiler) and cook for 1–2 minutes on each side until lightly golden.

3 Rub both sides of each piece of bread with the cut sides of the garlic. Top with strips of sun-dried tomato and olives.

4 Brush lightly with olive oil and season well. Sprinkle with the basil and Mozzarella cheese and return to the grill (broiler) for 1–2 minutes until the cheese is melted and bubbling. Transfer to a warmed serving platter and garnish with fresh basil.

VARIATIONS

Sun-dried tomatoes give a rich, full flavour to this dish, but thinly sliced fresh tomatoes can be used instead.

Use dry-packed sun-dried tomatoes, as these have no added oil. If the only type available are packed in oil, drain them, rinse well in warm water and drain again on paper towels to remove as much oil as possible.

STEAMED VEGETABLES WITH HOT TAHINI & GARLIC DIP

•••••••••••••••••••••••••••••••••••

SERVES 4

250 g/8 oz small broccoli florets
250 g/8 oz small cauliflower florets
250 g/8 oz asparagus, sliced into 5 cm/2
   in lengths
2 small red onions, quartered
1 tbsp lime juice
2 tsp toasted sesame seeds
1 tbsp chopped fresh chives to garnish

HOT TAHINI & GARLIC DIP:
1 tsp sunflower oil
2 garlic cloves, crushed
½–1 tsp chilli powder
2 tsp tahini paste
150 ml/ ¼ pint/ ⅔ cup low-fat natural
   fromage frais
2 tbsp chopped fresh chives
salt and pepper

1 Line the base of a steamer with baking parchment and arrange the vegetables on top. Bring a wok or large saucepan of water to the boil, and place the steamer on top. Sprinkle with lime juice and steam for 10 minutes.

2 To make the dip, heat the oil in a small non-stick saucepan, add the garlic, chilli powder and seasoning and fry gently for 2–3 minutes until the garlic is softened.

3 Remove from the heat and stir in the tahini paste and fromage frais. Return to the heat and cook gently for 1–2 minutes without boiling. Stir in the chives.

4 Remove the vegetables from the steamer and place on a warmed serving platter. Sprinkle with the sesame seeds and garnish with chopped chives. Serve with the hot dip.

TAHINI

Tahini is an oily paste made from roasted sesame seeds. It has a strong, nutty flavour and a high fat content. A little goes a long way, so use sparingly to keep the fat content down.

PASTA STARTERS

Quick, simple to prepare and highly nutritious, pasta has become increasingly popular with all age-groups. These attractive starters are all easy to make, and could perfectly well double up as a quick snack or light lunch dish, while the Vegetable Pasta Stir-fry (page 49) is substantial enough to serve as a supper dish, with French bread. Two of the recipes – the Chilled Noodles & Peppers (page 47) and the Vegetable & Pasta Salad (page 48) – are ideal starters for a dinner party when you are likely to be short of time, as both can be prepared in advance.

CHICKEN SCALLOPS

SERVES 4

175 g/6 oz short-cut macaroni, or other
   short pasta shapes
3 tbsp vegetable oil, plus extra for
   brushing
1 medium onion, finely chopped
3 rashers unsmoked collar or back bacon,
   rind removed, chopped
125 g/4 oz button mushrooms, thinly
   sliced or chopped
175 g/6 oz/ ¾ cup cooked chicken, diced
175 ml/6 fl oz/ ¾ cup crème fraîche
4 tbsp dry breadcrumbs
60 g/2 oz/ ½ cup Cheddar cheese, grated
salt and pepper
flat-leaved parsley sprigs, to garnish

1 Cook the pasta in a large pan of boiling salted water to which you have added 1 tablespoon of the oil. When the pasta is almost tender, drain in a colander, return to the pan and cover.

2 Heat the grill to medium. Heat the remaining oil in a pan over medium heat and fry the onion until it is translucent. Add the chopped bacon and mushrooms and cook for a further 3-4 minutes, stirring once or twice.

3 Stir in the pasta, chicken and crème fraîche and season.

4 Brush 4 large scallop shells with oil. Spoon in the chicken mixture and smooth to make neat mounds.

5 Mix together the breadcrumbs and cheese and sprinkle over the top of the shells. Press the topping lightly into the chicken mixture, and grill for 4-5 minutes, until golden brown and bubbling. Garnish with parsley, and serve hot.

ALTERNATIVE

If you do not have scallop shells, you can assemble this dish in four small ovenproof dishes, such as ramekin dishes, or in one large one.

SPICY SAUSAGE SALAD

Serves 4

*125g/4 oz small pasta shapes, such as
    elbow tubetti
3 tbsp olive oil
1 medium onion, chopped
2 cloves garlic, crushed
1 small yellow (bell) pepper, cored, seeded
    and cut into matchstick strips
175 g/6 oz spicy pork sausage such as
    chorizo, skinned and sliced
2 tbsp red wine
1 tbsp red wine vinegar
mixed salad leaves, chilled
salt*

1 Cook the pasta in a large pan
    of boiling salted water, adding
1 tablespoon of the oil. When almost
tender, drain it in a colander and set
aside.

2 Heat the remaining oil in a saucepan
    over a medium heat. Fry the onion
until it is translucent, stir in the garlic,
(bell) pepper and sliced sausage and cook
for 3-4 minutes, stirring once or twice.

3 Add the wine, wine vinegar and
    reserved pasta to the pan, stir to
blend well and bring the mixture just to
the boil.

4 Arrange the chilled salad leaves on 4
    individual serving plates and spoon
on the warm sausage and pasta mixture.
Serve at once.

SPAGHETTI WITH RICOTTA CHEESE

Serves 4

*350 g/12 oz spaghetti
3 tbsp olive oil
45 g/1½ oz/3 tbsp butter, cut into small
    pieces
2 tbsp chopped parsley*

*SAUCE:
125 g/4 oz/1 cup freshly ground almonds
125 g/4 oz/ ½ cup Ricotta
large pinch of grated nutmeg
large pinch of ground cinnamon
150 ml/ ¼ pint/ ⅔ cup crème fraîche
120 ml/4 fl oz/ ½ cup hot chicken stock
freshly ground black pepper
1 tbsp pine kernels
coriander leaves, to garnish*

1 Cook the spaghetti in a large pan of
    boiling salted water to which you
have added 1 tablespoon of the oil. When
it is almost tender, drain the pasta in a
colander. Return to the pan and toss with
the butter and parsley. Cover the pan and
keep warm.

2 To make the sauce, mix together the
    ground almonds, Ricotta, nutmeg,
cinnamon and crème fraîche to make a
thick paste. Gradually pour on the
remaining oil, stirring constantly until it is
well blended. Gradually pour on the hot
stock, stirring all the time, until the sauce
is smooth.

3 Transfer the spaghetti to a warmed
    serving dish, pour on the sauce and
toss well. Sprinkle each serving with pine
kernels and garnish with coriander leaves.
Serve warm.

TOSSING SPAGHETTI

To toss spaghetti and coat it
thoroughly with a sauce or dressing,
use the 2 largest forks you can find –
special forks are sold in some kitchen
shops just for this purpose. Holding
one fork in each hand, ease the prongs
under the spaghetti from each side
and lift them towards the centre.
Repeat evenly and rhythmically until
the pasta is well and truly tossed.

CHILLED NOODLES & PEPPERS

SERVES 4-6

250 g/8 oz ribbon noodles, or Chinese egg
   noodles
1 tbsp sesame oil
1 red (bell) pepper
1 yellow (bell) pepper
1 green (bell) pepper
6 spring onions (scallions), cut into
   matchstick strips
salt

DRESSING:
5 tbsp sesame oil
2 tbsp light soy sauce
1 tbsp tahini (sesame paste)
4-5 drops hot pepper sauce

1 Preheat the grill (broiler) to medium.
   Cook the noodles in a large pan of
boiling, salted water until they are almost
tender. Drain them in a colander, run cold
water through them and drain thoroughly.
Tip the noodles into a bowl, stir in the
sesame oil, cover and chill.

2 Cook the (bell) peppers under the
   grill (broiler), turning them
frequently, until they are blackened on all
sides. Plunge into cold water, then skin
them. Cut in half, remove the core and
seeds and cut the flesh into thick strips.
Set aside in a covered container.

3 To make the dressing, mix together
   the sesame oil, soy sauce, tahini and
hot pepper sauce.

4 Pour the dressing on the noodles,
   reserving 1 tablespoon, and toss
well. Turn the noodles into a serving dish,
arrange the grilled (bell) peppers over the
noodles and spoon on the reserved
dressing. Scatter on the spring onion
(scallion) strips.

ALTERNATIVE

If you have time, another way of
skinning peppers is to first grill (broil)
them, then place in a plastic bag, seal
and leave for about 20 minutes. The
skin will then peel off easily.

ORIENTAL VEGETABLE NOODLES

SERVES 4

175 g/6 oz/1½ cups green thread noodles
   or multi-coloured spaghetti
1 tsp sesame oil
2 tbsp crunchy peanut butter
2 tbsp light soy sauce
1 tbsp white wine vinegar
1 tsp clear honey
125 g/4 oz daikon (mooli), grated
125 g/4 oz/1 large carrot, grated
125 g/4 oz cucumber, shredded finely
1 bunch spring onions (scallions),
   shredded finely
1 tbsp dry-roasted peanuts, crushed

TO GARNISH:
carrot flowers
spring onion (scallion) tassels

1 Bring a large saucepan of water to
   the boil, add the noodles or
spaghetti and cook according to the
packet instructions. Drain well and rinse
in cold water. Leave in a bowl of cold
water until required.

2 Put the sesame oil, peanut butter,
   soy sauce, vinegar, honey and
seasoning into a small screw-top jar. Seal
and shake well to mix.

3 Drain the noodles or spaghetti well,
   place in a large serving bowl and
mix in half the peanut sauce.

4 Using 2 forks, toss in the daikon
   (mooli), carrot, cucumber and spring
onions (scallions). Sprinkle with crushed
peanuts and garnish with carrot flowers
and spring onion (scallion) tassels. Serve
with the remaining peanut sauce.

NOODLES

There are many varieties of oriental
noodles available from oriental
markets, delicatessens and
supermarkets. Try rice noodles, which
contain very little fat and require little
cooking; usually soaking in boiling
water is sufficient.

VEGETABLE & PASTA SALAD

SERVES 4

2 small aubergines (eggplant), thinly
    sliced
1 large onion, sliced
2 large beef-steak tomatoes, skinned and
    cut into wedges
1 red (bell) pepper, cored, seeded and
    sliced
1 fennel bulb, thinly sliced
2 garlic cloves, sliced
4 tbsp olive oil
175 g/6 oz small pasta shapes, such as
    stars
90 g/3 oz/ ½ cup feta cheese, crumbled
a few basil leaves, torn
salt and pepper
salad leaves, to serve

DRESSING:
5 tbsp olive oil
juice of 1 orange
1 tsp grated orange zest
¼ tsp paprika
4 canned anchovies, finely chopped

1 Place the sliced aubergines
(eggplant) in a colander, sprinkle
with salt and set them aside for about 1
hour to draw out some of the bitter juices.
Rinse under cold, running water to
remove the salt, then drain. Toss on paper
towels to dry.

2 Arrange the aubergines (eggplant),
onion, tomatoes, red (bell) pepper,
fennel and garlic in a single layer in an
ovenproof dish, sprinkle on 3 tablespoons
of the olive oil and season with salt and
pepper. Bake in the preheated oven,
uncovered, for 45 minutes, until the
vegetables begin to turn brown. Remove
from the oven and set aside to cool.

3 Cook the pasta in a large pan of
boiling salted water to which you
have added the remaining olive oil. When
the pasta is almost tender, drain it in a
colander, then transfer to a bowl.

4 To make the dressing, mix together
the olive oil, orange juice, orange
zest and paprika. Stir in the finely
chopped anchovies and season with
pepper. Pour the dressing over the pasta
while it is still hot, and toss well. Set the
pasta aside to cool.

5 To assemble the salad, line a shallow
serving dish with the salad leaves
and arrange the cold roasted vegetables in
the centre. Spoon the pasta in a ring
around the vegetables and scatter over the
feta cheese and basil leaves. Serve at
once.

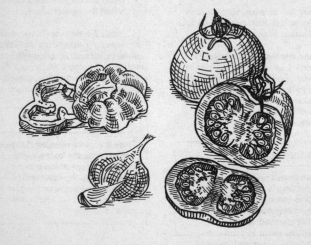

VEGETABLE PASTA STIR-FRY

SERVES 4

*400 g/14 oz wholewheat pasta shells, or
   other short pasta shapes*
1 tbsp olive oil
2 carrots, thinly sliced
125 g/4 oz baby sweetcorn
3 tbsp peanut oil
*2.5 cm/1 in ginger root, peeled and thinly
   sliced*
1 large onion, thinly sliced
1 garlic clove, thinly sliced
3 celery stalks, thinly sliced
*1 small red (bell) pepper, cored, seeded
   and sliced into matchstick strips*
*1 small green (bell) pepper, cored, seeded
   and sliced into matchstick strips*
salt

SAUCE:
1 tsp cornflour (cornstarch)
2 tbsp water
3 tbsp soy sauce
3 tbsp dry sherry
1 tsp clear honey
few drops of hot pepper sauce (optional)

steamed mangetout (snow peas), to serve

1 Cook the pasta in a large pan of
   boiling salted water, adding the
tablespoon of olive oil. When almost
tender, drain the pasta in a colander,
return to the pan, cover and keep the
pasta warm.

2 Cook the sliced carrot and baby
   sweetcorn in boiling, salted water for
2 minutes, then drain in a colander,
plunge into cold water to prevent further
cooking and drain again.

3 Heat the peanut oil in a wok or a
   large frying pan over medium heat
and fry the ginger for 1 minute, to flavour
the oil. Remove with a slotted spoon and
discard.

4 Add the onion, garlic, celery and
   (bell) peppers to the oil and stir-fry
for 2 minutes. Add the carrots and baby
sweetcorn and stir-fry for a further 2
minutes, then stir in the reserved pasta.

5 Put the cornflour (cornstarch) into a
   small bowl and gradually pour on
the water, stirring constantly. Stir in the
soy sauce, sherry and honey.

6 Pour the sauce into the pan, stir well
   and cook for 2 minutes, stirring once
or twice. Taste the sauce and season with
hot pepper sauce if liked. Serve with a
steamed green vegetable such as
mangetout (snow peas).

SALAD STARTERS

Salads make an ideal starter since they always look attractive and are generally quick and easy to prepare. They are not just a summer option either – some of the heartier, warm salads would be ideal for a chilly winter's day. When the thought of a cold salad makes you shiver, try the Goat's Cheese Salad (right) or the Hot Potato & Ham Salad (page 58). Some of the recipes – such as the Hot & Sour Duck Salad (right) or the Potato Skins with Guacamole Dip (page 58) – are more substantial, and could be served as a snack, or a light lunch.

TZATZIKI WITH PITTA (POCKET) BREADS & BLACK OLIVE DIP

SERVES 4

½ cucumber
250 g/8 oz/1 cup thick natural yogurt
1 tbsp chopped fresh mint
salt and pepper
4 pitta (pocket) breads

DIP:
2 garlic cloves, crushed
125 g/4 oz/¾ cup pitted black olives
4 tbsp olive oil
2 tbsp lemon juice
1 tbsp chopped fresh parsley

TO GARNISH:
sprigs of fresh mint
sprigs of fresh parsley

1 To make the tzatziki, peel the cucumber and chop roughly. Sprinkle it with salt and leave it to stand for 15–20 minutes. Rinse with cold water and drain well.

2 Mix the cucumber, yogurt and mint together. Season with salt and pepper and transfer to a serving bowl. Cover and chill for 20–30 minutes.

3 To make the dip, put the crushed garlic and olives into a blender or food processor and blend for 15–20 seconds. Alternatively, chop them very finely.

4 Add the olive oil, lemon juice and parsley to the blender or food processor and blend for a few more seconds. Alternatively, mix with the chopped garlic and olives and mash together. Season with salt and pepper.

5 Wrap the pitta (pocket) breads in foil and place over the barbecue for 2–3 minutes, turning once to warm through. Alternatively, heat in the oven or under the grill (broiler). Cut into pieces and serve with the tzatziki and black olive dip, garnished with sprigs of fresh mint and parsley.

GOAT'S CHEESE SALAD

SERVES 4

3 tbsp olive oil
1 tbsp white wine vinegar
1 tsp black olive paste
1 garlic clove, crushed
1 tsp chopped thyme
1 ciabatta loaf
4 small tomatoes
12 fresh basil leaves
2 x 125 g /4 oz logs goat's cheese
salad leaves including rocket (arugula)
 and radicchio to serve

1 Mix the oil, vinegar, olive paste, garlic and thyme together in a screw-top jar and shake vigorously.

2 Cut the ciabatta in half horizontally then in half vertically to make 4 pieces.

3 Drizzle some of the dressing over the bread then arrange the tomatoes and basil leaves over the top.

4 Cut each roll of goat's cheese into 6 slices and lay 3 slices on each piece of ciabatta.

5 Brush with some of the dressing and place in a preheated oven at 230 C/450 F/Gas Mark 8 for 5-6 minutes until turning brown at the edges.

6 Pour the remaining dressing over the salad leaves and serve with the baked bread.

GOAT'S CHEESE

Goat's cheese can either be fresh, which has a creamy flavour, or matured with a sharper, tangy flavour. Goat's cheeses are usually shaped into small round rolls or pyramids and are sometimes coated in ash.

HOT AND SOUR DUCK SALAD

SERVES 4

2 heads crisp salad lettuce, washed and
 separated into leaves
2 shallots, thinly sliced
4 spring onions (scallions), chopped
1 celery stick, finely sliced into julienne
 strips
5 cm/2 in piece cucumber, cut into
 julienne strips
125 g/4 oz bean-sprouts
1 x 200 g/7 oz can water chestnuts,
 drained and sliced
4 duck breast fillets, roasted and sliced
 (see page 429)
orange slices, to serve

DRESSING:
3 tbsp fish sauce
1½ tbsp lime juice
2 garlic cloves, crushed
1 red chilli pepper, seeded and very finely
 chopped
1 green chilli pepper, seeded and very
 finely chopped
1 tsp palm or demerara sugar

1 Mix the lettuce leaves with the shallots, spring onions (scallions), celery, cucumber, bean-sprouts and water chestnuts. Place the mixture on a large serving platter.

2 Arrange the duck breast slices on top of the salad in an attractive overlapping pattern.

3 To make the dressing, put the fish sauce, lime juice, garlic, chillies and sugar into a small pan. Heat gently, stirring constantly. Taste and adjust the piquancy if liked by adding more lime juice, or add more fish sauce to reduce the sharpness.

4 Drizzle the warm salad dressing over the duck salad and serve immediately.

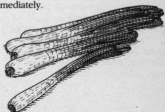

ARTICHOKE & PARMA HAM (PROSCIUTTO) SALAD

SERVES 4

275 g/9 fl oz bottle artichokes in oil,
  drained
4 small tomatoes
30 g/1 oz/ ¼ cup sun-dried tomatoes, cut
  into strips
30 g/1 oz/ ¼ cup black olives, halved and
  stoned (pitted)
30 g/1 oz/ ¼ cup Parma ham (prosciutto),
  cut into strips
1 tbsp chopped fresh basil

FRENCH DRESSING:
3 tbsp olive oil
1 tbsp wine vinegar
1 small garlic clove, crushed
½ tsp Dijon or Meaux mustard
1 tsp clear honey
salt and pepper

1 Drain the artichokes thoroughly, then
  cut them into quarters and place in a
bowl.

2 Cut each tomato into 6 wedges and
  place in the bowl with the sun-dried
tomatoes, olives and Parma ham
(prosciutto).

3 To make the dressing, put all the
  ingredients into a screw-top jar and
shake vigorously until the ingredients are
thoroughly blended.

4 Pour the dressing over the salad and
  toss well together.

5 Transfer to individual plates and
  sprinkle with the basil.

PARMA HAM (PROSCIUTTO)

This Italian ham is first dry cured and
then matured for about a year. Once it
is dried it can then be sliced very thinly
and is served raw. It can be found in
most supermarkets and in Italian
delicatessens.

SEAFOOD WITH TOMATO VINAIGRETTE

SERVES 4-6

1 red (bell) pepper
2 tomatoes
350 g/12 oz packet mixed seafood,
  defrosted and well drained
few sprigs of dill
lemon slices, to garnish

TOMATO VINAIGRETTE:
2 tomatoes, skinned and finely chopped
2 tsp tomato purée (paste)
4 tbsp olive oil
1 tsp wine vinegar
1 garlic clove, crushed
salt and pepper

1 Cut the red (bell) pepper in half and
  remove the seeds. Lay the red (bell)
pepper halves cut-side down on a grill
(broiler) pan and cook gently under a
preheated moderate grill (broiler) until
blackened.

2 Put the (bell) pepper into a plastic
  bag to cool, then remove the skin
and chop the flesh roughly.

3 Cut each tomato into 8 wedges and
  place in a bowl with the (bell)
pepper and drained seafood.

4 To make the vinaigrette, put all the
  ingredients in a bowl and whisk
together.

5 Pour the vinaigrette over the seafood
  and mix thoroughly.

6 Arrange the seafood salad on
  individual plates, sprinkle with dill
sprigs, and garnish with lemon slices.

SEAFOOD

If you cannot get hold of frozen mixed
seafood, buy the fish individually from
the fresh fish counter. Use a mixture of
prawns (shrimp), raw squid prepared
and cut into thin rings, and mussels.
The mussels should be cleaned and
cooked for 4 minutes before being
removed from their shells. A few
poached scallops cut into pieces would
make a really special addition.

MEDITERRANEAN (BELL) PEPPER SALAD

••

SERVES 4

1 onion
2 red (bell) peppers
2 yellow (bell) peppers
3 tbsp olive oil
2 large courgettes (zucchini), sliced
2 garlic cloves, sliced
1 tbsp balsamic vinegar
50 g/1¾ oz anchovy fillets, chopped
30 g/1 oz/ ¼ cup black olives, halved and pitted
1 tbsp chopped fresh basil
salt and pepper

TOMATO TOASTS:
small stick of French bread
1 garlic clove, crushed
1 tomato, skinned and chopped
2 tbsp olive oil
salt and pepper

1 Cut the onion into wedges. Core and deseed the (bell) peppers and cut into thick slices.

2 Heat the oil in a large heavy-based frying pan (skillet). Add the onion, (bell) peppers, courgettes (zucchini) and garlic, and fry gently for 20 minutes, stirring occasionally.

3 Add the vinegar, anchovies, olives and seasoning to taste, mix thoroughly and leave to cool.

4 Spoon on to individual plates and sprinkle with the basil.

5 To make the Tomato Toasts, cut the French bread diagonally into 1 cm/ ½ inch slices.

6 Mix the garlic, tomato and seasoning together, and spread thinly over each slice of bread.

7 Place on a baking sheet, drizzle with the olive oil and bake in a preheated oven at 220°C/425°F/Gas Mark 7 for 5–10 minutes until crisp.

PALM HEART & PAW-PAW (PAPAYA) VINAIGRETTE

••

SERVES 6

1 small paw-paw (papaya), halved and deseeded
400 g/13 oz can of palm hearts
1 bunch watercress
2 tbsp pine kernels (nuts), browned.

LIME & HONEY DRESSING:
grated rind of 1 lime
3 tbsp lime juice
2 tbsp olive oil
2 tbsp clear honey
salt and pepper

CHERVIL DRESSING:
2 tbsp caster (superfine) sugar
1 tbsp boiling water
2 tbsp chopped fresh chervil
2 tbsp olive oil
3 tbsp lemon juice

1 Peel the paw-paw (papaya) thinly and cut lengthways into thin slices. Arrange on individual plates.

2 Drain the can of palm hearts. Cut the palm hearts diagonally into rings and arrange over the paw-paw (papaya).

3 Break the watercress into sprigs and arrange around the edge of the plates.

4 To make the Lime & Honey Dressing, mix the grated lime rind and juice with the olive oil, honey and seasoning to taste.

5 To make the Chervil Dressing, mix the sugar, boiling water and chervil together, then mix in the olive oil and lemon juice.

6 Pour a little of the dressing over each salad and sprinkle the pine kernels (nuts) over the top.

PEAR & ROQUEFORT SALAD

SERVES 4

60 g/2 oz Roquefort cheese
150 ml/ ¼ pint/ ⅔ cup natural yogurt
milk (optional)
2 tbsp chopped chives
few lollo rosso leaves
few radiccio leaves
rocket (arugula) leaves
2 ripe pears
pepper
chopped chives to garnish

1 Mash the cheese with a fork and blend in the yogurt gradually until smooth, adding a little milk if necessary. Add the chives with pepper to taste.

2 Break the lollo rosso into manageable pieces. Arrange on individual plates with the radiccio and rocket (arugula) leaves.

3 Quarter and core the pears, and cut into slices.

4 Arrange some pear slices over the salad on each plate.

5 Drizzle the dressing over the top and garnish with chives.

ROQUEFORT CHEESE

A blue cheese from the southern Massif Central in France, Roquefort is creamy-white with blue-green veins running through it, and has a strong flavour.

If you prefer, you can cut the Roquefort cheese into cubes and add it to the salad leaves (greens) with the pears and pour a herb vinaigrette such as the one on page 15 over the salad.

SMOKED TROUT & APPLE SALAD

SERVES 4

2 orange-red dessert (eating) apples, such
   as Cox's Orange, quartered and cored
2 tbsp French Dressing (see page 56)
½ bunch watercress
1 smoked trout, skinned and boned, about
   175 g/6 oz

HORSERADISH DRESSING:
120 ml/4 fl oz/ ½ cup natural yogurt
½ – 1 tsp lemon juice
1 tbsp horseradish sauce
milk (optional)
salt and pepper

TO GARNISH:
1 tbsp chopped chives
chive flowers (optional)

1 Slice the apples into a bowl and toss in the French dressing to prevent them from browning.

2 Break the watercress into sprigs and arrange on 4 serving plates.

3 Flake the trout into fairly large pieces and arrange between the watercress with the apple.

4 To make the horseradish dressing, whisk all the ingredients together, adding a little milk if too thick, then drizzle over the trout. Sprinkle over the chives and flowers if you have them.

MELBA TOAST

To make Melba toast, toast thinly sliced bread then cut off the crusts and carefully slice in half horizontally using a sharp knife. Cut in half diagonally and place toasted side down in a warm oven for 15–20 minutes until the edges start to curl and the toast is crisp.

CAESAR SALAD

SERVES 4

4 tbsp olive oil
2 tbsp lemon juice
2 garlic cloves, crushed
1 tsp Worcestershire sauce
1 egg
6 quail's eggs
1 large cos (romaine) lettuce
30 g/1 oz block of Parmesan cheese
2 slices bread, crusts removed
4 tbsp corn oil
salt and pepper

1 Mix together the olive oil, lemon juice, garlic and Worcestershire sauce with salt and pepper to taste. Put the single egg in a blender or food processor and blend for 30 seconds. Add the oil mixture gradually through the feeder tube until the dressing thickens slightly.

2 If you do not have a food processor, you can make the dressing using a hand-held electric whisk, or a hand whisk. Put the egg in a small bowl and whisk in the garlic, Worcestershire sauce and seasoning. Gradually whisk in the oil and finally add the lemon juice.

3 Boil the quail's eggs for 5 minutes, then plunge into cold water to cool. Crack the shells and remove the eggs very carefully, then cut the eggs into quarters.

4 Tear the lettuce into manageable-sized pieces and put into a salad bowl with the quail's eggs.

5 Using a potato peeler, shave peelings off the Parmesan cheese.

6 Cut the bread into 5 mm/ ¼ in cubes and fry in the corn oil until golden. Drain well on paper towels.

7 Pour the dressing over the salad and toss thoroughly, then sprinkle the croûtons and Parmesan shavings over the top.

SPINACH & BACON SALAD

SERVES 4

250 g/8 oz young spinach leaves
1 avocado
3 tbsp French dressing (see page 56)
2 slices bread, crusts removed
3 tbsp olive oil
175 g/6 oz/5 slices thick back bacon, derinded
1 garlic clove, chopped
1 tbsp cider vinegar

1 Trim the stalks from the spinach and put the leaves into a salad bowl.

2 Halve the avocado and remove the stone (pit) by stabbing it with a sharp knife and twisting it to loosen. Peel the avocado, slice into a small bowl and toss in the French dressing until well coated. Add to the spinach and toss together.

3 Cut the bread into small triangles and fry in the olive oil until golden. Remove from the pan and drain well on paper towels.

4 Cut the bacon into strips.

5 Add the bacon to the pan and cook until it begins to brown, then add the garlic and fry for a further minute. Transfer the bacon to the salad bowl, using a perforated spoon.

6 Add the cider vinegar to the pan and stir to dissolve any juices, then pour over the salad. Sprinkle with the croûtons.

AVOCADOS

When ripe, an avocado should yield to gentle pressure at the pointed end. If you want to ripen them quickly, place them in a fruit bowl with ripe bananas. When halved, they will turn brown very quickly, so brush the cut surfaces with lemon juice.

MIXED LEAF SALAD WITH FLOWERS

••

SERVES 6

½ head frisée (chicory)
½ head feuille de chêne (oak leaf lettuce)
    or quattro stagione
few leaves of radiccio
1 head chicory (endive)
30 g/1 oz/ ½ cup rocket (arugula) leaves
few sprigs fresh basil or flat-leaf parsley
6 tbsp French Dressing (see right)
flowers of your choice (see below)

1   Tear the frisée (chicory), feuille de
    chêne (oak leaf lettuce) and radiccio
into manageable pieces.

2   Place the salad leaves (greens) into a
    large serving bowl, or individual
bowls if you prefer.

3   Cut the chicory (endive) into
    diagonal slices and add to the bowl
with the rocket (arugula) leaves, basil or
parsley.

4   Pour the dressing over the salad and
    toss thoroughly.

5   Scatter a mixture of flowers over the
    top of the salad.

EDIBLE FLOWERS

Violas, rock geraniums, nasturtiums,
chive flowers and pot marigolds add
vibrant colours and a sweet flavour to
any salad, and will turn this simple
salad into an unusual dish. Use it as a
centrepiece at a dinner party, or to
liven up a simple everyday meal.

ROCKET (ARUGULA)

The young green leaves of this plant
have a distinct warm, peppery flavour
and are delicious used in green salads.
It is extremely easy to grow and once
you have sown it in the garden or
greenhouse you will always have
plenty, as it re-seeds itself all over the
place!

CHICORY (ENDIVE) & AVOCADO SALAD

••

SERVES 4

1 pink grapefruit
1 avocado
1 packet lamb's lettuce (corn salad),
    washed thoroughly
2 heads chicory (endive), sliced
    diagonally
1 tbsp chopped fresh mint

FRENCH DRESSING:
3 tbsp olive oil
1 tbsp wine vinegar
1 small garlic clove, crushed
½ tsp Dijon or Meaux mustard
1 tsp clear honey
salt and pepper

1   Peel the grapefruit with a serrated-
    edge knife.

2   Cut the grapefruit into segments by
    cutting between the membranes.

3   To make the French dressing, put all
    the ingredients into a screw-top jar
and shake vigorously.

4   Halve the avocado and remove the
    stone (pit) by stabbing the stone
(pit) with a sharp knife and twisting to
loosen. Remove the skin.

5   Cut the avocado into small slices,
    put into a bowl and toss in the
French dressing.

6   Remove any stalks from the lamb's
    lettuce (corn salad) and put into a
bowl with the grapefruit, chicory (endive)
and mint.

7   Add the avocado and 2 tablespoons
    of the French dressing. Toss well
and transfer to serving plates.

LAMB'S LETTUCE (CORN SALAD)

This is so called because the shape of
its dark green leaves resembles a
lamb's tongue. It is also known as corn
salad and the French call it mâche.

ROCKET (ARUGULA) & ORANGE SALAD WITH LEMON DRESSING

SERVES 4

1 Frillice or frisée lettuce (chicory)
2 oranges
1 avocado, halved and stoned (pitted)
30 g/1 oz/ ¼ cup pine kernels (nuts)
30 g/1 oz/ ½ cup rocket (arugula) leaves

LEMON DRESSING:
finely grated rind of ½ lemon
2 tbsp lemon juice
2 tbsp olive oil
1 tsp clear honey
salt and pepper

1 Tear the lettuce into manageable pieces and place in a salad bowl.

2 Remove the pith and rind from the oranges and cut the flesh into segments. Put into flesh into the salad bowl.

3 Peel the avocado and cut into slices. Put the slices into the salad bowl.

4 Heat a heavy-based frying pan (skillet), add the pine kernels (nuts) and cook until they are golden, shaking the pan constantly.

5 Whisk all the dressing ingredients together with seasoning to taste.

6 Add the rocket (arugula) leaves to the salad bowl, pour over the dressing and toss thoroughly.

STONING (PITTING) AN AVOCADO

To stone (pit) an avocado, cut through to the stone (pit) lengthways then twist the two halves against each other to separate. Chop into the stone (pit) with a sharp knife so that it sticks in firmly then twist sharply; this will release the stone (pit), which will come away with the knife.

SALADE FRISÉE WITH NASTURTIUMS

SERVES 4

½ head frisée (chicory)
250 g/8 oz packet lamb's lettuce (corn salad), washed thoroughly
2 slices bread, crusts removed
4 tbsp corn oil for frying
nasturtium flowers

FRENCH DRESSING:
3 tbsp olive oil
1 tbsp wine vinegar
1 small garlic clove, crushed
½ tsp Dijon or Meaux mustard
1 tsp clear honey
salt and pepper

1 Tear the frisée (chicory) into manageable pieces and put into a bowl.

2 Trim the roots of the lamb's lettuce (corn salad) and add to the bowl.

3 Cut the bread into 10 mm/ ½ in cubes. Heat the corn oil in a frying-pan (skillet).

4 Fry the cubes of bread until golden brown. Remove from the pan and drain well on paper towels.

5 To make the French dressing, put all the ingredients in a screw-top jar and shake vigorously until blended. Pour 4 tablespoons of dressing over the salad and toss thoroughly.

6 Sprinkle the croûtons over the salad and arrange the nasturtium flowers on top.

TIPS

It is easier to cut bread into neat cubes if it is half-frozen. You can use either white or brown bread for croûtons.

For a slightly different dressing, add 1 tablespoon of chopped herbs such as chives and mint.

Nasturtium flowers have a peppery bite that enhances the flavour of any green salad. Nasturtiums are worth cultivating both for the leaves and flowers.

HOT POTATO & HAM SALAD

SERVES 4

175 g/6 oz smoked ham
500 g /1 lb salad potatoes
6 spring onions (scallions), white and
*   green parts sliced*
3 pickled dill cucumbers, sliced
4 tbsp mayonnaise
4 tbsp thick natural yogurt
2 tbsp chopped fresh dill
salt

1 Cut the ham into 3.5 cm/1½ in long strips

2 Cut the potatoes into 1 cm / ½ in cubes and cook in boiling salted water for 8 minutes until tender.

3 Drain the potatoes and return to the pan with the spring onions (scallions), ham and cucumber.

4 Mix in the mayonnaise, yogurt and dill and stir until the potatoes are coated.

5 Turn onto a warm dish.

POTATO SKINS WITH GUACAMOLE DIP

SERVES 4

4 x 250 g/8 oz baking potatoes
2 tsp olive oil
coarse sea salt and pepper
chopped fresh chives to garnish

GUACAMOLE DIP:
175 g/6 oz ripe avocado
1 tbsp lemon juice
2 ripe, firm tomatoes, chopped finely
1 tsp grated lemon rind
100 g/3½ oz/ ½ cup medium-fat soft cheese
*   with herbs and garlic*
4 spring onions (scallions), chopped finely
a few drops of Tabasco sauce
salt and pepper

1 Bake the potatoes directly on the oven shelf in a preheated oven at 200°C/400°F/Gas Mark 6 for 1¼ hours until tender. Remove from the oven and allow to cool for 30 minutes. Reset the oven to 220°C/425°F/Gas Mark 7.

2 Halve the potatoes lengthwise and scoop out 2 tablespoons of the flesh from the middle of each potato. Slice in half again. Place on a baking sheet and brush the flesh side lightly with oil. Sprinkle with salt and pepper. Bake for a further 25 minutes until golden and crisp.

3 Meanwhile make the guacamole dip. Halve the avocado and discard the stone (pit). Peel off the skin and mash the flesh with the lemon juice.

4 Transfer to a large bowl and mix with the remaining ingredients. Cover and chill until required.

5 Drain the potato skins on paper towels and transfer to a warmed serving platter. Garnish with chives. Pile the avocado mixture into a serving bowl.

TIPS

Mash the leftover potato flesh with natural yogurt and seasoning, and spoon the mixture onto meat, fish and vegetable fillings.

MEAT, POULTRY & FISH STARTERS

This varied assortment of starters should cater for most tastes. For heary appetites, try the traditional Potted Meat (page 60) which is served with crusty bread. For a touch of the exotic, serve Pork Satay (page 61) or Kaffir Lime Mussels with Lemon Grass (page 63), or impress your guests with a stunning presentation of Melon with Smoked Salmon Mousse (page 61). Simpler starters that could double as snacks or light lunches include Crab-meat Cakes (page 64) or the Tuna & Anchovy Pâté (page 65).

SPICY CHICKEN & NOODLE SALAD

SERVES 4

1 tsp finely grated fresh ginger root
½ tsp Chinese five-spice powder
1 tbsp plain (all-purpose) flour
½ tsp chilli powder
350 g/12 oz boned chicken breast, skinned and sliced thinly
60 g/2 oz rice noodles
125 g/4 oz/1½ cups Chinese leaves or hard white cabbage, shredded finely
7 cm/3 inch piece of cucumber, sliced finely
1 large carrot, pared thinly
1 tbsp olive oil
2 tbsp lime or lemon juice
2 tbsp sesame oil
salt and pepper

TO GARNISH:
lemon or lime slices
fresh coriander (cilantro) leaves

1 Mix together the ginger, five-spice powder, flour and chilli powder in a shallow mixing bowl. Season with salt and pepper. Add the strips of chicken and roll in the mixture until well coated.

2 Put the noodles into a large bowl and cover with warm water. Leave them to soak for about 5 minutes, then drain them well.

3 Mix together the Chinese leaves or cabbage, cucumber and carrot, and arrange them in a salad bowl. Whisk together the olive oil and lime or lemon juice, season with a little salt and pepper, and use to dress the salad.

4 Heat the sesame oil in a wok or frying pan (skillet) and add the chicken. Stir-fry for 5–6 minutes until well-browned and crispy on the outside. Remove from the wok or frying pan (skillet) with a perforated spoon and drain on paper towels.

5 Add the noodles to the wok or frying pan (skillet) and stir-fry for 3–4 minutes until heated through. Mix with the chicken and pile on top of the salad. Serve garnished with lime or lemon slices and coriander (cilantro) leaves.

TIPS

The easiest way to pare the carrot into fine strips is to use a potato peeler.
A few peanuts or cashew nuts, quickly stir-fried in a little sesame oil, add extra crunch and flavour to this delicious salad.

DUCKLING & RADISH SALAD

SERVES 4

350 g/12 oz boneless duckling breasts,
*   skinned*
2 tbsp plain (all-purpose) flour
1 egg
2 tbsp water
2 tbsp sesame seeds
3 tbsp sesame oil
½ head of Chinese leaves, shredded
3 celery sticks, sliced finely
8 radishes, trimmed and halved
salt and pepper
fresh basil leaves to garnish

DRESSING:
finely grated rind of 1 lime
2 tbsp lime juice
2 tbsp olive oil
1 tbsp light soy sauce
1 tbsp chopped fresh basil

1 Put each duckling breast between sheets of greaseproof paper (baking parchment) or clingfilm (plastic wrap). Use a meat mallet or rolling pin to beat them out and flatten them slightly.

2 Sprinkle the flour on to a large plate and season with salt and pepper. Beat the egg and water together in a shallow bowl, then sprinkle the sesame seeds on to a separate plate. Dip the duckling breasts first into the seasoned flour, then into the egg mixture and finally into the sesame seeds.

3 Heat the sesame oil in a wok or frying pan (skillet) and fry the duckling breasts over a medium heat for about 8 minutes, turning once. Insert a sharp knife into the thickest part – the juices should run clear. Lift them out and drain on paper towels.

4 To make the dressing for the salad, whisk together the lime rind and juice, olive oil, soy sauce and chopped basil. Season with a little salt and pepper.

5 Arrange the Chinese leaves, celery and radish on a serving plate. Slice the duckling breasts thinly and place on top of the salad. Drizzle with the dressing and garnish with fresh basil leaves. Serve at once.

POTTED MEAT

SERVES 4-6

250 g/8 oz cooked beef, lamb or any
*   boneless game or poultry*
125 g/4 oz/ ½ cup butter
1 onion, chopped very finely or minced
1-2 garlic cloves, crushed
2 tbsp sherry or port
about 4 tbsp good stock
good pinch of ground mace, nutmeg or
*   allspice*
pinch of dried mixed herbs
salt and pepper
sprigs of fresh thyme to garnish

TO SERVE:
watercress sprigs
cherry tomatoes or tomato slices or wedges
fingers of toast or crusty bread

1 Remove any skin, gristle and bone from the meat, game or poultry and then finely mince (grind) twice, or finely chop in a food processor.

2 Melt half the butter in a saucepan and fry the onion and garlic gently until soft but only lightly coloured.

3 Stir the meat into the pan, followed by the sherry or port and just enough stock to moisten.

4 Season to taste with salt, pepper, mace and herbs. Press the mixture into a lightly greased dish or several small individual dishes and level the top. Chill until firm.

5 Melt the remaining butter and pour a thin layer over the potted meat. Add a few sprigs of fresh herbs and chill thoroughly so the herbs set in the butter.

6 Serve the potted meat spooned on to plates, or in individual pots, garnished with watercress, tomatoes and fingers of toast or slices of crusty bread.

STORAGE

The potted meat will keep in the refrigerator for 2–3 days but no longer, as it does not contain any preservatives.

PORK SATAY

••

SERVES 4

8 bamboo satay sticks, soaked in warm
*   water*
500 g/1 lb pork fillet (tenderloin)

SAUCE:
125 g/4oz/1 cup unsalted peanuts
2 tsp hot chilli sauce
180 ml/6 fl oz/ ¾ cup coconut milk
2 tbsp soy sauce
1 tbsp ground coriander
pinch of ground turmeric
1 tbsp dark muscovado sugar
salt

TO GARNISH:
fresh flat leaf (Italian) parsley or
*   coriander (cilantro)*
cucumber leaves
red chillies

1 To make the sauce, scatter the
   peanuts on a baking (cookie) sheet
and toast under a preheated grill (broiler)
until golden brown, turning them once or
twice. Leave to cool, then grind them in a
food processor, blender or food mill.
Alternatively, chop them very finely.

2 Put the ground peanuts into a small
   saucepan with all the remaining
sauce ingredients. Heat gently, stirring
constantly. Reduce the heat to very low
and cook gently for 5 minutes.

3 Meanwhile, trim any fat from the
   pork. Cut the pork into small cubes
and thread it on to the bamboo satay
sticks. Place the kebabs on a rack covered
with foil in a grill (broiler) pan.

4 Put half the peanut sauce into a
   small serving bowl. Brush the
skewered pork with the remaining satay
sauce and place under a preheated grill
(broiler) for about 10 minutes, turning
and basting frequently, until cooked.

5 Serve the pork with the reserved
   peanut sauce and garnish with flat
leaf (Italian) parsley or coriander (cilantro)
leaves, cucumber leaves and red chillies.

MELON WITH SMOKED SALMON MOUSSE

••

SERVES 6

3 ripe small Charentais or Ogen melons

SMOKED SALMON MOUSSE:
175 g/6 oz smoked salmon pieces or slices
2–3 spring onions (scallions), trimmed
*   and sliced*
1–2 garlic cloves, crushed
175 g/6 oz/ ¾ cup light cream cheese
2–3 tsp lemon or lime juice
2–4 tbsp natural yogurt or natural
*   fromage frais*
salt and pepper

TO GARNISH:
pitted black olives
sprigs of fresh dill

1 Halve the melons and scoop out the
   seeds. For an attractive finish,
vandyke the edge by making short
slanting cuts into the centre of the melon
using a small sharp knife, creating a
zigzag design round the centre of the
melon.

2 To make the mousse, put the salmon
   pieces into a food processor with the
spring onions (scallions) and garlic, and
work until smoothly chopped.
Alternatively, chop the smoked salmon,
spring onions (scallions) and garlic very
finely, and mix together.

3 Add the cream cheese and process
   again until well blended, or beat into
the chopped salmon mixture. Add lemon
or lime juice to taste and sufficient yogurt
or fromage frais to give a piping
consistency. Season with salt and pepper.

4 Stand each melon half on a small
   plate, cutting a thin sliver off the
base if it will not stand evenly.

5 Put the salmon mousse into a piping
   bag fitted with a large star nozzle
(tip) and pipe a large whirl to fill the
centre of each melon.

6 Garnish each melon half with black
   olives and sprigs of fresh dill. When
prepared, the melons may be chilled for
up to 2 hours before serving.

SMOKED SALMON CHEESECAKE

SERVES 6

90 g/3 oz/6 tbsp butter
200 g/7 oz water biscuits (cookies),
*   crushed*
1 tbsp sesame seeds
salt and pepper

FILLING:
175 g/6 oz smoked salmon pieces, roughly
*   chopped*
grated rind and juice of 1 lemon
250 g/8 oz/1 cup full fat soft cheese
2 eggs, separated
150 ml/ ¼ pint/ ⅔ cup natural yogurt
freshly ground black pepper
4 tbsp warm water
1 sachet gelatine

TOPPING:
150 ml/ ¼ pint/ ⅔ cup Greek-style yogurt
4 thin slices lemon
a few sprigs of fresh dill
12 whole prawns (shrimp) (optional)

1   Grease a loose-bottomed 20 cm/
    8 in cake tin (pan).

2   Melt the butter in a pan. Remove
    from the heat, stir in the biscuit
(cookie) crumbs and sesame seeds and
season. Press the mixture evenly over the
base of the prepared tin (pan) and chill.

3   Process the smoked salmon and
    lemon juice briefly in a food
processor, then turn into a bowl and
beat in the cheese, egg yolks and
yogurt. Season well with pepper.

4   Pour the water into a small bowl
    and sprinkle on the gelatine. Place
the bowl in a pan of simmering water
and stir until the crystals have dissolved.
Remove from the heat and set aside to
cool. When the gelatine is syrupy and
on the point of setting, pour into the
salmon mixture and stir to blend
thoroughly.

5   Whisk the egg whites until stiff but
    not dry. Using a metal spoon, fold
them into the fish mixture until they are
well blended. Pour the filling into the
prepared tin (pan) and level the surface.
Chill for 3-4 hours until set.

6   Lift the cheesecake out of the tin
    (pan), keeping it on the metal
base, and place on a flat serving dish.
Spread the yogurt evenly over the top or
place in a piping bag and pipe swirls.
Cut the lemon slices in quarters and
arrange in pairs to form butterfly shapes
around the rim of the cheesecake .
Arrange the dill sprigs on top and
garnish with the prawns (shrimp), if
using. Serve chilled.

CELLOPHANE NOODLES WITH SHRIMPS & BEAN-SPROUTS

••

SERVES 4

2 tbsp light soy sauce
1 tbsp lime or lemon juice
1 tbsp fish sauce
125 g/4 oz firm tofu (bean curd), cut into chunks
125 g/4 oz cellophane noodles
2 tbsp sesame oil
4 shallots, sliced finely
2 garlic cloves, crushed
1 small red chilli, deseeded and chopped finely
2 celery sticks, sliced finely
2 carrots, sliced finely
125 g/4 oz/ ⅔ cup cooked, peeled (small) shrimps
60 g/2 oz/1 cup bean-sprouts

TO GARNISH:
carrot slices
celery leaves
fresh chillies

1 Mix together the soy sauce, lime or lemon juice and fish sauce in a shallow bowl. Add the tofu (bean curd) cubes and toss them in the mixture. Cover and set aside for 15 minutes.

2 Put the noodles into a large bowl and cover with warm water. Leave them to soak for about 5 minutes, and then drain them well.

3 Heat the sesame oil in a wok or large frying pan (skillet). Add the shallots, garlic and chilli, and stir-fry for 1 minute. Add the celery and carrots, and stir-fry for a further 2–3 minutes.

4 Tip the drained noodles into the wok or frying pan (skillet) and cook, stirring, for 2 minutes, then add the shrimps, bean-sprouts and tofu (bean curd), with the soy sauce mixture. Cook over a medium high heat for 2–3 minutes until heated through.

5 Transfer to a serving dish and garnish with carrot slices, celery leaves and chillies.

KAFFIR LIME MUSSELS WITH LEMON GRASS

••

SERVES 4

750 g/1½ lb live mussels
1 tbsp sesame oil
3 shallots, chopped finely
2 garlic cloves, chopped finely
1 stalk lemon grass
2 Kaffir lime leaves
2 tbsp chopped fresh coriander (cilantro)
finely grated rind of 1 lime
2 tbsp lime juice
300 ml/ ½ pint/1¼ cups hot vegetable stock
crusty bread to serve

TO GARNISH:
sprigs of fresh coriander (cilantro)
lime wedges

1 Using a small sharp knife, scrape the beards off the mussels under cold running water. Scrub them well, discarding any that are damaged or remain open when tapped. Keep rinsing until there is no trace of sand.

2 Heat the sesame oil in a large saucepan and fry the shallots and garlic until softened, about 2 minutes.

3 Bruise the lemon grass, using a meat mallet or rolling pin.

4 Add the lemon grass to the saucepan with the Kaffir lime leaves, coriander (cilantro), lime rind and juice, mussels and stock. Put the lid on the saucepan and cook over a moderate heat so that the mussels steam for 3–5 minutes. Shake the saucepan from time to time.

5 Check that the mussels have opened and discard any that remain shut. Lift them out into 4 warmed soup plates. Boil the remaining liquid rapidly so that it reduces slightly. Remove the lemon grass and Kaffir lime leaves, then pour the liquid over the mussels.

6 Garnish with the fresh coriander (cilantro) and lime wedges, and serve at once with chunks of crusty bread to soak up the juices.

THAI-STYLE SEAFOOD OMELETTE

SERVES 4

4 eggs
3 tbsp milk
1 tbsp fish sauce or light soy sauce
1 tbsp sesame oil
3 shallots, sliced finely
1 small red (bell) pepper, cored, deseeded and sliced very finely
1 small leek, trimmed and cut into matchstick pieces
125 g/4 oz squid rings
125 g/4 oz/⅔ cup cooked peeled prawns (shrimp)
1 tbsp chopped fresh basil
15 g/½ oz/1 tbsp butter
salt and pepper
sprigs of fresh basil to garnish

1 Beat the eggs, milk and fish sauce or soy sauce together.

2 Heat the sesame oil in a wok or large frying pan (skillet) and add all the vegetables. Stir-fry briskly for 2–3 minutes.

3 Add the squid, prawns (shrimp) and chopped basil to the wok or frying pan (skillet). Stir-fry for a further 2–3 minutes, until the squid looks opaque. Season with salt and pepper. Transfer to a warmed plate and keep warm.

4 Melt the butter in a large omelette pan or frying pan (skillet) and add the beaten egg mixture. Cook over a medium-high heat until just set.

5 Spoon the vegetable and seafood mixture in a line down the middle of the omelette, then fold each side of the omelette over. Transfer to a warmed serving dish and cut into 4 portions. Garnish with sprigs of fresh basil and serve at once.

VARIATIONS

Chopped, cooked chicken makes a delicious alternative to the squid.
Use fresh coriander (cilantro) instead of the basil for a change.

CRAB-MEAT CAKES

SERVES 4

90 g/3 oz/generous 1 cup long-grain rice
1 tbsp sesame oil
1 small onion, chopped finely
1 large garlic clove, crushed
2 tbsp chopped fresh coriander (cilantro)
200 g/7 oz can of crab meat, drained
1 tbsp fish sauce or light soy sauce
250 ml/8 fl oz/1 cup coconut milk
2 eggs
4 tbsp vegetable oil
salt and pepper
sliced spring onions (scallions), to garnish

1 Cook the rice in plenty of boiling, lightly salted water until just tender, about 12 minutes. Rinse with cold water and drain well.

2 Heat the sesame oil in a small frying pan (skillet) and fry the onion and garlic gently for about 5 minutes, until softened and golden brown.

3 In a large bowl, mix together the rice, onion, garlic, coriander (cilantro), crab meat, fish sauce or soy sauce and coconut milk. Season with salt and pepper. Beat the eggs together and add to the mixture.

4 Divide the mixture between 8 greased ramekin dishes or teacups and place them in a baking dish or roasting tin (pan) with enough warm water to come halfway up their sides. Place in a preheated oven at 180°C/350°F/Gas Mark 4 for about 25 minutes, until set. Leave to cool.

5 Turn the crab cakes out of the ramekin dishes or teacups. Heat the vegetable oil in a wok or frying pan (skillet) and fry the crab cakes in the oil until golden brown. Drain on paper towels and serve at once, garnished with sliced spring onions (scallions).

PREPARING AHEAD

If you want, you can prepare these crab cakes up to the point where they have been baked. Cool them, then cover and chill, ready for frying when needed.

SALMON MOUSSE

SERVES 6-8

30 g/1 oz/2 tbsp butter or margarine
30 g/1 oz/4 tbsp plain (all-purpose) flour
300 ml/ ½ pint/1¼ cups milk
½ tsp mustard
good pinch of chilli powder
2 tbsp white wine vinegar
2 eggs, separated
300–350 g/10–12 oz cooked salmon
150 ml/ ¼ pint/ ⅔ cup double (heavy) or
   soured cream
4 tsp powdered gelatine
3 tbsp water
salt and pepper
Melba Toast (see page 54) to serve

1 Melt the butter or margarine in a saucepan, stir in the flour and cook for a minute or so. Gradually stir in the milk and bring to the boil. Add the mustard, chilli powder, seasoning and vinegar and simmer for 2 minutes. Beat in the egg yolks and simmer for 1 minute, stirring constantly, then remove from the heat.

2 Flake the salmon, discarding any skin and bones, and stir into the sauce.

3 Lightly whip the double (heavy) cream, if using, until thick but not too stiff and fold this or the soured cream into the sauce.

4 Dissolve the gelatine in the water in a small bowl over a saucepan of hot water, or in a microwave oven set on Medium power. Cool slightly then stir evenly through the salmon mixture. Leave until on the point of setting.

5 Beat the egg whites until stiff then fold into the salmon mixture. Pour into an oiled fish mould, a serving dish or individual dishes. Chill until set.

6 If using a dish or individual dishes, garnish the top with slices of olive and cucumber. If the mousse has been set in a mould, loosen it from the mould and turn out carefully on to a flat dish. Serve with Melba Toast.

TUNA & ANCHOVY PÂTÉ WITH MELBA CROUTONS

SERVES 6

PÂTÉ:
50 g/1¾ oz can anchovy fillets, drained
about 400 g/13 oz can tuna fish in brine,
   drained
175 g/6 oz/ ¾ cup half-fat cottage cheese
125 g/4 oz/ ½ cup skimmed milk soft
   cheese
1 tbsp horseradish relish
½ tsp grated orange rind
white pepper

MELBA CROUTONS:
4 slices, thick sliced wholemeal
   (wholewheat) bread

1 To make the pâté, separate the anchovy fillets and pat well with paper towels to remove all traces of oil.

2 Place the anchovy fillets and remaining pâté ingredients into a blender or food processor. Blend for a few seconds until smooth. Alternatively, finely chop the anchovy fillets and flake the tuna, then beat together with the remaining ingredients; this will make a more textured pâté.

3 Transfer to a mixing bowl, cover and chill for 1 hour.

4 To make the melba croûtons, place the bread slices under a preheated medium grill (broiler) for 2–3 minutes on each side until lightly browned.

5 Using a serrated knife, slice off the crusts and slide the knife between the toasted edges of the bread.

6 Stamp out circles using a 5 cm/ 2 inch round cutter and place on a baking sheet. Alternatively, cut each piece of toast in half diagonally. Bake in a preheated oven at 150°C/300°F/Gas Mark 2 for 15–20 minutes until curled and dry.

7 Spoon the pâté on to serving plates and serve with the freshly baked Melba Croûtons.

BUTTERFLY PRAWNS (SHRIMP)

••

SERVES 2-4

8 wooden skewers
500 g/1 lb or 16 raw tiger prawns
(shrimp), shelled, leaving tails intact
juice of 2 limes
1 tsp cardamom seeds
2 tsp cumin seeds, ground
2 tsp coriander seeds, ground
½ tsp ground cinnamon
1 tsp ground turmeric
1 garlic clove, crushed
1 tsp cayenne
2 tbsp oil
cucumber slices to garnish

1 Soak 8 wooden skewers in water for 20 minutes. Cut the prawns (shrimp) lengthways in half down to the tail, so that they flatten out to a symmetrical shape.

2 Thread a prawn (shrimp) on to 2 wooden skewers, with the tail between them, so that, when laid flat, the skewers hold the prawn (shrimp) in shape. Thread another 3 prawns (shrimp) on to these 2 skewers in the same way. Repeat until you have 4 sets of 4 prawns (shrimp) each.

3 Lay the skewered prawns (shrimp) in a non-porous, non-metallic dish, and sprinkle over the lime juice.

4 Combine the spices and the oil, and coat the prawns (shrimp) well in the mixture.

5 Cover and chill for 4 hours.

6 Cook over a hot barbecue or in a grill (broiler) pan lined with foil under a preheated grill (broiler) for 6 minutes, turning once.

7 Serve immediately, garnished with cucumber and accompanied by a sweet chutney – walnut chutney is ideal.

PRAWNS (SHRIMP) WITH HOT & SWEET DIPPING SAUCE

••

SERVES 4

wooden skewers soaked in warm water for
20 minutes
500 g/1 lb/2½ cups uncooked prawns
(shrimp)
3 tbsp sesame oil
2 tbsp lime juice
1 tbsp chopped fresh coriander (cilantro)
sprigs of fresh coriander (cilantro) to
garnish

SAUCE:
4 tbsp light malt vinegar
2 tbsp Thai fish sauce or light soy sauce
2 tbsp water
2 tbsp light muscovado sugar
2 garlic cloves, crushed
2 tsp grated fresh ginger root
1 red chilli, deseeded and chopped finely
2 tbsp chopped fresh coriander (cilantro)
salt

1 Peel the prawns (shrimp), leaving the tails intact. Remove the black vein that runs along the back of each one, then skewer the prawns (shrimp) on to the wooden skewers.

2 Mix together the sesame oil, lime juice and chopped coriander (cilantro) in a shallow bowl. Lay the skewered prawns (shrimp) in this mixture. Cover and chill for 30 minutes, turning once, so that the prawns (shrimp) absorb the marinade.

3 Meanwhile, make the sauce. Heat the vinegar, fish sauce or soy sauce, water, sugar and salt until boiling. Remove from the heat and leave to cool.

4 Mix together the garlic, ginger, chilli and coriander (cilantro) in a small serving bowl. Add the cooled vinegar mixture and stir together.

5 Place the prawns (shrimp) on a foil-lined grill (broiler) pan under a preheated grill (broiler) for about 6 minutes, turning once and basting often with the marinade, until cooked. Transfer to a warmed serving platter. Garnish with coriander (cilantro) and serve with the dipping sauce.

·2·
Main Dishes

◆

Over one hundred pages of recipes
gives you an enormous choice, including
a variety of vegetarian dishes. Browsing
through, you will find plenty of ideas to
whet the appetite.

◆

PASTA DISHES – INTRODUCTION

Pasta means "paste" or "dough" in Italian, and many of the widely popular pasta dishes have their origins in Italy, where pasta has been produced at least as far back as the 13th century.

Its principal ingredients are modest, though more and more types of fresh and dried pasta are coming on to the market. By far the most widely available commercial type is made from hard durum wheat, milled to form fine semolina grains and then extruded through drums fitted with specially perforated discs. The production methods may not sound inspiring, but the end product certainly is. The wide variety of these discs makes it possible to produce an estimated 600 different pasta shapes and sizes including strands and shells, twists and spirals, rings and tubes.

VARIETIES OF PASTA
You can choose pasta which is made from just the endosperm of the wheat, as most of it is, or from the whole wheat; this type contains more dietary fibre. Other basic types are made from ground buckwheat, which gives the product a greyish colour and distinctively nutty flavour that combines especially well with vegetable and herb sauces; with the addition of spinach paste, which produces an attractive green colour – lasagne verde is a popular example; and with a proportion of tomato paste, which produces a deep coral-like colouring. Pasta all'uovo, which is made with the addition of eggs, is invariably produced in a range of flat shapes and those, too, are available in fresh and dried forms.

COLOURED PASTA
As well as green pasta, coloured with spinach, and red pasta, made with tomato paste, there are other colours available: saffron pasta is an attractive yellow-orange colour, beetroot-coloured pasta is a deep pink, and pasta coloured with squid ink is a dramatic black. You can also buy or make pasta flecked with chopped basil and other herbs.

THE PASTA FAMILY
Pasta is generally divided into three main categories, long and folded pasta, noodles, and short pasta, the group that offers, perhaps, the greatest scope for inspired presentation and recipe variation.

Since dried pasta has a shelf life of up to six months (see the panel on storage) and fresh pasta may be safely frozen for up to six months, it is a good idea to build up your own store cupboard of pasta selections to surprise and delight your family and friends.

Pasta Dictionary
The names of the various types and shapes of pasta have a romantic and evocative ring to them, conjuring up thoughts of warm, sunny climates and rich, herby sauces. But if you are not conversant with the similarities of tagliatelli and tagliarini, or the difference between cappelletti and conchiglie, you can find yourself longing for a translation. This glossary of some of the most popular pasta shapes should help you.

anelli and **anellini rings** small pasta used in soup

bozzoli deeply-ridged, cocoon-like shapes

bucatini long, medium-thick tubes

cappelletti wide-brimmed-hat shapes

INTRODUCTION

cappelli d'angelo "angel's hair", thinner than cappellini

cappellini fine strands of ribbon pasta, usually sold curled into a nest shape

casareccia short curled lengths of pasta twisted at one end

cavatappi short, thick corkscrew shapes

conchiglie ridged shells

conchigliette little shells used in soup

cornetti ridged shells

cresti di gallo curved shapes, resembling cocks' combs

ditali, ditalini short tubes

eliche loose spiral shapes

elicoidali short, ridged tubes

farfalle butterflies

fedeli, fedelini fine tubes twisted into "skeins"

festonati short lengths, like garlands

fettuccine ribbon pasta, narrower than tagliatelle

fiochette, fiochelli small bow shapes

frezine broad, flat ribbons

fusilli spindles, or short spirals

fusilli bucati thin spirals, like springs

gemelli "twins", two pieces wrapped together

gramigna meaning "grass" or "weed"; the shapes look like sprouting seeds

lasagne flat, rectangular sheets

linguini long, flat ribbons

lumache smooth, snail-like shells

lumachine U-shaped flat noodles

macaroni, maccheroni long or short-cut tubes, may be ridged or elbow shapes

maltagliati triangular-shaped pieces, traditionally used in bean soups

noodles fine, medium or broad flat ribbons

orecchiette dished shapes; the word means "ear"

orzi tiny pasta, like grains of rice, used in soups

pappardelle widest ribbons, either straight or sawtooth-edged

pearlini tiny discs

penne short, thick tubes with diagonal-cut ends

pipe rigate ridged, curved pipe shapes

rigatoni thick, ridged tubes

ruoti wheels

semini seed shapes

spaghetti fine, medium or thick rods

spirale two rods twisted together into spirals

INTRODUCTION

strozzapreti "priest strangler", double twisted strands

tagliarini flat, ribbon-like strips, thinner than tagliatelli

tagliatelli broad, flat ribbons

tortiglione thin, twisted tubes

vermicelli fine, slender strands usually sold folded into skeins

ziti tagliati short, thick tubes

PASTA SAUCES
Getting to know the individual pasta shapes is one of the delights of this form of cookery, and creative cooks will enjoy partnering their favourite sauces with first one and then another type of pasta. Although there are classic combinations such as Spaghetti Bolognese, when the pasta is tossed with the rich meat and tomato sauce of southern Italy, and Spaghetti Carbonara, when the eggs in the sauce are cooked on contact with the piping hot pasta, there are no hard and fast rules, just guidelines.

These guidelines are largely a matter of practicality. Long slender strands of pasta combine well with meat, fish and vegetable sauces, without absorbing the liquid element or concealing the shape and texture of the principal ingredient. Twisted, curved and hollow pasta shapes are ideal to serve with runny sauces, which get deliciously trapped in, say, the cavities of large pasta shells, and small shapes and fine strands are especially good for adding body and texture to clear meat, fish and vegetable soups.

Appearance is a factor in creating partnerships of pasta and sauce.

Shells are an obvious example, to evoke the appropriate mental image when combined with fish and seafoods. Taste comes into the decision-making process too. It may seem improbable, but it is a fact that spaghetti tossed with a green vegetable sauce does taste different from, say, pasta wagon wheels served with the identical sauce. And a calamares stew would lose much of its robust character if it were made with tiny pasta stars instead of macaroni.

Cheeses with Pasta
Some cheeses have a natural affinity with pasta dishes and appear frequently in recipes. It is always worth having a supply in store, handy for use at short notice. If you have difficulty in buying Parmesan in a whole piece, try a good Italian food store or delicatessen.

Ricotta A milky white, soft and crumbly Italian cheese which resembles cottage cheese. It is low in fat, being traditionally made from whey, but some varieties produced now have a proportion of whole milk added. If you cannot obtain Ricotta, use another low-fat soft cheese, or cottage cheese. To obtain a smooth-textured sauce or filling press cottage cheese through a sieve.

Parmesan A mature and exceptionally hard cheese produced in Italy. Parmesan, properly known as Parmigiano-reggiano, plays such an important part in the overall flavour of pasta dishes that it is worth exploiting its potential to the full. It may be useful to have a small carton of ready-grated Parmesan in the refrigerator, but you will find that it quickly loses its characteristic

INTRODUCTION

pungency and "bite". For that reason, it is better to buy small quantities of the cheese in one piece (it is usually very expensive) and grate it yourself as needed. Tightly wrapped in cling film and foil, it will keep in the refrigerator for several months. Grate it just before serving, for maximum flavour. To grate a large quantity by hand is time-consuming, as the cheese is so hard: you may find it easier to use a food processor.

Pecorino A hard sheep's milk cheese which resembles Parmesan and is often used for grating over dishes. It has a sharp flavour and is only used in small quantities. Best bought in the piece and stored, tightly wrapped in cling film and foil, in the refrigerator.

Mozzarella Another highly popular cheese, often found in pasta dishes. It is a soft, fresh cheese, with a piquant flavour, traditionally made from water buffalo's milk, and is usually sold surrounded by whey to keep it moist. Buffalo milk is now scarce, and so nowadays this cheese is often made with cow's milk. It can be used fresh, most popularly in tomato salads, and is also often added to provide a tangy, chewy layer to baked dishes.

OLIVE OIL

Olive oil, which is at the heart of so many pasta dishes, has a personality all of its own, and each variety has its own characteristic flavour. The main oil-producing countries are Italy, Greece and Spain. It is important to be able to recognize the different grades of oil.

Extra-virgin olive oil This is the finest grade, made from the first, cold

pressing of hand gathered olives. Always use extra-virgin oil for salad dressings.

Virgin olive oil This oil has a fine aroma and colour, and is also made by cold pressing. It may have a slightly higher acidity level than extra-virgin oil.

Refined or "pure" olive oil This is made by treating the paste residue from the pressings with heat or solvents to remove the residual oil.

Olive oil is a blend of refined and virgin olive oil.

TOMATO SAUCE
2 tbsp olive oil
1 small onion, chopped
1 garlic clove, chopped
1 x 424 g/15 oz can chopped
  tomatoes
2 tbsp chopped parsley
1 tsp dried oregano
2 bay leaves
2 tbsp tomato purée (paste)
1 tsp sugar

1. To make the tomato sauce, heat the oil in a pan over a medium heat and fry the onion until it is translucent. Add the garlic and fry for 1 further minute.

2. Stir in the chopped tomatoes, parsley, oregano, bay leaves, tomato purée (paste) and sugar and bring the sauce to the boil.

3. Simmer, uncovered, until the sauce has reduced by half, about 15-20 minutes. Taste the sauce and adjust the seasoning if necessary. Discard the bay leaves.

INTRODUCTION

BECHAMEL SAUCE

300 ml/ ½ pint/1¼ cups milk
2 bay leaves
3 cloves
1 small onion
60 g/2 oz/ ¼ cup butter, plus extra for greasing
45 g/1½ oz/6 tbsp flour
300 ml/ ½ pint/1¼ cups single cream
large pinch of grated nutmeg
salt and pepper

1. Pour the milk into a small pan and add bay leaves. Press the cloves into the onion, add to the pan and bring the milk to the boil. Remove from the heat and set it aside to cool.

2. Strain the milk into a jug and rinse the pan. Melt the butter in the pan and stir in the flour. Stir for 1 minute, then gradually pour on the milk, stirring constantly. Cook the sauce for 3 minutes, then pour on the cream and bring it to the boil. Remove from the heat and season with nutmeg, salt and pepper.

CHEESE SAUCE

30 g/1 oz/2 tbsp butter
1 tbsp flour
250 ml/8 fl oz/1 cup milk
2 tbsp single cream
pinch of grated nutmeg
45 g/1½ oz Cheddar cheese, grated
1 tbsp grated Parmesan cheese

1. Melt the butter in a pan, stir in the flour and cook for 1 minute.

2. Gradually pour on the milk, stirring all the time. Stir in the cream and season the sauce with nutmeg, salt and pepper.

3. Simmer the sauce for 5 minutes to reduce, then remove it from the heat and stir in the cheeses. Stir until the cheese has melted and blended into the sauce.

LAMB SAUCE

2 tbsp olive oil
1 large onion, sliced
2 celery stalks, thinly sliced
500 g/1 lb lean lamb, minced
3 tbsp tomato purée (paste)
150 g/5 oz bottled sun-dried tomatoes, drained and chopped
1 tsp dried oregano
1 tbsp red wine vinegar
150 ml/ ¼ pint/ ⅔ cup chicken stock
salt and pepper

1. Heat the oil in the frying pan over a medium heat and fry the onion and celery until the onion is translucent. Add the lamb, stirring frequently, and fry until it changes colour.

2. Stir in the tomato purée (paste), sun-dried tomatoes, oregano, wine vinegar and stock and season with salt and pepper.

3. Bring the sauce to the boil and cook, uncovered, for about 20 minutes until the meat has absorbed the stock. Taste the sauce and adjust the seasoning if necessary.

COURGETTE (ZUCCHINI) & AUBERGINE (EGGPLANT) LASAGNE

SERVES 6

1 kg/2 lb aubergines (eggplant)
4 tbsp salt
8 tbsp olive oil
30 g/1 oz/2 tbsp garlic and herb butter or
*   margarine*
500 g/1 lb courgettes (zucchini), sliced
250 g/8 oz/2 cups grated Mozzarella
*   cheese*
600 ml/1 pint/2½ cups passata
6 sheets pre-cooked green lasagne
600 ml/1 pint/2½ cups Béchamel Sauce
*   (see page 72)*
60 g/2 oz/ ½ cup freshly grated Parmesan
1 tsp dried oregano
black pepper

1 Thinly slice the aubergines (eggplant). Layer the slices in a bowl, sprinkling with the salt as you go. Set aside for 30 minutes. Rinse well in cold water and pat dry with paper towels.

2 Heat 4 tablespoons of the oil in a large frying pan (skillet) until very hot and gently fry half the aubergine (eggplant) slices for 6–7 minutes until lightly golden all over. Drain on paper towels. Repeat with the remaining aubergine slices and oil.

3 Melt the garlic and herb butter or margarine in the frying pan and fry the courgettes (zucchini) for 5–6 minutes until golden. Drain on paper towels.

4 Place half the aubergine (eggplant) and courgette (zucchini) slices in a large ovenproof dish. Season with pepper and sprinkle over half the Mozzarella. Spoon over half the passata and top with 3 sheets of lasagne.

5 Arrange the remaining aubergine (eggplant) and courgette (zucchini) slices on top. Season with pepper and top with the remaining Mozzarella and passata and another layer of lasagne.

6 Spoon over the béchamel sauce and top with Parmesan and oregano. Put on a baking sheet and bake in a preheated oven at 220°C/425°F/ Gas Mark 7 for 30–35 minutes until golden. Serve.

MEDITERRANEAN SPAGHETTI

SERVES 4

2 tbsp olive oil
1 large red onion, chopped
2 garlic cloves, crushed
1 tbsp lemon juice
4 baby aubergines (eggplant), quartered
600 ml/1 pint/2½ cups passata
2 tsp caster (superfine) sugar
2 tbsp tomato purée (paste)
400 g/14 oz can artichoke hearts, drained
*   and halved*
125 g/4 oz/ ¾ cup pitted black olives
350 g/12 oz wholewheat dried spaghetti
salt and pepper
sprigs of fresh basil to garnish
olive bread to serve

1 Heat 1 tablespoon of the oil in a large frying pan (skillet) and gently fry the onion, garlic, lemon juice and aubergines (eggplant) for 4–5 minutes until lightly browned.

2 Pour in the passata, season and add the sugar and tomato purée (paste). Bring to the boil, reduce the heat and simmer for 20 minutes.

3 Gently stir in the artichoke halves and olives and cook for 5 minutes.

4 Meanwhile, bring a large saucepan of lightly salted water to the boil and cook the spaghetti for 7–8 minutes until just tender. Drain well, toss in the remaining olive oil and season.

5 Pile into a warmed serving bowl and top with the vegetable sauce. Garnish with basil sprigs and serve with olive bread.

PASSATA

Passata is made from sieved tomatoes and makes an excellent base for sauces. It is available from supermarkets and delicatessens, usually in jars or cartons.

TRICOLOUR TIMBALLINI

SERVES 4

15 g/ ½ oz/1 tbsp butter or margarine,
softened
60 g/2 oz/ ½ cup dried white breadcrumbs
175 g/6 oz tricolour spaghetti
300 ml/ ½ pint/1¼ cups Béchamel Sauce
(see page 72)
1 egg yolk
125 g/4 oz/1 cup grated Gruyère (Swiss)
cheese
salt and pepper
fresh flat-leaf parsley leaves to garnish

SAUCE:
2 tsp olive oil
1 onion, chopped finely
1 bay leaf
150 ml/ ¼ pint/ ⅔ cup dry white wine
150 ml/ ¼ pint/ ⅔ cup creamed tomatoes
1 tbsp tomato purée (paste)

1 Grease 4x180 ml/6 fl oz/ ¾ cup
moulds or ramekins with the butter
or margarine. Evenly coat the insides with
half the breadcrumbs.

2 Break the spaghetti into 5 cm/
2 in lengths. Bring a saucepan of
lightly salted water to the boil and cook
the spaghetti for 5–6 minutes until just
tender. Drain well and put in a bowl.

3 Mix the béchamel sauce, egg yolk,
cheese and seasoning into the
cooked pasta and pack into the moulds.

4 Sprinkle with the remaining
breadcrumbs and put on a baking
sheet. Bake in a preheated oven at
220°C/425°F/Gas Mark 7 for 20 minutes.
Leave to stand for 10 minutes.

5 Meanwhile, make the sauce. Heat
the oil in a saucepan and gently fry
the onion and bay leaf for 2–3 minutes
until just softened.

6 Stir in the wine, tomatoes, tomato
purée (paste) and seasoning. Bring
to the boil and simmer for 20 minutes
until thickened. Discard the bay leaf.

7 Run a palette knife (spatula) around
the inside of the moulds or
ramekins. Turn on to serving plates,
garnish and serve with the tomato sauce.

GREEN GARLIC TAGLIATELLE

SERVES 4

2 tbsp walnut oil
1 bunch spring onions (scallions), sliced
2 garlic cloves, sliced thinly
250 g/8 oz mushrooms, sliced
500 g/1 lb fresh green and white tagliatelle
250 g/8 oz frozen chopped leaf spinach,
thawed and drained
125 g/4 oz/ ½ cup full-fat soft cheese with
garlic and herbs
4 tbsp single (light) cream
60 g/2 oz/ ½ cup chopped, unsalted
pistachio nuts
2 tbsp shredded fresh basil
salt and pepper
sprigs of fresh basil to garnish
Italian bread to serve

1 Gently heat the oil in a wok or
frying pan (skillet) and fry the spring
onions (scallions) and garlic for 1 minute
until just softened. Add the mushrooms,
stir well, cover and cook gently for 5
minutes until softened.

2 Meanwhile, bring a large saucepan
of lightly salted water to the boil and
cook the pasta for 3–5 minutes until just
tender. Drain well and return to the
saucepan.

3 Add the spinach to the mushrooms
and heat through for 1–2 minutes.
Add the cheese and allow to melt slightly.
Stir in the cream and continue to heat
without allowing to boil.

4 Pour over the pasta, season and mix
well. Heat gently, stirring, for 2–3
minutes.

5 Pile into a warmed serving bowl and
sprinkle over the pistachio nuts and
shredded basil. Garnish with basil sprigs
and serve with Italian bread.

NUT OILS

Choose any nut oil for this recipe, but
remember to keep the heat low as
they are much more delicate than
other oils.

THREE-CHEESE MACARONI BAKE

SERVES 4

600 ml/1 pint/2½ cups Béchamel Sauce
  (see page 72)
250 g/8 oz/2 cups macaroni
1 egg, beaten
125 g/4 oz/1 cup grated mature (sharp)
  Cheddar cheese
1 tbsp wholegrain mustard
2 tbsp chopped fresh chives
4 tomatoes, sliced
125 g/4 oz/1 cup grated Red Leicester
  cheese
60 g/2 oz/ ½ cup grated Cotswold cheese
  (see below)
2 tbsp sunflower seeds
salt and pepper
fresh chives to garnish

1 Make the béchamel sauce, put into a
  bowl and cover with clingfilm
(plastic wrap) to prevent a skin forming.
Set aside.

2 Bring a saucepan of lightly salted
  water to the boil and cook the
macaroni for 8–10 minutes until just
tender. Drain well and place in an
ovenproof dish.

3 Stir the egg, Cheddar cheese,
  mustard, chives and seasoning into
the béchamel sauce and spoon over the
macaroni, making sure it is well covered.
Top with a layer of sliced tomatoes.

4 Sprinkle over the Red Leicester and
  Cotswold cheeses and sunflower
seeds. Put on a baking sheet and bake in
a preheated oven at 190°C/375°F/Gas
Mark 5 for 25–30 minutes until bubbling
and golden. Garnish with chives and
serve immediately.

COTSWOLD CHEESE

Cotswold cheese is a tasty blend of
Double Gloucester, onion and chives.
It has a medium-soft creamy texture,
is pale orange-yellow in colour and is
perfect for melting as a topping.
If you can't find any, this recipe would
work just as well with any combination
of cheeses, so experiment with
whatever is available.

SPAGHETTI CARBONARA

SERVES 4

400 g/14 oz spaghetti
2 tbsp olive oil
1 large onion, thinly sliced
2 garlic cloves, chopped
175 g/6 oz streaky bacon rashers, rind
  removed, cut into thin strips
30 g/1 oz/2 tbsp butter
175 g/6 oz mushrooms, thinly sliced
300 ml/ ½ pint/1¼ cups double (heavy)
  cream
3 eggs, beaten
90 g/3 oz/ ¾ cup grated Parmesan, plus
  extra to serve, optional
freshly ground black pepper
sprigs of sage, to garnish

1 Heat a large serving dish or bowl.
  Cook the spaghetti in a large pan of
boiling salted water, adding 1 tablespoon
of the oil. When the pasta is almost
tender, drain in a colander. Return the
spaghetti to the pan, cover and leave it in
a warm place.

2 While the spaghetti is cooking, heat
  the remaining oil in a frying pan
over a medium heat. Fry the onion until it
is translucent, then add the garlic and
bacon and fry until the bacon is crisp.

3 Remove the onion, garlic and bacon
  with a slotted spoon and set it aside
to keep warm. Heat the butter in the pan
and fry the mushrooms for 3-4 minutes,
stirring them once or twice. Return the
bacon mixture to the mushrooms. Cover
and keep warm.

4 Stir together the cream, the beaten
  eggs and cheese and season with
salt and pepper.

5 Working very quickly to avoid
  cooling the cooked ingredients, tip
the spaghetti into the bacon and
mushroom mixture and pour on the eggs.
Toss the spaghetti quickly, using 2 forks,
and serve it at once. You can, if you wish,
hand round more grated Parmesan.

SPAGHETTI BOLOGNESE

SERVES 4

400 g/14 oz spaghetti
1 tbsp olive oil
salt
15 g/ ½ oz butter
2 tbsp chopped parsley, to garnish

RAGU SAUCE:
3 tbsp olive oil
45 g/1½ oz butter
2 large onions, chopped
4 celery stalks, thinly sliced
175 g/6 oz streaky bacon, chopped
2 garlic cloves, chopped
500 g/1 lb lean minced beef
2 tbsp tomato purée (paste)
1 tbsp flour
1 x 425 g/15 oz can chopped tomatoes
150 ml/ ¼ pint/ ⅔ cup beef stock
150 ml/ ¼ pint/ ⅔ cup red wine
2 tsp dried oregano
½ tsp grated nutmeg
salt and pepper

1 To make the Ragu sauce: heat the oil and the butter in a large frying pan over a medium heat. Add the onions, celery and bacon pieces and fry them together for 5 minutes, stirring.

2 Stir in the garlic and minced beef and cook, stirring, until the meat has lost its redness. Lower the heat and continue cooking for a further 10 minutes, stirring once or twice.

3 Increase the heat to medium, stir in the tomato purée (paste) and the flour and cook for 1-2 minutes. Stir in the chopped tomatoes and the beef stock and wine and bring to the boil, stirring. Season the sauce and stir in the oregano and nutmeg. Cover the pan and simmer for 45 minutes, stirring occasionally.

4 Cook the spaghetti in a large pan of boiling salted water, adding the olive oil. When it is almost tender, drain in a colander, then return to the pan. Dot the spaghetti with the butter and toss.

5 Taste the sauce and adjust the seasoning if necessary. Pour the sauce over the spaghetti and toss well. Sprinkle on the parsley to garnish and serve immediately.

LASAGNE VERDE

SERVES 6

Ragù Sauce (see left)
1 tbsp olive oil
250 g/8 oz lasagne verde
60 g/2 oz/ ½ cup Parmesan, grated
Bechamel sauce (see page 72)
salt and pepper
green salad, tomato salad or black olives,
  to serve

1 Begin by making the Ragù Sauce as described on the left. Cook the sauce for 10-12 minutes longer than the time given, in an uncovered pan, to allow the excess liquid to evaporate. To layer the sauce with lasagne, it needs to be reduced in this way until it has the consistency of a thick paste.

2 Have ready a large pan of boiling, salted water and add the olive oil. Drop the pasta sheets into the boiling water 2 or 3 at a time, and return the water to the boil before adding further pasta sheets. If you are using fresh lasagne, cook the sheets for a total of 8 minutes. If you are using dried or partly precooked pasta, cook it according to the directions given on the packet.

3 Spread a large, dampened tea towel on the working surface. Lift out the pasta sheets with a slotted spoon and spread them in a single layer on the tea towel. Use a second tea towel if necessary. Set the pasta aside while you make the Bechamel sauce, as described on page 72.

4 Grease a rectangular ovenproof dish, about 25-28 cm/10-11 in long. To assemble the dish, spoon a little of the meat sauce into the prepared dish, cover with a layer of lasagne, then spoon over a little Bechamel sauce and sprinkle on a little cheese. Continue making layers in this way, covering the final layer of lasagne with the remaining Bechamel sauce.

5 Sprinkle on the remaining cheese and bake in the preheated oven for 40 minutes, until the sauce is golden brown and bubbling. Serve with a chilled green salad, a tomato salad, or a bowl of black olives.

STUFFED CANNELLONI

SERVES 4

8 cannelloni tubes
1 tbsp olive oil
fresh herbs, to garnish

FILLING:
30 g/1 oz/2 tbsp butter
300 g/10 oz frozen spinach, defrosted and
    chopped
125 g/4 oz / ½ cup Ricotta
30 g/1 oz/ ¼ cup grated Parmesan
60 g/2 oz/ ¼ cup chopped ham
¼ tsp grated nutmeg
2 tbsp double (heavy) cream
2 eggs, lightly beaten
salt and pepper

SAUCE:
30 g/1 oz/2 tbsp butter
30 g/1 oz/ ¼ cup flour
300 ml/ ½ pint/1¼ cups milk
2 bay leaves
large pinch of grated nutmeg
30 g/1 oz / ¼ cup grated Parmesan

1 To prepare the filling, melt the butter
in a pan and stir in the spinach. Stir
for 2-3 minutes to allow the moisture to
evaporate, then remove the pan from the
heat. Stir in the cheeses and the ham.
Season with nutmeg, salt and pepper and
beat in the cream and eggs to make a
thick paste. Set aside to cool.

2 Cook the cannelloni in a large pan
of boiling salted water, adding the
olive oil. When almost tender, after 10-12
minutes, drain in a colander and set
aside to cool.

3 To make the sauce, melt the butter
in a pan, stir in the flour and, when
it has formed a roux, gradually pour on
the milk, stirring all the time. Add the
bay leaves, bring to simmering point,
and cook for 5 minutes. Season with
nutmeg, salt and pepper. Remove the
pan from the heat and discard the bay
leaves.

4 To assemble the dish, spoon the
filling into a piping bag and pipe it
into each of the cannelloni tubes.

5 Spoon a little of the sauce into a
shallow baking dish. Arrange the
cannelloni in a single layer, then pour
over the remaining sauce. Sprinkle on
the remaining Parmesan cheese and
bake in the preheated oven for 40-45
minutes, until the sauce is golden brown
and bubbling. Serve garnished with fresh
herb sprigs.

SEAFOOD LASAGNE

SERVES 6

8 sheets wholewheat lasagne
500 g/1 lb smoked cod
600 ml/1 pint/2½ cups milk
1 tbsp lemon juice
8 peppercorns
2 bay leaves
a few stalks of parsley
60 g/2 oz/½ cup Cheddar, grated
30 g/1 oz/¼ cup Parmesan, grated
salt and pepper
a few whole prawns (shrimp), to garnish
    (optional)

SAUCE:
60 g/2 oz/¼ cup butter, plus extra for
    greasing
1 large onion, sliced
1 green (bell) pepper, cored, seeded,and
    chopped
1 small courgette (zucchini), sliced
60 g/2 oz/½ cup flour
150 ml/¼ pint/⅔ cup white wine
150 ml/¼ pint/⅔ cup single cream
125 g/4 oz shelled prawns(shrimp)
60 g/2 oz/½ cup Cheddar, grated

1 Cook the lasagne in boiling, salted water until almost tender, as described on page 29. Drain and reserve.

2 Place the smoked cod, milk, lemon juice, peppercorns, bay leaves and parsley in a frying pan. Bring to the boil, cover and simmer for 10 minutes.

3 Remove the fish, skin and remove any bones. Flake the fish. Strain and reserve the liquor.

4 Make the sauce: melt the butter in a pan and fry the onion, (bell) pepper and courgette (zucchini) for 2-3 minutes. Stir in the flour and cook for 1 minute. Gradually add the fish liquor, then stir in the wine, cream and prawns (shrimp). Simmer for 2 minutes. Remove from the heat, add the cheese, and season.

5 Grease a shallow baking dish. Pour in a quarter of the sauce and spread evenly over the base. Cover the sauce with 3 sheets of lasagne, then with another quarter of the sauce. Arrange the fish on top, then cover with half the remaining sauce. Finish with the remaining lasagne, then the rest of the sauce. Sprinkle the Cheddar and Parmesan over the sauce.

6 Bake in the preheated oven for 25 minutes, or until the top is golden brown and bubbling. Garnish with a few whole prawns (shrimp), if liked.

TAGLIATELLE WITH CHICKEN

SERVES 4

250 g/8 oz fresh green ribbon noodles
1 tbsp olive oil
salt
basil leaves, to garnish
Tomato Sauce (see page 71)

CHICKEN SAUCE:
60 g/2 oz/ ¼ cup unsalted butter
400 g/14 oz boned, skinned chicken breast,
  thinly sliced
90 g/3 oz/ ¾ cup blanched almonds
300 ml/½ pint/1¼ cups double (heavy)
  cream
salt and pepper
basil leaves, to garnish

1 Make the Tomato Sauce, as described on page 71, and keep warm.

2 To make the Chicken Sauce, melt the butter in a pan over a medium heat and fry the chicken strips and almonds for 5-6 minutes, stirring frequently, until the chicken is cooked through.

3 Meanwhile, pour the cream into a small pan over a low heat, bring it to the boil and boil for about 10 minutes, until reduced by almost half. Pour the cream over the chicken and almonds, stir well, and season. Set it aside and keep it warm.

4 Cook the fresh pasta in a large pan of boiling salted water, first adding the oil. When the pasta is just tender, about 5 minutes, drain in a colander, then return it to the pan, cover and keep it warm.

5 To assemble the dish, turn the pasta into a warmed serving dish and spoon the tomato sauce over it. Spoon the chicken and cream over the centre, scatter the basil leaves over and serve at once.

TOMATO SAUCE

This tomato sauce used in the recipe above can be served with a variety of pasta dishes. Make double quantities and keep some in the freezer as a useful standby for quick and easy pasta dishes.

TAGLIATELLE TRICOLORE WITH BROCCOLI & BLUE CHEESE SAUCE

SERVES 4

300 g/10 oz tagliatelle tricolore (plain,
  spinach- and tomato-flavoured noodles)
250 g/8 oz broccoli, broken into small
  florets
350g/12 oz/1½ cups Mascarpone cheese
125 g/4 oz/1 cup Gorgonzola cheese,
  chopped
1 tbsp chopped fresh oregano
30 g/1 oz/2 tbsp butter
sprigs of fresh oregano to garnish
grated Parmesan cheese to serve
salt and pepper

1 Cook the tagliatelle in plenty of boiling, lightly salted water until just tender, according to the instructions on the packet. The Italians call this al dente, which literally means 'to the tooth'.

2 Meanwhile, cook the broccoli florets in a small amount of lightly salted, boiling water. Avoid overcooking the broccoli, so that it retains its colour and texture.

3 Heat the Mascarpone and Gorgonzola cheeses together gently in a large saucepan until they are melted. Stir in the oregano and season with salt and pepper.

4 Drain the pasta thoroughly. Return it to the saucepan and add the butter, tossing the tagliatelle to coat it. Drain the broccoli well and add to the pasta with the sauce, tossing gently to mix.

5 Divide the pasta between 4 warmed serving plates. Garnish with sprigs of fresh oregano and serve with Parmesan cheese.

ALTERNATIVES

Choose your favourite pasta shapes to use in this recipe as an alternative to tagliatelle. If you prefer, substitute a creamy blue Stilton for the Gorgonzola.

AUBERGINE (EGGPLANT) CAKE

SERVES 4

*1 medium aubergine (eggplant), thinly
   sliced*
5 tbsp olive oil
Lamb Sauce (see page 72)
*250 g/8 oz short pasta shapes, such as
   fusilli*
*60 g/2 oz/ ¼ cup butter, plus extra for
   greasing*
45 g/1½ oz/6 tbsp flour
300 ml/1/2 pint/1¼ cups milk
150ml/ ¼ pint/ ⅔ cup single cream
150 ml/ ¼ pint/ ⅔ cup chicken stock
large pinch of grated nutmeg
90 g/3 oz/ ¾ cup Cheddar cheese, grated
30 g/1 oz/ ¼ cup Parmesan, grated
artichoke heart and tomato salad, to serve

1 Put the aubergine (eggplant) slices in
a colander, sprinkle with salt and
leave for about 45 minutes, while the salt
draws out some of the bitter juices. Rinse
the aubergines (eggplant) under cold,
running water and drain. Toss them in
paper towels to dry.

2 Heat 4 tablespoons of the oil in a
frying pan over a medium heat. Fry
the aubergine (eggplant) slices for about 4
minutes on each side, until they are light
golden brown. Remove with a slotted
spoon and drain on paper towels.

3 Make the Lamb Sauce as described
on page 72 and keep warm.

4 Meanwhile, cook the pasta in a large
pan of boiling salted water, adding 1
tablespoon of olive oil. When the pasta is
almost tender, drain it in a colander and
return to the pan. Cover and keep warm.

5 Melt the butter in a small pan, stir in
the flour and cook for 1 minute.
Gradually pour on the milk, stirring all the
time, then stir in the cream and chicken
stock. Season with nutmeg, salt and
pepper, bring to the boil and simmer for 5
minutes. Stir in the Cheddar cheese and
remove from the heat. Pour half the sauce
over the pasta and mix well. Reserve the
remaining sauce.

6 Grease a shallow ovenproof dish.
Spoon in half the pasta, cover it with
half the meat sauce and then with the
aubergines (eggplant) in a single layer.
Repeat the layers of pasta and meat sauce
and spread the remaining cheese sauce
over the top. Sprinkle on the Parmesan
cheese. Bake in the preheated oven for 25
minutes, until the top is golden brown.
Serve hot or cold, with artichoke heart
and tomato salad.

7 A salad of canned artichoke hearts,
drained, sliced and tossed in a
lemon dressing is a good accompaniment.

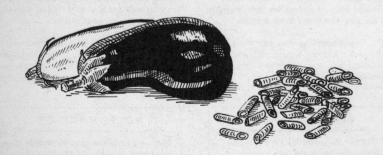

TAGLIATELLE WITH MEATBALLS

SERVES 4

500 g/1 lb lean minced beef
60 g/2 oz/1 cup soft white breadcrumbs
1 garlic clove, crushed
2 tbsp chopped parsley
1 tsp dried oregano
large pinch of grated nutmeg
1/4 tsp ground coriander
60 g/2 oz/ ½ cup Parmesan, grated
2-3 tbsp milk
flour, for dusting
4 tbsp olive oil
400 g/14 oz tagliatelli
30 g/1 oz/2 tbsp butter, diced
salt
2 tbsp chopped parsley, to garnish

SAUCE:
3 tbsp olive oil
2 large onions, sliced
2 celery stalks, thinly sliced
2 garlic cloves, chopped
1 x 425 g/15 oz can chopped tomatoes
125 g/4 oz bottled sun-dried tomatoes,
    drained and chopped
2 tbsp tomato purée (paste)
1 tbsp dark Muscovado sugar
150 ml/ ¼ pint/ ⅔ cup white wine, or water
salt and pepper
green salad, to serve

1 To make the sauce, heat the oil in a frying pan and fry the onion and celery until translucent. Add the garlic and cook for 1 minute. Stir in the tomatoes, tomato purée (paste), sugar and wine and season. Bring to the boil and simmer for 10 minutes.

2 Break up the meat in a bowl with a wooden spoon until it becomes a sticky paste. Stir in the breadcrumbs, garlic, herbs and spices. Stir in the cheese and enough milk to make a firm paste. Flour your hands, take large spoonfuls of the mixture and shape it into 12 balls. Heat the oil in a frying pan and fry the meatballs for 5-6 minutes until browned.

3 Pour the tomato sauce over the meatballs. Lower the heat, cover the pan and simmer for 30 minutes, turning once or twice. Add a little extra water if the sauce begins to dry.

4 Cook the pasta in a large saucepan of boiling salted water, adding the remaining oil. When almost tender, drain in a colander, then turn into a warmed serving dish, dot with the butter and toss with 2 forks. Spoon the meatballs and sauce over the pasta and sprinkle on the parsley. Serve with a green salad.

PASTICCIO

SERVES 6

250 g/8 oz fusilli, or other short pasta
   shapes
1 tbsp olive oil
4 tbsp double (heavy) cream
salt
rosemary sprigs, to garnish

SAUCE:
2 tbsp olive oil, plus extra for brushing
1 onion, thinly sliced
1 red (bell) pepper, cored, seeded and
   chopped
2 cloves garlic, chopped
625 g/1¼ lb lean beef, minced
1 x 425 g/15 oz can chopped tomatoes
125 ml/4 fl oz/ ½ cup dry white wine
2 tbsp chopped parsley
1 x 50 g/2 oz can anchovies, drained and
   chopped
salt and pepper

TOPPING:
300 ml/ ½ pint/1¼ cups plain yogurt
3 eggs
pinch of nutmeg
45 g/1½ oz/ ⅓ cup Parmesan, grated

1 To make the sauce, heat the oil in a large frying pan and fry the onion and red (bell) pepper for 3 minutes. Stir in the garlic and cook for 1 minute more. Stir in the beef and cook, stirring frequently, until it has changed colour.

2 Add the tomatoes and wine, stir well and bring to the boil. Simmer, uncovered, for 20 minutes, until the sauce is fairly thick. Stir in the parsley and anchovies and adjust the seasoning.

3 Cook the pasta in a large pan of boiling salted water, adding the oil. When it is almost tender, drain it in a colander, then transfer it to a bowl. Stir in the cream and set it aside.

4 To make the topping, beat together the yogurt and eggs and season the mixture with nutmeg, salt and pepper. Stir in the cheese.

5 Brush a shallow baking dish with oil. Spoon in half the macaroni and cover with half of the meat sauce. Repeat these layers, spread the topping evenly over the dish and sprinkle on the cheese.

6 Bake in the preheated oven for 25 minutes, until the topping is golden brown and bubbling. Garnish with rosemary and serve with a selection of raw vegetable crudités.

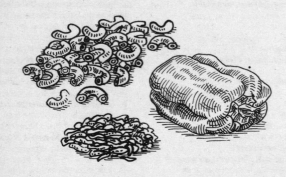

SPAGHETTI WITH SEAFOOD SAUCE

SERVES 4

*250 g/8 oz short-cut spaghetti, or long
    spaghetti broken into 15 cm/6 in lengths
2 tbsp olive oil
300 ml/ ½ pint/1¼ cups chicken stock
1 tsp lemon juice
1 small cauliflower, cut into florets
2 medium carrots, thinly sliced
125 g/4 oz mangetout (snow peas),
    trimmed
60 g/2 oz/ ¼ cup butter
1 onion, sliced
250 g/8 oz courgettes (zucchini), thinly
    sliced
1 garlic clove, chopped
350 g/12 oz frozen shelled prawns
    (shrimp), defrosted
2 tbsp chopped parsley
30 g/1 oz/ ¼ cup Parmesan, grated
salt and pepper
½ tsp paprika, to sprinkle
4 unshelled prawns (shrimp), to garnish
    (optional)*

1 Cook the spaghetti in a large pan of
boiling salted water, adding 1
tablespoon of the olive oil. When it is
almost tender, drain in a colander. Return
to the pan and stir in the remaining olive
oil. Cover the pan and keep warm.

2 Bring the chicken stock and lemon
juice to the boil in a pan over
medium heat and cook the cauliflower and
carrots for 3-4 minutes, until they are
barely tender. Remove with a slotted
spoon and set aside. Add the mangetout
(snow peas) to the stock and cook for 3-4
minutes, until they begin to soften.
Remove with a slotted spoon and add to
the other vegetables. Reserve the stock for
future use.

3 Melt half the butter in a frying pan
over medium heat and fry the onion
and courgettes (zucchini) for about 3
minutes. Add the garlic and prawns
(shrimp)and cook for a further 2-3
minutes, until they are thoroughly heated
through.

4 Stir in the reserved vegetables and
season well. When the vegetables are
heated through stir in the remaining butter.

5 Transfer the spaghetti to a warmed
serving dish. Pour on the sauce and
parsley and toss well, using 2 forks, until
thoroughly coated. Sprinkle on the grated
cheese and paprika and garnish with
unshelled prawns (shrimp), if using. Serve
immediately.

MACARONI & PRAWN (SHRIMP) BAKE

• •

SERVES 4

350 g/12 oz short pasta, such as short-cut
    macaroni
1 tbsp olive oil, plus extra for brushing
90 g/3 oz/6 tbsp butter, plus extra for
    greasing
2 small fennel bulbs, thinly sliced, leaves
    reserved
175 g/6 oz mushrooms, thinly sliced
175 g/6 oz shelled prawns (shrimp)
60 g/2 oz/ ½ cup Parmesan, grated
2 large tomatoes, sliced
1 tsp dried oregano
salt and pepper
Bechamel Sauce (see page 72)
pinch of cayenne

1   Cook the pasta in a large pan of
    boiling, salted water to which you
have added 1 tablespoon of olive oil.
When the pasta is almost tender, drain it
in a colander, return to the pan and dot
with 30g/1 oz/2 tablespoons of the butter.
Shake the pan well, cover and keep the
pasta warm.

2   Melt the remaining butter in a pan
    over medium heat and fry the fennel
for 3-4 minutes, until it begins to soften.
Stir in the mushrooms and fry for a
further 2 minutes. Stir in the prawns
(shrimp), remove the pan from the heat
and set it aside.

3   Make the Bechamel Sauce and add
    the cayenne. Remove the pan from
the heat and stir in the reserved
vegetables, prawns (shrimp) and the
pasta.

4   Grease a round, shallow baking
    dish. Pour in the pasta mixture and
spread evenly. Sprinkle on the Parmesan,
and arrange the tomato slices in a ring
around the edge of the dish. Brush the
tomato with olive oil and sprinkle on the
dried oregano.

5   Bake in the preheated oven for 25
    minutes, until the top is golden
brown. Serve hot.

PASTA SHELLS WITH MUSSELS

• •

SERVES 4-6

400 g/14 oz pasta shells
1 tbsp olive oil

SAUCE:
3.5 litres/6 pints mussels, scrubbed
2 large onions, chopped
250 ml/8 fl oz/1 cup dry white wine
125 g/4 oz/ ½ cup unsalted butter
6 large garlic cloves, finely chopped
5 tbsp chopped parsley
300 ml/ ½ pint/1¼ cups double (heavy)
    cream
salt and pepper
crusty bread, to serve

1   Pull off the "beards" from the
    mussels and rinse well in several
changes of water. Discard any mussels
that refuse to close when tapped. Put the
mussels in a large pan with one of the
onions and the white wine. Cover the
pan, shake and cook over a medium heat
for 2-3 minutes until the mussels open.

2   Remove the pan from the heat, lift
    out the mussels with a slotted
spoon, reserving the liquor, and set aside
until they are cool enough to handle.
Discard any mussels that have not
opened.

3   Melt the butter in a pan over
    medium heat and fry the remaining
onion until translucent. Stir in the garlic
and cook for 1 further minute. Gradually
pour on the reserved cooking liquor,
stirring to blend thoroughly. Stir in the
parsley and cream, season and bring to
simmering point. Taste and adjust the
seasoning if necessary.

4   Cook the pasta in a large pan of
    salted boiling water, adding the oil.
When it is almost tender, drain in a
colander. Return the pasta to the pan,
cover and keep warm.

5   Remove the mussels from their
    shells, reserving a few for garnish.
Stir the mussels into the cream sauce.
Tip the pasta into a warmed serving dish,
pour on the sauce and, using 2 large
spoons, toss it well. Garnish with a few
mussel shells. Serve hot, with warm,
crusty bread.

SPAGHETTI WITH SMOKED SALMON

SERVES 4

500 g/1 lb buckwheat spaghetti
2 tbsp olive oil
90 g/3 oz/ ½ cup feta cheese, crumbled

SAUCE:
300 ml/ ½ pint/1¼ cups double (heavy) cream
150 ml/ ¼ pint/ ⅔ cup whisky or brandy
125 g/4 oz smoked salmon
large pinch of cayenne pepper
2 tbsp chopped coriander, or parsley
salt and pepper

1 Cook the spaghetti in a large pan of salted boiling water, adding 1 tablespoon of the olive oil. When the pasta is almost tender, drain it in a colander. Return to the pan and sprinkle on the remaining oil. Cover and shake the pan and keep warm.

2 In separate small pans, heat the cream and the whisky or brandy to simmering point, but do not let them boil.

3 Combine the cream and whisky or brandy. Cut the smoked salmon into thin strips and add to the cream. Season with pepper and cayenne, and stir in the chopped herb.

4 Transfer the spaghetti to a warmed serving dish, pour on the sauce and toss thoroughly using 2 large forks. Scatter the crumbled cheese over the pasta and garnish with coriander leaves. Serve at once, while still piping hot.

ACCOMPANIMENTS

A green salad with a lemony dressing is a good accompaniment to this rich and luxurious dish.

VERMICELLI WITH CLAM SAUCE

SERVES 4

400 g/14 oz vermicelli, spaghetti, or other long pasta
1 tbsp olive oil
30 g/1 oz/2 tbsp butter
2 tbsp flaked Parmesan, to garnish
sprig of basil, to garnish

SAUCE:
1 tbsp olive oil
2 onions, chopped
2 garlic cloves, chopped
2 x 200 g/7 oz jars clams in brine
125 ml/4 fl oz/ ½ cup white wine
4 tbsp chopped parsley
½ tsp dried oregano
pinch of grated nutmeg
salt and pepper

1 Cook the pasta in a large pan of boiling salted water, adding the olive oil. When it is almost tender, drain in a colander, return to the pan and add the butter. Cover the pan. Shake it and keep it warm.

2 To make the clam sauce, heat the oil in a pan over a medium heat and fry the onion until it is translucent. Stir in the garlic and cook for 1 further minute.

3 Strain the liquid from one jar of clams, pour into the pan and add the wine. Stir well, bring to simmering point and simmer for 3 minutes. Drain the brine from the second jar of clams and discard. Add the shellfish and herbs to the pan and season with pepper and nutmeg. Lower the heat and cook until the sauce is heated through.

4 Transfer the pasta to a warmed serving dish, and pour on the sauce. Sprinkle on the Parmesan and garnish with the basil. Serve hot.

PARMESAN

You could use grated Parmesan for this dish, but flakes of fresh Parmesan, carved off the block, will give it an added depth of flavour.

SPAGHETTI WITH TUNA & PARSLEY

SERVES 4

500 g/1 lb spaghetti
1 tbsp olive oil
30 g/1 oz/2 tbsp butter
black olives, to garnish

SAUCE:
1 x 200 g/7 oz can tuna, drained
1 x 50 g/2 oz can anchovies, drained
250 ml/8 fl oz/1 cup olive oil
1 cup roughly chopped parsley
150 ml/ ¼ pint/ ⅔ cup crème fraîche
salt and pepper

1 Cook the spaghetti in a large pan of salted boiling water, adding the olive oil. When it is almost tender, drain in a colander and return to the pan. Add the butter, toss to coat and keep warm.

2 Remove any bones from the tuna. Put it into a blender or food processor with the anchovies, olive oil and parsley and process until the sauce is smooth. Pour in the crème fraîche and process for a few seconds to blend. Taste the sauce and season

3 Warm 4 plates. Shake the pan of spaghetti over medium heat until it is thoroughly warmed through. Pour on the sauce and toss quickly, using 2 forks. Garnish with the olives and serve immediately with warm, crusty bread.

KNOW YOUR OIL

Oils produced by different countries, mainly Italy, Spain and Greece, have their own characteristic flavours. Some olive varieties produce an oil which has a hot and peppery taste, while others, such as the Kalamata, grown in Greece, give a distinctly 'green' flavour. Get to know and recognize the different grades of oil, too, and use them appropriately (see page 71).

CALAMARES & MACARONI STEW

SERVES 4-6

250 g/8 oz short-cut macaroni, or other
   short pasta shapes
1 tbsp olive oil
2 tbsp chopped parsley
salt and pepper

SAUCE:
350 g/12 oz cleaned squid
6 tbsp olive oil
2 onions, sliced
250 ml/8 fl oz/1 cup fish stock
150 ml/ ¼ pint/ ⅔ cup red wine
350 g/12 oz tomatoes, skinned and thinly
   sliced
2 tbsp tomato purée (paste)
1 tsp dried oregano
2 bay leaves

1 Cook the pasta for only 3 minutes in a large pan of boiling salted water, adding the oil. When it is almost tender, drain the pasta in a colander, return to the pan, cover and keep warm.

2 Cut the squid into 4 cm/1½ in strips. Heat the oil in a pan over medium heat and fry the onion until translucent. Add the squid and stock and simmer for 5 minutes. Pour on the wine and add the tomatoes, tomato purée (paste), oregano and bay leaves. Bring the sauce to the boil, season and cook, uncovered, for 5 minutes.

3 Add the pasta, stir well, cover the pan and continue simmering it for 10 minutes, or until the macaroni and squid are almost tender. By this time the sauce should be thick and syrupy. If it is too liquid, uncover the pan and continue cooking for a few minutes. Taste the sauce and adjust the seasoning if necessary.

4 Remove the bay leaves and stir in most of the parsley, reserving a little to garnish. Transfer to a warmed serving dish. Sprinkle on the remaining parsley and serve hot. Serve with warm, crusty bread such as ciabatta.

NORTH SEA PASTA PUDDING

SERVES 4

125 g/4 oz short-cut macaroni, or other
*   short pasta shapes*
1 tbsp olive oil
15 g/ ½ oz/1 tbsp butter, plus extra for
*   greasing*
500 g/1 lb white fish fillets, such as cod,
*   haddock or coley*
a few parsley stalks
6 black peppercorns
125 ml/4 oz/ ½ cup double (heavy) cream
2 eggs, separated
2 tbsp chopped dill, or parsley
freshly ground black pepper
pinch of grated nutmeg
60 g/2 oz/ ½ cup Parmesan, grated
Tomato Sauce (see page 71), to serve
dill or parsley sprigs, to garnish

1 Cook the pasta in a large pan of salted boiling water, adding the oil. Drain in a colander, return to the pot, add the butter and cover the pan. Keep warm.

2 Place the fish in a frying pan with the parsley stalks and peppercorns and pour on just enough water to cover. Bring to the boil, cover, and simmer for 10 minutes. Lift out the fish with a fish slice, reserving the liquor. When the fish is cool enough to handle, skin and remove any remaining bones. Cut into bite-sized pieces.

3 Transfer the pasta to a large bowl and stir in the cream, egg yolks and dill. Stir in the fish, taking care not to break it up, and enough liquor to make a moist but firm mixture. It should fall easily from a spoon but not be too runny. Whisk the egg whites until stiff but not dry, then fold into the mixture.

4 Grease a heatproof bowl or pudding basin and spoon in the mixture to within 4 cm/1½ in of the rim. Cover the top with greased greaseproof paper and a cloth, or with foil, and tie firmly around the rim. Do not use foil if you cook the pudding in a microwave.

5 Stand the pudding on a trivet in a large pan of boiling water to come halfway up the sides. Cover and steam for 1½ hours, topping up the boiling water as needed, or cook in a microwave on maximum power for 7 minutes.

6 Run a knife around the inside of the bowl and invert on to a warmed serving dish. Pour some tomato sauce over the top and serve the rest separately. Garnish with the herb sprigs.

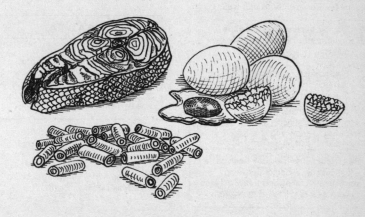

PASTA PROVENÇALE

SERVES 4

3 tbsp olive oil
1 onion, sliced
2 garlic cloves, chopped
3 red (bell) peppers, deseeded and cut into strips
3 courgettes (zucchini), sliced
425 g/14 oz can chopped tomatoes
3 tbsp sun-dried tomato paste
2 tbsp chopped fresh basil
250 g/8 oz fresh pasta spirals
125 g/4 oz/1 cup grated Gruyère (Swiss) cheese
salt and pepper
fresh basil sprigs to garnish

1 Heat the oil in a heavy-based saucepan or flameproof casserole. Add the onion and garlic and cook, stirring occasionally, until softened. Add the (bell) peppers and courgettes (zucchini) and fry for 5 minutes, stirring occasionally.

2 Add the tomatoes, sun-dried tomato paste, basil and seasoning, cover and cook for a further 5 minutes.

3 Meanwhile, bring a large saucepan of salted water to the boil and add the pasta. Stir and bring back to the boil. Reduce the heat slightly and cook, uncovered, for 3 minutes, until just tender. Drain thoroughly and add to the vegetables. Toss gently to mix well.

4 Put the mixture into a shallow ovenproof dish and sprinkle over the cheese.

5 Cook under a preheated grill (broiler) for 5 minutes until the cheese is golden brown. Garnish with basil sprigs and serve.

FRESH PASTA

Be careful not to overcook fresh pasta – it should be 'al dente' (retaining some bite). It takes only a few minutes to cook as it is still full of moisture.

PASTA WITH BROCCOLI

SERVES 4

500 g/1 lb broccoli
300 g/10 oz/1¼ cups garlic & herb cream cheese
4 tbsp milk
350 g/12 oz fresh herb tagliatelle
30 g/1 oz/ ¼ cup grated Parmesan cheese
chopped fresh chives to garnish

1 Cut the broccoli into even-sized florets. Cook the broccoli in boiling salted water for 3 minutes and drain thoroughly.

2 Put the soft cheese into a saucepan and heat gently, stirring, until melted. Add the milk and stir until well combined.

3 Add the broccoli to the cheese mixture and stir to coat.

4 Meanwhile, bring a large saucepan of salted water to the boil and add the tagliatelle. Stir and bring back to the boil. Reduce the heat slightly and cook the tagliatelle, uncovered, for 3–4 minutes until just tender.

5 Drain the tagliatelle thoroughly and divide among 4 warmed serving plates. Spoon the sauce on top. Sprinkle with grated Parmesan cheese, garnish with chives and serve.

PASTA

A herb-flavoured pasta goes particularly well with the broccoli sauce, but failing this, a *tagliatelle verde* or *'paglia e fieno'* (literally 'straw and hay' – thin green and yellow noodles) will fit the bill.

PASTA WITH PINE NUTS (KERNELS) & BLUE CHEESE

SERVES 4

60 g/2 oz/1 cup pine nuts (kernels)
350 g/12 oz dried pasta shapes
2 courgettes (zucchini), sliced
125 g/4 oz broccoli, broken into florets
200 g/7 oz/1 cup full-fat soft cheese
150 ml/ ¼ pint/ ⅔ cup milk
1 tbsp chopped fresh basil
125 g/4 oz button mushrooms, sliced
90 g/3 oz Stilton or Danish blue cheese, crumbled
salt and pepper
sprigs of fresh basil to garnish
green salad to serve

1 Scatter the pine nuts (kernels) on to a baking sheet and grill (broil), turning occasionally, until lightly browned all over. Set aside.

2 Cook the pasta in plenty of boiling, lightly salted water for 8–10 minutes until just tender. Meanwhile, cook the courgettes (zucchini) and broccoli in a small amount of boiling, lightly salted water for about 5 minutes until just tender.

3 Put the soft cheese into a saucepan and heat gently, stirring constantly. Add the milk and stir to mix.

4 Add the basil and mushrooms and cook gently for 2–3 minutes. Stir in the blue cheese and season to taste.

5 Drain the pasta and the vegetables and mix together. Pour over the cheese and mushroom sauce and add the pine nuts (kernels). Toss gently to mix. Garnish with basil sprigs and serve on warmed plates with a green salad.

LOW-FAT VERSION

Use low-fat soft cheese instead of full-fat soft cheese if you want to reduce the calories and fat of this recipe.

SMOKED FISH LASAGNE

SERVES 4

2 tsp olive or vegetable oil
1 garlic clove, crushed
1 small onion, chopped finely
125 g/4 oz mushrooms, sliced
425 g/14 oz can chopped tomatoes
1 small courgette (zucchini), sliced
150 ml/ ¼ pint/ ⅔ cup vegetable stock or water
30 g/1 oz/2 tbsp butter or margarine
300 ml/ ½ pint/1¼ cups skimmed milk
30 g/1 oz/ ¼ cup plain (all-purpose) flour
125 g/4 oz/1 cup grated mature (sharp) Cheddar cheese
1 tbsp chopped fresh parsley
125 g/4 oz (6 sheets) pre-cooked lasagne
350 g/12 oz skinned and boned smoked cod or haddock, cut into chunks
salt and pepper
fresh parsley sprigs to garnish

1 Heat the oil in a saucepan and fry the garlic and onion for about 5 minutes. Add the mushrooms and cook for 3 minutes.

2 Add the tomatoes, courgette (zucchini) and stock or water and simmer, uncovered, for 15–20 minutes until the vegetables are soft. Season.

3 Put the butter or margarine, milk and flour into a small saucepan and heat, whisking constantly, until the sauce boils and thickens. Remove from the heat and add half the cheese and all the parsley. Stir gently to melt the cheese and season to taste.

4 Spoon the tomato sauce mixture into a large, shallow ovenproof dish and top with half the lasagne sheets. Scatter the chunks of fish evenly over the top, then pour over half the cheese sauce. Top with the remaining lasagne sheets and spread the rest of the cheese sauce on top. Sprinkle with the remaining cheese.

5 Bake in a preheated oven at 190°C/375°F/Gas Mark 5 for 40 minutes, until the top is golden brown and bubbling. Garnish with parsley sprigs and serve.

CANNELLONI

SERVES 4

150 g/5 oz/2½ cups button mushrooms
250 g/8 oz/1 cup lean minced (ground)
    beef
1 large red onion, chopped finely
1 garlic clove, crushed
½ tsp ground nutmeg
1 tsp dried mixed herbs
2 tbsp tomato purée (paste)
4 tbsp dry red wine
12 dried 'quick cook' cannelloni tubes
salt and pepper
mixed salad to serve

TOMATO SAUCE:
1 red onion, chopped finely
1 large carrot, grated
1 celery stick, chopped finely
1 dried bay leaf
150 ml/ ¼ pint/ ⅔ cup dry red wine
about 400 g/13 oz can chopped tomatoes
2 tbsp tomato purée (paste)
1 tsp caster (superfine) sugar
salt and pepper

TO GARNISH:
plum tomato
fresh basil sprig
30g/1oz Parmesan cheese shavings

1 Finely chop the mushrooms. In a
non-stick frying pan (skillet), gently
dry-fry the minced (ground) beef, onion,
mushrooms and garlic for 3–4 minutes
until browned all over.

2 Stir in the nutmeg, mixed herbs,
seasoning, tomato purée (paste) and
wine. Simmer gently for 15–20 minutes,
until thick. Cool for 10 minutes.

3 To make the sauce, place the onion,
carrot, celery, bay leaf and wine in a
saucepan. Bring to the boil and simmer
for 5 minutes until the liquid is reduced
and the vegetables softened slightly.

4 Add the remaining ingredients and
bring to the boil. Simmer for 15
minutes. Discard the bay leaf.

5 Spoon ¼ of the sauce over the base
of an ovenproof dish. Using a
teaspoon, fill the cannelloni with the meat
mixture and place on the sauce.

6 Spoon over the remaining sauce.
Cover with foil and bake in a
preheated oven at 200°C/400°F/Gas Mark
6 for 35–40 minutes until tender.

7 Garnish with the Parmesan cheese,
plum tomato and basil sprig and
serve with a mixed salad.

SPRING VEGETABLE & TOFU (BEAN CURD) FUSILLI

SERVES 4

250 g/8 oz asparagus
125 g/4 oz mangetout (snow peas)
250 g/8 oz green beans
1 leek
250 g/8 oz shelled small broad (fava) beans
300 g/10 oz dried fusilli
2 tbsp olive oil
30 g/1 oz/2 tbsp butter or margarine
1 garlic clove, crushed
250 g/8 oz tofu (bean curd), cut into 2.5 cm/1 in cubes
60 g/2 oz/ ⅓ cup pitted green olives in brine, drained
salt and pepper
freshly grated Parmesan cheese to serve (optional)

1 Cut the asparagus into 5 cm/2 in lengths. Finely slice the mangetout (snow peas) diagonally and slice the green beans into 2.5 cm/1 in pieces. Finely slice the leek.

2 Bring a large saucepan of water to the boil and add the asparagus, green beans and broad (fava) beans. Bring back to the boil and cook for 4 minutes until just tender. Drain well and rinse in cold water. Set aside.

3 Bring a large saucepan of lightly salted water to the boil and cook the fusilli for 8–9 minutes until just tender. Drain well. Toss in 1 tablespoon of the oil and season well.

4 Meanwhile, in a wok or large frying pan (skillet), heat the remaining oil and the butter or margarine and gently fry the leek, garlic and tofu (bean curd) for 1–2 minutes until the vegetables have just softened.

5 Stir in the mangetout (snow peas) and cook for a further minute.

6 Add the boiled vegetables and olives to the pan and heat through for 1 minute. Carefully stir in the pasta and seasoning. Cook for 1 minute and pile into a warmed serving dish. Serve sprinkled with Parmesan cheese, if liked.

WARM PASTA WITH BASIL

SERVES 4

250 g/8 oz pasta spirals
4 tomatoes
60 g/2 oz/ ½ cup black olives
30 g/1 oz/ ¼ cup sun-dried tomatoes
2 tbsp pine kernels (nuts), browned
2 tbsp Parmesan cheese shavings
sprig of fresh basil to garnish

BASIL VINAIGRETTE:
4 tbsp chopped fresh basil
1 garlic clove, crushed
2 tbsp grated Parmesan cheese
4 tbsp olive oil
2 tbsp lemon juice
pepper

1 Cook the pasta in boiling salted water for 10–12 minutes until al dente. Drain and rinse well in hot water, then drain again thoroughly.

2 To make the vinaigrette, mix the basil, garlic, Parmesan cheese, olive oil, lemon juice and pepper together with a whisk until blended.

3 Put the pasta into a bowl, pour over the basil vinaigrette and toss thoroughly.

4 Skin the tomatoes and cut into wedges. Halve and pit the olives and slice the sun-dried tomatoes.

5 Add them all to the pasta and mix together thoroughly. Transfer to a salad bowl and scatter the nuts and Parmesan shavings over the top. Serve warm, garnished with a sprig of basil.

SUN-DRIED TOMATOES

Sun-dried tomatoes are, as their name indicates, tomatoes that have been halved and dried in the sun, leaving a wrinkled specimen with an extremely rich, concentrated flavour. They are usually covered with oil, and herbs and garlic are added to give extra flavour. When added to a sauce or salad they impart an added depth of flavour, and may also be used as a spread.

PASTA WITH GREEN VEGETABLES

SERVES 4

250 g/8 oz gemelli or other pasta shapes
1 tbsp olive oil
2 tbsp chopped parsley
salt and pepper

SAUCE:
1 head green broccoli, cut into florets
2 medium courgettes (zucchini), sliced
250 g/8 oz asparagus spears, trimmed
125 g/4 oz mangetout (snow peas),
*   trimmed*
125 g/4 oz frozen peas
30 g/1 oz/2 tbsp butter
3 tbsp vegetable stock
5 tbsp double (heavy) cream
large pinch of grated nutmeg
2 tbsp grated Parmesan

1 Cook the pasta in a large pan of salted boiling water, adding the olive oil. When almost tender, drain the pasta in a colander and return to the pan, cover and keep warm.

2 Steam the broccoli, courgettes (zucchini), asparagus spears and mangetout (snow peas) over a pan of boiling, salted water until they are just beginning to soften. Remove from the heat and plunge into cold water to prevent them from cooking further in the residual heat. Drain and set them aside.

3 Cook the frozen peas in boiling, salted water for 3 minutes, then drain. Refresh in cold water and drain again.

4 Put the butter and vegetable stock in a pan over a medium heat. Add all the vegetables except the asparagus spears and toss carefully with a wooden spoon to heat through, taking care not to break them up. Stir in the cream, allow the sauce just to heat through and season well with salt, pepper and nutmeg.

5 Transfer the pasta to a warmed serving dish and stir in the chopped parsley. Spoon the sauce over, and sprinkle on the Parmesan. Arrange the asparagus spears in a pattern on top. Serve hot.

SPANISH OMELETTE

SERVES 2

4 tbsp olive oil
1 small Spanish onion, chopped
1 fennel bulb, thinly sliced
125 g/4 oz raw potato, diced and dried
1 garlic clove, chopped
4 eggs
1 tbsp chopped parsley
pinch of cayenne pepper
90 g/3 oz short pasta, cooked weight
1 tbsp stuffed green olives, halved, plus
*   extra to garnish*
salt and pepper
marjoram sprigs, to garnish
tomato salad, to serve

1 Heat 2 tablespoons of the oil in a heavy frying pan over a low heat and fry the onion, fennel and potato for 8-10 minutes, stirring occasionally, until the potato is just tender. Do not allow it to break up. Stir in the garlic and cook for 1 further minute. Remove the pan from the heat, lift out the vegetables with a slotted spoon and set them aside. Rinse and dry the pan.

2 Break the eggs into a bowl and beat them until they are frothy. Stir in the parsley and season with salt, pepper and cayenne.

3 Heat 1 tablespoon of the remaining oil in a pan over medium heat. Pour in half the beaten eggs, then add the cooked vegetables, the pasta and the olives. Pour on the remaining egg and cook until the sides begin to set.

4 Lift up the edges with a spatula to allow the uncooked egg to spread underneath. Continue cooking the omelette, shaking the pan occasionally, until the underside is golden brown.

5 Slide the omelette out on to a large, flat plate and wipe the pan clean with paper towels. Heat the remaining oil in the pan and invert the omelette. Cook on the other side until it is also golden brown.

6 Slide the omelette on to a warmed serving dish. Garnish with a few olives and marjoram, and serve hot, cut into wedges, with a tomato salad.

VEGETARIAN DISHES – INTRODUCTION

Vegetarianism is becoming increasingly popular in the West. Some people choose not to eat meat because of their feelings about animal cruelty, while others believe that cutting out meat will help reduce the risk of heart disease caused by eating cholesterol-rich foods, and that eating more fibrous vegetables and pulses will help reduce the risk of cancers such as colonic cancer. Others may opt for a vegetarian diet – at least some of the time – for reasons of economy.

Whatever your reason for eating meals without meat, providing your meals are properly planned and varied, a vegetarian diet can be as interesting as it is healthy. So dispel the myth that vegetarian cooking can be complicated, time-consuming, heavy or stodgy. Choose recipes that are fun to cook as well as to eat, and which are full of vibrant colours and exciting flavours. Experiment with exotic fruit, vegetables, herbs and spices, as well as the vast range of grains and pulses that are staple foods in other countries, to provide meals for family and guests alike.

VEGETARIAN NUTRITION

When following a vegetarian diet, your food intake must be carefully thought out in order to ensure the diet is well balanced and provides the body with the correct nourishment. The use of milk, cheese, eggs, pulses and cereals should be maximized to provide sufficient protein, vitamins and minerals. Resist the temptation to eat large amounts of dairy produce in place of meat, however, as cream, butter and cheese contain cholesterol and a lot of fat. As with any diet, keep everything in moderation.

Proteins

Protein is made up of smaller units, called amino acids, which combine to help the body with growth, repair, maintenance and protection.

There are eight essential amino acids; some foods are better at providing these than others. The main sources of protein for vegetarians are dairy produce (which contains all the essential amino acids), and nuts and seeds, pulses, cereals and cereal products, each of which is deficient in at least one amino acid. Because of this, two or more of these sources must be eaten at the same meal or combined with dairy produce if they are to be of value to the body.

Carbohydrates

Used by the body for energy, the two main groups of carbohydrates are starches and sugars, which are present in cereals and grains and related products such as flour. They are also found in fruits, pulses and some vegetables.

Sugar: Whether white, brown or in the form of honey, syrup or molasses, sugar is purely a source of energy and has no other nutritional value. Use any type of sugar in moderation and avoid excessive intake.

Dietary fibre: Many carbohydrates in their natural, unrefined form, such as wholemeal (whole wheat) flour, contain dietary fibre. It does not have any nutritional value but is vital for the efficient working of the digestive system and the elimination of waste matter. Some types of fibre may also slow down the rate at which the body absorbs carbohydrates. A vegetarian diet is naturally high in

INTRODUCTION

fibre. There is no fibre in meat, poultry, fish or dairy produce. Good sources of fibre are pulses, whole grains, vegetables (especially sweetcorn, spinach and baked potatoes) dried fruits and fresh fruits. Try to include at least one high-fibre food per meal.

Fats

The most concentrated form of energy in the diet and a vital carrier of vitamins A and D. Fat comes in two forms: animal and vegetable. The only animal fats in the vegetarian diet are found in dairy produce and egg yolks.

Fats can be classified as saturated, monounsaturated and polyunsaturated. Saturated fats, such as butter, are solid at room temperature and are believed to raise the quantity of fat and cholesterol in the blood; monounsaturated fats, such as olive oil, are thought to decrease the risk of heart disease and may lower blood pressure; polyunsaturated fats, such as sunflower and corn oils, were at one time believed to be better than mono-unsaturated fats at lowering the amount of cholesterol in the blood, but latest research has found no difference between the two. Polyunsaturated margarines and fats are an exception, however. The oils are made solid by a process called hydrogenation and it is thought that this process can make the fats more harmful than saturated fats. It is important to be aware of this when choosing an alternative to butter. Whatever you choose, keep your intake of fat to a sensible level and cut down wherever possible. Always read labelling for 'hidden' fats.

Vitamins and minerals

Vegetables are lower in certain vitamins and minerals than animal products, so it is essential to plan your food intake to obtain the correct nutritional balance.

Vitamin B group: Important for the metabolism of other foods, the health of the nervous system and the production of red blood cells. You will obtain a good supply by eating grains, cereals, leafy green vegetables, nuts and seeds and dried fruits. Yeast extract, wheatgerm and brewer's yeast are also good sources.

There are three B vitamins which vegetarians may lack if they consume little or no dairy produce: vitamin B2 (riboflavin), vitamin B3 (nicotinic acid) and vitamin B12. Good sources of vitamins B2 and B3 are mushrooms, sesame seeds, sunflower seeds, almonds, prunes and dried peaches. Vitamin B12 is found mainly in animal products and supplementation is often advised for vegans, as deficiency can lead to anaemia and nerve damage. Yeast extract, alfalfa sprouts, seaweed, textured vegetable proteins and fortified soya milk are other sources of vitamin B12.

Calcium: Essential for bone and teeth formation, and for the functioning of nerves and muscles. The best sources are dairy produce and eggs. Vegans and those who don't eat many dairy foods need to eat more grains, pulses, nuts, seeds and dried fruits to obtain a good supply of calcium.

Iron: Lack of iron can lead to anaemia as it is essential for the production of red blood cells which carry oxygen around the body. Eggs are an excellent source, as are dark green leafy vegetables, broccoli, dried apricots and figs, pulses and nuts. However, as iron from vegetable

INTRODUCTION

sources is not readily absorbed by the body it is important to eat foods rich in vitamin C at the same meal as this aids the absorption of iron.

Zinc: An important trace element for growth, healing, reproduction and the digestion of protein and carbohydrate. Although wholegrains and pulses contain zinc, a substance called phytic acid inhibits its absorption. Other sources are wheatgerm, oats, nuts and seeds. Useful amounts also occur in yellow and green vegetables and fruits.

VEGETARIAN INGREDIENTS

At the heart of any balanced diet is an interesting variety of ingredients. This is especially true of the vegetarian diet, which may feature foodstuffs that are not very familiar to many people.

Nuts and seeds

Nuts and seeds provide valuable quantities of protein, B vitamins, iron and calcium but also have a high fat content. Nuts and seeds are often pressed for their oil or made into pastes and butters. They add a wealth of flavours to dishes as well as adding texture.

Pulses

Pulses are very important in the vegetarian diet. They provide not only fibre but are also one of the main sources of vegetable protein.

Pulses are the dried seeds of peas and beans, and there is a great variety to choose from. In their dry form, they are cheap to buy and, because they are very filling, offer an economical addition to the diet if you are on a tight budget. Except for lentils, most pulses require prior soaking before cooking. (Red kidney

beans should be boiled rapidly for the first 10 minutes of cooking, or they may lead to food poisoning.)

More expensive but more convenient are canned pulses. Because these are pre-cooked, they are much softer in texture than the dried types, and so only really need draining and thorough heating through before serving. If they are to be combined with other ingredients, add them towards the end of the cooking time.

Grains and cereals

Both cereals and grains are key ingredients of the vegetarian diet, not only in terms of variety of taste, texture and a source of fibre, but also because of the protein, vitamins and minerals they provide.

Pasta

A high carbohydrate food which, like grains and cereals, forms the basis of the vegetarian diet. Made from white, wholemeal (whole wheat) or rice flour. All types of fresh pasta, and some dried varieties, contain egg.

Vegetables

These can be categorized into different groups:
Leaves: Lettuces, spinach, watercress, chard, vine leaves. Contain calcium, iron and fibre.

Brassicas: Cabbage, broccoli, kale, Brussels sprouts, cauliflower, Chinese leaves. Rich in vitamins and minerals.

Pods and seeds: Fresh beans, sweetcorn, peas, mangetout (snow peas), okra. Full of fibre and a good source of protein.

Shoots: Asparagus, celery, chicory (endive), bamboo, artichoke, fennel.

INTRODUCTION

Shoots are better known for their flavour, texture and shape than their nutritional value.

Bulbs: Onions, garlic, leeks, shallots. Excellent for flavour.

Roots: Celeriac (celery root), carrots, turnips, swede (rutabaga), beetroot, daikon (mooli). Contain iron, calcium and protein. Carrots are also very rich in vitamin A.

Tubers: White and sweet potatoes, yams, Jerusalem artichokes. High in carbohydrate, and useful sources of vitamin C, iron and protein.

'Fruits': Tomatoes, avocado, (bell) peppers, chillies, aubergines (eggplants). Rich in vitamin C.

Cucumbers and squash: Including courgettes (zucchini), pumpkins and marrow. Very high water content, Contain some fibre.

Mushrooms: Rich in both vitamins B2 and B3.

Sea vegetables: Laver, samphire and dulse are increasingly popular and very nutritious. Rich in protein, iron, calcium and vitamin B12.

Fruits

From home-grown varieties such as apples, pears and soft fruits, to the more exotic imports such as lychees, mangoes and pineapples, fruits are a valuable source of vitamin C and fibre as well as specific trace elements: bananas, for example, are an excellent source of magnesium and vitamin B6, and mangoes provide zinc.

Dried fruits are higher in fibre and B vitamins and have a richer flavour than fresh fruit. Look out for sun-dried fruits, and those free from sulphur dioxide, which is used to prevent darkening during drying. Sulphur dioxide inhibits the absorption of vitamin B1 in the body. To cut down on its effect, wash dried fruit in warm water, boil for 5 minutes, then rinse again.

Dairy and non-dairy products

Cheeses, eggs, milk, yogurt, creams and tofu (bean curd) are valuable sources of protein, calcium, vitamins A and D and iron. Cheese adds an excellent flavour to many dishes. Many varieties of vegetarian cheeses, which are made from non-animal rennet, are available.

If you choose not to eat dairy products at all, check the nutritional content of non-dairy products such as soya milks and look out for fortified varieties. Tofu (bean curd) is made from soya milk and is available in many forms – firm, soft, dried or smoked. It is low in fat and high in protein. It can be fried or added to casseroles and soups. It has a neutral flavour and absorbs flavours from the foods it is cooked with. Smoked tofu, with a slightly stronger flavour, is also available.

Herbs and spices

Careful combining of fresh or dried herbs and spices can add zest to any dish: they help stimulate the taste buds and aid digestion as well as bringing out the flavour of the basic ingredients used.

Experiment with different flavours and read the packet if you are uncertain about strength – most show possible uses and suggested quantities. Don't let any one flavour dominate: what you are aiming for is a perfect blend of flavours.

INTRODUCTION

FRESH VEGETABLE STOCK

This stock can be kept chilled for up to 3 days or frozen for up to 3 months. Salt is not added when cooking the stock; it is better to season it according to the dish it is to be used in.

Makes 1.5 litres/2½ pints/1½ quarts
250 g/8 oz shallots
1 large carrot, diced
1 celery stick, chopped
½ fennel bulb
1 garlic clove
1 bay leaf
a few fresh parsley and tarragon
  sprigs
2 litres/3½ pints/2 quarts water
pepper

1. Put all the ingredients in a large saucepan and bring to the boil.

2. Skim off surface scum with a flat spoon. Reduce to a gentle simmer, partially cover and cook for 45 minutes. Leave to cool.

3. Line a sieve (strainer) with clean muslin (cheesecloth) and put over a large jug or bowl. Pour the stock through the sieve (strainer). Discard the herbs and vegetables. Cover and store in the refrigerator for up to 3 days or freeze in small quantities.

YOGURT CHEESE

Once you are in the habit of making your own yogurt, or if you buy yogurt in reasonably large quantities, the next step is to make your own soft cheese. You can use it in place of cottage cheese or commercially made low-fat soft cheese in sandwiches and snacks, salads and toppings, baked dishes and desserts.

The yield varies slightly according to the type of milk from which the yogurt was made, and the length of time it was left to drain. As a guide, any quantity of yogurt will provide just over half its volume in yogurt cheese. The whey that is drained off can be stored in the refrigerator and used in place of stock in soups and sauces.

To make 400 g/14 oz/1½ cups Yogurt Cheese
1 litre/1¾ pints/4 cups natural yogurt
salt (optional)

1. Line a colander with a double thickness of cheesecloth or muslin. Tip in the yogurt and draw the muslin over to cover it. Or tie the corners of the muslin to make a bag. Stand the colander in a bowl, or hang the bag over a bowl, to catch the whey.

2. Leave it to drain overnight. Transfer the yogurt to a bowl and, if you wish, beat in a little salt. Store in a covered container in the refrigerator for up to a week.

Storing yogurt cheese

You may like to store some of your yogurt cheese in the traditional Middle Eastern way. Scoop out small spoonfuls and roll them into walnut-sized balls. Pack them in a lidded jar and pour on olive oil to cover the cheese completely. Add any flavourings you wish, such as bay leaves, sprigs of thyme or rosemary, dried chillies, peppercorns or mustard seeds.

To serve, lift out the cheese as required with a draining spoon, drain off the excess oil and roll the balls in chopped walnuts. Serve these cheese balls with cocktail sticks, as an appetizer with drinks.

AVIYAL

SERVES 4

250 g/8 oz/2⅔ cups desiccated (shredded)
   coconut or 125 g (4 oz) creamed
   coconut
300 ml/ ½ pint/1¼ cups boiling water
2 tbsp sunflower oil
30 g/1 oz ginger root, grated
2 onions, finely chopped
1 garlic clove, crushed
2 tsp ground coriander
1 tbsp garam masala
1 tsp turmeric
2 green (bell) peppers, cored, seeded and
   sliced in thin rings
1 red or yellow (bell) pepper, cored, seeded
   and sliced in thin rings
2 carrots, cut into julienne strips
1 green chilli pepper, cored, seeded and
   sliced (optional)
125-175 g/4-6 oz French or fine beans,
   cut into 7 cm/3 in lengths
175 g/6 oz green broccoli, divided into
   florets
3 tomatoes, peeled, quartered and seeded
salt and pepper

1 Soak the coconut in the boiling
   water for 20 minutes, then process in
a food processor until smooth, or blend
the creamed coconut with the boiling
water until smooth.

2 Heat the oil in the wok, swirling it
   around until really hot. Add the
ginger, onions and garlic and stir-fry for
2-3 minutes until they are beginning to
colour lightly.

3 Add the coriander, garam masala and
   turmeric and continue to stir-fry for a
few minutes then add the peppers,
carrots, chilli, beans, broccoli and
tomatoes, and stir-fry for 4–5 minutes,
turning the heat down a little.

4 Add the coconut purée and plenty
   of seasoning and bring to the boil.
Continue to simmer and stir-fry for about
5–8 minutes, until tender but still with a
bite to the vegetables.

5 Serve as a main dish with boiled rice
   or noodles, or as a curry
accompaniment.

VEGETABLE MEDLEY

SERVES 4

150 g/5 oz young, tender green beans
8 baby carrots
6 baby turnips
½ small cauliflower
2 tbsp vegetable oil
2 large onions, sliced
2 garlic cloves, finely chopped
300 ml/ ½ pint/1¼ cups natural yogurt
1 tbsp cornflour (cornstarch)
2 tbsp tomato purée (paste)
large pinch of chilli powder
salt

1 Top and tail the beans and snap
   them in half. Cut the carrots in half
and the turnips in quarters. Divide the
cauliflower into florets, discarding the
thickest part of the stalk. Steam the
vegetables over boiling, salted water for 3
minutes, then turn them into a colander
and plunge them at once in a large bowl
of cold water to prevent further cooking.

2 Heat the oil in a pan and fry the
   onions until they are translucent. Stir
in the garlic and cook for 1 further
minute.

3 Mix together the yogurt, cornflour
   (cornstarch) and tomato purée
(paste) to form a smooth paste. Stir this
paste into the onions in the pan and cook
for 1-2 minutes until the sauce is well
blended.

4 Drain the vegetables well, then
   gradually stir them into the sauce,
taking care not to break them up. Season
with salt and chilli powder to taste, cover
and simmer gently for 5 minutes, until the
vegetables are just tender. Taste and
adjust the seasoning if necessary. Serve
immediately.

SWEET & SOUR VEGETABLES

SERVES 4

5-6 vegetables from the following:
1 (bell) pepper, red, green or yellow, cored,
*   seeded and sliced*
125 g/4 oz French beans, cut into 2-3
*   pieces*
125 g/4 oz mangetout (snow peas), cut
*   into 2-3 pieces*
250 g/8 oz green broccoli or cauliflower,
*   divided into tiny florets*
250 g/8 oz courgettes (zucchini), cut into
*   thin 5 cm/2 in lengths*
175 g/6 oz carrots, cut into julienne strips
125 g/4 oz baby sweetcorn, sliced thinly
2 leeks, sliced thinly and cut into
*   matchsticks*
175 g/6 oz parsnip, finely diced
175 g/6 oz celeriac, finely diced
3 celery sticks, thinly sliced crosswise
4 tomatoes, peeled, quartered and seeded
125 g/4 oz button or closed cup
*   mushrooms, thinly sliced*
7 cm/3 in length of cucumber, diced
1 x 200 g/7 oz can water chestnuts or
*   bamboo shoots, drained and sliced*
1 x 425 g/15 oz can bean-sprouts or
*   hearts of palm, drained and sliced*
4 spring onions (scallions) trimmed and
*   thinly sliced*
1 garlic clove, crushed
2 tbsp sunflower oil

SWEET & SOUR SAUCE:
2 tbsp wine vinegar
2 tbsp clear honey
1 tbsp tomato purée (paste)
2 tbsp soy sauce
2 tbsp sherry
1-2 tsp sweet chilli sauce (optional)
2 tsp cornflour (cornstarch)

1 Prepare the selected vegetables, cutting them into uniform lengths.

2 Combine the sauce ingredients in a bowl, blending well together.

3 Heat the oil in the wok, swirling it around until really hot. Add the spring onions (scallions) and garlic and stir-fry for 1 minute.

4 Add the prepared vegetables – the harder and firmer ones first – and stir-fry for 2 minutes. Then add the softer ones such as mushrooms, mangetout (snow peas) and tomatoes and continue to stir-fry for 2 minutes.

5 Add the sweet and sour mixture to the wok and bring to the boil quickly, tossing all the vegetables until they are thoroughly coated and the sauce has thickened. Serve hot.

CAULIFLOWER ROULADE

SERVES 6

1 small cauliflower, divided into florets
4 eggs, separated
90 g/3 oz/ ¾ cup Cheddar, grated
60 g/2 oz/ ¼ cup Yogurt Cheese (see
page 97), or cottage cheese
large pinch of grated nutmeg
½ tsp mustard powder
salt and pepper

FILLING:
1 bunch watercress, trimmed
60 g/2 oz/ ¼ cup butter
30 g/1 oz/ ¼ cup flour
175 ml/6 fl oz/ ¾ cup natural yogurt
30 g/1 oz/ ¼ cup Cheddar, grated
60 g/2 oz/ ¼ cup yogurt cheese (see
page 97), or cottage cheese

1 Line a Swiss roll tin (pan) with baking parchment.

2 Steam the cauliflower until just tender. Drain and run cold water on it, to prevent further cooking. Place the cauliflower in a food processor and chop finely.

3 Beat the egg yolks, then stir in the cauliflower, 60 g/2 oz/½ cup of the Cheddar and the yogurt cheese. Season with salt, nutmeg, mustard and pepper. Whisk the egg whites until stiff but not dry, then fold into the cauliflower mixture, using a metal spoon.

4 Spread the mixture evenly in the prepared tin (pan) and bake in the preheated oven for 20-25 minutes, until well risen and golden brown.

5 Finely chop the watercress, reserving a few sprigs for garnish. Melt the butter in a small pan and add the watercress. Cook for 3 minutes, stirring, until it has collapsed. Blend in the flour, then stir in the yogurt and simmer for 2 minutes. Stir in the cheeses.

6 Turn out the roulade on to a damp tea towel covered with baking parchment. Peel off the paper and leave 1 minute for the steam to escape. Roll up the roulade, including a new sheet of paper, starting from one narrow end.

7 Unroll the roulade, spread the filling to within 2.5 cm/1 in of the edges, and roll up tightly. Transfer to a baking sheet, sprinkle on the remaining Cheddar and return to the oven for 5 minutes. Serve hot or cold.

SAGE & ONION CHOWDER

∙∙

SERVES 4-6

60 g/2 oz/ ¼ cup butter or margarine
4 onions, sliced very thinly or chopped
1–2 garlic cloves, crushed
4 slices lean bacon, chopped
2 tbsp plain (all-purpose) flour
900 ml/1½ pints/3½ cups Fresh Vegetable
    Stock (see page 97)
500 g/1 lb potatoes, diced very finely
300 ml/ ½ pint/⅔ cup creamy milk
about 200 g/7 oz can sweetcorn, well
    drained
1 tbsp chopped fresh sage or 1½ tsp dried
    sage
2 tbsp white wine vinegar
salt and pepper
sprigs of fresh sage to garnish
Cheese Scones (see page 11), warmed, to
    serve

1 Melt the butter or margarine in a
large saucepan and fry the onions
and garlic very gently for about 15
minutes until soft but not coloured.

2 Add the bacon and continue to fry
for a few minutes, allowing the
onions to colour a little. Stir in the flour
and cook for a further minute or so.

3 Add the stock, bring to the boil, then
add the potatoes and seasoning and
simmer gently for 20 minutes.

4 Add the milk and sweetcorn and
bring back to the boil, then add the
sage and vinegar and simmer for a further
10–15 minutes until the potatoes are very
tender but not broken up.

5 Adjust the seasoning, garnish with
sprigs of sage and serve with
warmed cheese scones.

VARIATION

Frozen sweetcorn can be used instead
of the canned variety. Add directly to
the soup in step 4 — there's no need
to thaw it first.

SPLIT PEAS WITH VEGETABLES

∙∙

SERVES 4-5

250 g/8 oz/1 cup dried yellow split peas
1.25 litres/2 pints/5 cups cold water
½ tsp ground turmeric (optional)
500g/1 lb new potatoes, scrubbed
75 ml/5 tbsp/ ⅓ cup vegetable oil
2 onions, peeled and coarsely chopped
175 g/6 oz button mushrooms, wiped
1 tsp ground coriander
1 tsp ground cumin
1 tsp chilli powder
1 tsp garam masala
salt and freshly ground black pepper
450 ml/ ¾ pint/1¾ cups Fresh Vegetable
    Stock (see page 97)
½ cauliflower, broken into florets
90 g/3 oz frozen peas
175 g/6 oz cherry tomatoes and halved
    mint sprigs, to garnish

1 Place the split peas in a bowl, add
the cold water and leave to soak for
at least 4 hours or overnight.

2 Place the peas and the soaking
liquid in a fairly large saucepan, stir
in the turmeric, if using, and bring to the
boil. Skim off any surface scum, half-
cover the pan with a lid and simmer
gently for 20 minutes or until the peas are
tender and almost dry. Remove the pan
from the heat and reserve.

3 Meanwhile, cut the potatoes into 5
mm (¼ in) thick slices. Heat the oil
in a flameproof casserole, add the onions,
potatoes and mushrooms and cook gently
for 5 minutes, stirring frequently. Stir in
the spices and fry gently for 1 minute,
then add salt and pepper to taste, stock
and cauliflower florets.

4 Cover and simmer gently for 25
minutes or until the potato is tender,
stirring occasionally. Add the split peas
(and any of the cooking liquid) and the
frozen peas. Bring to the boil, cover and
continue cooking for 5 minutes.

5 Stir in the halved cherry tomatoes
and cook for 2 minutes. Taste and
adjust the seasoning, if necessary. Serve
hot, garnished with mint sprigs.

VEGETARIAN CASSOULET

••

SERVES 6

250 g/8 oz/generous 1 cup dried haricot
 beans, soaked and drained
250 g/8 oz penne, or other short pasta
 shapes
6 tbsp olive oil
900 ml/1½ pints/3½ cups Fresh Vegetable
 Stock (see page 97)
2 large onions, sliced
2 cloves garlic, chopped
2 bay leaves
1 tsp dried oregano
1 tsp dried thyme
5 tbsp red wine
2 tbsp tomato purée (paste)
2 celery stalks, sliced
1 fennel bulb, sliced
125 g/4 oz mushrooms, sliced
250 g/8 oz tomatoes, sliced
1 tsp dark Muscovado sugar
4 tbsp dry white breadcrumbs
salt and pepper
salad leaves and crusty bread, to serve

1 Put the beans in a large pan, cover
 them with water and bring to the
boil. Boil the beans rapidly for 20
minutes, then drain them.

2 Cook the pasta for only 3 minutes in
 a large pan of boiling salted water,
adding 1 tablespoon of the oil. When
almost tender, drain the pasta in a
colander and set it aside.

3 Place the beans in a large flameproof
 casserole, pour on the Vegetable
Stock and stir in the remaining olive oil,
the onions, garlic, bay leaves, herbs, wine
and tomato purée (paste).

4 Bring the stock to the boil, cover the
 casserole and cook it in the oven for
2 hours.

5 Add the reserved pasta, the celery,
 fennel, mushrooms and tomatoes,
and season with salt and pepper. Stir
in the sugar and sprinkle on the
breadcrumbs. Cover the casserole and
continue cooking it for 1 hour. Serve it
hot, with salad leaves and plenty of
crusty bread.

BAKED AUBERGINES (EGGPLANT)

••

SERVES 4

250 g/8 oz penne, or other short pasta
 shapes
4 tbsp olive oil, plus extra for brushing
2 medium aubergines (eggplant)
1 large onion, chopped
2 garlic cloves, crushed
1 x 425 g/15 oz can chopped tomatoes
2 tsp dried oregano
60 g/2 oz Mozzarella, thinly sliced
30 g/1 oz/ ¼ cup Parmesan, grated
2 tbsp dry breadcrumbs
salt and pepper
salad leaves, to serve

1 Cook the pasta in a large pan of
 salted boiling water, adding 1
tablespoon of the olive oil. When almost
tender, drain the pasta in a colander,
return to the pan, cover and keep warm.

2 Cut the aubergines (eggplant) in half
 lengthways. Score around the inside
with a knife, then scoop out the flesh
with a spoon, taking care not to pierce
the skin. Brush the insides of the
aubergine (eggplant) shells with olive oil.
Chop the aubergine (eggplant) flesh and
set it aside.

3 Heat the remaining oil in a frying
 pan over a medium heat and fry the
onion until it is translucent. Add the garlic
and fry for 1 further minute. Add the
chopped aubergine (eggplant) and fry for
5 minutes, stirring frequently. Add the
tomatoes and oregano and season with
salt and pepper. Bring to the boil and
simmer for 10 minutes, or until the
mixture is thick. Taste and adjust the
seasoning if necessary. Remove from the
heat and stir in the reserved pasta.

4 Brush a baking sheet with oil and
 arrange the aubergine (eggplant)
shells in a single layer. Divide half the
tomato mixture between the four shells.
Arrange the Mozzarella on top and cover
with the remaining mixture, piling it into
a mound. Mix together the Parmesan and
breadcrumbs, and sprinkle over the top.

5 Bake in the preheated oven at
 180º/350ºF/Gas Mark 4 for 25
minutes. Serve hot, with green salad.

AUBERGINE (EGGPLANT) & MUSHROOM SATAY WITH PEANUT SAUCE

SERVES 4

8 wooden or metal skewers.
2 aubergines (eggplants), cut into 2.5
cm/1 in pieces
175 g/6 oz small chestnut mushrooms

MARINADE:
1 tsp cumin seed
1 tsp coriander seed
2.5 cm/1 in piece ginger, grated
2 garlic cloves, crushed lightly
½ stalk lemon grass, chopped roughly
4 tbsp light soy sauce
8 tbsp sunflower oil
2 tbsp lemon juice

PEANUT SAUCE:
½ tsp cumin seed
½ tsp coriander seed
3 garlic cloves
1 small onion, quartered
1 tbsp lemon juice
1 tsp salt
½ red chilli, deseeded and sliced
120 ml/4 fl oz/ ½ cup coconut milk
250 g/8 oz/1 cup crunchy peanut butter
250 ml/8 fl oz/1 cup water

1 If using wooden skewers, soak in hand-hot water for 5 minutes.

2 Thread the aubergine (eggplant) and mushroom on to the skewers.

3 To make the marinade, grind the cumin and coriander seeds, ginger, garlic and lemon grass together. Put in a wok or a large frying pan (skillet). Stir over a high heat until fragrant. Remove from the heat and add the remaining marinade ingredients.

4 Place the skewers in a non-porous dish and spoon the marinade over the skewers. Leave to marinate for a minimum of 2 hours and up to 8 hours.

5 To make the peanut sauce, grind together the cumin and coriander seeds and the garlic. Switch on your food processor or blender and feed in the onion, or chop the onion finely by hand, then add to the cumin seed mixture. Add the rest of the ingredients in order, except the water.

6 Transfer to a saucepan and blend in the water. Bring to the boil and cook until the required thickness is reached. Transfer to a serving bowl.

7 Place the skewers on a baking sheet and cook under a preheated very hot grill (broiler) for 15–20 minutes. Brush with the marinade frequently and turn once. Serve with the peanut sauce.

THREE MUSHROOMS IN COCONUT MILK

••

SERVES 4

2 lemon grass stalks, sliced thinly
2 green chillies, deseeded and chopped finely
1 tbsp light soy sauce
2 garlic cloves, crushed
2 tbsp chopped fresh coriander (cilantro)
2 tbsp chopped fresh parsley
6 slices galangal, peeled
3 tbsp sunflower oil
1 aubergine (eggplant), cubed
60 g/2 oz/⅔ cup oyster mushrooms
60 g/2 oz/⅔ cup chestnut (crimini) mushrooms
60 g/2 oz/⅔ cup field mushrooms, quartered if large
125 g/4 oz green beans, cut into 5 cm/ 2 in lengths, blanched
300 ml/½ pint/1¼ cups coconut milk
1 tbsp lemon juice
2 tbsp chopped roasted peanuts to garnish

1 Grind together the lemon grass, chillies, soy sauce, garlic, coriander (cilantro), parsley and galangal in a large pestle and mortar or a food processor. Set aside.

2 Heat the sunflower oil in a wok or large, heavy frying pan (skillet). Add the aubergine (eggplant) and stir over a high heat for 3 minutes; then add the mushrooms, stir and add the beans. Cook for 3 minutes, stirring constantly. Add the ground spice paste.

3 Add the coconut milk and lemon juice to the pan, bring to the boil and simmer for 2 minutes.

4 Serve immediately over rice, and garnish with the roasted peanuts.

VARIATION

Any mixture of tasty mushrooms can be used in this recipe. If using dried mushrooms, use 15 g/ ½ oz/1 tbsp for every 60 g/2 oz/ ⅔ cup fresh.

INDONESIAN CHESTNUT & VEGETABLE STIR-FRY WITH PEANUT SAUCE

••

SERVES 4

SAUCE:
125 g/4 oz/1 cup unsalted peanuts, roasted and ground
2 tsp hot chilli sauce
180 ml/6 fl oz/ ¾ cup coconut milk
2 tbsp soy sauce
1 tbsp ground coriander
pinch of ground turmeric
1 tbsp dark muscovado sugar

STIR-FRY:
3 tbsp sesame oil
3–4 shallots, finely sliced
1 garlic clove, finely sliced
1–2 red chillies, deseeded and finely chopped
1 large carrot, cut into fine strips
1 yellow & 1 red (bell) pepper, deseeded and cut into fine strips
1 courgette (zucchini), cut into fine strips
125 g/4 oz sugar snap peas, trimmed
7.5 cm/3 in piece of cucumber, cut into strips
250 g/8 oz oyster mushrooms, wiped and torn into small pieces, if large
250 g/8 oz canned whole peeled chestnuts, drained
2 tsp grated fresh root ginger
finely grated rind and juice of 1 lime
1 tbsp chopped fresh coriander (cilantro)
salt and pepper
slices of lime, to garnish

1 To make the sauce, put all the ingredients into a small pan. Heat gently and simmer for 3–4 minutes.

2 Heat the sesame oil in a wok or large frying pan (skillet). Add the shallots, garlic and chillies and stir-fry for 2 minutes.

3 Add the carrot, (bell) peppers, courgette (zucchini) and sugar snap peas to the wok or pan (skillet) and stir-fry for 2 more minutes.

4 Add all the remaining ingredients to the wok or pan (skillet) and stir-fry briskly for about 5 minutes. Divide between 4 warmed serving plates, and garnish with slices of lime. Serve with the peanut sauce.

SPINACH PANCAKES

SERVES 4

90 g/3 oz/ ¾ cup wholewheat flour
1 egg
150 ml/ ¼ pint/ ⅔ cup natural yogurt
3 tbsp water
1 tbsp vegetable oil, plus extra for
   brushing
200 g/7 oz frozen leaf spinach, defrosted
   and liquidized
pinch of grated nutmeg
salt and pepper
lemon wedges and coriander, to garnish

FILLING:
1 tbsp vegetable oil
3 spring onions (scallions), thinly sliced
250 g/8 oz/1 cup Ricotta
4 tbsp plain yogurt
90 g/3 oz/ ¾ cup Gruyère, grated
1 egg, lightly beaten
250 g/8 oz shelled prawns (shrimp),
   chopped
2 tbsp chopped parsley
pinch of cayenne pepper

1 Sift the flour and salt into a bowl and tip in any bran remaining in the sieve. Beat together the egg, yogurt, water and oil. Gradually pour it on to the flour, beating all the time. Stir in the spinach purée and season with pepper and nutmeg.

2 To make the filling, heat the oil in a pan and fry the onions until translucent. Remove with a slotted spoon and drain on paper towels. Beat together the Ricotta, yogurt and half the Gruyère. Beat in the egg and stir in the prawns (shrimp) and parsley. Season with salt and cayenne pepper.

3 Lightly brush a small, heavy frying pan with oil and heat. Pour in 3-4 tablespoons of the pancake batter and tilt the pan so that it covers the base. Cook for about 3 minutes, until bubbles appear in the centre. Turn and cook the other side for about 2 minutes, until lightly browned. Slide the pancake on a warmed plate, cover with foil and keep warm while you cook the remainder. It should make 8-12 pancakes.

4 Spread a little filling over each pancake and fold in half and then half again, envelope style. Spoon the remaining filling into the opening.

5 Grease a shallow, ovenproof dish and arrange the pancakes in a single layer. Sprinkle on the remaining cheese and cook in the preheated oven for about 15 minutes. Serve hot, garnished with lemon and coriander.

TOMATO & COURGETTE (ZUCCHINI) FRITTATA

••

SERVES 4

3 tbsp olive oil
1 onion, chopped
250 g/8 oz courgettes (zucchini), sliced
  thinly
2 garlic cloves, chopped
4 eggs
about 425 g/14 oz can borlotti beans,
  drained
3 tomatoes, skinned and chopped
2 tbsp chopped fresh parsley
1 tbsp chopped fresh basil
60 g/2 oz/ ½ cup grated Gruyère (Swiss)
  cheese
salt and pepper

1 Heat 2 tablespoons of the oil in a
frying pan (skillet) and fry the onion,
courgettes (zucchini) and garlic for 7
minutes, stirring occasionally, until
softened.

2 Break the eggs into a bowl, add the
seasoning, fried vegetables, beans,
tomatoes and herbs.

3 Heat the remaining oil in a 23 cm/
9 in omelette pan, add the egg
mixture and fry gently for 5 minutes until
the underneath is brown.

4 Sprinkle the cheese over the top and
place the pan under a preheated
moderate grill (broiler) for 3–4 minutes
until set on the top but still moist in the
middle.

GRUYÈRE CHEESE

This famous Swiss cheese is made
from unpasturised cows' milk and has
a sweet, nutty flavour, which enhances
the taste of this frittata. Gruyère
(Swiss) cheese is close textured and
has small holes interspersed
throughout.

SAVOURY BREAD & BUTTER PUDDING

••

SERVES 4

60 g/2 oz/ ¼ cup butter or margarine
1 bunch spring onions (scallions), sliced
6 slices of white or brown bread, crusts
  removed
175g/6 oz/1½ cups grated mature (sharp)
  Cheddar cheese
2 eggs
450 ml/ ¾ pint/scant 2 cups milk
salt and pepper
fresh flat-leaf parsley sprigs to garnish

1 Grease a 1.5 litre/2½ pint/1½ quart
baking dish with a little of the butter
or margarine. Melt the remaining butter or
margarine in a small saucepan and fry the
spring onions (scallions) until softened
and golden.

2 Meanwhile, cut the bread into
triangles and layer half of them in
the baking dish. Top with the spring
onions (scallions) and half the cheese.

3 Beat together the eggs and milk and
season with salt and pepper. Layer
the remaining triangles of bread in the
dish and carefully pour over the milk
mixture. Leave to soak for 15–20 minutes.

4 Sprinkle the remaining cheese over
the soaked bread pudding. Bake in a
preheated oven at 190°C/375°F/Gas Mark
5 for 35–40 minutes until puffed up and
golden brown. Garnish with flat-leaf
parsley and serve at once.

BREAD

This is an excellent recipe for using up
bread that is slightly stale.

VARIATIONS

For a change, add 60 g/2 oz/⅓ cup
chopped cooked ham to the spring
onions (scallions), when layering them
in the baking dish.
  Use 1 large onion instead of the
spring onions (scallions), if preferred.

WINTER VEGETABLE COBBLER

SERVES 4

1 tbsp olive oil
1 garlic clove, crushed
8 small onions, halved
2 celery sticks, sliced
250 g/8 oz swede (rutabaga), chopped
2 carrots, sliced
½ small cauliflower, broken into florets
250 g/8 oz mushrooms, sliced
425 g/14 oz can chopped tomatoes
60 g/2 oz/ ¼ cup red lentils
2 tbsp cornflour (cornstarch)
3–4 tbsp water
300 ml/ ½ pint/1¼ cups Fresh Vegetable
 Stock (see page 96)
2 tsp Tabasco sauce
2 tsp chopped fresh oregano or parsley
oregano sprigs to garnish

COBBLER TOPPING:
250 g/8 oz/2 cups self-raising flour
60 g/2 oz/ ¼ cup butter
125 g/4 oz/1 cup grated mature (sharp)
 Cheddar cheese
2 tsp chopped fresh oregano or parsley
1 egg, beaten
150 ml/ ¼ pint/ ⅔ cup skimmed milk
salt

1 Heat the oil in a large saucepan and fry the garlic and onions for 5 minutes. Add the celery, swede (rutabaga), carrots and cauliflower and fry for 2–3 minutes.

2 Remove from the heat and add the mushrooms, tomatoes and lentils. Mix the cornflour (cornstarch) with the water and add to the pan with the vegetable stock, Tabasco sauce and oregano or parsley. Bring to the boil, stirring, until thickened. Transfer to an ovenproof dish, cover and bake in a preheated oven at 180°C/350°F/Gas Mark 4 for 20 minutes.

3 To make the topping, sift the flour and salt into a bowl. Rub in the butter, then stir in most of the cheese and the chopped herbs. Beat together the egg and milk and add enough to the dry ingredients to make a soft dough. Knead lightly, roll out to 1 cm/ ½ in thick and cut into 5 cm/2 in rounds.

4 Remove the casserole from the oven and increase the temperature to 200°C/400°F/Gas Mark 6. Arrange the rounds around the edge of the dish, brush with the remaining egg and milk and sprinkle with the reserved cheese. Cook for 10–12 minutes until the topping is risen and golden. Garnish and serve.

ELIZABETHAN ARTICHOKE PIE

SERVES 4-6

350 g/12 oz Jerusalem artichokes
30 g/1 oz/2 tbsp butter or margarine
1 onion, chopped
1-2 garlic cloves, crushed
125 g/4 oz white (green) seedless grapes,
* halved*
60 g/2 oz/⅓ cup dates, chopped coarsely
2 hard-boiled (hard-cooked) eggs, sliced
1 tbsp chopped fresh mixed herbs or 1 tsp
* dried herbs*
4-6 tbsp single (light) cream or natural
* yogurt*

SHORTCRUST PASTRY (PIE DOUGH):
350 g/12 oz/3 cups plain (all-purpose)
* flour*
good pinch of salt
90 g/3 oz/⅓ cup butter or margarine
90 g/3 oz/⅓ cup lard or white vegetable
* fat (shortening)*
4-6 tbsp cold water
beaten egg or milk to glaze

1 To make the pastry (pie dough), see
   Cornish Pasties (page 479).

2 Peel the artichokes, plunging them
   immediately into salted water to
prevent discolouration. Drain, cover with
fresh water, bring to the boil and simmer
for 10-12 minutes until just tender. Drain
well.

3 Heat the butter or margarine in a
   saucepan and fry the onion and
garlic until soft but not coloured. Remove
the pan from the heat and stir in the
grapes and dates.

4 Roll out almost two-thirds of the
   pastry (pie dough) and use to line a
20 cm/8 inch pie dish. Slice the artichokes
and arrange in the pie dish, cover with
slices of egg and then with the onion
mixture, seasoning and herbs.

5 Roll out the remaining pastry (pie
   dough), dampen the edges and use
to cover the pie; press the edges firmly
together, then trim and crimp. Roll out the
trimmings and cut into narrow strips.
Arrange a lattice over the top of the pie,
dampening the strips to attach them.

6 Glaze with beaten egg or milk and
   make 2-3 slits in the lid. Bake in a
preheated oven at 200°C/400°F/Gas Mark
6 for 40-50 minutes until golden. Gently
heat the cream or yogurt and pour into
the pie through the holes in the lid. Serve
hot or cold.

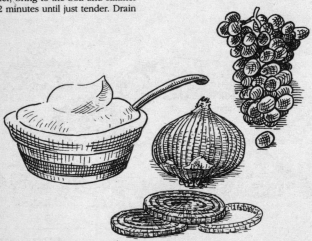

STUFFED AUBERGINES (EGGPLANT)

SERVES 6

250 g/8 oz/1⅓ cup continental lentils
900 ml/1½ pints/3¾ cups water
2 garlic cloves, peeled and crushed
3 well-shaped aubergines (eggplants), leaf
   ends trimmed
150 ml/ ¼ pint/ ⅔ cup vegetable oil
salt and freshly ground black pepper
2 onions, peeled and chopped
4 tomatoes, chopped
2 tsp cumin seeds
1 tsp ground cinnamon
2 tbsp mild curry paste
1 tsp minced chilli (from a jar)
2 tbsp chopped fresh mint
natural yogurt and mint sprigs, to serve

1 Rinse the lentils under cold running water. Drain and place in a saucepan with the water and garlic. Cover and simmer for 30 minutes.

2 Cook the aubergines (eggplants) in a saucepan of boiling water for 5 minutes. Drain, then plunge into cold water for 5 minutes. Drain again, then cut the aubergines (eggplants) in half lengthways and scoop out most of the flesh and reserve, leaving a 1 cm/ ½ in thick border to form a shell.

3 Place the aubergine (eggplant) shells in a shallow greased ovenproof dish, brush with a little oil and sprinkle with salt and pepper. Cook in the preheated oven for 10 minutes. Meanwhile, heat half the remaining oil in a frying pan, add the onions and tomatoes and fry gently for 5 minutes. Chop the reserved aubergine (eggplant) flesh, add to the pan with the spices and cook gently for 5 minutes. Season with salt.

4 Stir in the lentils, most of the remaining oil, reserving a little for later, and the mint. Spoon the mixture into the shells. Drizzle with remaining oil and bake for 15 minutes. Serve hot or cold topped with a spoonful of natural yogurt and mint sprigs.

FLAMENCO EGGS

SERVES 4

6 tbsp olive oil
2 thick slices white bread, cut into cubes
500 g/1 lb potatoes, cut into small cubes
1 onion, chopped
60 g/2 oz green beans, cut into ½ cm/1 in
   lengths
2 small courgettes (zucchini), halved and
   sliced
1 red (bell) pepper, deseeded and chopped
4 tomatoes, deseeded and sliced
2 chorizo sausages, sliced
chilli powder, to taste
4 eggs
salt
chopped fresh parsley to garnish

1 Heat the oil in a large frying pan (skillet) and add the cubes of bread. Fry until golden brown, then remove with a perforated spoon and drain on paper towels. Set aside.

2 Add the potatoes to the frying pan (skillet) and cook over a low heat, turning often, for about 15 minutes until just tender.

3 Add the onion to the frying pan (skillet) and cook for 3 minutes, then add the green beans, courgettes (zucchini), (bell) pepper and tomatoes. Cook gently for 3–4 minutes, stirring often. Stir in the chorizo sausage. Season with salt and a little chilli powder.

4 Grease 4 individual ovenproof dishes or 1 large ovenproof dish with olive oil. Transfer the vegetable mixture to the dishes and make a hollow in the mixture. Carefully crack 1 egg into each hollow. Bake in a preheated oven at 190°C/375°F/Gas Mark 5 for 10 minutes.

5 Sprinkle the cubes of fried bread over the surface and bake for a further 2 minutes. Serve immediately, garnished with chopped fresh parsley.

TIP

Slightly stale bread is best for making the fried bread cubes, as it absorbs less oil.

ROOT CROUSTADES WITH SUNSHINE (BELL) PEPPERS

SERVES 4

1 orange (bell) pepper
1 red (bell) pepper
1 yellow (bell) pepper
3 tbsp olive oil
2 tbsp red wine vinegar
1 tsp French mustard
1 tsp clear honey
salt and pepper
sprigs of fresh flat-leaf parsley to garnish
green vegetables to serve

CROUSTADES:
250 g/8 oz potatoes, grated coarsely
250 g/8 oz carrots, grated coarsely
350 g/12 oz celeriac (celery root), grated
   coarsely
1 garlic clove, crushed
1 tbsp lemon juice
30 g/1 oz/2 tbsp butter or margarine,
   melted
1 egg, beaten
1 tbsp vegetable oil

1 Place the (bell) peppers on a baking
sheet and bake in a preheated oven
at 190°C/375°F/Gas Mark 5 for 35
minutes, turning after 20 minutes.

2 Cover with a tea towel (dish cloth)
and leave to cool for 10 minutes.

3 Peel the skin from the cooked (bell)
peppers; cut in half and discard the
seeds. Thinly slice the flesh into strips and
place in a shallow dish.

4 Put the oil, vinegar, mustard, honey
and seasoning in a small screw-top
jar and shake well to mix. Pour over the
(bell) pepper strips, mix well and leave to
marinate for 2 hours.

5 To make the croustades, put the
potatoes, carrots and celeriac (celery
root) in a mixing bowl and toss in the
garlic and lemon juice.

6 Mix in the melted butter or
margarine and the egg. Season well.
Divide the mixture into 8 and pile on
to 2 baking sheets lined with baking
parchment, forming each into a 10 cm/
4 in round. Brush with oil.

7 Bake in a preheated oven at 220°C/
425°F/Gas Mark 7 for 30–35 minutes
until crisp around the edge and golden.
Carefully transfer to a warmed serving
dish. Heat the (bell) peppers and
marinade for 2–3 minutes until warmed
through. Spoon the (bell) peppers over
the croustades, garnish with parsley and
serve with green vegetables.

MUSHROOM & NUT CRUMBLE

••

SERVES 6

350 g/12 oz open-cup mushrooms, sliced
350 g/12 oz chestnut mushrooms, sliced
400 ml/14 fl oz/1¼ cups Fresh Vegetable
  Stock (see page 96)
60 g/2 oz/ ¼ cup butter or margarine
1 large onion, chopped finely
1 garlic clove, crushed
60 g/2 oz/ ½ cup plain (all-purpose) flour
4 tbsp double (heavy) cream
2 tbsp chopped fresh parsley
salt and pepper
fresh herbs to garnish

CRUMBLE TOPPING:
90 g/3 oz/ ¾ cup medium oatmeal
90 g/3 oz/ ¾ cup wholemeal (whole wheat)
  plain (all-purpose) flour
30 g/1 oz/ ¼ cup ground almonds
30 g/1 oz/ ¼ cup finely chopped walnuts
60 g/2 oz/ ½ cup finely chopped unsalted
  shelled pistachio nuts
1 tsp dried thyme
90 g/3 oz/ ⅓ cup butter or margarine,
  softened
1 tbsp fennel seeds

1 Put the mushrooms and stock in a large saucepan, bring to the boil, cover and simmer for 15 minutes until tender. Drain, reserving the stock.

2 In another saucepan, melt the butter or margarine, and gently fry the onion and garlic for 2–3 minutes until just softened but not browned. Stir in the flour and cook for 1 minute.

3 Remove from the heat and gradually stir in the reserved mushroom stock. Return to the heat and cook, stirring, until thickened. Stir in the mushrooms, seasoning, cream and parsley and spoon into a shallow ovenproof dish.

4 Mix together the oatmeal, flour, nuts, thyme and seasoning. Using a fork, work in the butter or margarine until the topping resembles coarse breadcrumbs.

5 Sprinkle over the mushrooms, add fennel seeds and bake in a preheated oven at 190°C/375°F/Gas Mark 5 for 25–30 minutes. Garnish and serve.

COCONUT VEGETABLE CURRY

••

SERVES 6

1 large aubergine (eggplant), cut into
  2.5 cm/1 in cubes
2 tbsp salt
2 tbsp vegetable oil
2 garlic cloves, crushed
1 fresh green chilli, deseeded and chopped
  finely
1 tsp grated ginger root
1 onion, finely chopped
2 tsp garam masala
8 cardamom pods
1 tsp ground turmeric
1 tbsp tomato purée (paste)
700 ml/1¼ pints/3 cups Fresh Vegetable
  Stock (see page 97)
1 tbsp lemon juice
250 g/8 oz potatoes, diced
250 g/8 oz small cauliflower florets
250 g/8 oz okra, trimmed
250 g/8 oz frozen peas
150 ml/ ¼ pint/ ⅔ cups coconut milk
salt and pepper
flaked coconut to garnish
naan bread to serve

1 Layer the aubergine (eggplant) in a bowl, sprinkling with salt as you go. Set aside for 30 minutes.

2 Rinse well under running water to remove all the salt. Drain and pat dry with paper towels. Set aside.

3 Heat the oil in a large saucepan and gently fry the garlic, chilli, ginger, onion and spices for 4–5 minutes until lightly browned.

4 Stir in the tomato purée (paste), stock, lemon juice, potatoes and cauliflower and mix well. Bring to the boil, cover and simmer for 15 minutes.

5 Stir in the aubergine (eggplant), okra, peas and coconut milk. Adjust the seasoning. Return to the boil and continue to simmer, uncovered, for a further 10 minutes until tender. Discard the cardamom pods.

6 Pile on to a warmed serving platter, garnish with flaked coconut and serve with naan bread.

WHITE NUT FILO PARCELS

SERVES 4

45 g/1½ oz/3 tbsp butter or margarine
1 large onion, chopped finely
275 g/9 oz/2¼ cups mixed white nuts, such
*   as pine kernels (nuts), unsalted cashew*
*   nuts, blanched almonds, unsalted*
*   peanuts, chopped finely*
90 g/3 oz/1½ cups fresh white
*   breadcrumbs*
½ tsp ground mace
1 egg, beaten
1 egg yolk
3 tbsp pesto sauce
2 tbsp chopped fresh basil
125 g/4 oz/ ½ cup melted butter or
*   margarine*
16 sheets filo pastry
salt and pepper
sprigs of fresh basil to garnish

TO SERVE:
cranberry sauce
steamed vegetables

1 Melt the butter or margarine in a
   frying pan (skillet) and gently fry the
onion for 2–3 minutes until just softened
but not browned.

2 Remove from the heat and stir in the
   nuts, 60 g/2 oz/1 cup of the

breadcrumbs, the mace, seasoning and
beaten egg. Set aside.

3 Place the remaining breadcrumbs in
   a bowl and stir in the egg yolk,
pesto sauce, basil, and 1 tablespoon of
the melted butter or margarine. Mix well.

4 Brush 1 sheet of filo with melted
   butter or margarine. Fold in half and
brush again. Repeat with a second sheet
and lay on top of the first one to form a
cross.

5 Divide the nut mixture and pesto
   mixture into 8 portions each. Put a
portion of nut mixture in the centre of the
pastry. Top with a portion of the pesto
mixture. Fold over the edges, brushing
with more butter or margarine, to form a
parcel. Brush the top with butter or
margarine and transfer to a baking sheet.

6 Continue with the remaining pastry
   and fillings to make 8 parcels. Brush
with the remaining butter or margarine
and bake in a preheated oven at
220°C/425°F/Gas Mark 7 for 15–20
minutes until golden. Garnish with basil
sprigs and serve with cranberry sauce and
steamed vegetables.

GREEN VEGETABLE GOUGÈRE

SERVES 6

150 g/5 oz/1¼ cups plain (all-purpose)
   flour
125 g/4 oz/ ½ cup butter or margarine
300 ml/ ½ pint/1¼ cups water
4 eggs, beaten
90 g/3 oz/ ¾ cup grated Gruyère (Swiss)
   cheese
1 tbsp milk
salt and pepper

FILLING:
30 g/1 oz/2 tbsp garlic and herb butter or
   margarine
2 tsp olive oil
2 leeks, shredded
250 g/8 oz green cabbage, shredded finely
125 g/4 oz beansprouts
½ tsp grated lime rind
1 tbsp lime juice
celery salt and pepper
lime slices to garnish

1 Sift the flour on to a piece of baking
   parchment and set aside. Cut the
butter or margarine into dice and put in a
saucepan with the water. Heat until the
butter has melted.

2 Bring the butter and water to the
   boil, then shoot in the flour all at

once. Beat until the mixture becomes
thick. Remove from the heat and beat
until the mixture is glossy and comes
away from the sides of the saucepan.

3 Transfer to a mixing bowl and cool
   for 10 minutes. Gradually beat in the
eggs, a little at a time, making sure they
are thoroughly incorporated after each
addition. Stir in 60 g/2 oz/ ½ cup of the
cheese and season.

4 Dampen a baking sheet. Place
   spoonfuls of the mixture in a
23 cm/9 in circle on the baking sheet.
Brush with milk and sprinkle with the
remaining cheese. Bake in a preheated
oven at 220°C/425°F/Gas Mark 7 for
30–35 minutes until golden and crisp.
Transfer to a warmed serving plate.

5 Make the filling about 5 minutes
   before the end of cooking time. Heat
the butter or margarine and the oil in a
large frying pan (skillet) and stir-fry the
leeks and cabbage for 2 minutes.

6 Add the beansprouts, lime rind and
   lime juice and cook for 1 minute,
stirring. Season and pile into the centre of
the cooked pastry ring. Garnish with lime
slices and serve.

CHEESY SEMOLINA FRITTERS WITH APPLE RELISH

SERVES 4

600 ml/1 pint/2½ cups milk
1 small onion
1 celery stick
1 bay leaf
2 cloves
125 g/4 oz/ ⅔ cup semolina
125 g/4 oz/1 cup grated mature (sharp)
Cheddar cheese
½ tsp dried mustard powder
2 tbsp plain (all-purpose) flour
1 egg, beaten
60 g/2 oz/ ½ cup dried white breadcrumbs
6 tbsp vegetable oil
salt and pepper
celery leaves to garnish
coleslaw to serve

RELISH:
2 celery sticks, chopped
2 small dessert (eating) apples, cored and
diced finely
90 g/3 oz/ ½ cup sultanas (golden raisins)
90 g/3 oz/ ½ cup no-need-to-soak dried
apricots, chopped
6 tbsp cider vinegar
pinch of ground cloves
½ tsp ground cinnamon

1 Pour the milk into a saucepan and add the onion, celery, bay leaf and cloves. Bring to the boil, remove from the heat and allow to stand for 15 minutes.

2 Strain into another saucepan, bring to the boil and sprinkle in the semolina, stirring constantly. Reduce the heat and simmer for 5 minutes until very thick, stirring occasionally to prevent it sticking.

3 Remove from the heat and beat in the cheese, mustard and seasoning. Place in a greased bowl and allow to cool.

4 To make the relish, put all the ingredients in a saucepan, bring to the boil, cover and simmer gently for 20 minutes, until tender. Allow to cool.

5 Put the flour, egg and breadcrumbs on separate plates. Divide the cooled semolina mixture into 8 and press into 6 cm/2½ inch rounds, flouring the hands if necessary.

6 Coat lightly in flour, then egg and breadcrumbs. Heat the oil in a large frying pan (skillet) and gently fry the fritters for 3–4 minutes on each side until golden. Drain on paper towels. Garnish with celery leaves and serve with the relish and coleslaw.

ORIENTAL-STYLE MILLET PILAFF

SERVES 4

300 g/10 oz/1½ cups millet grains
1 tbsp vegetable oil
1 bunch spring onions (scallions), white
  and green parts, chopped
1 garlic clove, crushed
1 tsp grated ginger root
1 orange (bell) pepper, deseeded and
  diced
600 ml/1 pint/2½ cups water
1 orange
125 g/4 oz/⅔ cup chopped pitted dates
2 tsp sesame oil
125 g/4 oz/1 cup roasted cashew nuts
2 tbsp pumpkin seeds
salt and pepper
oriental salad vegetables to serve

1 Place the millet in a large saucepan and put over a medium heat for 4–5 minutes to toast, shaking the pan occasionally until the grains begin to crack and pop.

2 Heat the oil in another saucepan and gently fry the spring onions (scallions), garlic, ginger and (bell) pepper for 2–3 minutes until just softened but not browned. Add the millet and pour in the water.

3 Using a vegetable peeler, pare the rind from the orange and add the rind to the pan. Squeeze the juice from the orange into the pan. Season well.

4 Bring to the boil, reduce the heat, cover and cook gently for 20 minutes until all the liquid has been absorbed. Remove from the heat, stir in the dates and sesame oil and leave to stand for 10 minutes.

5 Discard the orange rind and stir in the cashew nuts. Pile into a serving dish, sprinkle with pumpkin seeds and serve with oriental salad vegetables.

ORANGES

For extra orange flavour, peel and segment 2 oranges and stir the segments into the mixture with the cashew nuts.

MEXICAN CHILLI CORN PIE

SERVES 4

1 tbsp corn oil
2 garlic cloves, crushed
1 red (bell) pepper, deseeded and diced
1 green (bell) pepper, deseeded and diced
1 celery stick, diced
1 tsp hot chilli powder
400 g/14 oz can chopped tomatoes
325 g/11 oz can sweetcorn, drained
215 g/7½ oz can kidney beans, drained
  and rinsed
2 tbsp chopped fresh coriander (cilantro)
salt and pepper
sprigs of fresh coriander (cilantro) to
  garnish
tomato and avocado salad to serve

TOPPING:
125 g/4 oz/⅔ cup cornmeal
1 tbsp plain (all-purpose) flour
½ tsp salt
2 tsp baking powder
1 egg, beaten
90 ml/3½ fl oz/6 tbsp milk
1 tbsp corn oil
125 g/4 oz/1 cup grated Cheddar cheese

1 Heat the oil in a large frying pan (skillet) and gently fry the garlic, (bell) peppers and celery for 5–6 minutes until just softened.

2 Stir in the chilli powder, tomatoes, sweetcorn, beans and seasoning. Bring to the boil and simmer for 10 minutes. Stir in the coriander (cilantro) and spoon into an ovenproof dish.

3 To make the topping, mix together the cornmeal, flour, salt and baking powder. Make a well in the centre, add the egg, milk and oil and beat until a smooth batter is formed.

4 Spoon over the (bell) pepper and sweetcorn mixture and sprinkle with the cheese. Bake in a preheated oven at 220°C/425°F/Gas Mark 7 for 25–30 minutes until golden and firm.

5 Garnish with coriander (cilantro) sprigs and serve immediately with a tomato and avocado salad.

SPINACH PANCAKE LAYER

SERVES 4

125 g/4 oz/1 cup buckwheat flour
1 egg, beaten
1 tbsp walnut oil
300 ml/ ½ pint/1¼ cups milk
2 tsp vegetable oil

FILLING:
1 kg/2 lb young spinach leaves
2 tbsp water
1 bunch spring onions (scallions), white
*   and green parts, chopped*
2 tsp walnut oil
1 egg, beaten
1 egg yolk
250 g/8 oz/1 cup cottage cheese
½ tsp grated nutmeg
30 g/1 oz/ ¼ cup grated Cheddar cheese
30 g/1 oz/ ¼ cup walnut pieces
salt and pepper

1 Sift the flour into a bowl and add any husks that remain behind in the sieve (strainer).

2 Make a well in the centre and add the egg and walnut oil. Gradually whisk in the milk to make a smooth batter. Leave to stand for 30 minutes.

3 To make the filling, wash the spinach and pack into a saucepan with the water. Cover tightly and cook on a high heat for 5–6 minutes until soft.

4 Drain well and leave to cool. Gently fry the spring onions (scallions) in the walnut oil for 2–3 minutes until just soft. Drain on paper towels. Set aside.

5 Whisk the batter. Brush a small crêpe pan with oil, heat until hot and pour in enough batter to lightly cover the base. Cook for 1–2 minutes until set, turn and cook for 1 minute until golden. Turn on to a warmed plate. Repeat to make 8–10 pancakes, layering them with baking parchment.

6 Chop the spinach and dry with paper towels. Mix with the spring onions (scallions), egg, egg yolk, cottage cheese, nutmeg and seasoning.

7 Layer the pancakes and spinach mixture on a baking sheet lined with baking parchment, finishing with a pancake. Sprinkle with Cheddar cheese and bake in a preheated oven at 190°C/375°F/Gas Mark 5 for 20–25 minutes until firm and golden. Sprinkle with walnuts and serve.

CHILLI TOFU (BEAN CURD) ENCHILLADAS

SERVES 4

½ tsp chilli powder
1 tsp paprika
2 tbsp plain (all-purpose) flour
250 g/8 oz tofu (bean curd), cut into
    1 cm/ ½ in pieces
2 tbsp vegetable oil
1 onion, chopped finely
1 garlic clove, crushed
1 large red (bell) pepper, deseeded and
    chopped finely
1 large ripe avocado
1 tbsp lime juice
4 tomatoes, peeled, deseeded and chopped
125 g/4 oz/1 cup grated Cheddar cheese
8 soft flour tortillas
150 ml/ ¼ pint/ ⅔ cup soured cream
salt and pepper
sprigs of fresh coriander (cilantro) to
    garnish
pickled green jalapeño chillies to serve

SAUCE:
900 ml/1½ pints/3½ cups tomato sauce
3 tbsp chopped fresh parsley
3 tbsp chopped fresh coriander (cilantro)

1 Mix the chilli powder, paprika, flour
    and seasoning on a plate and coat
the tofu (bean curd) pieces.

2 Heat the oil in a frying pan (skillet)
    and gently fry the tofu (bean curd)
for 3–4 minutes until golden. Remove
with a perforated spoon, drain on paper
towels and set aside.

3 Add the onion, garlic and (bell)
    pepper to the oil and gently fry for
2–3 minutes until just softened. Drain and
set aside.

4 Halve the avocado, peel and remove
    the stone (pit). Slice lengthways, put
in a bowl with the lime juice and toss to
coat.

5 Add the tofu (bean curd) and onion
    mixture and gently mix in the
tomatoes and half the cheese. Spoon the
filling down the centre of each tortilla, top
with soured cream and roll up. Put in a
shallow ovenproof dish.

6 To make the sauce, mix together all
    the ingredients. Spoon over the
tortillas, sprinkle with the remaining
cheese and bake in a preheated oven at
190°C/375°F/Gas Mark 5 for 25 minutes
until golden and bubbling. Garnish with
coriander (cilantro) and serve with
jalapeño chillies.

117

RICE, PULSES AND GRAIN DISHES – INTRODUCTION

Rice, pulses and grains form an important part of the vegetarian diet, providing additional nutrition and a useful source of fibre, as well as variety in taste and texture. They can also add extra interest to a diet containing meat and fish, either as accompaniments or as dishes in their own right.

As well as the more familiar forms of rice, grains and pulses, many supermarkets now stock lesser-known varieties which you could try out. Even if you have never used some of these ingredients before, the recipes here will provide inspiration and will prove just how appetizing and delicious these basic and little-used foodstuffs can be.

RICE

There are several different varieties of rice, each with its own distinct characteristics and each suited to a different culinary purpose. You can choose from long-grain for general use, delicately flavoured basmati with its long, slender grains, Italian arborio which is ideal for making risotto, short-grain for puddings, wild rice to add interest.

Look out, too, for fragrant Thai rice, jasmine rice and combinations of different varieties to add colour and texture to your dishes. Easy-cook versions of several types of rice are now available.

Rice often needs rinsing before cooking to wash out the starch which it contains and to prevent it ending up a sticky mass, but check the instructions on the packet first.

PULSES

High in fibre and protein and low in fat, beans, peas and lentils come in all sizes and colours. They are cheap to buy in their dry form, but most require overnight soaking to soften them before boiling.

Pulses, such as soya beans, haricot (navy) beans, red kidney and cannellini beans, chick-peas (garbanzo beans), all types of lentils, split peas and butter beans are very important in a vegetarian diet as they are a good protein source, and contain vitamins and minerals. Buy them dried for soaking and cooking yourself or, if you are short of time, use canned pulses. Although canned pulses are more expensive, they are ready cooked and ready to use.

When you buy dried pulses, always check the package for any small stones or husks that should be removed before you cook them. Dried pulses keep for up to six months in an air-tight container, after which the skins begin to toughen, so buy your pulses from a store with a fast turnover. Do not season dried pulses until after cooking as the salt may cause them to become tough.

Types of pulses

Lentils are among the most familiar of the different varieties of pulses, and include both the small, split red lentils, and the slightly larger, green-brown types. All lentils have the advantage of not needing pre-soaking or boiling before cooking, which makes them the most convenient pulses to use. Take care, however, that you do not overcook them or they will be reduced to a pulpy mass.

Red kidney beans, with their nutty flavour, are another well-known pulse, and are an essential ingredient of the classic Chilli con Carne. If you are using dried kidney beans, soak them to soften them before cooking, and then boil them hard for the first 10 minutes. This

INTRODUCTION

last stage is vital in order to kill a poisonous enzyme contained in the beans (canned red kidney beans do not need boiling in this way).

Perhaps slightly less familiar than lentils and red kidney beans, but well worth including in your regular ingredient list (if you do not already do so) are chick-peas (garbanzo beans). Cream-coloured and resembling a hazelnut in appearance, these have a nutty flavour and slightly crunchy texture, and give an earthy quality reminiscent of robust peasant cookery to any dish in which they are used.

Pale cream and oval in shape, haricot (navy) beans are the key ingredient in that staple convenience food, baked beans. However, when bought dried and prepared in the home kitchen, these humble beans can be turned into a delicious dish that can form the centrepiece of a family meal.

Canned pulses
If you want to save time, you can now buy many different pulses in cans. Although these are more convenient, they do not however have the same texture and 'bite' as the dried variety.

Choose varieties that are canned in water without added sugar and salt. Always drain canned pulses and rinse well in cold water before use. Take care not to overcook as the canning process will already have softened them. For this reason, it is best to add them to a dish towards the end of the cooking time.

GRAINS
Very important components of the vegetarian diet, grains supply fibre, carbohydrates, protein, iron, zinc, calcium and B vitamins. They will also add bulk and texture to any diet.

Experiment with barley (whole grain or pearl), millet, bulgur wheat, polenta (made from maize) oats (oatmeal, oatflakes or oatbran), semolina – including couscous (from which it is made) – sago and tapioca.

Different grains produce very different end results when cooked, and so can add even more variety to the diet than rice or pulses. For example, polenta – which consists of minute grains when uncooked – coheres into a solid mass after cooking, which can be cut into slices and served with a rich tomato sauce. Barley is often included in hearty, winter soups to provide extra bulk, while couscous offers the cook the easy option of a 'meal-in-a-pot'. An ingredient of North African cookery, couscous is traditionally cooked in the steam from the stew with which it will be served, so that the whole dish can effectively be cooked in a single, large stewpot.

FLAVOURINGS
The delicate flavours of rice and grains in particular, and pulses to a lesser extent, make them the perfect accompaniment to stronger-tasting dishes. If served as dishes in their own right, they may need help to prevent them being too bland – such as a rich sauce, perhaps, or flavouring with herbs or spices, or a sprinkling of grated cheese.

Spices
A good selection of spices is important for adding variety and interest to your cooking, whatever the ingredients you are using. Try to add to your range each time you try a new recipe. There are some good and unusual spice mixtures available – try Cajun seasoning, Chinese five-

INTRODUCTION

spice powder, Indonesian piri-piri seasoning and various curry blends, depending on the dish you are cooking. Cumin is good for giving a Middle Eastern flavour to a dish, and cinnamon is the perfect complement to creamy, delicately flavoured dishes.

Herbs
Fresh herbs are always preferable to dried, but it is essential to have dried ones in stock as a useful back-up to use when fresh are unavailable. Keep the basics such as parsley, thyme, rosemary, bay leaves and some good Mediterranean mixtures for Italian and French cooking.

Nuts and seeds
As well as adding protein, vitamins and useful fats to the diet, nuts and seeds add important flavour and texture to vegetarian meals, and make an interesting addition to rice dishes, providing yet another contrast in texture. Make sure that you keep a good supply of almonds, brazils, cashews, chestnuts (in cans), hazelnuts, peanuts, pecans, pistachios, pine kernels (nuts) and

walnuts. Coconut – either creamed or desiccated (shredded) – is useful too.

For your seed collection, have sesame, sunflower, pumpkin and poppy. Pumpkin seeds, in particular, are an excellent source of zinc.

OILS AND FATS
Useful for adding subtle flavourings to foods, it is a good idea to have a selection in store. Have a light olive oil for cooking and an extra-virgin one for salad dressings. Use sunflower oil as a good general-purpose oil and select one or two speciality oils to add character to different dishes. Sesame oil is wonderful in stir-fries; hazelnut and walnut oils are superb in salad dressings.

Oils and fats add flavour to foods, and contain the important fat-soluble vitamins A, D, E and K. It is a good idea to keep an eye on how much you use, especially if you are watcing your weight, as all fats and oils are high in calories. It is worth pointing out that oils are simply fats that are liquid at room temperature, and they are higher in calories than butter or margarine. (Oils contain 100% fat; butter and margarine contain 80% fat.)

NASI GORENG

SERVES 4

300 g/10 oz/1½ cups long-grain rice
350-500 g/12 oz-1 lb pork fillet or lean
* pork slices*
3 tomatoes, peeled, quartered and seeded
2 eggs
4 tsp water
3 tbsp sunflower oil
1 onion, thinly sliced
1-2 garlic cloves, crushed
1 tsp medium or mild curry powder
½ tsp ground coriander
¼ tsp medium chilli powder or 1 tsp bottled
* sweet chilli sauce*
2 tbsp soy sauce
125 g/4 oz frozen peas, defrosted
salt and pepper

1 Cook the rice in boiling salted water, following the instructions given in Chinese Fried Rice (see page 122) and keep warm.

2 Meanwhile, cut the pork into narrow strips across the grain, discarding any fat. Slice the tomatoes.

3 Beat each egg separately with 2 teaspoons cold water and salt and pepper. Heat 2 teaspoons of oil in the wok, swirling it around until really hot. Pour in the first egg, swirl it around and cook undisturbed until set. Remove to a plate or board and repeat with the second egg. Cut the omelettes into strips about 1 cm/ ½ in wide.

4 Heat the remaining oil in the wok and when really hot add the onion and garlic and stir-fry for 1-2 minutes. Add the pork and continue to stir-fry for about 3 minutes or until almost cooked.

5 Add the curry powder, coriander, chilli powder or chilli sauce and soy sauce to the wok and cook for a further minute, stirring constantly.

6 Stir in the rice, tomatoes and peas and stir-fry for about 2 minutes until piping hot. Adjust the seasoning and turn into a heated serving dish. Arrange the strips of omelette on top and serve at once.

RICE WITH CRAB & MUSSELS

SERVES 4, OR 6 AS A STARTER

300 g/10 oz/1½ cups long-grain rice
175 g/6 oz crab meat, fresh, canned or
* frozen (defrosted if frozen), or 8 crab*
* sticks, defrosted if frozen*
2 tbsp sesame or sunflower oil
2.5 cm/1 in ginger root, grated
4 spring onions (scallions), thinly sliced
* diagonally*
125 g/4 oz mangetout (snow peas), cut
* into 2-3 pieces*
½ tsp turmeric
1 tsp ground cumin
2 x 200 g/7 oz jars mussels, well drained,
* or 350 g/12 oz frozen mussels, defrosted*
1 x 425 g/15 oz can bean-sprouts, well
* drained*
salt and pepper

TO GARNISH:
crab claws or legs (optional)
8 mangetout (snow peas), blanched

1 Cook the rice in boiling salted water, following the instructions given in Chinese Fried Rice (see page 1).

2 Meanwhile, extract the crab meat, if using fresh crab. Flake the crab meat or cut the crab sticks into 3 or 4 pieces.

3 Heat the oil in the wok, swirling it around until really hot. Add the ginger and spring onions (scallions) and stir-fry for a minute or so. Add the mangetout (snow peas) and continue to cook for a further minute.

4 Sprinkle the turmeric, cumin and seasoning over the vegetables and mix well. Add the crab meat and mussels and stir-fry for 1 minute.

5 Stir in the cooked rice and bean-sprouts and stir-fry for 2 minutes or until really hot and well mixed.

6 Adjust the seasoning and serve very hot, garnished with crab claws and mangetout (snow peas).

FRIED RICE WITH PRAWNS (SHRIMP)

SERVES 4

300 g/10 oz/1½ cups long-grain rice
2 eggs
4 tsp cold water
salt and pepper
3 tbsp sunflower oil
4 spring onions (scallions), thinly sliced
    diagonally
1 garlic clove, crushed
125 g/4 oz closed cup or button
    mushrooms, thinly sliced
2 tbsp oyster or anchovy sauce
1 x 200 g/7 oz can water chestnuts,
    drained and sliced
250 g/8 oz peeled prawns (shrimp),
    defrosted if frozen
½ bunch of watercress, roughly chopped
watercress sprigs, to garnish (optional)

1 Cook the rice in boiling salted water, following the instructions given in Chinese Fried Rice (see right) and keep warm.

2 Beat each egg separately with 2 teaspoons of cold water and salt and pepper. Heat 2 teaspoons of oil in a wok, swirling it around until really hot. Pour in the first egg, swirl it around and leave to cook undisturbed until set. Remove to a plate or board and repeat with the second egg. Cut the omelettes into 2.5 cm/1 in squares.

3 Heat the remaining oil in the wok and when really hot add the spring onions (scallions) and garlic and stir-fry for 1 minute. Add the mushrooms and continue to cook for a further 2 minutes.

4 Stir in the oyster or anchovy sauce and seasoning and add the water chestnuts and prawns (shrimp); stir-fry for 2 minutes.

5 Stir in the cooked rice and stir-fry for 1 minute, then add the watercress and omelette squares and stir-fry for a further 1-2 minutes until piping hot. Serve at once garnished with sprigs of watercress, if liked.

CHINESE FRIED RICE

SERVES 4 (OR 6 AS AN ACCOMPANIMENT)

750 ml/1¼ pints/3 cups water
1/2 tsp salt
300 g/10 oz/1½ cups long-grain rice
2 eggs
4 tsp cold water
3 tbsp sunflower oil
4 spring onions (scallions), sliced
    diagonally
1 red, green or yellow (bell) pepper, cored,
    seeded and thinly sliced
3-4 lean rashers bacon, rinded and cut
    into strips
200 g/7 oz fresh bean-sprouts
125 g/4 oz frozen peas, defrosted
2 tbsp soy sauce (optional)
salt and pepper

1 Pour the water into the wok with the salt and bring to the boil. Rinse the rice in a sieve under cold water until the water runs clear, drain well and add to the boiling water. Stir well, then cover the wok tightly with the lid or a lid made of foil, and simmer gently for 12-13 minutes. (Don't remove the lid during cooking or the rice will not be cooked.)

2 Remove the lid, give the rice a good stir and spread out on a large plate or baking sheet to cool and dry.

3 Beat each egg separately with salt and pepper and 2 teaspoons cold water. Heat 1 tablespoon of oil in the wok, swirling it around until really hot. Pour in the first egg, swirl it around and leave to cook undisturbed until set. Remove to a board or plate; repeat with the second egg. Cut the omelettes into thin slices.

4 Add the remaining oil to the wok and when really hot add the spring onions (scallions) and (bell) pepper and stir-fry for 1-2 minutes. Add the bacon and continue to stir-fry for a further 1-2 minutes. Add the bean-sprouts and peas and toss together thoroughly; stir in the soy sauce if using.

5 Add the rice and seasoning and stir-fry for a minute or so then add the strips of omelette and continue to stir for about 2 minutes or until the rice is piping hot. Serve at once.

MIXED BEAN STIR-FRY

SERVES 4

1 x 425 g/15 oz can red kidney beans
1 x 425 g/15 oz can cannellini beans
6 spring onions (scallions)
1 x 200 g/7 oz can pineapple rings or
*   pieces in natural juice, chopped*
2 tbsp pineapple juice
3-4 pieces stem ginger
2 tbsp ginger syrup from the jar
thinly pared rind of ½ lime or lemon, cut
*   into julienne strips*
2 tbsp lime or lemon juice
2 tbsp soy sauce
1 tsp cornflour (cornstarch)
1 tbsp sesame oil
125 g/4 oz French beans, cut into 4 cm/
*   1½ in lengths*
1 x 250 g/8 oz can bamboo shoots,
*   drained and thinly sliced*
salt and pepper

1   Drain all the beans, rinse under cold
    water and drain again very
thoroughly.

2   Cut 4 spring onions (scallions) into
    narrow slanting slices. Thinly slice
the remainder and reserve for garnish.

3   Combine the pineapple and juice,
    ginger and syrup, lime rind and
juice, soy sauce and cornflour
(cornstarch) in a bowl.

4   Heat the oil in the wok, swirling it
    around until really hot. Add the
spring onions (scallions) and stir-fry for a
minute or so. Add the French beans and
bamboo shoots and continue to stir-fry for
2 minutes.

5   Add the pineapple and ginger
    mixture and bring just to the boil.
Add the canned beans and stir until very
hot – about a minute or so.

6   Season to taste, and serve with
    freshly boiled rice sprinkled with the
reserved chopped spring onions
(scallions); or serve as a vegetable
accompaniment.

HOLLANDAISE OATMEAL CHOWDER

SERVES 4-6

60 g/2 oz/ ¼ cup butter or margarine
2 large onions, chopped finely or sliced
*   very thinly*
1 garlic clove, crushed
1 turnip
3 carrots
3 celery sticks and/or 175 g/6 oz celeriac
*   (celery root)*
1 leek
45 g/1½ oz/ ½ cup medium oatmeal
1 litre/1¾ pints/4 cups stock
150 ml/ ¼ pint/ ⅔ cup milk
about 2 tbsp white wine vinegar
1 egg yolk
150 ml/ ¼ pint/ ⅔ cup single (light) cream
2 tbsp mayonnaise
salt and pepper
chopped fresh herbs and herb sprigs to
*   garnish*
oatcakes to serve

1   Melt the butter or margarine in a
    saucepan and gently fry the onions
and garlic for about 10 minutes until very
soft but not coloured.

2   Finely chop the turnip, carrots and
    celery and/or celeriac (celery root).
Thinly slice the leek.

3   Add the vegetables to the pan and
    continue to fry, stirring from time to
time, for about 5 minutes. Add the
oatmeal and cook for a further minute.

4   Add the stock and then the milk and
    bring to the boil. Season well, add 2
tablespoons of vinegar, cover and simmer
for about 30 minutes until the vegetables
are very tender.

5   Mix the egg yolk with the cream,
    add a little of the soup to the cream
and then whisk it all back into the soup,
followed by the mayonnaise.

6   Bring slowly back just to the boil,
    adjust the seasoning and add extra
vinegar, if necessary, to sharpen the taste.
Garnish with herbs and serve with
oatcakes.

RED BEAN CHOWDER

••

SERVES 4-6

175 g/6 oz/1 cup dried red kidney beans,
    soaked overnight and drained or 425 g/
    14 oz can red kidney beans, drained
900 ml/1½ pints/3½ cups water if using
    dried beans
45 g/1½ oz/3 tbsp butter or margarine
1 large onion, chopped very finely
1 large carrot, chopped finely
1-2 celery sticks, chopped finely
1 small turnip, chopped finely
2 garlic cloves, crushed
175 g/6 oz/ ¾ cup extra lean finely
    minced (ground) beef
2 tbsp plain (all-purpose) flour
1-2 tsp chilli powder
900 ml/1½ pints/3½ cups Beef Stock (see
    page 8)
2 tsp tomato purée (paste)
4 tomatoes, skinned and chopped finely
1 tsp chopped fresh oregano or ½ tsp dried
    oregano
salt and pepper

1 If using dried kidney beans, put
    them in a saucepan with the water,
bring to the boil and boil hard for 10–15
minutes, reduce the heat and simmer for
about 1–1½ hours until tender; drain.

2 Melt the butter or margarine in a
    saucepan and fry the onion, carrot,
celery, turnip and garlic very slowly for
about 10 minutes until soft.

3 Add the beef and cook slowly,
    stirring frequently, for 10 minutes
until cooked and lightly browned.

4 Stir in the flour and chilli powder
    and cook for 2 minutes. Gradually
stir in the stock and tomato purée (paste)
and bring to the boil, stirring.

5 Season the chowder, cover the pan
    and simmer for 30 minutes. Stir in
the tomatoes, oregano and beans.

6 Return to the boil and simmer for 5
    minutes. If the soup seems very
thick add a little more boiling water or
stock. Adjust the seasoning and serve.

LAMB COUSCOUS

••

SERVES 4

2 tbsp olive oil
500 g/1 lb lamb fillet (tenderloin), sliced
    thinly
2 onions, sliced
2 garlic cloves, chopped
1 cinnamon stick
1 tsp ground ginger
1 tsp paprika
½ tsp chilli powder
600 ml/1 pint/2½ cups hot chicken stock
3 carrots, sliced thinly
2 turnips, halved and sliced
425 g/14 oz can chopped tomatoes
30 g/1 oz/2 tbsp raisins
425 g/14 oz can chick-peas (garbanzo
    beans), drained and rinsed
3 courgettes (zucchini), sliced
125 g/4 oz fresh dates, halved and pitted
    or 125 g/4 oz dried apricots
300 g/10 oz/1¾ cups couscous
600 ml/1 pint/2½ cups boiling water
salt

1 Heat the oil in a frying pan (skillet)
    and fry the lamb briskly for 3
minutes until browned. Remove the meat
from the pan with a perforated spoon or
fish slice and set aside.

2 Add the onions to the pan and cook,
    stirring, until soft. Add the garlic and
spices and cook for 1 minute.

3 Add the stock, carrots, turnips,
    tomatoes, raisins, chick-peas
(garbanzo beans) and lamb. Cover, bring
to the boil and simmer for 12 minutes.

4 Add the courgettes (zucchini), dates
    or apricots and season with salt.
Cover again and cook for 8 minutes.

5 Meanwhile, put the couscous in a
    bowl with 1 teaspoon of salt and
pour over the boiling water. Leave to soak
for 5 minutes, then fluff with a fork.

6 To serve, pile the couscous on to a
    warmed serving platter and make a
hollow in the centre. Put the meat and
vegetables in the hollow and pour over
some of the sauce. Serve the rest of the
sauce separately.

CHICK-PEA (GARBANZO BEAN) & PEANUT BALLS WITH HOT CHILLI SAUCE

SERVES 4

3 tbsp groundnut oil
1 onion, chopped finely
1 celery stick, chopped
1 tsp dried mixed herbs
250 g/8 oz/2 cups roasted unsalted
   peanuts, ground
175 g/6 oz/1 cup canned chick-peas
   (garbanzo beans), drained and
   mashed
1 tsp yeast extract
60 g/2 oz/1 cup fresh wholemeal (whole
   wheat) breadcrumbs
1 egg yolk
30 g/1 oz/ ¼ cup plain (all-purpose) flour
strips of fresh red chilli to garnish

HOT CHILLI SAUCE:
2 tsp groundnut oil
1 large red chilli, deseeded and chopped
   finely
2 spring onions (scallions) chopped finely
2 tbsp red wine vinegar
230 g/7½ oz can chopped tomatoes
2 tbsp tomato purée (paste)
2 tsp caster (superfine) sugar

TO SERVE:
rice
green salad

1 Heat 1 tablespoon of the oil in a frying pan (skillet) and gently fry the onion and celery for 3–4 minutes until softened but not browned.

2 Place all the other ingredients, except the remaining oil and the flour, in a mixing bowl and add the onion and celery. Mix well.

3 Divide the mixture into 12 portions and roll into small balls. Coat with the flour.

4 Heat the remaining oil in a frying pan (skillet). Add the chick-pea (garbanzo bean) balls and cook over a medium heat for 15 minutes, turning frequently, until cooked through and golden. Drain on paper towels.

5 Meanwhile, make the hot chilli sauce. Heat the oil in a small frying pan (skillet) and gently fry the chilli and spring onions (scallions) for 2–3 minutes. Sitr in the remaining ingredients and season. Bring to the boil and simmer for 5 minutes. Serve the chick-pea (garbanzo bean) and peanut balls with the hot chilli sauce, rice and a green salad.

EGG & CHICK-PEA (GARBANZO BEAN) CURRY

SERVES 4

2 tbsp vegetable oil
2 garlic cloves, crushed
1 large onion, chopped
1 large carrot, sliced
1 apple, cored and chopped
2 tbsp medium-hot curry powder
1 tsp finely grated fresh ginger root
2 tsp paprika
900 ml/1½ pints/3½ cups vegetable stock
2 tbsp tomato purée (paste)
½ small cauliflower, broken into florets
475 g/15 oz can chick-peas (garbanzo
    beans), rinsed and drained
30 g/1 oz/2 tbsp sultanas (golden raisins)
    or raisins
2 tbsp cornflour (cornstarch)
2 tbsp water
4 hard-boiled (hard-cooked) eggs,
    quartered
salt and pepper
paprika to garnish

CUCUMBER DIP:
7.5 cm/3 in piece of cucumber, chopped
    finely
1 tbsp chopped fresh mint
150 ml/¼ pint/⅔ cup natural yogurt
sprigs of fresh mint to garnish

1 Heat the oil in a large saucepan and fry the garlic, onion, carrot and apple for 4–5 minutes, until softened.

2 Add the curry powder, ginger and paprika and fry for 1 minute more.

3 Stir in the vegetable stock and tomato purée (paste).

4 Add the cauliflower, chick-peas (garbanzo beans) and sultanas (golden raisins) or raisins. Bring to the boil, then reduce the heat and simmer, covered, for 25–30 minutes until the vegetables are tender.

5 Blend the cornflour (cornstarch) with the water and add to the curry, stirring until thickened. Cook gently for 2 minutes. Season to taste.

6 To make the dip, in a small serving bowl, mix together the cucumber, mint and yogurt.

7 Ladle the curry onto 4 warmed serving plates and arrange the eggs on top. Sprinkle with a little paprika. Garnish the cucumber and mint dip with mint and serve with the curry.

MUSHROOM & PARMESAN RISOTTO

SERVES 4

2 tbsp olive or vegetable oil
250 g/8 oz/generous 1 cup arborio
    (risotto) rice
2 garlic cloves, crushed
1 onion, chopped
2 celery sticks, chopped
1 red or green (bell) pepper, deseeded and
    chopped
250 g/8 oz mushrooms, sliced
1 tbsp chopped fresh oregano or 1 tsp
    dried oregano
1 litre/1¾ pints/4 cups vegetable stock
60 g /2 oz sun-dried tomatoes in olive oil,
    drained and chopped (optional)
60 g/2 oz/ ½ cup finely grated Parmesan
    cheese
salt and pepper

TO GARNISH:
fresh flat-leaf parsley sprigs
fresh bay leaves

1 Heat the oil in a wok or large frying
   pan (skillet). Add the rice and cook,
stirring, for 5 minutes.

2 Add the garlic, onion, celery and
   (bell) pepper and cook, stirring, for
5 minutes. Add the mushrooms and cook
for a further 3–4 minutes.

3 Stir in the oregano and stock. Heat
   until just boiling, then reduce the
heat, cover and simmer gently for about
20 minutes until the rice is tender and
creamy.

4 Add the sun-dried tomatoes, if using,
   and season to taste. Stir in half the
Parmesan cheese. Top with the remaining
cheese, garnish with flat-leaf parsley and
bay leaves and serve.

ARBORIO RICE

This is an Italian short-grain rice used
specially for risottos – the starch it
contains is essential for the creamy
texture, so don't rinse it before cooking.
   Check the rice as it cooks from time
to time. If it has absorbed all the liquid
before it is tender, add a little extra
stock or water.

BROWN RICE WITH FRUIT & NUTS

SERVES 4-6

4 tbsp vegetable ghee or oil
1 large onion, peeled and chopped
2 garlic cloves, peeled and crushed
2.5 cm/1 in ginger root, peeled and
    chopped
1 tsp chilli powder
1 tsp cumin seeds
1 tbsp mild or medium curry powder or
    paste
300 g/10 oz/1½ cups brown rice
900 ml/1½ pints/3½ cups boiling vegetable
    stock
1 x 425 g/14 oz can chopped tomatoes
salt and freshly ground black pepper
175 g/6 oz ready-soaked dried apricots or
    peaches, cut into slivers
1 red (bell) pepper, cored, seeded and
    diced
90 g/3 oz frozen peas
1-2 small, slightly green bananas
60-90g/2-3 oz/ ⅓-½ cup toasted nuts
    (a mixture of almonds, cashews and
    hazelnuts, or pine kernels)
coriander sprigs, to garnish

1 Heat the ghee or oil in a large
   saucepan, add the onion and fry
gently for 3 minutes. Stir in the garlic,
ginger, spices and rice and cook gently
for 2 minutes, stirring all the time until the
rice is coated in the spiced oil.

2 Pour in the boiling stock and add
   the canned tomatoes and season
with salt and pepper to taste. Bring to the
boil, then reduce the heat, cover and
simmer gently for 40 minutes or until the
rice is almost cooked and most of the
liquid is absorbed.

3 Add the slivered apricots or peaches,
   diced red (bell) pepper and peas.
Cover and continue cooking for 10
minutes. Remove from the heat and allow
to stand for 5 minutes without
uncovering.

4 Peel and slice the bananas. Uncover
   the rice mixture and fork through to
mix the ingredients together. Add the
toasted nuts and sliced banana and toss
lightly. Transfer to a warm serving platter
and garnish with coriander sprigs. Serve
hot.

KOFTA KEBABS WITH TABBOULEH

SERVES 4

175 g/6 oz/1 cup aduki beans
175 g/6 oz/1 cup bulgur wheat
450 ml/ ¾ pint/scant 2 cups Fresh
   Vegetable Stock (see page 97)
3 tbsp olive oil
1 onion, chopped finely
2 garlic cloves, crushed
1 tsp ground coriander
1 tsp ground cumin
2 tbsp chopped fresh coriander (cilantro)
3 eggs, beaten
125 g/4 oz/1 cup dried wholemeal (whole
   wheat) breadcrumbs
salt and pepper
fresh coriander (cilantro) sprigs to garnish

TABBOULEH:
175 g/6 oz/1 cup bulgur wheat soaked in
   450 ml/ ¾ pint/scant 2 cups boiling
   water for 15 minutes
2 tbsp lemon juice
1 tbsp olive oil
6 tbsp chopped fresh parsley
4 spring onions (scallions), chopped finely
60 g/2 oz cucumber, chopped finely
3 tbsp chopped fresh mint
1 extra-large tomato, chopped finely

TO SERVE:
Tahini Cream (see below)
black olives
pitta bread

1 Cook the aduki beans in boiling
   water for 40 minutes until tender.
Drain, rinse and leave to cool. Cook the
bulgur wheat in the stock for 10 minutes
until the stock is absorbed. Set aside.

2 Heat 1 tablespoon of the oil in a
   frying pan (skillet) and fry the onion,
garlic and spices for 4–5 minutes.

3 Transfer to a bowl with the beans,
   coriander (cilantro), seasoning and
eggs and mash with a potato masher or
fork. Add the breadcrumbs and bulgur
wheat and stir well. Cover and chill for 1
hour, until firm.

4 Combine the tabbouleh ingredients.
   Cover and chill.

5 With wet hands, mould the kofta
   mixture into 32 oval shapes. Press
on to skewers, brush with oil and grill
(broil) for 5–6 minutes until golden. Turn,
re-brush, and cook for 5–6 minutes. Drain
on paper towels. Garnish and serve with
the tabbouleh, tahini cream, black olives
and pitta bread.

TAHINI CREAM

Tahini Cream is a nutty-flavoured sauce
that goes well with the Kofta Kebabs
above, and with other Middle Eastern
dishes such as falafel. To make it, blend
together 3 tbsp tahini and 6 tbsp water,
then stir in 2 tsp lemon juice and
1 crushed garlic clove. Season to taste
with salt and pepper, and serve.

LENTIL ROAST

SERVES 6

250 g/8 oz/1 cup split red lentils
500 ml/16 fl oz/2 cups Fresh Vegetable
  Stock (see page 97)
1 bay leaf
15 g/ ½ oz/1 tbsp butter or margarine,
  softened
2 tbsp dried wholemeal (whole wheat)
  breadcrumbs
250 g/8 oz/2 cups grated Cheddar cheese
1 leek, chopped finely
125 g/4 oz button mushrooms, chopped
  finely
90 g/3 oz/1½ cups fresh wholemeal (whole
  wheat) breadcrumbs
2 tbsp chopped fresh parsley
1 tbsp lemon juice
2 eggs, beaten lightly
salt and pepper
sprigs of fresh flat-leaf parsley to garnish
mixed roast vegetables to serve

1 Put the lentils, stock and bay leaf in a saucepan, bring to the boil, cover and simmer gently for 15–20 minutes until all the liquid is absorbed and the lentils have softened. Discard the bay leaf.

2 Meanwhile, base-line a 1 kg/2 lb loaf tin (pan) with baking parchment. Grease with the butter or margarine and sprinkle with the dried breadcrumbs.

3 Stir the cheese, leek, mushrooms, fresh breadcrumbs and parsley into the lentils.

4 Bind together with the lemon juice and eggs. Season well and spoon into the prepared loaf tin (pan). Smooth the top and bake in a preheated oven at 190°C/375°F/Gas Mark 5 for 1 hour until golden.

5 Loosen the loaf with a palette knife (spatula) and turn on to a warmed serving plate. Garnish with parsley and serve sliced, with roast vegetables.

VARIATIONS

Chopped onion or spring onions (scallions) would make a suitable substitute for leek. Try using different herbs in the mixture to vary the flavour.

RED BEAN STEW & DUMPLINGS

SERVES 4

1 tbsp vegetable oil
1 red onion, sliced
2 celery sticks, chopped
900 ml/1½ pints/3½ cups Fresh Vegetable
  Stock (see page 97)
250 g/8 oz carrots, diced
250 g/8 oz potatoes, diced
250 g/8 oz courgettes (zucchini), diced
4 tomatoes, skinned and chopped
125 g/4 oz/ ½ cup split red lentils
425 g/14 oz can kidney beans, rinsed and
  drained
1 tsp paprika
salt and pepper

DUMPLINGS:
125 g/4 oz/1 cup plain (all-purpose) flour
½ tsp salt
2 tsp baking powder
1 tsp paprika
1 tsp dried mixed herbs
30 g/1 oz/2 tbsp vegetable suet
7 tbsp water
sprigs of fresh flat-leaf parsley to garnish

1 Heat the oil in a flameproof casserole or a large saucepan and gently fry the onion and celery for 3–4 minutes until just softened.

2 Pour in the stock and stir in the carrots and potatoes. Bring to the boil, cover and cook for 5 minutes.

3 Stir in the courgettes (zucchini), tomatoes, lentils, kidney beans, paprika and seasoning. Bring to the boil, cover and cook for 5 minutes.

4 Meanwhile, make the dumplings. Sift the flour, salt, baking powder and paprika into a bowl. Stir in the herbs and suet. Bind together with the water to form a soft dough. Divide into 8 portions and roll gently to form balls.

5 Uncover the stew, stir, then add the dumplings, pushing them slightly into the stew. Cover, reduce the heat so the stew simmers and cook for a further 15 minutes until the dumplings have risen and are cooked through. Garnish with flat-leaf parsley and serve immediately.

BARBECUE BEAN BURGERS

••

SERVES 6

125 g/4 oz/ ⅓ cup aduki beans
125 g/4 oz/ ⅓ cup black-eye beans (peas)
6 tbsp vegetable oil
1 large onion, chopped finely
1 tsp yeast extract
125 g/4 oz grated carrot
90 g/3 oz/1½ cups fresh wholemeal (whole
  wheat) breadcrumbs
2 tbsp wholemeal (whole wheat) plain (all-
  purpose) flour
salt and pepper

BARBECUE SAUCE:
½ tsp chilli powder
1 tsp celery salt
2 tbsp light muscovado sugar
2 tbsp red wine vinegar
2 tbsp vegetarian Worcestershire sauce
3 tbsp tomato purée (paste)
dash of Tabasco sauce

TO SERVE:
6 wholemeal (whole wheat) baps, toasted
mixed green salad
jacket potato fries

1 Place the beans in separate
  saucepans, cover with water, bring to
the boil, cover and simmer the aduki
beans for 40 minutes and the black-eye
beans (peas) for 50 minutes, until tender.
Drain and rinse well.

2 Transfer to a mixing bowl and lightly
  mash together with a potato masher
or fork. Set aside.

3 Heat 1 tablespoon of the oil in a
  frying pan (skillet) and gently fry the
onion for 3–4 minutes until softened. Mix
into the beans with the yeast extract,
grated carrot, breadcrumbs and seasoning.
Bind together well.

4 With wet hands, divide the mixture
  into 6 portions and form into
burgers 8 cm/3½ in in diameter. Put the
flour on a plate and use to coat the
burgers.

5 Heat the remaining oil in a large
  frying pan (skillet) and cook the
burgers for 3–4 minutes on each side,
turning carefully, until golden and crisp.
Drain on paper towels.

6 Meanwhile, make the sauce. Mix all
  the ingredients together until well
blended. Put the burgers in the toasted
baps and serve with a mixed green salad,
jacket potato fries and a spoonful of the
barbecue sauce.

SPICED BASMATI PILAU

SERVES 6

500 g/1 lb/2½ cups basmati rice
175 g/6 oz broccoli, trimmed
6 tbsp vegetable oil
2 large onions, peeled and chopped
250 g/8 oz mushrooms, wiped and sliced
2 garlic cloves, peeled and crushed
6 cardamom pods, split
6 whole cloves
8 black peppercorns
1 cinnamon stick or piece of cassia bark
1 tsp ground turmeric
1.25 litres/2 pints/5 cups boiling vegetable stock or water
salt and freshly ground black pepper
60 g/2 oz/ ⅓ cup seedless raisins
60 g/2 oz/ ½ cup unsalted pistachios, coarsely chopped

1 Place the rice in a sieve and wash well under cold running water until the water runs clear. Drain. Trim off most of the broccoli stalk and cut into small florets, then quarter the stalk lengthways and cut diagonally into 1 cm/ ½ in pieces.

2 Heat the oil in a large saucepan, add the onions and broccoli stalks and cook gently for 3 minutes, stirring frequently. Add the mushrooms, rice, garlic and spices and cook gently for 1 minute, stirring frequently until the rice is coated in spiced oil.

3 Add the boiling stock and season with salt and pepper. Stir in the broccoli florets and return the mixture to the boil. Cover, reduce the heat and cook gently for 15 minutes without uncovering.

4 Remove from the heat and leave to stand for 5 minutes without uncovering. Add the raisins and pistachios and gently fork through to fluff up the grains. Serve hot.

VARIATION

For added richness, stir a spoonful of vegetable ghee through the rice mixture just before serving. A little diced red pepper and a few cooked peas or sweetcorn kernels forked through at step 4 add a colourful touch.

KITCHOURI

SERVES 4

2 tbsp ghee or butter
1 red onion, chopped finely
1 garlic clove, crushed
½ celery stick, chopped finely
1 tsp turmeric
½ tsp garam masala
1 green chilli, deseeded and chopped finely
½ tsp cumin seeds
1 tbsp chopped fresh coriander (cilantro)
125 g/4 oz/generous ½ cup basmati rice, rinsed under cold water until water runs clear
125 g/4 oz/ ½ cup green lentils
300 ml/ ½ pint/1¼ cups vegetable juice
600 ml/1 pint/2½ cups vegetable stock

1 Melt the ghee in a large saucepan. Add the onion, garlic and celery, and cook until soft, about 5 minutes.

2 Add the turmeric, garam masala, green chilli, cumin seeds and coriander (cilantro). Stir until fragrant over a moderate heat, about 1 minute.

3 Add the rice and green lentils, and stir until the rice is translucent, about 1 minute.

4 Pour the vegetable juice and vegetable stock into the saucepan, and bring to the boil. Cover and simmer over a low heat for about 20 minutes, or until the lentils are cooked. They should be tender when pressed between 2 fingers. Stir occasionally.

5 Transfer to a warmed serving dish and serve piping hot.

VEGETARIAN LUNCH

This is a versatile dish, and can be served as a great-tasting and satisfying one-pot meal for a vegetarian. I have also served it as a winter lunch dish with tomatoes and yogurt.

INDONESIAN HOT RICE SALAD

SERVES 4

300 g/10 oz/1½ cups brown rice
425 g/14 oz can pineapple pieces in
  natural juice, drained
1 bunch spring onions (scallions),
  chopped
1 red (bell) pepper, deseeded and chopped
125 g/4 oz/2 cups beansprouts
90 g/3 oz/ ¾ cup dry-roasted peanuts
125 g/4 oz radishes, sliced thinly

DRESSING:
2 tbsp crunchy peanut butter
1 tbsp groundnut oil
2 tbsp light soy sauce
2 tbsp white wine vinegar
2 tsp clear honey
1 tsp chilli powder
½ tsp garlic salt
pepper

1 Place the rice in a saucepan and cover with water. Bring to the boil, cover and simmer for 30 minutes until tender.

2 Meanwhile, make the dressing. Place all the ingredients in a small bowl and whisk for a few seconds until well combined.

3 Drain the rice and place in a heatproof bowl. Heat the dressing in a small saucepan for 1 minute and then toss into the rice and mix well.

4 Working quickly, stir in the pineapple, spring onions (scallions), (bell) pepper, beansprouts and peanuts.

5 Pile into a warmed serving bowl or dish, arrange the radish slices around the outside and serve immediately.

SERVING COLD

This salad is equally delicious served cold. Add the dressing to the rice while still warm, but allow the rice to cool before adding the remaining ingredients.

PESTO RICE WITH GARLIC BREAD

SERVES 4

300 g/10 oz/1½ cups mixed long-grain
  and wild rice
sprigs of fresh basil to garnish
tomato and orange salad to serve

PESTO DRESSING:
15 g/ ½ oz fresh basil
125 g/4 oz/1 cup pine kernels (nuts)
2 garlic cloves, crushed
90 ml/3½ fl oz/6 tbsp olive oil
60 g/2 oz/ ½ cup grated Parmesan cheese
salt and pepper

GARLIC BREAD:
2 small Granary or wholegrain sticks of
  French bread
90 g/3 oz/ ⅓ cup butter or margarine,
  softened
2 garlic cloves, crushed
1 tsp dried mixed herbs

1 Place the rice in a saucepan and cover with water. Bring to the boil and cook according to the packet instructions. Drain well and keep warm.

2 Meanwhile, make the pesto dressing. Remove the basil leaves from the stalks and finely chop the leaves. Reserve 30 g/1 oz/ ¼ cup of the pine kernels (nuts) and finely chop the remainder. Mix with the chopped basil and dressing ingredients. Alternatively, put all the ingredients in a food processor or blender and blend for a few seconds until smooth.

3 To make the garlic bread, slice the bread at 2.5 cm/1 in intervals, taking care not to slice all the way through. Mix the butter or margarine with the garlic, herbs and seasoning. Spread thickly between each slice. Wrap the bread in foil and bake in a preheated oven at 200°C/400°F/ Gas Mark 6 for 10–15 minutes.

4 To serve, toast the reserved pine kernels (nuts) under a preheated medium grill (broiler) for 2–3 minutes until golden. Toss the pesto dressing into the hot rice and pile into a warmed serving dish. Sprinkle with toasted pine kernels (nuts) and garnish with basil sprigs. Serve with the garlic bread and a tomato and orange salad.

MEDITERRANEAN VEGETABLE TART

SERVES 6

1 aubergine (eggplant), sliced
2 tbsp salt
4 tbsp olive oil
1 garlic clove, crushed
1 large yellow (bell) pepper, sliced
300 ml/ ½ pint/1¼ cups ready-made
  tomato pasta sauce
125 g/4 oz/ ⅔ cup sun-dried tomatoes in
  oil, drained and halved if necessary
175 g/6 oz Mozzarella cheese, drained
  and sliced thinly

PASTRY:
250 g/8 oz/2 cups plain (all-purpose) flour
pinch of celery salt
125 g/4 oz/ ½ cup butter or margarine
2 tbsp tomato purée (paste)
2–3 tbsp milk

1 To make the pastry, sift the flour and celery salt into a bowl and rub in the butter or margarine until the mixture resembles breadcrumbs.

2 Mix together the tomato purée (paste) and milk and stir into the mixture to form a firm dough. Knead gently on a lightly floured surface until smooth. Wrap and chill for 30 minutes.

3 Grease a 28 cm/11 in loose-bottomed flan tin. Roll out the pastry on a lightly floured surface and use to line the tin. Trim and prick all over with a fork. Chill for 30 minutes.

4 Meanwhile, layer the aubergine (eggplant) in a dish, sprinkling with the salt. Leave for 30 minutes.

5 Bake the pastry case in a preheated oven at 200°C/400°F/ Gas Mark 6 for 20–25 minutes until cooked and lightly golden. Set aside. Increase the oven temperature to 230°C/450°F/Gas Mark 8.

6 Rinse the aubergine (eggplant) and pat dry. Heat 3 tablespoons of the oil in a frying pan (skillet) and gently fry the garlic, aubergine (eggplant) and (bell) pepper for 5–6 minutes until just softened. Drain on paper towels.

7 Spread the pastry case with pasta sauce and arrange the cooked vegetables, sun-dried tomatoes and Mozzarella on top. Brush with the remaining oil and bake for 5 minutes until the cheese is just melting. Serve.

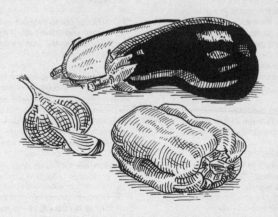

GREEN RICE

SERVES 4

2 large green (bell) peppers
2 fresh green chillies
2 tbsp plus 1 tsp vegetable oil
1 large onion, chopped finely
1 garlic clove, crushed
1 tbsp ground coriander
300 g/10 oz/1½ cups long-grain rice
700 ml/1¼ pints/3 cups Fresh Vegetable
   Stock (see page 97)
250 g/8 oz/2 cups frozen peas
6 tbsp chopped fresh coriander (cilantro)
1 egg, beaten
salt and pepper
fresh coriander (cilantro) to garnish

TO SERVE:
tortilla chips
lime wedges

1 Halve, core and deseed the (bell) peppers. Cut the flesh into small cubes. Deseed and finely chop the chillies.

2 Heat 2 tablespoons of the oil in a saucepan and gently fry the onion, garlic, (bell) peppers and chillies for 5–6 minutes until softened but not browned.

3 Stir in the ground coriander, rice, and vegetable stock. Bring to the boil, cover and simmer for 10 minutes. Add the frozen peas, bring back to the boil, cover again and simmer for a further 5 minutes until the rice is tender and the liquid has been absorbed. Remove from the heat and leave to stand, covered, for 10 minutes.

4 Season well and mix in the fresh coriander (cilantro). Pile into a warmed serving dish and keep warm.

5 Heat the remaining oil in a small omelette pan, pour in the egg and cook for 1–2 minutes on each side until set. Slide on to a plate, roll up and slice into thin rounds.

6 Arrange the omelette strips on top of the rice. Garnish with coriander (cilantro) and serve with tortilla chips and lime wedges.

THAI-STYLE CHICKEN FRIED RICE

SERVES 4

250 g/8 oz/generous 1 cup long-grain rice
4 tbsp vegetable oil
2 garlic cloves, chopped finely
6 shallots, sliced finely
1 red (bell) pepper, deseeded and diced
125 g/4 oz green beans, cut into 2.5 cm/
   1 in lengths
1 tbsp Thai red curry paste
350 g/12 oz cooked chicken, chopped
½ tsp ground coriander
1 tsp finely grated ginger root
2 tbsp Thai fish sauce
finely grated rind of 1 lime
3 tbsp lime juice
1 tbsp chopped fresh coriander (cilantro)
salt and pepper

TO GARNISH:
lime wedges
fresh coriander (cilantro) sprigs

1 Cook the rice in plenty of boiling, lightly salted water for 12–15 minutes until tender. Drain, rinse in cold water and drain thoroughly.

2 Heat the oil in a large frying pan (skillet) or wok and add the garlic and shallots. Fry gently for 2–3 minutes until golden.

3 Add the (bell) pepper and green beans and stir-fry for 2 minutes. Add the Thai curry paste and stir-fry for 1 minute.

4 Add the cooked rice to the pan then add the chicken, ground coriander, ginger, fish sauce, lime rind and juice and fresh coriander (cilantro). Stir-fry over a medium-high heat for about 4–5 minutes, until the rice and chicken are thoroughly reheated. Season to taste.

5 Garnish with lime wedges and coriander (cilantro) and serve.

THAI FISH SAUCE

Thai fish sauce is used to season many Thai dishes. It adds a salty flavour, rather than a seafood one, so take care when adding extra salt to the dish.

COUSCOUS ROYALE

....

SERVES 6

3 carrots
3 courgettes (zucchini)
350 g/12 oz pumpkin or squash
*1.25 litres/2¼ pints/5 cups Fresh Vegetable
    Stock (see page 97)*
2 cinnamon sticks, broken in half
2 tsp ground cumin
1 tsp ground coriander
pinch of saffron strands
2 tbsp olive oil
pared rind and juice of 1 lemon
2 tbsp clear honey
500 g/1 lb/2⅔ cups pre-cooked couscous
*60 g/2 oz/ ¼ cup butter or margarine,
    softened*
175 g/6 oz/1 cup large seedless raisins
salt and pepper
fresh coriander (cilantro) to garnish

1 Cut the carrots and courgettes
(zucchini) into 7 cm/3 in pieces and
cut in half lengthways.

2 Trim the pumpkin or squash and
discard the seeds. Peel and cut into
pieces the same size as the carrots and
courgettes (zucchini).

3 Put the stock, spices, saffron and
carrots in a large saucepan. Bring to
the boil, skim off any scum and add the
olive oil. Simmer for 15 minutes.

4 Add the lemon rind and juice to the
pan with the honey, courgettes
(zucchini) and pumpkin or squash.
Season well. Bring back to the boil and
simmer for a further 10 minutes.

5 Meanwhile, soak the couscous
according to the packet instructions.
Transfer to a steamer or large sieve
(strainer) lined with muslin (cheesecloth)
and place over the vegetable pan. Cover
and steam as directed. Stir in the butter or
margarine.

6 Pile the couscous on to a warmed
serving plate. Drain the vegetables,
reserving the stock, lemon rind and
cinnamon. Arrange the vegetables on top
of the couscous. Put the raisins on top
and spoon over 6 tablespoons of the
reserved stock. Keep warm.

7 Return the remaining stock to the
heat and boil for 5 minutes to
reduce slightly. Discard the lemon rind
and cinnamon. Garnish with the coriander
(cilantro) and serve with the sauce
handed separately.

FISH & SHELLFISH – INTRODUCTION

FISH

Fish is always popular and features in many classic dishes. Take care when buying fish; always make sure it is really fresh, check the 'use by' date on prepacked fish and, if you buy fish fresh to freeze yourself, make sure it has not previously been frozen. Fish is very perishable, but provided it is handled with care, kept chilled after purchase and used quickly, there is nothing better. When buying fish, check that it is fresh and clean with a low odour. Eyes should be bright, and flesh and skin should be firm and not too dry. Choose white-flesh fish as opposed to darker oily varieties, as the latter are high in fat. Include these oily fish in the diet occasionally, unless otherwise advised, as they contain valuable nutrients in their oils. If you have a specific cholesterol problem, then avoid prawns (shrimp) as they have a relatively high cholesterol content.

Nowadays, whole salmon are very reasonably priced, and are no longer the luxury they used to be, but they still make a very elegant and spectacular centrepiece to a buffet or special meal. To serve salmon hot, follow the method for Glazed Salmon (see page 633), but increase the cooking time to 10 minutes per 500 g/1 lb. When cooked, remove the fish carefully from the fish kettle and drain off all the liquid. Place the salmon on a serving dish and carefully strip off the skin. Serve with lemon wedges and hollandaise sauce (see Herrings in Oatmeal, page 155).

If you don't have a large fish kettle you can sometimes hire one from a fishmonger or from the wet fish counter of a large supermarket. Alternatively, the fish can be cooked in a large saucepan or preserving pan. Simply heat the water and other ingredients until just boiling, then hold the fish upright in two or three strips of folded foil and carefully lower it into the pan, curving it as you go. The fish will retain this shape and look very attractive when glazed. It is, however, not quite so easy to serve when it is cooked in this shape.

SHELLFISH

It is essential that all shellfish must be in prime condition, transported home as quickly as possible and, if fresh, stored in the refrigerator and used within 24 hours. Avoid shellfish that looks stale or has a strong, sour or unpleasant odour which will be quite apparent and different from the usual 'fishy' smell. Mussels need special attention; any that are open should be tapped sharply – if they don't close quickly they must be discarded, for they are dead and therefore poisonous. Mussels will open up during cooking; any that remain closed should be discarded.

Frozen shellfish is widely available and probably more frequently used. Again, take home quickly and store in the freezer if not to be used at once. Thaw out what is required either for a few hours at room temperature or overnight in the refrigerator. Once thawed, they should be well drained and used quickly. Do not leave them around for a further 24 hours before use.

When it comes to freezing cooked dishes using fish or shellfish, they can be frozen for 1–2 months, provided the dish has been properly cooked, even if the main ingredient has been frozen once before. If the ingredients have just been added to the dish at the end of cooking and warmed through, as prawns (shrimp) may be, do not freeze it.

SEAFOOD & AROMATIC RICE

SERVES 4

250 g/8 oz/1¼ cups basmati rice
2 tbsp ghee or vegetable oil
1 onion, peeled and chopped
1 garlic clove, peeled and crushed
1 tsp cumin seeds
½-1 tsp chilli powder
4 cloves
1 cinnamon stick or a piece of cassia bark
2 tsp curry paste
250 g/8 oz peeled prawns (shrimp)
500g/1 lb white fish fillets (such as
  monkfish, cod or haddock), skinned
  and boned and cut into bite-sized
  pieces
salt and freshly ground black pepper
600 ml/1 pint/2½ cups boiling water
60 g/2 oz/ ⅓ cup frozen peas
60 g/2 oz/ ⅓ cup frozen sweetcorn kernels
1-2 tbsp lime juice
2 tbsp toasted desiccated (shredded)
  coconut
coriander sprigs and lime slices, to
  garnish

1 Place the rice in a sieve and wash
  well under cold running water until
the water runs clear, then drain well. Heat
the ghee or oil in a saucepan, add the
onion, garlic, spices and curry paste and
fry very gently for 1 minute.

2 Stir in the rice and mix well until
  coated in the spiced oil. Add the
prawns (shrimp) and white fish and
season well with salt and pepper. Stir
lightly, then pour in the boiling water.

3 Cover and cook gently for 10
  minutes, without uncovering the
pan. Add the peas and corn, cover and
continue cooking for a further 8 minutes.
Remove from the heat and allow to stand
for 10 minutes.

4 Uncover the pan, fluff up the rice
  with a fork and transfer to a warm
serving platter. Sprinkle the dish with the
lime juice and toasted coconut, and serve
garnished with coriander sprigs and
lime slices.

MARINER'S PIE

SERVES 4

750 g/1½ lb potatoes
2 large leeks, sliced
300 ml/ ½ pint/1¼ cups + 2 tbsp milk
1 tbsp chopped fresh parsley
60 g/2 oz/ ¼ cup butter
60 g/2 oz/ ½ cup plain (all-purpose) flour
750 g/1½ lb skinned and boned coley, cut
  into chunks
1 egg
salt and pepper
chopped fresh parsley to garnish
green beans and tomatoes to serve

1 Boil the potatoes in lightly salted
  water for about 15 minutes until
tender. Meanwhile, cook the leeks in
lightly salted boiling water for about 8
minutes.

2 Drain the potatoes and leeks,
  reserving the cooking liquid. Mash
the potatoes with 2 tbsp of the milk and
half the butter. Make the remaining milk
up to 600 ml/1 pint/2½ cups with the
cooking liquid from the potatoes and
leeks. Add the parsley to the milk
mixture.

3 Melt the remaining butter in a
  saucepan. Add the flour and cook
gently, stirring, for 1 minute. Gradually
stir in the milk and parsley mixture. Heat,
stirring constantly, until thickened and
smooth. Season to taste.

4 Grease a large, shallow ovenproof
  dish. Put the fish in the dish and
arrange the cooked leeks on top. Pour
over the parsley sauce.

5 Pipe or spoon the potatoes on top.
  Bake in a preheated oven at
190°C/375°F/Gas Mark 5 for 25–30
minutes until golden. Garnish with parsley
and serve with beans and tomatoes.

VARIATIONS

For a treat, add a few cooked, peeled
prawns (shrimp) to the fish pie.
  Top the pie with sliced, cooked
potato if you prefer, brushing with a
little beaten egg and milk.

THAI PRAWN (SHRIMP) STIR-FRY

SERVES 4

½ cucumber
2 tbsp sunflower oil
6 spring onions (scallions), halved
    lengthways and cut into 4 cm/1½ inch
    lengths
1 stalk lemon grass, sliced thinly
1 garlic clove, chopped
1 tsp chopped fresh red chilli
125 g/4 oz oyster mushrooms
1 tsp chopped ginger root
350 g/12 oz cooked peeled prawns
    (shrimp)
2 tsp cornflour (cornstarch)
2 tbsp water
1 tbsp dark soy sauce
½ tsp fish sauce
2 tbsp dry sherry or rice wine
boiled rice to serve

1 Cut the cucumber into strips about 5 mm x 4 cm/ ¼ x 1¾ in.

2 Heat the oil in a wok or large frying pan (skillet), add the spring onions (scallions), cucumber, lemon grass, garlic, chilli, mushrooms and ginger and stir-fry for 2 minutes.

3 Add the prawns (shrimp) and stir-fry for a further minute.

4 Mix together the cornflour (cornstarch), water, soy sauce and fish sauce until smooth.

5 Stir the cornflour (cornstarch) mixture and dry sherry or rice wine into the pan and heat through, stirring, until the sauce has thickened. Serve immediately with boiled rice.

LEMON GRASS

Lemon grass is used extensively in South-East Asian cooking, particularly that of Thailand. You can thinly slice the white part of the stem and leave it in the cooked dish, or use the whole stem and remove it before serving. You can buy lemon grass chopped and dried, or preserved in jars, but neither has the fragrance or delicacy of the fresh variety.

SPICY FISH & POTATO FRITTERS

SERVES 4

500 g/1 lb potatoes, peeled and cut into
    even-sized pieces
500g/1 lb white fish fillets, such as cod or
    haddock, skinned and boned
6 spring onions (scallions), sliced
1 fresh green chilli, seeded
2 garlic cloves, peeled
1 tsp salt
1 tbsp medium or hot curry paste
2 eggs, beaten
150 g/5 oz/2½ cups fresh white
    breadcrumbs
vegetable oil, for shallow frying
mango chutney, to serve
lime wedges and coriander sprigs, to
    garnish

1 Cook the potatoes in a pan of boiling, salted water until tender. Drain well, return the potatoes to the pan and place over a moderate heat for a few moments to dry off. Cool slightly, then place in a food processor with the fish, onions, chilli, garlic, salt and curry paste. Process until the ingredients are very finely chopped and blended.

2 Turn the potato mixture into a bowl and mix in 2 tablespoons of beaten egg and 60 g/2 oz/1 cup of breadcrumbs. Place the remaining beaten egg and breadcrumbs in separate dishes.

3 Divide the fish mixture into 8 and, using a spoon to help you (the mixture is quite soft), dip first in the beaten egg and then coat in the breadcrumbs, and carefully shape the mixture into ovals.

4 Heat enough oil in a large frying pan for shallow frying and fry the fritters over moderate heat for 3-4 minutes, turning frequently, until golden brown and cooked through. Drain on absorbent paper towels and garnish with lime wedges and coriander sprigs. Serve hot, with mango chutney.

PRAWNS (SHRIMP) IN SAUCE

SERVES 4

20-24 large raw tiger prawns (shrimp)
45 g/1½ oz/ ½ cup desiccated (shredded)
*   coconut*
90 g/3 oz/1½ cups fresh white
*   breadcrumbs*
1 egg, beaten
600 ml/1 pint/2½ cups sunflower or
*   vegetable oil*
fresh sprigs of coriander, to garnish

PEANUT & COCONUT SAUCE:
60 g/2 oz creamed coconut (see page 336)
150 ml/ ¼ pint/ ⅔ cup hot water
125 g/4 oz crunchy peanut butter
2 spring onions (scallions), trimmed and
*   finely chopped*
1 tbsp dark soy sauce
1 tsp brown sugar
2 tsp sesame seeds
salt and pepper
½ small honeydew or Ogen melon

1 Peel the tiger prawns (shrimp), leaving the tails, and dry thoroughly on paper towels. Put the coconut and breadcrumbs into a food processor and process until well blended and finely chopped. Spread the coconut mixture on a plate. Dip the prawns (shrimp) in the beaten egg, then coat thoroughly in the coconut and breadcrumb mixture. Chill while making the sauce.

2 For the sauce, put the creamed coconut and water into the wok and blend thoroughly, then bring slowly up to the boil. Remove from the heat, stir in the peanut butter, spring onions (scallions), soy sauce, sugar, sesame seeds and seasoning and when blended put into a serving bowl and keep warm.

3 Cut the melon into 12 slices, removing the seeds.

4 Wash and dry the wok, add the oil and heat to 180°-190°C /350°-375°F, or until a cube of bread browns in 30 seconds. Deep-fry the prawns (shrimp) a few at a time for 2-3 minutes until golden brown. Remove with a slotted spoon and drain on paper towels. Keep warm while cooking the remainder.

5 Serve immediately on individual plates, with slices of melon, garnished with sprigs of coriander. Serve the warm sauce in its bowl.

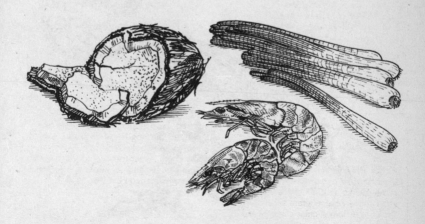

SHRIMP CURRY & FRUIT SAUCE

SERVES 4

2 tbsp vegetable oil
30 g/1 oz/2 tbsp butter
2 onions, finely chopped
2 garlic cloves, finely chopped
1 tsp cumin seeds, lightly crushed
1 tsp ground turmeric
1 tsp paprika
½ tsp chilli powder, or to taste
½ cucumber, thinly diced
60 g/2 oz creamed coconut
1 x 425 g/15 oz can chopped tomatoes
1 tbsp tomato purée (paste)
500 g/1 lb frozen shrimps, defrosted
150 ml/ ¼ pint/ ⅔ cup Greek-style yogurt
2 hard-boiled eggs, quartered
salt
coriander and onion rings, to garnish

FRUIT SAUCE:
300 ml/ ½ pint/1¼ cups natural yogurt
¼ tsp salt
1 garlic clove, crushed
2 tbsp chopped mint
4 tbsp seedless raisins
1 small pomegranate

1 Heat the oil and butter in a frying pan. Add the chopped onions and fry until translucent. Add the garlic and fry for a further minute, until softened but not browned.

2 Stir in the cumin seeds, turmeric, paprika and chilli powder and cook for 2 minutes, stirring. Stir in the creamed coconut, chopped tomatoes and tomato purée (paste) and bring to the boil. Simmer for 10 minutes, or until the sauce has thickened slightly. It should not be at all runny.

3 Remove the pan from the heat and set aside to cool. Stir in the shrimps, cucumber and yogurt. Taste the sauce and adjust the seasoning if necessary. Cover and chill until ready to serve.

4 To make the fruit sauce, place the yogurt in a bowl and stir in the salt, garlic, mint and raisins. Cut the pomegranate in half, scoop out the seeds and discard the white membrane. Stir the seeds into the yogurt, reserving a few for garnish.

5 Transfer the curry to a serving dish and arrange the hard-boiled egg, coriander and onion rings on top. Serve the sauce separately, sprinkled with the reserved pomegranate seeds.

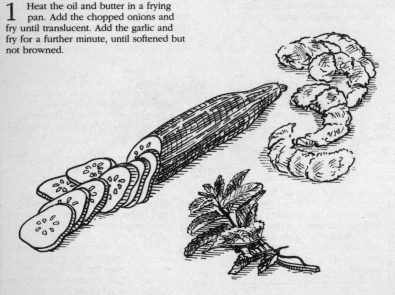

PRAWNS (SHRIMP) & CHILLI SAUCE

SERVES 4

4 tbsp ghee or vegetable oil
1 onion, peeled, quartered and sliced
1 bunch spring onions (scallions),
trimmed and sliced
1 garlic clove, peeled and crushed
1-2 fresh green chillies, seeded and finely
chopped
2.5 cm/1 in piece ginger root, finely
chopped
1 tsp ground turmeric
1 tsp ground cumin
1 tsp ground coriander
1½ tsp curry powder or paste
1 x 400 g/14 oz can chopped tomatoes
150 ml/ ¼ pint/ ⅔ cup water
150 ml/ ¼ pint/ ⅔ cup double (heavy)
cream
500 g/1 lb peeled prawns (shrimp)
1-2 tbsp chopped fresh coriander
salt
coriander sprigs, to garnish

1 Heat the ghee or vegetable oil in a saucepan and fry the onions, garlic and chilli over gentle heat for 3 minutes. Stir in the ginger, spices and curry powder or paste and cook very gently for a further 1 minute, stirring all the time.

2 Stir in the tomatoes and water and bring to the boil, stirring. Reduce the heat and simmer for 10 minutes, stirring occasionally.

3 Add the cream, mix well and simmer for 5 minutes, then add the prawns (shrimp) and coriander and season with salt to taste. Cook gently for 2-3 minutes. Taste and adjust the seasoning, if necessary. Serve garnished with coriander sprigs.

PREPARING EARLY

This dish may be prepared in advance to the end of step 2. A few minutes before the dish is required for serving, reheat the mixture until simmering then follow the instructions given in step 3.

STIR-FRIED PRAWNS (SHRIMP)

SERVES 4

170 g/6 oz raw prawns (shrimp), peeled
1 tsp salt
¼ tsp egg white
2 tsp cornflour (cornstarch) paste (see
page 376)
300 ml/ ½ pint/1¼ cups vegetable oil
1 spring onion (scallion), cut into short
sections
2.5 cm (1 in) ginger root, thinly sliced
1 small green (bell) pepper, cored, seeded
and cubed
½ tsp sugar
1 tbsp light soy sauce
1 tsp rice wine or dry sherry
a few drops of sesame oil

1 Mix the prawns (shrimp) with a pinch of the salt, the egg white and cornflour (cornstarch) paste until they are all well coated.

2 Heat the oil in a preheated wok and stir-fry the prawns (shrimp) for 30-40 seconds only. Remove and drain on paper towels.

3 Pour off the oil, leaving about 1 tablespoon in the wok. Add the spring onion (scallion) and ginger to flavour the oil for a few seconds, then add the green (bell) pepper and stir-fry for about 1 minute.

4 Add the remaining salt and the sugar followed by the prawns (shrimp). Continue stirring for another minute or so, then add the soy sauce and wine and blend well. Sprinkle with sesame oil and serve immediately.

COOK'S HINTS

1-2 small green or red hot chillies, sliced, can be added with the green (bell) pepper to create a more spicy dish. Leave the chillies unseeded for a very hot dish.

Fresh ginger root should be peeled and sliced, then finely chopped or shredded before use. It will keep for weeks in a cool, dry place. Dried ginger powder is no substitute – compared with fresh ginger root, it lacks flavour.

SPICED SCALLOPS

SERVES 4

12 large scallops with coral attached,
  defrosted if frozen, or 350 g/12 oz small
  scallops without coral, defrosted
4 tbsp sunflower oil
4-6 spring onions (scallions), thinly sliced
  diagonally
1 garlic clove, crushed
2.5 cm/1 in ginger root, finely chopped
250 g/8 oz mangetout (snow peas)
125 g/4 oz button or closed cup
  mushrooms, sliced
2 tbsp sherry
2 tbsp soy sauce
1 tbsp clear honey
¼ tsp ground allspice
salt and pepper
1 tbsp sesame seeds, toasted

1 Wash and dry the scallops,
  discarding any black pieces and
detach the corals, if using. Slice each
scallop into 3-4 pieces and if the corals
are large halve them.

2 Heat 2 tablespoons of oil in the
  wok, swirling it around until really
hot. Add the spring onions (scallions),
garlic and ginger and stir-fry for a minute
or so then add the mangetout (snow
peas) and continue to cook for 2-3
minutes, stirring continuously. Remove to
a bowl.

3 Add the remaining oil to the wok
  and when really hot add the scallops
and corals and stir-fry for a couple of
minutes. Add the mushrooms and
continue to cook for a further minute or
so.

4 Add the sherry, soy sauce, honey
  and allspice to the wok, with salt
and pepper to taste. Mix thoroughly, then
return the mangetout (snow peas) mixture
to the wok.

5 Season well and toss together over a
  high heat for a minute or so until
piping hot. Serve immediately, sprinkled
with sesame seeds.

SCALLOPS WITH WILD MUSHROOMS

SERVES 2

15 g/ ½ oz/1 tbsp butter
250 g/8 oz shelled queen scallops
1 tbp olive oil
125 g/4 oz oyster mushrooms, sliced
1 garlic clove, chopped
4 spring onions (scallions), white and
  green parts sliced
3 tbsp double (heavy) cream
1 tbsp brandy
salt and pepper

TO SERVE
boiled basmati rice
green salad

1 Heat the butter in a heavy-based
  frying pan (skillet) and fry the
scallops for 1 minute, turning
occasionally, then remove from the pan.

2 Add the oil to the pan and heat. Add
  the mushrooms, garlic and spring
onions (scallions) and cook for 2 minutes,
stirring constantly.

3 Return the scallops to the pan with
  the cream and brandy. Season to
taste and heat through gently.

4 Serve with basmati rice and a green
  salad.

SCALLOPS

The most delicious seafood in the
prettiest of shells. The rounded half
can be used as a dish in which to
serve the scallops. Scallops can grow
to about 18 cm/7 in across and consist
a large round white muscle with a
bright orange roe.

Small queen scallops, or queenies,
are smaller, only about 7 cm/3 in
across and are usually sold ready-
prepared, both fresh and frozen.

If you buy scallops on the shell,
slide a knife underneath the
membrane to loosen and cut off the
tough muscle that holds the scallop to
the shell. Discard the black stomach
sac and intestinal vein.

FISH WITH SAFFRON SAUCE

SERVES 4

*625-750 g/1¼ – 1½ lb white fish fillets (cod,
    haddock, whiting etc)*
pinch of Chinese five-spice powder
4 sprigs of fresh thyme
large pinch of saffron threads
*250 ml/8 fl oz/1 cup boiling fish or
    vegetable stock*
2 tbsp sunflower oil
*125 g/4 oz button mushrooms, thinly
    sliced*
grated rind of ½ lemon
1 tbsp lemon juice
*½ tsp freshly chopped thyme or ¼ tsp dried
    thyme*
½ bunch watercress, chopped
1½ tsp cornflour
3 tbsp single or double (heavy) cream
salt and pepper
lemon and watercress sprigs, to garnish

1 Skin the fish and cut into 4 even-
    sized portions. Season with salt and
pepper and five-spice powder. Arrange
the fish on a plate and place in the
bottom of a bamboo steamer, laying a
sprig of thyme on each piece of fish (if
the fillets are large you may need 2
steamers, one on top of the other).

2 Stand a low metal trivet in a wok
    and add water to come almost to the
top of it. Bring to the boil, stand the
bamboo steamer on the trivet and cover
with first the bamboo lid and then the lid
of the wok. If there is no wok lid, make
one out of a domed piece of foil pressed
tightly to the sides of the wok. Simmer for
about 20 minutes until the fish is tender,
adding more boiling water to the wok as
necessary.

3 Meanwhile, soak the saffron threads
    in the boiling stock.

4 When the fish is tender, remove and
    keep warm. Empty the wok and
wipe dry. Heat the oil in the wok, add the
mushrooms and stir-fry for about 2
minutes.

5 Add the saffron stock, lemon rind
    and juice and chopped thyme and
bring to the boil. Add the watercress and
simmer for a 1-2 minutes.

6 Blend the cornflour with the cream,
    add a little of the sauce from the
wok, mix well, then return to the wok
and heat gently until thickened. Remove
the sprigs of thyme from the fish and
serve surrounded by the sauce with a
little spooned over it and garnished with
lemon and watercress.

BAJAN FISH

500-625 g /1-1¼ lb monkfish tails, boned
   and cubed
2 large carrots
175-250 g/6-8 oz baby sweetcorn
3 tbsp sunflower oil
1 courgette (zucchini), sliced
1 yellow (bell) pepper, cored, seeded and
   thinly sliced
1 tbsp wine vinegar
150 ml/ ¼ pint/ ⅔ cup fish or vegetable
   stock
1 tbsp lemon juice
2 tbsp sherry
1 tsp cornflour (cornstarch)
salt and pepper
fresh herbs and lemon slices, to garnish

BAJAN SEASONING:
1 small onion, quartered
2 shallots
3-4 garlic cloves, crushed
4-6 large spring onions (scallions), sliced
small handful of fresh parsley
2-3 sprigs of fresh thyme
small strip of green chilli pepper, seeds
   removed, or ½ -¼ tsp chilli powder
½ tsp salt
¼ tsp freshly ground black pepper
2 tbsp brown rum or red wine vinegar

1 First make the Bajan seasoning. Place all the ingredients in a food processor and process very finely.

2 Put the fish in a shallow dish and spread the Bajan seasoning over it, turning to coat evenly. Cover with clingfilm and leave to marinate for at least 30 minutes and up to 24 hours.

3 Cut the carrots into narrow 4 cm/1½ in slices and slice the baby sweetcorn diagonally.

4 Heat 2 tablespoons of oil in the wok, swirling it around until really hot. Add the fish and stir-fry for 3-4 minutes until cooked through. Remove to a bowl and keep warm.

5 Add the remaining oil to the wok and when hot stir-fry the carrots and corn for 2 minutes, then add the (bell) pepper and stir-fry for another minute or so. Return the fish and juices to the wok and stir-fry for 1-2 minutes.

6 Blend the vinegar, stock, lemon juice, sherry and seasoning with the cornflour (cornstarch). Stir into the wok and boil until the sauce thickens. Serve garnished with herbs and lemon.

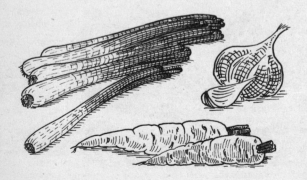

MUSSEL & SCALLOP SPAGHETTI

•••

SERVES 4

250 g/8 oz dried wholemeal (wholewheat)
  spaghetti
60 g/2 oz/2 slices rindless lean back
  bacon, chopped
2 shallots, chopped finely
2 celery stick, chopped finely
150 ml/ ¼ pint/ ⅔ cup dry white wine
150 ml/ ¼ pint/ ⅔ cup Fish Stock (see
  page 9)
500 g/1 lb fresh mussels, prepared
250 g/8 oz shelled queen scallops
1 tbsp chopped fresh parsley
salt and pepper

1 Cook the spaghetti in a saucepan of
  boiling water according to the packet
instructions, until the pasta is cooked but
'al dente', firm to the bite – about 10
minutes.

2 Meanwhile, gently dry-fry the bacon
  in a large non-stick frying pan
(skillet) for 2–3 minutes. Stir in the
shallots, celery and wine. Simmer gently,
uncovered, for 5 minutes until softened.

3 Add the stock, mussels and scallops,
  cover and cook for a further 6–7
minutes. Discard any mussels that remain
unopened.

4 Drain the spaghetti and add to the
  frying pan (skillet). Add the parsley,
season to taste and toss together.
Continue to cook for 1–2 minutes to heat
through. Pile on to warmed serving
plates, spooning over the cooking juices.

VARIATIONS

Most varieties of pasta work well in this
recipe, and strands look particularly
attractive. Wholemeal (wholewheat)
pasta doesn't have any egg added to
the dough, so it is low in fat, and higher
in fibre than other pastas.

  Prawns (shrimp) or chopped crab
meat would make a suitable alternative
to either mussels or scallops, and
350 g/12 oz/2 cups diced cooked
chicken would give a good alternative
for non-shellfish eaters.

SOLE PAUPIETTES

•••

SERVES 4

125 g/4 oz fresh young spinach leaves
2 Dover soles or large lemon soles or
  plaice, filleted
125 g/4 oz peeled prawns (shrimp),
  defrosted if frozen
2 tsp sunflower oil
2-4 spring onions (scallions), finely sliced
  diagonally
2 thin slices ginger root, finely chopped
150 ml/ ¼ pint/ ⅔ cup fish stock or water
2 tsp cornflour (cornstarch)
4 tbsp single cream
6 tbsp natural yogurt
salt and pepper
whole prawns (shrimp), to garnish
  (optional)

1 Strip the stalks off the spinach, wash
  and dry on paper towels. Divide the
spinach between the seasoned fish fillets,
laying the leaves on the skin side. Divide
half the prawns (shrimp) between them.
Roll up the fillets from head to tail and
secure with wooden cocktail sticks.
Arrange the rolls on a plate in the base of
a bamboo steamer.

2 Stand a low metal trivet in the wok
  and add enough water to come
almost to the top of it. Bring to the boil.
Place the bamboo steamer on the trivet,
cover with the steamer lid and then the
wok lid, or cover tightly with a domed
piece of foil. Steam gently for 30 minutes
until the fish is tender and cooked
through.

3 Remove the fish rolls and keep
  warm. Empty the wok and wipe dry.
Heat the oil in the wok, swirling it around
until really hot. Add the spring onions
(scallions) and ginger and stir-fry for
1-2 minutes. Add the stock and bring to
the boil.

4 Blend the cornflour (cornstarch)
  with the cream. Add the yogurt and
remaining prawns (shrimp) to the wok
and heat gently until boiling. Add a little
sauce to the blended cream and return it
all to the wok. Heat gently until
thickened. Adjust the seasoning. Serve the
paupiettes with the sauce spooned over
and garnished with whole prawns
(shrimp), if liked.

SESAME SALMON & CREAM SAUCE

SERVES 4

625-750 g/1¼ – 1½ lb salmon or pink trout
    fillets
2 tbsp light soy sauce
3 tbsp sesame seeds
3 tbsp sunflower oil
4 spring onions (scallions), thinly sliced
    diagonally
2 large courgettes (zucchini), diced, or
    2.5 cm/5 in piece of cucumber, diced
grated rind of ½ lemon
½ tsp turmeric
1 tbsp lemon juice
6 tbsp fish stock or water
3 tbsp double (heavy) cream or fromage
    frais
salt and pepper
curly endive, to garnish

1 Skin the salmon and cut into strips
    about 4 x 2 cm/1½ x ¾ in. Pat dry on
paper towels. Season lightly, then brush
with soy sauce and sprinkle all over with
sesame seeds.

2 Heat 2 tablespoons of oil in the
    wok, swirling it around until really
hot. Add the pieces of salmon and stir-fry
for 3-4 minutes until lightly browned all
over. Remove with a fish slice, drain on
paper towels and keep warm.

3 Add the remaining oil to the wok
    and when hot add the spring onions
(scallions) and courgettes (zucchini) or
cucumber and stir-fry for 1-2 minutes.
Add the lemon rind and juice, turmeric,
stock and seasoning and bring to the boil
for a minute or so. Stir the cream or
fromage frais into the sauce.

4 Return the salmon pieces to the wok
    and toss gently in the sauce until
they are really hot. Serve on warm plates
and garnish with curly endive, if using.

SKINNING FISH

Lay the fillet skin-side down. Insert a
sharp, flexible knife at one end
between the flesh and the skin. Hold
the skin tightly at the end and push the
knife along, keeping the knife blade as
flat as possible against the skin.

POACHED SALMON

SERVES 4

1 small onion, sliced
1 small carrot, sliced
1 stick celery, sliced
1 bay leaf
pared rind and juice of ½ orange
a few stalks of parsley
salt
5-6 black peppercorns
750 ml/1¼ pints/3 cups water
4 salmon steaks, about 350 g/12 oz each
salad leaves, to serve
lemon twists, to garnish

SAUCE:
1 large avocado, peeled, halved and
    stoned
125 ml/4 fl oz/ ½ cup Greek-style yogurt
grated zest and juice of ½ orange
black pepper
a few drops of hot red pepper sauce

1 Put the onion, carrot, celery, bay
    leaf, orange rind, orange juice,
parsley stalks, salt and peppercorns in a
pan just large enough to take the salmon
steaks in a single layer. Pour on the water,
cover the pan and bring to the boil.
Simmer the stock for 20 minutes.

2 Arrange the salmon steaks in the
    pan, return the stock to the boil and
simmer for 3 minutes. Cover the pan,
remove from the heat and leave the
salmon to cool in the stock.

3 To make the sauce, roughly chop
    the avocado and place it in a
blender or food processor with the
yogurt, orange zest and orange juice.
Process to make a smooth sauce, then
season to taste with salt, pepper and hot
pepper sauce.

4 Remove the salmon steaks from the
    stock (reserve it to make fish soup
or a sauce), skin them and pat dry with
paper towels.

5 Cover the serving dish with salad
    leaves, arrange the salmon steaks on
top and spoon a little of the sauce into
the centre of each one. Garnish the fish
with lemon twists, and serve the
remaining sauce separately.

BAKED RED SNAPPER

SERVES 4

*1 red snapper, sea bream, or other whole
  fish, about1.25 kg/2 lb, cleaned*
juice of 2 limes, or 1 lemon
*4-5 sprigs of thyme, lemon thyme or
  parsley*
3 tbsp olive oil
1 large onion, chopped
2 garlic cloves, finely chopped
1 x 425 g/14 oz can chopped tomatoes
2 tbsp tomato purée (paste)
2 tbsp red wine vinegar
5 tbsp Greek-style yogurt
2 tbsp chopped parsley
2 tsp dried oregano
6 tbsp dry breadcrumbs
*60 g/2 oz/ ¼ cup yogurt cheese (see page
  97), or feta cheese, crumbled*
salt and pepper
lime wedges and dill sprigs, to serve

SALAD:
1 small lettuce, thickly sliced
10-12 young spinach leaves, torn
½ small cucumber, sliced and quartered
4 spring onions (scallions), thickly sliced
3 tbsp chopped parsley
2 tbsp olive oil
2 tbsp plain yogurt
1 tbsp red wine vinegar

1 Wash the fish and dry with paper
towels. Sprinkle the lime or lemon
juice inside and over the fish, and season
well. Place the herbs inside the fish.

2 Heat the oil in a pan and fry the
onion until translucent. Stir in the
garlic and cook for 1 minute, then stir in
the chopped tomatoes, tomato purée
(paste) and wine vinegar. Bring to the
boil and simmer, uncovered, for 5 minutes
until it has thickened slightly.

3 Remove the pan from the heat,
allow the sauce to cool a little, then
stir in the yogurt, parsley and oregano.

4 Pour half the sauce into a shallow,
ovenproof dish just large enough to
take the fish. Pour the remainder of the
sauce over it, and sprinkle on the
breadcrumbs. Bake uncovered for 30-35
minutes, until it is firm. Sprinkle the
yogurt cheese or feta over the fish and
serve with lime wedges and dill sprigs.
Serve the salad separately.

5 Arrange the lettuce, spinach,
cucumber, spring onions (scallions)
and parsley in a bowl. Whisk the oil,
yogurt and wine vinegar until well
blended, and pour over the salad.

QUENELLES & WATERCRESS SAUCE

••

SERVES 4

750 g/1½ lb white fish fillets, such as cod,
  coley or whiting, skinned
2 small egg whites
½ tsp ground coriander
1 tsp ground mace
150 ml/ ¼ pint/ ⅔ cup natural yogurt
1 small onion, sliced
salt and pepper
mixture of boiled Basmati rice and wild
  rice, to serve

SAUCE:
1 bunch watercress, trimmed
300 ml/ ½ pint/1¼ cups chicken stock
2 tbsp cornflour (cornstarch)
150 ml/¼ pint/ ⅔ cup natural yogurt
2 tbsp crème fraîche

1 Cut the fish into pieces and process it in a food processor for about 30 seconds, until it is finely chopped.

2 Add the egg whites to the fish and process for a further 30 seconds until the mixture forms a stiff paste. Add the coriander and mace and season. Add the yogurt and process until well blended. Transfer the mixture to a covered container and chill it for at least 30 minutes.

3 Spoon the mixture into a piping bag, and pipe into sausage shapes about 10 cm/4 in long. Cut off each length with a knife. Alternatively, take rounded dessertspoons of the mixture and shape into ovals, using 2 spoons.

4 Bring about 5 cm/2 in of water to the boil in a frying pan and add the onion for flavouring. Lower the quenelles into the water, using a fish slice or spoon. Cover the pan, keep the water at a gentle rolling boil and poach the quenelles for 8 minutes, turning them once. Remove with a slotted spoon and drain on paper towels.

5 To make the sauce, roughly chop the watercress, reserving a few sprigs for garnish. Process the remainder with the chicken stock until well blended, then pour into a small pan. Stir the cornflour (cornstarch) into the yogurt and pour the mixture into the pan. Bring to the boil, stirring. Stir in the crème fraîche, season and remove from the heat. Pour the sauce into a warmed dish and serve it separately.

6 Garnish with the reserved watercress sprigs. Serve with a Basmati rice and wild rice mixture.

SALMON FILLETS WITH CAPER SAUCE

SERVES 4

4 salmon fillets, skinned
1 fresh bay leaf
few black peppercorns
1 tsp white wine vinegar
150 ml/ ¼ pint/ ⅔ cup fish stock
3 tbsp double (heavy) cream
1 tbsp capers
1 tbsp chopped fresh dill
1 tbsp chopped fresh chives
1 tsp cornflour (cornstarch)
2 tbsp milk
salt and pepper
new potatoes to serve

TO GARNISH:
fresh dill sprigs
chive flowers

1 Lay the salmon fillets in a shallow ovenproof dish. Add the bay leaf, peppercorns, vinegar and stock.

2 Cover with foil and bake in a preheated oven at 180°C/350°F/ Gas Mark 4 for 15–20 minutes until the flesh is opaque and flakes easily when tested with a fork.

3 Transfer the fish to warmed serving plates, cover and keep warm.

4 Strain the cooking liquid into a saucepan. Stir in the cream, capers, herbs and seasoning to taste.

5 Blend the cornflour (cornstarch) with the milk. Add to the saucepan and heat, stirring, until thickened slightly. Boil for 1 minute.

6 Spoon the sauce over the salmon, garnish with dill sprigs and chive flowers and serve with new potatoes.

LOW-FAT VERSION

If you want to cut down on fat and calories, use fromage frais or thick yogurt instead of the cream and omit the cornflour (cornstarch) and milk. Don't allow the sauce to boil.

KEDGEREE

SERVES 4

300 g/10 oz/scant 1½ cups long-grain rice
375 g/12 oz smoked haddock fillet
1 bay leaf
2–3 lemon slices
60 g/2 oz/ ¼ cup butter or margarine
1 large onion, chopped finely
125 g/4 oz/2 cups button mushrooms, sliced (optional)
good pinch of ground coriander
3 tbsp chopped fresh parsley or 2 tbsp chopped fresh tarragon
2–4 hard-boiled (hard-cooked) eggs, chopped
6–8 tbsp single (light) cream
salt and pepper

TO GARNISH:
sprigs of fresh parsley or tarragon
chopped fresh parsley

1 Cook the rice in boiling salted water until just tender. Drain, rinse under hot water and drain well.

2 Put the fish in a saucepan and barely cover with water. Add the bay leaf and lemon slices and poach gently for about 15 minutes until tender. Drain thoroughly, remove the skin and any bones from the fish and flake the fish.

3 Melt the butter or margarine in a saucepan and fry the onion gently until soft and just barely coloured. Add the mushrooms, if using, and cook for 2–3 minutes.

4 Add the flaked haddock, the coriander and plenty of seasoning and heat through, stirring frequently.

5 Add the cooked rice, parsley or tarragon and eggs and heat through, stirring from time to time. Pour the cream over, mix lightly and serve, garnished with sprigs of parsley or tarragon and chopped parsley.

FREEZING

Freeze for up to 2 months, but do not add the hard-boiled (hard-cooked) eggs and cream until just before serving.

FISH & SEAFOOD CHOWDER

SERVES 4

1 kg/2 lb mussels in their shells
1 large onion, thinly sliced
2 garlic cloves, chopped
3 bay leaves
a few stalks of parsley
a few stalks of thyme
300 ml/ ½ pint/1¼ cups water
250 g/8 oz smoked haddock fillets
500 g/1 lb potatoes, peeled and diced
4 celery stalks, thickly sliced
1 x 250 g/8 oz can sweetcorn kernels,
*   drained and rinsed*
150 ml/ ¼ pint/ ⅔ cup natural yogurt
1 tsp cornflour (cornstarch)
150 ml/ ¼ pint/ ⅔ cup dry white wine, or
*   dry cider*
½ tsp cayenne pepper, or to taste
black pepper
2 tbsp chopped parsley

1 Scrub the mussels, pull off the
   "beards" and rinse in several changes
of cold water. Discard any open shells
that remain open when tapped.

2 Put the onion, garlic, bay leaves,
   parsley and thyme in a large pan
and pour on the water. Add the mussels,
cover and cook over high heat for 5
minutes, shaking the pan once or twice.

3 Line a colander with muslin or
   cheesecloth and stand it in a bowl.
Strain the mussel liquor into the bowl.
Remove and shell the mussels and set
them aside. Discard the vegetables and
herbs and reserve the liquor.

4 Put the haddock, potatoes and
   celery into the rinsed pan, add
600 ml/1 pint/2½ cups of cold water and
bring to the boil. Cover the pan and
simmer for 10 minutes. Remove the
haddock with a fish slice and skin, bone
and flake it. Remove the vegetables with a
slotted spoon and strain the liquor into
the reserved seafood liquor.

5 Return the cooking liquor to the
   rinsed pan, add the sweetcorn and
bring to the boil. Stir together the yogurt
and cornflour (cornstarch) to make a
smooth paste. Stir in a little of the fish
liquor, then pour it into the pan. Stir until
the yogurt is well blended, then add the
reserved mussels, haddock, potatoes and
celery. Add the white wine, season with
cayenne and black pepper and heat the
soup gently, without boiling. Taste and
adjust the seasoning if necessary. Transfer
to a warm serving dish and sprinkle with
the chopped parsley. Serve hot, with
crusty bread.

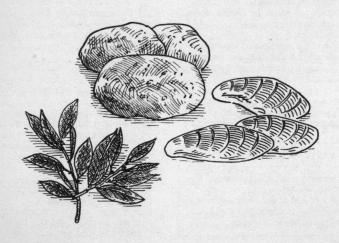

BOUILLABAISSE

•••

SERVES 4-6

750 g–1 kg/1½–2 lb mixed fish and
  shellfish such as whiting, mackerel, red
  or grey mullet, cod, eel, bass, crab,
  prawns (shrimp), lobster, squid and
  mussels
2 large onions, sliced thinly or chopped
2 celery sticks, sliced very thinly
1 carrot, chopped finely
2–3 garlic cloves, crushed
4 tbsp olive oil
425 g/14 oz can chopped tomatoes with
  mixed herbs or 350 g/12 oz fresh
  tomatoes, skinned and chopped
1 fresh or dried bay leaf
¼ tsp ground coriander
few sprigs of fresh mixed herbs, including
  parsley
1 tsp grated lemon rind
1–2 tbsp lemon juice
about 300 ml/ ½ pint/1¼ cups water
pinch of saffron threads or ground
  turmeric
salt and pepper
chopped mixed herbs to garnish

1 Clean the fish, removing any skin
   and bones, and cut into pieces about
5 x 2.5 cm/2 x 1 in. Remove the heads
from the prawns (shrimp). Cut the squid
into rings. Scrub the mussels.

2 Gently fry the onions, celery, carrot
   and garlic in the oil in a large
saucepan for about 5 minutes until soft
but not coloured. Stir in the tomatoes, bay
leaf, coriander, herbs, seasoning and
lemon rind and juice. Arrange all the fish
and shellfish in the pan over the
vegetables.

3 Put the measured water in another
   saucepan, add the saffron or
turmeric and bring to the boil. Pour into
the saucepan of fish, adding enough to
just cover the fish.

4 Bring to the boil, cover and simmer
   for about 20 minutes until the fish is
tender but not broken up.

5 Discard the bay leaf and herbs, then
   ladle the soup into bowls, sprinkle
with the chopped mixed herbs and serve.
Both a soup spoon and fork are needed
to eat this soup.

MOULES MARINIÈRE

•••

SERVES 4

about 3 litres/5 pints/12 cups fresh mussels
60 g/2 oz/ ¼ cup butter
1 large onion, chopped very finely
2–3 garlic cloves, crushed
350 ml/12 fl oz/1½ cups dry white wine
150 ml/ ¼ pint/⅔ cup water
2 tbsp lemon juice
good pinch of finely grated lemon rind
1 Bouquet Garni (see page 9)
1 tbsp plain (all-purpose) flour
4 tbsp single (light) or double (thick)
  cream
2–3 tbsp chopped fresh parsley
salt and pepper
warm crusty bread to serve

1 Scrub the mussels in several changes
   of cold water to remove all mud,
sand, barnacles, etc. Pull off all the
'beards'. All the mussels must be tightly
closed; if they don't close when given a
sharp tap, they must be discarded.

2 Melt half the butter in a large
   saucepan. Add the onion and garlic
and fry gently until soft but not coloured.

3 Add the wine, water, lemon juice
   and rind, bouquet garni and plenty
of seasoning and bring to the boil. Cover
and simmer for 4–5 minutes.

4 Add the mussels to the pan, cover
   tightly and simmer for 5 minutes,
shaking the pan frequently, until all the
mussels have opened. Discard any
mussels which have not opened and
remove the bouquet garni.

5 Remove the mussels from the pan,
   discarding any which did not open
during cooking and take the empty half
shell off each one. Blend the remaining
butter with the flour and whisk into the
soup, a little at a time. Simmer gently for
2–3 minutes until slightly thickened.

6 Add the cream and half the parsley
   to the soup and reheat gently. Adjust
the seasoning. Ladle the mussels and
soup into warmed large soup bowls,
sprinkle with the remaining parsley and
serve with plenty of warm crusty bread.

CURRIED COD CHOWDER

··

SERVES 4–6

30 g/1 oz/2 tbsp butter or margarine
1 tbsp olive oil
1 onion, chopped finely
2 celery sticks, chopped finely
1 garlic clove, crushed
1½ tsp medium curry powder
700 ml/1¼ pints/3 cups Fish or Vegetable
  Stock (see page 9)
1 fresh or dried bay leaf
350 g/12 oz haddock or cod fillet, skinned
  and chopped coarsely
425 g/14 oz can chopped tomatoes
1 tbsp tomato purée (paste)
60 g/2 oz/ ¼ cup long-grain rice
1 carrot, grated coarsely
2 tsp lemon juice
4 tbsp single (light) or double (heavy)
  cream or natural fromage frais
2 tsp chopped fresh mixed herbs
salt and pepper
crusty bread to serve

1 Heat the butter or margarine with the
   oil in a saucepan, add the onion,
celery and garlic and gently fry until soft
but not coloured.

2 Stir in the curry powder, cook for 1
   minute and then add the stock, bay
leaf and seasoning. Bring to the boil.

3 Add the fish, cover and simmer
   gently for about 10 minutes until the
flesh flakes easily.

4 Break up the fish, then add the
   tomatoes, tomato purée (paste), rice,
carrot and lemon juice. Bring back to the
boil, cover and simmer for 20 minutes
until the rice is tender.

5 Stir in the cream or fromage frais
   and the herbs and adjust the
seasoning. Reheat and serve with plenty
of crusty bread.

VARIATION

Prawns (shrimp), smoked fish or
salmon, or a mixture of fish may also
be used for this chowder.

ITALIAN FISH STEW

··

SERVES 4

2 tbsp olive oil
2 red onions, finely chopped
1 garlic clove, crushed
2 courgettes (zucchini), sliced
425 g/14 oz can chopped tomatoes
900 ml/1½ pints/3½ cups Fish or Vegetable
  Stock (see page 9)
90 g/3 oz dried pasta shapes
350 g/12 oz firm white fish, such as cod,
  haddock or hake
1 tbsp chopped fresh basil or oregano or
  1 tsp dried oregano
1 tsp grated lemon rind
1 tbsp cornflour (cornstarch)
1 tbsp water
salt and pepper
sprigs of fresh basil or oregano to garnish

1 Heat the oil in a large saucepan and
   fry the onions and garlic for 5
minutes. Add the courgettes (zucchini)
and cook for 2–3 minutes, stirring often.

2 Add the tomatoes and stock to the
   saucepan and bring to the boil. Add
the pasta, cover and reduce the heat.
Simmer for 5 minutes.

3 Skin and bone the fish, then cut it
   into chunks. Add to the saucepan
with the basil or oregano and lemon rind
and cook gently for 5 minutes until the
fish is opaque and flakes easily. Take care
not to overcook it.

4 Blend the cornflour (cornstarch)
   with the water and stir into the stew.
Cook gently for 2 minutes, stirring, until
thickened. Season to taste and ladle into 4
warmed soup bowls. Garnish with basil
or oregano sprigs and serve at once.

VARIATIONS

This recipe is a good way to use up a
little leftover wine. Add a couple of
tablespoons of dry white wine just
before serving.
  Canned chopped tomatoes can be
bought with various flavourings; those
with herbs are perfect for this stew.

MONKFISH KEBABS

SERVES 4

750 g/1½ lb monkfish tail
3 tbsp olive oil
2 garlic cloves, crushed
2 tbsp powdered coconut
120 ml/4 fl oz/ ½ cup boiling water
1 tsp ground coriander
½ tsp ground cumin
1 tsp ground turmeric
1 tsp ground ginger
3 tbsp double (heavy) cream
1 tbsp chopped fresh coriander (cilantro)

1 Remove the central bone from the fish and cut the fish into 2.5 cm/ 1 in cubes. Put in a bowl with the oil and garlic and mix until the fish is coated.

2 Remove the fish from the oil and garlic mixture and thread on to 8 wooden skewers. Set aside.

3 Blend the powdered coconut with the boiling water. Heat the oil and garlic mixture in a saucepan, add the spices and cook, stirring, for 30 seconds. Add the coconut mixture and boil for 5 minutes.

4 Add the cream and chopped coriander (cilantro) and boil for 1 minute.

5 Put the fish under a preheated hot grill (broiler) and cook for 5–6 minutes, turning once, until charred outside but still moist on the inside.

6 Arrange 2 kebabs on each warmed serving plate, pour over the sauce and serve.

MONKFISH

Monkfish has a single narrow, vertical bone along the back, and no other bones. The flesh is covered with a tough transparent membrane which should be removed before cooking. Ask the fishmonger to prepare the fish for you if you like.

PLAICE FILLETS WITH GRAPES

SERVES 4

500 g/1 lb plaice fillets, skinned
1 bunch spring onions (scallions), white
*   and green parts cut into strips*
120 ml/4 fl oz/ ½ cup dry white wine
2 tsp cornflour (cornstarch)
2 tbsp milk
2 tbsp chopped fresh dill
90 ml/3 fl oz/ ⅓ cup double (heavy) cream
125 g /4 oz seedless white (green) grapes
salt and pepper
boiled basmati rice to serve

1 Cut the fish into strips about 4 cm x 5 mm/1 ½ x ¼ in and put into a frying pan (skillet) with the spring onions (scallions), wine and seasoning.

2 Cover and simmer for 4 minutes, then carefully transfer the fish to a warm serving dish. Cover and keep warm.

3 Mix the cornflour (cornstarch) and milk together then add to the pan with the dill and cream and boil, stirring, for 2 minutes until thickened.

4 Add the grapes and heat through very gently for 1-2 minutes, then pour over the fish. Serve with basmati rice.

DILL

Dill has a fairly strong aniseed flavour that goes very well with fish. The feathery leaves are particularly attractive when used as a garnish. It is widely used in Scandinavian dishes such as gravadlax and also with cucumber.

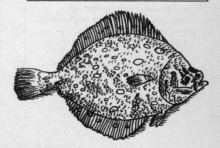

GRILLED PLAICE WITH MIXED MUSHROOMS

SERVES 4

4 x 150 g/5 oz white-skinned plaice fillets
2 tbsp lime juice
90 g/3 oz/ ⅓ cup low-fat spread
300 g/10 oz/2½ cups mixed small
 mushrooms such as button, oyster,
 shiitake, chanterelle or morel, sliced or
 quartered
4 tomatoes, skinned, seeded and chopped
celery salt and pepper
basil leaves to garnish
mixed salad to serve

1 Line a grill (broiler) rack with baking parchment and place the fish on top.

2 Sprinkle over the lime juice and season with celery salt and pepper. Place under a preheated moderate grill (broiler) and cook for 7–8 minutes without turning, until just cooked. Keep warm.

3 Meanwhile, gently melt the low fat spread in a non-stick frying pan (skillet), add the mushrooms and fry for 4–5 minutes over a low heat until cooked.

4 Gently heat the tomatoes in a small saucepan. Spoon the mushrooms, with any pan juices, and the tomatoes over the plaice.

5 Garnish with basil leaves and serve with a light salad.

MUSHROOMS

There are many varieties of mushrooms available now from greengrocers and supermarkets. Experiment with different mushrooms; they are ideal in a low-fat diet, as they are packed full of flavour and contain no fat. More 'meaty' types of mushroom like chestnut (crimini), will take slightly longer to cook.

SOUSED TROUT

SERVES 4

4 trout, about 250–350 g/8–12 oz each,
 filleted
1 onion, sliced very thinly
2 bay leaves, preferably fresh
sprigs of fresh parsley and dill or other
 fresh herbs
10–12 black peppercorns
4–6 cloves
good pinch of salt
150 ml/ ¼ pint/ ⅔ cup red wine vinegar
salad leaves to garnish

POTATO SALAD:
500 g/1 lb small new potatoes
2 tbsp French dressing
4 tbsp thick mayonnaise
3–4 spring onions (scallions), sliced

1 Trim the trout fillets, cutting off any pieces of fin. If preferred, remove the skin – use a sharp knife and, beginning at the tail end, carefully cut the flesh from the skin, pressing the knife down firmly as you go.

2 Lightly grease a shallow ovenproof dish and lay the fillets in it, packing them fairly tightly together but keeping in a single layer. Arrange the sliced onion, bay leaves and herbs over the fish.

3 Put the peppercorns, cloves, salt and vinegar into a saucepan and bring almost to the boil. Remove from the heat and pour evenly over the fish.

4 Cover with foil and cook in a preheated oven at 160°C/325°F/ Gas Mark 3 for 15 minutes. Leave until cold and then chill thoroughly.

5 Meanwhile, make the potato salad. Cook the potatoes in boiling salted water for 10–15 minutes until just tender. Drain. While still warm, cut into large dice and place in a bowl. Combine the French dressing and mayonnaise, add to the potatoes while warm and toss evenly. Leave until cold, then sprinkle with chopped spring onions (scallions).

6 Serve each portion of fish with a little of the juices, garnished with salad leaves and accompanied by the potato salad.

HERRINGS IN OATMEAL

SERVES 4

4 herrings, about 350 g/12 oz each, cleaned
1 egg, beaten
about 125 g/4 oz/1 cup fine or medium oatmeal or 150 g/5 oz/1¼ cups coarse oatmeal
60 g/2 oz/ ¼ cup butter or margarine (optional)
2 tbsp oil
salt and pepper

MUSTARD HOLLANDAISE SAUCE:
2 tbsp tarragon vinegar
1 tbsp water
2 egg yolks, lightly beaten
90–125 g/3–4 oz/ ⅓–½ cup butter, diced and softened slightly
1 tbsp chopped fresh mixed herbs
1 tbsp wholegrain mustard
grated rind of ½ small orange

TO GARNISH:
orange slices
fresh herbs

1 Cut the heads off the herrings then open out, flesh side down, on a flat surface. Press very firmly along the backbone of the fish with your thumbs or the heel of your hand; this loosens the backbone.

2 Turn the fish over and carefully ease out the backbone and any other loose bones. Cut each fish lengthways into 2 fillets, rinse in cold water and dry thoroughly. Season lightly, then dip in beaten egg and coat in oatmeal, pressing it on well. Set aside.

3 To make the sauce, put the vinegar and water into a saucepan and boil until reduced by half. Put the egg yolks into a bowl and stir in the vinegar. Stand the bowl over a pan of simmering water and heat gently, stirring, until the mixture thickens. (Don't let the water boil or the sauce will curdle.)

4 Whisk in the butter, a little at a time. Stir in the herbs, mustard, orange rind and seasoning.

5 Melt the butter and oil in a frying pan (skillet) and fry the fish for 4–5 minutes on each side until golden brown. Alternatively, place the fish in a greased baking tin (pan), drizzle over a little oil and cook in a preheated oven at 180°C/350°F/Gas Mark 4 for about 30 minutes.

6 Garnish with orange slices and herbs and serve with the mustard hollandaise sauce.

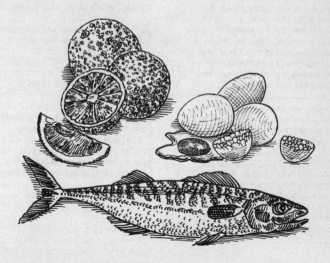

INDIAN GRILLED TROUT

••

SERVES 4

4 trout, each weighing about 250 g/8 oz,
  cleaned
salt
6 tbsp ghee or melted butter
1-2 garlic cloves, peeled and crushed
1 fresh green chilli, seeded and chopped,
  or use 1 tsp minced chilli (from a jar)
2.5 cm/1 in ginger root, peeled and finely
  chopped
1½ tsp cumin seeds
1 tsp garam masala
1 tsp ground cumin
finely grated rind of 1 lemon
juice of 2 lemons
coriander sprigs and lemon wedges, to
  garnish

1   Using a sharp knife, carefully make 3
    diagonal slashes (not too deep) on
each side of the trout. Season the trout
and place in a lightly greased grill
(broiler) pan.

2   Heat the ghee or butter in a small
    pan over a low heat, add the
crushed garlic, chilli, chopped ginger and
spices and cook very gently for 30
seconds, stirring. Remove the pan from
the heat and stir the lemon rind and juice
into the mixture.

3   Spoon half the mixture over the
    trout and cook under a moderately
hot grill (broiler) for 5-8 minutes or until
cooked on one side. Turn the fish over
and spoon the remaining mixture over the
fish and grill (broil) for a further 5-8
minutes, basting with the juices in pan
during cooking.

4   Arrange the trout on a hot serving
    plate, spoon the pan juices over the
fish and garnish with coriander sprigs and
lemon wedges. Serve hot.

SLASHING THE TROUT

Take care when making the diagonal
slashes on either side of the trout not
to cut too deeply or you will cut into
the bones and spoil the finished result.

SKATE WITH BLACK BUTTER

••

SERVES 4

4 skate wings, about 650g/1¼ lb each
60–90 g/2–3 oz/ ¼–⅓ cup butter
3 tbsp drained capers
2 tbsp wine vinegar
1 tbsp chopped fresh parsley
salt and pepper

TO GARNISH:
lime or lemon slices or wedges
sprigs of fresh parsley

1   Wash the skate wings, dry and then
    cut each in half. Place in a roasting
tin (pan) in a single layer and cover with
salted water.

2   Bring to the boil, cover with foil or a
    baking sheet (cookie sheet) and
simmer gently for 10–15 minutes until
tender.

3   Drain the fish thoroughly and place
    on a warm dish; keep warm.

4   Melt the butter in a small saucepan
    then continue to cook until it turns
golden brown (taking care it does not
burn and turn black).

5   Quickly add the capers and vinegar
    and cook until bubbling. Season
lightly and stir in the chopped parsley.

6   Spoon the sauce over the skate and
    serve garnished with lime or lemon
and parsley sprigs.

VARIATIONS

For a creamier sauce, stir in 4
tablespoons of single (light) cream or
fromage frais with the parsley.
    The sauce is excellent served with
other white fish, such as cod, haddock,
sole, halibut, turbot or plaice; they can
be poached, grilled (broiled) or baked.

BEEF, LAMB & PORK DISHES – INTRODUCTION

Most meat is bought fresh and prepackaged from a supermarket, often complete with cooking instructions and hints on storage and preparation. Once bought, large pieces of meat can be kept for two or three days before cooking (check the 'use by' date), but minced (ground) meat, offal, etc. must be cooked within 24 hours.

When buying from an independent butcher, hints on preparation and cooking methods will be given by the assistants if required, and they will suggest which types of meat need long slow cooking and which can be roasted or grilled (broiled).

Fresh meat should have a firm texture and not too much gristle or fat, although a certain amount of fat is needed to give flavour and keep the meat moist. If you want to reduce the fat content of a dish, it is better to skim it off the top before serving. Unpack any tightly wrapped meat, cover loosely so it can 'breathe', and store on a rimmed plate at the bottom of the refrigerator so any blood can't drip on to other foods.

When buying frozen meat, it is essential to thaw it slowly and completely, especially when it is to be roasted. It is possible to roast from frozen but it is rather tricky to ensure complete cooking and tenderness. Minced (ground) meat and chops can be cooked from frozen with care, but to my mind it is better to thaw all meat before cooking. Again meat that has been frozen raw can be frozen as a cooked dish, if thoroughly cooked, for up to two months. Defrost completely before reheating.

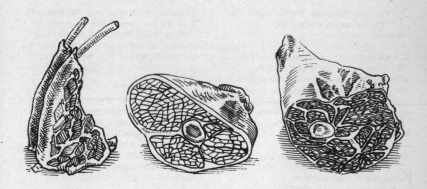

RED SPICED BEEF

SERVES 4

625 g/1¼ lb sirloin or rump steak
2 tbsp paprika
2-3 tsp mild chilli powder
½ tsp salt
6 celery sticks
4 tomatoes, peeled, seeded and sliced
6 tbsp stock or water
2 tbsp tomato purée (paste)
2 tbsp clear honey
3 tbsp wine vinegar
1 tbsp Worcestershire sauce
2 tbsp sunflower oil
4 spring onions (scallions), thinly sliced
    diagonally
1-2 garlic cloves, crushed
Chinese noodles, to serve
celery leaves, to garnish (optional)

1 Cut the steak across the grain into
  narrow strips 1cm/ ½in thick and
place in a bowl. Combine the paprika,
chilli powder and salt, add to the beef
and mix thoroughly until the meat strips
are evenly coated with the spices. Leave
the beef to marinate in a cool place for at
least 30 minutes.

2 Cut the celery into 5 cm/2 in
  lengths, then cut the lengths into
strips about 5 mm/ ¼ in thick.

3 Combine the stock, tomato purée
  (paste), honey, vinegar and
Worcestershire sauce.

4 Heat the oil in the wok, swirling it
  around until really hot. Add the
spring onion (scallions), celery and garlic
and stir-fry for about 1 minute until the
vegetables are beginning to soften, then
add the steak strips. Stir-fry over a high
heat for 3-4 minutes until the meat is well
sealed.

5 Add the sauce to the wok and
  continue to stir-fry briskly until
thoroughly coated and sizzling.

6 Serve with noodles and garnish with
  celery leaves, if liked.

SUKIYAKI BEEF

SERVES 4

2.5 cm/1 in ginger root, grated
1 garlic clove, crushed
4 tbsp sherry
4 tbsp teriyaki sauce
500-625 g/1-1¼ lb sirloin, rump or
    fillet steak
1 x 425 g/15 oz can hearts of palm
2 tbsp sesame or sunflower oil
125 g/4 oz button or closed cup
    mushrooms, thinly sliced
salt and pepper

TO GARNISH:
sesame seeds (optional)
spring onion (scallion) tassles

1 Blend the ginger in a shallow dish
  with the garlic, sherry and teriyaki
sauce, adding a little salt.

2 Cut the steak into narrow strips
  about 2.5-4 cm/1-1½ in long, across
the grain. Add the strips to the marinade
in the dish, mix thoroughly to coat, cover
and leave in a cool place for at least 1
hour and up to 24 hours.

3 Drain the hearts of palm and cut into
  slanting slices about 1 cm/ ½ in
thick.

4 Remove the beef from the marinade
  with a slotted spoon, reserving the
marinade. Heat the oil in the wok,
swirling it around until really hot. Add the
beef and stir-fry for 2 minutes, then add
the mushrooms and continue to cook for
a further minute.

5 Add the hearts of palm to the wok
  with the reserved marinade and stir-
fry for another minute, making sure the
meat is thoroughly coated in the sauce.
Adjust the seasoning and serve sprinkled
with sesame seeds (if using) and
garnished with spring onion (scallion)
tassles.

BEEF WITH BEANS

SERVES 4

500-625 g/1-1¼ lb sirloin, rump or fillet
    steak
1 orange
2 tbsp sesame oil
4 spring onions (scallions), thinly sliced
    diagonally
175 g/6 oz French or fine beans, cut into
    2-3 pieces
1 garlic clove, crushed
4 tbsp sherry
1½ tbsp teriyaki sauce
¼ tsp ground allspice
1 tsp sugar
1 x 425 g/15 oz can cannellini beans,
    drained
salt and pepper

TO GARNISH:
canelled orange slices (see 'Orange
    Shreds', page 250)
fresh bay leaves

1 Cut the steak into narrow strips,
   about 4 cm/1½ in long, cutting across
the grain.

2 Remove the peel from the orange
   using a citrus zester, or pare thinly
with a potato peeler, and cut the rind into
julienne strips. Squeeze the orange and
reserve the juice.

3 Heat 1 tablespoon of the oil in the
   wok, swirling it around until really
hot. Add the strips of beef and stir-fry
briskly for about 2 minutes, then remove
from the wok and keep warm.

4 Add the remaining oil to the wok
   and when hot add the spring onions
(scallions) and garlic and stir-fry for 1-2
minutes. Add the French beans and
continue to cook for 2 minutes.

5 Add the sherry, teriyaki, orange rind
   and 3 tablespoons of orange juice,
allspice, sugar and seasoning and when
well mixed return the beef and any juices
to the wok.

6 Stir-fry for 1-2 minutes then add the
   cannellini beans and stir until piping
hot. Adjust the seasoning. Serve garnished
with canelled orange twists and bay
leaves.

SPICY BEEF & YOGURT

SERVES 4

500 g/1 lb lean rump steak, trimmed
4 tbsp ghee or vegetable oil
2 onions, peeled and sliced
2 garlic cloves, peeled and crushed
2 tbsp mild, medium or hot curry paste
1 tsp minced chilli (from a jar)
150 ml/¼ pint/⅔ cup beef stock
1x227 g/8 oz can chopped tomatoes

AUBERGINE (EGGPLANT) YOGURT:
½ medium aubergine (eggplant)
150 ml/¼ pint/⅔ cup strained Greek
    yogurt
1 garlic clove, peeled and crushed
1 tbsp chopped fresh coriander or parsley
salt and freshly ground black pepper

1 First make the Aubergine (Eggplant)
   Yogurt. Peel the aubergine (eggplant)
and cut into 2.5 cm/1 in pieces. Place in
the top half of a steamer and steam over
boiling water for 10 minutes.

2 Meanwhile, whisk the yogurt with
   the garlic, coriander and salt and
pepper to taste. Allow the cooked
aubergine (eggplant) to cool slightly, then
mash with a fork. Stir the aubergine
(eggplant) into the yogurt.

3 Heat the ghee or oil in a large frying
   pan, add the beef and onions and
stir-fry for 5 minutes until the beef is
sealed all over.

4 Stir in the garlic, curry paste, chilli,
   stock and tomatoes and bring to the
boil. Cover, reduce the heat and simmer
gently for 5 minutes, stirring occasionally.
Serve hot with the aubergine (eggplant)
yogurt.

VARIATIONS

You could use thin strips of pork
tenderloin or chicken breast instead of
the rump steak, if preferred, and serve
with Raita rather than Aubergine
(Eggplant) Yogurt, for a change: see
recipe on page 350.

BEEF & MUSHROOM CURRY

SERVES 4

750 g/1½ lb lean braising beef, trimmed
3 tbsp vegetable oil
2 onions, peeled, quartered and sliced
2 garlic cloves, peeled and crushed
2.5 cm/1 in piece ginger root, peeled and chopped
2 fresh green chillies, seeded and chopped, or use 1-2 tsp minced chilli (from a jar)
1½ tbsp medium curry paste
1 tsp ground coriander
175-250 g/6-8 oz mushrooms, thickly sliced
900 ml/1½ pints/3½ cups stock or water
3 tomatoes, chopped
½-1 tsp salt
60 g/2 oz creamed coconut, chopped
2 tbsp ground almonds

TO FINISH:
2 tbsp vegetable oil
1 green or red (bell) pepper, seeded and cut into thin strips
6 spring onions (scallions), trimmed and sliced
1 tsp cumin seeds

1 Cut the beef into small bite-sized cubes. Heat the oil in a saucepan, add the beef and fry until sealed, stirring frequently. Remove from the pan.

2 Add the onions, garlic, ginger, chillies, curry paste and coriander to the pan and cook gently for 2 minutes. Stir in the mushrooms, stock and tomatoes and season with salt to taste. Return the beef to the pan, then cover and simmer very gently for 1¼ -1½ hours or until beef is tender.

3 Stir the chopped creamed coconut and ground almonds into the curry, then cover the pan and cook gently for 3 minutes.

4 Meanwhile, heat the remaining oil in a frying pan, add the (bell) pepper strips and spring onion (scallion) slices and fry gently until glistening and tender-crisp. Stir in the cumin seeds and fry gently for 30 seconds, then spoon the mixture over the curry and serve at once.

BEEF STROGANOFF

SERVES 4

350 g/12 oz sirloin steak slices about 5 mm/¼ inch thick
2 tbsp olive oil
250 g/8 oz/2 ⅔ cups button mushrooms, sliced
6 spring onions (scallions), white and green parts cut into strips
150 ml/5 fl oz/⅔ cup double (heavy) cream
2 tbsp brandy
2 tbsp chopped fresh parsley
salt and pepper

TO SERVE:
boiled basmati rice
green salad

1 Cut the meat across the grain into 4 cm x 5 mm/1 ½ x ¼ inch strips.

2 Heat 1 tablespoon of the oil in a wok or heavy-based frying pan (skillet) and stir-fry for 2 minutes until the meat is sealed then remove from the pan.

3 Add the remaining oil to the pan then fry the mushrooms and spring onions (scallions) for 2 minutes.

4 Return the meat to the pan with the cream, brandy, parsley and seasoning to taste and heat through.

5 Serve with basmati rice and a green salad.

TIP

Cut the meat into very fine strips across the grain so that there will be less shrinkage when it is cooked. A wok is especially suitable for this recipe because the meat will seal as soon as it touches the hot pan.

SPICY MEATBALLS

SERVES 4

4 tbsp olive oil
1 large onion, finely chopped
2 garlic cloves, finely chopped
500 g/1 lb lean minced beef
90 g/3 oz/ ¾ cup dry breadcrumbs
2 tbsp chopped coriander or parsley
1 tsp cayenne pepper
3 tbsp natural yogurt
juice of ½ lemon
salt and pepper
flour, for dusting
30 g/1 oz/2 tbsp butter
noodles, to serve

SAUCE:
1 tbsp plain flour
175 ml/6 fl oz/ ¾ cup chicken stock
150 g/ ¼ pint/ ⅔ cup natural yogurt
1 tbsp chopped coriander

1 Heat 2 tablespoons of the oil in a frying pan and fry the onion until it is transparent. Add the garlic, and fry for 1 minute more. Set aside to cool.

2 Put the meat in a bowl and mash with a wooden spoon until it forms a sticky paste. Add the onion mixture, breadcrumbs and coriander or parsley. Stir in the paprika and cayenne pepper and mix well. Stir in the yogurt and lemon juice, season and stir until it forms a thick, sticky paste. Cover and chill for at least 30 minutes.

3 Flour your hands and shape the mixture into rounds about the size of table-tennis balls. Roll each one in flour until evenly coated.

4 Heat the remaining oil and the butter in the frying pan and fry the meatballs for 7-8 minutes, until they are firm, and lightly coloured on all sides. Remove with a slotted spoon.

5 To make the sauce, stir the flour into the remaining oil and fat. When well blended, gradually pour on the chicken stock, stirring constantly. Season and bring to the boil. Add the meatballs, cover and simmer over low heat for 30 minutes, turning the meatballs once or twice.

6 Stir in the yogurt, and taste for seasoning. Slowly reheat without bringing it to the boil. Remove from the heat and stir in half the coriander. Transfer to a serving dish and sprinkle with remaining coriander. Serve with buttered noodles.

LAYERED MEAT LOAF

SERVES 6

30 g/1 oz/2 tbsp butter, plus extra for
  greasing
1 onion, finely chopped
1 small red (bell) pepper, cored, seeded
  and chopped
1 garlic clove, chopped
500 g/1 lb lean beef, minced
30 g/1 oz/ ½ cup soft white breadcrumbs
½ tsp cayenne pepper
1 tbsp lemon juice
½ tsp grated lemon rind
2 tbsp chopped parsley
4 bay leaves
90 g/3 oz short pasta, such as fusilli
175 g/6 oz streaky bacon rashers, rind
  removed
1 tbsp olive oil
Cheese Sauce (see page 72)
salt and pepper
salad leaves, to garnish

1 Melt the butter in a pan over a
  medium heat and fry the onion and
pepper for about 3 minutes, until the
onion is translucent. Stir in the garlic and
cook it for a further 1 minute.

2 Put the meat into a large bowl and
  mash it with a wooden spoon until it
becomes a sticky paste. Tip in the fried

vegetables and stir in the breadcrumbs,
cayenne, lemon juice, lemon rind and
parsley. Season the mixture with salt and
pepper and set it aside.

3 Cook the pasta in a large pan of
  boiling water to which you have
added salt and the olive oil. When it is
almost tender, drain in a colander.

4 Make the Cheese Sauce (see page
  72). Stir in the pasta.

5 Grease a 1 kg/2 lb loaf tin and
  arrange the bay leaves in the base.
Stretch the bacon rashers with the back of
a knife blade and arrange them to line the
base and the sides of the tin. Spoon in
half the meat mixture, level the surface
and cover it with the pasta. Spoon in the
remaining meat mixture, level the top and
cover the tin with foil.

6 Cook the meat loaf in the preheated
  oven for 1 hour, or until the juices
run clear and the loaf has shrunk away
from the sides of the tin. Pour off any
excess fat from the tin and turn the loaf
out on a warmed serving dish, loosening
the edges if necessary. Serve hot, with a
green salad.

BEEF GOULASH

•••

SERVES 4

2 tbsp vegetable oil
1 large onion, chopped
1 garlic clove, crushed
750 g/1½ lb stewing steak, cut into chunks
2 tbsp paprika
425 g/14 oz can chopped tomatoes
2 tbsp tomato purée (paste)
1 large red (bell) pepper, deseeded and
    chopped
175 g/6 oz mushrooms, sliced
600 ml/1 pint/2½ cups beef stock
1 tbsp cornflour (cornstarch)
1 tbsp water
4 tbsp crème fraîche or natural yogurt
salt and pepper
paprika for sprinkling
chopped fresh parsley to garnish
long grain rice and wild rice to serve

1 Heat the oil in a large frying pan
  (skillet) and cook the onion and
garlic for 3–4 minutes, until softened. Add
the meat and cook over a high heat for 3
minutes until browned all over.

2 Add the paprika and stir well, then
  add the tomatoes, tomato purée
(paste), (bell) pepper and mushrooms.
Cook for 2 minutes, stirring frequently.

3 Pour in the stock. Bring to the boil,
  then reduce the heat. Cover and
simmer for 1½–2 hours until the meat is
very tender.

4 Blend the cornflour (cornstarch)
  with the water, then add to the
saucepan, stirring until thickened and
smooth. Cook for 1 minute, then season
to taste.

5 Put the crème fraîche or natural
  yogurt in a bowl and sprinkle with a
little paprika. Garnish the goulash with
chopped parsley and serve with rice and
the crème fraîche or yogurt.

PAPRIKA

Paprika is quite a mild, sweet spice, so
you can add plenty without it being
overpowering.

BOILED BEEF & CARROTS WITH DUMPLINGS

•••

SERVES 6

about 1.75 kg/3½ lb joint of salted
    silverside or topside
2 onions, quartered, or 5–8 small onions
8–10 cloves
2 bay leaves
1 cinnamon stick
2 tbsp brown sugar
4 large carrots, sliced thickly
1 turnip, quartered
½ swede, sliced thickly
1 large leek, sliced thickly
30 g/1 oz/2 tbsp butter or margarine
30 g/1 oz/4 tbsp plain (all-purpose) flour
½ tsp dried mustard powder
salt and pepper

DUMPLINGS:
250 g/8 oz/2 cups self-raising flour
½ tsp dried sage
90 g/3 oz/generous ½ cup shredded suet
about 150 ml/¼ pint/⅔ cup water

1 Put the beef in a large saucepan, add
  the onions, cloves, bay leaves,
cinnamon and sugar and sufficient water
to cover the meat. Bring slowly to the
boil, remove any scum from the surface,
cover and simmer gently for 1 hour. Add
the carrots, turnip, swede and leeks, cover
and simmer for a further 1¼ hours until
the beef is tender.

2 Meanwhile, make the dumplings. Sift
  the flour into a bowl, season well
and mix in the herbs and suet. Add
sufficient water to mix to a softish dough.

3 Divide the dough into 8 pieces,
  roughly shape into balls and place
on top of the beef and vegetables.
Replace the lid and simmer for 15–20
minutes until the dumplings are well
puffed up and cooked.

4 Remove the dumplings, then place
  the beef and vegetables in a serving
dish. Measure 300 ml/½ pint/1¼ cups of
the cooking liquid into a saucepan. Blend
the butter or margarine with the flour
then gradually whisk into the pan. Bring
to the boil and simmer until thickened.
Stir in the mustard, adjust the seasoning
and serve with the beef.

STEAK & KIDNEY PUDDING

SERVES 4

500 g/1 lb best braising steak, trimmed
175 g/6 oz ox or lamb's kidneys
2 tbsp seasoned plain (all-purpose) flour
125 g/4 oz/2 cups button mushrooms,
sliced or quartered or a small can
oysters or smoked oysters, drained
about 4 tbsp red wine, beef stock or water
½ tsp Worcestershire sauce
½ tsp dried mixed herbs
salt and pepper
sprigs of fresh parsley to garnish

SUET CRUST PASTRY (PIE DOUGH):
250 g/8 oz/2 cups self-raising flour
½ tsp salt
125 g/4 oz/⅔ cup shredded suet
about 150 ml/¼ pint/⅔ cup cold water

1 Grease a 1 litre/2 pint/5 cup pudding basin (mold). To make the pastry (pie dough), sift the flour and salt into a bowl and stir in the suet. Add sufficient water to mix to a soft dough and knead lightly. Roll out three-quarters of the pastry (pie dough) to about 5 mm/¼ inch thick and use to line the basin (mold).

2 Cut the steak into 2 cm/¾ inch cubes. Skin the kidneys, remove the cores and cut into small cubes. Toss the meats in the seasoned flour.

3 Put the meat in the basin (mold), layering it with the mushrooms or oysters and seasoning, if required. Combine the wine, stock or water, Worcestershire sauce and herbs and add to the basin (mold).

4 Roll out the remaining pastry (pie dough) to form a lid, dampen the edges and position, pressing the edges firmly together. Trim.

5 Cover with a piece of pleated greased baking parchment and then with pleated foil, and tie very securely under the rim of the basin.

6 Put in a saucepan with enough boiling water to reach halfway up the basin (mold), or in the top of a steamer. Cover and steam for about 4 hours, adding more boiling water to the saucepan as necessary.

7 To serve the pudding, remove the cloth or foil and paper, tie a napkin around the bowl and serve from the basin (mold) – it may split open if you turn it out first.

FIVE-SPICE LAMB

SERVES 4

625 g/1¼ lb lean boneless lamb (leg or
  fillet)
2 tsp Chinese five-spice powder
3 tbsp sunflower oil
1 red (bell) pepper, cored, seeded and
  thinly sliced
1 green (bell) pepper, cored, seeded and
  thinly sliced
1 yellow or orange (bell) pepper, cored,
  seeded and thinly sliced
4–6 spring onions (scallions), thinly sliced
  diagonally
175 g/6 oz French or fine beans, cut into
  4 cm/1½ in lengths
2 tbsp soy sauce
4 tbsp sherry
salt and pepper
Chinese noodles, to serve

TO GARNISH:
strips of red and yellow (bell) pepper
fresh coriander leaves

1 Cut the lamb into narrow strips,
  about 4 cm/1½ in long, across the
grain. Place in a bowl, add the five-spice
powder and ¼ teaspoon salt, mix well and
leave to marinate, covered, in a cool
place for at least an hour and up to 24
hours.

2 Heat half the oil in the wok, swirling
  it around until really hot. Add the
lamb and stir-fry briskly for 3-4 minutes
until almost cooked through; remove from
the pan.

3 Add the remaining oil to the wok
  and when hot add the (bell) peppers
and spring onions (scallions). Stir-fry for
2-3 minutes, then add the beans and stir
for a minute or so.

4 Add the soy sauce and sherry to the
  wok and when hot replace the lamb
and any juices. Stir-fry for 1-2 minutes
until the lamb is really hot again and
thoroughly coated in the sauce. Season to
taste.

5 Serve with Chinese noodles,
  garnished with strips of red and
green (bell) pepper and fresh coriander.

SAVOURY HOTPOT

SERVES 4

8 middle neck lamb chops, neck of lamb
  or any stewing lamb on the bone
1–2 garlic cloves, crushed
2 lamb's kidneys (optional)
1 large onion, sliced thinly
1 leek, sliced
2–3 carrots, sliced
1 tsp chopped fresh tarragon or sage or
  ½ tsp dried tarragon or sage
1 kg/2 lb potatoes, sliced thinly
300 ml/ ½ pint/1¼ cups stock
30 g/1 oz/2 tbsp butter or margarine,
  melted, or 1 tbsp vegetable oil
salt and pepper
chopped fresh parsley to garnish

1 Trim the lamb of any excess fat,
  season well with salt and pepper
and arrange in a large ovenproof
casserole. Sprinkle with the garlic.

2 If using kidneys, remove the skin,
  halve the kidneys and cut out the
cores. Chop into small pieces and sprinkle
over the lamb.

3 Place the onion, leek and carrots
  over the lamb, allowing the pieces to
slip in between the meat, then sprinkle
with the herbs.

4 Arrange the potatoes evenly over the
  contents of the casserole. Bring the
stock to the boil, season and pour into
the casserole.

5 Brush the potatoes with melted
  butter or margarine, or oil, cover
with greased foil or a lid and cook in a
preheated oven at 180°C/350°F/Gas Mark
4 for 1½ hours.

6 Remove the foil or lid from the
  potatoes, increase the oven
temperature to 220°C/425°F/Gas Mark 7
and return the casserole to the oven for
about 30 minutes until the potatoes are
browned. Garnish with chopped parsley.

VARIATION

Try cooking small pieces of chicken,
such as thighs or drumsticks, this way.

ROAST LEG OF LAMB

Serves 6

1 x 50 g/1½ oz can anchovies, drained
1.8 kg/4 lb leg of lamb
2 tbsp coriander seeds
4 large garlic cloves, crushed
300 ml/ ½ pint/1¼ cups natural yogurt
6-8 tbsp chopped parsley
1 bottle dry white wine
juice of 1 lemon
500 g/1 lb small button onions, peeled
   and left whole
45 g/1½ oz/3 tbsp butter
30 g/1 oz/2 tbsp caster sugar
150 ml/ ¼ pint/ ⅔ cup water
salt and pepper
fresh herbs, to garnish
new potatoes tossed in butter and parsley,
   to serve

1 Cut the anchovies in half and split them lengthways. Using a small, sharp knife make slits all over the lamb and insert the anchovy pieces, folding if necessary to push them in.

2 Lightly crush the coriander seeds in a pestle and mortar. Tip them into a bowl, stir in the garlic, yogurt and parsley and season with pepper.

3 Spread the yogurt paste evenly over the lamb, using the back of a spoon to press it into the meat. Place the lamb in a shallow dish, cover loosely with foil and leave in the refrigerator for 1-2 days, turning it once or twice.

4 Transfer the lamb to a roasting pan. Pour in the wine and lemon juice and cook uncovered for 15 minutes. Lower the heat and continue roasting for a further 1-1¼ hours, basting frequently.

5 Remove the meat from the oven, cover with foil and leave to rest in a warm place for at least 15 minutes. Pour the juices into a small pan and boil rapidly to reduce. Taste for seasoning.

6 Blanch the onions in boiling, salted water for 3 minutes, then drain and dry on paper towels. Melt the butter in a pan and add the onions, sugar and water. Simmer, uncovered, for 15 minutes, turning frequently. Watch carefully towards the end, as the water evaporates and the sugar caramelizes.

7 Transfer the meat to a serving dish and spoon the onions around. Serve with new potatoes and serve the sauce separately.

LAMB KEBABS & CUCUMBER SAUCE

SERVES 4

1 kg/2 lb lean leg of lamb, trimmed of fat
3 tbsp olive oil
1 tbsp red wine vinegar
juice of ½ lemon
3 tbsp natural yogurt
1 tbsp dried oregano
2 large garlic cloves, crushed
2 dried bay leaves, crumbled
4 fresh bay leaves
2 tbsp chopped parsley
salt and pepper

SAUCE:
300 ml/ ½ pint/1¼ cups natural yogurt
1 garlic clove, crushed
¼ tsp salt
½ small cucumber, peeled and finely chopped
3 tbsp finely chopped mint
pinch of paprika

1 Cut the lamb into cubes about 4-5 cm/1½-2 in square. Pat dry with paper towels. This will help to ensure that the meat is crisp and firm on the outside when grilled (broiled).

2 Whisk together the olive oil, wine vinegar, lemon juice and yogurt. Stir in the oregano, garlic and crumbled bay leaves and season.

3 Place the meat cubes in the marinade and stir until well coated in the mixture. Cover and place in the refrigerator for at least 2 hours, for the meat to absorb the flavours.

4 Meanwhile, make the sauce. Place the yogurt in a large bowl. Stir in the garlic, salt, cucumber and mint. Cover and set aside in the refrigerator. If it is more convenient, the sauce may be made several hours in advance.

5 Heat the grill (broiler) to high. With a slotted spoon, lift the meat from the marinade and shake off any excess liquid. Divide the meat into 4 equal portions. Thread the meat and the fresh bay leaves on to 4 skewers.

6 Grill (broil) the kebabs for about 4 minutes on each side, basting frequently with the marinade. At this stage the meat should be crisp on the outside and slightly pink on the inside. If you prefer it well done, cook the kebabs for a little longer.

7 Sprinkle the kebabs with parsley and serve at once with a tomato salad. Sprinkle the paprika over the sauce and serve chilled.

MOUSSAKA

SERVES 6

*750 g/1½ lb aubergines (eggplant), thinly
    sliced*
6 tbsp olive oil, plus extra for brushing
2 large onions, finely chopped
2 large garlic cloves, finely chopped
750 g/1½ lb lean lamb, minced
2 tbsp tomato purée (paste)
½ tsp ground cumin
salt and pepper
5 tbsp chopped coriander, or parsley

TOPPING:
4 eggs
600 ml/1 pint/2½ cups natural yogurt
½ tsp ground cumin
60 g/2 oz/ ¼ cup feta cheese, crumbled
pepper
30 g/1 oz/ ¼ cup Gruyère, grated

1 Put the aubergines (eggplant) in a
   colander over a bowl and sprinkle
with salt. Leave for about 1 hour, while
the salt draws out the bitter juices, then
rinse under cold, running water. Drain
and pat dry with paper towels.

2 Heat 2 tablespoons of the oil in a
   frying pan. Fry half the aubergine
(eggplant) slices, turning them once, until
evenly brown on both sides. Remove and
keep warm. Heat another 2 tablespoons
of the oil and fry the remaining slices in
the same way. Remove and keep warm.

3 Add the remaining oil to the pan
   and fry the onions until they are a
light, golden brown. Stir in the chopped
garlic. Add the meat to the pan and fry,
stirring, until it changes colour.

4 Stir in the tomato purée (paste) and
   cumin and season. Remove the pan
from the heat and stir in the coriander or
parsley.

5 Brush a large ovenproof dish with
   olive oil. Arrange half the aubergine
(eggplant) slices in the dish. Cover with
the meat mixture, then arrange the
remaining aubergine (eggplant) on top.

6 To make the topping, beat the eggs,
   then beat in the yogurt. Add the
cumin and feta cheese, and season with
pepper. Pour the sauce over the dish, and
sprinkle on the grated cheese.

7 Bake in the preheated oven for 45-
   50 minutes, until the top is dark
golden brown and bubbling. Serve hot.

ACCOMPANIMENT

A green salad tossed with chopped
spring onions is a good
accompaniment to this dish.

(BELL) PEPPERS WITH LAMB

SERVES 4-6

4 tbsp vegetable oil
500 g/1 lb lean minced lamb
2 onions, peeled and finely chopped
2 garlic cloves, peeled and crushed
3.5cm/1½ in ginger root, peeled and finely
   chopped
2 tsp minced chilli (from a jar)
1 tsp ground coriander
1 tsp ground cumin
4 tbsp strained Greek yogurt
2 tbsp tomato purée (paste)
2 tbsp chopped fresh mint
90 g/3 oz frozen peas
1 x 227 g/8 oz can chopped tomatoes
salt and freshly ground black pepper
3 large red (bell) peppers
sprigs of mint, to garnish

1 Heat 3 tablespoons of oil in a
   saucepan, add the lamb and fry until
sealed all over. Stir in the onions, garlic,
ginger, chilli and spices and cook gently
for 5 minutes.

2 Stir in the yogurt, tomato purée
   (paste), mint, peas, tomatoes and
seasoning to taste. Cover and cook gently
for 15 minutes, stirring frequently. Place
in the preheated oven.

3 Meanwhile, cut the (bell) peppers in
   half lengthways, cutting through the
stalks and leaving them attached. Scoop
out the seeds and membranes from each
one. Add the (bell) pepper halves to a
pan of boiling water and simmer for 5-7
minutes or until only just tender – take
care not to overcook. Drain well, refresh
with cold water and drain well again. Pat
dry on absorbent paper towels.

4 Brush the (bell) peppers with the
   remaining oil and arrange in a
shallow, greased ovenproof dish. Spoon
the lamb mixture into the (bell) peppers.
Cover with greased foil and cook in the
oven for 15-20 minutes until piping hot.
Serve hot, garnished with mint sprigs.

LAMB & GINGER STIR-FRY

SERVES 4

500 g/1 lb lamb fillet (tenderloin)
2 tbsp sunflower oil
1 tbsp chopped ginger root
2 garlic cloves, chopped
6 spring onions (scallions), white and
   green parts diagonally sliced
250 g/8 oz shiitake mushrooms, sliced
175 g/6 oz mangetout (snow peas)
1 tsp cornflour (cornstarch)
2 tbsp dry sherry
1 tbsp light soy sauce
1 tsp sesame oil
1 tbsp sesame seeds, browned
Chinese egg noodles to serve

1 Cut the lamb fillets into 5 mm/
   ¼ inch thick discs.

2 Heat the oil in a wok or frying pan
   (skillet). Add the lamb and stir-fry
for 2 minutes.

3 Add the ginger, garlic, spring onions
   (scallions), mushrooms and
mangetout (snow peas) and stir-fry for a
further 2 minutes.

4 Mix the cornflour (cornstarch) with
   the sherry, add to the wok with the
soy sauce and sesame oil and cook,
stirring, for 1 minute until thickened.
Sprinkle over the sesame seeds and serve
with Chinese egg noodles.

SHIITAKE MUSHROOMS

An Oriental mushroom much used in
Chinese and Japanese cooking.
Shiitake mushrooms can be bought
both fresh and dried and have a
slightly meaty flavour. Their powerful
flavour will permeate more bland
mushrooms so they are excellent in
conjunction with button mushrooms.
Cook them briefly or they begin to
toughen.

MINCED (GROUND) LAMB & POTATO MOUSSAKA

SERVES 4

1 large aubergine (eggplant), sliced
1 tbsp olive or vegetable oil
1 onion, chopped finely
1 garlic clove, crushed
350 g/12 oz minced (ground) lamb
250 g/8 oz mushrooms, sliced
425 g/14 oz can chopped tomatoes
150 ml/ ¼ pint/ ⅔ cup vegetable stock
2 tbsp cornflour (cornstarch)
2 tbsp water
500 g/1 lb potatoes, par-boiled for 10
    minutes and sliced
2 eggs
125 g/4 oz/ ½ cup low-fat soft cheese
150 ml/ ¼ pint/ ⅔ cup natural yogurt
60 g/2 oz/ ½ cup grated Cheddar cheese
salt and pepper
flat-leaf parsley to garnish
green salad to serve

1 Lay the aubergine (eggplant) slices
on a clean surface and sprinkle
liberally with salt, to extract the bitter
juices. Leave for 10 minutes then turn the
slices over and repeat. Put in a colander,
rinse and drain well.

2 Meanwhile, heat the oil in a
saucepan and fry the onion and
garlic for 3–4 minutes. Add the lamb and
mushrooms and cook for 5 minutes, until
browned. Stir in the tomatoes and stock,
bring to the boil and simmer for 10
minutes. Mix the cornflour (cornstarch)
with the water and stir into the pan.
Cook, stirring, until thickened.

3 Spoon half the mixture into an
ovenproof dish. Cover with the
aubergine (eggplant) slices, then the
remaining lamb mixture. Arrange the
sliced potatoes on top.

4 Beat together the eggs, soft cheese,
yogurt and seasoning. Pour over the
potatoes to cover them completely.
Sprinkle with the grated cheese. Bake in a
preheated oven at 190°C/375°F/Gas Mark
5 for 45 minutes until the topping is set
and golden brown. Garnish with flat-leaf
parsley and serve with a green salad.

LAMB & POTATO MASALA

SERVES 4

750 g/1½ lb lean lamb (from the leg)
4 tbsp ghee or vegetable oil
500 g/1 lb potatoes, peeled and cut in
    large 2.5 cm/1 in pieces
1 large onion, peeled, quartered and
    sliced
2 garlic cloves, peeled and crushed
175 g/6 oz mushrooms, thickly sliced
1 x 283 g/10 oz can Tikka Masala Curry
    Sauce
300 ml/ ½ pint/1¼ cups water
salt
3 tomatoes, halved and cut into thin slices
125g/4 oz spinach, washed and stalks
    trimmed
sprigs of mint, to garnish

1 Cut the lamb into 2.5 cm/1 in cubes.
Heat the ghee or oil in a large pan,
add the lamb and fry over moderate heat
for 3 minutes or until sealed all over.
Remove from the pan.

2 Add the potatoes, onion, garlic and
mushrooms and fry for 3-4 minutes,
stirring frequently. Stir the curry sauce and
water into the pan, add the lamb, mix
well and season with salt to taste. Cover
and cook very gently for 1 hour or until
the lamb is tender and cooked through,
stirring occasionally.

3 Add the sliced tomatoes and the
spinach to the pan, pushing the
leaves well down into the mixture, then
cover and cook for a further 10 minutes
until the spinach is cooked and tender.
Garnish with mint sprigs and serve hot.

SPINACH LEAVES

Spinach leaves wilt quickly during
cooking, so if the leaves are young and
tender add them whole to the mixture;
larger leaves may be coarsely
shredded, if wished, before adding to
the pan.

ROSEMARY & REDCURRANT LAMB FILLET (TENDERLOIN) WITH LEEK & POTATO MASH

SERVES 4

500 g/1 lb lean lamb fillet (tenderloin)
4 tbsp redcurrant jelly
1 tbsp chopped fresh rosemary
1 garlic clove, crushed
500 g/1 lb potatoes, diced
500 g/1 lb leeks, sliced
150 ml/ ¼ pint/ ⅔ cup Fresh Vegetable
 Stock, (see page 97)
4 tsp low-fat natural fromage frais
salt and pepper
freshly steamed vegetables to serve

TO GARNISH:
chopped fresh rosemary
redcurrants

1 Put the lamb in a shallow baking tin (pan). Blend 2 tablespoons of the redcurrant jelly with the rosemary, garlic and seasoning. Brush over the lamb and cook in a preheated oven at 230°C/450°F/Gas Mark 8, brushing occasionally with any cooking juices, for 30 minutes.

2 Meanwhile, place the potatoes in a saucepan and cover with water. Bring to the boil, and cook for 8 minutes until softened. Drain well. Put the leeks in a saucepan with the stock. Cover and simmer for 7–8 minutes or until soft. Drain, reserving the cooking liquid.

3 Place the potato and leeks in a bowl and mash with a potato masher. Season to taste and stir in the fromage frais. Pile on to a warmed platter and keep warm.

4 In a saucepan, melt the remaining redcurrant jelly and stir in the leek cooking liquid. Bring to the boil for 5 minutes.

5 Slice the lamb and arrange over the mash. Spoon the sauce over the top. Garnish with rosemary and redcurrants and serve with freshly steamed vegetables.

SHEPHERD'S PIE

SERVES 4–5

750 g/1½ lb lean minced (ground) or
 lamb or beef
2 onions, chopped
250 g/8 oz carrots, diced
1–2 garlic cloves, crushed
1 tbsp plain (all-purpose) flour
200 ml/7 fl oz/scant 1 cup beef stock
200 g/7 oz can chopped tomatoes
1 tsp Worcestershire sauce
1 tsp chopped fresh sage or oregano or ½
 tsp dried sage or oregano
750 g–1 kg/1½–2 lb potatoes
30 g/1 oz/2 tbsp butter or margarine
3–4 tbsp milk
125 g/4 oz button mushrooms, sliced
 (optional)
salt and pepper

1 Place the meat in a heavy-based saucepan with no extra fat and cook gently, stirring frequently, until the meat begins to brown.

2 Add the onions, carrots and garlic and continue to cook gently for about 10 minutes. Stir in the flour and cook for a minute or so, then gradually stir in the stock and tomatoes and bring to the boil.

3 Add the Worcestershire sauce, seasoning and herbs, cover the pan and simmer gently for about 25 minutes, giving an occasional stir.

4 Cook the potatoes in boiling salted water until tender, then drain thoroughly and mash, beating in the butter or margarine, seasoning and sufficient milk to give a piping consistency. Place in a piping bag fitted with a large star nozzle (tip).

5 Stir the mushrooms, if using, into the meat and adjust the seasoning. Turn into a shallow ovenproof dish.

6 Pipe the potatoes evenly over the meat. Cook in a preheated oven at 200°C/400°F/Gas Mark 6 for about 30 minutes until piping hot and the potatoes are golden brown.

PORK BALLS WITH MINTED SAUCE

SERVES 4

500 g/1 lb lean minced pork
45 g/1½ oz/¾ cup fine fresh white
   breadcrumbs
½ tsp ground allspice
1 garlic clove, crushed
2 tbsp freshly chopped mint
1 egg, beaten
2 tbsp sunflower oil
1 red (bell) pepper, cored, seeded and
   thinly sliced
250 ml/8 fl oz/1 cup chicken stock
4 pickled walnuts, sliced
salt and pepper
rice or Chinese noodles, to serve
fresh mint, to garnish

1 Combine the pork, breadcrumbs, seasoning, allspice, garlic and half the chopped mint in a bowl, then bind together with the egg. Shape the meat mixture into 20 small balls with your hands, damping your hands if it is easier for shaping.

2 Heat the oil in the wok, swirling it around until really hot, then stir-fry the pork balls until browned all over, about 4-5 minutes. Remove from the wok with a slotted spoon as they are ready and drain on paper towels.

3 Pour off all but 1 tablespoon of fat and oil from the wok then add the red (bell) pepper and stir-fry for 2-3 minutes, or until it is beginning to soften, but not colour.

4 Add the stock and bring to the boil. Season well and replace the pork balls, stirring well to coat in the sauce; simmer for 7-10 minutes, turning them from time to time.

5 Add the remaining chopped mint and the pickled walnuts to the wok and continue to simmer for 2-3 minutes, turning the pork balls regularly to coat them in the sauce.

6 Adjust the seasoning and serve with rice or Chinese noodles, or with a stir-fried vegetable dish, garnished with sprigs of fresh mint.

ORCHARD PORK

SERVES 4

60 g/2 oz/ ¼ cup butter
1 onion, chopped
1 garlic clove, finely chopped
500 g/1 lb pork tenderloin (fillet)
1 tbsp paprika
150 ml/ ¼ pint/ ⅔ cup chicken stock
300 ml/ ½ pint/1¼ cups natural yogurt
2 tsp cornflour (cornstarch)
2 dessert apples
juice of ½ lemon
salt and pepper
parsley sprigs, to garnish
sautéd baby vegetables, to garnish
   (optional)

1 Heat half the butter in a frying pan over a medium heat. Fry the onion until it is translucent. Then stir in the garlic and fry for 1 minute more.

2 Trim the pork of excess fat and cut into small thin slices. Pat the meat dry with paper towels. Add the pork to the pan, sprinkle on the paprika and stir until the meat is coated with the spice. Cook for 3 minutes, stirring once or twice.

3 Pour in the chicken stock and stir well. Bring to the boil, cover the pan and simmer for 10 minutes.

4 Mix together the yogurt and cornflour (cornstarch) to make a smooth, thin paste. Stir it into the pork, season and continue cooking for 10 minutes, stirring occasionally. Do not overheat or it will curdle.

5 Heat the remaining butter in a frying pan. Core and slice the apples and fry until they are golden brown on both sides.

6 Stir the lemon juice into the sauce and taste to check the seasoning. Transfer the meat to a warmed serving dish, arrange the apple slices on top and garnish with parsley. Serve with baby vegetables, if liked.

VINDALOO CURRY

SERVES 4–6

100 ml/3½ fl oz/scant ½ cup oil
1 large onion, sliced into half rings
120 ml/4 fl oz/ ½ cup white wine vinegar
300 ml/ ½ pint/1¼ cups water
750 g/1½ lb boneless pork shoulder, diced
2 tsp cumin seeds
4 dried red chillies
1 tsp black peppercorns
6 green cardamom pods
2.5 cm/1 inch piece cinnamon stick
1 tsp black mustard seeds
3 cloves
1 tsp fenugreek seeds
2 tbsp ghee
4 garlic cloves, chopped finely
3.5 cm/1½ inch piece ginger root, chopped
    finely
1 tbsp coriander seeds, ground
2 tomatoes, peeled and chopped
250 g/8 oz potato, cut into 1 cm/ ½ inch
    cubes
1 tsp light brown sugar
½ tsp ground turmeric
salt
basmati rice, to serve

1 Heat the oil in a large saucepan and
  fry the onion until golden brown. Set
aside.

2 Combine 2 tablespoons of the
  vinegar with 1 tablespoon of the
water in a large bowl, add the pork and
stir together well. Set aside.

3 In a food processor or blender mix
  the onions, cumin, chillies, peppercorns, cardamom, cinnamon, mustard
seeds, cloves and fenugreek to a paste.
Alternatively, grind the ingredients
together in a pestle and mortar. Transfer
to a bowl and add the remaining vinegar.

4 Heat the ghee in a frying pan
  (skillet) or casserole and cook the
pork until it is browned on all sides.

5 Stir in the garlic, ginger and
  coriander, then add the tomatoes,
potato, brown sugar, turmeric and
remaining water. Add salt to taste and
bring to the boil. Stir in the spice paste,
cover and reduce the heat. Simmer for 1
hour until the pork is tender. Serve with
basmati rice.

PORK CHOPS & SPICY RED BEANS

SERVES 4

3 tbsp ghee or vegetable oil
4 pork chops, rind removed
2 onions, peeled and thinly sliced
2 garlic cloves, peeled and crushed
2 fresh green chillies, seeded and chopped
    or use 1-2 tsp minced chilli (from a jar)
2.5 cm/1 in piece ginger root, peeled and
    chopped
1½ tsp cumin seeds
1½ tsp ground coriander
600 ml/1 pint/2½ cups stock or water
2 tbsp tomato purée (paste)
1/2 aubergine (eggplant), trimmed and
    cut into 1 cm/ ½ in dice
salt
1 x 439 g/14 oz can red kidney beans,
    drained
4 tbsp double (heavy) cream
sprigs of coriander, to garnish

1 Heat the ghee or oil in a large frying
  pan, add the pork chops and fry
until sealed and browned on both sides.
Remove from the pan and reserve.

2 Add the sliced onions, garlic, chillies,
  ginger and spices and fry gently for
2 minutes. Stir in the stock, tomato purée
(paste), aubergine (eggplant) and salt to
taste.

3 Bring the mixture to the boil, place
  the chops on top, then cover and
simmer gently over medium heat for 30
minutes, or until the chops are tender and
cooked through.

4 Remove the chops for a moment
  and stir the red kidney beans and
cream into the mixture. Return the chops
to the pan, cover and heat through gently
for 5 minutes. Taste and adjust the
seasoning, if necessary. Serve hot,
garnished with coriander sprigs.

VARIATIONS

Use lamb chops instead of pork chops,
if wished. Canned chick-peas and
black-eyed beans are also delicious
cooked this way in place of the red
kidney beans (remember to drain them
first before adding to the pan).

HAM & CHICKEN PIE

SERVES 6

*250 g/8 oz/2 cups flour, plus extra for
    dusting*
½ tsp mustard powder
¼ tsp salt
*175 g/6 oz/ ¾ cup butter, cut into small
    pieces, plus extra for greasing*
about 3 tbsp natural yogurt
2 tbsp milk
dill sprigs, to garnish

FILLING:
60 g/2 oz/ ¼ cup butter
30 g/1 oz/ ¼ cup flour
150 ml/ ¼ pint/ ⅔ cup milk
150 ml/ ¼ pint/ ⅔ cup natural yogurt
2 small leeks, sliced
*250g/8 oz boned, skinned chicken breast,
    diced*
250 g (8 oz) diced ham
1 tsp mushroom ketchup, or soy sauce
black pepper

1 Grease a loose-bottomed flan tin, 4 cm/1¾ in deep. Sift together the flour, mustard powder and salt and rub in the butter until the mixture resembles fine breadcrumbs. Stir in just enough yogurt to make a firm and non-sticky dough. Wrap in foil and chill.

2 Melt 30 g/1 oz/2 tbsp of the butter in a small pan over a medium heat. Blend in the flour then pour on the milk and yogurt, stirring all the time. Simmer, uncovered, for 5 minutes, then remove from the heat, transfer the sauce to a bowl and leave to cool.

3 Melt the remaining butter in a small pan and fry the leeks for 2-3 minutes, until they begin to soften.

4 Stir the leeks into the white sauce, add the chicken and ham, and cook for 3 minutes, until the chicken has changed colour. Add the ketchup or soy sauce, and season, then leave to cool completely.

5 Roll out the pastry on a lightly-floured board. Use just over half of it to line the prepared tin. Pour in the cold filling. Roll out the remaining pastry and cover the pie. Trim the edges and press them together. Brush the top with milk. Re-roll the pastry trimmings and cut into decorative shapes such as leaves or stars. Arrange the shapes over the pie and brush with milk. Bake the pie in the preheated oven for 35 minutes, or until the pastry is golden brown. Serve hot or cold.

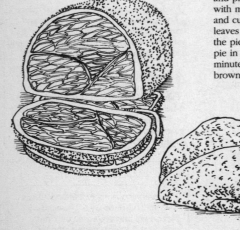

PORK WITH MUSTARD CREAM SAUCE

SERVES 4

2 tbsp olive oil
4 escalopes of pork, 150-175 g/5-6 oz each
1 garlic clove, chopped
6 spring onions (scallions), white and
  green parts sliced diagonally
120 ml/4 fl oz/ ½ cup white wine
1 tsp chopped fresh sage
2 tsp cornflour (cornstach)
2 tbsp milk
2 tbsp Meaux mustard
90 ml/3 fl oz/ ¼ cup double (heavy) cream
salt and pepper

TO SERVE:
fresh herb noodles
green salad

1 Heat the oil in a heavy-based frying pan (skillet) and fry the pork for 1-2 minutes until just turning brown, then turn over and fry the other side for 1-2 minutes.

2 Add the garlic and spring onions (scallions) and fry for 1 minute.

3 Pour in the wine, add the sage and seasoning, then cover and cook for 4 minutes.

4 Mix the cornflour (cornstarch) and milk together and add to the pan with the mustard and cream and boil, stirring, for 2 minutes until thickened.

5 Serve with fresh herb noodles and a green salad.

MEAUX MUSTARD

This delicious mustard from France is made from brown and white mustard seeds and has a grainy texture with a warm spicy flavour. Do not keep for more than 3 months as it will begin to darken and dry out.

BACON, ONION & POTATO HOTPOT

SERVES 4

60 g/2 oz/ ¼ cup butter or margarine
1 kg/2 lb old potatoes, sliced
500 g/1 lb onions, sliced
900 ml/1½ pints/3½ cups chicken stock
500 g/1 lb streaky bacon
salt and pepper
broccoli to serve

1 Grease a 2 litre/3½ pint/2 quart casserole with some of the butter or margarine. Layer the potatoes and onions alternately in the casserole dish, seasoning each layer. Finish with a layer of potatoes.

2 Pour the stock over the potatoes and dot the surface with the remaining butter or margarine. Cover and bake in a preheated oven at 190°C/ 375°F/Gas Mark 5 for 45 minutes.

3 Remove the lid from the casserole and return to the oven for a further 30 minutes until the potatoes are golden brown.

4 Meanwhile, cook the bacon under a preheated moderate grill (broiler) until cooked, but not too crisp.

5 Put the bacon on top of the potatoes and cook in the oven for a further 10 minutes. Serve at once on warmed plates, with broccoli.

ACCOMPANIMENTS

As an alternative to broccoli, hot, buttered cabbage seasoned with a pinch of nutmeg tastes just right with this tasty, economical hotpot. Homemade chutney or relish can also be served with this dish.

SAVOURY BATTER PUDDINGS WITH THYME & ONION SAUCE

SERVES 4

2 tbsp vegetable oil
175 g/6 oz/1½ cups plain (all-purpose)
    flour
2 small eggs
450 ml/¾ pint/scant 2 cups milk
salt and pepper
fresh thyme sprigs to garnish
leeks and carrots to serve

FILLING:
175 g/6 oz lean minced (ground) pork
1 very small onion, chopped finely
1 small carrot, grated finely
1 tbsp chopped fresh thyme or parsley
30 g/1 oz/½ cup fresh wholemeal (whole
    wheat) breadcrumbs

SAUCE:
1 tbsp vegetable oil
1 small onion, chopped finely
125 g/4 oz button mushrooms, sliced
300 ml/½ pint/1¼ cups chicken or
    vegetable stock
1 tbsp chopped fresh thyme or parsley
2 tbsp cornflour (cornstarch)
2 tbsp water

1 Spoon 2 teaspoons of the oil into
each of 4 individual shallow
ovenproof dishes.

2 Whisk together the flour, salt, eggs
and milk to make a smooth batter.
Allow to stand while making the pork
filling.

3 To make the filling, mix together the
pork, onion, carrot, thyme or
parsley, breadcrumbs and seasoning.
Form the mixture into 12 small balls and
place 3 in each dish. Bake in a preheated
oven at 200°C/400°F/Gas Mark 6 for 10
minutes.

4 Remove the dishes from the oven
and quickly pour an equal amount
of batter into each one. Bake for a further
20–25 minutes, until risen and golden
brown.

5 To make the sauce, heat the oil in a
saucepan and fry the onion and
mushrooms until browned. Add the stock
and thyme or parsley. Bring to the boil,
then reduce the heat and simmer for 5
minutes. Mix the cornflour (cornstarch)
with the water, stir into the pan and heat,
stirring, until the sauce boils and thickens.
Garnish the popovers with thyme sprigs
and serve with the sauce and vegetables.

BAKED HAM WITH CUMBERLAND SAUCE

SERVES 4-6

2-3 kg/4-6 lb gammon or prime collar
    joint of bacon
2 bay leaves
1-2 onions, quartered
2 carrots, sliced thickly
6 cloves

GLAZE:
1 tbsp redcurrant jelly
1 tbsp wholegrain mustard

CUMBERLAND SAUCE:
1 orange
3 tbsp redcurrant jelly
2 tbsp lemon or lime juice
2 tbsp orange juice
2-4 tbsp port
1 tbsp wholegrain mustard

TO GARNISH:
salad leaves
orange slices

1 Put the meat in a large saucepan. Add the bay leaves, onion, carrots and cloves and cover with cold water. Bring slowly to the boil, cover and simmer for half the cooking time, allowing 30 minutes per 500 g/1 lb plus 30 minutes.

2 Drain the meat and remove the skin. Put the meat in a roasting tin (pan) or dish and score the fat.

3 To make the glaze, combine the ingredients and spread over the fat. Cook in a preheated oven at 180°C/350°F/Gas Mark 4 for the remainder of the cooking time. Baste at least once.

4 To make the sauce, thinly pare the rind from half the orange and cut into narrow strips. Cook in boiling water for 3 minutes then drain.

5 Place all the remaining sauce ingredients in a small saucepan and heat gently until the redcurrant jelly dissolves. Add the orange rind and simmer gently for 3-4 minutes. Slice the gammon or bacon and serve with the Cumberland sauce, garnished with salad leaves and orange slices.

PORK WITH BLACKBERRIES & APPLE

SERVES 4

500 g/1 lb piece lean pork fillet
    (tenderloin)
2 tsp sunflower oil
150 ml/ ¼ pint/ ⅔ cup Fresh Vegetable
    Stock (see page 97)
150 ml/ ¼ pint/ ⅔ cup dry rosé wine
1 tbsp chopped fresh thyme
1 tbsp clear honey
2 green-skinned dessert apples, cored and
    sliced, and tossed in 1 tbsp lemon juice
175 g/6 oz/1¼ cups prepared fresh or
    frozen blackberries, or 213 g/7½ oz can
    blackberries in natural juice, drained
2 tsp cornflour (cornstarch) mixed with
    4 tsp cold water
salt and pepper
freshly cooked vegetables to serve

1 Trim away any fat and silvery skin from the pork fillet and cut into 1 cm/½ inch thick slices, taking care to keep the slices a good shape.

2 Heat the oil in a non-stick frying pan (skillet), add the pork slices and fry for 4-5 minutes until browned all over. Using a perforated spoon, transfer the pork to paper towels; reserve the pan juices.

3 Pour the stock and wine into the pan with the juices and add the thyme and honey. Mix well, bring to a simmer and add the pork and apples. Continue to simmer, uncovered, for 5 minutes.

4 Add the blackberries, season to taste and simmer for a further 5 minutes. Stir in the cornflour (cornstarch) mixture until thickened. Serve with freshly cooked vegetables.

BLACKBERRIES

This dish works very well with fresh blackberries, but the type that are frozen or canned in natural juice make a suitable substitute.

POULTRY & GAME DISHES – INTRODUCTION

POULTRY

All types of poultry can be bought fresh, chilled or frozen. Fresh birds should be stored in the refrigerator between purchase and cooking, with the giblets removed, if there are any, as soon as possible. Fresh birds can be stored in the refrigerator for up to 48 hours. Cover loosely so the bird can 'breathe', and keep on a rimmed plate at the bottom of the refrigerator so the juices can't drip on to other foods and contaminate them. Treat chilled birds in the same way, but frozen birds should be given the suggested time for thawing, whether this is done immediately after purchase or after further storage in the freezer. All frozen birds come with both thawing and roasting instructions. Thaw in the refrigerator and, once again, put on a plate to catch any juices. Make sure the bird, whatever type, is cooked as soon as possible after thawing.

All poultry must be thoroughly cooked to avoid the risk of food poisoning. To test if a bird is cooked, pierce the thickest part of the thigh with a skewer – the juices should run clear. Never put stuffing into the large cavity of a bird, as it may not reach a temperature high enough to kill any harmful bacteria. Stuff the smaller cavity at the neck end instead, and cook any remaining stuffing separately.

GAME

Game covers a wide variety of animals, from feathered game and water fowl to venison and hare. All game is subject to strict laws on shooting seasons, so is only available fresh at certain times of the year,

usually in the autumn and winter. Grouse is the first to become available – from 12th August – while the final dates for game are in February.

There are now many specialist game shops country wide and these and many of the larger supermarkets sell a limited amount of frozen game all year round.

All birds should be hung to improve the flavour of the game, help tenderize it and give the characteristic taste, but the weather conditions determine the length of hanging required. Usually 7–10 days is sufficient for pheasants and partridges while others need less time; water fowl for instance need only 1–3 days.

All game is very short of fat so needs extra fat or liquid to add moisture during cooking. Quarters of citrus fruit or onion added to the cavity add moisture as well as flavour. Take care not to overcook game as it will become tough and dry. If you want to roast a bird, it is advisable to buy a young one; mature birds should be cooked slowly and gently to ensure tenderness. When roasting, slices of bacon laid over the breast help protect the meat and add flavour, and also make a good accompaniment when serving the birds.

SPICED CHICKEN

SERVES 4

2 tbsp tomato purée (paste)
juice of 2 limes, or 1 lemon
4 portions of chicken, about 350 g/12 oz
*   each, skinned*
125 g/4 oz/ ½ cup Clarified Butter (see
*   right)*
2 tbsp paprika
Spiced Courgettes (Zucchini), to serve (see
*   right)*

1 Put the yogurt in a bowl and stir in the salt, turmeric, cumin seeds, ginger, garam masala and chilli powder. Stir until well blended, then stir in the garlic, bay leaves, tomato purée (paste) and lime or lemon juice.

2 Pour half the yogurt marinade into a shallow dish, spread evenly over the base and place the chicken pieces in a single layer on top. Spoon the remaining marinade over the chicken pieces to cover them completely. Loosely cover with foil and chill for at least 3 hours, or overnight. Spoon the marinade over the chicken from time to time.

3 Preheat the oven to 200°C/400°F/ Gas 6. Line a roasting tin with a piece of foil large enough to enclose it. Remove the chicken from the marinade and allow any excess to drain back into the bowl. Place the chicken pieces in the tin in a single layer. Pour the clarified butter over the chicken. Fold the foil over the tin and seal the edges so that no steam can escape.

4 Cook the chicken for 1 hour, then open the foil. Sprinkle the chicken evenly with paprika and return to the oven, uncovered, for a further 15 minutes.

5 Make the Spiced Courgettes (Zucchini) (see right).

6 Transfer the chicken to a warmed serving dish with the Spiced Courgettes (Zucchini). Strain the marinade into a small pan, bring to the boil and boil rapidly for 2-3 minutes to reduce. Serve separately.

SPICY COURGETTES

SERVES 4

4 tbsp vegetable oil
3 medium courgettes (zucchini), sliced
250 ml/8 fl oz/1 cup natural yogurt
2 garlic cloves, crushed
¹ tsp cumin seeds, lightly crushed
pinch of chilli powder
large pinch of paprika
salt

1 Heat the oil in a frying pan and fry the courgettes (zucchini), in a single layer, until light brown on all sides. Transfer to a warmed dish.

2 Place the yogurt in a bowl, stir in the garlic, cumin seeds and chilli powder and season. Just before serving, pour over the courgettes (zucchini) and sprinkle with paprika.

CLARIFIED BUTTER

To clarify butter, place 125 g/ 4 oz/ ½ cup unsalted butter in a small pan. Melt the butter over low heat, then strain into a bowl. Discard the sediment that collects at the base of the pan.

COCK-A-LEEKIE SOUP

SERVES 4-6

1–1.5 kg/2–3 lb oven-ready chicken plus
  giblets, if available
1.75 – 2 litres/3–3½ pints/8–9 cups
  Chicken Stock (see page 9)
1 onion, sliced
4 leeks, sliced thinly
good pinch of ground allspice or ground
  coriander
1 Bouquet Garni (see page 9)
12 no-need-to-soak prunes, halved and
  pitted
salt and pepper
warm crusty bread to serve

1 Put the chicken, giblets, if using,
  stock and onion in a large saucepan.

2 Bring to the boil and remove any
  scum from the surface.

3 Add the leeks, seasoning, allspice or
  coriander and bouquet garni to the
pan, cover and simmer gently for about
1½ hours until the chicken is falling off
the bones.

4 Remove the chicken and bouquet
  garni from the pan and skim any fat
from the surface of the soup.

5 Chop some of the chicken flesh and
  return to the pan. Add the prunes,
bring back to the boil and simmer,
uncovered, for about 20 minutes.

6 Adjust the seasoning and serve with
  warm crusty bread.

CHICKEN STOCK

You can replace the chicken stock with
3 chicken stock cubes dissolved in the
same amount of water, if you prefer.

CHICKEN WITH PEANUT SAUCE

SERVES 4

4 boneless, skinned chicken breasts, about
  625 g/1¼ lb
4 tbsp soy sauce
4 tbsp sherry
3 tbsp crunchy peanut butter
2 tbsp sunflower oil
4-6 spring onions (scallions), thinly sliced
  diagonally
350 g/12 oz courgettes (zucchini),
  trimmed
1 x 250 g/8 oz can bamboo shoots, well
  drained and sliced
salt and pepper
4 tbsp desiccated (shredded) coconut,
  toasted

1 Cut the chicken into thin strips
  across the grain and season lightly
with salt and pepper.

2 Stir the soy sauce in a bowl with the
  sherry and peanut butter until
smooth and well blended.

3 Cut the courgettes (zucchini) into 5
  cm/2 in lengths and then cut into
sticks about 5mm/¼ in thick.

4 Heat the oil in the wok, swirling it
  around until it is really hot. Add the
spring onions (scallions) and stir-fry for a
minute or so then add the chicken and
stir-fry for 3-4 minutes until well sealed
and almost cooked.

5 Add the courgettes (zucchini) and
  bamboo shoots and continue to stir-
fry for 1-2 minutes.

6 Add the peanut butter mixture and
  heat thoroughly, stirring all the time
so everything is coated in the sauce as it
thickens. Adjust the seasoning and serve
very hot, sprinkled with toasted coconut.

VARIATION

This dish can also be made with turkey
fillet or pork fillet. For coconut lovers
dissolve 30 g/1 oz creamed coconut in
2-3 tablespoons boiling water and add
to the soy sauce mixture before adding
to the wok.

CHICKEN & AROMATIC ALMONDS

SERVES 4

150 ml/ ¼ pint/ ⅔ cup strained Greek
    yogurt
½ tsp cornflour (cornstarch)
4 tbsp ghee or vegetable oil
4 boneless chicken breasts
2 onions, peeled and sliced
1 garlic clove, peeled and crushed
2.5 cm/1 in piece fresh root ginger, peeled
    and chopped
1½ tbsp garam masala
½ tsp chilli powder
2 tsp medium curry paste
300 ml/ ½ pint/1¼ cups chicken stock
salt and freshly ground black pepper
150 ml/ ¼ pint/ ⅔ cup double (heavy)
    cream
60 g/2 oz/ ½ cup ground almonds
125 g/4 oz French green beans, topped,
    tailed and halved
juice of ½ lemon
toasted flaked almonds, to garnish
boiled rice, to serve

1 Smoothly blend the yogurt in a small
   bowl with the cornflour (cornstarch).
Heat the ghee or oil in a large flameproof
casserole, add the chicken breasts and fry
until golden all over. Remove the chicken
from the casserole and reserve.

2 Add the onions, garlic and ginger to
   the casserole and fry gently for 3
minutes, then add the garam masala, chilli
powder and curry paste and fry gently for
1 minute. Stir in the stock, yogurt and salt
and pepper to taste and bring to the boil,
stirring all the time.

3 Return the chicken breasts to the
   casserole, then cover and simmer
gently for 25 minutes. Remove the
chicken to a dish and keep warm.

4 Blend the cream with the ground
   almonds and add to the sauce, then
stir in the green beans and lemon juice
and boil vigorously for 1 minute, stirring
all the time.

5 Return the chicken to the casserole,
   cover and cook gently for a further
10 minutes. Serve with rice and garnish
with toasted flaked almonds.

CHICKEN WITH CELERY & CASHEWS

SERVES 4

3-4 boneless, skinned chicken breasts,
    about 625g/1¼ lb
2 tbsp sunflower or vegetable oil
125 g/4 oz/1 cup cashew nuts (unsalted)
4-6 spring onions (scallions), thinly sliced
    diagonally
5-6 celery sticks, thinly sliced diagonally
1 x 175 g/6 oz jar stir-fry yellow bean
    sauce
salt and pepper
celery leaves, to garnish (optional)

1 Cut the chicken into thin slices
   across the grain.

2 Heat the oil in the wok, swirling it
   around until really hot. Add the
cashew nuts and stir-fry until they begin
to brown, then add the chicken and stir-
fry until well sealed and almost cooked
through.

3 Add the spring onions (scallions)
   and celery and continue to stir-fry
for 2–3 minutes, stirring the food well
around the wok.

4 Add the stir-fry yellow bean sauce,
   season lightly and toss until the
chicken and vegetables are thoroughly
coated with the sauce and piping hot.

5 Serve at once with plain boiled rice,
   garnished with celery leaves, if liked.

VARIATION

This recipe can be adapted to use
turkey fillets or steaks, or pork fillet or
boneless steaks. Cut the turkey or
pork lengthwise first, then slice thinly
across the grain. Alternatively, cut into
2 cm/ ¾ in cubes.

CHICKEN WITH LEMON & TARRAGON

SERVES 6

6 large boneless chicken breasts
¼ tsp saffron strands
250 ml/8 fl oz/1 cup boiling water
1 tbsp olive oil
30 g/1 oz/2 tbsp butter
1 garlic clove, crushed
125 ml/4 fl oz/ ½ cup dry white wine
grated rind of 1 small lemon
1 tbsp lemon juice
1–2 tbsp chopped fresh tarragon or 1 tsp
   dried tarragon
2 tsp cornflour (cornstarch)
1 egg yolk
6 tbsp soured cream or double (heavy)
   cream
4 tbsp thick mayonnaise
salt and pepper

TO GARNISH:
fresh tarragon
lemon twists

1 Remove the skin from the chicken
and cut each breast almost
horizontally into 3 thin slices. Season each
piece well with salt and pepper.

2 Put the saffron strands into a bowl,
pour on the boiling water and leave
to stand until they are needed.

3 Heat the oil, butter and garlic in a
frying pan (skillet). When foaming,
add the pieces of chicken and fry for a
few minutes on each side until well
sealed but only lightly coloured.

4 Add the saffron liquid, wine, lemon
rind and juice, and half the fresh
tarragon or all the dried tarragon. Bring to
the boil, then simmer gently for about 5
minutes or until tender. Lift out the
chicken pieces with a perforated spoon
and place on a serving dish in
overlapping slices. Leave to cool. Boil the
juices for 3–4 minutes to reduce slightly.

5 Blend the cornflour (cornstarch), egg
yolk and cream together in a bowl.
Whisk in a little of the cooking juices,
then return to the pan and heat gently,
stirring continuously until thickened and
just barely simmering. Remove from the
heat, adjust the seasoning and pour into a
bowl. Cover and leave until cool.

6 Beat the mayonnaise and remaining
fresh tarragon into the sauce and
spoon over the chicken. Cover and chill
thoroughly. Garnish with sprigs of fresh
tarragon and lemon twists.

DUCK BREAST WITH BEANS

Serves 4-6

4-6 duck breasts, about 175 g/6 oz each
2 tbsp olive oil
1 onion, chopped
2 garlic cloves, chopped
125 g/4 oz streaky bacon, chopped
300 ml/ ½ pint/1¼ cups red wine
2 tbsp tomato purée (paste)
2 tsp clear honey
1 fresh bay leaf
1 tbsp chopped fresh marjoram
425 g/14 oz can pinto beans or red kidney
  beans, drained and rinsed
425 g/14 oz can haricot (navy) beans,
  drained and rinsed
425 g/14 oz can flageolet (small navy)
  beans, drained and rinsed
425 g/14 oz can green lentils, drained
  and rinsed
1 tbsp balsamic vinegar
2 tbsp chopped fresh parsley
salt and pepper
fresh marjoram sprigs to garnish
green salad to serve

1 Prick the skin of the duck breasts
then put the breasts skin side down
on a rack in a grill (broiler) pan. Brush
with oil and cook under a preheated
moderate grill (broiler) for 3–4 minutes.
Turn the duck over and grill (broil) for a
further 5–10 minutes until most of the fat
has run out, the skin is crisp, but the flesh
is still pink.

2 Meanwhile, heat the remaining oil in
a heavy-based saucepan and fry the
onion, garlic and bacon, stirring
occasionally, for 5 minutes.

3 Add the wine, tomato purée (paste),
honey, bay leaf, marjoram, beans,
lentils and seasoning. Bring to the boil
and simmer for 5 minutes. Stir in the
vinegar and parsley, adding a little extra
wine or water if necessary.

4 Slice the duck breasts and divide
between warmed serving plates.
Spoon some beans and lentils next to the
duck. Garnish with marjoram sprigs and
serve with a green salad.

CHICKEN WITH SPICY CHICK-PEAS

Serves 4

3 tbsp ghee or vegetable oil
8 small chicken portions, such as thighs or
  drumsticks
1 large onion, peeled and chopped
2 garlic cloves, peeled and crushed
1-2 fresh green chillies, seeded and
  chopped, or use 1-2 tsp minced chilli
  (from a jar)
2 tsp ground cumin
2 tsp ground coriander
1 tsp garam masala
1 tsp ground turmeric
1 x 425 g/14 oz can chopped tomatoes
150 ml/ ¼ pint/ ⅔ cup water
1 tbsp chopped fresh mint
1 x 475 g/15 oz can chick-peas, drained
salt
1 tbsp chopped fresh coriander
natural yogurt, to serve (optional)

1 Heat the ghee or oil in a large
saucepan and fry the chicken pieces
all over until sealed and lightly golden.
Remove from the pan. Add the onion,
garlic, chilli and spices and cook very
gently for 2 minutes, stirring frequently.

2 Stir in the tomatoes, water, mint and
chick-peas. Mix well, return the
chicken portions to the pan, season with
salt to taste, then cover and simmer gently
for about 20 minutes or until the chicken
is tender and cooked through.

3 Taste and adjust the seasoning if
necessary, then sprinkle with the
chopped coriander and serve hot, drizzled
with yogurt, if using.

VARIATIONS

Canned black-eyed beans and red
kidney beans also make delicious
additions to this spicy chicken dish. Be
sure to drain the canned beans and to
rinse them, if necessary, before adding
to the pan.

CHICKEN & VEGETABLE RICE

SERVES 4-6

4 chicken drumsticks
3 tbsp mango chutney
1½ tbsp lemon juice
6 tbsp vegetable oil
1½-2 tbsp medium or hot curry paste
1½ tsp paprika
1 large onion, peeled and chopped
2 garlic cloves, peeled and crushed
125 g/4 oz button mushrooms, wiped and left whole
2 carrots, peeled and thinly sliced
2 celery sticks, trimmed and thinly sliced
½ aubergine (eggplant), quartered and sliced
¼ tsp ground cinnamon
250 g/8 oz/1¼ cups long-grain rice
600 ml/1 pint/2½ cups chicken stock or water
60 g/2 oz frozen peas or sliced green beans
60 g/2 oz/ ⅓ cup seedless raisins
salt and freshly ground black pepper
wedges of hard-boiled egg and lemon slices, to garnish (optional)

1 Slash the drumsticks twice on each side, cutting through the skin and deep into the flesh each time. Mix the chutney with the lemon juice, 1 tablespoon oil, curry paste and paprika. Brush over the drumsticks and reserve the remainder for later.

2 Heat 2 tablespoons of oil in the frying pan and fry the drumsticks over a moderate heat for about 5 minutes until sealed and golden brown all over.

3 Meanwhile, heat the remaining oil in a saucepan, add the onion, mushrooms, carrots, celery, aubergine (eggplant), garlic and cinnamon and fry lightly for 1 minute. Stir in the rice and cook gently for 1 minute, stirring until the rice is well coated with the oil. Add the stock and the remaining mango chutney mixture, peas, raisins and salt and pepper to taste. Mix well and bring to the boil.

4 Reduce the heat and add the drumsticks to the mixture, pushing them down into the liquid. Cover and cook gently for 25 minutes until the liquid has been absorbed, the drumsticks are tender and the rice is cooked.

5 Remove the drumsticks from the pan and keep warm. Fluff up the rice mixture and transfer to a warm serving plate. Arrange the rice into a nicely shaped mound and place the drumsticks around it. Garnish the dish with wedges of hard-boiled egg and lemon slices, if using.

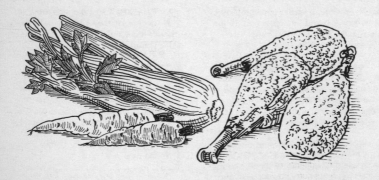

CHICKEN IN SPICED COCONUT

SERVES 4

4 boneless chicken breasts, skinned
6 tbsp vegetable oil
2 onions, peeled, quartered and thinly
    sliced
1 garlic clove, peeled and crushed
2.5 cm/1 in fresh ginger root, peeled and
    finely chopped
1-2 fresh green chillies, seeded and finely
    chopped, or use 1-2 tsp minced chilli (in
    a jar)
175 g/6 oz mushrooms, wiped and sliced
2 tsp medium curry powder
2 tsp ground coriander
½ tsp ground cinnamon
1 tbsp sesame seeds
150 ml/¼ pint/⅔ cup chicken stock or
    water
1 x 250 g/8 oz can chopped tomatoes
300 ml/½ pint/1¼ cups coconut milk
salt
coriander sprigs, to garnish

1 Cut each chicken breast into 3
diagonal pieces. Heat 4 tablespoons
of oil in a saucepan and fry the chicken
pieces until lightly sealed all over.
Remove from the pan and reserve.

2 Add the remaining oil to the pan
and gently fry the onions, garlic,
ginger, chillies, mushrooms, curry
powders, spices and sesame seeds for 3
minutes, stirring frequently. Stir in the
chicken stock, tomatoes and coconut
milk. Season with salt to taste and bring
to the boil.

3 Reduce the heat, return the chicken
pieces to the pan and simmer gently,
uncovered, for about 12 minutes, or until
the chicken is tender and cooked through
and the sauce has thickened, stirring
occasionally. Garnish with coriander
sprigs.

SPICES

Increase the pungency of the mixture
by adding more curry powder or chilli,
to taste. You can also leave the dish to
stand overnight to allow the flavours to
develop and reheat it gently when
required.

SPICED CHICKEN & GRAPE MAYONNAISE

SERVES 4

500 g/1 lb cooked chicken breast
2 celery sticks
250 g/8 oz/2 cups black grapes
60 g/2 oz/½ cup split almonds,
    browned
paprika
fresh coriander (cilantro) or flat-leaf
    parsley to garnish

CURRY MAYONNAISE:
150 ml/¼ pint/⅔ cup mayonnaise
125 g/4 oz/½ cup natural fromage frais
1 tbsp clear honey
1 tbsp curry sauce

1 Cut the chicken into fairly large
pieces and slice the celery finely.

2 Halve the grapes, remove the seeds
and place in a bowl with the
chicken and celery.

3 To make the curry mayonnaise, mix
all the ingredients together until
blended.

4 Pour the mayonnaise over the salad
and mix together carefully until well
coated.

5 Transfer to a shallow serving dish
and sprinkle with the almonds and
paprika. Garnish with the coriander
(cilantro) or parsley.

BROWNING ALMONDS

To brown almonds, place them on a
baking sheet and place in a hot oven
for 5–10 minutes until golden brown.

CRANBERRY TURKEY BURGERS WITH SAGE & ONION

••

SERVES 4

350 g/12 oz/1½ cups lean minced
   (ground) turkey
1 onion, chopped finely
1 tbsp chopped fresh sage
6 tbsp dry white breadcrumbs
4 tbsp cranberry sauce
1 egg white, size 2, lightly beaten
2 tsp sunflower oil
salt and pepper

TO SERVE:
4 toasted granary or wholemeal (whole
   wheat) burger buns
½ iceberg lettuce, shredded
4 tomatoes, sliced
4 tsp cranberry sauce

1 Mix together the turkey, onion, sage, seasoning, breadcrumbs and cranberry sauce, then bind with egg white. The mixture needs to be quite soft to prevent drying out during cooking.

2 Divide the mixture into 4 and press into 10 cm/4 inch rounds, about 2 cm/ ¾ inch thick; flour your hands with cornflour (cornstarch) if necessary. Line a plate with baking parchment, arrange the turkey burgers on top, cover and chill for 30 minutes.

3 Line a grill (broiler) rack with baking parchment, making sure the ends are secured underneath the rack to ensure they don't catch fire. Place the burgers on top and brush lightly with oil. Put under a preheated moderate grill (broiler) and cook for 10 minutes.

4 Carefully turn the burgers over, brush again with oil and cook for a further 12–15 minutes until cooked through. Drain on paper towels and keep warm.

5 Fill the burger rolls with lettuce, tomato and a burger, and top with cranberry sauce.

QUICK CHINESE CHICKEN WITH NOODLES

••

SERVES 4

175 g/6 oz Chinese thread egg noodles
2 tbsp sesame or vegetable oil
30 g/1 oz/ ¼ cup peanuts
1 bunch of spring onions (scallions),
   sliced
1 green (bell) pepper, deseeded and cut
   into thin strips
1 large carrot, cut into matchsticks
125 g/4 oz cauliflower, broken into small
   florets
350 g/12 oz skinless, boneless chicken, cut
   into strips
250 g/8 oz mushrooms, sliced
1 tsp finely grated ginger root
1 tsp Chinese five-spice powder
1 tbsp chopped fresh coriander (cilantro)
1 tbsp light soy sauce
salt and pepper
fresh chives to garnish

1 Put the noodles into a large bowl and cover with boiling water. Leave to soak for 6 minutes, or according to packet instructions.

2 Meanwhile, heat the oil in a wok or large frying pan (skillet). Add the peanuts and stir-fry for about 1 minute until browned. Lift them out with a perforated spoon and drain on paper towels.

3 Add the spring onions (scallions), (bell) pepper, carrot, cauliflower and chicken to the pan. Stir-fry over a high heat for 4–5 minutes, until the chicken is cooked. The vegetables should remain crisp and colourful.

4 Drain the noodles thoroughly and add them to the wok. Add the mushrooms and stir-fry for 2 minutes. Add the ginger, five-spice powder and coriander (cilantro) and stir-fry for 1 more minute.

5 Season with soy sauce and salt and pepper. Sprinkle with the peanuts, garnish with chives and serve on warmed plates.

CHICKEN & SWEETCORN PUFF

SERVES 4

CHOUX PASTRY:
75 g/2½ oz/generous ½ cup plain (all-
* purpose) flour*
60 g /2 oz/ ¼ cup butter or block
* margarine*
150 ml/ ¼ pint/ ⅔ cup water
2 eggs, beaten
salt

FILLING:
30 g/1 oz/2 tbsp butter or block margarine
30 g/1 oz/ ¼ cup plain (all-purpose) flour
300 ml/ ½ pint/1¼ cups skimmed milk
250 g/8 oz/1 cup cooked chicken,
* shredded*
125 g/4 oz/ ¾ cup canned sweetcorn,
* drained*
1 tbsp chopped fresh parsley
salt and pepper

1 To make the choux pastry, sift the flour and salt into a bowl. Put the butter or margarine and water into a saucepan, then heat gently to melt. Bring to the boil. Remove from the heat and quickly add the flour all at once. Beat with a wooden spoon until the mixture leaves the sides of the saucepan clean. Leave to cool slightly.

2 Gradually beat in the eggs, using an electric whisk if wished, until the mixture is thick and very glossy. Chill while making the filling.

3 To make the filling, put the butter or margarine, flour and milk into a saucepan. Heat, whisking constantly, until smooth and thickened.

4 Add the chicken, sweetcorn and parsley to the sauce. Season to taste. Pour into a 1 litre/1¾ pint/4 cup shallow baking dish.

5 Spoon the choux pastry around the edge of the dish. Bake in a preheated oven at 220°C/425°F/Gas Mark 7 for 35–40 minutes until puffed up and golden brown. Serve at once.

CHICKEN WITH BEAN-SPROUTS

SERVES 4

125 g/4 oz chicken breast fillet, skinned
1 tsp salt
¼ egg white, lightly beaten
2 tsp cornflour (cornstarch) paste (see
* page 376)*
about 300 ml/ ½ pint/1 ¼ cups vegetable
* oil*
1 small onion, thinly shredded
1 small green (bell) pepper, cored, seeded
* and thinly shredded*
1 small carrot, thinly shredded
125 g/4 oz fresh bean-sprouts
½ tsp sugar
1 tbsp light soy sauce
1 tsp rice wine or dry sherry
2-3 tbsp Chinese Stock (see page 376)
a few drops of sesame oil
chilli sauce, to serve

1 Thinly shred the chicken and mix with a pinch of the salt, the egg white and cornflour (cornstarch) paste.

2 Heat the oil in a preheated wok and stir-fry the chicken for about 1 minute, stirring to separate the shreds. Remove with a slotted spoon and drain on paper towels.

3 Pour off the oil, leaving about 2 tablespoons in the wok. Add all the vegetables except the bean-sprouts and stir-fry for about 2 minutes, then add the bean-sprouts and stir for a few seconds.

4 Add the chicken with the remaining salt, sugar, soy sauce and wine, blend well and add the stock or water. Sprinkle with the sesame oil and serve at once.

CHICKEN CHOP SUEY

Chop Suey actually originated in San Francisco at the turn of the century when Chinese immigrants were first settling there, and was first devised as a handy dish for using up leftovers.

CHICKEN & MANGO TIKKA KEBABS

SERVES 4

4 x 125 g/4 oz boneless, skinless chicken
  breasts, cut into 2.5 cm/1 inch cubes
1 garlic clove, crushed
1 tsp grated ginger root
1 fresh green chilli, seeded and chopped
  finely
6 tbsp low-fat natural yogurt
1 tbsp tomato purée (paste)
1 tsp ground cumin
1 tsp ground coriander
1 tsp ground turmeric
1 large ripe mango
1 tbsp lime juice
salt and pepper
fresh coriander (cilantro) leaves to
  garnish

TO SERVE:
boiled white rice
lime wedges
mixed salad
warmed naan bread

1 Place the chicken in a shallow dish.
  Mix together the garlic, ginger, chilli,
yogurt, tomato purée (paste), cumin,
ground coriander, turmeric and seasoning.
Spoon over the chicken, mix well, cover
and chill for 2 hours.

2 Using a vegetable peeler, peel the
  skin from the mango. Slice down
either side of the stone (pit) and cut the
mango flesh into cubes. Toss in lime
juice, cover and chill until required.

3 Thread the chicken and mango
  pieces alternately on 8 skewers.
Place the skewers on a grill (broiler) rack
and brush the chicken with the yogurt
marinade and the lime juice left from the
mango.

4 Place under a preheated moderate
  grill (broiler) for 6–7 minutes. Turn
over, brush again with the yogurt
marinade and lime juice and cook for a
further 6–7 minutes until the chicken
juices run clear when the cubes are
pierced with a sharp knife.

5 Serve on a bed of rice on a warmed
  platter, garnished with coriander
(cilantro) leaves, and accompanied by
lime wedges and a mixed salad.

CHICKEN WITH VERMOUTH, GRAPES & ARTICHOKES

SERVES 4

4 x 175 g/6 oz 'part-boned' chicken
  breasts, skinned
150 ml/ ¼ pint/ ⅔ cup dry white vermouth
150 ml/ ¼ pint/ ⅔ cup Chicken Stock (see
  page 9)
2 shallots, sliced thinly
about 400 g/13 oz can artichoke hearts,
  drained and halved
125 g/4 oz/ ¾ cup seedless green grapes
1 tbsp cornflour (cornstarch) mixed with
  2 tbsp cold water
salt and pepper
watercress sprigs to garnish
freshly cooked vegetables to serve

1 Cook the chicken in a heavy-based
  non-stick frying pan (skillet) for 2–3
minutes on each side until sealed. Drain
on paper towels.

2 Rinse out the pan, then add the dry
  vermouth and stock. Bring to the
boil and add the shallots and chicken.
Cover and simmer for 35 minutes.

3 Season to taste. Stir in the artichokes
  and grapes and heat through for 2–3
minutes.

4 Stir in the cornflour (cornstarch)
  mixture until thickened. Garnish
with watercress sprigs and serve with
freshly cooked vegetables.

ROAST BABY CHICKENS

SERVES 4

4 small poussins, weighing about 350-
    500 g/12 oz-1 lb each
coriander leaves and lime wedges, to
    garnish
a mixture of wild rice and Basmati rice,
    to serve

MARINADE:
4 garlic cloves, peeled
2 fresh coriander roots
1 tbsp light soy sauce
salt and pepper

STUFFING:
4 blades lemon grass
4 kaffir lime leaves
4 slices ginger root
about 6 tbsp coconut milk, to brush

1   Preheat the oven to 200°C/400°F/
    Gas 6. Wash the chickens and dry on
paper towels.

2   Place all the ingredients for the
    marinade in a small blender and
purée until smooth, or grind down in a
pestle and mortar. Season to taste with
salt and pepper. Rub this marinade
mixture into the skin of the chickens,
using the back of a spoon to spread it
evenly over the skins.

3   Place a blade of lemon grass, a lime
    leaf and a piece of ginger in the
cavity of each chicken.

4   Place the chickens in a roasting pan
    and brush lightly with the coconut
milk. Roast for 30 minutes in the
preheated oven.

5   Remove from the oven, brush again
    with coconut milk, return to the
oven and cook for a further 15-25
minutes, until golden and cooked
through, depending upon the size of the
chickens. The chickens are cooked when
the juices from the thigh run clear and are
not tinged at all with pink.

6   Serve with the pan juices poured
    over. Garnish with coriander leaves
and lime wedges.

DUCK WITH LIME & KIWI FRUIT

SERVES 4

4 boneless or part-boned duck breasts
2 large limes
2 tbsp sunflower oil
4 spring onions (scallions), thinly sliced
125 g/4 oz carrots, cut into matchsticks
6 tbsp dry white wine
60 g/2 oz/¼ cup white sugar
2 kiwi fruit, peeled, halved and sliced
salt and pepper

1   Remove any excess fat from the
    duck, then prick the skin all over
and lay in a shallow dish in a single layer.
Remove the rind from the limes using a
citrus zester or grate it coarsely. Squeeze
the juice from the limes (there should be
at least 3 tablespoons, if not make up
with lemon juice), and add half the strips
of lime and half the juice to the duck
breasts, rubbing in thoroughly. Leave to
stand in a cool place for at least 1 hour,
turning at least once.

2   Drain the duck breasts thoroughly.
    Heat 1 tablespoon of oil in the wok,
swirling it around until it is really hot.
Add the duck and fry quickly to seal all
over then lower the heat a little and
continue to cook for about 5 minutes,
turning several times until just cooked
through and well browned all over.
Remove and keep warm.

3   Wipe the wok clean with paper
    towels and heat the remaining oil in
it. Add the spring onions (scallions) and
carrots and stir-fry for 1 minute, then add
the remaining lime marinade, wine and
sugar. Bring to the boil and simmer for
2-3 minutes until slightly syrupy.

4   Replace the duck breasts in the
    sauce, season well and add the kiwi
fruit. Cook for about a minute or until
really hot and both the duck and kiwi
fruit are well coated in the sauce.

5   Cut each duck breast into slices,
    leaving a "hinge" at one end, open
out into a fan shape and arrange on
plates. Spoon the sauce over the duck,
sprinkle with the remaining pieces of lime
peel and garnish with parsley leaves and
lime halves.

CRISPY-COATED POUSSINS

SERVES 6

4 tbsp vegetable oil
60 g/2 oz/ ¼ cup butter
6 small poussins, trussed
1 large onion, sliced
500 g/1 lb baby carrots
1 tbsp flour
150 ml/ ¼ pint/ ⅔ cup white wine
juice of 2 oranges
2 fennel bulbs, quartered
300 ml/ ½ pint/1¼ cups chicken stock
1 tbsp green peppercorns, lightly crushed
½ tsp salt
1 tsp cornflour (cornstarch)
150 ml/ ¼ pint/ ⅔ cup Greek-style yogurt

COATING:
3 tbsp demerara sugar
1 tbsp green peppercorns, lightly crushed
3 tbsp coarse sea salt
150 ml/ ¼ pint/ ⅔ cup Greek-style yogurt

1 Heat the oil in a large frying pan and
add the butter. When bubbling, add
the poussins in batches and brown evenly
on all sides. Remove and keep warm.

2 Add the onion to the pan and fry
until translucent. Add the carrots ,
stir to coat evenly, then sprinkle on the
flour and blend well. Pour on the wine
and orange juice, stirring all the time. Add
the fennel, chicken stock and
peppercorns and season. Bring to the boil
then pour into a large roasting pan.

3 Arrange the poussins in the roasting
pan, cover loosely with foil and
cook in the preheated oven for 40
minutes.

4 To make the coating, stir together
the sugar, peppercorns, salt and
yogurt to make a thick paste.

5 Preheat the grill (broiler) to high.
Remove the poussins from the
roasting tin and place them on a rack.
Spread the paste evenly over the
poussins then grill (broil) for 3-4 minutes,
until the coating is crisp.

6 Arrange the drained vegetables on a
warm serving dish. Place the
roasting tin over medium heat and bring
the sauce to the boil. Stir the cornflour
(cornstarch) into the yogurt then blend
into the sauce. Taste for seasoning. Place
the poussins in the centre of the dish,
spoon a little sauce over the vegetables,
and serve the rest separately.

STIR-FRY CHICKEN CURRY

SERVES 4

4 boneless chicken breasts, skinned
6 tbsp strained Greek yogurt
juice of 1 lime
2 garlic cloves, peeled and crushed
5 cm/2 in piece ginger root, peeled and
 chopped
2 tbsp medium or hot curry paste, to taste
1 tbsp paprika
salt
5 tbsp ghee or vegetable oil
1 onion, peeled, quartered and separated
 into layers
1 red (bell) pepper, seeded and cut into
 1 cm/ ½ in pieces
1 green (bell) pepper, seeded and cut into
 1 cm/ ½ in pieces
60 g/2 oz/ ½ cup unsalted cashews
4 tbsp water
snipped chives or spring onion (scallion)
 leaves, to garnish

1 Cut the chicken breasts into 1 cm/½ in wide strips and place in a bowl. Add the yogurt, lime juice, garlic, ginger, curry paste and paprika. Season well and mix the ingredients together.

2 Heat the ghee or oil in a large frying pan, add the onion, red and green (bell) pepper and the cashews and stir-fry over a moderate heat for 2 minutes. Remove from the pan and reserve.

3 Stir the chicken mixture into the pan and stir-fry for 4-5 minutes until well sealed and cooked though.

4 Add the water and mix well, then return the vegetables to the pan, reduce the heat and cook gently for 2 minutes. Serve at once, sprinkled with chives or spring onion (scallion) leaves.

VARIATIONS

Thin strips of pork tenderloin or rump steak are also extremely good cooked this way. Add slices of courgette (zuccini) or celery instead of one of the (bell) peppers, if wished, and substitute blanched almonds for the cashews.

CHICKEN & CHILLI BEAN POT

SERVES 4

2 tbsp plain (all-purpose) flour
1 tsp chilli powder
8 chicken thighs or 4 chicken legs
3 tbsp olive or vegetable oil
2 garlic cloves, crushed
1 large onion, chopped
1 green or red (bell) pepper, deseeded and
 chopped
300 ml/ ½ pint/1¼ cups chicken stock
350 g/12 oz tomatoes, chopped
425 g/14 oz can red kidney beans, rinsed
 and drained
2 tbsp tomato purée (paste)
salt and pepper

1 together the flour, chilli powder and seasoning in a shallow dish. Rinse the chicken, but do not dry. Dip the chicken into the seasoned flour, turning to coat it on all sides.

2 Heat the oil in a large, deep frying pan (skillet) or saucepan and add the chicken. Cook over a high heat for 3–4 minutes, turning the pieces to brown them all over. Lift the chicken out of the pan with a perforated spoon and drain on paper towels.

3 Add the garlic, onion and (bell) pepper to the pan and cook for 2–3 minutes until softened.

4 Add the stock, tomatoes, kidney beans and tomato purée (paste), stirring well. Bring to the boil, then return the chicken to the pan. Reduce the heat and simmer, covered, for about 30 minutes, until the chicken is tender. Season to taste and serve at once.

VARIATIONS

When fresh tomatoes are expensive, use a 425 g/14 oz can of chopped tomatoes instead.

Choose a mild, medium or hot variety of chilli powder, depending on your preference.

For extra intensity of flavour, use sun-dried tomato paste instead of ordinary tomato purée (paste).

RABBIT WITH FRIED CHEESE

SERVES 4

1 kg/2 lb rabbit joints, washed and dried
salt
1 tbsp vegetable oil
45 g/1½ oz/3 tbsp butter
45 g/1½ oz/6 tbsp flour
300 ml/ ½ pint/1¼ cups chicken stock
2 tsp Dijon mustard
freshly ground black pepper
4 tbsp plain yogurt

MARINADE:
2 tbsp olive oil
1 small onion, sliced
150 ml/ ¼ pint/⅔ cup dry cider
2 tbsp white wine vinegar
2 sprigs each of rosemary and thyme
½ tsp juniper berries, crushed
½ tsp coriander seeds, crushed
150 ml/ ¼ pint/⅔ cup natural yogurt

TOPPING:
250g/8 oz/1 cup Yogurt Cheese (see
 page 97), cut into 4 slices
2 tbsp flour seasoned with 1 tsp dried
 thyme and freshly-ground black pepper
3 tbsp olive oil

1 Put all the marinade ingredients
 except the yogurt in a small pan.
Bring to the boil, remove from the heat
and allow to cool completely.

2 Beat the yogurt into the cold
 marinade, and pour into a shallow
dish. Put the rabbit in the dish and spoon
over the marinade. Cover and chill for
several hours.

3 Heat the oil and butter in a
 casserole. Drain the rabbit then fry
until golden brown. Remove with a
slotted spoon and stir in the flour. Pour
the marinade into the casserole and
blend. Stir in the stock and mustard, and
season.

4 Return the rabbit to the casserole,
 bring to the boil and cover. Cook in
the preheated oven for 1-1½ hours until
tender – test with a skewer. Strain the
sauce into a pan, stir in the yogurt and
check the seasoning. Pour the sauce over
the rabbit.

5 To make the topping, toss the yogurt
 cheese in the seasoned flour. Heat
the oil in a frying pan and fry the cheese
for 2 minutes on each side, until golden
brown. Place the cheese on the rabbit and
serve, garnished with rosemary.

SALADS - INTRODUCTION

Salads are such a versatile way of eating, and the variety of ingredients is so great, that they can be made to suit any occasion, from the light piquant starter designed to stimulate the taste buds to the more substantial dish served as a main course or the mixture of exotic fruits that makes a delicious dessert.

Salads can be fruity, fishy, meaty, eggy, cheesy or just fresh green. All are highly nutritious providing valuable minerals, vitamins and the necessary fibre. They are also generally low in calories, provided you go easy on the dressing, or use a fat-free dressing. It is easy to make a salad look attractive and appetizing, which will encourage your family to eat the fruits and vegetables which are so vital to their good health. It is also often a welcome dish to serve alongside richer offerings at a dinner party or celebration meal.

It is both worthwhile and interesting to take note of the various vegetables and fruits available in the shops at different seasons of the year. It is obviously best to use them when they are at their peak, and of course, when they are in season, as they will be plentiful and cheap. A bonus for the budget!

Supermarkets now stock many unusual ingredients, which can add interest to an ordinary salad. Experiment with new fruits and vegetables, buying them in small quantities to lend unusual flavours to salads made mostly from cheaper ingredients.

You will see from the recipes that I have been liberal in the use of herbs, which must be fresh. They add a unique 'zip' and it can be great fun trying them out to discover which are your favourites. Experiment each time you make a salad or a dressing; try marjoram, thyme, chives, basil, mint, fennel and dill as well as the ubiquitous parsley. Basil goes especially well with tomatoes, and fennel or dill are particularly good with cucumber, beetroot and fish salads.

A salad is the ideal emergency meal. It is quick to 'rustle up' and there are times when you might discover that you already have a really good combination of ingredients to hand when you need to present a meal-in-a-moment. A rapid check in the pantry might produce a can of beans or artichoke hearts. Add the couple of tomatoes and yellow (bell) pepper languishing in the salad drawer of the refrigerator, throw in a few sprigs of mint or basil that you have growing on the window sill, a few olives from that jar in the corner, a splash of dressing and you have a culinary inspiration, a super salad that you had no idea was lurking in your kitchen.

Dressings
All salads depend on being well dressed and so it is necessary to use the best ingredients, and the choice of oil is particularly important.

The principal ingredients in a salad dressing are oil and vinegar with a variety of other flavourings that can be varied to suit the particular ingredients in the salad.

Salad oils
Oils are produced from various nuts, seeds and beans and each has its own particular flavour. Unrefined oils have a superior taste and, although more expensive, they are definitely worth using for salad dressings.

Olive oil is the best oil for most salad dressings as its flavour is far

INTRODUCTION

superior to others. Choose a green-tinged, fruity oil which will be labelled 'extra virgin' or 'first pressing'.

Sesame oil has a strong nutty tang which gives an unusual flavour to dressings and is particularly good with oriental-type salads.

Sunflower and safflower oil are neutral-flavoured oils and can be mixed with olive oil or used alone to produce a lighter dressing. Mayonnaise made with a combination of one of these oils and olive oil has a lighter consistency.

Walnut and hazelnut oils have the most wonderful flavour and aroma, and are usually mixed with olive oil in a French dressing. It is especially good with slightly bitter salad plants such as chicory (endive), radiccio or spinach.

Vinegars

Vinegars such as wine, cider, sherry or herb-flavoured are essential for a good dressing. Malt vinegar is far too harsh and overpowers the subtle balance of the dressing. Lemon juice may be used if you prefer and is often preferable if the salad is fruit-based.

Cider vinegar is reputed to contain many healthy properties and valuable nutrients. It also has a light subtle flavour.

Wine vinegar is the one most commonly used for French dressing; either red or white will do.

Sherry vinegar has a rich mellow flavour which blends particularly well with walnut and hazelnut oils.

Flavoured vinegars can be made from cider and wine vinegar. To do this, steep your chosen ingredient in a small bottle of vinegar for anything up to 2 weeks. Particularly good additions are basil, tarragon, garlic,

thyme, mint or rosemary. Raspberry wine vinegar can be made by adding about 12 raspberries to a bottle of vinegar.

Balsamic vinegar is dark and mellow with a sweet/sour flavour. It is expensive but you need only a few drops or at most a teaspoonful to give a wonderful taste. It is made in the area around Modena in Italy and some, made by traditional methods, are aged for many years in oak barrels.

Mustards

Mustards are made from black, brown or white mustard seeds which are ground, mixed with spices and then, usually, mixed with vinegar.

There are many flavoured mustards available, including horseradish, honey, chilli and tarragon.

Meaux mustard is made from mixed mustard seeds and has a grainy texture with a warm spicy taste.

Dijon mustard, made from husked and ground mustard seeds, is a medium hot mustard with a sharp flavour and is the most versatile in salads. It is made in Dijon, France, and only mustard made there can be labelled as such.

German mustard is a mild sweet/sour tasting mustard and is best used in Scandinavian and German salads.

GREEK SALAD

SERVES 4

½ cucumber
1 small onion, sliced thinly into rings
1 green (bell) pepper, cored, deseeded and chopped
500 g/1 lb tomatoes
4 tbsp olive oil
1 tbsp cider vinegar
1 tbsp chopped fresh basil
1 tbsp chopped fresh oregano
250 g/8 oz Feta cheese
salt and pepper
60 g/2 oz/ ½ cup black olives, pitted, to garnish

1 Cut the cucumber into large dice and put into a bowl with the sliced onion and chopped green (bell) pepper.

2 Cut each tomato into 8 wedges and add to the bowl with the oil, vinegar, herbs, and salt and pepper to taste.

3 Toss all the ingredients thoroughly and turn into a salad bowl.

4 Cut the Feta cheese into cubes. Sprinkle the cheese evenly over the salad.

5 Garnish with the olives and serve with plenty of crusty bread to mop up the juices.

TIP

Use Greek kalamata olives if possible. They are a purple-brown colour and have a superior flavour to other varieties.

HOT & SPICY GOLDEN RICE SALAD

SERVES 4

2 tsp vegetable oil
1 onion, chopped finely
1 fresh red chilli, deseeded and chopped finely
8 cardamom pods
1 tsp ground turmeric
1 tsp garam masala
350 g/12 oz /1¼ cups basmati rice, rinsed
700 ml/1¼ pints/3cups boiling water
1 orange bell pepper, chopped
250 g/8 oz cauliflower florets, divided into small sprigs
4 ripe tomatoes, skinned, deseeded, and chopped
125 g/4 oz/ ¾ cup seedless raisins
30 g/1 oz/ ¼ cup toasted flaked (slivered) almonds
salt and pepper
salad of low-fat natural yogurt, onion, cucumber and mint to serve

1 Heat the oil in a large non-stick saucepan, add the onion, chilli, cardamom pods, turmeric and garam

2 masala and fry gently for 2–3 minutes until the vegetables are just softened.

3 Stir in the rice, boiling water, seasoning, (bell) pepper and cauliflower. Cover with a tight-fitting lid, bring to the boil, then cook over a low heat for 15 minutes without lifting the lid.

4 Uncover, fork through and stir in the tomatoes and raisins. Cover again, turn off the heat and leave for 15 minutes. Discard the cardamom pods.

5 Pile on to a warmed serving platter and sprinkle over the toasted flaked (slivered) almonds. Serve with the yogurt salad.

BASMATI RICE

Indian basmati rice is more expensive than long-grain, but it has a fragrant flavour and fluffy texture. Rinse or soak it before cooking to remove the excess starch.

SEEFOOD SALAD

SERVES 4

175 g/6 oz squid rings, defrosted if frozen
600 ml/1 pint/2½ cups water
150 ml/ ¼ pint/ ⅔ cup dry white wine
250 g/8 oz hake or monkfish, cut into
   cubes
16-20 fresh mussels, scrubbed and beards
   removed
20 clams in shells, scrubbed, if available
   (otherwise use extra mussels)
125-175 g/4-6 oz peeled prawns (shrimp)
3-4 spring onions (scallions) trimmed and
   sliced (optional)
radicchio and curly endive leaves, to serve
lemon wedges, to garnish

DRESSING
6 tbsp olive oil
1 tbsp wine vinegar
2 tbsp freshly chopped parsley
1-2 garlic cloves, crushed
salt and pepper

GARLIC MAYONNAISE
5 tbsp thick mayonnaise
2-3 tbsp fromage frais or natural yogurt
2 garlic cloves, crushed
1 tbsp capers
2 tbsp freshly chopped parsley or mixed
   herbs

1 Poach the squid in the water and wine for 20 minutes or until nearly tender. Add the fish cubes and continue to cook gently for 7-8 minutes or until tender. Strain, reserving the fish, and place the stock in a clean pan.

2 Bring the fish stock to the boil and add the mussels and clams. Cover the pan and simmer gently for about 5 minutes or until the shells open. Discard any that stay closed.

3 Drain the shellfish and remove from their shells. Put into a bowl with the cooked fish and add the prawns (shrimp) and onions (scallions) if using.

4 For the dressing, whisk together the oil, vinegar, parsley, garlic, salt and plenty of black pepper. Pour over the fish, mix well, cover and chill for several hours.

5 Arrange small leaves of radicchio and curly endive on 4 plates and spoon the fish salad into the centre. Garnish each plate with lemon wedges. Combine all the ingredients for the garlic mayonnaise and serve with the salad.

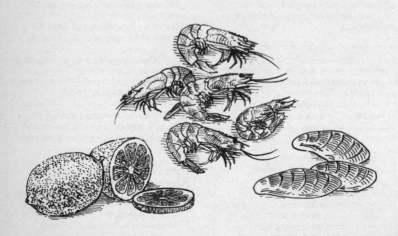

PASTA PROVENÇAL

SERVES 4

175 g/6 oz dried pasta shapes
4 tbsp French Dressing (see page 52)
350 g/12 oz chicken breast
2 tbsp olive oil
2 courgettes (zucchini)
1 red (bell) pepper
2 garlic cloves
4 tomatoes
60 g/2 oz can of anchovies, drained
30 g/1 oz/1/4 cup black olives
sprig of fresh parsley to garnish

1 Cook the pasta in boiling salted water for 10–12 minutes until al dente. Drain and rinse in hot water, then drain again thoroughly.

2 Put into a bowl with the dressing and mix together.

3 Cut the chicken breast into strips. Heat the oil in a frying pan (skillet). Add the chicken and stir-fry for 4–5 minutes, stirring occasionally until cooked, then remove from the pan.

4 Slice the courgettes (zucchini). Core and deseed the red (bell) pepper and cut into chunks. Slice the garlic, add to the pan with the courgettes (zucchini) and (bell) pepper and fry for 12–15 minutes, stirring occasionally, until softened.

5 Cut the tomatoes into wedges, chop the anchovies roughly, and halve and pit the olives. Add to the pasta with the chicken and fried vegetables, and mix together.

6 Transfer to a serving dish, garnish with parsley and serve immediately while warm.

PASTA SHAPES

For some suitable pasta shapes, choose from the following; farfalle (bow ties), conchiglie (shells), conchiglie rigate (ridged shells), penne (quill shapes), rigatoni (tubular pasta, usually ridged), fusilli (spiral shapes), rotelle (wheels) and orecchiette (little ears).

TURKISH LAMB SALAD

SERVES 4

2 red (bell) peppers, cored, and deseeded
1 yellow (bell) pepper, cored and deseeded
1 green (bell) pepper, cored and deseeded
4 tomatoes, skinned
1 small onion
500 g/1 lb lamb fillet (tenderloin)
3 pitta breads
4 tbsp Tomato Vinaigrette (see page 52)
120 ml/4 fl oz/½ cup thick, creamy yogurt
3 tbsp chopped fresh parsley

1 To skin the (bell) peppers, lay them cut-side down on a grill (broiler) pan and cook gently until blackened. Put in a plastic bag to cool.

2 Remove the (bell) pepper skin and chop roughly. Cut each tomato into 8 wedges and slice the onion. Put the onion into a bowl with the tomato wedges and (bell) pepper chunks.

3 Place the lamb fillet (tenderloin) under a preheated medium-hot grill (broiler) until charred on the outside but still pink in the middle.

4 Cut the bread into pieces and add to the bowl with the (bell) peppers, onion and tomato. Pour over the dressing, mix together thoroughly and arrange on individual plates.

5 Slice the lamb and arrange a few pieces over each salad. Drizzle over the yogurt and sprinkle with the parsley.

VARIATION

You may prefer to use a half leg of lamb instead of lamb fillet (tenderloin). If so, cut it into cubes, thread the meat on to skewers and cook for 3–4 minutes on each side under a hot grill (broiler). Then slide off the skewers and arrange over the salad.

WARM CALF'S LIVER SALAD

SERVES 2

250 g/8 oz packet of mixed salad leaves
   (greens)
250 g/8 oz calf's liver
1 orange, cut into segments
2 tbsp pine kernels (nuts)
3 tbsp olive oil
1 garlic clove, sliced
2 tsp chopped sage
2 tbsp balsamic vinegar
salt and pepper

1 Arrange the salad leaves (greens) on 2 individual plates. Cut the liver into large pieces.

2 Peel the orange using a serrated knife, then divide into segments.

3 Put the pine kernels (nuts) in a small heavy-based frying pan (skillet) and cook over a moderate heat, shaking the pan constantly so that the nuts do not burn. Remove the nuts from the pan.

4 Heat the oil in a heavy-based frying pan (skillet). Add the liver to the pan with the garlic and sage, and fry for 1–2 minutes, depending on the thickness of the liver, turning it once.

5 Remove the liver, using a perforated spoon, and arrange on the salad with the orange segments.

6 Add the vinegar to the frying pan (skillet) with any juices from the orange and stir well to deglaze the pan. Season to taste.

7 Sprinkle the pine kernels (nuts) over the salad, then pour over the juices and serve immediately.

CALF'S LIVER

Calf's liver is generally considered to be the finest in quality and flavour, but is also the most expensive. It should be thinly sliced and fried briefly so that it is still pink inside.

SALADE NIÇOISE

SERVES 4

1 small crisp lettuce
500 g/1 lb tomatoes
200 g/7 oz can of tuna fish, drained
2 tbsp chopped fresh parsley
½ cucumber
1 small red onion, sliced
250 g/8 oz French (green) beans, topped
   and tailed, cooked
1 small red (bell) pepper, cored and
   deseeded
6 tbsp French Dressing (see page 609)
3 hard-boiled (hard-cooked) eggs
60 g/2 oz can of anchovies, drained
12 black olives, pitted

1 Place the lettuce leaves in a mixing bowl.

2 Cut the tomatoes into wedges, flake the tuna fish and put both into the bowl with the parsley.

3 Cut the cucumber in half lengthways, then cut into slices. Slice the onion. Add the cucumber and onion to the bowl.

4 Cut the French (green) beans in half, chop the red (bell) pepper and add both to the bowl.

5 Pour over the French dressing and toss thoroughly, then spoon into a salad bowl to serve.

6 Cut the eggs into quarters, arrange over the top with the anchovies and scatter with the olives.

GARLIC BREAD

To make garlic bread, cream 90 g/3 oz/ ⅓ cup butter with 2 crushed garlic cloves and seasoning to taste. Slice a French stick diagonally without cutting right through, so the pieces stay attached. Spread both sides of each slice with the garlic butter. Wrap in foil and put in a hot oven for about 10 minutes. Unwrap and leave in the oven to crisp for 5 minutes.

LENTIL & FRANKFURTER SALAD

SERVES 8

250 g/8 oz/1 cup green lentils
4 tbsp sunflower oil
1 tbsp soy sauce
1 tbsp wine vinegar
1 garlic clove, crushed
4 frankfurters
1 onion
1 red (bell) pepper
2 celery sticks
4 tomatoes
2 tbsp chopped fresh parsley
1 tbsp chopped fresh marjoram
salt and pepper

1 Put the lentils into a pan of boiling salted water, bring back to the boil and cook for 35–40 minutes until softened. Drain well and put into a bowl.

2 Add the oil, soy sauce, vinegar and garlic with seasoning to taste, and mix with the lentils while still warm. Leave to cool.

3 Cut the frankfurters into diagonal slices and chop the onion finely.

4 Core and deseed the (bell) pepper and chop roughly.

5 Cut the celery into thin diagonal slices.

6 Skin the tomatoes and cut into slices, then add to the lentils with the frankfurters, onion, (bell) pepper, celery and herbs. Mix together well and transfer to a serving dish.

VARIATION

Instead of frankfurters, you could use cubes of smoked ham or chopped fried bacon.

MANGO & WILD RICE SALAD

SERVES 4

60 g/2 oz/ ⅓ cup wild rice
60 g/2 oz/ ⅓ cup basmati rice
3 tbsp hazelnut oil
1 tbsp sherry vinegar
1 small mango
2 celery sticks
60 g/2 oz/ ½ cup ready-to-eat dried
    apricots, chopped
60 g/2 oz/ ½ cup split almonds, browned
2 tbsp chopped fresh mint
salt and pepper

1 Cook the rice in separate saucepans in boiling salted water – the wild rice for 45–50 minutes, the basmati for 10–12 minutes. Drain, rinse well and drain again thoroughly.

2 Mix the oil, vinegar and seasoning together and pour over the rice in a bowl.

3 Cut the mango in half lengthways as close to the stone (pit) as possible. Remove the stone (pit), using a sharp knife.

4 Peel off the skin and cut the flesh into slices.

5 Slice the celery finely and add to the cooled rice with the apricots, mango, browned almonds and chopped mint. Mix together thoroughly and transfer to a serving bowl.

BROWNING ALMONDS

To brown almonds, place on a baking sheet in a moderate oven for 5–10 minutes until golden brown.

Alternatively, they can be browned under a moderate grill (broiler), turning frequently, as they burn quickly. Cool before adding to the salad so that they are crisp.

POTATOES IN OLIVE & TOMATO DRESSING

•••

SERVES 4

750 g/1½ lb waxy potatoes
1 shallot
2 tomatoes
1 tbsp chopped fresh basil
salt

TOMATO AND OLIVE DRESSING:
1 tomato, skinned and chopped finely
4 black olives, pitted and chopped finely
4 tbsp olive oil
1 tbsp wine vinegar
1 garlic clove, crushed
salt and pepper

1 Cook the potatoes in boiling salted water for 15 minutes until they are tender.

2 Drain the potatoes well, chop roughly and put into a bowl.

3 Chop the shallot. Cut the tomatoes into wedges and add the shallot and tomatoes to the potatoes.

4 To make the dressing, put all the ingredients into a screw-top jar and mix together thoroughly.

5 Pour the dressing over the potato mixture and toss thoroughly.

6 Transfer the salad to a serving dish and sprinkle with the chopped fresh basil.

TIPS

I often make this with floury (mealy) potatoes. It doesn't look so attractive, as the potatoes break up when they are cooked, but they absorb the dressing wonderfully.

Be sure to use an extra virgin olive oil for the dressing to give a really fruity flavour to the potatoes.

POTATO & SMOKED HAM MAYONNAISE

•••

SERVES 4

750 g/1½ lb new potatoes, scrubbed
4 spring onions (scallions), chopped
2 tbsp French Dressing (see page 52)
150 ml/ ¼ pint/ ⅔ cup mayonnaise
3 tbsp thick natural yogurt
1 tbsp Dijon mustard
2 eggs
250 g/8 oz slice of smoked ham
3 dill pickles
2 tbsp chopped fresh dill

1 Cook the potatoes in boiling salted water for 15 minutes until just tender, then drain.

2 Cut into pieces and put into a bowl while still warm with the spring onion (scallion) and dressing and mix together.

3 Mix the mayonnaise, yogurt and mustard together.

4 Boil the eggs for 12 minutes, then plunge into cold water to cool. Shell and chop roughly.

5 Cut the smoked ham into cubes and slice the dill pickles.

6 Add to the potatoes with the egg. Pour over the mayonnaise and mix together thoroughly, but carefully.

7 Transfer to a serving dish and sprinkle with the dill.

DILL

Dill is a very popular herb in Scandinavia, central Europe and Russia. It is particularly good with cucumber, beetroot, fish and potato dishes. It has very pretty delicate, feathery fronds which makes it an excellent garnish too. Fennel would be a good substitute, but has a stronger, more aniseedy flavour.

WARM BULGAR & CORIANDER (CILANTRO) SALAD

SERVES 4

175 g/6 oz/1½ cups bulgar wheat
1 onion
1 garlic clove
1 red (bell) pepper
3 tbsp olive oil
2 tsp ground cumin
2 tsp ground coriander
2 tomatoes
2 tbsp lemon juice
4 tbsp currants
2 tbsp chopped fresh coriander (cilantro)
4 tbsp pine kernels (nuts), browned

1 Soak the bulgar wheat in salted boiling water for 20 minutes. Chop the onion and garlic, and core, deseed and chop the red (bell) pepper.

2 Heat the oil in a pan and fry the onion, garlic and (bell) pepper for about 5 minutes until softened.

3 Add the spices and cook for a further 1 minute.

4 Drain the bulgar through a sieve (strainer), pressing out as much liquid as possible.

5 Chop the tomatoes, then add to the pan with the bulgar, lemon juice and currants and mix together thoroughly.

6 Transfer to a serving dish and sprinkle with the coriander (cilantro) and pine kernels (nuts). Serve while warm.

HELPFUL HINTS

Cous-cous can be used instead of bulgar wheat for this salad, and is prepared in a similar manner. Cous-cous is semolina grains that have been dampened and rolled in flour. Bulgar wheat is cracked wheat that has been partially cooked.

SWEET & SOUR TUNA SALAD

SERVES 4

2 tbsp olive oil
1 onion, chopped
2 garlic cloves, chopped
2 courgettes (zucchini), sliced
4 tomatoes, skinned
about 400 g/14 oz can flageolet (small navy) beans, drained
10 black olives, halved and pitted
1 tbsp capers
1 tsp caster (superfine) sugar
1 tbsp wholegrain mustard
1 tbsp white wine vinegar
200 g/7 oz can tuna fish, drained
2 tbsp chopped fresh parsley
ciabatta bread to serve

1 Heat the oil in a frying pan (skillet) and fry the onion, garlic and courgettes (zucchini) for 8 minutes, stirring occasionally.

2 Cut the tomatoes in half then into strips.

3 Add the tomatoes to the pan with the beans, olives, capers, sugar, mustard and vinegar to the pan. Simmer for 2 minutes then allow to cool for 15 minutes.

4 Flake the tuna fish and mix into the bean mixture with the parsley. Serve lukewarm with ciabatta bread.

CAPERS

Capers are the flower buds of the caper bush, which is native to the Mediterranean region. Capers are preserved in vinegar and salt and give a distinctive flavour to this salad. They are much used in Italian and Provençale cooking.

THREE-BEAN SALAD

••

SERVES 4–6

3 tbsp olive oil
1 tbsp lemon juice
1 tbsp tomato purée (paste)
1 tbsp light malt vinegar
1 tbsp chopped fresh chives
175 g/6 oz dwarf (thin) green beans
425 g/14 oz can soya beans, rinsed and
    drained
425 g/14 oz can red kidney beans, rinsed
    and drained
2 tomatoes, chopped
4 spring onions (scallions), trimmed and
    chopped
125 g/4 oz Feta cheese, cut into cubes
salt and pepper
mixed salad leaves (greens) to serve
chopped fresh chives to garnish

1 Put the olive oil, lemon juice, tomato
purée, vinegar and chives into a
large bowl and whisk together until
thoroughly combined.

2 Cook the dwarf (thin) green beans
in a little boiling, lightly salted water
until just cooked, about 4–5 minutes.
Drain, refresh under cold running water
and drain well.

3 Add the green beans, soya beans
and red kidney beans to the
dressing, stirring to mix together.

4 Add the tomatoes, spring onions and
Feta cheese to the bean mixture,
tossing gently to coat in the dressing.
Season well with salt and pepper.

5 Arrange the mixed salad leaves on 4
serving plates. Pile the bean salad on
to the plates and garnish with chopped
chives.

BEANS

You can substitute different types of
canned beans for the soya beans and
red kidney beans. Try haricot (navy)
beans, black-eye beans (peas) or chick-
peas (garbanzo beans) instead.

CHARGRILLED VEGETABLES WITH SIDEKICK DRESSING

••

SERVES 4

1 red (bell) pepper, cored and deseeded
1 orange or yellow (bell) pepper, cored
    and deseeded
2 courgettes (zucchini)
2 corn-on-the-cob
1 aubergine (eggplant)
olive oil for brushing
chopped fresh thyme, rosemary and
    parsley
salt and pepper

DRESSING:
2 tbsp olive oil
1 tbsp sesame oil
1 garlic clove, crushed
1 small onion, chopped finely
1 celery stick, chopped finely
1 small green chilli, deseeded and
    chopped finely
4 tomatoes, chopped
5 cm/2 inch piece cucumber, chopped
    finely
1 tbsp tomato purée (paste)
1 tbsp lime or lemon juice

1 To make the dressing, heat the olive
and sesame oils together in a
saucepan or frying pan (skillet). Add the
garlic and onion, and fry together gently
until softened, about 3 minutes.

2 Add the celery, chilli and tomatoes
to the pan and cook, stirring
occasionally, for 5 minutes over a medium
heat.

3 Stir in the cucumber, tomato purée
(paste) and lime or lemon juice, and
simmer for 8–10 minutes until thick and
pulpy. Season to taste with salt and
pepper.

4 Cut the vegetables into thick slices
and brush with a little olive oil.
Cook over the hot coals for about 5-8
minutes, sprinkling them with salt and
pepper and fresh herbs as they cook, and
turning once.

5 Divide the vegetables between
4 serving plates and spoon some of
the dressing on to the side. Serve at once,
sprinkled with chopped herbs.

THREE-WAY POTATO SALAD

EACH DRESSING SERVES 4

LIGHT CURRY DRESSING:
1 tbsp vegetable oil
1 tbsp medium curry paste
1 small onion, chopped
1 tbsp mango chutney, chopped
6 tbsp natural yogurt
3 tbsp single (light) cream
2 tbsp mayonnaise
salt and pepper
1 tbsp single (light) cream to garnish

WARM VINAIGRETTE DRESSING:
6 tbsp hazelnut oil
3 tbsp cider vinegar
1 tsp wholegrain mustard
1 tsp caster (superfine) sugar
few basil leaves, torn into shreds
salt and pepper

PARSLEY, SPRING ONION (SCALLION) &
   SOURED CREAM DRESSING:
150 ml/ ¼ pint/ ⅔ cup soured cream
3 tbsp light mayonnaise
4 spring onions (scallions), trimmed and
   chopped finely
1 tbsp chopped fresh parsley
salt and pepper
500 g/1lb new potatoes for each dressing
fresh herbs to garnish

1 To make the Light Curry Dressing, heat the vegetable oil in a saucepan and add the curry paste and onion. Fry together, stirring frequently, until the onion is soft, about 5 minutes. Remove from the heat and leave to cool slightly.

2 Mix together the mango chutney, yogurt, cream and mayonnaise. Add the curry mixture and blend together. Season with salt and pepper.

3 To make the Vinaigrette Dressing, whisk the hazelnut oil, cider vinegar, mustard, sugar and basil together in a small jug or bowl. Season with salt and pepper.

4 To make the Parsley, Spring Onion (Scallion) & Soured Cream Dressing, mix all the ingredients together until thoroughly combined. Season with salt and pepper.

5 Cook the potatoes in lightly salted boiling water until just tender. Drain well and leave to cool for 5 minutes, then add the chosen dressing, tossing to coat. Serve, garnished with fresh herbs, spooning a little single (light) cream on to the potatoes if using the curry dressing.

PIZZAS – INTRODUCTION

The pizza has become a universally popular food, in every form from the genuine article – thin, crisp and oven- baked – to frozen and fast-food pizza slices. The delightful aroma of freshly baked bread topped with tomatoes, fresh herbs and cheese rarely fails to have a mouthwatering effect. As well as being economical and popular, few other dishes are so versatile, thanks to the countless possible permutations of bases and toppings that can be served to suit every palate.

Although there is much speculation about where pizza in its simplest form was first invented, it is usually associated with the old Italian town of Naples. It was then a simple street food, richly flavoured and quickly made. It was not always round and flat as we know it today, but was originally folded up like a book, with the filling inside, and eaten by hand. Pizzas were usually sold on the streets by street criers who carried them around in copper cylindrical drums kept hot by coals from the pizza ovens.

The word pizza actually means any kind of pie. The classic Napoletana pizza is probably the best-known of the many varieties. This consists of a thin crust of dough topped simply with a fresh tomato sauce, Mozzarella cheese, olives, anchovies and a sprinkling of oregano. When baked, the flavours blend perfectly together to give the distinctive aromatic pizza. Another classic is the 'Margherita' pizza, named after the Italian Queen Margherita. Bored with their usual cuisine when on a visit to Naples, she asked to sample a local speciality. The local 'Pizzaiolo' created a pizza in the colours of the Italian flag – red tomatoes, green basil and white Mozzarella. The Queen was delighted, and it became widely celebrated.

THE BASIC INGREDIENTS
Pizzas are made from very basic ingredients and are very simple to cook. Although making your own base and topping can be a little time-consuming, it is very straightforward, and you end up with a delicious home-baked dish, as well as a sense of achievement.

Flour
Traditional pizza bases are made from bread dough, which is usually made with strong plain bread flour. However, for the best results use ordinary plain flour. A strong flour will make the dough very difficult to stretch into whatever shape you choose to make your pizza. For a brown bread base, use one of the many types of wholemeal flours available on the market, such as stoneground wholemeal , wheat meal and granary. Wheatgerm or bran can also be added to white flour for extra flavour, fibre and interest. Or you could mix equal quantities of wholemeal and white flour. Always sift the flour first, as this will remove any lumps and help to incorporate air, which will in turn help to produce a light dough. If you sift wholemeal flours, there will be some bran, etc. left in the sieve which is normally tipped back into the sifted flour so as to benefit from it.

Yeast thrives in warm surroundings, so all the ingredients for the bread dough base should be warm, as should the equipment used. If the yeast is added to a cold bowl containing cold flour, the tepid yeast liquid will quickly cool down and

INTRODUCTION

this will retard its growth, and the dough will take much longer to rise. If the flour is kept in a cool cupboard or larder, remember to get it out in plenty of time to allow it to warm to room temperature before you use it. Sift the flour into a large mixing bowl, then place it somewhere warm, such as an airing cupboard or even in a top oven on the lowest setting. Do not allow it to overheat, as this will kill the yeast.

Salt
Add the required amount of salt to the flour when sifting, as this will help to distribute it evenly. Salt is important, as it helps to develop the gluten in the flour. Gluten is the protein which produces the elasticity of the dough, but mostly it gives the dough its flavour.

Yeast
There are three types of yeast available: fresh, dried and easy-blend. Fresh is usually found in health-food shops and is not expensive. Dissolve 15g/½ oz fresh yeast in 90ml/3½ fl oz tepid water with 2.5ml/½ tsp sugar and allow it to froth before adding it to the flour about 5 minutes. The frothiness indicates that the yeast is working. Fresh yeast will keep for 4 to 5 days in the refrigerator. Make sure it is well covered, as it will dry out very quickly.

Dried yeast can be found in sachets or drums in most supermarkets and chemists. It has a shelf life of about 6 months, so buy only a small drum if you are not going to make bread dough on a regular basis. It is easy to make up a dough that won't rise, only to find out too late that the yeast has passed the sell-by date. Like fresh yeast, add it to the tepid water with a little

sugar, and stir to dissolve. Allow the mixture to stand for 10-15 minutes until froth develops on the surface.

Easy-blend yeast is the simplest to use, as it is simply stirred dry into the flour before the water is added. It is available in sachet form and can be found in most supermarkets.

Water
It has been said that Naples produces the best pizzas because of the quality of its water! But as that may be a bit far to travel just to make a pizza, your local water will suffice.

The water must be tepid, as this is the optimum temperature for the yeast to grow. Take care to add just the right amount of water stated in the recipe. If you add too much water, the dough will be difficult to handle and the cooked base will be too hard.

Kneading
This can be the most daunting procedure in bread-making but is a very necessary one. The best way of doing it is to take the edge of the dough that is furthest away from you and pull it into the centre towards you, then push it down with the heel of your hand, turning the dough round with your other hand as you go.

The kneading process mixes all the ingredients together and strengthens the gluten, which holds the bubbles of air created by the yeast, which in turn causes the dough to rise. The dough must be kneaded for at least 5 minutes or until it becomes smooth and pliable and is no longer sticky.

Try adding extra ingredients to the dough when kneading, such as chopped sun-dried tomatoes or olives to create a more interesting base.

INTRODUCTION

The tomato sauce

Every pizza must have tomato sauce of some kind as the basis of the topping. This can be made using either canned or fresh tomatoes. There are many types of canned tomato available – for example, plum tomatoes, or tomatoes chopped in water, or chopped, sieved tomato (passata). The chopped variety are often canned with added flavours such as garlic, basil, onion, chilli and mixed herbs, which will add more interest to your sauce. Make sure the sauce is well seasoned before adding it to your base, as a tasteless sauce will spoil your pizza.

Cheese

The cheese most often associated with the pizza is, of course, Mozzarella. It is a mild, white, delicate cheese traditionally made from buffalo milk. The best feature of this cheese as far as pizzas are concerned is its ability to melt and produce strings of cheese when a slice is cut and pulled away. It is sold in supermarkets, wrapped in small bags of whey to keep it moist. Slice, grate or cut Mozzarella into small pieces before placing it on the pizza. Many supermarkets stock bags of pre-grated Mozzarella cheese, which is a great timesaver.

The other cheeses most often found on pizzas are Parmesan and Cheddar. The recipes in this book use a variety of different cheeses. If you are using strongly flavoured topping ingredients such as anchovies and olives, a milder-tasting cheese may be more suitable.

TOPPING INGREDIENTS

There are a number of classic ingredients that are used regularly in pizza toppings, such as olives,

anchovies, capers, mushrooms, (bell) peppers, artichokes and chillies, but most ingredients are suitable, if used in complementary combinations. Be adventurous and experiment, but don't be afraid to stick to simple combinations of just two or three ingredients – often the simplest pizzas are the most delicious and the most memorable, as the flavours don't fight each other.

Herbs

Whenever possible, use fresh herbs. They are becoming more readily available, especially since the introduction of 'growing' herbs, small pots of herbs which you buy from the supermarket or greengrocer and grow at home. This not only ensures the herbs are as fresh as possible, but also provides a continuous supply.

If you use dried herbs, remember that you need only about one third of dried to fresh. The most popular pizza herbs are basil, oregano and parsley, although you can experiment with your favourite ones. Torn leaves of fresh basil on a tomato base is a simple but deliciously aromatic combination.

Baking

Traditionally pizzas are cooked in special ovens on a stone hearth. A large peel or paddle is used to slide them in and out. But at home it is best to place the dough on a baking sheet or in a pizza pan. The dough will expand while cooking, so make sure the baking sheet is big enough. Always push up the edge of the dough to form a rim to prevent the topping from spilling during cooking.

Time-savers

Fortunately for the busy cook, pizzas are an easy food to package and chill

INTRODUCTION

or freeze, ready to be cooked on demand. There is a wide range of ready-made pizza bases, either in packet form which only need to be mixed and shaped before they are ready for a topping, which can also be bought separately.

Pizzas are also sold complete with a variety of toppings, which you can bake as they are, or add more toppings yourself. Although they never seem to taste as good as a real homemade pizza, they can be very useful to keep on hand. Jars of peppers, sun-dried tomatoes and artichokes in olive oil make very good toppings, and will keep for quite a while in your larder.

Serving

Pizzas should be served as soon as they leave the oven. Cut the pizza into wedges or strips using a sharp knife or pizza cutter. As pizza slices are easy to eat by hand, they make great party food.

Crisp salads, coleslaw and garlic bread go well with pizzas and help to make a balanced meal. Due to their rich flavour pizzas are best served with a well-chilled Italian table wine such as Frascati, Valpolicella or Chianti. If you are not a wine drinker, beer will go with pizza just as well.

Freezing

Pizzas are ideal standby food, as you can make and freeze them in advance, and both the bread dough and the complete pizza can be frozen. Make up double quantities of dough and freeze the half that is unused after it has been kneaded. Wrap in clingfilm (plastic wrap) and place in a freezer bag. Defrost at room temperature and allow to rise as normal. Alternatively, rise and roll

out the dough, top with tomato sauce, cheese and any other topping ingredients and bake for only 10 minutes. Cool, wrap in a polythene bag and place in the freezer. Cook straight from the freezer in a hot oven for about 15 minutes.

The tomato sauce will keep well in a screw-topped jar in the refrigerator for up to a week, or can be placed in freezer-proof containers and frozen if you need to keep it for longer periods.

TIPS

Pizza bases and their ingredients
Buy fresh yeast in bulk and freeze in 15g/½ oz quantities ready to use whenever needed.

To give the base extra flavour and a different texture, try adding to the flour fresh or dried herbs, chopped nuts or seeds, such as poppy, sunflower and sesame.

Always use a good olive oil such as extra virgin for the best flavour.

If time is short, place the bread dough in a food processor for a few minutes to knead.

If you have made the bread dough or scone (biscuit) base too wet, add a little extra flour and work it in. If the base is too dry, add a little extra water or milk in the same way.

Bread dough bases can be kept for several days before being used. After kneading, carefully wrap in clingfilm (plastic wrap) to prevent them from drying out in the refrigerator. Allow extra time for the dough to rise, as it will take a while for the dough to warm up and for the yeast to work.

BREAD DOUGH BASE

MAKES ONE 25 CM/10 IN ROUND

15 g/ ½ oz fresh yeast or 1 tsp dried or
  easy-blend yeast
90 ml/3½ fl oz tepid water
½ tsp sugar
1 tbsp olive oil
175 g/6 oz plain flour
1 tsp salt

1 Combine the fresh yeast with the water and sugar in a bowl. If using dried yeast, sprinkle it over the surface of the water and whisk in until dissolved.

2 Leave the mixture to rest in a warm place for 10–15 minutes until frothy on the surface. Stir in the olive oil.

3 Sift the flour and salt into a large bowl. If using easy-blend yeast, stir it in at this point. Make a well in the centre and pour in the yeast liquid, or water and oil (without the sugar for easy-blend yeast).

4 Using either floured hands or a wooden spoon, mix together to form a dough. Turn out on to a floured work surface and knead for about 5 minutes until smooth and elastic.

5 Place in a large greased plastic bag and leave in a warm place for about 1 hour or until doubled in size. Airing cupboards are often the best places for this, as the temperature remains constant.

6 Turn out on to a lightly floured work surface and 'knock back' by punching the dough. This releases any air bubbles which would make the pizza uneven. Knead 4 or 5 times. The dough is now ready to use.

USING YEAST

Many people may be nervous about using yeast, but it is really quite simple, especially if you use an easy-blend variety. See page 205 for tips on cooking with yeast.

SCONE (BISCUIT) BASE

MAKES ONE 25 CM/10 IN ROUND

175 g/6 oz self-raising flour
½ tsp salt
30 g/1 oz butter
120 ml/4 fl oz milk

1 Sift the flour and salt into a bowl. Rub in the butter with your fingertips until it resembles fine breadcrumbs.

2 Make a well in the centre of the flour and butter mixture and pour in nearly all the milk at once. Mix in quickly with a knife. Add the remaining milk only if necessary to mix to a soft dough.

3 Turn the dough out on to a floured work surface and knead by turning and pressing with the heel of your hand 3 or 4 times.

4 Either roll out or press the dough into a 25 cm/10 in circle on a lightly greased baking sheet or pizza pan. Push up the edge all round slightly to form a ridge and use immediately.

ADDING TASTE

You can vary the taste of your biscuit base by adding a little grated cheese or ½ teaspoon dried oregano or mixed herbs to it for a more interesting flavour. Add your extra flavourings to the mixture after rubbing in the butter.

RUBBING IN

When rubbing in butter, it helps if your hands and the butter are very cold. Cut the butter into small dice first, then cut it into the flour with two knives held like scissors. Finally, rub in the remaining lumps of butter with your fingertips, remembering to keep your hands cool as you go.

POTATO BASE

MAKES ONE 25 CM/10 IN ROUND

250 g/8 oz boiled potatoes
60 g/2 oz butter or margarine
125 g/4 oz self-raising flour
½ tsp salt

1 If the potatoes are hot, mash them, then stir in the butter until it has melted and is distributed evenly throughout the potatoes. Leave to cool.

2 Sift the flour and salt together and stir into the mashed potato to form a soft dough.

3 If the potatoes are cold, mash them without adding the butter. Sift the flour and salt into a bowl. Rub in the butter with your fingertips until the mixture resembles fine breadcrumbs, then stir the flour and butter mixture into the mashed potatoes to form a soft dough.

4 Either roll out or press the dough into a 25 cm/10 in circle on a lightly greased baking sheet or pizza pan, pushing up the edge all round slightly to form a ridge before adding the topping. This base is tricky to lift before it is cooked, so you will find it easier to handle if you roll it out directly on the baking sheet.

5 If the base is not required for cooking immediately, you can cover it with clingfilm (plastic wrap) and chill it for up to 2 hours.

USING INSTANT COOKED POTATO

If time is short and you do not have any leftover cooked potato, make up a batch of instant dried mashed potato, keeping the consistency fairly dry, and use that instead.

TOMATO PIZZA SAUCE

MAKES ENOUGH TO COVER ONE 25 CM/10 IN PIZZA BASE

1 small onion, chopped
1 garlic clove, crushed
1 tbsp olive oil
220 g/7 oz can chopped tomatoes
2 tsp tomato purée
½ tsp sugar
½ tsp dried oregano
1 bay leaf
salt and pepper

1 Fry the onion and garlic gently in the oil for 5 minutes until softened but not browned.

2 Add the tomatoes, tomato purée, sugar, oregano, bay leaf and seasoning. Stir well.

3 Bring to the boil, cover and simmer gently for 20 minutes, stirring occasionally, until you have a thickish sauce.

4 Remove the bay leaf and adjust the seasoning to taste. Leave to cool completely before using. This sauce keeps well in a screw-top jar in the refrigerator for up to 1 week.

TOMATOES

Tomatoes are actually berries and are related to potatoes. There are many different shapes and sizes of this versatile fruit. The one most used in Italian cooking is the plum tomato. Large beefsteak tomatoes or small, sweet cherry tomatoes are ideal for use in accompanying salads.

SPECIAL TOMATO SAUCE

••

MAKES ENOUGH TO COVER ONE
25 CM/10 IN PIZZA BASE.

1 small onion, chopped
1 small red (bell) pepper, chopped
1 garlic clove, crushed
2 tbsp olive oil
250 g/8 oz tomatoes
1 tbsp tomato purée
1 tsp soft brown sugar
2 tsp chopped fresh basil
½ tsp dried oregano
1 bay leaf
salt and pepper

1 Fry the onion, (bell) pepper and
garlic gently in the oil for 5 minutes
until softened but not browned.

2 Cut a cross in the base of each
tomato and place them in a bowl.
Pour on boiling water and leave for about
45 seconds. Drain, and then plunge in
cold water. The skins will slide off easily.

3 Chop the tomatoes, discarding
any hard cores. Add the chopped
tomatoes, tomato purée, sugar, herbs and
seasoning to the onion mixture. Stir well.
Bring to the boil, cover and simmer gently
for 30 minutes, stirring occasionally, until
you have a thickish sauce.

4 Remove the bay leaf and adjust the
seasoning to taste. Leave to cool
completely before using.

5 This sauce will keep well in a screw-
top jar in the refrigerator for up to
a week.

SKINNING TOMATOES

You can skin tomatoes in another way
if you have a gas stove. Cut a cross in
the base of the tomato, push it on to a
fork and hold it over a gas flame,
turning it slowly so that the skin heats
evenly all over. The skin will start to
bubble and split, and should then slide
off easily.

CHICKEN SATAY

••

SERVES 2-4

2 tbsp crunchy peanut butter
1 tbsp lime juice
1 tbsp soy sauce
3 tbsp milk
1 red chilli, deseeded and chopped
1 garlic clove, crushed
175 g/6 oz cooked chicken, diced
1 quantity Bread Dough Base (see
  page 208)
1 quantity Special Tomato Sauce (see
  left)
4 spring onions (scallions), trimmed and
  chopped
60 g/2 oz Mozzarella cheese, grated
olive oil for drizzling
salt and pepper

1 Mix together the peanut butter, lime
juice, soy sauce, milk, chilli and
garlic in a bowl to form a sauce. Season
well.

2 Add the chicken to the peanut sauce
and stir until well coated. Cover and
leave to marinate in a cool place for
about 20 minutes.

3 Roll out or press the dough, using
a rolling pin or your hands, into
a 25 cm/10 in circle on a lightly floured
work surface. Place on a large greased
baking sheet or pizza pan and push up
the edge a little. Cover and leave to rise
slightly for 10 minutes in a warm place.

4 When the dough has risen, spread
with the tomato sauce almost to the
edge.

5 Top with the spring onions
(scallions) and chicken pieces,
spooning over the peanut sauce.

6 Sprinkle over the cheese. Drizzle
with a little olive oil and season
well. Bake in a preheated oven at
200°C/400°F/Gas Mark 6, for 18–20
minutes, or until the crust is golden.
Serve immediately with a simple
vegetable stir-fry.

AMERICAN HOT CHILLI BEEF

SERVES 2-4

FOR THE DOUGH BASE:
20 g/¼ oz fresh yeast or 1½ tsp dried or
*   easy-blend yeast*
125 ml/4 fl oz tepid water
1 tsp sugar
3 tbsp olive oil
250 g/8 oz plain flour
1 tsp salt

FOR THE TOPPING:
1 small onion, sliced thinly
1 garlic clove, crushed
½ yellow (bell) pepper, chopped
1 tbsp olive oil
175 g/6 oz lean minced (ground) beef
¼ tsp chilli powder
¼ tsp ground cumin
220 g/7 oz can red kidney beans, drained
1 quantity Tomato Pizza Sauce (see page
*   209)*
30 g/1 oz jalapeño chillies, sliced
60 g/2 oz Mozzarella cheese, sliced thinly
60 g/2 oz Monterey Jack cheese, grated
olive oil for drizzling
salt and pepper
chopped parsley to garnish

1 For the deep-pan dough base, use the same method as the Bread Dough Base recipe (see page 208).

2 Roll out or press the dough, using a rolling pin or your hands, into a 23 cm/9 in circle on a lightly floured work surface. Place on a pizza pan and push up the edge to fit and form a small ridge. Cover and leave to rise slightly for about 10 minutes.

3 Fry the onion, garlic and (bell) pepper gently in the oil for 5 minutes until softened but not browned. Increase the heat slightly and add the beef, chilli and cumin. Fry for 5 minutes, stirring occasionally. Remove from the heat and stir in the kidney beans. Season well.

4 Spread the tomato sauce over the dough almost to the edge and top with the meat mixture.

5 Top with the sliced chillies and Mozzarella cheese and sprinkle over the grated cheese. Drizzle with a little olive oil and season.

6 Bake in a preheated oven at 200°C/400°F/Gas Mark 6 for 18–20 minutes, or until the crust is golden. Serve sprinkled with chopped parsley.

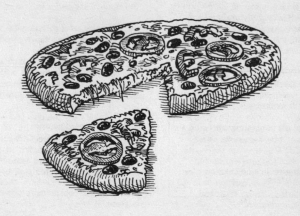

AUBERGINE (EGGPLANT) AND LAMB

SERVES 2–4

1 small aubergine (eggplant), diced
1 quantity Bread Dough Base (see page 208)
1 small onion, sliced thinly
1 garlic clove, crushed
1 tsp cumin seeds
1 tbsp olive oil
175 g/6 oz minced (ground) lamb
30 g/1 oz pimiento, sliced thinly
2 tbsp chopped fresh coriander (cilantro)
1 quantity Special Tomato Sauce (see page 210)
90 g/3 oz Mozzarella cheese, sliced thinly
olive oil for drizzling
salt and pepper

1 Sprinkle the diced aubergine (eggplant) with salt in a colander and let the bitter juices drain over a sink for about 20 minutes; then rinse and pat dry with paper towels.

2 Roll out or press the dough, using a rolling pin or your hands, into a 25 cm/10 in circle on a lightly floured work surface. Place on a large greased baking sheet or pizza pan and push up the edge a little to form a rim.

3 Cover and leave to rise slightly for 10 minutes in a warm place.

4 Fry the onion, garlic and cumin seeds gently in the oil for 3 minutes. Increase the heat slightly and add the lamb, aubergine (eggplant) and pimiento. Fry for 5 minutes, stirring occasionally. Add the coriander (cilantro) and season well.

5 Spread the tomato sauce over the dough base almost to the edge. Top with the lamb mixture.

6 Arrange the Mozzarella slices on top. Drizzle over a little olive oil and season.

7 Bake in a preheated oven at 200°C/400°F/Gas Mark 6 for 18–20 minutes, until the crust is crisp and golden. Serve immediately.

SMOKY BACON AND PEPPERONI

SERVES 2–4

1 quantity Bread Dough Base (see page 208)
1 tbsp olive oil
1 tbsp grated fresh Parmesan cheese
1 quantity Tomato Pizza Sauce (see page 209)
125 g/4 oz lightly smoked bacon, diced
½ green (bell) pepper, sliced thinly
½ yellow (bell) pepper, sliced thinly
60 g/2 oz pepperoni-style sliced spicy sausage
60 g/2 oz smoked Bavarian cheese, grated
½ tsp dried oregano
olive oil for drizzling
salt and pepper

1 Roll out or press the dough, using a rolling pin or your hands, into a 25 cm/10 in circle on a lightly floured work surface. Place on a large greased baking sheet or pizza pan and push up the edge a little with your fingers, to form a rim.

2 Brush the base with the olive oil and sprinkle the Parmesan cheese over it. Cover and leave to rise slightly in a warm place for about 10 minutes.

3 Spread the tomato sauce over the base almost to the edge. Top with the bacon and (bell) peppers. Arrange the pepperoni slices over and sprinkle with the smoked cheese.

4 Sprinkle over the oregano and drizzle with a little olive oil. Season.

5 Bake in a preheated oven at 200°C/400°F/Gas Mark 6 for 18–20 minutes, or until the crust is golden and crisp around the edge. Cut into wedges and serve immediately.

PEPPERONI

A spicy pepperoni-style sausage can be quite hot. If you prefer a milder taste, use slices of salami, chorizo or even sliced, cooked sausages in its place.

FOUR SEASONS

• •

SERVES 2-4

1 quantity Bread Dough Base (see page 208)
1 quantity Special Tomato Sauce (see page 210)
30 g/1 oz chorizo sausage, sliced thinly
30 g/1 oz button mushrooms, wiped and sliced thinly
45g/1½ oz artichoke hearts, sliced thinly
30 g/1 oz Mozzarella cheese, sliced thinly
3 anchovies, halved lengthways
2 tsp capers
4 pitted black olives, sliced
4 fresh basil leaves, shredded
olive oil for drizzling
salt and pepper

1 Roll out or press the dough, using a rolling pin or your hands, into a 25 cm/10 in circle on a lightly floured work surface. Place on a large greased baking sheet or pizza pan and push up the edge a little.

2 Cover and leave to rise slightly for 10 minutes in a warm place before spreading with tomato sauce almost to the edge.

3 Put the sliced chorizo on 1 quarter of the pizza, the sliced mushrooms on another, the artichoke hearts on a third and the Mozzarella cheese and anchovies on the fourth.

4 Dot the pizza with the capers, olives and basil leaves. Drizzle a little olive oil over the pizza and season. Do not put any salt on the anchovy section as the fish are very salty.

5 Bake in a preheated oven at 200°C/ 400°F/Gas Mark 6 for 18–20 minutes, or until the crust is golden and crisp. Serve immediately.

FISHY ALTERNATIVE

Fish-lovers could make a seafood four seasons pizza using prawns (shrimp), cockles, mussels and anchovies with one ingredient on each quarter, placed in a decorative arrangement.

MARINARA

• •

SERVES 2-4

1 quantity Potato Base (see page 209)
1 quantity Special Tomato Sauce (see page 210)
200 g/7 oz frozen seafood cocktail, defrosted
1 tbsp capers
1 small yellow (bell) pepper, chopped
1 tbsp chopped fresh marjoram
½ tsp dried oregano
60 g/2 oz Mozzarella cheese, grated
15g/½ oz Parmesan cheese, grated
12 black olives
olive oil for drizzling
salt and pepper
sprig of fresh marjoram or oregano to garnish

1 Roll out or press out the potato dough, using a rolling pin or your hands, into a 25 cm/10 in circle on a lightly floured work surface. Place on a large greased baking sheet or pizza pan and push up the edge a little with your fingers to form a rim.

2 Spread with the tomato sauce almost to the edge.

3 Arrange the seafood cocktail, capers and yellow (bell) pepper on the sauce.

4 Sprinkle over the herbs and cheeses. Arrange the olives on top. Drizzle over a little olive oil and season well.

5 Bake in a preheated oven at 200°C/400°F/Gas Mark 6 for 18–20 minutes until the edge of the pizza is crisp and golden.

6 Transfer to a warmed serving plate, garnish with a sprig of marjoram or oregano and serve immediately.

SEAFOOD TOPPING

If you prefer, you can replace any of the seafood with small pieces of monkfish, plaice, cod or slices of crabstick.

213

ALASKA PIZZA

••

SERVES 2-4

1 quantity Scone (Biscuit) Base (see page 208)
1 quantity Tomato Sauce (see page 209)
1 courgette (zucchini), grated
1 tomato, sliced thinly
100 g/3½ oz can red or pink salmon
60 g/2 oz button mushrooms, wiped and sliced
1 tbsp chopped fresh dill
½ tsp dried oregano
45 g/1½ oz Mozzarella cheese, grated
olive oil for drizzling
salt and pepper
sprig of fresh dill to garnish

1 Roll out or press the dough, using a rolling pin or your hands, into a 25 cm/10 in circle on a lightly floured work surface. Place on a large greased baking sheet or pizza pan and push up the edge a little with your fingers to form a rim.

2 Spread with the tomato sauce almost to the edge.

3 Top the tomato sauce with the grated courgette (zucchini), then lay the tomato slices on top.

4 Drain the can of salmon. Remove any bones and skin and flake the fish. Arrange on the pizza with the mushrooms. Sprinkle over the herbs and cheese. Drizzle with a little olive oil and season well.

5 Bake in a preheated oven at 200°C/400°F/Gas Mark 6, for 18–20 minutes, or until the edge is golden and crisp.

6 Transfer to a warmed serving plate and serve immediately, garnished with a sprig of dill.

ECONOMY VERSION

Tuna or sardines make a delicious and economical everyday fish pizza. Choose canned fish in brine for a healthier topping. If fresh dill is unavailable, use parsley instead.

FLORENTINE

••

SERVES 2-4

2 tbsp Parmesan cheese, grated
1 quantity Potato Base (see page 209)
1 quantity Tomato Sauce (see page 210)
175 g/6 oz fresh spinach leaves
1 small red onion, sliced thinly
2 tbsp olive oil
¼ tsp freshly grated nutmeg
2 hard-boiled eggs
15 g/ ½ oz fresh white breadcrumbs
60 g/2 oz Jarlsberg cheese, grated (or Emmental, Cheddar or Gruyère, if not available)
2 tbsp flaked (slivered) almonds
olive oil for drizzling
salt and pepper

1 Mix the Parmesan cheese with the potato base. Roll out or press the dough, using a rolling pin or your hands, into a 25 cm/10 in circle on a lightly floured work surface. Place on a large greased baking sheet or pizza pan and push up the edge slightly. Spread with the tomato sauce almost to the edge.

2 Remove the stalks from the spinach and wash the leaves thoroughly in plenty of cold water. Drain the spinach well and pat off the excess water with paper towels.

3 Fry the onion gently in the oil for 5 minutes until softened. Add the spinach and continue to fry until just wilted. Drain off any excess liquid produced. Place on the pizza and sprinkle over the nutmeg.

4 Remove the shells from the eggs and slice. Arrange on the spinach.

5 Mix together the breadcrumbs, cheese and almonds, and sprinkle over. Drizzle with a little olive oil and season well.

6 Bake in a preheated oven at 200°C/400°F/Gas Mark 6 for 18–20 minutes, or until the edge is crisp and golden. Serve immediately.

RATATOUILLE AND LENTIL

SERVES 2-4

60 g/2 oz green lentils
½ small aubergine (eggplant), diced
1 small onion, sliced
1 garlic clove, crushed
3 tbsp olive oil
½ courgette (zucchini), sliced
½ red (bell) pepper, sliced
½ green (bell) pepper, sliced
220 g/7½ oz can chopped tomatoes
1 tbsp chopped fresh oregano or 1 tsp dried
1 quantity Bread Dough Base made with wholemeal flour (see page 208)
60 g/2 oz vegetarian Cheddar cheese, sliced thinly
1 tbsp sunflower seeds
olive oil for drizzling
salt and pepper

1 Soak the lentils in hot water for 30 minutes. Drain and rinse; then simmer in a pan covered with fresh water for 10 minutes.

2 Sprinkle the aubergine (eggplant) with a little salt in a colander and allow the bitter juices to drain over a sink for about 20 minutes. Rinse and pat dry with paper towels.

3 Fry the onion and garlic gently in the oil for 3 minutes. Add the courgette (zucchini), (bell) peppers and aubergine (eggplant). Cover and leave to 'sweat' over a low heat for about 5 minutes.

4 Add the tomatoes, drained lentils, oregano, 2 tbsp water and seasoning. Cover and simmer for 15 minutes, stirring occasionally, adding more water if necessary.

5 Roll out or press the dough, using a rolling pin or your hands, into a 25 cm/10 in circle on a lightly floured work surface. Place on a large greased baking sheet or pizza pan and push up the edge slightly. Cover and leave to rise slightly for 10 minutes in a warm place.

6 Spread the ratatouille over the dough base almost to the edge. Arrange the cheese slices on top and sprinkle over the sunflower seeds. Drizzle with a little olive oil and season.

7 Bake in a preheated oven at 200°C/400°F/Gas Mark 6 for 18–20 minutes, or until the edge is crisp and golden. Serve immediately.

THREE CHEESE AND ARTICHOKE

SERVES 2-4

*1 quantity Bread Dough Base (see page
    208)*
*1 quantity Special Tomato Sauce (see page
    210)*
60 g/2 oz Dolcelatte cheese, sliced
125 g/4 oz artichoke hearts in oil, sliced
½ small red onion, chopped
45 g/1½ oz Cheddar cheese, grated
2 tbsp Parmesan cheese, grated
1 tbsp chopped fresh thyme
oil from artichokes for drizzling
salt and pepper

1 Roll out or press the dough, using
a rolling pin or your hands, into
a 25 cm/10 in circle on a lightly floured
work surface. Place the base on a large
greased baking sheet or pizza pan and
push up the edge slightly.

2 Cover and leave to rise for 10
minutes in a warm place. Spread
with the tomato sauce almost to the edge.

3 Arrange the Dolcelatte cheese on the
tomato sauce, followed by the
artichoke hearts and red onion.

4 Mix the Cheddar and Parmesan
cheeses together with the thyme and
sprinkle the mixture over the pizza.
Drizzle a little of the oil from the jar of
artichokes over the pizza and season to
taste.

5 Bake in a preheated oven at
200°C/400°F/Gas Mark 6 for 18–20
minutes, or until the edge is crisp and
golden and the cheese is bubbling.

6 Serve immediately with a fresh salad
of lettuce leaves and cherry tomato
halves.

CHEESES AND SALADS

You can use any cheese of your choice
but remember that a strongly flavoured
cheese will dominate the others. For
the accompanying salad, buy a bag of
mixed prepared lettuce leaves, as it
saves buying several whole lettuces of
different kinds.

GIARDINIERA

SERVES 2-4

6 fresh spinach leaves
1 quantity Potato Base (see page 209)
*1 quantity Special Tomato Sauce (see page
    210)*
1 tomato, sliced
1 celery stick, sliced thinly
½ green (bell) pepper, sliced thinly
1 baby courgette (zucchini), sliced
30 g/1 oz asparagus tips
30 g/1 oz sweetcorn, defrosted if frozen
30 g/1 oz peas, defrosted if frozen
*4 spring onions (scallions), trimmed and
    chopped*
*1 tbsp chopped fresh mixed herbs, such as
    tarragon and parsley*
60 g/2 oz Mozzarella cheese, grated
2 tbsp Parmesan cheese, grated
1 artichoke heart
olive oil for drizzling
salt and pepper

1 Remove any stalks from the spinach
and wash the leaves in plenty of
cold water. Pat dry with paper towels.

2 Roll out or press the potato base,
using a rolling pin or your hands,
into a large 25 cm/10 in circle on a lightly
floured work surface. Place the round on
a large greased baking sheet or pizza pan
and push up the edge a little to form a
rim. Spread with the tomato sauce.

3 Arrange the spinach leaves on the
sauce, followed by the tomato slices.
Top with the remaining vegetables and
herbs.

4 Mix together the cheeses and
sprinkle over. Place the artichoke
heart in the centre. Drizzle the pizza with
a little olive oil and season.

5 Bake in a preheated oven at
200°C/400°F/Gas Mark 6 for 18–20
minutes, or until the edges are crisp and
golden. Serve immediately.

SPINACH

Bags of pre-washed young spinach
leaves are available in most supermarkets. Use any surplus in a salad.

WILD MUSHROOM AND WALNUT

SERVES 2-4

1 quantity Scone (Biscuit) Base (see page 208)
1 quantity Special Tomato Sauce (see page 210)
125 g/4 oz soft cheese
1 tbsp chopped fresh mixed herbs, such as parsley, oregano and basil
250 g/8 oz wild mushrooms, such as oyster, shiitake or ceps, or 125 g/4 oz each wild and button mushrooms
2 tbsp olive oil
¼ tsp fennel seeds
30 g/1 oz walnuts, roughly chopped
45 g/1½ oz Roquefort cheese
olive oil to drizzle
salt and pepper
sprig of flat-leaf (Italian) parsley to garnish

1 Roll out or press the scone (biscuit) base, using a rolling pin or your hands, into a 25 cm/10 in circle on a lightly floured work surface. Place on a large greased baking sheet or pizza pan and push up the edge a little with your fingers to form a rim.

2 Spread with the tomato sauce almost to the edge. Dot with the soft cheese and herbs.

3 Wipe and slice the mushrooms. Heat the oil in a large frying pan or wok and stir-fry the mushrooms and fennel seeds for 2–3 minutes. Spread over the pizza with the walnuts.

4 Crumble the cheese over the pizza, drizzle with a little olive oil and season.

5 Bake in a preheated oven at 200°C/400°F/Gas Mark 6 for 18–20 minutes, or until the edge is crisp and golden. Serve immediately garnished with a sprig of flat-leaf (Italian) parsley.

MUSHROOMS

Wild mushrooms each have their own distinctive flavours but they can be expensive, so try using a mixture with crimini or button mushrooms instead.

ROASTED VEGETABLE AND GOAT'S CHEESE

SERVES 2-4

2 baby courgettes (zucchini), halved lengthways
2 baby aubergines (eggplant), quartered lengthways
½ red (bell) pepper, cut into 4 strips
½ yellow (bell) pepper, cut into 4 strips
1 small red onion, cut into wedges
2 whole garlic cloves
4 tbsp olive oil
1 tbsp red wine vinegar
1 tbsp chopped fresh thyme
1 quantity Bread Dough Base (see page 208)
1 quantity Tomato Pizza Sauce (see page 209)
90 g/3 oz goat's cheese
salt and pepper

1 Place all the prepared vegetables in a large roasting tin. Mix together the olive oil, vinegar, thyme and plenty of seasoning and pour over, coating all the vegetables well.

2 Bake in a preheated oven at 200°C/400°F/Gas Mark 6 for 15–20 minutes until the skins on the vegetables have started to blacken in places. Turn the vegetables over half-way through cooking. Leave the vegetables to rest for 5 minutes after roasting.

3 Carefully peel off the skins from the roast (bell) peppers and the garlic cloves. Slice the garlic.

4 Roll out or press the dough, using a rolling pin or your hands, into a 25 cm/10 in circle on a lightly floured work surface. Place on a large greased baking sheet or pizza pan and raise the edge a little. Cover and leave for 10 minutes to rise slightly in a warm place. Spread with the tomato sauce almost to the edge. Arrange the roasted vegetables on top and dot with the cheese. Drizzle the oil and juices from the roasting tin over the pizza and season.

5 Bake in a preheated oven at 200°C/400°F/Gas Mark 6 for 18–20 minutes, or until the edge is crisp and golden. Serve garnished with basil leaves.

TOFU CHINESE-STYLE

SERVES 2-4

1 litre/1¾ pints milk
1 tsp salt
250 g/8 oz semolina
1 tbsp soy sauce
1 tbsp dry sherry
½ tsp fresh grated ginger root
285 g/9½ oz pack tofu, cut into chunks
2 eggs
60 g/2 oz Parmesan cheese, grated
1 quantity Tomato Pizza Sauce (see page 209)
30 g/1 oz baby sweetcorn, cut into 4
30 g/1 oz mangetout (snow peas), trimmed and cut into 4
4 spring onions (scallions), trimmed and cut into 2.5 cm/1 in strips
60 g/2 oz Mozzarella cheese, sliced thinly
2 tsp sesame oil
salt and pepper

1 Bring the milk to the boil with the salt. Sprinkle the semolina over the surface, stirring all the time. Cook for 10 minutes over a low heat, stirring occasionally, taking care not to let it burn. Remove from the heat and leave to cool until tepid.

2 Mix the soy sauce, sherry and ginger together in a bowl, add the tofu and stir gently to coat. Leave to marinate in a cool place for about 20 minutes.

3 Beat the eggs with a little pepper. Add to the semolina with the Parmesan cheese and mix well. Place on a large greased baking sheet or in a pizza pan and pat into a 25 cm/10 in round, using the back of a metal spoon or wetted hands. Spread with the tomato sauce almost to the edge.

4 Blanch the sweetcorn and mangetout (snow peas) in boiling water for 1 minute, drain and place on the pizza with the drained tofu. Top with the spring onions (scallions) and slices of cheese. Drizzle over the sesame oil and season.

5 Bake in a preheated oven at 200°C/400°F/Gas Mark 6 for 18–20 minutes, or until the edge is crisp and golden. Serve immediately.

PISSALADIÈRE

MAKES 6 SQUARES

4 tbsp olive oil
3 onions, sliced thinly
1 garlic clove, crushed
1 tsp soft brown sugar
½ tsp crushed fresh rosemary
220 g/7½ oz can chopped tomatoes
1 quantity Bread Dough Base (see page 208)
2 tbsp grated Parmesan cheese
60 g/2 oz can anchovies
12–14 black olives
salt and black pepper

1 Heat 3 tbsp of the oil in a large saucepan and add the onions, garlic, sugar and rosemary. Cover the pan and fry gently for 10 minutes until the onions have softened but not browned, stirring occasionally. Add the tomatoes, stir and season well. Leave to cool slightly.

2 Roll out or press the dough, using a rolling pin or your hands, on a lightly floured work surface to fit a 30 x 18 cm/12 x 7 in greased Swiss roll tin. Place in the tin and push up the edges slightly.

3 Brush the remaining oil over the dough and sprinkle with the cheese. Cover and leave to rise slightly in a warm place for about 10 minutes.

4 Spread the onion and tomato topping over the base. Remove the anchovies from the can, reserving the oil. Split each anchovy in half lengthways and arrange on the pizza in a lattice pattern. Place olives in between the anchovies and drizzle over a little of the reserved oil. Season.

5 Bake in a preheated oven at 200°C/400°F/Gas Mark 6 for 18–20 minutes, or until the edges are crisp and golden. Cut into squares and serve immediately.

HAWAIIAN MUFFINS

••

SERVES 4

4 muffins
1 quantity Tomato Pizza Sauce (see page
209)
2 sun-dried tomatoes in oil, chopped
60 g/2 oz prosciutto ham
2 rings canned pineapple, chopped
½ green (bell) pepper, chopped
125 g/4 oz Mozzarella cheese, sliced thinly
olive oil for drizzling
salt and pepper
small fresh basil leaves to garnish

1 Cut the muffins in half and toast the cut side lightly.

2 Divide the sauce evenly between the muffins and spread over. Sprinkle over the sun-dried tomatoes.

3 Cut the ham into thin strips and place on the muffins with the pineapple and green (bell) pepper. Lay the Mozzarella slices on top.

4 Drizzle a little olive oil over each pizza, and season.

5 Place under a preheated medium grill and cook until the cheese melts and bubbles.

6 Serve immediately garnished with small basil leaves.

MUFFINS

You don't have to use plain muffins for your base; wholemeal or cheese muffins also make ideal pizza bases. Muffins freeze well, so keep some in the freezer for an instant pizza.

PREPARING PINEAPPLE

To prepare a fresh pineapple, slice off the skin from the top, bottom and sides. Remove the eyes with a sharp knife or the end of a potato peeler. Cut the pineapple into chunks. The pineapple will lose a lot of juice as you peel it – save this to drink later.

FRENCH BREAD PIZZAS

••

SERVES 4

2 baguettes
1 quantity Tomato Pizza Sauce (see page
209)
4 plum tomatoes, sliced thinly lengthways
150 g/5 oz Mozzarella cheese, sliced thinly
10 black olives, cut into rings
8 fresh basil leaves, shredded
olive oil for drizzling
salt and pepper

1 Cut the baguettes in half lengthways and toast the cut side of the bread lightly. Spread with the tomato sauce.

2 Arrange the tomato and Mozzarella cheese slices alternately along the length.

3 Top with the olive rings and half the basil. Drizzle over a little olive oil and season well.

4 Either place under a preheated medium grill (broiler) and cook until the cheese melts and is bubbling or bake in a preheated oven at 200°C/400°F/Gas Mark 6 for 15–20 minutes.

5 Sprinkle over the remaining basil and serve immediately.

INSTANT PIZZA

Make up double quantities and freeze half of the pizzas. Reheat them from frozen in the oven for about 15 minutes for an instant snack.

DIFFERENT BREAD BASES

There are many different types of bread available which would be suitable for these pizzas. Italian ciabatta bread is made with olive oil and is available both plain and with different ingredients, such as small pieces of black olives or sun-dried tomatoes, mixed in.

CALZONE

••

SERVES 2-4

1 quantity Bread Dough Base (see page
    208)
1 egg, beaten
1 tomato
1 tbsp tomato purée
30 g/1 oz Italian salami, chopped
30 g/1 oz mortadella ham, chopped
30 g/1 oz Ricotta cheese
2 spring onions (scallions), trimmed and
    chopped
¼ tsp dried oregano
salt and pepper

1 Roll out the dough into a 23 cm/
  9 in circle on a lightly floured work
surface.

2 Brush the edge of the dough with a
  little beaten egg.

3 To skin the tomato, cut a cross in
  the skin and immerse it in boiling
water for 45 seconds. Remove and rinse
in cold water; the skin should slide off
easily. Chop the tomato.

4 Spread the tomato purée over half
  the circle nearest to you. Scatter the
salami, mortadella and chopped tomato
on top. Dot with the Ricotta cheese and
sprinkle over the spring onions (scallions)
and oregano. Season well.

5 Fold over the other half of the
  dough to form a half moon. Press
the edges together well to prevent the
filling from coming out.

6 Place on a baking sheet and brush
  with beaten egg to glaze. Make a
hole in the top to allow steam to escape.

7 Bake in a preheated oven at
  200°C/400°F/Gas Mark 6 for 20
minutes, or until golden.

VEGETARIAN VERSION

For a vegetarian calzone, replace the
salami and mortadella with
mushrooms or cooked chopped
spinach.

CALIFORNIAN

••

MAKES 8

1 quantity Bread Dough Base (see page
    208)
2 tbsp olive oil
½ each red, green and yellow (bell) pepper,
    sliced thinly
1 small red onion, sliced thinly
1 garlic clove, crushed
1 quantity Tomato Pizza Sauce (see page
    209)
3 tbsp raisins
30 g/1 oz pine kernels
1 tbsp chopped fresh thyme
olive oil for drizzling
salt and pepper

1 Roll out or press the dough, using a
  rolling pin or your hands, on a
lightly floured work surface to fit a 30 x
18 cm/12 x 7 in greased Swiss roll tin.

2 Place in the tin and push up the
  edges slightly.

3 Cover and leave to rise slightly in a
  warm place for about 10 minutes.

4 Heat the oil in a large frying pan.
  Add the (bell) peppers, onion and
garlic, and fry gently for 5 minutes until
they have softened but not browned.
Leave to cool.

5 Spread the tomato sauce over the
  base almost to the edge.

6 Sprinkle over the raisins and top
  with the cooled (bell) pepper
mixture. Add the pine kernels and thyme.
Drizzle with a little olive oil and season
well.

7 Bake in a preheated oven at
  200°C/400°F/Gas Mark 6 for 18–20
minutes, or until the edges are crisp and
golden. Cut into fingers and serve
immediately.

RAISINS

Soak the raisins in some warm water
for 15 minutes before adding them to
the pizza, as this will keep them plump
and moist when they are baked.

MINI PITTA BREAD CANAPÉS

MAKES 16

8 thin asparagus spears
16 mini pitta breads
1 quantity Special Tomato Sauce (see page 210)
30 g/1 oz mild Cheddar cheese, grated
30 g/1 oz Ricotta cheese
60 g/2 oz smoked salmon
olive oil for drizzling
pepper

1 Cut the asparagus spears into 2.5 cm/1 in lengths; then cut each piece in half lengthways.

2 Blanch the asparagus in boiling water for 1 minute. Drain and plunge into cold water.

3 Place the pitta breads on 2 baking sheets. Spread about 1 tsp tomato sauce on each.

4 Mix the cheeses together and divide between the 16 pitta breads.

5 Cut the smoked salmon into 16 long thin strips. Arrange one strip on each pitta bread with the asparagus spears.

6 Drizzle over a little olive oil and season with pepper.

7 Bake in a preheated oven at 200°C/400°F/Gas Mark 6 for 8–10 minutes. Serve immediately.

ASPARAGUS

Blanching the asparagus helps to soften it before topping the canapes. Plunge it into cold water after blanching, as this helps it to keep its colour.

ECONOMY VERSIONS

Smoked salmon is expensive, so for a cheaper version, use smoked trout which tastes just as good. Experiment with other smoked fish, such as smoked mackerel, with its strong, distinctive flavour, for a bit of variety.

CORNED BEEF HASH

SERVES 2–4

500 g/1 lb potatoes
3 tbsp soured cream
325 g/11 oz can corned beef
1 small onion, chopped finely
1 green (bell) pepper, chopped
3 tbsp tomato and chilli relish
1 quantity Special Tomato Sauce (see page 210)
4 eggs
30 g/1 oz Mozzarella cheese, grated
30 g/1 oz Cheddar cheese, grated
paprika
salt and pepper
chopped fresh parsley to garnish

1 Peel the potatoes and cut into even-sized chunks. Parboil them for 5 minutes in boiling salted water. Drain, rinse in cold water and cool.

2 Grate the potatoes and mix with the soured cream and seasoning in a bowl. Place on a large greased baking sheet or pizza pan and pat out into a 25 cm/10 in circle, pushing up the edge slightly to form a rim.

3 Mash the corned beef roughly with a fork and stir in the onion, green (bell) pepper and relish. Season well.

4 Spread the tomato sauce over the potato base almost to the edge. Top with the corned beef mixture. Using a spoon, make 4 wells in the corned beef. Break an egg into each.

5 Mix the cheeses together and sprinkle over the pizza with a little paprika. Season well.

6 Bake in a preheated oven at 200°C/400°F/Gas Mark 6 for 20–25 minutes until the eggs have cooked but still have slightly runny yolks. Serve immediately garnished with chopped parsley.

SPICY MEATBALL

SERVES 2-4

250 g/8 oz lean minced (ground) beef
30 g/1 oz jalapeño chillies in brine,
   chopped
1 tsp cumin seeds
1 tbsp chopped fresh parsley
1 tbsp beaten egg
3 tbsp olive oil
1 quantity Scone (Biscuit) Base (see page
   208)
1 quantity Tomato Pizza Sauce (see page
   209)
30 g/1 oz pimiento, sliced
2 rashers streaky bacon, cut into strips
60 g/2 oz Cheddar cheese, grated
olive oil for drizzling
salt and pepper
chopped fresh parsley to garnish

1 Mix the beef, chillies, cumin seeds,
parsley and egg together in a bowl
and season. Form into 12 small meatballs.
Cover and chill for 1 hour.

2 Heat the oil in a large frying pan.
Add the meatballs and brown all
over. Remove with a perforated spoon or
fish slice and drain on paper towels.

3 Roll out or press the dough, using
a rolling pin or your hands, into a
25 cm/10 in circle on a lightly floured
work surface. Place on a greased baking
sheet or pizza pan and push up the edge
slightly to form a rim. Spread with the
tomato sauce almost to the edge.

4 Arrange the meatballs on the pizza
with the pimiento and bacon.
Sprinkle over the cheese and drizzle with
a little olive oil. Season.

5 Bake in a preheated oven at
200°C/400°F/Gas Mark 6 for 18–20
minutes, or until the edge is golden and
crisp.

6 Serve immediately garnished with
chopped parsley.

AVOCADO AND HAM

SERVES 2-4

1 quantity Bread Dough Base (see page
   208)
4 sun-dried tomatoes, chopped
30 g/1 oz black olives, chopped
1 quantity Special Tomato Sauce (see page
   210)
4 small chicory (endive) leaves, shredded
4 small radicchio lettuce leaves, shredded
1 avocado, peeled, pitted and sliced
60 g/2 oz wafer-thin smoked ham
60 g/2 oz Pipo Crème or other blue cheese,
   cut into small pieces
olive oil for drizzling
salt and pepper
chopped fresh chervil to garnish

1 Knead the dough gently, adding the
sun-dried tomatoes and olives until
mixed in.

2 Roll out or press the dough, using
a rolling pin or your hands, into a 25
cm/10 in circle on a lightly floured work
surface. Place on a greased baking sheet
or pizza pan and push up the edge a little
to form a rim.

3 Cover and leave to rise slightly in a
warm place for 10 minutes before
spreading with tomato sauce almost to the
edge.

4 Top the pizza with shredded lettuce
leaves and avocado slices.

5 Scrunch up the ham and add with
the cheese.

6 Drizzle with a little olive oil and
season well.

7 Bake in a preheated oven at
200°C/400°F/Gas Mark 6 for 18–20
minutes, or until the edge is crisp and
golden.

8 Sprinkle with chervil to garnish and
serve immediately.

MICROWAVE – INTRODUCTION

Microwave ovens have revolutionized cooking. Unlike conventional cookers, where you can feel the heat, microwave ovens appear to cook the food without any direct source of heat. There is a whole new set of guidelines and rules to be followed but common sense is the main requirement when using a microwave oven.

There are many advantages to cooking in a microwave oven instead of using conventional methods. Due to shorter cooking times and the small amount of water needed, vegetables, fish and white meats cook extremely well. The flavours and colours remain bright and fresh, while the textures are tender and the maximum number of nutrients are preserved.

Microwave ovens are safe, easy to use, economical and time-saving. No installation is required and, being relatively small appliances, they do not take up too much space in your kitchen. They can be placed on a work surface, a shelf, or be built in as part of a fitted kitchen. There is very little splatter or soiling in the oven, especially as most foods need to be covered during cooking. Any minor spills will not become baked on the insides of the oven, so they can be wiped away easily with a damp cloth. Running costs are low, as the energy concentrates on the food and not the surrounding areas. Microwave ovens work instantly and do not have to be preheated like conventional ovens.

Kitchens remain cool and free of steam, which is an added advantage when cooking in the summer. The microwave oven itself remains relatively cool, and there are no hot parts on which a user can be burnt. Microwave cooking contributes to a healthier diet. Firstly, more nutrients are retained in the food; secondly, foods can be cooked with little or no added fat; and thirdly, microwave ovens are wonderful for cooking low cholesterol foods such as poultry, fish and vegetables.

WHAT ARE MICROWAVES?

Microwaves are invisible, high-frequency, electromagnetic waves of energy that are present in the atmosphere. They occur naturally as well as from artificial sources, and are similar to the waves that convey radio, television and radar signals.

Microwaves are absorbed by the moisture molecules, such as water, fat and sugar, that are present in foods. They cause these molecules to vibrate at an intense rate, and as they vibrate they knock into each other, causing friction and therefore heat. Unlike conventional cooking, which starts heating the food from the outside and gradually works its way in, microwaves penetrate the food up to a depth of 5 cm/2 in over all the surface. The heat spreads rapidly throughout the food by conduction.

As microwaves are absorbed by moisture in food, they pass through materials such as glass, china, paper and some plastics. Microwaves are reflected by metal, therefore the microwaves bounce off the metal walls of the cavity until they are absorbed by the food.

Cooking Times

All the recipes in this book were tested on an 800-watt microwave oven. If your oven has a different output, adjust the cooking time as follows:

600 watt – add 20 seconds per minute
650 watt – add 15 seconds per minute

INTRODUCTION

700 watt – add 10 seconds per minute
750 watt – add 5 seconds per minute
850 watt – subtract 5 seconds per minute

The power levels vary on microwave ovens, but as a guide:

HIGH	= 100%
MEDIUM	= 50 – 60%
LOW	= 45 – 50%
DEFROST/SIMMER	= 30%
WARM	= 10%

GENERAL GUIDELINES

Arranging the food.
To ensure even cooking, space the foods evenly apart and never pile them on top of each other. Arrange smaller items of food, such as meatballs or broccoli florets, in a circle around the edge of a plate. Place denser, thicker items at the edge of a dish or on a plate so they receive the maximum microwave energy. Spread food out to give an even depth in the dish.

Rearranging the food
Some microwave ovens have hot spots. These are caused by microwaves being more concentrated in some areas than in others, which can result in food cooking unevenly. Microwaves are less concentrated in the centre of the oven, the corners and near the walls. Rearranging foods helps to get over this effect. Be sure to turn over larger items, such as joints of meat, to promote even cooking.

Shape
Cut food into small pieces to allow fast, even cooking. Choose similar-sized foods such as jacket potatoes and chops.

Quantity
Small quantities of food will cook faster than large quantities. Sometimes it may be necessary and more beneficial to cook food in smaller batches. If necessary, keep the first batch hot by covering or wrapping it in foil after cooking.

Prick or score
Foods which have a skin or membranes, such as sausages, unpeeled fruit, jacket potatoes or egg yolks, should be pricked or scored in several places. This allows the food to expand naturally and prevents it from bursting.

Covering food
Always cover foods when it is instructed in the recipe, as this reduces the cooking time, helps to retain moisture and prevents food splattering the oven walls. Dishes which are usually covered during conventional cooking generally require covering in a microwave oven. Foods which are meant to have a dry finish – such as cakes, biscuits (cookies) and breads – should not be covered.

Casserole dishes or specialized micro-wave dishes with lids are the most suitable containers to use for covered cooking. Alternatively, a plate or saucer may do just as well. Foods high in fat, such as bacon, can be covered with a paper towel. The towel soaks up splattering fat, and keeps the microwave oven free of debris inside. Remove the paper from the bacon after it has finished cooking, as paper has a habit of sticking to meat. Foods can also be cooked inside roasting bags. If the bag is too small to enclose the food, place it over the top like a tent.

SPICED KIDNEYS

SERVES 4

175 g/6 oz/scant cup long-grain rice
550 ml/18 fl oz/2¼ cups boiling water
8 lamb's kidneys, skinned, halved and
  cored
30 g/1 oz/2 tbsp butter
1 small onion, sliced
2 tbsp plain (all-purpose) flour
1 tsp chilli powder
2 slices back bacon, chopped
4 tbsp medium dry sherry
2 tbsp water
2 tbsp double (heavy) cream
salt and pepper
chopped fresh parsley to garnish

1 Place the rice in a large bowl. Pour over the boiling water. Add ½ teaspoon of salt. Cover and cook on HIGH power for 14 minutes, stirring from time to time until the rice is tender and the water has been absorbed. Leave to stand, covered, while cooking the kidneys.

2 Cut each kidney half into 3 and rinse in cold water. Drain well.

3 Place the butter and onion in a large bowl. Cover and cook on HIGH power for 2 minutes.

4 Mix the flour, chilli powder and seasoning in a bowl. Add the kidneys and toss well to coat. Add the kidneys and bacon to the onion. Cover and cook on HIGH power for 4 minutes.

5 Mix the sherry with the water. Stir into the kidney mixture, cover and cook on MEDIUM power for 15 minutes until the kidneys are tender.

6 Stir in the cream and adjust the seasoning. Garnish with parsley and serve with the rice.

TIP

Place the flour, chilli powder and seasonings in a large plastic bag, add the kidneys in batches and shake well to coat them evenly.

MUSSELS WITH TOMATO SAUCE

SERVES 2–4

½ small onion, chopped
1 garlic clove, crushed
1 tbsp olive oil
3 tomatoes
1 tbsp chopped fresh parsley
900 g/2 lb live mussels
1 tbsp freshly grated Parmesan cheese
1 tbsp fresh white breadcrumbs
salt and pepper
chopped fresh parsley to garnish

1 Place the onion, garlic and oil in a bowl. Cover and cook on HIGH power for 3 minutes.

2 Cut a cross in the base of each tomato and place them in a small bowl. Pour on boiling water and leave for about 45 seconds. Drain and then plunge into cold water. The skins will slide off easily. Chop the tomatoes, removing any hard cores.

3 Add the tomatoes to the onion mixture, cover and cook on HIGH power for 3 minutes. Stir in the parsley and season to taste.

4 Scrub the mussels well in several changes of cold water. Remove the beards and discard any open mussels and those which do not close when tapped smartly with the back of a knife.

5 Place the mussels in a large bowl. Add enough boiling water to cover them. Cover and cook on HIGH power for 2 minutes, stirring halfway through, until the mussels open. Drain well and remove the empty half of each shell. Arrange the mussels in 1 layer on a plate.

6 Spoon the tomato sauce over each mussel. Mix the Parmesan cheese with the breadcrumbs and sprinkle on top. Cook, uncovered, on HIGH power for 2 minutes. Garnish with parsley and serve.

FRUITY STUFFED BACON CHOPS

SERVES 4

60 g/2 oz/ ¼ cup green lentils, washed
1 celery stick, sliced
2 spring onions (scallions), chopped
4 thick cut tendersweet bacon chops
1 tbsp chopped fresh sage
4 apricot halves canned in natural juice,
   drained and chopped
1 tsp cornflour (cornstarch)
4 tbsp natural juice from can of apricots
2 tbsp fresh orange juice
1 tsp grated orange rind
1 tbsp crème fraîche or soured cream
salt and pepper
orange slices
sprigs of fresh sage

1 Place the lentils and celery in a
   bowl. Pour on boiling water to cover
them. Cover and cook on HIGH power
for 18–20 minutes until tender, adding
extra water if necessary. Add the spring
onions (scallions) for the last minute of
cooking. Leave to stand, covered, for 10
minutes.

2 Using a sharp knife, slit the meaty
   end of each chop nearly through to
the fat side, to form a pocket.

3 Drain the lentils and mix with half of
   the sage and the apricots. Season to
taste.

4 Spoon the lentil stuffing into the
   pockets in the bacon chops. Arrange
2 on a plate. Cover with a paper towel.
Cook on HIGH power for 4 minutes until
cooked through. Transfer to warmed
plates, cover and keep warm while
cooking the remaining stuffed chops.

5 Mix the cornflour (cornstarch) with a
   little water in a bowl, then stir in the
juice from the apricots, and the orange
juice and rind. Cover and cook on HIGH
power for 2 minutes, stirring every 30
seconds. Stir in the crème fraîche or
soured cream and remaining sage. Season
to taste and reheat on HIGH power for 30
seconds.

6 Serve the bacon chops with the
   sauce spooned over. Garnish with
orange slices and sprigs of fresh sage.

PASTA & LAMB LOAF

SERVES 3–4

15 g/ ½ oz/1 tbsp butter
½ small aubergine (eggplant), diced
60 g/2 oz multi-coloured fusilli
2 tsp olive oil
250 g/8 oz/1 cup minced (ground) lamb
½ small onion, chopped
½ red (bell) pepper, chopped
1 garlic clove, crushed
1 tsp dried mixed herbs
2 eggs, beaten
2 tbsp single (light) cream
salt and pepper

TO SERVE:
salad
pasta sauce of your choice

1 Place the butter in a 500 g/1 lb loaf
   dish. Cook on HIGH power for 30
seconds until melted. Brush over the
base and sides. Sprinkle the aubergine
(eggplant) with salt, put in a colander and
leave to drain over a sink for about 20
minutes. Rinse the aubergine (eggplant)
well and pat dry with paper towels.

2 Place the pasta in a bowl, add a little
   salt and boiling water to cover by
2.5 cm/1 inch. Cover and cook on HIGH
power for 8 minutes, stirring halfway
through. Leave to stand, covered, for a
few minutes.

3 Place the oil, lamb and onion in a
   bowl. Cover and cook on HIGH
power for 2 minutes.

4 Break up any lumps of meat using a
   fork. Add the (bell) pepper, garlic,
herbs and aubergine (eggplant). Cover
and cook on HIGH power for 5 minutes,
stirring.

5 Drain the pasta and add to the lamb
   with the eggs and cream. Season
well. Turn into the loaf dish and pat
down using the back of a spoon.

6 Cook on MEDIUM power for 10
   minutes until firm to the touch.
Leave to stand for 5 minutes before
turning out. Serve in slices with a salad
and a ready made pasta sauce.

SALMON & MUSHROOM LASAGNE ROLLS

••

SERVES 4

8 sheets green lasagne
1 onion, sliced
15 g/ ½ oz/1 tbsp butter
½ red (bell) pepper, chopped
1 courgette (zucchini), diced
1 tsp chopped ginger root
125 g/4 oz oyster mushrooms, preferably
  yellow, chopped coarsely
250 g/8 oz fresh salmon fillet, skinned,
  and cut into chunks
2 tbsp dry sherry
2 tsp cornflour (cornstarch)
20 g/ ¾ oz/3 tbsp plain (all-purpose) flour
20 g/ ¾ oz/1½ tbsp butter
300 ml/ ½ pint/1¼ cups milk
30 g/1 oz/ ¼ cup Cheddar cheese, grated
15 g/ ½ oz/ ¼ cup fresh white breadcrumbs
salt and pepper
salad to serve

1 Place the lasagne sheets in a large shallow dish. Cover with plenty of boiling water. Cook on HIGH power for 5 minutes. Leave to stand, covered, for a few minutes before draining. Rinse in cold water and lay the sheets out on a clean work surface.

2 Put the onion and butter into a bowl. Cover and cook on HIGH power for 2 minutes. Add the (bell) pepper, courgette (zucchini) and ginger root. Cover and cook on HIGH power for 3 minutes.

3 Add the mushrooms and salmon to the bowl. Mix the sherry into the cornflour (cornstarch) then stir into the bowl. Cover and cook on HIGH power for 4 minutes until the fish flakes when tested with a fork. Season to taste.

4 Whisk the flour, butter and milk in a bowl. Cook on HIGH power for 3–4 minutes, whisking every minute, to give a sauce of coating consistency. Stir in half the cheese and season to taste.

5 Spoon the salmon filling in equal quantities along the shorter side of each lasagne sheet. Roll up to enclose the filling. Arrange in a lightly oiled large rectangular dish. Pour over the sauce and sprinkle over the remaining cheese and the breadcrumbs.

6 Cook on HIGH power for 3 minutes until heated through. If possible, lightly brown under a preheated grill (broiler) before serving. Serve with salad.

MEXICAN BEEF

SERVES 4

250 g/8 oz/1 generous cup brown rice
700 ml/1¼ pints/3 cups boiling water
½ tsp salt
2 tbsp oil
1 onion, sliced into rings
1 carrot, cut into thin matchsticks
½ each red, green and yellow (bell)
  peppers, sliced
½–1 fresh green chilli, deseeded and
  chopped
1 garlic clove, crushed
500 g/1 lb rump steak, cut into strips
225 g/7 oz/scant 1 cup canned tomatoes
1 tbsp tomato purée (paste)
2 tsp cornflour (cornstarch)
sprigs of fresh coriander (cilantro) to
  garnish

SALSA:
2 tomatoes, skinned and chopped
2 spring onions (scallions), chopped
1 small fresh green chilli, deseeded and
  chopped
2 tbsp lime juice
1 tbsp chopped fresh coriander (cilantro)
8 flour tortillas
salt and pepper

1 Place the rice in a large bowl. Add
the boiling water and salt. Cover and
cook on HIGH power for 15 minutes.
Leave to stand, covered, for 5 minutes
before draining.

2 Place the oil, onion and carrot in a
large bowl. Cover and cook on
HIGH power for 2 minutes. Add the (bell)
peppers, chilli, garlic and steak. Cover
and cook on HIGH power for 4 minutes,
stirring once.

3 Add the canned tomatoes, tomato
purée (paste) and seasoning. Mix the
cornflour (cornstarch) with a little water,
then stir into the bowl. Cover and cook
on MEDIUM power for 10 minutes.

4 To make the salsa, mix together the
tomatoes, spring onions (scallions),
chilli, lime juice and coriander (cilantro).
Season to taste and leave to stand for 10
minutes.

5 Heat the tortillas on HIGH power for
40 seconds, covered or according to
the packet instructions.

6 Garnish the beef with fresh
coriander (cilantro) sprigs and serve
with the tortillas, rice and salsa.

PENNE WITH BUTTERNUT SQUASH & HAM

SERVES 4

2 tbsp olive oil
1 garlic clove, crushed
60 g/2 oz/1 cup fresh white breadcrumbs
500 g/1 lb peeled and deseeded butternut squash
8 tbsp water
500 g/1 lb fresh penne, or other pasta shape
15 g/ ½ oz/1 tbsp butter
1 onion, sliced
125 g/4 oz/ ½ cup ham, cut into strips
200 ml/7 fl oz/scant cup single (light) cream
60 g/2 oz/ ½ cup Cheddar cheese, grated
2 tbsp chopped fresh parsley
salt and pepper

1 Mix together the oil, garlic and breadcrumbs and spread out on a large plate. Cook on HIGH power for 4–5 minutes, stirring every minute, until crisp and beginning to brown. Set aside.

2 Dice the squash. Place in a large bowl with half the water. Cover and cook on HIGH power for 8–9 minutes, stirring occasionally. Leave to stand for 2 minutes.

3 Place the pasta in a large bowl, add a little salt and pour over boiling water to cover by 2.5 cm/1 inch. Cover and cook on HIGH power for 5 minutes, stirring once, until the pasta is just tender but still firm to the bite. Leave to stand, covered, for 1 minute before draining.

4 Place the butter and onion in a large bowl. Cover and cook on HIGH power for 3 minutes.

5 Coarsely mash the squash, using a fork. Add to the onion with the pasta, ham, cream, cheese, parsley and remaining water. Season generously and mix well. Cover and cook on HIGH power for 4 minutes until heated through.

6 Serve the pasta sprinkled with the crisp garlic crumbs.

BABY CAULIFLOWERS WITH POPPY SEED SAUCE

SERVES 4

4 cloves
½ onion
½ carrot
1 bouquet garni
250 ml/8 fl oz/1 cup milk
4 baby cauliflowers
3 tbsp water
15 g/ ½ oz/1 tbsp butter
15 g/ ½ oz/1 tbsp plain (all-purpose) flour
60 g/2 oz/ ½ cup red Leicester cheese, grated
1 tbsp poppy seeds
large pinch of paprika
salt and pepper

1 Stick the cloves into the onion. Place in a bowl with the carrot, bouquet garni and milk. Heat on HIGH power for 2½–3 minutes. Leave to stand for 20 minutes to allow the flavours to infuse.

2 Trim the base and leaves from the cauliflowers and scoop out the stem using a small sharp knife, leaving the cauliflowers intact. Place the cauliflowers upside down in a large dish. Add the water, cover and cook on HIGH power for 5 minutes until just tender. Leave to stand for 2–3 minutes.

3 Put the butter in a bowl and cook on HIGH power for 30 seconds until melted. Stir in the flour. Cook on HIGH power for 30 seconds.

4 Strain the milk into a jug, discarding the vegetables. Gradually add to the flour and butter, beating well between each addition. Cover and cook on HIGH power for 3 minutes, stirring every 30 seconds after the first minute, until the sauce has thickened.

5 Stir the cheese and poppy seeds into the sauce and season. Cover and cook on HIGH power for 30 seconds.

6 Drain the cauliflowers and arrange on a plate or in a shallow dish. Pour over the sauce and sprinkle with a little paprika. Cook on HIGH power for 1 minute to reheat.

STUFFED GLOBE ARTICHOKES

SERVES 4

4 globe artichokes
8 tbsp water
4 tbsp lemon juice
1 onion, chopped
1 garlic clove, crushed
2 tbsp olive oil
250 g/8 oz/2 cups button mushrooms,
   chopped
40 g/1½ oz pitted black olives, sliced
60 g/2 oz/¼ cup sun-dried tomatoes in oil,
   drained and chopped
1 tbsp chopped fresh basil
60 g/2 oz/1 cup fresh white breadcrumbs
30 g/1 oz/¼ cup pine kernels (nuts),
   toasted
oil from the jar of sun-dried tomatoes for
   drizzling
salt and pepper

1 Cut the stalks and lower leaves off
   the artichokes. Snip off the leaf tips
using scissors. Place 2 artichokes in a
large bowl with half the water and half
the lemon juice. Cover and cook on
HIGH power for 10 minutes, turning the
artichokes over halfway through, until a
leaf pulls away easily from the base.
Leave to stand, covered, for 3 minutes
before draining. Turn the artichokes
upside down and leave to cool. Repeat
with the remaining artichokes.

2 Place the onion, garlic and oil in a
   bowl. Cover and cook on HIGH
power for 2 minutes, stirring once. Add
the mushrooms, olives and sun-dried
tomatoes. Cover and cook on HIGH
power for 2 minutes.

3 Stir in the basil, breadcrumbs and
   pine kernels (nuts). Season to taste.

4 Turn the artichokes the right way up
   and carefully pull the leaves apart.
Remove the purple-tipped central leaves.
Using a teaspoon, scrape out the hairy
choke and discard.

5 Spoon the stuffing into the centre of
   each artichoke. Push the leaves back
around the stuffing. Arrange in a shallow
dish and drizzle over a little oil from the
sun-dried tomatoes. Cook on HIGH
power for 7–8 minutes to reheat, turning
the artichokes around halfway through.

SPINACH & NUT PILAU

SERVES 4

10 g/⅓ oz pack dried porcini (cep)
   mushrooms
300 ml/½ pint/1¼ cups hot water
1 onion, chopped
1 garlic clove, crushed
1 tsp grated ginger root
½ fresh green chilli, deseeded and chopped
2 tbsp oil
250 g/8 oz generous 1 cup basmati rice1
   large carrot, grated
175 ml/6 fl oz/¾ cup vegetable stock
½ tsp ground cinnamon
4 cloves
½ tsp saffron strands
250 g/8 oz/6 cups fresh spinach, long
   stalks removed
60 g/2 oz/½ cup pistachio nuts
1 tbsp chopped fresh coriander (cilantro)
salt and pepper
fresh coriander (cilantro) leaves to
   garnish

1 Place the porcini (cep) mushrooms
   in a small bowl. Pour over the hot
water and leave to soak for 30 minutes.

2 Place the onion, garlic, ginger, chilli
   and oil in a large bowl. Cover and
cook on HIGH power for 2 minutes.
Rinse the rice, then stir it into the bowl
with the carrot. Cover and cook on HIGH
power for 1 minute.

3 Strain and coarsely chop the
   mushrooms. Add the mushroom
liquid to the stock to make 450 ml/
¾ pint/scant 2 cups. Pour on to the rice.
Stir in the mushrooms, cinnamon, cloves,
saffron and ½ teaspoon salt. Cover and
cook on HIGH power for 10 minutes,
stirring once. Leave to stand, covered, for
10 minutes.

4 Place the spinach in a large bowl.
   Cover and cook on HIGH power for
3½ minutes, stirring once. Drain well and
chop coarsely.

5 Stir the spinach, nuts and coriander
   (cilantro) into the rice. Season to
taste and garnish with coriander (cilantro)
leaves.

·3·

International Cooking

◆

Bored with humdrum meals? Cruise the world with this global selection of international favourites. There is plenty here to inspire and challenge the imaginative cook.

◆

CARIBBEAN DISHES – INTRODUCTION

There are over 200 islands in the Caribbean, including the Greater Antilles (Cuba, Jamaica, Haiti and Puerto Rico), the smaller islands of the Lesser Antilles, the Leeward and Windward Islands and the Virgin Islands. The turbulent history of this area has left its mark on the culture, customs and, most importantly, the food and cooking. Caribbean cuisine has been influenced by peoples from Europe, India, Africa and China and over the years these influences have combined with the native foods to create a cuisine that is quite unique. The word 'creole' is often used with reference to Caribbean food – the term indicates a dish with mixed African and European influence.

The Amerindians

The food of the islands owes much to the native Amerindians – the Arawak – who cultivated crops such as chillies, corn, garlic, yams, sweet potatoes, pineapples, guava and cassava, and made spices by grinding berries, leaves and buds. They concocted a preservative from cassava and added it to a meat and chilli stew that is still eaten throughout the islands today, and known as Pepperpot. The Arawak also preserved meat by rubbing in spices and chillies then cooking it slowly over a fire until the meat was dry but full of flavour. This method of cooking, or barbecuing (an Arawak word), was adopted by the Mexicans and the West Indians, who described food cooked in this way as 'jerky'. Although the need to preserve meat has disappeared, the tenderizing and flavouring qualities are still popular and jerked dishes are now the very essence of Caribbean cooking – they have even become popular as a fast food.

Colonial influences

Slaves from the west coast of Africa were brought to the islands in the seventeenth century to work on the sugar cane plantations. They brought with them okra, greens such as callaloo, black-eyed peas (beans) and pigeon peas.

Of the many European nations that colonized the islands in the seventeenth and eighteenth centuries, the most influential were the British, Spanish and French, who brought with them foodstuffs from all over the world. The British brought Worcestershire sauce and rum; the French introduced herbs such as chives as well as some of the more complex cooking techniques; from the Spanish came onions, sugar cane, oranges, bananas and limes. It was also the Europeans who first introduced salted fish and meats, which were used to feed the slaves.

As the islands frequently changed hands, the cooking of any one island and the names of the local dishes can be seen to have several influences. Jamaica's Caveached Fish, for example, comes from the Spanish dish known as escabeche, and Sancoche started life as the South American sancocho. But it was the last controlling power of each island that really left its mark. Flamed Baked Bananas is a typical French dish from Martinique; the British influence in Jamaica can be seen in the Jamaican Patty – a spiced meat parcel that is a descendant of the Cornish pasty; the cuisine of India is reflected in the curries and roti (a type of flat bread) of Trinidad, and in their use of ghee.

Island specialities

Despite the colonial influences, many dishes and ingredients are shared by

INTRODUCTION

more than one island, although they often have different names, and recipes may contain slightly different ingredients. On some islands, for example, avocado is known as zaboca; christophene is chayote or cho-cho; and salt-fish fritters are called 'Stamp and Go' in Jamaica but on Martinique they are known as accra.

Ingredients are also used in diverse ways: Cubans prefer black beans although most islands used red beans; Virgin islanders use spinach instead of callaloo; in Jamaica, chillies are used to preserve foods while elsewhere they are mixed with herbs and spices to tenderize tough cuts of meat. The use of chillies for their flavour, however, is widespread and on all the islands they are added to marinades, rubs, sauces, curries, stews and salads. Cakes and desserts made from coconuts or bananas are also popular.

CARIBBEAN TECHNIQUES
Seasoning-up or marinating meats, fish and poultry is essential to authentic Caribbean dishes, although basic ingredients can be altered according to personal taste. The range of seasoning ingredients available is so vast that most cooks vary them every time they cook.

Caribbean cooks are quite fastidious about the appearance of a finished dish, so herbs that will leave specks in a sauce are often tied in muslin (cheesecloth) before being added to the pot.

Whole chillies, with the stem left on, are sometimes added to the pot to impart their flavour without the heat. They should be removed before serving. Chopped chillies may also be tied in muslin (cheesecloth).

Many recipes use fresh herbs, as their flavour is so much better than that of dried ones. Fresh herbs need not always be chopped first, sometimes the stems are crushed, to release the flavour, then the whole sprig added to the pot. The sprig should be removed before serving.

COOKING EQUIPMENT
No specialist equipment is required. For best results, use good quality, heavy-based pans. Casseroles that are both flameproof and ovenproof are a good choice. As many creole dishes contain acids such as vinegar or lime or lemon juice, use non-metallic dishes and pans that have a non-metallic coating, as the acid can react with the metal.

THE SPIRIT OF CARIBBEAN COOKING
Caribbean cooking comes from the soul, and most dishes have an informal, home-made feel without any fancy techniques or ingredients, relying more on the overall look, feel and flavour of a dish. Most islanders use recipes that have been handed down through the generations; recipes and quantities are used only for guidance and most cooks add their own secret ingredients or special touches to their favourite dishes. The basic rule of this unique, exotic cuisine is to be inventive and not afraid of adapting the recipes to suit your own tastes. Spice them up and down as you feel and vary the ingredients according to what is available, but above all, enjoy it!

CARIBBEAN INGREDIENTS
As people from the Caribbean now live all over the world, ingredients that were once unheard of outside the area are quite widely available. You should be able to find all of the

INTRODUCTION

following in street markets, ethnic stores or large supermarkets.

Ackee, akee, achee
This fruit is used as a vegetable in Jamaica and served with salt cod. It is dark red on the outside and has creamy white flesh with shiny black seeds. Only the flesh should be eaten as the seeds, skin and pink membrane are poisonous. Unripe and overripe fruits are also poisonous, so eat when just ripe.

Avocado
Known in Trinidad as zaboca and in other parts of the Caribbean as alligator pear, midshipman's butter or guacate. To test the ripeness, apply gentle pressure to the top – if it yields, it is ready for use.

Bananas and banana leaves
Both green and ripe bananas are used in vast quantities and are one of the main exports of the Caribbean. Green bananas are used as a vegetable. Foods are sometimes wrapped in banana leaves before cooking, which gives the food a delicate flavour.

Breadfruit
Breadfruit is a large fruit with mottled, green, rough skin and a yellowish white flesh. It is not edible until it has been cooked. It tastes like potato with a slightly nutty flavour, and can be boiled, fried, roasted or barbecued and served in salads, soups, stews or as fritters. When buying, look for firm, heavy fruit.

Callaloo
The West Indian and Creole name for the tops of the taro plant, or Caribbean spinach. The leaves are used like spinach.

Cho-cho, christophene or chayote
This pear-shaped, pale green, slightly prickly squash has a single edible seed (pit) and white flesh with a delicate flavour. It is usually boiled or fried then stuffed and baked. Also available canned.

Coconut milk
Cans of coconut milk are available in ethnic stores and supermarkets. Creamed coconut, which comes in the form of a solid bar, can be grated or chopped and mixed with water to give coconut milk.

Cornmeal
Cornmeal is ground corn. It can be made into porridge (or 'pap', as it is known), puddings, bread or dumplings.

Ghee
Ghee is a type of clarified butter which can be heated to much higher temperatures than ordinary butter.

Herbs & spices
Many of the herbs and spices used in Caribbean cooking are now grown in abundance and exported all over the world, so they are quite easy to find.

Mango
The skin of ripe mangoes varies in colour from green to a deep rose red and the flesh from pale yellow to bright orange. The fruit is ripe when the flesh yields to a gentle pressure.

Okra, ochro, ladies' fingers, bamie
Okra is a green, slightly hairy pod that is available fresh or canned. It is served as an accompaniment, or added to stews and soups for its thickening qualities as well as its flavour. They are best left uncut, otherwise they have a slimy texture.

INTRODUCTION

Paw-paw (papaya)
This elongated, pear-shaped fruit is hard and green when unripe, when it is used as a vegetable in chutneys and relishes. When ripe it has a yellow to orange skin. The seeds are edible but have a peppery taste. It is available fresh and canned.

Peppers & chillies
Sweet peppers, also known as bell peppers or capsicums, and hot chillies characterize all island cooking. The chilli peppers are among the hottest in the world and are used in many sauces and relishes. They are sometimes available crushed and preserved in vinegar or as bottled sauces. Scotch bonnet chillies, which are small and lantern-shaped, are very hot indeed. The seeds of a chilli are the hottest part, so remove them if you don't want your dish to be too fiery.

Plantain
Plantains are a member of the banana family, but must be cooked before eating. They look like large green bananas and are usually used when unripe (green).

Rice
This is the staple diet of the islands and forms the basis of most meals. Use good-quality long-grain rice.

Soursop
Soursop is a large, heart-shaped, spiny, dark green fruit, with an edible white pulp and black seeds. Soursop has a refreshing taste and is used mainly in ices, drinks and sherbets. It is available canned.

Sweet potato
The skin colour of this root vegetable is reddish brown, pink or white. The flesh ranges from deep orange through yellow to white. Although it is a vegetable, it is used in both sweet and savoury dishes. The sweet potato is very versatile and can be boiled, roasted, fried, or cooked over a barbecue.

Yam
This root vegetable has a bark-like skin, creamy yellow flesh and a nutty flavour. It is cooked in the same way as potatoes.

Yard-long beans
Yard-long beans are also known as Chinese beans and asparagus beans. These delicately flavoured narrow beans can grow up to 100 cm/40 in long. They are available from Caribbean and Chinese food stores.

ACCOMPANIMENT
Cornmeal Dumplings
These dumplings may also be cooked in a soup or stew.

Makes 24

125 g/4 oz/1 cup plain (all-purpose) flour
125 g/4 oz/scant 1 cup fine cornmeal
1 tsp baking powder
1 tsp finely chopped fresh chives
45 g/1½ oz/3 tbsp lard or white vegetable fat (shortening)
about 6 tbsp water
salt

Put the flour, cornmeal, baking powder, chives and a pinch of salt in a bowl. Rub in the fat until the mixture resembles fine breadcrumbs. Stir in enough water to make a stiff dough. Roll into 24 balls. Place in a pan of boiling salted water. Reduce the heat, cover and simmer for 10–15 minutes. Drain and serve.

STARTERS

PEPPERPOT SOUP

SERVES 6-8

500 g/1 lb shin of beef, cubed
250 g/8 oz salt beef, cubed
500 g/1 lb callaloo, trimmed and chopped
2 onions, chopped finely
2 garlic cloves, crushed
4 spring onions (scallions), chopped
1 tsp dried thyme
1 fresh green chilli
250 g/8 oz yam, sliced
250 g/8 oz coco, sliced
250 g/8 oz unshelled raw prawns (shrimp)
1 litre/1¾ pints/4½ cups beef stock
15 g/ ½ oz/1 tbsp unsalted butter
125 g/4 oz okra, trimmed and sliced
salt and pepper

1 Put the beef and salt beef into a large saucepan, pour over enough cold water to cover, and bring to the boil. Reduce the heat, cover and simmer for 1½ hours.

2 Put the callaloo in another saucepan and cover with cold water. Bring to the boil. Cook for 10 minutes, drain and purée in a food processor or blender for 30 seconds, or press through a sieve.

3 Add the callaloo purée, onions, garlic, spring onions (scallions), thyme, chilli, yam, coco, prawns (shrimp) and seasoning to the meat. Add the stock and bring to the boil, then simmer for 20 minutes, until the coco and yam are soft.

4 Melt the butter in a small frying pan (skillet) and fry the okra until golden brown. Add to the soup and cook for a further 5 minutes.

5 Discard the chilli, pour the soup into warm soup bowls or a tureen and serve.

VARIATIONS

Coco is very similar to potato, so you could use potatoes if coco is not available. Alternatively double the quantity of yam.

CALLALOO

SERVES 6-8

30 g/1 oz/2 tbsp butter
125 g/4 oz salt pork, cubed
1 onion or 4 spring onions (scallions), chopped
1 garlic clove, crushed
1 celery stick, sliced
250 g/8 oz callaloo, shredded
1 sprig fresh thyme
1.25 litres/2¼ pints/5½ cups chicken stock or water
5 cm/2 in piece creamed coconut, chopped
175 g/6 oz/ ¾ cup white crab meat, shredded
125 g/4 oz okra, sliced
West Indian hot pepper sauce (optional)
salt and pepper
bread to serve

1 Melt the butter in a frying pan (skillet) and gently fry the salt pork for 2-3 minutes.

2 Add the onion or spring onions (scallions) and garlic and fry until soft and golden. Transfer to a saucepan.

3 Stir in the celery, callaloo, thyme, stock or water and coconut. Bring to the boil, cover, reduce the heat and simmer for 10 minutes.

4 Add the crab meat and okra and simmer, covered, for a further 10 minutes. Season to taste and add a dash of West Indian hot pepper sauce if liked. Serve with bread.

CRAB MEAT

Fresh, canned or frozen crab meat (frozen meat must be defrosted before using) can be used in this soup. Crab claws or crab meat in the shells may be used for a more authentic soup.

CALLALOO

Callaloo may be replaced by spinach, Swiss chard, Chinese spinach or finely shredded greens.

CORNMEAL & SEAFOOD PARCELS

MAKES 18

2 tbsp sunflower oil
1 onion, chopped finely
1 garlic clove, crushed
1 fresh red chilli, chopped
2 tomatoes, skinned and chopped
1 small red (bell) pepper, chopped finely
2 tbsp capers, chopped
250 g/8 oz/1½ cups peeled cooked prawns
  (shrimp)
250 g/8 oz/1 cup white crab meat,
  shredded
1 tbsp finely chopped fresh chives
1 tsp finely grated ginger root
1 tsp chopped fresh coriander (cilantro)
pared rind of 1 lime
salt and pepper

CORNMEAL WRAPPERS:
500 g/1 lb/3 cups coarse cornmeal
30 g/1 oz/2 tbsp margarine, diced
5 tbsp sunflower oil
2 tsp salt
650 ml/22 fl oz/2¾ cups boiling water
3–4 banana leaves

1 Heat the oil in a frying pan (skillet) and gently fry the onion until soft. Stir in the garlic and chilli and cook for 3 minutes. Stir in the tomatoes, red (bell) pepper, capers, prawns (shrimp), crab meat, chives, ginger and coriander (cilantro) and cook for 1–2 minutes. Add the lime rind, season and leave to cool.

2 To make the cornmeal wrappers, place the cornmeal in a bowl, add the margarine and rub in with 2 tablespoons of the oil and the salt. Add the boiling water and mix well to make a smooth dough. Roll into 18 balls.

3 Cut the banana leaves into 36 rectangles, 20 x 25 cm/8 x 10 in. Place in a bowl and pour over the boiling water. Drain and refresh under cold water. Pat dry with paper towels.

4 Brush a leaf with a little of the remaining oil. Place a cornmeal ball in the centre and pat down to form a circle about 5 mm/ ¼ in thick. Spread 1½ tablespoons of filling in the centre.

5 Fold half the leaf over the filling, then fold over the other half. Fold in the ends to make a parcel. Place the parcel folded side down on a second leaf, on the opposite grain, and repeat the folding to enclose it. Secure with string.

6 Repeat to make 18 parcels. Place in a large saucepan of boiling salted water and simmer for 1 hour. Drain the parcels and serve.

CRAB & POTATO BALLS

••

MAKES 30

500 g/1 lb potatoes, cut into chunks
45 g/1½ oz/3 tbsp butter
2 egg yolks
60 g/2 oz/ ½ cup Edam cheese, grated
1 tbsp finely chopped fresh flat-leaf parsley
1 onion, chopped finely
500 g/1 lb/2 cups crab meat, shredded
plain (all-purpose) flour for coating
1 egg, beaten
60 g/2 oz/ ½ cup dry white breadcrumbs
oil for deep-frying
salt and pepper

TO GARNISH:
lemon or lime wedges
spinach leaves

1 Cook the potatoes in boiling salted water until tender. Drain and mash with 30 g/1 oz/2 tablespoons of the butter, the egg yolks, cheese, parsley and seasoning. Set aside.

2 Heat the remaining butter in a small frying pan (skillet) and gently fry the onion until soft but not brown. Transfer to a bowl and leave to cool.

3 Add the crab meat and mashed potato to the onion and combine well. Form into 30 small balls. Place on a baking sheet lined with baking parchment and refrigerate for at least 30 minutes.

4 Roll the balls in the flour, dip in the beaten egg and then coat with the breadcrumbs.

5 Half fill a deep-fat fryer or saucepan with oil and heat to 190°C/375°F, or until a cube of bread turns brown in 40 seconds. Deep fry the balls in batches for 5–6 minutes until golden brown all over. Remove with a perforated spoon and drain on paper towels. Keep warm until all the balls have been cooked.

6 Serve garnished with lemon or lime wedges and spinach leaves.

PLANTAIN & BREADFRUIT CRISPS WITH AVOCADO DIP

••

SERVES 4–6

1 breadfruit
1 green plantain
soya oil for deep frying
coarse sea salt

AVOCADO DIP:
1 large ripe avocado
2 tsp lime juice
1 garlic clove, crushed
2 tsp finely chopped spring onion
(scallion)
90 g/3 oz/⅓ cup full-fat soft cheese,
softened
1 tbsp coconut milk
pinch of chilli powder
dash of West Indian hot pepper sauce
salt and pepper

TO GARNISH:
spring onion (scallion) slices
chilli powder

1 Peel the breadfruit and cut into quarters. Cook in boiling salted water for 20 minutes until just tender. Dry on paper towels then slice thinly.

2 Peel the plantain and slice very thinly.

3 Half fill a deep-fat fryer or saucepan with oil and heat to 190°C/375°F or until a cube of bread turns brown in 40 seconds. Deep fry the plantain and breadfruit slices in batches for 2–3 minutes until crisp and golden. Remove with a perforated spoon and drain on paper towels. Sprinkle with salt and leave to cool.

4 To make the avocado dip, peel the avocado and mash the flesh with a fork or blend in a food processor until smooth.

5 Mix in the lime juice, garlic, spring onion (scallion), soft cheese, coconut milk, chilli powder and pepper sauce. Season to taste.

6 Garnish the dip with spring onions (scallions) and chilli powder and serve with the crisps.

CHORIZO, CORIANDER (CILANTRO) & GINGER FRITTERS

••

MAKES 20–24

125 g/4 oz/1 cup plain (all-purpose) flour
1½ tsp baking powder
4 eggs, beaten
2 tsp melted unsalted butter
2 tsp corn or groundnut oil
2 tsp white rum
90 g/3 oz chorizo sausage, chopped
2 tsp chopped fresh coriander (cilantro)
1 tsp finely grated ginger root
corn or groundnut oil for deep frying
salt and pepper
sprigs of fresh coriander (cilantro) to garnish
West Indian hot pepper sauce to serve

1 Sift the flour and baking powder into a bowl.

2 Make a well in the centre and add the eggs, butter, oil and rum and beat until the batter is smooth. Leave to stand for 1 hour.

3 Stir in the chorizo sausage, chopped coriander (cilantro), ginger and seasoning.

4 Half fill a deep-fat fryer or saucepan with oil and heat to 190°C/375°F, or until a teaspoon of the batter sizzles on contact. Drop tablespoons of the batter into the oil and deep fry for 6–8 minutes until golden brown all over. Remove with a perforated spoon and drain on paper towels.

5 Serve garnished with sprigs of coriander (cilantro) and with hot pepper sauce for dipping.

CHORIZO SAUSAGE

Chorizo is a Spanish sausage. It is lightly smoked and made from coarsely chopped pork seasoned with chilli pepper and garlic. It is available from supermarkets and delicatessens. Italian sausage, garlic sausage or smoked ham make good alternatives.

FISH & SHELLFISH

SALT FISH & ACKEE

••

SERVES 4–6

250 g/8 oz salt cod, soaked overnight
30 g/1oz/2 tbsp butter
2 tbsp olive oil
2 slices streaky bacon, chopped
4 spring onions (scallions), sliced
1 onion, sliced
½ tsp dried thyme
2 fresh green chillies, sliced finely
1 green (bell) pepper, sliced
2 tomatoes, skinned and chopped
350 g/12 oz can ackee, drained
pepper

FRIED PLANTAIN:
30 g/1 oz/2 tbsp butter
2 ripe plantains, sliced lengthways

1 Drain the salt cod and rinse under cold water. Put in a saucepan, cover with cold water and bring to the boil. Cover and simmer for 10 minutes. Drain, rinse and remove the skin and bones and flake the flesh.

2 Heat the butter with the oil in a frying pan (skillet), add the bacon and fry for 5 minutes until crisp. Remove with a perforated spoon and drain on paper towels.

3 Fry the spring onions (scallions), onion, thyme, chillies and (bell) pepper for 5 minutes. Add the tomatoes and cook for a further 5 minutes. Stir in the salt cod, ackee and bacon and cook for a further 2–3 minutes.

4 Meanwhile, make the fried plantain. Heat the butter in a frying pan (skillet) and cook the plantains for 2–3 minutes per side. Drain on paper towels and serve with the cod and ackee.

ACKEE

Canned ackee is available from West Indian stores and markets. The skin, seeds and membrane of fresh ackee are poisonous. Both unripe and overripe ackee are poisonous.

SALT-FISH FRITTERS WITH SEAFOOD SAUCE

•••

MAKES 24

250 g/8 oz salt cod, soaked overnight
125 g/4 oz/1 cup plain (all-purpose) flour
1 tsp baking powder
½ tsp salt
1 egg, lightly beaten
180 ml/6 fl oz/¾ cup milk
15 g/½ oz/1 tbsp butter, melted
1 onion, grated finely
1 fresh red chilli, chopped finely
corn oil, for frying
basil sprigs
chicory (endive) leaves

SEAFOOD SAUCE:
150 ml/¼ pint/⅔ cup mayonnaise
2 tbsp tomato purée (paste)
½ tsp chilli powder
1 tbsp lemon juice
1 tsp wholegrain mustard

1 Drain the salt cod and rinse under cold water. Put in a saucepan, cover with cold water and bring to the boil. Cover and simmer for 10 minutes.

2 Drain, rinse and remove the skin and bones and flake the flesh.

3 Mix together the flour, baking powder and salt. Make a well in the centre and pour in the egg, milk and butter. Mix to a smooth batter. Stir in the onion, chilli and salt cod.

4 Heat about 1 cm/½ in of oil in a large deep frying pan (skillet). Drop tablespoons of the mixture, spaced well apart, into the oil and fry for 3–4 minutes until golden on one side.

5 Turn over the fritters and cook for a further 3–4 minutes until the second side is golden. Remove and drain on paper towels. Keep warm. Repeat with the remaining batter.

6 To make the seafood sauce, mix together all the ingredients

7 Serve the fritters with the sauce, garnished with basil sprigs and chicory (endive) leaves.

SEA BREAM & SWEET POTATO PIE

•••

SERVES 6

15 g/½ oz/1 tbsp butter
3 tbsp groundnut oil
250 g/8 oz sweet potatoes, unpeeled, sliced thinly
1 onion, chopped finely
750 g/1½ lb sea bream fillets, skinned and cut into large pieces
2 hard-boiled (hard-cooked) eggs, chopped
sprigs of fresh parsley to garnish

CURRY SAUCE:
45 g/1½ oz/3 tbsp butter
2 tbsp plain (all-purpose) flour
300 ml/½ pint/1¼ cups milk
90 g/3 oz/¾ cup mature (sharp) Cheddar cheese, grated
1 tsp curry powder
2 tbsp chopped fresh flat-leaf parsley
salt and pepper

1 Melt the butter with 2 tablespoons of the oil in a frying pan (skillet). Fry the sweet potatoes in batches for 1–2 minutes on each side, without allowing to soften. Remove with a perforated spoon and drain on paper towels.

2 Add the onion to the pan and fry for 5 minutes. Add the sea bream and cook for a further 5 minutes.

3 Remove the pan from the heat and stir in the eggs. Transfer the fish mixture to an ovenproof dish.

4 To make the sauce, melt the butter in a saucepan, add the flour and stir over a low heat for 1–2 minutes. Remove from the heat and gradually stir in the milk. Return to the heat and stir for a further 2–3 minutes. Add two-thirds of the cheese, the curry powder, parsley and seasoning.

5 Pour the sauce over the fish and mix gently. Layer the sweet potato over the top, overlapping the slices. Brush with the remaining oil and sprinkle with the remaining cheese. Bake in a preheated oven at 180°C/350°F/Gas Mark 4 for 30 minutes until golden. Garnish with parsley and serve.

ESCOVITCH FISH

••••••••••••••••••••••••••••••••••••••

SERVES 4

4 red snapper, scaled
juice of 1 lime
3 green (bell) peppers, sliced
2 onions, sliced
3 carrots, cut into matchsticks
1 fresh bay leaf
1 tbsp finely chopped ginger root
6 black peppercorns
pinch of ground mace
500 ml/16 fl oz/2 cups water
5 tbsp olive oil
6 tbsp malt or white wine vinegar
salt and pepper
lime wedges to garnish

DUMPLINGS:
250 g/8 oz/2 cups self-raising flour
pinch of salt
cold water
oil for frying

1 Put the fish in a shallow non-metallic dish or dishes and season with salt, pepper and lime juice. Leave for 20 minutes.

2 Place the peppers, onions, carrots, bay leaf, ginger, peppercorns, mace, water and salt in a saucepan. Cover and simmer for 30 minutes.

3 Add 2 tablespoons of the olive oil and the vinegar and simmer for a further 1–2 minutes.

4 Heat the remaining oil in a large frying pan (skillet) and fry the fish in batches for 6–8 minutes on each side. Transfer to a serving dish.

5 Meanwhile, make the dumplings. Sift the flour and salt into a bowl. Add enough cold water to make a soft dough. Knead lightly, shape into balls and flatten.

6 Heat 1 cm/½ in oil in a frying pan (skillet). Fry the dumplings in batches for 3–4 minutes on each side, until golden. Remove with a perforated spoon and drain on paper towels. Keep warm while frying the remainder.

7 Pour the sauce over the fish, garnish with lime wedges and serve with the dumplings.

RED MULLET & COCONUT LOAF WITH PEPPER SAUCE

••••••••••••••••••••••••••••••••••••••

SERVES 4–6

250 g/8 oz red mullet fillets, skinned
2 small tomatoes, deseeded and chopped
  finely
2 green (bell) peppers, chopped finely
1 onion, chopped finely
1 fresh red chilli, chopped finely
150 g/5 oz/2½ cups breadcrumbs
600 ml/1 pint/2½ cups coconut liquid
salt and pepper

HOT PEPPER SAUCE:
120 ml/4 fl oz/ ½ cup tomato ketchup
1 tsp West Indian hot pepper sauce
¼ tsp hot mustard

TO GARNISH:
lemon twists
sprigs of fresh chervil

1 Finely chop the fish and mix with the tomatoes, (bell) peppers, onion and chilli.

2 Stir in the breadcrumbs, coconut liquid and seasoning.

3 Grease and base-line a 500 g/1 lb loaf tin (pan) and add the fish. Bake in a preheated oven at 200°C/400°F/Gas Mark 6 for 1–1¼ hours until set.

4 To make the hot pepper sauce, mix together the tomato ketchup, hot pepper sauce and mustard until smooth and creamy.

5 To serve, cut the loaf into slices, garnish with lemon twists and chervil and serve hot or cold with the hot pepper sauce.

COCONUT LIQUID

Coconut liquid is the juice found inside a coconut. Use a hammer and screwdriver or the tip of a sturdy knife to poke out the three 'eyes' in the top of the coconut and pour out the liquid.

STUFFED BAKED CRAB

SERVES 4

4 small cooked crabs, weighing about
    350 g/12 oz each
90 g/3 oz/1½ cups fresh breadcrumbs
1 fresh red chilli, preferably Scotch bonnet,
    deseeded and chopped finely
3 tbsp chopped fresh chives
2 tbsp chopped fresh parsley
2 garlic cloves, crushed
1 tbsp lemon juice
¼ tsp ground allspice
3 tbsp dark rum or Madeira
45 g/1½ oz/⅓ cup grated Parmesan cheese
15 g/½ oz/1 tbsp butter
salt and pepper
green salad to serve

TO GARNISH:
lime wedges
fresh chives

1 Pull away the 2 flaps between the
large claws of the crab, stand it
upside down where the flaps were and
bang down firmly on the rounded end
with the heel of your hand.

2 Separate the crab from its top shell.
Remove the mouth and the stomach
sac, which lies immediately below the
mouth, and discard.

3 Pull out the feathery gills and
discard. Scrape out the brown and
white meat from both sides of the shell
and reserve. Crack the claws using a
rolling pin and remove the meat. Scrub
the shells.

4 Finely chop the crab meat and mix
with 60 g/2 oz/1 cup of the
breadcrumbs, the chilli, chives, parsley,
garlic, lemon juice, allspice, rum or
Madeira and seasoning.

5 Spoon the crab mixture back into
the shells. Sprinkle with the
remaining breadcrumbs mixed with the
cheese. Dot with butter and bake in a
preheated oven at 180°C/350°F/Gas Mark
4 for 25–30 minutes until golden brown.
Garnish with lime wedges and chives and
serve with a green salad.

MEAT & POULTRY

JERK CHICKEN

SERVES 6

1.5 kg/3 lb chicken pieces
cherry tomatoes to garnish
salad to serve

MARINADE:
6 spring onions (scallions)
2 fresh red chillies, preferably Scotch
    bonnet
2 tbsp dark soy sauce
2 tbsp lime juice
3 tsp ground allspice
½ tsp ground bay leaves
1 tsp ground cinnamon
2 garlic cloves, chopped
2 tsp brown sugar
1 tsp dried thyme
½ tsp salt

1 To make the marinade, chop the
spring onions (scallions). Deseed and
finely chop the chillies.

2 Put the spring onions (scallions),
chillies, soy sauce, lime juice,
allspice, ground bay leaves, cinnamon,
garlic, sugar, thyme and salt in a food
processor or blender and blend until
smooth. Alternatively, finely chop the
spring onions (scallions) and chillies, add
to the remaining ingredients and, using a
pestle and mortar, work to a paste.

3 Place the chicken in a shallow dish
and spoon over the marinade. Cover
and refrigerate for 24 hours, turning the
chicken several times.

4 Brush a grill (broiler) rack with oil
and place the chicken on it. Grill
(broil) under a preheated medium grill
(broiler) for about 15–20 minutes on each
side until the chicken juices run clear
when the thickest part of each piece is
pierced with a sharp knife.

5 Garnish with cherry tomatoes and
serve with a salad.

CHICKEN WITH RICE & PEAS

SERVES 6

1 onion, chopped
2 garlic cloves
1 tbsp chopped fresh chives
1 tbsp chopped fresh thyme
2 celery sticks with leaves, chopped
350 ml/12 fl oz/1½ cups water
½ fresh coconut, chopped
liquid from 1 fresh coconut
500 g/16 oz can pigeon peas, drained
1 fresh red chilli, deseeded and cut into
  strips
2 tbsp groundnut oil
2 tbsp caster (superfine) sugar
1.5 kg/3 lb chicken pieces
250 g/8 oz/generous 1 cup long-grain rice,
  rinsed and drained
salt and pepper
celery leaves to garnish

1 Put the onion, garlic, chives, thyme, celery and 4 tablespoons of the water into a food processor or blender and blend until smooth. Alternatively, chop the onion and celery very finely, then grind with the garlic and herbs in a pestle and mortar, gradually mixing in the water. Pour into a pan and set aside.

2 Put the chopped coconut and liquid into the food processor or blender and mix to a thick milk, adding water if necessary. Alternatively, finely grate the coconut and mix with the liquid. Add to the onion and celery mixture in the pan.

3 Stir in the pigeon peas and chilli and cook over a low heat for 15 minutes. Season to taste.

4 Put the oil and sugar in a heavy-based saucepan or flameproof casserole and cook over a moderate heat until the sugar begins to caramelize.

5 Add the chicken and cook for 15–20 minutes, turning frequently, until browned all over.

6 Stir in the coconut mixture, the rice and remaining water. Bring to the boil, then reduce the heat, cover and simmer for 20 minutes until the chicken and rice are tender and the liquid has been absorbed. Garnish with celery leaves and serve.

CURRIED LAMB

SERVES 6

2–3 tbsp corn or groundnut oil
1.5 kg/3 lb lean boneless lamb, cut into
  5 cm/2 in cubes
2 large onions, chopped
2 fresh red chillies, sliced (optional)
3 tbsp mild or hot curry powder
300 ml/ ½ pint/1¼ cups coconut milk
1 fresh bay leaf
½ tsp ground allspice
300 ml/ ½ pint/1¼ cups lamb or chicken
  stock
2 tbsp lime or lemon juice
salt and pepper

TO GARNISH:
lime rind
fresh red chillies

TO SERVE:
rice or roti
banana leaves (optional)

1 Heat the oil in a frying pan (skillet) and fry the lamb until brown. Remove with a perforated spoon and place in a large flameproof casserole. Fry the onions and chillies, if using, in the frying pan (skillet) until golden brown.

2 Add the curry powder and cook for a further 2–3 minutes, stirring.

3 Add the fried onion to the casserole with the coconut milk, bay leaf, allspice, seasoning and just enough stock to barely cover the meat. Cover and simmer for 2 hours until the lamb is tender.

4 Just before serving, add the lime or lemon juice and cook for a further 2–3 minutes. Garnish with lime rind and chillies and serve on banana leaves, if liked, with rice or roti.

ROTI

Roti is a flat Indian-style bread that can sometimes be found in supermarkets and West Indian stores. This curry is sometimes served spooned into the centre of a large roti, which is then folded over the filling like an envelope.

LAMB KEBABS WITH YARD-LONG BEANS

SERVES 4

2 tbsp grated onion
1 tbsp hot paprika
1 tbsp grated ginger root
2 garlic cloves, crushed
1 tbsp curry powder
6 tbsp lime juice
3 tbsp peanut oil
1 kg/2 lb lean lamb, cubed
16 pickling onions
8 slices streaky bacon, halved
2 red (bell) peppers, cut into 16 squares
16 cherry tomatoes
4 yard-long beans, parboiled for 1–2
  minutes
salt and pepper
rice to serve

1 In a large bowl, mix the onion, paprika, ginger, garlic, curry powder, lime juice, oil and seasoning. Stir in the lamb, cover and refrigerate for at least 2 hours, or overnight.

2 Cover the onions with boiling water and leave for 5 minutes. Drain, leave to cool, then peel.

3 Wrap a piece of bacon around each (bell) pepper square.

4 Lift the lamb from the marinade, reserving the marinade. Thread the lamb, onions, bacon and (bell) pepper squares and tomatoes alternately on to 4 long skewers.

5 Wrap the beans around the skewers, securing in place with string. Brush on all sides with the marinade.

6 Cook the kebabs under a preheated medium grill (broiler) for 10–15 minutes, turning and brushing them frequently with the marinade, until the lamb is cooked.

7 Discard the string and serve the kebabs with rice.

SANCOCHE

SERVES 6

250 g/8 oz salt beef, cubed
250 g/8 oz salt pork, cubed
4–5 tbsp oil
275 g/9 oz stewing beef, cubed
2 onions, chopped
250 g/8 oz/1¼ cups red lentils or split peas,
  rinsed
600 ml/1 pint/2½ cups boiling water
250 g/8 oz green bananas, sliced thickly
250 g/8 oz yam, sliced thickly
250 g/8 oz sweet potatoes, sliced thickly
125 g/4 oz okra, trimmed
1 fresh red chilli
salt and pepper

1 Place the salt beef and salt pork in a large bowl. Pour over enough cold water to cover and leave to soak for 1 hour. Drain and pat the meat dry with paper towels.

2 Heat 2 tablespoons of the oil in a large deep saucepan or flameproof casserole and fry the salt beef for 6–8 minutes until brown on all sides. Remove with a perforated spoon and transfer to a plate. Add the salt pork and stewing beef to the pan and cook until browned, adding more oil if necessary. Remove with a perforated spoon.

3 Add the onions and cook for 5 minutes. Return the meat to the pan, add the lentils or split peas and pour over the boiling water. Bring to the boil. Reduce the heat, cover and simmer for 1½ hours.

4 Add the green bananas, yam, sweet potatoes, okra, chilli and seasoning. Cook for a further 25–30 minutes.

5 To serve, discard the chilli and transfer to a warmed serving dish.

VARIATION

Use unsalted pork and beef if you cannot find the salted versions.

STUFFED PAW-PAWS (PAPAYAS)
•••

SERVES 4

2 tbsp oil
6 spring onions (scallions), sliced
1 garlic clove, crushed
300 g/10 oz/1¼ cups minced (ground)
   beef
1 fresh red chilli, chopped finely
2 ripe tomatoes, skinned and chopped
2 tbsp sultanas (golden raisins)
1 tbsp cashew nuts, toasted and chopped
2 tbsp freshly grated Parmesan cheese
2 ripe but firm paw-paws (papayas),
   halved lengthways and deseeded
1 tbsp fine fresh breadcrumbs
salt and pepper
sprigs of fresh flat-leaf parsley to garnish

1 Heat the oil in a frying pan (skillet),
   add the spring onions (scallions) and
cook for 5 minutes until soft. Add the
garlic and cook for 2 minutes. Stir in the
beef and cook until brown.

2 Add the chilli, tomatoes, sultanas
   (golden raisins) and cashew nuts
and cook until the mixture is quite dry.
Remove the pan from the heat and stir in
half the Parmesan cheese and the
seasoning.

3 Place the paw-paw (papaya) shells
   in a shallow ovenproof dish and
spoon the beef mixture into the shells.

4 Pour boiling water into the dish to
   come a quarter of the way up the
paw-paws (papayas). Mix the remaining
cheese with the breadcrumbs and sprinkle
over the paw-paws (papayas). Bake in a
preheated oven at 180°C/350°F/Gas Mark
4 for 30 minutes.

5 Carefully lift the paw-paws (papayas)
   from the dish with a perforated
spoon. Garnish with flat-leaf parsley and
serve.

VARIATION

Ring the changes by using (bell)
peppers in place of paw-paws
(papayas); slice in half through the
stalks, remove the seeds, and fill and
bake in the same way.

VEGETABLES & SALADS

BREADFRUIT COO-COO
•••

SERVES 6

1 kg/2 lb breadfruit, or a 760 g/25 oz can
250 g/8 oz salt beef, chopped finely
1 onion, chopped finely
½ tsp dried thyme
1 fresh bay leaf
1 sprig fresh parsley
3 fresh chive stalks
125 g/4 oz/ ½ cup unsalted butter
2 tbsp olive oil
salt and pepper

TO GARNISH:
cherry tomatoes
sprigs of fresh parsley

1 Peel the breadfruit, cut out the core
   and roughly chop the flesh. If using
canned breadfruit, drain and chop
coarsely. Place in a saucepan with the salt
beef and onion.

2 Wrap the thyme, bay leaf, parsley
   and chives in a piece of muslin
(cheesecloth) and add to the pan with
enough cold water to cover. Bring to the
boil, cover and simmer for 25–30 minutes
until the breadfruit is tender.

3 Drain, reserving the liquid, and
   return the ingredients to the pan.
Discard the muslin (cheesecloth) bag.

4 Mash half the butter into the pan,
   adding a little of the reserved liquid
if necessary to make a smooth but slightly
stiff consistency like mashed potatoes.
Season to taste.

5 Butter a shallow dish and turn the
   breadfruit mixture into it. Smooth
down and refrigerate for a few hours.

6 Turn out on to a lightly floured
   surface and cut into triangles.

7 Heat the remaining butter with the
   oil in a large frying pan (skillet) and
fry the triangles a few at a time for 2–3
minutes on each side until golden.
Remove with a perforated spoon and
drain on paper towels. Garnish with
cherry tomatoes and parsley and serve.

OKRA IN SPICY TOMATO SAUCE

SERVES 4

2 tbsp extra-virgin olive oil
1 large onion, chopped
2 garlic cloves, crushed
6 large ripe tomatoes, skinned and
  chopped
1 fresh red chilli, deseeded and chopped
3–4 fresh basil leaves, torn into fine shreds
large pinch of curry powder
1 tbsp tomato purée (paste)
175 ml/6 fl oz/ ¾ cup water
500 g/1 lb okra, trimmed
salt and pepper
fresh basil leaves, torn, to garnish

1 Heat the oil in a large saucepan, add the onion and fry for 5 minutes until soft but not brown. Add the garlic and fry for a further 2 minutes.

2 Stir in the tomatoes, chilli, basil, curry powder, tomato purée (paste), water and seasoning.

3 Bring to the boil, reduce the heat and simmer for 5 minutes.

4 Add the okra and cook for 15–20 minutes, stirring occasionally, until the okra is tender.

5 Transfer to a warmed serving dish and garnish with basil leaves.

OKRA

Okra, or ladies' fingers, is available fresh or canned. Fresh okra is available from supermarkets, while canned okra can be found in specialist stores and markets. Use a 350 g/12 oz can for this recipe; drain well and heat for 10 minutes in step 4.

RICE & PEAS

SERVES 6

175 g/6 oz/scant 1 cup dried red kidney
  beans, soaked overnight in cold water
2 tbsp groundnut oil
4 spring onions (scallions), sliced
1 small fresh red chilli, sliced
2 garlic cloves, crushed
125 g/4 oz creamed coconut, chopped
400 ml/14 fl oz/1¾ cups boiling water
1 sprig fresh thyme
500 g/1 lb/2½ cups long-grain rice
salt and pepper

1 Drain the beans. Rinse and place in a large saucepan with enough cold water to cover by about 5 cm/2 in. Bring to the boil and boil rapidly for 10 minutes. Reduce the heat to simmering and cook, covered, for 1–1½ hours until the beans are almost tender.

2 Drain the beans, reserving the cooking liquid. Make the liquid up to 500 ml/16 fl oz/2 cups with cold water if necessary.

3 Return the beans and liquid to the saucepan.

4 Heat the oil in a frying pan (skillet) and fry the spring onions (scallions), chilli and garlic for 1–2 minutes. Add to the beans.

5 Dissolve the creamed coconut in the boiling water. Stir into the pan with the thyme, rice and seasoning. Cover and cook over a very low heat for about 20 minutes until the rice and beans are tender and all the liquid has been absorbed. Discard the thyme sprigs and transfer to a warmed serving dish. Serve with meat or chicken.

KIDNEY BEANS

Kidney beans, also known as red peas, must be soaked, boiled and simmered according to the recipe to remove the poisonous toxins they contain.

A 425 g/14 oz can of beans may be used for this recipe; do not cook them beforehand, simply add with the rice.

CHEESE-STUFFED YAM BALLS

MAKES 18

1 kg/2 lb yams, chopped coarsely
60 g/2 oz/¼ cup butter
2 eggs, beaten
2 spring onions (scallions), chopped
125 g/4 oz Mozzarella or Edam cheese,
*   cut into 18 cubes*
18 pimento-stuffed olives
175 g/6 oz/1½ cups dry fine breadcrumbs
corn oil for deep frying
salt and pepper
watercress to garnish

1 Put the yams into a large saucepan. Pour in enough cold water to cover. Bring to the boil, cover and simmer for 15 minutes until soft. Drain well and add the butter, half the eggs and the seasoning. Mash with a potato masher to a smooth purée. Mix in the spring onions (scallions).

2 Shape the mixture into 18 balls. Push a piece of cheese and an olive into the centre of each ball and reshape the yam mixture around them.

3 Roll the yam balls in the remaining egg, then in the breadcrumbs until coated on all sides.

4 Heat the oil in a deep-fat fryer or saucepan to 190°C/375°F or until a cube of bread turns brown in 40 seconds. Deep-fry the yam balls in batches for about 2 minutes until golden brown. Remove with a perforated spoon and drain on paper towels. Keep warm while frying the remaining balls.

5 Place on a warm serving plate and garnish with watercress.

YAMS

Yams have a flavour similar to potatoes although the yam is slightly nuttier. Potatoes or sweet potatoes may be used in this recipe instead.

STUFFED CHO-CHO

SERVES 6

3 large cho-chos, each weighing about
*   350 g/12 oz*
60 g/2 oz/¼ cup butter
1 large Spanish onion, chopped
1 large red (bell) pepper, chopped
3 spring onions (scallions), sliced
350 g/12 oz/3 cups cashew nuts, toasted
125 g/4 oz/2 cups fresh breadcrumbs
1 egg, lightly beaten
125 g/4 oz/1 cup mature (sharp) Cheddar
*   cheese, grated*
1 fresh green chilli, chopped
salt and pepper

TO GARNISH:
sprigs of fresh parsley
fresh red chillies

1 Cook the whole cho-chos in boiling salted water for 30 minutes until tender. Drain and leave until cool enough to handle. Halve lengthways. Scoop out the pulp, including the edible seed (pit), and set aside. Arrange the shells in a shallow ovenproof dish.

2 Heat half the butter in a frying pan (skillet), add the cho-cho pulp, the onion and (bell) pepper and cook for 5 minutes. Stir in the spring onions (scallions) and cook for a further 2 minutes, stirring frequently.

3 Add the cashews, breadcrumbs, egg, cheese, chilli and seasoning and stir well.

4 Pack into the cho-cho shells, dot with the remaining butter and bake in a preheated oven at 180°C/350°F/Gas Mark 4 for 15 minutes until lightly browned.

5 Transfer to a warmed serving plate, garnish with parsley and red chillies and serve.

VARIATION

Courgettes (zucchini) and marrow may also be stuffed and cooked in this way.

CARIBBEAN YAM SALAD

••

SERVES 6

750 g/1½ lb yam, unpeeled
¼ cucumber, peeled and chopped
2 hard-boiled (hard-cooked) eggs,
*   quartered*
8 cherry tomatoes, halved
2 dill pickles, sliced
3 spring onions (scallions), sliced
2 celery sticks, sliced
1 tbsp chopped fresh chives
1 tsp paprika
salt and pepper
celery leaves to garnish

DRESSING:
150 ml/ ¼ pint/ ⅔ cup mayonnaise
4 tbsp natural fromage frais
2 tbsp white wine vinegar
1 tsp finely grated lemon rind

1 To make the dressing, mix together the mayonnaise, fromage frais, vinegar, lemon rind and seasoning. Chill until required.

2 Place the yam in a large saucepan, cover with water and bring to the boil. Cook for 20–25 minutes until tender. Drain and leave until cool enough to handle.

3 Peel the yam and cut into 2.5 cm/ 1 in cubes.

4 Place the yam in a bowl and pour over the dressing. Mix well to coat.

5 Carefully fold in the cucumber, eggs, tomatoes, dill pickles, spring onions (scallions), celery, chives and paprika. Adjust the seasoning.

6 Spoon into a serving bowl, cover and refrigerate for at least 1 hour. Serve garnished with celery leaves.

VARIATION

Cooked meats, such as shredded chicken, chopped ham or beef, may be added to this salad for a more substantial meal.

DESSERTS

TROPICAL FRUIT ICE CREAMS

••

SERVES 6-8

4 eggs
125 g/4 oz/1¼ cups caster (superfine)
*   sugar*
250 ml/8 fl oz/1 cup single (light) cream
125 ml/ ¼ pint/ ⅔ cup milk
125 ml/ ¼ pint/ ⅔ cup evaporated milk
½ tsp vanilla flavouring (extract)
125 g/4 oz/ ½ cup canned crushed
*   pineapple, drained*
175 g/6 oz/ ¾ cup caster (superfine) sugar
125 g/4 oz/ ½ cup puréed canned or ripe
*   paw-paw (papaya)*
1 tbsp lemon juice

SOURSOP ICE CREAM:
450 ml/ ¾ pint/2 cups canned soursop
*   juice*
300 ml/ ½ pint/1½ cups double (heavy)
*   cream*
90 g/3oz/ ⅓ cup caster (superfine) sugar

1 Beat the eggs with the sugar in a large heatproof bowl. Heat the cream, milk and evaporated milk to scalding point and stir into the eggs.

2 Place the bowl over a saucepan half-filled with simmering water. Cook over a low heat, stirring constantly, until the mixture is thick enough to coat the back of a spoon. Leave to cool, then stir in the vanilla flavouring (extract).

3 Pour half the custard into another bowl. Add the pineapple and 125 g/4 oz/ ½ cup of the sugar to one bowl and the paw-paw (papaya), remaining sugar and lemon juice to the other bowl. Stir until the sugar dissolves.

4 Pour into freezerproof containers and freeze for 2–3 hours until just firm. Remove and beat well. Return to the containers and freeze until frozen.

5 To make the soursop ice cream, mix the soursop juice with the cream and sugar. Freeze as in step 4.

6 Remove the ice creams from the freezer 1 hour before serving and place in the refrigerator to soften slightly.

FLAMED BAKED BANANAS

SERVES 4

125 g/4 oz/ ½ cup unsalted butter
4 large ripe bananas, halved lengthways
250 g/8 oz/1½ cups soft light brown sugar
120 ml/4 fl oz/ ½ cup orange juice
250 ml/8 fl oz/1 cup white rum
2 tsp ground allspice
double (heavy) cream, lightly whipped, to serve
orange shreds to decorate (see page 250)

1 Use a little of the butter to grease a shallow ovenproof dish. Arrange the banana halves in a single layer in the dish.

2 Sprinkle with the sugar. Mix together the orange juice, half the rum and the allspice. Pour over the bananas.

3 Dot the bananas with the remaining buttter. Bake in a preheated oven at 200°C/400°F/Gas Mark 6 for 15 minutes, basting halfway through.

4 Remove the bananas from the oven and transfer to a flameproof serving dish, if wished. Warm the remaining rum in a small saucepan.

5 Top the bananas with whipped cream and decorate with orange shreds. Pour over the warmed rum and carefully set alight. Serve as soon as the flames have died down. If preferred, the bananas can be flamed in the baking dish, then transferred to serving dishes and decorated when the flames die down.

VARIATION

You can vary the flavour of the sauce in this dish by using lime or lemon juice instead of orange juice. Add another 30 g/1 oz/2 tablespoons sugar as these fruits are sharper than oranges. Remember to decorate with lime or lemon shreds, made as the orange shreds on page 250.

LIME MERINGUE PIE

SERVES 6

3 tbsp cornflour (cornstarch)
150 ml/ ¼ pint/ ⅔ cup water
grated rind and juice of 4 limes
125 g/4 oz/ ½ cup caster (superfine) sugar
2 egg yolks
lime slices to decorate

MERINGUE:
2 egg whites
60 g/2 oz/ ¼ cup caster (superfine) sugar

PASTRY:
125 g/4 oz/1 cup plain (all-purpose) flour
60 g/2 oz/ ¼ cup butter, diced
about 1½ tbsp cold water

1 To make the pastry, sift the flour into a bowl, add the butter and rub in until the mixture resembles fine breadcrumbs. Mix in enough cold water to form a soft but not sticky dough. Wrap in clingfilm (plastic wrap) and refrigerate for 15 minutes.

2 Knead the pastry lightly then roll out and use to line a deep 20 cm/ 8 in flan tin (quiche pan). Line with foil, weight with baking beans and bake at 200°C/400°F/Gas Mark 6 for 10–15 minutes. Remove the foil and beans and bake for a further 5 minutes. Reduce the oven temperature to 180°C/350°F/Gas Mark 4.

3 Mix the cornflour (cornstarch) with the water and lime rind and juice, put in a saucepan and bring slowly to the boil, stirring until the mixture thickens. Add the sugar.

4 Remove from the heat and cool slightly. Add the egg yolks and cook over a low heat, stirring constantly, for 2–3 minutes; do not allow to boil. Pour into the pastry case.

5 To make the meringue, whisk the egg whites until stiff, then whisk in half the sugar until soft peaks form. Fold in the remaining sugar.

6 Spread the meringue on top of the pie and bake for 10–15 minutes until the meringue is lightly browned. Serve hot or cold, decorated with lime slices.

GINGER & COCONUT BREAD

MAKES 1 KG/2 LB LOAF

300 g/10 oz/2½ cups plain (all-purpose)
    flour
2 tsp baking powder
2 tsp ground ginger
1 tsp bicarbonate of soda (baking soda)
1 tsp ground allspice
60 g/2 oz/⅔ cup unsweetened desiccated
    (shredded) coconut
125 g/4 oz/⅔ cup soft dark brown sugar
175 g/6 oz/¾ cup dark molasses
125 g/4 oz/½ cup unsalted butter
175 ml/6 fl oz/¾ cup evaporated milk
2 eggs, beaten
2 tbsp sieved warmed apricot jam
fresh coconut shreds to decorate (optional)

1 Lightly grease and line the bottom of a 1 kg/2 lb loaf tin (pan). Sift the flour, baking powder, ground ginger, bicarbonate of soda (baking soda) and allspice into a large bowl. Stir in the coconut.

2 Place the sugar, molasses and butter in a saucepan and heat gently until the butter has melted and the molasses and sugar dissolved. Remove from the heat, leave to cool, then stir in the evaporated milk and eggs and mix well.

3 Pour into the flour and coconut mixture and mix well. Pour into the loaf tin (pan) and bake in a preheated oven at 170°C/325°F/Gas Mark 3 for 50 minutes until a skewer inserted into the centre comes out clean.

4 Allow to cool in the tin (pan). Turn out and brush the top with the jam. Slice and serve as it is, or spread with butter, and decorated with coconut, if liked.

COCONUT SHREDS

To make coconut shreds, use a potato peeler to 'peel' strips from the flesh of a fresh coconut.

ORANGE TEACAKE

MAKES 1 KG/2 LB LOAF

250 g/8 oz/2 cups plain (all-purpose) flour
2 tsp baking powder
½ tsp salt
125 g/4 oz/ ½ cup caster (superfine) sugar
1 tbsp finely grated orange rind
2 eggs, beaten
250 ml/8 fl oz/1 cup orange juice,
    strained
45 g/1½ oz/3 tbsp unsalted butter, melted
orange shreds to decorate

1 Grease and line the bottom of a 1 kg/2 lb loaf tin (pan). Sift the flour, baking powder and salt into a bowl. Stir in the sugar and orange rind.

2 In a separate bowl, whisk together the eggs, orange juice and butter.

3 Carefully fold the egg mixture into the dry ingredients.

4 Pour into the loaf tin (pan) and bake in a preheated oven at 180°C/350°F/Gas Mark 4 for 45 minutes until a skewer inserted in the centre comes out clean.

5 Allow to cool in the tin (pan) for 10 minutes. Turn out on to a wire rack and leave to cool.

6 Serve sliced, decorated with orange shreds. Store any remaining cake in an airtight container.

VARIATION

Try using lemon or lime rind and juice for a lemon or lime teacake. Decorate with lemon or lime shreds, as above.

ORANGE SHREDS

Use a cannelle knife to peel away thin strips of rind from the fruit, taking care not to include any bitter pith. Alternatively, use a potato peeler to peel off the rind. Slice very finely into shreds, blanch in boiling water for 1 minute and refresh under cold water.

JAMAICAN SPICED BUNS

MAKES 12–14

275 g/9 oz/generous 1 cup butter or
   margarine, melted
150 g/5 oz/scant 1 cup soft light brown
   sugar
1 egg, beaten
500 g/1 lb/4 cups strong plain (all-
   purpose) flour
60 g/2 oz fast-action dried yeast
275 g/9 oz/1½ cups mixed dried fruit
2 tsp ground allspice
½ tsp vanilla flavouring (extract)
2 tbsp dark molasses
150 ml/5 fl oz/ ⅔ cup milk
pinch of salt

GLAZE:
3 tbsp caster (superfine) sugar
3 tbsp water

1 Mix together the butter or margarine, sugar and egg. Sift the flour and salt and stir in the yeast.

2 Stir the butter mixture, dried fruit, allspice, vanilla and molasses into the flour mixture and gradually stir in the milk. Mix well.

3 Knead into a soft dough, then place in a clean, lightly oiled bowl. Cover with a damp cloth and leave to rise in a warm place for about 2 hours until doubled in volume.

4 Turn out the dough and knock back (punch down). Knead again on a lightly floured work surface for about 10 minutes until smooth.

5 Divide the dough into 12–14 pieces and shape into small buns using the palm of the hand. Lightly oil and flour a baking sheet and put the buns on it, spaced well apart. Leave to rise in a warm place for about 30 minutes.

6 Bake in a preheated oven at 190°C/375°F/Gas Mark 5 for 30 minutes until golden and firm to the touch.

7 To make the sugar glaze, put the sugar and water in a small saucepan, bring to the boil and boil for 2 minutes. Brush over the buns while they are still warm. Cool on a wire rack. Serve warm or cold, split and buttered and accompanied by a slice of cheese if liked.

CAJUN & CREOLE DISHES – INTRODUCTION

Cajun and Creole cuisines originated in Louisiana. These cooking styles are a melting pot of varied cultures, among them Indian, French, Spanish and African. They evolved as each new ethnic group combined the best of its own traditions with ingredients that were available locally. Tradition has it that Cajun cuisine was for poor folk and Creole for aristocrats.

Another way to describe the difference between Creole and Cajun food is to explain that a Creole would use ten chickens in a dish for one person, whilst a Cajun would use one chicken to feed ten people. That is not to say that Cajuns are mean. Far from it. They are generous, warm-hearted people. However, traditionally they were poor, southern Louisiana country folk, very unlike their rich, privileged, New Orleans city dwelling cousins.

Creole food is therefore the sophisticated city food of New Orleans, based on the French culinary traditions appplied to local delicacies, and Cajun is the cookery of the rugged people who lived in the bayous – the waterways and swamps that dot Louisiana. These people lived off the land, being mostly trappers and fishermen, and cooked their daily catch in a big black iron pot over an open fire. It was, and still is, hearty, robust cookery.

Over the centuries, the difference between Cajuns and Creoles evened out and today they live harmoniously together on equal terms, sharing food, music, culture and hospitality.

Cajun cuisine relies on what can be grown or hunted in the immediate locality. That is why it makes such good use of locally grown rice, seafood, freshwater fish from the bayous (rivers) and wild or farmed hogs and pigs. The Cajuns love their food spicy and most dishes are pepped up to the required standards with Tabasco sauce and Cajun Spice Mix (see page 258).

Many of the names of foods, recipes and traditions are in a form of pure or adapted French. This is because the Cajuns were originally from southern France. A number of French emigrated to Nova Scotia at the beginning of the 17th century and founded a colony which they named Acadia. Unfortunately, due to religious persecution the settlers were driven out and forced to seek a new home. Eventually the Cajuns arrived in southern Louisiana where they settled and can be found today still speaking their adapted mother tongue. The name Cajun evolved from Acadian. Music plays an important part in their life and today's Cajun bands still produce the traditional distinctive sound heard by their ancestors.

Today, Louisiana is an old traditional world nestling comfortably inside a newer more vibrant one. It is a foot-tapping, hand-clapping, song-humming kind of place where jazz still beats out its soul some 24 hours a day. The jewel in its crown is New Orleans – famed and feted for its fine restaurants, cocktail bars, showy festivals and markets that boast the very finest in succulent seafood, exotic vegetables, fine patisssserie and more. Intermingling with this fine culture is more than a hint of the best of Southern country style or Cajun cuisine. This is a marriage of cultures and cuisines made in heaven!

INTRODUCTION

CAJUN AND CREOLE BASICS
Cooking terms, ingredients and other Cajun-Creole essentials:

Blackened This is not a traditional Cajun cooking technique but one invented by the famous New Orleans chef, Paul Prudhomme. A prime piece of meat, poultry or fish is coated in a spice and herb mixture then cooked quickly in a white hot, smoking cast-iron pan. The intense heat creates a blackened exterior whilst the flesh inside stays moist.

Boudin A spicy, open-textured sausage made from rice, pork, pork liver, onion and seasonings. When hard to find use any other spicy, coarse-textured sausage.

Bread Pudding A favourite Cajun dessert not unlike our own but served with a hot, whisky or bourbon sauce.

Cajun Popcorn These are prawns that have been sprinkled with Cajun seasoning then coated in batter and deep fried. They are eaten in New Orleans as a hot snack or starter with a remoulade dipping sauce.

Cayenne Pepper Pepper made from a type of chilli pepper that is cooked with flour then dried and finely ground for use in dishes that need a "kick".

Crawfish Or crayfish, these are crustaceans which look like small lobsters. Only the tail meat is eaten. Lobster, scampi or large green prawns can be used instead.

Etouffé This is a term that means smothered and refers to a dish that is smothered with plenty of sauce.

Fish Stock Many Cajun-Creole fish or seafood dishes require fish stock. This is easiest made by simmering fish bones and heads in water for about 15-20 minutes, then straining for use. Alternatively, canned seafood bisque of the condensed variety will also make an excellent alternative.

Grillades Pronounced "gree-ards", these are served at breakfast or brunch. Basically they are slices of beef or veal in thick gravy. Traditionally, they are always served with a sort of cornmeal porridge called grits.

Grits Hominy grits are a creamy white cereal that looks like coarse semolina, made from corn with the husks removed. You can find it in specialist stores but cooked couscous makes a good, if not authentic, alternative.

Gumbo A hearty, rich, thick soup, almost a stew. It is made by combining any variety of poultry, seafood and spiced sausage, with Tabasco sauce. Cajuns enjoy arguing over whether it should be thickened with filé or okra. The name gumbo is thought to derive from a similar African word meaning okra. Gumbo is always served with hot cooked rice.

Gumbo Filé Filé is sassafras leaves ground to a fine powder which is used to thicken gumbos. It is added prior to serving rather than during cooking because it turns stringy when cooked. Very hard to find outside the USA.

Hush Puppies Fried cornmeal fritters that are usually served with fried fish.

INTRODUCTION

Jambalaya A spicy rice dish, usually made with several types of meat and traditionally almost always with the highly seasoned smoked ham known as tasso. Tasso is virtually unobtainable outside Louisiana. A good home-made substitute can be made by coating smoked gammon cubes in Cajun seasoning mix.

Maque Choux This is a corn dish made with sweetcorn, (bell) peppers, onion and tomato and was introduced to the Cajuns by the local Native Americans.

Mirlitons These are pear-shaped vegetables from the same family as the marrow or squash that are traditionally stuffed and also used in sweet and savoury dishes. They are also known as chayote or christophene.

Po-Boys Short for poor boy. These are hearty sandwiches made on French bread. In days gone by these were considered the cheapest lunch possible; they were just a huge sandwich filled fit-to-burst with anything from the usual ham and cheese to meatballs, fried chicken or fried oysters. They have always been consumed by rich and poor alike but are not so cheap to purchase in Louisiana today.

Pralines Pralines are a cross between a sweet and a cookie and have the texture of softish fudge. They are usually very sweet and crammed with pecans. They are generally served with tea alongside other cakes or after a meal with coffee like mints.

Red Beans 'n' Rice A hearty mixture of red kidney beans and rice, flavoured traditionally with pickled pork or ham hock, bay leaves and Tabasco. It is slow-cooked and traditionally served on a Monday. It would be left simmering on the stove whilst the women washed clothes in the Mississippi river.

Redfish This is the favourite fish for blackening. The flesh is mild and sweet and the fish has a black spot on the tail. Many fishmongers now stock redfish fillets but when unavailable you can use red snapper, salmon or haddock fillets instead.

Remoulade Sauce A sauce made from mayonnaise, hot Creole mustard and Tabasco sauce. It is used as a dip for shrimp or as a salad dressing.

Roux A roux is one of the most important mixtures required in Cajun-Creole cooking. It is a mixture of flour and oil that is cooked slowly, sometimes for hours to produce a deeply-coloured paste which gives a characteristic nutty, toasty flavour to the finished dish. A roux is also required to thicken the juices of a dish. As a general rule, the darker the roux the less its thickening ability. The Cajuns prepare a light, medium or dark roux depending upon whether it is to be used for thickening or flavour.

Sauce Piquante A tomato sauce, served hot and spiced very liberally with Tabasco sauce.

Soft Shell Crabs These are small crabs that are caught after they moult and before they can grow their new shells. They are sautéed in butter or deep-fried in batter for eating.

Tabasco Sauce This is the Cajun-Creole cooking essential. A true

INTRODUCTION

Cajun cannot tolerate bland food. Tabasco sauce is a combination of red pepper (called Tabasco pepper), vinegar and salt. It is made by the McIlhenny family at their home on Avery Island, Louisiana. Originally Edmund McIlhenny, who created the sauce in 1868, made it for his family and close friends but it proved so popular that he began to sell it to local people. News of this unique sauce quickly spread, and now Tabasco is the world's best known pepper sauce.

The Trinity Also called the holy trinity, it is a combination of onion, green peppers and celery. The Trinity is essential to Cajun cuisine and appears in virtually every recipe.

CAJUN AND CREOLE FESTIVALS
Cajuns love to party so it is not surprising that their favourite saying is *laissez les bon temps roulez* (let the good times roll). To this end they have devised a number of party and festival occasions, a few of which are described below:

Boucherie Before refrigeration there was no way of preserving slaughtered livestock for future use. Therefore, the whole animal had to be cooked or preserved immediately to avoid waste. The boucherie came around once a month. Everyone would gather together, the men would butcher and clean and the women would prepare tasso, boudin, sausage and hogshead cheese. Following a long day's work the event would become a celebration.

Couchon de Lait This a dining festival and involved the slaughtering of a suckling pig which was then cooked over a slow fire until crispy and tender.

Crayfish Boil This is a serious outdoor eating party. Enormous quantities of crayfish are boiled in enormous tubs over an open fire. Guests sit around and simply eat and talk until they disappear from view under a pile of shells!

Fais Do Do This is the ultimate good time party. Translated, it means time for babies and young children to sleep while the adults have fun. The fun consists of dancing to a Cajun band, lots of eating, drinking, laughter and much merry-making.

CAJUN SEASONING
This is a combination of the main herbs and seasonings used in Cajun-Creole cooking. The spices should be mixed together and stored in a screw-topped jar. Cajun seasoning mix can be bought ready-made from specialist shops but here is a recipe for a good home-made one:

1 tbsp garlic powder or salt
1 tbsp onion powder or onion salt
2 tsp ground white pepper
2 tsp ground black pepper
1½ tsp cayenne pepper
2 tsp dried thyme
½ tsp dried oregano
pinch of dried cumin
pinch of dried basil

STARTERS

CAJUN BEAN SOUP

SERVES 6

2 tbsp vegetable oil
125 g/4 oz streaky bacon, rinded and
  chopped
1 large onion, chopped
1 red (bell) pepper, cored, seeded and
  chopped
5 celery sticks, chopped
1 x 425 g/14 oz can chopped tomatoes
600 ml/1 pint/2½ cups vegetable stock
2 bay leaves
½ tsp Tabasco
1 tsp salt
2 x 475 g/15 oz cans butter beans,
  drained
chopped parsley, to garnish

1 Heat the oil in a large, heavy-based
  pan. Add the bacon and cook
quickly until crisp.

2 Add the onion, (bell) pepper and
  celery and cook until just beginning
to turn golden.

3 Add the chopped tomatoes, stock,
  bay leaves, Tabasco and salt, mixing
well. Bring to the boil, reduce the heat
and cook for 10 minutes.

4 Add the butter beans, stir well, cover
  and simmer for about 30 minutes,
stirring occasionally, until the vegetables
are tender.

5 Remove and discard the bay leaves.

6 Serve the soup, ladled into warm
  soup bowls, sprinkled with parsley.

VARIATION

This soup could be made with other
varieties of canned beans – black-eyed
beans, cannellini beans, borlotti beans
or red kidney beans. Some canned
beans contain brine – rinse before
using.

LOUISIANA SEAFOOD GUMBO

SERVES 4

1 tbsp plain flour
1 tsp paprika
350 g/12 oz monkfish fillets, cut into
  chunks
2 tbsp olive oil
1 onion, chopped
1 green (bell) pepper, cored, seeded and
  chopped
3 celery sticks, finely chopped
2 garlic cloves, crushed
175 g/6 oz okra, sliced
600 ml/1 pint/2½ cups vegetable stock
1 x 425 g/14 oz can chopped tomatoes
1 bouquet garni
125 g/4 oz peeled prawns (shrimp)
juice of 1 lemon
dash of Tabasco
2 tsp Worcestershire sauce
175 g/6 oz/generous 1 cup cooked long-
  grain American rice

1 Mix the flour with the paprika. Add
  the monkfish and toss to coat well.

2 Heat the olive oil in a large, heavy-
  based pan. Add the monkfish pieces
and fry until browned on all sides.
Remove from the pan with a slotted
spoon and set aside. Add the onion,
green (bell) pepper, celery, garlic and
okra and fry gently for 5 minutes until
softened.

3 Add the stock, tomatoes and
  bouquet garni. Bring to the boil,
reduce the heat and simmer for 15
minutes.

4 Return the monkfish to the pan with
  the prawns (shrimp), lemon juice,
Tabasco and Worcestershire sauces.
Simmer for a further 5 minutes.

5 To serve, place a mound of cooked
  rice in each warmed, serving bowl,
then ladle over the seafood gumbo.

VARIATION

In the South filé powder is used to
flavour and thicken the gumbo. Filé
powder is made from sassafras leaves
and is very hard to find outside the US.

EGGS SARDOU

SERVES 4

2 warm muffins
4 canned or cooked artichoke hearts,
  heated until warm
8 anchovy fillets
4 eggs

HOLLANDAISE SAUCE:
150 g/5 oz/ ⅔ cup butter
1 tbsp white wine vinegar
1 tbsp lemon juice
3 large egg yolks
¼ tsp caster sugar
¼ tsp salt
pinch of white pepper

1 To make the sauce, melt the butter in a pan and skim off the white foam that collects on top.

2 Heat the vinegar and lemon juice separately in small pans. .

3 Put the egg yolks in a blender goblet with the sugar, salt, hot vinegar and hot lemon juice. Cover and blend for 5-6 seconds. Remove the lid, set the blender to maximum speed, then add the butter in a steady slow stream. The sauce will thicken and emulsify in about 45 seconds. Season with pepper to taste.

4 Split the muffins in half and place each half on a warmed serving plate. Top with a warm artichoke heart.

5 Arrange two anchovy fillets in a cross over the top of each artichoke heart on the muffins.

6 Poach the eggs in water until just cooked then place on top of each prepared muffin. Spoon or pour over the warm Hollandaise sauce and serve immediately.

VARIATION

The anchovy fillets can be replaced with anchovy paste (such as Gentleman's Relish) if liked. Spread over the muffins before topping with the artichoke hearts.

BAKED CRAB SHELLS

SERVES 4

60 g/2 oz/ ¼ cup butter
2 garlic cloves, crushed
1 small onion, chopped
1 celery stick, finely chopped
½ green (bell) pepper, cored, seeded and
  chopped
½ red (bell) pepper, cored, seeded and
  chopped
½ fresh chilli, seeded and finely chopped
½ tsp chopped fresh thyme
150 ml/ ¼ pint/ ⅔ cup double (heavy)
  cream
salt and pepper
500 g/1 lb fresh or frozen crab meat,
  defrosted if frozen, flaked
60 g/2 oz/1 cup fresh breadcrumbs
celery leaves, to garnish

1 Melt the butter in a large, heavy-based frying pan. Add the garlic, onion, celery, green and red (bell) peppers, and chilli. Stir-fry for about 5 minutes, or until softened.

2 Add the thyme, cream and salt and pepper to taste, stirring constantly. Reduce the heat and simmer gently for about 4-5 minutes until slightly thickened.

3 Add the crab meat with half of the breadcrumbs, increase the heat and cook for about 1-2 minutes.

4 Remove from the heat and spoon into 4 scrubbed and oiled crab shells, ramekins or small gratin dishes and level the surfaces.

5 Sprinkle the remaining breadcrumbs over the tops then bake in the preheated oven at 200ºC/400ºF/Gas Mark 6 for about 15 minutes until crisp and golden. Garnish with celery to serve.

ALTERNATIVE

The cream in the recipe could be replaced with a condensed soup such as chicken, prawn (shrimp) bisque or celery. Use 150 ml/¼ pint/⅔ cup undiluted soup.

FISH & SHELLFISH

LOUISIANA SEAFOOD PAELLA

SERVES 4

2 tbsp vegetable oil
1 green (bell) pepper, cored, seeded and
    chopped
1 onion, chopped
1 celery stick, chopped
½ tsp dried thyme
creole sauce (see page 263)
150 ml/ ¼ pt/ ⅔ cup fish stock or water
75 ml/3 fl oz/5 tbsp double (heavy) cream
300 g/10 oz/scant 2 cups cooked
    long-grain rice
250 g/8 oz peeled prawns (shrimp)
125 g/4 oz cooked mussels
175 g/6 oz crab meat
2 tbsp snipped chives or spring onion
    (scallion) tops
salt
wedges of lime, to garnish

1 Heat the oil in a large heavy-based
pan. Add the (bell) pepper, onion
and celery and fry gently for 10 minutes
until soft but not brown.

2 Stir in the thyme, Creole sauce and
stock or water and simmer for 5
minutes over gentle heat.

3 Add the cream and mix well to
blend. Simmer for 5 minutes.

4 Add the rice, prawns (shrimp),
mussels, crab meat, chives and salt
to taste. Stir in carefully so that the crab
meat remains in chunky pieces. Cook for
2-3 minutes until hot.

5 Turn on to a warmed serving dish
and garnish with wedges of lime to
serve. Serve immediately.

FISH STOCK

You can make your own fish stock by
simmering fish heads, bones and
trimmings in water for 15-20 minutes.
Do not cook for longer or the stock will
be bitter. Freeze any surplus stock –
it is very useful for making fish soups
and chowders.

BLACKENED CAJUN FISH

SERVES 4

4 fish fillets (red fish or bass for example),
    cut about 1 cm/ ½ in thick
60 g/2 oz/ ¼ cup butter, melted

CAJUN SPICE MIXTURE:
1 tbsp salt
2 tsp garlic powder
2 tsp ground black pepper
1½ tsp ground cumin
½-1 tsp cayenne pepper (to taste)
1½ tsp paprika
1½ tsp barbecue seasoning powder
boiled rice with spicy butter dressing, to
    serve (see variation, below)

1 Blend the ingredients for the spice
mixture together. Dip the fish fillets
in the melted butter then sprinkle each
side evenly with the seasoning mixture.

2 Meanwhile, put a heavy-based cast
iron frying pan on to heat slowly
and steadily until very hot indeed. Don't
heat too fast – the heat needs to be
steady and even. Hold the palm of your
hand just above the surface of the pan –
the pan will be hot enough when you can
feel a strong rising heat.

3 Press the fish fillets down firmly on
to the very hot surface with a fish
slice. There should be an almighty hiss
and a great deal of smoke and steam.
Cook for 1-2 minutes until blackened.

4 Turn the fish over, using the slice,
and cook the other side. The surface
should be well charred on both sides
when cooked. Serve hot, with any
remaining melted butter poured over, and
with cooked rice.

VARIATION

Blackened fish is delicious served with
rice tossed in a hot butter dressing.
Melt 60 g/2 oz/ ¼ cup butter in a pan,
add 1-2 sliced red chillies, 2 teaspoons
cumin or poppy seeds and fry for 1
minute. Stir in a squeeze of lemon
juice, cooked rice and 2 tablespoons
chopped mixed parsley and coriander.
Stir into hot rice and serve.

AUBERGINE (EGGPLANT) PIROGUES

SERVES 4

2 large aubergines (eggplant)
60 g/2 oz/ ¼ cup butter
1 large onion, chopped
1 green (bell) pepper, cored, seeded and
 chopped
1 celery stick, finely chopped
175 g/6 oz peeled prawns (shrimp)
90 g/3 oz button mushrooms, chopped
60 g/2 oz/1 cup soft white breadcrumbs
salt and cayenne pepper
125 g/4 oz/1 cup Cheddar, grated

1 Halve the aubergines (eggplant) and
 cut out the centres, leaving a 1 cm/½
in thick shell. Chop the flesh coarsely and
set aside. Cook the aubergines (eggplant)
halves in boiling salted water for about 5
minutes, then drain thoroughly.

2 Meanwhile, melt the butter in a pan,
 add the onion, green (bell) pepper
and celery until softened. Add the
chopped aubergine (eggplant) flesh and
cook until golden. Add the prawns
(shrimp) and mushrooms and cook for a
further 3-4 minutes.

3 Remove the vegetable mixture from
 the heat and stir in the breadcrumbs.
Season with salt and cayenne pepper to
taste. Pile into the aubergine (eggplant)
halves and sprinkle with the cheese.

4 Arrange the aubergine (eggplant)
 halves in an ovenproof dish and
bake in the preheated oven at
200ºC/400ºF/Gas Mark 6 for 20-25 minutes
until golden and bubbly.

VARIATION

This mixture is often used to stuff
mirlitons, mild-flavoured, pear-shaped
squashes, which can be found in good
supermarkets. Boil 4 whole mirlitons in
boiling salted water for about 45
minutes until tender. Drain, cool and
halve lengthwise. Remove the seeds,
scoop out the flesh to leave a shell and
chop the flesh. Use the flesh instead
of the aubergine (eggplant) flesh and
fill the halved shells in the same way.
Bake for about 15-20 minutes.

LOUISIANA RICE & SHRIMP

SERVES 4

60 g/2 oz/ ¼ cup butter or margarine
4 celery sticks, finely chopped
1 large onion, chopped
½ green (bell) pepper, cored and chopped
1 x 295 g/10¼ oz can condensed cream
 of mushroom soup
150 ml/ ¼ pt/ ⅔ cup water
500 g/1 lb peeled crayfish tails or shrimps
2 tbsp chopped parsley
750 g/1½ lb/4¼ cups hot cooked American
 long-grain rice
cayenne and black pepper, to taste
shrimps and celery leaves, to garnish

1 Melt the butter or margarine in a
 large, heavy-based pan. Add the
celery and cook until tender, but not
brown, for about 10-15 minutes.

2 Add the onion and (bell) pepper
 and cook for a further 5 minutes.

3 Blend the soup with the water then
 stir into the vegetables.

4 Add the crayfish tails or shrimps and
 cook over a low heat for about 10
minutes, stirring frequently. Add the
chopped parsley and cook for a further
5 minutes.

5 Stir in the cooked rice, season to
 taste with cayenne and black pepper
and heat through for 2-3 minutes before
serving.

CRAYFISH

Crayfish look like miniature lobsters –
they are about 7-10 cm/3-4 in. A dark
greeny-brown, they become deep red
or bright pink when cooked and have a
sweet, delicate flavour. They are found
in freshwater lakes and streams in
many parts of the US and Europe.

CRAYFISH PIES

••

SERVES 4

PASTRY:
175 g/6 oz/1½ cups plain flour
pinch of salt
90 g/3 oz/6 tbsp butter
1 egg yolk
3-4 tbsp cold water

FILLING:
2 tbsp vegetable oil
15 g/ ½ oz/2 tbsp plain flour
½ green (bell) pepper, cored, seeded and
*   finely chopped*
½ small onion, finely chopped
1 celery stick, finely chopped
250 ml/8 fl oz/1 cup double (heavy)
*   cream*
90 g/3 oz/6 tbsp unsalted butter
6 spring onions (scallions), finely chopped
1 garlic clove, crushed
350 g/12 oz peeled crayfish tails
1½-2 tsp Cajun Spice Mixture (see
*   page 258)*

1 To make the pastry, sift the flour with the salt, then rub in the butter until the mixture resembles fine breadcrumbs. Make a well in the centre and add the egg yolk with the water. Mix to a firm dough. Roll out the pastry thinly and use to line 4 x 10 cm/4 in fluted flan tins. Chill for 20 minutes then bake 'blind' for 10 minutes at 200ºC/400ºF/Gas Mark 6. Remove the paper and beans and bake for a further 5 minutes until golden.

2 To make the filling, heat the oil until it begins to smoke. Stir in the flour and cook, stirring briskly, for about 2-3 minutes or until a dark-red/brown roux is formed.

3 Remove from the heat and immediately add the (bell) peppers, onion and celery. Stir briskly until the mixture cools.

4 Meanwhile, heat the cream to a simmer, gradually add to the roux mixture, bring to the boil and whisk to make a thickened sauce.

5 Heat the butter in a frying pan. Add the spring onions (scallions) and garlic and cook for 1 minute. Add the crayfish tails (reserving 4 for garnish) and the spice mixture. Sauté for about 3 minutes until hot and cooked through. Stir in the sauce and mix well.

6 Spoon the mixture into the tartlet cases, garnish with the reserved tails and serve at once.

MEAT & POULTRY

BATON ROUGE CHICKEN GUMBO

SERVES 4-6

30 g/1 oz/2 tbsp butter
1 tbsp corn oil
30 g/1 oz/ ¼ cup plain flour
90 g/3 oz belly of pork, sliced
1 large onion, sliced
2 celery sticks, chopped
500 g/1 lb okra, trimmed and sliced
1 x 425 g/14 oz can peeled tomatoes
2 garlic cloves, crushed
1 litre/1¾ pints/4½ cups chicken stock or water
250 g/8 oz peeled prawns (shrimp)
500 g/1 lb cooked chicken, skinned and cut into bite-sized pieces
1 tsp Tabasco
500 g/1 lb/3 cups hot cooked rice, to serve

1 Heat the butter and oil in a small, heavy-based pan. Add the flour and cook, stirring frequently, over a low heat until the roux turns a rich brown colour (but be careful not to burn or it will taste bitter). Set aside.

2 Meanwhile, in a large pan, sauté the pork slices, without extra fat, until they are golden brown on all sides and the fat has been rendered. Add the sliced onion and celery and cook for a further 5 minutes.

3 Stir in the okra and sauté for a further 3 minutes. Stir in the tomatoes and garlic and simmer over gentle heat for 15 minutes.

4 Gradually add the stock to the browned roux, mixing and blending well, then add to the okra mixture. Cover and simmer for 1 hour.

5 Add the prawns (shrimp) and chicken to the okra mixture, cook for a further 5 minutes, then stir in the Tabasco.

6 Spoon the gumbo into individual serving bowls and top with a scoop of hot cooked rice.

JAMBALAYA

SERVES 4

60 g/2 oz/ ¼ cup butter
2 onions, chopped
2 garlic cloves, crushed
5 celery sticks, chopped
1 red (bell) pepper, cored, seeded and chopped
1 green (bell) pepper, cored, seeded and chopped
1 tsp Cajun Spice Mixture (see page 258)
250 g/8 oz/1 cup long-grain rice
1 x 425 g/14 oz can tomatoes, drained and chopped
500 g/1 lb cooked assorted meats (chicken, duck, ham or sausage), sliced or diced
250 ml/8 fl oz/1 cup vegetable stock or white wine
1 tsp salt
parsley sprigs, to garnish

1 Melt the butter in a large, heavy-based pan. Add the onions, garlic, celery, (bell) peppers and spice mixture and mix well.

2 Add the rice and stir well to coat the grains in the butter mixture.

3 Add the tomatoes, diced meat, stock or wine and salt. Bring to the boil, stirring well.

4 Reduce the heat, cover and simmer for about 15 minutes or until the rice is cooked and fluffy and has absorbed all the liquid. If the mixture seems to be too dry then add a little boiling water, tablespoon by tablespoon, towards the end of the cooking time.

5 Serve the jamabalaya on warm plates, garnished with parsley.

SEAFOOD JAMBALAYA

Prepare and cook as above but use 500 g/ 1 lb assorted seafood, such as shrimps, prawns (shrimp), crab, lobster meat and cooked oysters.

CHICKEN ETOUFFÉ

SERVES 4-6

60 g/2 oz/ ¼ cup butter
1 small onion, chopped
1 small green (bell) pepper, cored, seeded and chopped
1 celery stick, chopped
1 red (bell) pepper, cored, seeded and chopped
1 small red chilli, seeded and finely chopped
1 tsp Cajun Spice Mixture (see page 258)
1 tsp chopped fresh basil
salt
2 tbsp vegetable oil
2 tbsp flour
475 ml/16 fl oz/2 cups rich chicken stock
500 g/1 lb skinless, boned chicken breasts, cut into strips or bite-sized pieces
4 spring onions (scallions), chopped

1 Melt the butter in a large, heavy-based pan. Add the onion, green (bell) pepper, celery, red (bell) pepper and chilli and cook over gentle heat until softened, about 5 minutes.

2 Add the Cajun Spice Mixture, basil and salt to taste and cook for a further 2 minutes.

3 Meanwhile, heat the oil in a pan, add the flour and cook, slowly, until a rich red/brown roux is formed, whisk constantly to prevent the roux from scorching and becoming bitter.

4 Gradually add the stock and whisk well to make a smooth thickened sauce. Pour the sauce over the vegetable mixture and allow to simmer for about 15 minutes.

5 Add the chicken strips and the spring onions (scallions) and cook for a further 10 minutes, stirring occasionally until the chicken is cooked and tender.

6 Serve with cooked long-grain rice or freshly cooked fluffy couscous.

GRILLADES (WITH GRITS)

SERVES 6

4 tbsp olive oil
1 kg/2 lb veal fillet, pork tenderloin or turkey breast, cut into 7 x 10 cm/3 x 4 in strips
60 g/2 oz/ ½ cup plain flour
3 onions, chopped
2 green (bell) peppers, cored, seeded and chopped
4 celery sticks, finely chopped
1 garlic clove, crushed
500 g/1 lb ripe tomatoes, skinned, seeded and chopped
2 tbsp tomato purée (paste)
1 tsp chopped fresh thyme
½-1 tsp Tabasco
1½ tsp paprika
¼ tsp cayenne pepper
1 tsp salt
150 ml/ ¼ pint/ ⅔ cup vegetable stock
150 ml/ ¼ pint/ ⅔ cup white wine
grits, to serve (see below)

1 Heat the oil in a large, heavy-based pan. Add the meat strips and fry quickly on both sides until it changes colour. Remove with slotted spoon.

2 Add the flour to the pan juices and mix well. Cook over a gentle heat, stirring constantly, until the roux changes to a rich brown colour. Add the onions, (bell) peppers, celery and garlic and mix well. Cover and cook over a gentle heat for about 15 minutes.

3 Return the meat to the pan with the tomatoes, tomato purée (paste), thyme, Tabasco, paprika, cayenne, salt, stock and wine, mixing well. Cover and simmer gently for a further 40-45 minutes, or until the meat and vegetables are tender. Serve hot with grits, if liked.

GRITS

Place 600 ml/1 pint/2½ cups milk, and water or stock in a pan. Add 165 g/ 5½ oz hominy grits (or 175 g/6 oz couscous) and bring to the boil, stirring constantly. Add 1 tbsp butter and 1 tsp salt, partially cover and cook over a very gentle heat for 15 minutes.

LOUISIANA DUCK WITH BISCUITS

••

SERVES 6

BISCUITS:
250 g/8 oz/2 cups self-raising flour
½ tsp Cajun Spice Mixture (see page 258)
125 g/4 oz/ ½ cup chilled butter
175 ml/6 fl oz/ ¾ cup single cream

FILLING:
1 tbsp vegetable oil
1 tbsp plain flour
150ml/ ¼ pint/ ⅔ cup chicken or duck
    stock
2 tbsp dry vermouth
30 g/1 oz/2 tbsp butter
500 g/1 lb cooked duck, cut into bite-sized
    pieces
2 rashers bacon, rinded and chopped
2 tbsp chopped red (bell) pepper
6 tbsp double (heavy) cream
3 spring onions (scallions), finely chopped
milk, to glaze

1 To make the biscuits, place the flour
  and spice mixture in a blender or
food processor with the butter and
process until it is finely mixed and
resembles breadcrumbs. Add the cream
and process again to make a soft dough.
Form the dough into a ball, wrap in foil
and chill for 30 minutes.

2 Meanwhile, to make the filling, heat
  the oil in a pan, add the flour and
cook gently for about 4-5 minutes to
make a straw-coloured roux, stirring
constantly. Gradually blend in the stock
and vermouth to make a smooth sauce.

3 Heat the butter in a pan, add the
  duck, bacon and red pepper and
cook until well coloured. Stir in the sauce,
cream and spring onions (scallions). Cook
the mixture gently for about 2 minutes
then pour into a shallow pie dish.

4 Roll out the dough to a thickness
  of about 1 cm/½ in, then stamp
out about 18 rounds with a 5 cm/2 in
scone cutter.

5 Prick the pastry rounds with a
  fork then arrange in overlapping
rows over the duck mixture. Brush with
milk to glaze then bake in the preheated
oven at 220º/425ºF/Gas Mark 7 for about
15 minutes until cooked and golden.

MARDI GRAS MEATBALLS

••

SERVES 6

MEATBALLS:
500 g/1 lb minced beef or pork
1 onion, chopped
60 g/2 oz/1 cup breadcrumbs
1 egg, beaten
salt and pepper
flour, to dust
2 tbsp vegetable oil
chopped parsley, to garnish
boiled rice or pasta, to serve

CREOLE SAUCE:
2 tbsp vegetable oil
1 onion, finely chopped
3 celery sticks, chopped
1 garlic clove, crushed
1 green (bell) pepper, cored, seeded and
    chopped
1 red (bell) pepper, cored, seeded and
    chopped
1 x 425 g/14 oz can chopped tomatoes
1 tsp molasses
1 tbsp lemon juice
pinch of ground bay leaves
Tabasco, to taste

1 To make the meatballs, mix the
  mince with the onion, breadcrumbs,
egg and salt and pepper to taste. Divide
and form into 24 meatballs, shaping them
with your hands. Spread some flour on a
flat plate and roll the meatballs in the
flour to coat. Set aside.

2 To make the sauce, heat the oil in a
  pan, add the onion, celery, garlic
and (bell) peppers and cook for about 10
minutes until softened.

3 Add the tomatoes, molasses, lemon
  juice, bay leaves, Tabasco and salt
and pepper to taste. Bring to the boil,
cover and simmer for 15 minutes.

4 Meanwhile, heat the oil in a large
  frying pan and fry the meatballs
until brown on all sides.

5 Remove the meatballs from the pan
  with a slotted spoon and add to the
sauce. Simmer gently for 20 minutes, then
serve with rice or pasta. Sprinkle with
chopped parsley to garnish.

CAJUN ROAST BEEF

•••

SERVES 4

2 ribs of beef, each weighing about 950 g/
1¾ lb, trimmed

STUFFING:
15 g/ ½ oz/1 tbsp butter
½ onion, chopped
½ small green (bell) pepper, cored, seeded
*   and chopped*
1 small celery stick, finely chopped
2 garlic cloves, crushed
1 tsp chopped fresh thyme
¼-½ tsp cayenne pepper (to taste)
60 g/2 oz/1 cup soft white breadcrumbs
2 bay leaves
salt and pepper
2 tbsp olive oil
1 tbsp flour
175 ml/6 fl oz/ ¾ cup red wine
175 ml/6 fl oz/ ¾ cup beef stock

1 Preheat the oven to 220ºC/425ºF/Gas
   Mark 7. Using a sharp knife, cut a
pocket deeply into the thickest part of
each rib roast for the stuffing.

2 To make the stuffing, melt the butter
   in a pan, add the chopped onion,
green (bell) pepper, celery and garlic and
cook until golden, about 10 minutes.

3 Add the thyme, cayenne and
   breadcrumbs and mix well. Use half
of the mixture to stuff each rib roast. Tie
the roasts firmly with string, tucking in the
bay leaves, to enclose the stuffing. Season
with salt and pepper.

4 Heat the oil in a large, heavy-based
   frying pan and fry the ribs over a
high heat, for 2 minutes on each side.
Transfer ribs and juices to a roasting pan.

5 Cook in the preheated oven for 15
   minutes, turning the meat halfway
through, for rare beef. Cook for a further
5-7 minutes for medium beef. Remove
from the pan and leave to rest in a warm
place while preparing the sauce.

6 Add the flour to the pan juices and
   cook for 1 minute, stirring
constantly, gradually add the wine and
stock, bring to the boil and simmer to
make a smooth sauce. Serve the ribs with
a little of the sauce poured over.

BEEF DAUBE

•••

SERVES 6-8

2 tbsp olive oil
1 large onion, cut into wedges
2 celery sticks, chopped
1 green (bell) pepper, cored, seeded and
*   chopped*
1.15 kg/2¼ lb braising steak, cubed
60 g/2 oz/ ½ cup plain flour, seasoned with
*   salt and pepper*
600 ml/1 pint/2½ cups beef stock
2 garlic cloves, crushed
150 ml/ ¼ pint/ ⅔ cup red wine
2 tbsp red wine vinegar
2 tbsp tomato purée (paste)
½ tsp Tabasco
1 tsp chopped fresh thyme
2 bay leaves
½ tsp Cajun Spice Mixture (see page 258)

1 Heat the oil in a large heavy-based,
   flameproof casserole. Add the onion
wedges and cook until browned on all
sides. Remove with a slotted spoon and
set aside.

2 Add the celery and (bell) pepper to
   the pan and cook until softened.
Remove the vegetables with a slotted
spoon and set aside.

3 Coat the meat in the seasoned flour,
   add to the pan and sauté until
browned on all sides.

4 Add the stock, garlic, wine, vinegar,
   tomato purée (paste), Tabasco and
thyme and heat gently, scraping up any
sediment.

5 Return the onions, celery and
   peppers to the pan. Tuck in the bay
leaves and sprinkle with the Cajun
seasoning. Bring to the boil, transfer to
the preheated oven at 160ºC/325ºF/Gas
Mark 3 and cook for 2½-3 hours, or until
the meat and vegetables are tender.

TABASCO

Tabasco sauce, made with red chilli
pepper, vinegar and salt, is an essential
ingredient in Cajun-Creole cooking. It
was first manufactured in Louisiana in
the 19th century and is now the
world's best-known pepper sauce.

CAJUN MEATLOAF

Serves 6

2 tbsp vegetable oil
1 onion, finely chopped
1 green (bell) pepper, cored, seeded and
    finely chopped
2 celery sticks, finely chopped
1 garlic clove, crushed
4 tbsp snipped chives
1 kg/2 lb lean minced beef
2 tbsp tomato purée (paste)
2 tsp molasses
¼ tsp Tabasco
½ tsp Worcestershire sauce
1 tsp salt
2 large eggs
60 g/2 oz/1 cup soft white breadcrumbs
Creole Sauce (see page 263)

1 Heat the oil in a large, heavy-based pan, add the onion, green (bell) pepper, celery, garlic and chives, mixing well. Cook over a gentle heat until tender and just beginning to turn golden, about 10-15 minutes.

2 Meanwhile, place the beef in a bowl and break down with a fork. Add the tomato purée (paste), molasses, Tabasco, Worcestershire sauce and salt, mixing well.

3 Add the cooked vegetable mixture, eggs and breadcrumbs and mix well to combine thoroughly.

4 Using wetted hands, shape the mixture into a loaf and place on a baking tray lined with greased foil.

5 Bake for about 1½ hours in the preheated oven at 180ºC/350ºF/Gas Mark 4 until brown and cooked all the way through.

6 Serve hot cut into thick slices with seasonal vegetables and the hot Creole Sauce.

VARIATION

Brush the meatloaf with 2 tablespoons tomato purée (paste) or tomato ketchup before baking to get a really good rich colour, if liked.

PIQUANTE (BELL) PEPPERS

Serves 4

4 large (bell) peppers, red, green or yellow
30 g/1 oz/2 tbsp butter
1 onion, finely chopped
1 large celery stick, finely chopped
150 g/5 oz/1¼ cups cooked long-grain rice
2 tbsp chopped spring onions (scallions)
1 tbsp chopped mixed herbs
250 g/8 oz/1 cup chopped cooked meat,
    such as ham, chicken or sausage
1 large egg, beaten
salt and pepper

SAUCE:
1 x 425 g/14 oz can chopped tomatoes
    with herbs
1 garlic clove, crushed
½ tsp Tabasco
1 tsp sugar
1 tsp paprika

1 Cut the tops off the (bell) peppers, then remove the core and seeds.

2 Place the (bell) pepper shells and caps in a saucepan of boiling water and cook for about 6 minutes until softened but not limp. Remove with a slotted spoon and leave to drain upside down while preparing the filling.

3 To make the filling, melt the butter in a heavy-based pan, add the onion and celery and cook until softened. Remove from the heat.

4 Stir in the rice, spring onions (scallions), herbs, meat, egg and salt and pepper to taste, mixing well.

5 Pack the mixture into the par-cooked (bell) pepper shells and replace the par-cooked caps. Place in a baking dish so that the (bell) peppers are packed snugly together.

6 To make the sauce, mix all the ingredients well with salt and pepper to taste and spoon around and between the (bell) peppers. Bake in the preheated oven at 180ºC/350ºF/Gas Mark 4 for about 40-45 minutes until tender. Serve hot.

VEGETABLES & BOUDIN SAUSAGES

SERVES 4

15 g/ ½ oz/1 tbsp butter or margarine
500 g/1 lb Boudin or other spicy sausage
250 g/8 oz bacon or gammon pieces,
    sliced
2 large onions, chopped
3 celery sticks, chopped
1 red (bell) pepper, cored, seeded and cut
    into bite-sized pieces
1 green (bell) pepper, cored, seeded and
    cut into bite-sized pieces
125 g/4 oz okra (optional)
2-3 tsp Cajun Spice Mixture (see page 258)
3 tomatoes, skinned and chopped
300 ml/ ½ pt/1¼ cups chicken stock
chopped parsley, to garnish

1 Cut the sausages into bite-sized
    pieces. Melt the butter in a large,
heavy-based pan. Add the bacon or
gammon followed by the sausages and
cook quickly until browned on all sides.
Remove from the pan with a slotted
spoon and set aside.

2 Add the onions, celery, (bell)
    peppers and okra to the pan and
sauté until softened.

3 Add the spice mixture to the pan,
    stirring well. Cook for 5 minutes
over low heat.

4 Add the tomatoes and stock, mixing
    well.

5 Return the bacon pieces and
    sausages to the pan. Cover and
simmer for about 35 minutes until
cooked. Serve with rice.

BOUDIN SAUSAGES

These are spicy, open-textured
sausages made from pork, rice, pork
liver and seasonings and are well
worth seeking out. If you can't find
them use any other spicy sausage
instead.

HUSH PUPPIES

MAKES ABOUT 24

150 g/5 oz/1 cup cornmeal
60 g/2 oz/ ½ cup self-raising flour
2 tbsp cornflour (cornstarch)
1 tbsp baking powder
1 tsp Cajun Spice Mixture (see page 258)
¼ tsp chilli powder
1 garlic clove, crushed
2 tbsp grated onion
2 eggs, beaten
175 ml/6 fl oz/ ¾ cup milk
vegetable oil, for deep frying

1 Mix the cornmeal with the flour,
    cornflour (cornstarch), baking
powder, spice mixture and chilli powder.

2 Mix the garlic with the onion and
    eggs and stir into the flour mixture.

3 Heat the milk until hot but not
    boiling then pour over the cornmeal
mixture and stir well to mix. Allow to
cool.

4 Heat the oil in a large, heavy-based
    pan until hot. Carefully add about 5
heaped teaspoonfuls of the mixture to the
oil and deep-fry until puffy and a light
golden colour, about 1 minute, turning
over occasionally.

5 Remove with a slotted spoon and
    drain on paper towels. Keep warm.

6 Repeat with the remaining mixture,
    cooking about 5 hush puppies at a
time, for best results. Serve immediately,
as an accompaniment to fried fish fillets.

VARIATION

These fried cornmeal fritters are crisp
and golden on the outside and mellow,
soft and fluffy on the inside. These are
traditionally served with fried fish, but
are also good as finger fare with
drinks. To be really Southern, the Hush
Puppies should be fried in the pan
after the fish has been fried, using the
same fat or oil.

MAQUE CHOUX

••••••••••••••••••••••••••••••••••

SERVES 4-6

1 large tomato
15 g/ ½ oz/1 tbsp butter or margarine
½ onion, chopped
1 small green (bell) pepper, cored, seeded and chopped
750 g/1½ lb/generous 4 cups sweetcorn kernels, defrosted if frozen
½ tsp salt
½ tsp Tabasco sauce

1 Skin, seed and chop the tomato. Melt the butter or margarine in a large heavy-based pan. Add the onion and (bell) pepper and cook for 5 minutes until tender.

2 Stir in the corn, tomato, salt and Tabasco, stirring well.

3 Reduce the heat to a gentle simmer and cook the mixture for 10-15 minutes or until the corn is tender.

4 Serve hot with meat, poultry, rice and pasta dishes.

FRESH CORN

Fresh corn kernels undoubtedly make the best Maque Choux. To remove the kernels from fresh cobs, pull away the leaves and all the silks clinging to the corn, then trim the stems level with the base of the cobs. Stand each cob upright, pointed end uppermost, then slice away the kernels with a sharp knife as close to the cob as possible. Fresh corn kernels can be frozen for up to 12 months for convenience.

RED BEANS 'N' RICE

••••••••••••••••••••••••••••••••••

SERVES 4

175 g/6 oz streaky bacon, rinded and chopped
1 large onion, chopped
2 celery sticks, chopped
1 green (bell) pepper, cored and chopped
2 garlic cloves, crushed
½ tsp ground bay leaves
dash of Tabasco
2 tbsp tomato purée (paste)
4 tsp chopped parsley
1 x 475 g/15 oz can red kidney beans, undrained
salt and pepper
boiled rice, to serve

1 Place the bacon in a pan over a gentle heat and cook until the fat starts to run. Add the onion, celery, (bell) pepper and garlic and mix well. Cover and cook gently for about 15 minutes or until well softened.

2 Add the bay leaves, Tabasco, tomato purée (paste), parsley, kidney beans and salt and pepper to taste. Stir well to mix.

3 Cover the pan and simmer for a further 30 minutes, stirring occasionally.

4 Serve hot with freshly cooked rice for a main meal, or as an accompaniment to a meat dish.

ALTERNATIVE

Some of the bacon may be replaced with smoked pork sausage if liked. Reduce the amount of bacon to 60 g/2 oz and add 1 tablespoon of oil to cook the vegetables, then add 125 g/4 oz thickly sliced smoked pork sausage with the beans.

CORNBREAD

MAKES 1 LOAF

175 g/6 oz/1½ cups self-raising flour
150 g/5 oz/1 cup fine cornmeal
30 g/1 oz/¼ cup cornflour (cornstarch)
pinch of salt
1 tsp baking powder
60 g/2 oz/¼ cup caster sugar
350 ml/12 fl oz/1½ cups milk
90 g/3 oz/6 tbsp butter
1 egg, beaten

1 Place a 30 x 20 cm/12 x 8 in shallow oblong baking tin in the preheated oven at 180ºC/350ºF/Gas Mark 4 for 5 minutes.

2 To make the cornbread, mix the flour in a bowl with the cornmeal, cornflour (cornstarch), salt, baking powder and sugar.

3 Warm the milk in a small pan with 60 g/2 oz/¼ cup of the butter until it is slightly hot and the butter has melted. Remove the milk and butter mixture from the heat and beat in the egg. Melt the remaining butter and set aside.

4 Stir the milk and egg mixture into the flour mixture and mix well.

5 Remove the hot tin from the oven, brush with butter to grease then pour in the batter. Smooth the top to level the mixture.

6 Bake in the oven for 25 minutes, remove from the oven, brush with the melted butter and cook for a further 15 minutes until golden and firm to the touch. Serve hot, cut into squares.

SERVING

Cornbread is traditionally served with butter for breakfast or eaten with main dishes like fried chicken or fish, as a side dish.

DESSERTS

CREOLE ICE-CREAM

SERVES 6

200 g/7 oz/generous cup crème fraîche
600 ml/1 pint/2½ cups custard, lightly
*   sweetened to taste*
few drops of vanilla essence
90 g/3 oz/6 tbsp caster sugar

1 Mix the crème fraîche with the custard, vanilla essence to taste and caster sugar, mixing well.

2 Pour into a freezer-proof container and place in the freezer or freezing compartment of the refrigerator. Freeze until almost firm.

3 Remove the ice-cream from the freezer and beat or whisk until smooth – this breaks down the large ice crystals that form and will keep the ice-cream smooth and creamy. Return to the freezer and freeze until firm, about 2 hours.

4 Remove the ice-cream from the freezer about 15 minutes before serving to soften slightly – this will make scooping or slicing easier.

5 Scoop or slice into chilled glasses and serve at once.

VARIATIONS

Chocolate Creole Ice-cream: Prepare as above but add 125 g/4 oz/4 squares melted plain chocolate to the basic mixture.

Creole Fudge Ice-cream: Prepare as above but add 250 g/8 oz fudge that has been gently melted over a low heat with 3 tablespoons milk.

MISSISSIPPI MUD PIE

SERVES 6-8

PASTRY:
250 g/8 oz/2 cups plain flour
125 g/4 oz/ ½ cup butter, softened
30 g/1 oz/2 tbsp caster sugar
1 tbsp cocoa powder, sifted (optional)
4-5 tbsp iced water

FILLING:
½ recipe Creole Ice-cream (see left)
½ recipe Chocolate Creole Ice-cream

TOPPING:
3 egg whites
175 g/6 oz/ ¾ cup caster sugar

1 To make the pastry, sift the flour into a bowl, then rub in the butter until the mixture resembles fine breadcrumbs. Stir in the sugar and cocoa powder, if using (to make a chocolate-flavoured pie crust), until well mixed. Add the water and mix to a firm but pliable dough. Roll out the pastry thinly. Grease a 23 cm/9 in loose-bottomed fluted flan tin or dish and line with the pastry. Trim off surplus pastry level with the top of the tin.

2 Bake "blind" in the preheated oven at 200ºC/400ºF/Gas Mark 6 for 25 minutes. Remove the paper and beans and bake for a further 10-15 minutes or until crisp and golden. Remove from the oven and allow to cool completely.

3 About 15 minutes before required, remove the ice-creams from the freezer and allow to soften slightly.

4 Scoop the ice-creams into the pastry case then return to the freezer while making the meringue topping.

5 To make the topping, whisk the egg whites until they stand in firm peaks. Gradually whisk in the sugar, 1 tablespoon at a time, until the meringue is very thick and glossy. Swirl or pipe over the frozen ice-cream mixture to completely enclose.

6 Bake in the oven at 230ºC/450ºF/Gas Mark 8 for about 5 minutes or until the meringue is tinged golden. Serve the pie at once, cut into wedges.

AMBROSIA

SERVES 6

1 pineapple
6 oranges
125 g/4 oz/ ¾ cup maraschino cherries
60 g/2 oz/ ⅔ cup desiccated (shredded) coconut
2 bananas (optional)
soured cream or crème fraîche, to serve

1 Peel and core the pineapple then cut the flesh into bite-sized pieces. Place in a mixing bowl.

2 Peel the oranges, remove the pith then segment the flesh. Add to the pineapple.

3 Thoroughly drain the cherries and add to the fruit mixture, mixing well.

4 Stir in the coconut, cover and chill for at least 8 hours or overnight.

5 Just before serving, peel and thinly slice the bananas (if used). Stir into the fruit and coconut mixture.

6 Serve the fruit in individual bowls topped with a dollop of the soured cream or crème fraîche.

AMBROSIA

This is a very old, traditional US recipe and many variations exist. Maraschino cherries are a modern addition, but they add a splash of colour to the dish.

BELLE OF THE SOUTH PECAN TART

SERVES 8-10

PASTRY:
250 g/8 oz/2 cups plain flour
125 g/4 oz/ ½ cup butter, softened
2 tbsp finely chopped pecans (optional)
4-5 tbsp iced water

FILLING:
200 g/7 oz/1 cup pecans
3 large eggs, beaten
250 g/8 oz/1 cup caster sugar
250 g/8 oz/ ¾ cup golden syrup
30 g/1 oz/2 tbsp butter, melted
1 tsp vanilla essence
whipped cream, to serve

1 To make the pastry, sift the flour into
a bowl, then rub in the butter until
the mixture resembles fine breadcrumbs.
Stir in the chopped pecans, if using, then
the water, and mix to a firm but pliable
dough.

2 Roll out the pastry thinly. Grease a
25 cm/10 in fluted flan tin or dish
and line with the pastry. Trim off the
surplus pastry from the edge.

3 Sprinkle the pecans evenly over the
base of the tart.

4 To make the filling, beat the eggs
with the sugar, golden syrup, butter
and vanilla essence, mixing well. Pour or
spoon over the pecans.

5 Bake in the preheated oven at
190ºC/375ºF/Gas Mark 5 for about
45 minutes or until the pastry is crisp
and golden and the filling is firm.

6 Allow to cool slightly before cutting
into wedges. Serve with softly
whipped cream.

PECANS

Pecan nuts grow in profusion in the
South – it is a wild tree native to the
US. Pecan nuts are now widely
available, though if unobtainable
walnuts can also be used.

BREAD PUDDING WITH BOURBON

SERVES 6

100 g/3½ oz stale French bread, broken
into pieces
300 ml/ ½ pint/1¼ cups milk or half milk
and half double (heavy) cream
125 g/4 oz/ ½ cup sugar
45 g/1½ oz/3 tbsp butter, melted
1 egg, lightly beaten
60 g/2 oz/ ⅓ cup raisins
30 g/1 oz/ ⅓ cup desiccated (shredded)
coconut
45 g/1½ oz/ ⅓ cup chopped pecans
¼ tsp ground cinnamon
large pinch grated nutmeg

BOURBON SAUCE:
60 g/2 oz/ ¼ cup butter
90 g/3 oz/ ⅔ cup icing (confectioner's)
sugar
1 small egg yolk (size 4)
50 ml/2 fl oz/ ¼ cup Bourbon

1 To make the pudding, mix all the
ingredients together in a large mixing
bowl – the mixture should be very moist
but not soupy.

2 Pour the pudding mixture into a
buttered 900 ml/1½ pint/3½ cup
baking dish.

3 Bake in the middle of the preheated
oven at 180ºC/350ºF/Gas Mark 4 for
about 45 minutes or until the pudding is
set and the top is a dark golden colour.

4 Meanwhile, to make the sauce,
cream the butter with the sugar in a
small saucepan over a gentle heat until all
the butter has been absorbed.

5 Remove from the heat and blend in
the egg yolk. Gradually beat in the
Bourbon. Serve warm poured over the
pudding – the sauce thickens as it cools.

ALTERNATIVE

Malt whisky can be used instead of
Bourbon if liked.

COCONUT PIE

•••

SERVES 8-10

PASTRY:
250 g/8 oz/2 cups plain flour
125 g/4 oz/ ½ cup butter, softened
2 tbsp desiccated (shredded) coconut
4-5 tbsp iced water

FILLING:
5 large eggs, beaten
150 g/5 oz/1⅔ cups desiccated (shredded)
* coconut*
350 g/12 oz/1½ cups caster sugar
125 g/4 oz/ ½ cup butter, melted
150 ml/ ¼ pint/ ⅔ cup buttermilk or 4 tbsp
* natural yogurt mixed with 4 tbsp*
* skimmed milk*
1 tsp vanilla essence

1 To make the pastry, sift the flour into a bowl, then rub in the butter in pieces until the mixture resembles fine breadcrumbs. Stir in the coconut and water and mix to a firm but pliable dough.

2 Roll out the pastry thinly and use to line a 25 cm/10 in greased fluted flan tin or dish. Bake 'blind' in the preheated oven at 200ºC/400ºF/Gas Mark 6 for 25 minutes. Remove the paper and beans and bake for a further 10-15 minutes or until crisp and golden. Remove from the oven then reduce the oven temperature.

3 To make the filling, beat the eggs with the coconut, sugar, butter, buttermilk and vanilla, mixing well.

4 Pour into the baked pastry case. Return to the oven and cook at 180ºC/350ºF/Gas Mark 4 for about 45 minutes or until the filling has set and is firm to the touch.

5 Turn off the heat and leave the pie to stand in the oven, with the door open, for a further 15 minutes.

6 Serve warm or when just cold, but not chilled.

VARIATIONS

There are many variations of the coconut pie, a favourite in the South. In some versions the pastry case is filled with a sweet coconut custard and allowed to set. When cold the top is sprinkled with toasted coconut and decorated with whipped cream.

MEXICAN DISHES – INTRODUCTION

The cuisine of Mexico, though it has changed over the years, remains one that is based on age-old recipes that use the staple foods of the old country – chiefly corn, beans of all kinds, potatoes and sweet potatoes, avocados, tomatoes, chillies, pumpkin, turkey and duck, a wealth of fish from the long coastline, and the delicious cinnamon-flavoured chocolate. Over the centuries, traditional Mexican recipes were combined with the comparatively new influences brought by the conquering Spaniards in the sixteenth century, who arrived with the cattle (for milk and meat), poultry, pigs, wheat, rice, citrus fruits and spices. The combination of the two methods of cooking soon brought forth a wonderful array of new dishes, though they were still based on the old ideas of the Aztecs and Mayans, enhanced with Spanish touches and produce.

SIMPLE RECIPES

Mexican food is easy to prepare at home. With a few exceptions, most of the recipes are uncomplicated and fairly quick to put together. Garnishes and decorations are kept to a minimum, and the food is prepared in a relaxed manner that is reflected in the informal nature of Mexican cuisine. Of course there are certain skills required for a few of the dishes, and the making of the tortilla is probably the most important to master.

Tortillas

The tortilla is really the staple bread of Mexico. Traditionally, it is made with maize flour (masa harina) but can also be made with wheat flour or a combination of the two, which is becoming more popular in the north of the country near to the US border. Maize meal is finely ground corn, pale yellow in colour and available in health-food shops and some supermarkets. It is sometimes called cornmeal but is not the same thing as either polenta or cornflour.

The dough must be properly prepared, rested and then rolled out thickly into a circle, or you can use a tortilla press to make the perfect tortilla. If you have problems rolling the dough into a circle, trim around a suitably sized plate.

Tortillas are cooked for the minimum length of time on a heated 'cormal' or heavy-based frying pan, which should be heated slowly and evenly before the tortilla is added; the tortilla is cooked until just speckled brown, then flipped over to cook the second side. If bubbles appear in the surface, they should be pressed down with a rolled-up tea towel or pad of paper towels. The pan should not be greased unless the tortillas stick – normally they do not – and then only lightly with a touch of oil.

Once made, wrap in a clean tea towel. If left uncovered, they will immediately firm up. To store them for future use, layer a piece of non-stick baking paper between each tortilla, wrap in a clean tea towel, then put in either a polythene bag or airtight container and chill for up to 3 days. If they become firm they can be reheated in a pan, fried, or dipped briefly in boiling water to soften, so that they can then be further shaped or rolled and used for making other dishes. Tortillas are eaten as a dish in themselves and are also used as the base for a variety of dishes, including Burritos, Tostados, Tacos, Tortilla Chips, Nachos, Enchiladas and Quesadillas.

INTRODUCTION

Chillies

Many people think that all Mexican food is red-hot and almost inedible unless you have a stomach of iron. True, it is highly spiced, and chillies certainly appear in abundance in recipes, but the amount and type of chillies used governs both the spiciness and 'hotness' of the dish, so it is up to the cook to decide just how much or how little to add. There are several types of chilli that are commonly used. However, some of them are readily available only in Mexico and similar countries, so in the recipes I have only stipulated chillis – you can use whichever you prefer or is available.

Beans

Another important ingredient in the Mexican diet is the bean, particularly the pinkish pinto bean, the black bean and the red kidney bean. Both fresh and dried beans are used widely to serve as 'stewed' or 'pot' beans as an everyday dish. Long, slow cooking is essential to make the beans digestible, and salt should be added only when they are tender, or the beans will take forever to tenderize. Many flavours can be added during cooking, including onions, chillies, bacon, garlic, and many others, which the beans readily absorb.

Each type of bean has its own special quality and flavour, and every family will have its own particular way of cooking them, either to be eaten as they are, or to be turned into Refried Beans. This is another traditional (and famous) Mexican dish, which can be eaten as a dish in its own right, or it can form part of many other Mexican dishes, particularly in combination with tortillas and their various fillings and toppings. Stewed or pot beans (or drained canned beans) are added to fried onion, garlic and chilli, mashed as they are added and then cooked to a thick paste to serve either hot or cold.

Salads

Guacamole and Tomato Salsa are regular accompaniments to many Mexican dishes, and are flavoured with chillies and onions; they are very attractive and tasty and can be eaten alone as well as being presented as a side dish to other foods. Other salads tend to use a mixture of fruit and vegetables, often combining flavours we may not be used to, but which turn out to blend extremely well. For instance, beetroot, bananas, mangoes and pomegranates are often mixed with a range of vegetables, giving the finished dish colour, texture and an original flavour.

Peppers

Peppers feature extensively in Mexican cookery, in all varieties and colours, including red, green, orange and yellow.

Some people find the taste of pepper can be harsh and almost bitter. To remove this, the Mexicans always roast or toast the pepper to peel the skin, which in turn takes away any bitterness. It is simple to do. First cut the pepper in half from stem to tip and lay the pieces cut-side down on a foil-lined grill rack and cook under a moderate heat until the skin chars and turns completely black. Remove and leave to cool a little and then the skin will peel off easily. Finally, turn over the pepper and remove the stem, membrane and any seeds and it is ready for use. Peppers may also be dry-fried by placing each half skin-side down in a 'cormal' or heavy-based frying pan and cooked slowly over a low heat until the skin blisters and chars.

Tomatoes

Tomatoes are an important part of Mexican cuisine, as they are used in salads – including the indispensable Tomato Salsa – as well as in a great many main-course dishes and a wide range of sauces. If they are to be cooked or added to cooked dishes, the skins are always removed first. This can be done in either of two ways. One is to place the tomatoes in a bowl and cover them with boiling water for a minute, then make a nick in the skin with a knife and transfer them quickly to a bowl of cold water. The skin will then peel off easily. Alternatively, if you have a gas hob, impale the tomato on a long fork and hold it carefully over the flame, turning it so that it heats evenly, until the skin chars and splits, after which it will peel off easily. This can also be done by placing the tomato under a hot grill until the skin just chars and splits.

Coriander (cilantro)

Also known as Chinese parsley, coriander (cilantro) is used in many Mexican recipes, either as a flavouring ingredient or as a garnish. It has a fairly potent but refreshing flavour, and is a true taste of Mexico. However, it does wilt extremely easily, so should be picked fresh or kept in cold water.

Coriander seeds and ground coriander are also used in Mexican cuisine, but the flavours are quite different which means that seed coriander and ground coriander are not interchangeable.

Spices

Several spices feature frequently in Mexican recipes, particularly cumin and cinnamon. Cumin, either in seed or powdered form, gives a touch of the oriental flavour brought by Indian settlers; cinnamon, used both ground and in stick form, is found in both sweet and savoury dishes.

Mexican chocolate is flavoured with cinnamon also, and if you use any other type of chocolate for a Mexican recipe, it is advisable to add a pinch of ground cinnamon for an authentic taste. Cloves too are used frequently in Mexican dishes, often in their ground form.

Pumpkin seeds

When the skin is removed from pumpkin seeds, the familiar green seeds are revealed, which are known as 'pepitas'. They can be added to dishes as they are, or they can be toasted or roasted first.

Often ground up to make a dip or dressing, they have a delicious nutty flavour and are extremely nutritious. If you cannot find them in your local supermarket, they are usually available from health-food shops.

Tacos

These can be bought ready-made in airtight packets and are often eaten as a snack – the Mexican version of potato crisps. They can easily be made at home simply by cutting homemade tortillas into wedges and frying them in deep or shallow fat until they are crispy.

Tacos are ideal for serving with dips such as Guacamole, as the dips complement the dry hot taste of the tacos. Once they have been fried, they can be kept for up to a week in an airtight container.

INTRODUCTION

Mexican Drinks

There are several drinks associated with Mexico, most of which are pretty, and ideal for a party.
Everyone knows the famous Tequila Sunrise – a mixture of tequila, orange juice, a touch of grenadine and lime juice, served with crushed ice. The Margarita is perhaps equally famous; it is a blend of tequila, lime juice, clear orange liqueur such as Cointreau and crushed ice.

Every country has its own version of fresh lemonade and in Mexico it is particularly refreshing; but whether or not you ever visit Mexico and try the lemonade, you must sample their hot chocolate. Put 750ml/1¼ pints of milk into a saucepan with 3 thin strips of orange rind, bring barely to the boil, remove from the heat, cover and leave to stand for 5 minutes; then discard the rind. Blend 90g/3½ oz Mexican chocolate or plain dark chocolate with a good pinch of ground cinnamon with the milk until dissolved and whisk until the mixture is really frothy. Serve at once, topped with a pinch of ground cinnamon – quite delicious!

Freezing

On the whole, Mexican food is not very suitable for freezing, mainly because of the strong flavours involved – particularly chillies and chilli sauces, which are widely used. When strong flavours are frozen they tend to intensify, and if left for more than a couple of weeks, a musty flavour can develop which spoils the dish, although it is not harmful. So before you decide to freeze a dish, consider whether it is really going to be helpful, and do so only if necessary and then for just a couple of weeks or so. Tortillas, which are widely used in the Mexican diet, cannot be frozen, so this does make many of the recipes unsuitable for freezing as they feature in them so frequently.

Mexican food is very distinctive, but with its simplicity and the wide use of fresh local produce you will find, as many people do, that the flavours and spiciness can quickly become almost addictive. Whether you want to serve a complete Mexican meal, or intersperse your cooking with a starter, main dish or dessert with a Mexican flavour, or just serve one of the delicious snacks, you are sure to be pleasantly surprised by the simplicity of the preparation and the mouth-watering results.

SALSA VERDE

An alternative to tomato salsa (see page 280), this salad makes an attractive and different accompaniment to Mexican dishes.

500g/1lb tomatillos or green tomatoes, chopped
½ medium onion, chopped very finely
1 level tbsp fresh coriander (cilantro), chopped
salt and pepper

Mix well, turn into a bowl and cover with clingfilm (plastic food wrap). Chill for at least 30 minutes.

STARTERS

VEGETABLE & CHICK-PEA (GARBANZO BEAN) SOUP

SERVES 4-6

3 tbsp olive oil
1 large onion, chopped finely
2–3 garlic cloves, crushed
½–1 red chilli, deseeded and chopped very finely
1 chicken breast (about 150 g/5 oz)
2 celery sticks, chopped finely
175 g/6 oz carrots, grated coarsely
1.25 litres/2¼ pints chicken stock
2 bay leaves
½ tsp dried oregano
¼ tsp ground cinnamon
salt and pepper
425 g/14 oz can chick-peas (garbanzo beans), drained
250 g/8 oz tomatoes, peeled, deseeded and chopped
1 tbsp tomato purée (paste)
chopped fresh coriander (cilantro) or parsley, to garnish

1 Heat the oil in a large saucepan and fry the onion, garlic and chilli very gently until softened but not coloured.

2 Slice the chicken thickly, add to the pan and continue to cook until it is well sealed all over.

3 Add the celery, carrots, stock, bay leaves, oregano, cinnamon and seasoning. Bring to the boil, then cover and simmer gently for about 20 minutes, or until the chicken is tender.

4 Remove the chicken from the soup and chop it finely, or cut it into narrow strips

5 Return the chicken to the pan with the chick-peas (garbanzo beans), tomatoes and tomato purée (paste) and cover the pan.

6 Simmer for a further 15–20 minutes, then discard the bay leaves, adjust the seasoning and serve very hot sprinkled with coriander (cilantro) or parsley and with warmed tortillas.

BEAN SOUP

SERVES 4

175 g/6 oz pinto beans
1.25 litres/2¼ pints water
175–225 g/6–8 oz carrots, chopped finely
1 large onion, chopped finely
2–3 garlic cloves, crushed
½–1 chilli, deseeded and chopped finely
1 litre /1¾ pints chicken or vegetable stock
2 tomatoes, peeled and chopped finely
2 celery sticks, sliced very thinly
salt and pepper
1 tbsp chopped fresh coriander (cilantro) (optional)

CROUTONS:
3 slices white bread
fat or oil for deep-frying
1–2 garlic cloves, crushed

1 Soak the beans overnight in cold water; drain and place in a pan with the water. Bring to the boil and boil fast for 10 minutes. Cover and simmer for 2 hours, or until the beans are tender and most of the liquid has evaporated.

2 Add the carrots, onion, garlic, chilli and stock, and bring back to the boil. Cover and simmer for a further 30 minutes or so until very tender.

3 Remove half the beans and vegetables with the cooking juices and press through a sieve or purée in a food processor or blender until smooth.

4 Return the bean purée to the saucepan and add the tomatoes and celery to the soup. Simmer for a further 10–15 minutes or until the celery is just tender, adding a little more stock or water if the soup is too thick.

5 Add seasoning to taste and stir in the chopped coriander (cilantro), if using. Serve with the croûtons.

6 To make the croûtons, remove the crusts from the bread and cut into small cubes. Heat the oil with the garlic in a small frying pan and fry the croûtons until golden brown. Drain on paper towels. The croûtons may be made up to 48 hours in advance and stored in an airtight container.

TORTILLAS

MAKES 10

WHEAT TORTILLAS:
300 g/10 oz plain (all-purpose) white flour
1 tsp salt
60 g/2 oz white vegetable fat (shortening)
150–175 ml/5–6 fl oz warm water

CORN TORTILLAS:
150 g/5 oz plain (all-purpose) white flour
1 tsp salt
150 g/5 oz maize meal
45 g/1½ oz white vegetable fat (shortening)
150–175 ml/5–6 fl oz warm water

1 To make the wheat tortillas, sift the flour and salt into a bowl and rub the fat into the flour with your fingertips until the mixture resembles very fine breadcrumbs.

2 Add sufficient warm water to mix to a softish pliable dough; turn out on to a lightly floured work surface and knead until smooth (2–3 minutes). Place in a plastic bag and leave to rest for about 15 minutes. [Steps 1 and 2 may be done in a food processor.]

3 Divide the dough into 10 equal pieces and keep covered with a damp cloth to prevent it from drying out. Roll out each piece of dough on a lightly floured work surface to a circle of 18–20 cm/7–8 in. Place the tortillas between sheets of paper towel as they are made to prevent them from drying out.

4 Heat a griddle or heavy-based frying pan until just beginning to smoke. Brush off all excess flour from each tortilla, place in the pan and cook for 20–30 seconds only on each side until just speckled brown. They will quickly bubble from the heat and should be pressed down lightly with a spatula occasionally during cooking. Take care not to burn or brown them too much. If black deposits appear in the pan, scrape them off; they are excess burnt flour from the tortillas. Do not grease the pan.

5 Wrap the tortillas in a clean tea towel or place between sheets of paper towel when cooked to keep them pliable. When cold, wrap in clingfilm if they are not to be used at once. They will keep in the refrigerator for several days.

6 Corn tortillas are made in a similar way, except the flour and salt is sifted into a bowl, the maize meal is mixed in and then the fat is rubbed in finely; continue as for wheat tortillas.

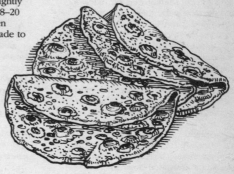

NACHOS

MAKES 30

5 tortillas (wheat or corn – see page 277)
oil for frying
1 red (bell) pepper, halved and deseeded
300 g/10 oz jar tomato salsa dip
4 spring onions (scallions), trimmed and
    chopped
4 tomatoes, peeled and chopped
500 g/1 lb can refried beans or 1 quantity
    Refried Beans (see page 282)
175 g/6 oz mature Cheddar cheese, grated
3 tbsp grated Parmesan cheese
chopped fresh coriander (cilantro) to
    garnish

1 Stack the tortillas neatly and cut in
half with a sharp knife, and then cut
each half into 3 wedges to give 6 nachos
from each tortilla.

2 Heat about 2.5 cm/1 in oil in a large
frying pan until just smoking. Fry the
pieces of tortilla – a few at a time – until
crispy and lightly browned, turning once.
Remove and drain on paper towels before
transferring to baking sheets.

3 Put the (bell) pepper cut-side
downwards into a grill pan and
place under a preheated moderate grill
until the skin is charred. Remove and
leave to cool slightly. Peel off the skin
and then chop the (bell) pepper.

4 Put the chopped (bell) pepper in a
bowl with the salsa dip, spring
onions (scallions) and tomatoes, and mix
together well.

5 Mash the refried beans and spread
an even layer over each nacho, then
top with the tomato salsa mixture.

6 Sprinkle with the cheeses and place
under a preheated moderate grill
until the cheese bubbles. Alternatively,
place in a preheated oven at
200°C/400°F/Gas Mark 6 for about 10
minutes until the cheese is bubbling.
Serve hot or cold sprinkled with chopped
coriander (cilantro).

GUACAMOLE

SERVES 4

4–6 spring onions (scallions), trimmed
2 large ripe avocados, quartered, stoned
    and peeled
1 tbsp lime juice
2–3 garlic cloves, crushed
few drops of Tabasco sauce
2–4 tomatoes, peeled, deseeded and
    chopped finely
1–2 tbsp soured cream (optional)
salt and pepper
1 tbsp chopped fresh coriander (cilantro)
    or chives

1 Put the spring onions (scallions) into
a food processor and chop finely.
Cut the avocado into slices, add to the
food processor and work until smooth.
Alternatively, chop the onions finely with
a knife and mash the avocados and
onions together thoroughly with a fork.

2 Add the lime juice, garlic and
Tabasco sauce to the avocado
mixture and work or mash until smoothly
blended. Turn out into a bowl.

3 Stir in the chopped tomatoes and the
soured cream, if using, and season
the mixture to taste. Then mix in half the
chopped fresh coriander (cilantro) or
chives.

4 Turn the guacamole into a serving
bowl, and if it is not to be used
immediately, bury one of the avocado
stones in it as this will help it to keep its
colour. Cover the guacamole tightly with
clingfilm until you are ready to use it,
removing the avocado stone at the last
minute, and sprinkling with the remaining
coriander (cilantro) or chives.

5 Serve as a starter with tacos or
tortillas; or serve as an
accompaniment to such dishes as Chilli
Lamb Chops (see page 287) or Chilli con
Carne (see page 290); or use with other
ingredients as a topping for tortillas or as
part of other recipes.

TOSTADOS

MAKES 8

½ quantity Tortillas (wheat or corn – see page 277)
oil for frying
500 g/1 lb can refried beans, mashed or 1 quantity Refried Beans (see page 282)
finely shredded lettuce
200 g/7 oz can prawns (shrimp) or tuna fish in brine, well drained, or 4–6 hard-boiled eggs, grated coarsely
2–3 tsp sweet chilli sauce
¼ tsp ground cumin
5–6 tbsp soured cream
3 tomatoes, sliced
2 small ripe avocados
3–4 spring onions (scallions), trimmed and sliced
1–2 garlic cloves, crushed
1 tbsp lime juice
salt and pepper

TO GARNISH:
stoned black olives, halved
fresh coriander (cilantro) or parsley

1 Make up the tortilla recipe and divide into 8 pieces, keeping them covered with a damp cloth. Roll out each piece to a thin circle of about 12 cm/5 in, on a lightly floured work surface. Cook as for large tortillas.

2 Heat about 2.5 cm/1 inch oil in a large frying pan and when just smoking fry the tortillas, one at a time, for a minute or so until a pale golden brown on each side and just crispy. Drain on paper towels and leave to cool.

3 Mash the refried beans and spread a layer over each tortilla, then sprinkle with shredded lettuce.

4 Combine the drained prawns (shrimp) or tuna fish (mashing if necessary), or eggs, chilli sauce, cumin and soured cream, and place a spoonful to one side of each tortilla on the lettuce; then arrange the tomato slices down the other side.

5 Mash the avocados thoroughly with the spring onions (scallions), garlic and lime juice, or process in a food processor until smooth. Season to taste. Place a spoonful of the avocado sauce on top of the other ingredients.

6 Garnish each with halved and stoned black olives and coriander (cilantro) leaves or parsley sprigs. Serve within an hour of preparing or the tortilla may become soggy and the avocado will lose its colour.

VEGETABLES & SALADS

TOMATO SALSA

SERVES 4

4 ripe red tomatoes
1 medium red-skinned onion or 6 spring
    onions (scallions)
1–2 garlic cloves, crushed (optional)
2 tbsp chopped fresh coriander (cilantro)
½ red or green chilli (optional)
finely grated rind of ½–1 lemon or lime
1–2 tbsp lemon or lime juice
pepper

1 Chop the tomatoes fairly finely and
evenly, and put into a bowl. They
must be firm and a good strong red
colour for the best results, but if
preferred, they may be peeled by placing
them in boiling water for about 20
seconds and then plunging into cold
water. The skins should then slip off
easily when they are nicked with a knife.

2 Peel and slice the red onions thinly,
or trim the spring onions (scallions)
and cut into thin slanting slices; add to
the tomatoes with the garlic and coriander
(cilantro) and mix lightly.

3 Remove the seeds from the red or
green chilli, if using, chop the flesh
very finely and add to the salad. Treat the
chillies with care; do not touch your eyes
or face after handling them until you have
washed your hands thoroughly. Chilli
juices can burn.

4 Add the lemon or lime rind and
juice to the salsa, and mix well.
Transfer to a serving bowl and sprinkle
with pepper.

VARIATION

If you don't like the distinctive flavour
of fresh coriander (cilantro), you can
replace it with flat-leaf parsley instead.

CHRISTMAS SALAD

SERVES 4

1 cos (romaine) lettuce
125 g/4 oz cooked beetroot
2 oranges
1 green-skinned dessert (eating) apple
1–2 bananas
1 tbsp lime or lemon juice
1 carrot, peeled
1 pomegranate or paw-paw
60 g/2 oz roasted peanuts or flaked
    almonds, toasted

DRESSING:
1 tbsp lime or lemon juice
finely grated rind of ¼ lime or lemon
    (optional)
1 garlic clove, crushed
4 tbsp light olive oil or sunflower oil
1 tsp sugar
salt and pepper

1 Shred the lettuce and arrange on a
flat dish.

2 Peel the beetroot if necessary and
cut into dice or small slices; then
arrange around the edge of the lettuce.

3 Cut away the peel and pith from the
oranges and ease out the segments
carefully from between the membranes.
Arrange the orange segments over the
lettuce.

4 Core and chop the apple and put
into a bowl with the sliced bananas.
Add the lime or lemon juice and toss,
then drain off the excess juice.

5 Cut the carrot into julienne strips or
peel off in thin strips, using a potato
peeler, add to the apple mixture and
spoon over the salad.

6 Cut the pomegranate into quarters
and ease out the seeds, or halve the
paw-paw, discard the seeds and peel and
dice. Sprinkle over the salad with the
peanuts or almonds.

7 Whisk all the ingredients together for
the dressing and either spoon over
the salad or serve in a jug.

MEXICAN SALAD

••

SERVES 4

500 g/1 lb small new potatoes, scraped
salt
250 g/8 oz small cauliflower florets
1–2 carrots, peeled
3 large gherkins
2–3 spring onions (scallions), trimmed
1–2 tbsp capers
12 pitted black olives
1 iceberg lettuce or other lettuce leaves

DRESSING:
1½–2 tsp Dijon mustard
1 tsp sugar
2 tbsp olive oil
4 tbsp thick mayonnaise
1 tbsp wine vinegar
salt and pepper

TO GARNISH:
1 ripe avocado
1 tbsp lime or lemon juice

1 Cook the potatoes in salted water until they are just tender; drain, cool and either dice or slice. Cook the cauliflower in boiling salted water for 2 minutes. Drain, rinse in cold water and drain again.

2 Cut the carrots into narrow julienne strips and mix with the potatoes and cauliflower.

3 Cut the gherkins and spring onions (scallions) into slanting slices and add them to the salad together with the capers and black olives.

4 Arrange the lettuce leaves on a plate or in a bowl and spoon the salad over the lettuce.

5 To make the dressing, whisk all the ingredients together until completely emulsified. Drizzle the dressing over the salad.

6 Cut the avocado into quarters, then remove the stone and peel. Cut into slices and dip immediately in the lime or lemon juice. Use to garnish the salad just before serving.

MEXICAN RICE

••

SERVES 6

300 g/10 oz long-grain rice
3 tbsp oil
1 large onion, chopped
½ chilli, deseeded and chopped finely
2 large garlic cloves, crushed
4 tomatoes (about 250 g/8 oz), peeled and chopped
125 g/4 oz carrots, peeled and chopped
900 ml /1½ pints chicken or vegetable stock
125 g/4 oz frozen peas (optional)
salt and pepper
chopped fresh coriander (cilantro) or parsley to garnish

1 Put the rice in a heatproof bowl, cover with boiling water and leave to rest for 10 minutes; then drain very thoroughly.

2 Heat the oil in a pan, add the rice and fry gently, stirring almost constantly for about 5 minutes, or until just beginning to colour.

3 Add the onion, chilli, garlic, tomatoes and carrots, and continue to cook for a minute or so before adding the stock and bringing to the boil.

4 Stir the rice well, cover the pan and simmer gently for 20 minutes without removing the lid.

5 Stir in the peas, if using, and seasoning; continue to cook, covered, for about 5 minutes, or until all the liquid has been absorbed and the rice is tender.

6 If time allows, leave the covered pan to rest for 5–10 minutes, then fork up the rice and serve sprinkled generously with chopped fresh coriander (cilantro) or parsley.

NOTE

The chilli content of this dish can be increased to give a hotter 'Mexican' taste, but be warned – once it has been added, it cannot be removed!

BASIC STEWED BEANS

SERVES 4

225 g/8 oz pinto beans or cannellini
   beans
1 large onion, sliced
2 garlic cloves, crushed
1 litre /1¾ pints water
salt
chopped fresh coriander (cilantro) or
   parsley to garnish

BEAN STEW:
1 large onion, sliced
2 garlic cloves, crushed
8 rashers streaky bacon, rinded and diced
2 tbsp oil
425 g/14 oz can chopped tomatoes
1 tsp ground cumin
1 tbsp sweet chilli sauce

REFRIED BEANS:
1 onion, chopped
2 garlic cloves, crushed
2 tbsp oil

1 Soak the beans in cold water
   overnight; or if time is short, cover
the beans with boiling water and leave
until cold – about 2 hours.

2 Drain the beans and put into a
   saucepan with the onion, garlic and
water, bring to the boil, cover and simmer

gently for 1½ hours. Stir well, add more
boiling water if necessary, and simmer,
covered, for a further 30–90 minutes, or
until the beans are tender.

3 When the beans are tender, add salt
   to taste (about 1 tsp) and continue
to cook, uncovered, for about 15 minutes
to allow most of the liquor to evaporate
to form a thick sauce.

4 Serve the basic beans hot sprinkled
   with chopped coriander (cilantro) or
parsley; or cool, chill and reheat to serve
next day; or use in another dish.

5 To make a bean stew, fry the onion,
   garlic and bacon for 3–4 minutes in
the oil, add the canned tomatoes, the
basic beans, cumin and chilli sauce, and
bring to the boil. Cover and simmer very
gently for 30 minutes. Adjust the
seasoning and serve.

6 To make refried beans, fry the onion
   and garlic in the oil until golden
brown. Add a quarter of the basic beans
with a little of their liquor and mash.
Continue adding and mashing the beans,
while simmering gently until thick. Adjust
the seasoning and serve hot, or cool and
chill for up to 1 week.

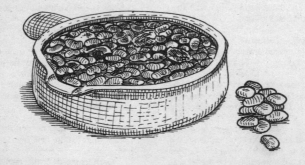

LIGHT MEALS

QUESADILLAS

••

SERVES 4

8 tortillas (corn or wheat – see page 277)

FILLING:
175 g/6 oz Feta cheese or white Cheshire
* cheese*
175 g/6 oz Mozzarella cheese
6 tbsp grated Parmesan cheese
6 spring onions (scallions), trimmed and
* chopped*
1–2 garlic cloves, crushed
1 tbsp sweet chilli sauce
1 tbsp chopped fresh coriander (cilantro)
1 cooked potato, grated coarsely
salt and pepper
beaten egg or egg white
oil for brushing

TO SERVE:
shredded lettuce
Tomato Salsa (see page 280)

1 To make the filling, grate the Feta
   and Mozzarella cheeses coarsely into
a bowl and mix in the Parmesan cheese,
spring onions (scallions), garlic, sweet
chilli sauce, coriander (cilantro), grated
potato and seasoning.

2 If the tortillas are too firm to bend in
   half, dip each one into a pan of
gently simmering water until just soft and
drain on paper towels.

3 Place about 1½ tbsp of the cheese
   filling on one side of each tortilla
and fold in half. Brush the edges with
beaten egg or egg white.

4 Fold over and press the edges
   together well. Place the quesadillas
on lightly greased baking sheets and
brush each one with a little oil. Cook in a
preheated oven at 190°C/375°F/Gas Mark
5 for 12–15 minutes, or until they are
lightly browned.

5 Serve the quesadillas either hot or
   warm with shredded lettuce and
tomato salsa as accompaniments.

YUCATAN FISH

••

SERVES 4

4 cod cutlets or steaks or hake cutlets
* (about 175 g/6 oz each)*
2 tbsp lime juice
salt and pepper
1 green (bell) pepper
1 tbsp olive oil
1 onion, chopped finely
1–2 garlic cloves, crushed
45 g/1½ oz green pumpkin seeds
grated rind of ½ lime
1 tbsp fresh coriander (cilantro) or
* parsley, chopped*
1 tbsp fresh mixed herbs, chopped
60g/2oz button mushrooms, sliced thinly
2–3 tbsp fresh orange juice or white wine

TO GARNISH:
lime wedges
fresh mixed herbs

1 Wipe the fish, place in a shallow
   ovenproof dish and pour the lime
juice over. Turn the fish in the juice,
season with salt and pepper, cover and
leave in a cool place for 15–30 minutes.

2 Halve the (bell) pepper, remove the
   seeds and place under a preheated
moderate grill, skin-side upwards, until
the skin burns and splits. Leave to cool
slightly, then peel off the skin and chop
the flesh.

3 Heat the oil in a pan and fry the
   onion, garlic, (bell) pepper and
pumpkin seeds gently for a few minutes
until the onion is soft.

4 Stir in the lime rind, coriander
   (cilantro) or parsley, mixed herbs,
mushrooms and seasoning, and spoon
over the fish.

5 Spoon or pour the orange juice or
   wine over the fish, cover with foil
or a lid and place in a preheated oven at
180°C/350°F/Gas Mark 4 for about 30
minutes, or until the fish is just tender.

6 Garnish the fish with lime wedges
   and fresh herbs and serve with
Mexican Rice (see page 281) or plain
boiled rice and tortillas.

PRAWNS (SHRIMP) IN BACON WITH SOURED CREAM

SERVES 4

16–20 king prawns or large tiger prawns
   (jumbo shrimp)
16–20 lean rashers streaky bacon,
   derinded
60 g/2 oz butter
finely grated rind of 1 lime
2 garlic cloves, crushed

CORIANDER (CILANTRO) AND SOURED
   CREAM SAUCE:
150 ml/ ¼ pint soured cream
2–3 garlic cloves, crushed
½ small red chilli, deseeded and chopped
   very finely
2 tbsp chopped fresh coriander (cilantro)
2 spring onions (scallions), trimmed and
   chopped finely
salt and pepper
1–2 tsp lime juice

TO GARNISH:
fresh coriander (cilantro)
lime wedges

1 Remove the heads and shells from the prawns (shrimp) but leave the tails in place. Remove the black vein which runs down the length of the prawn (shrimp).

2 Wrap a rasher of bacon around each prawn (shrimp), securing with a piece of wooden cocktail stick. Place on a foil-lined grill pan.

3 Melt the butter and mix in half the grated lime rind and the garlic. Use to brush over the bacon-wrapped prawns (shrimp).

4 To make the sauce, put the soured cream into a bowl and mix in the garlic, chilli, coriander (cilantro), spring onions (scallions), remaining grated lime rind, seasoning and finally lime juice to taste, which will thicken up the sauce. Transfer to a serving bowl.

5 Cook the prawns (shrimp) under a preheated grill for about 2 minutes on each side, or until the bacon is lightly browned and the prawns (shrimp) are hot. Remove and discard the wooden cocktail sticks.

6 Serve the prawns (shrimp) on a large plate or 4 individual plates, together with the soured cream sauce and a garnish of fresh coriander (cilantro) and lime wedges.

ENCHILLADA LAYERS

••

SERVES 4

CHICKEN FILLING:
500 g/1 lb boneless chicken breasts
2 tbsp olive oil
1 large onion, sliced thinly
3 garlic cloves, crushed
1 tsp ground cumin
2 tbsp stock or water
salt and pepper
1 tbsp chopped fresh coriander (cilantro)
chopped fresh coriander (cilantro) to
*   garnish*

TOMATO SAUCE:
2 tbsp oil
1 onion, chopped very finely
3 garlic cloves, crushed
1 red chilli, deseeded and chopped finely
425 g/14 oz can chopped tomatoes with
*   herbs*
250 g/8 oz can peeled tomatoes, chopped
3 tbsp tomato purée (paste)
2 tbsp lime juice
2 tsp caster (superfine) sugar
salt and pepper
6 tortillas (wheat or corn – see page 277)
175 g/6 oz Feta or white Cheshire cheese,
*   coarsely grated*

1 Remove the skin from the chicken and chop the flesh finely. Heat the oil in a pan and fry the onion and garlic gently until soft.

2 Add the chicken and fry for about 5 minutes, or until well sealed and almost cooked, stirring frequently. Add the cumin, stock or water and seasoning, and continue to cook for 2–3 minutes until tender; then stir in the coriander (cilantro) and remove from the heat.

3 To make the tomato sauce, heat the oil in a pan and fry the onion, garlic and chilli gently until softened.

4 Add both cans of tomatoes, the tomato purée (paste), lime juice, sugar and seasoning. Bring to the boil and simmer gently for 10 minutes.

5 Place 1 tortilla on a greased ovenproof dish, cover with a fifth of the chicken mixture and 2 tbsp tomato sauce and sprinkle with cheese. Continue to layer in this way, finishing with a tortilla, the remaining sauce and cheese.

6 Place, uncovered, in a preheated oven at 190°C/375°F/Gas Mark 5 for about 25 minutes, or until lightly browned. Serve cut into wedges and sprinkle with coriander (cilantro).

PICADILLO

••

SERVES 4

350 g/12 oz lean minced beef
225 g/8 oz minced pork (or beef)
2 onions, sliced thinly
3 garlic cloves, crushed
1 large carrot, chopped finely
1 green chilli, deseeded and chopped
    finely
425 g/14 oz can tomatoes
2 tbsp tomato purée (paste)
90 g/3 oz raisins
150 ml / ¼ pint red wine
1 tbsp vinegar
1 tsp cumin
½ tsp ground allspice
½ tsp ground cinnamon
60 g/2 oz blanched flaked almonds
salt and pepper
chopped fresh coriander (cilantro) to
    garnish

1 Put the meats into a heavy-based
  saucepan with no extra fat and cook
over a low heat until well sealed, stirring
frequently.

2 Add the onions, garlic, carrot and
  chilli to the pan and continue to
cook for 3–4 minutes, or until they have
softened. Drain off any excess fat.

3 Add the tomatoes, tomato purée
  (paste), raisins, wine, vinegar, cumin,
allspice, cinnamon, half the almonds and
seasoning. Stir into the meat mixture.

4 Bring to the boil, cover the pan
  and simmer gently, stirring
occasionally, for 20–30 minutes, or until
the meat is tender and most of the liquid
has evaporated.

5 Adjust the seasoning and serve
  sprinkled with the remaining
almonds and chopped coriander
(cilantro).

STUFFING FOR VEGETABLES

This recipe is excellent topped with a
layer of creamed potatoes, or it can be
used as a stuffing for peppers,
courgettes or aubergines (eggplants).

SPICED PORK RIBS WITH APRICOTS

••

SERVES 4

1.75–2 kg/3½–4 lb American-style pork ribs
salt
1 tbsp coarsely ground black pepper
1 tbsp ground cumin
4 garlic cloves, crushed
2 tbsp chopped fresh coriander (cilantro)
1 tsp ground coriander
1 tbsp oil
chopped fresh coriander (cilantro) to
    garnish (optional)

APRICOT SAUCE:
450 ml/ ¾ pint chicken or beef stock
175 g/6 oz ready-to-eat dried apricot
    halves
4 garlic cloves, crushed
1 tbsp hot chilli sauce or ½–1 tsp chilli
    powder
2 tbsp oil
1 large onion, chopped

1 Cut the pork into 5 cm/2 in pieces
  and place in an ovenproof dish or
tin in a single layer. Season with salt and
pepper. Combine the cumin, garlic, fresh
coriander (cilantro) and ground coriander,
and sprinkle over the pork, rubbing in
and turning the pieces so they are evenly
coated. Leave to marinate for at least
2 hours.

2 Drizzle the oil over the pork and
  place in a preheated oven at
200°C/400°F/Gas Mark 6 for 45 minutes,
or until lightly browned.

3 Prepare the sauce. Put the stock,
  apricots, garlic and chilli sauce or
powder into a food processor or blender
and work until puréed, or chop finely.

4 Heat the 2 tbsp oil and fry the onion
  until softened but only lightly
coloured. Add the apricot purée, bring to
the boil and simmer gently for 10
minutes. (If necessary add a little hot
water, but the sauce should be thick.)

5 Drain off any excess fat from the
  pork, then pour the apricot sauce
over the ribs and return to the oven for
about 20 minutes, or until well browned.

6 Serve hot sprinkled with chopped
  coriander (cilantro), if liked.

CHILLI LAMB CHOPS

SERVES 4

4 large lamb leg chops (about 175 g/6 oz
each)
150 ml / ¼ pint red wine
3 large garlic cloves, crushed
½ small onion, chopped
1 small chilli, deseeded and chopped
finely
2 small thin slices fresh root ginger,
chopped
1 tbsp paprika
1½ tsp ground cumin
½ tsp salt
pepper
grated rind of ½ lime
2 tbsp lime juice
oil for frying

TO GARNISH:
lime slices, twisted
2 spring onions (scallions), trimmed and
sliced
chopped fresh coriander (cilantro) or
coriander (cilantro) leaves

1 Cover the chops with clingfilm and
beat out a little thinner with a meat
cleaver or rolling pin.

2 Put the wine into a food processor
or blender with the garlic, onion,
chilli, ginger, paprika, cumin, salt, pepper,
and lime rind and juice. and work until
smooth. Alternatively, chop the onion,
chilli and garlic very finely by hand and
mix well with the other ingredients.

3 Pour a thin layer of the sauce into a
container that is just large enough to
hold the lamb chops in a single layer, add
the chops and cover with the remaining
sauce.

4 Cover the lamb with clingfilm and
leave in a cool place to marinate for
at least 2 hours, preferably 3–4 hours.

5 Heat the oil in a pan. Drain the
pieces of lamb and fry each one
gently for 3–4 minutes on each side until
browned and just cooked through. Pour
off any excess fat from the pan, then add
the remaining marinade to the pan and
cook for 3–4 minutes. Adjust the
seasoning to taste.

6 Serve the lamb chops on a platter
with the sauce spooned over and
garnished with twisted lime slices, sliced
spring onions (scallions) and chopped
fresh coriander (cilantro) or coriander
(cilantro) leaves. Serve with fried or
boiled potatoes, tortillas and a salad.

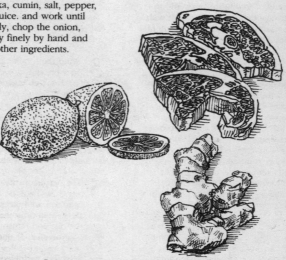

PORK TACOS

MAKES 8

oil for frying
350 g/12 oz lean minced pork
2 rashers bacon, derinded and chopped
1 onion, chopped very finely
2 garlic cloves, crushed
1 tbsp sweet chilli sauce
1–2 tbsp tomato purée (paste)
½ tsp ground cumin
½ tsp dried oregano
salt and pepper
60 g/2 oz button mushrooms, chopped
2 tbsp stock or water
8 small tortillas (wheat or corn – see page 277), about 15 cm/6 in
salad leaves to garnish

1 Heat the oil in a saucepan, add the pork, bacon, onion and garlic and cook gently, stirring frequently, for about 10 minutes, until almost cooked.

2 Add the chilli sauce, tomato purée (paste), cumin, oregano and seasoning, and continue to cook for a few minutes more; then add the mushrooms and stock or water and cook for a further 2–3 minutes. Adjust the seasoning and leave to cool.

3 Divide the pork mixture between the tortillas, fold in the ends and roll them up tightly; then secure each with a wooden cocktail stick to prevent them unrolling while cooking.

4 Heat about 2.5 cm/1 in oil in a large frying pan and when just smoking, add the taco rolls, 2 at a time, and fry until a light golden brown all over, turning in the oil as necessary. Alternatively, they may be cooked in deep fat at 180°C/350°F until a light golden brown.

5 Drain thoroughly on paper towels and remove the cocktail sticks carefully. Keep warm while frying the remaining tacos. Serve with a garnish of salad leaves.

BURRITOS

SERVES 4

60 g/2 oz pumpkin seeds, toasted
3–4 spring onions (scallions), trimmed and sliced
1 chilli, deseeded and chopped finely
4 tbsp chopped fresh parsley
1 tbsp chopped fresh coriander (cilantro)
6 tbsp natural yogurt
salt and pepper
4 wheat or corn tortillas (see page 277)
30 g/1 oz butter
4 tbsp milk
1 garlic clove, crushed
6 eggs
60 g/2 oz cooked ham or bacon, chopped, or 125 g/4 oz cooked white or smoked fish, flaked
2 tomatoes, peeled and sliced

TO GARNISH:
shredded lettuce
Tomato Salsa (see page 280)

1 Toast the pumpkin seeds lightly (under a moderate grill or in a heavy-based frying pan with no added fat) and chop finely. Put into a food processor with the spring onions (scallions) and chilli and work until well blended.

2 Add the chopped parsley and coriander (cilantro), followed by the yogurt, and blend until well mixed. Season to taste.

3 Wrap the tortillas in foil and warm in a preheated oven at 180°C/350°F/Gas Mark 4 for a few minutes.

4 Melt the butter in a pan with the milk, garlic and seasoning. Remove from the heat and beat in the eggs. Cook over a gentle heat, stirring, until just scrambled. Stir in the ham, bacon or fish.

5 Lay out the tortillas, spoon the scrambled egg down the centre of each and top with the pumpkin seed mixture followed by the sliced tomatoes.

6 Roll up the tortillas and serve as they are, garnished with the shredded lettuce and tomato salsa.

MEXICAN TACOS

SERVES 4

350 g/12 oz lean minced beef
1 onion, chopped finely
3 garlic cloves, crushed
1 chilli, deseeded and chopped
    very finely
1 celery stick, chopped finely
1 red (bell) pepper
3 tomatoes, peeled and chopped
1 tbsp tomato purée (paste)
½ tsp ground cumin
½ tsp ground cinnamon
salt and pepper
1 tbsp vinegar
2 tbsp stock or water
1 tbsp chopped fresh coriander (cilantro)
    (optional)
oil for frying
4 tortillas (wheat or corn)

TO SERVE:
500 g/1 lb can refried beans
shredded lettuce
4 tbsp soured cream
Guacamole (see page 278)
Tomato Salsa (see page 280)

1 Put the beef into a saucepan with the onion, garlic, chilli and celery, and cook gently, stirring frequently, for about 10 minutes until cooked through.

2 Halve the (bell) pepper, remove the seeds and place in the grill pan, cut-side down. Place under a preheated moderate grill until charred. Cool slightly, then peel off the skin and chop the flesh.

3 Add the (bell) pepper and tomatoes to the beef mixture, followed by the tomato purée (paste), spices, seasoning, vinegar and stock. Simmer for 10 minutes, until tender, and all the liquid has evaporated. Stir in the coriander (cilantro), if using.

4 If making your own taco shells, heat 2.5 cm/1 inch oil in a frying pan and when just smoking, add a tortilla and fry briefly until beginning to colour, folding in half during cooking. Remove quickly and drain on paper towels, placing crumpled paper towels in the centre of the taco so it sets in a shell shape. If using bought taco shells, warm in the oven.

5 Mash the refried beans and put a layer in the base of each taco; then cover with the beef mixture, dividing it equally between each taco. Sprinkle with shredded lettuce and drizzle with soured cream. Serve on warmed plates with guacamole and tomato salsa.

CHICKEN FAJITAS

SERVES 4

2 red (bell) peppers
2 green (bell) peppers
2 tbsp olive oil
2 onions, chopped
3 garlic cloves, crushed
1 chilli, deseeded and chopped finely
2 boneless chicken breasts (about
*   350 g/12 oz)*
60 g/2 oz button mushrooms, sliced
2 tsp freshly chopped coriander (cilantro)
grated rind of ½ lime
2 tbsp lime juice
salt and pepper
4 wheat or corn tortillas (see page 277)
4–6 tbsp soured cream

TO GARNISH:
Tomato Salsa (see page 280)
lime wedges

1 Halve the (bell) peppers, remove the seeds and place skin-side upwards under a preheated moderate grill until well charred. Leave to cool slightly and then peel off the skin; cut the flesh into thin slices.

2 Heat the oil in a pan, add the onions, garlic and chilli, and fry them for a few minutes just until the onion has softened.

3 Cut the chicken into narrow strips, add to the vegetable mixture in the pan and fry for 4–5 minutes until almost cooked through, stirring occasionally.

4 Add the peppers, mushrooms, coriander, lime rind and juice, and continue to cook for 2–3 minutes. Season to taste.

5 Heat the tortillas, wrapped in foil, in a preheated oven at 180°C/350°F/ Gas Mark 4 for a few minutes. Bend them in half and divide the chicken mixture between them.

6 Top the chicken filling in each tortilla with a spoonful of soured cream and serve garnished with tomato salsa and lime wedges.

CHILLI CON CARNE

SERVES 4

750 g/1½ lb braising or best stewing steak
2 tbsp oil
1 large onion, sliced
2–4 garlic cloves, crushed
1 tbsp plain (all-purpose) flour
450 ml/ ¾ pint tomato juice
425 g/14 oz can tomatoes
1–2 tbsp sweet chilli sauce
1 tsp ground cumin
salt and pepper
425 g/14 oz can red kidney beans,
*   drained*
½ teaspoon dried oregano
1–2 tbsp chopped fresh parsley
chopped fresh herbs to garnish

1 Cut the beef into cubes of about 2 cm/¾ in. Heat the oil in a flameproof casserole and fry the beef until well sealed all over. Remove from the casserole.

2 Add the onion and garlic to the casserole and fry in the same oil until lightly browned; then stir in the flour and cook for 1–2 minutes.

3 Stir in the tomato juice and tomatoes gradually and bring to the boil. Replace the beef and add the chilli sauce, cumin and seasoning. Cover and place in a preheated oven at 160°C/325°F/Gas Mark 3 for 1½ hours, or until almost tender.

4 Stir in the kidney beans, oregano and parsley, and adjust the seasoning to taste. Cover the casserole and return to the oven for 45 minutes, or until the meat is very tender and the sauce is fairly thick.

5 Serve the chilli con carne sprinkled with chopped fresh herbs and with boiled rice and tortillas.

CHILLI MEATBALLS

SERVES 4

750 g/1½ lb minced beef
1 small onion, chopped finely
30 g/1 oz ground almonds
60 g/2 oz fresh white breadcrumbs
1 tsp ground cumin
¼ tsp mild chilli powder
1 tsp freshly chopped thyme or ½ tsp dried
*   thyme*
salt and pepper
1 egg, beaten
3–4 tbsp oil for frying
sprigs of fresh thyme or parsley to garnish

SAUCE:
1 onion, sliced
250 g/8 oz tomatoes, peeled
2 garlic cloves, crushed
300 ml / ½ pint tomato juice
½–1 red chilli, deseeded and chopped
*   finely*
1 tsp sweet chilli sauce
1 red pepper

1 To make the meatballs, combine the beef, onion, ground almonds, breadcrumbs, cumin, chilli powder, herbs and seasoning, and bind together with the beaten egg. Divide into 16–20 pieces and shape into round balls.

2 Heat the oil in a pan and fry the meatballs until lightly browned; transfer to a casserole.

3 Purée the onion, tomatoes and garlic in a food processor or blender. or chop finely and mix well; pour into a saucepan with the tomato juice, chilli, chilli sauce and seasoning. Bring to the boil and simmer gently for 10 minutes.

4 Cut the pepper in half, remove the seeds and place under a preheated moderate grill, skin-side up, and cook until the skin chars. Leave to cool slightly, then peel off the skin and cut into strips.

5 Add the pepper to the sauce and pour over the meatballs. Cover and place in a preheated oven at 160°C/325°F/Gas Mark 3 for 35 minutes.

6 Adjust the seasoning and serve garnished with thyme or parsley. Serve with rice or potatoes and a salad.

DESSERTS

FRUIT CHIMICHANGAS

SERVES 4

1 large paw-paw, or 4 apricots,
*   or 1 large mango*
8–12 strawberries
1 large orange
2 tbsp caster (superfine) sugar
¼ tsp ground cinnamon
4 wheat tortillas (see page 277)
60 g/2 oz butter
sifted icing (confectioners') sugar
30 g/1 oz flaked almonds (optional)

1 Halve the paw-paw, scoop out the seeds, peel and cut into small dice; or stone and slice the apricots; or peel the mango, remove the stone and dice the flesh. Slice the strawberries. Put the fruit into a bowl.

2 Finely grate half the rind from the orange and add to the fruit. Cut away the peel and pith from the orange and ease out the segments from between the membranes. Cut the segments in half and mix with the fruit, adding the sugar and cinnamon.

3 Divide the mixture between the tortillas, placing on one side; then fold in half, and in half again to make a quarter or pocket.

4 Melt half the butter in a small pan and fry the chimichangas 2 at a time for 1–2 minutes on each side until golden brown, turning them over carefully. Place on warmed plates, then add the remaining butter to the pan and fry the other 2 chimichangas in the same way.

5 Sift icing (confectioners') sugar over the chimichangas and sprinkle them with the toasted almonds, if using. Serve hot.

OTHER FRUITS

Other fruits such as cherries, strawberries and raspberries can be used for this recipe instead of the tropical fruits.

SWEET TORTILLA FRITTERS

••

SERVES 4-6

2 eggs
45 g/1½ oz caster (superfine) sugar
125 g/4 oz plain (all-purpose) flour
90 g/3 oz self-raising flour
pinch of salt
¼ tsp ground cinnamon
oil for shallow frying

CINNAMON SUGAR:
90 g/3 oz caster (superfine) sugar
½ tsp ground cinnamon
good pinch of ground ginger

TO DECORATE:
clear honey (optional)
mixed fresh fruits

1 Put the eggs and sugar into a bowl
and whisk together until very thick
and pale in colour, with the whisk leaving
a distinct trail. It is best to use an electric
hand mixer if you have one.

2 Sift the two flours together with the
salt and ground cinnamon. Whisk
half of the flour gradually into the egg
mixture, then work in the remainder to
make a dough.

3 Turn the dough out on a lightly
floured work surface and knead until
smooth and no longer sticky. (This may
be done in a large electric mixer fitted
with a dough hook.) Wrap in clingfilm
and leave to rest for about 30 minutes.

4 Divide the dough into 6 and roll
each piece out to a thin circle of
about 20 cm/8 in; then cut each circle
into quarters.

5 Heat about 2.5 cm/1 in of oil in a
pan until a cube of bread will brown
in about 1 minute. Fry the fritters, a few
at a time, for about 1 minute on each
side, until golden brown and bubbly.
Drain on paper towels and toss quickly in
a mixture of the sugar, cinnamon and
ginger.

6 Serve the fritters (hot or cold) on a
plate, and, if liked, drizzle a little
clear honey over them. Decorate with
fresh fruits such as sliced mango, figs,
passion-fruit, nectarines, etc.

VANILLA & CINNAMON ICE CREAM

••

SERVES 4-6

4 eggs
60 g/2 oz caster (superfine) sugar
450 ml / ¾ pint milk
few drops of vanilla flavouring (extract)
1 tsp ground cinnamon
200 g/7 oz crème fraîche or 300 ml/ ½ pint
  double (heavy) cream
45 g/1½ oz toasted chopped hazelnuts or
  almonds (optional)
fresh fruits to decorate

1 To make the custard, whisk the eggs
with the sugar until thick in a
heatproof bowl. Heat the milk to just
below boiling point and whisk into the
egg mixture gradually.

2 Stand the bowl over a pan of gently
simmering water and cook gently,
stirring almost constantly until thickened
sufficiently to coat the back of a spoon
quite thickly. Remove from the heat and
stir in the vanilla and cinnamon. Cover
with clingfilm and leave until cold.

3 If using crème fraîche, mix evenly
through the custard; or if using
double (heavy) cream, whip until thick
but not stiff and fold into the custard.
Cover and freeze until just firm.

4 Remove the ice cream from the
freezer and whisk until smooth,
turning into a bowl if necessary. This
breaks down the ice crystals in the ice
cream. Beat in the nuts, if using. Cover,
return to the freezer and freeze until firm.

5 Serve the ice cream decorated with
fresh fruits such as raspberries or
mangoes; or top with chocolate sauce.

CHOCOLATE SAUCE

To make the chocolate sauce, melt
125 g/4 oz plain chocolate with 30 g/
1 oz butter in a bowl and beat in 125
ml/4 fl oz of evaporated milk and a few
drops of vanilla flavouring (extract) until
smooth, heating a little if necessary to
remove any lumps. 1–2 tbsp brandy
may also be added.

MEXICAN BREAD PUDDING

Serves 6

1 small French stick loaf
60 g/2 oz butter

SYRUP:
175 g/6 oz soft brown sugar
200 ml/7 fl oz water
1 cinnamon stick
6 whole cloves or a pinch of ground cloves
¼ tsp mixed (apple pie) spice
300 ml/ ½ pint milk
3–4 wheat or corn tortillas (18–20 cm/
7–8 in) (see page 277)
175 g/6 oz raisins
90 g/3 oz almonds, flaked or chopped
grated rind of 1 orange
75 g/2½ oz mature (sharp) Cheddar
cheese, grated

1 Cut the French bread into 1 cm/
½ in slices (about 14) and spread
each side lightly with some of the butter.
Place on a baking sheet and cook in a
preheated oven at 180°C/350°F/Gas Mark
4 for about 10 minutes, or until golden
brown.

2 Meanwhile make the syrup: put the
sugar and water into a saucepan
with the cinnamon stick, cloves and
mixed (apple pie) spice. Heat gently until
dissolved and then simmer for 2 minutes.
Strain into a jug, discarding the spices,
and mix in the milk.

3 Use the remaining butter to grease
an ovenproof dish of about 1.7
litre/3 pint capacity. Use the tortillas to
line the dish, cutting them to fit neatly.

4 Dip half the baked bread slices into
the syrup and lay over the tortillas.

5 Combine the raisins, almonds and
orange rind and sprinkle half over
the bread, followed by half the cheese.

6 Dip the remaining bread in the
syrup and lay over the raisin
mixture; then sprinkle with the remaining
raisins, nuts, orange rind and cheese.

7 Pour the remaining syrup into the
dish, and place in a preheated oven
at 200°C/400°F/Gas Mark 6 for 20
minutes. Reduce the temperature to
160°C/325°F/Gas Mark 3, cover with a
sheet of greaseproof paper or foil and
continue to cook for about 30 minutes.
Serve hot, warm or cold cut into wedges,
with cream, ice cream or natural yogurt.

CINNAMON BAKED CUSTARD

SERVES 6

175 g/6 oz caster (superfine) sugar
3 tbsp water

CUSTARD:
5 eggs
45 g/1½ oz caster (superfine) sugar
600 ml /1 pint milk
3 tbsp double (heavy) cream
few drops of vanilla flavouring (extract)
good pinch of ground allspice
½ tsp ground cinnamon
pouring or whipped cream to serve
(optional)

1 Prepare a 15–18 cm/6–7 in deep round cake tin or 6 individual ramekin dishes or dariole moulds by rinsing with cold water. Put the sugar into a heavy-based saucepan with the water and mix together. Heat gently, stirring constantly until the sugar has dissolved. Bring to the boil, increase the heat and boil, uncovered and without further stirring, until the sugar turns a golden brown.

2 Pour the caramel quickly into the large container or divide between the individual ones, tipping so the caramel evenly coats the base and a little way up the sides of the container(s). Leave for a few minutes to set.

3 To make the custard, whisk the eggs together lightly with the sugar, then whisk in the milk and cream and strain into a jug. Whisk the vanilla, allspice and cinnamon into the custard and pour over the caramel.

4 Place the container(s) in a baking tin and add boiling water to come half-way up the sides of the container(s). Lay a sheet of greased greaseproof paper or foil over the custard.

5 Place in a preheated oven at 150°C/300°F/Gas Mark 2, allowing about 45 minutes for the individual custards or 1–1¼ hours for the large one, cooking until set and until a knife inserted in the custard comes out clean. Remove from the water bath and leave to cool; then chill thoroughly.

6 Dip each container briefly in hot water, leave to rest for a minute or so, then shake gently to loosen and invert on to a serving dish or individual plates, allowing the caramel to flow around the custard. Serve plain or with pouring or whipped cream, if liked.

CHURROS

••

SERVES 4-6

60 g/2 oz butter
150 ml/ ¼ pint water
75 g/2½ oz plain (all-purpose) flour, sifted
2 eggs, beaten
grated rind of ½ orange
oil for deep-frying

ANISEED SUGAR:
5 star anise
90 g/3 oz caster (superfine) sugar

CINNAMON SYRUP:
125 g/4 oz soft brown sugar
150 ml / ¼ pint water
2 star anise
½ tsp ground cinnamon
2 tbsp orange juice

1 To make the choux paste, melt the butter in the water in a saucepan over a gentle heat; then bring to the boil. Add the flour all at once, stirring vigorously over a gentle heat until the mixture forms a ball, leaving the sides of the pan clean. Remove from the heat and leave to cool for 4–5 minutes.

2 To make the aniseed sugar, put the star anise and sugar into a pestle and mortar, a food processor or a blender, and grind until well mixed. Sift the sugar mixture into a bowl.

3 To make the cinnamon syrup, put the brown sugar into a small pan with the water, star anise and cinnamon, and heat until the sugar dissolves; then boil for about 2 minutes. Stir in the orange juice and strain into a jug.

4 Add the beaten eggs gradually to the cooling choux paste, beating hard (preferably with an electric hand mixer) until smooth and glossy. The mixture may not take quite all the egg. Beat in the orange rind and fill the choux paste into a large piping bag fitted with a large star nozzle.

5 Heat the oil to 180°C/350°F or until a cube of bread browns in about 1 minute. Pipe 2.5–4 cm/1–1½ in lengths of the choux paste carefully into the hot oil, cutting each one off with a knife, and fry about 6 at a time for about 3–4 minutes, or until golden brown and crisp all over.

6 Drain the churros on paper towels, then toss thoroughly in the aniseed sugar and serve hot, warm or cold with the cinnamon syrup.

ITALIAN DISHES – INTRODUCTION

There are two main culinary zones in Italy: the wine and olive zone, which lies around Umbria, Liguria and the South; and the cattle country, where the olive tree will not flourish – Emilia-Romagna, Lombardy and Veneto – but where milk and butter are widely produced. Tuscany uses both butter and oil in its cooking because cattle flourish in the area and so do the olive trees.

PIEDMONT

The name means "at the foot of the mountain", which it is, bordering on both France and Switzerland. Its fertile arable fields are irrigated by the many canals which flow through the region.

The food is substantial, peasant-type fare, though the fragrant white truffle is found in this region. Truffles can be finely flaked or grated and added to many of the smarter dishes, but they are wildly expensive. There is also an abundance of wild mushrooms throughout the region. Garlic features strongly in the recipes and polenta, gnocchi and rice are eaten in larger quantities than pasta, the former offered as a first course when soup is not served. A large variety of game is also widely available in the area.

LOMBARDY

The mention of the capital, Milan, produces immediate thoughts of the wonderful risotto named after the city and also the Milanese soufflé flavoured strongly with lemon. Veal dishes, including vitello tonnato and osso buco, are specialties of the region and other excellent meat dishes, particularly pot roasts, feature widely.

The lakes of the area produce a wealth of fresh fish. Rice and polenta are again popular but pasta also appears in many guises. The famous sweet yeasted cake Panettone is a product of this region.

TRENTINO-ALTO-ADIGE

This is a double area with a strong Germanic influence, particularly when it comes to the wines. There are also several liqueurs produced, still with a German influence, such as Aquavit, Kümmel and Slivovitz.

The foods are robust and basic in this mountainous area with rich green valleys and lakes where fish are plentiful. In the Trentino area particularly, pasta and simple meat and offal dishes are popular, while in the Adige soups and pot roasts are favoured, often with added dumplings and spiced sausages.

VENETO

The cooking in this north-east corner is straightforward, with abundant servings of polenta with almost everything. The land is intensely farmed, providing mostly cereals and wine. Pasta is more in the background with polenta, gnocchi and rice more favoured. Fish, particularly seafood, is in abundance and especially good seafood salads are widely available. There are also excellent robust soups and risottos flavoured withthe seafood and sausages of the area.

LIGURIA

The Genoese are excellent cooks, and all along the Italian Riviera coast can be found fantastic trattoria which produce amazing fish dishes flavoured with the local olive oil. Pesto sauce flavoured with basil, cheese and pine kernels comes from this area, along with other excellent sauces. The aroma of fresh herbs

INTRODUCTION

abounds, widely used in many dishes, including their famous pizzas.

EMILIA-ROMAGNA

This is a special region of high gastronomic importance, with an abundance of everything, and rich food is widely served. Tortellini and lasagne feature widely, along with many other pasta dishes, as do saltimbocca and other veal dishes. Parma is famous for its ham, prosciutto di Parma, thought to be the best in the world. Balsamic vinegar, which has grown in popularity over the past decade, is also produced here, from wine which is distilled until it is dark brown and extremely strongly flavoured.

TUSCANY

The Tuscans share a great pride in cooking and eating with the Emilians, and are known to have hefty appetites. Tuscany has everything: an excellent coastal area providing splendid fish, and hills covered in vineyards and fertile plains where every conceivable vegetable and fruit happily grows. There is plenty of game in the region, providing many interesting recipes; tripe cooked in a thick tomato sauce is popular along with many liver recipes; beans in many guises appear frequently, as well as pot roasts, steaks and full-bodied soups, all of which are well favoured.

Florence has a wide variety of specialties, while Siena boasts the famous candied fruit cake called Panforte di Siena.

UMBRIA/MARCHES

Inland Umbria is famous for its pork, and the character of the cuisine is marked by the use of the local fresh ingredients, including lamb, game

and fish from the lakes, but is not spectacular on the whole. Spit-roasting and grilling is popular, and the excellent local olive oil is used both in cooking and to pour over dishes before serving. Black truffles, olives, fruit and herbs are plentiful and feature in many recipes. Eastwards to the Marches the wealth of fish from the coast adds even more to the variety and the food tends to be more on the elaborate side, with almost every restaurant noted for its excellent cuisine. First-class sausages and cured pork come from the Marches, particularly on the Umbrian border, and pasta features widely all over the region.

LAZIO

Rome is the capital of both Lazio and Italy and thus has become a focal point for specialities from all over Italy. Food from this region tends to be fairly simple and quick to prepare, hence the many pasta dishes with delicious sauces, gnocchi in various forms and plenty of dishes featuring lamb and veal (saltimbocca being just one), and offal, all with plenty of herbs and seasonings giving really robust flavours and delicious sauces. Vegetables feature along with the fantastic fruits which are always in abundance in the local markets; and beans appear both in soups and many other dishes. The main theme of this region is strongly flavoured food with robust sauces.

ABRUZZI AND MOLISE

Another divided region with an interior of mountains with river valleys, high plateaux, densely forested areas and a coastal plain. The cuisine here is deeply traditional, with local hams and cheeses from the mountain areas, interesting

INTRODUCTION

sausages with plenty of garlic and other seasonings, cured meats, wonderful fish and seafood, which is the main produce of the coastal areas, where fishing boats abound on the beaches. Lamb features widely: tender, juicy and well-flavoured with herbs.

CAMPANIA
Naples is the home of pasta dishes, served with a splendid tomato sauce (with many variations) whose fame has spread worldwide. Pizza is said to have been created in Naples and now has spread to the north of the country and indeed worldwide.

Fish abounds, with fritto misto and fritto pesce being great favourites, varying daily depending on the catch. Fish stews are robust and varied and shellfish in particular is often served with pasta. Cutlets and steaks are excellent, served with strong sauces usually flavoured with garlic, tomatoes and herbs: pizzaiola steak is one of the favourites. Excellent Mozzarella cheese is produced locally and used to create the crispy Mozarella in Carozza, again served with a garlicky tomato sauce. Sweet dishes are popular too, often with flaky pastry and Ricotta cheese, and the seasonal fruit salads laced with wine or liqueur take a lot of beating.

PUGLIA (APULIA)
The ground is stony but it produces good fruit, olive groves, vegetables and herbs, and, of course, there is a large amount of seafood from the sea. Puglians are said to be champion pasta eaters: many of the excellent pasta dishes are exclusive to the region both in shape and ingredients. Mushrooms abound and are always added to the local pizzas.

Oysters and mussels are plentiful, and so is octopus. Brindisi is famous for its shellfish – both the seafood salads and risottos are truly memorable. But it is not all fish or pasta: lamb is roasted and stewed to perfection and so is veal, always with plenty of herbs.

BASILICATA
This is a sheep-farming area, mainly mountainous, where potent wines are produced to accompany a robust cuisine largely based on pasta, lamb, pork, game and abundant dairy produce. The salamis and cured meats are excellent, as are the mountain hams. Lamb is flavoured from the herbs and grasses on which it feeds. Wonderful thick soups – true minestrone – are produced in the mountains, and eels and fish are plentiful in the lakes. Chilli peppers are grown in this region and appear in many of the recipes. They are not overpoweringly strong, although the flavours of the region in general tend to be quite strong and intense. The cheeses are excellent, with good fruits grown and interesting local bread baked in huge loaves.

CALABRIA
This is the toe of Italy, where orange and lemon groves flourish along with olive groves and a profusion of vegetables, especially aubergines (eggplant) which are cooked in a variety of ways.

Chicken, rabbit and guinea fowl are often on the menu. Pizzas feature largely, often with a fishy topping. Mushrooms grow well in the Calabrian climate and feature in many dishes from sauces and stews to salads. Pasta comes with a great variety of sauces including baby artichokes, eggs, meat, cheese, mixed

INTRODUCTION

vegetables, the large sweet (bell) peppers of the region and of course garlic. The fish is excellent too and here fresh tunafish and swordfish are available with many other varieties.

Like most southern Italians, the Calabrians are sweet-toothed and many desserts and cakes are flavoured with aniseed, honey and almonds and featuring the plentiful figs of the region.

SICILY

This is the largest island in the Mediterranean and the cuisine is largely based on fish and vegetables. Fish soups, stews and salads appear in unlimited forms, including tuna, swordfish, mussels and many more; citrus fruits are widely grown along with almonds and pistachio nuts, and the local wines, including Marsala, are excellent.

Meat is often given a long, slow cooking, or else is minced and shaped before cooking. Game is plentiful and is often cooked in sweet-sour sauces containing the local black olives.

Pasta abounds again with more unusual sauces as well as the old favourites. All Sicilians have a love of desserts, cakes and especially ice-cream. Cassata and other ice-creams from Sicily are famous all over the world, and the huge variety of flavours of both cream ices and granita makes it difficult to decide which is your favourite.

SARDINIA

A pretty island with a wealth of flowers in the spring, but the landscape dries out in the summer from the hot sun. The national dish is suckling pig. or newborn lamb cooked on an open fire or spit; game and offal dishes are very popular.

The sweet dishes are numerous and often extremely delicate, and for non-sweet eaters there is fresh fruit of almost every kind in abundance.

Fish is top quality, with excellent sea bass, lobsters, tuna, mullet, eels and mussels in good supply.

The island has a haunting aroma which drifts from many kitchens – it is myrtle (mirto), a local herb which is added to anything and everything from chicken to the local liqueur; and along with the wonderful cakes and breads of Sardinia, myrtle will long remain a memory of the island when you have returned home.

STARTERS

FISH SOUP

SERVES 4-6

1 kg/2 lb assorted prepared fish (including mixed fish fillets, squid, etc.)
2 onions, peeled and thinly sliced
a few sprigs of parsley
2 bay leaves
2 celery sticks, thinly sliced
150 ml/ ¼ pint/ ⅔ cup white wine
1 litre/1¾ pints/4 cups water
2 tbsp olive oil
1 garlic clove, crushed
1 carrot, peeled and finely chopped
1 x 425 g/15 oz can peeled tomatoes, puréed
2 potatoes, peeled and chopped
1 tbsp tomato purée (paste)
1 tsp freshly chopped oregano or ½ tsp dried oregano
350 g/12 oz fresh mussels
175 g/6 oz peeled prawns (shrimp)
2 tbsp freshly chopped parsley
salt and pepper
crusty bread, to serve

1 Cut the cleaned and prepared fish into slices or cubes and put into a large saucepan with 1 sliced onion, the parsley sprigs and bay leaves, 1 sliced celery stick, the wine and the water. Bring to the boil, cover and simmer for about 25 minutes.

2 Strain the fish stock and discard the vegetables. Skin the fish, remove any bones and reserve.

3 Heat the oil in a pan, finely chop the remaining onion and fry with the garlic, remaining celery and carrot until soft but not coloured. Add the puréed canned tomatoes, potatoes, tomato purée (paste), oregano, reserved stock and seasonings. Bring to the boil and simmer for about 15 minutes or until the potato is almost tender.

4 Meanwhile, thoroughly scrub the mussels. Add to the pan with the prawns (shrimp) and simmer for about 5 minutes or until the mussels have opened (discard any that stay closed).

5 Return the fish to the soup with the chopped parsley, bring back to the boil and simmer for 5 minutes. Adjust the seasoning.

6 Serve the soup in warmed bowls with chunks of fresh crusty bread, or put a toasted slice of crusty bread in the bottom of each bowl before adding the soup. If possible, remove a few half shells from the mussels before serving.

RED BEAN SOUP

SERVES 4-6

175 g/6 oz/scant 1 cup dried red kidney
  beans, soaked overnight
1.7 litres/3 pints/7½ cups water
1 large ham bone or bacon knuckle
2 carrots, peeled and chopped
1 large onion, peeled and chopped
2 celery sticks, thinly sliced
1 leek, trimmed, washed and sliced
1-2 bay leaves
2 tbsp olive oil
2-3 tomatoes, peeled and chopped
1 garlic clove, crushed
1 tbsp tomato purée (paste)
60 g/2 oz/4 tbsp arborio or Italian rice
125-175 g/4-6 oz green cabbage, finely
  shredded
salt and pepper

1 Drain the beans and put into a
saucepan with enough water to
cover. Bring to the boil and boil hard for
15 minutes, then reduce the heat and
simmer for 45 minutes. The hard boiling
is essential with red beans for safety
reasons. Drain.

2 Put the beans into a clean saucepan
with the measured amount of water,
ham bone or knuckle, carrots, onion,
celery, leek, bay leaves and olive oil.
Bring to the boil, cover and simmer for an
hour or until the beans are very tender.

3 Discard the bay leaves and bone,
reserving any ham pieces from the
bone. Remove a small cupful of the beans
and reserve. Purée or liquidize the soup
in a food processor or blender and return
to a clean pan.

4 Add the tomatoes, garlic, tomato
purée (paste), rice and plenty of
seasoning, bring back to the boil and
simmer for about 15 minutes or until the
rice is tender.

5 Add the cabbage and reserved beans
and ham and continue to simmer for
5 minutes. Adjust the seasoning and serve
very hot. If liked, a piece of toasted crusty
bread may be put in the base of each
soup bowl before ladling in the soup. If
the soup is too thick, add a little boiling
water or stock.

MINESTRONE WITH PESTO

SERVES 6

175 g/6 oz/scant 1 cup dried cannellini
  beans, soaked overnight
2.5 litres/4 pints/10 cups water or stock
1 large onion, peeled and chopped
1 leek, trimmed and thinly sliced
2 celery stalks, very thinly sliced
2 carrots, peeled and chopped
3 tbsp olive oil
2 tomatoes, peeled and roughly chopped
1 courgette (zucchini), trimmed and
  thinly sliced
2 potatoes, peeled and diced
90 g/3 oz elbow macaroni (or other small
  macaroni)
salt and pepper
4-6 tbsp Parmesan, grated

PESTO:
2 tbsp pine kernels
5 tbsp olive oil
2 bunches fresh basil, stems removed
4-6 garlic cloves, crushed
90 g /3 oz/ ¾ cup Pecorino or Parmesan,
  grated
salt and pepper

1 Drain the beans, rinse and place in a
saucepan with the measured water
or stock. Bring to the boil, cover and
simmer gently for 1 hour.

2 Add the onion, leek, celery, carrots,
and oil. Cover and simmer for 4-5
minutes.

3 Add the tomatoes, courgette
(zucchini), potatoes and macaroni
and seasoning, cover again and continue
to simmer for about 30 minutes or until
very tender.

4 Meanwhile, make the pesto. Fry the
pine kernels in 1 tablespoon of the
oil until pale brown, then drain. Put the
basil into a food processor or blender
with the nuts and garlic. Process until well
chopped. Gradually add the oil until
smooth. Turn into a bowl, add the cheese
and seasoning and mix thoroughly.

5 Stir 1½ tablespoons of the pesto into
the soup until well blended, simmer
for a further 5 minutes and adjust the
seasoning. Serve very hot, sprinkled with
the cheese.

AUBERGINE (EGGPLANT) SALAD

SERVES 4

2 large aubergines (eggplant), about 1 kg/
*   2 lb*
salt
6 tbsp olive oil
1 small onion, peeled and finely chopped
2 garlic cloves, crushed
6-8 celery sticks
2 tbsp capers
12-16 green olives, pitted and sliced
2 tbsp pine kernels
30 g/1 oz bitter or plain chocolate, grated
4 tbsp wine vinegar
1 tbsp brown sugar
salt and pepper
2 hard-boiled eggs, sliced, to serve
celery leaves or curly endive, to garnish

1 Cut the aubergines (eggplant) into 2.5 cm/1 in cubes and sprinkle liberally with 2-3 tablespoons salt. Leave to stand for an hour, to extract the bitter juices, then rinse off the salt thoroughly under cold water, drain and dry on paper towels.

2 Heat most of the oil in a frying pan and fry the aubergines (eggplant) cubes until golden brown all over. Drain on paper towels then transfer them to a large bowl.

3 Add the onion and garlic to the pan with the remaining oil and fry very gently until just soft. Cut the celery into 1 cm/½ in slices, add to the pan and fry for a few minutes, stirring frequently, until lightly coloured but still crisp.

4 Add the celery to the aubergines (eggplant) with the capers, olives and pine kernels and mix lightly.

5 Add the chocolate and vinegar to the residue in the pan with the sugar. Heat gently until melted, then bring up to the boil. Season with a little salt and plenty of freshly ground black pepper and pour over the salad. Mix lightly, cover, leave until cold and then chill thoroughly.

6 Serve with sliced hard-boiled eggs and garnish with celery leaves or curly endive.

CROSTINI ALLA FIORENTINA

SERVES 4

3 tbsp olive oil
1 onion, peeled and chopped
1 celery stick, chopped
1 carrot, peeled and chopped
1-2 garlic cloves, crushed
125 g/4 oz chicken livers
125 g/4 oz calf's, lamb's or pig's liver
150 ml/ ¼ pint/ ⅔ cup red wine
1 tbsp tomato purée (paste)
2 tbsp freshly chopped parsley
3-4 canned anchovy fillets, finely chopped
2 tbsp stock or water
30-45 g/1-1½ oz/2-3 tbsp butter
1 tbsp capers
salt and pepper
small pieces of fried crusty bread
chopped parsley, to garnish

1 Heat the oil in a pan, add the onion, celery, carrot and garlic and cook gently for 4-5 minutes or until the onion is soft, but not coloured.

2 Meanwhile, rinse and dry the chicken livers. Dry the calf's or other liver, and slice into strips. Add the liver to the pan and fry gently for a few minutes until the strips are well sealed on all sides.

3 Add half the wine and cook until mostly evaporated then add the rest of the wine, tomato purée (paste), half the parsley, anchovy fillets, stock or water, a little salt and plenty of black pepper.

4 Cover the pan and simmer for 15-20 minutes or until tender and most of the liquid has been absorbed.

5 Cool the mixture a little then either coarsely mince or put into a food processor and process until coarsely blended.

6 Return to the pan and add the butter, remaining parsley and capers and heat through gently until the butter melts. Adjust the seasoning and turn into a bowl. Serve warm or cold spread on the slices of crusty bread and sprinkled with chopped parsley.

MOZZARELLA IN CAROZZA

SERVES 4

200 g/7 oz Mozzarella
4 slices, about 90 g/3 oz, Parma ham
8 slices white bread, preferably 2 days old,
  crusts removed
a little butter for spreading
2 -3 eggs
3 tbsp milk
vegetable oil, for deep frying
salt and pepper

TOMATO AND PEPPER SAUCE:
1 onion, peeled and chopped
2 garlic cloves, crushed
3 tbsp olive oil
1 red (bell) pepper, cored, seeded and
  chopped
1 x 425 g/15 oz can peeled tomatoes
2 tbsp tomato purée (paste)
3 tbsp water
1 tbsp lemon juice
flat-leaf parsley, to garnish (optional)

1 First make the sauce: fry the onion and garlic in the oil until soft. Add the (bell) pepper and continue to cook for a few minutes. Add the tomatoes, tomato purée (paste), water, lemon juice and seasoning, bring up to the boil, cover and simmer for 10-15 minutes or until tender. Cool the sauce a little, then purée or liquidize until smooth and return to a clean pan.

2 Cut the Mozzarella into 4 slices so they are as large as possible; if a square piece of cheese cut into 8 slices. Trim the Parma ham slices to the same size as the cheese.

3 Lightly butter the bread and use the cheese and ham to make 4 sandwiches, pressing the edges well together. If liked, they may be cut in half at this stage. Chill.

4 Lightly beat the eggs with the milk and seasoning in a shallow dish.

5 Carefully dip the sandwiches in the egg mixture until well coated all over, and if possible leave to soak for a few minutes.

6 Heat the oil in a large pan or deep-frier until it just begins to smoke, or until a cube of bread browns in about 30 seconds. Fry the sandwiches in batches until golden brown on both sides. Drain well on crumpled paper towels and keep warm. Serve the sandwiches hot, with the reheated tomato and pepper sauce, and garnished with parsley.

MAIN DISHES

TORTELLINI

•••

SERVES 4

FILLING:
125 g/4 oz boneless, skinned chicken
*   breast*
60 g/2 oz prosciutto or Parma ham
45 g/1½ oz cooked spinach, well drained
1 tbsp finely chopped onion
2 tbsp grated Parmesan
good pinch of ground allspice
1 egg, beaten
salt and pepper
1 quantity Pasta Dough (see below)

SAUCE:
300 ml/ ½ pint/1¼ cups single cream
1-2 garlic cloves, crushed
125 g/4 oz button mushrooms, thinly
*   sliced*
4 tbsp grated Parmesan
1-2 tbsp freshly chopped parsley

1 Poach the chicken in well-seasoned water until tender, about 10 minutes; drain and chop roughly. When cool put into a food processor with the prosciutto, spinach and onion and process until finely chopped, then add the Parmesan, allspice, seasonings and egg.

2 Roll out the pasta dough, half at a time, on a lightly floured surface until as thin as possible. Cut into 4-5 cm/ 1½-2 in rounds using a plain cutter.

3 Place ½ teaspoon of the filling in the centre of each dough circle, fold the pieces in half to make a semi-circle and press the edges firmly together. Wrap the dough semi-circle around your index finger and cross over the 2 ends, pressing firmly together, curling the rest of the dough backwards to make a "tummy button" shape. Slip the tortellini off your finger and lay on a lightly floured tray. Repeat with the rest of the dough, re-rolling the trimmings.

4 Cook the tortellini in batches: heat a large pan of salted boiling water and add some tortellini. Bring back to the boil and once they rise to the surface cook for about 5 minutes, giving an occasional stir. Remove with a slotted spoon, drain on paper towels and keep warm in a serving dish while cooking the remainder.

5 To make the sauce, heat the cream with the garlic in a pan and bring to the boil; simmer for a few minutes. Add the mushrooms, half the Parmesan and seasoning and simmer for 2-3 minutes. Stir in the parsley and pour over the warm tortellini. Sprinkle the tortellini with the remaining Parmesan and serve immediately.

PASTA DOUGH

Sift 325 g/11 oz/generous 2½ cups plain flour and a pinch of salt onto a flat surface and make a well in the centre. Beat together 3 large eggs, 1 tbsp olive oil and 1 tbsp water, then slowly pour this mixture into the centre of the flour, gradually working in the flour by hand until you have formed a dough. Knead the dough for about 5 minutes until smooth. Cover with a damp cloth or put into a lightly oiled polythene bag and leave to rest for 5-15 minutes.

SICILIAN SPAGHETTI

••

SERVES 4

2 aubergines (eggplant), about 650 g/
1¼ lb
150 ml/ ¼ pint/ ⅔ cup olive oil
350 g/12 oz finely minced lean beef
1 onion, peeled and chopped
2 garlic cloves, crushed
2 tbsp tomato purée (paste)
1 x 425 g/15 oz can peeled tomatoes,
chopped
1 tsp Worcestershire sauce
1 tsp freshly chopped oregano or
marjoram or ½ tsp dried oregano or
marjoram
45 g/1½ oz pitted black olives, sliced
1 green, red or yellow (bell) pepper, cored,
seeded and chopped
175 g/6 oz spaghetti
125 g/4 oz/1 cup grated Parmesan
salt and pepper
oregano or parsley, to garnish (optional)

1 Brush a 20 cm/8 in loose-based
round cake tin with olive oil, place a
disc of baking parchment in the base and
oil. Trim the aubergines (eggplant) and
cut into slanting slices approx 5 mm/ ¼ in
thick. Heat some of the oil in a frying
pan. Fry a few slices at a time in hot oil
until lightly browned, turning once, and
adding more oil as necessary. Drain on
paper towels.

2 Put the minced beef, onion and
garlic into a saucepan and cook,
stirring frequently, until browned all over.
Add the tomato purée (paste), tomatoes,
Worcestershire sauce, herbs and seasoning
and simmer for 10 minutes, stirring
occasionally, then add the olives and
(bell) pepper and continue for a further
10 minutes.

3 Heat a large pan of salted water and
cook the spaghetti for12-14 minutes
until tender. Drain thoroughly.

4 Turn the spaghetti into a bowl and
mix in the meat mixture and
Parmesan, combining thoroughly using
two forks.

5 Lay overlapping slices of aubergine
(eggplant) evenly over the base of
the cake tin and up the sides. Add the
meat mixture, pressing it down, and cover
with the remaining slices of aubergine
(eggplant).

6 Stand in a baking tin and cook in a
preheated oven at 200ºC/400ºF/Gas
Mark 6 for 40 minutes. Leave to stand for
5 minutes then loosen around the edges
and invert onto a warmed serving dish,
releasing the tin clip. Remove the paper.
Sprinkle with herbs before serving, if
liked. Extra Parmesan cheese may be
offered, if liked.

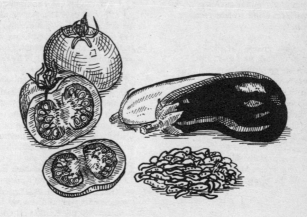

GNOCCHI ROMANA

SERVES 4

750 ml/1¼ pints/3 cups milk
¼ tsp grated nutmeg
90 g/3 oz/6 tbsp butter, plus extra for
    greasing
250 g/8 oz/1½ cups semolina
125 g/4 oz/1 cup Parmesan, finely grated
2 eggs, beaten
60 g/ 2 oz/ ½ cup Gruyère, grated
salt and pepper
basil sprigs, to garnish

1 Bring the milk to the boil, remove
  from the heat and stir in seasoning,
nutmeg and 30 g/1 oz/2 tablespoons
butter. Gradually whisk in the semolina to
prevent lumps forming and return to a
low heat. Simmer gently for about 10
minutes, stirring constantly, until very
thick.

2 Beat 60 g/2 oz/½ cup of Parmesan
  into the semolina, followed by the
eggs. Continue beating until it is quite
smooth.

3 Spread out the semolina mixture in
  an even layer on a sheet of baking
parchment or in a large oiled baking tin
(pan), smoothing the surface with a wet
spatula – it should be about1 cm/½ in
thick. Leave until cold, then chill for
about an hour until firm.

4 Cut the gnocchi into circles of about
  4 cm/1½ in, using a plain greased
pastry cutter.

5 Thoroughly grease a shallow
  ovenproof dish, or 4 individual
dishes. Lay the gnocchi trimmings in the
base of the dish and cover with
overlapping circles of gnocchi. Melt the
remaining butter and drizzle all over the
gnocchi, then sprinkle first with the
remaining Parmesan and then with the
grated Gruyère.

6 Cook in a preheated oven at
  200ºC/400ºF/Gas Mark 6 for 25-30
minutes until the top is crisp and golden
brown.

POLENTA

SERVES 4

1.5 litres/ 2⅔ pints/7 cups water
1½ tsp salt
300 g/10 oz/2 cups polenta or cornmeal
    flour
2 beaten eggs (optional)
125 g/4 oz/2 cups fresh fine white
    breadcrumbs (optional)
vegetable oil, for frying and oiling

MUSHROOM SAUCE:
250 g/8 oz mushrooms, sliced
3 tbsp olive oil
2 garlic cloves, crushed
150 ml/¼ pint/⅔ cup dry white wine
4 tbsp double (heavy) cream
2 tbsp freshly chopped mixed herbs
salt and pepper

1 Bring the water and salt to the boil
  in a large pan and gradually sprinkle
in the polenta or cornmeal flour, stirring
all the time to make sure the mixture is
smooth and there are no lumps.

2 Simmer the mixture very gently,
  stirring frequently, until the polenta
becomes very thick, about 30-35 minutes.
It is likely to splatter, in which case
partially cover the pan with a lid. The
mixture should become thick enough for
a wooden spoon to almost stand upright
in it on its own.

3 Thoroughly oil a shallow tin, about
  28 x 18 cm/ 11 x 7 in, and spoon in
the polenta. Spread out evenly, using a
wet spatula if necessary. Leave until cold
then leave for a few hours at room
temperature, if possible.

4 Cut the polenta into 30-36 squares.
  Heat the oil in a frying pan and fry
the pieces until golden brown all over,
turning several times – about 5 minutes.
Alternatively, dip each piece of polenta in
beaten egg and coat in breadcrumbs
before frying in the hot oil.

5 To make the sauce: heat the oil in a
  pan and fry the mushrooms with the
crushed garlic for 3-4 minutes. Add the
wine, season well and simmer for 5
minutes. Add the cream and chopped
herbs and simmer for another minute or
so. Serve the polenta with the sauce.

TAGLIATELLE WITH PUMPKIN

SERVES 4

500 g/1 lb pumpkin or butternut squash
2 tbsp olive oil
1 onion, peeled and finely chopped
2 garlic cloves, crushed
4–6 tbsp freshly chopped parsley
good pinch of ground or grated nutmeg
about 250 ml/8 fl oz/1 cup chicken or
* vegetable stock*
125 g/4 oz Parma ham, cut into narrow
* strips*
275 g/9 oz tagliatelle, green or white
* (fresh or dried)*
150 ml/ ¼ pint/ ⅔ cup double (heavy)
* cream*
salt and pepper
freshly grated Parmesan, to serve

1 Peel the pumpkin or butternut squash, removing the hard layer directly under the skin and scoop out the seeds and membrane around them. Cut the flesh into 1 cm/½ in dice.

2 Heat the oil in a pan and fry the onion and garlic gently until soft. Add half the parsley and continue for a minute or so longer.

3 Add the pumpkin or squash and continue to cook for 2-3 minutes, then season well with salt, pepper and nutmeg and add half the stock. Bring to the boil, cover and simmer for about 10 minutes or until the pumpkin is tender, adding more stock as necessary. Add the Parma ham and continue to cook for a further 2 minutes, stirring frequently.

4 Meanwhile, cook the tagliatelle in a large saucepan of boiling salted water, allowing 3-4 minutes for fresh pasta or about 12 minutes for dried (or follow the directions on the packet). When al dente, drain thoroughly and turn into a warmed dish.

5 Add the cream to the ham mixture and heat gently until really hot. Adjust the seasoning and spoon over the pasta. Sprinkle with the remaining parsley and hand grated Parmesan cheese separately.

MILANESE RISOTTO

SERVES 4-5

2 good pinches of saffron threads
1 large onion, finely chopped
1-2 garlic cloves, crushed
90 g/3 oz/6 tbsp butter
350 g/12 oz/1⅔ cups Arborio or other
* short-grain Italian rice*
150 ml/¼ pint/⅔ cup dry white wine
1.25 litres/2 pints/5 cups boiling stock
* (chicken, beef or vegetable)*
90 g/3 oz/¾ cup grated Parmesan
salt and pepper

1 Put the saffron in a small bowl, cover with 3-4 tablespoons boiling water and leave to soak.

2 Fry the onion and garlic in 60 g/2 oz of the butter until soft but not coloured, then add the rice and continue to cook for a few minutes until all the grains are coated in oil and beginning to colour lightly.

3 Add the wine to the rice and simmer gently, stirring from time to time until it is all absorbed.

4 Add the boiling stock a little at a time, about 150 ml/¼ pint/⅔ cup, cooking until the liquid is fully absorbed before adding more, and stirring frequently.

5 When all the stock is absorbed the rice should be tender but not soggy. Add the saffron liquid, Parmesan, remaining butter and seasoning and simmer for a minute until piping hot.

6 Cover the pan tightly and leave to stand for 5 minutes off the heat. Give a good stir and serve at once.

COOKING RISOTTO

The finished dish should have moist but separate grains. This is achieved by adding the hot stock a little at a time, only adding more when the last addition is fully absorbed. Don't leave the risotto to cook by itself: it needs constant watching to see when more liquid is required.

CALABRIAN PIZZA

••

SERVES 4-6

400 g/14 oz/3½ cups plain flour
½ tsp salt
1 sachet easy-blend yeast
2 tbsp olive oil
about 275 ml/9 fl oz/1 cup warm water

FILLING:
2 tbsp olive oil
2 garlic cloves , crushed
*1 red (bell) pepper, cored, seeded and
sliced*
*1 yellow (bell) pepper, cored, seeded and
sliced*
125 g/4 oz Ricotta
*1 x 175 g/6 oz jar sun-dried tomatoes,
drained*
3 hard-boiled eggs, thinly sliced
1 tbsp freshly chopped mixed herbs
125 g/4 oz salami, cut into strips
150-175 g/5-6 oz Mozzarella, grated
a little milk, to glaze
salt and pepper

1 Sift the flour and salt into a bowl
and mix in the easy-blend yeast then
add the olive oil and enough warm water
to mix to a smooth pliable dough. Knead
for 10-15 minutes by hand, or process
for 5 minutes in a mixer fitted
with a dough hook.

2 Shape the dough into
a ball, place in a
lightly oiled polythene bag
and put in a warm place
for 1-1½ hours or until
doubled in size.

3 For the filling: heat the oil in a frying
pan and fry the garlic and (bell)
peppers slowly in the oil until soft. Knock
back the dough and roll out half to fit the
base of a 30 x 25 cm/12 x 10 in oiled
roasting tin. Season the dough and spread
with the Ricotta, then cover with sun-
dried tomatoes, hard-boiled eggs, herbs
and the pepper mixture. Arrange the
salami strips on top and sprinkle with the
grated cheese.

4 Roll out the remaining dough and
place over the filling, pressing the
edges well together, or use to make a
second pizza. Put to rise for about an
hour in a warm place until well puffed
up. An uncovered pizza will only take
about 30-40 minutes to rise.

5 Prick the double pizza with a fork
about 20 times, brush the top with
milk and cook in a preheated oven at
180°C/350°F/Gas Mark 4 for about 50
minutes or until lightly browned and firm
to the touch. The uncovered pizza will
take only 35-40 minutes. Serve hot.

BAKED SEA BASS

•••

SERVES 4

1.4 kg/3 lb fresh sea bass or 2 x 750 g/1½ lb
    sea bass, gutted
2-4 sprigs fresh rosemary
½ lemon, thinly sliced
2 tbsp olive oil

GARLIC SAUCE:
2 tsp coarse sea salt
2 tsp capers
2 garlic cloves, crushed
4 tbsp water
2 fresh bay leaves
1 tsp lemon juice or wine vinegar
2 tbsp olive oil
black pepper

1 Scrape off the fish scales and cut off
   the fins. Make diagonal cuts along
both sides. Wash and dry thoroughly.

2 Place a sprig of rosemary in the
   cavity of each of the smaller fish
with half the lemon slices; or 2 sprigs and
all the lemon in the large fish. To grill
(broil), place in a foil-lined pan, brush
lightly with 1-2 tablespoons oil and grill
(broil) under a moderate heat for about 5
minutes each side or until cooked
through, turning carefully.

3 To bake: place the fish in a foil-lined
   dish or roasting tin brushed with oil,
and brush the fish with the rest of the oil.
Cook in a preheated oven at
190ºC/375ºF/Gas Mark 5 for about 30
minutes for the small fish or 45-50
minutes for the large fish, until tender
when tested with a skewer.

4 For the sauce: crush the salt and
   capers with the garlic in a pestle and
mortar if available and then gradually
work in the water. Alternatively, put it all
into a food processor or blender and
switch on until smooth. Bruise the bay
leaves and remaining sprigs of rosemary
and put in a bowl. Add the garlic mixture,
lemon juice or vinegar and oil and pound
together until the flavours are released.
Season with black pepper.

5 Place the fish on a serving dish.
   Spoon some of the sauce over the
fish and serve the rest separately.

SARDINE AND POTATO BAKE

•••

SERVES 4

1 kg/2 lb potatoes, peeled
1 kg/2 lb sardines, defrosted if frozen
1 tbsp olive oil, plus extra for oiling
1 onion, peeled and chopped
2-3 garlic cloves, crushed
2 tbsp freshly chopped parsley
350 g/12 oz ripe tomatoes, peeled and
    sliced or 1 x 425 g/15 oz can peeled
    tomatoes, partly drained and chopped
1-2 tbsp freshly chopped Italian herbs (e.g.
    oregano, thyme, rosemary, marjoram)
150 ml/ ¼ pint/ ⅔ cup dry white wine
salt and pepper

1 Put the potatoes in a pan of salted
   water, bring to the boil, cover and
simmer for 10 minutes then drain. When
cool enough to handle, cut into slices
about 5 mm/¼ in thick.

2 Gut and clean the sardines: cut off
   their heads and tails and then slit
open the length of the belly. Turn the fish
over so the skin is upwards and press
firmly along the backbone to loosen the
bones. Turn over again and carefully
remove the backbone. Wash the fish in
cold water, drain well and dry them on
paper towels.

3 Heat the oil in a pan and fry the
   onion and garlic until soft, but not
coloured.

4 Arrange the potatoes in a well-oiled
   ovenproof dish and sprinkle with the
onions and then the parsley and plenty of
seasoning.

5 Lay the open sardines over the
   potatoes, skin-side down, then cover
with the tomatoes and the rest of the
herbs. Pour on the wine and season
again.

6 Cook uncovered in a preheated
   oven at 190ºC/375ºF/Gas Mark 5 for
about 40 minutes until the fish is tender.
If the casserole seems to be drying out,
add another couple of tablespoons of
wine.

TROUT IN RED WINE

••

SERVES 4

4 fresh trout, about300 g/10 oz each
250 ml/8 fl oz/1 cup red or white wine
  vinegar
300 ml/ ½ pint/1¼ cups red or dry white
  wine
150 ml/ ¼ pint/ ⅔ cup water
1 carrot, peeled and sliced
2-4 bay leaves
thinly pared rind of 1 lemon
1 small onion, peeled and very thinly
  sliced
4 sprigs fresh parsley
4 sprigs fresh thyme
1 tsp black peppercorns
6-8 whole cloves
90 g/3 oz/6 tbsp butter
1 tbsp freshly chopped mixed herbs or
  parsley
salt and pepper
herbs and lemon slices, to garnish

1 Gut the trout but leave their heads
  on. Dry on paper towels and lay the
fish head to tail in a shallow container or
baking tin just large enough to hold them.

2 Bring the wine vinegar to the boil
  and pour slowly all over the fish.
Leave the fish to marinate for about
20 minutes.

3 Put the wine, water, carrot, bay
  leaves, lemon rind, onion, herbs,
peppercorns and cloves into a pan with a
good pinch of sea salt and heat gently.

4 Drain the fish thoroughly, discarding
  the vinegar. Place the fish in a fish
kettle or large frying pan so they touch.
When the wine mixture boils, strain
gently over the fish so they are about half
covered. Cover the pan and simmer very
gently for 15 minutes.

5 Carefully remove the fish from the
  liquid, draining off as much as
possible, and arrange on a serving dish.

6 Boil the cooking liquid hard until
  reduced to about 4-6 tablespoons.
Melt the butter in a small saucepan and
strain in the cooking liquor. Adjust the
seasoning and spoon over the fish.
Sprinkle with chopped mixed herbs and
garnish with lemon and sprigs of herbs.

SQUID CASSEROLE

••

SERVES 4

1 kg/2 lb whole squid or 750 g/1½ lb squid
  rings, defrosted if frozen
3 tbsp olive oil
1 large onion, thinly sliced
2 garlic cloves, crushed
1 red (bell) pepper, cored, seeded and
  sliced
1-2 sprigs fresh rosemary
150 ml/ ¼ pint/ ⅔ cup dry white wine and
  250 ml/8 fl oz/1 cup water, or 350 ml/
  12 fl oz/1½ cups water or fish stock
1 x 425 g/15 oz can tomatoes, chopped
2 tbsp tomato purée (paste)
1 tsp paprika
salt and pepper
fresh sprigs of rosemary or parsley, to
  garnish

1 Prepare the squid (see below) and
  cut into 1 cm/½ in slices; cut the
tentacles into lengths of about 5 cm/2 in.

2 Heat the oil in a flameproof
  casserole and fry the onion and
garlic gently until soft. Add the squid
rings, increase the heat and cook for
about 10 minutes until beginning to
colour lightly. Add the red (bell) pepper,
rosemary and wine (if using), and water
or stock and bring up to the boil. Cover
and simmer gently for 45 minutes.

3 Discard the sprigs of rosemary (but
  don't take out any leaves that have
come off). Add the tomatoes, tomato
purée (paste), seasonings and paprika.
Continue to simmer gently for 45-60
minutes, or cover the casserole tightly and
cook in a moderate oven for 45-60
minutes until tender. Stir well, adjust the
seasoning and serve with crusty bread.

TO PREPARE SQUID

Peel off as much as possible of the
fine outer skin, using your fingers, then
cut off the head and tentacles. Extract
the transparent flat oval bone from the
body and discard. Carefully remove the
sac of black ink, then turn the body sac
inside out. Wash thoroughly in cold
water. Cut off the tentacles from the
head and discard the rest; wash well.

PIZZAIOLA STEAK

SERVES 4

2 x 425 g/15 oz cans peeled tomatoes or
   750 g/1½ lb fresh tomatoes
4 tbsp olive oil
2-3 garlic cloves, crushed
1 onion, finely chopped
1 tbsp tomato purée (paste)
1½ tsp freshly chopped marjoram or
   oregano or ¼ tsp dried marjoram or
   oregano
4 thin sirloin or rump steaks
2 tbsp freshly chopped parsley
1 tsp sugar
salt and pepper
fresh herbs, to garnish (optional)
sauté potatoes, to serve

1 If using canned tomatoes, purée
them in a food processor, then sieve
to remove the seeds. If using fresh
tomatoes, peel, remove the seeds and
chop finely.

2 Heat half the oil in a pan and fry the
garlic and onions very gently until
soft – about 5 minutes.

3 Add the tomatoes, seasoning, tomato
purée (paste) and chopped herbs to
the pan. If using fresh tomatoes add
4 tablespoons water too, and then simmer
very gently for 8-10 minutes, giving an
occasional stir.

4 Meanwhile, trim the steaks if
necessary and season with salt and
pepper. Heat the remaining oil in a frying
pan and fry the steaks quickly on both
sides to seal, then continue until cooked
to your liking – 2 minutes for rare, 3-4
minutes for medium, or 5 minutes for well
done. Alternatively, cook the steaks under
a hot grill after brushing lightly with oil.

5 When the sauce has thickened a
little, adjust the seasoning and stir in
the chopped parsley and sugar to taste.

6 Pour off the excess fat from the pan
with the steaks and add the tomato
sauce. Reheat gently and serve at once,
with the sauce spooned over and around
the steaks. Garnish with fresh herbs, if
liked. Sauté potatoes make a good
accompaniment with a green vegetable.

SALTIMBOCCA

SERVES 4

4 thin veal escalopes
8 fresh sage leaves
4 thin slices prosciutto or Parma ham
   (same size as the veal)
flour, for dredging
2 tbsp olive oil
30 g/1 oz/2 tbsp butter
4 tbsp white wine
4 tbsp chicken stock
4 tbsp Marsala
salt and pepper
fresh sage leaves, to garnish

1 Either leave the escalopes as they are
or cut in half. Place the pieces of
veal on a sheet of clingfilm or baking
parchment, keeping well apart, and cover
with another piece.

2 Using a meat mallet or rolling pin
beat the escalopes gently until at
least twice their size and very thin.

3 Lightly season the veal escalopes
with salt and pepper and lay 2 fresh
sage leaves on the large slices, or one on
each of the smaller slices. Then lay the
prosciutto slices evenly over the escalopes
to cover the sage and fit the size of the
veal almost exactly.

4 Secure the prosciutto to the veal
with wooden cocktail sticks. If
preferred, the large slices can be folded in
half first. Dredge lightly with a little flour.

5 Heat the olive oil and butter in a
large frying pan and fry the
escalopes until golden brown each side
and just cooked through – about 4
minutes for single slices or 5-6 minutes
for double ones. Take care not to
overcook. Remove to a serving dish and
keep warm.

6 Add the wine, stock and Marsala to
the pan and bring to the boil,
stirring well to loosen all the sediment
from the pan. Boil until reduced by
almost half. Adjust the seasoning and
quickly pour over the saltimbocca. Serve
at once, garnished with fresh sage leaves.

VITELLO TONNATO

SERVES 4

750 g/1½ lb boned leg of veal, rolled
2 bay leaves
10 black peppercorns
2-3 whole cloves
½ tsp salt
2 carrots, sliced
1 onion, sliced
2 celery sticks, sliced
about 750 ml/1¼ pints /3 cups stock or
    water
150 ml/ ¼ pint/ ⅔ cup dry white wine
    (optional)
90 g/3 oz canned tuna fish, well drained
1 x 50 g (1½ oz) can anchovy fillets,
    drained
150 ml/ ¼ pint/ ⅔ cup olive oil
2 tsp bottled capers, drained
2 egg yolks
1 tbsp lemon juice
salt and pepper

TO GARNISH:
capers
lemon wedges
fresh herbs

1 Put the veal in a saucepan with the bay leaves, peppercorns, cloves, salt and vegetables. Add sufficient stock or water and the wine (if using) to barely cover the veal. Bring to the boil, remove any scum from the surface, then cover the pan and simmer gently for an hour or so until tender. Leave in the water until cold, then drain thoroughly. If time allows, chill the veal to make it easier to carve.

2 For the tuna sauce: thoroughly mash the tuna fish with 4 anchovy fillets and 1 tablespoon oil and the capers, then add the egg yolks and press through a sieve or purée in a food processor or liquidizer until smooth.

3 Stir in the lemon juice then gradually whisk in the rest of the oil a few drops at a time until the sauce is smooth and has the consistency of thick cream. Season to taste.

4 Slice the veal thinly and arrange on a flat platter in overlapping slices. Spoon the tunafish sauce over the veal to cover. Then cover the dish and chill overnight.

5 Before serving, uncover the veal carefully. Arrange the remaining anchovy fillets and the capers in a decorative pattern on top, and garnish with lemon wedges and herbs.

POT ROAST LEG OF LAMB

SERVES 4

1.75 kg/3½ lb leg of lamb
3-4 sprigs fresh rosemary
125 g/4 oz streaky bacon rashers
4 tbsp olive oil
2-3 garlic cloves, crushed
2 onions, sliced
2 carrots, sliced
2 celery sticks, sliced
300 ml/ ½ pint/1¼ cups dry white wine
1 tbsp tomato purée (paste)
300 ml/ ½ pint/1¼ cups stock
*350 g/12 oz tomatoes, peeled, quartered
    and seeded*
1 tbsp freshly chopped parsley
*1 tbsp freshly chopped oregano or
    marjoram*
salt and pepper
fresh rosemary sprigs, to garnish

1   Wipe the joint of lamb all over, trimming off any excess fat, then season well with salt and pepper, rubbing well in. Lay the sprigs of rosemary over the lamb, cover evenly with the bacon rashers and tie in place with fine string.

2   Heat the oil in a frying pan and fry the lamb until browned all over, turning several times – about 10 minutes. Remove from the pan.

3   Transfer the oil from the frying pan to a large fireproof casserole and fry the garlic and onion together for 3-4 minutes until beginning to soften, then add the carrots and celery and continue to cook for a few minutes longer.

4   Lay the lamb on top of the vegetables and press well to partly bury. Pour the wine over the lamb, add the tomato purée (paste) and simmer for 3-4 minutes. Add the stock, tomatoes and herbs and plenty of seasoning and bring back to the boil for a further 3-4 minutes.

5   Cover the casserole tightly and cook in a preheated oven at 180ºC/350ºF/Gas Mark 4 for 2-2½ hours.

6   Remove the lamb from the casserole and if liked, take off the bacon and herbs along with the string. Strain the juices, skimming off any fat, and serve in a jug. Garnish with sprigs of rosemary.

CHICKEN WITH GREEN OLIVES

SERVES 4

4 chicken breasts, part boned
30 g/1 oz/2 tbsp butter
2 tbsp olive oil
1 large onion, finely chopped
2 garlic cloves, crushed
*2 (bell) peppers, red, yellow or green,
    cored, seeded and cut into large pieces*
*250 g/8 oz large closed cup mushrooms,
    sliced or quartered*
175 g/6 oz tomatoes, peeled and halved
150 ml/ ¼ pint/ ⅔ cup dry white wine
125-175 g/4-6 oz green olives, pitted
4-6 tbsp double (heavy) cream
salt and pepper
flat-leaf parsley, chopped, to garnish

1   Season the chicken with salt and pepper. Heat the oil and butter in a frying pan, add the chicken and fry until browned all over. Remove from the pan.

2   Add the onion and garlic to the pan and fry gently until beginning to soften. Add the (bell) peppers to the pan with the mushrooms and continue to cook for a few minutes longer.

3   Add the tomatoes and plenty of seasoning to the pan and then transfer the vegetable mixture to an ovenproof casserole. Place the chicken on the bed of vegetables.

4   Add the wine to the frying pan and bring to the boil. Pour the wine over the chicken and cover the casserole tightly. Cook in a preheated oven at 180ºC/350ºF/Gas Mark 4 for 50 minutes.

5   Add the olives to the chicken, mix lightly then pour on the cream. Re-cover the casserole and return to the oven for 10-20 minutes or until the chicken is very tender.

6   Adjust the seasoning and serve the pieces of chicken, surrounded by the vegetables and sauce, with pasta or tiny new potatoes. Sprinkle with parsley to garnish.

LIVER WITH WINE SAUCE

••

SERVES 4

4 slices calf's liver or 8 slices lamb's liver,
*   about 500 g/1 lb*
flour, for coating
1 tbsp olive oil
30 g/1 oz/2 tbsp butter
1garlic clove, crushed
125 g/4 oz lean bacon rashers, rinded
1 onion, chopped
1 celery stick, thinly sliced
150 ml/ ¼ pint/ ⅔ cup red wine
150 ml/ ¼ pint/ ⅔ cup beef stock
good pinch of ground allspice
1 tsp Worcestershire sauce
1 tsp freshly chopped sage or ½ tsp
*   dried sage*
3-4 tomatoes, peeled
salt and pepper
fresh sage leaves, to garnish
sauté potatoes, to serve

1 Wipe the liver, season with salt and pepper and coat lightly in flour, shaking off the surplus.

2 Heat the oil and butter in a pan and fry the liver until well sealed on both sides and just cooked through – take care not to overcook. Remove the liver from the pan, cover and keep warm, but do not allow to dry out.

3 Cut the bacon into narrow strips and add to the fat left in the pan with the onion and celery. Fry gently until soft.

4 Add the wine and stock, allspice, Worcestershire sauce and seasonings, bring to the boil and simmer for 3-4 minutes.

5 Quarter the tomatoes, discard the seeds and cut each piece in half. Add to the sauce and continue to cook for a couple of minutes.

6 Serve the liver on a little of the sauce, with the remainder spooned over. Garnish with fresh sage leaves and serve with tiny new potatoes or sauté potatoes.

DESSERTS

ZABAGLIONE

••

SERVES 4

6 egg yolks
90 g/3 oz/6 tbsp caster sugar
6 tbsp Marsala
amaretti biscuits or sponge fingers, to serve
strawberries or raspberries, to decorate
*   (optional)*

1 Put the egg yolks into a heatproof bowl and whisk until a pale yellow colour, using a rotary, balloon or electric whisk.

2 Whisk in the sugar, followed by the Marsala, continuing to whisk all the time.

3 Stand the bowl over a saucepan of very gently simmering water, or transfer to the top of a double boiler, and continue to whisk continuously. Whisk until the mixture thickens sufficiently to stand in soft peaks. On no account allow the water to boil or the zabaglione will over-cook and turn into scrambled eggs.

4 Scrape around the sides of the bowl from time to time while whisking. As soon as the mixture is really thick and foamy, take from the heat and continue to whisk for a couple of minutes longer.

5 Pour immediately into stemmed glasses and serve warm; or leave until cold and serve chilled.

6 Fruits such as strawberries or raspberries or crumbled sponge fingers or amaretti biscuits may be placed in the base of the glasses before adding the zabaglione.

ALTERNATIVE

Any other type of liqueur may be used in place of Marsala, for a change.

CLASSIC TIRAMISU

•••

SERVES 4-6

20-24 sponge fingers (boudoir biscuits),
    about 150 g/5 oz
2 tbsp cold black coffee
2 tbsp coffee essence
2 tbsp Amaretto or brandy
4 egg yolks (size 2 or 3)
90 g/3 oz/6 tbsp caster sugar
few drops of vanilla essence
grated rind of ½ lemon
350 g/12 oz/1½ cups Mascarpone
2 tsp lemon juice
250 ml/8 fl oz/1 cup double (heavy) cream
1 tbsp milk
30 g/1 oz/¼ cup flaked almonds, lightly
    toasted
2 tbsp cocoa powder
1 tbsp icing (confectioner's) sugar

1 Arrange almost half the sponge
   fingers in the base of a glass bowl or
serving dish. Combine the black coffee,
coffee essence and Amaretto or brandy
and sprinkle just over half the mixture
over the fingers.

2 Put the egg yolks into a heatproof
   bowl with the sugar, vanilla essence
and lemon rind. Stand over a saucepan of
gently simmering water and whisk until
very thick and creamy and the whisk
leaves a very heavy trail when lifted from
the bowl.

3 Put the Mascarpone cheese into a
   bowl, add the lemon juice and beat
until smooth.

4 Combine the egg mixture and
   Mascarpone cheese and when
evenly blended pour half over the sponge
fingers and spread out evenly.

5 Add another layer of sponge fingers,
   sprinkle with the remaining coffee
and then cover with the rest of the cheese
mixture. Chill for at least 2 hours and
preferably longer, or overnight.

6 To serve, whip the cream and milk
   together until fairly stiff and spread
or pipe over the dessert. Sprinkle with the
flaked almonds and then sift an even
layer of cocoa powder so the top is
completely covered. Finally sift a very
light layer of icing sugar over the cocoa.

PANFORTE DI SIENA

•••

SERVES 12

125 g/4 oz/1 cup split whole almonds
125 g/4 oz/ ¾ cup hazelnuts
90 g/3 oz/ ½ cup cut mixed peel
60 g/2 oz/ ⅓ cup no-need-to-soak dried
    apricots
60 g/2 oz glacé or crystallized pineapple
grated rind of 1 large orange
60 g/2 oz/ ½ cup plain flour
2 tbsp cocoa powder
2 tsp ground cinnamon
125 g/4 oz/ ½ cup caster sugar
175 g/6 oz/ ½ cup honey
icing (confectioner's) sugar, for dredging

1 Toast the almonds until lightly
   browned and place in a bowl. Toast
the hazelnuts under the grill until the
skins split. Place the hazelnuts on a tea
towel and rub off the skins with the
towel. Roughly chop the hazelnuts and
add to the almonds with the mixed peel.

2 Chop the apricots and pineapple
   fairly finely, add to the nuts with the
orange rind and mix well.

3 Sift the flour with the cocoa and
   cinnamon, add to the nut mixture
and mix evenly.

4 Line a round 20 cm/8 in cake tin or
   deep loose-based flan tin with
baking parchment.

5 Put the sugar and honey into a
   saucepan and heat until the sugar
dissolves, then boil gently for about
5 minutes or until the mixture thickens
and begins to turn a deeper shade of
brown. Quickly add to the nut mixture
and stir through it evenly. Turn into the
prepared tin and level the top with the
help of a damp spoon.

6 Cook in a preheated oven at
   150ºC/300ºF/Gas Mark 2 for an hour.
Remove from the oven and leave in the
tin until cold. Take out of the tin and
carefully peel off the paper. Before
serving, dredge the cake heavily with
sifted icing (confectioner's) sugar. Serve
cut into very thin slices.

INDIAN DISHES – INTRODUCTION

It's never been easier to create quick and authentic tasting Indian dishes thanks to the marvellous range of exciting spices, tempting ingredients and ready-prepared products so widely available. All the ingredients used in the recipes in this book are easy to find from the larger supermarkets.

SPICES

Spices play an essential part in Indian cooking, but don't be put off by the vast array of jars and packets on the supermarket shelves, remember that you only need a few to give characteristic flavour to your Indian cooking.

It is best to buy whole spices (they keep their flavour and aroma much longer than the ready ground spice) and to grind them as you need them. A small coffee grinder, electric mill or a pestle and mortar does the job easily. If you cook a lot of Indian dishes, it may well be worth grinding the various spices in small quantities at a time: store them in small, airtight containers and use up quickly.

When time is short, however, do make the most of the excellent range of commercially prepared products widely available in supermarkets. Spice mixtures such as curry powders, garam masala and tandoori spices and the jars of ready-made curry pastes, etc. are extremely convenient and make light work of adding flavour and authenticity to Indian-style dishes. Useful too, are the jars of ready-minced chilli and chopped fresh ginger – and the varied selection of canned curry sauces (ranging from mild to medium and hot) ensure there is something to please most palates.

Here is a suggestion of just a handful of spices well worth buying to give your Indian meals that special flavour and aroma:

Cardamom These small pods contain numerous tiny black seeds which have a warm, highly aromatic flavour – green cardamoms are considered the best. Cardamom pods (used in savoury and sweet dishes) are often lightly crushed prior to adding to dishes to allow the full flavour of the seeds to be appreciated.

When the whole or crushed pods are used they are not meant to be eaten and should either be removed before serving or simply left on the side of the plate by the diner.

When the seeds only are required, the pods should be lightly crushed to break them open and the seeds removed for using whole or crushed, according to the recipe. Use a pestle and mortar or the end of a rolling pin for crushing either pods or seeds.

Cinnamon Available in stick and ground form. Shavings of bark from the cinnamon tree are processed and curled to form cinnamon sticks and these will keep almost indefinitely in an airtight container. This fragrant spice is used to flavour savoury and sweet dishes and drinks. The sticks are not edible and should be removed before serving, or may be used as a garnish or decoration.

Cassia Cassia comes from the bark of the cassia tree. It is not as uniform in shape as cinnamon sticks, but has a similar, less delicate flavour.

Cloves These dried unopened flower buds are used to give flavour and aroma to foods, but should be used with care as the flavour can become overpowering. When whole cloves

INTRODUCTION

are used they are not meant to be eaten and may be removed before serving, if wished.

Coriander An essential spice in Indian cooking, coriander has a mild and spicy flavour with a slight hint of orange peel. It is available as seeds or ground.

Cumin These caraway-like seeds are used extensively in Indian dishes either in their whole or ground form. Cumin has a warm, pungent and aromatic flavour.

Garam masala This is a ground aromatic spice mix that generally includes cardamom, cinnamon, cumin, cloves, peppercorns and nutmeg. It may be used during and towards the end of cooking, or sprinkled over dishes as an aromatic garnish just before serving. You can buy this spice ready-mixed or prepare your own quite simply: finely grind together 1 tsp each black peppercorns and cumin seeds with 1 tbsp cardamom seeds, 8 whole cloves, a 5 cm/2 in piece of cinnamon stick or cassia bark and about 1/4 teaspoon freshly grated nutmeg. Store the mixture in an airtight container and use within 3 weeks. This quantity makes about 3 tablespoonfuls.

Ginger Fresh root ginger is now widely available from supermarkets and green grocers. It looks like a knobbly brown stem and should be peeled and chopped, sliced or grated before use. It is also now available ready-minced in jars.

Paprika This ground, bright red pepper, although similar in colour to fiery cayenne pepper, has a mild

flavour and is used for colouring as well as flavouring dishes.

Saffron This spice (the most expensive of all) has a distinctive flavour and gives a rich yellow colouring to dishes. It is available in small packets and jars, either powdered or in strands – the strands have by far the better flavour.

Turmeric Is an aromatic root which is dried and ground to produce a bright, orangey-yellow powder. It has a warm, distinctive smell and a delicate, aromatic flavour. It is frequently used to give dishes an attractive yellow colouring.

CHILLIES

Fresh chillies, used extensively in Indian dishes to give them their hot and fiery flavour, vary considerably in size, shape and hotness – it really depends on the variety. It's worth remembering that all chillies are hot, so use caution when adding them to a dish, it is wise to start with small amounts – you can always add more to taste at a later stage according to personal preference. Take care too, when preparing chillies. The cream-coloured seeds inside are the hottest part and may be removed before using, if wished: generally, the seeds are only left in if you like your spicy dishes very hot indeed! Chillies contain a pungent oil which can cause an unpleasant burning sensation to eyes and skin, so it is advisable to wear thin polythene or rubber gloves when handling them and to be sure not to touch your face or eyes during preparation.

To prepare a chilli: cut the chilli in half lengthways, cut off the stalk end, then scrape out the seeds with a pointed knife and discard. Rinse the

INTRODUCTION

chilli under cold running water and pat dry before chopping or slicing as required. Once you have finished, thoroughly wash your hands, utensils and surfaces with soapy water.

Dried red chillies are sold whole or ground and are used to make cayenne pepper, chilli and curry powders. Again, remove the seeds from dried chillies. Chilli powders come in varying degrees of strength, so check the label before you buy, as many are a blend of chilli and other spices, such as "chilli seasoning" – a popular blend that is quite mild.

You can also buy ready-minced red chilli in a jar from many supermarkets – this is an excellent and most convenient way of adding a fiery touch to Indian dishes without any hassle.

Green chillies, too, are available in brine or pickled in sweetened vinegar – these should be drained and dried on paper towels before using.

FRESH CORIANDER (DHANIA)
This pretty green herb has leaves rather similar in appearance to flat-leaf parsley. It is frequently used in Indian dishes both as a garnish and for its delicate flavour.

COCONUT
Many Indian dishes are flavoured with coconut and the ready prepared desiccated (shredded) type is convenient and easy to use, however, you really do get the very best flavour from fresh grated coconut. It freezes well too, so is well worth preparing to freeze away in handy quantities to use when required.

To prepare for freezing: choose a fresh coconut that is heavy with liquid (best way to check is to give it a good shake before buying). Break

it in half, drain off the liquid and prise the coconut from its shell. Using a potato peeler, peel off the brown skin and break the flesh into smallish pieces. Place in a food processor and process until finely grated, or, if preferred grate larger pieces on a cheese grater. Freeze in small usable quantities for up to 3 months. It thaws quickly and can be used as required.

Coconut milk too, is a popular ingredient in Indian cooking and is available in liquid form in cans, or as coconut milk powder in sachets, to make up into a liquid following the packet instructions.

You can also make your own delicious version very easily: chop 1 x 198 g/7 oz packet creamed coconut and place in a heatproof measuring jug. Pour in enough boiling water to come to the 600 ml/1 pint/2½ cup mark and stir until dissolved. Cool and use as required. This will keep in the refrigerator for up to 1 week.

GHEE
Indian recipes often call for ghee (or clarified butter) for cooking. It can be cooked at high temperatures without burning, gives a delicious rich, nutty flavour to all manner of dishes and a glossy sheen to sauces. You can buy ghee in cans from supermarkets and Indian food shops and a vegetarian ghee is also available. Vegetable oil may be used instead of ghee, as preferred.

RICE
The two types of rice most frequently used in Indian cooking are long-grain rice (also called American long-grain or Patna rice) and basmati rice which, although rather more expensive, is prized for its slender grains and fine aromatic flavour. This

INTRODUCTION

is the one to use whenever possible, but if you can't afford this variety every time, save it for special occasions.

It is essential to rinse rice, particularly basmati, in a sieve under cold running water, before cooking to get rid of the starchy residue left from the milling process. Easy-cook rice, including basmati, is now widely available in supermarkets and always gives good results. It is also now possible to buy brown basmati rice, which will take a little longer to cook.

YOGURT
Homemade yogurt (dahi) is used extensively in Indian cooking for marinading meats and poultry to tenderise and flavour them and also as an ingredient in various dishes and sauces. It is also widely used as a cooling accompaniment to spicy dishes, such as Raita, see recipe on page xx. Strained Greek yogurt, with its tart, creamy flavour, most closely resembles the homemade yogurt eaten by Indian families. A brief whisk before using will thin the consistency, if necessary. Any natural yogurt of your choice may be used instead, if preferred.

SUPERMARKET ADDITIONS TO A HOMEMADE INDIAN MEAL
There's a wonderful selection of ready-prepared products available from supermarkets that you could include with your homemade dishes. A basket of poppadums, for example, is always favourite as a starter. Other traditional and popular accompaniments could include parathas, chapatis or naan, plus a bowl of yogurt or Raita (see above) and a selection of shop bought pickles or chutneys such as lime or mango.

DRINKS TO SERVE
You will need a supply of cooling and refreshing drinks to accompany an Indian meal: the best ones are ice-cold water, chilled lagers or beers and fruit juices. Fine wine is rather wasted since its taste is overpowered by the strong flavours of the food.

STARTERS

PRAWN (SHRIMP) POORIS

• •

SERVES 6

POORIS:
60 g/2 oz/ ½ cup plain wholemeal flour
60 g/2 oz/ ½ cup plain white flour
1 tbsp ghee or vegetable oil
2 good pinches of salt
75 ml/3 fl oz/ ⅓ cup hot water

TOPPING:
250 g/8 oz fresh spinach, washed and
  stalks trimmed
4 tbsp ghee or vegetable oil, plus extra oil
  for shallow frying
1 onion, peeled and chopped
1 garlic clove, peeled and crushed
½-1 tsp minced chilli (from a jar)
1-1½ tbsp medium curry paste, to taste
250 g/8 oz canned chopped tomatoes
150 ml/ ¼ pint/ ⅔ cup coconut milk
250 g/8 oz peeled tiger prawns (shrimp)

1 To make the pooris, put the flours in a bowl and make a well in the centre. Add the ghee or oil, salt and hot water and mix to form a dough. Leave to stand for 1 hour.

2 Meanwhile, prepare the topping. Cut the spinach crossways into wide strips – do this by making bundles of leaves and slicing with a sharp knife. Heat the ghee or oil in a frying pan, add the onion, garlic, chilli and spinach and cook gently for 4 minutes, shaking the pan and stirring frequently. Add the curry paste, tomatoes and coconut milk and simmer for 10 minutes, stirring occasionally. Remove from the heat, stir in the prawns (shrimp) and season with salt to taste.

3 Knead the dough well on a floured surface, divide into 6 pieces and shape into 6 balls. Roll out each one to a 12 cm/5 in round. Heat about 2.5 cm/1 in oil in a deep frying pan until smoking hot. Take one poori at a time, lower into the hot oil and cook for 10-15 seconds on each side until puffed up and golden. Remove the poori with a slotted spoon, drain on absorbent paper towels and keep warm while cooking the remainder in the same way.

4 Reheat the prawn (shrimp) mixture, stirring until piping hot. Arrange a poori on each serving plate and spoon the prawn (shrimp) and spinach mixture on to each one. Serve immediately.

SPINACH POORI

••

SERVES 6

125 g/4 oz/1 cup wholemeal flour
125 g/4 oz/1 cup plain (all-purpose) flour
½ tsp salt
2 tbsp vegetable oil
125 g/4 oz/½ cup chopped spinach, fresh
 or frozen, blanched, puréed and all
 excess water squeezed out
50 ml/2 fl oz/ ¼ cup water
oil for deep-frying

RELISH:
2 tbsp chopped fresh mint
2 tbsp natural yogurt
½ red onion, sliced and rinsed
½ tsp cayenne

1 Sift the flours and salt together into a
  bowl. Drizzle over the oil and rub in
until the mixture resembles fine
breadcrumbs. Add the spinach and water,
and stir in to make a stiff dough. Knead
for 10 minutes until smooth.

2 Form the dough into a ball. Put into
  an oiled bowl and turn to coat.
Cover with clingfilm (plastic wrap) and
set aside for 30 minutes.

3 Make the relish. Combine the mint,
  yogurt and onion, place in a serving
bowl and sift cayenne over the top.

4 Knead the dough again and divide
  into 12 small balls. Remove 1 ball
and keep the rest covered. Roll this ball
out into a 12 cm/5 in circle.

5 Put the oil into a wok or wide frying
  pan (skillet) to 2.5 cm/1 in depth.
Heat it until a haze appears. It must be
very hot.

6 Put 1 poori on the surface of the
  oil – if it sinks, it should rise up
immediately and sizzle; if it doesn't,
the oil isn't hot enough. Keep the poori
submerged in the oil, using the back of
a fish slice or a perforated spoon. The
poori will puff up immediately. Turn it
over and cook the other side for 5–10
seconds. Drain on paper towels. Repeat
with the remaining balls of dough. Serve
with the relish.

BRINDIL BHAJI

••

SERVES 4

500 g/1 lb aubergines (eggplant), cut into
 1 cm/ ½ in slices
2 tbsp ghee
1 onion, thinly sliced
2 garlic cloves, sliced
2.5 cm/1 in piece ginger root, grated
½ tsp ground turmeric
1 dried red chilli
½ tsp salt
425 g/14 oz can tomatoes
1 tsp Garam Masala (see page 317)
fresh coriander (cilantro) sprigs to garnish

1 Cut the aubergine (eggplant) slices
  into finger-width strips using a sharp
knife.

2 Heat the ghee in a saucepan and
  cook the onion over a medium heat
for 7–8 minutes, stirring constantly, until
very soft.

3 Add the garlic and aubergine
  (eggplant), increase the heat and
cook for 2 minutes.

4 Stir in the ginger, the turmeric,
  chilli, salt and the contents of
the can of tomatoes. Use the back of a
wooden spoon to break up the tomatoes.
Simmer uncovered for 15–20 minutes until
the aubergine (eggplant) is very soft.

5 Stir in the garam masala. Simmer for
  a further 4–5 minutes.

6 Serve garnished with fresh coriander
  (cilantro) sprigs.

VARIATION

Other vegetables can be used instead
of the aubergines (eggplants). Try courgettes (zucchini), potatoes or (bell)
peppers, or any combination of these
vegetables, using the same sauce.

MINTED ONION BHAJIS

MAKES 12

125 g/4 oz/1 cup gram flour
¼ tsp cayenne pepper
¼–½ tsp ground coriander
¼–½ tsp ground cumin
1 tbsp chopped fresh mint
salt and freshly ground black pepper
4 tbsp strained Greek yogurt
65 ml/2½ fl oz/¼ cup cold water
1 large onion, peeled, quartered and
*   thinly sliced*
vegetable oil, for frying
mint sprigs, to garnish

1 Put the gram flour into a bowl, add the cayenne pepper, coriander, cumin and mint and season with salt and pepper to taste. Stir in the yogurt, water and sliced onion and mix well together.

2 One-third fill a large, deep frying pan with oil and heat until hot. Drop heaped spoonfuls of the mixture, a few at a time, into the hot oil and use two forks to neaten the mixture into rough ball-shapes.

3 Fry the bhajis until rich golden brown and cooked through, turning frequently. Drain on absorbent paper towels and keep warm while cooking the remainder in the same way. Serve hot or warm.

VARIATION

For a more fiery flavour, add 1 seeded and chopped fresh green chilli (or 1 teaspoon ready prepared minced chilli, from a jar) to the above ingredients and omit the cayenne pepper, if wished.

ALOO CHAT

SERVES 4

125 g/4 oz/generous ½ cup chick-peas
*   (garbanzo beans), soaked overnight in*
*   cold water and drained*
1 dried red chilli
500 g/1 lb waxy potatoes, such as red-
*   skinned or Cyprus potatoes, boiled in*
*   their skins and peeled*
1 tsp cumin seeds
1 tsp black peppercorns
2 tsp salt
½ tsp dried mint
½ tsp chilli powder
½ tsp ground ginger
2 tsp mango powder
120 ml/4 fl oz/½ cup natural yogurt
oil for deep frying
4 poppadoms

TO SERVE:
Cucumber Raita (see page 350)

1 Boil the chick-peas (garbanzo beans) with the chilli in plenty of water for about 1 hour until tender. Drain.

2 Cut the potatoes into 2.5 cm/ 1 in dice and mix into the chick-peas (garbanzo beans) while they are still warm. Set aside.

3 Grind together the cumin, peppercorns and salt in a spice grinder or pestle and mortar. Stir in the mint, chilli powder, ginger and mango powder.

4 Put a small dry saucepan or frying pan (skillet) over a low heat and add the spice mix. Stir until fragrant and immediately remove from the heat.

5 Stir half of the spice mix into the chick-peas (garbanzo beans) and potatoes, and stir the yogurt into the other half.

6 Cook the poppadoms according to the pack instructions. Drain on plenty of paper towels. Break into bite-size pieces and stir into the potatoes and chick-peas (garbanzo beans), spoon over the spiced yogurt and serve with the cucumber raita.

PAKORAS

SERVES 4-6

125g/4 oz broccoli
1 onion
2 potatoes
175 g/6 oz/1½ cups gram flour
1 tsp garam masala
1½ tsp salt
½ tsp cayenne pepper
1 tsp cumin seeds
200 ml/7 fl oz/just under 1 cup water
vegetable oil, for deep frying
coriander sprigs, to garnish

1 Cut the broccoli into small florets, discarding most of the stalk and cook in a pan of boiling, salted water for 4 minutes. Drain well, return to the pan and shake dry over a low heat for a few moments. Place the broccoli on absorbent paper towels to completely dry while preparing the other vegetables.

2 Peel and thinly slice the onion and separate into rings. Peel and thinly slice the potatoes and pat dry.

3 Place the gram flour in a bowl with the garam masala, salt, cayenne pepper and cumin seeds. Make a well in the centre, add the water and mix to form a smooth batter.

4 One-third fill a deep fat fryer or pan with oil and heat to 190°C/375°F or until a cube of day-old bread browns in 30 seconds. Dip the vegetables into the batter to coat, then lower into the hot oil and fry, in batches, for 3-4 minutes or until golden brown and crisp. Drain on absorbent paper towels and keep warm while cooking the remainder in the same way. Serve the pakoras hot, garnished with coriander sprigs.

VARIATIONS

Small cauliflower florets, strips of red or green (bell) pepper and slices of courgette (zucchini) are also very good cooked this way. The cauliflower should be par-cooked in the same way as broccoli (see step 1) before dipping in the batter. Use up the leftover stalks in a soup, rice or main course dish.

PARATHAS

MAKES 6

90 g/3 oz/ ¾ cup plain wholemeal flour
90 g/3 oz/ ¾ cup plain white flour
a good pinch of salt
1 tbsp vegetable oil, plus extra for greasing
75 ml/3 fl oz/ ⅓ cup tepid water

1 Place the flours and the salt in a bowl. Drizzle 1 tablespoon of oil over the flour, add the tepid water and mix to form a soft dough, adding a little more water, if necessary. Knead on a lightly floured surface until smooth, then cover and leave for 30 minutes.

2 Knead the dough on a floured surface and divide into 6 equal pieces. Shape each one into a ball. Roll out on a floured surface to a 15 cm/6 in round and brush very lightly with oil.

3 Fold in half, and then in half again to form a triangle. Roll out to form an 18 cm/7 in triangle (when measured from point to centre top), dusting with extra flour as necessary.

4 Brush a large frying pan with a little oil and heat until hot, then add one or two parathas and cook for about 1-1½ minutes. Brush the surfaces very lightly with oil, then turn and cook the other sides for 1½ minutes until cooked through.

5 Place the cooked parathas on a plate and cover with foil, or place between a clean tea towel to keep warm, while cooking the remainder in the same way, greasing the pan between cooking each batch.

ALTERNATIVE

If the parathas puff up a lot during cooking, press down lightly with a fish slice. Make parathas in advance, if wished: wrap in kitchen foil and reheat in a hot oven for about 15 minutes when required.

VEGETABLE & CASHEW SAMOSAS

MAKES 12

*350 g/12 oz potatoes, peeled and diced
salt
125 g/4 oz frozen peas
45 ml/3 tbsp vegetable oil
1 onion, peeled and chopped
2.5 cm/1 in ginger root, peeled and
   chopped
1 garlic clove, peeled and crushed
1 tsp garam masala
2 tsp mild curry paste
½ tsp cumin seeds
2 tsp lemon juice
60 g/2 oz/½ cup unsalted cashews,
   coarsely chopped
vegetable oil, for shallow frying
coriander sprigs, to garnish
mango chutney, to serve*

*PASTRY:
250 g/8 oz/2 cups plain flour
60 g/2 oz/¼ cup butter
75 ml/6 tbsp/⅓ cup warm milk*

1 Cook the potatoes in a saucepan of
  boiling, salted water for 5 minutes.
Add the peas and cook for a further 4
minutes or until the potato is tender.
Drain well. Heat the oil in a frying pan,
add the onion, potato and pea mixture,
ginger, garlic and spices and fry for
2 minutes. Stir in the lemon juice and
cook gently, uncovered, for 2 minutes.
Remove from the heat, slightly mash the
potato and peas, then add the cashews,
mix well and season with salt.

2 To make the pastry, put the flour in
  a bowl and rub in the butter finely.
Mix in the milk to form a dough. Knead
lightly and divide into 6 portions. Form
each into a ball and roll out on a lightly
floured surface to an 18 cm/7 in round.
Cut each one in half.

3 Divide the filling equally between
  each semi-circle of pastry, spreading
it out to within 5 mm/¼ in of the edges.
Brush the edges of pastry all the way
round with water and fold over to form
triangular shapes, sealing the edges well
together to enclose the filling completely.

4 One-third fill a large, deep frying
  pan with oil and heat to 180°C/
350°F/Gas 4 or until hot enough to brown
a cube of bread in 30 seconds.
Fry the samosas, a few at a time, turning
frequently until golden brown and heated
through. Drain on papertowels and keep
warm while cooking the remainder in the
same way. Garnish with coriander sprigs
and serve hot.

PESHWARI NAAN

SERVES 4-6

50 ml/2 fl oz/ ¼ cup warm water
pinch of sugar
½ tsp active dried yeast
500 g/1 lb/4 cups strong bread flour
½ tsp salt
50 ml/2 fl oz/ ¼ cup natural yogurt
2 Granny Smith apples, peeled and diced
60 g/2 oz/ ⅓ cup sultanas (golden raisins)
60 g/2 oz/ ½ cup flaked (slivered) almonds
1 tbsp coriander (cilantro) leaves
2 tbsp grated coconut

1 Combine the water and sugar in a bowl and sprinkle over the yeast. Leave for 5–10 minutes, until the yeast has dissolved and the mixture is foamy.

2 Put the flour and salt into a large bowl and make a well in the centre. Add the yeast mixture and yogurt to the bowl. Draw the flour into the liquid, until all the flour is absorbed. Mix together, adding enough tepid water to form a soft dough, about 150 ml/¼pint/⅔ cup.

3 Turn out on to a floured board and knead for 10 minutes until smooth and elastic. Put into an oiled bowl, cover with a cloth and leave for 3 hours in a warm place, or in the fridge overnight.

4 Line the grill (broiler) pan with foil, shiny side up.

5 Put the apples into a saucepan with a little water. Bring to the boil, mash them down, reduce the heat and continue to simmer for 20 minutes, mashing occasionally.

6 Divide the dough into 4 pieces and roll each piece out to a 20 cm/8 in oval.

7 Pull one end out into a teardrop shape, about 5 mm/ ¼ in thick. Lay on a floured surface and prick all over with a fork.

8 Brush both sides of the bread with oil. Place under a preheated grill (broiler) at the highest setting. Cook for 3 minutes, turn the bread over and cook for a further 3 minutes. It should have dark brown spots all over.

9 Spread a teaspoonful of the apple purée all over the bread, then sprinkle over a quarter of the sultanas (golden raisins), the flaked (slivered) almonds, the coriander (cilantro) leaves and the coconut. Repeat with the remaining 3 ovals of dough.

SPICY OVEN BREAD

●●

SERVES 8

½ tsp active dried yeast
300 ml/ ½ pint/1¼ cups warm water
500 g/1 lb/4 cups strong white flour
1 tsp salt
250 g/8 oz/1 cup butter, melted and
* cooled*
½ tsp garam masala
½ tsp coriander seeds, ground
1 tsp cumin seeds, ground

1 Mix the yeast with a little of the warm water until it starts to foam and is completely dissolved.

2 Put the flour and salt into a large bowl, make a well in the centre and add the yeast mixture, and 125 g/4 oz/ ½ cup of the melted butter. Blend the yeast and butter together before drawing in the flour and kneading lightly. Add the water gradually until a firm dough is obtained; you may not need it all.

3 Turn the dough out and knead until smooth and elastic, about 10 minutes. Put the dough into an oiled bowl and turn it over so that it is all coated. Cover and leave in a warm place to rise until doubled, about 30 minutes. Alternatively, leave in the refrigerator overnight.

4 Knock back (punch down) the dough and divide into 8 balls. Roll each ball out to about a 15 cm/6 in round. Put on to a floured baking sheet. Sprinkle with flour and leave for 20 minutes.

5 Mix the spices together with the remaining melted butter.

6 Brush each bread with the spice and butter mixture and cover with foil. Place on the middle shelf of a preheated oven at 220°C/425°F/Gas mark 7 for 5 minutes. Remove the foil, brush with the butter once again and cook for a further 5 minutes.

7 Remove from the oven and wrap in a clean tea towel (dish cloth) until ready to eat.

PALAK PANEER

●●●

SERVES 4-6

2 tbsp ghee
1 onion, sliced
1 garlic clove, crushed
1 dried red chilli
1 tsp ground turmeric
500 g/1 lb waxy potatoes, such as red-
* skinned or Cyprus potatoes, cut into*
* 2.5 cm/1 in cubes*
425 g/14 oz can tomatoes, drained
150 ml/ ¼ pint/ ⅔ cup water
250 g/8 oz/6 cups fresh spinach
500 g/1 lb/2 cups curd cheese, cut into
* 2.5 cm/1 in cubes*
1 tsp Garam Masala (see page 317)
1 tbsp chopped fresh coriander (cilantro)
1 tbsp chopped fresh parsley
salt and pepper
naan bread to serve

1 Heat the ghee in a saucepan, add the onion and cook over a low heat for 10 minutes until very soft. Add the garlic and chilli and cook for 5 minutes.

2 Add the turmeric, salt, potatoes, tomatoes and water and bring to the boil. Simmer for 10 –15 minutes until the potatoes are cooked.

3 Stir in the spinach, cheese cubes, garam masala, coriander (cilantro) and parsley. Simmer for 5 minutes and season well. Serve with naan bread.

CURD CHEESE

Indian paneer is a homemade fresh cheese. To make it, pour 2.25 litres/4 pints/2½ quarts of very creamy milk into a large saucepan. Heat until the surface of the milk is quivering, stirring occasionally to prevent the milk from catching on the bottom of the pan. Remove the pan from the heat and add 4 tablespoons of vinegar. Do not stir. The milk will separate. When cool, pour through a clean tea towel, and tie up the remaining solids in the cloth. Put on a draining board, cover with a strong board and stand a heavy weight on top (several food cans, or a large saucepan full of water). Leave for 4 hours. Cut into 2.5 cm/1 in cubes.

MAIN DISHES

GREEN FISH CURRY

SERVES 4

1 tbsp oil
2 spring onions (scallions), sliced
1 tsp cumin seeds, ground
2 fresh green chillies, choppped
1 tsp coriander seeds, ground
4 tbsp chopped fresh coriander (cilantro)
4 tbsp chopped fresh mint
1 tbsp chopped chives
150 ml / ¼ pint/ ⅔ cup coconut milk
4 white fish fillets, about 250 g/8 oz each
salt and pepper

TO SERVE:
basmati rice
mint to garnish

1 Heat the oil in a large frying pan (skillet) or shallow saucepan and add the spring onions (scallions).

2 Stir-fry the spring onions (scallions) over a medium heat until they are softened but not coloured. Stir in the cumin, chillies and ground coriander, and cook them until fragrant.

3 Add the fresh coriander (cilantro), mint, chives and coconut milk and season liberally.

4 Carefully place the fish in the pan and poach for 10–15 minutes until the flesh flakes when tested with a fork.

5 Serve the fish fillets in the sauce with basmati rice.

FISH

Any white fish can be used for this dish. In most supermarkets a wide range of frozen fish is available; it is cheaper than fresh fish and is fine for this dish because the flavour of the fish is not as important as the sauce it is cooked in.

PRAWN (SHRIMP) BHUNA

SERVES 4–6

2 dried red chillies, deseeded if liked
3 fresh green chillies, finely chopped
1 tsp ground turmeric
2 tsp white wine vinegar
½ tsp salt
3 garlic cloves, crushed
½ tsp ground black pepper
1 tsp paprika
500 g/1 lb uncooked peeled king prawns (shrimp)
4 tbsp oil
1 onion, chopped very finely
180 ml/6 fl oz/ ¾ cup water
2 tbsp lemon juice
2 tsp Garam Masala (see page 317)
fresh coriander (cilantro) sprigs to garnish

1 Combine the chillies, turmeric, vinegar, salt, garlic, pepper and paprika in a non-metallic bowl. Stir in the prawns and set aside for 10 minutes.

2 Heat the oil in a large frying pan (skillet) or wok, add the onion and fry for 3–4 minutes until the onion is soft.

3 Add the prawns (shrimp) and the contents of the bowl to the pan and stir-fry over a high heat for 2 minutes.

4 Reduce the heat, add the water and boil for 10 minutes, stirring occasionally, until the water is evaporated and the curry is fragrant.

5 Stir in the lemon juice and garam masala. Serve garnished with fresh coriander (cilantro) sprigs.

FLAVOUR FROM HERBS AND SPICES

To get the full flavour from any spices they must be heated first. This also applies to dried herbs. To make raita with dried herbs, take 3 tsp of dried mint and put it into a dry pan, warm it through very gently until you can start to smell the mint. Remove it from the heat and add 120 ml/4 fl oz/ ½ cup natural yogurt and salt to taste. Transfer to a serving dish.

PRAWN (SHRIMP) DANSAK

SERVES 4–6

*750 g/1½ lb uncooked tiger prawns
   (shrimp) in their shells or 650 g/
   1 lb 5 oz peeled tiger prawns (shrimp),
   or cooked, peeled Atlantic
   prawns(shrimp)*
1 tsp salt
1 dried bay leaf
3 garlic cloves
*90 g/3 oz/ ⅓ cup split yellow peas, soaked
   for 1 hour in cold water and drained*
60 g/2 oz/ ¼ cup red lentils
1 carrot, chopped
1 potato, cut into large dice
3 tbsp drained canned sweetcorn
3 tbsp oil
2 onions, chopped
½ tsp yellow mustard seeds
1½ tsp coriander seeds, ground
½ tsp cumin seeds, ground
½ tsp fenugreek seeds, ground
1½ tsp ground turmeric
1 dried red chilli
425 g/14 oz can tomatoes
½ tsp Garam Masala (see page 317)
3 tbsp chopped fresh coriander (cilantro)
2 tbsp chopped fresh mint

1 Reserve a few of the prawns
   (shrimp) for garnish and peel the
rest. Set aside. Cook those for the garnish
in boiling water for 3–5 minutes.

2 Fill a large saucepan with water and
   add the salt, bay leaf, 1 garlic clove
and the split yellow peas. Bring to the
boil and cook for 15 minutes. Add the red
lentils, carrot and potato and cook,
uncovered, for a further 15 minutes.
Drain, discarding the garlic and bay leaf.

3 Purée the cooked vegetables with
   the sweetcorn in a blender or food
processor. Alternatively, use a potato
masher to break down the lumps.

4 Crush the remaining garlic. Heat the
   oil in a large saucepan and cook the
onion and garlic for 3–4 minutes. Add the
mustard seeds and when they start to
pop, stir in the ground coriander, cumin,
fenugreek, turmeric and chilli. Add the
peeled prawns (shrimp) and stir over a
high heat for 1–2 minutes.

5 Add the tomatoes and the puréed
   vegetables, and gently simmer. Cook,
uncovered, for 30–40 minutes. Stir in the
garam masala and taste for seasoning.

6 Serve, sprinkled with the fresh
   coriander (cilantro) and mint, and
garnished with reserved prawns (shrimp).

PRAWN (SHRIMP) BIRIANI

•••

SERVES 6-8

250 g/8 oz/generous 1 cup basmati rice,
* rinsed and drained*
1 tsp saffron strands
50 ml/2 fl oz/4 tbsp tepid water
2 shallots, chopped coarsely
3 garlic cloves, crushed
1 tsp chopped ginger root
2 tsp coriander seeds
½ tsp black peppercorns
2 cloves
2 green cardamom pods
2.5 cm/1 in piece cinnamon stick
1 tsp ground turmeric
1 fresh green chilli, chopped
½ tsp salt
2 tbsp ghee
1 tsp whole black mustard seeds
500 g/1 lb uncooked tiger prawns (shrimp)
* in their shells, or 425 g/14 oz peeled*
* uncooked tiger prawns (shrimp), or*
* cooked and peeled Atlantic prawns*
* (shrimp)*
300 ml/ ½ pint/1¼ cups coconut milk
300 ml/ ½ pint/1¼ cups natural yogurt
1 tbsp sultanas (golden raisins)

TO GARNISH:
3 tbsp flaked (slivered) almonds, toasted
1 spring onion (scallion), sliced and
* rinsed*

1 Soak the rice in cold water for 2 hours. Combine the saffron with the tepid water and soak for 10 minutes.

2 Put the shallots, garlic, ginger, coriander, peppercorns, cloves, cardamom, cinnamon, turmeric, chilli and salt into a spice blender or pestle and mortar and grind to a paste.

3 Heat the ghee in a large saucepan and add the mustard seeds. When they start to pop, add the prawns (shrimp) and stir over a high heat for 1 minute. Stir in the spice mix, then the coconut milk and yogurt. Simmer for 20 minutes.

4 Meanwhile, bring a large saucepan of salted water to the boil. Drain the rice and slowly add to the pan. Boil for 12 minutes. Drain. Carefully pile the rice on the prawns. Spoon over the sultanas (golden raisins) and trickle the saffron and water over the rice in lines.

5 Cover the pan with a clean tea towel or dish towel and put the lid on tightly. Remove the pan from heat and leave to stand for 5 minutes to infuse. Serve, garnished with the toasted almonds and spring onion (scallion).

MASALA FRIED FISH

SERVES 4-8

8 plaice or other white fish fillets, about
  125–150 g/4–5 oz each
1 tbsp ground turmeric
2 tbsp plain (all-purpose) flour
salt
½ tsp black peppercorns, ground
1 tsp chilli powder
1 tbsp coriander seeds, ground
1 garlic clove, crushed
2 tsp Garam Masala (see page 317)
oil for deep frying

TO GARNISH:
chilli powder
lemon wedges

1 To skin the fish fillets, lay the fillet
   skin side down with the tail nearest
you. Hold the tail end between your
thumb and forefinger. Hold a sharp knife
at a shallow angle to the fish in your
other hand. Holding the fish firmly, make
an angled cut between the flesh and the
skin, then continue to cut the flesh away
from the skin until it is free.

2 In a shallow dish, combine the
   turmeric, flour, salt, peppercorns,
chilli powder, coriander seeds, garlic and
garam masala. Mix well.

3 Fill a shallow saucepan or a deep
   frying pan (skillet) with oil to a
depth of 5–7 cm/2–3 in, and heat to 180°
C/350° F.

4 Coat the fish fillets in the spice mix
   either by shaking gently in a paper
bag or turning over in the dish of spice
mix until well coated.

5 Deep fry the fish fillets for about
   3–5 minutes, turning often until the
fish flakes with a fork. Drain on plenty of
paper towels.

6 Serve sprinkled with chilli powder,
   garnished with lemon wedges, and
accompanied by a selection of pickles
and chutneys.

INDIAN COD WITH TOMATOES

SERVES 4

3 tbsp vegetable oil
4 cod steaks, about 2.5 cm/1 in thick
salt and freshly ground black pepper
1 onion, peeled and finely chopped
2 garlic cloves, peeled and crushed
1 red (bell) pepper, seeded and chopped
1 tsp ground coriander
1 tsp ground cumin
1 tsp ground turmeric
½ tsp garam masala
1 x 400 g/14 oz can chopped tomatoes
150 ml/ ¼ pint/ ⅔ cup coconut milk
1-2 tbsp chopped fresh coriander or
  parsley

1 Heat the oil in a frying pan, add the
   fish steaks, season with salt and
pepper and fry until browned on both
sides (but not cooked through). Remove
from the pan and reserve.

2 Add the onion, garlic, red (bell)
   pepper and spices and cook very
gently for 2 minutes, stirring frequently.
Add the tomatoes, bring to the boil and
simmer for 5 minutes.

3 Add the fish steaks to the pan and
   simmer gently for 8 minutes or until
the fish is cooked through. Remove from
the pan and keep warm on a serving
dish. Add the coconut milk and coriander
to the pan and reheat gently. Spoon the
sauce over the cod steaks and serve
immediately.

VARIATIONS

The mixture may be flavoured with a
tablespoonful of curry powder or curry
paste (mild, medium or hot, according
to personal preference) instead of the
mixture of spices at step 2, if wished.

CURRIED CRAB

••

SERVES 4

2 tbsp mustard oil
1 tbsp ghee
1 onion, chopped finely
5 cm/2 in piece ginger root, grated
2 garlic cloves, peeled but left whole
1 tsp ground turmeric
1 tsp salt
1 tsp chilli powder
2 fresh green chillies, chopped
1 tsp paprika
125 g/4 oz/½ cup brown crab meat
350 g/12 oz/1½ cups white crab meat
250 ml/8 fl oz /1 cup natural yogurt
1 tsp Garam Masala (see page 317)

TO SERVE:
basmati rice
fresh coriander (cilantro) to garnish

1 Heat the mustard oil in a large, preferably non-stick, frying pan (skillet), wok or saucepan. When it starts to smoke add the ghee and onion. Stir for 3 minutes over a medium heat until the onion is soft.

2 Stir in the ginger and whole garlic cloves.

3 Add the turmeric, salt, chilli powder, chillies and paprika. Stir to mix thoroughly.

4 Increase the heat and add the crab meat and yogurt. Simmer, stirring occasionally, for 10 minutes until the sauce is thickened slightly. Add garam masala to taste.

5 Serve hot, over plain basmati rice, with the fresh coriander (cilantro) either chopped or in sprigs.

CRAB MEAT

If you cannot buy fresh crab meat, frozen crab meat is a good substitute. It can be bought frozen in packs, which usually contain half brown meat and half white meat. Use canned crab meat as a last resort, as it has less flavour.

SAFFRON CHICKEN

••

SERVES 4

large pinch of saffron strands, about
  30 strands
50 ml/2 fl oz/4 tbsp boiling water
4 chicken supremes
3 tbsp ghee
½ tsp coriander seeds, ground
1 dried bay leaf
2.5 cm/1 in piece cinnamon stick
30 g/1 oz/1½ tbsp sultanas (golden raisins)
300 ml/ ½ pint/1¼ cups natural yogurt
15 g/ ½ oz/2 tbsp flaked (slivered)
  almonds, toasted
salt and pepper

1 Combine the saffron with the boiling water, and leave to steep for 10 minutes.

2 Season the chicken pieces well. Heat the ghee in a large frying pan (skillet), add the chicken pieces and brown on both sides. Cook in batches if necessary. Remove the chicken from the pan.

3 Reduce the heat to medium and add the coriander to the pan, stir once and add the bay leaf, cinnamon stick, sultanas (golden raisins) and the saffron with the soaking water all at once.

4 Return the chicken to the pan. Cover and simmer gently for 40–50 minutes or until the chicken juices run clear when the thickest part of each piece is pierced with a sharp knife. Remove the pan from the heat and gently stir the yogurt into the sauce.

5 Discard the bay leaf and cinnamon stick. Scatter over the toasted almonds and serve.

CHICKEN

The chicken supreme is the breast on the bone, with part of the wing bone still attached; it does not dry out as much as the breast fillet during long cooking, and, in my opinion, has more flavour. Chicken supremes are available from butchers and most supermarkets.

SHAHI MURG

SERVES 4

1 tsp cumin seeds
1 tsp coriander seeds
2 tbsp ghee
1 onion, sliced finely
8 small–medium chicken pieces
½ tsp salt
350 ml/12 fl oz/1½ cups natural yogurt
120 ml/4 fl oz/ ½ cup double cream
1 tbsp ground almonds
½ tsp Garam Masala (see page 317)
3 cloves
seeds from 3 green cardamom pods
1 dried bay leaf
60 g/2 oz/ ⅓ cup sultanas (golden raisins)
fresh coriander (cilantro) sprigs to garnish

1 Grind together the cumin and coriander seeds in a spice grinder or a pestle and mortar.

2 Heat half the ghee in a large saucepan and cook the onion over a medium heat for 15 minutes, stirring occasionally, until the onion is very soft and sweet.

3 Meanwhile, heat the remaining ghee in a large frying pan (skillet) and brown the chicken pieces well. Add to the onions.

4 Add the ground cumin, ground coriander, salt, yogurt, cream, almonds and garam masala.

5 Bring to a gentle simmer, and add the cloves, cardamom, bay leaf and sultanas (golden raisins).

6 Simmer for 40 minutes until the chicken juices run clear when the thickest part of each piece is pierced with a sharp knife, and the sauce has reduced and thickened. Serve garnished with coriander (cilantro) sprigs.

HANDY HINT

The cloves and bay leaf are not meant to be eaten, but it is easier to put them to one side of the plate than to discard them before serving.

CHICKEN JALFREZI

SERVES 4

1 tsp mustard oil
3 tbsp vegetable oil
1 large onion, chopped finely
3 garlic cloves, crushed
1 tbsp tomato purée (paste)
2 tomatoes, peeled and chopped
1 tsp ground turmeric
½ tsp cumin seeds, ground
½ tsp coriander seeds, ground
½ tsp chilli powder
½ tsp Garam Masala (see page 317)
1 tsp red wine vinegar
1 small red (bell) pepper, chopped
125 g/4 oz/1 cup frozen broad (fava) beans
500 g/1 lb cooked chicken, cut into bite-sized pieces
½ tsp salt
fresh coriander (cilantro) sprigs to garnish

1 Heat the mustard oil in a large, frying pan (skillet) set over a high heat for about 1 minute until it begins to smoke. Add the vegetable oil, reduce the heat and then add the onion and the garlic. Fry oil, garlic and onion until they are golden.

2 Add the tomato purée (paste), chopped tomatoes, turmeric, ground cumin, ground coriander, chilli powder, garam masala and vinegar to the frying pan (skillet). Stir the mixture until fragrant.

3 Add the red (bell) pepper and broad (fava) beans and stir for 2 minutes until the pepper is softened.

4 Stir in the chicken, and salt to taste. Simmer gently for 6–8 minutes until the chicken is heated through and the beans are tender. Serve garnished with coriander (cilantro) sprigs.

USING LEFTOVERS

This dish is an ideal way of making use of leftover poultry – turkey, duck or quail. Any variety of bean works well, but vegetables are just as useful, especially root vegetables, courgettes, potatoes or broccoli.

CHICKEN TIKKA MASALA

SERVES 4

½ onion, chopped coarsely
60 g/2 oz/3 tbsp tomato purée (paste)
1 tsp cumin seeds
2.5 cm/1 in piece ginger root, chopped
3 tbsp lemon juice
2 garlic cloves, crushed
2 tsp chilli powder
750 g/1½ lb boneless chicken
salt and pepper

MASALA SAUCE:
2 tbsp ghee
1 onion, sliced
1 tbsp black onion seeds
3 garlic cloves, crushed
2 fresh green chillies, chopped
200 g/7 oz can tomatoes
120 ml/4 fl oz/ ½ cup natural yogurt
120 ml/4 fl oz/ ½ cup coconut milk
1 tbsp chopped fresh coriander (cilantro)
1 tbsp chopped fresh mint
2 tbsp lemon or lime juice
½ tsp Garam Masala (see page 317)

1 Combine the onion, tomato purée (paste), cumin, ginger, lemon juice, garlic, chilli powder and salt and pepper in a food processor or blender and then transfer to a bowl. Alternatively, grind the cumin in a pestle and mortar and transfer to a bowl. Finely chop the onion and ginger and stir into the bowl with the tomato purée (paste), lemon juice, salt and pepper, garlic and chilli powder.

2 Cut chicken into 4 cm/1½ in cubes. Stir into the bowl and leave to marinate for 2 hours.

3 Heat the ghee in a large saucepan, add the onion and stir over a medium heat for 5 minutes. Add the onion seeds, garlic and chillies and cook until fragrant. Add the tomatoes, yogurt and coconut milk, bring to the boil, then simmer for 20 minutes.

4 Meanwhile, divide the chicken evenly between 8 oiled skewers and cook under a preheated very hot grill (broiler) for 15 minutes, turning frequently. Remove the chicken from the skewers and add to the sauce. Stir in the fresh coriander (cilantro), mint, lemon or lime juice, and garam masala.

KARAHI CHICKEN

SERVES 4-6

2 tbsp ghee
3 garlic cloves, crushed
1 onion, chopped finely
2 tbsp Garam Masala (see page 317)
1 tsp coriander seeds, ground
½ tsp dried mint
1 dried bay leaf
750 g/1½ lb boneless chicken meat, diced
200 ml/7 fl oz/scant 1 cup chicken stock
  or water
1 tbsp finely chopped fresh coriander
  (cilantro)
salt
naan bread or chapatis to serve

1 Heat the ghee in a karahi or wok, or a large, heavy frying pan (skillet) and add the garlic and onion. Stir for about 4 minutes until the onion is golden.

2 Stir in the garam masala, ground coriander, mint and bay leaf.

3 Add the chicken and cook over a high heat, stirring occasionally, for about 5 minutes.

4 Add the stock or water and simmer for 10 minutes, until the sauce has thickened and the chicken juices run clear when the meat is tested with a sharp knife.

5 Stir in the fresh coriander (cilantro), salt to taste and serve immediately with naan bread or chapatis.

SERVING SUGGESTIONS

Take the sizzling curry to the table in the pan on which it was cooked, and serve a huge pile of naan bread or chapatis for scooping up the curry from the dish.

333

TANDOORI CHICKEN

SERVES 4

8 small chicken portions, skinned
3 dried red chillies
1 tsp salt
2 tsp coriander seeds
2 tbsp lime juice
2 garlic cloves, crushed
2.5 cm/1 in piece ginger root, grated
1 clove
2 tsp Garam Masala (see page 317)
2 tsp chilli powder
½ onion, chopped and rinsed
300 ml/ ½ pint/1¼ cups natural yogurt
1 tbsp chopped fresh coriander (cilantro)
lemon slices to garnish
Cucumber Raita (see page 350) to serve

1 Make 2–3 slashes with a sharp knife in the flesh of the chicken pieces.

2 Crush together the chillies, salt, coriander seeds, lime juice, garlic, ginger and clove. Stir in the garam masala and chilli powder. Transfer to a small saucepan and heat gently until aromatic.

3 Add the onion and fry. Then stir in yogurt and remove pan from heat.

4 Arrange the chicken in a non-metallic dish and pour over the yogurt mixture. Cover and put in the refrigerator to marinate for 4 hours or overnight.

5 Arrange the chicken on a grill (broiler) tray and cook under a preheated very hot grill (broiler) or over a barbecue for 20–30 minutes, turning once, until the chicken juices run clear when the thickest parts of the portions are pierced with a sharp knife.

6 Sprinkle the chicken with chopped fresh coriander (cilantro). Serve hot or cold, garnished with the lemon slices and accompanied by cucumber raita.

LAMB DO PYAZA

SERVES 4

2 tbsp ghee
2 large onions, sliced finely
4 garlic cloves, 2 of them crushed
750 g/1½ lb boneless lamb shoulder, cut
*   into 2.5 cm/1 in cubes*
1 tsp chilli powder
2.5 cm/1 in piece ginger root, grated
2 fresh green chillies, chopped
½ tsp ground turmeric
½ tsp salt and ground black pepper
180 ml/6 fl oz/ ¾ cup natural yogurt
2 cloves
2.5 cm/1 in piece cinnamon stick
300 ml/ ½ pint/1¼ cups water
2 tbsp chopped fresh coriander (cilantro)
3 tbsp lemon juice
naan bread to serve

1 Heat the ghee in a large saucepan and add 1 of the onions and the garlic. Cook for 2–3 minutes, stirring constantly. Add the lamb and brown all over. Remove and set aside.

2 Add the chilli powder, ginger, chillies and turmeric and stir for a further 30 seconds.

3 Add plenty of salt and pepper, the yogurt, cloves, cinnamon and water. Return the lamb to the pan. Bring to the boil then simmer for 10 minutes.

4 Transfer to an ovenproof dish and place uncovered in a preheated oven at 180°C/350°F/Gas mark 4 for 40 minutes. Check the seasoning.

5 Stir in the remaining onion and cook uncovered for a further 40 minutes. Add the fresh coriander (cilantro) and lemon juice. Serve with naan bread.

ADVANCE PREPARATION

This curry definitely improves if made in advance and then reheated before serving. This develops the flavours and makes them deeper. The dish will also freeze successfully for up to 6 weeks.

LAMB BIRIANI

SERVES 4

250 g/8 oz/generous 1 cup basmati rice,
  washed and drained
½ tsp salt
2 garlic cloves, peeled and left whole
2.5 cm/1 in piece ginger root, grated
4 cloves
½ tsp black peppercorns
2 green cardamom pods
1 tsp cumin seeds
1 tsp coriander seeds
2.5 cm/1 in piece cinnamon stick
1 tsp saffron strands
50 ml/2 fl oz/4 tbsp tepid water
2 tbsp ghee
2 shallots, sliced
¼ tsp grated nutmeg
¼ tsp chilli powder
500 g/1 lb boneless leg of lamb, cut into
  2.5 cm/1 in cubes
180 ml/6 fl oz/¾ cup natural yogurt
30 g/1 oz/ 2 tbsp sultanas (golden raisins)
30 g /1 oz/ ¼ cup flaked (slivered)
  almonds, toasted

1 Bring a large saucepan of salted
  water to the boil. Add the rice and
boil for 6 minutes. Drain and set aside.

2 Grind together the garlic, ginger,
  cloves, peppercorns, cardamom
pods, cumin, coriander and cinnamon.

3 Combine saffron and water, and set
  aside. Heat the ghee in a large
saucepan and add shallots. Fry until
golden brown then add the ground spice
mix, nutmeg and chilli powder. Stir for
1 minute and add the lamb. Cook until
evenly browned.

4 Add the yogurt, stirring constantly,
  then the sultanas (golden raisins)
and bring to a simmer. Cook for
40 minutes, stirring occasionally.

5 Carefully pile the rice on the sauce,
  in a pyramid shape. Trickle the
saffron and soaking water over the rice in
lines. Cover the pan with a clean tea
towel or dish towel and put the lid on.
Reduce the heat to low and cook for
10 minutes. Remove the lid and tea towel,
and quickly make 3 holes in the rice with
a wooden spoon handle, to the level of
the sauce, but not touching it. Replace the
tea towel and the lid and leave to stand
for 5 minutes.

6 Remove the lid and tea towel, lightly
  fork the rice and serve, sprinkled
with the toasted almonds.

LAMB PASANDA

SERVES 4

500 g/1 lb boneless lamb shoulder
150 ml/ ¼ pint/ ⅔ cup red wine
75 ml/3 fl oz/ ⅓ cup oil
3 garlic cloves, crushed
5 cm/2 in piece ginger root, grated
1 tsp coriander seeds, ground
1 tsp cumin seeds, ground
2 tbsp ghee
1 large onion, chopped
1 tsp Garam Masala (see page 317)
2 fresh green chillies, halved
300 ml/ ½ pint/1¼ cups natural yogurt
2 tbsp ground almonds
20 whole blanched almonds
salt

1 Cut the lamb into strips 2.5 cm/ 1 in across and 10 cm/4 in long. Set aside.

2 Combine the red wine, oil, garlic, ginger, coriander and cumin in a large non-metallic bowl. Stir in the lamb and leave to marinate for 1 hour.

3 Heat the ghee in a frying pan (skillet) and fry the onion until brown. Drain the lamb, reserving the contents of the bowl. Pat dry with paper towels. Add to the frying pan (skillet) and stir over a high heat until it is evenly sealed and browned.

4 Add the contents of the bowl to the pan, and bring to a gentle boil. Add the garam masala, chillies, yogurt, ground almonds, whole almonds, and salt to taste. Cover and simmer for 12–15 minutes until the lamb is tender.

MUTTON

In India mutton is often used for curries; it has a lovely full flavour and stands up well to the long cooking of most curries. It is well worth searching for. If you would like to use it for this recipe, marinate boneless shoulder, uncovered, in the refrigerator for 4–5 hours or overnight. Simmer for 1 hour, skimming the surface to remove any fat, before adding the garam masala, chillies, yogurt and almonds.

LAMB BHUNA

SERVES 4-6

1 onion, chopped
2 garlic cloves
3 tomatoes, peeled and chopped
1 tsp malt vinegar
1 tbsp oil
750 g/1½ lb lean boneless lamb, cut into 4 cm/1½ in cubes
2 tsp coriander seeds, ground
1 tsp cumin seeds, ground
2 dried red chillies, chopped
3 fresh green chillies, chopped
½ tsp ground turmeric
30 g/1 oz/2 tbsp creamed coconut
50 ml/2 fl oz/4 tbsp water
1 tsp Garam Masala (see page 317)
salt and pepper

1 Purée the onion, garlic, tomatoes and vinegar in a food processor or blender. Alternatively, chop the vegetables finely by hand, then mix with the vinegar. Set aside.

2 Heat the oil in a large frying pan (skillet) and brown the meat for 5–10 minutes. Remove and set aside.

3 Reduce the heat beneath the pan and add the ground coriander seeds, cumin, chillies and turmeric. Stir continuously until the spices are fragrant.

4 Increase the heat again and add the onion mixture. Stir-fry for 5 minutes until nearly dry.

5 Return the meat to the pan. Combine the coconut and water and add to the pan. Simmer for 45–60 minutes until the meat is tender. Stir in the garam masala and season to taste.

CREAMED COCONUT

Creamed coconut can be bought in block form and is extremely convenient to keep on hand. Coconut milk can be made by dissolving creamed coconut in an equal quantity of tepid water. Creamed coconut or coconut milk adds richness to a dish and, if used in small quantities, gives a good depth of flavour.

LAMB TIKKA MASALA

SERVES 6

1 tsp cumin seeds, ground
½ tsp ground turmeric
5 cm/2 in piece ginger root, grated
2 garlic cloves, crushed
½ tsp salt
120 ml/4 fl oz/½ cup natural yogurt
1 kg/2 lb boneless lamb, cut into
    2.5 cm/1 in cubes
1–2 drops edible red food colouring
1 tsp water
fresh mint leaves to garnish

MASALA SAUCE:
1 tbsp ghee
3 tomatoes, peeled and chopped
½ tsp yellow mustard seed
2 fresh green chillies, chopped
120 ml/4 fl oz/½ cup coconut milk
3 tbsp chopped fresh mint
3 tbsp chopped fresh coriander (cilantro)
salt

1   Combine the cumin, turmeric, ginger, garlic, salt and yogurt in a bowl. Stir in the lamb until evenly coated with the sauce. Dilute the food colouring with the water, and add to the bowl, stirring well. Marinate in the refrigerator for 2 hours. Soak 6 wooden skewers in warm water for 15 minutes.

2   Make the masala sauce. Heat the ghee in a large saucepan and add the tomatoes, mustard seeds, green chillies and coconut milk. Bring to the boil, then simmer for 20 minutes until the tomatoes have broken down. Stir occasionally.

3   Thread the pieces of lamb on to 6 oiled skewers. Set on a grill (broiler) pan and cook under a preheated very hot grill for 15–20 minutes, turning occasionally.

4   Stir the mint and fresh coriander (cilantro) into the sauce, and season with salt.

5   Carefully remove the lamb from the skewers. Stir the lamb into the sauce and serve garnished with mint leaves.

LAMB PHALL

SERVES 4–6

8 fresh or dried red chillies, or to taste
4 tbsp ghee
1 onion, chopped finely
6 garlic cloves, chopped finely
5 cm/2 in piece ginger root, chopped finely
1 tsp cumin seeds, ground
1 tsp coriander seeds, ground
1 tsp fenugreek seeds, ground
1 tsp Garam Masala (see page 317)
425 g/14 oz can tomatoes
1 tbsp tomato ketchup
 1 tbsp tomato purée (paste)
750 g/1½ lb boneless lamb shoulder, cut
    into 5 cm/2 in cubes

TO SERVE:
Cucumber Raita (see page 350)
pickles

1   Chop 4 of the chillies and leave the other 4 whole.

2   Heat half of the ghee in a saucepan and add the onion, garlic and ginger. Stir over a medium heat until golden.

3   Stir the cumin, coriander, fenugreek and garam masala into the onion. Cook over a medium heat for 10 minutes.

4   Stir the canned tomatoes, tomato ketchup, tomato purée (paste) and the whole and chopped chillies into the pan, and bring to a gentle boil. Cook over a low heat for 10 minutes.

5   Meanwhile, heat the remaining ghee in a flameproof casserole and cook the meat until evenly sealed. Cook in batches if necessary.

6   Transfer the sauce to the casserole with the meat, cover and cook in a preheated oven at 180°C/350°F/Gas mark 4 for 1½ hours until the meat is tender.

7   Serve with cucumber raita and pickles.

MASALA KEBABS

•••

SERVES 4–6

1 dried bay leaf
2.5 cm/1 in piece ginger root, chopped
2.5 cm/1 in cinnamon stick
1 tsp coriander seeds
½ tsp salt
1 tsp fennel seeds
1 tsp chilli powder
1 tsp Garam Masala (see page 317)
1 tsp lemon juice
1 tsp ground turmeric
1 tbsp oil
750 g/1½ lb lamb neck fillet

TO GARNISH:
fresh coriander (cilantro) sprigs
lemon wedges

TO SERVE:
bread
chutney

1   Use a food processor, blender or
    pestle and mortar to grind together
the bay leaf, ginger, cinnamon, coriander
seeds, salt, fennel seeds and chilli
powder.

2   Combine this spice mix with the
    garam masala, lemon juice, turmeric
and oil in a large bowl.

3   Cut the lamb into 5mm/¼ in slices.

4   Add to the spice mix and leave to
    marinate at room temperature for
about 1 hour, or in the refrigerator for
3 hours or overnight.

5   Spread out the pieces of lamb on a
    baking sheet and cook in a
preheated oven at 200°C/400°F/Gas mark
6 for 20 minutes until well done. Transfer
to paper towels to drain any excess fat.

6   Thread 3 or 4 pieces of meat on to
    each skewer and garnish with fresh
coriander (cilantro) sprigs and lemon
wedges. Serve hot with bread and
chutney.

RASHMI KEBABS

•••

SERVES 4

1 red (bell) pepper, deseeded and chopped
   coarsely
1 tsp chilli powder
2 tsp coriander seeds
2 tsp cumin seeds
½ tsp salt
2 cloves garlic
½ tsp ground black pepper
500 g/1 lb/2 cups minced (ground) lamb
4 eggs
oil for deep frying

1   Grind the red (bell) pepper, chilli
    powder, coriander seeds, cumin
seeds, salt, garlic and black pepper in a
food processor or blender. Alternatively,
grind the coriander and cumin in a pestle
and mortar, chop the red (bell) pepper
and garlic very finely and mix with the
ground spices, salt, chilli powder and
black pepper.

2   Transfer the spice mixture to a bowl
    and add the lamb and 1 of the eggs.
Mix well to evenly distribute the egg and
bind the mixture together.

3   Divide the lamb mixture into 8.
    Shape 1 piece into a ball. Put the
ball on a clean plate and gently squash
the top with the palm of your hand, to
form a patty. Repeat with the remaining
pieces. If possible, refrigerate the kebabs
for at least 30 minutes.

4   Cook the kebabs under a preheated
    hot grill (broiler) for 15 minutes,
turning once.

5   Meanwhile, make the egg nets. Beat
    together the remaining eggs. Fill a
large frying pan (skillet) with oil to a
depth of 5–7.5 cm/2–3 in. Heat until a
cube of bread that is dropped in sizzles in
1 minute.

6   Trickle the egg off the end of a
    spoon into the oil, crisscrossing the
lines in a grid shape. It will take only
seconds to cook. Remove and drain on
plenty of paper towels. Repeat until all
the egg is used. Wrap each kebab in 1–2
egg nets. Serve warm.

STUFFED PARATHAS

• •

SERVES 4–8

250 g/8 oz/2 cups wholemeal
(wholewheat) flour
250 g/8 oz/2 cups plain (all-purpose) flour
120–180 ml/4–6 fl oz/ ½–¾ cup water
1 tbsp ghee
1 onion, chopped
2.5 cm/1 in piece cinnamon stick
1 dried bay leaf
1 dried red chilli
¼ tsp ground turmeric
1 tsp coriander seeds, ground
1 tsp cumin seeds, ground
500 g/1 lb/2 cups lean minced (ground)
beef
150 ml/ ¼ pint/ ⅔ cup natural yogurt
125 g/4 oz/ ¾ cup frozen peas
60 g/2 oz/ ¼ cup butter, melted
salt and pepper
chopped fresh coriander (cilantro) to
garnish

1 Sift the two flours and a pinch of salt together into a bowl and make a well in the centre.

2 Gradually add water to make a soft dough, and knead until smooth and no longer sticky. Set aside.

3 Heat the ghee in a large frying pan (skillet) and fry the onion until golden brown. Stir in the cinnamon, bay leaf, chilli, turmeric, ground coriander, cumin and minced (ground) beef for 1 minute. Add the yogurt and cook over a high heat until the beef is dry. Add the peas, season to taste and simmer for 8–10 minutes.

4 To make the parathas, divide the dough into 6 or 8 pieces. Roll each piece into a ball, then roll out to a 25 cm/ 10 in round.

5 Brush the upper side with melted butter. Fold in half, and spoon 1 tablespoon of the stuffing into the centre of each folded piece. Fold each half in half again so that you are left with cone shapes.

6 Gently heat a large frying pan (skillet) and place a paratha in it. Brush each side lightly with a little melted butter and cook over a medium heat for 3–4 minutes. Do not let the pan get too hot. Turn over and cook the other side for 3–4 minutes. Keep warm and repeat

SHEEK KEBABS

SERVES 4-8

1 tsp coriander seeds
1 tsp cumin seeds
1 clove
2.5 cm/1 in piece ginger root, chopped
1 tsp ground turmeric
1 fresh red chilli, deseeded and chopped
½ tsp ground cinnamon
1 tsp ground black pepper
½ tsp salt
125 g/4 oz/½ cup minced (ground) beef
350 g/12 oz/1½ cups minced (ground) lamb
1 onion, chopped finely
1 egg

TO SERVE:
salad
Cucumber Raita (see page 350)

1 Grind together the coriander, cumin, clove and ginger in a pestle and mortar. Mix in the turmeric, chilli, cinnamon, pepper and salt.

2 Combine the spice mixture with the beef, lamb and onion.

3 Make a well in the centre of the meat mixture, add the egg and mix in thoroughly.

4 Press one-eighth of the meat mixture around an oiled skewer, to form a shape about 10 cm/4 in long and 2.5 cm/1 in thick. Repeat with the remaining meat mixture.

5 If possible, leave to rest in the refrigerator for at least 1 hour.

6 Cook the kebabs under a preheated medium grill (broiler) for about 20 minutes, turning once or twice, until the meat juices run clear when the thickest part of the meat balls is pierced with the point of a sharp knife. Serve with salad and cucumber raita.

ROGAN JOSH

SERVES 6

2 tbsp ghee
1 kg/2 lb braising steak, cut into 2.5 cm/1 in cubes
1 onion, chopped finely
3 garlic cloves
2.5 cm/1 in piece ginger root, grated
4 fresh red chillies, chopped
4 green cardamom pods
4 cloves
2 tsp coriander seeds
2 tsp cumin seeds
1 tsp paprika
1 tsp salt
1 dried bay leaf
120 ml /4 fl oz/ ½ cup natural yogurt
2.5 cm/1 in piece cinnamon stick
150 ml/ ¼ pint/ ⅔ cups hot water
¼ tsp Garam Masala (see page 317)
pepper

1 Heat the ghee in a large flameproof casserole and brown the meat in batches. Set aside in a bowl. Add the onion to the ghee and stir over a high heat for 3–4 minutes.

2 Grind together the garlic, ginger, chillies, cardamom, cloves, coriander, cumin, paprika and salt. Add the spice paste and bay leaf to the casserole and stir until fragrant.

3 Return the meat and any juices in the bowl to the casserole and simmer for 2–3 minutes.

4 Gradually stir the yogurt into the casserole so that the sauce keeps simmering. Stir in the cinnamon and hot water, and pepper to taste.

5 Cover and cook in a preheated oven at 180°C/350°F/Gas mark 4 for 1¼ hours, stirring frequently, until the meat is very tender and the sauce is slightly reduced.

6 Discard the cinnamon stick and stir in the garam masala. Remove surplus oil from the surface of the casserole before serving.

TARKA DAL

SERVES 4

2 tbsp ghee
2 shallots, sliced
1 tsp yellow mustard seeds
2 garlic cloves, crushed
8 fenugreek seeds
1 cm/ ½ in piece ginger root, grated
½ tsp salt
125 g/4 oz/ ½ cup red lentils
1 tbsp tomato purée (paste)
600 ml/1 pint/2½ cups water
2 tomatoes, peeled and chopped
1 tbsp lemon juice
4 tbsp chopped fresh coriander (cilantro)
½ tsp chilli powder
½ tsp Garam Masala (see page 317)
naan bread to serve

1 Heat half of the ghee in a large saucepan, and add the shallots. Cook for 2–3 minutes over a high heat, then add the mustard seeds. Cover the pan until the seeds begin to pop.

2 Immediately remove the lid from the pan and add the garlic, fenugreek, ginger and salt. Stir once and add the lentils, tomato purée (paste) and water and simmer gently for 10 minutes.

3 Stir in the tomatoes, lemon juice, and coriander (cilantro) and simmer for a further 4–5 minutes until the lentils are tender.

4 Transfer to a serving dish. Heat the remaining ghee in a small saucepan until it starts to bubble. Remove from the heat and stir in the garam masala and chilli powder. Immediately pour over the tarka dal and serve.

DALS

The flavours in a dal can be altered to suit your personal taste; for example, for added heat, add more chilli powder or chillies, or add fennel seeds for a pleasant aniseed flavour.

To make a dal stew into a single-dish meal, add a combination of vegetables, such as fried aubergine cubes (eggplant), courgettes (zucchini), carrots, or any firm vegetable.

MURKHA DAL

SERVES 4

60 g/2 oz/ ¼ cup butter
2 tsp black mustard seeds
1 onion, chopped finely
2 garlic cloves, chopped finely
1 tbsp grated ginger root
1 tsp turmeric
2 green chillies, deseeded and chopped finely
250 g/8 oz/1 cup red lentils
1 litre/1¾ pints/4 cups water
300 ml/ ½ pint/1¼ cups coconut milk
1 tsp salt

1 Melt the butter in a large saucepan over a moderate heat. Add the mustard seeds and cover the pan. When you can hear the seeds popping, add the onion, garlic and ginger. Cook, uncovered, until they are soft and the garlic is brown, about 7–8 minutes.

2 Stir in the turmeric and green chillies and cook for 1–2 minutes until the chillies soften.

3 Add the lentils and cook for 2 minutes, stirring frequently, until the lentils begin to turn translucent.

4 Add the water, coconut milk and salt. Stir well. Bring to the boil, then reduce the heat and simmer for 40 minutes or until the desired consistency is reached. Cook it for longer if you prefer a thicker consistency. (However, if you intend to reheat it later rather than eat it straight away, cook for only 30 minutes to allow for reheating time.) Serve immediately, while piping hot.

LENTILS

There are many types of lentil used in India, but the two most commonly used are red lentils and green or beige lentils. The red lentils are particularly useful, as they cook in a relatively short time down to a homogeneous mass. The green and beige lentils stay more separate when cooked.

SPICY CAULIFLOWER

SERVES 4

500 g/1 lb cauliflower, cut into florets
1 tbsp sunflower oil
1 garlic clove
½ tsp turmeric
1 tsp cumin seeds, ground
1 tsp coriander seeds, ground
1 tsp yellow mustard seeds
12 spring onions (scallions), sliced finely
salt and pepper

1 Blanch the cauliflower in boiling water, drain and set aside. Cauliflower holds a lot of water, which tends to make it over-soft, so turn the florets upside-down at this stage and you will end up with a crisper result.

2 Heat the oil gently in a large, heavy frying pan (skillet) or wok. Add the garlic clove, turmeric, ground cumin, ground coriander and mustard seeds. Stir well and cover the pan.

3 When you hear the mustard seeds popping, add the spring onions (scallions) and stir. Cook for 2 minutes, stirring constantly, to soften them a little. Season to taste.

4 Add the cauliflower and stir for 3–4 minutes until coated completely with the spices and thoroughly heated.

5 Remove the garlic clove and serve immediately.

BABY CAULIFLOWERS

For a weekend feast or a special occasion this dish looks great made with baby cauliflowers instead of florets. Baby vegetables are more widely available nowadays, and the baby cauliflowers look very appealing on the plate. Peel off most of the outer leaves, leaving a few small ones for decoration. Blanch the baby cauliflowers whole for 4 minutes and drain. Continue as in step 2.

LENTIL & VEGETABLE BIRYANI

SERVES 6

125 g/4 oz/ ⅔ cup continental lentils
4 tbsp vegetable ghee or oil
2 onions, peeled, quartered and sliced
2 garlic cloves, peeled and crushed
2.5 cm/1 in ginger root, peeled and chopped
1 tsp ground turmeric
¼ tsp chilli powder
1 tsp ground coriander
2 tsp ground cumin
3 tomatoes, skinned and chopped
1 aubergine (eggplant), trimmed and cut in 1 cm/ ½ in pieces
1.75 litres/2½ pints/6¼ cups boiling vegetable stock
1 red pepper, cored, seeded and diced
350 g/12 oz/1¾ cups basmati rice
125 g/4 oz/1 cup French beans, topped, tailed and halved
250 g/8 oz/1⅓ cups cauliflower florets
125 g/4 oz/1½ mushrooms, sliced
60 g/2 oz/ ½ cup unsalted cashews
3 hard-boiled eggs, shelled, to garnish
coriander sprigs, to garnish

1 Rinse the lentils under cold running water and drain. Heat the ghee or oil in a saucepan, add the onions and fry gently for 2 minutes. Stir in the garlic, ginger and spices and fry gently for 1 minute, stirring frequently. Add the lentils, tomatoes, aubergine (eggplant) and 600 ml/1 pint/2½ cups of the stock, mix well, then cover and simmer gently for 20 minutes. Add the red or green (bell) pepper and cook for a further 10 minutes or until the lentils are tender and all the liquid has been absorbed.

2 Meanwhile, place the rice in a sieve and rinse under cold running water until the water runs clear. Drain and place in another pan with the remaining stock. Bring to the boil, add the French beans, cauliflower and mushrooms, then cover and cook gently for 15 minutes or until rice and vegetables are tender. Remove from the heat and leave, covered, for 10 minutes.

3 Add the lentil mixture and the cashews to the cooked rice and mix lightly together. Pile onto a warm serving platter and garnish with wedges of hard-boiled egg and coriander sprigs.

CHICK-PEAS & AUBERGINE (EGG-PLANT)

••••••••••••••••••••••••••••••••••

SERVES 4

1 large aubergine (eggplant)
2 courgettes (zucchini)
6 tbsp vegetable ghee or oil
1 large onion, sliced
2 garlic cloves, peeled and crushed
1–2 fresh green chillies, seeded and
*   chopped*
2 tsp ground coriander
2 tsp cumin seeds
1 tsp ground turmeric
1 tsp garam masala
1 x 425 g/14 oz can chopped tomatoes
300 ml/ ½ pint/1¼ cups vegetable stock
salt and freshly ground black pepper
1 x 425 g/14 oz can chick-peas, drained
*   and rinsed*
2 tbsp chopped fresh mint
150 ml/ ¼ pint/⅔ cup double (heavy) cream

1 Trim the leaf end off aubergine (eggplant) and cut into cubes. Trim and slice the courgettes (zucchini). Heat the ghee or oil in a saucepan and gently fry the aubergine (eggplant), courgettes (zucchini), onion, garlic and chillies for about 5 minutes, stirring frequently and adding a little more oil to the pan, if necessary.

2 Stir in the spices and cook for 30 seconds. Add the tomatoes, stock and salt and pepper to taste and cook for 10 minutes.

3 Add the chick-peas to the pan and continue cooking for a further 5 minutes. Stir in the mint and cream and reheat gently. Taste and adjust the seasoning if necessary. Serve hot with plain or pilau rice, or with parathas.

YOGURT

You could use natural yogurt instead of cream in this dish, in which case first blend it with ½ teaspoon cornflour (cornstarch) before adding to the pan and heating gently, stirring constanty. The cornflour (cornstarch) helps stabilize the yogurt to prevent it separating during cooking.

SIDE DISHES

KASHMIRI SPINACH

••••••••••••••••••••••••••••••••••

SERVES 4

500g/1lb spinach, washed (Swiss chard or
*   baby leaf spinach may be substituted –*
*   baby leaf spinach needs no*
*   preparation)*
2 tbsp mustard oil
¼ tsp garam masala
1 tsp yellow mustard seeds
2 spring onions (scallions), sliced

1 Remove the tough stalks from the spinach.

2 Heat the mustard oil in a wok or large heavy frying pan (skillet) until it smokes. Add the garam masala and mustard seeds. Cover the pan quickly – you will hear the mustard seeds popping inside.

3 When the popping has ceased, remove the cover, add the spring onions (scallions) and stir in the spinach until wilted.

4 Continue cooking the spinach, uncovered, over a medium heat for 10–15 minutes, until most of the water has evaporated. If using frozen spinach, it will not need as much cooking – cook it until most of the water has evaporated.

5 Remove the spinach and spring onions (scallions) with a perforated spoon in order to drain off any remaining liquid. This dish is more pleasant to eat when it is served as dry as possible. Serve immediately while it is piping hot.

MUSTARD OIL

Mustard oil is made from mustard seeds and is very fiery when raw. However, when it is heated to this smoking stage, it loses a lot of the fire and takes on a delightful sweet quality. It is quite common in Asian cuisine, and you should find it in any Indian or oriental store.

BOMBAY POTATOES

SERVES 4

1 kg/2 lb waxy potatoes, peeled
2 tbsp ghee
1 tsp panch poran spice mix (see below)
3 tsp ground turmeric
2 tbsp tomato purée (paste)
300 ml/ ½ pint/1¼ cups natural yogurt
salt
chopped fresh coriander (cilantro) to
* garnish*

1 Put the whole potatoes into a large saucepan of salted cold water, bring to the boil, then simmer until the potatoes are just cooked but not tender; the time depends on the size of the potato, but an average-sized one should take about 15 minutes.

2 Put the ghee into a saucepan over a medium heat, and add the panch poran, turmeric, tomato purée (paste), yogurt and salt. Bring to the boil, and simmer, uncovered, for 5 minutes.

3 Drain the potatoes and cut each into 4 pieces.

4 Add the potatoes to the pan and cook with a lid on. Transfer to an ovenproof casserole, cover and cook in a preheated oven at 180°C/350°F/Gas mark 4 for about 40 minutes, until the potatoes are tender and the sauce has thickened a little.

5 Sprinkle liberally with fresh chopped coriander (cilantro) and serve immediately.

PANCH PORAN SPICE MIX

Panch poran spice mix can be bought from Asian or Indian grocery stores, or make your own from equal quantities of cumin seeds, fennel seeds, mustard seeds, nigella seeds and fenugreek seeds.

ROASTED AUBERGINE (EGGPLANT) CURRY

SERVES 6

2 whole aubergines (eggplants)
250 ml/8 fl oz/1 cup natural yogurt
2 cardamom pods
½ tsp ground turmeric
1 dried red chilli
½ tsp coriander seeds
½ tsp ground black pepper
1 tsp garam masala
1 clove
2 tbsp sunflower oil
1 onion, sliced lengthways
2 garlic cloves, crushed
1 tbsp grated ginger root
6 ripe tomatoes, peeled, deseeded and
* quartered*
fresh coriander (cilantro) to garnish

1 If you have a gas cooker, roast the 2 aubergines (eggplants) over a naked flame, turning frequently, until charred and black all over (for other methods see box, right). This should take about 5 minutes. Peel under running cold water. Cut off the stem end and discard.

2 Put the peeled aubergines (eggplants) into a large bowl and mash lightly with a fork. Stir in the yogurt. Set aside.

3 Grind together the cardamom pods, turmeric, red chilli, coriander seeds, black pepper, garam masala and clove in a large pestle and mortar or spice grinder.

4 Heat the oil in a wok or heavy frying pan (skillet) over a moderate heat and cook the onion, garlic and ginger root until soft. Add the tomatoes and ground spices, and stir well.

5 Add the aubergine (eggplant) mixture to the pan and stir well. Cook for 5 minutes over a gentle heat, stirring constantly, until all the flavours are combined, and some of the liquid has evaporated. Serve immediately, garnished with coriander (cilantro).

LONG BEANS WITH TOMATOES

SERVES 4–6

500 g/1 lb green beans, cut into
5 cm/2 in lengths
2 tbsp ghee
2.5 cm/1 in piece ginger root, grated
1 garlic clove, crushed
1 tsp turmeric
½ tsp cayenne
1 tsp ground coriander
4 tomatoes, peeled, deseeded and diced
150 ml/ ¼ pint/ ⅔ cup vegetable stock

1 Blanch the beans quickly in boiling water, drain and refresh under cold running water.

2 Melt the ghee in a large saucepan. Add the grated ginger root and crushed garlic, stir and add the turmeric, cayenne and ground coriander. Stir until fragrant, about 1 minute.

3 Add the tomatoes, tossing them until they are thoroughly coated in the spice mix.

4 Add the vegetable stock to the pan, bring to the boil and cook over a medium-high heat for 10 minutes, until the sauce has thickened, stirring occasionally.

5 Add the beans, reduce the heat to moderate and heat through for 5 minutes, stirring.

6 Transfer to a serving dish and serve immediately.

GINGER GRATERS

Ginger graters are an invaluable piece of equipment to have when cooking Indian food. These small flat graters, made of either bamboo or china, can be held directly over the pan while you grate. They have an ingenious way of dealing with ginger, which leaves most of the tough stringy bits behind.

EGG & LENTIL CURRY

SERVES 4

3 tbsp vegetable ghee or oil
1 large onion, peeled and chopped
2 garlic cloves, peeled and chopped
2.5 cm/1 in ginger root, peeled and
chopped
½ tsp minced chilli (from a jar), or use
chilli powder
1 tsp ground coriander
1 tsp ground cumin
1 tsp paprika
90 g/3 oz split red lentils
450 ml / ¾ pint/1¾ cups vegetable stock
1 x 250 g/8 oz can chopped tomatoes
6 eggs
50 ml/2 fl oz/ ¼ cup coconut milk
salt
2 tomatoes, cut into wedges, and
coriander sprigs, to garnish
parathas, chapatis or naan bread, to serve

1 Heat the ghee or oil in a saucepan, add the onion and fry gently for 3 minutes. Stir in the garlic, ginger, chilli and spices and cook gently for 1 minute, stirring frequently. Stir in the lentils, stock and chopped tomatoes and bring to the boil. Reduce the heat, cover and simmer gently for 30 minutes, stirring occasionally until the lentils and onion are tender.

2 Meanwhile, place the eggs in a saucepan of cold water and bring to the boil. Reduce the heat and simmer for 10 minutes. Drain and cover immediately with cold water.

3 Stir the coconut milk into the lentil mixture and season well with salt to taste. Purée the mixture in a blender or food processor until smooth. Return to the pan and heat through.

4 Shell and cut the hard-boiled eggs in half lengthways. Arrange 3 halves, in a petal design, on each serving plate. Spoon the hot lentil sauce over the eggs, adding enough to flood the serving plate. Arrange a tomato wedge and a coriander sprig between each halved egg. Serve hot with parathas, chapatis or naan bread to mop up the sauce.

FRIED SPICED POTATOES

•••

SERVES 4-6

2 onions, peeled and quartered
5 cm/2 in ginger root, peeled and finely
    chopped
2 garlic cloves, peeled
2-3 tbsp mild or medium curry paste
4 tbsp water
750 g/1½ lb new potatoes
vegetable oil, for deep frying
3 tbsp vegetable ghee or oil
150 ml/ ¼ pint/ ⅔ cup strained Greek
    yogurt
150 ml/ ¼ pint/ ⅔ cup double (heavy)
    cream
3 tbsp chopped fresh mint
salt and freshly ground black pepper
½ bunch spring onions (scallions),
    trimmed and chopped, to garnish

1 Place the onions, ginger, garlic, curry
   paste and water in a blender or food
processor and process until smooth,
scraping down the sides of machine and
blending again, if necessary.

2 Cut the potatoes into quarters – the
   pieces need to be about 2.5 cm/
1 in in size – and pat dry with absorbent
kitchen paper. Heat the oil in a deep-fat
fryer to 180°C/350°F/Gas 4 and fry the
potatoes, in batches, for about 5 minutes
or until golden brown, turning frequently.
Remove from the pan and drain on paper
towels.

3 Heat the ghee or oil in a large frying
   pan, add the curry and onion
mixture and fry gently for 2 minutes,
stirring all the time. Add the yogurt, cream
and 2 tablespoons of mint and mix well.

4 Add the fried potatoes and stir until
   coated in the sauce. Cook for a
further 5-7 minutes or until heated
through and sauce has thickened, stirring
frequently. Season with salt and pepper to
taste and sprinkle with the remaining mint
and sliced spring onions (scallions). Serve
immediately.

SPINACH & AUBERGINE (EGGPLANT)

•••

SERVES 4

250 g/8 oz/1 cup split red lentils
750 ml/1¼ pints/3 cups water
1 onion
1 aubergine (eggplant)
1 red (bell) pepper
2 courgettes (zucchini)
125 g/4 oz mushrooms, wiped
250 g/8 oz leaf spinach
4 tbsp vegetable ghee or oil
1 fresh green chilli, seeded and chopped,
    or use 1 tsp minced chilli (from a jar)
1 tsp ground cumin
1 tsp ground coriander
2.5 cm/1 in ginger root, peeled and
    chopped
150 ml/ ¼ pint/ ⅔ cup vegetable stock
salt
coriander or flat-leaved parsley sprigs, to
    garnish

1 Wash the lentils and place in a
   saucepan with the water. Cover and
simmer for 15 minutes until the lentils are
soft but still whole.

2 Meanwhile, peel, quarter and slice
   the onion. Trim leaf end and cut the
aubergine (eggplant) into 1 cm/ ½ in
pieces. Remove stalk end and seeds from
the (bell) pepper and cut into 1 cm/ ½ in
pieces. Trim and cut courgettes (zucchini)
into 1 cm/ ½ in thick slices. Thickly slice
the mushrooms. Discard coarse stalks
from spinach leaves and wash spinach
well.

3 Heat the ghee or oil in a large
   saucepan, add the onion and red
(bell) pepper and fry gently for 3 minutes,
stirring frequently. Stir in the aubergine
(eggplant), mushrooms, chilli, spices and
ginger and fry gently for 1 minute. Add
the spinach and stock and season with
salt to taste. Stir and turn until the spinach
leaves wilt down. Cover and simmer for
10 minutes or until the vegetables are just
tender.

4 Make a border of the lentils on a
   warm serving plate and spoon the
vegetable mixture into the centre. (The
lentils may be stirred into the vegetable
mixture, instead of being used as a
border, if wished.) Garnish with coriander
or flat-leaved parsley sprigs.

AUBERGINE (EGGPLANT) IN SAFFRON

SERVES 4

a good pinch of saffron strands, finely
  crushed
1 tbsp boiling water
1 large aubergine (eggplant)
3 tbsp vegetable oil
1 large onion, peeled and coarsely
  chopped
2 garlic cloves, peeled and crushed
2.5 cm/1 in ginger root, peeled and
  chopped
1½ tbsp mild or medium curry paste
1 tsp cumin seeds
150 ml/ ¼ pint/ ⅔ cup double (heavy)
  cream
150 ml/ ¼ pint/ ⅔ cup strained Greek
  yogurt
2 tbsp mango chutney, chopped if
  necessary
salt and freshly ground black pepper

1 Place the saffron in a small bowl,
add the boiling water and leave to
infuse for 5 minutes. Trim the leaf end off
the aubergine (eggplant), cut lengthways
into quarters, then into 1 cm/½ in thick
slices.

2 Heat the oil in a large frying pan,
add the onion and cook gently for
3 minutes. Stir in the aubergine (eggplant),
garlic, ginger, curry paste and cumin and
cook gently for 3 minutes.

3 Stir in the saffron water, cream,
yogurt and chutney and cook gently
for 8-10 minutes, stirring frequently, until
the aubergine (eggplant) is cooked
through and tender. Season with salt and
pepper to taste and serve hot.

YOGURT

You will find that yogurt adds a creamy
texture and pleasant tartness to this
sauce. If you are worried about it
curdling on heating, add a
tablespoonful at a time and stir it in
well before adding another. A little
cornflour (cornstarch), blended with
the yogurt before cooking, also helps
to prevent it from separating when
it is heated.

VEGETABLE, NUT & LENTIL KOFTAS

SERVES 4-5

6 tbsp vegetable ghee or oil
1 onion, peeled and finely chopped
2 carrots, peeled and finely chopped
2 celery sticks, finely chopped
2 garlic cloves, peeled and crushed
1 fresh green chilli, seeded and finely
  chopped
1½ tbsp curry powder or paste
250 g/8 oz/1¼ cups split red lentils
600 ml/1 pint/2½ cups vegetable stock
30 ml/2 tbsp tomato purée (paste)
125 g/4 oz/2 cups fresh wholewheat
  breadcrumbs
90 g/3 oz/ ¾ cup unsalted cashews, finely
  chopped
2 tbsp chopped fresh coriander or parsley
1 egg, beaten
salt and freshly ground black pepper
garam masala, for sprinkling

YOGURT DRESSING:
250 g/8 oz natural yogurt
1-2 tbsp chopped fresh coriander
1-2 tbsp mango chutney, chopped

1 Heat 4 tablespoons of ghee or oil in
a large saucepan and gently fry the
onion, carrots, celery, garlic and chilli for
5 minutes, stirring frequently. Add the
curry powder or paste and the lentils and
cook gently for 1 minute, stirring.

2 Add the stock and tomato purée
(paste) and bring to the boil. Reduce
the heat, cover and simmer for 20 minutes
or until the lentils are tender and all the
liquid is absorbed.

3 Remove from the heat and cool
slightly. Add the breadcrumbs, nuts,
coriander, egg and seasoning to taste. Mix
well and leave to cool. Shape into rounds
about the size of golf balls.

4 Place the balls on a greased baking
sheet, drizzle with the remaining oil
and sprinkle with a little garam masala, to
taste. Cook in the preheated oven at
180°C/350°F/Gas Mark 4 for 15-20
minutes or until piping hot and golden.

5 To make the yogurt dressing, mix all
the ingredients together in a bowl.
Serve the koftas with the dressing.

KABLI CHANNA SAG

SERVES 6

250 g/8 oz/generous cup whole chick-
peas (garbanzo beans), rinsed, soaked
overnight and drained
5 cloves
2.5 cm/1 in piece cinnamon stick
2 garlic cloves
3 tbsp sunflower oil
1 small onion, sliced
3 tbsp lemon juice
1 tsp coriander seeds
2 tomatoes, peeled, deseeded and
chopped
500 g/1 lb spinach, rinsed and any tough
stems removed
1 tbsp chopped fresh coriander (cilantro)

TO GARNISH:
fresh coriander (cilantro) sprigs
lemon slices

1 Put the chick-peas (garbanzo beans) into a saucepan with enough water to cover. Add the cloves, cinnamon and 1 whole unpeeled garlic clove that has been lightly crushed with the back of a knife to release the juices. Bring to the boil, reduce the heat and simmer for 40–50 minutes, or until the chick-peas (garbanzo beans) are tender when tested with a skewer. Skim off any foam that comes to the surface.

2 Meanwhile, heat 1 tablespoon of the oil in a saucepan. Crush the remaining garlic clove. Put this into the pan with the oil and the onion, and cook over a moderate heat until soft, about 5 minutes.

3 Remove the cloves, cinnamon and garlic from the pan of chick-peas (garbanzo beans). Drain the chick-peas (garbanzo beans). Using a food processor or a fork, blend 90 g/3 oz/ ½ cup of the chick-peas (garbanzo beans) until smooth with the onion and garlic, the lemon juice and 1 tablespoon of the oil. Stir this purée into the remaining chick-peas (garbanzo beans).

4 Heat the remaining oil in a large frying pan (skillet), add the coriander seeds and stir for 1 minute. Add the tomatoes, stir and add the spinach. Cover and cook for 1 minute over a moderate heat. The spinach should be wilted, but not soggy. Stir in the chopped coriander (cilantro) and remove from the heat.

5 Transfer the chick-peas (garbanzo beans) to a serving dish, and spoon over the spinach. Garnish with the coriander (cilantro) and lemon.

SAFFRON RICE

SERVES 8

12 saffron threads, crushed lightly
2 tbsp warm water
270 ml/14 fl oz/1¼ cups water
250 g/8 oz basmati rice
1 tbsp toasted, flaked (slivered) almonds

1 Put the saffron threads into a bowl with the warm water and leave for 10 minutes. They need to be crushed before soaking to ensure that the maximum flavour and colour is extracted at this stage.

2 Put the water and rice into a medium saucepan and set it over the heat to boil. Add the saffron and saffron water and stir.

3 Bring back to a gentle boil, stir again and let the rice simmer, uncovered, for about 10 minutes, until all the water has been absorbed.

4 Cover tightly, reduce the heat as much as possible and leave for 10 minutes. Do not remove the lid. This ensures that the grains separate and that the rice is not soggy.

5 Remove from the heat and transfer to a serving dish. Fork through the rice gently and sprinkle on the toasted almonds before serving.

SAFFRON

Saffron is the most ancient of spices and continues to be the most expensive – literally worth its weight in gold. It is still harvested and sorted by hand and is a treasured commodity. The purest, strongest saffron – La Mancha grade – is not easily found. Saffron is grown in Europe and the Middle East and is found worldwide in food and drinks. It is used in England for Cornish saffron cake, in Italy for risotto, in France for bouillabaisse and in Spain for paella.

Saffron stigmas are wiry, 2.5 cm/1 in long and a vibrant reddish-orange or sometimes yellow colour – the deeper colour is the better quality.

HYDERABAD RICE PILAU

SERVES 6

3 tbsp sunflower oil
1 onion, sliced finely
3 shallots, chopped finely
1 garlic clove, crushed
1 tsp grated ginger root
425 g/14 oz/2 cups basmati rice
½ tsp cayenne
250 g/8 oz/2 cups okra, trimmed
1 litre/1¾ pints/4 cups chicken stock
1 tsp saffron, crushed lightly
rind of ½ orange, with pith shaved off
60 g/2 oz/ ⅓ cup sultanas (golden raisins)
1 tbsp lemon juice

TO GARNISH:
30 g/1 oz flaked (slivered) almonds, toasted
1 tsp chopped fresh mint
1 tsp chopped fresh coriander (cilantro)

1 Heat the oil in a wok or large frying pan (skillet) until quite hot. Fry the onions until golden brown, then remove and drain on paper towels. Do not cook them all at once, as they won't be crispy.

2 Reduce the heat under the wok. Cook the shallots in the remaining oil until soft, about 5 minutes. Add the garlic and ginger, and stir. Stir in the rice, cayenne and okra.

3 Pour in the chicken stock, saffron and orange rind. Bring to the boil and simmer over a moderate heat for 15 minutes.

4 Add the sultanas (golden raisins) at the end of this time and stir in the lemon juice.

5 Remove the piece of orange rind if you prefer, then transfer to a serving dish and garnish with the fried onion, toasted almonds, mint and coriander (cilantro).

TOMATO, ONION & CUCUMBER KACHUMBER

EACH SERVES 6

*TOMATO, ONION & CUCUMBER
KACHUMBER:*
3 ripe tomatoes, peeled
¼ cucumber, peeled
1 small onion, quartered
1 tsp lime juice
*2 green chillies, deseeded and chopped
(optional)*

1   Cut the tomatoes into quarters and
cut each quarter in half. The seeds
can be removed at this stage, if you
prefer.

2   Cut the cucumber lengthways into
quarters.

3   Remove the seeds from the
cucumber, and cut into cubes.

4   Cut each onion quarter into slices.

5   Combine all the ingredients in a
bowl and sprinkle with the lime
juice.

6   Add the chillies, if using, and serve.

MANGO KACHUMBER:
½ mango, peeled and chopped
1 small onion, chopped
1 tbsp chopped fresh coriander (cilantro)
2 tomatoes, chopped

Combine all the ingredients in a bowl,
and serve.

RADISH KACHUMBER:
8 large radishes, sliced
½ cucumber, peeled and chopped
1 small onion, chopped
1 tbsp chopped fresh coriander (cilantro)
1 tbsp oil
1 tbsp vinegar

Combine all the ingredients in a bowl,
and serve.

CUCUMBER RAITA

SERVES 4

CUCUMBER RAITA:
2 tsp fresh mint
½ cucumber
250 ml/8 fl oz/1 cup natural yogurt
salt and pepper
grated nutmeg to serve

1   Chop the fresh mint finely. Peel the
cucumber, deseed it and cut into
matchsticks.

2   Combine the yogurt, mint and
cucumber. Season to taste. Turn into
a serving dish and sprinkle over nutmeg
to serve.

GRAPEFRUIT RAITA:
1 tsp sugar
1 tsp finely grated grapefruit rind
½ grapefruit, segmented
250 ml/8 fl oz/1 cup natural yogurt
salt and pepper

Combine all the ingredients and serve
immediately. This version should be eaten
on the day you make it, as it does not
keep for more than a day.

MELON RAITA:
*¼ honeydew or firm melon, peeled and
cut into 1 cm/ ½ in cubes*
*¼ medium pineapple, peeled and cut into
1 cm/ ½ in cubes*
1 tsp cayenne
1 tsp ground coriander seeds
250 ml/8 fl oz/1 cup natural yogurt
salt and pepper

Combine the melon and pineapple cubes,
cayenne, ground coriander seeds and salt
and pepper in a bowl. Stir in the yogurt
and serve. This will keep for 1–2 days in
the refrigerator.

DATE RAITA:
6 dates, chopped
1 tbsp raisins
1 Granny Smith apple, chopped
250 ml/8 fl oz/1 cup natural yogurt
salt and pepper

Combine all these ingredients in a bowl
and serve. This will keep for 1–2 days in
the refrigerator.

LIME PICKLE

MAKES ENOUGH FOR 2 X 500 G/1 LB JARS

6 limes, rinsed
60 g/2 oz/ ½ cup salt
1 tbsp yellow mustard seeds
1 tsp fenugreek seeds
seeds from 2 star anise
4 small green chillies, chopped finely
125 g/4 oz/ ⅔ cup light muscovado sugar
1 tbsp ground ginger
3–4 tbsp water

1 Cut the limes into quarters, put them into a wide bowl and sprinkle over the salt. Leave for 24 hours.

2 Next day, put the mustard seeds, fenugreek, star anise seeds and chillies into a dry saucepan and cover. Place over a high heat and roast the spices, shaking the pan constantly until the mustard seeds start to pop. Remove from the heat.

3 Strain the liquid from the limes into a small pan. Add the sugar, ginger and water. Boil for 2 minutes or until the sugar has dissolved.

4 Combine the limes and spices thoroughly and put into 2 clean, dry preserving jars. Pour over the sugar mixture, making sure that it covers the limes. If it doesn't, cram the limes further down into the jar, or remove one or two quarters.

5 Cover the jars loosely, and when quite cool, screw on the lids tightly. Label each jar, adding the date on which the pickle was made. Keep for 4 weeks before using.

FENUGREEK

Fenugreek can be bought quite easily in supermarkets and Indian stores. It adds rather a bitter taste to recipes, which is sometimes needed – here I have used it to offset the sweetness of the sugar.

CHILLI CHUTNEY

SERVES 6

1 lime, rinsed and halved, sliced very
  thinly
1 tbsp salt
2 red chillies, chopped finely
2 green chillies, chopped finely
1 tbsp white wine vinegar
1 tbsp lemon juice
½ tsp sugar
2 shallots, chopped finely and rinsed
1 tbsp oil

1 Combine the lime slices and salt. Leave for 30 minutes.

2 Rinse the chillies in the vinegar briefly. Drain.

3 Combine the chillies, lemon juice, sugar, shallots and oil.

4 Stir the salted limes into the other ingredients.

5 Transfer to a non-staining serving dish. Serve this chutney with any mild or rich curry.

CHILLIES

The outward appearance of a chilli is no guide to the heat content: large chillies can be blisteringly hot, and small ones can be sweet and mild. There are a number of ways to reduce the heat in chillies.

The chilli seeds are the hottest part, so leave out the seeds altogether. Chillies give up more heat when they are chopped, so if you use them whole and remove them from the dish before serving, they will impart less heat. However, if you do want to slice or chop them, rinse in cold water before use, which removes a little heat. Rinsing in vinegar removes more. Blanching chopped chillies in boiling water washes out the heat.

Above all, use caution – it is easier to increase the heat than to reduce it. If you do overdo it, try eating rice or bread to cool your mouth, as this is more effective than drinking water.

LASSI YOGURT DRINK

SERVES 4

SWEET VERSION:
600 ml/1 pint/2½ cups natural yogurt
600 ml/1 pint/2½ cups water
1 tsp rosewater
4 tsp caster (superfine) sugar
4 cardamom pods, crushed, pods
  discarded
1 tbsp pistachio nuts

SAVOURY VERSION:
600 ml/1 pint/2½ cups natural yogurt
600 ml/1 pint/2½ cups water
¼ tsp salt
1 tsp sugar
¼ tsp cumin seeds, ground and roasted
fresh mint sprigs to garnish

1 For both versions, put the yogurt and water in a bowl or jug and whisk together until smooth.

2 For the sweet version, stir in the rosewater, caster sugar and cardamom pods. Add more sugar if required. Mix together well.

3 Chop the pistachio nuts. Serve over ice and decorate with chopped pistachios.

4 For the savoury version, stir the salt, sugar and cumin into the yogurt and water.

5 Mix together well, serve over ice and garnish with mint sprigs.

ROSEWATER

Rosewater has acquired very romantic connotations, not least because it was precious enough to be offered up to the gods in times past. It is made from the extracts of rose petals, and is not too expensive to buy in small quantities. It is available from good supermarkets, health food stores and delicatessens.

DESSERTS

INDIAN ICE-CREAM (KULFI)

SERVES 6-8

4 cardamom pods, crushed and seeds
  removed
75 ml/3 fl oz/ ⅓ cup boiling water
1 x 405 g/14 oz can sweetened condensed
  milk
75 ml/3 fl oz/ ⅓ cup cold water
30 g/1 oz/ ¼ cup unsalted pistachio nuts
30 g/1 oz/ ¼ cup blanched almonds
2 drops almond essence (optional)
150 ml/ ¼ pint/ ⅔ cup double (heavy) cream
  lime zest and rose petals, to decorate

1 Pour the boiling water into a bowl, stir in the cardamom seeds and leave for 15 minutes to infuse. Meanwhile, put the condensed milk into a blender or food processor together with the cold water, pistachio nuts, almonds and almond essence, if using. Process the mixture for about 30 seconds until very finely mixed.

2 Add the cooled and strained cardamom water and pour into a bowl. Whip the cream until softly peaking and whisk into the mixture. Pour the mixture into a shallow metal or plastic container and freeze for about 3 hours or until semi-frozen around the edges and mushy in the centre.

3 Transfer the mixture to a bowl and mash well with a fork (to break up the ice crystals). Divide the mixture evenly between 6-8 small moulds (see below) and freeze for at least 4 hours or overnight until firm.

4 To serve, dip the base of each mould quickly into hot water and run a knife around the top edge. Turn out on to serving plates and decorate with lime zest and rose petals, if using.

MOULDING THE KULFI

Traditionally this dessert is frozen in special conical-shaped moulds, but you can use dariole moulds, small yogurt pots or fromage frais cartons instead.

MANGO & YOGURT CREAM

SERVES 6

2 large ripe mangoes
2 tbsp lime juice
2 tbsp caster sugar
150 ml/ ¼ pint/ ⅔ cup double (heavy)
 cream
150 ml/ ¼ pint/ ⅔ cup strained Greek
 yogurt
4 cardamom pods, crushed, and seeds
 removed and crushed
lime twists or zest, to decorate

1 To prepare each mango, cut along either side of the large central stone, to give two halves of mango. Remove the seed, scoop out the flesh and discard the skin.

2 Place the flesh in a blender or food processor with the lime juice and sugar and process until the mixture forms a smooth purée. Turn the mixture into a bowl.

3 Whip the cream in a bowl until stiff, then fold in the yogurt and the crushed cardamom seeds. Reserve 4 tablespoons of the mango purée for decoration, and mix the remaining mango purée into the cream and yogurt mixture.

4 Spoon the mixture into pretty serving glasses. Drizzle a little of the reserved mango sauce over each dessert and serve chilled, decorated with lime twists.

MANGOES

When choosing mangoes, select ones that are shiny with unblemished skins. To test if they are ripe for eating, gently cup the mango in your hand and squeeze it gently – it should give slightly to the touch if ready for eating.

SWEET CARROT HALVA

SERVES 6

750 g/1½ lb carrots, peeled and grated
750 ml/1¼ pints/3 cups milk
1 cinnamon stick or piece of cassia bark
 (optional)
4 tbsp vegetable ghee or oil
60 g/2 oz/ ¼ cup granulated sugar
30 g/1 oz/ ¼ cup unsalted pistachio nuts,
 chopped
30-50 g/1-2 oz/ ¼-½ cup blanched
 almonds, slivered or chopped
60 g/2 oz/ ⅓ cup seedless raisins
8 cardamom pods, split and seeds
 removed and crushed
thick cream or yogurt, to serve

1 Put the grated carrots, milk and cinnamon or cassia, if using, into a large, heavy-based saucepan and bring to the boil. Reduce the heat to a simmer and cook, uncovered, for 35-40 minutes, or until the mixture is thick (with no milk remaining). Stir the mixture frequently during cooking to prevent it sticking.

2 Discard the cinnamon. Heat the ghee or oil in a non-stick frying pan, add the carrot mixture and stir-fry over a medium heat for about 5 minutes or until the carrots take on a glossy sheen.

3 Add the sugar, pistachios, almonds, raisins and crushed cardamom seeds, mix well and continue frying for a further 3-4 minutes, stirring frequently. Serve warm or cold with thick cream or yogurt.

GRATING

The quickest and easiest way to grate this quantity of carrots is by using a food processor fitted with the appropriate blade. This mixture may be prepared ahead of time and reheated in the microwave when required. Use green cardamoms as these have the best flavour.

BALTI DISHES – INTRODUCTION

Balti cooking developed in mountainous areas of northern Pakistan, where there is a region called Baltistan. The translation of Balti literally means 'cooking bucket', which refers to the traditional Pakistani deep, two-handled cooking pot with a rounded bottom. Balti curries are quick to cook using the stir-fry method, and can be served in the traditional cooking pot. They typically use ground or whole spices and fresh coriander (cilantro).

HISTORY
Pakistan borders India, China, Afghanistan and Iran, so its cuisine has been subject to a varied cross-section of influences throughout the centuries. For example, the Balti pan has arguably developed from the Chinese wok. The Moguls have also played a part in influencing the food and cooking of northern Pakistan; they spent the hot summer months in the cool hills of Kashmir, bringing with them new recipes, foods and spices. Spices were traded on the silk route from China and made their way down into Pakistan over the Karakoram mountains, on their way to India. Spices were a vital link in overland trading, which in itself was a far more treacherous method of transport than the later sea routes.

Balti curries are traditionally eaten with naan bread or chapatis, instead of rice. The naan bread or chapati is used to scoop up the sauce and meat, straight from the Balti pan in which it is served; this is how you will find it served in authentic Balti curry houses. Naan bread and chapatis can be bought in Asian food stores and most supermarkets, and are best served warm.

One of the great things about Balti curries is that you can mix and match them, and add your own choice of ingredients. This is particularly the case with spices, so you can alter the curry to suit your particular tastes. The heat of the curry can be altered depending whether you like a hot, fiery curry or a milder, spicy one. Chillies, whether they are powdered, dried or fresh, are one of the main hot ingredients, and should be used with caution until you discover just how hot you like your curry. If your guests' spice tolerance differs, the best policy is to divide the curry during the final stages of cooking and add dried chillies or extra garam masala as appropriate.

EQUIPMENT
Most well-equipped kitchens will have the necessary equipment for cooking Balti curries, such as good heavy-based saucepans with tight-fitting lids, sharp knives, a chopping board, sieves (strainers) and spoons. However, there are a few items which could prove useful and will also be time-saving:

Balti pan
The main item you will need is a Balti pan or a good quality wok. A Balti pan, or Karahi, is the traditional cooking pan used throughout Pakistan and India. It is a real all-purpose pan, as it is used for stir-frying, deep-frying and slow simmering. Originally, the pans were made of cast iron and had a rounded base, but now they come in a variety of metals and, in order to fit modern cookers, have a flattened base. A Balti pan or wok should always be heated before the oil or spices are added.

A new pan needs to be seasoned before it is used for cooking for the

INTRODUCTION

first time. To do this, wash the pan, then heat some oil until nearly smoking; maintain this temperature for 10 minutes, making sure you swirl the oil carefully around the insides of the pan. Discard the oil and wipe out the pan with paper towels; it is now ready to use. To clean a Balti pan it is best to use a bamboo wok-cleaning brush.

Electric coffee grinder or spice mill
Either an electric coffee grinder or spice mill will greatly cut down the time taken to grind the spices. If using a coffee grinder that is also used for coffee, always remember to clean the grinder thoroughly afterwards, otherwise you will end up with strange tasting coffee, or coffee-tasting curries.

If you don't have an electric coffee grinder or spice mill, use a pestle and mortar, which will take longer and is not so good for finely ground spices or large quantities.

Food processor or blender
A food processor or blender will really help to save time in the preparation of a Balti curry because they are able to purée, chop and grate ingredients more quickly and with far less effort than doing these tasks manually.

A food processor or blender will also grind spices, but not as finely as a coffee grinder or spice mill, and it is not very good for small quantities.

BALTI INGREDIENTS
Most of the ingredients needed for Balti cooking can be found in supermarkets, which now have a large range of different foods from around the world. If there are any ingredients that you cannot find in a supermarket, visit a specialist Asian store. Many of the special ingredients can be substituted, or you can make up your own combination using the spices you have and the recipes as a guide.

Meat, poultry, fish and vegetables should be cut into bite-size pieces to make them quicker to cook and easier to scoop up with naan bread. It is best to use good quality ingredients in Balti cooking. Balti dishes are only cooked for a short time, so the dishes will only be as good as the ingredients used.

Fat is an essential part of a Balti curry, and traditionally ghee is used. Ghee is clarified butter and gives a much richer taste to a curry than ordinary butter or oil. However, many people today are health-conscious, so may prefer to use vegetable oil or corn oil.

Whole spices, such as whole curry leaves, bay leaves, cinnamon sticks, cloves, cardamom pods and black peppercorns, are fried in oil to release their flavour and aroma. They should not be eaten.

Garam Masala
Garam masala means 'hot mixed' and will be needed for most of the recipes. It can be bought ready-prepared in supermarkets and Asian food stores, or you can make your own. Store it in an airtight container for no longer than 3 months.

3 cm/1¼ inch piece cinnamon stick
¾ tsp black peppercorns
8 green cardamom pods
1 tsp cloves
1 tsp cumin seeds
1 tsp coriander seeds
½ small nutmeg

1. Heat a dry Balti pan or heavy frying pan (skillet), add the spices

INTRODUCTION

and roast until they have darkened slightly. Alternatively, roast the spices in a preheated oven at 180°C/350°F/Gas mark 4 for 5 minutes until they turn a slightly darker colour. Leave to cool.

2. Put the roast spices into a coffee grinder, spice mill or pestle and mortar, and grind to a fine powder. Use straight away or store for later use.

Par-cooked Balti meat

Balti dishes are stir-fried so it is necessary to cook tougher cuts of meat, such as braising steak, beforehand. If you don't want to do this, you will have to cook the Balti curry for about 1 hour, preferably in a covered dish in a preheated oven at 180°C/350°F/Gas mark 4. Here is a recipe for par-cooked meat.

Par-cooked lamb or beef

1 tbsp oil
250 g/8 oz/2 cups chopped onion
2 garlic cloves, crushed
1 tsp ground ginger
1 fresh green chilli, chopped
1 tsp Garam Masala
1 tbsp tomato purée (paste)
1 tsp salt
½ tsp brown onion seeds
200 ml/7 fl oz/1 scant cup water
750 g/1½ lb braising steak or lamb, cubed

1. Heat the oil in a flameproof casserole, add the onion and fry until softened. Add the garlic and fry for 1 minute.

2. Stir in the remaining ingredients and bring to the boil. Put the lid on the casserole and cook in a preheated oven at 200°C/400°F/Gas mark 6, allowing 40 minutes for lamb

and 1 hour for beef. The meat should be tender but still pink in the centre. Remove the meat with a perforated spoon and keep the contents of the casserole to make a Balti sauce.

Balti sauce

The sauce from the par-cooked meat is used to add extra liquid and flavour to some of the recipes. To make the sauce, put all the ingredients into a food processor or blender and blend to a smooth purée. Alternatively, push the ingredients through a sieve (strainer). It is a good idea is to make double the quantity of sauce and freeze it in portions. Use the sauce as required in a recipe or add it to any of the curries that need a little extra liquid.

A vegetarian Balti sauce can be made by omitting the meat from the par-cooked meat recipe; cook the sauce in the oven or on the hob for 40 minutes.

If you don't have time to make the sauce, use stock instead.

BALTI CURRY PREPARATION

Adding the ingredients in quick succession is very much a part of Balti cooking, so before you start to cook a curry, have all the ingredients ready and the spices roasted and ground, if necessary.

The ingredient list may look long on some of the recipes, but don't be put off, as most of the ingredients are spices so do not take a lot of preparation.

Marinating

Meat, poultry, fish and seafood can all be marinated to give them a wonderful flavour. Where marinating is called for in the recipes, it should be done after grinding the spices. All the marinade ingredients should be

INTRODUCTION

mixed together in a bowl, the meat, poultry, fish or seafood stirred in, then the bowl covered and left in the refrigerator to marinate, ideally overnight. Marinating needs a bit of forward planning, but if you don't have time to leave it overnight, leave it for a minimum of 1 hour.

Stir-frying

Stir-frying for Balti cooking can be done in a Balti pan or wok. The pan should be heated before you add the oil. The oil should be heated over a high heat before the food is added. This is usually cooked over high heat, and is kept on the move, to ensure it does not stick. Then the heat can be turned down to cook the food as required for the rest of the recipe.

SPICES

The best spices to buy are whole spices, as they will keep for much longer than ground spices. If you do buy ground, purchase small quantities at a time. A wide selection of spices can be found in the supermarkets and the more unusual ones can be bought from specialist Asian food stores. It is best to store spices in airtight containers in a cool cupboard, rather than in a spice rack in the kitchen, because light and warmth will affect the colour and freshness. A good idea is to have racks on the inside of a cupboard door, so you can find the spices easily.

Freshly ground spices have a stronger aroma and flavour than bought ground spices. Store ground spices in an airtight container. No ground spice should be stored for longer than 3 months.

Roasting spices

Roasting brings out the flavour of spices, but be careful not to burn them. The spices can be roasted in a preheated oven at 180°C/350°F/Gas mark 4 for 5 minutes until they turn a slightly darker colour, but the easiest way to roast them is to dry-fry them in a Balti pan or heavy-based frying pan (skillet). Heat the pan then add the spices and cook for 2–5 minutes, depending on the quantity, until they have darkened slightly.

STARTERS

BALTI KING PRAWNS (JUMBO SHRIMP)

SERVES 4

1 garlic clove, crushed
2 tsp freshly grated ginger root
2 tsp ground coriander
2 tsp ground cumin
½ tsp ground cardamom
¼ tsp chilli powder
2 tbsp tomato purée (paste)
5 tbsp water
3 tbsp chopped fresh coriander (cilantro)
500 g/1 lb peeled cooked king prawns
  (jumbo shrimp)
2 tbsp oil
2 small onions, sliced
1 fresh green chilli, chopped
salt

1 Put the garlic, ginger, ground coriander, cumin, cardamom, chilli powder, tomato purée (paste), 4 tablespoons of the water and 2 tablespoons of the fresh coriander (cilantro) into a bowl. Mix all the ingredients together.

2 Add the prawns (shrimp) to the bowl and leave to marinate for 2 hours.

3 Heat the oil in a Balti pan or wok, add the onions and stir-fry until golden brown.

4 Add the prawns (shrimp), marinade and the chilli and stir-fry over a medium heat for 5 minutes. Add the salt, and the remaining tablespoon of water if the mixture is very dry. Stir-fry over a medium heat for a further 5 minutes.

5 Serve immediately with the remaining fresh chopped coriander (cilantro).

PRAWNS (SHRIMP)

Smaller prawns (shrimp) can be substituted for the same weight in king prawns (jumbo shrimp), if wished.

GREEN CHILLI & GALANGAL PRAWNS (SHRIMP)

SERVES 4

2 tbsp oil
4 garlic cloves, crushed
2.5 cm/1 inch fresh galangal root, grated
500 g/1 lb peeled cooked king prawns
  (jumbo shrimp)
2 fresh green chillies, sliced
1 tbsp lemon juice
1 tbsp tomato purée (paste)
180 ml/6 fl oz/ ¾ cup coconut milk
¾ tsp Garam Masala (see page 355)
1 tsp salt
1 tbsp chopped fresh coriander (cilantro)

1 Heat the oil in a Balti pan or wok, add the garlic and galangal and stir-fry until golden brown.

2 Add the prawns (shrimp) and green chillies and stir-fry for 3 minutes.

3 Stir in the lemon juice, tomato purée (paste), coconut milk, garam masala and salt. Simmer for 8–10 minutes until the prawns (shrimp) are cooked.

4 Add the fresh coriander (cilantro) and serve at once.

GALANGAL

Galangal is related to ginger. The root resembles ginger root, but it has a more peppery taste. It is used chopped or sliced. Galangal will probably only be found in Asian food stores. Ginger root can be used as a substitute.

DEEP-FRIED BATTERED FISH WITH FENUGREEK DIP

••

SERVES 4

125 g/4 oz/1 cup gram flour or plain (all-
   purpose) flour
2 tsp Garam Masala (see page 355)
4 tsp brown mustard seeds
2 eggs
1 tbsp oil
120–150 ml/4 –5 fl oz/ ½–⅔ cup coconut
   milk
500 g/1 lb plaice fillets, skinned, and cut
   into 1.5 cm/ ½ inch strips
300 ml/ ½ pint/1¼ cups oil for deep-frying
lemon wedges to serve

DIP:
150 ml/ ¼ pint/ ⅔ cup thick creamy yogurt
2 tbsp chopped fresh fenugreek
½ tsp Garam Masala (see page 355)
1 tsp tomato purée (paste)

1 Sift the flour into a bowl and add the
   garam masala and mustard seeds.
Make a well in the centre and gradually
add the eggs, 1 tablespoon of oil and
enough coconut milk to make a batter
which has the consistency of thick cream.

2 Coat the fish in the batter and set
   aside.

3 To make the dip, put the yogurt,
   fenugreek, garam masala and tomato
purée (paste) into a bowl and mix
together.

4 Heat the oil in a Balti pan or wok.
   Add the fish in batches so the pan is
not crowded, and deep-fry for 3–4
minutes until golden brown. Transfer the
fish on to paper towels to drain then
keep warm in a low oven while you cook
the rest of the fish.

5 Serve the fish hot with lemon
   wedges and the dip.

SPICED CHICKEN KOFTAS WITH LIME PICKLE

••

SERVES 4

500 g/1lb skinned and boned chicken,
   chopped coarsely
1 garlic clove
2.5 cm/1 inch piece ginger root, grated
4 tsp Garam Masala (see page 355)
½ tsp ground turmeric
2 tbsp chopped fresh coriander (cilantro)
½ green (bell) pepper, chopped coarsely
2 fresh green chillies, deseeded
½ tsp salt
6 tbsp oil
1 jar lime pickle to serve
lime wedges to garnish

1 Put all the ingredients except the oil
   and lime pickle into a food
processor or blender and process until the
mixture is chopped finely. Alternatively,
finely chop the chicken, garlic, ginger,
(bell) pepper and chillies, and mix
together in a bowl with the garam masala,
turmeric, coriander (cilantro) and salt.

2 Shape the mixture into 16 small
   balls.

3 Heat the oil in a Balti pan or wok
   and fry the koftas for 8–10 minutes,
turning them occasionally to ensure they
cook evenly. If you cannot fit all the
koftas into the pan at once, keep the first
batch warm in a low oven, while you fry
the remaining koftas.

4 Drain the koftas on paper towels and
   serve hot with lime pickle.

VEGETARIAN KOFTAS

You could make these into vegetarian
koftas by substituting the chicken with
500 g/1 lb of mixed vegetables, such
as potatoes, carrots or pumkin. Add
the vegetables in place of the chicken
in step 1 with 1 egg to bind the
ingredients together.

BALTI MUSHROOM PANEER

•••

SERVES 4

2 tbsp oil
2 small onions, sliced
2 tsp brown mustard seeds
1 garlic clove, crushed
2.5 cm/1 inch piece ginger root, grated
½ tsp chilli powder
500 g/1lb mixed mushrooms, such as
   oyster, shiitake, brown cap (crimini),
   and flat
125 g/4 oz paneer, cut into 1 cm/½ inch
   cubes
150 ml/¼ pint/⅔ cup Balti Sauce (see
   page 356) or chicken stock
¼ tsp salt
2 tsp Garam Masala (see page 355)
1 tbsp chopped fresh coriander (cilantro)

1   Heat the oil in a Balti pan or wok.
    Add the onions and mustard seeds
and fry until the onions have softened.

2   Stir in the garlic, ginger and chilli
    powder and stir-fry for 1 minute.

3   Add the mushrooms and paneer and
    stir-fry for 2 minutes.

4   Stir in the Balti sauce or stock, the
    salt and garam masala and simmer
for 5–7 minutes.

5   Stir in the chopped coriander
    (cilantro) and serve.

MINTY LAMB KEBABS WITH CUCUMBER & YOGURT

•••

SERVES 4

2 tsp coriander seeds
2 tsp cumin seeds
3 cloves
3 green cardamom pods
6 black peppercorns
1 cm/½ inch piece ginger root
2 garlic cloves
2 tbsp chopped fresh mint
1 small onion, chopped
425 g/14 oz/1¾ cups minced (ground)
   lamb
½ tsp salt
lime slices to serve

DIP:
150 ml/5 fl oz/⅔ cup natural yogurt
2 tbsp chopped fresh mint
7 cm/3 inch piece of cucumber, grated
1 tsp mango chutney

1   Dry-fry the coriander, cumin, cloves,
    cardamom pods and peppercorns
until they turn a shade darker and release
a roasted aroma.

2   Grind the roasted spices in a coffee
    grinder, spice mill or a pestle and
mortar.

3   Put the ginger and garlic into a food
    processor or blender and process to
a purée. Add the ground spices, mint,
onion, lamb and salt and process until
chopped finely. Alternatively, finely chop
the garlic and ginger and mix with the
ground spices and remaining kebab
ingredients.

4   Mould the kebab mixture into small
    sausage shapes on 4 kebab skewers.
Cook under a preheated hot grill (broiler)
for 10–15 minutes, turning the skewers
occasionally.

5   To make the dip, mix together the
    ingredients.

6   Serve the kebabs with lime slices
    and the dip.

MAIN DISHES

TRADITIONAL BALTI CHICKEN

••••••••••••••••••••••••••••••••••••

Serves 4

3 tbsp oil
4 green cardamom pods
2 tsp cumin seeds
2 onions, sliced
2 garlic cloves, crushed
1.25 kg/2½ lb chicken, skinned and
  jointed into 8 pieces, or 8 small chicken
  portions
1 tsp chilli powder
½ tsp salt
1 tsp Garam Masala (see page 355)
90 ml/3½ fl oz/6 tbsp water
10 tomatoes, chopped coarsely
2 tbsp chopped fresh coriander (cilantro)

1 Heat the oil in a Balti pan or wok,
add the cardamom pods and cumin
seeds and fry until the seeds pop.

2 Stir in the onions and garlic and fry
until golden brown.

3 Add the chicken and stir-fry for
5–6 minutes until brown.

4 Stir in the chilli powder, salt, garam
masala, water and tomatoes. Bring to
the boil, then turn the heat down and
simmer for 20–25 minutes, until the
chicken juices run clear when the thickest
parts of the pieces are pierced with a
sharp knife. Turn the chicken over
halfway through cooking.

5 Stir in the coriander (cilantro) and
serve at once.

VARIATIONS

The traditional Balti chicken recipe is a
good basis for trying out your own
combination of ingredients to make
your own original curry. At step 4 you
could add: par-cooked diced vegetables
such as okra, aubergine, potato, (bell)
pepper, etc. Pulses could also be used
– add a 425 g/14 oz can of beans or
lentils with the vegetables at step 4.

CHICKEN, CORIANDER (CILANTRO), GINGER & LEMON STIR-FRY

••••••••••••••••••••••••••••••••••••

Serves 4

3 tbsp oil
750 g/1½ lb chicken breast, skinned,
  boned and cut in 5 cm/2 inch strips
3 garlic cloves, crushed
3.5 cm/1½ inch piece ginger root, cut into
  strips
1 tsp pomegranate seeds, crushed
½ tsp ground turmeric
1 tsp Garam Masala (see page 355)
2 fresh green chillies, sliced
½ tsp salt
4 tbsp lemon juice
grated rind of 1 lemon
6 tbsp chopped fresh coriander (cilantro)
120 ml/4 fl oz/ ½ cup chicken stock

1 Heat the oil in a Balti pan or wok
and stir-fry the chicken until golden
brown on both sides. Remove the chicken
from the pan and set aside.

2 Fry the garlic, ginger and
pomegranate seeds in the oil for
1 minute.

3 Stir in the turmeric, garam masala
and chillies and fry for 30 seconds.

4 Return the chicken to the pan and
add the salt, lemon juice, lemon
rind, coriander (cilantro) and stock. Stir
the chicken to ensure it is coated in the
sauce. Bring to the boil, then lower the
heat and simmer for 10–15 minutes until
the chicken juices run clear when the
thickest part of the chicken is pierced
with a sharp knife.

5 Serve with naan bread or aromatic
basmatic rice (see page 372).

SUMMER DISH

This dish can be served cold in the
summer with a spicy rice salad or a
mixed lettuce salad.

BALTI CHICKEN PANEER

SERVES 4

60 g/2 oz/ ½ cup ground almonds
250 g/8 oz/1 cup chopped tomatoes
2 fresh green chillies, chopped
1 tsp poppy seeds
1 garlic clove
150 ml/ ¼ pint/ ⅔ cup natural yogurt
90 g/3 oz/ ⅖ cup butter
750 g/1½ lb chicken breast meat, cut into
    2.5 cm/1 inch cubes
175 g/6 oz paneer (see page 326), cut into
    1 cm/ ½ inch cubes
1 tsp ground cumin
1 tsp paprika
1 tsp Garam Masala (see page 355)
¼ tsp ground cinnamon
½ tsp salt

To GARNISH:
1 tbsp chopped fresh coriander (cilantro)
30 g/1 oz/ ¼ cup flaked slivered almonds,
    toasted

1 Put the ground almonds, tomatoes,
chillies, poppy seeds and garlic in a
food processor or blender and blend to a
smooth paste. Alternatively, push the
tomatoes through a sieve (strainer), finely
chop the chillies and garlic, crush the
poppy seeds, then mix together the
tomatoes, chillies, garlic, poppy seeds and
ground almonds. Stir the yogurt into the
tomato mixture.

2 Heat the butter in a Balti pan or
wok, add the chicken and stir-fry for
5 minutes.

3 Add the paneer, cumin, paprika,
garam masala, cinnamon and salt
and stir-fry for 1 minute.

4 Slowly add the tomato and yogurt
mixture to prevent the yogurt
curdling. Simmer for 10–15 minutes until
the chicken juices run clear when the
chicken is pierced with a sharp knife.

5 Serve garnished with the coriander
(cilantro) and flaked almonds.

CHICKEN & BLACK-EYE BEANS (PEAS)

SERVES 4

250 g/8 oz/1 generous cup dried black-eye
    beans (peas), soaked overnight and
    drained
1 tsp salt
2 onions, chopped
2 garlic cloves, crushed
1 tsp ground turmeric
1 tsp ground cumin
1.25 kg/2½ lb chicken, jointed into 8 pieces
1 green (bell) pepper, chopped
2 tbsp oil
2.5 cm/1 inch piece ginger root, grated
2 tsp coriander seeds
½ tsp fennel seeds
2 tsp Garam Masala (see page 355)
1 tbsp chopped fresh coriander (cilantro)
    to garnish

1 Put the beans into a Balti pan, wok
or saucepan with the salt, onions,
garlic, turmeric and cumin. Cover the
beans with water, bring to the boil and
cook for 15 minutes.

2 Add the chicken and green (bell)
pepper to the pan and bring to the
boil. Lower the heat and simmer gently
for 30 minutes until the beans are tender
and the chicken juices run clear when the
thickest parts of the pieces are pierced
with a sharp knife.

3 Heat the oil in a Balti pan, wok or
frying pan (skillet) and fry the
ginger, coriander seeds and fennel seeds
for 30 seconds.

4 Stir the ginger, coriander seeds and
fennel seeds into the chicken and
add the garam masala. Simmer for a
further 5 minutes and serve garnished
with fresh coriander (cilantro).

CANNED BEANS

For convenience, use 425 g/14 oz can
of black-eye beans (peas) instead of
dried beans (peas). Add at step 2.

BALTI QUAIL

SERVES 4

4 quail, roughly jointed
1.5 cm/ ⅔ inch piece ginger root, grated
2 garlic cloves, crushed
1 tsp ground cumin
2 tsp Garam Masala (see page 355)
2 tsp paprika
1 tsp ground turmeric
1 tbsp chopped fresh mint
⅔ tsp salt
250 ml/8 fl oz/1 cup natural yogurt
2 tbsp oil
8 baby onions, total weight about
    250 g/8 oz
4 courgettes (zucchini), sliced thickly
1 fresh green chilli, chopped
4 lime wedges to garnish

1   Using a sharp knife, make cuts in several places in the skin and flesh of each quail joint.

2   Mix together the ginger, garlic, cumin, garam masala, paprika, turmeric, mint, salt and yogurt. Add the quail and coat in the sauce.

3   Cover and leave in the refrigerator to marinate for 2 hours or overnight.

4   Put the quail on a rack over a roasting tin (pan) containing about 2.5 cm/1 inch depth of water; this keeps the quail moist during cooking. Roast the quail in a preheated oven at 200°C/ 400°F/ Gas mark 6 for 30 minutes, until the quail juices run clear when the thickest part of each piece is pierced with a sharp knife.

5   Heat the oil in a Balti pan or wok and fry the onions, courgettes (zucchini) and chilli for 5–6 minutes until golden brown and tender.

6   Add the cooked quail to the pan and serve with lime wedges.

SWEET & SOUR BALTI DUCK

SERVES 4

4 tbsp oil
½ tsp cumin seeds
½ tsp brown mustard seeds
½ tsp crushed dried pomegranate seeds
1 onion, sliced
1 garlic clove, chopped
1 cm/ ½ inch piece ginger root, shredded
2 fresh green chillies, sliced
4 duck breasts, boned and sliced into
    5 cm/2 inch strips
½ tsp salt
150 ml/ ¼ pint / ⅔ cup orange juice
1 orange, quartered and sliced
2 tsp ground turmeric
½ tsp Garam Masala (see page 355)
1 tbsp white wine vinegar
shredded orange rind to garnish

1   Heat the oil in a Balti pan or wok and fry the cumin seeds, mustard seeds and pomegranate seeds until they start popping.

2   Add the onion, garlic, ginger and chillies and stir-fry until the onions are golden brown.

3   Add the duck and stir-fry for 5 minutes until it is brown on both sides.

4   Stir in the salt, orange juice, orange slices, turmeric, garam masala and vinegar and bring to the boil. Lower the hear and simmer for 15–20 minutes until the duck is tender but still pinkish inside; if you prefer duck to be well done, cook for longer. Serve garnished with shredded orange rind.

POMEGRANATE SEEDS

Dried pomegranate seeds can be bought at Asian stores and will give a very individual tangy taste.
   Alternatively, you could use the seeds from the fresh fruit.

PATHAN BEEF STIR-FRY

•••

SERVES 4

750 g/1½ lb fillet of beef, cut into
   2.5 cm/ 1 inch strips
2 tbsp oil
1 onion
2.5 cm/1 inch piece ginger root, cut into
   strips
1 fresh red chilli, deseeded and sliced
2 carrots, cut into strips
1 green (bell) pepper, cut into strips
1 tsp Garam Masala (see page 355)
1 tbsp toasted sesame seeds

MARINADE:
1 tsp dried fenugreek
1 tsp brown mustard seeds, ground
1 tsp ground cinnamon
1 tsp ground cumin
1 garlic clove, crushed
150 ml/ ¼ pint/ ⅔ cup natural yogurt

1 To make the marinade, mix all the
marinade ingredients in a bowl.

2 Add the beef to the marinade, stir to
coat, then cover and leave to
marinate for 1–2 hours, or overnight in
the refrigerator.

3 Heat the oil in a Balti pan or wok,
add the onion and stir-fry until
softened.

4 Stir in the ginger, chilli, carrots and
green (bell) pepper and stir-fry for
1 minute. Add the garam masala and beef
with the marinade liquids, and stir-fry for
8–10 minutes until the beef is tender; it is
best if it is still pinkish inside.

5 Stir in the toasted sesame seeds and
serve.

VARIATIONS

Any selection of vegetables can be
added to the stir-fry, which is a good
way to use up any vegetables left over
in the refrigerator, but add them to the
beef for just long enough to heat
through.

TAMARIND BEEF BALTI

•••

SERVES 4

125 g/4 oz tamarind block, broken into
   pieces
150 ml/ ¼ pint/ ⅔ cup water
2 tbsp tomato purée (paste)
1 tbsp granulated sugar
2.5 cm/1 inch piece ginger root, chopped
1 garlic clove, chopped
½ tsp salt
1 onion, chopped
2 tbsp oil
1 tsp cumin seeds
1 tsp coriander seeds
1 tsp brown mustard seeds
4 curry leaves
750 g/1½ lb braising steak, cut into
   2.5 cm/1 inch cubes and par-cooked
   (see page 356)
1 red (bell) pepper, cut in half, sliced
2 fresh green chillies, deseeded, sliced
1 tsp Garam Masala (see page 355)
1 tbsp chopped fresh coriander (cilantro)
   to garnish

1 Soak the tamarind overnight in the
water. Strain the soaked tamarind,
keeping the liquid.

2 Put the tamarind, tomato purée
(paste), sugar, ginger, garlic, salt and
onion into a food processor or blender
and mix to a smooth purée. Alternatively,
mash the ingredients together in a bowl.

3 Heat the oil in a Balti pan or wok,
add the cumin, coriander seeds,
mustard seeds and curry leaves, and cook
until the spices start popping.

4 Stir the beef into the spices and stir-
fry for 2–4 minutes until the meat is
browned.

5 Add the red (bell) pepper, chillies,
garam masala, tamarind mixture and
reserved tamarind liquid and cook for
20–25 minutes. Serve garnished with fresh
coriander (cilantro).

LAMB KOFTAS WITH SPINACH & CARDAMOM

SERVES 4

5 tbsp oil
2 tsp cardamom seeds
6 black peppercorns, crushed
1 tsp cumin seeds
1 onion, chopped finely
1 garlic clove, crushed
150 ml/ ¼ pint/ ⅔ cup natural yogurt
500 g/1 lb chopped fresh spinach
½ tsp grated nutmeg
1 tsp Garam Masala (see page 355)
1 tsp salt
90 g/3 oz/ ¾ cup split almonds, shredded

KOFTAS:
1 onion, quartered
1 garlic clove
1 fresh green chilli, deseeded
1 tsp Garam Masala (see page 355)
1 tsp salt
750 g/1½ lb minced/3 cups (ground) lamb

1 To make the koftas, put the onion, garlic and chilli into a food processor or blender and process until chopped finely, then add the garam masala, salt and lamb and process to combine the ingredients. Alternatively, finely chop the onion, garlic and chilli, then mix with the garam masala, salt and lamb in a bowl.

2 Shape the lamb mixture into small balls. Heat 3 tablespoons of the oil in a Balti pan or wok, add the koftas in batches and cook, turning frequently, until evenly browned. Remove the koftas from the pan with a perforated spoon, drain on paper towels and keep warm.

3 Heat the remaining oil in the pan and fry the cardamom seeds, peppercorns and cumin seeds until they start popping. Add the onion and garlic and cook until golden brown.

4 Gradually add the yogurt, stirring to prevent it curdling. Stir in the spinach, nutmeg, garam masala, salt, two-thirds of the almonds and the koftas and simmer for 30 minutes. Sprinkle over the remaining almonds and serve.

BALTI LAMB ROGAN JOSH

SERVES 4

3 tbsp fennel seeds
1 cm/ ½ inch piece cinnamon stick
4 black peppercorns
3 tbsp oil
2 onions, sliced
2 garlic cloves, crushed
2.5 cm/1 inch piece ginger root, grated
750 g/1½ lb lamb, cut into 2.5 cm/1 inch cubes and par-cooked (see page 356)
8 tomatoes, chopped
1 green (bell) pepper, sliced
150 ml/ ¼ pint/ ⅔ cup natural yogurt
3 tsp paprika
½ tsp chilli powder
½ tsp Garam Masala (see page 355)
300 ml/ ½ pint/1¼ cups Balti Sauce (see page 356) or lamb stock

TO GARNISH :
2 tbsp chopped fresh coriander (cilantro)
2 tbsp natural yogurt

1 Grind the fennel seeds, cinnamon and peppercorns to a fine powder in a coffee grinder, spice mill or pestle and mortar.

2 Heat the oil in a Balti pan or wok, add the onions and stir-fry until softened. Add the garlic and ginger and stir-fry for 1 minute.

3 Add the par-cooked lamb, stir-fry for 3 minutes, then add the tomatoes and green (bell) pepper. Stir-fry for 1 minute.

4 Slowly stir in the yogurt, then add the paprika, chilli powder, ground spices, garam masala and Balti sauce or stock. Simmer for 30 minutes until the sauce is reduced to the consistency of a thick gravy.

5 Serve garnished with fresh coriander (cilantro) and yogurt.

MASALA LAMB & LENTILS

SERVES 4

2 tbsp oil
1 tsp cumin seeds
2 bay leaves
2.5 cm/1 inch piece cinnamon stick
1 onion, chopped
750 g/1½ lb lean, boneless lamb, cut into
  2.5 cm/1 inch cubes
125 g/4 oz/ ½ cup split gram lentils,
  soaked for 6 hours and drained
1 tsp salt
1 fresh green chilli, sliced
1.25 litres/2¼ pints/5 cups water
1 garlic clove, crushed
¼ tsp ground turmeric
1 tsp chilli powder
½ tsp Garam Masala (see page 355)
  (optional)
1 tbsp chopped fresh coriander (cilantro)
  (optional)

1 Heat the oil in a Balti pan or wok
  and add the cumin seeds, bay leaves
and cinnamon and fry until the seeds start
popping.

2 Add the onion to the pan and stir-fry
  until golden brown.

3 Stir the lamb into the onion and stir-
  fry until browned.

4 Add the lentils, salt, chilli, water,
  garlic, turmeric and chilli powder.
Bring to the boil, then simmer for 1 hour
until the meat and lentils are tender.

5 Taste and stir the garam masala into
  the pan, if liked, and cook for a
further 5 minutes. Stir in the coriander
(cilantro), if using, and serve.

TIMESAVER

To save time on soaking, use a 425 g/
14 oz can of lentils. These should be
added at the end of stage 4 and
cooked for 15 minutes. The meat still
needs the same cooking time.

BALTI KEEMA WITH SWEET POTATOES, OKRA & SPINACH

SERVES 4

250 g/8 oz sweet potatoes, cut into chunks
175 g/6 oz okra
2 tbsp oil
2 onions, sliced
2 garlic cloves, crushed
1 cm/ ½ inch piece ginger root, chopped
500 g/1 lb/2 cups minced (ground) lamb
250 g/8 oz/6 cups fresh spinach, chopped
300 ml/ ½ pint/1¼ cups lamb stock
½ tsp salt
125 g/4 oz/1 cup pine nuts
125 g/4 oz/ ¾ cup sultanas (golden
  raisins)
1 tbsp granulated sugar
3 tsp Garam Masala (see page 355)
rice or naan bread to serve

1 Bring 2 saucepans of water to the
  boil. Add the sweet potatoes to one
and the okra to the other. Boil both for
4–5 minutes, then drain well. Cut the okra
into 1 cm/½ inch slices. Set aside both
vegetables.

2 Heat the oil in a Balti pan or wok,
  add the onions and stir-fry until
golden brown. Stir in the garlic and
ginger and fry for 1 minute.

3 Add the lamb to the pan and stir-fry
  for 5 minutes.

4 Stir in the sweet potato, okra and
  spinach and stir-fry for 2 minutes.

5 Add the stock, salt, pine nuts,
  sultanas (golden raisins), sugar and
garam masala and simmer for 10–15
minutes until the sauce has thickened.
Serve with rice or naan bread.

ALTERNATIVES

Sweet potato gives a wonderful
flavour to the dish, but you could use
pumpkin, which has a sweetish taste
similar to that of sweet potatoes, or
ordinary potatoes.

BALTI SCALLOPS WITH CORIANDER (CILANTRO) & TOMATO

SERVES 4

750 g/1½ lb shelled scallops
2 onions, chopped
3 tomatoes, quartered
2 fresh green chillies, sliced
2 tbsp oil
4 lime wedges to garnish

MARINADE:
3 tbsp chopped fresh coriander (cilantro)
2.5 cm/1 inch piece ginger root, grated
1 tsp ground coriander
3 tbsp lemon juice
grated rind of 1 lemon
¼ tsp ground black pepper
½ tsp salt
½ tsp ground cumin
1 garlic clove, crushed

1 To make the marinade, mix all the ingredients together in a bowl.

2 Put the scallops into a bowl. Add the marinade and turn the scallops until they are well coated. Then cover and leave to marinate for 1 hour or overnight in the fridge.

3 Heat the oil in a Balti pan or wok, add the onions and stir-fry until softened. Add the tomatoes and chillies and stir-fry for 1 minute.

4 Add the scallops and stir-fry for 6–8 minutes until the scallops are cooked through, but still succulent inside. Serve garnished with lime wedges.

SCALLOPS

It is best to buy the scallops fresh in the shell with the roe – you will need 1.5 kg/3 lb – a fishmonger will clean them and remove the shell for you.

KING PRAWNS (JUMBO SHRIMP) WITH SPICED COURGETTES (ZUCCHINI)

SERVES 4

3 tbsp oil
2 onion, chopped
3 garlic cloves, chopped
1 cm/½ inch piece ginger root, chopped
250 g/8 oz courgettes (zucchini), sliced
1 tsp dried pomegranate seeds, crushed
8 tomatoes, chopped
1 tbsp tomato purée (paste)
150 ml/¼ pint/⅔ cup coconut milk
2 tbsp chopped fresh coriander (cilantro)
1 tsp chilli powder
1 tsp ground cumin
½ tsp salt
500 g/1 lb peeled cooked king prawns
   (jumbo shrimp)
fresh coriander (cilantro) to garnish

1 Heat the oil in a Balti pan or wok, add the onions and stir-fry until golden brown. Add the garlic and ginger and stir-fry for 1 minute.

2 Stir the courgettes (zucchini) and pomegranate seeds into the pan and stir-fry for 2 minutes.

3 Add the tomatoes, tomato purée (paste), coconut milk, fresh coriander (cilantro), chilli powder, cumin and salt and stir-fry for a further 2 minutes.

4 Stir in the prawns, bring to the boil then simmer for 6 minutes. Serve garnished with fresh coriander (cilantro).

ADDING SPICE

If you want a more spicy dish, add more chilli powder or 2 teaspoons Garam Masala.

BALTI COD & RED LENTILS

••

SERVES 4

2 tbsp oil
¼ tsp ground asafoetida (optional)
1 tbsp crushed aniseed
1 tsp ground ginger
1 tsp chilli powder
¼ tsp ground turmeric
250 g/8 oz/1 cup split red lentils, washed
1 tsp salt
500 g/1 lb cod, skinned, filleted and cut
into 2.5 cm/1 inch cubes
1 fresh red chilli, chopped
3 tbsp natural yogurt
2 tbsp chopped fresh coriander (cilantro)

1 Heat the oil in a Balti pan or wok, add the asafoetida, if using, and fry for about 10 seconds to burn off the smell of the asafoetida. Add the aniseed, ginger, chilli powder and turmeric and fry for 30 seconds.

2 Stir in the lentils and salt and add enough water to cover the lentils. Bring to the boil, then simmer gently for 45 minutes, until the lentils are soft but not mushy.

3 Add the cod and chilli, bring to the boil and simmer for a further 10 minutes.

4 Stir in the yogurt and fresh coriander (cilantro) and serve straight away.

ASAFOETIDA

Asafoetida is a digestive, so will help in the digestion of the lentils.

Ground asafoetida is easier to use than the type that comes on a block. It should only be used in small quantities. Do not be put off by the smell which is very pungent.

CREAMY FISH & PRAWN (SHRIMP) MASALA

••

SERVES 4

1 tsp ground coriander
250 ml/8 fl oz/1 cup natural yogurt
1 tsp ground turmeric
1 tsp salt
500 g/1 lb firm white fish such as cod or
haddock, skinned, filleted and cut into
2.5 cm/1 inch cubes
250 g/8 oz/¼ cup peeled cooked king
prawns (jumbo shrimp)
2 tbsp oil
1 tsp brown mustard seeds
1 onion, chopped
1 garlic clove, crushed
2 tsp Garam Masala (see page 355)
2 tbsp chopped fresh coriander (cilantro)
120 ml/4 fl oz/½ cup double (heavy)
cream

TO GARNISH:
1 tbsp crushed dried red chillies
sprigs of fresh coriander (cilantro)

1 Put the ground coriander, yogurt, turmeric and salt into a bowl and stir together. Add the fish and prawns (shrimp) and leave to marinate for 1 hour.

2 Heat the oil in a Balti pan or wok, add the mustard seeds and fry until they start popping.

3 Add the onion to the pan, stir-fry until golden brown, then add the garlic and stir-fry for 1 minute.

4 Stir in the garam masala, fresh coriander (cilantro), marinated fish and prawns (shrimp). Simmer for 10–15 minutes until the fish flakes easily when tested with a fork. Stir in the cream during the last few minutes of cooking.

5 Serve garnished with crushed red chillies and fresh coriander (cilantro) sprig.

DELICATELY SPICED TROUT

SERVES 4

4 trout, each weighing 175–250 g/6–8 oz,
   cleaned
3 tbsp oil
1 tsp fennel seeds
1tsp onion seeds
1 garlic clove, crushed
150 ml/ ¼ pint/ ⅔ cup coconut milk or fish
   stock
3 tbsp tomato purée (paste)
60 g/2 oz/ ⅛ cup sultanas (golden raisins)
½ tsp Garam Masala (see page 355)

TO GARNISH:
30 g/ 1 oz/ ¼ cup chopped cashew nuts
lemon wedges
sprigs of fresh coriander (cilantro)

MARINADE:
4 tbsp lemon juice
2 tbsp chopped fresh coriander (cilantro)
1 tsp ground cumin
½ tsp salt
½ tsp ground black pepper

1 Slash the trout skin in several places on both sides to ensure the marinade is absorbed into the fish faster.

2 To make the marinade, mix all the ingredients together in a bowl.

3 Put the trout in a shallow dish and pour over the marinade. Leave to marinate for 30–40 minutes; turn the fish over during the marinating time.

4 Heat the oil in a Balti pan or wok and fry the fennel seeds and onion seeds until they start popping. Add the garlic, coconut milk or fish stock, and tomato purée (paste) and bring to the boil.

5 Add the sultanas (golden raisins), garam masala and trout with the juices from the marinade. Cover the pan with foil and simmer for 5 minutes. Turn the trout over carefully and simmer for a further 10 minutes. Serve garnished with cashew nuts, lemon wedges and coriander (cilantro) sprigs.

MONKFISH & OKRA BALTI

SERVES 4

750 g/1½ lb monkfish, cut into
   3 cm/1¼ inch cubes
250 g/8 oz okra
2 tbsp oil
1 onion, sliced
1 garlic clove, crushed
2.5 cm/1 inch piece ginger root, sliced
150 ml/ ¼ pint/ ⅔ cup coconut milk or fish
   stock
2 tsp Garam Masala (see page 355)

MARINADE:
3 tbsp lemon juice
grated rind of 1 lemon
¼ tsp aniseed
½ tsp salt
½ tsp ground black pepper

TO GARNISH :
4 lime wedges
sprigs of fresh coriander (cilantro)

1 To make the marinade, mix the ingredients together in a bowl.

2 Stir the monkfish into the bowl and leave to marinate for 1 hour.

3 Bring a large saucepan of water to the boil, add the okra and boil for 4–5 mnutes. Drain well and cut into 1 cm/ ½ inch slices.

4 Heat the oil in a Balti pan or wok, add the onion and stir-fry until golden brown. Add the garlic and ginger and fry for 1 minute.

5 Add the fish with the marinade juices to the pan and stir-fry for 2 minutes.

6 Stir in the okra, coconut milk or stock, and the garam masala and simmer for 10 minutes. Serve garnished with lime wedges and fresh coriander (cilantro).

SIDE DISHES

MUSTARD & ONION POTATOES

SERVES 4

350 g/12 oz small new potatoes
3 tbsp oil
2 tbsp brown mustard seeds
1 tsp cumin seeds
1 tsp crushed dried red chillies
250 g/8 oz baby onions
1 garlic clove, chopped
1 cm/ ½ inch piece ginger root
¼ tsp Garam Masala (see page 355)

1 Boil the potatoes in salted water for 10–15 minutes until just tender. Drain the potatoes, cut in half if they are on the largish side, and set aside.

2 Heat the oil in a Balti pan or wok, add the mustard seeds, cumin, and chillies and fry until the seeds start popping.

3 Add the onions to the pan and stir-fry until golden brown. Add the garlic and ginger and fry for 1 minute.

4 Stir in the potatoes and garam masala and stir-fry for 4–5 minutes until the potatoes are golden brown. Serve hot.

VARIATIONS

This recipe can be made with any combination of vegetable to make a tasty dry stir-fry dish, to go with any of the curries in this book. One of my favourites is to substitute the new potatoes with the sweet variety. These make a wonderful potato salad if served cold and are ideal with barbecues in the summer. If you like a moist potato salad add 3 tbsp of yogurt stirred into the potatoes. You could also add 1 tbsp of chopped mint to the yogurt.

MIXED VEGETABLE BALTI

SERVES 4

250 g/8 oz/1 cup split yellow peas, washed
3 tbsp oil
1 tsp onion seeds
2 onions, sliced
125 g/4 oz courgettes (zucchini), sliced
125 g/4 oz potatoes, cut into 1 cm/ ½ inch cubes
125 g/4 oz carrots, sliced
1 small aubergine (eggplant), sliced
250 g/8 oz tomatoes, chopped
300 ml/ ½ pint/1¼ cups water
3 garlic cloves, chopped
1 tsp ground cumin
1 tsp ground coriander
1 tsp salt
2 fresh green chillies, sliced
½ tsp Garam Masala (see page 355)
2 tbsp chopped fresh coriander (cilantro)

1 Put the split peas into a saucepan and cover with salted water. Bring to the boil and simmer for 30 minutes. Drain the peas and keep warm.

2 Heat the oil in a Balti pan or wok, add the onion seeds and fry until they start popping. Add the onions and stir-fry until golden brown.

3 Add the courgettes (zucchini), potatoes, carrots and aubergine (eggplant) to the pan and stir-fry for 2 minutes.

4 Stir in the tomatoes, water, garlic, cumin, ground coriander, salt, chillies, garam masala and reserved split peas. Bring to the boil, then simmer for 15 minutes until all the vegetables are tender. Stir the fresh coriander (cilantro) into the vegetables and serve.

TIP

The split peas can be cooked in the Balti pan or wok. After draining the split peas, remove them and keep them warm, wipe out the pan and continue from step 2.

SWEET POTATOES & SPINACH

SERVES 4

500 g/1lb sweet potatoes, cut into
  2.5 cm/ 1 inch cubes
4 tbsp oil
2 onions, sliced
1 garlic clove, crushed
125 g/4 oz/1 cup pine nuts, toasted
500 g/1 lb fresh spinach
1 tsp Garam Masala (see page 355)
2 tbsp chopped dried red chillies
2 tsp water
freshly grated nutmeg to serve

1 Boil the sweet potatoes in salted
   water for 5 minutes until half
cooked. Drain and set aside.

2 Heat the oil in a Balti pan or wok,
   add the onions and stir-fry until
golden brown.

3 Add the garlic, sweet potatoes and
   pine nuts to the pan and stir-fry for
2 minutes until the sweet potatoes have
absorbed the oil.

4 Stir in the spinach, garam masala
   and dried chillies and stir-fry for
2 minutes. Add the water and stir-fry for
4 minutes until the sweet potatoes
and spinach are tender.

5 Serve with freshly
   grated nutmeg
sprinkled over.

QUICK TIP

Fresh spinach can be substituted with
1kg/ 2 lb of frozen leaf spinach. Fresh
chillies can be used instead of dried
chilles if you do not have any.

BALTI DAL

SERVES 4

250 g/8 oz/1 cup chang dal or split yellow
  peas, washed
½ tsp ground turmeric
1 tsp ground coriander
1 tsp salt
4 curry leaves
2 tbsp oil
½ tsp asafoetida powder (optional)
1 tsp cumin seeds
2 onions, chopped
2 garlic cloves, crushed
1 cm/ ½ inch piece ginger root, grated
½ tsp Garam Masala (see page 355)

1 Put the chang dal in a saucepan and
   pour in enough water to cover by
2.5 cm/1 inch. Bring to the boil and
spoon off the scum that has formed.

2 Add the turmeric, ground coriander,
   salt and curry leaves and simmer for
1 hour. The chang dal should be tender,
but not mushy.

3 Heat the oil in a Balti pan or wok,
   add the asafoetida, if using, and
fry for 30 seconds. Add the cumin seeds
and fry until they start popping. Add
the onions and stir-fry until golden
brown.

4 Add the garlic, ginger, garam masala
   and chang dal and stir-fry for
2 minutes. Serve hot with one of the Balti
curries.

DAL

Dal reheats and keeps well, so it is a
good idea to make a large amount and
store in the refrigerator, or freeze in
portions.

PUMPKIN KORMA

SERVES 4

4 tbsp oil
½ tsp onion seeds
4 curry leaves
2 onions, chopped
500 g/1 lb peeled and deseeded pumpkin,
    cut into 2.5 cm/1 in cubes
150 ml/ ¼ pint/ ⅔ cup natural yogurt
1 cm/ ½ in piece ginger root, grated
2 garlic cloves, crushed
125 g/4 oz/1 cup ground almonds
½ tsp ground turmeric
½ tsp chilli powder
½ tsp Garam Masala (see page 355)
1 tsp salt
150 ml/ ¼ pint/ ⅔ cup coconut milk
1 tbsp chopped fresh coriander (cilantro)

TO GARNISH:
1 tbsp chopped toasted almonds
1 tbsp chopped fresh coriander (cilantro)

1   Heat the oil in a Balti pan or wok,
    add the onion seeds and curry leaves
and fry until the seeds start popping.

2   Add the onions to the pan and stir-
    fry until golden brown.

3   Stir in the pumpkin and stir-fry until
    golden brown.

4   Stir in the yogurt gradually to
    prevent it curdling. Add the ginger,
garlic, almonds, turmeric, chilli powder,
garam masala, salt, coconut milk and
fresh coriander (cilantro) and simmer for
10–15 minutes until the pumpkin is
tender. Serve garnished with toasted
almonds and fresh coriander (cilantro).

PUMPKIN

There are many varieties of pumpkin
available in supermarkets. It is not only
the flesh of the pumpkin that is used
in cooking but also the seeds. If these
are toasted, they make a nutty topping
to vegetables. Pumpkin seeds are left
to dry on the balconies and roofs of
the houses in Pakistan.

AROMATIC BASMATI RICE & SPICY SAFFRON RICE

SERVES 4

AROMATIC BASMATI RICE:
1 tbsp oil
1 cinnamon stick
2 dried bay leaves
4 green cardamom pods
4 black peppercorns
250 g/8 oz/1 cup basmati rice, washed
    and soaked
1 tsp salt

1   Heat the oil in a heavy-based
    saucepan and fry the cinnamon, bay
leaves, cardamom pods and black
peppercorns for 30 seconds.

2   Add the rice and salt and enough
    water to cover the rice by
2.5 cm/1 inch. Cover with a tight-fitting
lid, bring to the boil and simmer for
20 minutes or until all the water has been
absorbed and the rice is tender.

SPICY SAFFRON RICE:
60 g/2 oz/ ¼ cup butter or ghee
1 onion, chopped
½ teaspoon saffron strands
1 tsp cumin seeds
250 g/8 oz/1 cup basmati rice, washed
    and soaked
1 tsp salt
90 g/3 oz/ ⅔ cup split almonds,
    ¾ cut in slivers and toasted

1   Heat the butter or ghee in a heavy-
    based saucepan, add the onion and
stir-fry. Add the saffron strands and cumin
seeds and fry for 30 seconds.

2   Add the rice and fry for 2 minutes
    until it has absorbed the oil and the
saffron colour. Add the salt and enough
water to cover the rice by 2.5 cm/1 in.
Cover with a tight-fitting lid and simmer
for 20 minutes until all the water has been
absorbed and the rice is tender. Stir in
the almonds.

CHINESE – INTRODUCTION

China is a vast country – about the same size as the United States – and its climate and food products are similarly varied. Consequently, each region has a distinctive style of cooking: no wonder China can claim to have the world's most diverse cuisine. Yet the fundamental character of Chinese cooking remains the same throughout the land: from Peking in the north to Canton in the south, and Shanghai in the east to Szechuan in the west, different ingredients are prepared, cooked and served in accordance with the same centuries-old principles. Some of the cooking methods may vary a little from one region to another, and the emphasis on seasonings may differ, but basically dishes from different regions are all unmistakably "Chinese".

The principles of Chinese cooking
What distinguishes Chinese cooking from all other food cultures is the emphasis on the harmonious blending of colour, aroma, flavour, and texture both in a single dish and in a course of dishes for a meal. Balance and contrast are the key words, based on the ancient Taoist philosophy of yin and yang. Consciously or unconsciously, Chinese cooks from the housewife to the professional chef all work to this yin-yang principle: harmonious balance and contrast in conspicuous juxtaposition of different colours, aromas, flavours and textures by varying the ingredients, cutting shapes, seasonings and cooking methods.

In order to achieve this, two most important factors should be observed: heat and timing – the degree of heat and duration of cooking, which means the right cooking method for the right food. This is why the size and shape of the cut ingredient must, first of all, be suitable for a particular method of cooking. For instance, ingredients for quick stir-frying should be cut into small, thin slices or shreds of uniform size, never large, thick chunks. This is not just for the sake of appearance, but also because ingredients of the same size and shape require about the same amount of time in cooking.

EQUIPMENT AND UTENSILS
There are only a few basic implements in the Chinese batterie de cuisine that are considered essential in order to achieve the best results. Equivalent equipment is always available in a Western kitchen, but Chinese cooking utensils are of an ancient design, usually made of inexpensive materials; they have been in continuous use for several thousand years and do serve a special function. Their more sophisticated and much more expensive Western counterparts prove rather inadequate in contrast.

Chinese cleaver An all-purpose cook's knife that is used for slicing, shredding, peeling, crushing and chopping. Different sizes and weights are available.

Wok The round-bottomed iron wok conducts and retains heat evenly, and because of its shape, the ingredients always return to the centre, where the heat is most intense, however vigorously you stir. The wok is also ideal for deep-frying – its conical shape requires far less oil than the flat-bottomed deep-fryer, and has more depth (which means more heat) and more cooking surface (which means more food can be

INTRODUCTION

cooked at one go). Besides being a frying-pan, a wok is also used for braising, steaming, boiling and poaching, etc. – in other words, the whole spectrum of Chinese cooking methods can be executed in a single utensil.

Ladle and spatula Some wok sets come with a pair of stirrers in the form of a ladle and spatula. Of the two, the flat ladle or scooper (as it is sometimes called) is more versatile. It is used by the Chinese cook for adding ingredients and seasonings to the wok as well as for stirring.

Strainers There are two basic types of strainers – one is made of copper or steel wire with long bamboo handles, the other of perforated iron or stainless steel. Several different sizes are available.

Steamers The traditional Chinese steamer is made of bamboo, and the modern version is made of aluminium. Of course, the wok can be used as a steamer with a rack or trivet and the dome-shaped wok lid.

Chopsticks Does Chinese food taste any better when eaten with chopsticks? This is not merely an aesthetic question, but also a practical point, partly because all Chinese food is prepared in such a way that it is easily picked up by chopsticks.

Learning to use chopsticks is quite simple and easy – place one chopstick in the hollow between thumb and index finger and rest its lower end below the first joint of the third finger. This chopstick remains stationary. Hold the other chopstick between the tips of the index and middle finger, steady its upper half against the base of the index finger, and use the tip of the thumb to keep it in place. To pick up food, move the upper chopstick with index and middle fingers.

GLOSSARY OF INGREDIENTS USED IN CHINESE COOKING

Baby sweetcorn Baby corn cobs have a wonderfully sweet fragrance and flavour, and an irresistible texture. They are available both fresh and canned.

Bamboo shoots Available in cans only. Once opened, the contents may be kept in fresh water in a covered jar for up to a week in the refrigerator.

Bean-sprouts Fresh bean-sprouts, from mung or soya beans, are widely available from Oriental stores and supermarkets. They can be kept in the refrigerator for two to three days.

Black bean sauce Sold in jars or cans. Salted beans are crushed and mixed with flour and spices (such as ginger, garlic or chilli) to make a thickish paste. Once opened, keep in the refrigerator.

Chilli bean sauce Fermented bean paste made from soy beans and mixed with hot chilli and other seasonings. Sold in jars, some sauces are quite mild, but others are very hot. You will have to try out the various brands to see which one is to your taste.

Chilli sauce Very hot sauce made from chillis, vinegar, sugar and salt. Usually sold in bottles and should be used sparingly in cooking or as a dip. Tabasco sauce can be a substitute.

INTRODUCTION

Chinese leaves Also known as Chinese cabbage, there are two widely available varieties in supermarkets and greengrocers. The most commonly seen one is a pale green colour and has a tightly wrapped, elongated head – about two-thirds of the cabbage is stem, which has a crunchy texture. The other variety has a shorter, fatter head with curlier, pale yellow or green leaves, also with white stems.

Coriander Fresh coriander leaves, also known as Chinese parsley or cilantro, are widely used in Chinese cooking as a garnish.

Dried Chinese mushrooms (Shiitake) Highly fragrant dried mushrooms which add a special flavour to Chinese dishes. There are many different varieties, but Shiitake are the best. They are not cheap, but a small amount will go a long way, and they will keep indefinitely in an airtight jar. Soak them in warm water for 20-30 minutes (or in cold water for several hours), squeeze dry and discard the hard stalks before use.

Egg noodles There are many varieties of noodles in China, ranging from flat, broad ribbons to long narrow strands. Both dried and fresh noodles are available.

Five-spice powder A mixture of star anise, fennel seeds, cloves, cinnamon bark and Szechuan pepper. It is very pungent, so should be used sparingly. It will keep in an airtight container indefinitely.

Ginger root Fresh ginger root, sold by weight, should be peeled then sliced, finely chopped or shredded before use. It will keep for weeks in

a dry, cool place. Dried ginger powder is no substitute.

Hoi-sin sauce Also known as barbecue sauce, this is made from soy beans, sugar, flour, vinegar, salt, garlic, chilli and sesame seed oil. Sold in cans or jars, it will keep in the refrigerator for several months.

Oyster sauce A thickish soy-based sauce used as a flavouring in Cantonese cooking. Sold in bottles, it will keep in the refrigerator for months.

Plum sauce Plum sauce has a unique, fruity flavour – a sweet and sour sauce with a difference.

Rice wine Chinese rice wine, made from glutinous rice, is also known as "Yellow wine" (Huang jiu or chiew in Chinese) because of its golden amber colour. The best variety is called Shao Hsing or Shaoxing from south-east China. A good dry or medium sherry can be a good substitute.

Rice vinegar There are two basic types of rice vinegar. Red vinegar is made from fermented rice and has a distinctive dark colour and depth of flavour. White vinegar is stronger in taste as it is distilled from rice wine.

Sesame oil Aromatic oil sold in bottles and widely used as a finishing touch, added to dishes just before serving. The refined yellow sesame oil sold in Middle-Eastern stores is not so aromatic, has less flavour and therefore is not a very satisfactory substitute.

Soy sauce Sold in bottles or cans, this popular Chinese sauce is used both for cooking and at the table. Light

INTRODUCTION

soy sauce has more flavour than the sweeter dark soy sauce, which gives the food a rich, reddish colour.

Straw mushrooms Grown on beds of rice straw, these have a pleasant slippery texture, and a subtle taste. Canned straw mushrooms should be rinsed and drained after opening.

Szechuan peppercorns Also known as *farchiew*, these are wild reddish-brown peppercorns from Szechuan. More aromatic but less hot than either white or black peppercorns, they do impart a unique flavour.

Szechuan preserved vegetables The pickled mustard root, sold in cans, is very hot and salty. Once opened, it will keep for many months in a tightly sealed jar in the refrigerator.

Tofu (bean curd) This custard-like preparation of puréed and pressed soya beans is exceptionally high in protein. It is usually sold in cakes about 7.5 cm/3 in square and 2.5 cm/1 in thick in Oriental and health-food stores. Will keep for a few days if submerged in water and placed in the refrigerator

Water chestnuts The roots of the plant *Heleocharis tuberosa*. Also known as horse's hooves in China because of their appearance before the skin is peeled off. They are available fresh or canned. Will keep for about a month in the refrigerator in a covered jar if the water is changed every couple of days.

Wood ears Also known as cloud ears, this is a dried black fungus. Sold in plastic bags in Oriental stores, it should be soaked in cold or warm water for 20 minutes, then rinsed in fresh water before use. It has a crunchy texture and subtle flavour.

Wonton skins Thin discs of dough used to wrap savoury or sweet mixtures, then steamed or fried.

Yellow bean sauce A thick paste made from salted, fermented yellow soya beans, crushed with flour and sugar. Sold in cans or jars. It will keep in the refrigerator for months if stored in a screw-top jar.

CHINESE STOCK
This stock is used in soup-making, and to replace water in cooking.

Makes 2.5 litres/4 pints/10 cups

750 g/1½ lb chicken pieces
750 g/1½ lb pork spare ribs
3.75 litres/6 pints/15 cups cold water
3-4 pieces of ginger root, crushed
3-4 spring onions (scallions), each tied into a knot
3-4 tbsp Chinese rice wine or dry sherry

Trim excess fat from the chicken and spare ribs, and chop into large pieces. Place in a large pan with water, and add the ginger and spring onions (scallions). Bring to the boil, and skim off the scum. Reduce heat and simmer uncovered for at least 2–3 hours. Strain the stock, discarding the **chicken, pork, ginger and spring onions (scallions)**; add the wine and return to the boil, and simmer for 2–3 minutes. The stock will keep in the refrigerator for 4–5 days, or it can be frozen.

CORNFLOUR PASTE
Cornflour paste is made by mixing 1 part cornflour (cornstarch) with about 1½ parts of cold water, and stirring until smooth. The paste is used to thicken sauces.

STARTERS

CRISPY SEAWEED

••••••••••••••••••••••••••••••••••

SERVES 4

250 g/8 oz spring greens
vegetable oil for deep-frying
1½ tsp caster (superfine) sugar
1 tsp salt
30 g/1 oz/¼ cup flaked (slivered) almonds

1 Wash the spring greens thoroughly. Trim off the excess tough stalks. Place on paper towels or a dry tea towel (dish cloth) and leave to drain thoroughly.

2 Using a sharp knife, shred the spring greens finely and spread out on paper towels for about 30 minutes to dry.

3 Heat the oil in a wok or deep-fat fryer. Remove the pan from the heat and add the spring greens in batches. Return the pan to the heat and deep-fry until the greens begin to float to the surface and become translucent and crinkled. Remove the spring greens, using a perforated spoon, and drain on paper towels. Keep each batch warm.

4 Mix the sugar and salt together, sprinkle over the 'seaweed' and toss together to mix well.

5 Add the flaked (slivered) almonds to the hot oil and fry until lightly golden. Remove with a perforated spoon and drain on paper towels.

6 Serve the crispy 'seaweed' with the flaked (slivered) almonds.

TIME-SAVER

As a time-saver you can use a food processor to shred the greens finely.

Make sure you use only the best of the leaves; sort through the spring greens and discard any tough outer leaves, as these will spoil the overall taste and texture if they are included.

SPRING ROLLS

••••••••••••••••••••••••••••••••••••••

MAKES 12

5 Chinese dried mushrooms (if
   unavailable, use open-cup mushrooms)
1 large carrot
60 g/2 oz/1 cup canned bamboo shoots
2 spring onions (scallions)
60 g/2 oz Chinese leaves
2 tbsp vegetable oil
250 g/8 oz/4 cups bean-sprouts
1 tbsp soy sauce
12 spring roll wrappers
1 egg, beaten
vegetable oil for deep-frying
salt

1 Place the dried mushrooms in a small bowl and cover with warm water. Leave to soak for 20–25 minutes.

2 Drain the mushrooms and squeeze out the excess water. Remove the tough centres and slice the mushrooms thinly. Cut the carrot and bamboo shoots into very thin julienne strips. Chop the spring onions (scallions) and shred the Chinese leaves.

3 Heat the 2 tablespoons of oil in a wok or frying pan (skillet). Add the mushrooms, carrot and bamboo shoots, and stir-fry for 2 minutes. Add the spring onions (scallions), Chinese leaves, bean-sprouts and soy sauce. Season with salt and stir-fry for 2 minutes. Leave to cool.

4 Divide the mixture into 12 equal portions and place one portion on the edge of each spring roll wrapper. Fold in the sides and roll each one up, brushing the join with a little beaten egg to seal.

5 Deep-fry the spring rolls in batches in hot oil in a wok or large saucepan for 4–5 minutes, or until golden and crispy. Take care that the oil is not too hot or the spring rolls will brown on the outside before cooking on the inside. Remove and drain on paper towels. Keep each batch warm while the others are being cooked. Serve at once. Serve the crispy 'seaweed' with the flaked (slivered) almonds.

CRISPY WONTONS WITH PIQUANT DIPPING SAUCE

SERVES 4

8 wooden skewers
1 tbsp vegetable oil
1 tbsp chopped onion
1 small garlic clove, chopped
½ tsp chopped ginger root
60 g/2 oz/ ½ cup flat mushrooms, chopped
16 wonton skins (see page 376)
vegetable oil for deep-frying
salt

SAUCE:
2 tbsp vegetable oil
2 spring onions (scallions), shredded
   thinly
1 red and 1 green chilli, deseeded and
   shredded thinly
3 tbsp light soy sauce
1 tbsp vinegar
1 tbsp dry sherry
pinch of sugar

1 Heat the oil in a wok or frying pan (skillet). Add the onion, garlic and ginger root, and stir-fry for 2 minutes. Stir in the mushrooms and fry for a further 2 minutes. Season well with salt and leave to cool.

2 Place 1 teaspoon of the cooled mushroom filling in the centre of each wonton skin. Bring two opposite corners together to cover the mixture and pinch together to seal. Repeat with the remaining corners.

3 Thread 2 wontons on to each skewer. Heat enough oil in a large saucepan to deep-fry the wontons in batches until golden and crisp. Remove with a perforated spoon and drain on paper towels.

4 To make the sauce, heat the oil in a small saucepan until quite hot, i.e. until a small cube of bread dropped in the oil browns in a few seconds. Put the spring onions (scallions) and chillies in a bowl and pour the hot oil slowly on top. Then mix in the remaining ingredients and serve with the crispy wontons.

DEEP-FRIED PRAWNS (SHRIMP)

SERVES 4

250-300 g/8-10 oz raw prawns (shrimp)
   in their shells, defrosted if frozen
1 tbsp light soy sauce
1 tsp Chinese rice wine or dry sherry
2 tsp cornflour (cornstarch)
vegetable oil, for deep-frying
2-3 spring onions (scallions), to garnish

SPICY SALT AND PEPPER:
1 tbsp salt
1 tsp ground Szechuan peppercorns
1 tsp five-spice powder

1 Pull the soft legs off the prawns (shrimp), but keep the body shell on. Dry well on paper towels.

2 Place the prawns (shrimp) in a bowl with the soy sauce, wine and cornflour (cornstarch). Turn to coat and leave to marinate for about 25-30 minutes.

3 To make the Spicy Salt and Pepper, mix the salt, pepper and five-spice powder together. Place in a dry frying pan and stir-fry for about 3-4 minutes over a low heat, stirring constantly. Remove from the heat and allow to cool.

4 Heat the oil in a preheated wok until smoking, then deep-fry the prawns (shrimp) in batches until golden brown. Remove with a slotted spoon and drain on paper towels.

5 Place the spring onions (scallions) in a bowl, pour on 1 tablespoon of the hot oil and leave for 30 seconds. Serve the prawns (shrimp) garnished with the spring onions (scallions), and with Spicy Salt and Pepper as a dip.

ROASTING SPICES

The roasted spice mixture made with Szechuan peppercorns is used throughout China as a dip for deep-fried food. The peppercorns are sometimes roasted first and then ground. Dry-frying is a way of releasing the flavours of the spices. You can make the dip in advance and store in a tightly sealed jar until ready to use.

LETTUCE-WRAPPED MINCED MEAT

SERVES 4

250 g/8 oz minced pork or chicken
1 tbsp finely chopped Chinese mushrooms
1 tbsp finely chopped water chestnuts
salt and pepper
pinch of sugar
1 tsp light soy sauce
1 tsp Chinese rice wine or dry sherry
1 tsp cornflour (cornstarch)
2-3 tbsp vegetable oil
½ tsp finely chopped ginger root
1 tsp finely chopped spring onions
   (scallions)
1 tbsp finely chopped Szechuan preserved
   vegetables (optional)
1 tbsp oyster sauce
a few drops of sesame oil
8 crisp lettuce leaves, to serve

1 Mix the minced meat with the mushrooms, water chestnuts, salt, pepper, sugar, soy sauce, wine and cornflour (cornstarch).

2 Heat the oil in a preheated wok or pan and add the ginger and spring onions (scallions) followed by the meat. Stir-fry for 1 minute.

3 Add the Szechuan preserved vegetables and continue stirring for 1 more minute. Add the oyster sauce and sesame oil, blend well and cook for 1 more minute. Remove to a warmed serving dish.

4 To serve, place about 2-3 tablespoons of the mixture on a lettuce leaf and roll it up tightly to form a small parcel. Eat with your fingers.

SZECHUAN PRESERVED VEGETABLES

These pickled mustard roots are hot and salty, with a peppery flavour, and are often used to intensify the spiciness of a dish. Once opened, store in the refrigerator in a tightly sealed jar.

PORK WITH CHILLI & GARLIC

SERVES 4

500 g/1 lb leg of pork, boned but not
   skinned

SAUCE:
1 tsp finely chopped garlic
1 tsp finely chopped spring onions
   (scallions)
2 tbsp light soy sauce
1 tsp red chilli oil
½ tsp sesame oil

1 Place the pork, tied together in one piece, in a large pan, add enough cold water to cover, and bring to a rolling boil over a medium heat.

2 Skim off the scum that rises to the surface, cover and simmer gently for 25-30 minutes.

3 Leave the meat in the liquid to cool, under cover, for at least 1-2 hours. Lift out the meat with 2 slotted spoons and leave to cool completely, skin-side up, for 2-3 hours.

4 To serve, cut off the skin, leaving a very thin layer of fat on top like a ham joint. Cut the meat in small thin slices across the grain, and arrange neatly on a plate. Mix together the sauce ingredients, and pour the sauce evenly over the pork.

SZECHUAN CHILLI

One of the local Szechuan plants that contributes most to the typical character of the region's cooking is the small red fagara chilli, which is used both fresh and dried. The chilli has a delayed action on the palate; at first it seems to have little taste, but suddenly it burns the mouth with great ferocity, so it is used with much respect. It is claimed that instead of burning the taste-buds, the chilli actually makes them more sensitive to other flavours.

This is a very simple dish, but beautifully presented. Make sure you slice the meat as thinly and evenly as possible to make an elegant dish.

DEEP-FRIED SPARE RIBS

SERVES 4

8-10 finger spare ribs
1 tsp five-spice powder or 1 tbsp mild curry
    powder
1 tbsp rice wine or dry sherry
1 egg
2 tbsp flour
vegetable oil, for deep-frying
1 tsp finely shredded spring onions
    (scallions)
1 tsp finely shredded fresh green or red
    hot chillies, seeded
salt and pepper
Spicy Salt and Pepper (see page 378), to
    serve

1 Chop the ribs into 3-4 small pieces. Place the ribs in a bowl with salt, pepper, five-spice or curry powder and the wine. Turn to coat the ribs in the spices and leave them to marinate for 1-2 hours.

2 Mix the egg and flour together to make a batter.

3 Dip the ribs in the batter one by one to coat well.

4 Heat the oil in a preheated wok until smoking. Deep-fry the ribs for 4-5 minutes, then remove with a slotted spoon and drain on paper towels.

5 Reheat the oil over a high heat and deep-fry the ribs once more for another minute. Remove and drain again on paper towels.

6 Pour 1 tablespoon of the hot oil over the spring onions (scallions) and chillies and leave for 30-40 seconds. Serve the ribs with Spicy Salt and Pepper, garnished with the shredded spring onions (scallions) and chillies.

FINGER RIBS

To make finger ribs, cut the sheet of spare ribs into individual ribs down each side of the bones. These ribs are then chopped into bite-sized pieces for deep-frying.

BANG-BANG CHICKEN

SERVES 4

1 litre/1¾ pints/4 cups water
2 chicken quarters (breast half and leg)
1 cucumber, cut into matchstick shreds

SAUCE:
2 tbsp light soy sauce
1 tsp sugar
1 tbsp finely chopped spring onions
    (scallions)
1 tsp red chilli oil
¼ tsp pepper
1 tsp white sesame seeds
2 tbsp peanut butter, creamed with a little
    sesame oil

1 Bring the water to a rolling boil in a wok or a large pan. Add the chicken pieces, reduce the heat, cover and cook for 30-35 minutes.

2 Remove the chicken from the pan and immerse it in a bowl of cold water for at least 1 hour to cool it, ready for shredding.

3 Remove the chicken pieces and drain well. Dry the chicken pieces on absorbent kitchen paper (paper towels), then take the meat off the bone.

4 On a flat surface, pound the chicken with a rolling pin, then tear the meat into shreds with 2 forks. Mix with the shredded cucumber and arrange in a serving dish.

5 To serve, mix together all the sauce ingredients and pour over the chicken and cucumber.

THE CHOICEST CHICKEN

This dish is also known as Bon-bon Chicken – bon is a Chinese word for stick, so again the tenderizing technique inspires the recipe name.

Take the time to tear the chicken meat into similar-sized shreds, to make an elegant-looking dish. You can do this quite efficiently with 2 forks, although Chinese cooks would do it with their fingers.

SWEET & SOUR CUCUMBER

SERVES 4

1 cucumber
1 tsp salt
2 tsp honey
2 tbsp rice vinegar
3 tbsp chopped fresh coriander (cilantro)
2 tsp sesame oil
¼ tsp crushed red peppercorns
strips of red and yellow (bell) pepper to
    garnish

1 Peel thin strips off the cucumber along the length. This gives a pretty striped effect. Cut the cucumber in quarters lengthways and then into 2.5 cm/1 in long pieces. Place in a colander.

2 Sprinkle the salt over the cucumber and leave to rest for 30 minutes to allow the salt to draw out the excess water from the cucumber. Wash the cucumber thoroughly to remove the salt, drain and pat dry with paper towels.

3 Place the cucumber in a bowl. Combine the honey with the vinegar and pour over. Mix together and leave to marinate for 15 minutes.

4 Stir in the coriander (cilantro) and sesame oil, and place in a serving bowl.

5 Sprinkle over the crushed red peppercorns. Serve garnished with strips of red and yellow (bell) pepper.

RICE VINEGAR

Rice vinegar is a common Chinese cooking ingredient. White rice vinegar is made from rice wine, whereas red rice vinegar is made from fermented rice. Both have a distinctive flavour, but the white version tends to be used more often, as it will flavour but not colour all kinds of food. If rice vinegar is unavailable, use white wine vinegar instead.

VEGETARIAN HOT & SOUR SOUP

SERVES 4

4 Chinese dried mushrooms (if
    unavailable, use open-cup mushrooms)
125 g/4 oz firm tofu (beancurd)
60 g/2 oz/1 cup canned bamboo shoots
600 ml/1 pint/2½ cups vegetable stock or
    water
60 g/2 oz/⅓ cup peas
1 tbsp dark soy sauce
2 tbsp white wine vinegar
2 tbsp cornflour (cornstarch)
salt and pepper
sesame oil to serve

1 Place the Chinese dried mushrooms in a small bowl and cover with warm water. Leave to soak for 20–25 minutes.

2 Drain the mushrooms and squeeze out the excess water, reserving this. Remove the tough centres and cut the mushrooms into thin shreds. Shred the tofu (beancurd) and bamboo shoots.

3 Bring the stock or water to the boil in a large saucepan. Add the mushrooms, tofu (beancurd), bamboo shoots and peas. Simmer for 2 minutes.

4 Mix together the soy sauce, vinegar and cornflour (cornstarch) with 2 tablespoons of the reserved mushroom liquid. Stir into the soup with the remaining mushroom liquid. Bring to the boil and season with salt and plenty of pepper. Simmer for 2 minutes.

5 Serve in warmed bowls with a few drops of sesame oil in each.

MUSHROOMS

If you use open-cup mushrooms instead of dried mushrooms, add an extra 150 ml/ ¼ pint/ ⅔ cup vegetable stock or water to the soup, as these mushrooms do not need soaking.

WONTON SOUP

SERVES 4

Wonton skins:
1 egg
6 tbsp water
250 g/8 oz/2 cups plain (all-purpose)
 flour

FILLING:
125 g/4 oz/ ½ cup frozen chopped spinach,
 defrosted
15 g/ ½ oz/1 tbsp pine kernels (nuts),
 toasted and chopped
30 g/1 oz/ ¼ cup minced quorn (TVP)
salt

SOUP:
600 ml/1 pint/2½ cups vegetable stock
1 tbsp dry sherry
1 tbsp light soy sauce
2 spring onions (scallions), chopped

1 Beat the egg lightly in a bowl and mix with the water. Stir in the flour to form a stiff dough. Knead lightly, then cover with a damp cloth and leave to rest for 30 minutes.

2 Roll the dough out into a large sheet about 1.5 mm/ ¼ in thick. Cut out 24 x 7 cm/3 in squares. Dust each one lightly with flour. Only 12 squares are required for the soup so freeze the remainder.

3 To make the filling, squeeze out the excess water from the spinach. Mix the spinach with the pine kernels (nuts) and quorn (TVP). Season with salt.

4 Divide the mixture into 12 equal portions and place one portion in the centre of each square. Seal by bringing the opposite corners of each square together and squeezing well.

5 To make the soup, bring the stock, sherry and soy sauce to the boil, add the wontons and boil rapidly for 2–3 minutes. Add the spring onions (scallions) and serve in warmed bowls immediately.

THREE-FLAVOUR SOUP

SERVES 4

125 g/4 oz skinned, boned chicken breast
125 g/4 oz raw peeled prawns (shrimp)
salt
½ egg white, lightly beaten
2 tsp cornflour (cornstarch) paste
 (see page 376)
125 g/4 oz honey-roast ham
750 ml/1¼ pints/3 cups Chinese Stock
 (see page 376) or water
finely chopped spring onions (scallions), to
 garnish

1 Thinly slice the chicken into small shreds. If the prawns (shrimp) are large, cut each in half lengthways, otherwise leave whole. Place the chicken and prawns (shrimps) in a bowl and mix with a pinch of salt, the egg white and cornflour (cornstarch) paste until well coated.

2 Cut the ham into small thin slices roughly the same size as the chicken pieces.

3 Bring the stock or water to a rolling boil, add the chicken, the raw prawns (shrimps) and the ham. Bring the soup back to the boil, and simmer for 1 minute.

4 Adjust the seasoning and serve the soup hot, garnished with the spring onions (scallions).

COOKING TIPS

Soups such as this are improved enormously in flavour if you use a well-flavoured stock. Either use a stock cube, or find time to make Chinese Stock – see the recipe on page 376. Better still, make double quantities and freeze some for future use.

 Fresh, uncooked prawns (shrimp) impart the best flavour. If these are not available, you can use ready-cooked prawns (shrimp). They must be added at the last moment before serving to prevent them becoming tough and over-cooked.

SWEETCORN & LENTIL SOUP

SERVES 4

30 g/1 oz/2 tbsp green lentils
1 litre/1¾ pints/4 cups vegetable stock
1cm/½ in piece ginger root, chopped finely
2 tsp soy sauce
1 tsp sugar
1 tbsp cornflour (cornstarch)
3 tbsp dry sherry
325 g/11 oz can of sweetcorn
1 egg white
1 tsp sesame oil
salt and pepper

TO GARNISH:
strips spring onion (scallion)
strips red chilli

1 Wash the lentils in a sieve (strainer). Place in a saucepan with the stock, ginger root, soy sauce and sugar. Bring to the boil and boil rapidly, uncovered, for 10 minutes. Skim off any froth on the surface. Reduce the heat, cover and simmer for 15 minutes.

2 Mix the cornflour (cornstarch) with the sherry in a small bowl. Add the sweetcorn with the liquid from the can and cornflour (cornstarch) mix to the saucepan. Simmer for 2 minutes.

3 Whisk the egg white lightly with the sesame oil. Pour the egg mixture into the soup in a thin stream, remove from the heat and stir. The egg white will form white strands.

4 Season to taste. Pour into 4 warmed soup bowls and garnish with strips of spring onion (scallion) and chilli before serving.

USING CANNED LENTILS

As a time-saver use a 425 g/14 oz can of green lentils instead of dried ones. Place the lentils and sweetcorn together in a large saucepan with the stock and flavourings, bring to the boil and simmer for 2 minutes, then continue the recipe from step 2.

SWEETCORN & CRAB MEAT SOUP

SERVES 4

125 g/4 oz crab meat
¼ tsp finely chopped ginger root
2 egg whites
2 tbsp milk
1 tbsp cornflour (cornstarch) paste (see page 376)
600 ml/1 pint/2 ½ cups Chinese Stock (see page 376)
1 x 250 g/8 oz can American-style creamed sweetcorn
salt and pepper
finely chopped spring onions (scallions), to garnish

1 Flake the crab meat (or coarsely chop the chicken breast) and mix with the ginger.

2 Beat the egg whites until frothy, add the milk and cornflour (cornstarch) paste and beat again until smooth. Blend in the crab or chicken.

3 In a wok or large frying pan (skillet), bring the stock to the boil, add the creamed sweetcorn and bring back to the boil.

4 Stir in the crab meat or chicken pieces and egg-white mixture, adjust the seasoning and stir gently until the mixture is well blended. Serve hot, garnished with chopped spring onions (scallions).

CHOOSING CRAB

Always obtain the freshest possible crab; fresh is best, though frozen or canned will work for this recipe.

CREAMED SWEETCORN

Be sure to use proper creamed sweetcorn for this soup, as it has quite a different texture from sweetcorn kernels. Creamed sweetcorn has a thick, slightly mushy consistency, makng a thick, creamy soup.

SEAFOOD & TOFU SOUP

SERVES 4

250 g/8 oz seafood: peeled prawns
(shrimp), squid, scallops, etc. defrosted
if frozen
½ egg white, lightly beaten
1 tbsp cornflour (cornstarch) paste (see
page 376)
1 cake tofu (bean curd)
750 ml/1¼ pints/3 cups Chinese Stock (see
page 376)
1 tbsp light soy sauce
salt and pepper
fresh coriander leaves, to garnish
(optional)

1 Small prawns (shrimp) can be left
whole; larger ones should be cut
into smaller pieces; cut the squid and
scallops into small pieces.

2 If raw, mix the prawns (shrimp) and
scallops with the egg white and
cornflour (cornstarch) paste to prevent
them from becoming tough when they
are cooked.

3 Cut the cake of tofu into about
24 small cubes.

4 Bring the stock to a rolling boil. Add
the tofu and soy sauce, bring back
to the boil and simmer for 1 minute.

5 Stir in the seafood, raw pieces first,
pre-cooked ones last. Bring back to
boil and simmer for just 1 minute. Adjust
the seasoning and serve garnished with
coriander leaves, if liked.

LETTUCE & TOFU (BEANCURD) SOUP

SERVES 4

200 g/7 oz tofu (beancurd)
2 tbsp vegetable oil
1 carrot, sliced thinly
1 cm/ ½ in piece ginger root, cut into thin
shreds
3 spring onions (scallions), sliced
diagonally
1.25 litres/2 pints/5 cups vegetable stock
2 tbsp soy sauce
2 tbsp dry sherry
1 tsp sugar
125 g/4 oz/1½ cups cos (romaine) lettuce,
shredded
salt and pepper

1 Cut the tofu (beancurd) into small
cubes. Heat the oil in a wok or large
saucepan, add the tofu (beancurd) and
stir-fry until browned. Remove with a
perforated spoon and drain on paper
towels.

2 Add the carrot, ginger root and
spring onions (scallions) to the wok
or saucepan and stir-fry for 2 minutes.

3 Add the stock, soy sauce, sherry and
sugar. Bring to the boil and simmer
for 1 minute.

4 Add the lettuce and stir until it has
just wilted.

5 Return the tofu (beancurd) to the
pan to reheat. Season with salt and
pepper and serve in warmed bowls.

DECORATIVE CARROTS

For a prettier effect, score grooves
along the length of the carrot with a
sharp knife before slicing. This will
create a flower effect as the carrot is
cut into rounds. You could also try
slicing the carrot on the diagonal to
make longer slices. Try garnishing the
soup with carrot curls – very fine strips
of carrot that have been placed in iced
water to make them curl up.

FISH DISHES

PORK & SZECHUAN VEGETABLE
••

SERVES 4

250 g/8 oz pork fillet
2 tsp cornflour (cornstarch) paste
  (see page 376)
125 g/4 oz Szechuan preserved vegetable
750 ml/1¼ pints/3 cups Chinese stock
  (see page 376) or water
salt and pepper
a few drops of sesame oil (optional)
2-3 spring onions (scallions), sliced, to
  garnish

1 Cut the pork across the grain into
thin shreds and mix with the
cornflour (cornstarch) paste.

2 Wash and rinse the Szechuan
preserved vegetable, then cut into
thin shreds the same size as the pork.

3 Bring the stock or water to a rolling
boil, add the pork and stir to
separate the shreds. Return to the boil.

4 Add the Szechuan preserved
vegetable and bring back to the boil
once more. Adjust the seasoning and
sprinkle with sesame oil. Serve hot,
garnished with spring onions (scallions).

SZECHUAN PRESERVED VEGETABLE

The Chinese are fond of pickles, and
there are many varieties of pickled
vegetables. In the Szechuan region in
particular, preserved vegetables are
important because the region is over
1,600 km (1,000 miles) from the coast.
One of the most popular is Szechuan
preserved vegetable, a speciality of the
province, available in cans from
specialist Chinese supermarkets. It is
actually mustard green root, pickled in
salt and chillies. It gives a crunchy,
spicy taste to dishes. Rinse in cold
water before use. Once opened the
vegetable should be stored in a tightly
sealed jar and kept in the refrigerator.

SWEET & SOUR PRAWNS (SHRIMP)
••

SERVES 4

175-250 g/6-8 oz peeled raw tiger prawns
pinch of salt
1 tsp egg white
1 tsp cornflour (cornstarch) paste (see
  page 376)
300 ml/ ½ pint/1¼ cups vegetable oil

SAUCE:
1 tbsp vegetable oil
½ small green (bell) pepper, cored, seeded
  and thinly sliced
½ small carrot, thinly sliced
125 g/4 oz canned water chestnuts,
  drained and sliced
½ tsp salt
1 tbsp light soy sauce
2 tbsp sugar
3 tbsp rice or sherry vinegar
1 tsp rice wine or dry sherry
1 tbsp tomato sauce
½ tsp chilli sauce
3-4 tbsp Chinese Stock (see page 376) or
  water
2 tsp cornflour (cornstarch) paste (see
  page 376)
a few drops of sesame oil

1 Mix the prawns (shrimp) with the
salt, egg white and cornflour
(cornstarch) paste.

2 Heat the oil in a preheated wok and
stir-fry the prawns (shrimp) for
30-40 seconds only. Remove and drain
on paper towels.

3 Pour off the oil and wipe the wok
clean with paper towels. To make
the sauce, first heat the tablespoon of oil.
Add the vegetables and stir-fry for about
1 minute, then add the seasonings with
the stock or water and bring to the boil.

4 Add the prawns (shrimp) and stir
until blended well. Thicken the
sauce with the cornflour (cornstarch)
paste and stir until smooth. Sprinkle with
sesame oil and serve hot.

SZECHUAN PRAWNS (SHRIMP)

••

SERVES 4

250-300 g/8-10 oz raw tiger prawns
(shrimp)
pinch of salt
½ egg white, lightly beaten
1 tsp cornflour (cornstarch) paste (see
page 376)
600 ml/1pint/2½ cups vegetable oil
fresh coriander leaves, to garnish

SAUCE:
1 tsp finely chopped ginger root
2 spring onions (scallions), finely chopped
1 garlic clove, finely chopped
3-4 small dried red chillies, seeded and
chopped
1 tbsp light soy sauce
1 tsp rice wine or dry sherry
1 tbsp tomato purée (paste)
1 tbsp oyster sauce
2-3 tbsp Chinese Stock (see page 376) or
water
a few drops of sesame oil

1 Peel the raw prawns (shrimp), then mix with the salt, egg white and cornflour (cornstarch) paste until well coated.

2 Heat the oil in a preheated wok until it is smoking, then deep-fry the prawns (shrimp) in hot oil for about 1 minute. Remove with a slotted spoon and drain on paper towels.

3 Pour off the oil, leaving about 1 tablespoon in the wok. Add all the ingredients for the sauce, bring to the boil and stir until smooth and well blended.

4 Add the prawns (shrimp) to the sauce and stir until blended well. Serve garnished with coriander leaves.

CHILLIES

In Szechuan dishes chillies are often left unseeded, giving an extremely hot flavour to dishes. If you dislike very hot food, make sure the dried chillies are carefully seeded before use.

FRIED SQUID FLOWERS

••

SERVES 4

350-400 g/12-14 oz prepared and cleaned
squid (see below)
1 medium green (bell) pepper, cored and
seeded
3-4 tbsp vegetable oil
1 garlic clove, finely chopped
¼ tsp finely chopped ginger root
2 tsp finely chopped spring onions
(scallions)
½ tsp salt
2 tbsp crushed black bean sauce
1 tsp Chinese rice wine or dry sherry
a few drops of sesame oil

1 If ready-prepared squid is not available, prepare as instructed below right.

2 Open up the squid and score the inside of the flesh in a criss-cross pattern.

3 Cut the squid into pieces about the size of an oblong postage stamp. Blanch in a bowl of boiling water for a few seconds. Remove and drain; dry well on paper towels.

4 Cut the (bell) pepper into small triangular pieces. Heat the oil in a preheated wok and stir-fry the (bell) pepper for about 1 minute. Add the garlic, ginger, spring onion (scallion), salt and squid. Continue stirring for another minute.

5 Finally add the black bean sauce and wine, and blend well. Serve hot, sprinkled with sesame oil.

TO CLEAN THE SQUID

Clean the squid by first cutting off the head. Cut off the tentacles and reserve. Remove the small soft bone at the base of the tentacles and the transparant backbone, as well as the ink bag. Peel off the thin skin, then wash and dry well.

BAKED CRAB WITH GINGER

SERVES 4

*1 large or 2 medium crabs, weighing
    about 750 g/1½ lb in total*
2 tbsp Chinese rice wine or dry sherry
1 egg, lightly beaten
1 tbsp cornflour (cornstarch)
3-4 tbsp vegetable oil
1 tbsp finely chopped ginger root
*3-4 spring onions (scallions), cut into
    sections*
2 tbsp light soy sauce
1 tsp sugar
*about 75 ml/5 tbsp/ ⅓ cup Chinese Stock
    (see page 376) or water*
½ tsp sesame oil
coriander leaves, to garnish

1 Cut the crab in half from the underbelly. Break off the claws and crack
them with the back of the cleaver or a
large kitchen knife.

2 Discard the legs and crack the shell,
breaking it into several pieces.
Discard the feathery gills and the stomach
sac. Place in a bowl with the wine, egg
and cornflour (cornstarch) and leave to
marinate for 10-15 minutes.

3 Heat the oil in a preheated wok and
stir-fry the crab with ginger and
spring onions (scallions) for 2-3 minutes.

4 Add the soy sauce, sugar and stock
or water, blend well and bring to the
boil. Cover and cook for 3-4 minutes,
then remove the cover, sprinkle with
sesame oil and serve.

TECHNIQUES

The term "baked" may be used on
Chinese restaurant menus to describe
dishes such as this one, which are
actually cooked in a wok. "Pot-
roasted" may be a more accurate way
to describe this cooking technique.

FISH WITH BLACK BEAN SAUCE

SERVES 4-6

*1 sea bass, trout or turbot, weighing about
    675g/1½ lb, cleaned*
1 tsp salt
1 tbsp sesame oil
*2-3 spring onions (scallions), cut in half
    lengthways*
1 tbsp light soy sauce
1 tbsp Chinese rice wine or dry sherry
1 tbsp finely shredded ginger root
1 tbsp oil
2 tbsp crushed black bean sauce
2 finely shredded spring onions (scallions)
*fresh coriander leaves, to garnish
    (optional)*
lemon slices, to garnish

1 Score both sides of the fish with
diagonal cuts at 2.5cm (1in) intervals.
Rub both the inside and outside of the
fish with salt and sesame oil.

2 Place the fish on top of the spring
onions (scallions) on a heat-proof
platter. Blend the soy sauce and wine
with the ginger shreds and pour evenly all
over the fish.

3 Place the fish on the platter in a very
hot steamer (or inside a wok on a
rack), cover and steam vigorously for 12-
15 minutes.

4 Heat the oil until hot, then blend in
the black bean sauce. Remove the
fish from the steamer and place on a
serving dish. Pour the hot black bean
sauce over the whole length of the fish
and place the shredded spring onions
(scallions) on top. Serve garnished with
coriander leaves and lemon slices.

FISH STEAKS

If using fish steaks, rub them with the
salt and sesame oil, but do not score
with a knife. The fish may require less
cooking, depending on the thickness
of the steaks – test for doneness with
a skewer after about 8 minutes.

BRAISED FISH FILLETS

••

SERVES 4

3-4 small Chinese dried mushrooms
300-350 g/10-12 oz fish fillets
1 tsp salt
½ egg white, lightly beaten
1 tsp cornflour (cornstarch) paste (see
* page 376)*
600 ml/1 pint/2½ cups vegetable oil
1 tsp finely chopped ginger root
2 spring onions (scallions), finely chopped
1 garlic clove, finely chopped
½ small green (bell) pepper, cored, seeded
* and cut into small cubes*
½ small carrot, thinly sliced
60 g/2 oz canned sliced bamboo shoots,
* rinsed and drained*
½ tsp sugar
1 tbsp light soy sauce
1 tsp rice wine or dry sherry
1 tbsp chilli bean sauce
2-3 tbsp Chinese Stock (see page 376) or
* water*
a few drops of sesame oil

1 Soak the Chinese mushrooms in
  warm water for 30 minutes, then
drain on paper towels, reserving the
soaking water for stock or soup. Squeeze
the mushrooms to extract all the moisture,
cut off and discard any hard stems and
slice thinly.

2 Cut the fish into bite-sized pieces,
  then place in a shallow dish and mix
with a pinch of salt, the egg white and
cornflour (cornstarch) paste, turning the
fish to coat well.

3 Heat the oil and deep-fry the fish
  pieces for about 1 minute. Remove
with a slotted spoon and drain on paper
towels.

4 Pour off the oil, leaving about
  1 tablespoon in the wok. Add the
ginger, spring onions (scallions) and garlic
to flavour the oil for a few seconds, then
add the vegetables and stir-fry for about
1 minute.

5 Add the salt, sugar, soy sauce, wine,
  chilli bean sauce and stock or water
and bring to the boil. Add the fish pieces,
stir to coat well with the sauce, and braise
for another minute. Sprinkle with sesame
oil and serve immediately.

FISH IN SZECHUAN HOT SAUCE

••

SERVES 4

1 carp, bream, sea bass, trout, grouper or
* grey mullet, about 750g/1½ lb, gutted*
1 tbsp light soy sauce
1 tbsp Chinese rice wine or dry sherry
vegetable oil, for deep-frying
flat-leaf parsley or coriander sprigs, to
* garnish*

SAUCE:
2 garlic cloves, finely chopped
2-3 spring onions (scallions), finely
* chopped*
1 tsp finely chopped ginger root
2 tbsp chilli bean sauce
1 tbsp tomato purée (paste)
2 tsp sugar
1 tbsp rice vinegar
125 ml/4 fl oz/ ½ cup Chinese Stock
* (see page 376) or water*
1 tbsp cornflour (cornstarch) paste
* (see page 376)*
½ tsp sesame oil

1 Wash the fish and dry well on paper
  towels. Score both sides of the fish
to the bone with a sharp knife, making
diagonal cuts at intervals of about
2.5 cm/1 in. Rub the fish with the soy
sauce and wine on both sides, then leave
on a plate in the refrigerator to marinate
for 10-15 minutes.

2 Heat the oil in a preheated wok until
  smoking. Deep-fry the fish in the hot
oil for about 3-4 minutes on both sides, or
until golden brown.

3 Pour off the oil, leaving about
  1 tablespoon in the wok. Push the
fish to one side of the wok and add the
garlic, white parts of the spring onions
(scallions), ginger, chilli bean sauce,
tomato purée (paste), sugar, vinegar and
stock. Bring to the boil and braise the fish
in the sauce for 4-5 minutes, turning it
over once.

4 Add the green parts of the spring
  onions (scallions) and stir in the
cornflour (cornstarch) paste to thicken the
sauce. Sprinkle with sesame oil and serve
immediately, garnished with parsley or
coriander.

MEAT & POULTRY

DUCK WITH PINEAPPLE

SERVES 4

125-175 g/4-6 oz cooked duck meat
3 tbsp vegetable oil
1 small onion, thinly shredded
2-3 slices ginger root, thinly shredded
1 spring onion (scallion), thinly shredded
1 small carrot, thinly shredded
125 g/4 oz canned pineapple, cut into small slices
½ tsp salt
1 tbsp red rice vinegar
2 tbsp syrup from the pineapple
1 tbsp cornflour (cornstarch) paste (see page 376)
black bean sauce, to serve (optional)

1 Cut the cooked duck meat into thin strips.

2 Heat the oil in a preheated wok, add the shredded onion and stir-fry until the shreds are opaque. Add the ginger, spring onion (scallion) and carrot shreds. Stir-fry for about 1 minute.

3 Add the duck shreds and pineapple to the wok together with the salt, rice vinegar and the pineapple syrup. Stir until the mixture is blended well.

4 Add the cornflour (cornstarch) paste and stir for 1–2 minutes until the sauce has thickened. Serve hot.

CANNED PINEAPPLE

Fortunately, most canned fruit is now available preserved in juice rather than syrup. The sugared syrup once used exclusively for this purpose was cloyingly sweet. To prepare this dish, be sure to choose pineapple in juice rather than syrup, so that the sauce is pleasantly tangy rather than overwhelmingly sugary.

KUNG PO CHICKEN WITH CASHEW

SERVES 4

250-300 g/8-10 oz chicken meat, boned and skinned
¼ tsp salt
⅓ egg white
1 tsp cornflour (cornstarch) paste (see page 376)
1 medium green (bell) pepper, cored and seeded
4 tbsp vegetable oil
1 spring onion (scallion), cut into short sections
a few small slices of ginger root
4-5 small dried red chillies, soaked, seeded and shredded
2 tbsp crushed yellow bean sauce
1 tsp rice wine or dry sherry
125 g/4 oz roasted cashew nuts
a few drops of sesame oil
boiled rice, to serve

1 Cut the chicken into small cubes about the size of sugar lumps. Place the chicken in a small bowl and mix with a pinch of salt, the egg white and the cornflour (cornstarch) paste, in that order.

2 Cut the green (bell) pepper into cubes or triangles about the same size as the chicken pieces.

3 Heat the oil in a preheated wok, add the chicken cubes and stir-fry for about 1 minute, or until the colour changes. Remove with a slotted spoon and keep warm.

4 Add the spring onion (scallion), ginger, chillies and green (bell) pepper. Stir-fry for about 1 minute, then add the chicken with the yellow bean sauce and wine. Blend well and stir-fry for another minute. Finally stir in the cashew nuts and sesame oil. Serve hot.

5 Add the cornflour (cornstarch) paste and stir for 1-2 minutes until the sauce has thickened. Serve hot.

VARIATIONS

Any nuts can be used in place of the cashew nuts. The important feature is their crunchy texture.

AROMATIC & CRISPY DUCK

SERVES 4

2 large duckling quarters
1 tsp salt
3-4 pieces star anise
1 tsp Szechuan red peppercorns
1 tsp cloves
2 cinnamon sticks, broken into pieces
2-3 spring onions (scallions), cut into
*   short sections*
4-5 small slices ginger root
3-4 tbsp rice wine or dry sherry
vegetable oil, for deep-frying

TO SERVE:
12 ready-made pancakes or 12 crisp
*   lettuce leaves*
hoi-sin or plum sauce
¼ cucumber, thinly shredded
3-4 spring onions (scallions), thinly
*   shredded*

1 Rub the duck pieces with the salt
   and arrange the star anise,
peppercorns, cloves and cinnamon on
top. Sprinkle with the spring onions
(scallions), ginger and wine and leave to
marinate for at least 3-4 hours.

2 Arrange the duck pieces (with the
   marinade spices) on a plate that will
fit inside a bamboo steamer. Pour
some hot water into a wok,
place the bamboo steamer
in the wok, sitting on a
trivet. Put in the duck
and cover with the
bamboo lid. Steam
the duck pieces
(with the marinade)
over high heat for
at least 2-3 hours,
until tender and cooked
through. Top up the hot
water from time to time as required.

3 Remove the duck and leave to cool
   for at least 4-5 hours – this is very
important, for unless the duck is cold and
dry, it will not be crispy.

4 Pour off the water and wipe the
   wok dry. Pour in the oil and heat
until smoking. Deep-fry the duck pieces,
skin-side down, for 4-5 minutes or until
crisp and brown. Remove and drain on
paper towels.

5 To serve, scrape the meat off the
   bone, place about 1 teaspoon of
hoi-sin or plum sauce on the centre of a
pancake (or lettuce leaf), add a few
pieces of cucumber and spring onion
(scallion) with a portion of the duck meat.
Wrap up to form a small parcel and eat
with your fingers. Provide plenty of paper
napkins for your guests.

CHICKEN FOO-YUNG

SERVES 4

175 g/6 oz chicken breast fillet, skinned
½ tsp salt
pepper
1 tsp rice wine or dry sherry
1 tbsp cornflour (cornstarch)
3 eggs, beaten
½ tsp finely chopped spring onions
  (scallions)
3 tbsp vegetable oil
125 g/4 oz green peas
1 tsp light soy sauce
salt
few drops of sesame oil

1 Cut the chicken across the grain into very small, paper-thin slices, using the cleaver. Place the slices in a shallow dish, add the ½ teaspoon salt, pepper, wine and cornflour (cornstarch) and turn in the mixture until they are well coated.

2 Beat the eggs in a small bowl with a pinch of salt and the spring onions (scallions).

3 Heat oil in a preheated wok, add chicken slices and stir-fry for about 1 minute, making sure that the slices are kept separated. Pour the beaten eggs over the chicken, and lightly scramble until set. Do not stir too vigorously, or the mixture will break up in the oil. Stir the oil from the bottom of the wok so that the foo-yung rises to the surface.

4 Add the peas, salt and soy sauce and blend well. Sprinkle with sesame oil and serve.

VARIATION

If available, chicken goujons can be used for this dish: these are small, delicate strips of chicken which require no further cutting and are very tender.

LEMON CHICKEN

SERVES 4

350 g/12 oz chicken breast fillets, skinned
1 tbsp rice wine or dry sherry
1 egg, beaten
4 tbsp plain flour blended with 2 tbsp
  water
vegetable oil, for deep-frying
readymade lemon sauce, or homemade
  sauce (see below)
salt and pepper
slices of fresh lemon, to garnish

1 Cut the chicken into thin slices and place in a shallow dish with wine, salt and pepper. Leave to marinate for 25-30 minutes.

2 Make a batter with the egg and flour paste. Place the chicken slices in the batter and turn to coat well.

3 Heat the oil in a wok or deep-fryer. Deep-fry the chicken slices until golden brown, remove with a slotted spoon and drain on paper towels. Cut the chicken slices into bite-sized pieces.

4 Heat about 1 tablespoon of oil in a wok or pan. Stir in the lemon sauce until well blended and pour evenly over the chicken. Garnish with lemon slices and serve.

LEMON SAUCE:
1 tbsp vegetable oil
250 ml/8 fl oz/1 cup Chinese Stock (see
  page 376)
1 tbsp caster sugar
1 tbsp lemon juice
1 tbsp cornflour (cornstarch)
1 tsp salt
1 tsp lemon rind

1 Heat the oil in a wok until hot, reduce the heat and add all the other ingredients. Blend well, then bring to the boil and stir until smooth.

SZECHUAN CHILLI CHICKEN

SERVES 4

500 g/1 lb chicken thighs
¼ tsp pepper
1 tbsp sugar
2 tsp light soy sauce
1 tsp dark soy sauce
1 tbsp rice wine or dry sherry
2 tsp cornflour (cornstarch)
2-3 tbsp vegetable oil
1-2 garlic cloves, crushed
2 spring onions (scallions), cut into short
  sections, with the green and white parts
  separated
4-6 small dried red chillies, soaked and
  seeded
2 tbsp crushed yellow bean sauce
about 150 ml/ ¼ pint/ ⅔ cup Chinese Stock
  (see page 376) or water

1 Cut or chop the chicken thighs into bite-sized pieces and marinate with the pepper, sugar, soy sauce, wine and cornflour (cornstarch) for 25-30 minutes.

2 Heat the oil in a pre-heated wok, add the chicken pieces and stir-fry until lightly brown for about 1-2 minutes. Remove the chicken pieces with a slotted spoon, remove to a warm dish and reserve.

3 Add the garlic, the white parts of the spring onions (scallions), the chillies and yellow bean sauce to the wok and stir-fry for about 30 seconds, blending well.

4 Return the chicken pieces to the wok, stirring constantly for about 1-2 minutes, then add the stock or water, bring to the boil and cover. Braise over medium heat for 5-6 minutes, stirring once or twice. Garnish with the green parts of the spring onions (scallions) and serve immediately.

CHILLIES

One of the striking features of Szechuan cooking is the quantity of chillies used. Food here is much hotter than elsewhere in China – people tend to keep a string of dry chillies hanging from the eaves of their houses.

CHICKEN OR PORK CHOW MEIN

SERVES 4

250 g/8 oz egg noodles
4-5 tbsp vegetable oil
125g/4 oz French beans
250 g/8 oz chicken breast meat, or pork
  fillet, cooked
2 tbsp light soy sauce
1 tsp salt
½ tsp sugar
1 tbsp Chinese rice wine or dry sherry
2 spring onions (scallions), finely
  shredded
a few drops of sesame oil
chilli sauce, to serve (optional)

1 Cook the noodles in boiling water according to the instructions on the packet, then drain and rinse under cold water. Drain again then toss with 1 tablespoon of the oil.

2 Slice the meat into thin shreds and top and tail the beans.

3 Heat 3 tablespoons of oil in a preheated wok until hot, add the noodles and stir-fry for 2-3 minutes with 1 tablespoon soy sauce, then remove to a serving dish. Keep warm.

4 Heat the remaining oil and stir-fry the beans and meat for about 2 minutes. Add the salt, sugar, wine, the remaining soy sauce and about half the spring onions (scallions) to the wok.

5 Blend the meat mixture well and add a little stock if necessary, then pour on top of the noodles, and sprinkle with sesame oil and the remaining spring onions (scallions). Serve hot or cold with or without chilli sauce.

CHOW MEIN

Chow Mein literally means "stir-fried noodles" and is highly popular in the West as well as in China. Almost any ingredient can be added, such as fish, meat, poultry or vegetables. It is very popular for lunch and makes a tasty salad served cold.

CHICKEN WITH MUSHROOMS

SERVES 4

*300-350 g/10-12 oz chicken, boned and
    skinned*
½ tsp sugar
1 tbsp light soy sauce
1 tsp rice wine or dry sherry
2 tsp cornflour (cornstarch)
*4-6 dried Chinese mushrooms, soaked in
    warm water*
1 tbsp finely shredded ginger root
salt and pepper
a few drops of sesame oil
coriander leaves, to garnish

1 Cut the chicken into small bite-sized
pieces and place in a bowl. Add the
sugar, soy sauce, wine and cornflour
(cornstarch) and leave to marinate for
25-30 minutes.

2 Drain the mushrooms and dry on
paper towels. Slice the mushrooms
into thin shreds, discarding any hard
pieces of stem.

3 Place the chicken pieces on a heatproof dish that will fit inside a
bamboo steamer. Arrange the mushroom
and ginger shreds on top of the chicken
and sprinkle with salt, pepper and sesame
oil.

4 Place the dish on the rack inside a
hot steamer or on a rack in a wok
filled with hot water and steam over high
heat for 20 minutes. Serve hot, garnished
with coriander leaves.

CHINESE MUSHROOMS

Chinese mushrooms come in many
varieties: Shiitake are the best, and the
two terms are often used
synonymously. These fragrant
mushrooms are most readily available
at Oriental food stores and
supermarkets but are also seasonally
available.

Do not throw away the soaking
water from the dried Chinese
mushrooms. It is very useful, as it can
be added to soups and stocks to give
extra flavour.

STIR-FRIED PORK WITH VEGETABLES

SERVES 4

250 g/8 oz pork fillet, sliced
1 tsp sugar
1 tbsp light soy sauce
1 tsp rice wine or dry sherry
*1 tsp cornflour (cornstarch) paste (see
page 376)*
1 small carrot
*1 small green (bell) pepper, cored and
    seeded*
about 175 g/6 oz Chinese leaves
4 tbsp vegetable oil
*1 spring onion (scallion), cut into short
    sections*
a few small slices of peeled ginger root
1 tsp salt
*2-3 tbsp Chinese Stock (see page 376) or
    water*
a few drops of sesame oil

1 Thinly slice the pork fillet into small
pieces and place in a shallow dish.
Add half the sugar and the soy sauce, the
wine and cornflour (cornstarch) paste,
and leave in the refrigerator to marinate
for 10-15 minutes.

2 Cut the carrot, green (bell) pepper
and Chinese leaves into thin slices
roughly the same length and width as the
pork pieces.

3 Heat the oil in a preheated wok and
stir-fry the pork for about 1 minute
to seal in the flavour. Remove with a
slotted spoon and keep warm.

4 Add the carrot, (bell) pepper,
Chinese leaves, spring onion
(scallion) and ginger and stir-fry for about
2 minutes.

5 Add the salt and remaining sugar,
followed by the pork and remaining
soy sauce, and the stock or water. Blend
well and stir for another 1-2 minutes until
hot. Sprinkle with the sesame oil and
serve.

CHICKEN WITH (BELL) PEPPERS

•••

SERVES 4

300 g/10 oz boned, skinned chicken
* breast*
1 tsp salt
½ egg white
2 tsp cornflour (cornstarch) paste (see
* page 376)*
1 medium green (bell) pepper, cored and
* seeded*
300 ml/ ½ pint/1¼ cups vegetable oil
1 spring onion (scallion), finely shredded
a few strips of ginger root, thinly shredded
1-2 red chillies, seeded and thinly
* shredded*
½ tsp sugar
1 tbsp rice wine or dry sherry
a few drops of sesame oil

1 Cut the chicken breast into strips,
  then mix in a bowl with a pinch of
the salt, the egg white and cornflour
(cornstarch), in that order.

2 Cut the green (bell) pepper into thin
  shreds the same size and length as
the chicken strips.

3 Heat the oil in a preheated wok, and
  deep-fry the chicken strips in
batches for about 1 minute, or until the
colour of the chicken changes. Remove
the chicken strips with a slotted spoon
and keep warm.

4 Pour off the excess oil from the
  wok, leaving about 1 tablespoon.
Add the spring onion (scallion), ginger,
chillies and green (bell) pepper. Stir-fry
for about 1 minute, then return the
chicken to the wok together with the
remaining salt, the sugar and wine. Stir-fry
for another minute, sprinkle with sesame
oil and serve.

RICE WINE

Rice wine is used in China for both
cooking and drinking. The best variety
is called Shao Hsing or Shaoxing, and
comes from the south-east of China.
Rice wine is more powerful than wines
in the West – about 16° proof – and
sherry is the best substitute as a
cooking ingredient.

FISH-FLAVOURED SHREDDED PORK

•••

SERVES 4

about 2 tbsp dried wood ears
250-300 g/8-10 oz pork fillet
1 tsp salt
2 tsp cornflour (cornstarch) paste
* (see page 376)*
3 tbsp vegetable oil
1 garlic clove, finely chopped
½ tsp finely chopped ginger root
2 spring onions (scallions), finely chopped,
* with the white and green parts*
* separated*
2 celery stalks, thinly sliced
½ tsp sugar
1 tbsp light soy sauce
1 tbsp chilli bean sauce
2 tsp rice vinegar
1 tsp rice wine or dry sherry
a few drops of sesame oil

1 Soak the wood ears in warm water
  for about 20 minutes, then rinse in
cold water until the water is clear. Drain
well, then cut into thin shreds.

2 Cut the pork into thin shreds, then
  mix in a bowl with a pinch of salt
and about half the cornflour (cornstarch)
paste until well coated.

3 Heat 1 tablespoon of oil in a
  preheated wok. Add the pork strips
and stir-fry for about 1 minute, or until
the colour changes, then remove with a
slotted spoon.

4 Add the remaining oil to the wok
  and heat. Add the garlic, ginger, the
white parts of the spring onions
(scallions), the wood ears and celery. Stir-
fry for about 1 minute, then return the
pork strips together with the salt, sugar,
soy sauce, chili bean sauce, vinegar and
wine. Blend well and continue stirring for
another minute.

5 Finally add the green parts of the
  spring onions (scallions) and blend
in the remaining cornflour (cornstarch)
paste and sesame oil. Stir until the sauce
has thickened and serve hot.

TWICE-COOKED PORK

SERVES 4

250-300 g/8-10 oz shoulder or leg of pork, in one piece
1 small green (bell) pepper, cored and seeded
1 small red (bell) pepper, cored and seeded
125 g/4 oz canned sliced bamboo shoots, rinsed and drained
3 tbsp vegetable oil
1 spring onion (scallion), cut into short sections
1 tsp salt
½ tsp sugar
1 tbsp light soy sauce
1 tsp chilli bean sauce or freshly minced chilli
1 tsp rice wine or dry sherry
a few drops of sesame oil

1 Immerse the pork in a pot of boiling water to cover. Return to the boil and skim the surface. Reduce the heat, cover and simmer for 15-20 minutes. Turn off the heat and leave the pork in the water to cool for at least 2-3 hours.

2 Remove the pork from the water and drain well. Trim off any excess fat, then cut into small, thin slices. Cut the green and red (bell) peppers into pieces about the same size as the pork and the sliced bamboo shoots.

3 Heat the oil in a preheated wok and add the vegetables together with the spring onion (scallion). Stir-fry for about 1 minute.

4 Add the pork, followed by the salt, sugar, soy sauce, chilli bean sauce and wine. Blend well, continue stirring for another minute, then sprinkle with sesame oil and serve.

PREPARING THE MEAT

For ease of handling, buy a boned piece of meat, and roll into a compact shape. Tie securely with string before placing in the boiling water.

SWEET & SOUR PORK

SERVES 4

250-300 g/8-10 oz lean pork
2 tsp brandy or whisky
vegetable oil, for deep-frying
1 egg, beaten
2 tbsp plain flour
salt and pepper

SAUCE:
1 tbsp vegetable oil
1 small onion, diced
1 small carrot, diced
½ small green (bell) pepper, cored, seeded and diced
1 tbsp light soy sauce
3 tbsp sugar
3 tbsp wine vinegar
1 tbsp tomato purée (paste)
about 3-4 tbsp Chinese Stock (see page 376) or water
1 tbsp cornflour (cornstarch) paste (see page 376)

1 Cut the pork into small bite-sized cubes. Place in a dish with the salt, pepper and brandy and leave to marinate for 15-20 minutes.

2 Heat the oil in a wok or deep-fryer. Place the pork cubes in a bowl with the beaten egg and turn to coat. Sprinkle on the flour and turn the pork cubes until they are well coated.

3 Deep-fry the pork cubes in batches for about 3-4 minutes, stirring gently to separate the pieces. Remove with a slotted spoon or strainer and drain on paper towels. Reheat the oil until hot, and return the meat to the wok for another minute or so or until golden brown. Remove with a slotted spoon and drain on paper towels.

4 To make the sauce, heat the oil in a pre-heated wok or pan, add the vegetables and stir-fry for about 1 minute. Add the seasonings and tomato purée (paste) with stock or water, bring to the boil and thicken with the cornflour (cornstarch) paste.

5 Add the pork and blend well so that each piece of meat is coated with the sauce. Serve hot.

SPARE RIBS WITH CHILLI

SERVES 4

500 g/1 lb pork spare ribs
1 tsp sugar
1 tbsp light soy sauce
1 tsp rice wine or dry sherry
1 tsp cornflour (cornstarch)
about 600 ml/1pint/2½ cups vegetable oil
1 garlic clove, finely chopped
1 spring onion (scallion), cut into short
   sections
1 small hot chilli pepper (green or red),
   thinly sliced
2 tbsp black bean sauce
about 150 ml/¼ pint/⅔ cup Chinese Stock
   (see page 376) or water
1 small onion, diced
1 medium green (bell) pepper, cored,
   seeded and diced

1 Trim excess fat from the ribs, and chop each one into 3-4 bite-sized pieces. Place the ribs in a shallow dish with the sugar, soy sauce, wine and cornflour (cornstarch) and leave to marinate for 35-45 minutes.

2 Heat the oil in a preheated wok. Add the spare ribs and deep-fry for 2-3 minutes until light brown. Remove with a slotted spoon and drain on paper towels.

3 Pour off the oil, leaving about 1 tablespoon in the wok. Add the garlic, spring onion (scallion), chilli pepper and black bean sauce and stir-fry for 30-40 seconds.

4 Add the spare ribs, blend well, then add the stock or water. Bring to the boil, then reduce the heat, cover and braise for 8-10 minutes, stirring once or twice.

5 Add the onion and green (bell) pepper, increase the heat to high, and stir uncovered for about 2 minutes to reduce the sauce a little. Serve hot.

OYSTER SAUCE BEEF

SERVES 4

300 g/10 oz beef steak
1 tsp sugar
1 tbsp light soy sauce
1 tsp rice wine or dry sherry
1 tsp cornflour (cornstarch) paste (see
   page 376)
½ small carrot
60 g/2 oz mangetout (snow peas)
60 g/2 oz canned bamboo shoots
60 g/2 oz canned straw mushrooms
about 300 ml/ ½ pint/1¼ cups vegetable oil
1 spring onion (scallion), cut into short
   sections
2-3 small slices ginger root
½ tsp salt
2 tbsp oyster sauce
2-3 tbsp Chinese Stock (see page 376)
   or water

1 Cut the beef into small, thin slices. Place in a shallow dish with the sugar, soy sauce, wine and cornflour (cornstarch) paste and leave to marinate for 25-30 minutes.

2 Slice the carrots, mangetout (snow peas), bamboo shoots and straw mushrooms so that as far as possible the vegetable pieces are of uniform size and thickness.

3 Heat the oil in a preheated wok and add the beef slices. Stir-fry for about 1 minute, then remove with a slotted spoon and keep warm.

4 Pour off the oil, leaving about 1 tablespoon in the wok. Add the sliced vegetables with the spring onion (scallion) and ginger and stir-fry for about 2 minutes. Add the salt, beef, and the oyster sauce with stock or water. Blend well until heated through, and serve with a dip sauce, if liked.

VARIATIONS

You can use whatever vegetables are available for this dish, but it is important to get a good contrast of colour – don't use all red or all green for example.

CRISPY SHREDDED BEEF

SERVES 4

300-350 g/10-12 oz beef steak (such as
    topside or rump)
2 eggs
¼ tsp salt
4-5 tbsp plain flour
vegetable oil for deep-frying
2 medium carrots, finely shredded
2 spring onions (scallions), thinly
    shredded
1 garlic clove, finely chopped
2-3 small fresh green or red chillies,
    seeded and thinly shredded
4 tbsp sugar
3 tbsp rice vinegar
1 tbsp light soy sauce
2-3 tbsp Chinese Stock (see page 376) or
    water
1 tsp cornflour (cornstarch) paste (see
    page 376)

1 Cut the steak across the grain into
thin strips. Beat the eggs in a bowl
with the salt and flour, adding a little
water if necessary. Add the beef strips
and mix well until coated with the batter.

2 Heat the oil in a preheated wok until
smoking. Add the beef strips and
deep-fry for 4-5 minutes, stirring to
separate the shreds. Remove with a
slotted spoon and drain on paper towels.

3 Add the carrots to the wok and
deep-fry for about 1-1½ minutes,
then remove with a slotted spoon and
drain on paper towels.

4 Pour off the excess oil, leaving
about 1 tablespoon in the wok.
Add the spring onions (scallions), garlic,
chillies and carrots, stir-fry for about 1
minute, then add the sugar, vinegar, soy
sauce and stock or water, blend well and
bring to the boil.

5 Stir in the cornflour (cornstarch)
paste and simmer for a few minutes
to thicken the sauce. Return the beef to
the wok and stir until the shreds of meat
are well coated with the sauce. Serve hot.

BEEF & CHILLI BLACK BEAN SAUCE

SERVES 4

250-300 g/8-10 oz beef steak (such as
    rump)
1 small onion
1 small green (bell) pepper, cored and
    seeded
about 300 ml/ ½ pint/1¼ cups vegetable oil
1 spring onion (scallion), cut into short
    sections
a few small slices of ginger root
1-2 small green or red chillies, seeded and
    sliced
2 tbsp crushed black bean sauce

MARINADE:
½ tsp bicarbonate of soda or baking
    powder
½ tsp sugar
1 tbsp light soy sauce
2 tsp rice wine or dry sherry
2 tsp cornflour (cornstarch) paste (see
    page 376)
2 tsp sesame oil

1 Cut the beef into small thin strips.
Mix together the marinade
ingredients in a shallow dish, add the
beef strips, turn to coat and leave to
marinate for at least 2-3 hours – the
longer the better.

2 Cut the onion and green (bell)
pepper into small cubes.

3 Heat the oil in a pre-heated wok.
Add the beef strips and stir-fry for
about 1 minute, or until the colour
changes. Remove with a slotted spoon
and drain on paper towels. Keep warm.

4 Pour off the excess oil, leaving
about 1 tablespoon in the wok. Add
the spring onion (scallion), ginger, chillies,
onion and green (bell) pepper and stir-fry
for about 1 minute. Add the black bean
sauce, stir until smooth then return the
beef strips to the wok. Blend well and
stir-fry for another minute. Serve hot.

VEGETABLE DISHES

VEGETABLE & NUT STIR-FRY

••

SERVES 4

3 tbsp crunchy peanut butter
150 ml/ ¼ pint/ ⅔ cup water
1 tbsp soy sauce
1 tsp sugar
1 carrot
½ red onion
4 baby courgettes (zucchini)
1 red (bell) pepper
250 g/8 oz egg thread noodles
30 g/1 oz/ ¼ cup peanuts, chopped roughly
2 tbsp vegetable oil
1 tsp sesame oil
1 small green chilli, deseeded and sliced
    thinly
1 garlic clove, sliced thinly
225 g/7½ oz can of water chestnuts,
    drained and sliced
175 g/6 oz/3 cups bean-sprouts
salt

1 Blend the peanut butter with the
   water gradually in a small bowl.
Stir in the soy sauce and sugar.

2 Cut the carrot into thin matchsticks
   and slice the onion. Slice the
courgettes (zucchini) on the diagonal
and cut the (bell) pepper into chunks.

3 Bring a large pan of water to the
   boil and add the egg noodles.
Remove from the heat immediately and
leave to rest for 4 minutes, stirring
occasionally to divide the noodles.

4 Heat a wok or large frying pan
   (skillet), add the peanuts and dry-fry
until they are beginning to brown.
Remove and set aside.

5 Add the oils to the pan and heat.
   Add the carrot, onion, courgette
(zucchini), (bell) pepper, chilli and garlic,
and stir-fry for 2–3 minutes. Add the
water chestnuts, bean-sprouts and peanut
sauce. Bring to the boil and heat
thoroughly. Season to taste. Drain the
noodles and serve with the stir-fry.
Sprinkle with the peanuts.

AUBERGINES (EGGPLANTS) IN BLACK BEAN SAUCE

••

SERVES 4

60 g/2 oz/generous ⅓ cup dried black
    beans
450 ml/ ¾ pint/scant 2 cups vegetable
    stock
1 tbsp malt vinegar
1 tbsp dry sherry
1 tbsp soy sauce
1 tbsp sugar
1½ tsp cornflour (cornstarch)
1 red chilli, deseeded and chopped
1 cm/ ½ in piece ginger root, chopped
2 aubergines (eggplants)
2 tsp salt
3 tbsp vegetable oil
2 garlic cloves, sliced
4 spring onions (scallions), cut diagonally
shredded radishes to garnish

1 Soak the beans overnight in plenty
   of cold water. Drain and place in a
saucepan. Cover with cold water, bring to
the boil and boil rapidly, uncovered, for
10 minutes. Drain. Return the beans to the
saucepan with the stock and bring to the
boil.

2 Blend together the vinegar, sherry,
   soy sauce, sugar, cornflour
(cornstarch), chilli and ginger in a small
bowl. Add to the saucepan, cover and
simmer for 40 minutes, or until the beans
are tender and the sauce has thickened.
Stir occasionally.

3 Cut the aubergines (eggplants) into
   chunks and place in a colander.
Sprinkle over the salt and leave to drain
for 30 minutes. Rinse well to remove the
salt and dry on paper towels.

4 Heat the oil in a wok or large frying
   pan (skillet). Add the aubergine
(eggplant) and garlic. Stir-fry for 3–4
minutes until the aubergine (eggplant) has
started to brown.

5 Add the sauce to the aubergine
   (eggplant) with the spring onions
(scallions). Heat thoroughly and garnish
with radish shreds.

STIR-FRIED MUSHROOMS, CUCUMBER & SMOKED TOFU (BEANCURD)

●●●●●●●●●●●●●●●●●●●●●●●●●●●●●●●●●●●●

SERVES 4

1 large cucumber
1 tsp salt
225 g/7½ oz smoked tofu (beancurd)
2 tbsp vegetable oil
60 g/2 oz mangetout (snow peas)
125 g/4 oz/8 baby corn
1 celery stick, sliced diagonally
425 g/14 oz can of straw mushrooms, drained
2 spring onions (scallions), cut into strips
1 cm/ ½ in piece ginger root, chopped
1 tbsp yellow bean sauce
1 tbsp light soy sauce
1 tbsp dry sherry

1 Halve the cucumber lengthways. Remove the seeds, using a teaspoon. Cut into cubes, place in a colander and sprinkle over the salt. Leave to drain for 10 minutes. Rinse thoroughly in cold water to remove the salt and drain thoroughly.

2 Cut the tofu (beancurd) into cubes. Heat the oil in a wok or large frying pan (skillet). Add the tofu (beancurd), mangetout (snow peas), baby corn and celery. Stir until the tofu (beancurd) is lightly browned.

3 Add the straw mushrooms, spring onions (scallions) and ginger, and stir-fry for a further minute.

4 Stir in the cucumber, yellow bean sauce, soy sauce, sherry and 2 tablespoons of water.

5 Stir-fry the mixture for 1 minute before serving.

STRAW MUSHROOMS

Straw mushrooms are available in cans from oriental suppliers and some supermarkets. If unavailable, substitute 250 g/8 oz baby button mushrooms.

MONEY BAGS

●●●●●●●●●●●●●●●●●●●●●●●●●●●●●●●●●●●●

SERVES 4

3 Chinese dried mushrooms (if unavailable, use thinly sliced open-cup mushrooms)
250 g/8 oz/2 cups plain (all-purpose) flour
1 egg, beaten
75 ml/3 fl oz/ ⅓ cup water
1 tsp baking powder
¾ tsp salt
2 tbsp vegetable oil
2 spring onions (scallions), chopped
90 g/3 oz/ ½ cup sweetcorn kernels
½ red chilli, deseeded and chopped
1 tbsp brown bean sauce

1 Place the dried mushrooms in a small bowl, cover with warm water and leave to soak for 20–25 minutes.

2 To make the wrappers, sift the flour into a bowl. Add the egg and mix in lightly. Stir in the water, baking powder and salt. Mix to make a soft dough. Knead lightly until smooth on a floured board. Cover with a damp cloth and set aside for 5–6 minutes. This allows the baking powder time to activate, so that the dumplings swell when steaming.

3 Drain the mushrooms, squeezing them dry. Remove the tough centres and chop the mushrooms.

4 Heat the oil in a wok or large frying pan (skillet) and stir-fry the mushrooms, spring onions (scallions), sweetcorn and chilli for 2 minutes. Stir in the brown bean sauce and remove from the heat.

5 Roll the dough into a large sausage and cut into 24 even-sized pieces. Roll each piece out into a thin round and place a teaspoonful of the filling in the centre. Gather up the edges to a point, pinch together and twist to seal.

6 Stand the dumplings in an oiled steaming basket. Place over a saucepan of simmering water, cover and steam for 12–14 minutes before serving.

CARROTS & PARSNIPS WITH COCONUT

SERVES 2

90 g/3 oz/⅓ cup creamed coconut
300 ml/½ pint/1¼ cups hot water
15 g/½ oz/2 tbsp flaked (slivered) almonds
4 tbsp vegetable oil
5 cardamom pods
4 thin slices ginger root
350 g/12 oz/2½ cups carrots, sliced
350 g/12 oz/2½ cups parsnips, cut into
   small chunks
¼ tsp five-spice powder
15 g/½ oz/2 tbsp ground almonds
200 g/7 oz/4 cups young spinach leaves
½ red onion, sliced thinly
1 garlic clove, sliced
salt

1 Crumble the creamed coconut into a
   bowl or jug, add the hot water and
stir until dissolved.

2 Heat a saucepan and dry-fry the
   flaked (slivered) almonds until
golden. Remove and set aside.

3 Heat half the oil in the saucepan.
   Add the cardamom pods and ginger
root. Fry for 30 seconds to flavour the oil.
Add the carrots and parsnips. Stir-fry for
2–3 minutes.

4 Stir in the five-spice powder and
   ground almonds, and pour in the
coconut liquid. Bring to the boil and
season with salt to taste. Cover and
simmer for 12–15 minutes until the
vegetables are tender. Stir occasionally,
adding extra water if necessary.

5 Wash the spinach and drain
   thoroughly. Remove any stalks. Heat
the remaining oil in a wok or large frying
pan (skillet). Add the onion and garlic,
and stir-fry for 2 minutes. Add the spinach
and stir-fry until it has just wilted. Drain
off any excess liquid formed. Season with
salt.

6 Remove the cardamom pods and
   ginger root from the carrots and
parsnips, and adjust the seasoning. Serve
on a bed of the spinach sprinkled with
the almonds.

BROCCOLI IN OYSTER SAUCE

SERVES 4

250-300 g/8-10 oz broccoli
3 tbsp vegetable oil
3-4 small slices ginger root
½ tsp salt
½ tsp sugar
3-4 tbsp Chinese Stock (see page 376) or
   water
1 tbsp oyster sauce

1 Cut the broccoli spears into small
   florets. Trim the stalks, peel off the
rough skin, and cut the stalks diagonally
into diamond-shaped chunks.

2 Heat the oil in a preheated wok and
   add the pieces of stalk and the
ginger. Stir-fry for half a minute then add
the florets and continue to stir-fry for
another 2 minutes.

3 Add the salt, sugar and stock or
   water, and continue stirring for
another minute or so.

4 Blend in the oyster sauce. Serve hot
   or cold.

BROCCOLI STALKS

The broccoli stalks have to be peeled
and cut diagonally to ensure that they
will cook evenly. If they are thin stalks,
the pieces can be added to the wok at
the same time as the florets, but
otherwise add the stalks first, to
ensure that they will be tender.

VARIATION

Any crunchy-textured vegetable can be
used in this recipe. If preferred, you
could use cauliflower, celery,
courgettes, French beans, etc., making
sure that they are cut into even-sized
pieces.

BRAISED CHINESE VEGETABLES

SERVES 4

5 g/ ¼ oz dried wood ears
1 cake tofu (bean curd)
60 g/2 oz mangetout (snow peas)
125 g/4 oz Chinese leaves
1 small carrot
90 g/3 oz canned baby sweetcorn,
  drained
90 g/3 oz canned straw mushrooms,
  drained
60 g/2 oz canned water chestnuts,
  drained
300 ml/ ½ pint/1¼ cups vegetable oil
1 tsp salt
½ tsp sugar
1 tbsp light soy sauce or oyster sauce
2-3 tbsp Chinese Stock (see page 376) or
  water
a few drops of sesame oil

1 Soak the wood ears in warm water
for 15-20 minutes, then rinse and
drain, discarding any hard bits, and dry
on paper towels.

2 Cut the cake of tofu into about
18 small pieces. Top and tail the
mangetout (snow peas). Cut the Chinese
leaves and the carrot into slices roughly
the same size and shape as the mangetout
(snow peas). Cut the baby sweetcorn, the
straw mushrooms and the water chestnuts
in half.

3 Heat the oil in a preheated wok.
Add the tofu and deep-fry for about
2 minutes until it turns slightly golden.
Remove with a slotted spoon and drain
on paper towels.

4 Pour off the oil, leaving about
2 tablespoons in the wok. Add the
carrot, Chinese leaves and mangetout
(snow peas) and stir-fry for about
1 minute.

5 Now add the sweetcorn, mushrooms
and water chestnuts. Stir gently for
2 more minutes, then add the salt, sugar,
soy sauce and stock or water. Bring to the
boil and stir-fry for 1 more minute.

6 Sprinkle with sesame oil and serve
hot or cold.

STIR-FRIED BEAN-SPROUTS

SERVES 4

250 g/8 oz fresh bean-sprouts
2-3 spring onions (scallions)
1 medium red chilli pepper (optional)
3 tbsp vegetable oil
½ tsp salt
½ tsp sugar
1 tbsp light soy sauce
a few drops of sesame oil (optional)

1 Rinse the bean-sprouts in cold water,
discarding any husks or small pieces
that float to the top. Drain well on paper
towels.

2 Cut the spring onions (scallions) into
short sections. Thinly shred the red
chilli pepper, if using, discarding the
seeds.

3 Heat the oil in a preheated wok.
Add the bean-sprouts, spring onions
(scallions) and chilli pepper, if using, and
stir-fry for about 2 minutes.

4 Add the salt, sugar, soy sauce and
sesame oil, if using, to the mixture
in the wok. Stir well to blend. Serve hot
or cold.

TO GROW BEAN-SPROUTS

It is very easy to grow bean-sprouts. If
you find it difficult to buy fresh ones,
this could be the answer. Use dried
mung beans, obtainable from
supermarkets and health-food shops.
Wash the beans thoroughly in several
changes of water. Place in a lidded jar,
or a seed sprouter if you have one, and
place in a warm, dark place (the airing
cupboard is ideal). Check daily and
rinse with a little water to keep them
moist. You should have sprouts ready
to use in 3-4 days.

AUBERGINES (EGGPLANTS) IN CHILLI SAUCE

••

SERVES 4

1 large aubergine (eggplant)
vegetable oil for deep-frying
2 carrots
4 spring onions (scallions)
2 large garlic cloves
1 tbsp vegetable oil
2 tsp chilli sauce
1 tbsp soy sauce
1 tbsp dry sherry

1 Slice the aubergine (eggplant) and then cut into strips about the size of potato chips (French fries).

2 Heat enough oil in a large heavy-based saucepan to deep-fry the aubergine (eggplant) in batches until just browned. Remove the strips with a perforated spoon and drain them on paper towels.

3 Cut the carrots into thin matchsticks. Trim and slice the spring onions (scallions) diagonally. Slice the garlic cloves.

4 Heat 1 tablespoon of oil in a wok or large frying pan (skillet). Add the carrot matchsticks and stir-fry for 1 minute; then add the chopped spring onions (scallions) and garlic and stir-fry for a further minute.

5 Stir in the chilli sauce, soy sauce and sherry, then stir in the drained aubergine (eggplant). Mix well to ensure that the vegetables are heated through thoroughly before serving.

MILDER FLAVOUR

For a milder dish, substitute hoisin sauce for the chilli sauce. This can be bought ready-made from all supermarkets.

FISH AUBERGINE (EGGPLANT)

••

SERVES 4

500 g/1 lb aubergine (eggplant)
vegetable oil, for deep-frying
1 garlic clove, finely chopped
½ tsp finely chopped ginger root
2 spring onions (scallions), finely chopped,
   with the white and green parts
   separated
125 g/4 oz pork, thinly shredded
   (optional)
1 tbsp light soy sauce
2 tsp rice wine or dry sherry
1 tbsp chilli bean sauce
½ tsp salt
½ tsp sugar
1 tbsp rice vinegar
2 tsp cornflour (cornstarch) paste (see
   page 376)
a few drops of sesame oil

1 Cut the aubergine (eggplant) into rounds and then into thin strips about the size of potato chips – the skin can either be peeled or left on.

2 Heat the oil in a preheated wok until smoking. Add the aubergine (eggplant) chips and deep-fry for about 3-4 minutes, or until soft. Remove and drain on paper towels.

3 Pour off the hot oil, leaving about 1 tablespoon in the wok. Add the garlic, ginger and the white parts of the spring onions (scallions), followed by the pork (if using). Stir-fry for about 1 minute or until the colour of the meat changes, then add the soy sauce, wine and chilli bean sauce, blending them in well.

4 Return the aubergine (eggplant) chips to the wok together with the salt, sugar and vinegar. Continue stirring for another minute or so, then add the cornflour (cornstarch) paste and stir until the sauce has thickened.

5 Add the green parts of the spring onions (scallions) to the wok and sprinkle on the sesame oil. Serve hot.

STIR-FRIED SEASONAL VEGETABLES

Serves 4

*1 medium red (bell) pepper, cored and
    seeded*
125 g/4 oz courgettes (zucchini)
125 g/4 oz cauliflower
125 g/4 oz French beans
3 tbsp vegetable oil
a few small slices ginger root
½ tsp salt
½ tsp sugar
Chinese Stock (see page 376) or water
1 tbsp light soy sauce
a few drops of sesame oil (optional)

1 Cut the red (bell) pepper into small
    squares. Thinly slice the courgettes
(zucchini). Trim the cauliflower and
divide into small florets, discarding any
thick stems. Make sure the vegetables are
cut into roughly similar shapes and sizes
to ensure even cooking.

2 Top and tail the French beans, then
    cut them in half.

3 Heat the oil in a pre-heated wok,
    add the vegetables and stir-fry with
the ginger for about 2 minutes.

4 Add the salt and sugar to the wok,
    and continue to stir-fry for
1-2 minutes, adding a little Chinese stock
or water if the vegetables appear to be
too dry. Do not add liquid unless it seems
necessary.

5 Add the light soy sauce and sesame
    oil (if using) blend well to lightly
coat the vegetables and serve
immediately.

VEGETABLES

Almost any vegetables could be used
in this dish: other good choices would
be mangetout (snow peas), broccoli
florets, carrots, baby corn cobs, green
peas, Chinese cabbage and young
spinach leaves. Either white or black
(oyster) mushrooms can also be used
to give a greater diversity of textures.
Make sure there is a good variety of
colour, and always include several crisp
vegetables such as carrots.

GINGERED BROCCOLI WITH ORANGE

Serves 4

750 g/1½ lb broccoli
2 thin slices ginger root
2 garlic cloves
1 orange
2 tsp cornflour (cornstarch)
1 tbsp light soy sauce
½ tsp sugar
2 tbsp vegetable oil

1 Divide the broccoli into small florets.
    Peel the stems, using a vegetable
peeler, and then cut the stems into thin
slices. Cut the ginger root into matchsticks
and slice the garlic.

2 Peel 2 long strips of zest from the
    orange and cut into thin strips. Place
the strips in a bowl, cover with cold water
and set aside. Squeeze the juice from the
orange and mix with the cornflour
(cornstarch), soy sauce, sugar and 4
tablespoons water.

3 Heat the oil in a wok or large frying
    pan (skillet). Add the broccoli stem
slices and stir-fry for 2 minutes. Add the
ginger root slices, garlic and broccoli
florets, and stir-fry for a further 3 minutes.

4 Stir in the orange
    sauce mixture and
cook, stirring constantly,
until the sauce has
thickened and coated
the broccoli.

5 Drain the
    reserved orange
rind and stir in before
serving.

VARIATION

This dish could be made with
cauliflower, if you prefer, or a mixture
of cauliflower and broccoli.

LEMON CHINESE LEAVES

••

SERVES 4

500 g/1 lb Chinese leaves
3 tbsp vegetable oil
1 cm/ ½ in piece ginger root, grated
1 tsp salt
1 tsp sugar
120 ml/4 fl oz/ ½ cup water or vegetable
    stock
1 tsp grated lemon rind
1 tbsp cornflour (cornstarch)
1 tbsp lemon juice

1   Separate the Chinese leaves, wash
    and drain thoroughly. Pat dry with
paper towels. Cut into 5 cm/2 in wide
slices.

2   Heat the oil in a wok or large frying
    pan (skillet). Add the grated ginger
root, followed by the Chinese leaves, stir-
fry for 2–3 minutes or until the leaves
begin to wilt. Add the salt and sugar, and
mix well until the leaves soften. Remove
the leaves with a perforated spoon and
set aside.

3   Add the water or vegetable stock to
    the pan with the grated lemon zest
and bring to the boil. Meanwhile, mix the
cornflour (cornstarch) to a smooth paste
with the lemon juice, then add to the
water or stock in the pan. Simmer, stirring
constantly, for about 1 minute to make a
smooth sauce.

4   Return the cooked leaves to the pan
    and mix thoroughly. Arrange on a
serving plate and serve immediately.

CHINESE LEAVES

If Chinese leaves are unavailable,
substitute slices of savoy cabbage.
Cook for 1 extra minute to soften the
leaves.

GOLDEN NEEDLES WITH BAMBOO SHOOTS

••

SERVES 4

30 g/1 oz/ ¼ cup dried lily flowers
2 x 225 g/7½ oz cans of bamboo shoots,
    drained
60 g/2 oz/ ½ cup cornflour (cornstarch)
vegetable oil for deep-frying
1 tbsp vegetable oil
450ml/ ¾ pint/scant 2 cups vegetable stock
1 tbsp dark soy sauce
1 tbsp dry sherry
1 tsp sugar
1 large garlic clove, sliced
½ each red, green and yellow (bell)
    peppers

1   Soak the lily flowers in hot water for
    30 minutes.

2   Coat the bamboo shoots in cornflour
    (cornstarch). Heat enough oil in a
large heavy-based saucepan to deep-fry
the bamboo shoots in batches until just
beginning to colour. Remove with a
perforated spoon and drain on paper
towels.

3   Drain the lily flowers and trim off
    the hard ends. Heat 1 tablespoon
oil in a wok or large frying pan (skillet). Add
the lily flowers, bamboo shoots, stock,
soy sauce, sherry, sugar and garlic.

4   Slice the (bell) peppers thinly and
    add to the pan. Bring to the boil,
stirring constantly, then reduce the heat
and simmer for 5 minutes. Add extra
water or stock if necessary.

COATING THE
BAMBOO SHOOTS

To coat the bamboo shoots easily with
cornflour (cornstarch), place the
cornflour (cornstarch) in a plastic bag,
add the bamboo shoots in batches and
shake well.

SPINACH WITH STRAW MUSHROOMS

SERVES 4

30 g/1 oz/ ¼ cup pine kernels (nuts)
500 g/1 lb fresh spinach leaves
3 tbsp vegetable oil
1 red onion, sliced
2 garlic cloves, sliced
425 g/14 oz can of straw mushrooms,
    drained
30 g/1 oz/3 tbsp raisins
2 tbsp soy sauce
salt

1 Heat a wok or large frying pan (skillet) and dry-fry the pine kernels (nuts) until lightly browned. Remove and set aside.

2 Wash the spinach thoroughly, picking the leaves over and removing long stalks. Drain and pat dry with paper towels.

3 Heat the oil in the wok or frying pan (skillet). Add the onion and garlic, and stir-fry for 1 minute.

4 Add the spinach and mushrooms, and continue to stir-fry until the leaves have wilted. Drain off any excess liquid.

5 Stir in the raisins, reserved pine kernels (nuts) and soy sauce. Stir-fry until thoroughly heated and well-mixed. Season to taste with salt before serving.

ADDING FLAVOUR

Soak the raisins in 2 tablespoons dry sherry before using. This helps to plump them up as well as adding extra flavour to the stir-fry.

MA-PO TOFU

SERVES 4

3 cakes tofu (bean curd)
3 tbsp vegetable oil
125 g/4 oz coarsely minced (ground) beef
½ tsp finely chopped garlic
1 leek, cut into short sections
½ tsp salt
1 tbsp black bean sauce
1 tbsp light soy sauce
1 tsp chilli bean sauce
3-4 tbsp Chinese Stock (see page 376) or
    water
2 tsp cornflour (cornstarch) paste (see
    page 376)
a few drops of sesame oil
black pepper
finely chopped spring onions (scallions), to
    garnish

1 Cut the tofu into 1 cm/ ½ in cubes, handling it carefully. Bring some water to the boil in a small pan or a wok, add the tofu and blanch for 2-3 minutes to harden. Remove and drain well.

2 Heat the oil in a preheated wok. Add the minced (ground) beef and garlic and stir-fry for about 1 minute, or until the colour of the beef changes. Add the chopped leek, salt and sauces and blend well.

3 Add the stock or water followed by the tofu. Bring to the boil and braise gently for 2-3 minutes.

4 Add the cornflour (cornstarch) paste, and stir until the sauce has thickened. Sprinkle with sesame oil and black pepper and garnish with spring onions (scallions). Serve hot.

TOFU (BEAN CURD)

Tofu has been an important element in Chinese cooking for more than 1000 years. It is made of yellow soya beans, which are soaked, ground and mixed with water. Tofu is highly nutritious, being rich in protein, and has a very bland taste. Solid cakes of tofu can be cut up with a sharp knife. Cook carefully as too much stirring can cause it to disintegrate.

RICE & NOODLES

SEAFOOD CHOW MEIN

•••

SERVES 4

90 g/3 oz squid, cleaned
3-4 fresh scallops
90 g/3 oz raw prawns (shrimp), shelled
½ egg white, lightly beaten
1 tbsp cornflour (cornstarch) paste (see
    page 376)
275 g/9 oz egg noodles
5-6 tbsp vegetable oil
2 tbsp light soy sauce
60 g/2 oz mangetout (snow peas)
½ tsp salt
½ tsp sugar
1 tsp Chinese rice wine or dry sherry
2 spring onions (scallions), finely
    shredded
a few drops of sesame oil

1 Open up the squid and score the
    inside in a criss-cross pattern, then
cut into pieces about the size of a postage
stamp. Soak the squid in a bowl of
boiling water until all the pieces curl up.
Rinse in cold water and drain.

2 Cut each scallop into 3-4 slices. Cut
    the prawns (shrimp) in half
lengthways if large. Mix the scallops and
prawns with the egg white and cornflour
(cornstarch) paste.

3 Cook the noodles in boiling water
    according to the packet instructions,
then drain and rinse under cold water.
Drain, then toss in 1 tablespoon of oil.

4 Heat 3 tablespoons of oil in a
    preheated wok. Add the noodles
and 1 tablespoon of soy sauce and stir-fry
for 2-3 minutes. Remove to a serving dish.

5 Heat the remaining oil in the wok
    and add the mangetout (snow peas)
and seafood. Stir-fry for about 2 minutes,
then add the salt, sugar, wine, remaining
soy sauce and about half the spring
onions (scallions). Blend well and add a
little stock or water if necessary.

6 Pour the seafood mixture on top of
    the noodles and sprinkle with
sesame oil. Garnish with the remaining
spring onions (scallions).

MUSHROOM & CUCUMBER NOODLE SOUP

•••

SERVES 4

125 g/4 oz flat or open-cup mushrooms
½ cucumber
2 spring onions (scallions)
1 garlic clove
2 tbsp vegetable oil
30 g/1 oz/¼ cup Chinese rice noodles
¾ tsp salt
1 tbsp soy sauce

1 Wash the mushrooms and slice
    thinly. Do not remove the peel as
this adds more flavour. Halve the
cucumber lengthways. Scoop out the
seeds, using a teaspoon, and slice the
cucumber thinly.

2 Chop the spring onions (scallions)
    finely and cut the garlic clove into
thin strips.

3 Heat the oil in a large saucepan
    or wok. Add the spring onions
(scallions) and garlic, and stir-fry for
30 seconds. Add the mushrooms and
stir-fry for 2-3 minutes.

4 Stir in 600 ml/1 pint/2½ cups water.
    Break the noodles into short lengths
and add to the soup. Bring to the boil.

5 Add the cucumber slices, salt and
    soy sauce, and simmer for
2-3 minutes.

6 Serve the soup in warmed bowls,
    distributing the noodles and
vegetables evenly.

CUCUMBER SEEDS

Scooping the seeds out from the
cucumber gives it a prettier effect
when sliced, and also helps to reduce
any bitterness, but if you prefer, you
can leave them in.

HOMEMADE NOODLES WITH STIR-FRIED VEGETABLES

SERVES 2–4

NOODLES:
125 g/4 oz/1 cup plain (all-purpose) flour
2 tbsp cornflour (cornstarch)
½ tsp salt
120 ml/4 fl oz/ ½ cup boiling water
5 tbsp vegetable oil

STIR-FRY:
1 courgette (zucchini)
1 celery stick
1 carrot
125 g/4 oz open-cup mushrooms
1 leek
125 g/4 oz broccoli
125 g/4 oz/2 cups bean-sprouts
1 tbsp soy sauce
2 tsp rice wine vinegar (if unavailable, use white wine vinegar)
½ tsp sugar

1 To prepare the noodles, sift the flour, cornflour (cornstarch) and salt into a bowl. Make a well in the centre and pour in the boiling water and 1 teaspoon of the oil. Mix quickly, using a wooden spoon, to make a soft dough. Cover and leave for 5–6 minutes.

2 Prepare the vegetables for the stir-fry. Cut the courgette (zucchini), celery and carrot into thin sticks. Slice the mushrooms and leek. Divide the broccoli into small florets, peel and thinly slice the stalks.

3 Make the noodles by breaking off small pieces of dough and rolling into balls. Then roll each ball across a very lightly oiled work surface (counter) with the palm of your hand to form thin noodles. Do not worry if some of the noodles break into shorter lengths. Set the noodles aside.

4 Heat 3 tablespoons of oil in a wok or large frying pan (skillet). Add the noodles in batches and fry over a high heat for 1 minute. Reduce the heat and cook for a further 2 minutes. Remove and drain on paper towels. Set aside.

5 Heat the remaining oil in the pan. Add the courgette (zucchini), celery and carrot, and stir-fry for 1 minute. Add the mushrooms, broccoli and leek, and stir-fry for a further minute. Stir in the remaining ingredients and mix well until thoroughly heated.

6 Add the noodles and toss to mix together over a high heat. Serve immediately.

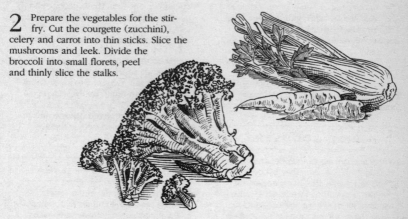

SINGAPORE-STYLE RICE NOODLES

••

SERVES 4

200 g/7 oz rice vermicelli
125 g/4 oz cooked chicken or pork
60 g/2 oz peeled prawns (shrimp),
  defrosted if frozen
4 tbsp vegetable oil
1 medium onion, thinly shredded
125 g/4 oz fresh bean-sprouts
1 tsp salt
1 tbsp mild curry powder
2 tbsp light soy sauce
2 spring onions (scallions), thinly
  shredded
1-2 small fresh green or red chilli peppers,
  seeded and thinly shredded

1 Soak the rice vermicelli in boiling
  water for 8-10 minutes, then rinse in
cold water and drain well.

2 Thinly slice the cooked meat. Dry
  the prawns (shrimp) on paper
towels.

3 Heat the oil in a preheated wok.
  Add the onion and stir-fry until
opaque. Add the bean-sprouts and stir-fry
for 1 minute.

4 Add the noodles with the meat and
  prawns (shrimp), and continue
stirring for another minute.

5 Blend in the salt, curry powder and
  soy sauce, followed by the spring
onions (scallions) and chilli peppers. Stir-
fry for one more minute, then serve
immediately.

┌─────────────────────────────────────┐
│   RICE NOODLES   │
│ ─────────────────────────────────── │
│ Rice noodles are very delicate noodles │
│ made from rice flour. They become   │
│ soft and pliable after being soaked for│
│ about 15 minutes. If you wish to store │
│ them after they have been soaked,   │
│ toss them in a few drops of sesame oil │
│ then place them in a sealed container │
│ in the refrigerator.   │
└─────────────────────────────────────┘

SPECIAL FRIED RICE

••

SERVES 2–4

175 g/6 oz/generous ¾ cup long-grain rice
60 g/2 oz/ ½ cup cashew nuts
1 carrot
½ cucumber
1 yellow (bell) pepper
2 spring onions (scallions)
2 tbsp vegetable oil
1 garlic clove, crushed
125 g/4 oz/ ¾ cup frozen peas, defrosted
1 tbsp soy sauce
1 tsp salt
coriander (cilantro) leaves to garnish

1 Bring a large pan of water to the
  boil. Add the rice and simmer for
15 minutes. Tip the rice into a sieve
(strainer) and rinse; drain thoroughly.

2 Heat a wok or large frying pan
  (skillet), add the cashew nuts and
dry-fry until lightly browned. Remove and
set aside.

3 Cut the carrot in half along the
  length, then slice thinly into semi-
circles. Halve the cucumber and remove
the seeds, using a teaspoon; dice the
cucumber. Slice the (bell) pepper and
chop the spring onions (scallions).

4 Heat the oil in the wok or large
  frying pan (skillet). Add the
prepared vegetables and the garlic. Stir-fry
for 3 minutes. Add the rice, peas, soy
sauce and salt. Continue to stir-fry until
well mixed and thoroughly heated.

5 Stir in the reserved cashew nuts and
  serve garnished with coriander
(cilantro) leaves.

┌─────────────────────────────────────┐
│   LAST-MINUTE MEAL   │
│ ─────────────────────────────────── │
│ You can replace any of the vegetables │
│ in this recipe with others suitable for a │
│ stir-fry, and using leftover rice makes │
│ this a perfect last-minute dish.   │
└─────────────────────────────────────┘

EGG-FRIED RICE

SERVES 4

3 eggs
1 tsp salt
2 spring onions (scallions), finely chopped
2-3 tbsp vegetable oil
500 g/1 lb/3 cups cooked rice, well
  drained and cooled (see note in step 3)
125 g/4 oz cooked peas

1 Lightly beat the eggs with a pinch of salt and 1 tablespoon of the spring onions (scallions).

2 Heat the oil in a preheated wok, add the eggs and stir until lightly scrambled. (The eggs should only be cooked until they start to set, so they are still moist.)

3 Add the rice and stir to make sure that each grain of rice is separated. Note: the cooked rice should be cool, preferably cold, so that much of the moisture has evaporated. This ensures that the oil will coat the grains of rice and prevent them sticking. Store the cooked rice in the refrigerator until ready to cook. Make sure the oil is really hot before adding the rice, to avoid the rice being saturated with oil otherwise it will be heavy and greasy.

4 Add the remaining salt, spring onions (scallions) and peas. Blend well and serve hot or cold.

PERFECT FRIED RICE

Use rice with a fairly firm texture. Ideally, the raw rice should be soaked in water for a short time before cooking. The two main varieties of rice available are long-grain and short-grain. While it used to be necessary to wash rice, processing now makes this unnecessary. Short-grain Oriental rice can be substituted for long-grain.

Fried rice lends itself to many variations. You may choose to add other vegetables as well as the spring onions (scallions), if desired, as well as prawns (shrimp), ham or chicken.

FRAGRANT STEAMED RICE IN LOTUS LEAVES

SERVES 4

2 lotus leaves
4 Chinese dried mushrooms
  (if unavailable, use thinly sliced open-
  cup mushrooms)
175 g/6 oz/generous ¾ cup long-grain rice
1 cinnamon stick
6 cardamom pods
4 cloves
1 tsp salt
2 eggs
1 tbsp vegetable oil
2 spring onions (scallions), chopped
1 tbsp soy sauce
2 tbsp sherry
1 tsp sugar
1 tsp sesame oil

1 Unfold the lotus leaves carefully and cut along the fold to divide each leaf in half. Lay on a large baking sheet and pour over enough hot water to cover. Leave to soak for about 30 minutes.

2 Place the dried mushrooms in a small bowl and cover with warm water. Leave to soak for 20–25 minutes.

3 Cook the rice in boiling water with the cinnamon stick, cardamom pods, cloves and salt for about 10 minutes. Drain. Remove the cinnamon stick.

4 Beat the eggs lightly. Heat the oil in a wok or frying pan (skillet) and cook the eggs quickly, stirring constantly until set; then remove and set aside.

5 Drain the mushrooms, squeezing out the excess water. Remove the tough centres and chop the mushrooms. Place the drained rice in a bowl. Stir in the mushrooms, cooked egg, spring onions (scallions), soy sauce, sherry, sugar and sesame oil. Season with salt to taste.

6 Drain the lotus leaves and divide the rice mixture into four portions. Place a portion in the centre of each lotus leaf and fold up to form a parcel (package). Place in a steamer, cover and steam over simmering water for 20 minutes. To serve, cut the tops of the lotus leaves open to expose the fragrant rice inside.

SPICY COCONUT RICE WITH GREEN LENTILS

SERVES 2-4

90 g/3 oz/ ⅓ cup green lentils
250 g/8 oz/generous 1 cup long-grain rice
2 tbsp vegetable oil
1 onion, sliced
2 garlic cloves, crushed
3 curry leaves
1 stalk lemon grass, chopped
  (if unavailable, use grated rind of
  ½ lemon)
1 green chilli, deseeded and chopped
½ tsp cumin seeds
1½ tsp salt
90 g/3 oz/ ⅓ cup creamed coconut
600 ml/1 pint/2½ cups hot water
2 tbsp chopped fresh coriander (cilantro)

TO GARNISH:
shredded radishes
shredded cucumber

1 Wash the lentils and place in a saucepan. Cover with cold water, bring to the boil and boil rapidly for 10 minutes. Wash the rice thoroughly and drain well.

2 Heat the oil in a large saucepan, which has a tight-fitting lid, and fry the onion for 3–4 minutes. Add the garlic, curry leaves, lemon grass, chilli, cumin seeds and salt, and stir well.

3 Drain the lentils and rinse. Add to the onion and spices with the rice and mix well. Add the creamed coconut to the hot water and stir until dissolved. Stir into the rice mixture and bring to the boil. Turn down the heat to low, put the lid on tightly and leave to cook undisturbed for 15 minutes.

4 Without removing the lid, remove the pan from the heat and leave to rest for 10 minutes to allow the rice and lentils to finish cooking in their own steam.

5 Stir in the coriander (cilantro) and remove the curry leaves. Serve garnished with shredded radishes and cucumber.

CREAMED COCONUT

If creamed coconut is unavailable, use 60 g/2 oz/ ⅔ cup desiccated (shredded) coconut. Infuse it in the hot water for 20 minutes, drain well and squeeze out any excess water. Discard the coconut and use the liquid.

THAI DISHES – INTRODUCTION

Thailand has a richly abundant and totally unique cuisine that has changed little over the centuries, despite regular foreign intervention Today, it still stands independent, with head held high, to critical gastronomic scrutiny and fares the better for it.

It is not difficult to spot the influence of near neighbours like China and India in stir-fries and curries but somehow they are given the unmistakeable Thai treatment with herbs, spices and coconut milk. So it is easy to see how on the one hand Thai cuisine can be described as light, aromatic and zestful, yet on the other hot, handsome, robust and full-blooded!

CHARACTERISTICS

Thai cuisine is dependent upon the rich harvests of rice, green vegetables, herbs, spices and fruit. A lavish supply of fish means that normally at least one fish dish, be it sizzled prawns (shrimp), a fish curry or banana-wrapped baked whole fish, features in every Thai meal. Meat, of all types, also makes for a varied cuisine where there are few religious restrictions to the basic diet.

Rice is the staple food and is served at every meal with many main-course meat, fish, poultry and vegetable dishes in a sauce. Noodles are generally served as snack or "fast" foods to supplement the main meal. Soups also feature frequently and are typically flavoured with Thai staples like lemon grass, lime juice and fish sauce.

Creamy curries, ranging from mild and aromatic to fierce and fiery, are prepared daily with care from some of the finest fresh ingredients and spicy curry pastes whose bases are red or green chilli peppers.

SPECIAL INGREDIENTS

Such has been the popularity of Thai food that nearly every supermarket boasts the ingredients required to cook a Thai meal. Only a few special foods will have to be purchased from specialist and oriental food stores and, fortunately, every town now seems to have at least one good supplier.

Bamboo shoots Still only available canned and sometimes dried (which need soaking before use), bamboo shoots are the crunchy cream-coloured shoots of the bamboo plant.

Banana leaves These are the large green, inedible leaves of the banana tree that are principally used for wrapping food and for making containers for steaming purposes. They give the food a slightly aromatic delicate flavour but cannot be eaten.

Holy basil or Thai basil, available from specialist stores, has a stronger, more pungent and sharper flavour than our domestic or "sweet" basil. When unavailable use ordinary basil in the same proportions.

Bean sauce A thick sauce made from yellow or black soy beans. The crushed beans are mixed with flour, vinegar, spices and salt to make a spicy, sometimes salty and definitely aromatic sauce. It is usually sold in cans or jars.

Bean sprouts The tiny, crunchy shoots of mung beans. These are widely available fresh and should be used on the day of purchase. Canned beansprouts are available but generally lack flavour and crunchiness.

INTRODUCTION

Chilli paste This is a paste of roast ground chillies mixed with oil. Depending upon the chillies used, the colour and flavour will differ appreciably so only add a small amount to err on the side of safety. It is sold in small jars and may be called "Ground Chillies in Oil". A small jar will last a long time if stored in the refrigerator.

Fresh chillies Fresh chillies come in varying degrees of hotness. Cooking helps to mellow the flavour but a degree of caution should be exercised when using them. If you do not like your food too hot then discard the seeds when you prepare them. Remember, at all costs, to make sure that you wash your hands thoroughly after touching them as they contain an irritant which will sting the eyes and mouth harshly on contact. Fresh chopped hot chillies can be replaced with chilli paste or cayenne pepper but the result will be slightly different. As a general guide for buying - the smaller the chilli the hotter it will be. Most supermarkets stock the larger, milder chilli and this is perhaps the best starting point for the novice Thai cook.

Dried chillies These add a surprisingly good kick to a dish, especially if they are tossed in oil with other spices at the beginning of cooking. Generally the chillies are added whole but can sometimes be halved. In most cases they should be removed from the dish before serving. Again, the smaller the dried chilli, the hotter the flavour.

Coconut The coconut is used in a good many sweet and savoury Thai dishes and is infinitely better to use than desiccated coconut. Many supermarkets now stock them fresh at little cost.

Coconut milk Coconut milk is an infusion used to flavour and thicken many Thai dishes. Perhaps the best and easiest type to use comes in cans from Oriental stores but remember to check that it is unsweetened for savoury dishes.

Coriander This is a delicate and fragrant herb that is widely used in Thai cooking. The roots and the leaves are used, the former having a more intense flavour. The roots are generally used for cooking and the leaves are used more for flavouring the cooked and finished dish. Chopped leaves are frequently stirred into a cooked dish or scattered over the surface just prior to serving.

Curry leaves Rather like bay leaves but not quite so thick and luscious, these are highly aromatic leaves that are chopped, torn or left whole and added to many Thai curries and slow-simmered dishes. Olive-green in colour they can be bought fresh or dried from specialist shops.

Fish paste This is a thick fish paste made from fermented fish or shrimps and salt. It is used only in small amounts since it has enormous flavouring power. Anchovy paste makes a good if not authentic alternative.

Fish sauce/nam pla This is a thin, brown salty sauce that is widely used in Thai cooking instead of salt. It is made by pressing salted fish and is available in many Oriental food stores. There is really no good available substitute so is worth hunting for.

INTRODUCTION

Galangal Galangal is a spice very similar to ginger and is used to replace the latter in Thai cuisine. It can be bought fresh from Oriental food stores but is also available dried and as a powder. The fresh root, which is not as pungent as ginger, needs to be peeled before slicing to use whilst dried pieces need to be soaked in water before using and discarded from the dish before serving. If fresh galangal is unavailable for a recipe then substitute 1 dried slice or 1 teaspoon powder for each 1.5 cm/½ in fresh.

Ginger root Root ginger is also often used in Thai cooking. Always peel before using then chop, grate or purée to a paste to use. Buy root ginger in small quantities to ensure freshness and store in a plastic bag in the refrigerator.

Kaffir lime leaves These are dark green, glossy leaves that have a lemony-lime flavour that can be bought from specialist shops either fresh or dried. Fresh leaves impart the most delicious flavour to a dish so are worth seeking out. Most recipes call for the leaves to be left whole or shredded. This is best done with a pair of scissors. When stocks cannot be found then substitute 1 leaf with about 1 teaspoon finely grated lime zest.

Lemon grass Known also as citronelle, lemon grass is a tropical grass with a pungent, aromatic lemon flavour. It is fairly easy to buy fresh from supermarkets. When chopped lemon grass is specified then use the thick bulky end of the spring onion (scallions) like stem. Alternatively, if the whole stem is required then beat well to bruise so that the flavour can be imparted. Stalks keep well in the refrigerator for up to about 2 weeks. When unavailable used grated lemon zest instead of a pared piece of lemon peel. Dried lemon grass is also available as a powder called sereh.

Noodles Many different varieties.

Oyster sauce Oriental oyster sauce, a light sauce made from oysters and soy sauce, is frequently used as a flavouring in Thai cooking. It is often used to flavour meat and vegetables during cooking. Despite its name, oyster sauce, it is entirely free from the flavour of oysters, or indeed fish!

Palm sugar This is a thick, coarse brown sugar that has a slightly caramel taste. It is sold in round cakes or in small round, flat containers. It is not strictly necessary and can be replaced with dark soft brown or demerara sugar.

Rice Check your recipe to see whether you require long-grain fragrant Thai rice or 'sticky' glutinous rice before preparation. Most recipes call for the long-grain fragrant variety labelled as Thai but when unavailable then replace with a good-quality basmati or other long-grain rice. When the shorter stickier rice is required then opt for Italian, arborio or medium-round-grain rice. Wash both types very well before use until the water runs clear. This gets rid of any dirt, dust and starch which can ruin the final appearance of the dish.

Rice vinegar This is vinegar made from rice but with a far less acidic flavour than Western varieties. Cider vinegar makes a good alternative.

413

INTRODUCTION

Sesame oil A nutty-flavoured oil, generally used in small quantities at the end of cooking for flavour. Sometimes sesame oil is used with groundnut or sunflower oil for stir-frying.

Shrimp paste Thai shrimp paste is a dark brown, dry paste made from prawns and salt and is used in small amounts to flavour sauces. Anchovy paste makes a good substitute.

Shrimps, dried These are strongly-flavoured dried prawns available whole or in powder form. Whole ones should be rinsed before use.

Soy sauce Choose from light and dark types. The light variety, harder to find, is light in colour but saltier in taste and still full of flavour. It is the best type to use in cooking. The dark variety is darker in colour and often a little thicker than the light type.

Star anise A Chinese spice with a distinctive liquorice flavour. It is a spice that is shaped like a star with eight points and is used to flavour meat and poultry dishes in particular.

Tofu Also called beancurd, this is a food made from puréed and pressed soy beans. Sold in flat cakes it has the texture and consistency of soft cheese. Available plain and bland or smoked it is highly nutritious and does take on the flavour of the things it is being cooked with. The type used for stir-frying should be firm so that it does not crumble during cooking and is best cut into cubes.

Waterchestnuts Only available in cans but quite acceptable. These give a lovely crunch to a stir-fry, salad or vegetable accompaniment.

Wonton skins These are thin, yellow discs of dough generally packed in cellophane for easy use. Store in the refrigerator before use and do not allow to dry out or they will become dry and brittle and unsuitable for wrapping around sweet and savoury mixtures that are steamed or fried. Filo pastry makes a good alternative when unavailable.

COOKING EQUIPMENT AND METHODS

In Thailand, there are few gas and electric ovens or grills as Westerners know them, most cooking being done on an open charcoal stove. Meat and fish are frequently barbecued or grilled and woks are set upon their surfaces to stir-fry, boil, steam or simmer dishes. A wok is therefore the most necessary piece of equipment required for cooking - although a heavy-duty, deep frying pan may suffice. There is really very little need for specialist equipment although the following special items may be worth the investment to the avid Thai cook:

Pestle and mortar An absolute must to crush spices, herbs and other flavourings to make pastes for flavouring a whole host of dishes. A small electric herb grinder or coffee grinder, specifically reserved for spices, could be employed instead.

Steamer A steamer, with a good tight-fitting lid, is necessary to cook foods gently above boiling water. Chinese bamboo steamers are ideal solutions at very little cost and can be purchased cheaply from Chinese supermarkets. An improvised set-up could use a metal colander over a saucepan with tight-fitting lid to cover.

STARTERS

HOT & SOUR SOUP
• •

SERVES 4

1 tbsp sunflower oil
250 g/8 oz smoked tofu (bean curd),
    sliced
90 g/3 oz/1 cup shiitake mushrooms,
    sliced
2 tbsp chopped fresh coriander (cilantro)
125 g/4 oz/2 cups watercress
1 red chilli, sliced finely, to garnish

STOCK:
1 tbsp tamarind pulp
2 dried red chillies, chopped
2 kaffir lime leaves, torn in half
2.5 cm/1 in piece ginger, chopped
5 cm/2 in piece galangal, chopped
1 stalk lemon grass, chopped
1 onion, quartered
1 litre/1¾ pints/4 cups cold water

1 Put all the ingredients for the stock
   into a saucepan and bring to the
boil. Simmer for 5 minutes. Remove from
the heat and strain, reserving the stock.

2 Heat the oil in a wok or large, heavy
   frying pan (skillet) and cook the tofu
(bean curd) over a high heat for about
2 minutes, stirring constantly. Add the
strained stock.

3 Add the mushrooms and coriander
   (cilantro), and boil for 3 minutes.
Add the watercress and boil for 1 minute.

4 Serve immediately, garnished with
   red chilli slices.

MUSHROOMS

You might like to try a mixture of
different types of mushroom. Oyster,
button and straw mushrooms are all
suitable.

FILLED CUCUMBER CUPS
• •

SERVES 6

1 cucumber
4 spring onions (scallions), chopped finely
4 tbsp lime juice
2 small red chillies, deseeded and chopped
    finely
3 tsp sugar
150 g/5 oz/1¼ cups ground roasted
    peanuts
¼ tsp salt
3 shallots, sliced finely and deep-fried, to
    garnish

1 To make the cucumber cups, cut the
   ends off the cucumber, and divide it
into 3 equal lengths. Mark a line around
the centre of each one as a guide.

2 Make a zigzag cut all the way
   around the centre of each section,
always pointing the knife towards the
centre of the cucumber. Pull apart the two
halves.

3 Scoop out the centre of each cup
   with a melon baller or teaspoon.

4 Put the remaining ingredients,
   except for the shallots, in a bowl
and mix well to combine.

5 Divide the filling between the
   6 cucumber cups and arrange on a
serving plate. Garnish with the deep-fried
shallots.

CHERRY TOMATOES

Cherry tomatoes can also be hollowed
out very simply with a melon baller and
filled with this mixture. The two
look very pretty arranged together on a
serving dish.

THAI CHICKEN SPRING ROLLS

••

SERVES 4

2 tbsp vegetable oil
4 spring onions (scallions), trimmed and
* sliced very finely*
1 carrot, cut into matchstick pieces
1 small green or red (bell) pepper, cored,
* deseeded and sliced finely*
60 g/2 oz/⅔ cup button mushrooms, sliced
60 g/2 oz/1 cup bean-sprouts
175 g/6 oz/1 cup cooked chicken,
* shredded*
1 tbsp light soy sauce
1 tsp sugar
2 tsp cornflour (cornstarch), blended in
* 2 tbsp cold water*
12 x 20 cm/8 in spring roll wrappers
oil for deep-frying
salt and pepper
spring onion (scallion) slices to garnish

SAUCE:
50 ml/2 fl oz/ ¼ cup light malt vinegar
2 tbsp water
60 g/2 oz/ ¼ cup light muscovado sugar
½ tsp salt
5 cm/2 in piece of cucumber, peeled and
* chopped finely*
4 spring onions (scallions), trimmed and
* sliced finely*
1 small red or green chilli, deseeded and
* chopped very finely*

1 Heat the oil in a wok or frying pan (skillet) and add the spring onions (scallions), carrot and (bell) pepper. Stir-fry for 2–3 minutes. Add the mushrooms, bean-sprouts and chicken and cook for a further 2 minutes. Season to taste.

2 Mix together the soy sauce, sugar and blended cornflour (cornstarch). Add to the stir-fry and cook, stirring continuously for about 1 minute, until thickened. Leave to cool slightly.

3 Place spoonfuls of the chicken and vegetable mixture on the spring roll wrappers. Dampen the edges and roll them up to enclose the filling completely.

4 To make the dipping sauce, heat the vinegar, water, sugar and salt in a saucepan. Boil for 1 minute. Mix the cucumber, spring onions (scallions) and chilli in a small serving bowl and pour over the vinegar mixture. Leave to cool.

5 Heat the oil and fry the rolls until crisp and golden brown. Drain on paper towels, then serve the rolls, garnished with spring onion (scallion) slices and accompanied by the cucumber dipping sauce.

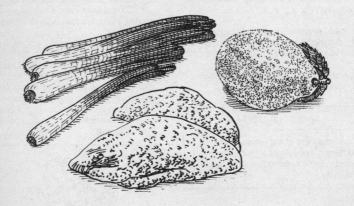

PORK & PRAWN (SHRIMP) SESAME TOASTS

••

SERVES 4

250 g/8 oz lean pork
250 g/8 oz/ ⅔ cup uncooked peeled prawns
   (shrimp), deveined
4 spring onions (scallions), trimmed
1 garlic clove, crushed
1 tbsp chopped fresh coriander (cilantro)
   leaves and stems
1 tbsp fish sauce
1 egg
8–10 slices of thick-cut white bread
3 tbsp sesame seeds
150 ml/ ¼ pint/ ⅔ cup vegetable oil
salt and pepper

TO GARNISH:
sprigs of fresh coriander (cilantro)
red (bell) pepper, sliced finely

1 Put the pork, prawns (shrimp),
   spring onions (scallions), garlic,
coriander (cilantro), fish sauce, egg and
seasoning into a food processor or
blender. Process for a few seconds to
chop the ingredients finely. Transfer the
mixture to a bowl. Alternatively, chop the
pork, prawns (shrimp) and spring onions
(scallions) very finely, and mix with the
garlic, coriander (cilantro), fish sauce,
beaten egg and seasoning until well
combined.

2 Spread the pork and prawn (shrimp)
   mixture thickly over the bread so
that it reaches right up to the edges. Cut
off the crusts and slice each piece of
bread into 4 squares or triangles. Sprinkle
with sesame seeds.

3 Heat the oil in a wok or frying pan
   (skillet). Fry a few pieces of the
bread, topping side down first so that it
sets the egg, for about 2 minutes or until
golden brown. Turn the pieces over to
cook on the other side, about 1 minute.

4 Drain the pork and prawn (shrimp)
   toasts and place them on paper
towels. Fry the remaining pieces in
batches until they are all cooked. Serve
garnished with sprigs of fresh coriander
(cilantro) and strips of red (bell) pepper.

CHICKEN & MUSHROOM WONTONS

••

SERVES 4

250 g/8 oz boneless chicken breast,
   skinned
60 g/2 oz/ ⅔ cup mushrooms
1 garlic clove
2 shallots
1 tbsp fish sauce or mushroom ketchup
1 tbsp chopped fresh coriander (cilantro)
2 tbsp vegetable oil
about 50 wonton wrappers
oil for deep-frying
salt and pepper
sliced spring onion (scallion) to garnish
sweet chilli sauce to serve

1 Put the chicken, mushrooms, garlic,
   shallots, fish sauce or mushroom
ketchup and coriander (cilantro) into a
blender or food processor. Blend for
10–15 seconds. Alternatively, chop all the
ingredients finely and mix together well.

2 Heat the vegetable oil in a wok or
   frying pan (skillet) and add the
chicken mixture. Stir-fry for about 8
minutes, breaking up the mixture as it
cooks, until it browns. Transfer to a bowl
and leave to cool for 10–15 minutes.

3 Place the wonton wrappers on a
   clean, damp tea towel (dish cloth).
Layering 2 wrappers together at a time,
place teaspoonfuls of the chicken mixture
into the middle. Dampen the edges with
water, then make small pouches, pressing
the edges together to seal. Repeat with
the remaining wrappers until all the
mixture is used.

4 Heat the oil in a wok or deep fat
   fryer. Fry the wontons, a few at a
time, for about 2–3 minutes until golden
brown. Lift them from the oil with a
perforated spoon and drain on paper
towels. Keep warm while frying the
remaining wontons.

5 Transfer the wontons to a warmed
   serving platter and garnish with
sliced spring onion (scallion). Serve at
once, accompanied by sweet chilli sauce.

417

RED CURRY FISHCAKES

MAKES ABOUT 24 (TO SERVE 4-6)

*1 kg/2 lb fish fillets or prepared seafood,
  such as cod, haddock, prawns (shrimp),
  crab meat or lobster*
1 egg, beaten
2 tbsp chopped fresh coriander
Red Curry Paste (see page 426)
*1 bunch spring onions (scallions), finely
  chopped*
vegetable oil, for deep-frying
chilli flowers, to garnish

CUCUMBER SALAD:
1 large cucumber, peeled and grated
2 shallots, peeled and grated
*2 red chillies, seeded and very finely
  chopped*
2 tbsp fish sauce
2 tbsp dried powdered shrimps
1½-2 tbsp lime juice

1 Place the fish in a blender or food
  processor with the egg, coriander
and curry paste and purée until smooth
and well blended.

2 Turn the mixture into a bowl, add
  the spring onions (scallions) and mix
well to combine.

3 Taking 2 tablespoons of the fish
  mixture at a time, shape into balls,
then flatten them slightly with your fingers
to make fishcakes.

4 Heat the oil in a wok or pan until
  hot, add a few of the fishcakes and
deep-fry for a few minutes until brown
and cooked through. Remove with a
slotted spoon and drain on paper towels.
Keep warm while cooking the remaining
fishcakes.

5 Meanwhile, to make the cucumber
  salad, mix the cucumber with the
shallots, chillies, fish sauce, dried shrimps
and lime juice.

6 Serve the salad immediately, with
  the warm fishcakes.

CRUDITÉS WITH SHRIMP SAUCE

SERVES 6

*about 750 g/1½ lb prepared raw fruit and
  vegetables, such as broccoli, cauliflower,
  apple, pineapple, cucumber, celery,
  (bell) peppers and mushrooms*

SAUCE:
60 g/2 oz dried shrimps
1 cm/ ½ in cube shrimp paste
3 garlic cloves, crushed
4 red chillies, seeded and chopped
6 stems fresh coriander, coarsely chopped
juice of 2 limes
fish sauce, to taste
brown sugar, to taste

1 Soak the dried shrimps in warm
  water for 10 minutes.

2 To make the sauce, place the shrimp
  paste, drained shrimps, garlic,
chillies and coriander in a food processor
or blender and process until well
chopped but not smooth.

3 Turn the sauce mixture into a bowl
  and add the lime juice, mixing well.

4 Add fish sauce and brown sugar to
  taste to the sauce, mixing to blend
well. Cover the bowl tightly and chill the
sauce in the refrigerator for at least
12 hours, or overnight.

5 To serve, arrange the fruit and
  vegetables attractively on a large
serving plate. Place the prepared sauce in
the centre for dipping.

ALTERNATIVE

Hard-boiled quail's eggs are often
added to this traditional fruit and
vegetable platter and certainly would
be offered on a special occasion.

SWEET & SOUR TOFU SALAD

SERVES 4-6

2 tbsp vegetable oil
1 tbsp sesame oil
1 garlic clove, crushed
500 g/1 lb tofu (bean curd), cubed
1 onion, sliced
1 carrot, cut into julienne strips
1 stick celery, sliced
*2 small red (bell) peppers, cored, seeded
    and sliced*
*250 g/8 oz mangetout (snow peas),
    trimmed and halved*
*125 g/4 oz broccoli, trimmed and divided
    into florets*
125 g/4 oz thin green beans, halved
2 tbsp oyster sauce
1 tbsp tamarind concentrate
1 tbsp fish sauce
1 tbsp tomato purée (paste)
1 tbsp light soy sauce
1 tbsp chilli sauce
2 tbsp sugar
1 tbsp white vinegar
pinch of ground star anise
1 tsp cornflour (cornstarch)
300 ml/ ½ pint/1¼ cups water

1 Heat the vegetable oil in a large, heavy-based frying pan or wok until hot. Add the crushed garlic and cook for a few seconds.

2 Add the tofu in batches and stir-fry over a gentle heat, until golden on all sides. Remove with a slotted spoon and keep warm.

3 Add the onion, carrot, celery, red (bell) pepper, mangetout (snow peas), broccoli and green beans to the pan and stir-fry for about 2-3 minutes or until tender-crisp.

4 Add the oyster sauce, tamarind concentrate, fish sauce, tomato purée (paste), soy sauce, chilli sauce, sugar, vinegar and star anise, mixing well to blend. Stir-fry for a further 2 minutes.

5 Mix the cornflour (cornstarch) with the water and add to the pan with the fried tofu. Stir-fry gently until the sauce boils and thickens slightly.

6 Serve the salad immediately, on warm plates.

CHICKEN OR BEEF SATAY

SERVES 4-6

*4 boneless, skinned chicken breasts or
    750 g/1½ lb rump steak, trimmed*

MARINADE:
1 small onion, finely chopped
1 garlic clove, crushed
*2.5 cm/1 in piece ginger root, peeled and
    grated*
2 tbsp dark soy sauce
2 tsp chilli powder
1 tsp ground coriander
2 tsp dark brown sugar
1 tbsp lemon or lime juice
1 tbsp vegetable oil

SAUCE:
300 ml/ ½ pint/1¼ cups coconut milk
4 tbsp/ ⅓ cup crunchy peanut butter
1 tbsp fish sauce
1 tsp lemon or lime juice
salt and pepper

1 Trim any fat from the chicken or beef then cut into thin strips, about 7 cm/3 in long.

2 To make the marinade, place all the ingredients in a shallow dish and mix well. Add the chicken or beef strips and turn in the marinade until well coated. Cover and leave to marinate for 2 hours or stand overnight in the refrigerator.

3 Remove the meat from the marinade and thread the pieces, concertina style, on bamboo or thin wooden skewers.

4 Grill the chicken and beef satays for 8-10 minutes, turning and brushing occasionally with the marinade, until cooked through.

5 Meanwhile, to make the sauce, mix the coconut milk with the peanut butter, fish sauce and lemon juice in a pan. Bring to the boil and cook for 3 minutes. Season to taste and serve with the cooked satays.

FAT HORSES

SERVES 6

30 g/1 oz/2 tbsp creamed coconut
125 g/4 oz lean pork
125 g/4 oz chicken breast, skin removed
125 g/4 oz/ ½ cup canned crab meat,
   drained
2 eggs
2 garlic cloves, crushed
4 spring onions (scallions), trimmed and
   chopped
1 tbsp fish sauce
1 tbsp chopped fresh coriander (cilantro)
   leaves and stems
1 tbsp dark muscovado sugar
salt and pepper

TO GARNISH:
finely sliced white radish (mooli) or turnip
chives
red chilli
sprigs of fresh coriander (cilantro)

1 Put the coconut into a bowl and
  pour over 3 tablespoons of hot
water. Stir to dissolve the coconut.

2 Put the pork, chicken and crab meat
  into a food processor or blender and
process for 10–15 seconds until minced
(ground), or chop them finely by hand
and put in a mixing bowl.

3 Add the coconut mixture to the food
  processor or blender with the eggs,
garlic, spring onions (scallions), fish
sauce, coriander (cilantro) and sugar.
Season with salt and pepper and process
for a few more seconds. Alternatively, mix
these ingredients into the chopped pork,
chicken and crab meat.

4 Grease 6 ramekin dishes with a little
  butter. Spoon in the minced
(ground) mixture, levelling the surface.
Place them in a steamer, then set the
steamer over a pan of gently boiling
water. Cook until set – about 30 minutes.

5 Lift out the dishes and leave to cool
  for a few minutes. Run a knife
around the edge of each dish, then invert
on to warmed plates. Serve garnished
with finely sliced white radish (mooli) or
turnip, chives, red chilli and sprigs of
fresh coriander (cilantro).

MEATBALLS IN SPICY PEANUT SAUCE

SERVES 4

500 g/1 lb/2 cups lean minced (ground)
   beef
2 tsp finely grated fresh ginger root
1 small red chilli, deseeded and chopped
   finely
1 tbsp chopped fresh basil or coriander
   (cilantro)
1 tbsp sesame oil
1 tbsp vegetable oil
salt and pepper

SAUCE:
2 tbsp Thai red curry paste
300 ml/ ½ pint/1¼ cups coconut milk
125 g/4 oz/1 cup ground peanuts
1 tbsp fish sauce

TO GARNISH:
chopped fresh basil
sprigs of fresh basil or coriander (cilantro)

1 Put the beef, ginger, chilli and basil
  or coriander (cilantro) into a food
processor or blender. Add ½ teaspoon of
salt and plenty of pepper. Process for
about 10–15 seconds until finely chopped.
Alternatively, chop the ingredients finely
and mix together.

2 Form the beef mixture into about
  12 balls. Heat the sesame oil and
vegetable oil in a wok or frying pan
(skillet) and fry the meatballs over a
medium-high heat until well browned on
all sides, about 10 minutes. Lift them out
and drain on paper towels.

3 To make the sauce, stir-fry the red
  curry paste in the wok or frying pan
(skillet) for 1 minute. Add the coconut
milk, peanuts and fish sauce. Heat,
stirring, until just simmering.

4 Return the meatballs to the wok or
  frying pan (skillet) and cook gently
in the sauce for 10–15 minutes. If the
sauce begins to get too thick, add a little
extra coconut milk or water. Season with
a little salt and pepper, if needed.

5 Serve garnished with chopped fresh
  basil and sprigs of fresh basil or
coriander (cilantro).

ROAST RED PORK

SERVES 4

750 g/1½ lb pork fillet (tenderloin)
1 tsp red food colouring
4 garlic cloves, crushed
1 tsp Chinese five-spice powder
1 tbsp light soy sauce
1 tbsp fish sauce
1 tbsp dry sherry
1 tbsp dark muscovado sugar
1 tbsp sesame oil
1 tbsp finely grated fresh ginger root

TO GARNISH:
lettuce
spring onions (scallions), finely sliced

1 Rinse the pork fillet (tenderloin) and trim off any fat. Place in a large clear plastic food bag or freezer bag and add the red food colouring. Roll the pork around in the bag to coat it in the colouring.

2 Mix all the remaining ingredients together in a bowl.

3 Add the mixture to the pork in the plastic bag. Secure the opening and chill overnight, or for at least 12 hours, turning the bag over occasionally.

4 Place the pork on a rack over a roasting tin (pan) and cook in a preheated oven at 220°C/425°F/Gas Mark 7 for 15 minutes. Remove from the oven and baste with the remaining marinade.

5 Reduce the oven temperature to 180°C/350°F/Gas Mark 4 and return the pork to the oven to roast for a further 25 minutes, basting occasionally with any remaining marinade. Leave to cool for at least 10 minutes before slicing.

6 Slice thinly, arrange on a serving platter and garnish with lettuce and finely sliced spring onions (scallions).

THAI STUFFED COURGETTES (ZUCCHINI)

SERVES 4

8 medium courgettes (zucchini)
1 tbsp sesame or vegetable oil
1 garlic clove, crushed
2 shallots, chopped finely
1 small red chilli, deseeded and chopped finely
250 g/8 oz/1 cup lean minced (ground) beef
1 tbsp fish sauce or mushroom ketchup
1 tbsp chopped fresh coriander (cilantro) or basil
2 tsp cornflour (cornstarch), blended with a little cold water
90 g/3 oz / ½ cup cooked long-grain rice
salt and pepper

TO GARNISH:
sprigs of fresh coriander (cilantro) or basil
carrot slices

1 Slice the courgettes (zucchini) in half horizontally and scoop out a channel down the middle, discarding all the seeds. Sprinkle with salt and set aside for 15 minutes.

2 Heat the oil in a wok or frying pan (skillet) and add the garlic, shallots and chilli. Stir-fry for 2 minutes, until golden. Add the minced (ground) beef and stir-fry briskly for about 5 minutes. Stir in the fish sauce or mushroom ketchup, the chopped coriander (cilantro) or basil and the blended cornflour (cornstarch), and cook for 2 minutes, stirring until thickened. Season with salt and pepper, then remove from the heat.

3 Rinse the courgettes (zucchini) in cold water and arrange them in a greased shallow ovenproof dish, cut side uppermost. Mix the cooked rice into the minced (ground) beef, then use this mixture to stuff the courgettes (zucchini).

4 Cover with foil and bake in a preheated oven at 190°C/375°F/Gas Mark 5 for about 20–25 minutes, removing the foil for the last 5 minutes of cooking time. Serve at once, garnished with sprigs of fresh coriander (cilantro) or basil, and carrot slices.

RICE CUBES WITH DIPPING SAUCE

SERVES 4-6

300 g/10 oz/1½ cups Thai jasmine rice
1.25 litres/2¼ pints/5 cups water

CORIANDER (CILANTRO) DIPPING SAUCE:
1 garlic clove
2 tsp salt
1 tbsp black peppercorns
60 g/2 oz/1 cup washed coriander
(cilantro), including roots and stem
3 tbsp lemon juice
180 ml/6 fl oz/¾ cup coconut milk
2 tbsp peanut butter
2 spring onions (scallions), chopped
roughly
1 red chilli, deseeded and sliced

1 Grease and line a 20 x 10 x 2.5 cm/
8 x 4 x 1 in tin.

2 To make the sauce, put the garlic,
salt, peppercorns, coriander
(cilantro) and lemon juice into a pestle
and mortar or blender. Grind finely.

3 Add the coconut milk, peanut butter,
spring onions (scallions) and chilli.
Grind finely. Transfer to a saucepan and
bring to the boil. Leave to cool. This
sauce will keep for 3–5 days in a
refrigerator.

4 To cook the rice, do not rinse. Bring
the water to the boil and add the
rice. Stir and return to a medium boil.
Cook, uncovered, for 14–16 minutes until
very soft. Drain thoroughly.

5 Put 125 g/4 oz/ ⅔ cup of the cooked
rice in a blender and purée, or grind
to a paste in a pestle and mortar. Stir into
the remaining cooked rice and spoon into
the lined tin (pan). Level the surface and
cover with clingfilm (plastic wrap).
Compress the rice by using either a
similar-sized tin (pan) which will fit into
the filled tin (pan), or a small piece of
board, and weigh this down with cans.
Chill for at least 8 hours or preferably
overnight.

6 Invert the tin (pan) on to a board.
Cut the rice into cubes with a wet
knife. Serve with the Coriander (Cilantro)
Dipping Sauce.

SON-IN-LAW EGGS

••

SERVES 4

6 eggs, hard-boiled (hard-cooked) and
  shelled
4 tbsp sunflower oil
1 onion, sliced thinly
2 fresh red chillies, sliced
2 tbsp sugar
1 tbsp water
2 tsp tamarind pulp
1 tbsp liquid seasoning, such as Maggi

1 Prick the hard-boiled (hard-cooked)
  eggs 2 or 3 times with a cocktail
stick (toothpick).

2 Heat the oil in a wok or large, heavy
  frying pan (skillet) and fry the eggs
until crispy and golden. Drain on paper
towels.

3 Halve the eggs lengthways and put
  on a serving dish.

4 Reserve one tablespoon of the oil,
  pour off the rest, then heat the
tablespoonful in the wok or pan (skillet).
Cook the onion and chillies over a high
heat until golden and slightly crisp. Drain
on paper towels.

5 Combine the sugar, water, tamarind
  pulp and liquid seasoning. Simmer
for 5 minutes until thickened.

6 Pour the sauce over the eggs and
  spoon over the onion and chillies.
Serve immediately with rice.

TAMARIND PULP

Tamarind pulp is sold in oriental stores,
and is quite sour. If it is not available,
use twice the amount of lemon juice in
its place.

PERFECT EGGS

When hard-boiling (hard-cooking) eggs,
stir the water gently one way, then the
other, and you will have beautifully
centred yolks.

MAIN DISHES

FRIED RICE & PRAWNS (SHRIMP)

••

SERVES 4

60 g/2 oz/ ¼ cup butter
3 tbsp vegetable oil
500 g/1 lb/3 cups cooked basmati rice
6 spring onions (scallions), finely sliced
125 g/4 oz mangetout (snow peas), halved
1 carrot, cut into fine julienne strips
125 g/4 oz canned water chestnuts,
  drained and sliced
1 small crisp lettuce, shredded
350 g/12 oz peeled tiger prawns (shrimp)
1 large red chilli, seeded and sliced
  diagonally
3 egg yolks
4 tsp sesame oil
salt and pepper

1 Heat the butter and the oil in a large,
  heavy-based frying pan or wok. Add
the cooked rice and stir-fry for 2 minutes.

2 Add the spring onions (scallions),
  mangetout (snow peas), carrot, water
chestnuts and salt and pepper to taste,
mixing well. Stir-fry over medium heat for
a further 2 minutes.

3 Add the shredded lettuce, prawns
  (shrimp) and chilli and stir-fry for a
further 2 minutes.

4 Beat the egg yolks with the sesame
  oil and stir into the pan, coating the
rice and vegetable mixture. Cook for
about 2 minutes to set the egg mixture.

5 Serve the rice and prawns (shrimp)
  at once on warmed plates.

FRIED RICE

For perfect fried rice, it is best to cook
the rice ahead of time and allow it to
cool completely before adding to the
hot oil. In that way the rice grains will
remain separate, and the rice will not
become lumpy or heavy.

SIZZLED CHILLI PRAWNS (SHRIMP)

SERVES 4

5 tbsp soy sauce
5 tbsp dry sherry
3 dried red chillies, seeded and chopped
2 garlic cloves, crushed
2 tsp grated ginger root
5 tbsp water
625 g/1¼ lb shelled tiger prawns (shrimp)
1 large bunch spring onions (scallions),
    chopped
90 g/3 oz/⅔ cup salted cashew nuts
3 tbsp vegetable oil
2 tsp cornflour (cornstarch)

1 Mix the soy sauce with the sherry, chillies, garlic, ginger and water in a large bowl.

2 Add the prawns (shrimp), spring onions (scallions) and cashews and mix well. Cover tightly and leave to marinate for at least 2 hours, stirring occasionally.

3 Heat the oil in a large, heavy-based frying pan or wok. Drain the prawns (shrimp), spring onions (scallions) and cashews from the marinade with a slotted spoon and add to the pan, reserving the marinade. Stir-fry over a high heat for 1-2 minutes.

4 Mix the reserved marinade with the cornflour (cornstarch), add to the pan and stir-fry for about 30 seconds, until the marinade forms a slightly thickened shiny glaze over the prawn (shrimp) mixture.

5 Serve the prawns (shrimp) immediately, with rice.

VARIATION

For an attractive presentation serve this dish on mixed wild rice and basmati or other long-grain rice. Start cooking the wild rice in boiling water. After 10 minutes, add the basmati rice or other rice and continue boiling until all grains are tender. Drain well and adjust the seasoning.

PINEAPPLE & FISH CURRY

SERVES 4

2 pineapples
7 cm/3 in piece galangal, sliced
2 blades of lemon grass, bruised then
    chopped
5 sprigs fresh basil
500 g/1 lb firm white fish fillets, cubed
    (monkfish, halibut or cod, for example)
125 g/4 oz peeled prawns (shrimp)
2 tbsp vegetable oil
2 tbsp Red Curry Paste (see page 426)
125 ml/4 fl oz/ ½ cup thick coconut milk
    or cream
2 tbsp fish sauce
2 tsp palm or demarara sugar
2-3 red chillies, seeded and cut into thin
    julienne strips
about 6 kaffir lime leaves, torn into pieces
coriander sprigs, to garnish

1 Cut the pineapples in half lengthways. Remove the flesh, reserving the shells if using (see right). Remove the core from the pineapple flesh then dice into bite-sized pieces.

2 Place the galangal in a large shallow pan with the lemon grass and basil. Add the fish cubes and just enough water to cover. Bring to the boil, reduce the heat and simmer for about 2 minutes. Add the prawns (shrimp) and cook for a further 1 minute or until the fish is just cooked. Remove from the flavoured stock with a slotted spoon and keep warm.

3 Heat the oil in a heavy-based pan or wok. Add the curry paste and cook for 1 minute. Stir in the coconut milk or cream, fish sauce, brown sugar, chillies and lime leaves.

4 Add the pineapple and cook until just heated through. Add the cooked fish and mix gently to combine.

5 Spoon into the reserved pineapple shells, if liked, and serve immediately, garnished with sprigs of coriander.

WRAPPED FISH WITH GINGER

SERVES 4

4 x 250 g/8 oz whole trout or mackerel,
  gutted
4 tbsp chopped fresh coriander
5 garlic cloves, crushed
2 tsp grated lemon or lime zest
2 tsp vegetable oil
banana leaves, for wrapping (optional)
90 g/3 oz/6 tbsp butter
1 tbsp grated ginger root
1 tbsp light soy sauce
salt and pepper
coriander sprigs and lemon or lime
  wedges, to garnish

1 Wash and dry the fish. Mix the
coriander with the garlic, lemon or
lime zest and salt and pepper to taste.
Spoon into the fish cavities.

2 Brush the fish with a little oil, season
well and place each fish on a double
thickness sheet of baking parchment or
foil and wrap up well to enclose.
Alternatively, wrap in banana leaves
(see right).

3 Place on a baking tray and bake in
the preheated oven at
190ºC/375ºF/Gas Mark 5 for about 25
minutes or until the flesh will flake easily.

4 Meanwhile, melt the butter in a
small pan. Add the grated ginger
and stir until well mixed, then stir in the
soy sauce.

5 To serve, unwrap the fish parcels,
drizzle over the ginger butter and
garnish with coriander and lemon or lime
wedges.

BANANA LEAVES

For a really authentic touch, wrap the
fish in banana leaves, which can be
ordered from specialist oriental
supermarkets. They are not edible, but
impart a delicate flavour to the fish.

KING PRAWNS (JUMBO SHRIMP) IN RED CURRY SAUCE

SERVES 4

1 tbsp vegetable oil
6 spring onions (scallions), trimmed and
  sliced
1 stalk lemon grass
1 cm/ ½ in piece of fresh ginger root
250 ml/8 fl oz/1 cup coconut milk
2 tbsp Thai red curry paste
1 tbsp fish sauce
500 g/1 lb/3 cups uncooked king prawns
  (jumbo shrimp)
1 tbsp chopped fresh coriander (cilantro)
fresh chillies to garnish

1 Heat the vegetable oil in a wok or
large frying pan (skillet) and fry the
spring onions (scallions) gently until
softened, about 2 minutes.

2 Bruise the stalk of lemon grass using
a meat mallet or rolling pin. Peel
and finely grate the piece of fresh ginger
root.

3 Add the bruised lemon grass and
grated ginger root to the wok or
frying pan (skillet) with the coconut milk,
Thai red curry paste and fish sauce. Heat
until almost boiling.

4 Peel the prawns (shrimp), leaving
the tails intact. Remove the black
vein running down the back of each
prawn (shrimp). Add the prawns (shrimp)
to the wok or frying pan (skillet) with the
chopped coriander (cilantro) and cook
gently for 5 minutes.

5 Serve the prawns (shrimp) with the
sauce, garnished with fresh chillies.

VARIATIONS

Try this recipe using Thai green curry
sauce instead of red. Both varieties are
obtainable from many supermarkets –
look for them in the oriental foods
section.

Use 3 shallots or ½ small onion
instead of the spring onions (scallions),
if you prefer.

RED CHICKEN CURRY

SERVES 6

4 tbsp vegetable oil
2 garlic cloves, crushed
400 ml/14 fl oz/1¾ cups coconut milk
6 chicken breast fillets, skinned and cut
into bite-sized pieces
125 ml/4 fl oz/ ½ cup chicken stock
2 tbsp fish sauce
kaffir lime leaves, sliced red chillies and
chopped coriander, to garnish

RED CURRY PASTE:
8 dried red chillies, seeded and chopped
2.5 cm/1 in galangal or ginger root,
peeled and sliced
3 stalks lemon grass, chopped
1 garlic clove, peeled
2 tsp shrimp paste
1 kaffir lime leaf, chopped
1 tsp ground coriander
¾ tsp ground cumin
1 tbsp chopped fresh coriander
1 tsp salt and black pepper

1 To make the curry paste, place all
the ingredients in a food processor
or blender and process until smooth.

2 Heat the oil in a large, heavy-based
pan or wok. Add the garlic and cook
for 1 minute or until it turns golden.

3 Stir in the curry paste and cook for
10-15 seconds then gradually add
the coconut milk, stirring constantly (don't
worry if the mixture starts to look curdled
at this stage).

4 Add the chicken pieces and turn in
the sauce mixture to coat. Cook
gently for about 3-5 minutes or until
almost tender.

5 Stir in the chicken stock and fish
sauce, mixing well, then cook for a
further 2 minutes.

6 Transfer to a warmed serving dish
and garnish with lime leaves, sliced
red chillies and chopped coriander. Serve
with rice.

SESAME SKEWERED CHICKEN WITH GINGER BASTE

SERVES 4

4 wooden satay sticks, soaked in warm
water
500 g/1 lb boneless chicken breasts
sprigs of fresh mint to garnish

MARINADE:
1 garlic clove, crushed
1 shallot, chopped very finely
2 tbsp sesame oil
1 tbsp fish sauce or light soy sauce
finely grated rind of 1 lime or ½ lemon
2 tbsp lime juice or lemon juice
1 tsp sesame seeds
2 tsp finely grated fresh ginger root
2 tsp chopped fresh mint
salt and pepper

1 To make the marinade, put the
garlic, shallot, sesame oil, fish sauce
or soy sauce, lime or lemon rind and
juice, sesame seeds, ginger and chopped
mint into a large non-metallic bowl.
Season with a little salt and pepper.

2 Remove the skin from the chicken
breasts and cut the flesh into
chunks. Add them to the marinade,
stirring to coat them in the mixture. Cover
and chill for at least 2 hours so that the
flavours are absorbed.

3 Thread the chicken on to wooden
satay sticks. Place them on the rack
of a grill (broiler) pan and baste with the
marinade.

4 Place the kebabs under a preheated
grill (broiler) for about 8–10 minutes.
Turn them frequently, basting them with
the remaining marinade.

5 Serve at once, garnished with sprigs
of fresh mint.

VARIATIONS

Pork fillet (tenderloin) or turkey breasts
can be used instead of the chicken.
The kebabs taste delicious if dipped
into an accompanying bowl of hot chilli
sauce.

BARBECUED CHICKEN LEGS

SERVES 6

12 chicken drumsticks

SPICED BUTTER:
175 g/6 oz/ ¾ cup butter
2 garlic cloves, crushed
1 tsp grated ginger root
2 tsp ground turmeric
4 tsp cayenne pepper
2 tbsp lime juice
3 tbsp mango chutney

1 Prepare a barbecue with medium coals or preheat a conventional grill (broiler) to moderate.

2 To make the Spiced Butter mixture, beat the butter with the garlic, ginger, turmeric, cayenne pepper, lime juice and chutney until it is blended well.

3 Using a sharp knife, slash each chicken leg to the bone 3-4 times.

4 Cook the drumsticks over the barbecue for about 12-15 minutes or until almost cooked. Alternatively, grill (broil) the chicken for about 10-12 minutes until almost cooked, turning halfway through.

5 Spread the chicken legs liberally with the butter mixture and continue to cook for a further 5-6 minutes, turning and basting frequently with the butter until golden and crisp.

6 Serve hot or cold with a crisp green salad and rice.

VARIATION

This spicy butter mixture would be equally effective on grilled chicken or turkey breast fillets. Skin before coating with the mixture.

GREEN CHILLI CHICKEN

SERVES 4

5 tbsp vegetable oil
500 g/1 lb boneless chicken breasts, sliced
*   into thin strips*
50 ml/2 fl oz/ ¼ cup coconut milk
3 tbsp brown sugar
3 tsp fish sauce
3 tbsp sliced red and green chillies, seeded
4-6 tbsp chopped fresh basil
3 tbsp thick coconut milk or cream
finely chopped fresh chillies, seeded, lemon
*   grass and lemon slices, to garnish*

GREEN CURRY PASTE:
2 tsp ground ginger
2 tsp ground coriander
2 tsp caraway seeds,
2 tsp ground nutmeg
2 tsp shrimp paste
2 tsp salt
2 tsp black pepper
pinch of ground cloves
1 stalk lemon grass, finely chopped
2 tbsp chopped coriander
2 garlic cloves, peeled
2 onions, peeled
grated rind and juice of 2 limes
4 fresh green chillies, about 5 cm/2 in long,
*   seeded*

1 To make the curry paste, place all the ingredients and 2 tablespoons of the oil in a food processor or blender and process to a smooth paste.

2 Heat the remaining oil in a heavy-based pan or wok. Add the curry paste and cook for about 30 seconds.

3 Add the chicken strips to the wok and stir-fry over a high heat for about 2-3 minutes.

4 Add the coconut milk, brown sugar, fish sauce and chillies. Cook for 5 minutes, stirring frequently. Remove from the heat, add the basil and toss.

5 Transfer the chicken to a warmed serving dish. To serve, spoon on a little of the thick coconut milk or cream and garnish with chopped chillies, lemon grass and lemon slices. Serve with steamed or boiled rice.

PEANUT SESAME CHICKEN

SERVES 4

2 tbsp vegetable oil
2 tbsp sesame oil
*500g/1 lb boneless, skinned chicken
    breasts, sliced into strips*
*250 g/8 oz broccoli, divided into small
    florets*
*250 g/8 oz baby or dwarf corn, halved if
    large*
*1 small red (bell) pepper, cored, seeded
    and sliced*
2 tbsp soy sauce
250 ml/8 fl oz/1 cup orange juice
2 tsp cornflour (cornstarch)
2 tbsp toasted sesame seeds
*60 g/2 oz/⅓ cup roasted, shelled, unsalted
    peanuts*

1 Heat the oils in a large, heavy-based
    frying pan or wok, add the chicken
strips and stir-fry until browned, about
4-5 minutes.

2 Add the broccoli, corn and red (bell)
    pepper and stir-fry for a further
1-2 minutes.

3 Meanwhile, mix the soy sauce with
    the orange juice and cornflour
(cornstarch). Stir into the chicken and
vegetable mixture, stirring constantly until
the sauce has slightly thickened and a
glaze develops.

4 Stir in the sesame seeds and
    peanuts, mixing well. Heat for a
further 3-4 minutes then serve at once,
with rice or noodles.

PEANUTS

Make sure you use the unsalted
variety of peanuts or the dish will be
too salty, as the soy sauce adds
saltiness.

CHICKEN & NOODLE ONE-POT

SERVES 4

1 tbsp sunflower oil
1 onion, sliced
1 garlic clove, crushed
2.5 cm/1 in root ginger, peeled and grated
*1 bunch spring onions (scallions), sliced
    diagonally*
*500 g/1 lb chicken breast fillet, skinned
    and cut into bite-sized pieces*
2 tbsp mild curry paste
475 ml/16 fl oz/2 cups coconut milk
300 ml/ ½ pint/1¼ cups chicken stock
250 g/8 oz Chinese egg noodles
2 tsp lime juice
salt and pepper
basil sprigs, to garnish

1 Heat the oil in a wok or large,
    heavy-based pan. Add the onion,
garlic, ginger and spring onions (scallions)
and stir-fry for 2 minutes until softened.

2 Add the chicken pieces and curry
    paste and stir-fry until the vegetables
and chicken are golden brown, about
4 minutes.

3 Stir in the coconut milk, stock and
    salt and pepper to taste, mixing until
well blended.

4 Bring to the boil, break the noodles
    into large pieces, if necessary, add to
the pan, cover and simmer for about
6-8 minutes until the noodles are just
tender, stirring occasionally.

5 Add the lime juice, taste and adjust
    the seasoning, if necessary, then
serve at once in deep soup bowls.

COOK'S TIP

If you enjoy the hot flavours of Thai
cooking then substitute the mild curry
paste in the above recipe with Thai hot
curry paste (found in most
supermarkets) but reduce the quantity
to 1 tablespoon.

DUCK WITH GINGER & LIME

SERVES 6

3 boneless Barbary duck breasts, about
250 g/8 oz each
salt

DRESSING:
125 ml/4 fl oz/ ½ cup olive oil
2 tsp sesame oil
2 tbsp lime juice
grated rind and juice of 1 orange
2 tsp fish sauce
1 tbsp grated ginger root
1 garlic clove, crushed
2 tsp light soy sauce
3 spring onions (scallions), finely chopped
1 tsp sugar
about 250 g/8 oz assorted salad leaves
orange slices, to garnish, optional

1 Wash the duck breasts, dry on paper towels, then cut in half. Prick the skin all over with a fork and season well with salt. Place the duck pieces, skin-side down, on a wire rack or trivet over a roasting tin. Cook the duck in the preheated oven for 10 minutes, then turn over and cook for a further 12-15 minutes, or until the duck is cooked, but still pink in the centre, and the skin is crisp.

2 To make the dressing, beat the oils with the lime juice, orange rind and juice, fish sauce, ginger, garlic, soy sauce, spring onions (scallions) and sugar until well blended.

3 Remove the duck from the oven, allow to cool, then cut into thick slices. Add a little of the dressing to moisten and coat the duck.

4 To serve, arrange assorted salad leaves on a serving dish. Top with the sliced duck breasts and drizzle with the remaining salad dressing.

5 Garnish with orange twists, if using, then serve at once.

BEEF & BOK CHOY

SERVES 4

1 large head of bok choy, about 250-275 g/
8-9 oz, torn into large pieces
2 tbsp vegetable oil
2 garlic cloves, crushed
500 g/1 lb rump or fillet steak, cut into
thin strips
150 g/5 oz mangetout (snow peas),
trimmed
150 g/5 oz baby or dwarf corn
6 spring onions (scallions), chopped
2 red (bell) peppers, cored, seeded and
thinly sliced
2 tbsp oyster sauce
1 tbsp fish sauce
1 tbsp sugar

1 Steam the bok choy leaves over boiling water until just tender. Keep warm.

2 Heat the oil in a large, heavy-based frying pan or wok, add the garlic and steak strips and stir-fry until just browned, about 1-2 minutes.

3 Add the mangetout (snow peas), baby corn, spring onions (scallions), red (bell) pepper, oyster sauce, fish sauce and sugar to the pan, mixing well. Stir-fry for a further 2-3 minutes until the vegetables are just tender, but still crisp.

4 Arrange the bok choy leaves in the base of a heated serving dish and spoon the beef and vegetable mixture into the centre.

5 Serve the stir-fry immediately, with rice or noodles.

VARIATION

Bok choy is one of the most important ingredients in this dish. If unavailable, use Chinese leaves, kai choy (mustard leaves) or pak choy.

GREEN BEEF CURRY

SERVES 4

1 aubergine (eggplant), peeled and cubed
2 onions, cut into thin wedges
2 tbsp vegetable oil
Green Curry Paste (see page 427)
500 g/1 lb beef fillet, cut into thin strips
475 ml/16 fl oz/2 cups thick coconut milk
  or cream
2 tbsp fish sauce
1 tbsp brown sugar
1 red chilli, seeded and very finely
  chopped
1 green chilli, seeded and very finely
  chopped
2.5 cm/1 in ginger root, finely chopped
4 kaffir lime leaves, torn into pieces
chopped fresh basil, to garnish

1 Blanch the aubergine (eggplant)
  cubes and onion wedges in boiling
water for about 2 minutes, to soften.
Drain thoroughly.

2 Heat the oil in a large heavy-based
  pan or wok, add the curry paste and
cook for 1 minute.

3 Add the beef strips and stir-fry, over
  a high heat, for about 1 minute, to
brown on all sides.

4 Add the coconut milk or cream, fish
  sauce and sugar to the pan and
bring the mixture to the boil, stirring
constantly.

5 Add the aubergine (eggplant) and
  onion, chillies, ginger and lime
leaves. Cook for a further 2 minutes.

6 Sprinkle with chopped basil to serve.
  Accompany with rice.

COCONUT MILK

Coconut milk is sold in cans, or you
can make your own. Pour 300 ml/
½ pint /1¼ cups boiling water over
250 g/8 oz shredded coconut and
simmer over low heat for 30 minutes.
Strain the milk into a bowl through a
piece of muslin. Gather the ends of
muslin together and squeeze tightly to
extract as much liquid as possible.

PEPPERED BEEF CASHEW

SERVES 4

1 tbsp groundnut or sunflower oil
1 tbsp sesame oil
1 onion, sliced
1 garlic clove, crushed
1 tbsp grated ginger root
500 g/1 lb fillet or rump steak, cut into
  thin strips
2 tsp palm or demerara sugar
2 tbsp light soy sauce
1 small yellow (bell) pepper, cored, seeded
  and sliced
1 red (bell) pepper, cored, seeded and
  sliced
4 spring onions (scallions), chopped
2 celery sticks, chopped
4 large open-cap mushrooms, sliced
4 tbsp roasted cashew nuts
3 tbsp stock or white wine

1 Heat the oils in a large, heavy-based
  frying pan or wok. Add the onion,
garlic and ginger and stir-fry for about
2 minutes until softened and lightly
coloured.

2 Add the steak strips and stir-fry for a
  further 2-3 minutes, until the meat
has browned.

3 Add the sugar and soy sauce, mixing
  well.

4 Add the (bell) peppers, spring
  onions (scallions), celery,
mushrooms and cashews, mixing well.

5 Add the stock or wine and stir-fry
  for 2-3 minutes until the beef is
cooked through and the vegetables are
tender-crisp.

6 Serve the stir-fry immediately with
  rice noodles.

PALM SUGAR

Palm sugar is a thick brown sugar with
a slightly caramel taste. It is sold in
cakes, or in small containers. If not
available, use soft dark brown or
demerara sugar.

GARLIC PORK & SHRIMPS

SERVES 4

250 g/8 oz packet medium egg noodles
3 tbsp vegetable oil
2 garlic cloves, crushed
350 g/12 oz pork fillet, cut into strips
4 tbsp/ ⅓ cup dried shrimps, or 125 g/4 oz peeled prawns (shrimp)
1 bunch spring onions (scallions), finely chopped
90 g/3 oz/ ¾ cup chopped roasted and shelled unsalted peanuts
3 tbsp fish sauce
1½ tsp palm or demerara sugar
1-2 small red chillies, seeded and finely chopped (to taste)
3 tbsp lime juice
3 tbsp chopped fresh coriander
coriander sprigs, to garnish

1 Place the noodles in a large pan of boiling water, then immediately remove from the heat. Cover and leave to stand for 6 minutes, stirring once halfway through the time. At the end of 6 minutes the noodles will be perfectly cooked. Alternatively, follow the packet instructions. Drain the noodles thoroughly and keep warm.

2 Heat the oil in a large, heavy-based pan or wok, add the garlic and pork and stir-fry until the pork strips are browned, about 2-3 minutes.

3 Add the dried shrimps or shelled prawns (shrimp), spring onions (scallions), peanuts, fish sauce, sugar, chillies to taste and lime juice. Stir-fry for a further 1 minute.

4 Add the cooked noodles and coriander and stir-fry until heated through, about 1 minute. Serve the stir-fry immediately, garnished with coriander sprigs. If you prefer, the dish can be prepared with rice as an accompaniment rather than adding in the noodles.

VEGETABLE DISHES

RED CURRY WITH CASHEWS

SERVES 4

3 tbsp Curry Paste (see below)
250 ml/8 fl oz/1 cup coconut milk
1 kaffir lime leaf, mid-rib removed
¼ tsp light soy sauce
60 g/2 oz/4 baby corn, halved lengthways
125 g/4 oz/1¼ cups broccoli florets
125 g/4 oz green beans, cut into 5 cm/2 in pieces
30 g/1 oz/ ¼ cup cashew nuts
15 fresh basil leaves
1 tbsp chopped fresh coriander (cilantro)
1 tbsp chopped roast peanuts to garnish

CURRY PASTE:
7 fresh red chillies, halved, deseeded and blanched (use dried if fresh are not available)
2 tsp cumin seeds
2 tsp coriander seeds
2.5 cm/1 in piece galangal, peeled and chopped
½ stalk lemon grass, chopped
1 tsp salt
grated rind of 1 lime
4 garlic cloves, chopped
3 shallots, chopped
2 kaffir lime leaves, mid-rib removed, shredded
1 tbsp oil to blend

1 To make the curry paste, grind all the ingredients together in a large pestle and mortar, food processor or grinder. The paste will keep for up to 3 weeks in a sealed jar in the refrigerator.

2 Put a wok or large, heavy frying pan (skillet) over a high heat, add the red curry paste and stir until fragrant. Reduce the heat.

3 Add the coconut milk, lime leaf, light soy sauce, baby corn, broccoli, beans and cashew nuts. Bring to the boil and simmer for about 10 minutes until the vegetables are cooked, but still firm.

4 Remove the lime leaf and stir in the basil leaves and coriander (cilantro). Serve over rice, garnished with peanuts.

GREEN CURRY WITH TEMPEH

SERVES 4

1 tbsp sunflower oil
175 g/6 oz marinated or plain tempeh, cut
   into diamonds
6 spring onions (scallions), cut into
   2.5 cm/1 in pieces
150 ml/ ¼ pint/ ⅔ cup coconut milk
6 tbsp Green Curry Paste (see below)
grated rind of 1 lime
15 g/½ oz/ ¼ cup fresh basil leaves
¼ tsp liquid seasoning, such as Maggi

GREEN CURRY PASTE:
2 tsp coriander seeds
1 tsp cumin seeds
1 tsp black peppercorns
4 large green chillies, deseeded
2 shallots, quartered
2 garlic cloves, peeled
2 tbsp chopped fresh coriander (cilantro),
   including root and stalk
grated rind of 1 lime
1 tbsp roughly chopped galangal
1 tsp ground turmeric
salt
2 tbsp oil

TO GARNISH:
fresh coriander (cilantro) leaves
2 green chillies, sliced thinly

1 To make the green curry paste, grind together the coriander and cumin seeds and the peppercorns in a food processor or pestle and mortar.

2 Blend the remaining ingredients together and add the ground spice mixture. Store in a clean, dry jar for up to 3 weeks in the refrigerator, or freeze in a suitable container. Makes 6 tbsp.

3 Heat the oil in a wok or large, heavy frying pan (skillet). Add the tempeh and stir over a high heat for about 2 minutes until sealed on all sides. Add the spring onions (scallions) and stir-fry for 1 minute. Remove the tempeh and spring onions (scallions) and reserve.

4 Put half the coconut milk into the wok or pan (skillet) and bring to the boil. Add the curry paste and lime rind, and cook until fragrant, about 1 minute. Add the reserved tempeh and spring onions (scallions).

5 Add the remaining coconut milk and simmer for 7–8 minutes. Stir in the basil leaves and liquid seasoning. Simmer for one more minute before serving, garnished with coriander (cilantro) and chillies.

MASSAMAN CURRIED RICE

SERVES 4

PASTE:
1 tsp coriander seeds
1 tsp cumin seeds
1 tsp ground cinnamon
1 tsp cloves
1 whole star anise
1 tsp cardamom pods
1 tsp white peppercorns
1 tbsp oil
6 shallots, chopped very roughly
6 garlic cloves, chopped very roughly
5 cm/2 in piece lemon grass, sliced
4 fresh red chillies, deseeded and chopped
grated rind of 1 lime
1 tsp salt
1 tbsp chopped roast peanuts to garnish

CURRY:
3 tbsp sunflower oil
250 g/8 oz/1 cup marinated tofu (bean curd), cut into 2.5 cm/1 in cubes
125 g/4 oz green beans, cut into 2.5cm/1 in lengths
1 kg/2 lb/6 cups cooked rice (300 g/10 oz/1½ cups raw weight)
3 shallots, diced finely and deep-fried
1 spring onion (scallion),chopped finely
2 tbsp chopped roast peanuts
1 tbsp lime juice

1 First, make the paste. Grind together the seeds and spices in a pestle and mortar or spice grinder.

2 Heat the oil in a saucepan and add the shallots, garlic and lemon grass. Cook over a low heat until soft, about 5 minutes, and then add the chilli and grind together with the dry spices. Stir in the lime rind and salt.

3 To make the curry, heat the oil in a wok or large, heavy frying pan (skillet). Cook the tofu (bean curd) over a high heat for 2 minutes to seal. Add the curry paste and beans, and stir. Add the rice and, using 2 spoons, lift and stir over a high heat for about 3 minutes.

4 Transfer to a warmed serving dish. Sprinkle with the deep-fried shallots, spring onion (scallion) and peanuts. Squeeze over the lime juice.

MIXED VEGETABLES IN COCONUT MILK

SERVES 4–6

1 red chilli, deseeded and chopped
1 tsp coriander seeds
1 tsp cumin seeds
2 garlic cloves, crushed
juice of 1 lime
250 ml/8 fl oz/1 cup coconut milk
125 g/4 oz/2 cups bean-sprouts
125 g/4 oz/2 cups white cabbage, shredded
125 g/4 oz mangetout (snow peas), trimmed
125 g/4 oz/1¼ cups carrots, sliced thinly
125 g/4 oz/1¼ cups cauliflower florets
3 tbsp peanut butter
grated or shaved coconut, to garnish

1 Grind together the chilli, coriander and cumin seeds, garlic and lime juice in a pestle and mortar or food processor.

2 Put into a medium saucepan and heat gently until fragrant, about 1 minute. Add the coconut milk and stir until just about to boil.

3 Meanwhile, mix all the vegetables together in a large bowl.

4 Stir the peanut butter into the coconut mixture and combine with the vegetables. Sprinkle over slivers of grated or shaved coconut. Serve immediately.

TIPS

If you prefer, the cauliflower, carrots and mangetout (snow peas) can be blanched before being mixed with the dressing, to give them less bite.

This dish is ideal as a buffet dish as the quantity of dressing is quite sparse, and is only intended to coat, so you don't need too much of it to cover a large bowlful of vegetables.

MANGO SALAD

SERVES 4

1 lollo rosso lettuce, or any crunchy lettuce
15 g/ ½ oz coriander (cilantro) leaves
1 large unripe mango, peeled and cut into
long thin shreds
1 small red chilli, deseeded and chopped
finely
2 shallots, chopped finely
2 tbsp lemon juice
1 tbsp light soy sauce
6 roasted canned chestnuts, quartered

1 Line a serving plate with the lettuce and coriander (cilantro).

2 Soak the mango briefly in cold water, in order to remove any syrup, while you prepare the dressing.

3 Combine the chilli, shallots, lemon juice and soy sauce. Drain the mango, combine with the chestnuts and spoon on to the serving plate. Pour over the dressing and serve immediately.

HANDY HINT

This would look wonderful if served in a watermelon basket. To make a watermelon basket, stand a watermelon on one end on a level surface. Holding a knife level and in one place, turn the watermelon on its axis so that the knife marks an even line all around the middle. Mark a 2.5 cm/1 in wide handle across the top and through the centre stem, joining the middle line at either end.

Take a sharp knife and, following the marks made for the handle, make the first vertical cut. Then cut down the other side of the handle. Now follow the middle line and make your cut, taking care that the knife is always pointing towards the centre of the watermelon, and is level with the work surface (counter), as this ensures that when you reach the handle cuts, the cut out piece of melon will pull away cleanly. Hollow out the flesh with a spoon, leaving a clean edge, and fill as required.

SWEETCORN PATTIES

MAKES 12

325 g/11 oz can sweetcorn, drained
1 onion, chopped finely
1 tsp curry powder
1 garlic clove, crushed
1 tsp ground coriander
2 spring onions (scallions), chopped
3 tbsp plain (all-purpose) flour
½ tsp baking powder
salt
1 large egg
4 tbsp sunflower oil

1 Mash the drained sweetcorn lightly in a medium-sized bowl. Add all the remaining ingredients, except for the oil, one at a time, stirring after each addition.

2 Heat the sunflower oil in a frying pan (skillet). Drop tablespoonfuls of the mixture carefully on to the hot oil, far enough apart for them not to run into each other as they cook.

3 Cook for 4–5 minutes, turning each patty once, until they are golden brown and firm. Take care not to turn them too soon, or they will break up in the pan.

4 Remove from the pan with a slice and drain on paper towels. Serve quickly while still warm.

PRESENTATION

To make this dish more attractive, you can serve the patties on large leaves. Be sure to cut the spring onions (scallions) on the slant, for a more elegant appearance.

THAI BRAISED VEGETABLES

SERVES 4-6

3 tbsp sunflower oil
1 garlic clove, crushed
1 Chinese cabbage, thickly shredded
2 onions, peeled and cut into wedges
250 g/8 oz broccoli florets
2 large carrots, peeled and cut into thin
  julienne strips
12 baby or dwarf corn, halved if large
60 g/2 oz mangetout (snow peas), halved
90 g/3 oz Chinese or oyster mushrooms,
  sliced
1 tbsp grated ginger root
175 ml/6 fl oz/ ¾ cup vegetable stock
2 tbsp light soy sauce
1 tbsp cornflour (cornstarch)
salt and pepper
½ tsp sugar

1 Heat the oil in a large, heavy-based frying pan or wok. Add the garlic, cabbage, onions, broccoli, carrots, corn, mangetout (snow peas), mushrooms and ginger and stir-fry for 2 minutes.

2 Add the stock, cover and cook for a further 2-3 minutes.

3 Blend the soy sauce with the cornflour (cornstarch) and salt and pepper to taste.

4 Remove the braised vegetables from the pan with a slotted spoon and keep warm. Add the soy sauce mixture to the pan juices, mixing well. Bring to the boil, stirring constantly, until the mixture thickens slightly. Stir in the sugar.

5 Return the vegetables to the pan and toss in the slightly thickened sauce. Cook gently to just heat through then serve immediately.

VARIATION

This dish also makes an ideal vegetarian main meal. Double the quantities, to serve 4-6, and serve with rice or noodles.

THAI SALAD

SERVES 4-6

250 g/8 oz white cabbage, finely shredded
2 tomatoes, skinned, seeded and chopped
250 g/8 oz cooked green beans, halved if
  large
125 g/4 oz peeled prawns (shrimp)
1 papaya, peeled, seeded and chopped
1-2 fresh red chillies, seeded and very
  finely sliced
60 g/2 oz/scant ⅓ cup roasted salted
  peanuts, crushed
handful of lettuce or baby spinach leaves,
  shredded or torn into small pieces

DRESSING:
4 tbsp lime juice
2 tbsp fish sauce
sugar, to taste
pepper
coriander sprigs, to garnish

1 Mix the cabbage with the tomatoes, green beans, prawns (shrimp), three-quarters of the papaya and half the chillies in a bowl. Stir in two-thirds of the crushed peanuts and mix well.

2 Line the rim of a large serving plate with the lettuce or spinach and pile the salad mixture into the centre.

3 To make the dressing, beat the lime juice with the fish sauce and add sugar and pepper to taste. Drizzle over the salad.

4 Scatter the top with the remaining papaya, chillies and crushed peanuts. Garnish with coriander leaves and serve at once.

SKINNING TOMATOES

To skin tomatoes, make a cross at the base with a very sharp knife, then immerse in a bowl of boiling water for a few minutes. Remove with a slotted spoon and peel off the skin.

RICE & NOODLES

THAI JASMINE RICE

SERVES 3-4

1: OPEN PAN METHOD
250 g/8 oz/generous 1 cup Thai jasmine rice
1 litre/1¾ pints/4 cups water

1 Rinse the rice in a sieve (strainer) under cold running water and leave to drain.

2 Bring the water to the boil. Add the rice, stir and return to a medium boil. Cook, uncovered, for 8–10 minutes.

3 Drain and fork through lightly before serving.

2: ABSORPTION METHOD
250 g/8 oz/generous 1 cup Thai jasmine rice
450 ml/ ¾ pint/scant 2 cups water

1 Rinse the rice in a sieve (strainer) under cold running water.

2 Put the rice and water into a saucepan and bring to the boil. Stir once and then cover the pan tightly. Lower the heat as much as possible. Cook for 10 minutes. Leave to rest for 5 minutes.

3 Fork through lightly and serve immediately.

MICROWAVING AND FREEZING

Thai jasmine rice can also be cooked in a microwave oven. Use 250 g/8 oz/ generous 1 cup rice to 450 ml/ ¾ pint/ scant 2 cups boiling water. Combine in a bowl, cover and cook on High for 5 minutes. Stir, cover and cook on Defrost for 6 minutes. Leave to stand for 3 minutes. Fork through lightly and serve. Freeze in a plastic sealed container. Frozen rice is ideal for stir-fry dishes, as the process seems to separate the grains.

CHILLI FRIED RICE

SERVES 4

250 g/8 oz/generous 1 cup long-grain rice
4 tbsp vegetable oil
2 garlic cloves, chopped finely
1 small red chilli, deseeded and chopped finely
8 spring onions (scallions), trimmed and sliced finely
1 tbsp Thai red curry paste or 2 tsp chilli sauce
1 red (bell) pepper, cored, deseeded and chopped
90 g/3 oz/ ¾ cup dwarf green beans, chopped
250 g/8 oz/1½ cups cooked peeled prawns (shrimp) or chopped cooked chicken
2 tbsp fish sauce

TO GARNISH:
cucumber slices
shredded spring onion (scallion)

1 Cook the rice in plenty of boiling, lightly salted water until tender, about 12 minutes. Drain, rinse with cold water and drain thoroughly.

2 Heat the vegetable oil in a wok or large frying pan (skillet) and add the garlic. Fry gently for 2 minutes until golden. Add the chilli and spring onions (scallions) and cook, stirring, for 3–4 minutes.

3 Add the Thai curry paste or chilli sauce to the wok or frying pan (skillet) and fry for 1 minute, then add the red (bell) pepper and green beans. Stir-fry briskly for 2 minutes.

4 Tip the cooked rice into the wok or frying pan (skillet) and add the prawns (shrimp) or chicken. Stir-fry over a medium-high heat for about 4–5 minutes, until the rice is hot.

5 Serve garnished with cucumber slices and shredded spring onion (scallion).

MANGOES WITH STICKY RICE

SERVES 4

125 g/4 oz/generous ½ cup glutinous
  (sticky) rice
250 ml/8 fl oz/1 cup coconut milk
60 g/2 oz / ⅓ cup light muscovado sugar
¼ tsp salt
1 tsp sesame seeds, toasted
4 ripe mangoes, peeled, halved, stoned
  (pitted) and sliced

1 Put the rice into a colander and rinse
  well with plenty of cold water until
the water runs clear. Transfer the rice to
a large bowl, cover with cold water and
leave to soak overnight, or for at least
12 hours. Drain well.

2 Line a bamboo basket or steamer
  with muslin (cheesecloth) or finely
woven cotton cloth. Add the rice and
steam over a pan of gently simmering
water until the rice is tender, about
40 minutes. Remove from the heat and
transfer the rice to a bowl.

3 Reserve 4 tablespoons of the
  coconut milk and put the remainder
into a small saucepan with the sugar and
salt. Heat and simmer gently for about
8 minutes until reduced by about one third.

4 Pour the coconut milk mixture over
  the rice, fluffing up the rice so that
the mixture is absorbed. Set aside for
10–15 minutes.

5 Pack the rice into individual moulds
  and then invert them on to serving
plates. Pour a little reserved coconut milk
over each mound and sprinkle with the
sesame seeds. Arrange the sliced mango
on the plates and serve, decorated with
pieces of mango cut into shapes with tiny
cutters.

COCONUT MILK

Canned coconut milk is widely
available from supermarkets, or you
can buy packets of coconut cream,
which can be mixed with milk or water
to make coconut milk. Dried coconut
milk, which can be reconstituted with
water, is also available.

LIME & CORIANDER (CILANTRO) CHICKEN FRIED RICE

SERVES 4

250 g/8 oz/generous 1 cup long-grain rice
4 tbsp vegetable oil
2 garlic cloves, chopped finely
1 small green chilli, deseeded and
  chopped finely
5 shallots, sliced finely
1 tbsp Green Curry Paste (see page 432)
1 yellow or green (bell) pepper, cored,
  deseeded and chopped
2 celery sticks, sliced finely
250 g/8 oz/1½ cups cooked chicken,
  chopped
2 tbsp light soy sauce
finely grated rind of 1 lime
2 tbsp lime juice
1 tbsp chopped fresh coriander (cilantro)
30 g/1 oz/ ¼ cup unsalted peanuts, toasted

TO GARNISH:
fresh coriander (cilantro)
finely sliced shallots
lime slices

1 Cook the rice in plenty of boiling,
  lightly salted water until tender,
about 12 minutes. Drain, rinse with cold
water and drain thoroughly.

2 Heat the oil in a wok or large frying
  pan (skillet) and add the garlic. Fry
gently for 2 minutes until golden. Add the
chilli and shallots, and cook, stirring, for a
further 3–4 minutes.

3 Add the Thai curry paste to the wok
  or frying pan (skillet) and fry for
1 minute, then add the yellow or green
(bell) pepper and celery. Stir-fry briskly
for 2 minutes.

4 Tip the cooked rice into the wok or
  frying pan (skillet) and add the
chicken, soy sauce, lime rind and juice
and chopped coriander (cilantro). Stir-fry
over a medium-high heat for about
4–5 minutes, until the rice is hot.

5 Serve sprinkled with the peanuts and
  garnished with sprigs of fresh
coriander (cilantro), sliced shallots and
lime slices.

FRIED RICE IN PINEAPPLE

SERVES 4-6

1 large pineapple
1 tbsp sunflower oil
1 garlic clove, crushed
1 small onion, diced
½ celery stick, sliced
1 tsp coriander seeds, ground
1 tsp cumin seeds, ground
150 g/5 oz/1½ cups button mushrooms, sliced
250 g/8 oz/1⅓ cups cooked rice
2 tbsp light soy sauce
½ tsp sugar
½ tsp salt
30 g/1 oz/¼ cup cashew nuts

TO GARNISH:
1 spring onion (scallion), sliced finely
fresh coriander (cilantro) leaves
mint sprig

1 Halve the pineapple lengthways and cut out the flesh to make 2 boat-shaped shells. Cut the flesh into cubes and reserve 125 g/4 oz/1 cup to use in this recipe. (Any remaining pineapple cubes can be served separately.)

2 Heat the oil in a wok or large, heavy frying pan (skillet). Cook the garlic, onion and celery over a high heat, stirring constantly, for 2 minutes. Stir in the coriander and cumin seeds, and the mushrooms.

3 Add the pineapple cubes and cooked rice to the pan and stir well. Stir in the soy sauce, sugar, salt and cashew nuts.

4 Using 2 spoons, lift and stir the rice for about 4 minutes until it is thoroughly heated.

5 Spoon the rice mixture into the pineapple boats. Garnish with spring onion (scallion), coriander (cilantro) leaves and chopped mint.

THAI FRAGRANT COCONUT RICE

SERVES 4-6

2.5 cm/1 in piece ginger root, peeled and sliced
2 cloves
1 piece lemon grass, bruised and halved
2 tsp ground nutmeg
1 cinnamon stick
1 bay leaf
2 small thin strips lime zest
1 tsp salt
30 g/1 oz creamed coconut, chopped
600 ml/1 pint/2½ cups water
350 g/12 oz/1¾ cups basmati rice
ground pepper

1 Place the ginger, cloves, lemon grass, nutmeg, cinnamon stick, bay leaf, lime zest, salt, creamed coconut and water in a large, heavy-based pan and bring slowly to the boil.

2 Add the rice, stir well, then cover and simmer, over a very gentle heat, for about 15 minutes or until all the liquid has been absorbed and the rice is tender but still has a bite to it.

3 Remove from the heat, add pepper to taste, then fluff up the rice with a fork. Remove the large pieces of spices before serving.

COOKING RICE

An alternative method of cooking the rice – the absorption method – leaves you free to concentrate on other dishes. Add the rice to the pan as in step 1, then bring back to the boil. Stir well, then cover tightly and turn off the heat. Leave for 20-25 minutes before removing the lid – the rice will be perfectly cooked.

THAI-STYLE STIR-FRIED NOODLES

SERVES 4

250 g/8 oz dried rice noodles
2 red chillies, deseeded and chopped finely
2 shallots, chopped finely
2 tbsp sugar
2 tbsp tamarind water
1 tbsp lime juice
2 tbsp light soy sauce
black pepper
1 tbsp sunflower oil
1 tsp sesame oil
175 g/6 oz/ ¾ cup smoked tofu (bean curd), diced
2 tbsp chopped roasted peanuts

1 Cook the rice noodles as directed on the pack, or soak them in boiling water for 5 minutes.

2 Grind together the chillies, shallots, sugar, tamarind water, lime juice, light soy sauce and black pepper.

3 Heat both the oils together in a wok or large, heavy frying pan (skillet) over a high heat. Add the tofu (bean curd) and stir for 1 minute.

4 Add the chilli mixture, bring to the boil, and stir for about 2 minutes until thickened.

5 Drain the rice noodles and add them to the chilli mixture. Use 2 spoons to lift and stir them until they are no longer steaming. Serve immediately, garnished with the peanuts.

ONE-DISH MEAL

This is a quick one-dish meal that is very useful if you are catering for a single vegetarian in the family.

SESAME HOT NOODLES

SERVES 6

2 x 250 g/8 oz pkts medium egg noodles
3 tbsp sunflower oil
2 tbsp sesame oil
1 garlic clove, crushed
1 tbsp smooth peanut butter
1 small green chilli, seeded and very finely chopped
3 tbsp toasted sesame seeds
4 tbsp light soy sauce
1-2 tbsp lime juice
salt and pepper
4 tbsp chopped fresh coriander

1 Place the noodles in a large pan of boiling water, then immediately remove from the heat. Cover and leave to stand for 6 minutes, stirring once halfway through the time. At the end of 6 minutes the noodles will be perfectly cooked. Otherwise follow packet instructions.

2 Meanwhile, to make the dressing, mix the oils with the garlic and peanut butter until smooth.

3 Add the chilli, sesame seeds, soy sauce and lime juice, according to taste and mix well. Season with salt and pepper.

4 Drain the noodles thoroughly then place in a heated serving bowl. Add the dressing and coriander and toss well to mix. Serve immediately.

COOKING NOODLES

If you are cooking noodles ahead of time, toss the cooked, drained noodles in 2 teaspoons sesame oil, then turn into a bowl. Cover and keep warm.

CRISPY NOODLES WITH CORIANDER (CILANTRO) & CUCUMBER

SERVES 4

250 g/8 oz rice noodles
oil for deep-frying
2 garlic cloves, chopped finely
8 spring onions (scallions), trimmed and
    chopped finely
1 small red or green chilli, deseeded and
    chopped finely
2 tbsp fish sauce
2 tbsp light soy sauce
2 tbsp lime or lemon juice
2 tbsp molasses sugar

TO GARNISH:
spring onions (scallions), shredded
cucumber, sliced thinly
fresh chillies
fresh coriander (cilantro)

1 Break the noodles into smaller
   pieces with your hands.

2 Heat the oil for deep-frying in a wok
   or large frying pan (skillet). Add
small batches of the noodles and fry them
until pale golden brown and puffed up.
Make sure that the oil is hot enough, or
they will be tough. As each batch cooks,
lift the noodles out with a perforated
spoon on to paper towels.

3 When all the noodles are cooked,
   carefully pour off the oil into a
separate container, then return
 3 tablespoons of it to the wok or frying
pan (skillet). Add the garlic, spring onions
(scallions) and chilli, and stir-fry for about
2 minutes.

4 Mix together the fish sauce, soy
   sauce, lime or lemon juice and
sugar. Add to the wok or frying pan
(skillet) and cook for about 2 minutes,
until the sugar has dissolved. Tip all the
noodles back into the wok or frying pan
(skillet) and toss lightly to coat with the
sauce mixture. Avoid breaking them up
too much.

5 Serve the noodles garnished with
   shredded spring onions (scallions),
thinly sliced cucumber, chillies and fresh
coriander (cilantro).

CRISPY DEEP-FRIED NOODLES

SERVES 4

175 g/6 oz thread egg noodles
600 ml/1 pint/2½ cups sunflower oil for
    deep-frying
2 tsp grated lemon peel
1 tbsp light soy sauce
1 tbsp rice vinegar
1 tbsp lemon juice
1½ tbsp sugar
250 g/8 oz/1 cup marinated tofu (bean
    curd), diced
2 garlic cloves, crushed
1 red chilli, sliced finely
1 red (bell) pepper, diced
4 eggs, beaten
red chilli, sliced, to garnish

1 Blanch the egg noodles briefly in hot
   water, to which a little of the oil has
been added. Drain and spread out to dry
for at least 30 minutes. Cut into threads
about 7 cm/3 in long.

2 Combine the lemon peel, light soy
   sauce, rice vinegar, lemon juice and
sugar in a small bowl.

3 Heat the oil in a wok or large, heavy
   frying pan (skillet), and test the
temperature with a few strands of
noodles. They should swell to many times
their size, but if they do not, wait until
the oil is hot enough; otherwise they will
be tough and stringy, not puffy and light.
Cook them in batches. As soon as they
turn a pale gold colour, scoop them out
and drain on plenty of paper towels.
Leave to cool.

4 Reserve 2 tbsp of the oil and drain
   off the rest. Heat the 2 tbsp of oil in
the wok or pan (skillet). Cook the tofu
(bean curd) quickly over a high heat to
seal. Add the garlic, chilli and diced (bell)
pepper. Stir for 1–2 minutes. Add the
vinegar mixture to the pan, stir and add
the eggs, stirring until they are set.

5 Serve with the crispy fried noodles,
   garnished with sliced red chilli.

STIR-FRIED NOODLES WITH THAI HOT SAUCE

••••••••••••••••••••••••••••••••••

SERVES 4

125 g/4 oz rice noodles
2 tbsp sesame oil
1 large garlic clove, crushed
125 g/4 oz pork fillet (tenderloin), sliced
  into strips
125 g/4 oz / ⅔ cup large prawns (shrimp),
  peeled and deveined
15 g/ ½ oz/1 tbsp dried shrimp (optional)
60 g/2 oz / ½ cup white radish (mooli),
  grated
2 tbsp fish sauce
2 tbsp dark muscovado sugar
2 tbsp lime or lemon juice
60 g/2 oz/1 cup bean-sprouts
30 g/1 oz/ ¼ cup peanuts, chopped
3–4 tbsp Thai hot sauce to serve

TO GARNISH:
2 shallots, sliced
fresh coriander (cilantro) leaves

1 Put the noodles into a large bowl and cover them with just-boiled water. Leave to soak for 15 minutes.

2 Heat the oil in a wok or large frying pan (skillet) and add the garlic, stir-frying for 2 minutes until golden brown. Add the strips of pork and stir-fry for a further 4–5 minutes.

3 Add the prawns (shrimp), dried shrimp (if using) and white radish (mooli) to the wok or frying pan (skillet) and stir-fry briskly for 2 minutes.

4 Stir in the fish sauce, sugar and lime or lemon juice.

5 Drain the noodles well and stir into the wok or frying pan (skillet) with the bean-sprouts and peanuts. Cook for 2–3 minutes, then serve.

6 Drizzle the Thai hot sauce over the noodles and garnish with the sliced shallot and coriander (cilantro) leaves.

DEEP-FRIED VEGETABLES WITH SWEET & SOUR SAUCE

••••••••••••••••••••••••••••••••••

SERVES 4

500 g/1 lb selection of fresh vegetables,
  such as red and green (bell) peppers,
  courgettes (zucchini), carrots, spring
  onions (scallions), cauliflower, broccoli
  and mushrooms
oil for deep-frying

BATTER:
125 g/4 oz/1 cup plain (all-purpose) flour
½ tsp salt
1 tsp caster (superfine) sugar
1 tsp baking powder
3 tbsp vegetable oil
200 ml/7 fl oz/scant 1 cup tepid water

SAUCE:
1 tbsp light muscovado sugar
2 tbsp soy sauce
4 tbsp cider vinegar
4 tbsp medium sherry
1 tbsp cornflour (cornstarch)
1 tsp finely grated fresh ginger root

TO GARNISH:
spring onion (scallion) brushes
chopped spring onions (scallions)

1 To make the batter, sift the flour, salt, sugar and baking powder into a large bowl. Add the oil and most of the water. Whisk together to make a smooth batter, adding extra water to give it the consistency of single (light) cream. Chill for 20–30 minutes.

2 To make the sauce, put all the ingredients into a small saucepan. Heat, stirring, until thickened and smooth.

3 Cut all the vegetables into even, bite-sized pieces.

4 Heat the oil in a wok or deep fat fryer. Dip the vegetables into the batter and fry them in the hot oil, a few at a time, until golden brown and crispy, about 2 minutes. Drain on paper towels.

5 Serve the vegetables on a warmed platter, garnished with spring onion (scallion) brushes and chopped spring onions (scallions), accompanied by the sauce.

BAMBOO SHOOTS WITH CUCUMBER

SERVES 4

½ cucumber
2 tbsp sesame oil
4 shallots, chopped finely
1 garlic clove, sliced finely
350 g/12 oz can of bamboo shoots,
    drained
1 tbsp dry sherry
1 tbsp soy sauce
2 tsp cornflour (cornstarch)
1 tsp sesame seeds
salt

TO GARNISH:
2 red chilli flowers
sliced spring onions (scallions)

1 Slice the cucumber thinly and
sprinkle with salt. Leave for
10–15 minutes, then rinse with cold water.
To make chilli flowers for garnishing,
hold the stem of the chilli and cut down
its length several times with a sharp knife.
Place in a bowl of chilled water and chill
so that the 'petals' turn out. Remove the
chilli seeds when the 'petals' have
opened.

2 Heat the sesame oil in a wok or
frying pan (skillet) and add the
shallots and garlic. Stir-fry for 2 minutes,
until golden.

3 Add the bamboo shoots and
cucumber to the wok or frying pan
(skillet) and stir-fry for 2–3 minutes.

4 Blend together the sherry, soy sauce
and cornflour (cornstarch). Add to
the bamboo shoots and cucumber, stirring
to combine. Cook for 1–2 minutes to
thicken slightly, then add the sesame
seeds and stir them through.

5 Transfer the vegetables to a warmed
serving dish. Garnish with the chilli
flowers and chopped spring onion
(scallion). Serve at once.

LITTLE GOLDEN PARCELS

MAKES 30

1 garlic clove, crushed
1 tsp chopped coriander (cilantro) root
1 tsp pepper
250 g/8 oz/1 cup boiled mashed potato
175 g/6 oz/1 cup water chestnuts, chopped
    finely
1 tsp grated ginger root
2 tbsp ground roast peanuts
2 tsp light soy sauce
½ tsp salt
½ tsp sugar
30 wonton sheets, defrosted
1 tsp cornflour (cornstarch), made into a
    paste with a little water
vegetable oil for deep-frying
fresh chives to garnish
sweet chilli sauce, to serve

1 Combine all the ingredients
thoroughly, except the wonton
sheets, cornflour (cornstarch) and oil.

2 Keeping the remainder of the
wonton sheets covered with a damp
cloth, lay 4 sheets out on a work surface
(counter). Put a teaspoonful of the
mixture on each.

3 Make a line of the cornflour
(cornstarch) paste around each
sheet, about 1 cm/½ in from the edge.

4 Bring all four corners to the centre
and press together to form little
bags. Continue the process until all the
wonton sheets are used.

5 Meanwhile, heat 5 cm/2 ines of the
oil in a deep saucepan until a light
haze appears on top and lower the
parcels in, in batches of 3. Fry until
golden brown, and remove with a slotted
spoon, to drain on paper towels.

6 Tie a chive around the neck of each
bag to garnish, and serve with a
sweet chilli sauce for dipping.

DESSERTS

THAI-STYLE BANANAS

SERVES 6

3 tbsp shredded fresh coconut
60 g/2 oz/ ¼ cup unsalted butter
1 tbsp grated ginger root
grated zest of 1 orange
6 bananas
60 g/2 oz/ ¼ cup caster sugar
4 tbsp fresh lime juice
6 tbsp orange liqueur (Cointreau or
   Grand Marnier, for example)
3 tsp toasted sesame seeds
lime slices, to decorate
ice-cream, to serve (optional)

1 Heat a small non-stick frying pan
   until hot. Add the coconut and cook,
stirring constantly, for about 1 minute
until lightly coloured. Remove from the
pan and allow to cool.

2 Heat the butter in a large frying pan
   until it melts. Add the ginger and
orange zest and mix well.

3 Peel and slice the bananas
   lengthways (and halve if they are
very large). Place the bananas cut-side
down in the butter mixture and cook for
1-2 minutes or until the sauce mixture
starts to become sticky. Turn to coat in
the sauce.

4 Remove the bananas from the pan
   and place on heated serving plates.
Keep warm.

5 Return the pan to the heat and add
   the orange liqueur, stirring well to
blend. Ignite with a taper, allow the
flames to die down, then pour over the
bananas.

6 Sprinkle with the coconut and
   sesame seeds and serve at once,
decorated with slices of lime.

VARIATION

For a very special treat try serving with
a flavoured ice-cream such as coconut,
ginger or praline.

MANGO PARFAIT

SERVES 4

1 large ripe mango
juice of 1 lime
about 1 tbsp caster sugar
3 egg yolks
60 g/2 oz/ ½ cup icing (confectioner's)
   sugar, sifted
150 ml/ ¼ pint/ ⅔ cup double (heavy)
   cream
lime zest, to decorate
fried wontons dusted with sugar, to serve
   (optional)

1 Peel the mango and slice the flesh
   away from the stone. Purée in a food
processor or blender with the lime juice
and caster sugar to taste, until the mixture
is smooth.

2 Beat the egg yolks with the icing
   (confectioner's) sugar until the
mixture is pale and thick, then fold in the
mango purée.

3 Whip the cream until it stands in soft
   peaks. Fold into the mango mixture
with a metal spoon.

4 Pour the mango mixture into
   4 freezerproof serving glasses and
freeze until firm, about 4-6 hours.

5 Serve the parfaits straight from the
   freezer (they will be soft enough to
scoop) with crisp dessert biscuits or warm
fried wontons (see instructions below)
dusted with sugar.

FRIED WONTONS

Allow about 2 wontons per person.
Deep-fry the wonton skins in hot oil for
about 30 seconds until crisp and
golden. Drain on paper towels, then
dust with icing (confectioner's) sugar
to serve.

BAKED COCONUT RICE PUDDING

••

SERVES 4-6

*90 g/3 oz/scant ⅓ cup short or round-
   grain pudding rice
600 ml/1 pint/2½ cups coconut milk
300 ml/ ½ pint/1¼ cups milk
1 large strip lime rind
60 g/2 oz/ ¼ cup caster sugar
knob of butter
pinch of ground star anise (optional)
fresh or stewed fruit, to serve*

1 Mix the rice with the coconut milk,
   milk, lime rind and sugar.

2 Pour the rice mixture into a lightly-
   greased 1.4 litre/2½ pint shallow
ovenproof dish and dot the surface with
a little butter. Bake in the preheated oven
at 170ºC/250ºF/Gas Mark 2 for about
30 minutes.

3 Remove and discard the strip of
   lime. Stir the pudding well, add the
pinch of ground star anise, if using, return
to the oven and cook for a further
1-2 hours or until almost all the milk has
been absorbed and a golden brown skin
has baked on the top of the pudding.
Cover the top of the pudding with foil if it
starts to brown too much towards the end
of the cooking time.

4 Serve the pudding warm or chilled
   with fresh or stewed fruit.

COOK'S TIP

As the mixture cools it thickens. If you
plan to serve the rice chilled then fold
in about 3 tbsp cream or extra coconut
milk before serving to give a thinner
consistency.

FRUIT SALAD WITH GINGER SYRUP

••

SERVES 6-8

*2.5 cm/1 in ginger root, peeled and
   chopped
60 g/2 oz/ ¼ cup caster sugar
150 ml/ ¼ pint/ ⅔ cup water
grated rind and juice of 1 lime
4 tbsp/ ⅓ cup ginger wine
1 fresh pineapple, peeled, cored and cut
   into bite-sized pieces
2 ripe mangoes, peeled, stoned and diced
4 kiwi fruit, peeled and sliced
1 papaya, peeled, seeded and diced
2 passion fruit, halved and flesh removed
350 g/12 oz lychees, peeled and stoned
¼ fresh coconut, grated
60 g/2 oz Cape gooseberries, to decorate
   (optional)
coconut ice-cream, to serve (optional)*

1 Place the ginger, sugar, water and
   lime juice in a small pan and bring
slowly to the boil. Simmer for 1 minute,
remove from the heat and allow the syrup
to cool slightly.

2 Pass the sugar syrup through a fine
   sieve then add the ginger wine and
mix well. Allow to cool completely.

3 Place the prepared pineapple,
   mango, kiwi, papaya, passion fruit
and lychees in a serving bowl. Add the
cold syrup and mix well. Cover and chill
for 2-4 hours.

4 Just before serving, add half of the
   grated coconut to the salad and mix
well. Sprinkle the remainder on the top of
the fruit salad.

5 If using Cape gooseberries to
   decorate the fruit salad, peel back
each calyx to form a flower. Wipe the
berries with a damp cloth, then arrange
them around the side of the fruit salad
before serving.

PANCAKES POLAMAI

SERVES 4

BATTER:
125 g/4 oz/1 cup plain flour
pinch of salt
1 egg
1 egg yolk
300 ml/ ½ pint/1¼ cups coconut milk
4 tsp vegetable oil, plus oil for frying

FILLING:
1 banana
1 papaya
juice of 1 lime
2 passion fruit
1 mango, peeled, stoned and sliced
4 lychees, stoned and halved
1-2 tbsp honey
flowers or mint sprigs, to decorate

1 To make the batter, sift the flour into a bowl with the salt. Make a well in the centre, add the egg and egg yolk and a little of the coconut milk. Gradually draw the flour into the egg mixture, beating well and gradually adding the remaining coconut milk to make a smooth batter. Add the oil and mix well. Cover and chill for 30 minutes.

2 To make the filling, peel and slice the banana and place in a bowl. Peel and slice the papaya, remove and discard the seeds then cut into bite-sized chunks. Add to the banana with the lime juice and mix well to coat.

3 Cut the passion fruit in half and scoop out the flesh and seeds into the fruit bowl. Add the mango, lychees and honey and mix well.

4 To make the pancakes, heat a little oil in a 15 cm/6 in crêpe or frying pan. Pour in just enough of the pancake batter to cover the base of the pan and tilt so that it spreads thinly and evenly. Cook until the pancake is just set and the underside is lightly browned, turn and briefly cook the other side. Remove from the pan and keep warm. Repeat with the remaining batter to make a total of 8 pancakes.

5 To serve, place a little of the prepared fruit filling along the centre of each pancake and then, using both hands, roll it into a cone shape. Lay seam-side down on warmed serving plates, allowing 2 pancakes per serving.

6 Serve the stuffed pancakes at once, decorated with flowers and mint sprigs, if liked.

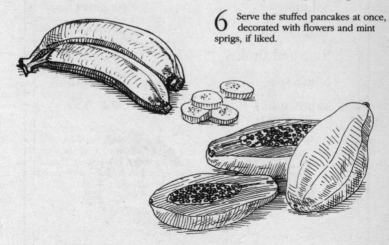

·4·

Snacks and Accompaniments

Looking for ideas for the kids' lunchbox, or something quick and tasty for supper? Take your pick from healthy salads, spicy tit-bits, sandwiches for hearty appetites and delicious side dishes.

SALADS – INTRODUCTION

SALAD LEAVES (GREENS)
Round or cabbage lettuce is the one most familiar to us all. I try to avoid the hothouse variety as the leaves are limp and floppy. There are a number of salad leaves now available, and it is worth experimenting with different varieties to find your favourite.

Chicory (endive)
This is available from autumn (fall) to spring and with its slightly bitter flavour makes an interesting addition to winter salads. Choose firm, tightly packed cones with yellow leaf tips. Avoid any with damaged leaves or leaf tips that are turning green as they will be rather too bitter. Red chicory (endive) is also available.

Chinese leaves
These are a most useful salad ingredient available in the the autumn (fall) and winter months. I like to shred them fairly finely and use them as a base, adding bean shoots and leaves such as watercress.

Cos (romaine) lettuce
This is a superb crisp variety used especially in Caesar salad. It has long, narrow, bright green leaves.

Endive (chicory)
A slightly bitter-tasting but most attractive curly-leaved salad plant. There are two varieties; the curly endive (frisée) which has a mop head of light green frilly leaves and the Batavia endive (escarole) which has broader, smoother leaves. Both have their leaves tied together to blanch and tenderize the centres.

Feuille de chêne (oak leaf)
This red-tinged, delicately flavoured lettuce is good when mixed with other leaves.

Iceberg lettuce
This has pale green, densely packed leaves. It is extremely good value when compared with other lettuces by weight. It has a fresh crisp texture and keeps well in the refrigerator, wrapped in a polythene bag.

Lamb's lettuce (corn salad)
This is so called because its dark green leaves resemble a lamb's tongue. It is also known as corn salad and the French call it mâche. It is easy to grow in the garden and will even withstand the frost. It is well worth looking out for when it is in season.

Purslane
This has fleshy stalks and rosettes of succulent green leaves which have a sharp, clean flavour. It is an excellent addition to green salads.

Radiccio
This is a variety of chicory (endive) originating in Italy. It looks rather like a small, tightly packed red lettuce and is widely available. It is quite expensive but comparatively few leaves are needed, as it has quite a bitter flavour. The leaves are a deep purple with a white contrasting rib, and add character and interest to any green salad.

Rocket (arugula, Roquette)
The young green leaves of this plant have a distinctive warm peppery flavour, delicious in green salads.

Watercress
This has a fresh peppery taste that recommends it to many salads. It is available throughout the year, though it is less good when flowering, or early in the season when the leaves are very small.

CHINESE HOT SALAD

SERVES 4

1 tbsp dark soy sauce
1½-2 tsp bottled sweet chilli sauce
2 tbsp sherry
1 tbsp brown sugar
1 tbsp wine vinegar
2 tbsp sunflower oil
1 garlic clove, crushed
4 spring onions (scallions), thinly sliced
    diagonally
250 g/8 oz courgettes (zucchini) cut into
    julienne strips about 4 cm/1½ in long
250 g/8 oz carrots, cut into julienne strips
    about 4 cm/1½ in long
1 red or green (bell) pepper, cored, seeded
    and thinly sliced
1 x 400 g/14 oz can bean-sprouts, well
    drained
125 g/4 oz French or fine beans, cut into
    5 cm/2 in lengths
1 tbsp sesame oil
salt and pepper
1-2 tsp sesame seeds, to garnish

1 Blend the soy sauce, chilli sauce, sherry, sugar, vinegar and seasonings together in a jug.

2 Heat the 2 tablespoons of sunflower oil in a wok, swirling it around until it is really hot.

3 Add the garlic and spring onions (scallions) to the wok and stir-fry for 1-2 minutes.

4 Add the courgettes (zucchini), carrots and (bell) peppers and stir-fry for 1-2 minutes, then add the soy sauce mixture and bring to the boil.

5 Add the bean-sprouts and French beans and stir-fry for 1-2 minutes, making sure all the vegetables are thoroughly coated with the sauce.

6 Drizzle the sesame oil over the vegetables in the wok, stir-fry for about 30 seconds and serve hot sprinkled with sesame seeds.

GOAT'S CHEESE WITH WALNUTS IN WARM OIL & VINEGAR DRESSING

SERVES 4

90 g/3 oz/1 cup walnut halves
mixed salad leaves (greens)
125 g/4 oz soft goat's cheese
snipped fresh chives to garnish

DRESSING:
6 tbsp walnut oil
3 tbsp white wine vinegar
1 tbsp clear honey
1 tsp Dijon mustard
pinch of ground ginger
salt and pepper

1 To make the dressing, whisk together the walnut oil, wine vinegar, honey, mustard and ginger in a small saucepan. Season to taste.

2 Heat the dressing on the hob (stove top) or over the barbecue, stirring occasionally, until warm. Add the walnut halves to the warm dressing and continue to heat for 3–4 minutes.

3 Arrange the salad leaves on 4 serving plates and place spoonfuls of goat's cheese on top. Lift the walnut halves from the dressing with a perforated spoon, and scatter them over the salads.

4 Transfer the warm dressing to a small jug, for sprinkling over the salads when ready.

5 Sprinkle chives over the salads and serve them, accompanied by the warm walnut oil dressing.

TIPS

Hazelnut oil makes a delicious alternative to walnut oil; if you use it, you can also replace the walnuts with hazelnuts if you wish.

If you are heating the dressing over the barbecue, choose an old saucepan, as it may become blackened on the outside.

CARROT & CASHEW NUT COLESLAW

SERVES 4

1 large carrot, grated
1 small onion, chopped finely
2 celery sticks, chopped
¼ small, hard white cabbage, shredded
1 tbsp chopped fresh parsley
4 tbsp sesame oil
½ tsp poppy seeds
60 g/2 oz/ ½ cup cashew nuts
2 tbsp white wine or cider vinegar
salt and pepper
sprigs of fresh parsley to garnish

1 In a large salad bowl, mix together the carrot, onion, celery and cabbage. Stir in the chopped parsley.

2 Heat the sesame oil in a saucepan that has a lid. Add the poppy seeds and cover the pan. Cook over a medium high heat until the seeds start to make a popping sound. Remove from the heat and leave to cool.

3 Scatter the cashew nuts on to a baking sheet. Place them under a medium-hot grill (broiler) and toast until lightly browned, being careful not to burn them. Leave to cool.

4 Add the vinegar to the oil and poppy seeds, then pour over the carrot mixture. Add the cooled cashew nuts. Toss together to coat the salad ingredients with the dressing.

5 Garnish the salad with sprigs of parsley and serve.

VARIATIONS

Sesame seeds or sunflower seeds can be used in place of poppy seeds.
Substitute peanuts for cashew nuts if you prefer – they are more economical and taste every bit as good when lightly toasted.

HONEYDEW & STRAWBERRY SALAD WITH COOL CUCUMBER DRESSING

SERVES 4

½ iceberg lettuce, shredded
1 small honeydew melon
250 g/8 oz/1½ cups strawberries, hulled
and sliced
5 cm/2 in piece of cucumber, sliced thinly
sprigs of fresh mint to garnish

DRESSING:
200 g/7 oz/scant 1 cup natural yogurt
5 cm/2 in piece of cucumber, peeled
a few fresh mint leaves
½ tsp finely grated lime or lemon rind
pinch of caster (superfine) sugar
3–4 ice cubes

1 Arrange the shredded lettuce on 4 serving plates.

2 Cut the melon lengthways into quarters. Scoop out the seeds and cut through the flesh down to the skin at 2.5 cm/1 in intervals. Cut the melon close to the skin and detach the flesh.

3 Place the melon chunks on the bed of lettuce with the strawberries and cucumber.

4 To make the dressing, put the yogurt, cucumber, mint leaves, lime or lemon rind, caster (superfine) sugar and ice cubes into a blender or food processor. Blend together for about 15 seconds. Alternatively, chop the mint and cucumber finely, crush the ice cubes and combine with the other ingredients.

5 Serve the salad with a little dressing poured over it. Garnish with sprigs of fresh mint.

VARIATIONS

Omit the ice cubes in the dressing if you prefer, but make sure that the ingredients are well-chilled. This will ensure that the finished dressing is really cool.
Charentais, cantaloup or ogen melon can be substituted for honeydew.

CARROT AND CORIANDER (CILANTRO) SALAD

SERVES 4

4 large carrots
2 celery sticks, cut into matchsticks
2 tbsp roughly chopped fresh coriander
  (cilantro)

DRESSING:
1 tbsp sesame oil
1½ tbsp rice vinegar
½ tsp sugar
½ tsp salt

1 To create flower-shaped carrot slices, as shown, cut several grooves lengthways along each carrot before slicing it.

2 Slice each carrot into very thin slices, using the slicing cutter of a grater.

3 Combine the carrot, celery and coriander (cilantro) in a bowl. Combine the dressing ingredients thoroughly.

4 Just before serving, toss the carrot, celery and coriander mixture in the dressing and transfer to a serving dish.

GARNISHES

You can make this salad look even more appealing with a simple garnish. Cut very fine strips of carrot with a vegetable peeler and curl into a spiral, or drop in iced water to make them curl up. Alternatively make thin cuts through a chunk of celery from the top almost to the bottom, and leave in iced water until the fronds curl up.

SESAME OIL

Sesame oil is a very aromatic oil used in small quantities in a lot of oriental cooking, to impart a special flavour to salad dressings and sauces. If it is not available, you can substitute any high quality oil, though the dressing will not have the distinctive Thai flavour.

CUCUMBER SALAD

SERVES 4

½ cucumber
1 tbsp rice vinegar
2 tbsp sugar
2 tbsp hot water
½ tsp salt
1 small shallot, sliced thinly

1 Peel the cucumber, halve it lengthways, and deseed it, using a teaspoon or a melon baller.

2 Slice the cucumber thinly, and arrange the cucumber slices on a serving plate.

3 To make the dressing, combine the vinegar, sugar and salt in a bowl. Pour on the hot water and stir until the sugar has dissolved.

4 Pour the dressing evenly over the cucumber slices.

5 Sprinkle the shallot slices over the cucumber. Chill the salad before serving with a Chinese meal.

RICE VINEGAR

There are two kinds of rice vinegar, each of which is less acidic than Western vinegars. Red vinegar is made from fermented rice, and has a dark colour and depth of flavour. White rice vinegar is distilled from rice wine and has a stronger flavour than red vinegar. Because of its distinctive flavour, white rice vinegar is preferred by many Western cooks. If unavailable, use white wine vinegar or cider vinegar.

CUCUMBERS

Some people dislike the bitter taste that cucumbers can have – I find that peeling off the skin and deseeding the cucumber often eliminates this problem.

Using a melon baller is the neatest method of deseeding a cucumber, although a rounded teaspoon will do instead.

GRAPEFRUIT & COCONUT SALAD

SERVES 4

125 g/4 oz/1 cup grated coconut
2 tsp light soy sauce
2 tbsp lime juice
2 tbsp water
2 tsp sunflower oil
1 garlic clove, halved
1 onion, chopped finely
2 large ruby grapefruits, peeled and
  segmented
90 g/3 oz/1½ cups alfalfa sprouts

1 Toast the coconut in a dry frying pan (skillet), stirring constantly, until golden brown, about 3 minutes. Transfer to a bowl.

2 Add the light soy sauce, lime juice and water.

3 Heat the oil in a saucepan and fry the garlic and onion until soft. Stir the onion into the coconut mixture. Remove the garlic.

4 Divide the grapefruit segments between 4 plates. Sprinkle each with a quarter of the alfalfa sprouts and spoon over a quarter of the coconut mixture.

ALFALFA SPROUTS

Alfalfa sprouts can be bought in trays or packets from most supermarkets, but you can easily grow your own, if you like to have a constant and cheap supply.

Soak a couple of tablespoons of alfalfa seeds overnight in warm water. Drain the seeds and place them in a jam jar, or a sprouting tray if you have one. Cover the neck of the jar with a piece of muslin or fine netting. Leave in a dark, warm place. Once a day, fill the jar with warm water, then turn it upside down and allow the water to drain out through the muslin. After 3 or 4 days, the seeds will be ready to eat.

You can sprout almost any seeds and beans in this way, including mung beans, which turn into bean-sprouts, and are usually much crunchier than the shop-bought variety.

CELERY & GREEN (BELL) PEPPER WITH SESAME DRESSING

SERVES 4

125 g/4 oz/2 cups bean-sprouts
1½ tbsp chopped coriander (cilantro)
3 tbsp fresh lime juice
½ tsp mild chilli powder
1 tsp sugar
½ tsp salt
3 celery sticks, cut into 2.5 cm/1 in pieces
1 large green (bell) pepper, chopped
1 large Granny Smith apple
2 tbsp sesame seeds to garnish

1 Rinse and drain the bean-sprouts. Pick them over and remove any that seem a little brown or limp – it is essential that they are fresh and crunchy for this recipe.

2 To make the dressing, combine the coriander (cilantro), lime juice, chilli powder, sugar and salt in a small bowl and mix thoroughly.

3 In a larger bowl, combine the celery, (bell) pepper, bean-sprouts and apple.

4 To prepare the garnish, toast the sesame seeds in a dry skillet until they are just turning colour.

5 Stir the dressing into the mixed vegetables just before serving. Garnish with the toasted sesame seeds.

MARINATED VEGETABLE SALAD

SERVES 4-6

175 g/6 oz baby carrots, trimmed
2 celery hearts, cut into 4 pieces
125g/4 oz sugar snap peas or mangetout
(snow peas)
1 bulb fennel, sliced
175 g/6 oz small asparagus spears
15 g/ ½ oz/1½ sunflower seeds
sprigs of fresh dill to garnish

DRESSING:
4 tbsp olive oil
4 tbsp dry white wine
2 tbsp white wine vinegar
1 tbsp chopped fresh dill
1 tbsp chopped parsley
salt and pepper

1 Steam the carrots, celery, sugar snap peas or mangetout (snow peas), fennel and asparagus over gently boiling water until just tender. It is important that they retain a little 'bite'.

2 Meanwhile, mix together the olive oil, wine, vinegar and chopped herbs. Season well with salt and pepper.

3 When the vegetables are cooked, transfer them to a serving dish and pour over the dressing at once. The hot vegetables will absorb the flavour of the dressing as they cool.

4 Scatter the sunflower seeds on a baking sheet and toast them under a preheated grill (broiler) until lightly browned. Sprinkle them over the vegetables.

5 Serve the salad while the vegetables are still slightly warm, garnished with sprigs of fresh dill.

VARIATION

Sesame seeds or pine kernels can be used instead of sunflower seeds for sprinkling over the vegetables. Keep an eye on them while grilling, as they can burn easily.

RED ONION, CHERRY TOMATO & PASTA SALAD

SERVES 4

175 g/6 oz/1½ cups pasta shapes
1 yellow (bell) pepper, halved, cored and
deseeded
2 small courgettes (zucchini), sliced
1 red onion, sliced thinly
125 g/4 oz cherry tomatoes, halved
a handful of fresh basil leaves, torn into
small pieces
salt and pepper
sprigs of fresh basil to garnish

DRESSING:
60 ml/4 tbsp olive oil
30 ml/2 tbsp red wine vinegar
2 tsp lemon juice
1 tsp Dijon mustard
½ tsp caster (superfine) sugar

1 Cook the pasta in plenty of boiling, lightly salted water for about 8 minutes, or until just tender.

2 Meanwhile, place the (bell) pepper halves, skin-side uppermost, under a preheated grill (broiler) until they just begin to char. Leave them to cool, then peel and slice them into strips.

3 Cook the courgettes (zucchini) in a small amount of boiling, lightly salted water for 3–4 minutes, until cooked, yet still crunchy. Drain and refresh under cold running water to cool quickly.

4 To make the dressing, mix together the olive oil, red wine vinegar, lemon juice, mustard and sugar. Season well with salt and pepper. Add the basil leaves.

5 Drain the pasta well and tip it into a large serving bowl. Add the dressing and toss well. Add the pepper, courgettes (zucchini), onion and cherry tomatoes, stirring to combine. Cover and leave at room temperature for about 30 minutes to allow the flavours to develop.

6 Serve as a side dish, garnished with sprigs of fresh basil.

MELON, MANGO & GRAPE SALAD WITH GINGER & HONEY DRESSING

SERVES 4

1 cantaloup melon
60 g/2 oz/ ½ cup black grapes, halved and
   pipped
60 g/2 oz/ ½ cup green grapes
1 large mango
1 bunch of watercress, trimmed
iceberg lettuce leaves, shredded
2 tbsp olive oil
1 tbsp cider vinegar
1 passion fruit
salt and pepper

DRESSING:
150 ml/ ¼ pint/ ⅔ cup natural thick, full-
   fat yogurt
1 tbsp clear honey
1 tsp grated fresh root ginger

1 To make the dressing for the melon,
   mix together the yogurt, honey and
ginger in a bowl.

2 Halve the melon and scoop out the
   seeds. Slice, peel and cut into
chunks. Mix with the grapes.

3 Slice the mango on each side of its
   large flat stone (pit). On each mango
half, slash the flesh into a criss-cross
pattern down to, but not through, the
skin. Push the skin from underneath to
turn the mango halves inside out. Now
remove the squares of flesh and add to
the melon mixture.

4 Arrange the watercress and lettuce
   on 4 serving plates. Make the
dressing for the salad leaves (greens) by
mixing together the olive oil and cider
vinegar with a little salt and pepper.
Drizzle over the watercress and lettuce.

5 Divide the melon mixture between
   the 4 plates and spoon over the
yogurt dressing. Scoop the seeds out of
the passion fruit and sprinkle them over
the salads.

MOROCCAN ORANGE & COUSCOUS SALAD

SERVES 4–6

175 g/6 oz/2 cups couscous
1 bunch spring onions (scallions),
   trimmed and chopped finely
1 small green (bell) pepper, deseeded and
   chopped
10 cm/4 in piece of cucumber, chopped
175 g/6 oz can chick-peas (garbanzo
   beans), rinsed and drained
60 g/2 oz/ ⅓ cup sultanas (golden raisins)
   or raisins
2 oranges
salt and pepper
lettuce leaves to serve
sprigs of fresh mint to garnish

DRESSING:
finely grated rind of 1 orange
1 tbsp chopped fresh mint
150 ml/ ¼ pint/ ⅔ cup natural yogurt

1 Put the couscous into a bowl and
   cover with boiling water. Leave it to
soak for about 15 minutes to swell the
grains, then stir lightly with a fork to
separate them.

2 Add the spring onions (scallions),
   green (bell) pepper, cucumber,
chick-peas (garbanzo beans) and sultanas
(golden raisins) or raisins to the couscous, stirring to combine. Season well
with salt and pepper.

3 To make the dressing, mix together
   the orange rind, mint and yogurt.
Pour the dressing over the couscous
mixture and stir well.

4 Using a sharp serrated knife, remove
   the peel and pith from the oranges.
Cut them into segments, removing all the
membrane.

5 Arrange the lettuce leaves on
   4 serving plates. Divide the couscous mixture between the plates and
arrange the orange segments on top.
Garnish with sprigs of fresh mint and
serve immediately.

PINK GRAPEFRUIT, AVOCADO & DOLCELATTE SALAD

•••

SERVES 4

½ cos (romaine) lettuce
½ oak leaf lettuce
2 pink grapefruit
2 ripe avocados
175 g/6 oz Dolcelatte cheese, sliced thinly
sprigs of fresh basil to garnish

DRESSING:
4 tbsp olive oil
1 tbsp white wine vinegar
salt and pepper

1 Arrange the lettuce leaves on 4 serving plates or in a salad bowl.

2 Remove the peel and pith from the grapefruit with a sharp serrated knife, catching the juice in a bowl.

3 Segment the grapefruit by cutting down each side of the membrane. Remove all the membrane. Arrange the segments on the serving plates.

4 Peel, stone (pit) and slice the avocados, dipping them in the grapefruit juice to prevent them from going brown. Arrange the slices on the salad with the Dolcelatte cheese.

5 To make the dressing, combine any remaining grapefruit juice with the olive oil and wine vinegar. Season with salt and pepper, mixing well.

6 Drizzle the dressing over the salads. Garnish with fresh basil leaves and serve at once.

TIPS

Pink grapefruit segments make a very attractive colour combination with the avocados, but ordinary grapefruit will work just as well.

To help avocados to ripen, keep them at room temperature in a brown paper bag.

GADO GADO SALAD

•••

SERVES 4

250 g/8 oz new potatoes, scrubbed
125 g/4 oz green beans
125 g/4 oz cauliflower, broken into small florets
125 g/4 oz/1½ cups white cabbage, shredded
1 carrot, cut into thin sticks
¼ cucumber, cut into chunks
125 g/4 oz/2 cups bean-sprouts
2 hard-boiled (hard-cooked) eggs

SAUCE:
6 tbsp crunchy peanut butter
300 ml/ ½ pint/1¼ cups cold water
1 garlic clove, crushed
1 fresh red chilli, deseeded and finely chopped
2 tbsp soy sauce
1 tbsp dry sherry
2 tsp sugar
1 tbsp lemon juice

1 Halve the potatoes and place in a saucepan of lightly salted water. Bring to the boil and then simmer for 12–15 minutes, or until cooked through. Drain and plunge into cold water to cool.

2 Bring another pan of lightly salted water to the boil. Add the green beans, cauliflower and cabbage, and cook for 3 minutes. Drain and plunge the vegetables into cold water to cool and prevent any further cooking.

3 Drain the potatoes and other cooked vegetables. Arrange in piles on a large serving platter with the carrot, cucumber and bean-sprouts.

4 Remove the shells from the hard-boiled (hard-cooked) eggs, cut into quarters and arrange on the salad. Cover and set aside.

5 To make the sauce, place the peanut butter in a bowl and blend in the water gradually, followed by the remaining ingredients.

6 Uncover the salad, place the sauce in a separate serving bowl and drizzle some over each serving.

ORIENTAL SALAD

SERVES 4-6

30 g/1 oz/ ¼ cup dried vermicelli
½ head Chinese leaves
125 g/4 oz/2 cups bean-sprouts
6 radishes
125 g/4 oz mangetout (snow peas)
1 large carrot
125 g/4 oz sprouting beans

DRESSING:
juice of 1 orange
1 tbsp sesame seeds, toasted
1 tsp honey
1 tsp sesame oil
1 tbsp hazelnut oil

1 Break the vermicelli into small strands. Heat a wok or frying pan (skillet) and dry-fry the vermicelli until lightly golden. Remove from the pan and set aside.

2 Shred the Chinese leaves and wash with the bean-sprouts. Drain thoroughly and place in a large bowl. Slice the radishes. Trim the mangetout (snow peas) and cut each into 3. Cut the carrot into thin matchsticks. Add the sprouting beans and prepared vegetables to the bowl.

3 Place all the dressing ingredients in a screw-top jar and shake until well-blended. Pour over the salad and toss.

4 Transfer the salad to a serving bowl and sprinkle over the reserved vermicelli before serving.

SPROUTING BEANS

If you are unable to buy sprouting beans, you can make your own. Use a mixture of mung and aduki beans and chick-peas (garbanzo beans). Soak the beans overnight in cold water, drain and rinse. Place in a large glass jam jar and cover the mouth of the jar with a piece of muslin tied on to secure it. Lay the jar on its side and place in indirect light. For the next 2–3 days rinse the beans once each day in cold water until they are ready to eat.

PAW-PAW (PAPAYA) SALAD

SERVES 4

DRESSING:
4 tbsp olive oil
1 tbsp fish sauce or light soy sauce
2 tbsp lime or lemon juice
1 tbsp dark muscovado sugar
1 tsp finely chopped fresh red or green
  chilli

SALAD:
1 crisp lettuce
¼ small white cabbage
2 paw-paws (papayas)
2 tomatoes
30 g/1 oz/ ¼ cup roast peanuts, chopped
  roughly
4 spring onions (scallions), trimmed and
  sliced thinly
basil leaves, to garnish

1 To make the dressing, whisk together the olive oil, fish sauce or soy sauce, lime or lemon juice, sugar and chopped chilli. Set aside, stirring occasionally to dissolve the sugar.

2 Shred the lettuce and cabbage and toss them together. Arrange on a large serving plate.

3 Peel the paw-paws (papayas) and slice them in half. Scoop out the seeds, then slice the flesh thinly. Arrange on top of the shredded lettuce and cabbage.

4 Put the tomatoes into a small bowl and cover them with boiling water. Leave them to stand for 1 minute, then lift them out with a fork and peel them. Remove the seeds and chop the flesh. Arrange them on the salad leaves. Scatter the peanuts and spring onions (scallions) over the top.

5 Whisk the salad dressing to distribute the ingredients and pour over the salad. Garnish with basil leaves and serve at once.

CHICK-PEA (GARBANZO BEAN), TOMATO & AUBERGINE (EGGPLANT) SALAD

••

SERVES 4

500 g/1 lb aubergines (eggplant)
4 tbsp salt
1 tbsp olive oil
1 large onion, chopped
1 garlic clove, crushed
150 ml/ ¼ pint/ ⅔ cup Fresh Vegetable
    Stock (see page 97)
about 400 g/13 oz can chopped tomatoes
2 tbsp tomato purée (paste)
1 tsp ground cinnamon
2 tsp caster (superfine) sugar
1 tbsp chopped fresh coriander (cilantro)
1 tbsp lemon juice
about 425 g/14 oz can chick-peas
    (garbanzo beans), drained
freshly ground black pepper
fresh coriander (cilantro) sprigs to garnish

1 Cut the aubergines (eggplant) into
1 cm/ ½ in thick slices and then
cube. Layer in a bowl, sprinkling well
with salt as you go. Set aside for
30 minutes to allow the bitter juices to
drain out.

2 Transfer to a colander and rinse well
under running cold water to remove
the salt. Drain well and pat dry with
paper towels.

3 Heat the oil in a large non-stick
frying pan (skillet), add the onion
and garlic and fry gently for 2–3 minutes
until slightly softened.

4 Pour in the stock and bring to the
boil. Add the aubergines (eggplant),
canned tomatoes, tomato purée (paste),
cinnamon, sugar and pepper. Mix well
and simmer gently, uncovered, for
20 minutes until softened. Set aside to
cool completely.

5 Stir in the fresh coriander (cilantro),
lemon juice and chick-peas (garbanzo
beans), cover and chill for 1 hour.

6 Serve garnished with coriander
(cilantro) sprigs.

CARROT, CELERIAC (CELERY ROOT), CELERY & ORANGE SALAD

••

SERVES 6

500 g/1 lb celeriac (celery root)
2 tbsp orange juice
350 g/12 oz/4 carrots, sliced finely
2 celery sticks, chopped finely
30 g/1 oz/1 cup celery leaves
4 oranges
30 g/1 oz/ ¼ cup walnut pieces

DRESSING:
1 tbsp walnut oil
½ tsp grated orange rind
3 tbsp orange juice
1 tbsp white wine vinegar
1 tsp clear honey
salt and pepper

1 Trim and peel the celeriac (celery
root) and slice or grate finely into a
bowl. Add the orange juice and toss
together into the celeriac.

2 Mix in the carrots, celery and celery
leaves. Cover and chill while
preparing the oranges.

3 Slice off the tops and bottoms from
the oranges. Using a sharp knife,
slice off the skin, taking the pith away at
the same time. Cut out the orange flesh
by slicing along the side of the
membranes dividing the segments. Gently
mix the segments into the celeriac (celery
root) mixture.

4 To make the dressing, place all the
ingredients in a small screw-top jar.
Seal and shake well to mix.

5 Pile the vegetable mixture on to a
plate. Sprinkle over the walnut
pieces and serve with the dressing.

CELERIAC (CELERY ROOT)

Celeriac (celery root) is a variety of
celery with a bulbous, knobbly root. It
has a rough, light brown skin and
creamy white flesh. It is delicious raw
or cooked. In this salad, it combines
well with carrots and celery.

VEGETABLE DISHES – INTRODUCTION

Fresh vegetables are essential to successful cooking. If in a good condition, they will keep in the refrigerator or a cool place for 2–3 days, but for the best flavour and nutritional content, they should be used as soon as possible. Never store vegetables in an enclosed polythene bag: they will 'sweat' and quickly deteriorate. It is best to take them out of the bag and store in a net or paper bag which allows them to 'breathe' and thus prolongs their life. If they have to stay in polythene, make several large holes in the bag to allow the air to circulate. Root vegetables will keep longer than green ones, and green vegetables and salads will last longer if kept in the salad drawer at the bottom of the refrigerator.

CARROTS WITH PINEAPPLE

SERVES 4

1 tbsp sunflower oil
1 tbsp olive oil
1 small onion, finely sliced
2.5 cm/1 in piece ginger root, peeled and grated
1-2 garlic cloves, crushed
500 g/1 lb carrots, thinly sliced
1 x 200 g/7 oz can pineapple in natural juice, chopped, or 250 g/8 oz fresh pineapple, chopped
2-3 tbsp pineapple juice (from the can or fresh)
salt and pepper
freshly chopped parsley or dill, to garnish

1 Heat the oil in the wok, swirling it around until it is really hot. Add the onion, ginger and garlic and stir-fry briskly for 2-3 minutes, taking care not to allow it to colour.

2 Add the carrots and continue to stir-fry, lowering the heat a little, for about 5 minutes, spreading the slices out evenly over the surface of the wok as you stir.

3 Add the pineapple and juice and plenty of seasoning and continue to stir-fry for 5-6 minutes, or until the carrots are tender-crisp and the liquid has almost evaporated.

4 Adjust the seasoning, adding plenty of black pepper (the extra-coarse type is good to use here) and turn into a warmed serving dish. Sprinkle with chopped parsley or dill and serve as a vegetable accompaniment. Alternatively, you can allow the carrots to cool and serve as a salad, dressed with 2-4 tablespoons French dressing.

CANNED FRUIT

If using canned pineapple make sure it is in natural juice, not syrup: the sweet taste of the syrup will ruin the fresh flavour of this dish. Most fruits can now be bought canned in natural juice, which gives them a much fresher, lighter taste.

CARAWAY CABBAGE
••••••••••••••••••••••••••••••••••

SERVES 4

500 g/1 lb white cabbage
1 tbsp sunflower oil
4 spring onions (scallions), thinly sliced
  diagonally
60 g/2 oz/ 6 tbsp raisins
60 g/2 oz/ ½ cup walnut pieces or pecan
  nuts, roughly chopped
5 tbsp milk or vegetable stock
salt and pepper
1 tbsp caraway seeds
1-2 tbsp freshly chopped mint
mint sprigs, to garnish

1 Remove any outer leaves from the
cabbage and cut out the stem, then
shred the leaves very finely, either by
hand or using the fine slicing blade on a
food processor.

2 Heat the oil in a wok, swirling it
around until it is really hot. Add the
spring onions (scallions) and stir-fry for a
minute or so.

3 Add the shredded cabbage and stir-
fry for 3-4 minutes, keeping the
cabbage moving all the time and stirring
from the outside to the centre of the wok.
Make sure the cabbage does not catch or
go brown.

4 Add the raisins and walnuts and the
milk and continue to stir-fry for
3-4 minutes until the cabbage begins to
slightly soften but is still crisp.

5 Season well, add the caraway seeds
and 1 tablespoon of the chopped
mint and continue to stir-fry for a minute
or so. Serve sprinkled with the remaining
chopped mint and garnish with sprigs of
fresh mint.

VARIATION

Red cabbage may also be cooked in the
wok, but substitute 2 tablespoons red or
white wine vinegar and 3 tablespoons
water for the milk and add 1 tablespoon
brown sugar. The caraway seeds may be
omitted and a finely chopped dessert
apple added with the cabbage. Replace
the chopped mint with chopped parsley.

BRAISED CHINESE LEAVES
••••••••••••••••••••••••••••••••••

SERVES 4

500 g/1 lb Chinese leaves or white cabbage
3 tbsp vegetable oil
½ tsp Szechuan red peppercorns
5-6 small dried red chillies, seeded and
  chopped
½ tsp salt
1 tbsp sugar
1 tbsp light soy sauce
1 tbsp rice vinegar
a few drops of sesame oil (optional)

1 Shred the Chinese leaves or cabbage
crosswise into thin pieces. (If
Chinese leaves are unavailable, the best
alternative is a firm-packed white
cabbage, not the dark green type. Cut out
the thick core of the cabbage with a sharp
knife before shredding.)

2 Heat the oil in a pre-heated wok,
add the Szechuan red peppercorns
and dried red chillies and stir-fry for a few
seconds.

3 Add the Chinese leaves or shredded
cabbage to the peppercorns and
chillies, stir-fry for about 1 minute, then
add salt and continue stirring for another
minute.

4 Add the sugar, soy sauce and
vinegar, blend well and braise for
one more minute. Finally sprinkle on the
sesame oil, if using. Serve hot or cold.

PEPPERCORNS

It is important to use the correct type
of peppercorns in preparing this dish.
Szechuan red peppercorns are also
known as farchiew. They are not true
peppers, but reddish brown dry berries
with a pungent, aromatic odour which
distinguishes them from the hotter
black peppercorns. Roast them briefly
in the oven or sauté them in a dry
frying pan (skillet). Grind the
peppercorns in a blender and store in a
jar until needed.

STIR-FRIED GREENS

SERVES 4

1 tbsp sunflower oil
1 garlic clove, halved
2 spring onions (scallions), sliced finely
227 g/7½ oz can water chestnuts, drained
  and sliced finely (optional)
500 g/1 lb spinach, any tough stalks
  removed
1 tsp sherry vinegar
1 tsp light soy sauce
pepper

1 Heat the oil in a wok or large, heavy
  frying pan (skillet) over a high heat.

2 Add the garlic and cook, stirring, for
  1 minute. If the garlic should brown,
remove it immediately.

3 Add the spring onions (scallions)
  and water chestnuts, if using, and
stir for 2–3 minutes. Add the spinach and
stir well.

4 Add the sherry vinegar, soy sauce
  and a sprinkling of pepper. Cook,
stirring, until the spinach is tender.
Remove the garlic.

5 Use a slotted spoon in order to drain
  off the excess liquid and serve
immediately.

TIPS

These stir-fried greens are delicious
served as an accompaniment to the
Red Curry with Cashews (see page
431).

Several types of oriental greens (for
example, choi sam and pak choi) are
widely available and any of these can
be successfully substituted for the
spinach.

CAULIFLOWER WITH THAI SPINACH

SERVES 4

175 g/6 oz cauliflower, cut into florets
1 garlic clove
½ tsp turmeric
1 tbsp coriander (cilantro) root or stem
1 tbsp sunflower oil
2 spring onions (scallions), cut into
  2.5 cm/1 in pieces
125 g/4 oz Thai spinach, tough stalks
  removed, or oriental greens
1 tsp yellow mustard seeds

1 Blanch the cauliflower, rinse in cold
  running water and drain. Set aside.

2 Grind the garlic, turmeric and
  coriander (cilantro) together in a
pestle and mortar or spice grinder.

3 Heat the oil in a wok or large, heavy
  frying pan (skillet). Add the spring
onions (scallions) and stir over a high
heat for 2 minutes. Add the Thai spinach,
or greens, and stir for 1 minute. Set aside.

4 Return the wok or frying pan
  (skillet) to the heat and add the
mustard seeds. Stir until they start to pop,
then add the turmeric mixture and the
cauliflower, and stir until all the
cauliflower is coated.

5 Serve with the spinach or greens on
  a warmed serving plate.

SUBSTITUTES

Oriental greens are now available in
many of the larger supermarkets;
however, English spinach or chard is
equally good with the cauliflower.

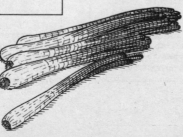

CURRIED ROAST POTATOES

SERVES 4

2 tsp cumin seeds
2 tsp coriander seeds
90 g/3 oz/ ⅓ cup salted butter
1 tsp ground turmeric
1 tsp black mustard seeds
2 garlic cloves, crushed
2 dried red chillies
750 g/1½ lb baby new potatoes

1 Grind the cumin and coriander seeds together in a pestle and mortar or spice grinder. Grinding them fresh like this captures all of the flavour before it has a chance to dry out.

2 Melt the butter gently in a roasting tin (pan) and add the turmeric, mustard seeds, garlic and chillies and the ground cumin and coriander seeds. Stir well to combine evenly. Place in a preheated oven at 200°C/400°F/Gas mark 6 for 5 minutes.

3 Remove the tin (pan) from the oven – the spices should be very fragrant at this stage – and add the potatoes. Stir well so that the butter and spice mix coats the potatoes completely.

4 Put back in the preheated oven and bake for 20–25 minutes. Stir occasionally to ensure that the potatoes are coated evenly. Test the potatoes with a skewer – if they drop off the end of the skewer when lifted, they are done. Serve immediately.

POTATOES

Baby new potatoes are now available all year round from supermarkets. However, they are not essential for this recipe. Red or white old potatoes can be substituted, cut into 2.5 cm/1 in cubes. You can also try substituting parsnips, carrots or turnips, peeled and cut into 2.5 cm/1 in cubes. Peel 250 g/ 8 oz pickling onions and mix in with the vegetables for a tasty variation.

SPICY INDIAN-STYLE POTATOES

SERVES 4

750 g/1½ lb potatoes
salt
60 g/2 oz/ ¼ cup ghee or butter
2 tbsp vegetable oil
1 tsp ground turmeric
1 large onion, peeled, quartered and sliced
2-3 garlic cloves, peeled and crushed
5 cm/2 in piece ginger root, peeled and chopped
1½ tsp cumin seeds
¼-½ tsp cayenne pepper
2 tsp lemon juice
1 tbsp shredded mint leaves
sprigs of mint, to garnish

1 Peel the potatoes and cut into 2-2.5 cm/ ¾-1 in cubes and cook in a pan of boiling, salted water for 6-8 minutes or until knife-tip tender (do not overcook). Drain well, return to the pan and shake dry over a moderate heat for a few moments.

2 Heat the ghee or butter and oil in a large frying pan over medium heat. Stir in the turmeric, then add the sliced onion and the cooked potatoes and fry for 4-5 minutes or until the mixture is beginning to brown, stirring and turning the vegetables frequently.

3 Stir in the garlic, ginger, cumin seeds, cayenne and salt to taste. Fry over gentle heat for 1 minute, stirring all the time.

4 Transfer the potatoes to a warm serving dish. Add the lemon juice to the juices in the pan and spoon the mixture over the potatoes. Sprinkle with the shredded mint leaves, garnish with sprigs of mint and serve hot.

POTATOES

This method of cooking potatoes is perfect for using up leftover potatoes – in fact if you've time, par-boil the potatoes in advance and leave them to cool before frying for even tastier results.

(BELL) PEPPERS WITH ROSEMARY BASTE

•••

SERVES 4

4 tbsp olive oil
finely grated rind of 1 lemon
4 tbsp lemon juice
1 tbsp balsamic vinegar
1 tbsp crushed fresh rosemary, or 1 tsp
   dried rosemary
2 red (bell) peppers, halved, cored and
   deseeded
2 yellow (bell) peppers, halved, cored and
   deseeded
2 tbsp pine kernels
salt and pepper
sprigs of fresh rosemary to garnish

1 Mix together the olive oil, lemon
   rind, lemon juice, vinegar and
crushed rosemary in a bowl. Season with
salt and pepper.

2 Place the (bell) peppers, skin-side
   uppermost, on the rack of a grill
(broiler) pan, lined with foil. Brush the
olive oil mixture over them.

3 Cook the (bell) peppers until the
   skin begins to char, basting
frequently with the lemon juice mixture.
Remove from the heat, cover with foil to
trap the steam and leave for 5 minutes.

4 Meanwhile, scatter the pine kernels
   on to the grill (broiler) rack and
toast them lightly.

5 Peel the (bell) peppers, slice them
   into strips and place them in a
warmed serving dish. Sprinkle with the
pine kernels and drizzle any remaining
lemon juice mixture over them. Garnish
the peppers with sprigs of fresh rosemary
and serve at once.

PEELING PEPPERS

Covering the hot (bell) peppers with a
piece of foil after grilling (broiling) traps
the escaping steam. This loosens their
skins, so that they are easy to peel,
and it helps to keep them warm.

CREAMY BAKED FENNEL

•••

SERVES 4

2 tbsp lemon juice
2 bulbs fennel, trimmed
125 g/4 oz/ ¼ cup low-fat soft cheese
150 ml/ ¼ pint/ ⅔ cup single (light)
   cream
150 ml/ ¼ pint/ ⅔ cup milk
1 egg, beaten
60 g/2 oz/ ¼ cup butter
2 tsp caraway seeds
60 g/2 oz/1 cup fresh white breadcrumbs
salt and pepper
sprigs of parsley to garnish

1 Bring a large saucepan of water to
   the boil and add the lemon juice.
Slice the bulbs of fennel thinly and add
them to the saucepan. Cook for
2–3 minutes to blanch, and then drain
them well, and arrange in a buttered
ovenproof baking dish.

2 Beat the soft cheese in a bowl until
   smooth. Add the cream, milk and
beaten egg, and whisk together until
combined. Season with salt and pepper
and pour over the fennel.

3 Melt 15 g/ ½ oz of the butter in a
   small frying pan (skillet) and fry the
caraway seeds gently for 1–2 minutes, to
release their flavour and aroma. Sprinkle
over the fennel.

4 Melt the remaining butter in a frying
   pan (skillet). Add the breadcrumbs
and fry gently until lightly browned.
Sprinkle evenly over the surface of the
fennel.

5 Place in a preheated oven at
   180°C/350°F/Gas Mark 4 and bake
for 25–30 minutes, or until the fennel is
tender. Serve, garnished with parsley.

ALTERNATIVE

If you cannot find any fennel in the
shops, leeks make a delicious
alternative. Use about 750 g/1½ lb,
washing them thoroughly to remove
all traces of sand.

COURGETTE (ZUCCHINI), CARROT & FETA CHEESE PATTIES

••••••••••••••••••••••••••••••••••••••

SERVES 4

2 large carrots
1 large courgette (zucchini)
1 small onion
60 g/2 oz Feta cheese
30 g/1 oz/ ¼ cup plain (all-purpose) flour
½ tsp cumin seeds
½ tsp poppy seeds
1 tsp medium curry powder
1 tbsp chopped fresh parsley
1 egg, beaten
30 g/1 oz/2 tbsp butter
2 tbsp vegetable oil
salt and pepper
sprigs of fresh herbs to garnish

1 Grate the carrots, courgette (zucchini), onion and Feta cheese coarsely, either by hand or using a food processor.

2 Mix together the flour, cumin seeds, poppy seeds, curry powder and parsley in a large bowl. Season well with salt and pepper.

3 Add the carrot mixture to the seasoned flour, tossing well to combine. Stir in the beaten egg and mix well together.

4 Heat the butter and oil in a large frying pan (skillet). Place heaped tablespoonfuls of the carrot mixture in the pan, flattening them slightly with the back of the spoon. Fry gently for about 2 minutes on each side, until crisp and golden brown. Drain on paper towels and keep warm until all the mixture is used.

5 Serve the patties, garnished with sprigs of fresh herbs.

VARIATION

If you want to vary the flavour of these patties, omit the cumin seeds and curry powder and substitute 1 tbsp chopped fresh oregano for the parsley.

SAUTÉ OF SUMMER VEGETABLES WITH TARRAGON DRESSING

••••••••••••••••••••••••••••••••••••••

SERVES 4

250 g/8 oz baby carrots, scrubbed
125 g/4 oz runner (green) beans
2 courgettes (zucchini), trimmed
1 bunch large spring onions (scallions), trimmed
1 bunch radishes, trimmed
60 g/2 oz/ ¼ cup butter
2 tbsp light olive oil
2 tbsp white wine vinegar
4 tbsp dry white wine
1 tsp caster (superfine) sugar
1 tbsp chopped fresh tarragon
salt and pepper
sprigs of fresh tarragon to garnish

1 Trim and halve the carrots, slice the beans and courgettes (zucchini), and halve the spring onions (scallions) and radishes, so that all the vegetables are cut to even-sized pieces.

2 Melt the butter in a large frying pan (skillet) or wok. Add all the vegetables and fry them over a medium heat, stirring frequently.

3 Gently heat the olive oil, vinegar, white wine and sugar in a small saucepan. Remove from the heat and add the tarragon.

4 When the vegetables are just cooked, but still retain their crunchiness, pour over the 'dressing'. Stir through, and then transfer to a warmed serving dish. Garnish with sprigs of fresh tarragon and serve at once.

ALTERNATIVES

Use any combination of fresh vegetables for this dish, but remember to serve them while still slightly crunchy for the best texture and flavour. The vegetables also retain more of their nutrients when cooked this way.

If you cannot find any fresh tarragon, substitute a different herb. Marjoram, basil, oregano, chives or chervil would make delicious alternatives.

SPICY STUFFED CHINESE LEAVES

SERVES 4

8 large Chinese leaves
60 g/2 oz/ ⅓ cup long-grain rice
½ vegetable stock (bouillon) cube
60 g/2 oz/ ¼ cup butter
1 bunch spring onions (scallions),
  trimmed and chopped finely
1 celery stick, chopped finely
125 g/4 oz/1¼ cups button mushrooms,
  sliced
1 tsp Chinese five-spice powder
300 ml/ ½ pint/1¼ cups passatta (sieved
  tomato sauce)
salt and pepper
fresh chives to garnish

1 Blanch the Chinese leaves in boiling
  water for 1 minute. Refresh them
under cold running water and drain well.
Be careful not to tear them.

2 Cook the rice in plenty of boiling
  water, flavoured with the stock
(bouillon) cube, until just tender. Drain.

3 Meanwhile, melt the butter in a
  frying pan (skillet) and fry the spring
onions (scallions) and celery gently for
3–4 minutes until softened, but not
browned. Add the mushrooms and cook
for a further 3–4 minutes, stirring often.

4 Add the cooked rice to the pan with
  the five-spice powder. Season with
salt and pepper and stir well to combine
the ingredients.

5 Lay out the Chinese leaves on a
  work surface (counter) and divide
the rice mixture between them. Roll each
leaf into a neat parcel to enclose the
stuffing. Place them, seam-side down, in a
greased ovenproof dish. Pour the passatta
over them and cover with foil.

6 Bake in a preheated oven at
  190°C/375°F/Gas Mark 5 for
  25–30 minutes. Serve
  immediately, garnished
  with chives.

STIR-FRIED WINTER VEGETABLES WITH CORIANDER (CILANTRO)

SERVES 4

3 tbsp sesame oil
30 g/1 oz/ ¼ cup blanched almonds
1 large carrot, cut into thin strips
1 large turnip, cut into thin strips
1 onion, sliced finely
1 garlic clove, crushed
3 celery sticks, sliced finely
125 g/4 oz Brussels sprouts, trimmed and
  halved
125 g/4 oz cauliflower, broken into florets
125 g/4 oz/2 cups white cabbage,
  shredded
2 tsp sesame seeds
1 tsp grated fresh root ginger
½ tsp medium chilli powder
1 tbsp chopped fresh coriander (cilantro)
1 tbsp light soy sauce
salt and pepper
sprigs of fresh coriander (cilantro) to
  garnish

1 Heat the sesame oil in a wok or
  large frying pan (skillet). Stir-fry the
almonds until lightly browned, then lift
them out and drain on paper towels.

2 Add all the vegetables to the wok or
  frying pan (skillet), except for the
cabbage. Stir-fry briskly for 3–4 minutes.

3 Add the cabbage, sesame seeds,
  ginger and chilli powder to the
vegetables and cook, stirring, for
2 minutes.

4 Add the chopped coriander
  (cilantro), soy sauce and almonds to
the mixture, stirring them through gently.
Serve the vegetables, garnished with
sprigs of fresh coriander (cilantro).

SESAME OIL

Sesame oil is not essential for this
stir-fry, but it does give an excellent
flavour and is a typical ingredient of
oriental cookery, though it is generally
used for sprinkling over food or
flavouring sauces. Vegetable or olive
oil could be used instead, or groundnut
or corn oil.

STIR-FRIED GREENS

SERVES 4

8 spring onions (scallions)
2 celery sticks
125 g/4 oz white radish (mooli)
125 g/4 oz sugar snap peas or mangetout
(snow peas)
175 g/6 oz Chinese leaves or cabbage
175 g/6 oz bok choy or spinach
2 tbsp vegetable oil
1 tbsp sesame oil
2 garlic cloves, chopped finely
1 tbsp fish sauce
2 tbsp oyster sauce
1 tsp finely grated fresh ginger root
pepper

1 Slice the spring onions (scallions) and celery finely. Cut the white radish (mooli) into matchstick strips. Trim the sugar snap peas or mangetout (snow peas). Shred the Chinese leaves or cabbage and shred the bok choy or spinach.

2 Heat the vegetable oil and sesame oil together in a wok or large frying pan (skillet). Add the garlic and fry for about 1 minute.

3 Add the spring onions (scallions), celery, white radish (mooli) and sugar snap peas or mangetout (snow peas) to the wok or frying pan (skillet) and stir-fry for about 2 minutes.

4 Add the Chinese leaves or cabbage and bok choy or spinach. Stir-fry for 1 minute.

5 Stir the fish sauce and oyster sauce into the vegetables with the grated ginger. Cook for 1 minute. Season with pepper and serve at once.

VARIATIONS

Any variety – and any amount – of fresh vegetables can be used in this dish. Just make sure that harder vegetables, such as carrots, are cut very finely so that they cook quickly.
    Use light soy sauce as an alternative to the fish sauce, if you prefer.

SHREDDED VEGETABLE OMELETTE

SERVES 4

4 eggs
3 tbsp milk
1 tbsp fish sauce or light soy sauce
1 tbsp sesame oil
1 small red onion, very finely sliced
1 small courgette (zucchini), trimmed
and cut into matchstick pieces
1 small leek, trimmed and cut into
matchstick pieces
1 small carrot, trimmed and cut into
matchstick pieces
5 cm/2 in piece of cucumber, cut into
matchstick pieces
1 tbsp chopped fresh coriander (cilantro)
15 g/ ½ oz/1 tbsp butter
salt and pepper

TO GARNISH:
sprigs of fresh basil
celery leaves

1 Beat the eggs, milk and fish sauce or soy sauce together.

2 Heat the sesame oil in a wok or large frying pan (skillet) and add all the vegetables. Stir-fry them briskly for 3–4 minutes, then add the chopped coriander (cilantro). Season with salt and pepper. Transfer to a warmed plate and keep warm.

3 Melt the butter in a large omelette pan or frying pan (skillet) and add the beaten egg mixture. Cook over a medium-high heat until just set.

4 Tip the vegetable mixture along one side of the omelette, then roll up the omelette. Slice into 4 portions and arrange on a warmed serving plate. Garnish with fresh basil and celery leaves, and serve at once.

VEGETABLES

Substitute other vegetables for the ones in the recipe as you wish – spring onions (scallions), mangetout (snow peas), small broccoli or cauliflower florets, for example.

LAYERED ROOT VEGETABLE GRATIN

SERVES 6

250 g/8 oz/2 large carrots
250 g/8 oz baby parsnips
1 fennel bulb
500 g/1 lb/3 potatoes
90 g/3 oz/⅛ cup low-fat spread
30 g/1 oz/¼ cup plain (all-purpose) flour
300 ml/½ pint/1¼ cups skimmed milk
½ tsp ground nutmeg
1 egg, beaten
30 g/1 oz/¼ cup freshly grated Parmesan
* cheese*
salt and pepper

TO SERVE:
crusty bread
tomatoes

1 Cut the carrots and parsnips into thin lengthwise strips. Cook in boiling water for 5 minutes. Drain well and transfer to an ovenproof baking dish.

2 Thinly slice the fennel lengthways and cook in boiling water for 2–3 minutes. Drain well and add to the carrots and parsnips. Season.

3 Peel and dice the potatoes into 2 cm/¾ in cubes. Cook in boiling water for 6 minutes. Drain well.

4 Gently melt half the low-fat spread and stir in the flour. Remove from the heat and gradually mix in the milk. Return to the heat and stir until thickened. Season and stir in the nutmeg. Cool for 10 minutes.

5 Beat in the egg and spoon over the vegetables. Arrange the potatoes on top and sprinkle over the cheese. Dot with the remaining low-fat spread. Bake in a preheated oven at 180°C/350°F/Gas Mark 4 for 1 hour, or until the vegetables are tender.

6 Serve as a light meal with crusty bread and a salad, or as an accompaniment to a light main course, such as steamed fish or grilled chicken.

RICE & GRAIN DISHES – INTRODUCTION

FLOURS, GRAINS, PASTA AND PULSES
You will need to keep a selection of
flours – plain (all-purpose) and self-
raising (self-rising), strong flour if you
want to make your own bread and
yeast bakes, and buy wholemeal
(whole wheat) flour too, for using on
its own or for combining with white
flour for cakes and pastries. You may
also like to keep some rice flour and
cornflour (cornstarch) (from maize)
for thickening sauces and to add to
cakes, biscuits and puddings.
Buckwheat, chick-pea (garbanzo
bean) and soya flours can also be
bought – useful for pancakes and for
combining with other flours to add
different flavours and textures.

Keep a good variety of grains –
for rice choose from long-grain,
basmati, Italian arborio for making
risotto, short-grain for puddings, wild
rice to add interest. Look out for
fragrant Thai rice, jasmine rice and
combinations of different varieties to
add colour and texture to your
dishes.

Other grains add variety to the
diet – try to include some barley
(whole grain or pearl), millet, bulgur
wheat, polenta (made from maize)
oats (oatmeal, oatflakes or
oatbran), semolina – including
cous-cous (from which it is
made), sago and tapioca.

Pasta has become
much more popular
recently, and there
are many types and
shapes to choose
from. Keep a good

selection, and always make sure you
have the basic lasagne sheets,
tagliatelle or fettucine (noodles) and
spaghetti. Try spinach or tomato
varieties for a change and sample
some of the fresh pastas that you can
now buy.

Pulses, such as soya beans,
haricot (navy) beans, red kidney and
cannellini beans, chick-peas
(garbanzo beans), all types of lentils,
split peas and butter beans are very
important in a vegetarian diet as they
are a good protein source, and
contain vitamins and minerals. Buy
them dried for soaking and cooking
yourself, or buy canned varieties for
speed and convenience.

TIPS
It is important to cook dried red and
black kidney beans in plenty of
vigorously boiling water for 15
minutes to destroy harmful toxins in
the outer skin. Drain and rinse the
beans, and then continue to simmer
until the beans are tender. Soya
beans should be boiled for 1 hour, as
they contain a substance that inhibits
protein from being
absorbed.

If you are short of
time, canned beans will
do just as well. If you prefer,
choose brands that contain no
added sugar or salt, and rinse
them well before using. Once
opened, they will keep in the
fridge for several days, but don't
leave them in the tin – transfer
them to a bowl, and cover them up.

COCONUT RICE

SERVES 4

90 g/3 oz creamed coconut
750 ml/1¼ pints/3 cups boiling water
1 tbsp sunflower oil (or olive oil for a
    stronger flavour)
1 onion, thinly sliced or chopped
250 g/8 oz/generous 1 cup long-grain rice
¼ tsp turmeric
6 whole cloves
1 cinnamon stick
½ tsp salt
60-90 g/2-3 oz/ ½ cup raisins or sultanas
60 g/2 oz/ ½ cup walnut or pecan halves,
    roughly chopped
2 tbsp pumpkin seeds (optional)
watercress sprigs, to garnish (optional)

1 Blend the creamed coconut with half
the boiling water until smooth, then
mix in the remainder and stir with a
wooden spoon until well blended.

2 Heat the oil in the wok, add the
onion and stir-fry gently for
3-4 minutes until the onion begins to
soften but not brown.

3 Rinse the rice thoroughly under cold
running water, drain well and add to
the wok with the turmeric. Cook for
1-2 minutes, stirring all the time.

4 Add the coconut milk, cloves,
cinnamon stick and salt and bring to
the boil. Cover with the wok lid, or a lid
made of foil, and simmer very gently for
10 minutes.

5 Add the raisins, nuts and pumpkin
seeds, if using, and mix well. Cover
the wok again and continue to cook for a
further 5-8 minutes or until all the liquid
has been absorbed and the rice is tender.

6 Remove from the heat and leave to
stand, still tightly covered, for
5 minutes before serving. Remove the
cinnamon stick. Serve garnished with
watercress sprigs, if liked.

DEEP SOUTH SPICED RICE & BEANS

SERVES 4

175 g/6 oz/scant 1 cup long-grain rice
4 tbsp olive oil
1 small green (bell) pepper, cored,
    deseeded and chopped
1 small red (bell) pepper, cored, deseeded
    and chopped
1 onion, chopped finely
1 small red or green chilli, deseeded and
    chopped finely
2 tomatoes, chopped
125 g/4 oz/ ½ cup canned red kidney
    beans, rinsed and drained
1 tbsp chopped fresh basil
2 tsp chopped fresh thyme (or 1 tsp dried)
1 tsp Cajun spice
salt and pepper
fresh basil leaves to garnish

1 Cook the rice in plenty of boiling,
lightly salted water until just tender,
about 12 minutes. Rinse with cold water
and drain well.

2 Meanwhile, heat the olive oil in a
frying pan (skillet) and fry the green
and red (bell) peppers and onion together
gently until softened, about
5 minutes.

3 Add the chilli and tomatoes, and
cook for a further 2 minutes.

4 Add the vegetable mixture and red
kidney beans to the rice. Stir well to
combine thoroughly.

5 Stir the chopped herbs and Cajun
spice into the rice mixture. Season
well with salt and pepper, and serve,
garnished with basil leaves.

CHILLIES

The fresh red or green chilli can be
replaced by 1 tsp chilli powder, for
speed and convenience.
    Take care when handling fresh
chillies, as the residue from them can
burn or irritate the skin. Be especially
careful to avoid rubbing your eyes
when preparing them, and rinse your
hands well after handling them.

GREEN RICE

SERVES 4

2 tbsp olive oil
500 g/1 lb/2¼ cups Basmati or Thai
  jasmine rice, soaked for 1 hour, washed
  and drained
750 ml/1¼ pints/3 cups coconut milk
1 tsp salt
1 bay leaf
2 tbsp chopped fresh coriander (cilantro)
2 tbsp chopped fresh mint
2 green chillies, deseeded and chopped
  finely

1 Heat the oil in a saucepan, add the
  rice and stir until it becomes
translucent.

2 Add the coconut milk, salt and bay
  leaf. Bring to the boil and cook until
all the liquid is absorbed.

3 Lower the heat as much as possible,
  cover the saucepan tightly and cook
for 10 minutes.

4 Remove the bay leaf and stir in the
  coriander (cilantro), mint and green
chillies. Fork through the rice gently and
serve.

COOKING IN A MICROWAVE

To save time, or to make some room
on your stove, step 3 can be done in a
microwave. Transfer the rice to a
microwave container, cover tightly and
cook on High for 4–5 minutes. Remove
the bay leaf, and stir in the herbs and
chillies. Fork through the rice gently
and serve.

GARNISHES

The contrasting colours of this dish
make it particularly attractive, and it
can be made to look even more
interesting with a carefully chosen
garnish. Two segments of fresh lime
complement the coriander (cilantro)
perfectly. Alternatively, use some small
sprigs of whole fresh coriander leaves.

CHATUCHAK FRIED RICE

SERVES 4

1 tbsp sunflower oil
3 shallots, chopped finely
2 garlic cloves, crushed
1 red chilli, deseeded and chopped finely
2.5 cm/1 in piece ginger, shredded finely
½ green (bell) pepper, sliced finely
150 g/5 oz/2–3 baby aubergines
  (eggplants), quartered
90 g/3 oz sugar snap peas or mange tout
  (snow peas), trimmed and blanched
90 g/3 oz/6 baby corn, halved lengthways
  and blanched
1 tomato, cut into 8 pieces
90 g/3 oz/1½ cups bean-sprouts
500 g/1 lb/3 cups cooked Thai jasmine rice
  (see page 436)
2 tbsp tomato ketchup
2 tbsp light soy sauce

TO GARNISH:
coriander (cilantro) leaves
lime wedges

1 Heat the oil in a wok or large, heavy
  frying pan (skillet) over a high heat.
Add the shallots, garlic, chilli and ginger.
Stir until the shallots have softened.

2 Add the green (bell) pepper and
  baby aubergines (eggplants) and stir.
Add the sugar snap peas or mange tout
(snow peas), baby corn, tomato and
bean-sprouts. Stir for 3 minutes.

3 Add the rice, and lift and stir with
  2 spoons for 4–5 minutes, until no
more steam is released. Stir in the tomato
ketchup and soy sauce.

4 Serve immediately, garnished with
  coriander (cilantro) leaves and lime
wedges to squeeze over.

VARIATION

Almost any vegetable, such as celery,
aubergine (eggplant), water chestnuts,
bamboo shoots, carrots, beans,
cauliflower or broccoli can be used.
Harder vegetables may need blanching
first, to ensure all the vegetables will
cook in the same amount of time.

FRIED NOODLES WITH BEAN-SPROUTS, CHIVES & CHILLI

SERVES 4

500 g/1 lb medium egg noodles
60 g/2 oz/1 cup bean-sprouts
15 g/½ oz chives
3 tbsp sunflower oil
1 garlic clove, crushed
4 green chillies, deseeded, sliced and
    soaked in 2 tbsp rice vinegar
salt

1 To cook the noodles, soak in boiling water for 10 minutes. Drain and set aside.

2 Soak the bean-sprouts in cold water while you cut the chives into 2.5cm/1 in pieces. Reserve a few whole chives for garnish. Drain the bean-sprouts.

3 Heat the oil in a wok or large, heavy frying pan (skillet). Add the crushed garlic and stir; then add the chillies and stir until fragrant, about 1 minute.

4 Add the bean-sprouts, stir and then add the noodles. Stir in some salt and the chives. Using 2 spoons, lift and stir the noodles for 1 minute.

5 Garnish the finished dish with the reserved chives, and serve at once.

CHILLIES

Soaking a chilli in rice vinegar has the effect of distributing the hot chilli flavour throughout the dish. To reduce the heat, you can slice the chilli more thickly before soaking, or soak it once, discard the vinegar, then soak again in a second batch of vinegar before adding the vinegar and chilli to the dish.

AROMATIC PILAU

SERVES 4-5

250 g/8 oz/1¼ cups basmati rice
2 tbsp ghee or vegetable oil
1 onion, peeled and chopped
3 cardamom pods, crushed
3 black peppercorns
3 cloves
1 tsp cumin seeds
½ cinnamon stick or piece of cassia bark
½ tsp ground turmeric
600 ml/1 pint/2½ cups boiling water or
    stock
60 g/2 oz/⅓ cup seedless raisins or
    sultanas
60 g/2 oz frozen peas
30 g/1 oz/¼ cup toasted, flaked almonds
crisp fried onion rings, to garnish
    (optional)

1 Place the rice in a sieve and wash well under cold running water until the water runs clear. Drain well.

2 Heat the oil in a large saucepan, add the onion and spices and fry gently for 1 minute, stirring all the time. Stir in the rice and mix well until coated in the spiced oil, then add the boiling water or stock and season with salt and pepper.

3 Bring to the boil, stir well, then cover, reduce the heat and cook gently for 15 minutes without uncovering. Add the raisins and peas, re-cover and leave to stand for 15 minutes.

4 Uncover, fluff up with a fork and stir the toasted flaked almonds into the mixture. Serve hot, garnished with crisp fried onion rings, if liked.

SPICES

The whole spices used for flavouring the rice are not meant to be eaten and may be removed from the mixture, if wished, before serving. Simply double up the quantities given for serving 8-10 portions for a party.

PRAWN (SHRIMP) PILAU

∙∙∙

SERVES 4-6

2.5 cm/1 in piece ginger root, peeled
4 garlic cloves, peeled
3 green chillies, deseeded
1 tsp cumin seeds
2 tsp coriander seeds
2 tbsp oil
2 shallots, chopped finely
250 g/8 oz/generous 1 cup basmati rice
10 cloves
5 cm/2 in piece cinnamon stick
5 cardamom pods
1 bay leaf
120 ml/4 fl oz/ ½ cup coconut milk
400 ml/14 fl oz/1¼ cups fish stock
175 g/6 oz/1 cup cooked, peeled prawns
 (shrimp)
2 tbsp cashew nuts, chopped and toasted
2 tbsp chopped fresh coriander (cilantro)
2 tbsp grated or desiccated (shredded)
 coconut, toasted

TO GARNISH:
lemon and tomato wedges

1 Grind together the ginger, garlic and green chillies in a coffee grinder or pestle and mortar.

2 Toast the cumin and coriander seeds and then grind them also.

3 Heat the oil in a wok or large frying pan (skillet). Add the shallots and cook over a medium heat until soft, about 5 minutes. Add the garlic mixture and stir until fragrant, about 1 minute. Add the cumin and coriander. Add the rice and stir until translucent.

4 Put the cloves, cinnamon, cardamom and bay leaf into a piece of muslin (cheesecloth). This is not essential but it makes them easier to remove at the end. Add the bag of spices to the pan.

5 Stir in the coconut milk and fish stock. Bring to the boil, stir once and simmer for 15–18 minutes, or until all the liquid is absorbed.

6 Add the prawns (shrimp), cashew nuts and coriander (cilantro). Cover with a close-fitting lid or a piece of foil, reduce the heat to the lowest setting and leave undisturbed for 10 minutes.

7 Discard the muslin (cheesecloth) bag of spices. Transfer the pilau to a serving dish and fork through lightly. Sprinkle over the toasted coconut and garnish with the lemon and tomato.

CHANNA DAL

SERVES 4–6

2 tbsp ghee
1 large onion, chopped finely
1 garlic clove, crushed
1 tbsp grated ginger root
1 tbsp cumin seeds, ground
2 tsp coriander seeds, ground
1 dried red chilli
2.5 cm/1 in piece cinnamon stick
1 tsp salt
½ tsp ground turmeric
250 g/ ½ lb/1 cup split yellow peas, soaked
  in cold water for 1 hour and drained
425 g /14 oz can plum tomatoes
300 ml/ ½ pint/1¼ cups water
2 tsp Garam Masala (see page 317)

1 Heat the ghee in a large saucepan, add the onion, garlic and ginger and fry for 3–4 minutes until the onion has softened slightly.

2 Add the cumin, coriander, chilli, cinnamon, salt and turmeric, then stir in the split peas until well mixed.

3 Add the contents of the can of tomatoes, breaking the tomatoes up slightly with the back of the spoon.

4 Add the water and bring to the boil. Reduce the heat to very low and simmer, uncovered, for about 40 minutes, stirring occasionally, until most of the liquid has been absorbed and the split peas are tender. Skim the surface occasionally with a perforated spoon to remove any scum.

5 Gradually stir in the garam masala, tasting after each addition, until it is of the required flavour.

HANDY HINTS

Use a non-stick saucepan if you have one, because the mixture is quite dense and does stick to the bottom of the pan occasionally. If the dal is overstirred the split peas will break up and the dish will not have much texture or bite.

EGG FU-YUNG WITH RICE

SERVES 2–4

175 g/6 oz/generous ¾ cup long-grain rice
2 Chinese dried mushrooms (if
  unavailable, use thinly sliced open-cup
  mushrooms)
3 eggs, beaten
3 tbsp vegetable oil
4 spring onions (scallions), sliced
½ green (bell) pepper, chopped
60 g/2 oz/ ⅓ cup canned bamboo shoots
60 g/2 oz/ ⅓ cup canned water chestnuts,
  sliced
125 g/4 oz/2 cups bean-sprouts
2 tbsp light soy sauce
2 tbsp dry sherry
2 tsp sesame oil
salt and pepper

1 Cook the rice in lightly salted boiling water according to the instructions on the packet.

2 Place the dried mushrooms in a small bowl, cover with warm water and leave to soak for 20–25 minutes.

3 Mix the beaten eggs with a little salt. Heat 1 tablespoon of the oil in a wok or large frying pan (skillet). Add the eggs and stir until just set. Remove and set aside.

4 Drain the mushrooms and squeeze out the excess water. Remove the tough centres and chop the mushrooms.

5 Heat the remaining oil in a clean wok or frying pan (skillet). Add the mushrooms, spring onions (scallions) and green (bell) pepper, and stir-fry for 2 minutes. Add the bamboo shoots, water chestnuts and bean-sprouts. Stir-fry for 1 minute.

6 Drain the rice thoroughly and add to the pan with the remaining ingredients. Mix well, heating the rice thoroughly. Season to taste, stir in the reserved eggs and serve.

YELLOW SPLIT PEA CASSEROLE

SERVES 6

2 tbsp ghee
1 tsp black mustard seeds
1 onion, chopped finely
2 garlic cloves, crushed
1 carrot, grated
2.5 cm/1 in piece ginger root, grated
1 green chilli, deseeded and chopped
finely
1 tbsp tomato purée (paste)
250 g/8 oz/1 cup yellow split peas, soaked
in water for 2 hours
400 g/13 oz can chopped tomatoes
500 ml/16 fl oz/2 cups vegetable stock
250 g/8 oz/1½ cups pumpkin, cubed
250 g/8 oz cauliflower, cut into florets
2 tbsp oil
1 large aubergine (eggplant), cubed
1 tbsp chopped fresh coriander (cilantro)
1 tsp garam masala
salt and pepper

1 Melt the ghee over a medium heat in a large pan. Add the mustard seeds, and when they start to splutter, add the onion, garlic, carrot, and ginger. Cook until soft, about 5 minutes. Add the green chilli and stir in the tomato purée (paste). Stir in the split peas.

2 Add the tomatoes and stock, and bring to the boil. Season well.

3 Simmer for 40 minutes, stirring occasionally. Add the pumpkin cubes and cauliflower florets, and simmer for a further 30 minutes, covered, until the split peas are soft.

4 Meanwhile, heat the oil in a frying pan (skillet) over a high heat. Add the aubergine (eggplant), and stir until sealed on all sides; remove and drain on paper towels.

5 Stir the aubergine (eggplant) into the split pea mixture with the coriander (cilantro) and garam masala. Check for seasoning. Transfer to a serving dish and serve immediately.

TIPS

When cooking with pulses and legumes, be sure that you do not over-stir, as this will break up the individual peas or beans.

To transform this recipe into a one-pot meal, simply add some cooked meat such as bacon, lamb or duck.

SNACKS – INTRODUCTION

THE STORE CUPBOARD
Dried, canned and preserved foods are ideal for making a quick meal and should always be kept to hand. They keep well in a cool, dark cupboard, but check the use-by dates of all store-cupboard goods.

Dried pasta
Keep a selection such as spaghetti, tagliatelle and, if you can find it, papardelle – a wider variety of tagliatelle. Shell-shaped conchiglie, spiral-shaped fusilli and bow-shaped farfalle are good for holding sauces.

Chinese egg noodles
These vary in size; thread noodles are the quickest to use as they only need to be soaked in boiling water for 3 minutes before serving.

Canned pulses
Pinto, haricot (navy), flageolet (small navy), cannellini and red kidney beans are excellent in casseroles and salads. Drain and rinse before use.

Canned tomatoes
The most useful of all canned products; quicker to prepare than fresh tomatoes and often having more flavour than the poor-quality tomatoes available in the winter.

Sun-dried tomatoes
Drying tomatoes in the sun concentrates their flavour. Most are sold in jars of olive oil which keeps them moist. Sun-dried tomatoes enliven pasta, rice or tomato sauces and give them great depth of flavour.

Sunflower oil
A good general-purpose oil, best used when you don't want to overpower the food with a strong flavour such as that of olive oil.

Olive oil
Olive oil is an essential ingredient in many dishes. Cold-pressed extra virgin oil enhances the flavour of almost any dish.

Wine vinegar
Wine vinegar is invaluable for dressings. White wine vinegar is more versatile, but keep a red wine vinegar and a flavoured one too, such as raspberry or sherry vinegar.

Olives
Both black and green olives are excellent for adding to salads, stews, pizzas and nibbles. When buying black olives, look for unpitted ones.

Chilli, coriander (cilantro), ginger and garlic pastes
These are convenient to use but don't have as good a flavour as the fresh equivalents. After opening, store in the refrigerator and use within 3 weeks.

Spices
Spices give exotic flavours to foods and can be varied according to your taste. Store in a cool, dark place and buy in small quantities as spices deteriorate over time. For the most aromatic flavour, grind your own in a pestle and mortar or spice grinder.

Coconut powder and creamed coconut
These are useful for Thai and Indian dishes. Creamed coconut is sold in blocks and is best grated or finely chopped before use.

Mustard
French mustards such as Dijon and Meaux are the ones I use most frequently because they are milder than English mustard.

PINWHEELS

••

MAKES 24

8 rashers streaky bacon
2 tsp oil
½ small onion, finely chopped
1 tbsp tomato purée
1 tsp yeast extract
4 slices of white or brown bread
15 g/½ oz/1 tbsp butter, melted

1 Heat the oven to 190°C/375°F/Gas
Mark 5. Lightly grease a large baking
sheet. Remove any rind from the bacon
and chop it very finely. Heat the oil in a
pan, add the onion and bacon and fry
together gently until cooked and turning
golden but not brown, as it will be
cooked further in the oven.

2 Remove the pan from the heat, then
stir in the tomato purée and yeast
extract.

3 Trim the crusts from the bread, then
flatten each slice very lightly with a
rolling pin.

4 Spread the slices of bread with the
prepared filling. Roll up each slice
widthways like a Swiss roll (jelly roll),
then cut each roll into 1-cm/ ½-in lengths.
Secure with cocktail sticks (toothpicks).
Place on the baking sheet and brush with
the melted butter.

5 Bake in the oven for about
10–12 minutes or until golden
brown. Remove the pinwheels from the
oven and leave to stand on the sheet for
5 minutes until firm and set.

6 Transfer to a wire rack to cool
further. Serve warm or cold.

FINISHING TOUCHES

Add a touch of elegance to a dish of
pinwheels with garnishes. Little
bouquets of watercress can be made
by trimming the ends of a small bunch
fairly short. Arrange these around the
edges of a plate to give it a fresh and
inviting appearance.

TOFU (BEANCURD) SANDWICHES

••

MAKES 28

4 Chinese dried mushrooms (if
unavailable, use thinly sliced open-cup
mushrooms)
275 g/9 oz tofu (beancurd)
½ cucumber, grated
1 cm/ ½ in piece ginger root, grated
60 g/2 oz/ ¼ cup cream cheese
salt and pepper

BATTER:
125 g/4 oz/1 cup plain (all-purpose)
flour
1 egg, beaten
120 ml/4 fl oz/ ½ cup water
½ tsp salt
2 tbsp sesame seeds
vegetable oil for deep-frying

SAUCE:
150 ml/ ¼ pint/ ⅔ cup natural yogurt
2 tsp honey
2 tbsp chopped fresh mint

1 Place the dried mushrooms in a
small bowl and cover with warm
water. Leave to soak for 20–25 minutes.
Drain and squeeze out the excess water.
Remove the tough centres and chop the
mushrooms.

2 Drain the tofu (beancurd) and slice
thinly. Then cut each slice to make
2.5 cm/1 in squares.

3 Squeeze the excess liquid from the
cucumber and mix the cucumber
with the mushrooms, grated ginger and
cream cheese. Season well. Use as a
filling to sandwich slices of tofu
(beancurd) together to make about
28 sandwiches.

4 To make the batter, sift the flour into
a bowl. Beat in the egg, water and
salt to make a thick batter. Stir in the
sesame seeds. Heat the oil in a large
saucepan or wok. Coat the sandwiches in
the batter and deep-fry in batches until
golden. Remove with a perforated spoon
and drain on paper towels.

5 To make the dipping sauce, blend
together the yogurt, honey and mint.
Serve the sauce with the tofu (beancurd)
sandwiches.

MELTING CHEESE & ONION BAGUETTES

••

SERVES 4

4 part-baked baguettes
2 tbsp tomato relish
60 g/2 oz/ ¼ cup butter
8 spring onions (scallions), trimmed and
*   chopped finely*
125 g/4 oz/ ½ cup cream cheese
125 g/4 oz/1 cup Cheddar cheese, grated
1 tsp snipped fresh chives
pepper

TO SERVE:
mixed salad leaves (greens)
fresh herbs

1 Split the part-baked baguettes in half lengthways, without cutting right through. Spread a little tomato relish on each split baguette.

2 Melt the butter in a frying pan (skillet) and add the spring onions (scallions). Fry them gently until softened and golden. Remove from the heat and leave to cool slightly.

3 Beat the cream cheese in a mixing bowl to soften it. Mix in the spring onions (scallions), with any remaining butter. Add the grated cheese and snipped chives, and mix well. Season.

4 Divide the cheese mixture between the baguettes, spread it over the cut surfaces and sandwich together. Wrap each baguette tightly in foil.

5 Heat the baguettes over a barbecue for about 10–15 minutes, turning them occasionally, or bake them in a preheated oven at 200°C/400°F/Gas Mark 6 for 15 minutes. Peel back the foil to check that they are cooked and the cheese mixture has melted. Serve with salad leaves (greens) and garnished with fresh herbs.

CHEESEBURGERS IN BUNS WITH BARBECUE SAUCE

••

SERVES 4

150 g/5 oz/ ⅔ cup dehydrated soya mince
300 ml/ ½ pint/1¼ cups vegetable stock
1 small onion, chopped finely
125 g/4 oz/1 cup plain (all-purpose) flour
1 egg, beaten
1 tbsp chopped fresh herbs
1 tbsp mushroom ketchup or soy sauce
2 tbsp vegetable oil
4 burger buns
4 cheese slices
salt and pepper

TO GARNISH:
Tasty Barbecue Sauce (see page 476)
dill pickle
tomato slices

TO SERVE:
lettuce, cucumber & spring onion
*   (scallion) salad*

1 Put the soya mince into a large bowl. Pour over the vegetable stock and leave to soak for about 15 minutes until it has been absorbed.

2 Add the onion, flour, beaten egg and chopped herbs. Season with the mushroom ketchup or soy sauce and a little salt and pepper.

3 Form the mixture into 8 burgers. Cover and chill until ready to cook.

4 Brush the burgers with vegetable oil and barbecue them over hot coals, turning once. Allow about 5 minutes on each side.

5 Split the buns and top with a burger. Lay a cheese slice on top and garnish with barbecue sauce, dill pickle and tomato slices. Serve with a green salad made with lettuce, spring onion (scallion) and cucumber.

TASTY BARBECUE SAUCE

SERVES 4

30 g/1 oz/2 tbsp butter or margarine
1 garlic clove, crushed
1 onion, chopped finely
400 g/13 oz can of chopped tomatoes
1 tbsp dark muscovado sugar
1 tsp hot chilli sauce
15 g/ ½ oz/1–2 gherkins
1 tbsp capers, drained
salt and pepper

1 Melt the butter or margarine in a saucepan and fry the garlic and onion until well browned, about 8–10 minutes.

2 Add the chopped tomatoes, sugar and chilli sauce. Bring to the boil, then reduce the heat and simmer gently for 20–25 minutes, until thick and pulpy.

3 Chop the gherkins and capers finely. Add to the sauce, stirring well to mix. Cook the sauce for a further 2 minutes.

4 Taste the sauce and season with a little salt and pepper. Use as a baste for vegetarian kebabs and burgers, or as an accompaniment to barbecued food.

TIPS

To make sure that the sauce has a good colour, it is important to brown the onions really well to begin with.

When fresh tomatoes are cheap and plentiful, they can be used instead of canned ones. Peel and chop 500 g/ 1 lb, and add them as before.

Substitute chilli powder instead of chilli sauce, according to taste. If you prefer a milder version of barbecue sauce, leave it out altogether.

PITTA (POCKET) BREADS WITH GREEK SALAD & HOT ROSEMARY DRESSING

SERVES 4

½ iceberg lettuce, chopped roughly
2 large tomatoes, cut into wedges
7.5 cm/3 in piece of cucumber, cut into chunks
30 g/1 oz/ ¼ cup pitted black olives
125 g/4 oz Feta cheese
4 pitta (pocket) breads

DRESSING:
6 tbsp olive oil
3 tbsp red wine vinegar
1 tbsp crushed fresh rosemary
½ tsp caster (superfine) sugar
salt and pepper

1 To make the salad, combine the lettuce, tomatoes, cucumber and olives in a bowl.

2 Cut the Feta cheese into chunks and add to the salad. Toss gently.

3 To make the dressing, whisk together the olive oil, red wine vinegar, rosemary and sugar. Season to taste with salt and pepper. Place in a small saucepan or heatproof bowl and heat gently or place over the barbecue to warm through.

4 Wrap the pitta (pocket) breads tightly in foil and place over the hot barbecue for 2–3 minutes, turning once, to warm through.

5 Unwrap the breads and split them open. Fill with the salad mixture and drizzle over the warm dressing. Serve immediately.

TIPS

Substitute different herbs for the rosemary – either oregano or basil would make a delicious alternative.

Pack plenty of the salad into the pitta (pocket) breads – they taste much better when packed full to bursting!

TOMATO & CHORIZO PIZZA

SERVES 2

23 cm/9 in pizza base with olive oil
1 tbsp black olive paste
1 tbsp olive oil
1 onion, sliced
1 garlic clove, crushed
4 tomatoes, sliced
2 chorizo sausages, sliced
1 tsp fresh oregano
125 g/4 oz Mozzarella cheese, chopped
6 black olives, pitted
black pepper

1 Place the pizza base on a baking sheet (cookie sheet) and spread the olive paste to the edges.

2 Heat the oil in a frying pan (skillet) and cook the onion briskly for 2 minutes. Add the garlic and fry for 1 minute further.

3 Spread over the pizza base and arrange the tomato slices over the top with slices of chorizo.

4 Sprinkle with the oregano and black pepper and then arrange the Mozzarella cheese and olives over the top.

5 Bake in a preheated oven at 230ºC/450ºF/Gas Mark 8 for 10 minutes.

PIZZA BASES

There are several varieties of pizza base available. I prefer the ones with added olive oil because the dough is much lighter and more tasty.

GOLDEN CHEESE & LEEK POTATO CAKES

SERVES 4

1 kg/2 lb potatoes
4 tbsp milk
60 g/2 oz/ ¼ cup butter or margarine
2 leeks, chopped finely
1 onion, chopped finely
175 g/6 oz/1½ cups grated Caerphilly or Cheddar cheese
1 tbsp chopped fresh parsley or chives
1 egg, beaten
2 tbsp water
90 g/3 oz/1½ cups fresh white or brown breadcrumbs
vegetable oil for shallow frying
salt and pepper
fresh flat-leaf parsley sprigs to garnish
mixed salad to serve

1 Cook the potatoes in lightly salted boiling water until tender. Drain and mash them with the milk and the butter or margarine.

2 Cook the leeks and onion in a small amount of salted boiling water for about 10 minutes until tender. Drain.

3 In a large mixing bowl, combine the leeks and onion with the mashed potato, cheese and parsley or chives. Season to taste.

4 Beat together the egg and water in a shallow bowl. Sprinkle the breadcrumbs into a separate shallow bowl. Shape the potato mixture into 12 even-sized cakes, brushing each with the egg mixture, then coating with the breadcrumbs.

5 Heat the oil in a large frying pan (skillet) and fry the potato cakes gently for about 2–3 minutes on each side until light golden brown. Garnish the potato cakes with flat-leaf parsley and serve with a mixed salad.

MIXED VEGETABLE BHAJI

Serves 4-6

1 small cauliflower
125 g/4 oz French green beans
2 potatoes
4 tbsp ghee or vegetable oil
1 onion, peeled and chopped
2 garlic cloves, peeled and crushed
5 cm/2 in ginger root, peeled and cut into
    fine slivers
1 tsp cumin seeds
2 tbsp medium curry paste
1 x 425 g/14 oz can chopped tomatoes
150 ml/ ¼ pint/ ⅔ cup water
4 tbsp strained Greek yogurt
chopped fresh coriander, to garnish

1 Break the cauliflower into neat florets. Top, tail and halve the beans. Peel and quarter the potatoes lengthways, then cut each quarter into 3 pieces. Cook all the prepared vegetables in a pan of boiling, salted water for 8 minutes. Drain well, return to the pan and shake dry over a low heat for a few moments.

2 Heat the ghee or oil in a large frying pan, add the onion, garlic, ginger and cumin seeds and stir-fry gently for 3 minutes. Stir in the curry paste, tomatoes and water and bring to the boil. Reduce the heat and simmer the spicy mixture for 2 minutes.

3 Stir in the par-cooked vegetables and mix lightly. Cover and cook gently for 5-8 minutes until just tender and cooked through. Whisk the yogurt to soften and drizzle the vegetable mixture with the yogurt. Sprinkle with the chopped coriander. Serve hot.

POTATO ALTERNATIVES

New potatoes are ideal for this dish as they have a more waxy texture and retain their shape better than old (main crop) potatoes which, when overcooked, become floury and lose their shape. You could use turnip or pumpkin instead of potatoes, if preferred.

TOAD IN THE HOLE

Serves 4

125 g/4 oz/1 cup plain (all-purpose) flour
½ tsp salt
2 eggs
275 ml/9 fl oz/scant 1¼ cups milk
¼ tsp dried mixed herbs or an individual
    herb (optional)
2 tbsp vegetable oil or dripping
1 onion, chopped finely
8 sausages, about 500 g/1 lb

1 Sift the flour and salt into a bowl and make a well in the centre. Add the eggs and about one-third of the milk and gradually work in the flour, beating until smooth.

2 Gradually beat in the rest of the milk. Add the herbs, if using.

3 Use the oil or dripping to thoroughly grease 8 x 10–12 cm/4–4½ in individual Yorkshire pudding tins (muffin pans) or a shallow ovenproof dish or roasting tin (pan).

4 Divide the onion between the tins (pans) then put a sausage in each tin (pan) and prick well. If using a large dish or tin (pan), add the onion and arrange the sausages in it.

5 Cook in a preheated oven at 220°C/425°F/Gas Mark 7 for 8–10 minutes until the sausages are beginning to colour a little, then stir the batter well and divide between the tins (pans) or pour evenly into the dish or tin (pan).

6 Return to the oven for 20–25 minutes until the batter is well risen and golden brown. The larger dish or tin (pan) will take 40–45 minutes.

ACCOMPANIMENTS

Gravy or a white or parsley sauce, creamed potatoes and a green vegetable are good accompaniments.

SCALLOPED POTATOES

••••••••••••••••••••••••••••••••••••••

SERVES 4

1.25 kg/2½ lb potatoes
2 large onions, chopped finely
2 garlic cloves, crushed (optional)
175–250 g/6–8 oz lean bacon, derinded
    and diced
2 tbsp chopped fresh dill or ¼ tsp dried dill
450 ml/ ¾ pint/scant 2 cups stock, milk or
    single (light) cream
15 g/ ½ oz/1 tbsp butter or margarine,
    melted
60 g/2 oz/ ½ cup mature (sharp) Cheddar,
    Gouda (Dutch) or Emmenthal (Swiss)
    cheese, grated
salt and pepper

1 Slice the potatoes, either by hand or using a food processor.

2 Thoroughly grease a large ovenproof dish or roasting tin (pan). Arrange a layer of sliced potatoes in the dish or tin (pan) and sprinkle with half the onions. Season lightly.

3 Add a second layer of potatoes, then the rest of the onions, the garlic, if using, the bacon, dill and seasoning, sprinkling evenly. Add a final layer of potatoes, arranging them in an attractive, overlapping pattern.

4 Gently heat the stock, milk or cream and pour over the potatoes. Brush the top layer of potatoes with the melted butter or margarine and cover with greased foil or a lid.

5 Cook in a preheated oven at 200°C/400°F/Gas Mark 6 for 1 hour.

6 Remove the foil or lid and sprinkle the cheese over the potatoes. Return, uncovered, to the oven for a further 30–45 minutes until well browned on top and the potatoes are tender.

VARIATIONS

Chopped salami, garlic sausage, diced smoked salmon or sliced button mushrooms may be used in place of the bacon in this dish.

CORNISH PASTIES

••••••••••••••••••••••••••••••••••••••

SERVES 4

175 g/6 oz/ ¾ cup extra lean minced
    (ground) beef or lamb
1 onion, chopped finely
1 garlic clove, crushed
1 small carrot, chopped very finely
125 g/4 oz potato, chopped very finely or
    grated coarsely
½ tsp dried mixed herbs or thyme,
    tarragon, sage or oregano
salt and pepper

SHORTCRUST PASTRY (PIE DOUGH):
250 g/8 oz/2 cups plain (all-purpose) flour
good pinch of salt
60 g/2 oz/ ¼ cup butter or margarine
60 g/2 oz/ ¼ cup lard or white vegetable
    fat (shortening)
about 4 tbsp cold water
beaten egg or milk to glaze

TO SERVE:
salad leaves
cherry tomatoes

1 To make the pastry (pie dough), sift the flour and salt into a bowl, rub in the butter or margarine and lard or white fat (shortening) until the mixture resembles fine breadcrumbs, then add sufficient water to mix to a pliable dough. Knead lightly. Wrap in foil or clingfilm (plastic wrap) and chill for 30 minutes.

2 Combine the meat, onion, garlic, carrot, potato, herbs and seasoning. Divide into 4 portions.

3 Roll out the pastry (pie dough) and, using a saucer or plate, cut into 4 x 18–20 cm/7–8 in rounds.

4 Place a portion of the meat mixture in the centre of each round.

5 Dampen the edges of the pastry (pie dough) and bring together at the top. Press the edges together and crimp.

6 Put the pasties on a greased baking sheet (cookie sheet) and glaze with beaten egg or milk. Bake in a preheated oven at 220°C/425°F/Gas Mark 7 for about 30 minutes until golden. Serve hot or cold, with salad leaves and tomatoes.

FISH CAKES WITH SPICY SAUCE

••

SERVES 4

1 kg/2 lb potatoes, cut into chunks
350–500 g/ ¾–1 lb smoked haddock or cod
fillet, skinned
1 bay leaf
2 hard-boiled (hard-cooked) eggs,
chopped finely
2–3 tbsp chopped fresh parsley
1 tbsp chopped fresh tarragon or 1 tsp
dried tarragon
2–3 spring onions (scallions), chopped
(optional)
30 g/1 oz/2 tbsp butter or margarine
1 egg, beaten
dried white or golden breadcrumbs
salt and pepper
vegetable oil for brushing or frying

SPICY SAUCE:
150 ml/ ¼ pint/ ⅔ cup dry white wine
150 ml/ ¼ pint/ ⅔ cup tomato ketchup
1–2 garlic cloves, crushed
good dash of Worcestershire sauce

TO GARNISH:
sprigs of fresh parsley
lemon slices

1 Cook the potatoes in boiling salted water until tender.

2 Meanwhile, put the fish and bay leaf in a saucepan and barely cover with water. Bring to the boil, cover and simmer for 15 minutes until tender.

3 Drain the fish, remove the skin and any bones and flake. Put in a bowl with the eggs, herbs, spring onions (scallions), if using, and seasoning and mix well.

4 Drain the potatoes and mash with the butter and seasoning. Add to the fish and mix thoroughly.

5 Divide the mixture into 8 and shape into cakes. Brush with beaten egg then coat in breadcrumbs. Put on a greased baking sheet (cookie sheet), brush with oil and cook in a preheated oven at 200°C/400°F/Gas Mark 6 for about 30 minutes until golden. Alternatively, fry for about 5 minutes on each side.

6 To make the spicy sauce, put all the ingredients in a saucepan, bring to the boil and simmer, uncovered, for about 15 minutes until thickened and smooth. Adjust the seasoning. Serve with the fish cakes, garnished with parsley and lemon.

BUCK RAREBIT

SERVES 4

350 g/12 oz mature (sharp) Cheddar
cheese
125 g/4 oz Gouda (Dutch), Gruyère or
Emmenthal (Swiss) cheese
1 tsp mustard powder
1 tsp wholegrain mustard
2–4 tbsp brown ale, cider or milk
½ tsp Worcestershire sauce
4 thick slices white or brown bread
4 eggs
salt and pepper

TO GARNISH:
tomato wedges
watercress sprigs

1 Grate the cheeses and place in a
saucepan, preferably non-stick.

2 Add the mustards, seasoning, brown
ale, cider or milk and Worcestershire
sauce and mix well.

3 Heat the cheese mixture gently,
stirring, until it has melted and is
completely creamy and thick. Remove
from the heat and leave to cool a little.

4 Toast the slices of bread on each
side under a preheated grill (broiler)
then spread the rarebit mixture evenly
over each piece. Put under a moderate
grill (broiler) until the cheese is golden
brown and bubbling.

5 Meanwhile, poach the eggs. If using
a poacher, grease the cups, heat the
water in the pan and, when just boiling,
break the eggs into the cups. Cover and
simmer for 4–5 minutes until just set.
Alternatively, bring about 4 cm/1½ in of
water to the boil in a frying pan (skillet)
or large saucepan and for each egg
quickly swirl the water with a knife and
drop the egg into the 'hole' created. Cook
for about 4 minutes until just set.

6 Top the rarebits with a poached egg
and serve garnished with tomato and
sprigs of watercress.

POTATO FRITTERS WITH RELISH

MAKES 8

60 g/2 oz/ ½ cup plain wholemeal flour
½ tsp ground coriander
½ tsp cumin seeds
¼ tsp chilli powder
½ tsp ground turmeric
¼ tsp salt
1 egg
3 tbsp milk
350 g/12 oz potatoes, peeled
1-2 garlic cloves, peeled and crushed
4 spring onions (scallions), trimmed and
chopped
60 g/2 oz sweetcorn kernels
vegetable oil for shallow frying

ONION AND TOMATO RELISH:
1 onion, peeled
250 g/8 oz tomatoes
2 tbsp chopped fresh coriander
2 tbsp chopped fresh mint
2 tbsp lemon juice
½ tsp roasted cumin seeds
¼ tsp salt
a few pinches of cayenne pepper, to taste

1 First make the relish. Cut the onion
and tomatoes into small dice and
place in a bowl with the remaining
ingredients. Mix well and leave to stand
for at least 15 minutes before serving to
allow time for the flavours to blend.

2 Place the flour in a bowl, stir in the
spices and salt and make a well in
the centre. Add the egg and milk and mix
to form a fairly thick batter.

3 Coarsely grate the potatoes, place in
a sieve and rinse well under cold
running water. Drain and squeeze dry,
then stir into the batter with the garlic,
spring onions (scallions)and corn.

4 Heat about 5 mm/ ¼ in oil in a
large frying pan and add a few
tablespoonfuls of the mixture at a time,
flattening each one to form a thin cake.
Fry gently for 2-3 minutes or until golden
brown and cooked through, turning the
fritters frequently.

5 Drain on paper towels and keep hot
while frying the remaining mixture.
Serve hot with onion and tomato relish.

481

CHEESE SHRIMPY

SERVES 2

75 g/3 oz semi-hard cheese, such as
*   Samsoe or Edam*
175 g/6 oz/1 cup peeled shrimps (small
*   prawns)*
2 tbsp mayonnaise
1 tbsp soured cream or natural yoghurt
juice of ½ lemon
salt and pepper
40 g/1½ oz/3 tbsp butter
4 slices close-textured white Danish bread
2 egg whites
parsley sprigs and 4 unpeeled shrimps
*   (prawns), to garnish*

1 Heat the oven to 200°C/400°F/Gas
   Mark 6. Grate the cheese and set
aside, together with a few shrimps
(prawns) for the garnish.

2 Mix the remaining shrimps (prawns)
   with the mayonnaise, soured cream
and lemon juice. Season to taste.

3 Butter the slices of bread and divide
   the shrimp mixture between the
slices to cover each slice evenly.

4 Whisk the egg whites until they
   stand in stiff peaks. Fold in the
grated cheese. Spread the egg and cheese
mixture onto the bread, being sure to
completely cover the shrimp and
mayonnaise mixture.

5 Place on a baking sheet and cook in
   the oven for about 20–25 minutes
until golden brown.

6 Transfer to a warmed serving plate,
   garnish with the reserved shrimps
and the parsley sprigs and serve while
still hot.

LIGHT OPTIONS

If you are watching your weight, try
substituting low-calorie mayonnaise
and low-fat yoghurt or sour cream in
this recipe. It still tastes sensational,
without being too high in fat.

SAVOURY CHEESE FLUFFS

SERVES 2

2 slices of toasted bread
15 g/ ½ oz butter or margarine
50 g/ 2 oz Cheddar or Lancashire cheese,
*   grated*
2-3 tablespoons thick double (heavy)
*   cream*
¼ teaspoon mustard
1 tablespoon snipped chives
salt and pepper
1 egg white
sprigs of parsley and tomato wedges, to
*   garnish (optional)*

1 Coat the slices of toasted bread with
   the butter, spread thinly.

2 Mix the cheese with the cream,
   mustard, snipped chives and salt and
pepper to taste.

3 Whisk the egg white until it stands
   in stiff peaks then fold into the
cheese mixture with a metal spoon.

4 Pile the mixture evenly over the
   prepared toast slices.

5 Cook under a preheated low to
   moderate grill until the topping is
golden and fluffy.

6 Serve at once, garnished with
   parsley sprigs and tomato wedges,
if you like.

7 Like many hot sandwiches, this one
   is best eaten immediately; it quickly
goes limp and the cheese filling will lose
its fluffiness if left.

SOFT BUTTER

Before spreading butter, let it stand at
room temperature for 30 minutes or so
before sandwich preparation (although
there are now some varieties of butter
that claim to spread 'straight from the
refrigerator'). Alternatively, cream in a
bowl until soft before spreading.

GRILLED PITTA POCKETS

SERVES 2

2 pitta breads
2 generous handfuls of mixed salad leaves
  (such as lamb's lettuce, frisée, endive,
  rocket/arugala and radicchio)
5-cm/2-in piece cucumber
2 tomatoes
2 spring onions (scallions)
2 tbsp French or yoghurt salad dressing
50 g/2 oz/ ½ cup cooked cubed lamb
  (optional)
1 tsp chopped fresh mint (optional)
75 g/3 oz/ ¾ cup cheese, grated

1 Carefully cut an opening into the centre of each pitta bread but not through to the base. Open out the bread pockets by gently pulling the bread apart.

2 Wash and tear the salad leaves into small pieces. Slice the cucumber, tomatoes and spring onions. Mix the salad ingredients together and toss with the prepared dressing. Add the lamb and mint, if using, and mix well.

3 Stuff the bread pockets with the salad mixture.

4 Sprinkle with the cheese so that the salad mixture is covered.

5 Cook under a preheated moderate grill (broiler) until the cheese is golden and bubbly, about 5–6 minutes.

6 Transfer to plates and serve at once while still hot. Serve with tomato and onion salad.

FILLING OPTIONS

Lamb is popular in Greece, Turkey and throughout the Middle East, where pitta bread is eaten several times a day. But this filling is an also an excellent way to make the most of leftover roast beef, pork or chicken. To make your own yogurt salad dressing, beat 150 ml/ ¼ pint/ ⅔ cup natural yogurt with 1 tbsp lemon juice, 1 tsp clear honey, ¼ tsp mustard and salt and pepper, until smooth and creamy. Flavour with chopped herbs.

LAMB & TOMATO KOFTAS

SERVES 4

250 g/8 oz finely minced lean lamb
1½ onions, peeled
1-2 garlic cloves, peeled and crushed
1 dried red chilli, finely chopped
  (optional)
2-3 tsp garam masala
2 tbsp chopped fresh mint
2 tsp lemon juice
salt
2 tbsp vegetable oil
4 small tomatoes, quartered
mint sprigs, to garnish

YOGURT DRESSING:
150 ml/ ¼ pint/ ⅔ cup strained Greek
  yogurt
5 cm/2 in piece cucumber, grated
2 tbsp chopped fresh mint
½ tsp toasted cumin seeds (optional)

1 Place the minced lamb in a bowl. Finely chop 1 onion and add to the bowl with the garlic and chilli, if using. Stir in the garam masala, mint and lemon juice and season well with salt. Mix the ingredients well together. Divide the mixture in half, then divide each half into 10 equal portions and form each into a small ball. Roll balls in the oil to coat. Quarter the remaining onion half and separate into layers.

2 Thread 5 of the balls, 4 tomato quarters and some of the onion layers onto each of 4 bamboo or metal skewers. Brush the vegetables with the remaining oil and cook under a hot grill for about 10 minutes, turning frequently until browned and cooked through.

3 Meanwhile, prepare the yogurt dressing. Mix the yogurt with the cucumber, mint and toasted cumin seeds, if using. Garnish the koftas with mint sprigs and serve hot with the dressing.

SHAPING KOFTAS

It is important that the lamb is finely minced and the onion finely chopped or the mixture will not shape neatly into balls. The mixture could be finely ground in a food processor, if wished.

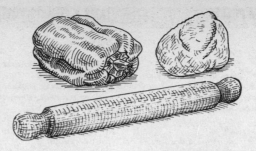

MIXED (BELL) PEPPER POORIS

SERVES 6

POORIS:
125 g/4 oz/ 1 cup plain wholemeal flour
1 tbsp vegetable ghee or oil
2 good pinches of salt
75 ml/3 fl oz/ ⅓ cup hot water
vegetable oil, for shallow frying
natural yogurt, to serve
coriander sprigs, to garnish

TOPPING:
4 tbsp vegetable ghee or oil
1 large onion, peeled, quartered and
    thinly sliced
½ red (bell) pepper, seeded and thinly
    sliced
½ green (bell) pepper, seeded and thinly
    sliced
¼ aubergine (eggplant), cut lengthways
    into 6 wedges and sliced thinly
1 garlic clove, peeled and crushed
2.5 cm/1 in ginger root, peeled and
    chopped
½-1 tsp minced chilli (from a jar)
2 tsp mild or medium curry paste
1 x 250 g/8 oz can chopped tomatoes
salt

1 To make the pooris, put the flour in
  a bowl with the ghee or oil and salt.
Add hot water and mix to form a fairly
soft dough. Knead gently, cover with a
damp cloth and leave for 30 minutes.

2 Meanwhile, prepare the topping.
  Heat the ghee or oil in a large
saucepan, add the onion, (bell) peppers,
aubergine (eggplant), garlic, ginger, chilli
and curry paste and fry gently for
5 minutes. Stir in the tomatoes and salt to
taste and simmer gently, uncovered, for
5 minutes, stirring occasionally until the
sauce thickens. Remove from the heat.

3 Knead the dough on a floured
  surface and divide into 6. Roll each
one to a round about 15 cm/6 in in
diameter. Cover each one as you finish
rolling, to prevent drying out.

4 Heat about 1 cm/ ½ in oil in a large
  frying pan. Add a poori, one at a
time, and fry for about 15 seconds on
each side until puffed and golden, turning
frequently. Drain on paper towels and
keep warm while cooking the remainder
in the same way.

5 Reheat the vegetable mixture. Place
  a poori on each serving plate and
top with the vegetable mixture. Add a
spoonful of yogurt to each one and
garnish with coriander sprigs. Serve hot.

SANDWICHES – INTRODUCTION

THE BREAD

Bread is the major part of a sandwich, so make sure it is fresh. A new crusty loaf can be put in the refrigerator for a few hours to make it easier to slice. Ready-sliced bread is handy because you have a choice of thicknesses and the wrapping keeps it fresh longer.

To vary sandwiches use different types of bread. Some of the lighter rye breads are particularly delicious, especially those sprinkled with caraway seeds. Breads flavoured with nuts, olives, sun-dried tomatoes and herbs make a welcome entrance when combined with suitable fillings.

Brown breads These basically differ with the flour used rather than with their shape. Choose from wheatmeal, wheatgerm, wholemeal and stoneground wholemeal. Some brown varieties also have nuts and seeds added for extra flavour, nutrition and interest.

White breads This is made from milled flour where most of the bran particles have been removed. Some bleaching of the flour also takes place to give the characteristic white appearance. The choices here are also wide, as some flours are then enriched with vitamins and paradoxically some have bran added back to the basic mixture.

Crusty loaves These loaves are mostly made with white flour, and open-baked on the floor of the oven to give a golden crusty casing. There are basically six main varieties of crusty loaf: the bloomer, coburg, cottage, Danish, French and plait.

Enriched loaves These breads are enriched by the addition of eggs and/or fat and/or milk. They include fruit loaf; malt loaf (made with malt meal, sometimes with added fruit); milk loaf; cholla (a version of the Jewish Ritriel Bread that is enriched with butter and eggs); and Vienna (enriched with milk).

Proprietary breads These are white and brown breads made from special flours and recipes, and sold under brand names. They include bran loaves (available in both brown and white varieties); brown breads (some have added wheatgerm or malted meal, while others are made from branded flours); and scofa (bicarbonate of soda is used as a raising agent instead of yeast, and the bread is usually cut into quarters from a large, flat loaf).

Tin loaves This category covers all types of bread baked in tins or containers and includes the Barrel, Farmhouse, Pan or Batch, Sandwich and Split Tin. The description refers to the shape of the loaf; many can be made with brown or white flours.

Rolls and buns

In just the same way as there are dozens of varieties of loaves, there are just as many varieties of rolls and buns. Some of the most popular include brown, crusty white, fruited, rich such as brioche and croissants), soft white and wholemeal.

THE FILLING

Always fill sandwiches generously and do not forget the seasonings. Fillings should be more highly seasoned than the same ingredients without bread. If a smooth filling is used such as cream cheese or potted meat, leave it at room temperature for about 1 hour – it will then be

INTRODUCTION

easier to spread. Remember, too, that diffferent tastes are obtained by spreading each filling separately. For instance, if you are using peanut butter and jam, the two flavours will be more pronounced if the peanut butter is spread on one slice of bread and the jam on the other than if the two were blended and spread on both sides.

There is a host of sandwich ideas in the recipes in this book, but for added inspiration, why not try some of the following additional ideas.

Banana Mash with lemon juice and single cream. Try adding desiccated coconut or crispy snippets of bacon.

Beef Cut into very thin slices and use on bread spread with horseradish sauce or mustard. Add coleslaw, sliced gherkins or cucumber.

Blue cheese spread on brown or granary bread. Try adding crisp Cos or Webb's lettuce, thin slices of apple or grated carrot.

Cheese Slice or grate hard types. Try adding pickle, mustard, sliced raw onions, tomato, ham, pineapple, chopped celery in mayonnaise, yeast extract, lettuce or cucumber.

Chicken or turkey Best finely chopped and mixed with mayonnaise, soured cream, thick yogurt or natural fromage frais. Try adding flaked almonds, spring onions, pineapple titbits, sultanas, crisp lettuce or mustard.

Corned beef Slice or break up by mashing. Try adding horseradish relish, chopped gherkin or capers in mayonnaise, tomato, coleslaw, parsley or chive butter.

Cream cheese Spread onto bread or mix with flavourings first. Try adding chives, spring onions, dates, raisins, sultanas, celery, apple, walnuts, diced cucumber, prawns or smoked salmon, crispy bacon or capers.

Egg Hard-boil and slice, or mash with a little milk, or scramble. Try adding chopped gherkin, peppers, diced prawns or smoked salmon, chives, parsley, curry powder and cucumber.

Lamb Trim away any fat from thin slices. Try adding tomato, gherkins, mint jelly, coleslaw, orange-flavoured mayonnaise, shredded lettuce or sliced cucumber.

Liver sausage Slice finely or spread. Try adding grated carrot, coleslaw, fine slices of raw onion or apple, gherkins or tomato.

Pork Dice or slice finely. Try adding shredded lettuce, tomato, apple sauce, pickle, chutney or pineapple in a thick mayonnaise.

Prawns and crab Shell and chop. Try adding cream cheese, chives in mayonnaise, diced avocado tossed in lemon juice, crisp lettuce or anchovy butter.

Sardines, tuna or mackerel Drain and mash. Try adding lemon-flavoured salad dressing, tomato, crisp cucumber, lettuce or celery salt.

Salami, ham or luncheon meat Slice and add pickles, chutney, coleslaw, tomato, lettuce or cucumber.

ITALIAN HEROES

SERVES 4

12 Italian sausages
4 tbsp water
2 tbsp olive or vegetable oil
2 onions, sliced
4 or 5 red or green peppers, or a mixture
* of both, cored and cut into strips*
4 long, crusty hero-type rolls

1 Put the sausages in a pan with the water. Cover and simmer gently for about 5 minutes. Remove the lid and continue to cook for about 15 minutes or until the sausages are browned, turning them occasionally.

2 Meanwhile, heat the oil in another pan and sauté the sliced onions for about 5–8 minutes until they are soft but not coloured.

3 Add the pepper strips and continue cooking, stirring occasionally, for about 10 minutes or until tender.

4 Add the sausages and cook for a further 3 minutes.

5 Split the rolls in half lengthways. Spoon some of the cooked pepper and onion mixture onto the bottom half of each roll.

6 Top each roll base with three of the sausages, then replace the top half of each roll. Cut each roll in half crossways to serve.

ITALIAN SAUSAGES

Choose from meaty frying sausages such as luganega, spicy pork sausages from Romagna in the north (salsiccia al metro), which are sold in lengths; or salamelle, small, spicy sausages linked in a chain. Although the Italians would make these rolls spicy by using hot sausages, you may like to use plain sausages then spice up the onion mixture by adding 1-2 tbsp sun-dried or plain tomato purée mixed with a generous pinch of chilli powder or a dash of chilli sauce.

CROQUE MONSIEUR

SERVES 4

8 thick slices white bread, crusts removed
prepared mustard, to taste
100 g/4 oz Gruyère cheese, sliced
100 g/4 oz cooked ham, thinly sliced
40 g/1½ oz/3 tbsp butter, melted

1 Heat the oven to 230°C/450°F/Gas Mark 8. Spread half of the slices of white bread with mustard to taste. (Dijon mustard is the traditional choice, but you may prefer to use a hotter mustard, or one of the many herbed mustard varieties that are now widely available.)

2 Trim the cheese slices to fit and put them on the bread. Trim the ham slices to fit and place them on top of the cheese.

3 Top with the remaining slices of bread to make sandwiches, and place them on a baking sheet.

4 Brush the sandwiches lightly with some of the melted butter, setting the remaining butter aside.

5 Cook in the top of the oven for about 5 minutes or until lightly browned. Turn the sandwiches over with a spatula, brush with the remaining butter and cook for a further 3–5 minutes.

6 Cut the sandwiches in half and serve them hot, wrapped in small paper napkins.

ADAPTING CROQUE MONSIEUR

Brown or wholegrain bread can be used instead of white bread to create Croque Monsieur, if you prefer. You may even like to add tomato slices. If you prefer to cook these sandwiches on the hob, then fry in 50 g/2 oz/ ¼ cup butter with 2 tsp olive or corn oil until golden brown on both sides – about 1-2 minutes. Drain well on absorbent kitchen paper (paper towels) before halving to serve as above.

PO'-BOY SANDWICH

SERVES 4

16 fresh oysters
3 tbsp olive oil
25 g/1 oz/2 tbsp unsalted butter
1 clove garlic, crushed
1 tbsp chopped fresh parsley
freshly ground black pepper
1 tsp lemon juice
4 rashers streaky bacon, rinds removed
2 small (demi) baguettes, or French loaves
Tabasco sauce

1 Grill the oysters, flat shells
uppermost, until the shells open
slightly. The oyster liquid will start to
bubble out of the shells after about
3–5 minutes. Hold the oysters in a cloth,
insert a knife between the shells and twist
off the top shell. Slip the knife under the
oyster to release it from the bottom shell.
Put the oysters in a bowl with their juices.

2 Stretch the bacon with the back of a
knife, cut each rasher into 4 pieces
and make 4 small bacon rolls from each.

3 Heat the oil and butter with the
garlic in a small pan. Add the
parsley, black pepper to taste and lemon
juice, mixing well.

4 Thread the oysters and bacon rolls
onto 4 lightly oiled skewers. Brush
with the buttery sauce and grill (broil) for
2 minutes on each side, basting frquently
until cooked.

5 Halve each baguette lengthways, and
toast the cut sides until golden.
Drizzle with the remaining garlic butter.

6 Remove the oysters and bacon from
the skewers and arrange on the
bread. Sprinkle a little Tabasco sauce on
top and serve at once.

SOUTHERN CLASSIC

This is the famous Louisiana sandwich,
packed with any number of fillings, from
the more usual ham, cheese and turkey
to soft-shelled crab and oysters. So
experiment with your favourite fillings.

FRIED REUBEN SANDWICH

SERVES 4

6 tbsp mayonnaise
1 tbsp finely chopped green pepper
1 tbsp mild chilli sauce
8 slices rye bread
225 g/8 oz canned or bottled sauerkraut
75 g/3 oz Gruyère or Emmenthal (Swiss)
   cheese
225 g/8 oz salt (corned) beef, sliced
50 g/2 oz/¼ cup butter or margarine
1 tbsp oil
sliced gherkins, to garnish

1 Mix the mayonnaise with the
chopped green pepper and chilli
sauce, blending well.

2 Spread about 1 tablespoon of the
pepper mixture onto each slice of
rye bread.

3 Drain the sauerkraut and slice the
cheese into 8 pieces.

4 Place a piece of cheese (sliced quite
thickly) on four slices of the bread.
Top each slice with a quarter of the salt
(corned) beef and a quarter of the
sauerkraut. Cover each with another slice
of cheese, then sandwich together with
the remaining slices of bread, mayonnaise
side down.

5 Melt the butter or margarine and oil
in a large, heavy-based frying-pan.
Add the sandwiches one by one and cook
on one side for about 3–4 minutes until
golden. Turn over and cook for a further
3–4 minutes until crisp and brown.

6 Drain on absorbent kitchen paper
(paper towels). Cut in half and serve
at once, garnished with sliced gherkins.

A MILD CHANGE

Not surprisingly, these sandwiches
originated in Germany, where chilli
sauce was not part of the original
recipe. If you have a sensitive palate,
you may wish to leave out the chilli
sauce for a milder flavour.

ITALIAN MOZZARELLA LOAF

SERVES 4-6

1 tsp oil
1 x 450 g/1 lb rye and caraway seed loaf,
*   not sliced*
225 g/8 oz mozzarella cheese
50 g/2 oz/ ¼ cup butter, softened
10–12 anchovy fillets
12 black olives, halved and stoned
½ tsp dried marjoram
1 tsp fresh chopped basil or ½ tsp dried

1 Heat the oven to 220°C/425°F/Gas
Mark 7. Lightly grease a baking sheet
with the oil. On a bread board, slice the
loaf of bread at 2.5 cm/1 in intervals
almost through to the base, being careful
not to cut it all the way through.

2 Cut the mozzarella into thin slices
and insert each slice between the
slices of bread.

3 Using a flat-bladed knife, spread the
top of the loaf of bread with the
softened butter.

4 Place the anchovies over the top of
the bread in a criss-cross pattern.
Scatter the olives on top and sprinkle with
the herbs.

5 Place the loaf on the greased baking
sheet and bake in the oven for
15 minutes until it is crisp and golden
brown, and the cheese is bubbly.

6 Allow the loaf to stand for a few
minutes before serving. Pull the
slices of bread apart to eat.

MARINATED OLIVES

It is easy to marinate your own olives,
for added flavour in this recipe. Drain a
jar of black olives and place in a clean
screwtop jar. Add peeled garlic cloves,
orange rind and a sprig of fresh
rosemary or thyme. Add olive oil to
just cover the olives, cover the jar and
leave the olives to marinate for at least
a day.

GREEK FETA CROÛTES

SERVES 4

150 ml/ ¼ pint/ ⅔ cup olive oil
1 large clove garlic, crushed
1 tsp chopped fresh thyme
1 tbsp lemon juice
salt and pepper
1 small aubergine (eggplant), sliced, then
*   cut into bite-sized pieces*
1 large courgette (zucchini), thickly sliced
1 small bulb fennel, sliced and cut into
*   bite-sized chunks*
1 small red pepper, cored, seeded and cut
*   into pieces*
1 small yellow pepper, cored, seeded and
*   cut into pieces*
1 onion, cut into thin wedges
4 large thick slices country-style white
*   crusty bread*
100 g/4 oz Greek cheese (Halloumi or feta,
*   for example), sliced or broken into*
*   pieces*
8 black olives, stoned and cut into strips

1 Beat the oil with the garlic, thyme,
lemon juice, and salt and pepper to
taste in a large bowl.

2 Add the prepared aubergine
(eggplant), courgette (zucchini),
fennel, peppers and onion, mixing well.
Cover and leave to stand for about
1 hour, stirring occasionally.

3 Spread the vegetable mixture on a
grill pan or baking sheet with
upturned edges. Cook under a preheated
moderate grill (broiler) for about
15 minutes, turning over frequently, until
the vegetables are tender and lightly
charred around the edges. Keep warm.

4 Meanwhile, brush the bread with a
little of the cooking juices from the
vegetables and toast lightly on both sides
until just crisp and golden.

5 Top each slice of bread with the
cheese slices or pieces, then cover in
turn with a generous amount of the
cooked vegetable mixture.

6 Return to the grill (broiler) and cook
for a further 3–5 minutes or until the
cheese is bubbly. Serve at once, garnished
with the black olive strips.

SALAD DAYS

••

SERVES 1

25 g/1 oz/2 tbsp butter
1 tsp snipped fresh chives
1 tsp lemon juice
4 slices granary bread
a little shredded crisp lettuce
2 hard-boiled eggs
2 tbsp mayonnaise or natural fromage
  frais
½ avocado, stoned
salt and pepper

1 Beat the butter with the chives and half of the lemon juice to make a smooth spread.

2 Spread the slices of bread with the prepared chive butter, then cover two slices with shredded lettuce.

3 Shell and chop the hard-boiled eggs and place in a bowl with the mayonnaise or fromage frais and mix gently to coat.

4 Peel and stone the avocado, cut into chunky slices or bite-sized cubes and toss with the remaining lemon juice to prevent discoloration.

5 Add the avocado to the egg mixture and fold gently to mix.

6 Spoon the mixture onto the shredded lettuce and place the remaining slices of bread on top. Press lightly to seal, then cut into halves or quarters to serve.

VARIATIONS

Avocado adds a creamy texture to this filling, as well as colour, but it is loaded with calories. For a low-fat option, replace it with two finely chopped potatoes and use low-fat yoghurt instead of mayonnaise. For a crunchy texture, add a very finely chopped celery stick.

In this recipe, you can make good use of the wide variety of crisp lettuce and salad greens now on the market.

CIABATTA PIZZA TOASTS

••

SERVES 2-4

1 ciabatta loaf
6 tbsp/ ½ cup sun-dried-tomato and herb
  spread
150 g/5 oz/ ⅔ cup Cheddar cheese, roughly
  grated
1 red onion, sliced
225 g/8 oz tomatoes, sliced
100 g/4 oz mozzarella cheese, sliced quite
  finely
fresh basil sprigs, to garnish

1 Heat the oven to 220°C/425°F/Gas Mark 7. Split the ciabatta loaf in half lengthways.

2 Spread the sun-dried-tomato and herb paste evenly over both of the cut surfaces of the loaf.

3 Top the sun-dried-tomato and herb paste with the grated Cheddar cheese, followed by the red onion separated into rings, tomatoes, and finally the sliced mozzarella cheese.

4 Place both halves of the loaf on a large baking sheet and cook in the oven for 10–15 minutes, or until it is browned and crisp on top, and the cheese is bubbling.

5 Remove from the oven and garnish with the basil sprigs.

6 Cut into thick slices or leave in halves to serve.

QUICK TOPPINGS

The joy of this recipe is that it uses a prepared spread from the supermarket, so it is very quick to prepare. This example uses ready-prepared chopped sun-dried tomatoes with herbs and oil as its base, but this can be replaced with pesto sauce for a more gutsy flavour. You can also use a prepared tomato sauce with garlic and herbs. Look at the delicatessen section of your supermarket for other ideas.

WALNUT FINGER SANDWICH

••••••••••••••••••••••••••••••••••••

SERVES 1

25 g/1 oz/2 tbsp butter or margarine
1 tsp finely grated onion
½ tsp snipped chives or chopped fresh
  parsley
salt and pepper
4 slices walnut bread
75 g/3 oz Roquefort cheese
about 6 black grapes
sprigs of parsley or watercress to garnish,
  if liked

1 Beat the butter with the grated onion
  and parsley or chives to make a
smooth spread. Season to taste with salt
and pepper.

2 Spread the slices of bread with the
  prepared butter.

3 Slice the Roquefort cheese thinly and
  layer the cheese onto two of the
slices of bread so that the pieces of
cheese overlap slightly.

4 Halve the grapes and remove any
  seeds. Place on top of the cheese
slices, cut sides down.

5 Cover with the remaining slices of
  bread and press gently to seal.

6 Cut into thick finger sandwiches to
  serve. Garnish with parsley or
watercress, if liked.

7 A blue cheese is the best companion
  for the nutty bread and grapes in
this recipe. If you do not like blue cheese,
replace it with a hard cheese with a sharp
flavour, such as Leicester.

NEW BREADS

These days, supermarket shelves and
bakeries all boast imaginative varieties
of bread, from simple onion, nut and
seeded to special olive and sun-dried-
tomato studded types.

VEGETARIAN MUNCH AND CRUNCH

••••••••••••••••••••••••••••••••••••

MAKES 2

50 g/2 oz smooth peanut butter
50 g/2 oz/ ¼ cup cream cheese
1 small carrot
1 celery stick
4 green olives
small handful of alfalfa sprouts or
  beansprouts
½ small red apple
2 tsp lemon juice
2 large wholemeal rolls or baps (buns)

1 In a small bowl mix the peanut
  butter with the cream cheese to
make a smooth spread.

2 Grate the carrot, finely chop the
  celery and dice the olives. Add to
the spread and, using a wooden spoon,
mix gently but thoroughly to combine.

3 Place the alfalfa sprouts or
  beansprouts in another bowl. Core
but do not peel the apple, then dice. Add
to the sprouts with the lemon juice and
toss well to mix.

4 Cut the rolls or baps (buns) in half
  and spread each half generously
with the vegetable, peanut butter and
cream cheese mixture.

5 Top each roll with half of the sprout-
  and-apple mixture, replace the lids
and press gently to seal.

6 Wrap in foil to transport in a lunch
  box if required.

ALTERNATIVES

For a change, try replacing butter with
other spreads such as mayonnaise,
savoury pastes or spreads, bouillon-
based spreads or well-seasoned
vegetable purées.

  Any number of different fruits can
be used in this sandwich filling to
produce a delicious variation on a
theme. Consider adding diced pear,
snipped dried apricot, diced fresh
peach or nectarine, chopped fresh
apricot or chopped banana to the
sprout mixture instead of diced apple.

NIÇOISE (PROVENÇAL) SANDWICH

SERVES 2

*1 French loaf, ideally round, about
 18 cm/7 ines in diameter
1 clove garlic, cut in half
5 tbsp olive oil
4 firm tomatoes, sliced
½ green pepper, cored and sliced
50 g/2 oz canned anchovy fillets
50 g/2 oz canned tuna, flaked
4 black or green olives, stoned
2 tsp capers
salt and pepper
1 tbsp lemon juice or wine vinegar*

1 Cut the bread in half horizontally and rub the cut surfaces with the clove of garlic.

2 Sprinkle about 3 tablespoons of the olive oil over each bread half, drizzling it lightly but evenly.

3 Top the base with the sliced tomatoes. Arrange the pepper slices, anchovy fillets, tuna, olives and capers on top, then season to taste

4 Beat the remaining oil with the lemon juice or vinegar to make a dressing and sprinkle over the top of the sandwich filling.

5 Place the remaining bread half on top of the filling and press down lightly so that the juices mix.

6 Leave to stand for 30 minutes before slicing to serve.

ORIGINS OF THE NIÇOISE

The Niçoise sandwich is derived from the days when peasants simply soaked their bread in oil and vinegar and filled it with an assortment of salad ingredients not unlike Salade Niçoise. This 'sandwich of the people' is also known as Pan Bagnat.

BOOKMAKER'S SANDWICH

SERVES 4

*1 long crusty Vienna or Danish loaf
100 g/4 oz/ ½ cup butter
675 g/1½ lb fillet, rump or sirloin steak,
 cut 2.5 cm/1 in thick
salt and pepper
3 tbsp/ ¼ cup horseradish mustard (or see
 boxed note below for alternatives)
small sprigs of watercress to garnish
 (optional)*

1 Slice the loaf in half lengthways and butter it thickly.

2 Grill the steaks under a very hot grill (broiler) for 2–3 minutes on each side, according to whether you would prefer your steaks to be rare, medium or well-done.

3 Place the hot steaks on one half of the loaf. Sprinkle with salt and pepper to taste.

4 Spread the mustard over the meat, then top with the remaining loaf half. Press down lightly to seal the sandwich and enclose the meat.

5 Wrap the loaf in foil, then set it aside until the meat is completely cold. (By wrapping the loaf, you will ensure that the meat doesn't dry out.)

6 Slice the sandwiched loaf into wedges for serving, garnished with watercress sprigs, if liked.

HERB AND PEPPER ALTERNATIVES

Although horseradish is the classic flavouring for the mustard used with this sandwich, try experimenting with other tastes: there are also prepared mustards flavoured with herbs.

For a steak sandwich with extra kick, prepare the steak au poivre before grilling. About one hour before grilling, press 2 tbsp crushed black peppercorns (use a rolling pin for crushing) well into the steaks with the palm of your hand. Leave in a cool place until ready to cook.

PICNIC SANDWICH

SERVES 8

1 small uncut bloomer loaf
75 g/3 oz/6 tbsp butter, melted
225 g/8 oz/1 cup pork sausage meat
100 g/4 oz/ ½ cup cooked tongue, diced
1 small onion, finely chopped
2 eggs
150 ml/ ½ pint/ ⅔ cup milk
2 hard-boiled eggs, shelled and halved
salt and pepper

1 Heat the oven to 200°C/400°F/Gas Mark 6. Cut horizontally across the loaf, two-thirds of the way up. and remove the 'lid'. Gently ease away the bread from around the edge of the crust. Make 100 g/4 oz/2 cups breadcrumbs from the bread.

2 Brush the cavity of the loaf and the lid with some of the melted butter.

3 Mix the sausage meat with the diced tongue, breadcrumbs and onion. Beat the eggs and milk together and stir into the meat mixture.

4 Place one-third of the filling in the bread case and arrange the halved hard-boiled eggs on top. Season to taste with salt and pepper. Pack the bread case with the remaining filling, then top with the bread lid.

5 Secure the loaf in a parcel-like fashion with string. Use the remaining butter to brush all over the loaf. Place on a baking sheet and cook in the oven for 15 minutes.

6 Cover the entire loaf with foil and continue to cook for a further 45 minutes. Remove and allow to cool. When cool, remove the string and cut into thick slices to serve. If you are packing this sandwich for a picnic, leave it unsliced and prepare it on the spot.

SUPER CLUB SANDWICH

SERVES 1

3 slices white or brown bread
50 g/2 oz/ ¼ cup butter
100 g/4 oz crabmeat, flaked
3 tbsp lemon mayonnaise
salt and pepper
4 small crisp lettuce leaves
1 tomato, sliced
5-cm/2-in piece cucumber, sliced
lemon wedges and watercress sprigs, to
   garnish

1 Toast the slices of bread on both sides until golden, then spread each slice with butter.

2 In a small bowl, mix the crabmeat with the mayonnaise, and salt and pepper to taste.

3 Cover the first slice of toast with 2 of the lettuce leaves, then half of the crab mixture and the tomato slices.

4 Cover with the second slice of toast, then the remaining crab mayonnaise and the sliced cucumber.

5 Place the third slice of toast on top, buttered side down, and press gently to seal.

6 Cut the whole sandwich into two large triangles or into quarters, and secure each with a cocktail stick (toothpick), if liked. Serve garnished with watercress sprigs and lemon wedge.

SANDWICH HISTORY

Legend has it that a man came home late and hungry from his club one night, raided the refrigerator and made himself a super sandwich, which he dubbed 'club'. Another says that the chef of a club made himself a reputation by devising a special sandwich. Either way, it is now known as the king of sandwiches.

HARLEQUIN BUFFET SANDWICH

MAKES 18

8 hard-boiled eggs
225 g/8 oz/1 cup butter or margarine
2 tbsp mayonnaise
salt and pepper
50 g/2 oz/ ⅓ cup peeled prawns or shrimps
juice of ½ lemon
2 tsp tomato purée
1 tsp Worcestershire sauce
50 g/2 oz liver pâté
6 slices brown bread
6 slices white bread

1 Shell the eggs and separate the yolks from the whites. Sieve the egg yolks and chop the whites very finely.

2 In a bowl, cream together 55 g/2 oz/ ¼ cup of the butter with the egg yolks, mayonnaise and salt and pepper to taste. Divide the mixture into 3 portions.

3 Finely chop the prawns or shrimps, add the lemon juice and half the chopped egg white and mix with one-third of the creamed egg mixture. Save the remaining egg whites and use them later in another recipe, or discard them if they won't be needed.

4 Stir the tomato purée and Worcestershire sauce into another third of the creamed egg, butter and mayonnaise mixture.

5 Mash the liver pâté and blend with the remaining one-third of the egg mixture. Butter the sliced white and brown bread. Using alternate layers of brown and white bread, sandwich together with the three fillings using four slices of bread per sandwich. Press well together, wrap in foil and chill until required.

6 Remove the crusts from the sandwiches and cut into 5 mm/ ¼ in slices. Arrange on a plate to serve.

NEW YORK BAGELS

SERVES 2

4 plain or onion bagels
15 g/ ½ oz butter (optional)
100 g/4 oz cream cheese
1 tsp grated lemon zest
1 tbsp capers
a little shredded crisp lettuce (iceberg is best for this)
100 g/4 oz smoked salmon

1 Slice the bagels in half and spread with a little butter if liked.

2 Mix the cream cheese with the grated lemon zest, beating well until the mixture becomes smooth and creamy. Finely chop 1 teaspoon of the capers and add to the cheese mixture, mixing well.

3 Divide the cream cheese mixture equally between the bagels, spreading evenly.

4 Cover the cream cheese mixture with a little shredded lettuce.

5 Cut the smoked salmon into thick strips and divide between the bagels. Scatter the remaining capers on top.

6 Replace the bagel tops and press down on them gently to seal. Serve as soon as possible.

BAGELS AND SALMON

Bagels come in all guises – plain, sprinkled and flavoured with onion seeds, speckled with caraway seeds, and even studded with raisins and flavoured with cinnamon. Plain or flavoured varieties are also delicious with cream cheese alone.

Other cured or smoked fish can be used instead of smoked salmon in this recipe. Try using smoked eel, gravad lax (cured salmon with a dill coating), smoked sturgeon or smoked halibut. Thinly slice and cut into strips before adding to the bagels. Gravad lax strips can be topped with a mustardy dill sauce instead of capers, if you prefer.

DANISH OPEN TRIO

MAKES 3

For all three sandwiches use 3 slices of close-textured Danish bread, spread with butter or margarine. Serve all the open sandwiches as soon as possible after assembling.

BLUE BOY

1 small lettuce leaf (one of the green varieties, such as iceberg or butter lettuce)
3 slices blue brie cheese
3 black grape halves, seeds removed

1 To make the Blue Boy sandwich, place the lettuce leaf at one end of a slice of bread. Arrange the slices of cheese on the bread so that they overlap.

2 Garnish each slice of the blue cheese with a black grape half.

COPENHAGEN

25 g/1 oz roast beef, thinly sliced
1 small lettuce leaf
2 tsp mayonnaise
1 tsp fried onions
1 tsp grated horseradish
1 gherkin fan
1 slice tomato

1 To make the Copenhagen open sandwich, arrange the beef slices to cover one slice of bread. Place the lettuce leaf at one end of the sandwich and spoon on the mayonnaise to secure but not cover the lettuce leaf. Add a scattering of onion and horseradish.

2 Position the gherkin fan opposite the lettuce leaf and top the entire sandwich with a tomato twist.

TIVOLI

1 large lettuce leaf
4 slices hard-boiled egg
4 slices tomato
1–2 tbsp mayonnaise
15 g/ ½ oz Danish-style caviare or lumpfish roe

1 To make the Tivoli open sandwich, cover the final slice of bread with the lettuce leaf. Arrange the egg and tomato slices in two rows lengthwise on the lettuce.

2 Pipe or spoon the mayonnaise down the centre of the egg and tomato slices, and spoon the caviare along the mayonnaise.

CITY TOASTS

••

SERVES 6

100 g/4 oz/ ½ cup butter, softened over hot
water or in the microwave
50 g/2 oz/ ½ cup Gruyère cheese, grated
50 g/2 oz/ ½ cup fresh Parmesan cheese,
grated
2 tsp double (heavy) cream
salt and cayenne pepper
6 x 8.5 cm/3½ in rounds (slices) of white
or brown bread
3 slices garlic, ham or liver sausage,
halved
3 slices Gruyère cheese, halved
6 gherkins, to garnish

1 In a bowl, blend the butter together
with the grated Gruyère cheese,
Parmesan cheese and cream, using a
wooden spoon. Season the mixture to
taste with salt and cayenne pepper.

2 Lightly toast the bread on both sides
until golden and crisp.

3 Divide the cheese mixture equally
between the pieces of toast,
spreading lightly to cover.

4 Place a halved slice of sausage and
cheese on top of the filling on each
slice of toast, setting them at an angle so
that they look like 'wings'.

5 Slice the gherkins to make fans,
cutting each one several times along
its length without cutting through fully at
the end. Garnish each toast with a
gherkin, and serve.

A COFFEE HOUSE
FAVOURITE

The name of these toasts derives from
a London tradition. Platters of City
Toasts were served at some of the
most famous City of London coffee
houses in the 19th century while the
gentlemen guests played chess.
   Create variety by varying the garnish
on these sandwiches. Instead of
decorating with gherkin fans, try spring
onion curls, cucumber twists, carrot
curls, sliced olives, small tomato roses
or herb bows and bundles.

WAGONS ROLL

••

SERVES 1

2 round brown bread rolls
25 g/1 oz/2 tbsp butter or margarine
a little yeast extract
225 g/8 oz canned baked beans in tomato
sauce
1 tsp raisins
salt and pepper

VARIATIONS
Add a sprinkling of any of the following
ingredients for a more 'adult' version of
this roll:

grilled bacon pieces
chopped mushrooms
chopped cooked ham
onion, chopped and fried in butter

1 Cut the rolls in half, scoop out the
soft bread from the top and bottom
roll halves.

2 Make the soft bread that you have
scooped out into crumbs by rubbing
it against a coarse grater, then set it aside.

3 Spread the insides of the rolls with
the butter or margarine and smear
lightly with yeast extract to taste.

4 Mash the baked beans lightly with
the scooped out and reserved
breadcrumbs, then add the raisins, and
salt and pepper to taste. Mix in any
additional ingredients you also wish to
include in the roll.

5 Pile the filling back into the roll
bases, replace the lids and wrap in
foil for transporting.

THE WHOLEMEAL
OPTION

Wholemeal rolls are also ideal for this
recipe. Wholemeal or wholewheat
flour is made from the whole wheat
grain which has been milled with
nothing added or taken away.
Stoneground wholemeal flour is much
the same, but it is made in the
traditional way using grinding stones.

·5·

Desserts

There is something here for all tastes and all seasons: fruity trifles, creamy mousses, traditional favourites like bread and butter pudding and apple pie, and sorbets and ice-creams galore.

COLD PUDDINGS

Light, creamy mousses, enticing syllabubs and rich, fruity trifles are just some of the delights in this entrancing collection. There is something here for all tastes and all seasons. When soft fruit is at its best make traditional Summer Pudding (see page 501) or Strawberry Romanoff (see page 508). Serve delicate Coeurs à la Crème (see page 505) after a rich, heavy dinner, Strawberry Meringues (see page 511) when you want to impress, and Brandy Mocha Cups (see page 507) to please the chocaholics.

BANANAS WITH SPICED YOGURT

SERVES 4-6

3 good pinches saffron strands
2 tbsp creamy milk
6 cardamom pods, crushed and seeds removed and crushed
45 g/1½ oz/3 tbsp butter
45 g/1½ oz/3 tbsp soft brown sugar
½ tsp ground cinnamon
2 bananas
500 g/1 lb strained Greek yogurt
2-3 tbsp clear honey, to taste
30 g/1 oz/ ¼ cup toasted, flaked almonds

1 Place the saffron strands on a small piece of foil and toast very lightly. Crush the saffron strands finely and place in a small bowl. Add the milk and crushed cardamom seeds, stir well and leave to cool.

2 Meanwhile, melt the butter in a frying pan, add the brown sugar and cinnamon and stir well. Peel and slice the bananas and fry gently for about 1 minute, turning halfway through cooking. Remove from the pan and place the fried banana slices in decorative serving glasses.

3 Mix the yogurt with the cold spiced milk and the honey. Spoon the mixture on top of the bananas and liberally sprinkle the surface of each serving with toasted, flaked almonds. Chill before serving, if preferred.

VARIATIONS

The flavour of saffron strands is improved by lightly toasting before use, but do take care not to overcook them or the flavour is spoilt and becomes bitter.

This delicious dessert may also be made using half cream and half yogurt and the tops could be sprinkled with unsalted, chopped pistachios instead of almonds, if wished.

CARAMELIZED ORANGES

••

SERVES 6

6 large oranges
250 g/8 oz/1 cup caster or granulated
  sugar
250 ml/8 fl oz/1 cup water
6 whole cloves (optional)
2-4 tbsp Grand Marnier, Curaçao or
  brandy

1 Use a citrus zester or potato peeler to pare off the rind from 2 oranges, to give narrow strips of peel without any of the white pith attached. If using a potato peeler, cut the peel into very thin julienne strips using a very sharp knife.

2 Put the strips into a small saucepan and barely cover with water. Bring to the boil and simmer for 5 minutes until tender. Drain the strips and reserve the water.

3 Cut away all the white pith and peel from the oranges using a very sharp knife and then cut horizontally into 4 slices. Reassemble the oranges and hold in place with wooden cocktail sticks. Stand in a heatproof dish.

4 Put the sugar and water into a heavy-based saucepan with the cloves, if using. Bring to the boil and simmer gently until the sugar has dissolved, then boil hard without stirring until the syrup thickens and begins to turn brown. Continue to cook until a light golden brown, then quickly remove from the heat and pour in the reserved liquor from cooking the orange rind.

5 Return to a gentle heat until the caramel has fully dissolved again, then remove from the heat, add the liqueur or brandy. When mixed pour over the oranges.

6 Sprinkle the orange strips over the oranges, cover with clingfilm and leave until cold. Chill for at least 3 hours and preferably for 24-48 hours before serving. If time allows, spoon the syrup over the oranges several times while they are marinating. Discard the cocktail stick before serving.

CHOCOLATE COCONUT LAYER

••

SERVES 6-8

200 g/7 oz/7 squares dark chocolate,
  broken into pieces
300 g/10 oz/1¼ cups full-fat soft cheese
60 g/2 oz/ ⅔ cup grated or desiccated
  (shredded) coconut
250 g/8 oz/2 cups digestive biscuits
  (graham crackers), crumbled

TO DECORATE:
icing (confectioners') sugar
coconut curls or desiccated (shredded)
  coconut

1 Melt the chocolate in a heatproof bowl set over a saucepan of barely simmering water for 10 minutes. Do not let the water splash into the bowl, as it will affect the texture of the chocolate.

2 Turn off the heat. Add the soft cheese to the chocolate and stir till well blended and smooth.

3 Stir in the grated or desiccated (shredded) coconut.

4 Place half of the biscuit (cracker) crumbs on the bottom of a shallow 1.1 litre/2 pint/4½ cup dish.

5 Layer with half the chocolate mixture, then another layer of the remaining biscuit (cracker) crumbs, finishing with a layer of the remaining chocolate mixture. Chill for 2 hours.

6 Dust with icing (confectioners') sugar and coconut curls or desiccated (shredded) coconut before serving.

COCONUT CURLS

If using a fresh coconut, drain the milk and split the coconut apart using a hammer. Remove the flesh from the shell in large pieces. To make the curls, peel down one side of each piece of coconut flesh with a peeler and use the resulting curls for decoration.

RUM & RAISIN CRUNCH

SERVES 4

BRANDYSNAPS:
125 g/4 oz/ ½ cup butter
125 g/4 oz/ ½ cup caster (superfine) sugar
125 g/4 oz/ ⅓ cup golden (light corn) syrup
90 g/3 oz/ ¾ cup plain (all-purpose) flour,
*   sifted*
½ tsp ground ginger

RUM & RAISIN CREAM:
125 g/4 oz/ ⅔ cup raisins
5 tbsp dark rum
5 tbsp water
150 ml/ ¼ pint/ ⅔ cup whipping cream
60 g/2 oz/ ¼ cup Ricotta or full-fat soft
*   cheese*
30 g/1 oz/ ¼ cup sifted icing
*   (confectioners') sugar*
30 g/1 oz/ ¼ cup ground almonds
¼ tsp almond flavouring (extract)
2 egg whites
6 brandysnaps, lightly crushed

1 To make the brandysnaps, put the butter, sugar and syrup into a saucepan and heat gently until melted.

2 Remove from the heat and mix in the flour and ginger until blended. Drop teaspoonfuls of the mixture on to a baking (cookie) sheet, leaving space to spread. Bake in a preheated oven at 180°C/350°F/Gas Mark 4 for about 8 minutes until golden brown.

3 Chill 4 ramekins or a serving bowl. Put the raisins, rum and water into a saucepan and bring to the boil. Simmer for 5 minutes, then leave to rest for 20 minutes.

4 Whip the cream. Press the soft cheese through a sieve (strainer) and stir in the icing (confectioners') sugar. Fold in the whipped cream, ground almonds and flavouring (extract). Whisk the egg whites and fold them into the mixture.

5 Drain the raisins and stir them into the mixture with the crushed brandysnaps. Spoon into the chilled dishes. Chill for at least 30 minutes.

SUMMER PUDDING

SERVES 4–6

*1 kg/2 lb mixed summer fruit, such as
    blackberries, redcurrants,
    blackcurrants, raspberries, loganberries
    and cherries*
175 g/6 oz/ ¾ cup caster (superfine) sugar
8 small slices white bread
*clotted cream or single (light) cream, to
    serve*

1 Stir the fruit and sugar together in a
    large saucepan, cover and bring to
the boil. Simmer for 10 minutes, stirring.

2 Cut the crusts off the bread slices.
    Line a 1.1 litre/2 pint/4½ cup
pudding basin with the bread.

3 Add the fruit and as much of the
    cooking juices as will fit into the
bread-lined bowl. Cover the fruit with the
remaining bread slices.

4 Put the pudding basin on to a large
    plate or a shallow baking (cookie)
sheet. Place a plate on top and weigh it
down with cans. Chill overnight, or for up
to 6 days.

5 When ready to serve, turn the
    pudding out on to a serving plate or
shallow bowl and serve cold with clotted
cream or single (light) cream.

VARIATION

To give the pudding a more lasting set,
dissolve 2 sachets (envelopes) or
2 tablespoons of powdered gelatine in
water and stir into the fruit mixture.
This enables you to turn it out on to
the serving plate a couple of hours
before serving.

CRÈME AUX MARRONS

SERVES 6

60 g/2 oz/ ⅓ cup sultanas (golden raisins)
3 tbsp orange-flavoured liqueur
finely grated rind of 1 orange
50 g/1¾ oz/scant ¼ cup granulated sugar
75 ml/3 fl oz/ ⅓ cup orange juice
*150 g/5 oz/1½ cups peeled chestnuts
    (canned or vacuum-packed)*
*300 ml/ ½ pint/1¼ cups double (heavy)
    cream*
*30 g/1 oz/ ¼ cup icing (confectioners')
    sugar*

TO DECORATE:
candied oranges

1 Put the sultanas (golden raisins) into
    a small saucepan with the liqueur
and the orange rind. Cover and bring to
a gentle boil. Remove from the heat
immediately and leave to steep for
10 minutes.

2 Put the granulated sugar and orange
    juice into a clean saucepan and
bring to the boil, stirring until the sugar
has dissolved. Add the chestnuts and
poach over a low to medium heat for
10 minutes. Drain the chestnuts and
reserve the cooking liquid.

3 Put the chestnuts into a blender with
    3 tbsp of the cooking liquid. Blend
until smooth; add more liquid if necessary.
Alternatively, chop and mash the chestnuts
and press them through a sieve (strainer)
with 3 tablespoons of the cooking liquid.
Add more liquid if necessary.

4 Whip the cream and sift in the icing
    (confectioners') sugar.

5 Put the cream into 1 piping bag and
    the chestnut mixture into another.
Pipe alternate layers of whipped cream
and chestnut mixture into 6 glasses,
reserving a little of the cream for
decoration. Alternatively, spoon into the
glasses. If you prefer, spoon the chestnut
mixture into the glasses first, and top with
the cream.

6 Spoon the raisins over the top.
    Decorate with chopped, candied
orange and a rosette of the whipped
cream.

WHITE & DARK CHOCOLATE MOUSSE

SERVES 6-8

100 g/3½ oz/3½ squares dark chocolate
100 g/3½ oz/3½ squares good quality white chocolate
4 egg yolks
2 tbsp brandy
1 sachet (envelope) or 1 tbsp powdered gelatine
50 ml/2 fl oz/ ¼ cup hot water
300 ml/ ½ pint/1¼ cups double (heavy) cream
4 egg whites

TO DECORATE:
100 g/3½ oz/3½ squares good quality white or dark chocolate
1 tbsp lard (shortening)
cocoa powder

1 Break the dark and white chocolate into pieces and put them into separate heatproof bowls. Set the bowls over saucepans of barely simmering water and melt the chocolate.

2 When melted, remove the bowls and beat 2 egg yolks into each, until smooth. Stir the brandy into the dark chocolate mixture. Set aside to cool, stirring the chocolate frequently.

3 Heat the gelatine and hot water in a heatproof bowl, set over a pan of barely simmering water, until it is clear, about 10 minutes. Stir half of the gelatine into each chocolate mixture until smooth.

4 Whip the cream until softly stiff, and whisk the egg whites until stiff.

5 Stir half of the cream into each chocolate mixture, then fold half of the egg whites into each mixture.

6 Pour or spoon both mousses at the same time into a 900 ml/1½ pint/3½ cup soufflé dish, one in each half of the dish, so that they meet in the middle but do not run into each other. Chill until ready to serve.

7 Break the chocolate for decorating into pieces and put into a heatproof bowl. Set over a pan of barely simmering water until melted, then stir in the lard (shortening) and pour into a small loaf tin (pan). Chill until set, then turn out.

8 To decorate, shave large curls of chocolate from the block with a vegetable peeler. Arrange attractively on the mousse, and dust with cocoa powder.

SHERRY TRIFLE

SERVES 4-6

60 g/2 oz/ ½ cup cornflour (cornstarch)
1.1 litres/2 pints/4½ cups milk
10 egg yolks
½ tsp almond flavouring (extract)
125 g/4 oz/ ½ cup caster (superfine) sugar
200 g/7 oz/6 inches Madeira (pound)
    cake, sliced
2 tbsp raspberry jam
250 ml/8 fl oz/1 cup sherry, sweet or dry,
    depending on taste
1½ tbsp chopped mixed nuts
2 x 425 g/14 oz cans of pineapple rings
10 glacé (candied) cherries

TO DECORATE:
300 ml/ ½ pint/1¼ cups whipping cream
chopped angelica
flaked (slivered) almonds, toasted

1 First make the custard. Blend the
  cornflour (cornstarch) in a saucepan
with a little of the milk to make a paste.
Add the remaining milk and place over a
medium heat. When it reaches boiling
point, remove from the heat.

2 Meanwhile, beat together the egg
  yolks, almond flavouring (extract)
and caster (superfine) sugar until pale.
Pour on the hot milk while beating
continuously. Transfer to a clean pan and
stir over a low heat until thickened.

3 Put the slices of cake in the base of
  a glass trifle bowl. Spread thinly with
the raspberry jam. Sprinkle the sherry and
then the nuts over the cake.

4 Arrange the pineapple rings around
  the edge of the bowl, flat against the
glass. Put one glacé (candied) cherry in
the centre of each pineapple ring.

5 Pour in the cooled custard without
  disturbing the pineapple rings, and
chill until the custard is set.

6 To decorate, whip the cream until it
  is of piping consistency and pipe
rosettes around the top of the trifle. Cut
the angelica into squares and top each
rosette with a square. Sprinkle the toasted
flaked (slivered) almonds over the top,
and serve.

BANOFFI PIE

SERVES 6-8

400 g/14 oz can condensed milk
250 g/8 oz/2 cups plain (all-purpose) flour
125 g/4 oz/ ½ cup unsalted butter
8 tsp cold water
3 bananas
300 ml/ ½ pint/1¼ cups double (heavy)
    cream
1 tsp instant coffee powder
1 tsp hot water

1 Leave the can of milk unopened and
  place it in a saucepan of water, so
that it is submerged. Bring the water to
the boil and boil the can for 4 hours.

2 Sift the flour into a bowl and rub in
  the butter until the mixture
resembles breadcrumbs. Mix in the water
and bring the mixture together lightly
with your fingertips. Wrap in clingfilm
(plastic wrap) or baking parchment and
chill for at least 30 minutes.

3 Line a 25 cm/10 inch flan tin (pan)
  with baking parchment. Roll out the
pastry into a 25 cm/10 inch circle and line
the flan tin (pan) with it.

4 Bake the pastry base in a preheated
  oven at 190°C/375°F/Gas Mark 5 for
15 minutes. Leave to cool in the tin (pan).

5 Open the boiled can of condensed
  milk – if it is still hot, open it under
a tea towel (dishcloth). The milk will have
turned to a toffee-like consistency. Spread
a single layer of the 'toffee' over the
cooked pastry base. Slice the bananas and
spread out over the toffee layer.

6 Whip the cream until softly stiff.
  Dissolve the instant coffee powder
in the hot water and fold into the cream.
Spoon or pipe the cream over the
bananas. Chill until ready to serve.

TIRAMISU

SERVES 6–8

24 sponge fingers (lady-fingers) or
   savoiardi
5 tbsp instant coffee powder
300 ml/ ½ pint/1¼ cups hot water
3 tbsp rum
300 ml/ ½ pint/1¼ cups double (heavy)
   cream
250 g/8 oz/1 cup Mascarpone cheese
60 g/2 oz/ ⅓ cup icing (confectioners')
   sugar
2 tbsp cocoa powder

1 Cover the bottom of a pretty serving
dish with half the sponge fingers
(lady-fingers) or savoiardi.

2 Combine the instant coffee powder
and hot water and soak the sponge
fingers (lady-fingers) in half of the coffee
and half of the rum for a few minutes.

3 Whip the cream, stir in the
Mascarpone cheese and sift in the
icing (confectioners') sugar.

4 Spoon half the Mascarpone cheese
mixture in a layer over the sponge
fingers (lady-fingers).

5 Sift half of the cocoa powder over
the Mascarpone cheese mixture.
Make another layer of sponge fingers
(lady-fingers) in the same way, using the
remaining coffee and rum, Mascarpone
cheese mixture and cocoa powder.

6 Chill the tiramisù for at least 4 hours
before serving.

HANDY HINT

Liquid instant coffee is ideal to use in
place of instant coffee powder when
baking. It can also be added to cakes
to provide an instant coffee flavour.

QUICK TIRAMISU

SERVES 4

250 g/8 oz/1 cup Mascarpone or full-fat
   soft cheese
1 egg, separated
2 tbsp natural yogurt
2 tbsp caster (superfine) sugar
2 tbsp dark rum
2 tbsp strong black coffee
8 sponge fingers (lady-fingers)
2 tbsp grated dark chocolate

1 Put the cheese in a bowl, add the
egg yolk and yogurt and beat the
mixture until smooth.

2 Whisk the egg white until stiff but
not dry, then whisk in the sugar and
carefully fold into the cheese mixture.
Spoon half the mixture into 4 sundae
glasses.

3 Mix together the rum and coffee in a
shallow dish. Dip the sponge fingers
(lady-fingers) into the rum mixture, break
them in half, or into smaller pieces if
necessary, and divide among the glasses.

4 Stir any remaining coffee mixture
into the remaining cheese and spoon
over the top. Sprinkle with grated
chocolate. Serve immediately or chill until
required.

MASCARPONE CHEESE

An Italian soft cream cheese made
from cow's milk. It has a rich, silky
smooth texture and a deliciously
creamy flavour. It can be eaten as it is
with fresh fruits or flavoured with
coffee or chocolate. I usually lighten it
slightly by mixing it with an equal
quantity of fromage frais or natural
thick yogurt.

MOULDS WITH MANGO LIME

SERVES 4

250 g/8 oz/1 cup fromage frais
grated rind of 1 lime
1 tbsp caster (superfine) sugar
120 ml/4 fl oz/ ½ cup double (heavy)
* cream*
4 cape gooseberries (ground cherries)
Mango sauce
1 mango
juice of 1 lime
4 tsp caster (superfine) sugar

1 Put the fromage frais, lime rind and
  sugar in a bowl and mix together.

2 Whisk the cream and fold into the
  fromage frais.

3 Line 4 moulds with muslin
  (cheesecloth) and divide the mixture
evenly between them. Fold the muslin
(cheesecloth) over the top place on a
plate and leave for 5 minutes.

4 To make the sauce, cut the mango
  in half discarding the stone (pit) and
peel each half.

5 Cut off 12 thin slices and set aside.
  Chop the remaining mango and put
into a food processor with the lime juice
and sugar. Blend until smooth.
Alternatively, push the mango through a
non-metallic sieve (strainer) then mix with
the lime juice and sugar.

6 Turn out the moulds onto individual
  plates. Arrange 3 slices of mango on
each plate, pour some sauce around and
decorate with cape gooseberries (ground
cherries).

CAPE GOOSEBERRIES
(GROUND CHERRIES)

Cape gooseberries (ground cherries)
are excellent decoration for many
desserts. The papery husks must be
peeled back to expose the bright
orange fruits. They have a tart and
mildly scented flavour.

COEURS À LA CRÈME

SERVES 4–6

250 g/8 oz/1 cup 20 per cent fat soft
* cheese (extra light) or Quark*
300 ml/ ½ pint/1¼ cups double (heavy)
* cream*
few drops vanilla flavouring (extract)
30 g/1 oz/ ¼ cup icing (confectioners')
* sugar*
2 egg whites
400 g/13 oz can apricots in syrup

1 Line 4 moulds (or whatever you are
  using) with damp muslin
(cheesecloth). Press the soft cheese
through a sieve (strainer).

2 Whip the cream until softly stiff and
  add the vanilla flavouring (extract)
and sugar. Blend well and stir into the
soft cheese.

3 Whisk the egg whites until stiff.
  Spoon a quarter of them into the
cream and blend well. Fold in the
remaining whites.

4 Divide the mixture between the
  moulds and put them on a tray or
plate. Leave to drain overnight in the
refrigerator. At this stage they can be
stored for up to 2 days in the refrigerator.

5 Blend the apricots and their syrup in
  a blender or food processor.
Alternatively, press them through a sieve
(strainer). Turn the moulds out on to a
serving plate and serve with a little
apricot coulis.

VARIATION

Raspberry coulis is also delicious with
this dessert. Blend or process a
400 g/14 oz can of raspberries in syrup
and sieve (strain). If fresh raspberries
are available, put 250 g/8 oz/1½ cups
into a saucepan with 2 tablespoons
icing (confectioners') sugar. Simmer to
dissolve the sugar, and sieve (strain).
Serve when cooled.

STRAWBERRY MASCARPONE WITH SABLE BISCUITS (COOKIES)

SERVES 4

BISCUITS (COOKIES):
150 g/5 oz/1¼ cups plain (all-purpose)
*   flour*
5 tbsp caster (superfine) sugar
90 g/3 oz/ ⅓ cup unsalted butter, softened
1 tbsp water
1 egg yolk

STRAWBERRY MASCARPONE:
2 egg yolks
60 g/2 oz/ ¼ cup caster (superfine) sugar
500 g/1 lb/2 cups Mascarpone cheese
300 g/10 oz/2 cups strawberries, hulled
2 egg whites
icing (confectioners') sugar, to decorate

1 First, make the biscuits (cookies). Sift
   the flour into a bowl and stir in the
sugar. Make a well in the centre and add
the butter, water and egg yolk. Work with
the fingertips until well blended, about
3 minutes. Roll into a ball and wrap in
greaseproof paper (baking parchment).
Chill for 1 hour.

2 Roll out the dough on a floured
   work surface until it is 5 mm/ ¼ inch
thick. Using a 6 cm/2½ inch cutter, stamp
out about 20 biscuits (cookies).

3 Transfer the biscuits (cookies) to
   greased and floured or lined baking
(cookie) sheets. Bake in a preheated oven
at 180°C/350°F/Gas Mark 4 for
15–20 minutes. Transfer to a wire rack
immediately.

4 Meanwhile, make the Strawberry
   Mascarpone. Beat together the egg
yolks and sugar until pale. Add the
Mascarpone cheese and beat well.

5 Blend the strawberries in a blender
   or food processor. Sieve (strain) into
a large bowl. Alternatively, mash the
strawberries with a wooden spoon and
press through a sieve (strainer). Stir in the
Mascarpone cheese mixture. Whisk the
egg whites until stiff and fold into the
Mascarpone cheese mixture.

6 To serve, place a spoonful or two of
   the strawberry Mascarpone on each
plate, with a few biscuits by the side.
Dust with icing (confectioners') sugar.

MANGO MOUSSE

••••••••••••••••••••••••••••••••••••••

SERVES 6–8

4 large ripe mangoes
1 passion-fruit
90 g/3 oz/⅓ cup caster (superfine) sugar
600 ml/1 pint/2½ cups thick natural
*   yogurt or 300 ml/½ pint/1¼ cups thick*
*   natural yogurt and 300 ml/½ pint/1¼*
*   cups double (heavy) cream*

1 To prepare the mango, set it on its
   side on a chopping board and cut a
thick slice from each side as near to the
stone (pit) as possible. Cut as much flesh
away from the stone (pit) as possible, in
large chunks. Take the 2 side slices and
make 3 cuts through the skin but not the
flesh, and make 3 more at right angles to
make a lattice pattern. Push the skin
inside out so that the cubed flesh is
exposed and you can easily cut it off in
large chunks.

2 Cut the passion-fruit in half and
   scoop out the flesh with a teaspoon.
Sieve (strain) this and add it to the mango
flesh. Sprinkle the fruit with the sugar and
leave to stand for 15–20 minutes.

3 Mash the fruit or blend it in a food
   processor or blender until smooth.
Set aside a few spoonfuls for decoration.

4 Fold in the yogurt and blend well.
   Whip the cream, if using, and fold it
into the mixture.

5 Chill the mousse for at least 2 hours
   until set. Spoon the reserved fruit
purée over the mousse to serve.

MANGOES

Mangoes are usually imported under-
ripe and, as they don't have a chance
to mature in the sun, may lose some
of their sweetness and flavour. The
flesh may be disappointingly stringy or
chalky. Look for Bombay mangoes,
which are available all year round,
although they are at their peak in
March and April. Canned mangoes in
syrup are a very good alternative if
fresh ones are hard to find.

BRANDY MOCHA CUPS

••••••••••••••••••••••••••••••••••••••

SERVES 4

250 ml/8 fl oz/1 cup double (heavy)
*   cream*
1 tsp coffee granules
125 g/4 oz dark chocolate, broken into
*   pieces*
2 tbsp brandy
75 ml/3 fl oz/⅓ cup double (heavy) cream
chocolate curls to decorate
amaretti biscuits (cookies) to serve

1 Put the cream, coffee and chocolate
   into a saucepan and heat gently,
stirring occasionally, until the chocolate
has melted.

2 Add the brandy and stir well until it
   is completely smooth. Remove from
the heat and leave to cool.

3 Pour into 4 individual glass dishes
   and chill until set.

4 Pile a spoonful of cream on to each
   cup, decorate with chocolate curls
and serve with amaretti biscuits (cookies).

VARIATIONS

You can use all kinds of flavourings in
this dessert. Try replacing the brandy
with almond liqueur to reflect the
flavour of the amaretti biscuits
(cookies), or use cherry brandy, orange
liqueur or, for a non-alcoholic version,
orange juice and a little grated orange
rind.

CHOCOLATE CURLS

Use a vegetable peeler to scrape curls
directly off the edge of a block of
chocolate. The chocolate should be at
room temperature; if it is too cold the
curls will break into small pieces.

STRAWBERRY ROMANOFF

••

SERVES 4

300 ml/ ½ pint/1¼ cups whipping (heavy)
  cream
2 tbsp orange liqueur
350 g/12 oz strawberries, hulled
1 egg white
25 g/1 oz/2 tbsp caster (superfine) sugar
strawberry leaves to decorate

1 Put the cream and orange liqueur in
  a bowl and whisk until the cream
holds its shape.

2 Put half the strawberries in a food
  processor or blender and blend to
a purée. Alternatively, press through a
non-metallic sieve (strainer). Halve the
remaining strawberries.

3 Whisk the egg white until stiff then
  whisk in the sugar. Carefully fold
into the cream.

4 Set aside a few strawberry halves for
  decoration. Fold the rest into the
cream mixture with the purée.

5 Spoon the cream into glasses and
  decorate with the reserved
strawberries and the leaves.

TIP

When folding the egg white into the
cream use a large metal spoon so that
you do not knock out so much air.
When you fold in the fruit purée, stop
when it looks pleasantly marbled.

AMARETTI FIGS WITH RASPBERRY COULIS

••

SERVES 4

120 ml/4 fl oz/ ½ cup double (heavy)
  cream
4 amaretti biscuits (cookies)
4 figs
175 g/6 oz raspberries
2 tbsp icing (confectioners') sugar, sifted
raspberry leaves to decorate

1 Set aside 1 tablespoon of the cream
  then lightly whip the remainder until
stiff enough to hold its shape.

2 Put the amaretti biscuits in a plastic
  bag and crush with a rolling pin
until they form fine crumbs. Fold into the
whipped cream.

3 Slice each fig into 6 pieces and
  arrange on 4 serving plates. Put a
spoonful of the amaretti cream in the
centre of each plate.

4 Press the raspberries through a
  non-metallic sieve (strainer) then
stir in the icing (confectioners') sugar.

5 Spoon the raspberry sauce around
  the figs and amaretti cream.

6 Put drops of the reserved cream
  on to the sauce and drag a skewer
through the drops to make an attractive
pattern. Decorate with raspberry leaves
and serve.

RASPBERRY COULIS

The raspberries can be puréed in a
food processor if preferred, but they
should still be passed through a sieve
(strainer) to remove the seeds. Be sure
to use a non-metallic sieve (strainer) as
metal ones react with the acid in the
raspberries and may taint the flavour.

COFFEE CREAM TRIFLE

•••••••••••••••••••••••••••••••••••••••

SERVES 6

175 g/6 oz ginger cake, sliced
3 tbsp coffee essence
5 tbsp hot water
4 tbsp dark rum
60 g/2 oz/ ⅓ cup cornflour (cornstarch)
60 g/2 oz/3 tbsp light muscovado sugar
15 g/ ½ oz/1 tbsp butter or margarine
600 ml/1 pint/2½ cups milk
150 ml/ ¼ pint/ ⅔ cup whipping (heavy)
   cream

TO DECORATE:
1 tbsp demerara (brown crystal) sugar
grated chocolate
flaked almonds

1 Arrange the slices of ginger cake in the base of a glass serving dish. Mix together the coffee essence, water and rum. Pour half over the ginger cake.

2 Put the cornflour (cornstarch), sugar, butter or margarine and milk in a saucepan. Heat gently, whisking constantly until thickened and smooth. Cook gently for 2 minutes. Remove from the heat.

3 Add the remaining coffee mixture, stirring well to blend. Pour over the ginger cake. Allow to cool completely.

4 In a large chilled bowl, whip the cream until it holds its shape. Spoon into a large piping bag fitted with a star nozzle (tip).

5 Pipe swirls of cream around the edge of the trifle. Sprinkle with demerara (brown crystal) sugar and decorate with grated chocolate and flaked almonds.

VARIATIONS

Use plain sponge cake instead of ginger cake, if preferred.

   To make this trifle more economical, use 2 teaspoons rum essence in place of the rum.

WINTER PUDDINGS

•••••••••••••••••••••••••••••••••••••••

SERVES 4

325 g/11 oz fruit malt loaf
150 g/5 oz/1 cup no-need-to-soak dried
   apricots, chopped coarsely
90 g/3 oz/ ½ cup dried apple, chopped
   coarsely
450 ml/ ¾ pint/2 cups orange juice
1 tsp grated orange rind
2 tbsp orange liqueur
grated orange rind to decorate
low-fat crème fraîche or low-fat natural
   fromage frais to serve

1 Cut the malt loaf into 5mm/ ¼ inch thick slices.

2 Place the apricots, apple and orange juice in a saucepan. Bring to the boil, then simmer for 10 minutes. Remove the fruit using a perforated spoon and reserve the liquid. Place the fruit in a shallow dish and leave to cool. Stir in the orange rind and liqueur.

3 Line 4 x 180 ml/6 fl oz/ ¾ cup pudding basins or ramekin dishes with baking parchment. Cut 4 circles from the malt loaf slices to fit the tops of the moulds and cut the remaining slices to line the moulds.

4 Soak the malt loaf slices in the reserved fruit syrup, then arrange around the base and sides of the moulds. Trim away any crusts which overhang the edges. Fill the centres of the moulds with the chopped fruit, pressing down well, and place the malt loaf circles on top.

5 Cover the tops with baking parchment and weigh each basin down with a 250 g/8 oz weight or a food can. Chill overnight.

6 Remove the weight and baking parchment. Carefully turn the puddings out on to 4 serving plates. Remove the lining paper. Decorate with grated orange rind and serve with low-fat crème fraîche or natural fromage frais.

SYLLABUB WITH BRANDY SNAPS

SERVES 4

finely grated rind of 1 lemon
2 tbsp lemon juice
60–90 g/2–3 oz/ ⅓–½ cup caster
  (superfine) sugar
6 tbsp white wine
1–2 tbsp rum, brandy or sherry (optional)
300 ml/ ½ pint/1¼ cups double (heavy)
  cream

BRANDY SNAPS:
60 g/2 oz/ ¼ cup butter
60 g/2 oz/ ⅓ cup caster (superfine) sugar
2 tbsp golden (light corn) syrup
60 g/2 oz/ ½ cup plain (all-purpose) flour
½ tsp ground ginger
finely grated rind of ½ lemon

TO DECORATE:
fine strips of lemon rind, blanched
sprigs of mint

1 Put the lemon rind and juice into a bowl, add the sugar and wine and mix well. Leave to stand for at least 30 minutes, preferably 2–3 hours.

2 Add the rum, brandy or sherry, if using. Pour in the cream and whisk with a balloon whisk or electric mixer until it stands in soft peaks. Divide among 4 tall glasses, decorate with lemon strips and mint sprigs and chill for 3–4 hours.

3 To make the brandy snaps, line 2–3 large baking sheets (cookie sheets) with baking parchment. Gently heat the butter, sugar and syrup until melted, then remove from the heat and stir in the flour, ginger and lemon rind.

4 Drop 4–6 teaspoons of the mixture, spaced well apart, onto each baking sheet (cookie sheet). Cook in a preheated oven at 180°C/350°F/Gas Mark 4 for 7–8 minutes until golden brown and firm.

5 Quickly remove from the baking sheets (cookie sheets) using a palette knife (spatula) and immediately roll around a greased wooden spoon handle or greased cream horn tins (molds). Leave to cool on a wire rack. Remove from the handles or tins (molds) and store in an airtight container until required.

ORANGE SYLLABUB WITH SPONGE HEARTS

SERVES 4

4 oranges
600 ml/1 pint/2½ cups low-fat natural
  yogurt
6 tbsp low-fat skimmed milk powder
4 tbsp caster (superfine) sugar
1 tbsp grated orange rind
4 tbsp orange juice
2 egg whites
fresh orange zest to decorate

SPONGE HEARTS:
2 eggs, size 2
90 g/3 oz/6 tbsp caster (superfine) sugar
45 g/1½ oz/6 tbsp plain (all-purpose) flour
45 g/1½ oz/6 tbsp wholemeal flour
1 tbsp hot water
1 tsp icing (confectioners') sugar

1 Slice off the tops and bottoms of the oranges and the skin. Then cut out the segments, removing the zest and membranes between each one. Divide the orange segments between 4 dessert glasses, then chill.

2 In a large mixing bowl, combine the yogurt, milk powder, sugar, orange rind and juice. Cover and chill for 1 hour until thickened.

3 Whisk the egg whites until stiff, then fold into the orange yogurt mixture. Pile on to the orange slices and chill for an hour. Decorate with fresh orange rind and sponge hearts.

4 To make the sponge hearts, line a 15 x 25 cm/6 x 10 inch baking tin (pan) with baking parchment. Whisk the eggs and sugar until thick and pale. Sieve in the flours, then fold in with a metal spoon and add the hot water.

5 Pour into the tin (pan) and bake in a preheated oven at 220°C/425°F/Gas Mark 7 for 9–10 minutes until golden and firm to the touch. Turn on to a sheet of baking parchment. Using a 5 cm/2 inch heart-shaped cutter, stamp out hearts. Transfer to a wire rack to cool. Lightly dust with icing (confectioners') sugar before serving with the syllabub.

STRAWBERRY ROSE BROWN SUGAR MERINGUES

SERVES 6

3 egg whites, size 2
pinch of salt
175 g/6 oz/1 cup light muscovado sugar, crushed to be free of lumps
250 g/8 oz/1½ cups strawberries, hulled
2 tsp rose water
150 ml/ ¼ pint/ ⅔ cup low-fat natural fromage frais
extra strawberries to serve (optional)

TO DECORATE:
rose-scented geranium leaves
rose petals

1 In a large grease-free bowl, whisk the egg whites and salt until very stiff and dry. Gradually whisk in the sugar a spoonful at a time, until the mixture is stiff again.

2 Line a baking sheet with baking parchment and drop 12 spoonfuls of the meringue mixture on to the sheet. Bake in a preheated oven at 120°C/250°F/ Gas Mark ½ for 3–3½ hours, until completely dried out and crisp. Allow to cool.

3 Reserve 60 g/2 oz/ ⅓ cup of the strawberries. Place the remaining strawberries in a blender or food processor and blend for a few seconds until smooth. Alternatively, mash the strawberries with a fork and press through a sieve (strainer) to form a purée paste. Stir in the rose water. Chill until required.

4 To serve, slice the reserved strawberries. Sandwich the meringues together with fromage frais and sliced strawberries. Spoon the strawberry rose purée paste on to 6 serving plates and top with a meringue. Decorate with rose petals and rose- scented geranium leaves, and serve with extra strawberries.

TIP

The brown sugar gives a treacley caramelized flavour. If preferred, you can use unbleached granulated sugar.

TROPICAL FRUIT RICE MOULD

SERVES 8

250 g/8 oz/1 cup + 1 tbsp short-grain or pudding rice, rinsed
900 ml/1½ pints/3¾ cups skimmed milk
1 tbsp caster (superfine) sugar
4 tbsp white rum with coconut or unsweetened pineapple juice
180 ml/6 fl oz/ ¾ cup low-fat natural yogurt
about 425 g/14 oz can pineapple pieces in natural juice, drained and chopped
1 tsp grated lime rind
1 tbsp lime juice
1 sachet/1 envelope powdered gelatine dissolved in 3 tbsp boiling water
lime wedges to decorate
mixed tropical fruits such as passion-fruit, baby pineapple, paw-paw (papaya), mango, carambola (star fruit) to serve

1 Place the rice and milk in a saucepan. Bring to the boil, then simmer gently, uncovered, for 20 minutes until the rice is soft and the milk is absorbed. Stir the mixture occasionally and keep the heat low to prevent sticking. Transfer to a mixing bowl and leave to cool.

2 Stir the sugar, white rum with coconut or pineapple juice, yogurt, pineapple pieces, lime rind and juice into the rice. Fold into the gelatine mixture.

3 Rinse a 1.5 litre/2½ pint/1½ quart non-stick ring mould or ring cake tin (pan) with water and spoon in the rice mixture. Press down well and chill for 2 hours until firm.

4 To serve, loosen the rice from the mould with a small palette knife (spatula) and invert on to a serving plate. Decorate with lime wedges and fill the centre with assorted tropical fruits.

VARIATION

Try serving this dessert with a light sauce made from 300 ml/ ½ pint/1¼ cups tropical fruit or pineapple juice thickened with 2 tsp arrowroot.

COCONUT CREAM MOULDS

SERVES 8

CARAMEL:
125 g/4 oz/ ½ cup granulated sugar
150 ml/ ¼ pint/ ⅔ cup water

CUSTARD:
300 ml/ ½ pint/1¼ cups water
90g/3 oz creamed coconut, chopped
2 eggs
2 egg yolks
1½ tbsp caster sugar
300 ml/ ½ pint/1¼ cups single cream
sliced banana or slivers of fresh pineapple
1-2 tbsp freshly grated or desiccated
(shredded) coconut

1 Have ready 8 small ovenproof dishes about 150 ml/ ¼ pint/ ⅔ cup capacity. To make the caramel, place the sugar and water in a saucepan and heat gently to dissolve the sugar, then boil rapidly, without stirring, until the mixture turns a rich golden brown.

2 Remove at once from the heat and dip the base of the pan into a basin of cold water (this stops it cooking). Quickly but carefully pour the caramel into the ovenproof dishes to coat the bases.

3 To make the custard, place the water in the same saucepan, add the coconut and heat until coconut dissolves, stirring all the time. Place the eggs, egg yolks and caster sugar in a bowl and beat well with a fork. Add the hot coconut milk and stir well to dissolve the sugar. Stir in the cream and strain mixture into a jug.

4 Arrange the dishes in a roasting tin and fill with enough cold water to come halfway up the sides of the dishes. Pour the custard mixture into the caramel-lined dishes, cover with greaseproof paper or foil and cook in the preheated oven at 140ºC/275ºF/Gas Mark 1 for about 40 minutes or until set.

5 Remove the dishes from the roasting tin and leave to cool. Chill overnight in the refrigerator. To serve, run a knife around the edge of each dish and turn out on to a serving plate. Serve with slices of banana or slivers of fresh pineapple sprinkled with freshly grated or desiccated coconut.

RUM & GINGER TRIFLE

SERVES 6

about 24 boudoir biscuits (lady-fingers)
6–8 pieces stem (candied) ginger, chopped
grated rind and juice of 1 orange
2–3 tbsp stem (candied) ginger syrup
(from the jar)
4–6 tbsp rum
250 g/8 oz/1½ cups raspberries, fresh or
frozen

CUSTARD:
450 ml/ ¾ pint/scant 2 cups milk
3 egg yolks
1 egg
few drops of vanilla flavouring (extract)
2 tbsp caster (superfine) sugar
1 tsp cornflour (cornstarch)

TO DECORATE:
300 ml/ ½ pint/1¼ cups whipping cream,
whipped
few pieces stem (candied) or crystallized
ginger, chopped
gold dragées
strips of angelica

1 Break each biscuit into 3 or 4 pieces, divide between 6 individual serving bowls and sprinkle with the chopped ginger and grated orange rind. Combine the orange juice, ginger syrup and rum, and spoon over the biscuits.

2 Arrange the raspberries over the biscuits (lady-fingers), leaving the fruit to thaw, if frozen, when the juices will seep into the biscuits (lady-fingers).

3 To make the custard, heat all but 2 tablespoons of the milk to just below boiling. Blend the remaining milk with the egg yolks, egg, vanilla flavouring (extract), sugar and cornflour (cornstarch). Pour the hot milk on to the egg mixture and return to a heatproof bowl. Stand it over a pan of gently simmering water and cook gently, stirring until the custard thickens sufficiently to coat the back of a spoon. Do not let it boil, or it will curdle.

4 Cool the custard a little then pour it over the fruit. Chill.

5 Pipe the cream over the custard with a large star nozzle (tip). Decorate with the ginger, dragées and angelica.

HOT PUDDINGS

There are plenty of old favourites here to delight the traditional-minded: Steamed Pudding (see page 515), Spotted Dick (see page 519), Apple Pie (see page 527) and three different versions of Bread and Butter Pudding (see pages 518 and 523). The more adventurous can try Cherry Clafoutis (see below) or Crêpes Suzette (see page 517) for a delicious after-dinner treat.

CHERRY CLAFOUTIS

SERVES 4-6

3 eggs
3 tbsp flour
pinch of salt
½ tbsp ground cinnamon
4 tbsp caster sugar, plus extra for
  sprinkling
300 ml/ ½ pint/1¼ cups milk
150 ml/ ¼ pint/ ⅔ cup natural yogurt
2 tbsp dark rum (optional)
750 g/1½ lb black cherries, stalks removed,
  and pitted
15 g/ ½ oz/1 tbsp butter, plus extra for
greasing

1 Grease a shallow, ovenproof dish. Lightly beat the eggs in a bowl. Put the flour, salt and cinnamon in a sieve, sift the dry ingredients over the eggs and beat the mixture until pale and creamy.

2 Pour the milk, yogurt and rum, if using, into a small pan and heat to simmering point. Pour over the egg mixture and beat thoroughly.

3 Place the cherries in the base of the prepared dish and spoon the batter over them. Dot the butter over the top of the pudding.

4 Bake the pudding in the preheated oven at 190ºC/375ºF/Gas Mark 5 for 30 minutes, or until it is well risen and golden brown on top. To test, insert a fine skewer into the centre: it should come out clean. Sprinkle the pudding with caster sugar, and serve hot or warm.

VARIATION

Clafoutis limousin is a traditional French batter pudding (they leave the stones in the cherries). Make in the same way, let cool until just warm – it will sink slightly – then sprinkle with 2-3 tablespoons of Armagnac and a little icing (confectioner's) sugar.

APRICOT BRULÉE

SERVES 6

125 g/4 oz/ ⅔ cup unsulphured apricots
150 ml/ ¼ pint/ ⅔ cup orange juice
4 egg yolks
2 tbsp caster sugar
150 ml/ ¼ pint/ ⅔ cup yogurt
150 ml/ ¼ pint/ ⅔ cup double (heavy)
  cream
1 tsp vanilla flavouring
90 g/3 oz/ ½ cup demerara sugar
caramelized meringues to serve, optional

1 Soak the apricots in the orange juice for at least 1 hour. Pour into a small pan, bring slowly to the boil and simmer for 20 minutes. Purée in a blender.

2 Beat together the egg yolks and sugar until the mixture is light and fluffy. Place the yogurt in a small pan, add the vanilla and bring to the boil over a low heat. Pour the yogurt mixture over the eggs and add the cream, beating all the time, then transfer to the top of a double boiler, or place the bowl over a pan of simmering water. Stir until the custard thickens.

3 Place the apricot mixture in 6 ramekins and carefully pour on the custard. Cool, then leave to chill.

4 Heat the grill (broiler) to high. Sprinkle the demerara sugar evenly over the custard and grill (broil) until the sugar caramelizes. Set aside to cool. To serve the brûlée, crack the hard caramel topping with the back of a tablespoon.

CARAMELIZED MERINGUES:
4 egg whites
90 g/3 oz/6 tbsp caster sugar
60 g/2 oz/4 tbsp granulated sugar
30 g/1 oz/ ¼ cup blanched almonds, toasted

Whisk the egg whites until stiff. Whisk in the caster sugar a little at a time, then whisk until the mixture is glossy and forms peaks. Pour water into a shallow frying pan until 1 cm/ ½ in deep and bring to simmering point. Take scoops of meringue, using 2 tablespoons, and place in the gently simmering water. Poach for 2 minutes, turning them over once: do not allow the water to boil. Remove with a slotted spoon and place on baking parchment. For the caramel, place the granulated sugar in a small, heavy pan over a low heat. Shake the pan to distribute the sugar evenly, then leave it to caramelize, without stirring. Do not leave the pan unattended. Transfer the meringues to a serving dish, pour on the caramel and scatter the almonds on top.

BAKED SEMOLINA PUDDING WITH SPICED PLUMS

SERVES 4

30 g/1 oz/2 tbsp butter or margarine
600 ml/1 pint/2½ cups milk
finely pared rind and juice of 1 orange
60 g/2 oz/⅓ cup semolina
pinch of grated nutmeg
30 g/1 oz/2 tbsp caster (superfine) sugar
1 egg, beaten

TO SERVE:
knob of butter
grated nutmeg

SPICED PLUMS:
250 g/8 oz plums, halved and stoned
150 ml/¼ pint/⅔ cup orange juice
30 g/1 oz/2 tbsp caster (superfine) sugar
½ tsp ground mixed spice

1 Grease a 1 litre/1¾ pint/4 cup ovenproof dish with a little of the butter or margarine. Put the milk, the remaining butter or margarine and the orange rind in a saucepan. Sprinkle in the semolina and heat until boiling, stirring constantly. Simmer gently for 2–3 minutes. Remove from the heat.

2 Add the nutmeg, orange juice and sugar to the semolina mixture, stirring well. Add the egg and stir to mix.

3 Transfer the mixture to the prepared dish and bake in a preheated oven at 190°C/375°F/Gas Mark 5 for about 30 minutes until lightly browned.

4 To make the spiced plums, put the plums, orange juice, sugar and spice into a saucepan and simmer gently for about 10 minutes until just tender. Leave to cool slightly.

5 Top the semolina pudding with a knob of butter and grated nutmeg and serve with the spiced plums.

SPICED STEAMED PUDDING

SERVES 4–6

2 tbsp golden (light corn) syrup
125 g/4 oz/½ cup butter or margarine
125 g/4 oz/generous ½ cup caster
   (superfine) or light soft brown sugar
2 eggs
175 g/6 oz/1½ cups self-raising flour
¾ tsp ground cinnamon or mixed spice
grated rind of 1 orange
1 tbsp orange juice
90 g/3 oz/½ cup sultanas (golden raisins)
   or raisins
45 g/1½ oz/5 tbsp stem (candied) ginger,
   chopped finely
1 dessert (eating) apple, peeled, cored and
   grated coarsely
extra golden (light corn) syrup, warmed,
   to serve

1 Thoroughly grease a 900 ml/1½ pint/ 3¾ cup pudding basin (mold). Put the golden (light corn) syrup into the basin (mold).

2 Cream the butter or margarine and sugar together until very light and fluffy and pale in colour. Beat in the eggs, one at a time, following each with a spoonful of the flour.

3 Sift the remaining flour with the cinnamon or spice and fold into the mixture, followed by the orange rind and juice. Fold in the sultanas (golden raisins) or raisins then the ginger and apple.

4 Turn the mixture into the basin (mold) and level the top. Cover with a piece of pleated greased baking parchment, tucking the edges under the rim of the basin (mold).

5 Cover with a sheet of pleated foil. Tie in place with string, with a piece of string tied over the top for a handle.

6 Put the basin (mold) into a saucepan half filled with boiling water, cover and steam for 1½ hours, adding more boiling water to the pan as necessary during cooking.

7 To serve, remove the foil and baking parchment, turn the pudding on to a warmed serving plate and serve with warmed golden (light corn) syrup.

SCOTCH MIST

••

SERVES 4-6

500 g/1 lb/generous 3 cups raspberries,
  fresh or frozen
3 tbsp Scotch whisky
300 ml/ ½ pint/1¼ cups double (heavy)
  cream
4 tbsp heather honey (if not available, use
  clear honey)
60 g/2 oz/ ⅓ cup oatmeal

1 Reserve 175 g/6 oz/scant 1 cup of
  the raspberries and put the rest into
a bowl with the Scotch whisky. Set aside.

2 Whip the cream until softly stiff. Stir
  in the honey and oatmeal. If the
cream turns soft, whip again until stiff.

3 Spoon a few raspberries into the
  bottom of each serving glass, or
spoon half the raspberries into the bottom
of a large glass bowl. Spoon half the
cream mixture over the raspberries, then
add the remaining raspberries. Spoon the
remaining cream over the top. Chill for at
least 1 hour, preferably overnight.

4 Mash the reserved raspberries with a
  wooden spoon, or blend them in a
blender or food processor. Press them
through a sieve (strainer).

5 When ready to serve, pour a little of
  the sieved (strained) raspberries over
each glass or over the whole bowl.

OATMEAL

Although there are different types of
oatmeal available, they are all made
from the same thing; the only
difference is how much the oats have
been milled. I always use the medium-
cut one that still has some fine, floury
content, as opposed to the slightly
more gritty version with no 'dust'.

MAGIC LEMON PUDDING

••

SERVES 4-6

90 g/3 oz/ ⅓ cup granulated sugar
30 g/1 oz/ ¼ cup plain (all-purpose) flour
2 egg yolks
15 g/ ½ oz/1 tbsp butter
finely grated rind of 1 lemon
4 tbsp lemon juice
250 ml/8 fl oz/1 cup milk
2 egg whites

TO DECORATE:
icing (confectioners') sugar
grated lemon rind

1 Sift the sugar and flour together into
  a bowl. Stir in the egg yolks, butter
and lemon rind and juice. Beat together
thoroughly.

2 Stir in the milk and whisk well.
  Whisk the egg whites until stiff and
fold in well.

3 Spoon the mixture into an attractive
  1 litre/1¾ pint/4 cup ovenproof
serving dish.

4 Put the dish into a roasting tin (pan)
  half-filled with water and bake in a
preheated oven at 180°C/ 350°F/Gas Mark
4 for 35 minutes.

5 Sprinkle with grated lemon rind and
  dust with icing (confectioners')
sugar. Serve immediately from the dish.

WHISKING EGG WHITES

When whisking egg whites, start
slowly, using a figure-of-eight motion,
until the whites are a mass of bubbles,
then speed up gradually. If using a
balloon whisk, you may find it
comfortable to sit the bowl on your left
hip and whisk with the right arm, or
vice versa. Electric whisks are a lot
quicker but they do not achieve such a
large volume from the egg whites as a
traditional hand whisk would. Make
sure the bowl is completely dry'.

CRÊPES SUZETTE

SERVES 4-6

125 g/4 oz/1 cup plain (all-purpose) flour
1 egg
1 egg yolk
300 ml/½ pint/1¼ cups milk
60 g/2 oz/¼ cup butter, melted
grated rind of 1 orange
250 g/8 oz/1 cup granulated sugar
150 ml/¼ pint/⅔ cup water
pared rind of 1 orange
melted butter, for frying
juice of 1 orange
250 ml/8 fl oz/1 cup orange-flavoured
  liqueur
1 orange, peeled and segmented

1 Sift the flour into a bowl and make a well in the centre. Add the egg, egg yolk, milk and butter, and draw in the flour. Whisk to a smooth batter. Stir in the orange rind. Leave the pancake batter to rest for 30 minutes.

2 Put the sugar and water into a saucepan and bring to a gentle boil. Add the orange rind and cook gently until the syrup coats the back of a spoon, about 5 minutes. Set aside.

3 Meanwhile, brush a frying pan (skillet) or pancake pan with a little melted butter and place over a medium heat. Tilt the pan (skillet) to one side and pour in about 50 ml/2 fl oz/¼ cup of the batter. Tilt the pan in the opposite direction immediately, so that the whole base is covered in batter.

4 After about 1 minute, or when the pancake is dry on top, turn it and cook the other side. Make 8–12 pancakes and keep warm in a low oven. Place 2 pancakes on each warmed serving plate, either flat or folded.

5 Reheat the syrup and stir in the orange juice, 150 ml/¼ pint/⅔ cup of the liqueur and the segmented orange. Pour a little over each serving plate.

6 Heat the remaining liqueur gently in a small pouring pan. It may ignite itself, but if it does not, set a lighted match to it and pour over the pancakes immediately. This is most effective if done at the serving table. You can warm the liqueur gently in the kitchen, take it to the table and ignite it. Blow out the flames immediately.

BREAD & BUTTER PUDDING

SERVES 4-6

about 60 g/2 oz/ ¼ cup butter, softened
4–5 slices white or brown bread
4 tbsp chunky orange marmalade
grated rind of 1 lemon
90–125 g/3–4 oz/½–¾ cup raisins or
*   sultanas (golden raisins)*
45 g/1½ oz/ ¼ cup chopped mixed
*   (candied) peel*
1 tsp ground cinnamon or mixed spice
1 cooking apple, peeled, cored and grated
*   coarsely*
90 g/3 oz/scant ½ cup demerara (golden
*   crystal) or light soft brown sugar*
3 eggs
500 ml/16 fl oz/2 cups milk
2 tbsp demerara (brown crystal) sugar

1 Use the butter to grease an ovenproof dish and to spread on the slices of bread, then spread the bread with the marmalade.

2 Place a layer of bread in the base of the dish and sprinkle with the lemon rind, half the raisins or sultanas (golden raisins), half the peel, half the spice, all of the apple and half the sugar.

3 Add another layer of bread, cutting so it fits the dish.

4 Sprinkle over most of the remaining raisins or sultanas (golden raisins) and the remaining peel, spice and sugar, sprinkling it evenly over the bread. Top with a final layer of bread, again cutting to fit the dish.

5 Beat together the eggs and milk and then strain over the bread in the dish. If time allows, leave to stand for 20–30 minutes.

6 Sprinkle with·the demerara (brown crystal) sugar and the remaining rasins or sultanas (golden raisins) and cook in a preheated oven at 200°C/400°F/Gas Mark 6 for 50–60 minutes until risen and golden brown. Serve hot or cold.

ITALIAN BREAD & BUTTER PUDDING

SERVES 4-6

90 g/3 oz/ ⅓ cup unsalted butter, softened
200 g/7 oz/7 slices white bread
90 g/3 oz/ ½ cup raisins
2 tbsp almond liqueur, such as Amaretto
125 g/4 oz/1 cup coarsely crushed
*   ratafias, macaroons, or amaretti*
*   biscuits (cookies)*
30 g/1 oz/3 tbsp cut mixed (candied) peel
600 ml/1 pint/2½ cups milk
¼ tsp vanilla flavouring (extract)
90 g/3 oz/ ⅓ cup caster (superfine) sugar
2 eggs, lightly beaten
45 g/1½ oz/ ⅓ cup soft light brown sugar

1 Grease a 25 x 20 cm/10 x 8 inch baking dish with some of the butter.

2 Spread the remaining butter on to the bread.

3 Combine the raisins, liqueur and 2 tablespoons of water in a small saucepan and bring to a gentle boil, then set aside for 30 minutes.

4 Leave the crusts on the bread slices and cut each slice diagonally into 4. Use half of the bread to make a layer in the bottom of the dish, overlapping in rows.

5 Sprinkle with half of the ratafias, half the soaked raisins and half the mixed (candied) peel. Repeat with the remaining half of the ingredients.

6 Heat the milk through gently with the vanilla flavouring (extract), until the surface quivers and it is nearly boiling. Remove from the heat and stir in the caster (superfine) sugar and eggs. Spoon the milk mixture over the whole bread dish. Sprinkle over the brown sugar.

7 Bake in a preheated oven at 180°C/350°F/Gas Mark 4 for 30 minutes. Serve immediately, piping hot from the dish.

NEW AGE SPOTTED DICK

SERVES 6–8

140 g/4½ oz/¾ cup raisins
140 ml/4½ fl oz/generous ½ cup corn oil,
plus a little for brushing
140 g/4½ oz/generous ½ cup caster
(superfine) sugar
30 g/1 oz/ ¼ cup ground almonds
2 eggs, lightly beaten
175 g/6 oz/1½ cups self-raising flour

SAUCE:
60 g/2 oz/ ½ cup chopped walnuts
60 g/2 oz/ ½ cup ground almonds
300 ml/ ½ pint/1¼ cups milk (semi-
skimmed may be used)
4 tbsp granulated sugar

1   Put the raisins in a saucepan with
    120 ml/4 fl oz/ ½ cup water. Bring to
the boil, then remove from the heat.
Leave to steep for 10 minutes, then drain.

2   Whisk together the oil, sugar and
    ground almonds until thick and
syrupy; this will need about 8 minutes of
beating (on medium speed if using an
electric whisk).

3   Add the eggs, one at a time, beating
    well after each addition. Combine
the flour and raisins. Stir into the mixture.

4   Brush a 1 litre/1¾ pint/4 cup
    pudding basin with oil, or line with
baking parchment.

5   Put all the sauce ingredients into a
    saucepan. Bring to the boil, stir and
simmer for 10 minutes.

6   Transfer the sponge mixture to the
    greased basin and pour on the hot
sauce. Place on a baking (cookie) sheet.

7   Bake in a preheated oven at
    170°C/340°F/Gas Mark 3½ for about
1 hour. Lay a piece of baking parchment
across the top if it starts to brown too fast.

8   Leave to cool for 2–3 minutes in the
    basin before turning out on to a
serving plate.

WARM CURRANTS IN CASSIS

SERVES 4

375 g/12 oz blackcurrants
250 g/8 oz redcurrants
4 tbsp caster (superfine) sugar
grated rind and juice of 1 orange
2 tsp arrowroot
2 tbsp Crème de cassis
whipped cream to serve

1   Using a fork strip the currants from
    their stalks and place in a saucepan.

2   Add the sugar and orange rind and
    juice and heat gently until the sugar
has dissolved. Bring to the boil and
simmer gently for 5 minutes.

3   Strain the currants and place in a
    bowl then return the juice to the
pan. Blend the arrowroot with a little
water and mix into the juice then boil
until thickened. Leave to cool slightly then
stir in the cassis.

4   Serve in individual dishes with
    whipped cream

TIP

Be sure not to overcook the currants
otherwise they will become mushy.

VARIATION

If you don't have any Crème de cassis
you could use port or an orange
flavoured liqueur.

ALMOND PANCAKES WITH FRUIT COULIS

SERVES 4–8

30 g/1 oz/¼ cup flaked (slivered) almonds
125 g/4 oz/1 cup plain (all-purpose) flour
1 egg
1 egg yolk
300 ml/½ pint/1¼ cups milk
30 g/1 oz/2 tbsp butter, melted
4 tbsp ground almonds, lightly toasted
¼ tsp almond flavouring (extract)
oil for brushing
250 g/8 oz/1½ cups frozen mixed summer
  fruits, such as redcurrants,
  blackcurrants and raspberries
2 tbsp icing (confectioners') sugar
400 g/14 oz can of guavas in syrup, or
  other fruit of your choice

1 Spread out the flaked (slivered) almonds on a baking sheet and toast them in a preheated oven at 180°C/350°F/ Gas Mark 4 for 3 minutes.

2 Sift the flour into a bowl and make a well in the centre. Add the egg, egg yolk, milk, melted butter, ground almonds and almond flavouring (extract). Whisk well to combine. Leave to rest for 30 minutes.

3 Brush a frying pan (skillet) or pancake pan with oil and place over a medium heat. Tilt the pan (skillet) in one direction and pour in 50 ml/2 fl oz/ ¼ cup of the batter. Tilt in the opposite direction immediately, so that the batter covers the whole base. After 1–2 minutes, or when the top of the pancake starts to dry out, toss it and cook on the other side for about 1 minute. Repeat with the remaining batter.

4 Transfer the pancakes to a baking (cookie) sheet lined with baking parchment, cover and keep warm in a preheated oven at 150°C/300°F/Gas Mark 3.

5 Blend the fruit in a blender or food processor, or mash it well by hand, with 2 tablespoons of water. Press through a sieve (strainer) and stir in the icing (confectioners') sugar. Warm the fruit coulis through over a medium heat.

6 Warm the guavas through, in their own syrup, over a medium heat.

7 Fold each pancake twice and place 1 or 2 on each serving plate. Lift the top layer of each pancake and spoon in the warmed guavas and decorate with the toasted almonds. Pour a little fruit coulis over the top.

BANANA & MARSHMALLOW MELTS WITH BUTTERSCOTCH SAUCE

SERVES 4

4 wooden skewers
4 bananas
4 tbsp lemon juice
250 g/8 oz pkt marshmallows

SAUCE:
125 g/4 oz/ ½ cup butter
125 g/4 oz/ ⅔ cup light muscovado sugar
125 g/4 oz/ ⅓ cup golden (light corn) syrup
4 tbsp hot water

1 Soak the wooden skewers in hand-hot water for 30 minutes.

2 Slice the bananas into large chunks and dip them into the lemon juice to prevent them from going brown.

3 Thread the marshmallows and pieces of banana alternately on to kebab sticks or bamboo skewers, placing 2 marshmallows and 1 piece of banana on to each one.

4 To make the sauce, melt the butter, sugar and syrup together in a small saucepan. Add the hot water, stirring until blended and smooth. Do not boil or else the mixture will become toffee-like. Keep the sauce warm, stirring from time to time.

5 Sear the kebabs over a flame for 30–40 seconds, turning constantly, so that the marshmallows just begin to brown and melt.

6 Serve the kebabs with some of the butterscotch sauce spooned over.

SERVING SUGGESTIONS

The warm butterscotch sauce tastes wonderful with vanilla ice cream. Make double the quantity of sauce if you plan to serve ice cream at the barbecue.

Prepare the kebabs just before they are cooked to prevent the bananas from turning brown. The sauce can be prepared in advance, though.

CHAR-COOKED PINEAPPLE WITH GINGER & BROWN SUGAR BUTTER

SERVES 4

1 fresh pineapple

BUTTER:
125 g/4 oz/ ½ cup butter
90 g/3 oz/ ½ cup light muscovado sugar
1 tsp finely grated fresh root ginger

TOPPING:
250 g/8 oz/1 cup natural fromage frais
½ tsp ground cinnamon
1 tbsp light muscovado sugar

1 Prepare the fresh pineapple by cutting off the spiky top. Peel the pineapple with a sharp knife and cut into thick slices.

2 To make the ginger-flavoured butter, put the butter, sugar and ginger into a small saucepan and heat gently until melted. Transfer to a heatproof bowl and keep warm, ready for basting the fruit.

3 To prepare the topping, mix together the fromage frais, cinnamon and sugar. Cover and chill until ready to serve.

4 Grill the pineapple slices for about 2 minutes on each side, brushing them with the ginger butter.

5 Serve the pineapple with a little extra ginger butter sauce poured over. Top with a spoonful of the spiced fromage frais.

VARIATIONS

If you prefer, substitute ½ teaspoon ground ginger for the grated fresh root ginger.

Light muscovado sugar gives the best flavour, but you can use ordinary soft brown sugar instead.

LIME FILO PARCELS

SERVES 4–8

3 lemons, rinsed
3 limes, rinsed
1 tbsp finely chopped stem (candied)
  ginger
120 ml/4 fl oz/ ½ cup water
90 g/3 oz/ ⅛ cup granulated sugar
1 tsp cornflour (cornstarch)
3 sheets filo pastry
90 g/3 oz/ ¾ cup pineapple, diced finely
90 g/3 oz/ ¾ cup mango, diced finely
1 tbsp cornflour (cornstarch), mixed with
  enough cold water to make a paste
oil for deep frying (not olive oil)
desiccated (shredded) coconut, lightly
  toasted

1 First, make the syrup. Finely grate the rind and extract the juice from the lemons and limes, and put into a saucepan with the ginger, water and sugar. Bring to the boil and simmer for 5 minutes.

2 Put the 1 teaspoon of cornflour (cornstarch) into a small bowl and add a little water to make a paste. Stir in about 50 ml/2 fl oz/ ¼ cup of the syrup, combine well and return to the saucepan. Bring to the boil, stirring. Remove from the heat and cover.

3 Spread out 1 sheet of the filo pastry on a work surface (counter), keeping the other 2 covered. Cut into 10 cm/4 inch squares.

4 Put a teaspoonful of the fruit in the middle of each square and roll up into a sausage shape, tucking the ends in. Seal the ends with the cornflour (cornstarch) paste.

5 Pour the oil to a depth of 6 cm/ 2½ inches into a deep frying pan (skillet) or wok and heat until it is 180°–190°C/350°–375°F or a cube of bread browns in 30 seconds. Have ready a plate or baking sheet lined with paper towels. Deep-fry the parcels until golden brown, 2–3 minutes, remove with a perforated spoon and drain on the paper towels. Keep warm while you fry the remaining parcels.

6 Put the desiccated (shredded) coconut on a plate and roll each parcel in it.

7 To serve, put 2 or 3 parcels on each plate, surrounded by the lemon and lime syrup.

CHOCOLATE BREAD PUDDING

SERVES 4

6 thick slices white bread, crusts removed
450 ml/ ¾ pint/2 cups milk
175 g/6 oz can evaporated milk
2 tbsp unsweetened cocoa powder
2 eggs
30 g/1 oz/2 tbsp dark muscovado sugar
1 tsp vanilla flavouring (extract)
icing (confectioners') sugar for dusting

HOT FUDGE SAUCE:
60 g/2 oz/2 squares dark chocolate,
  broken into pieces
1 tbsp unsweetened cocoa powder
2 tbsp golden (light corn) syrup
60 g/2 oz/ ¼ cup butter or margarine
30 g/1 oz/2 tbsp dark muscovado sugar
150 ml/ ¼ pint/⅔ cup milk
1 tbsp cornflour (cornstarch)

1 Grease a shallow ovenproof dish. Cut the bread into squares and layer them in the dish.

2 Heat the milk, evaporated milk and cocoa powder until lukewarm, stirring occasionally.

3 Whisk together the eggs, sugar and vanilla flavouring (extract). Add the warm milk mixture and beat well.

4 Pour into the baking dish, making sure that all the bread is covered. Cover the dish with clingfilm (plastic wrap) and chill for 1–2 hours.

5 Bake the pudding in a preheated oven at 180°C/350°F/Gas Mark 4 for about 35–40 minutes until set. Allow to stand for 5 minutes.

6 To make the sauce, put the chocolate, cocoa powder, syrup, butter or margarine, sugar, milk and cornflour (cornstarch) into a saucepan. Heat gently, stirring until smooth.

7 Dust the pudding with icing (confectioners') sugar and serve with the hot fudge sauce.

QUICK SYRUP SPONGE

SERVES 4

125 g/4 oz/ ½ cup butter or margarine
4 tbsp golden (light corn) syrup
90 g/3 oz/ ⅓ cup caster (superfine) sugar
2 eggs
125 g/4 oz/1 cup self-raising flour
1 tsp baking powder
about 2 tbsp warm water
custard to serve

1 Grease a 1.5 litre/2½ pint/1½ quart pudding basin (mold) with a small amount of the butter or margarine. Spoon the syrup into the basin (mold).

2 Cream the remaining butter or margarine with the sugar until light and fluffy. Gradually add the eggs, beating well between each addition.

3 Sift the flour and baking powder together, then fold into the creamed mixture using a large metal spoon. Add enough water to give a soft, dropping consistency. Spoon into the pudding basin (mold) and level the surface.

4 Cover with microwave-safe film, leaving a small space to allow air to escape. Microwave on Full Power for 4 minutes, then remove from the microwave and allow the pudding to stand for 5 minutes.

5 Turn the pudding out onto a serving plate. Serve with custard.

STEAMING

If you don't have a microwave, this pudding can be steamed. Cover the pudding with a piece of pleated baking parchment then a piece of pleated foil, secure with string and place in a large saucepan. Add enough boiling water to come halfway up the sides of the basin (mold), cover and steam for 1½ hours, topping up with more boiling water as necessary.

PANCAKES WITH APPLES & BUTTER-SCOTCH SAUCE

••

SERVES 4

125 g/4 oz/1 cup plain (all-purpose) flour
1 tsp finely grated lemon rind
1 egg
300 ml/ ½ pint/1¼ cups milk
1–2 tbsp vegetable oil
salt
pared lemon rind to garnish

FILLING:
250 g/8 oz cooking apples, peeled, cored
  and sliced
30 g/1 oz/2 tbsp sultanas (golden raisins)

SAUCE:
90 g/3 oz/⅓ cup butter
3 tbsp golden (light corn) syrup
90 g/3 oz/½ cup light muscovado sugar
1 tbsp rum or brandy (optional)
1 tbsp lemon juice

1   Sift the flour and salt into a large
    mixing bowl. Add the lemon rind,
egg and milk and whisk together to make
a smooth batter.

2   Heat a few drops of oil in a heavy-
    based frying pan (skillet). Make
8 thin pancakes, using a few drops of oil
for each one. Stack the cooked pancakes,
layering them with paper towels.

3   To make the filling, cook the apples
    with the sultanas (golden raisins) in
a little water until soft. Divide the mixture
between the pancakes and roll up or fold
into triangles. Place them in a buttered
ovenproof dish and bake in a preheated
oven at 160°C/325°F/Gas Mark 3 for
15 minutes to warm through.

4   To make the sauce, melt the butter,
    syrup and sugar together in a
saucepan, stirring well. Add the rum or
brandy, if using, and the lemon juice.
Do not allow the mixture to boil.

5   Serve the pancakes on warm plates,
    with a little sauce poured over and
garnished with lemon rind.

APRICOT & BANANA QUEEN OF PUDDINGS

••

SERVES 4

125 g/4 oz/2 cups fresh white
  breadcrumbs
600 ml/1 pint/2½ cups milk
3 eggs
½ tsp vanilla flavouring (extract)
60 g/2 oz/ ¼ cup caster (superfine) sugar
2 bananas
1 tbsp lemon juice
3 tbsp apricot jam

1   Sprinkle the breadcrumbs into a
    1 litre/1¾ pint/4 cup ovenproof dish.
Heat the milk until lukewarm, then pour
it over the breadcrumbs.

2   Separate 2 of the eggs and beat the
    yolks with the remaining whole egg.
Add to the baking dish with the vanilla
flavouring (extract) and half the sugar,
stirring well to mix. Allow to stand for
10 minutes.

3   Bake in a preheated oven at
    180°C/350°F/Gas Mark 4 for 40
minutes until set. Remove from the oven.

4   Slice the bananas and sprinkle with
    the lemon juice. Spoon the apricot
jam on to the pudding and spread out to
cover the surface. Arrange the bananas on
top of the apricot jam.

5   Whisk the egg whites until stiff, then
    add the remaining sugar. Whisk until
very stiff and glossy.

6   Pile on top of the pudding, return to
    the oven and cook for a further
10–15 minutes until set and golden
brown. Serve immediately.

+---+
| MERINGUE |
| |
| The meringue will have a soft, |
| marshmallow-like texture, unlike a hard |
| meringue which is cooked slowly for |
| 2–3 hours until dry. |
| Always use a grease-free bowl and |
| whisk for beating egg-whites, |
| otherwise they will not whip properly. |
+---+

TARTE TATIN

SERVES 4-6

PASTRY:
125 g/4 oz/ ½ cup unsalted butter, softened
90 g/3 oz/ ⅓ cup caster (superfine) sugar
1 egg, lightly beaten
250 g/8 oz/2 cups plain (all-purpose) flour
salt

PEAR TOPPING:
30 g/1 oz/2 tbsp butter
60 g/2 oz/ ⅓ cup light brown sugar
1 tbsp lemon juice
1 kg/2 lb dessert (eating) pears

1 First make the pastry. Beat the butter and caster (superfine) sugar together until light and fluffy.

2 Add the egg and beat well. Add the flour gradually with a pinch of salt and mix to a smooth dough. Knead lightly for 5 minutes. Wrap and chill for at least 2 hours.

3 Line the base of a 23 cm/9 inch cake tin (pan) with baking parchment. Spread half the butter and brown sugar over the bottom.

4 Add the lemon juice to a large bowl of water. Peel, core and quarter the pears, putting them into the acidulated water as you go. When all the pears are prepared, drain off the water thoroughly, and pat the fruit dry with paper towels. Pack them tightly into the bottom of the cake tin (pan).

5 Sprinkle with the remaining brown sugar and butter. Bake in a preheated oven at 220°C/425°F/Gas Mark 7 for 20 minutes, or until a light caramel forms on top.

6 When the pears are cooked, roll out the chilled dough into a 25 cm/ 10 inch circle on a floured work surface (counter). Work quickly at this stage, so that the butter in the dough does not melt. Use plenty of flour on both the work surface (counter) and the rolling pin. Do not worry about making the circle very neat as the tart is inverted, so any wrinkles will not show. Place the dough over the pears.

7 Bake in a preheated oven at 200°C/400°F/Gas Mark 6 for about 20 minutes, or until well browned.

8 Remove from the oven and invert on a warmed serving plate. Serve at once with clotted cream or ice cream.

RHUBARB & ORANGE CRUMBLE

SERVES 4-6

500 g/1 lb rhubarb
500 g/1 lb cooking apples
grated rind and juice of 1 orange
½–1 tsp ground cinnamon
about 90 g/3 oz/scant ½ cup light soft
 brown sugar

CRUMBLE:
250 g/8 oz/2 cups plain (all-purpose) flour
125 g/4 oz/ ½ cup butter or margarine
125 g/4 oz/generous ½ cup light soft brown
 or demerara (brown crystal) sugar
45–60 g/1½–2 oz/ ⅓–½ cup toasted
 chopped hazelnuts
2 tbsp demerara sugar (optional)

1 Cut the rhubarb into 2.5 cm/1 inch
 lengths and place in a large saucepan.

2 Peel, core and slice the apples and
 add to the rhubarb with the grated
orange rind and juice. Bring to the boil
and simmer for 2–3 minutes until the fruit
begins to soften.

3 Add the cinnamon and sugar to taste
 and turn the mixture into an ovenproof dish, so it is not more than two-
thirds full.

4 Sift the flour into a bowl and rub in
 the butter or margarine until the
mixture resembles fine breadcrumbs (this
can be done by hand or in a food
processor). Stir in the sugar followed by
the nuts.

5 Spoon the crumble mixture evenly
 over the fruit in the dish and level
the top. Sprinkle with demerara (brown
crystal) sugar, if liked. Cook in a
preheated oven at 200°C/ 400°F/Gas Mark
6 for 30–40 minutes until the topping is
browned. Serve hot or cold.

VARIATIONS

Other flavourings, such as 60 g/2 oz
chopped stem (candied) ginger, can be
added to the fruit. Any fruit such as
apple, blackberry, apricot, raspberry,
cherry, blackcurrant or gooseberry, can
be topped with crumble.

GRANNY BOB'S CHOCOLATE PUDDING

SERVES 4-6

60 g/2 oz/ ¼ cup butter, softened
125 g/4 oz/ ½ cup caster (superfine) sugar
60 g/2 oz/2 squares dark chocolate,
 broken into pieces
2 eggs, lightly beaten
125 g/4 oz/1 cup self-raising flour

SAUCE:
300 ml/ ½ pint/1¼ cups milk
60 g/2 oz/ ¼ cup butter
60 g/2 oz/2 squares dark chocolate,
 broken into pieces
3 tbsp granulated sugar
2 tbsp golden (light corn) syrup

1 Grease a 1.1 litre/2 pint/4½ cup
 pudding basin. In a separate bowl,
beat the butter and sugar together until
pale and fluffy.

2 Meanwhile, melt the chocolate in a
 bowl set over a pan of barely
simmering water. This should take about
10 minutes. Stir into the butter mixture.

3 Beat in the eggs, one at a time,
 beating well after each addition.

4 Sift the flour into the bowl and fold
 in thoroughly.

5 Put all the sauce ingredients into a
 saucepan and heat through gently,
without boiling, for about 10 minutes,
until the chocolate has melted. Whisk well
to combine.

6 Pour the sponge mixture into the
 greased pudding basin and pour the
sauce over the top.

7 Bake in a preheated oven at 190°C/
 375°F/Gas Mark 5 for about 40
minutes, and serve piping hot from the
bowl, or turned out on to a serving dish.

MELTING CHOCOLATE

Chocolate must be melted slowly in
order to prevent it from 'seizing',
which results in the chocolate being
very granular and unworkable.

TRADITIONAL APPLE PIE

SERVES 4-6

*750 g–1 kg/1½–2 lb cooking apples, peeled,
cored and sliced*
*about 125 g/4 oz/generous ½ cup brown
or white sugar, plus extra for sprinkling*
*½–1 tsp ground cinnamon, mixed spice or
ginger*
1–2 tbsp water

SHORTCRUST PASTRY (PIE DOUGH):
*350 g/12 oz/3 cups plain (all-purpose)
flour*
good pinch of salt
90 g/3 oz/⅓ cup butter or margarine
*90 g/3 oz/⅓ cup lard or white vegetable
fat (shortening)*
about 6 tbsp cold water
beaten egg or top of the milk for glazing

1 To make the pastry (pie dough), see
Cornish Pasties (page 479). If time
allows, wrap in foil or clingfilm (plastic
wrap) and chill for 30 minutes.

2 Roll out almost two-thirds of the
pastry (pie dough) thinly and use to
line a 20–23 cm/8–9 inch deep pie plate
or shallow pie tin (pan).

3 Mix the apples with the sugar and
spice and pack into the pastry case
(pie shell); the filling can come up above
the rim. Add the water if liked, particularly
if the apples are a dry variety.

4 Roll out the remaining pastry (pie
dough) to form a lid (top). Dampen
the edges of the pie rim with water and
position the lid (top), pressing the edges
firmly together. Trim and crimp the edges.

5 Use the trimmings to cut out leaves
or other shapes to decorate the top
of the pie; dampen and attach. Glaze the
top of the pie with beaten egg or milk,
make 1–2 slits in the top and put the pie
on a baking sheet (cookie sheet).

6 Bake in a preheated oven at
220°C/425°F/Gas Mark 7 for
20 minutes then reduce the temperature
to 180°C/350°F/Gas Mark 4 and cook for
about 30 minutes until the pastry is a light
golden brown. Serve hot or cold,
sprinkled with sugar.

CINNAMON PEARS WITH MAPLE & RICOTTA CREAM

SERVES 4

1 lemon
4 firm ripe pears
*300 ml/ ½ pint/1¼ cups dry cider or
unsweetened apple juice*
1 cinnamon stick, broken in half
mint leaves to decorate

MAPLE RICOTTA CREAM:
*125 g/4 oz/ ½ cup medium-fat Ricotta
cheese*
*125 g/4 oz/ ½ cup low-fat natural fromage
frais*
½ tsp ground cinnamon
½ tsp grated lemon rind
1 tbsp maple syrup
lemon rind to decorate

1 Using a vegetable peeler, remove the
rind from the lemon and place in a
non-stick frying pan (skillet). Squeeze the
lemon and pour into a shallow bowl.

2 Peel the pears, and halve and core
them. Toss them in the lemon juice
to prevent discolouration. Place in the
frying pan (skillet) and pour over the
remaining lemon juice.

3 Add the cider or apple juice and
cinnamon stick halves. Gently bring
to the boil, lower the heat so the liquid
simmers and cook for 10 minutes.
Remove the pears using a perforated
spoon; reserve the cooking juice. Put the
pears in a warm heatproof serving dish,
cover with foil and keep warm.

4 Return the pan to the heat, bring
to the boil, then simmer for 8–10
minutes until reduced by half. Spoon
over the pears.

5 To make the maple Ricotta cream,
mix together all the ingredients.
Decorate with lemon rind and serve with
the pears.

ICE-CREAMS

Home-made ice-cream is a very special treat, and not nearly as difficult as you might imagine. You do need to allow enough time for the various stages of beating and freezing, and it is probably best to make it the day before. Ice-cream makers are now available, which speed up the process considerably, and some of these recipes, such as the Chocolate Chip Ice-Cream (see below), could be adapted to a machine: always follow the manufacturer's instructions.

CHOCOLATE CHIP ICE-CREAM

SERVES 6

300 ml/ ½ pint/1¼ cups milk
1 vanilla pod
2 eggs
2 egg yolks
60 g/2 oz/ ¼ cup caster sugar
300 ml/ ½ pint/1¼ cups natural yogurt
125 g/4 oz chocolate chip cookies, broken into small pieces

1 Pour the milk into a small pan, add the vanilla pod and bring slowly to the boil. Remove from the heat, cover the pan and leave to cool.

2 Beat the eggs and egg yolks in a double boiler, or in a bowl over a pan of simmering water. Add the sugar and continue beating until the mixture is pale and creamy.

3 Reheat the milk to simmering point and strain it over the egg mixture. Stir continuously until the custard is thick enough to coat the back of a spoon. Remove the custard from the heat and stand the pan or bowl in cold water to prevent any further cooking. Wash and dry the vanilla pod for future use. (See right for advice on using and storing vanilla pods.)

4 Stir the yogurt into the cooled custard and beat until it is well blended. When the mixture is thoroughly cold, stir in the broken cookies.

5 Transfer the mixture to a chilled metal cake tin or polythene container, cover and freeze for 4 hours. Remove from the freezer every hour, transfer to a chilled bowl and beat vigorously to prevent ice crystals forming. Alternatively, use an ice-cream maker, following the manufacturer's instructions.

6 To serve the ice-cream, transfer it to the main part of the refrigerator for 1 hour. Serve in scoops.

VANILLA PODS

Vanilla pods can be used to flavour any hot liquid. For a stronger flavour, split the pod lengthwise with a sharp knife before infusing it in the hot liquid for 20-30 minutes. For a very strong flavour, scrape the seeds out of the pod and add to the liquid when infusing. Rinse and dry the pod after use. It can be stored in a jar of sugar, to which it will impart its flavour.

PASHKA

· ·

SERVES 8

900 ml/1½ pints/3½ cups natural yogurt
2 eggs
125 g/4 oz/ ½ cup golden caster sugar
150 g/5 oz/ ⅔ cup unsalted butter, softened
150 ml/ ¼ pint/ ⅔ cup double (heavy) cream
60 g/2 oz/ ⅓ cup candied orange peel,
  chopped
60 g/2 oz/ ⅓ cup dried apricots, chopped
90 g/3 oz/ ½ cup seedless raisins
90 g/3oz/ ¼ cup blanched almonds,
  chopped
1 tsp orange-flower water

TO DECORATE:
A selection of candied stalks and fruits,
  such as angelica, pineapple, greengages,
  pears and glacé cherries

1 Begin by making the yogurt cheese.
  Tip the yogurt into a colander lined
with muslin or cheesecloth. Draw up the
ends, tie firmly and hang up the bag to
drain overnight.

2 Turn the drained yogurt cheese into
  a large bowl. Beat together the eggs
and sugar until they are light and fluffy,
then gradually beat the mixture into the
yogurt cheese. Beat in the butter, then stir
in the double (heavy) cream.

3 Stir the candied peel, apricots, raisins
  and almonds into the cheese
mixture, then sprinkle on the orange-
flower water and stir it in.

4 Thoroughly wash and dry a flower
  pot and line it with 2 layers of
muslin or cheesecloth. Spoon the mixture
into the pot and fold over the ends of the
cloth to enclose it. Stand the pot in a dish
and place a small plate on top so that it
fits just inside the rim. Place a heavy
weight or some food cans on top and
place the pot in the refrigerator for at
least 12 hours.

5 To turn out the dessert, unfold the
  cheesecloth, place a serving dish
over the top of the container and invert it.
When the dessert has been released,
carefully ease away the cloth.

6 Decorate the top and sides of the
  dessert with slices of candied fruits
arranged in a pattern. The bright green
angelica can be used to represent leaves
or stalks. Serve the dessert chilled, cut
into wedge-shaped slices.

COUPE AU CHOCOLAT

•••

EACH RECIPE SERVES 4

COUPE BELLE HELENE:
250 g/8 oz/1 cup granulated sugar
250 ml/8 fl oz/1 cup water
3 pears, peeled, quartered and cored
125 g/4 oz/4 squares dark chocolate
chocolate ice cream
whipped double (heavy) cream (optional)

1 Put the sugar and water into a
saucepan and bring to the boil.
Simmer for 5 minutes and add the pears.
Simmer gently for 10 minutes, or until the
pears are tender. Very ripe pears will not
take as long. Set the pears aside and drain
off half of the syrup.

2 Break up the chocolate and add it to
the syrup in the saucepan. Stir until
smooth, about 3–4 minutes.

3 To serve, put 3 scoops of ice cream
into each serving dish or coupe, and
spoon over 3 pear quarters. Pour a little
chocolate syrup over the whole and pipe
some cream on top, if liked.

COUPE AUX FRAMBOISES:
250 g/8 oz can raspberries in syrup or
*   250 g/8 oz/1½ cups raspberries, fresh or*
*   frozen*
about 3 tbsp icing (confectioners') sugar
chocolate ice cream
whipped double (heavy) cream (optional)
ice cream wafers

1 If you are using canned raspberries,
purée them in a blender or food
processor, or mash them well with a
wooden spoon.

2 If using fresh raspberries, purée
them in a blender or food processor,
or mash them well with a wooden spoon,
and press through a sieve (strainer). Sift in
icing (confectioners') sugar to taste.

3 To serve, put 3 scoops of ice cream
in each chilled serving dish or
coupe, and pour the raspberry sauce over
the top. Pipe whipped cream on the top if
liked and serve with wafers.

MANGO ICE-CREAM

•••

SERVES 4-6

150 ml/ ¼ pint/ ⅔ cup single cream
2 egg yolks
½ tsp cornflour (cornstarch)
1 tsp water
2 x 439 g/14 oz cans mango slices in
*   syrup, drained*
1 tbsp lime or lemon juice
150 ml/ ¼ pint/ ⅔ cup double (heavy) cream
mint sprigs, to decorate

1 Heat the single cream in a saucepan
until hot (but do not allow it to
boil). Place the egg yolks in a bowl with
the cornflour (cornstarch) and water and
mix together until smooth. Pour the hot
cream on to the egg yolk mixture, stirring
all the time.

2 Return the mixture to the pan and
place over a very low heat, whisking
or stirring all the time until the mixture
thickens and coats the back of a wooden
spoon. (Do not try and hurry this process
or the mixture will overcook and spoil.)
Pour into a bowl.

3 Purée the drained mango slices in
a blender or food processor until
smooth. Mix with the custard and stir in
the lime juice. Whip the double (heavy)
cream until softly peaking and fold into
the mango mixture until thoroughly
combined.

4 Transfer the mixture to a loaf tin or
shallow freezerproof container.
Cover and freeze for 2-3 hours or until
half-frozen and still mushy in the centre.
Turn the mixture into a bowl and mash
well with a fork until smooth. Return to
the container, cover and freeze until firm.

5 Transfer the container of ice cream
to the main compartment of the
refrigerator for about 30 minutes before
serving to allow it to soften slightly.
Scoop or spoon the ice cream into serving
dishes and decorate with mint sprigs.

ALTERNATIVE

Use the drained mango syrup for
adding to fruit salads or drinks.

COCONUT ICE-CREAM

•••

SERVES 6

150 g/5 oz/ ⅔ cup granulated sugar
300 ml/ ½ pint/1¼ cups water
2 x 400 ml/14 fl oz cans coconut milk
300 ml/ ½ pint/1¼ cups double (heavy)
   cream
2 tbsp desiccated (shredded) coconut
sprigs of mint or rose petals, to decorate

1 Place the sugar and water in a
   saucepan and heat gently, stirring
occasionally until the sugar dissolves.
Boil gently for 10 minutes without stirring,
then remove from the heat and allow to
cool slightly.

2 Mix the cooled syrup with the
   coconut milk and pour into a
shallow freezer container. Cover and
freeze for about 3 hours or until semi-
frozen around the edges and mushy in
the centre.

3 Transfer the mixture to a bowl and
   cut up with a knife, then place (half
the quantity at a time) in a food processor
and process until smooth.

4 Turn the mixture into a bowl. Whip
   the cream until softly peaking and
fold into the ice-cream, then stir in the
desiccated coconut. Return the mixture to
the container and freeze again until solid.

5 Before serving, remove the container
   of ice-cream to the refrigerator and
leave in the main compartment for
30 minutes (or at room temperature for
15 minutes) to soften. Scoop or spoon the
ice-cream into serving dishes and decorate
with sprigs of mint.

SERVING ICE-CREAM

For easy serving, scoop the ice-cream
into portions the night before required
and place on a chilled baking tray, then
freeze until ready to serve.

RICOTTA ICE-CREAM

•••

SERVES 4-6

30 g/1 oz/ ¼ cup pistachio nuts
30 g/1 oz/ ¼ cup walnuts or pecan nuts
30 g/1 oz/ ¼ cup toasted chopped hazelnuts
grated rind of 1 orange
grated rind of 1 lemon
30 g/1 oz/2 tbsp crystallized or stem ginger
30 g/1 oz/2 tbsp glacé cherries
30 g/1 oz/ ¼ cup no-need-to-soak dried
   apricots
30 g/1 oz/3tbsp raisins
500 g/1 lb/1½ cups Ricotta
2 tbsp Maraschino, Amaretto or brandy
1 tsp vanilla essence
4 egg yolks
125 g/4 oz/ ½ cup caster sugar

TO DECORATE:
whipped cream
few glacé cherries, pistachio nuts or mint
   leaves

1 Roughly chop the pistachio nuts and
   walnuts and mix with the toasted
hazelnuts, orange and lemon rind. Finely
chop the ginger, cherries, apricots and
raisins and add to the bowl.

2 Mix the ricotta evenly through the
   fruit mixture, then beat in the
liqueur and vanilla essence.

3 Put the egg yolks and sugar in a
   bowl and whisk hard until very thick
and creamy – they may be whisked over
a pan of gently simmering water to speed
up the process. Leave to cool.

4 Carefully fold the ricotta mixture
   evenly through the beaten eggs and
sugar until smooth.

5 Line a 18 x 12 cm/ 7 x 5 in loaf tin
   (pan) with a double layer of
clingfilm or baking parchment, pour in
the ricotta mixture, level the top, cover
with clingfilm and chill in the freezer until
firm – at least overnight.

6 To serve, carefully remove the ice-
   cream from the tin (pan) and peel
off the paper. Stand on a serving dish and
decorate with whipped cream using a
piping bag and star vegetable nozzle, and
glacé cherries and/or pistachio nuts. Serve
in slices, with mint leaves.

FRUIT SALADS

On a hot day, or after a heavy meal, these is nothing so delicious as a fruit salad. For something different, try the Green Fruit Salad (see right), the Tropical Salad (see page 535) or the Exotic Fruit Salad (see page 536) to delight the taste buds.

AROMATIC FRUIT SALAD

SERVES 6

60 g/1½ oz/3 tbsp granulated sugar
150 ml/ ¼ pint/ ⅔ cup water
1 cinnamon stick or large piece of cassia bark
4 cardamom pods, crushed
1 clove
juice of 1 orange
juice of 1 lime
½ honeydew melon
a good-sized wedge of watermelon
2 ripe guavas
3 ripe nectarines
about 18 strawberries
a little toasted, shredded coconut for sprinkling
sprigs of mint or rose petals, to decorate
strained Greek yogurt, for serving

1 First prepare the syrup. Put the sugar, water, cinnamon, cardamom pods and cloves into a pan and bring to the boil, stirring to dissolve the sugar. Simmer for 2 minutes, then remove from heat, add the orange and lime juices and leave to cool and infuse while preparing the fruits.

2 Peel and remove the seeds from the melons and cut the flesh into neat slices. Cut the guavas in half, scoop out the seeds, then peel and slice the flesh neatly. Cut the nectarines into slices and hull and slice the strawberries.

3 Arrange the slices of fruit attractively on 6 serving plates. Strain the prepared cooled syrup and spoon over the sliced fruits. Sprinkle with a little toasted coconut. Decorate each serving with sprigs of mint or rose petals and serve with yogurt, if wished.

VARIATIONS

Use any exotic fruits of your choice, or those that are in season. You can, of course, cut up the fruits and serve them in a bowl, in the usual way, if you prefer.

GREEN FRUIT SALAD WITH MINT & LEMON SYRUP

....

SERVES 4

1 small Charentais or honeydew melon
2 green apples
2 kiwi fruit
125 g/4 oz/1 cup seedless white (green) grapes
sprigs of fresh mint to decorate

SYRUP:
1 lemon
150 ml/ ¼ pint/ ⅔ cup white wine
150 ml/ ¼ pint /⅔ cup water
4 tbsp clear honey
few sprigs of fresh mint

1 To make the syrup, pare the rind from the lemon using a potato peeler. Put the lemon rind into a saucepan with the wine, water and honey. Heat and simmer gently for 10 minutes. Remove from the heat. Add the mint and leave to cool.

2 Slice the melon in half and scoop out the seeds. Use a melon baller or a teaspoon to make melon balls. Core and chop the apples. Peel and slice the kiwi fruit.

3 Strain the cooled syrup into a serving bowl. Remove and reserve the lemon rind and discard the mint sprigs. Add the apple, grapes, kiwi and melon. Stir through gently to mix.

4 Serve, decorated with sprigs of fresh mint and some of the reserved lemon rind.

SERVING SUGGESTION

Serve the fruit salad in an attractive glass dish. Chill the dish for 20 minutes first, then keep the fruit salad cold by placing the dish in a large bowl of crushed ice or ice cubes.

BLACKBERRY, APPLE & FRESH FIG COMPOTE WITH HONEY YOGURT

....

SERVES 4

1 lemon
60 g/2 oz/ ¼ cup caster (superfine) sugar
4 tbsp elderflower cordial
300 ml/ ½ pint/1¼ cups water
4 dessert (eating) apples
250 g/8 oz/2 cups blackberries
2 fresh figs

TOPPING:
150 g/5 oz/ ⅔ cup thick, creamy natural yogurt
2 tbsp clear honey

1 Pare the rind from the lemon using a potato peeler. Squeeze the juice. Put the lemon rind and juice into a saucepan with the sugar, elderflower cordial and water. Heat gently and simmer, uncovered, for 10 minutes.

2 Peel, core and slice the apples, and add them to the saucepan. Simmer gently for about 4–5 minutes until just tender. Leave to cool.

3 Transfer the apples and syrup to a serving bowl and add the blackberries. Slice and add the figs. Stir gently to mix. Cover and chill until ready to serve.

4 Spoon the yogurt into a small serving bowl and drizzle the honey over the top. Cover and chill, then serve with the fruit salad.

ELDERFLOWERS AND CREAM

Elderflower cordial is easy to obtain from supermarkets, health-food shops and delicatessens. Alternatively, you can use a blackberry or apple cordial.

Fresh whipped cream is delicious served with this fruit salad. If you are choosing cream for whipping, buy either double (heavy) cream or whipping cream. Double cream labelled as 'extra thick' is only suitable for spooning, and will not whip.

SUMMER FRUIT SALAD

SERVES 6

90 g/3 oz/ ⅓ cup caster (superfine) sugar
75 ml/3 fl oz/ ⅓ cup water
grated rind and juice of 1 small orange
250 g/8 oz/2 cups redcurrants, stripped
  from their stalks
2 tsp arrowroot
2 tbsp port
125 g/4 oz/1 cup blackberries
125 g/4 oz/1 cup blueberries
125 g/4 oz/ ¾ cup strawberries
250 g/8 oz/1½ cups raspberries

1 Put the sugar, water and grated orange rind into a pan and heat gently, stirring until the sugar has dissolved. Add the redcurrants and orange juice, bring to the boil and simmer gently for 2–3 minutes.

2 Strain the fruit, reserving the syrup, and put into a bowl. Blend the arrowroot with a little water. Return the syrup to the pan, add the arrowroot and bring to the boil, stirring until thickened.

3 Add the port and mix together well. Then pour over the redcurrants in the bowl. Add the blackberries, blueberries, strawberries and raspberries. Mix together and leave to cool.

4 Serve in individual glass dishes with natural fromage frais or cream.

USING FROZEN FRUIT

Although this salad is really best made with fresh fruits in season, you can achieve an acceptable result with frozen equivalents, with perhaps the exception of strawberries. You can buy frozen fruits of the forest in most supermarkets, which would be ideal.

MELON & KIWI SALAD

SERVES 6

½ Galia melon
2 kiwi fruit
125 g/4 oz/1 cup white (green) seedless
  grapes
1 paw-paw (papaya), halved
3 tbsp orange-flavoured liqueur such as
  Cointreau
1 tbsp chopped lemon verbena, lemon
  balm or mint
sprigs of lemon verbena or physalis
  (ground cherries) to decorate

1 Remove the seeds from the melon, cut into 4 slices and cut away the skin. Cut the flesh into cubes and put into a bowl.

2 Peel the kiwi fruit and cut across into slices. Add to the melon with the grapes.

3 Remove the seeds from the paw-paw (papaya) and cut off the skin. Slice thickly and cut into diagonal pieces.

4 Mix together the liqueur and lemon verbena, pour over the fruit and leave for 1 hour, stirring it occasionally.

5 Spoon into glasses, pour over the juices and decorate with lemon verbena sprigs or physalis.

LEMON BALM

Lemon balm or sweet balm is a fragrant lemon-scented plant with slightly hairy serrated leaves and a pronounced lemon flavour. Lemon verbena can also be used – this has an even stronger lemon flavour and smooth elongated leaves. Both can be used as a herbal infusion, which is soothing, refreshing and delicious.

MANGO & PASSION-FRUIT SALAD WITH MASCARPONE CREAM

SERVES 4

1 large mango
2 oranges
4 passion-fruit
2 tbsp orange-flavoured liqueur such as
*   Grand Marnier*
mint or geranium leaves to decorate

MASCARPONE CREAM
125 g/4 oz/ ½ cup Mascarpone cheese
1 tbsp clear honey
4 tbsp thick, natural yogurt
few drops of vanilla flavouring (extract)

1 Cut the mango in half lengthwise as close to the stone (pit) as possible. Remove the stone (pit), using a sharp knife. Peel off the skin, cut the flesh into slices and put into a bowl.

2 Peel the oranges, removing all the pith, and cut into segments. Add to the bowl with any juices.

3 Halve the passion-fruit, scoop out the flesh and add to the bowl with the liqueur. Mix well and chill for 1 hour. Turn into glass dishes.

4 To make the Mascarpone cream, blend the Mascarpone cheese and honey together. Stir in the yogurt and vanilla flavouring (extract) until thoroughly blended.

5 Serve the fruit salad with the Mascarpone cream, decorated with mint or geranium leaves.

MASCARPONE

Mascarpone is a deliciously rich, soft cream cheese from Italy. It has a smooth silky texture with the flavour of cream. As it has a close texture, I usually add a liqueur or some yogurt to give it a softer consistency.

TROPICAL SALAD

SERVES 8

1 paw-paw (papaya)
2 tbsp fresh orange juice
3 tbsp rum
2 bananas
2 guavas
1 small pineapple or 2 baby pineapples
2 passion-fruit, halved
pineapple leaves to decorate

1 Cut the paw-paw (papaya) in half and remove the seeds. Peel and slice the flesh into a bowl. Pour over the orange juice together with the rum.

2 Slice the bananas, peel and slice the guavas, and add both to the bowl.

3 Cut the top and base from the pineapple, then cut off the skin. Slice the pineapple flesh, discard the core, cut into pieces and add to the bowl.

4 Halve the passion-fruit, scoop out the flesh with a teaspoon, add to the bowl and stir well to mix.

5 Spoon the salad into glass bowls and decorate with pineapple leaves.

PINEAPPLES

If you are using baby pineapples, cut them in half lengthways and scoop out the flesh after loosening with a grapefruit knife. Cut the flesh into pieces and use the shells to serve the salad in.

GUAVAS

Guavas come from the Caribbean, Thailand and Central America. They have a heavenly smell when ripe – their scent will fill a whole room. They should give to gentle pressure when ripe, and their skins should be yellow. If you cannot buy them fresh, the canned ones are very good and have a pink tinge to the flesh.

EXOTIC FRUIT SALAD

SERVES 6

3 passion-fruit
125 g/4 oz/ ½ cup caster (superfine) sugar
150 ml/ ¼ pint/ ⅔ cup water
1 mango
10 lychees, canned or fresh
1 star-fruit

1 Halve the passion-fruit and press the flesh through a sieve (strainer) into a saucepan. Add the sugar and water to the saucepan and bring to a gentle boil, stirring frequently.

2 Put the mango on a chopping board and cut a thick slice from either side, cutting as near to the stone (pit) as possible. Cut away as much flesh as possible in large chunks from the stone (pit) section.

3 Take the 2 side slices and make 3 cuts through the flesh but not the skin, and 3 more at right angles to make a lattice pattern. Push inside out so that the cubed flesh is exposed and you can easily cut it off.

4 Peel and stone (pit) the lychees and cut the star-fruit into 12 slices.

5 Add all the mango flesh, the lychees and the star-fruit to the passion-fruit and sugar syrup and poach gently for 5 minutes. Remove the fruit with a perforated spoon. Bring the sugar syrup to the boil and cook or 5 minutes until it thickens slightly.

6 To serve, transfer all the fruit to a warmed serving bowl or individual serving glasses, pour over the sugar syrup, and serve warm, but not hot.

CARDAMOM CREAM

A delicious accompaniment to any exotic fruit dish is cardamom cream. Crush the seeds from 8 cardamom pods, add 300 ml/ ¼ pint/1¼ cups whipping cream and whip until soft peaks form.

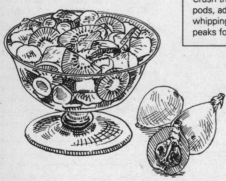

·6·

Cakes

Y ou are spoilt for choice here with luscious cheesecakes, elegant gâteaux, feather-light sponges and traditional fruit cakes, as well as lots of unusual ideas for that special birthday treat.

CAKES – INTRODUCTION

MAKING CAKES

The most important point to remember when making cakes is to read the recipe carefully before you begin, then follow it accurately. Making cakes and decorating them is enjoyable and should cause you few problems provided you follow a few basic rules and guidelines.

Always follow one set of ingredient measurements, either all metric, all imperial or all cup measures; mixing the systems may cause the recipe to fail, as the conversions are not exact.

Cookers with fan ovens are a little hotter than conventional electric ovens, so the temperatures must be adjusted. I suggest that where the recipe states 180°C/350°F, you lower the temperature to 160°C/ 325°F and check the cake at least 5 minutes before the suggested cooking time for a small one or 20–30 minutes for a large one. Lower all oven temperatures in the same way.

LINING CAKE TINS (PANS)

When baking a rich fruit cake, it is necessary to line the cake tin (pan) with a double thickness of non-stick baking parchment (which does not need greasing) to prevent the cake from over-browning and drying out during baking. Other cake mixtures need only a single thickness. Greased greaseproof paper can be used in place of baking parchment.

Cut one or two double strips of baking parchment long enough to go round the whole tin (pan) with a little extra for overlapping, and wide enough to come 2.5 cm/1 inch above the rim. Fold up the bottom edge of the strip about 2 cm/ ¾ inch and crease it firmly. Open the strip out and snip into it at 1 cm/ ½ inch intervals. This enables the paper to fit the inside of any shape of tin (pan).

Place the tin (pan) on a double thickness of baking parchment and draw around the base of it, then cut out just inside the line. Grease the inside of the tin (pan), position one circle of paper in the base and grease just around the edge. Put the long strips in around the inside of the tin (pan) with the cut edges spread out over the bottom (fold into corners with square or rectangular tins (pans)), press the strips against the sides of the tin (pan) and grease all over. Finally, position the second circle of paper in the base of the tin (pan) (which keeps the snipped edges of the band in place) and grease again.

To line a loaf tin (pan), cut a piece of baking parchment about 15 cm/6 inches larger than the base of the tin (pan). Place the tin (pan) on the paper and make a cut from each corner of the paper to the corner of the tin (pan). Grease the inside of the tin (pan) and put in the paper so that it fits neatly, overlapping the paper at the corners to give sharp angles. Brush the paper with fat or oil. This method can also be used to line shallow rectangular tins (pans).

MAKING PAPER PIPING BAGS

Use either greaseproof paper or baking parchment for making piping bags, as follows:

1. Cut the paper into a 25 cm/10 inch square. Fold the square in half to make a triangle. Fold in half again to make a smaller triangle and press the folds firmly.

2. Open out the smaller triangle and fold one of the bottom corners up to the central fold line, creasing firmly.

INTRODUCTION

3. Continue to fold the bag over, creasing it firmly, to make a cone.

4. Either secure the join with some adhesive tape or fold the top point over twice to secure. Cut off the top of the bag and open out before inserting the nozzle (tip).

FLAN PASTRY
Makes a 23 cm/9 inch flan
150 g/5 oz/1¼ cups plain (all-purpose)
flour
pinch of salt
90 g/3 oz/ ⅓ cup butter
1 tbsp caster (superfine) sugar
1 egg yolk
about 2–3 tsp cold water

1. Sift the flour and salt into a bowl and rub in the butter until the mixture resembles fine breadcrumbs. Stir in the sugar.

2. Mix the egg yolk with 1 tablespoon of the water and add to the dry ingredients with enough of the remaining water to mix to a firm pliable dough.

3. Wrap in foil or clingfilm (plastic wrap) and chill until required.

RICH FRUIT CAKE
Makes 23 cm/9 inch round cake
300 g/10 oz/2½ cups plain (all-purpose) flour
pinch of salt
2 tbsp cocoa powder
1½ tsp cinnamon
1 tsp mixed (apple pie) spice
generous pinch of ground nutmeg
500 g/1 lb/3 cups raisins
350 g/12 oz/2 cups sultanas (golden raisins)
250 g/8 oz/1½ cups currants
175 g/6 oz/ ¾ cup glacé (candied)

cherries, halved, washed and dried
60 g/2 oz/ ⅓ cup cut mixed (candied) peel
125 g/4 oz/1 cup blanched almonds, chopped, or other chopped nuts
grated rind and juice of 1 lemon
grated rind and juice of 1 orange
250 g/8 oz/1 cup butter or margarine
250 g/8 oz/1 ⅓ cups dark soft brown sugar
4 eggs
1 tbsp black treacle (molasses)
3–4 tbsp brandy or rum

1. Grease a 23 cm/9 inch round cake tin (pan) and line with a double layer of baking parchment.

2. Sift the flour, salt, cocoa powder and spices together. Combine the dried fruits, glacé (candied) cherries, mixed (candied) peel, nuts and fruit rinds.

3. Cream the butter or margarine and sugar together until very light and fluffy. Beat in the eggs, one at a time, adding a tablespoonful of the flour mixture after each egg, then fold in the remaining flour mixture, followed by the treacle and lemon and orange juice.

4. Fold in the fruit mixture evenly and spoon into the tin (pan). Level the top. Tie a band of several thicknesses of folded newspaper around the outside of the tin (pan) for protection during cooking.

5. Bake in a preheated oven at 140°C/ 275°F/Gas Mark 1 for 1 hour. Reduce the temperature to 120°C/ 250°F/Gas Mark ½ and cook for a further 2–2½ hours until firm and a skewer inserted in the centre comes out clean.

INTRODUCTION

6. Leave to cool in the tin (pan); then remove and pierce all over the top of the cake with a skewer. Spoon the brandy or rum over the top of the cake, and when it has seeped in, wrap the cake completely in foil and leave for at least 2 weeks before decorating or eating.

NOTE: For an 18 cm/7 inch round cake use half the mixture. After the first hour's cooking, lower the temperature and continue for 1½–1¾ hours until cooked.

MARZIPAN
Makes 1 kg/2 lb

250 g/8 oz/1 cup caster (superfine) sugar
250 g/8 oz/1¼ cups icing (confectioners') sugar, sifted
500 g/1 lb/4 cups ground almonds
1 tsp lemon juice
few drops of almond flavouring (extract)
1 egg or 2 egg yolks, beaten

1. Combine the sugars and ground almonds in a bowl and make a well in the centre. Add the lemon juice, almond flavouring (extract) and enough egg to mix to a firm but pliable dough.

2. Transfer to a lightly sugared work surface (counter) and knead until just smooth. It can be wrapped in clingfilm (plastic wrap) or foil and stored for 2 days before use.

TO COVER A CAKE WITH MARZIPAN
1. Place almost half the marzipan on a sheet of baking parchment dredged lightly with icing (confectioners') sugar and roll out the marzipan evenly until it is a little larger than the top of the cake.

2. Cut out a circle or square about 1 cm/ ½ inch larger than the cake. Set aside. Roll out the remaining marzipan to a rectangle.

3. Cut two lengths of string, one the circumference of the cake and the other the exact height of the cake. Using the string as a guide, cut the marzipan into a strip or strips to fit the sides of the cake.

4. Place the cake on a board and glaze the sides with apricot glaze or thinned apricot preserve. Position the marzipan strips around the cake, pressing the ends together with a blunt knife to secure. Brush the top of the cake with apricot glaze and position the circle or square on top. Press the edges together with the blunt knife. If the marzipan seems moist, rub it with sifted icing (confectioners') sugar.

5. Leave the marzipan to dry for at least 2 days. Brush off surplus icing (confectioners') sugar before adding the icing (frosting).

NOTE: If the cake is very uneven before you begin, first roll the top evenly with a rolling pin and then 'patch' it by filling in any dips with small pieces of marzipan, to make it neat and evenly shaped.

MARZIPAN CHRISTMAS TREES
Draw a pattern for a simple Christmas tree to the size required (about 4 cm/1½ inches) on a piece of stiff paper or card and cut out the shape. Using the pattern as a guide, cut out Christmas trees from thinly rolled out green marzipan (coloured with a dark green paste food colouring) and leave to dry.

A tub can be added, made from a

INTRODUCTION

small piece of red marzipan (coloured with Christmas red paste food colouring). To complete, add tiny silver or coloured balls to the tips of the branches with a dab of icing. Leave to dry.

MARZIPAN DAFFODILS

Colour about 60 g/2 oz marzipan a deep yellow daffodil colour with yellow paste or liquid food colouring.

Roll out the marzipan thinly on clean baking parchment. Either use a 5-petal metal flower cutter – about 3 cm/1¼ inches across – or draw and cut out a template in thick paper. Place the cutter or template on the marzipan and cut out 8–10 daffodil bases. Use the remaining marzipan to cut out a similar number of 1.5 cm/ ½ inch circles. Bend these into a cup and attach to the centre of each daffodil. Leave to dry, then using a fine paintbrush and orange paste or liquid food colouring paint around the rims of the centre of each flower.

MINIATURE CHOCOLATE CURLS

You will need a bar of chocolate and a potato peeler. Make sure the chocolate is not too cold, or the flakes will not peel off easily. Simply pare off curls with the potato peeler until you have enough. When made, they may be stored in an airtight container for several weeks.

CHOCOLATE CARAQUE

1. Melt about 125–175 g/4–6 oz/4–6 squares (or more if preferred) dark chocolate either in a bowl over a pan of gently simmering water or in a microwave oven on Full Power for about 45 seconds, taking care not to get any water into it. Stir gently until smooth and completely melted

2. Using a palette knife (spatula),

spread the melted chocolate out thinly over a cool flat surface, such as marble, and leave until on the point of setting.

3. Either push a sharp knife held at an angle over the surface, scraping off long scrolls of chocolate. When it becomes too hard, melt the chocolate again, then repeat the process on a clean surface. It can take a little practice to get the angle of the knife just right. Alternatively, pare off the chocolate with a cheese slice. Store the caraque in a rigid container between layers of baking parchment in the refrigerator or other cool place for up to 2–3 weeks.

BUTTER CREAM

125 g/4 oz/ ½ cup butter or soft margarine
250 g/8 oz/1¾ cups icing (confectioners') sugar, sifted
few drops of vanilla flavouring (extract)
1–2 tbsp milk

1. Beat the butter or margarine until soft, then cream in the sugar gradually. Add the vanilla flavouring (extract) and sufficient milk to give a fairly firm spreading consistency.

Variations:
Coffee: Omit the vanilla and replace 1 tablespoon of the milk with 1 tablespoon coffee flavouring (extract) or very strong black coffee.

Chocolate: Add either 30 g/1 oz/ 1 square melted chocolate or 2–3 tablespoons sifted cocoa powder.

Lemon or orange: Omit the vanilla and replace the milk with orange or lemon juice and the finely grated rind of 1 orange or lemon.

INTRODUCTION

WHITE (BOILED) FROSTING
*750 g/1½ lb/3 cups
granulated sugar
150 ml/ ¼ pint/ ⅔ cup water
pinch of cream of tartar
3 egg whites*

1. Put the sugar and water into a large heavy-based saucepan and heat gently until the sugar has dissolved. Add the cream of tartar. If you have one, place a sugar thermometer in the saucepan. Bring to the boil and boil until the sugar syrup reaches a temperature of 115°C/240°F, or until a small amount placed on a saucer makes a strand when rolled between finger and thumb.

2. Whisk the egg whites until very stiff. Pour the sugar syrup in a thin stream on to the egg whites, beating briskly all the time until standing in fairly firm peaks. Use at once.

ROYAL ICING
*3 egg whites
about 750 g/1½ lb/5 cups
icing (confectioners') sugar,
sifted
1 tbsp lemon juice, strained
1–1½ tsp glycerine (optional)*

1. Whisk the egg whites until frothy, but not at all stiff, then gradually beat in half the icing (confectioners') sugar.

2. Add the lemon juice and glycerine and gradually beat in the rest of the icing (confectioners') sugar, beating thoroughly after each addition until the icing stands in soft peaks. Cover the bowl with a damp cloth and place in an airtight container. Leave for 1–2 hours for any bubbles to come to the surface before using. The icing may be stored in an airtight plastic container for 4–5 days in a cool place.

Note: To colour royal icing, add either liquid or paste food colouring by dipping the tip of a cocktail stick (toothpick) into the colouring and then adding to the icing. Add the colouring in tiny amounts – it is easy to use too much and impossible to remove it! Beat well until evenly blended.

PASTRY CREAM
*300 ml/ ½ pint/1¼ cups milk
60 g/2 oz/4 tbsp caster
(superfine) sugar
1 tbsp plain (all-purpose) flour,
sifted
2 tbsp cornflour (cornstarch)
1 egg
1 egg yolk
few drops of vanilla flavouring
(extract)
knob of butter*

1. Heat the milk gently in a saucepan. Beat the sugar, flour, cornflour (cornstarch), egg and egg yolk together until quite smooth and creamy, then beat in a little of the hot milk. Return the mixture to the saucepan and cook gently, stirring all the time until the mixture thickens and just comes to the boil.

2. Add a few drops of vanilla and the butter, and heat gently for a minute longer. Turn into a bowl. Place a piece of wet baking parchment on the surface to prevent a skin forming.

PASTRY CREAM VARIATION
For lemon- or orange-flavoured pastry cream, omit the vanilla and replace the milk with orange or lemon juice and the finely grated rind of 1 orange or lemon.

CHEESECAKES

Cheesecakes originated in the Middle East, where they have been made for centuries. These cheesecakes were always cooked, and usually consisted of a pastry base, and a filling of soft cheese enriched with eggs and sugar and flavoured with spices. European cooks introduced new ingredients, such as fresh and candied fruits, nuts and liqueurs, while in the United States a new development was uncooked cheesecakes. Uncooked cakes usually have a crumb base and a creamy, set filling. They are very rich, and make an ideal dessert for a special occasion.

FRUITS OF THE FOREST CHEESECAKE MOUSSE

SERVES 6–8

1½ tsp powdered gelatine
4 tbsp water
2 tbsp caster (superfine) sugar
150 ml/ ¼ pint /⅔ cup red wine
250 g/8 oz/1¾ cups frozen fruits of the
    forest (raspberries, blackberries,
    redcurrants, blackcurrants), just
    thawed

CHEESECAKE LAYER:
500 g/1 lb/2 cups natural fromage frais
200 g/7 oz/scant 1 cup light cream cheese
finely grated rind of 1 lemon
finely grated rind of ½ orange
1 egg
60 g/2 oz/ ¼ cup caster (superfine) sugar
1 tbsp lemon juice
1 tbsp powdered gelatine
3 tbsp water

TO DECORATE (OPTIONAL):
whipped cream
fresh raspberries and/or blackberries

1 Line a 23 x 12 cm/9 x 5 inch loaf tin
(pan) with a double layer of food
wrap (plastic wrap).

2 Dissolve the gelatine in the water
either in a microwave oven set on
Medium Power for 40 seconds or in a
basin over a pan of gently simmering
water. Leave to cool slightly, stir in the
sugar and then mix into the red wine.

3 Pour a thin (about 5 mm/ ¼ inch)
layer of the wine jelly into the
prepared tin (pan) and leave until just set.
Add the fruits and any juice to the
remaining jelly and spoon over the set
layer, arranging the fruits attractively. Chill
until set.

4 To make the cheesecake layer, beat
the fromage frais, cream cheese and
fruit rinds together until smooth. Put the
egg, sugar and lemon juice into a heatproof bowl over a pan of simmering
water. Cook gently, stirring continuously
until thickened sufficiently to coat the
back of the spoon. Remove from the heat.

5 Dissolve the gelatine in the water
and stir into the lemon mixture, then
fold this through the cheese mixture. Pour
over the set jelly and chill, preferably
overnight, until very firm.

6 To serve, turn out carefully and
remove the food wrap (plastic
wrap). Decorate with whipped cream and
raspberries if liked.

GRAPE & RICOTTA CHEESECAKE

•••

SERVES 6

90 g/3 oz/ ¾ cup digestive biscuits
(graham crackers), crushed
125 g/4 oz/1 cup ratafia or amaretti
biscuits (cookies), crushed
90 g/3 oz/⅛ cup unsalted butter, melted
and cooled
1 tbsp or 1 sachet (envelope) powdered
gelatine
120 ml/4 fl oz/ ½ cup double (heavy)
cream
300 g/10 oz/1¼ cups Ricotta cheese
2 tbsp mixed (candied) peel
2 tbsp clear honey
¼ tsp vanilla flavouring (extract)
350 g/12 oz/3 cups white (green) seedless
grapes, washed

1 Combine the biscuits (crackers and
cookies) and the butter. Press into
the bottom of 6 ramekins or glasses, or
into a 20 cm/8 inch springform tin (pan),
and chill.

2 Put 3 tablespoons of hot water into a
heatproof bowl, sprinkle on the
powdered gelatine and stir. Set over a pan
of barely simmering water and leave to
dissolve. When it becomes clear, it is
ready to use.

3 Whip the cream until stiff. Combine
the Ricotta cheese, mixed (candied)
peel, honey and vanilla flavouring
(extract) in a separate bowl. Stir this
mixture into the double (heavy) cream.
Do not over-stir.

4 Stir the dissolved gelatine into the
Ricotta mixture.

5 Halve the grapes. Divide half of
them between the ramekins, glasses
or tin (pan), arranging neatly on top of
the biscuit (cracker and cookie) layer.

6 Spoon the Ricotta mixture over the
top. Arrange the remaining grapes
attractively on the top. Chill for 2 hours or
until set.

7 To serve, remove the outer ring from
the springform tin (pan), or put the
ramekins on small plates.

TRUFFLE CHEESECAKE

•••

SERVES 8

60 g/2 oz/ ¼ cup unsalted butter
125 g/4 oz Amaretti biscuits, crushed
250 g/8 oz/1 cup yogurt cheese (see
page 97) or low-fat soft cheese
250 g/8 oz/1 cup Mascarpone
150 ml/ ¼ pint/⅔ cup crème fraîche
½ tsp vanilla flavouring
90 g/3 oz/6 tbsp golden caster sugar
2 eggs, plus 1 egg yolk
1 tbsp flour
1 tbsp instant coffee granules
125 ml/4 fl oz/ ½ cup boiling water
2 tbsp coffee liqueur, or brandy
7 sponge finger (boudoir) biscuits

TOPPING:
15 g/ ½ oz/1 tbsp unsalted butter
150 ml/ ¼ pint/⅔ cup natural yogurt
60 g/2oz/ ¼ cup golden caster sugar
125 g/4 oz plain chocolate, broken up
1 tbsp coffee liqueur or brandy
1 tbsp cocoa powder

1 Grease and line a 18 cm/7 in loose-
bottomed cake tin (pan). Melt the
butter over low heat. Remove from the
heat, stir in the crumbs and tip them into
the prepared tin (pan). Press the crumbs
to cover the base evenly and chill.

2 Beat together the yogurt cheese,
mascarpone, crème fraîche and
vanilla. Beat in the sugar, eggs, egg yolk
and flour. Pour half into the tin (pan).

3 Dissolve the coffee in the boiling
water, add the liqueur and pour into
a bowl. Dip the sponge biscuits in the
coffee. Lay the biscuits over the cheese
mixture and spoon on the remainder.

4 Bake in the preheated oven
at 200ºC/400ºF/Gas Mark 6 for
20 minutes, then lower the heat to
140ºC/275ºF/Gas Mark 1 and cook for a
further 1½ hours, or until a fine skewer
inserted in the centre comes out clean.
Allow the cake to cool completely.

5 Bring the butter, yogurt and sugar to
the boil. Add the chocolate and
liqueur and melt over low heat. Remove
from the heat and beat. When cold, use
to pipe lines over the cheesecake. Just
before serving, dust with cocoa powder.

POLISH CHEESECAKE

MAKES 25 CM/10 INCH CHEESECAKE

SWEET SHORTCRUST (PLAIN) PASTRY:
175 g/6 oz/1½ cups plain (all-purpose)
   flour
pinch of salt
90 g/3 oz/⅓ cup caster (superfine) sugar
90 g/3 oz/⅓ cup butter, slightly softened
3 egg yolks

FILLING:
350 g/12 oz/1½ cups full-fat soft cheese
3 eggs
60 g/2 oz/¼ cup butter, melted
175 g/6 oz/¾ cup caster (superfine) sugar
grated rind of 1 lemon
grated rind of ½ orange
½ tsp ground cinnamon
few drops of vanilla flavouring (extract)

TOPPING:
300 ml/½ pint/1¼ cups double (heavy)
   cream
selection of fresh fruits

1 To make the pastry, sift together the flour and salt on to a work surface (counter). Make a well in the centre and add the sugar, butter and egg yolks. Using the fingertips, pinch and work the ingredients together, then gradually work in the flour to give a smooth pliable dough. Wrap in clingfilm (plastic wrap) or foil and chill for 1 hour.

2 Roll out the pastry carefully on a floured work surface (counter) and use to line either a deep 25 cm/10 inch round fluted flan tin (quiche pan) or a rectangular tin (pan), about 28 x 18 x 4 cm/11 x 7 x 1½ inches, lightly greased. Trim and crimp the edges.

3 To make the filling, beat the cheese until smooth, then beat in the eggs, butter, sugar, citrus rinds, cinnamon and vanilla. Spoon the cheese mixture into the pastry case (pie shell) and spread out evenly.

4 Bake in a preheated oven at 180°C/ 350°F/Gas Mark 4 for 50–60 minutes, until quite firm. Leave to cool in the tin (pan). The cheesecake will sink slightly as it cools.

5 Whip the cream until thick, then spread a layer over the top of the cheesecake, marking attractively with a round-bladed knife. Put the remaining cream into a piping bag fitted with a star nozzle (tip). Decorate the cheesecake with piped cream and fresh fruit, and cut into squares or wedges to serve.

SPONGE CAKES

The basic creamed butter sponge mixture that makes the classic Victoria Sandwich (see page 570), also lends itself to innumerable attractive variations, as these recipes show. There are a few golden rules to follow for perfect, light sponges: cream the butter and sugar until light and fluffy; take the eggs out of the refrigerator ahead of time to bring them up to room temperature; and add the eggs one by one, beating well after each addition. When baked, the sponge cake should be well risen and just firm to the touch.

CHOCOLATE ROULADE

MAKES 25 CM/10 INCH ROULADE

175 g/6 oz/6 squares dark chocolate
5 eggs, separated
175 g/6 oz/¾ cup caster (superfine) sugar
few drops of vanilla flavouring (extract)
icing (confectioners') sugar
coarsely grated chocolate or miniature
  chocolate curls to decorate (see
  page 541)

CREAM FILLING:
300 ml/ ½ pint/1¼ cups double (heavy)
  cream
2–4 tbsp rum, brandy or liqueur

1 Melt the chocolate in a bowl over a saucepan of gently simmering water, or in a microwave oven on Full Power for about 45 seconds. Stir until smooth.

2 Line a Swiss (jelly) roll tin (pan), about 30 x 25 cm/12 x 10 inches, with non-stick baking parchment. Whisk the egg yolks and sugar until very thick and creamy. Fold the melted chocolate through the egg yolk mixture with the vanilla.

3 Whisk the egg whites until very stiff and dry, and fold through the egg yolk mixture until blended. Spread out evenly in the prepared tin (pan), especially into the corners.

4 Bake in a preheated oven at 190°C/ 375°F/Gas Mark 5 for about 15–20 minutes, or until firm and crusty on top. Sprinkle a sheet of baking parchment very liberally with the sifted icing (confectioners') sugar. Invert the cake on to the paper and leave to cool slightly; then lay a damp tea towel (dish cloth) over the cake and leave until cold.

5 To make the filling, whip the cream until thick but not too stiff and fold in the alcohol. Put about 3–4 tablespoons of the filling into a piping bag fitted with a large star nozzle (tip).

6 Peel the lining paper off the cake and spread evenly with the cream.

7 Roll up the cake carefully with the help of the paper and transfer to a serving plate. Pipe a line of the filling along the top of the cake and decorate with grated chocolate or chocolate curls.

DANISH LEMON CAKE

SERVES 6-8

175 g/6 oz/ ¾ cup butter or margarine,
softened, plus extra for greasing
175 g/6 oz/ ¾ cup golden caster sugar
3 eggs
175 g/6 oz/1½ cups self-raising flour,
sifted, plus extra for dusting
2 tsp grated lemon rind
1 tbsp lemon juice
2 tbsp natural yogurt
8 cardamom pods

FILLING:
4 tbsp natural yogurt
4 tbsp icing (confectioner's) sugar, sifted,
plus extra for dusting
4 tbsp lemon curd

1 Grease 2 x 18 cm/7 in diameter sponge sandwich tins (pans) and dust them with flour. In a bowl beat together the butter or margarine and the sugar until the mixture is pale and golden. Beat in the eggs one at a time, beating in a tablespoon of the sifted flour after each addition to prevent the mixture from curdling. Fold in the remaining flour with a metal spoon, then stir in the lemon rind, lemon juice and yogurt.

2 Split the cardamom pods with a small, sharp knife. Remove the hard, black seeds and crush them with a pestle and mortar, or tap them lightly with a small hammer. Discard the pods and stir the crushed seeds into the cake mixture.

3 Divide between the prepared tins and level the surface. Bake in the preheated oven at 190ºC/375ºF/Gas Mark 5 for 25 minutes, until the cakes are well risen and feel springy to the touch. Stand the tins on a wire rack to cool, then turn the cakes out on to the rack to cool completely.

4 To make the filling, mix together the yogurt and icing (confectioner's) sugar, then beat in the lemon curd. Beat in a little more sifted sugar if necessary, to make a stiff, spreadable consistency.

5 Sandwich the 2 halves of the cake with the filling, and dust the top with sifted icing (confectioner's) sugar.

MARBLED CAKE

MAKES 20 CM/8 INCH SQUARE OR
23 CM/9 INCH ROUND CAKE

60 g/2 oz/2 squares dark chocolate
1 tbsp water
175 g/6 oz/ ¾ cup butter or margarine
175 g/6 oz/ ¾ cup caster (superfine) sugar
275 g/9 oz/2¼ cups plain (all-purpose)
flour
2 tsp baking powder
3 eggs
2 tbsp milk or water
grated rind of 1 orange
1 tsp orange flower water
few drops of orange food colouring
1 tsp vanilla flavouring (extract)
icing (confectioners') sugar for dredging

1 Line a 20 cm/8 inch square or 23 cm/9 inch round cake tin (pan) with non-stick baking parchment. Melt the chocolate and water in a bowl over simmering water or in a microwave oven set on Full Power for about 45 seconds.

2 Cream the fat and sugar together until very light and fluffy. Sift the flour and baking powder together. Beat the eggs one at a time into the sugar mixture, following each with a spoonful of the flour, then fold in the remainder with the milk or water.

3 Put one third of the mixture into another bowl and beat in the orange rind, orange flower water and colouring. Add the vanilla flavouring (extract) to the remaining mixture, then transfer half to another bowl and beat in the melted chocolate.

4 Place large spoonfuls of the 3 different cake mixtures alternately into the cake tin (pan).

5 Cut through the mixture with a knife several times to swirl the colours and flavours together, then level the top. Bake in a preheated oven at 180ºC/350ºF/ Gas Mark 4 for about an hour, or until well risen and firm to the touch.

6 Leave to cool slightly in the tin (pan), then invert on to a wire rack to cool completely. Before serving dredge the top with sifted icing (confectioners') sugar.

ORANGE CREAM CAKE

MAKES 23 CM/9 INCH ROUND CAKE

250 g/8 oz/1 cup butter or margarine
250 g/8 oz/1 cup caster (superfine) sugar
4 eggs
250 g/8 oz/2 cups self-raising flour, sifted
grated rind of 1 large or 2 small oranges
1 tbsp orange juice

MOUSSE:
1 egg
90 g/3 oz/ ⅓ cup caster (superfine) sugar
grated rind of 1 orange
125 g/4 oz/ ½ cup low-fat soft cheese
2 tsp powdered gelatine
2 tbsp orange juice

TOPPING:
4 tbsp orange shred marmalade
60 g/2 oz/ ¼ cup butter
125 g/4 oz/scant 1 cup icing
  (confectioners') sugar, sifted
1 tsp orange flower water
jellied orange slices to decorate

1 Grease and line a 23 cm/9 inch round springform cake tin (pan) with non-stick baking parchment. Make up the cake mixture as for Victoria Sandwich (Sponge Layer Cake) (see page 570), adding the orange rind and juice instead of water.

2 Transfer to the tin (pan), level the top and bake in a preheated oven at 180°C/350°F/Gas Mark 4 for about 45 minutes, or until well risen, golden brown and firm to the touch. Invert on to a wire rack and leave to cool.

3 When cold, peel off the paper and cut the cake in half horizontally. Line the cake tin (pan) with fresh non-stick baking parchment and place the bottom half of the cake in the tin (pan).

4 For the mousse, whisk the egg and sugar together until thick. Whisk in the orange rind, then the soft cheese. Dissolve the gelatine in the orange juice over a saucepan of simmering water until it looks clear.

5 Leave to cool slightly and stir into the cheese mixture. When almost setting, spread over the cake and press the top layer in place. Chill until set.

6 Remove the cake from the tin (pan). Spread marmalade over the top. Cream the butter and sugar together and add the orange flower water. Put into a piping bag with a large star nozzle (tip) and pipe shells around the top of the cake. Decorate with orange slices.

SMALL CAKES

Follow these recipes for a tempting array of assorted small cakes to serve at a special occasion tea-party. Vary the selection by making batches of different flavours and colours – see Butterfly Cakes (see page 551) for ideas. Most of these little cakes are best made as required, as they tend not to keep well, however carefully you store them. The exceptions are Eccles Cakes (see page 551) which store well and can also be frozen, and American Brownies (see below) which can be stored for a week in a tin.

AMERICAN BROWNIES

MAKES 20

125 g/4 oz/4 squares dark chocolate,
  broken into pieces
150 g/5 oz/ ⅔ cup butter or margarine
350 g/12 oz/1½ cups caster (superfine)
  sugar
½ tsp vanilla flavouring (extract)
4 eggs, beaten
150 g/5 oz/1¼ cups self-raising flour
90 g/3 oz/ ¾ cup pecans, walnuts,
  hazelnuts or almonds, chopped
60 g/2 oz/ ⅓ cup raisins
icing (confectioners') sugar for dredging

1 Line a rectangular tin (pan), about 28 x 18 x 4 cm/11 x 7 x 1½ inches, with non-stick baking parchment.

2 Put the chocolate and butter or margarine into a heatproof bowl and either place over a saucepan of gently simmering water and heat until melted, or melt in a microwave oven set on Full Power for about 1 minute. Stir until quite smooth.

3 Remove from the heat and beat in the sugar and flavouring (extract) until smooth, followed by the eggs.

4 Sift the flour and fold through the mixture, followed by the chopped nuts and raisins.

5 Pour into the prepared tin (pan) and bake in a preheated oven at 180°C/350°F/Gas Mark 4 for about 45–50 minutes, or until well risen, firm to the touch, and just beginning to shrink away from the sides of the tin (pan). Leave to cool in the tin (pan).

6 Dredge heavily with sifted icing (confectioners') sugar and cut into 20 squares or fingers (bars). Store in an airtight container. The brownies will keep well for a week.

NOTE

Brownies can be frozen successfully for up to 3 months. Add the icing (confectioners') sugar after thawing.

If preferred, the Brownies may be topped with chocolate butter cream (see page 541) sprinkled with grated dark or white chocolate; or simply be swirled with melted dark or white chocolate.

CHOCOLATE ÉCLAIRS

MAKES 12–14

CHOUX PASTE:
75 g/2½ oz/ ½ cup plus 2 tbsp plain
(all-purpose) flour
pinch of salt
60 g/2 oz/ ¼ cup butter or margarine
150 ml/ ¼ pint/ ⅔ cup water
2 eggs, beaten

FILLING:
300 ml/ ½ pint/1¼ cups double (heavy)
cream or 1 quantity of Pastry Cream
(see page 542)

TOPPING:
125 g/4 oz/4 squares dark chocolate
or white chocolate

1 Grease 2 baking sheets. Sift the flour and salt together. Put the butter or margarine and water into a saucepan and heat gently until the fat melts, then bring to the boil.

2 Add the flour all at once and beat vigorously until the paste is smooth and forms a ball that leaves the sides of the saucepan clean. Remove from the heat and spread the paste out over the base of the saucepan. Leave to cool for about 10 minutes.

3 Beat in the eggs gradually until the mixture is smooth, glossy and gives a piping consistency. It may not need quite all of the egg. A hand-held electric mixer is ideal for this.

4 Put the choux paste into a piping bag fitted with a plain 2 cm/ ¾ inch nozzle (tip) and pipe in straight lines about 6 cm/2½ inches long, spaced well apart on the baking sheets. Cut the ends of the paste from the nozzle (tip).

5 Bake in a preheated oven at 220°C/ 425°F/Gas Mark 7 for about 20–25 minutes, or until well risen, firm and a pale golden brown. Make a slit in the side of each éclair to let the steam escape, and return to the oven to dry out for a few minutes. Transfer to a wire rack to cool.

6 Whip the cream until stiff and use to fill each éclair, or use the pastry cream to fill the éclairs. Melt the chocolate in a bowl over simmering water, or in a microwave oven set on Full Power for 45 seconds. Remove from the heat and leave to cool until just beginning to thicken. Dip the top of each éclair into the chocolate, or spread with a palette knife (spatula). Leave to set.

ECCLES CAKES

MAKES 8–10

300 g/10 oz puff pastry, thawed if frozen
beaten egg white for glazing
caster (superfine) sugar for dredging

FILLING:
30 g/1 oz/2 tbsp butter, softened
30 g/1 oz/3 tbsp dark soft brown sugar
30 g/1 oz/3 tbsp chopped mixed
(candied) peel
125 g/4 oz/⅔ cup currants
generous pinch of grated nutmeg
¼–½ tsp mixed (apple pie) spice
grated rind of ½–1 orange (optional)

1 To make the filling, beat the butter until soft, then work in the sugar, peel, currants, nutmeg, spice and orange rind, if using.

2 Roll out the pastry thinly on a lightly floured work surface (counter) and cut into circles of about 13 cm/5½ inches – a saucer is a good guide.

3 Put a tablespoonful of the filling in the centre of each circle.

4 Dampen the edges of the pastry and gather together like a bag, pressing the edges well together to seal.

5 Turn each one over and, keeping the round shape, flatten gently with a rolling pin until the currants just begin to show through.

6 Brush each one liberally with egg white and dredge with sugar.

7 Transfer to a lightly greased baking sheet and make 2–3 small cuts in the top of each one. Bake in a preheated oven at 220°C/425°F/Gas Mark 7 for about 10–15 minutes, or until well puffed up and golden brown. Transfer to a wire rack to cool. Store in an airtight container. They will keep for up to a week; or freeze for up to 2 months.

BUTTERFLY CAKES

MAKES 16

1 quantity Victoria Sandwich (Sponge
Layer Cake) mixture (see page 570)
grated rind of 1 orange or lemon or 2 tbsp
sifted cocoa powder or 1 tbsp coffee
flavouring (extract)
icing (confectioners') sugar for dredging

BUTTER CREAM:
125 g/4 oz/ ½ cup butter or margarine
250 g/8 oz/1¾ cups icing (confectioners')
sugar, sifted
1–2 tbsp coffee flavouring (extract) or
2 tbsp sifted cocoa powder or grated
rind of 1 orange or lemon
1–2 tbsp milk, lemon or orange juice

1 Line 16 patty tins (muffin pans) with paper cake cases or grease them thoroughly with butter.

2 Make up the cake mixture using one of the flavourings and divide between the paper cases or patty tins (muffin pans).

3 Bake in a preheated oven at 190°C/375°F/Gas Mark 5 for about 15–20 minutes, or until well risen and just firm to the touch. Place on a wire rack and leave to cool.

4 Make up the butter cream in a flavour to complement the sponge mixture and put into a piping bag fitted with a small star nozzle (tip).

5 Neatly cut a small piece out of the top of each bun, leaving about 1 cm/ ½ inch all round the top surface uncut; and cut the removed piece in half to form the 'wings'.

6 Pipe a whirl of butter cream to fill the hole which has been cut out of each bun. Place the 'wings' in position, tilting them up at the edges. Either leave the 'wings' as they are or pipe a little butter cream between and around them. Dredge lightly with icing (confectioners') sugar before serving.

MOCHA BOXES

Makes 16

350 g/12 oz dark chocolate
16 chocolate matchsticks to decorate

CAKE MIXTURE:
175 g/6 oz/ ¾ cup butter or margarine
175 g/6 oz/1 cup light soft brown sugar
3 eggs
175 g/6 oz/1½ cups self-raising flour
90 g/3 oz/ ¾ cup plain (all-purpose) flour
1 tbsp sifted cocoa powder
1 tbsp coffee flavouring (extract)

MOCHA BUTTER CREAM:
125 g/4 oz/ ½ cup butter or margarine
250 g/8 oz/1¼ cups icing (confectioners')
  sugar, sifted
1 tbsp sifted cocoa powder
2–3 tsp coffee flavouring (extract)

1 Line a 20 cm/8 inch deep square
cake tin (pan) with non-stick baking
parchment. Make up the cake as on page
571 (Madeira Cake). Put into the tin (pan),
level the top and bake in a preheated
oven at 160°C/325°F/Gas Mark 3 for
about 1–1¼ hours, until well risen and
firm and a skewer inserted in the centre
comes out clean. Invert on a wire rack.

2 When cool, trim and level the cake
and cut into 16 even-sized squares
(a little less than 5 cm/2 inches each).

3 Melt the chocolate in a bowl over a
saucepan of simmering water, then
spread out thinly on a sheet of baking
parchment to a square of 40 cm/16
inches. Pick up one corner of the paper
and shake lightly to level the chocolate.
Leave until barely set. Using a knife and a
ruler, cut the chocolate into 64 x 5 cm/
2 inch squares. Chill until completely set.

4 For the butter cream, cream the
butter, sugar, cocoa powder and
coffee flavouring (extract) to give a
spreading consistency. Mask the sides and
top of each cake square with butter cream
and put the remainder into a piping bag
with a large star nozzle (tip).

5 Press a square of chocolate to each
side of the squares, then pipe a large
whirl of butter cream on top of each box.
Decorate with 2 or 3 chocolate matchsticks.

MAIDS OF HONOUR

Makes about 20

SHORTCRUST (PLAIN) PASTRY:
175 g/6 oz/1½ cups plain (all-purpose)
  flour
pinch of salt
45 g/1½ oz/3 tbsp butter or block
  margarine
45 g/1½ oz/3 tbsp lard (shortening)
  or white vegetable fat
about 4 tbsp cold water to mix

FILLING:
150 g/5 oz/ ⅔ cup curd (smooth cottage)
  cheese
90 g/3 oz/ ⅓ cup softened butter
2 eggs
1 tbsp brandy
30 g/1 oz/ ¼ cup blanched flaked
  (slivered) almonds, chopped
few drops of almond flavouring (extract)
  (optional)
2 tbsp caster (superfine) sugar
60 g/2 oz/ ⅓ cup currants

1 To make the pastry dough, sift the
flour and salt into a bowl and rub in
the fat until the mixture resembles fine
breadcrumbs. Add sufficient cold water to
mix to a pliable dough, knead lightly and
wrap in clingfilm (plastic wrap) or foil;
chill while making the filling.

2 To make the filling, work the curd
(smooth cottage) cheese and butter
together carefully. Whisk the eggs and
brandy together, and work into the cheese
mixture with the almonds, almond
flavouring (extract) and sugar.

3 Roll out the pastry thinly on a lightly
floured work surface (counter) and
cut into about 20 fluted circles about
7 cm/3 inches in diameter. Place each
circle carefully in a patty tin (muffin pan).

4 Divide the cheese mixture between
the pastry cases and then sprinkle
each with a few currants. Bake in a
preheated oven at 200°C/400°F/Gas Mark
6 for about 15–20 minutes, or until well
risen and lightly browned.

5 Transfer to a wire rack and leave to
cool. Before serving, dredge each
lightly with sifted icing (confectioners')
sugar and decorate as you wish.

FRUIT & SPICE CAKES

Most of these rich, traditional cakes, redolent with fruit and spices, improve in flavour with keeping, and mellow if stored even for a few days before cutting. This is particularly true of the Scottish Gingerbread (see below), Bara Brith (see page 554) and Dundee Cake (see page 558). Stored in an airtight tin, these cakes will mature and develop in flavour. The Christmas Cake (see page 558) is the perfect example. This is made from a fruit cake recipe (see page 539) and stored for a month at least before decorating.

SCOTTISH GINGERBREAD

SERVES 8

150 g/5 oz/1¼ cups wholewheat flour
½ tsp salt
2 tsp ground ginger
1 tsp ground cinnamon
grated nutmeg
2 tsp baking powder
175 g/6 oz/1 cup dark brown Muscovado sugar
150 g/ 5 oz/1½ cups rolled oats
6 tbsp black treacle (see below)
125 g/4 oz/ ½ cup butter
1 egg, beaten
150 ml/ ¼ pint/ ⅔ cup natural yogurt
125 g/4 oz/ ¾ cup sultanas
125 g/4 oz crystallized ginger, chopped
60 g/2 oz/ ½ cup blanched almond halves
about 150 ml/ ¼ pint/ ⅔ cup milk

1 Grease and line a 18 cm/7 in round cake tin (pan). Sift the flour, salt, ground ginger, cinnamon, nutmeg and baking powder into a bowl and tip in any bran remaining in the sieve. Stir in the sugar and rolled oats.

2 Put the treacle and butter into a small pan and warm it over low heat. Remove from the heat and stir with a wooden spoon to blend thoroughly.

3 Stir the butter mixture into the dry ingredients, then beat in the egg and yogurt. Stir in the sultanas and crystallized ginger. Stir in just enough milk to give a stiff, dropping consistency.

4 Spoon the mixture into the prepared tin (pan) and level the surface. Arrange the nuts over the surface. Bake in the preheated oven at 180°C/350°F/Gas Mark 4 for 1½ hours, or until a fine skewer inserted in the centre of the cake comes out clean.

5 Leave the cake to cool in the tin (pan), then turn it out and stand on a wire rack to cool completely. Wrap closely in foil to store. Serve sliced, with yogurt cheese and honey, or with well-matured hard cheese and fresh fruit such as apples and pears.

BARA BRITH

MAKES 900 G/2 LB LOAF

250 g/8 oz/2 cups self-raising flour
pinch of salt
¾ tsp mixed (apple pie) spice
60g/2 oz/ ¼ cup butter or margarine
60 g/2 oz/ ¼ cup caster (superfine) sugar
* or 90 g/3 oz/ ½ cup light soft brown sugar*
grated rind of 1 lemon
125 g/4 oz/ ⅔ cup sultanas (golden raisins)
1 egg, beaten
90 g/3 oz/ ¼ cup black treacle (molasses)
120 ml/4 fl oz/ ½ cup milk
½ tsp bicarbonate of soda (baking soda)

1 Line a 900 g/2 lb loaf tin (pan) with non-stick baking parchment.

2 Sift the flour, salt and spice into a bowl. Add the butter or margarine and rub in finely until the mixture resembles fine breadcrumbs.

3 Add the sugar, lemon rind and sultanas (golden raisins) to the mixture and mix evenly.

4 Add the egg to the mixture, followed by the black treacle (molasses).

5 Measure the milk into a jug or cup and sprinkle in the bicarbonate of soda (baking soda). Mix well and add to the other ingredients. Mix thoroughly until well blended. Spoon into the prepared tin (pan) and level the top.

6 Bake in a preheated oven at 180°C/ 350°F/Gas Mark 4 for about 1¼ hours, or until well risen, firm to the touch and a skewer inserted in the centre comes out clean. Invert on a wire rack to cool. Store wrapped in foil or in an airtight container for 24 hours before serving in slices with butter and jam, if liked.

MEASURING TREACLE (MOLASSES)

The best way to measure black treacle (molasses) or golden (light corn) syrup is to oil a bowl or measuring cup lightly, add the treacle (molasses) or syrup and it will slide out easily without sticking.

CARROT CAKE

MAKES 20 CM/8 INCH ROUND CAKE

250 g/8 oz/2 cups self-raising flour
2 tsp baking powder
1 tsp ground cinnamon
150 g/5 oz/generous ¾ cup light soft brown
* sugar*
125 g/4 oz/1 cup carrots
2 dessert (eating) apples, peeled and cored
60 g/2 oz/ ½ cup pecan nuts, chopped
2 eggs
150 ml/ ¼ pint/ ⅔ cup vegetable or corn oil

TOPPING:
90 g/3 oz/ ⅓ cup full-fat soft cheese
90 g/3 oz/ ⅓ cup softened butter or
* margarine*
175 g/6 oz/1⅓ cups icing (confectioners')
* sugar, sifted*
grated rind of ½ – 1 orange

TO DECORATE:
pecan halves
orange jelly slices

1 Grease a 20 cm/8 inch round cake tin (pan) and line with non-stick baking parchment.

2 Sift the flour, baking powder and spice into a bowl. Mix in the sugar until evenly blended.

3 Grate the carrots and apples. Add the nuts, carrot and apples to the flour mixture, and mix together lightly, then make a well in the centre. Add the eggs and oil, and beat well until thoroughly blended.

4 Spoon into the tin (pan) and level the top. Bake in a preheated oven at 180°C/350°F/Gas Mark 4 for about 1 hour, or until the cake is golden brown and just slightly shrinking from the sides of the tin (pan). Test by inserting a skewer in the centre of the cake; it should come out clean. Invert on to a wire rack and leave until cold.

5 To make the topping, put all the ingredients together in a bowl and beat well until smooth. Spread over the top of the cake and swirl with a round-bladed knife or palette knife (spatula). As it sets, decorate with pecan halves and orange jelly slices.

SHERRY & SPICE CAKE

MAKES 20 CM/8 INCH SANDWICH
(LAYER) CAKE

6 tbsp sherry
175 g/6 oz/1 cup sultanas (golden raisins)
125 g/4 oz/ ½ cup butter or margarine
125 g/4 oz/ ⅔ cup light soft brown sugar
2 eggs
175 g/6 oz/1½ cups plain (all-purpose)
* flour*
1 tsp bicarbonate of soda (baking soda)
½ tsp ground cloves
¼ tsp ground or grated nutmeg
½ tsp ground cinnamon
60 g/2 oz/ ½ cup walnuts, chopped

TO DECORATE:
1 egg yolk
1 tbsp sherry
1 quantity Butter Cream (see page 541)
icing (confectioners') sugar for dredging
walnut or pecan halves

1 Grease 2 x 20 cm/8 inch sandwich
tins (layer pans) and line the bases
with non-stick baking parchment. Bring
the sherry, sultanas (golden raisins) and
4 tablespoons water to the boil. Cover
and simmer for 15 minutes. Strain off the
liquid and make it up to 5 tablespoons
with cold water.

2 Cream the butter and sugar until
pale and fluffy. Beat in the eggs one
at a time, following each with a spoonful
of flour. Sift the remaining flour with the
bicarbonate of soda (baking soda) and
spices, and fold into the mixture, with the
cooled sultana (golden raisin) liquor.

3 Add the nuts and sultanas (golden
raisins), and mix lightly. Divide
between the tins (pans). Level the tops.

4 Bake in a preheated oven at
180°C/350°F/Gas Mark 4 for
25–35 minutes, until firm to the touch.
Cool briefly in the tin (pan), loosen the
edges and invert on to a wire rack to cool.

5 Beat the egg yolk and sherry into
the butter cream. Add a little sifted
icing (confectioners') sugar, if necessary.
Use half to sandwich the cakes together,
then sift icing (confectioners') sugar lightly
over the top of the cake.

6 Place the remaining butter cream in
a piping bag fitted with a large star
nozzle (tip) and pipe a row of elongated
shells around the top about 2.5 cm/1 inch
in from the edge. Complete the
decoration with pecan or walnut halves.

KUGELHUPF

●●

MAKES 18 CM/7 INCH CAKE

175 g/6 oz/ ¾ cup butter or margarine
175 g/6 oz/ ¾ cup caster (superfine) sugar
3 eggs
175 g/6 oz/1½ cups self-raising flour
60 g/2 oz/ ½ cup plain (all-purpose) flour
½ tsp ground allspice
1 tsp mixed (apple pie) spice
grated rind of 2 oranges
45 g/1½ oz/ ¼ cup cut mixed (candied) peel
45 g/1½ oz/ ¼ cup stem or glacé (candied)
   ginger, chopped
finely pared rind of 1 orange
60 g/2 oz/ ¼ cup caster (superfine) sugar

SYRUP:
60 g/2 oz/ ½ cup icing (confectioners')
   sugar, sifted
4 tbsp orange juice

ICING (FROSTING):
125 g/4 oz/scant 1 cup icing
   (confectioners') sugar, sifted
1 tsp orange flower water

1 Grease a 1.5 litre/2¾ pint/7½ cup ring mould and dust with flour.

2 Cream together the butter and sugar until very light, fluffy and pale. Beat in the eggs one at a time, following each with a spoonful of the plain (all-purpose) flour. Sift the remaining flours together with the spices and fold into the mixture, followed by the grated orange rind, mixed (candied) peel, ginger and 1 tablespoon of cold water. Spoon into the mould and level the top.

3 Bake in a preheated oven at 180°C/ 350°F/Gas Mark 4 for 50–60 minutes, or until well risen and firm to the touch. Leave to cool briefly, then loosen and invert on a wire rack.

4 For the syrup, blend the sugar and orange juice and spoon over the warm cake. Leave to cool, then store in an airtight container for 24 hours.

5 Cut the orange rind into fine strips and put in a saucepan. Cover with water, add the sugar and simmer for 5 minutes until tender and syrupy. Drain.

6 To make the icing (frosting), put the sugar into a bowl with the orange flower water and enough tepid water to mix to a spreading consistency. Spread over the top of the cake, letting it run down the sides. Sprinkle with the orange strips and leave to set.

AMERICAN FRUIT & NUT RING

MAKES 25 CM/10 INCH RING

175 g/6 oz/1 cup no-need-to-soak prunes
125 g/4 oz/⅔ cup no-need-to-soak dried
    apricots
6–8 tbsp brown rum
175 g/6 oz/¾ cup butter or margarine
175 g/6 oz/1 cup dark soft brown sugar
3 eggs
250 g/8 oz/2 cups plain (all-purpose) flour
¾ tsp baking powder
¾ tsp ground allspice
½ tsp each ground ginger and cinnamon
125 g/4 oz/1 cup chopped mixed nuts
175 g/6 oz/1 cup raisins
90 g/3 oz/⅔ cup glacé (candied) cherries,
    quartered, washed and dried
grated rind of 1 orange
grated rind of 1 lemon
1 tbsp black treacle (molasses)

TOPPING:
about 5 tbsp apricot jam, sieved (strained)
selection of shelled mixed nuts
9 no-need-to-soak prunes
18 no-need-to-soak apricots
halved glacé (candied) cherries
glacé (candied) pineapple or ginger
angelica

1 Finely chop the dried fruit and soak in 4 tablespoons of the rum for 30 minutes. Line a 25 cm/10 inch springform cake tin (pan) fitted with a tubular base with non-stick baking parchment.

2 Cream the fat and sugar until light and fluffy. Beat in the eggs, one at a time, following each with a tablespoonful of the flour. Sift the rest of the flour with the baking powder and spices, and fold into the mixture. Add the rest of the ingredients, and the prunes and apricots with any excess rum, and mix evenly.

3 Spoon into the tin (pan), level the top and tie several layers of folded newspaper around the outside. Bake in a preheated oven at 150°C/300°F/Gas Mark 2 for 1¾ hours, or until a skewer inserted in the cake comes out clean.

4 Leave the cake in the tin (pan) until cold, then remove carefully and peel off the lining paper. Pierce all over with a skewer and pour the remaining rum over the cake, then wrap securely in foil and store for up to a month.

5 Glaze the cake with some of the jam, then arrange the topping ingredients on top. Glaze again and leave to set.

CHRISTMAS CAKE

••

MAKES 23 CM/9 INCH CAKE

23 cm/9 inch rich fruit cake (see page 539)
    using half the recipe quantity
1 kg/2 lb marzipan (see page 540)
silver balls to decorate
875 g/1¾ lb sugarpaste (see page 571)
125 g/4 oz/ ⅓ cup apricot jam, sieved
    (strained) and mixed with 2 tbsp water
1.25 metres/1½ yards wide satin ribbon
⅓ quantity Royal Icing (see page 542)
green and red paste food colourings

1 Cover the cake with marzipan (see page 540), using 875 g/1½ lb, and leave for 2–3 days to dry. Colour the rest red and green and make 10 Christmas trees (see page 540). Decorate with silver balls.

2 Attach the cake to a 30 cm/12 inch cake board with a dab of icing. Knead the sugarpaste until smooth. Roll out on baking parchment to a circle 15 cm/6 inches larger than the cake. Brush the marzipan lightly with the apricot glaze and position the sugarpaste over the cake.

3 Using fingers dipped in icing (confectioners') sugar, mould the sugarpaste to fit the cake, making sure there are no air bubbles. Trim round the base. Use your fingers and the side of a clean bottle, to roll the sides and top until smooth. Trim and leave to set.

4 Attach the ribbon over the cake with dabs of icing and pins. Half fill a piping bag fitted with a No. 2 plain writing nozzle (tip) with royal icing and pipe lines parallel to the ribbon at 1 cm/½ inch intervals to the edge of the cake. Repeat on the other side. Pipe across the first lines at right angles. Add a second line close to the first, then leave a space. Write 'Happy Christmas' between the ribbons, and, when dry, overpipe to make it stand out.

5 Fit a piping bag with a small star nozzle (tip). Fill with royal icing. Pipe a line of shells inside the ribbon and round the top edge of the cake. Add a twisted coil of royal icing round the base to attach the cake to the board. Add 2 dots below alternate shells on the top edges and some stars on the sides. Attach 8 Christmas trees to the sides with a dab of royal icing and attach the last 2 on the top. Leave to dry.

DUNDEE CAKE

••

MAKES 20 CM/8 INCH CAKE

250 g/8 oz/1⅓ cups seedless raisins
125 g/4 oz/ ⅔ cup stoned raisins
125 g/4 oz/ ⅔ cup currants
150 g/5 oz/ ¾ cup sultanas (golden raisins)
125 g/4 oz/ ⅔ cup cut mixed (candied) peel
60 g/2 oz/ ½ cup blanched almonds, finely
    chopped
grated rind of 1 orange
grated rind of 1 lemon
250 g/8 oz/2 cups plain (all-purpose) flour
1 tsp mixed (apple pie) spice
1 tsp ground cinnamon
generous pinch of ground nutmeg
250 g/8 oz/1 cup butter
250 g/8 oz/1⅓ cups light soft brown sugar
4 eggs
1 tbsp brandy, rum, orange or lemon juice
about 60 g/2 oz/ ½ cup whole blanched
    almonds to decorate

1 Grease a 20 cm/8 inch deep round cake tin (pan) and line with a double layer of non-stick baking parchment. Mix together the dried fruits, mixed (candied) peel, chopped almonds and grated fruit rinds.

2 Sift the flour and the spices into a bowl. Cream the butter until soft, add the sugar, and cream together until very light and fluffy and pale in colour.

3 Beat in the eggs, one at a time, following each with a spoonful of the flour, then fold in the remaining flour, followed by the fruit mixture and brandy.

4 Spoon into the prepared tin (pan) and level the top. Arrange the whole almonds in circles all over the top of the cake, beginning at the outside and working into the centre. Tie several thicknesses of folded newspaper around the outside of the tin (pan).

5 Bake in a preheated oven at 150°C/300°F/Gas Mark 2 for about 3½ hours, or until a skewer inserted into the centre of the cake comes out clean. Leave to cool completely in the tin (pan). When cold, remove carefully and wrap in foil until required.

GÂTEAUX

Gâteaux are very much special-occasion cakes, flamboyant creations designed to impress, such as the Malakoff Gâteau (see page 562). Yet these elaborate cakes can be quite easy to make, and are often founded on a simple sponge mixture – see the Orange Caraque Gâteau (below) for example. The art lies in the decoration, often with whipped cream, butter cream, or frosting, and in the presentation, which must be immaculate. Use a chef's tip to achieve a perfect layer cake, such as the Black Forest Gâteau (see page 563): mark the side of the cake into layers, inserting 3-4 cocktail sticks at intervals around the cake, one for each layer. Then cut the layers evenly with a long, sharp, thin-bladed knife.

ORANGE CARAQUE GÂTEAU

SERVES 8-10

175 g/6 oz/ ¾ cup butter or soft margarine
90 g/3 oz/ ⅓ cup caster (superfine) sugar
90 g/3 oz/ ½ cup light soft brown sugar
3 eggs
175 g/6 oz/1½ cups self-raising flour, sifted
grated rind of 1 large or 1½ small oranges
3 tbsp orange juice
4 tbsp orange-flavoured liqueur
1 quantity Orange Pastry Cream (see page 542)
1 tsp orange flower water
grated rind of ½–1 orange
250 g/8 oz/8 squares dark chocolate
1 quantity Chocolate Butter Cream (see page 541)
icing (confectioners') sugar for dredging

1 Grease a rectangular tin (pan), about 28 x 18 x 4 cm/11 x 7 x 1½ inches, and line with non-stick baking parchment. Make the cake as for Victoria Sandwich (Sponge Layer Cake) (see page 570), adding the orange rind and using 1 tablespoon of the orange juice instead of the water. Spoon into the tin (pan), level the top and bake in a preheated oven at 190°C/ 375°F/Gas Mark 5 for 25–30 minutes, or until well risen and firm to the touch.

2 Invert the cake on a wire rack and leave to cool, then peel off the baking parchment. Combine the remaining orange juice with the liqueur and sprinkle over the cake.

3 Simmer the orange pastry cream for 1 minute, then remove from the heat and beat in the orange flower water and orange rind. Cover with clingfilm (plastic wrap) and leave until cold.

4 Cut the cake in half lengthways to give 2 slabs and sandwich together with the orange pastry cream.

5 Use 90–125 g/3–4 oz/3–4 squares of the chocolate to make Miniature Chocolate Curls (see page 541). Use the remaining chocolate to make Chocolate Caraque (see page 541).

6 Cover the whole cake with the chocolate butter cream and then use the chocolate curls to cover the sides of the gâteau. Arrange the caraque along the top of the gâteau and then dust lightly with icing (confectioners') sugar before serving.

PASSION CAKE

SERVES 8-10

150 ml/ ¼ pint/ ⅔ cup corn oil
175 g/6 oz/ ¾ cup golden caster sugar
4 tbsp natural yogurt
3 eggs, plus 1 extra yolk
1 tsp vanilla flavouring
125 g/4 oz/1 cup walnut pieces, chopped
175 g/6 oz carrots, grated
1 banana, mashed
175 g/ 6 oz/1½ cups flour
90 g/3 oz/ ½ cup fine oatmeal
1 tsp bicarbonate of soda
1 tsp baking powder
1 tsp ground cinnamon
½ tsp salt

FROSTING:
150 g/5 oz/generous ½ cup yogurt cheese
  (see page 97), or low-fat soft cheese
4 tbsp natural yogurt
90 g/3 oz/ ¾ cup icing (confectioner's)
  sugar
1 tsp grated lemon rind
2 tsp lemon juice

DECORATION:
a few primroses and violets
45 g/1½ oz/3tbsp caster sugar
1 egg white, lightly beaten

1 Grease and line a 23 cm/9 in round cake tin (pan). Beat together the oil, sugar, yogurt, eggs, egg yolk and vanilla flavouring. Beat in the chopped walnuts, grated carrot and banana.

2 Sift together the remaining ingredients and gradually beat into the mixture.

3 Pour the mixture into the tin (pan) and level the surface. Bake in the preheated oven at 160ºC/350ºF/Gas Mark 4 for 1½ hours, or until the cake is firm. To test, insert a fine skewer into the centre: it should come out clean. Leave to cool in the tin (pan) for 15 minutes, then turn out on a wire rack.

4 To make the frosting, beat together the cheese and yogurt. Sift in the icing (confectioner's) sugar and stir in the lemon rind and juice. Spread over the top and sides of the cake.

5 To prepare the decoration, dip the flowers quickly in the beaten egg white, then sprinkle with caster sugar to cover the surface completely. Place well apart on baking parchment. Leave in a warm, dry place for several hours until they are dry and crisp. Arrange the flowers in a pattern on top of the cake.

SACHERTORTE

MAKES 23CM/9 INCH CAKE

150 g/5 oz/5 squares dark chocolate
150 g/5 oz/⅔ cup caster (superfine) sugar
150 g/5 oz/⅔ cup butter
5 eggs, separated
few drops of vanilla flavouring (extract)
150 g/5 oz/1¼ cups plain (all-purpose)
    flour
1 tsp baking powder
300 g/10 oz/generous ¾ cup apricot jam,
    sieved (strained)
1 quantity Chocolate Butter Cream (see
    page 541)

CHOCOLATE ICING (FROSTING):
175 g/6 fl oz/6 squares dark chocolate
175 ml/6 fl oz/¾ cup water
good knob of butter
125 g/4 oz/½ cup caster (superfine) sugar

1 Grease a 23 cm/9 inch springform tin
   (pan) and line with non-stick baking
parchment. Dust with flour. Melt the
chocolate with 1 tablespoon water in a
bowl over a pan of simmering water.

2 Cream the sugar and butter together
   until light and fluffy. Beat in the egg
yolks one at a time, then beat in the
melted chocolate and vanilla. Fold the
sifted flour and baking powder into the
mixture. Whisk the egg whites until very
stiff and beat a tablespoonful into the
mixture, then fold in the rest evenly.

3 Spoon the mixture into the lined tin
   (pan), level the top and bake in a
preheated oven at 150°C/300°F/Gas Mark
2 for about 1 hour, or until well risen and
firm. Cool in the tin (pan) for 3 minutes,
then invert on a wire rack.

4 When it is cold, split the cake in half
   and spread with half the jam.
Reassemble the cake and spread the
remaining jam all over the cake.

5 To make the icing (frosting), melt
   the chocolate with 2 tablespoons of
the water, as above. Stir in the butter until
melted. Boil the remaining water with the
sugar until syrupy. Carefully pour over the
chocolate and beat until smooth. Leave to
cool, beating occasionally, until thick
enough to stick to the cake. Pour over the
cake and spread to cover the sides and
top evenly.

6 Use a piping bag and small star
   nozzle (tip) to pipe chocolate butter
cream stars around the edge and base of
the cake. Use a plain writing nozzle (tip)
to write 'SACHER' across the top.

MALAKOFF GÂTEAU

••

SERVES 8

90 g/3 oz/ ¾ cup blanched almonds,
  roughly chopped
250 g/8 oz/1 cup caster (superfine) sugar
175 g/6 oz/ ¾ cup butter
2 egg yolks
150 ml/ ¼ pint/ ⅔ cup milk
4 tbsp brandy or rum
2 tbsp coffee flavouring (extract) or
  extremely strong black coffee
about 40 boudoir biscuits or sponge
  fingers (lady-fingers)
300 ml/ ½ pint/1¼ cups double (heavy)
  cream
1 tbsp milk

TO DECORATE:
strawberries, sliced
1 kiwi fruit, sliced

1 Gently heat the almonds and half the sugar in a saucepan until they turn a caramel colour, shaking the pan frequently. Do not over-brown. Pour quickly on to some baking parchment and leave to set in a solid block.

2 Line a 900g/2 lb loaf tin (pan) with non-stick baking parchment. Crush the almond caramel until powdery with a rolling pin.

3 Beat the butter until soft, then add the remaining sugar, and cream until light and fluffy. Beat in the egg yolks, followed by the crushed almonds.

4 Combine the milk, alcohol and coffee flavouring (extract). Arrange a layer of boudoir biscuits (lady-fingers) in the base of the lined tin (pan), sugared-side downwards, and sprinkle with 3 tablespoons of the milk mixture.

5 Spread with one third of the nut mixture, cover with a layer of biscuits (lady-fingers) and sprinkle with milk. Layer the rest of the nut mixture and biscuits (lady-fingers) soaked in milk to make 3 layers of the former and 4 of the latter. Press down evenly, cover with baking parchment and weight lightly. Chill for at least 12 hours.

6 Invert the gâteau on to a plate and peel off the paper. Whip the cream and milk together until just stiff. Use most of it to cover the gâteau; put the remainder into a piping bag fitted with a large star nozzle (tip) and pipe diagonal lines across the top. Mark wavy lines around the sides and add piped cream to the corners and sides. Decorate with sliced strawberries and kiwi fruit.

BLACK FOREST GÂTEAU

SERVES 8–10

3 eggs
140 g/4½ oz/ ½ cup plus 1 tbsp caster
(superfine) sugar
90 g/3 oz/ ¾ cup plain (all-purpose) flour
20 g/¾ oz/3 tbsp cocoa powder
450 ml/ ¾ pint /2 cups double (heavy)
cream
90 g/3 oz/3 squares dark chocolate
3–4 tbsp Kirsch, brandy or other liqueur
1 quantity Chocolate Butter Cream (see
page 541)

FILLING:
425 g/14 oz can of stoned (pitted) black
cherries, drained and juice reserved
2 tsp arrowroot

1 Grease a deep 23 cm/9 inch cake tin
(pan) and line with non-stick baking
parchment. Whisk the eggs and sugar
together until the mixture is very thick
and pale in colour and the whisk leaves a
heavy trail when lifted.

2 Sift the flour and cocoa powder
together twice, then fold evenly and
lightly through the mixture. Pour into the
prepared tin (pan) and bake in a
preheated oven at 190°C/375°F/Gas Mark
5 for about 30 minutes, or until well risen
and firm to the touch. Invert on a wire
rack and cool.

3 To make the filling, mix the cherries
and 150 ml/ ¼ pint/ ⅔ cup of the
juice with the arrowroot. Bring slowly to
the boil, stirring continuously, and boil
until clear and thickened. Reserve 8
cherries for decoration. Halve the rest and
add to the sauce, then cool.

4 Whip the cream until thick enough
to pipe and put 4 tablespoons into a
piping bag with a large star nozzle (tip).
Pare the chocolate into curls. Split the
cake horizontally into 3 layers. Spread the
first layer with some of the cream and
half the cherry mixture.

5 Cover with the second cake layer,
sprinkle with the liqueur, then
spread with some of the butter cream and
the remaining cherry mixture. Top with
the final layer of cake. Cover the sides
with the rest of the butter cream.

6 Spread the remaining whipped
cream over the top of the gâteau
and press the chocolate curls around the
sides of the gâteau. Pipe 8 whirls of
cream on the top. Add a cherry to each
whirl. Chill for 2–3 hours.

LINZERTORTE

••

SERVES 8

PASTRY:
175 g/6 oz/ ¾ cup butter or margarine
90 g/3 oz/ ⅓ cup caster (superfine) sugar
finely grated rind of 1 orange (optional)
1 egg
250 g/8 oz/2 cups plain (all-purpose) flour
½ tsp baking powder
¾ tsp mixed (apple pie) spice
60 g/2 oz/ ½ cup blanched almonds,
*   walnuts or pecan nuts, finely chopped*

FILLING:
250 g/8 oz/1½ cups fresh raspberries (or
*   thawed, if frozen)*
250 g/8 oz/ ⅔ cup raspberry preserve
1–2 tbsp brandy
icing (confectioners') sugar for dredging

1 To make the pastry, cream the butter and sugar together until light and creamy, then beat in the orange rind, if using, and egg. Sift the flour with the baking powder and spice and work into the mixture, followed by the chopped nuts. Wrap in clingfilm (plastic wrap) or foil and chill until firm.

2 Lightly grease a loose-based flan tin (quiche pan) or ring about 20 cm/ 8 inches in diameter. Combine the raspberries, jam and brandy.

3 Roll out about two thirds of the pastry with great care, for it is very crumbly, and use to line the flan tin (quiche pan); trim and level the edges.

4 Spoon the raspberry mixture evenly into the pastry-lined tin (pan).

5 Roll out the remaining pastry and cut into narrow strips. Lay these strips evenly over the raspberry filling in a lattice design, attaching the ends to the flan case (pie shell). Bake in a preheated oven at 190°C/375°F/Gas Mark 5 for 40–50 minutes or until firm and a light golden brown.

6 Remove from the oven and leave until cold. Remove carefully from the flan tin (quiche pan) and place on a serving dish. Dredge evenly with sifted icing (confectioners') sugar and serve with whipped cream.

BOSTON CHOCOLATE PIE

••

SERVES 6

250 g/8 oz shortcrust pastry

FILLING:
3 eggs
125 g/4 oz/½ cup caster sugar
60 g/2 oz/½ cup flour, plus extra for
*   dusting*
1 tbsp icing (confectioner's) sugar
pinch of salt
1 tsp vanilla flavouring
400 ml/14 fl oz/1¾ cups milk
150 ml/ ¼ pint/ ⅔ cup natural yogurt
150 g/5 oz plain chocolate, broken into
*   pieces*
2 tbsp kirsch
150 ml/ ¼ pint/⅔ cup crème fraîche
Chocolate Caraque (see page 541)

1 Grease a 23 cm/9 in loose-bottomed flan tin. Roll out the pastry on a lightly-floured board and lower into the flan ring. Press into the ring and around the sides and trim neatly. Prick the base with a fork, line with baking parchment and fill it with dried beans. Bake "blind" for 20 minutes at 200ºC/400ºF/Gas Mark 6, then remove the beans and paper and return to the oven for 5 minutes to dry. Cool on a wire rack.

2 To make the filling, beat the eggs and sugar until light and fluffy. Sift the flour, icing (confectioner's) sugar and salt over the beaten eggs and stir until blended. Stir in the vanilla flavouring.

3 Put the milk and yogurt in a small pan, bring slowly to the boil, then strain on to the egg mixture. Pour into the top of a double boiler, or a bowl over a pan of simmering water, and stir until thick enough to coat the back of a spoon.

4 Melt the chocolate and kirsch over a low heat and stir into the custard. Remove the custard from the heat and stand in cold water to prevent further cooking. Leave to cool.

5 Make the Chocolate Caraque (see page 541). Pour the chocolate mixture into the pastry case. Spread the crème fraîche over the chocolate, and arrange the caraque rolls on top.

SIMNEL CAKE

••

MAKES 18–20 CM/7–8 INCH CAKE

250 g/8 oz/2 cups plain (all-purpose) flour
pinch of salt
1 tsp ground cinnamon
½ tsp each ground allspice and nutmeg
175 g/6 oz/1 cup sultanas (golden raisins)
125 g/4 oz/⅔ cup currants
125 g/4 oz/⅔ cup raisins
60 g/2 oz/⅓ cup cut mixed (candied) peel
60 g/2 oz/¼ cup glacé (candied) cherries,
  quartered, washed and dried
45 g/1½ oz/¼ cup stem ginger, chopped
grated rind of 1 orange
175 g/6 oz/¾ cup butter or margarine
175 g/6 oz/1 cup light soft brown sugar
3 eggs
1–2 tbsp orange juice
625 g/1¼ lb marzipan (see page 540)
apricot jam

1 Line an 18–20 cm/7–8 inch round
cake tin (pan) with a double layer of
non-stick baking parchment.

2 Sift the flour, salt and spices into a
bowl. Mix the dried fruits with the
peel, cherries, ginger and orange rind.

3 Cream the fat and sugar together
until light, fluffy and pale. Beat in
the eggs one at a time following each
with a spoonful of flour, then fold in the
remaining flour, followed by the fruit
mixture and orange juice. Spoon half the
cake mixture evenly into the tin (pan).

4 Roll out one third of the marzipan to
a circle the size of the tin (pan), lay
over the mixture and cover with the
remaining mixture. Tie several layers of
newspaper around the tin (pan).

5 Bake in a preheated oven at
160°C/325°F/Gas Mark 3 for 2–2½
hours until the sides are just shrinking
away from the tin (pan). Leave to cool for
10 minutes, then invert on to a wire rack
and leave until completely cold.

6 Roll out half the marzipan into a
circle to fit the cake and attach with
jam. Decorate the edge and mark a criss-
cross pattern with a knife. Roll the
remaining marzipan into 11 small balls
and arrange around the edge. Leave to
set. Tie a yellow ribbon around the cake.

BELGIAN APRICOT TORTE

••

MAKES 8–10

175 g/6 oz/¾ cup butter
60 g/2 oz/¼ cup caster (superfine) sugar
1½ tbsp oil
½ tsp vanilla flavouring (extract)
1 egg, beaten
350 g/12 oz/3 cups plain (all-purpose)
  flour
1½ tsp baking powder
grated rind of 1 lemon
grated rind of 1 orange
175 g/6 oz/½ cup apricot jam
90 g/3 oz/½ cup no-need-to-soak dried
  apricots, chopped finely
icing (confectioners') sugar for dredging

1 Line an 18–20 cm/7–8 inch round
cake tin (pan) with non-stick baking
parchment.

2 Cream the butter until soft then beat
in the sugar and continue until light
and fluffy. Beat in the oil, then add the
vanilla flavouring (extract) and egg and
beat well.

3 Sift the flour with the baking powder
and gradually work into the creamed
mixture with the grated lemon and orange
rinds. Knead together as for a shortbread
dough. Divide the dough in half and
coarsely grate one portion of it into the
tin (pan) so it covers the base evenly.

4 Beat the jam until smooth then beat
in the chopped apricots. Spread the
apricot mixture evenly over the dough,
taking it right to the edges.

5 Grate the remaining dough evenly
over the jam and cook in a
preheated oven at 150°C/300°F/Gas Mark
2 for about 1–1¼ hours or until lightly
browned and just firm. Remove from the
oven and leave until cold.

6 Remove the torte from the tin (pan)
and strip off the paper, then dredge
heavily with sifted icing (confectioners')
sugar. Either wrap in foil or place in an
airtight plastic container to transport.

HALLOWE'EN DEVIL'S FOOD CAKE

MAKES 25 CM/10 INCH CAKE

90 g/3 oz/ ⅓ cup butter or soft margarine
125 g/4 oz/ ½ cup caster (superfine) sugar
150 g/5 oz/ ¾ cup light soft brown sugar
300 g/10 oz/2½ cups plain (all-purpose)
  flour
2 tsp bicarbonate of soda (baking soda)
2 tbsp cocoa powder
4 eggs
125 g/4 oz/4 squares dark chocolate,
  melted
1 tbsp black treacle (molasses)
1 tsp vanilla flavouring (extract)
200 ml/7 fl oz/scant 1 cup milk
1 quantity White (Boiled) Frosting (see
  page 542)

TO DECORATE:
125 g/4 oz marzipan (see page 540)
orange paste food colouring
black paste food colouring

1 Grease 3 x 25 cm/10 inch deep
  sandwich tins (layer pans) and line
with non-stick baking parchment. Cream
the butter and sugars until light and fluffy.
Sift together the flour, bicarbonate of soda
(baking soda) and cocoa powder.

2 Beat the eggs into the creamed
  mixture one at a time, following
each with a spoonful of the flour mixture.
Beat in the melted chocolate, treacle
(molasses) and flavouring (extract).

3 Fold in the remaining flour,
  alternating with the milk, until
smooth. Divide equally between the tins
(pans) and level the tops. Bake in a preheated oven at 180°C/350°F/Gas Mark 4
for about 25–30 minutes, or until well
risen and firm to the touch. Invert
carefully on wire racks. Strip off the paper
and leave to cool.

4 Colour two thirds of the marzipan
  orange and shape it into 8 small
pumpkins and a larger one. Colour the
remaining marzipan black.

5 Draw and cut out a template of a
  witch on a broomstick. Roll out the
black marzipan, position the template and
cut out 5–6 witches.

6 Use a little of the frosting to
  sandwich the cakes together and
transfer to a plate or board. Use the
remaining frosting to cover the whole
cake, swirling it attractively before it sets.
Attach the witches and pumpkins to
decorate the cake and leave to set.

CHILDREN'S PARTY CAKES – INTRODUCTION

Decorating cakes is an art which is increasing in popularity, and this book aims to provide you with a wide range of novelty Children's Party Cakes to suit a wide range of ages, for both boys and girls and including simpler butter cream cakes, more ambitious sculptured designs and numeral cakes and Christmas party cakes to name just a few.

None of the designs is very difficult, but they do all require a little concentration and quite a few hours to complete satisfactorily. The flavour and type of cake is usually up to you, and the icings (frostings) can be coloured and flavoured to suit your personal taste.

If this is your first attempt at a novelty cake, do try one of the simpler designs first, but with a little practice and a lot of patience you will soon be able to attempt any of these cakes, and quickly be able to design your own party cakes.

Whatever cake you choose to make, leave it to rest on a wire rack for at least 12, and preferably 24, hours before you cut or decorate it. When the cake has been allowed to 'set' it will firm up slightly, and icing and decorating will be a lot easier.

VARIATIONS OF FLAVOURS
For Quick Mix Cakes:
Orange or Lemon: omit vanilla and add 3 teaspoons finely grated orange or lemon rind for the 3-egg mix; 4 teaspoons for the 4-egg mix; and 5 teaspoons for the 5-egg mix.

Chocolate: add 2 tablespoons sifted cocoa powder for the 3-egg mix; 2½ tablespoons for the 4-egg mix; and 3 tablespoons for the 5-egg mix.

Coffee: add 1 tablespoon instant coffee powder for the 3 egg mix; 1½ tablespoons for the 4 egg mix; or 2 tablespoons for the 5 egg mix.

For Madeira (Pound) Cakes:
Omit the lemon rind and juice and for Coffee replace lemon juice with coffee essence; for Chocolate replace the lemon juice with water and add 1½ tablespoons sifted cocoa powder for the 3-egg mix; 2 tablespoons for the 4-egg mix; and 3 tablespoons for the 6-egg mix.

DECORATIONS
Here are the methods for making the animals, flowers, leaves and other shapes featured in the recipes. They can all be made from sugarpaste either homemade (see page 571) or bought ready made from specialist cake decorating shops or large supermarkets; or marzipan again homemade (see page 540) or bought.

HOLLY LEAVES AND IVY LEAVES
(see page 579)
Special cutters in various sizes can be bought to cut out these leaves. Colour the sugarpaste or marzipan a suitable green and roll out thinly on non-stick baking parchment. Either stamp out the shapes, remove from cutters, mark in veins with a knife and lay over a lightly greased rolling pin or spoon handles, so they dry in realistic curves. Or cut sugarpaste into strips about 2 cm/ ¾ in wide and 2.5–4 cm/1–1½ inches long, and using the sharp rounded end of a piping nozzle (tip) take 'cuts' out each side of the strips to give holly leaves. Ivy leaves have 5 rounded points. Holly berries are tiny scraps of red sugarpaste or marzipan simply rolled out in the palms of your hands into balls and left to dry.

SUGARPASTE FLOWERS (see page 650)
Colour sugarpaste or marzipan as required and then roll out on non-

INTRODUCTION

Basic Cake Mixtures and Quantities

QUICK MIX CAKES

eggs	3	4	6
soft margarine	175g/6oz/ ¾ cup	250g/8oz/1 cup	350g/12oz/1½ cups
caster sugar	175g/6oz/ ¾ cup	250g/8oz/1 cup	350g/12oz/1½ cups
self-raising flour	175g/6oz/1½ cups	250g/8oz/2 cups	350g/12oz/3 cups
baking powder	1½ tsp	2 tsp	3 tsp
vanilla flavouring	½ tsp	½ tsp	½–¾ tsp

VICTORIA SANDWICH (SPONGE LAYER CAKE)

eggs	2	3	4
butter or margarine	125g/4oz/ ½ cup	175g/6oz/ ¾ cup	250g/8oz/1 cup
caster sugar	125g/4oz/ ½ cup	175g/6oz/ ¾ cup	250g/8oz/1 cup
self-raising flour	125g/4oz/1 cup	175g/6oz/1½ cup	250g/8oz/2 cups
cold water	2–3 tsp	1 tbsp	1½ tbsp
vanilla flavouring	few drops	few drops	few drops

VICTORIA SANDWICH (SPONGE LAYER CAKE)

eggs	5	6	7
butter or margarine	300g/10oz/1¼ cups	350g/12oz/1½ cups	425g/14oz/1¾ cups
caster sugar	300g/10oz/1¼ cups	350g/12oz/1½ cups	425g/14oz/1¾ cups
self-raising flour	300g/10oz/2½ cups	350g/12oz/3 cups	425g/14oz/3½ cups
cold water	2 tbsp	2 tbsp	2½ tbsp
vanilla flavouring	½ tsp	¾ tsp	¾–1 tsp

MADEIRA (POUND) CAKE

eggs	2	3	4
butter or margarine	125g/4oz/ ½ cup	175g/6oz/ ¾ cup	250g/8oz/1 cup
caster sugar	125g/4oz/ ½ cup	175g/6oz/ ¾ cup	250g/8oz/1 cup
self-raising flour	125g/4oz/1 cup	175g/6oz/1½ cups	250g/8oz/2 cups
plain flour	60g/2oz/ ½ cup	90g/3oz/ ¾ cup	125g/4oz/1 cup
grated lemon rind	½–1 lemon	1 lemon	1½–2 lemons

MADEIRA (POUND) CAKE

eggs	5	6	7
butter or margarine	300g/10oz/1¼ cups	350g/12oz/1½ cups	425g/14oz/1¾ cups
caster sugar	300g/10oz/1¼ cups	350g/12oz/1½ cups	425g/14oz/1¾ cups
self-raising flour	300g/10oz/2½ cups	350g/12oz/3 cups	425g/14oz/3½ cups
plain flour	150g/5oz/1¼ cups	175g/6oz/1½ cups	200g/7oz/1¾ cups
grated lemon rind	2 large lemons	2 large lemons	2–2½ lemons
lemon juice	2 tbsp	2 tbsp	2½ tbsp

INTRODUCTION

stick baking parchment. Using a multi-petal flower cutter, stamp out the flowers. If liked press a sugared mimosa ball in the centre of each. Leave to dry. For piped flowers in the grass, simply pipe large stars using a star nozzle (tip) and butter cream or royal icing and place a mimosa ball in the centre.

BELLS AND SHELLS FOR OPEN BOOK (see page 649)
Bells are simply shaped out of scraps of coloured sugarpaste by rolling them in the palms of the hands and then pressing a hole in the base with a rounded plastic skewer. Leave to dry.

Shells are made from coloured royal icing placed in a piping bag fitted with a large star nozzle (tip) and piping single shells on to non-stick baking parchment. Leave to dry.

MICE FOR HICKORY DICKORY DOCK CAKE (see page 577)
These can be made in any colour you like but the ears should be lined with white or pale pink sugarpaste and a scrap of black sugarpaste is needed for the noses. Use 30–90 g/1–3 oz sugarpaste for the mouse body, removing a scrap for the ears, and piece for the tail; shape into a teardrop shape with a point for the nose. Mark in 2 eyes with a cocktail stick and make 2 slits above the eyes for ears. Shape the ear scraps of sugarpaste into 2 very thin circles, then attach a slightly smaller circle of white or pink sugarpaste. Pinch together at the base and inset in the slits, tipping the ears forward slightly. Roll out the tail piece into a very thin sausage, make a tiny hole at the rear of the mouse and insert the tail. Add a scrap of black sugarpaste for the nose and then add 3 or 4 short lengths of flower stamens (available from specialist cake decorating

shops) for the whiskers and leave in a cool place to set.

PANDA BEARS FOR PANDA'S PICNIC CAKE (see page 578)
These need 45–90 g/1½–3 oz sugarpaste for each panda, two-thirds of which should be white and the remainder coloured black. For each panda shape just over two-thirds of the white sugarpaste into a ball for the body and the rest into a smaller ball for the head. Remove a tiny piece of black sugarpaste to make 2 eyes, 2 ears and a nose; halve the remainder and roll each piece into a sausage about 7–10 cm/3–4 in long, depending on the size of the panda. Bend 1 piece into a U shape for feet and legs and place the body on top. Insert half a wooden cocktail stick (toothpick) through the body and impale the head on top. Attach the arms around the body, then slot ears into slits in the top of the head, and add 2 eye patches and a nose.

CHRISTMAS PARCELS
Cut squares and rectangles approx 2.5–5 cm/1–2 in from coloured fondant paste or marzipan, and leave to dry. Tie with very narrow ribbons.

TEDDY BEARS
Make these in a similar way to the pandas, but all in one colour. Each bear will take 45–90 g/1½–3 oz/⅓–¾ cup sugarpaste or marzipan. Pinch out the ears, mark the eyes with a cocktail stick (toothpick), and add a scrap of black for the nose.

TEMPLATES
A template is a cutting guide used to cut out a cake in a particular shape, such as a teddy bear or stocking, or to cut shapes to decorate a cake. Cut templates from card or very stiff paper.

VICTORIA SANDWICH (SPONGE LAYER CAKE) & QUICK MIX

••

MAKES 30 x 25 CM/12 x 10 IN CAKE

*350 g/12 oz/1½ cups butter or margarine
  for Victoria Sandwich (Sponge Layer
  Cake) or 350 g/12 oz/1½ cups soft
  margarine for Quick Mix Cake*
*350 g/12 oz/1½ cups caster (superfine)
  sugar; or light soft brown; or half each
  caster (superfine) and soft brown*
6 eggs
350 g/12 oz/3 cups self-raising flour, sifted
*2 tbsp water for Victoria Sandwich
  (Sponge Layer Cake) only*
few drops of vanilla flavouring (extract)
*3 tsp baking powder for Quick Mix Cake
  only*
apricot jam, sieved (strained)
butter cream (see page 541) to decorate

1 For either cake, grease and line a
  rectangular cake or roasting tin (pan)
about 30 x 25 cm/12 x 10 in with baking
parchment.

2 For the Victoria Sandwich (Sponge
  Layer Cake), cream the butter and
sugar together until light, fluffy and pale.
Beat in the eggs, one at a time, following
each with a tablespoonful of the flour.
Fold in the remaining flour, then the
water and vanilla
flavouring (extract).

3 To make the
  Quick Mix
Cake, put the fat,
sugar, eggs, flour,
vanilla flavouring
(extract) and baking
powder into a bowl and beat
vigorously for 2 minutes either by hand,
using a hand-held electric mixer, or in a
large free-standing mixer.

4 Spread either cake mixture evenly
  into the prepared tin (pan), level the
top and make sure there is plenty of
mixture in the corners. Bake in a
preheated oven at 180°C/350°F/Gas Mark
4 for about 50–60 minutes for the Victoria
Sandwich (Sponge Layer Cake), or about
1–1¼ hours for the Quick Mix Cake, until
well risen and firm to the touch. Invert
carefully on a wire rack and leave to cool.
If possible leave for 12–24 hours to 'set'
(see page 567).

5 Use this size cake for the following
  numeral cakes: 2, 5, 6, 7 and 9.
Make a template (see page 569) and place
on the cake.

6 Cut carefully around the template
  with a serrated knife. Transfer the
cake to a suitable-sized cake board, brush
with sieved (strained) jam and decorate
with butter cream (see page 541).

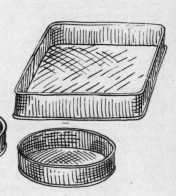

MADEIRA (POUND) CAKE

MAKES 23 CM/9 IN DEEP ROUND OR SQUARE CAKE OR 25 CM/10 IN SHALLOW ROUND OR SQUARE CAKE

300 g/10 oz/1¼ cups butter or margarine
300 g/10 oz/1¼ cups caster (superfine) sugar
5 eggs
300 g/10 oz/2½ cups self-raising flour
150 g/5 oz/1¼ cups plain (all-purpose) flour
grated rind of 2 large lemons
2 tbsp lemon juice

1 Grease and line a 23 cm/9 in round or square cake tin (pan); or a 25 cm/10 in round or square cake tin (pan) with baking parchment.

2 Cream the butter and sugar together until very light, fluffy and pale, then beat in the eggs, one at a time, following each with a tablespoonful of flour.

3 Sift the remaining flours together and fold them into the creamed mixture, followed by the grated lemon rind and juice. Spoon the mixture into the prepared tin (pan) and level the top, making sure there is plenty of mixture in the corners.

4 Bake in a preheated oven at 160°C/325°F/Gas Mark 3 for about 1¼–1½ hours for the 25 cm/10 in tin (pan); or about 1½–1¾ hours for the 23 cm/9 in tin (pan), until the cake is well risen, golden brown and firm to the touch. Cool in the tin (pan) for a few minutes, then invert on a wire rack to cool. Leave to set (see page 567).

5 Use a 23–25 cm/9–10 in square cake for a 0 or 4 numeral cake. Draw a template and cut it out (see page 569). Position the template on the cake and cut carefully around it, using a serrated knife.

6 Use 2 x 20 cm/8 in round cakes (using the 4-egg mixture: see page 568) for a 3 or 8 numeral cake. The template for the number 3 cake can be made by drawing a figure of 8, then cutting out a section of the card to make the 8 into a 3. Decorate the cake on the cake board with butter cream, sugarpaste and/or royal icing.

SUGARPASTE

MAKES 500 G/1 LB/4 CUPS

500 g/1 lb/4 cups icing (confectioners') sugar, sifted
1 egg white
50 ml/2 fl oz/4 tbsp liquid glucose or glucose syrup
icing (confectioners') sugar and cornflour (cornstarch) to knead
paste food colourings

1 Put the icing (confectioners') sugar in a bowl and make a well in the centre. Add the egg white and liquid glucose or glucose syrup.

2 Beat with a wooden spoon, gradually drawing in the icing (confectioners') sugar from the side of the bowl until the mixture is stiff.

3 Dip your hands in a mixture of icing (confectioners') sugar and cornflour (cornstarch), then knead the sugarpaste in a bowl, using the fingertips and kneading in a circular movement until smooth.

4 To colour the paste, add the paste food colouring sparingly from the tip of a skewer or cocktail stick (toothpick). Even deep colours need only ½–¾ teaspoon. Knead again until smooth and evenly blended. If the colour is not blended properly, it will be streaky when rolled out. Store in an airtight container or sealed thick polythene (plastic) bag for up to 2–3 days in a cool place.

5 To cover a cake, first brush the cake with jam or apricot glaze (see page 573). Roll out the sugarpaste on baking parchment dredged with sifted icing (confectioners') sugar so it is 13–15 cm/5–6 in larger than the cake (depending on the depth of the cake). Support the sugarpaste on a rolling pin, remove from the parchment, and position centrally on top of the cake.

6 Using fingertips dipped in a mixture of icing (confectioners') sugar and cornflour (cornstarch), press the sugarpaste to fit the cake, working from the centre to the edge, then down the sides in a circular movement. Trim off the excess sugarpaste from around the base and leave to set.

MY PONY

6-egg chocolate-flavoured Victoria
Sandwich (Sponge Layer Cake) or
Quick Mix Cake mixture (see pages 568
and 570)
6 tbsp apricot jam, sieved (strained)
875 g/1¾ lb/7 cups sugarpaste (see page
571)
green, blue, black and brown liquid or
paste food colouring
1 quantity butter cream (see page 541)
few long chocolate matchsticks

1 Grease and line a roasting tin (pan)
30 × 25 cm/12 × 10 in. Spread the
cake mixture evenly in it. Bake in a
preheated oven at 160°C/325°F/Gas Mark
3 for about 50–60 minutes (1–1¼ hours
for Quick Mix Cake). Invert on a wire
rack and leave to set for 24 hours.

2 Trim the cake, place upside-down
on a cake board, and brush all over
with the apricot jam. Colour 250 g/8 oz/
2 cups of the sugarpaste sky blue, roll out
and lay over the top third of the cake,
giving it a slightly uneven edge. Trim off
around the bottom neatly.

3 Colour about 425 g/14 oz/3½ cups
of the sugarpaste grass green. Roll
out and use to cover the rest of the cake,

matching it evenly to the sky, and trim off
neatly around the base.

4 Draw a picture of a horse on thick
paper or card and cut out. Colour
about 175 g/6 oz/1½ cups of the
sugarpaste the colour of the pony and roll
it out large enough to place the template
on. Cut carefully around the template.
Remove the template carefully and then
even more carefully move the horse to
the top of the cake, dampening in places
so it will stick.

5 Roll out the trimmings and make a
mane and forelock, marking them
and the tail with a knife to make them
look realistic. Mark in the eyes, nostrils
and mouth with a cocktail stick
(toothpick). Place the chocolate
matchsticks on the cake to form a fence,
attaching with butter cream.

6 Colour the butter cream grass green
and put into a piping bag fitted with
a star nozzle (tip). Pipe squiggly lines to
make a hedge at each end of the fence
plus a couple of trees (adding chocolate
matchsticks for trunks). Use the remaining
butter cream to pipe uneven lengths of
grass up the sides of the cake to attach to
the board, and random patches of grass
on the cake.

LUXURY BATH

3-egg and 2-egg Victoria Sandwich or
  Madeira Cake mixture, any flavour (see
  pages 568, 570 and 571)
5 tbsp apricot jam. sieved (strained)
625 g/1 ¼ lb/5 cups sugarpaste (see page
  571)
blue and yellow liquid or paste food
  colourings
250 g/8 oz//2 cups royal icing (see page
  542) or 1 quantity butter cream (see
  page 541)

1 Grease and line a 28 x 18 x 4 cm/11
  x 7 x 1 ½ in cake tin (pan) and a 23
x 13 cm/9 x 5 in loaf tin (pan). Spread
the 3-egg cake mixture evenly in the
rectangular tin (pan) and the 2-egg
mixture in the loaf tin (pan). Bake the
larger cake in a preheated oven at
160°C/325°F/Gas Mark 3 for about 45–50
minutes; and the smaller cake for about
35–40minutes. Invert on wire racks and
leave to set for 12–24 hours.

2 Place the rectangular cake upside-
  down on a cake board and brush
with jam. Roll out about 250 g/8 oz/
2 cups sugarpaste and use to cover the
cake, trimming off evenly at the base.

3 Turn the loaf cake upside-down and
  scoop out the centre so it represents a
bath. Trim the base evenly and brush all
over with jam. Roll out about 250 g/8 oz/
2 cups of sugarpaste and use to cover the
bath, carefully moulding it to fit the curves.
Trim off around the base and place on the
rectangular cake. Mould taps (faucets) from
the trimmings and attach to the bath. Add a
plug and overflow outlet.

4 Colour about 60 g/2 oz/⅓ cup of the
  sugarpaste trimmings yellow and use
to mould 3 or 4 ducks for the bath, and a
pair of slippers.

5 Colour the remaining sugarpaste
  2 shades of blue. Roll out about 60 g/
2 oz/generous ½ cup of the darker blue
sugarpaste to make a towel, add a fringe
of the paler blue, and drape over the bath.
Make a pale blue bath mat, adding a fringe
of dark blue and a couple of dark blue
stripes. A few stripes may be added to the
towel, if liked.

6 Colour the royal icing pale blue.
  Using a piping bag fitted with a star
nozzle (tip), pipe stars around the base of
the bath and the cake to attach it to the
board. Use the remaining royal icing and
a writing nozzle (tip) to write 'Happy
Birthday' and the name of the person on
the side of the bath. Leave to set.

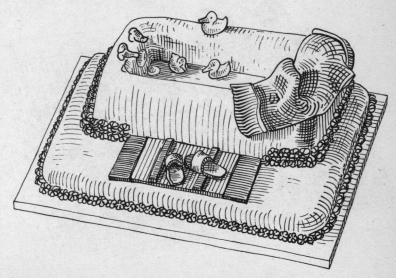

BABA THE LAMB

6-egg Victoria Sandwich or Madeira Cake
   mixture (see pages 568, 570 and 571)
6 tbsp apricot jam, sieved (strained)
350 g/12 oz/3 cups sugarpaste (see page
   571)
black, green, blue, yellow and pink liquid
   or paste food colourings
3 quantities vanilla-flavoured butter
   cream (see page 541)
few sugar mimosa balls

1 Grease and line a 30 x 25 cm/12 x 10
   in roasting tin (pan). Spread the cake
mixture evenly in it. Bake in a preheated
oven at 160°C/325°F/Gas Mark 3 for
about 50–60 minutes (1–1¼ hours for
Madeira Cake) or until firm to the touch.
Invert on a wire rack and leave to set for
12–24 hours.

2 Trim the cake and place upside-
   down on a cake board. Draw the
shape of a lamb on a piece of stiff paper
or card, cut out and position on the cake.
The ears and tail can be cut from the
cake trimmings. Cut round the template.
Cut out and attach the ears and tail with
jam. Then brush all over with jam.

3 Colour 90 g/3 oz/ ¾ cup of the
   sugarpaste green and roll out thinly.
Use to cover the board around the lamb's
legs and body up to sky level, attaching
with jam. Colour 60 g/2 oz/ ½ cup
sugarpaste blue for the sky, roll out and
use to cover the rest of the cake board.

4 Colour the remaining sugarpaste
   black or brownish-black and roll out
thinly. Use to cover the head and ears of
the lamb, and then the legs, pressing
evenly to the cake. Trim off where it
meets the grass and sky.

5 Add a touch of yellow colouring to
   three-quarters of the butter cream.
Put it into a piping bag fitted with a small
star nozzle (tip) and pipe stars all over
the body and tail to touch the head, legs,
sky and grass. Add a small star for each
eye and put a dot of black sugarpaste in
the centre. Add a black sugarpaste nose.

6 Colour a tablespoon of the
   remaining butter cream pink, and
the remainder grass green. Put both into
piping bags fitted with star nozzles (tips).
Pipe rough patches of grass on the cake
board as in the photograph. Add stars of
pink butter cream for daisies and
complete with a mimosa ball.

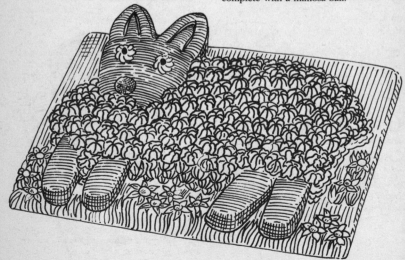

PINKY THE ELEPHANT

5-egg Victoria Sandwich or Madeira Cake
mixture, any flavour (see pages 568,
570 and 571)
4 tbsp apricot jam, sieved (strained)
3 quantities butter cream (see page 541)
pink, yellow and green liquid or paste
food colourings
2 black or chocolate sweets (candies), for
eyes

1 Grease and line a 25 cm/10 in deep
round cake tin (pan). Spread the
cake mixture evenly in it. Bake in a
preheated oven at 160°C/325°F/Gas Mark
3 for about 1 hour (1¼–1½ hours for
Madeira Cake) or until firm to the touch.
Invert on a wire rack and leave to set for
12–24 hours.

2 Draw a 25 cm/10 in round on a
piece of card and draw a pattern for
the head, ears and tusks of an elephant.
Cut out, position on the cake, and cut out
the pieces carefully.

3 Assemble the cake on a cake board,
sticking together with jam. Brush the
apricot jam all over the cake.

4 Colour about three-quarters of the
remaining butter cream bright pink
and put into a piping bag fitted with a
star nozzle (tip). Pipe either stars or lines
all over the cake, including the sides,
marking a defining line around the ears.

5 Colour about 4 tablespoons of the
butter cream pale yellow, put into a
piping bag fitted with a star nozzle (tip)
and use to cover the tusks, either with
stars or lines.

6 Pipe rounds of cream-coloured
butter cream for eyes on the head
and complete with the sweets (candies).

7 Colour the remaining butter cream
grass green and again using a star
nozzle (tip), pipe stars over the cake
board to cover. Add candles if required.
Leave to set.

TEDDY THE BEAR

6-egg Victoria Sandwich mixture (see page
568 and 570)
6 tbsp apricot jam, sieved (strained)
3 quantities butter cream (see page 541)
5 tbsp sifted cocoa powder or brown liquid
or paste food colouring
sweets (candies) for eyes
60 g/2 oz/ ½ cup sugarpaste (see page 571)
black and red, green or yellow liquid or
paste food colouring

1 Grease and line a roasting tin (pan)
about 30 x 25 cm/12 x 10 in. Spread
the cake mixture evenly in it and bake in
a preheated oven at 160°C/325°F/ Gas
Mark 3 for 50–60 minutes. Invert
on a wire rack and leave to set for
12–24 hours.

2 Draw a template for a teddy bear on
a piece of card, allowing enough
trimmings to make the ears, nose and
tummy. Place on the cake and cut out.
From the trimmings, cut out the ears, a
nose and a rounded tummy. Place the
cake on a board and attach the ears,
nose, and tummy with jam. Then brush
the whole cake with the jam.

3 Put about one-third of the butter
cream into a piping bag fitted with
a large star nozzle (tip) and pipe stars all
over the nose, paws, and tummy of the
bear, reserving a little butter cream for
the ears.

4 Colour the remaining butter cream
brown with the cocoa powder or
brown food colouring. Put into a piping
bag fitted with a large star nozzle (tip)
and pipe curved lines all over the head,
tummy, ears and paws of the bear, making
sure the butter cream reaches down the
sides of the cake.

5 Use the reserved butter cream to pipe
the centres of the ears. Add sweets
(candies) for the bear's eyes and nose.

6 Colour a scrap of sugarpaste black,
roll into very thin sausages and use
to complete the bear's nose and mouth
and claws to the tips of the paws. Colour
the remaining sugarpaste a bright colour
and use to make a bow to place around
the bear's neck. Leave to set.

BEAUTIFUL BUTTERFLY

*4-egg Victoria Sandwich mixture (see
  pages 568 and 570)*
3 quantities butter cream (see page 541)
4 tbsp apricot jam, sieved (strained)
*pink and purple liquid or paste food
  colourings*
scarlet balls
candles and holders (optional)

1 Grease and line the bottom of
  2 x 23 cm/9 in round sandwich tins
(layer pans). Divide the cake mixture
between the tins (pans) and bake in a
preheated oven at 180°C/350°F/Gas Mark
4 for about 30–35 minutes, or until firm to
the touch. Invert on a wire rack and let
set for 12–24 hours.

2 Use a little of the butter cream to
  sandwich the 2 cakes together, then
cut the cake evenly in half. If liked, a
small dip can be cut out of the base of
each wing.

3 Position the 2 halves back to back
  on a cake board at a slightly slanting
angle so the wings are wider apart at the
top. Brush all over with apricot jam.

4 Colour about two-thirds of the butter
  cream pale pink and spread all over
the cake. Using a serrated icing (frosting)
comb or fork, mark wavy lines around the
sides of the cake.

5 Tint some of the remaining butter
  cream mauve. Put it into a piping
bag fitted with a small star nozzle (tip)
and pipe a shell outline around the top
and base of the butterfly. Then divide
each wing in half by piping shapes about
2 cm/ ¾ in in from the edge of the cake
and pipe a wavy line between the wings
to make a body.

6 Put the remaining butter cream into
  a piping bag fitted with a fairly fine
writing nozzle (tip). Use to pipe wavy
lace patterns on the butterfly wings.

7 Add scarlet balls to complete the
  decoration of the butterfly. If liked,
add candles in holders for the antennae.
Leave to set.

HOUSEBOAT

*6-egg Victoria Sandwich mixture (see
  pages 568 and 570)*
8 tbsp apricot jam, sieved (strained)
1.25 kg/2½ lb sugarpaste (see page 571)
*red, blue, black and yellow liquid or paste
  food colourings*
250 g/8 oz royal icing (see page 542)

1 Grease and line a 30 x 25 cm/12 x
  10 in roasting tin (pan). Spread the
cake mixture evenly in it. Bake in a
preheated oven at 160°C/325°F/Gas Mark
3 for 50–60 minutes until firm. Invert on a
rack and leave to set for 12–24 hours.

2 Trim the cake neatly, then cut in half
  lengthwise so one piece is about
2.5 cm/1 in wider than the other. Slightly
round 1 end of the larger piece for the
stern and place on a cake board. Cut
about 7 cm/3 in off the other piece of
cake and cut this piece to a point for the
bow of the boat. Attach with jam. Brush
the cake all over with jam. Use
125 g/4 oz/1 cup of sugarpaste to build
up the bow so it is higher than the rest.

3 Colour 750 g/1½ lb/6 cups of the
  sugarpaste bright red; roll out part of
it and use to cover the whole of the base
of the boat, pressing it evenly to fit.

4 Colour 300 g/10 oz/2½ cups of the
  sugarpaste deep blue and the rest
pale grey. Attach the other piece of cake
on the boat at the stern end with jam, and
brush all over with jam. Roll out the blue
sugarpaste and use to cover the sides of
the cabin. Dampen and attach the rest
around the base of the boat.

5 Roll out the remaining red sugarpaste and make a roof for the cabin,
with an attractive edging, as shown.

6 Roll out the grey sugarpaste and cut
  out 4 long windows for the sides of
the cabin and 1 shorter (for the stern end)
and a door. Attach with jam.

7 Colour the royal icing yellow and
  put some into a piping bag fitted
with a No. 2 writing nozzle (tip). Pipe a
design around the sides of the boat, and
between the windows. Pipe the child's
name on the bows. Use the rest of the
royal icing to write a message on the roof.

HICKORY DICKORY DOCK CAKE

*3-egg and 4-egg Quick Mix Cake mixture
(see pages 568 and 570)*
10 tbsp apricot jam, sieved (strained)
1 kg/2 lb/8 cups sugarpaste (see page 571)
blue, green and black food colourings
250 g/8 oz/2 cups royal icing (see page 542)

1 Grease and line a 23 cm/9 in square cake tin (pan) and a 23 cm/9 in deep round cake tin (pan). Spread the 3-egg cake mixture in the square tin (pan) and the 4-egg mixture in the round tin (pan). Bake in a preheated oven at 160°C/325°F/Gas Mark 3, about 1¼–1½ hours for the round cake and 50–60 minutes for the square. Invert on wire racks and leave to set for 12–24 hours.

2 Halve the square cake and sandwich together with 4 tablespoons of the jam. Place on a cake board and cut out a deep dip so the round cake fits into it. Trim the round cake evenly. Brush both cakes with jam.

3 Colour half the sugarpaste pale blue. Roll it and use part to cover the cake on the board, moulding evenly. Cover the other cake's sides with two-thirds of the remaining blue sugarpaste and push it into the dip in the first cake.

4 Colour a third of the remaining sugarpaste dark blue and half green. Roll out some of the green sugarpaste and use to cover the face of the clock, just overlapping the edge; then crimp it attractively. Roll the blue and the rest of the green sugarpaste into long sausage shapes. Twist together and place around the base of the clock face.

5 Use a scrap of the pale blue sugarpaste to form clock hands and attach to the face. Use the remaining pieces of sugarpaste to shape into mice with 2 ears, a long tail and a black nose, and mark the eyes with a cocktail stick (toothpick) (see page 569). Leave to dry.

6 Using royal icing and a piping bag fitted with a star nozzle (tip), pipe a border of stars around the base of the bottom end of the clock. Pipe small stars on the sides of the clock face and base, and a twisted circle on the face about 2.5 cm/1 in from the edge. With a No. 2 writing nozzle (tip), pipe the numbers on the clock and write 'Happy Birthday' and the child's name on the base of the cake. Pipe any extra decorations you might like on the clock. Leave to set, then attach the mice on and around the clock. Leave to set.

PANDA'S PICNIC

....

4-egg Madeira (Pound) Cake or Quick
   Mix Cake mixture (see pages 568 and
   571)
5 tbsp apricot jam, sieved (strained)
1.5 kg/3 lb/12 cups sugarpaste (see page
   571)
green, black, orange, yellow, blue and
   brown liquid or paste food colourings
red icing (frosting) pen
1 quantity butter cream (see page 541)

1 Grease and line a 23 cm//9 in deep
   round cake tin (pan). Spread the
cake mixture evenly in it. Bake in a
preheated oven at 160°C/325°F/Gas Mark
3 for about 1–1¼ hours, or until firm.
Invert on a wire rack and leave to set for
12–24 hours. Trim the cake and place
upside-down on a 28 cm/11 in cake
board. Brush all over with the jam.

2 Colour 625 g/1¼ lb/5 cups of the
   sugarpaste green. Roll out and use to
cover the cake. Trim around the base.

3 Colour 90 g/3 oz/ ¾ cup of the
   sugarpaste pale yellow and another
90 g/3 oz/ ¾ cup orange. Roll them out
separately and cut each into 18 pieces,
2.5 cm/1 in square. Arrange the coloured
squares alternately on the grass to make a
square tablecloth, dampening each slightly
so they stick.

4 Colour 375 g/12 oz/3 cups of the
   sugarpaste black and leave 175 g/
6 oz/1½ cups of the sugarpaste white for
the pandas. Make 6 pandas (see page
569). Each panda needs about 90 g/3 oz/
¾ cup sugarpaste. Leave to dry.

5 Colour about 90 g/3 oz/ ¾ cup of
   the sugarpaste bright blue. Roll out
thinly and cut out 3 plates of about 4 cm/
1½ in and 6 of 2 cm/ ¾ in. Using a finger,
press into the centre of the plates to give
a rim. Mould 6 cups or mugs out of the
trimmings. Roll out a little of the white
sugarpaste and cut into sandwiches. Draw
around the sides with an icing (frosting)
pen for the filling and place on one of the
large plates. Colour the rest of the sugarpaste brown and shape into a cake. Cut
or slice and put some pieces on the small
plates. Arrange the plates and mugs on
the tablecloth, dampening them to attach.

6 Colour the butter cream grass green
   and put into a piping bag fitted with
a small star nozzle (tip). Pipe strands of
butter cream part way up on the sides of
the cake from the base upwards to
represent grass. Arrange the pandas on
top of the cake and by the side.

NOAH'S ARK

7-egg Victoria Sandwich mixture (see
   pages 568 and 570)
2 quantities butter cream (see page 541)
6 tbsp apricot jam, sieved (strained)
750 g/1½ lb/6 cups sugarpaste (see page
   571)
yellow, orange, red and blue liquid or
   paste food colourings
1 packet long matchstick chocolates
plastic toy animal pairs

1 Grease and line 3 cake tins (pans)
28 x 18 x 4 cm/11 x 7 x 1½ in.
Divide the cake mixture evenly between
the tins (pans). Bake in a preheated oven
at 160°C/325°F/Gas Mark 3 for about
35–40 minutes until well risen and firm.
Invert on wire racks and leave to set for
12–24 hours.

2 Sandwich 2 cakes together with
butter cream, then round one end of
the cake and cut the corners off the other
end to shape it into a point from about
7.5 cm/3 in back. Place on a cake board.
Reserve the cut-off corners.

3 Cut the third cake into 2 pieces about
11 cm/4½ in wide and sandwich
together with butter cream. Place on top
of the first cake to form the cabin. Use
the cut-off corners to form a roof and
attach. Brush the whole ark with jam.

4 Colour 500 g/1 lb of the sugarpaste
brown. Roll out and cover the bows
of the ark. Tint about a third of the butter
cream yellow and spread over the deck.
Colour the remaining sugarpaste orange.
Roll out and cover the sides of the cabin.
Spread butter cream over the roof.

5 Cover the roof of the cabin with
chocolate matchsticks. Place matchsticks all round the edge of the deck, and
make a gangplank with 3 or 4 chocolate
matchsticks. Cut circles in the brown sugarpaste and attach for windows and a door.
Make portholes out of orange sugarpaste.

6 Colour the remaining butter cream
blue and put into a piping bag fitted
with a star nozzle (tip). Pipe stars over
the cake board to represent water. Place
the animals on the deck and gangplank
of the ark.

CHRISTMAS CRACKER

3-egg Madeira (Pound) Cake mixture (see
   pages 568 and 571)
4 tbsp apricot jam, sieved (strained)
875 g/1¾ lb/7 cups sugarpaste (see page
   571)
green, red, yellow and brown liquid or
   paste food colourings
1.5 metres/1½ yards red and silver ribbon,
   about 1–2.5 cm/ ½–1 in wide
1 quantity butter cream (see page 541)

TO DECORATE:
holly leaves and berries (see page 567)
ivy leaves (see page 567)
teddy bears (see page 569)
parcels (see page 569)

1 Grease 2 special cylindrical loaf cake
tins (pans) about 18 cm/7 in long,
7 cm/3 in in diameter and with a capacity
of about 900 ml/1½ pints/3½ cups.

2 Divide the cake mixture evenly
between the tins (pans), filling each
two-thirds full. Place the tins (pans) on a
baking sheet, and bake in a preheated
oven at 160°C/325°F/Gas Mark 3 for
about 50–60 minutes until firm. Cool for
10 minutes before inverting on a rack.

3 Cut one cake in half and trim
diagonally around each edge.

4 Using 175 g/6 oz/1½ cups of the
white sugarpaste, roll out and cut
discs to fit one end of the two short
cakes. Roll a strip about 4 cm/1½ in wide
and place to overlap the ends by about
2.5 cm/1 in, attaching with jam. Snip the
edges with scissors. Attach one piece to
each end of the long cake with butter
cream and insert a plastic skewer through
the centre to hold in place.

5 Colour the remaining sugarpaste
bright green. Roll out so it is large
enough to enclose the cake completely,
overlapping 2.5 cm/1 in at each end.
Brush with jam, place the cake on it and
wrap around. Place on a cake board with
the seam underneath. Snip the edges.

6 Tie the ribbons around the cracker
and arrange holly leaves and berries,
teddy bears. parcels and ivy leaves on the
cracker, attaching with butter cream.
Leave to set.

HAPPY LION

4-egg Victoria Sandwich mixture (see pages 568 and 570)
4 tbsp apricot jam, sieved (strained)
350 g/12 oz/3 cups yellow marzipan or sugarpaste (see pages 540 or 571)
yellow, brown and red liquid or paste food colourings
3 quantities coffee butter cream (see page 541)
2 chocolate buttons or beans
few pieces of thin spaghetti

1 Grease and line a 23 cm/9 in deep round cake tin (pan). Spoon in the cake mixture. Bake in a preheated oven at 160°C/325°F/Gas Mark 3, allowing about 50–60 minutes. Invert on a wire rack and leave for 12–24 hours.

2 Using a sharp serrated knife, pare off a piece from the top edge of the cake and place it around the base, attaching with jam; then brush the whole cake with jam.

3 Cover the top of the cake with 250 g/8 oz/2 cups sugarpaste or marzipan coloured yellow. Keep the trimmings for step 6.

4 Put the butter cream into a piping bag fitted with a large star nozzle (tip) and pipe a circle of elongated stars, beginning about 2.5 cm/1 in up the side of the cake and taking them out toward the edge of the cake board. Then pipe 2 more circles, the third row beginning about 2.5 cm/1 in from the top edge on the lion's face, taking it part way down the side of the cake.

5 Roll out half the remaining marzipan or sugarpaste and cut out 2 circles of about 5 cm/2 in for the ears. Colour a scrap of the trimmings red for a mouth. Colour the remainder deep brown, roll it out and cut out 2 x 2.5 cm/ 1 in circles. Place one in each ear circle. Cut out 2 x 4 cm/1½-in rounds for eyes and mould the rest into a pointed nose.

6 Squeeze the base of the ears together and attach to the cake, with butter cream. Position the eyes, the mouth, the nose, and 2 wedges (made from the yellow trimmings) beneath the nose, and attach them all with butter cream. Use chocolate buttons for eyes, add a small dot of butter cream to each, then stick pieces of spaghetti into the yellow wedges for whiskers. Leave to set.

·7·

Special Occasions

◆

Whether you have the boss coming to dinner, endless Christmas meals, a riotous children's party or an elegant summer party to cater for, this section will provide all the inspiration you need.

◆

BARBECUES – INTRODUCTION

BARBECUES

For centuries people have built fires and cooked food over the flames or in the embers. Even though it is no longer necessary for most people to cook in this fashion, it remains an enjoyable way to cook, producing succulent food with an incomparable flavour. Barbecuing now takes slightly different forms all around the world but the principles remain the same. In Australia and New Zealand the fire is in a pit; in the Middle East lamb is spit-roasted over white-hot embers. In the Mediterranean countries fish is grilled over an open wood fire on the beach, while a charcoal burner is fired up in Greece. A terracotta burner is also used in India, but it is sunk into the ground and known as a tandoor. And finally, the Americans adapted gas to use as a cooking fuel for barbecues and gave us the quick and easy barbecue that many people use today.

The word 'barbecue' comes from the Spanish barbacoa, which describes the process of grilling meat over an open wood fire on bars of wet green wood. Today it has also come to mean the cooking apparatus, and the social gathering at which food is barbecued.

TYPES OF BARBECUE

There are many types of barbecue to choose from, and you should consider a number of things before you decide which to buy or build. As the life of any barbecue will be shortened if it is left outside for the winter months, you will need some storage space, not to mention enough space to use the barbecue easily. Another factor is the number of people you cook for regularly – it is easier to cook for small numbers on a large barbecue than vice versa.

The safety factor must be considered – if you have young children, you may not want to use hot charcoal or anything portable, and the height of the grill will have to be considered too. The following types of barbecue are commonly available:

Disposable

Sturdy foil trays enclose a rack and enough charcoal to cook a meal for two people; ideal for the beach and also for where space is limited, such as on balconies. Be sure to put them on a heatproof surface – for example, a concrete floor or sand.

Hibachi-type

Japanese in origin, they are made of cast iron and stand on four legs. They have air vents in the front to control the heat, and different height settings for the racks. They are ideal for cooking for one or two.

Charcoal burners

These are small free-standing, attractive round terracotta structures. They have air holes in the sides and a grid over the charcoal. They are rather small, but ideal for one or two people, and quite cheap.

Portable gas or charcoal

These are either table-top or floor-standing and are designed for camping trips or larger picnic parties. Some models are better than others and features to look for are adjustable air vents and rack height. They are also ideal for barbecue cooking at home if you have only limited storage space.

Kettle barbecues

The purpose of covering the food as you cook it is to get a more even finish – especially important for large cuts of meat. Some kettle barbecues have a water tray above the coals in order to semi-steam the meat; this retains a lot of moisture and avoids shrinkage. I once had a Christmas turkey that was cooked in a kettle barbecue, and it tasted marvellous and was very moist.

Counter height
This is one of the most popular types of barbecue, and a selection of models is available with a range of extras. Your choice of the latter depends on for what and how often you intend to use the barbecue. Make a priority of adjustable rack height and air vents. There are other options that are not essential but once you have them, you will find indispensable – these include a work-table, warming rack, rôtisserie, lid with viewing window, wheels, ash drainer and adjustable temperature settings. This type of barbecue is the most sturdy and ideal for families with children.

Brick-built
They can be built in many different sizes on ground level, slightly raised, or at counter height. A deluxe version can be decorated to match its surroundings and might have a built-in chimney to take the smoke away. The solid iron grid is quite large – around 100 x 60 cm/40 x 24 in.

Oil drums
These are very useful for large parties. The drum is cut in half lengthways and supported on a metal construction or bricks. Air holes must be drilled along the side at regular intervals, e.g.10 cms/ 4 in, The charcoal is piled inside on top of lava rocks or stones, and the grid rested across the top of the drum.

FUELS
Once you have selected a barbecue, you have to decide the kind of fuel you wish to use, unless you can link up to natural gas or plug in an electric 'barbecue'. Your choices are:

Portable gas
Butane is more widely available, but some people believe that propane burns hotter. If you buy an American barbecue, you will not be able to link up to either of these – do not buy an American gas barbecue for use in Europe.

Wood
Dried-out hardwoods are the best, as softwoods tend to impart resin flavours to the food. Fruit woods give a nice flavour, as do olive woods and vines. Hickory and mesquite chips are natural wood products that are used alongside other fuels to flavour the food. Mesquite is very strong and is usually used to 'smoke' the food as opposed to flaming it.

Charcoal
In the absence of wood this is the most popular fuel. Natural charcoal needs a bit of care in constructing the fire. Break up the large unmanageable pieces and put the smaller pieces at the bottom and larger ones on top, ensuring there is plenty of air circulation all around and that it comes to the right height. See lighting methods below.

Charcoal briquettes
These are a convenient form of charcoal, but the quality varies. An artificial resin is used to compact the briquettes and in some brands it is stronger than others. Try a few brands to discover the one that gives the best flavour to the food.

INTRODUCTION

Charcoal bags

These are quite a modern invention and have charcoal inside, which I find better than briquettes. A pack contains two 1 kg/2 lb paper bags. The paper bag of charcoal is simply placed in the barbecue and a match is set to it. The paper acts as kindling to stoke the fire.

Lava rocks

As these are the molten matter that flows from a volcano, they have an extremely high melting point. Once heated they will retain and radiate that heat, and are useful if used with charcoal. Gas barbecues and indoor chargrills often use these to supply a little genuine flavour.

LIGHTING THE BARBECUE

All fires need oxygen to enable them to burn and barbecues are no exception, so make sure that the air vents are working properly and that the structure has plenty of air circulation, and you will be well on your way to a blazing barbecue.

The tried and tested method of lighting it is to put kindling – tightly rolled and knotted paper is a good substitute – underneath the charcoal. Starter fluid or firelighters can be used but these do tend to leave a chemical flavour, however long they are left to burn – they are, however, the most convenient and the cleanest to use.

A blowtorch is a useful gadget to have at this point, but must be used with great care. Heat can be applied to the base of the fire which will permeate throughout the coals without leaving any unwanted aromas, as with firelighters.

Another useful gadget to have is a hand-held battery-operated fan – the kind that one uses in the summer

to cool down – as this can push air through the fire to oxygenate it, and increase the heat. The barbecue is ready when the embers are white hot, or the charcoal is covered in a fine white-grey ash.

Always have extra fuel on standby to stoke the fire and do as much advance preparation on the food as possible, as the barbecue will need regular tending in order to get the best, most constant heat from it.

Levels of heat

I have specified the different levels of heat needed for different foods throughout the recipes. These levels can be measured by holding your hand over the barbecue, about 15 cm/6 in away from the coals. If you can bear to hold it there

– for 4 seconds, the heat is low-medium

– for 3 seconds, the heat is medium

– for 2 seconds, the heat is high

– for 1 second, the heat is very high

The heat can be adjusted by raising or lowering the rack. I find that a pair of charcoal tongs is useful for tending the barbecue – special charcoal tongs can be bought, but a pair of standard metal tongs is sufficient, as long as the tongs are reserved for this purpose.

TOOLS

Other tools that you may find useful – in order of necessity – are:

Metal tongs

Preferably long-handled, for turning the food over. They do not pierce flesh and thus drain juices in the same way as a fork would.

Gloves

Heavy-duty gardening gloves or

INTRODUCTION

welders' gloves are best, if available, both for picking up jacket potatoes and for building the fire.

Work table
A small work table next to the barbecue is most useful for storing equipment and ingredients.

Apron
A plastic wipe-clean apron is ideal.

Basting brush
To keep everything moist with oil or sauce while cooking.

Water pistol
This is the easiest thing to use to extinguish or prevent flare-ups. However, this should not be used on electric barbecues in any circumstances, nor on gas barbecues, as you might extinguish the gas flames, leaving the gas seeping out without burning.

Wire brush
To brush down the barbecue after use. It is essential to start cooking with a clean rack, so that the meat does not stick.

Long fork
Useful to turn things, and used together with the tongs, to turn large cuts of meat.

Warming rack
This is a useful addition while waiting for everything else to finish cooking.

Rôtisserie
Not essential, but it does make cooking large joints of meat a great deal easier.

Potato rack
Four spikes arranged in a circle conduct heat through the potatoes and cook them quickly. A skewer is a good substitute.

Skewers
Metal skewers are the best type to have. All sorts of food can be skewered and cooked quickly with only a little basting needed. Wooden skewers can be used but they will need to be soaked in water first in order to prevent them from burning.

SWEET TREATS
Marshmallows are a popular barbecue finale. Stick one on the end of a metal skewer or soaked wooden skewer and hold over the hottest part of the barbecue for a maximum of 1 minute, after which they will drip off the stick. Eat with care – they are very hot when first removed from the flame.

Other post-barbecue treats include bananas in their skins tossed on to the dying fire and cooked for 15–30 minutes. When you peel off the skin, the banana falls out, as if it were relieved to be out of the heat!

Pineapple can be cubed and skewered to be grilled, while apples and pears can be wrapped in foil and cooked slowly – delicious with whipped cream! Try popping a piece of fudge into the cored apple before baking in foil.

A favourite is to prepare a variety of fruits – melon, pineapple, kiwi, strawberries – peeled and cut into bite-sized pieces. Arrange on a couple of large plates with cocktail sticks (toothpicks) to make them into finger food.

FILLED JACKET POTATOES

EACH FILLING SERVES 4

4 large or 8 medium baking potatoes

MEXICAN SWEETCORN RELISH:
250 g/8 oz can of sweetcorn, drained
½ red (bell) pepper, cored, deseeded and
* chopped finely*
5 cm/2 in piece cucumber, chopped finely
½ tsp chilli powder
salt and pepper

BLUE CHEESE, CELERY & CHIVE FILLING:
125 g/4 oz/ ½ cup full-fat soft cheese
125 g/4 oz/ ½ cup natural fromage frais
125 g/4 oz Danish blue cheese, cut into
* cubes*
1 celery stick, chopped finely
2 tsp snipped fresh chives
celery salt and pepper

MUSHROOMS IN SPICY TOMATO SAUCE:
30 g/1 oz/2 tbsp butter or margarine
250 g/8 oz button mushrooms
150 g/5 oz/ ⅔ cup natural yogurt
1 tbsp tomato purée (paste)
2 tsp mild curry powder
salt and pepper
paprika or chilli powder, or chopped fresh
* herbs, to garnish*

1 Scrub the potatoes and prick them with a fork. Bake in a preheated oven at 200°C/400°F/Gas Mark 6 for about 1 hour, until just tender.

2 To make the Mexican Sweetcorn Relish, put half the sweetcorn into a bowl. Put the remainder into a blender or food processor for 10–15 seconds or chop and mash roughly by hand. Add the puréed sweetcorn to the sweetcorn kernels with the (bell) pepper, cucumber and chilli powder. Season to taste.

3 To make the Blue Cheese, Celery & Chive Filling, mix the soft cheese and fromage frais together until smooth. Add the blue cheese, celery and chives. Season with pepper and celery salt.

4 To make the Mushrooms in Spicy Tomato Sauce, melt the butter or margarine in a small frying pan (skillet). Add the mushrooms and cook gently for 3–4 minutes. Remove from the heat and stir in the yogurt, tomato purée (paste) and curry powder. Season to taste.

5 Wrap the cooked potatoes in foil and keep warm at the edge of the barbecue. Serve the fillings sprinkled with paprika or chilli powder or herbs.

MOZZARELLA WITH BARBECUED RADICCHIO

••

SERVES 4

1 tbsp red or green pesto sauce
6 tbsp virgin olive oil
3 tbsp red wine vinegar
handful of fresh basil leaves
500 g/1 lb Mozzarella cheese
4 large tomatoes, sliced
2 radicchio
salt and pepper
fresh basil leaves to garnish

1 To make the dressing, mix the pesto sauce, olive oil and red wine vinegar together in a bowl.

2 Tear the fresh basil leaves into tiny pieces and add them to the dressing. Season with a little salt and pepper.

3 Slice the Mozzarella cheese thinly and arrange it on 4 serving plates with the tomatoes.

4 Leaving the root end on the radicchio, slice each one into quarters. Barbecue them quickly, so that the leaves singe on the outside. Place two quarters on each serving plate.

5 Drizzle the dressing over the radicchio, cheese and tomatoes.

6 Garnish with extra basil leaves and serve immediately.

TIPS

When singeing the radicchio, it is a good idea to barbecue each quarter individually, holding it over the hot coals with tongs and turning it constantly.

If you can't find fresh basil, substitute oregano or marjoram instead. Tearing the basil leaves instead of chopping them helps to retain their peppery fragrance.

Pesto sauce is an aromatic olive oil, basil and pine kernel (nut) paste that can be bought in jars from supermarkets or delicatessens.

NAAN BREAD WITH CURRIED VEGETABLE KEBABS

••

SERVES 4

4 metal or wooden skewers (soak wooden
*   skewers in warm water for 30 minutes)*

YOGURT BASTE:
150 ml/ ¼ pint/ ⅔ cup natural yogurt
1 tbsp chopped fresh mint (or 1 tsp dried)
1 tsp ground cumin
1 tsp ground coriander
½ tsp chilli powder
pinch of turmeric
pinch of ground ginger
salt and pepper

KEBABS:
8 small new potatoes
1 small aubergine (eggplant)
1 courgette (zucchini), cut into chunks
8 chestnut (crimini) or closed-cup
*   mushrooms*
8 small tomatoes
naan bread to serve
sprigs of fresh mint to garnish

1 To make the spiced yogurt baste, mix together the yogurt, mint, cumin, coriander, chilli powder, turmeric and ginger. Season with salt and pepper. Cover and chill.

2 Boil the potatoes until just tender. Meanwhile, chop the aubergine (eggplant) into chunks and sprinkle them liberally with salt. Leave for 10–15 minutes to extract the bitter juices. Rinse and drain them well. Drain the potatoes.

3 Thread the vegetables on to the skewers, alternating the different types. Place them in a shallow dish and brush with the yogurt baste, coating them evenly. Cover and chill until ready to cook.

4 Wrap the naan bread in foil and place towards one side of the barbecue to warm through.

5 Cook the kebabs over the barbecue, basting with any remaining spiced yogurt, until they just begin to char slightly. Serve with the warmed Indian bread, garnished with sprigs of fresh mint.

MEDITERRANEAN STUFFED (BELL) PEPPERS

••••••••••••••••••••••••••••••••••

SERVES 4

1 red (bell) pepper
1 green (bell) pepper
1 yellow (bell) pepper
1 orange (bell) pepper
6 tbsp olive oil
1 small red onion, sliced
1 small aubergine (eggplant), chopped roughly
125 g/4 oz button mushrooms, wiped
125 g/4 oz/1 cup cherry tomatoes, halved
few drops of mushroom ketchup
handful of fresh basil leaves, torn into pieces
2 tbsp lemon juice
salt and pepper
sprigs of fresh basil to garnish
lemon wedges to serve

1 Halve the (bell) peppers, remove the cores and deseed them. Sprinkle over a few drops of olive oil and season with a little salt and pepper.

2 Heat the remaining olive oil in a frying pan (skillet). Add the onion, aubergine (eggplant) and mushrooms, and fry for 3–4 minutes, stirring frequently. Remove from the heat and transfer to a mixing bowl.

3 Add the cherry tomatoes, mushroom ketchup, basil leaves and lemon juice to the aubergine (eggplant) mixture. Season well with salt and pepper.

4 Spoon the aubergine (eggplant) mixture into the (bell) pepper halves. Enclose in foil parcels (packages) and cook over the hot coals for about 15–20 minutes, turning once.

5 Unwrap carefully and serve garnished with sprigs of fresh basil. Serve with lemon wedges.

SMOKED TOFU (BEAN CURD) & MUSHROOM BROCHETTES

••••••••••••••••••••••••••••••••••

SERVES 4

8 wooden skewers
1 lemon
1 garlic clove, crushed
4 tbsp olive oil
4 tbsp white wine vinegar
1 tbsp chopped fresh herbs, such as rosemary, parsley and thyme
300 g/10 oz smoked tofu (bean curd)
350 g/12 oz/ cup mushrooms, wiped
salt and pepper
fresh herbs to garnish

TO SERVE:
mixed salad leaves (greens)
cherry tomatoes, halved

1 Soak the wooden skewers in hand-hot water for 30 minutes.

2 Grate the rind from the lemon finely and squeeze out the juice. Add the garlic, olive oil, vinegar and herbs to the lemon rind and juice, mixing well. Season to taste.

3 Slice the tofu (bean curd) into large chunks. Thread the pieces on to kebab sticks or wooden skewers, alternating them with the mushrooms.

4 Lay the kebabs in a shallow dish and pour over the marinade. Cover and chill for 1–2 hours, turning the kebabs in the marinade from time to time.

5 Cook the kebabs over the barbecue, brushing them with the marinade and turning often, for about 6 minutes.

6 Garnish with fresh herbs and serve with mixed salad leaves (greens) and cherry tomatoes.

EXTRA FLAVOUR

Firm tofu (bean curd) can be substituted for the smoked variety if you prefer.
   Thread small fresh bay leaves on to the skewers. They will help to give the kebabs a good flavour.

VINE (GRAPE) LEAF PARCELS WITH SOFT CHEESE & ALMONDS

••

SERVES 4

300 g/10 oz/1¼ cups full-fat soft cheese
60 g/2 oz/ ¼ cup ground almonds
30 g/1 oz/2 tbsp dates, stoned (pitted) and
* chopped*
30 g/1 oz/2 tbsp butter
30 g/1 oz/ ¼ cup flaked (slivered) almonds
12 –16 vine (grape) leaves
salt and pepper

TO GARNISH:
sprigs of rosemary
tomato wedges

1 Beat the soft cheese in a large bowl to soften it.

2 Add the ground almonds and chopped dates, and mix together thoroughly. Season with salt and pepper.

3 Melt the butter in a small frying pan. Add the flaked (slivered) almonds and fry them gently for 2–3 minutes until golden brown. Remove from the heat and leave to cool for a few minutes.

4 Mix the fried nuts with the soft cheese mixture, stirring well to combine thoroughly.

5 Soak the vine (grape) leaves in water to remove some of the saltiness, if specified on the packet. Drain them, lay them out on a work surface (counter) and spoon an equal amount of the soft cheese mixture on to each one. Fold over the leaves to enclose the filling.

6 Wrap the vine (grape) leaf parcels in foil, 1 or 2 per foil package. Place over the barbecue to heat through for about 8–10 minutes, turning once.

7 Serve with barbecued baby corn and garnish with sprigs of rosemary and tomato wedges.

TURKISH VEGETABLE KEBABS WITH SPICY CHICK-PEA (GARBANZO BEAN) SAUCE

••

SERVES 4

4 metal or wooden skewers (soak wooden
* skewers in warm water for 30 minutes)*

SAUCE:
4 tbsp olive oil
3 garlic cloves, crushed
1 small onion, chopped finely
475 g/15 oz can of chick-peas (garbanzo
* beans), rinsed and drained*
300 g/10 oz/1¼ cups natural yogurt
1 tsp cumin
½ tsp chilli powder
lemon juice
salt and pepper

KEBABS:
1 aubergine (eggplant)
1 red (bell) pepper, cored and deseeded
1 green (bell) pepper, cored and deseeded
4 plum tomatoes
1 lemon, cut into wedges
8 small fresh bay leaves
olive oil for brushing

1 To make the sauce, heat the olive oil in a small frying pan (skillet) and fry the garlic and onion gently until softened and golden brown, about 5 minutes.

2 Put the chick-peas (garbanzo beans) and yogurt into a blender or food processor and add the cumin, chilli powder and onion mixture. Blend for about 15 seconds until smooth. Alternatively, mash the chick-peas (garbanzo beans) and mix with the yogurt, cumin, chilli powder and onion.

3 Tip the puréed mixture into a bowl and season to taste with lemon juice, salt and pepper. Cover and chill until ready to serve.

4 To prepare the kebabs, cut the vegetables into large chunks and thread them on to the skewers, placing a bay leaf and lemon wedge at both ends of each kebab. Brush with olive oil and cook over the barbecue, turning frequently, for about 5–8 minutes. Heat the sauce and serve with the kebabs.

BARBECUED BEAN POT

SERVES 4

60 g/2 oz/ ¼ cup butter or margarine
1 large onion, chopped
2 garlic cloves, crushed
2 carrots, sliced
2 celery sticks, sliced
1 tbsp paprika
2 tsp ground cumin
425 g/14 oz can of chopped tomatoes
475 g/15 oz can of mixed beans, rinsed
  and drained
150 ml/ ¼ pint/ ⅔ cup vegetable stock
1 tbsp molasses sugar or black treacle
  (molasses)
350 g/12 oz Quorn or soya cubes
salt and pepper

1 Melt the butter or margarine in a
large flameproof casserole and fry
the onion and garlic gently for about
5 minutes, until golden brown.

2 Add the carrots and celery, and cook
for a further 2 minutes, then stir in
the paprika and cumin.

3 Add the tomatoes and beans. Pour in
the stock and add the sugar or
treacle (molasses). Bring to the boil, then
reduce the heat and simmer, uncovered,
for 30 minutes, stirring occasionally.

4 Add the Quorn to the casserole and
cook, covered, for a further 20
minutes. Stir the mixture occasionally.

5 Season to taste, then transfer the
casserole to the barbecue, keeping it
to one side to keep hot.

6 Ladle on to plates and serve with
crusty French bread.

ALTERNATIVES

If you prefer, cook the casserole in a
preheated oven at 190°C/375°F/Gas
Mark 5 from step 3, but keep the dish
covered.

Instead of mixed beans you could
use just one type of canned beans.
Choose from red kidney beans, black
eye beans (black-eyed peas), chick-
peas (garbanzo beans) or soya beans.

GRILLED CYPRIOT CHEESE WITH TOMATO & RED ONION SALAD

SERVES 4

500 g/1 lb Haloumi cheese
½ quantity Orange, Chive & Marjoram
  Marinade (see page 596)

SALAD:
250 g/8 oz plum tomatoes
1 small red onion
4 tbsp olive oil
2 tbsp cider vinegar
1 tsp lemon juice
pinch of ground coriander
2 tsp chopped fresh coriander (cilantro)
salt and pepper
fresh basil leaves to garnish

1 Slice the cheese quite thickly and
place it in a shallow dish.

2 Pour the marinade over the cheese.
Cover and chill for at least
30 minutes.

3 To make the salad, slice the
tomatoes and arrange them on a
serving plate. Slice the onion thinly and
scatter over the tomatoes.

4 Whisk together the olive oil, vinegar,
lemon juice, ground coriander and
fresh coriander (cilantro). Season to taste
with salt and pepper, then drizzle the
dressing over the tomatoes and onions.
Cover and chill.

5 Drain the marinade from the cheese.
Cook the cheese over hot coals for
2 minutes, turning once. Lift onto plates
and serve with the salad.

SERVING SUGGESTIONS

Warmed pitta (pocket) breads taste
wonderful stuffed with the salad and
topped with the barbecued Haloumi.

If Haloumi cheese is not available,
you can use Feta cheese instead.

Serve the cheese and salad with
crusty bread or potato salad to make it
more filling.

FILIPINO CHICKEN

SERVES 4

1 can lemonade or lime-and-lemonade
2 tbsp gin
4 tbsp tomato ketchup
2 tsp garlic salt
2 tsp Worcestershire sauce
4 chicken supremes or breast fillets
salt and pepper

TO SERVE:
thread egg noodles
1 green chilli, chopped finely
2 spring onions (scallions), sliced

1 Combine the lemonade or lime-and-lemonade, gin, tomato ketchup, garlic salt, Worcestershire sauce and seasoning in a large non-porous dish.

2 Put the chicken supremes into the dish and make sure that the marinade covers them completely.

3 Leave to marinate in the refrigerator for 2 hours. Remove and leave, covered, at room temperature for 30 minutes.

4 Place the chicken over a medium barbecue and cook for 20 minutes. Turn the chicken once, halfway through the cooking time.

5 Remove the chicken from the barbecue and leave to rest for 3–4 minutes before serving.

6 Serve with egg noodles, tossed with a little green chilli and spring onions (scallions).

PERFECT CHICKEN

Cooking the meat on the bone after it has reached room temperature means that it cooks in a shorter time, which ensures that the meat remains moist right through to the bone.

MEDITERRANEAN GRILLED CHICKEN

SERVES 4

4 tbsp natural yogurt
3 tbsp sun-dried tomato paste
1 tbsp olive oil
15 g/ ½ oz/ ¼ cup fresh basil leaves, lightly crushed
2 garlic cloves, chopped roughly
4 chicken quarters

1 Combine the yogurt, tomato paste, olive oil, basil leaves and garlic in a small bowl and stir well to mix.

2 Put the marinade into a bowl large enough to hold the chicken quarters in a single layer. Add the chicken quarters. Make sure that the chicken pieces are thoroughly coated in the marinade by turning them in it, and spooning it over them.

3 Leave to marinate in the refrigerator for 2 hours. Remove and leave, covered, at room temperature for 30 minutes.

4 Place the chicken over a medium barbecue and cook for 30–40 minutes, turning frequently. Test for readiness by piercing the flesh at the thickest part – usually at the top of the drumstick. If the juices that run out are clear, it is cooked through, but cook for 10 minutes longer if the juices have blood in them.

5 Serve hot with a green salad. It is also delicious eaten cold.

VARIATION

For a marinade with an extra zingy flavour combine 2 garlic cloves, coarsely chopped, the juice of 2 lemons and 3 tbsp olive oil, and cook in the same way.

Whether you cook the chicken with the skin on or off is up to you. The chicken will be higher in fat if the skin is left on, but many people like the rich taste and a crispy skin, especially when it is blackened by the barbecue.

TASMANIAN DUCK

SERVES 4

4 duck breasts
60 g/2 oz/ ½ cup dried cherries
120 ml/4 fl oz/ ½ cup water
4 tbsp lemon juice
2 large leeks, quartered, or 8 baby leeks
2 tbsp olive oil
2 tbsp balsamic vinegar
2 tbsp port
2 tsp pink peppercorns

1 Make 3 slashes in the fat of the duck breasts in one direction, and 3 in the other.

2 Put the dried cherries, water and lemon juice into a small saucepan. Bring to the boil. Remove from the heat and leave to cool.

3 Turn a large foil tray upside-down, make several holes in the bottom with a skewer and put it over a hot barbecue. Put the duck into the tray. Cover with foil and cook for 20 minutes.

4 Brush the leeks with oil and cook on the open barbecue for 5–7 minutes, turning constantly.

5 Remove the duck from the tray and cook on the open barbecue for 5 minutes, skin-side down, while you make the sauce.

6 Stir the balsamic vinegar into the cooking sauces in the tray, scraping any bits from the bottom. Add to the cherries in the saucepan. Return to the heat – either the hob (stove top) or barbecue – and stir in the port and pink peppercorns. Bring to the boil and cook for 5 minutes, until the sauce has thickened slightly.

7 Serve the duck piping hot, pour over the cherries and sauce, and accompany with the leeks.

BLACKENED CHICKEN WITH GUACAMOLE

SERVES 4

4 skinned chicken breasts
60 g/2 oz/ ¼ cup butter, melted

SPICE MIX:
1 tsp salt
1 tbsp sweet paprika
1 tsp dried onion granules
1 tsp dried garlic granules
1 tsp dried thyme
1 tsp cayenne
½ tsp cracked black pepper
½ tsp dried oregano

GUACAMOLE:
1 avocado
1 tbsp lemon juice
2 tbsp soured cream
½ red onion, chopped and rinsed
1 garlic clove, halved

1 Put each chicken breast between 2 pieces of clingfilm (plastic wrap), and pound with a mallet or rolling pin until it is an even thickness. It will be about 1 cm/ ½ in thick.

2 Brush each chicken breast all over with the melted butter. Combine the spice mix ingredients in a shallow bowl. Coat the chicken breasts with the spice mix, ensuring that they are covered completely. Set aside.

3 Mash the avocado thoroughly with the lemon juice in a small bowl. Stir in the soured cream and red onion.

4 Wipe the garlic clove around the guacamole serving dish, pressing hard. Spoon in the guacamole.

5 Place the chicken breasts over the hottest part of a very hot barbecue and cook for 8–10 minutes, turning once. Slice the breasts and serve immediately with the guacamole.

CHARGRILLED CHICKEN SALAD

SERVES 4

2 chicken breasts
1 red onion, peeled
oil for brushing
1 avocado, peeled and stoned (pitted)
1 tbsp lemon juice
120 ml/4 fl oz/ ½ cup mayonnaise
¼ tsp chilli powder
½ tsp pepper
¼ tsp salt
4 tomatoes, quartered
½ loaf sun-dried tomato-flavoured
  focaccia bread

1 Cut the chicken breasts into 1 cm/ ½ in strips. Cut the red onion into 8 pieces, held together at the root. Rinse and brush them with oil.

2 Purée or mash the avocado and lemon juice together. Whisk in the mayonnaise. Add in the chilli powder, pepper and salt.

3 Put the chicken and onion over a hot barbecue and grill for 3–4 minutes on each side. Mix the chicken, onion, tomato and avocado together.

4 Cut the bread in half twice, so that you have quarter-circle-shaped pieces, then in half horizontally. Toast on the hot barbecue for about 2 minutes on each side.

5 Spoon the chicken mixture onto the toasts and serve with a green salad.

STONING (PITTING) AVOCADOS

Hold the avocado in one hand and, using a vegetable knife, cut around the middle, so that you are left with two symmetrical halves. Put one half on a tea towel (dish cloth) in one hand and rap the vegetable knife sharply across the avocado stone (pit). The knife will embed itself and it will be simple to lift the stone (pit) out with the knife. If you are puréeing the avocado, spoon out the flesh; otherwise peel off the skin.

CHARGRILLED TUNA WITH ROASTED (BELL) PEPPERS

SERVES 4

4 tuna steaks, about 250 g/8 oz each
3 tbsp lemon juice
1 litre/1¾ pints/4 cups water
6 tbsp olive oil
2 orange (bell) peppers
2 red (bell) peppers
12 black olives
1 tsp balsamic vinegar
salt and pepper

1 Put the tuna steaks into a bowl with the lemon juice and water. Leave for 15 minutes.

2 Drain and brush the steaks all over with olive oil and season well.

3 Halve, core and deseed the (bell) peppers. Put them over a hot barbecue and cook for 12 minutes until they are charred all over. Put them into a plastic bag and close it.

4 Meanwhile, cook the tuna over a hot barbecue for 12–15 minutes, turning once.

5 When the (bell) peppers are cool enough to handle, peel them and cut each piece into 4 strips. Toss them with the remaining olive oil, olives and balsamic vinegar.

6 Serve the tuna steaks piping hot, with the roasted (bell) pepper salad.

PEELING (BELL) PEPPERS

Red, orange and yellow (bell) peppers can also be peeled by cooking them in a hot oven for 30 minutes, turning them frequently, or roasting them straight over a naked gas flame, again turning them frequently. In both methods, deseed the (bell) peppers after peeling.

SALMON FILLET ON A BED OF HERBS

SERVES 4

½ large bunch dried thyme
5 fresh rosemary branches, 15–20 cm/
    6–8 in long
8 bay leaves
1 kg/2 lb salmon fillet
1 bulb fennel, cut into 8 pieces
2 tbsp lemon juice
2 tbsp olive oil

1 Make a base on a hot barbecue with
the dried thyme, rosemary branches
and bay leaves, overlapping them so that
they cover a slightly bigger area than the
salmon.

2 Place the salmon on top of the
herbs. Arrange the fennel around the
edge of the fish.

3 Combine the lemon juice and oil
and brush the salmon with it. Cover
the salmon loosely with a piece of foil, to
keep it moist. Cook for about 20–30
minutes, basting frequently with the
lemon juice mixture.

4 Remove the salmon from the
barbecue, cut it into slices and serve
with the fennel.

PARTY DISH

If you find that a whole 1 kg/2 lb
salmon fillet is difficult to get hold of,
you can use a 1 kg/2 lb salmon 'steak'
split in half. Place the pieces on the
grill close together, so that the fish
does not dry out as it cooks.

Use whatever combination of herbs
you may have to hand – but avoid the
stronger tasting herbs, such as sage and
marjoram, which are unsuitable for fish.

While the salmon is cooking, keep
your guests' appetites keen by serving
some miniature corn-on-the-cob or
another light first course, such as
toasted pitta bread and some yogurt-
based dips.

Serve the salmon with fresh bread
and a crunchy green salad, which will
enhance the subtle flavour of the fish.
This salmon is also good eaten cold,
with a herb-flavoured mayonnaise.

SCALLOP SKEWERS

SERVES 4

8 wooden skewers
grated zest and juice of 2 limes
2 tbsp finely chopped lemon grass or 1 tbsp
    lemon juice
2 garlic cloves, crushed
1 green chilli, deseeded and chopped
16 scallops, with corals
2 limes, each cut into 8 segments
2 tbsp sunflower oil
1 tbsp lemon juice
salt and pepper

TO SERVE:
60 g/2 oz/1 cup rocket (arugula) salad
200 g/7 oz/3 cups mixed salad leaves
    (greens)

1 Soak the skewers in warm water for
at least 20 minutes.

2 Combine the lime juice and zest,
lemon grass, garlic and chilli
together in a pestle and mortar or spice
grinder to make a paste.

3 Thread 2 scallops on to each of the
soaked skewers, alternating with
2 lime segments.

4 Whisk together the oil, lemon juice,
salt and pepper thoroughly to make
the salad dressing.

5 Coat the scallops with the spice
paste and place over a medium
barbecue, basting occasionally. Cook for
10 minutes, turning once.

6 Toss the rocket (arugula), mixed
salad leaves (greens) and dressing
together well. Put into a serving bowl.

7 Serve the scallops piping hot,
2 skewers on each plate.

SEABASS BAKED IN FOIL

SERVES 4-6

*2 seabass, about 1 kg/2 lb each, cleaned
    and scaled
2 spring onions (scallions), green part
    only, cut into strips
5 cm/2 in piece ginger, peeled and cut
    into strips
2 garlic cloves, unpeeled, crushed lightly
2 tbsp mirin or dry sherry
salt and pepper*

*TO SERVE:
pickled sushi ginger (optional)
soy sauce*

1 For each fish lay out a double
thickness of foil and oil the top
piece well, or lay a piece of silicon paper
over the foil. Place the fish in the middle
and expose the cavity.

2 Divide the spring onion (scallion)
and ginger between each cavity. Put
a garlic clove in each cavity. Pour over the
mirin or dry sherry. Season the fish well.

3 Close the cavities and lay each fish
on its side. Bring over the foil and
fold the edges together to seal. Fold
each end neatly. Cook over a medium
barbecue for 15 minutes, turning once.

4 To serve, remove the foil and cut
each fish into 2 or 3 pieces. Serve
with the pickled ginger and soy sauce.

BONING THE FISH

To bone the fish, cover a chopping
board with greaseproof paper and lay
the fish on it. Open up the cavity and
locate the rib bones. Insert a sharp
vegetable knife under each bone on
both sides of the backbone and
dislodge it from the flesh. Cut these
bones off with kitchen scissors. To
remove the backbone, sever it near
the tail, and as near to the head as
possible. Open the fish out as wide as
possible without tearing the flesh and
run the knife down either side of the
spine, freeing the flesh from the
backbone without cutting through the
skin. Remove the backbone.

SWORDFISH STEAK WITH ROAST GARLIC

SERVES 4

*4 swordfish steaks, about 200 g/7 oz each
4 tbsp olive oil
2 whole garlic heads
pepper*

1 Brush the swordfish steaks with the
olive oil and season well. Set aside.

2 Put the whole unpeeled garlic heads
over a very hot barbecue and cook
for about 25 minutes until they are soft to
the touch. It is difficult to overcook the
garlic, but keep an eye on it nevertheless.

3 After the garlic has been cooking for
about 15 minutes, put the steaks on
the barbecue and cook for 5–6 minutes
on each side, until the flesh is firm and
comes away from the bone easily. Brush
once or twice with the olive oil.

4 When the garlic is soft to the touch,
cut across the top of it, exposing all
the cloves.

5 When the swordfish steaks are
cooked, place on a serving plate and
squeeze the garlic straight out of the
cloves across the top. Smear it all over
liberally. Season with pepper and serve
immediately.

GARLIC

When garlic is cooked like this, the
sweetness of it comes to the fore.
Although it does retain some of its
pungency, it can be used more liberally
than raw or slightly cooked garlic.

BABY OCTOPUS & SQUID WITH CHILLI SAUCE

•••••••••••••••••••••••••••••••••••••

SERVES 4–6

150 ml/ ¼ pint/²⁄₃ cup rice vinegar
50 ml/2 fl oz/ ¼ cup dry sherry
2 red chillies, chopped
1 tsp sugar
4 tbsp oil
12 baby octopus
12 small squid tubes, cleaned
2 spring onions (scallions), sliced
1 garlic clove, crushed
2.5 cm/1 in piece ginger, grated
4 tbsp sweet chilli sauce
salt

1 Combine the vinegar, dry sherry, red chillies, sugar, 2 tbsp of the oil and a pinch of salt in a large bowl.

2 Wash each octopus under cold running water and drain. Discard the head and beak, and put the tentacles, all in one piece, into the vinegar mixture.

3 Put the squid tubes into the vinegar mixture. Cover and chill overnight.

4 Put the remaining oil into a frying pan (skillet) or wok and add the spring onions (scallions), garlic and ginger. Stir for 1 minute over a very hot barbecue. Remove from the heat and add the chilli sauce. Set aside.

5 Drain the fish from the marinade. Cut the pointed bottom end off each squid tube, so that you are left with tubes of even width all the way down. Make a cut down one side and open out the squid so that it is flat. Make four cuts in one direction, and four in the other, taking care not to cut all the way through. You will have a lattice pattern.

6 Put all the octopus and squid over the hottest part of the barbecue for 4–5 minutes, turning them constantly. The octopus tentacles will curl up, and are cooked when the flesh is no longer translucent. The squid tubes will curl back on themselves, revealing the lattice cuts.

7 When cooked, toss them into the pan with the chilli sauce to coat completely and serve immediately.

CITRUS & FRESH HERB MARINADES

•••••••••••••••••••••••••••••••••••••

Keep the marinades covered with clingfilm (plastic wrap) or store in screw-top jars, ready for using as marinades or bastes.

ORANGE, CHIVE & MARJORAM:
1 orange
120 ml/4 fl oz/ ½ cup olive oil
4 tbsp dry white wine
4 tbsp white wine vinegar
1 tbsp snipped fresh chives
1 tbsp chopped fresh marjoram
salt and pepper

1 Remove the rind from the orange with a zester, or grate it finely, then squeeze the juice.

2 Mix the orange rind and juice with all the remaining ingredients in a small bowl, whisking together to combine. Season with salt and pepper.

THAI-SPICED LIME & CORIANDER (CILANTRO):
1 stalk lemon grass
finely grated rind and juice of 1 lemon
4 tbsp sesame oil
2 tbsp light soy sauce
pinch of ground ginger
1 tbsp chopped fresh coriander (cilantro)
salt and pepper

Bruise the lemon grass by crushing it with a rolling pin. Mix the remaining ingredients together and add the lemon grass.

BASIL, LEMON & OREGANO:
finely grated rind of 1 lemon
4 tbsp lemon juice
1 tbsp balsamic vinegar
2 tbsp red wine vinegar
2 tbsp virgin olive oil
1 tbsp chopped fresh oregano
1 tbsp chopped fresh basil
salt and pepper

Whisk all the ingredients together in a small bowl. Season the marinade with salt and pepper.

PERSIAN LAMB

SERVES 4–6

2 tbsp chopped fresh mint
250 ml/8 fl oz/1 cup natural yogurt
4 garlic cloves, crushed
¼ tsp pepper
6 lamb chops
2 tbsp lemon juice

TABBOULEH:
250 g/8 oz/2 cups couscous
500 ml/16 fl oz/2 cups boiling water
2 tbsp olive oil
2 tbsp lemon juice
½ onion, chopped finely
4 tomatoes, chopped
30 g/1 oz/¼ cup fresh coriander
  (cilantro), chopped
2 tbsp chopped fresh mint
salt and pepper

1 Combine the mint, yogurt, garlic and pepper. Put the chops into a non-porous dish and rub all over with the lemon juice. Pour over the yogurt marinade. Cover and marinate for 2–3 hours.

2 Meanwhile, make the tabbouleh. Put the couscous into a heatproof bowl and pour over the boiling water. Leave to steep for 5 minutes. Drain and put into a sieve (strainer). Set over a pan of barely simmering water and steam for 8 minutes.

3 Toss in the oil and lemon juice. Add the onion, tomato, coriander (cilantro) and mint. Season well and set aside.

4 Cook the lamb over a medium barbecue for 15 minutes, turning once. Serve with the tabbouleh.

YOGURT

Yogurt is a useful ingredient as a base for a marinade. The bland taste is a good medium for many flavours such as herbs, citrus fruit, spices and oils.

LAMB FILLET WITH ROASTED BABY ONIONS

SERVES 6–8

500 g/1 lb lamb neck fillet
500 g/1 lb pickling (pearl) onions
1 tbsp olive oil
3 tbsp chopped fresh thyme
2 lemons, rinsed and sliced thickly

MARINADE:
4 tbsp olive oil
3 garlic cloves, well crushed
½ tsp salt
½ tsp pepper

1 To make the marinade, mix the ingredients together to form a paste.

2 Smear the paste all over the lamb fillet and leave to marinate overnight in the refrigerator.

3 Cook the onions in a saucepan of boiling water for about 15 minutes, until almost cooked through. Peel them.

4 Heat the oil and thyme in a frying pan (skillet) and add the onions to reheat them and coat them in the oil and thyme. Set aside.

5 Lay enough lemon slices over a very hot barbecue for the lamb to sit on.

6 Place the lamb on top and cook for 10 minutes on each side, basting frequently.

7 Meanwhile, put the onions on the grid around the lamb and cook for 10 minutes, turning often until they are quite soft but charred on the outside. Serve the lamb with the onions and a green bean salad.

HANDY HINT

The lamb should be hot all the way through but still slightly pink and juicy in the centre. However, if you prefer your lamb to be cooked for longer, barbecue it for 25 minutes. The marinade will keep the meat moist.

KLEFTIKO

SERVES 6-8

1 kg/2 lb leg of lamb, boned and
*   butterflied*
6 tbsp olive oil
4 tbsp lemon juice
2 tbsp chopped fresh mint
½ tsp pepper
5 garlic cloves, sliced
2 large rosemary sprigs, broken into
*   20 short lengths*
½ onion, chopped
2 tbsp extra virgin olive oil
175 g/6 oz/1 cup basmati rice
300 ml/ ½ pint/1¼ cups chicken stock
1 tbsp pine kernels (nuts)
1 tbsp chopped fresh oregano
2 aubergines (eggplants), sliced
*   lengthways*
salt and pepper

1 Roll the lamb into a leg shape. Tuck in the shank (thin) end. Fasten in place with skewers, preferably metal.

2 Make 20 small nicks in the skin of the lamb with the tip of a knife.

3 Combine 4 tbsp of the olive oil with the lemon juice, mint and pepper in a saucepan. Bring to a slow boil. Pour the barely simmering marinade over the lamb and rub in all over.

4 Insert a garlic slice and rosemary sprig into each nick. Place the lamb on a piece of double foil or in a large foil tray on the grid over a medium barbecue.

5 Cook the lamb for 15 minutes, turning frequently. Then turn every 10–15 minutes for about 1 hour, until the lamb is cooked through. You may need to change the foil during this time to avoid flare-ups. Because the lamb is an uneven shape, the shank end will be more well cooked than the large end.

6 Make the rice pilau. Cook the onion and 2 tablespoons of the olive oil in a saucepan over a gentle heat until the onion is softened, about 5 minutes. Add the rice and stir until translucent. Add the stock and bring to the boil. Season well and simmer over a gentle heat for 15 minutes. Stir in the pine kernels (nuts) and oregano. Keep warm.

7 Cut a lattice pattern in the aubergine (eggplant) slices. Brush with the extra virgin olive oil and cook on the grid for 10 minutes, turning once.

8 Slice the lamb and serve with the aubergine (eggplant) and pilau.

SWEET & SOUR PORK RIBS

••••••••••••••••••••••••••••••••••••

SERVES 4–6

2 garlic cloves, crushed
5 cm/2 in piece ginger, grated
150 ml/ ¼ pint/ ⅔ cup soy sauce
2 tbsp sugar
4 tbsp sweet sherry
4 tbsp tomato purée (paste)
300 g/10 oz/2 cups pineapple, cubed
2 kg/4 lb pork spare ribs
3 tbsp clear honey
300 g/10 oz/5 pineapple rings, fresh or
    canned

1 Combine the garlic, ginger, soy
  sauce, sugar, sherry, tomato purée
(paste) and cubed pineapple in a non-
porous dish.

2 Put the spare ribs into the dish and
  make sure that they are coated
completely with the marinade. Cover the
dish.

3 Leave at room temperature for
  2 hours only.

4 Cook the ribs over a medium
  barbecue for 30–40 minutes,
brushing with the honey after 20–30
minutes. Baste with the reserved marinade
frequently until cooked.

5 Cook the pineapple rings over the
  barbecue for 10 minutes, turning
once. Serve the ribs with the pineapple
rings on the side.

MARINATING

If a marinade contains soy sauce, the
marinating time should be limited,
usually to 2 hours. If allowed to
marinate for too long, the meat will dry
out and become tough.

SAUSAGES

••••••••••••••••••••••••••••••••••••

SERVES 4

4 barbecue pork sausages, the double-
    length kind, or 8 standard size sausages
oil for brushing

TO SERVE:
1 onion
1 French baguette, cut into 4
French mustard

1 Prick the sausages all over with a
  fork. This not only ensures that the
skin does not split, but also allows the
excess fat to run out. Pork and beef
sausages work very well on a barbecue as
they are quite firm.

2 Brush the sausages all over with oil
  – this also protects the skin.

3 Cook the sausages over a hot
  barbecue for 10 minutes, turning
frequently. If you are using standard-sized
pork sausages, they will cook in less time,
and chipolatas will only take
5–7 minutes.

4 Cut the onion into 8 pieces, each
  piece held together by a bit of onion
root. Brush with oil and cook over the
barbecue for 2–3 minutes.

5 Meanwhile, insert a bread knife
  through the inside of each piece of
baguette. Without breaking the crust,
hollow out enough bread for the sausage
to fit in.

6 Spread a line of mustard through the
  middle of the bread. Put 2 pieces of
onion in each piece of baguette and push
the cooked sausage through the middle. If
using standard-sized sausages, put one in
each end.

HANDY HINT

For an emergency barbecue recipe,
defrost a packet of frozen sausages
and then marinate them in a shop-
bought marinade. They are ready in
minutes and guaranteed to be popular!

TEX-MEX RIBS

••

SERVES 4–6

250 ml/8 fl oz/1 cup tomato ketchup
50 ml/2 fl oz/ ¼ cup cider vinegar
60 g/2 oz/ ⅓ cup light muscovado sugar
1 onion, chopped
3 garlic cloves, crushed
1 tbsp dried chilli flakes
2 tbsp Dijon mustard
1 tsp Worcestershire sauce
2 kg/4 lb beef ribs

TO SERVE:
1 French baguette, sliced
125 g/4 oz/ ½ cup butter
3 garlic cloves, crushed
1 tbsp chopped fresh parsley
1 avocado
lemon juice
250 g/8 oz/4 cups mixed salad leaves
salt and pepper

1 Combine the ketchup, vinegar, sugar, onion, garlic, chilli flakes, mustard and Worcestershire sauce in a saucepan. Bring to the boil, and simmer for 10 minutes.

2 Wrap the ribs in foil, either in one piece or 3–4 smaller parcels. Cook over a medium barbecue for 10 minutes, turning once or twice.

3 Meanwhile, place the sliced French baguette in foil. Combine the butter, garlic and parsley with plenty of salt and pepper. Spread a little butter between each slice of the baguette and close the foil.

4 Peel and dice the avocado. Sprinkle over the lemon juice and mix together with the salad leaves.

5 Unwrap the ribs and place over the hot barbecue. Baste with the ketchup mixture. Cook for 20 minutes, turning occasionally.

6 Cook the garlic bread alongside the ribs, for 15–20 minutes.

7 Serve the ribs piping hot, with any leftover barbecue sauce for dipping, the garlic bread and the green salad.

PROVENÇAL GRILLED BEEF

••

SERVES 6–8

1 kg/2 lb rump skirt or rump steak
½ tsp pepper
4 tbsp French olive oil
6 anchovies, chopped finely
2 garlic cloves, chopped finely
2 tbsp chopped fresh flat-leafed (Italian) parsley
2 tsp sea salt
French bread to serve

1 With a sharp knife, trim any excess fat from the meat. Pare off any membrane or connective tissue, which will misshape the meat as it cooks.

2 Rub in pepper and 1 tbsp of the olive oil all over the meat. Cover and chill for about 2 hours.

3 Combine the anchovies, garlic, parsley, sea salt and remaining olive oil.

4 Remove the meat from the refrigerator 30 minutes before cooking. Place the beef over a hot barbecue. Cook for 8 minutes, then turn over and spread the anchovy mix on the top side. Cook for 6 minutes on the other side.

5 When the beef is cooked, remove to a chopping board. Leave to rest for 1 minute before slicing thinly. Transfer to a warmed serving platter and serve with the French bread.

OLIVE OIL

In Italian homes, seed oil is usually used for cooking, while the olive oil and extra virgin olive oil are used only as a table condiment. Extra virgin olive oil is a highly priced commodity, and has a delicate balance. Its structure and taste change upon heating, as well as its nutritional content; for this reason it should be used only as a dressing. Olive oil has a higher resilience to heat, being a coarser product, and is suitable for barbecuing and delicious for deep-frying. I have chosen French olive oil for this recipe, but Italian would do just as well.

STEAK IN A RED WINE MARINADE

SERVES 4

4 rump steaks, about 250 g/8 oz each
600 ml/1 pint/2½ cups red wine
1 onion, quartered
2 tbsp Dijon mustard
2 garlic cloves, crushed
salt and pepper
4 large field mushrooms
olive oil for brushing
branch of fresh rosemary (optional)

1 Snip through the fat strip on the steaks in 3 places, so that the steak retains its shape when barbecued.

2 Combine the red wine, onion, mustard, garlic, salt and pepper. Lay the steaks in a shallow non-porous dish and pour over the marinade. Cover and chill for 2–3 hours.

3 Remove the steaks from the refrigerator 30 minutes before you intend to cook them to let them come to room temperature. This is especially important if the steak is thick, so that it cooks more evenly and is not well done on the outside and raw in the middle.

4 Sear both sides of the steak – about 1 minute on each side – over a hot barbecue. If it is about 2.5 cm/1 in thick, keep it over a hot barbecue, and cook for about 4 minutes on each side. This will give a medium-rare steak – cook it more or less, to suit your taste. If the steak is a thicker cut, move it to a less hot part of the barbecue or further away from the coals. To test the readiness of the meat while cooking, simply press it with your finger – the more the meat yields, the less it is cooked.

5 Brush the mushrooms with the olive oil and cook them alongside the steak, for 5 minutes, turning once. When you put the mushrooms on the barbecue, put the rosemary branch in the fire to flavour the meat slightly.

6 Remove the steak and leave to rest for a minute or two before serving. Slice the mushrooms and serve alongside.

BEEF PATTIES

SERVES 4

500 g/1 lb/2 cups minced (ground) beef
250 g/8 oz/1 cup minced (ground) lamb
1 onion, chopped finely
6 tomatoes, halved
1 red onion, chopped finely
1 red chilli, deseeded and chopped
2 tbsp dark brown sugar
50 ml/2 fl oz/ ¼ cup cider vinegar
1 tsp balsamic or sherry vinegar
2 tbsp chopped fresh chervil (optional)
4 soft hamburger buns
½ iceberg lettuce, shredded
4 gherkins
mustard
salt and pepper

1 Combine the beef, lamb and onion in a large bowl with plenty of salt and pepper.

2 It is important that the patties do not have any air pockets. To ensure this, divide the mixture into 4 and make 1 ball from each quarter. Put each ball in a cupped hand and throw it into the other hand to compact the mixture, repeating a few times until you have a dense ball of meat. Put this on a plate and press down gently with the palm of your hand to make the ball into a patty. Chill.

3 Put the tomato halves on a rack over a baking sheet. Bake in a pre-heated oven at 180°C/350°F/Gas Mark 4 for 40–50 minutes until quite collapsed.

4 Chop the tomato coarsely and combine with the red onion, chilli, sugar and vinegars. Season and add chervil. Transfer to a serving dish.

5 Cook the patties over a hot barbecue for 10 minutes, turning once. This will give a medium-rare burger – for a well-done burger, cook for 15 minutes. Towards the end of cooking time, split the soft buns and toast lightly for 1–2 minutes on the cut side.

6 Put some shredded lettuce, the beefburger, a gherkin and mustard to taste on the bottom half of the toasted bun, and cover with the top half. Serve with the salsa.

PAN BAGNA

SERVES 4

1 red (bell) pepper, halved, cored and
    deseeded
250 g/8 oz sirloin steak, 2.5 cm/1 in thick
1 small white bloomer loaf or French stick
4 tbsp olive oil
2 extra-large tomatoes, sliced
10 black olives, halved
½ cucumber, peeled and sliced
6 anchovies, chopped
salt and pepper

1 Cook the (bell) pepper over a hot
   barbecue for 15 minutes, turning
once. Put it into a plastic bag and seal.

2 Sear both sides of the steak first and
   then grill for 8 minutes, turning
once. Cut the steak into thin strips.

3 When the (bell) pepper is cool
   enough to handle, peel and slice it.

4 Cut the loaf of bread lengthways and
   hollow out each half, leaving a
2.5 cm/1 in crust. Brush both halves very
liberally with olive oil.

5 Lay the tomatoes, olives, cucumber,
   steak strips, anchovies and red (bell)
pepper strips on the bottom half. Season
and cover with the top half.

6 Put the Pan Bagna on top of a piece
   of greaseproof paper (baking
parchment). Squash the whole loaf and its
filling down well and wrap tightly in
clingfilm (plastic wrap). Secure with
adhesive tape if necessary. Chill for at
least 2 hours. If made in the morning, by
lunchtime it will be ready to eat and all
the flavours will have combined.

VARIATIONS

Different fillings, such as pâtés,
sausages and other salad items, can
be used according to appetite and
taste. Mozzarella cheese is good, as it
is so moist. Onions give a bit of a zing
to the other ingredients.

FAJITAS

SERVES 4

4 tbsp corn oil
4 tbsp lime juice
2 tbsp chopped fresh coriander (cilantro)
2 garlic cloves, crushed
1 tbsp chilli flakes
500 g/1 lb topside steak
4 flour tortillas
1 avocado, peeled, halved and sliced
½ iceberg lettuce, shredded
salt and pepper

SALSA:
2 plum tomatoes, deseeded and chopped
    finely
¼ red onion, chopped finely
1 tbsp chopped fresh coriander (cilantro)
2 tsp sunflower oil
1 tsp white wine vinegar
1 green chilli, deseeded and chopped
    finely

1 Combine the corn oil, lime juice,
   coriander (cilantro), garlic, chilli
flakes, salt and pepper in a large non-
porous dish.

2 Add the meat to this mixture and
   make sure that it is coated all over.

3 Cover and leave in the refrigerator to
   marinate for 8 hours or overnight.

4 Next day, combine the salsa ingredients and transfer to a serving dish.

5 Cook the meat over a hot barbecue
   for 10–15 minutes, turning once. It
should be slightly pink in the middle, and
not completely firm when pressed. The
time will depend on the thickness of the
meat. Remove from the grill and slice
thinly, across the grain. Divide between
the 4 tortillas, alternating with the
avocado slices and putting a little
shredded lettuce into each one.

6 Wrap the tortilla around the filling.
   Serve immediately, with the salsa
and any other desired accompaniments.
Serve with a cold Mexican beer if liked.

STUFFED RED (BELL) PEPPERS

SERVES 4

2 red (bell) peppers, halved lengthways
and deseeded
2 tomatoes, halved
2 courgettes (zucchini), sliced thinly
lengthways
1 red onion, cut into 8 sections, each
section held together by the root
4 tbsp olive oil
2 tbsp fresh thyme leaves
60 g/2 oz/ ⅓ cup mixed basmati and wild
rice, cooked
salt and pepper

1   Put the halved (bell) peppers, halved
    tomatoes, sliced courgettes (zucchini)
and onion sections on to a baking sheet.

2   Brush the vegetables with olive oil
    and sprinkle over the thyme leaves.

3   Cook the (bell) pepper, onion and
    courgette (zucchini) over a medium
barbecue for 6 minutes, turning once.

4   When the (bell) peppers are cooked,
    put a spoonful of the cooked rice
into each one, and the onion and
courgette (zucchini) on top.

5   Cook the tomato halves for
    2–3 minutes only, before adding a
half to each stuffed (bell) pepper. Season
with plenty of salt and pepper and serve.

(BELL) PEPPERS

When chargrilled, red, orange and
yellow (bell) peppers all take on a
remarkable sweet quality. They are
often peeled in order to highlight this.
Orange (bell) peppers are worth
experimenting with as they do have a
different flavour from red and green
(bell) peppers. Both red and orange
(bell) peppers complement lamb
beautifully, and rice is a good foil to
both of these. Try the Stuffed Red
(Bell) Peppers with Lamb Fillet with
Roasted Baby Onions (page 597), or
Persian Lamb (page 597).

CORN-ON-THE-COB

SERVES 4–6

4–6 corn-on-the-cobs
oil for brushing

TO SERVE:
butter (optional)
salt (optional)

1   Soak the cobs in hand-hot water for
    20 minutes. Drain them thoroughly.

2   If the cobs have no green leaves,
    brush with oil and cook over a hot
barbecue for 30 minutes, brushing
occasionally with the oil and turning
frequently.

3   If your cobs have green leaves, tear
    off all but the last two layers and
brush with oil.

4   Cook over a hot barbecue for
    40 minutes, brushing with oil once
or twice and turning occasionally.

5   Serve hot, without the husks. If you
    like, add a knob of butter and salt
to taste.

CORN COBS

Try to buy the cobs with the husk still
on, as they will retain more moisture
when barbecued this way.

Corn-on-the-cob is an excellent
accompaniment to any American- or
South American-style dish such as
Blackened Chicken (page 592), Beef
Patties (page 600) and Tex-Mex Ribs
(page 600).

While you are barbecuing the corn-
on-the-cob, you may like to flavour it
with oils or herbs. Try tucking some
rosemary, coriander (cilantro) or thyme
inside the husk for a deliciously
aromatic flavour. A wide variety of
herbed and flavoured oils can be
bought – my favourite is hazelnut oil,
which really adds something to corn-
on-the-cob. You may also like to try a
chilli oil, or any of the oils that are
flavoured with herbs such as
rosemary, thyme or basil.

ROASTED VEGETABLES ON ROSEMARY SKEWERS

SERVES 6

1 small red cabbage
1 head fennel
1 orange (bell) pepper, cut into 3.5 cm/
    1½ in dice
1 aubergine (eggplant), halved and sliced
    into 1 cm/ ½ in pieces
2 courgettes (zucchini), sliced thickly
    diagonally
olive oil for brushing
6 rosemary twigs, about 15 cm/6 in long,
    soaked in water for 8 hours
salt and pepper

1 Put the red cabbage on its side on a chopping board and cut through the middle of its stem and heart. Divide each piece into four, each time including a bit of the stem in the slice to hold it together.

2 Prepare the fennel in the same way. Blanch the red cabbage and fennel in boiling water for 3 minutes, then drain well.

3 With a wooden skewer, pierce a hole through the middle of each piece of vegetable.

4 On to each rosemary twig, thread a piece of orange (bell) pepper, fennel, red cabbage, aubergine (eggplant) and courgette (zucchini), pushing the rosemary through the holes.

5 Brush liberally with olive oil and season with plenty of salt and pepper.

6 Cook over a hot barbecue for 8–10 minutes, turning occasionally. Serve hot.

FRUIT SKEWERS

Fruit skewers are a deliciously quick and easy dessert. Thread pieces of banana, mango, peach, strawberry, apple and pear on to soaked wooden skewers and cook over the dying embers. Brush with sugar syrup towards the end of cooking.

DEVILLED NEW POTATOES

SERVES 6–8

20 cocktail sticks (toothpicks)
500 g/1 lb baby new potatoes
olive oil for brushing
10 rashers (slices) streaky bacon
20 small sage leaves

1 Soak the cocktail sticks (toothpicks) in hand-hot water for 20 minutes before using.

2 Bring a pan of water to the boil and add the potatoes. Boil for 10 minutes and drain.

3 Brush the potatoes all over with olive oil.

4 Cut each bacon rasher (slice) in half widthways. Holding each piece at one end, smooth and stretch it with the back of a knife.

5 Wrap a piece of bacon around each potato enclosing a sage leaf and securing with a cocktail stick (toothpick).

6 Cook over a hot barbecue for 6–7 minutes, turning occasionally. Serve hot or cold.

VARIATIONS

Green bacon or smoked bacon may be used to wrap the vegetables. I favour the smoked variety as it tends to keep its shape for longer than green bacon.

All manner of root vegetables can be wrapped in bacon and grilled this way. Baby onions (the pickling variety) are especially delicious, as the outside skin turns crispy, golden and sweet. Carrots, parsnips and turnips will all need peeling and cutting down to 2.5 cm/1 in cubes.

Any variety of pumpkin or squash should be peeled, deseeded and cut down to 2.5 cm/1 in cubes. The pumpkin family of vegetables turns remarkably sweet when heated. The same recipe can be used to cook leeks – peel and parboil as in the recipe, cut into 2.5 cm/1 in cubes, wrap in bacon and tuck in the sage leaf.

ROASTED RED (BELL) PEPPER TERRINE

SERVES 6-8

olive oil, to oil the terrine
500 g/1 lb/3 cups broad (fava) beans
6 red (bell) peppers, halved and deseeded
3 small courgettes (zucchini), sliced
lengthways
1 aubergine (eggplant), sliced lengthways
3 leeks, halved lengthways
6 tbsp olive oil
6 tbsp single (light) cream
2 tbsp chopped fresh basil
salt and pepper

1 Oil a 1.5 litre/2½ pint/5 cup terrine. Blanch the broad (fava) beans in boiling water for 1–2 minutes and pop them out of their skins. It is not essential to do this, but the effort is worthwhile as the beans taste a lot sweeter.

2 Roast the red (bell) peppers over a hot barbecue until the skin is black – about 10–15 minutes. Remove and put into a plastic bag. Seal and set aside.

3 Brush the courgette (zucchini), aubergine (eggplant) and leeks with 5 tbsp of the olive oil, and season. Cook over the hot barbecue until tender, about 8–10 minutes, turning once.

4 Meanwhile, purée the broad (fava) beans in a blender or food processor with a tablespoon of the olive oil, the cream and seasoning. Alternatively, chop and then press through a sieve (strainer).

5 Remove the red (bell) peppers from the bag and peel.

6 Put a layer of red (bell) pepper along the bottom and up the sides of the terrine.

7 Spread a third of the bean purée over this. Cover with the aubergine (eggplant) slices and spread over half of the remaining bean purée.

8 Sprinkle over the basil. Top with courgettes (zucchini) and the remaining bean purée. Lay the leeks on top. Add any remaining pieces of red (bell) pepper. Put a piece of foil, folded 4 times, on the top and weigh down the layers with cans.

9 Chill until required. Turn out on to a serving platter, slice and serve with Italian bread and green salad.

ROAST LEEKS

SERVES 4-6

4 leeks
3 tbsp olive oil
2 tsp balsamic vinegar
sea salt and pepper

1 Halve the leeks lengthways, making sure that your knife goes straight, so that the leek is held together by the root.

2 Brush each leek liberally with the olive oil.

3 Cook over a hot barbecue for 6–7 minutes, turning once.

4 Remove the leeks from the barbecue and brush with the balsamic vinegar.

5 Sprinkle with salt and pepper and serve hot or warm.

SEA SALT

Sea salt or *gros sel* (bay salt in some older cookery books) is a very inexpensive ingredient that will add another dimension to your dishes. It is made by panning on salt marshes near the coast and contains more magnesium and calcium than other salts. When scattered over a simple dish such as these leeks it will bring out all the flavours and will look attractive too, crumbled between the fingertips. Because of the sharp taste you will not need to use as much sea salt as you would rock salt.

SUBSTITUTES

If in season, 8 baby leeks may be used instead of 4 standard-sized ones.
  Sherry vinegar makes a good substitute for the expensive balsamic vinegar and would work as well in this recipe.

TOASTED TROPICAL FRUIT KEBABS WITH HOT CHOCOLATE DIP

SERVES 4

4 wooden skewers

DIP:
125 g/4 oz/4 squares plain (dark) chocolate, broken into pieces
2 tbsp golden (light corn) syrup
1 tbsp cocoa powder
1 tbsp cornflour (cornstarch)
200 ml/7 fl oz /generous ¾ cup milk

KEBABS:
1 mango
1 paw-paw (papaya)
2 kiwi fruit
½ small pineapple
1 large banana
2 tbsp lemon juice
150 ml/ ¼ pint/ ⅔ cup white rum

1 Soak the wooden skewers in hand-hot water for 30 minutes.

2 Put all the ingredients for the chocolate dip into a saucepan. Heat, stirring constantly, until thickened and smooth. Keep warm at the edge of the barbecue.

3 Slice the mango on each side of its large, flat stone (pit). Cut the flesh into chunks, removing the peel. Halve, deseed and peel the paw-paw (papaya) and cut it into chunks. Peel the kiwi fruit and slice into chunks. Peel and cut the pineapple into chunks. Peel and slice the banana and dip the pieces in the lemon juice.

4 Thread the pieces of fruit alternately on to the wooden skewers. Place them in a shallow dish and pour over the rum. Leave to soak up the flavour of the rum until ready to barbecue, at least 30 minutes.

5 Cook the kebabs over the hot coals, turning frequently, until seared, about 2 minutes. Serve, accompanied by the hot chocolate dip.

PICNICS – INTRODUCTION

A picnic can vary from a simple and impromptu affair, to a well-organized and thoughtfully planned outing. The occasion can vary: you might take a picnic to a sporting event, such as a cricket match or baseball game, to save having to find food when you get there. At the other end of the scale, you might organize a truly stylish, sophisticated and elegant picnic, which includes a proper table set with china, silver and glass.

PLANNING THE MENU
If possible, a selection of food is best for a picnic, as appetites are always more healthy in 'the great outdoors' and even the most modest of eaters seem to consume enormous amounts of food.

For impromptu picnics, sandwiches and rolls are excellent, as they can be assembled quickly, either before you leave, or at the picnic site, when people can choose their own combination of bread and filling. Most store cupboards and refrigerators will reveal something suitable for sandwich fillings, and if you have time, you could even take the opportunity to create something really special in addition to the classic standbys such as eggs, cheese and cold meat. You could even pick up freshly baked bread and rolls on the way to the picnic, especially as there are nearly always some shops open, wherever you are and whatever the day of the week.

Take salad ingredients cut into chunky pieces; carrots, cucumber, celery and courgettes (zucchini) are ideal, and so are the small hearty little gem type of lettuce, as the tiny leaves are strong enough to use for scooping up dips. Salad dressings can easily be taken separately in screw-top containers for dunking or spooning into a salad sandwich. Unless you are eating quite near to your home, it is better to add the dressing to a salad when you actually arrive and set up the picnic, as the dressing may make the salad soggy if left for too long.

Something sweet to finish off a picnic is always popular, but it needn't be an elaborate dessert; it can just as easily be fresh fruit, cakes and cookies, although pies and tarts always go down well. You could consider taking individual yogurts, ice creams or sorbets, or even a frozen gâteau, if you have a freezer box to keep them in while the savoury food is being eaten.

PACKING AND TRANSPORTING THE FOOD
Packing and transporting a picnic has been made much easier thanks to the huge range of rigid plastic and other containers with securely fitting lids that is now available. Along with clingfilm (plastic wrap) and foil, it is possible to transport almost anything, although some kinds of food will inevitably travel better than others. Lids and coverings are also important, for wherever you choose to picnic, a number of flies or wasps are almost certain to join you!

Foil is best for closely wrapping such things as meat, pastry items, pâtés, etc, but if the food is at all acidic this may cause pitting to the foil, and a layer of food wrap or greaseproof paper (baking parchment) should be used first, under the foil. If it is a food with a high-fat content, such as cheese, you should use a suitable food wrap and not just ordinary clingfilm (plastic wrap) for wrapping. Even rolls and sandwiches will arrive as if they have

INTRODUCTION

been freshly made when they are wrapped properly.

One or more good, sturdy insulated 'cold' boxes or picnic baskets will of course help greatly with the transporting of the food. Obviously begin by placing the heavier items at the bottom, but also try to put the desserts, fruit and sweet food there, so it can be unpacked and used more or less in the order it is to be eaten. Always stand up anything that might seep if it tipped over, wedging it between other items. It may be an idea to carry chilled wines, beers and other drinks in a separate cold box, as often these are required first and it will avoid turning the food upside-down in the haste to find the drinks!

OTHER ESSENTIALS

Depending on the type of picnic you are having, you will need one or two thick rugs or blankets to sit on or portable chairs, perhaps a portable table and tablecloth, along with paper napkins or a roll of paper towels. If the ground is a little damp, use a groundsheet under the rugs or the plastic bin liners to be used later for collecting the rubbish.

Whether to use paper, plastic or china plates is your own choice; food always tastes better off china, but of course paper is easier to dispose of and plastic is lighter and safer to carry than china.

Don't take the best cutlery unless you are dining out in style (and probably will then have someone to help clear up afterwards!), but make sure you have at least one really sharp or serrated knife, condiments, scissors (most useful), a corkscrew and a bottle opener, and a damp cloth carried in a polythene bag with a couple of clean tea towels (dish

cloths). It's not as if you are going to do the washing-up, but a clean cloth always comes in handy, particularly if there are small children around, who seem always to be covered in food, sand or dirt!

COOKED SALAD DRESSING

For those who like salad dressing rather than mayonnaise, this is an easy way to produce a delicious dressing. It will keep in an airtight container in the refrigerator for about 5 days.

1¼ level tbsp plain (all-purpose) flour
1½ tsp caster (superfine) sugar
1 tsp dried mustard powder
salt and white pepper
6 tbsp milk
30 g/1 oz/2 tbsp butter
1 egg, beaten
3–4 tbsp wine or tarragon vinegar
4 tbsp sunflower or vegetable oil

1. Mix together the flour, sugar, mustard and seasonings and stir in the milk gradually until the mixture is smoothly blended.

2. Bring slowly to the boil, stirring all the time and simmer for 1 minute.

3. Remove from the heat and cool slightly, then beat in the butter until melted, followed by the egg. Return to a low heat and cook to just below boiling point, stirring continuously. Do not allow to boil or it may curdle.

4. Remove from the heat and beat in the vinegar gradually to taste, followed by the oil. Adjust the seasonings. Cover and leave to cool. Transfer to a container and chill.

INTRODUCTION

FRENCH DRESSING

The amount of olive oil used may be varied to suit your taste. Once made, store in a bottle or airtight container and keep in a cool place for up to 10 days. Shake vigorously before use.

4 tbsp olive oil
4 tbsp sunflower, corn or
vegetable oil
1 tbsp lemon juice (fresh or
bottled)
salt and pepper
½ tsp dried mustard powder
½ tsp caster (superfine) sugar
1 garlic clove, crushed

1. Put all the ingredients either into a screw-top jar and shake vigorously until completely emulsified; or place in a bowl and whisk thoroughly until emulsified.

2. Taste and adjust the seasonings and store.

MAYONNAISE

Mayonnaise is not as difficult to make as it is often thought to be, but it is essential that all the ingredients are at room temperature before you start – chilled ingredients make curdling much more likely. The flavour can be varied widely by using a flavoured vinegar in place of wine or cider vinegar, and many flavourings can be added for variations. Once made, pack in a plastic, glass or other container with a secure lid and chill until required. It will keep in the refrigerator for about a week in prime condition.

Use a fairly mild oil, but if you want to use olive oil, it is best to use only half olive and the remainder a lighter flavoured oil.

2 egg yolks
about 1 tbsp white wine
vinegar or lemon juice
½ tsp made mustard
300 ml/ ½ pint/1¼ cups oil
(vegetable, sunflower or
olive oil)
salt and pepper
good pinch of caster (superfine)
sugar

1. Put the egg yolks into a bowl with 1 teaspoon of the vinegar or lemon juice and the mustard and beat until thoroughly blended.

2. Whisk in the oil a drop at a time, definitely no faster, until about one third of the oil has been added and the mixture begins to thicken.

3. Add another teaspoon of vinegar or lemon juice and then continue to whisk in the oil, but now in a very thin trickle. It must be whisked briskly all the time, and when it begins to really thicken, the oil can be added a little faster.

4. Season to taste with salt, pepper and sugar, and add more vinegar or lemon juice if wished to give the desired flavour. If too thick, whisk in 1–2 tablespoons hot water. Store in in the refrigerator.

CRAB BISQUE

••••••••••••••••••••••••••••••••••••••

SERVES 4-6

1 fresh crab (about 500 g/1 lb) or 250 g/
*   8 oz/1 cup frozen crab meat, thawed*
1 onion, chopped
2 carrots, chopped
2 celery sticks, sliced thinly
1 bouquet garni
1.5 litres/2½ pints/6¼ cups water
45 g/1½ oz/3 tbsp butter or margarine
45 g/1½ oz/⅓ cup flour
1 tbsp lemon or lime juice
150 ml/¼ pint/⅔ cup dry white wine
¼ tsp ground allspice
30 g/1 oz/2 tbsp long-grain rice
3-4 tbsp brandy
6 tbsp double (heavy) cream or natural
*   fromage frais*
chopped fresh parsley
salt and pepper

1 Remove the brown and white crab
meat carefully from the cleaned
shell, smashing the claws to remove the
meat from them; then chop the meat
finely. Chill until required.

2 Break up the shell and put into a
saucepan with the onion, carrots,
celery, bouquet garni and water. Bring to
the boil, cover and simmer for about
45 minutes. Strain the liquid and reserve
1 litre/1¾ pints/4 cups. If using frozen
crab meat, use fish stock (bouillon) cubes.

3 Melt the fat in a pan, stir in the flour
and cook for 1-2 minutes without
browning. Add the crab stock gradually
and bring to the boil. Add the lemon or
lime juice, wine, allspice and rice, and
simmer for 10 minutes, stirring occasionally.

4 Add the crab meat and simmer for a
further 10-15 minutes, or until the
rice is tender, stirring from time to time.

5 Add the brandy, reheat and adjust
the seasoning. Finally, stir in the
cream or fromage frais and 1-2 tablespoons chopped parsley, reheat and pour
into a warmed vacuum flask for
transporting. Serve the soup in mugs,
sprinkled with more parsley.

RUSTIC CHEESE SCONES WITH CASHEW NUTS

••••••••••••••••••••••••••••••••••••••

MAKES 8-10

175 g/6 oz/1½ cups self-raising flour
175 g/6 oz/1½ cups granary flour
½ tsp baking powder
pinch of salt
90 g/3 oz/⅛ cup butter or margarine
60 g/2 oz/½ cup cashew nut kernels,
*   chopped*
4 spring onions (scallions), trimmed and
*   thinly sliced*
3 tbsp freshly grated Parmesan cheese
*   or 90 g/3 oz/¾ cup mature (sharp)*
*   Cheddar cheese, grated*
1 egg, beaten
about 120 ml/4 fl oz/½ cup milk
1 tsp lemon juice
1 tbsp sesame seeds

1 Sift the white flour into a bowl and
mix in the granary flour, baking
powder and salt. Rub in the fat until the
mixture resembles fine breadcrumbs.

2 Stir in the nuts and spring onions
(scallions) followed by the cheese.

3 Add the egg and enough of the milk
mixed with the lemon juice to mix
to a soft but pliable dough. Turn on to a
floured work surface (counter) and knead
lightly until smooth.

4 Shape the dough into an oblong bar
about 2.5 cm/1 in thick and
10 cm/4 in wide. Transfer to a well-
floured baking sheet.

5 Mark the bar into 8 or 10 slices with
the back of a knife, then brush
lightly with milk or water and sprinkle
liberally with the sesame seeds.

6 Bake in a preheated oven at
220°C/425°F/Gas Mark 7 for 20-25
minutes, or until well risen, golden brown
and firm to the touch. Transfer to a wire
rack to cool. When cold, wrap in foil for
transporting, or until ready to serve,
broken or cut into slices.

SAMOSAS WITH SPICY DIP

MAKES 16

FILLING:

1 onion, chopped finely
1 garlic clove, crushed
1 tsp freshly grated raw ginger root
2 tbsp oil
1 carrot, grated coarsely
1½ tsp garam masala
125 g/4 oz/ ½ cup cooked beef, pork or
ham, minced (ground)
125 g/4 oz/ ¾ cup cooked peas
175 g/6 oz/1 cup cooked potatoes, diced
finely
salt and pepper

PASTRY:

250 g/8 oz/2 cups plain (all-purpose) flour
½ tsp salt
30 g/1 oz/2 tbsp butter or margarine
about 100 ml/3½ fl oz/scant ½ cup cold
water
oil for deep-frying

CURRIED DIP:

150 ml/ ¼ pint/ ⅔ cup thick mayonnaise
3 tbsp soured cream or fromage frais
1½ tsp curry powder
½ tsp ground coriander
1 tsp tomato purée (paste)
2 tbsp mango chutney, chopped
1 tbsp chopped fresh parsley

1 To make the filling, fry the onion, garlic and ginger root in the oil until soft. Add the carrot and fry for 2–3 minutes. Stir in the garam masala and 4 tablespoons water, season, and simmer gently until the liquid is almost absorbed. Remove from the heat, stir in the meat, peas and potatoes and leave to cool.

2 To make the pastry, sift the flour and salt into a bowl and rub in the butter. Add sufficient of the water to mix to a smooth, elastic dough, kneading continually. Cut the dough into 16 pieces and keep covered. Dip each piece into a little oil or coat lightly with flour and roll out to a 12 cm/5 in circle.

3 Put 1–2 tablespoons of the filling on one side of each circle, dampen the edge, fold over and seal firmly. Keep the samosas covered with a damp cloth.

4 Heat the oil to 180–190°C/350–375°F, or until a cube of bread browns in about 30 seconds. Fry the samosas a few at a time for 3–4 minutes until golden brown, turning once or twice. Drain on paper towels.

5 To make the dip, combine all the ingredients, and pack separately.

CRUDITÉS WITH DIPS

....

SERVES 6

¼ cucumber
2–3 carrots
3 celery sticks
1 green (bell) pepper, halved, cored and
    deseeded
½ small cauliflower or head broccoli
1 bunch radishes, trimmed
1 x 250 g/8 oz packet tortilla chips
1 packet breadsticks, about 30

CURRIED DIP:
2 hard-boiled (hard-cooked) eggs, grated
    or chopped finely
4 tbsp natural fromage frais
2 tbsp thick mayonnaise
1 garlic clove, crushed
1 tsp curry powder
good pinch of ground mixed spice (apple
    pie spice)
salt and pepper

GARLIC CHEESE DIP:
200 g/7 oz/scant 1 cup light cream cheese
2 garlic cloves, crushed
2–3 tsp lemon or lime juice
4 spring onions (scallions), trimmed and
    chopped finely

SMOKED MACKEREL DIP:
1 tbsp very finely chopped onion
175 g/6 oz/ ¾ cup smoked mackerel fillet,
    skinned and flaked

finely grated rind of ¼ –½ lemon
2 tsp lemon juice
4 tbsp natural fromage frais or soured
    cream
1 tbsp chopped fresh parsley

1 Cut the cucumber, carrots and celery
    into sticks about 5 cm/2 in long. Cut
the (bell) pepper into strips and divide
the cauliflower or broccoli into small
florets. Put each vegetable separately into
a small plastic bag for transportation.

2 To make the Curried Dip, combine
    all the ingredients and season to taste.

3 To make the Garlic Cheese Dip,
    combine all the ingredients and
season to taste.

4 To make the Smoked Mackerel Dip,
    blend all the ingredients together
until well mixed and season to taste with
salt and pepper.

5 To serve, stand the bowls of dips in
    the centre of a large platter and
arrange the vegetables, tortilla chips and
breadsticks around the bowls.

THREE FILLET PARCEL (PACKAGE)

SERVES 8

300–350 g/10–12 oz pork fillet or
tenderloin
about 12 fresh sage leaves
250–300 g/8–10 oz lamb neck fillet
2 boneless chicken breast fillets (total
weight about 300 g/10 oz)
2 tbsp oil
125 g/4 oz large spinach leaves
350 g/12 oz puff pastry, thawed if frozen
250 g/8 oz/1 cup plain cottage cheese
pinch of ground allspice
pinch of garlic powder
beaten egg or milk to glaze
salt and pepper
sage leave and cucumber slices, to garnish

1 Layer the fillets beginning with the pork fillet, cover with half the sage leaves, then add the lamb fillet, more sage leaves and finally the chicken fillets. Secure with fine string and/or skewers.

2 Heat the oil in a frying pan (skillet) and fry the layered fillets for about 15 minutes, turning regularly until browned and partly cooked. Remove from the pan (skillet) and leave until cold.

3 Blanch the spinach in boiling water for 2 minutes and drain thoroughly.

4 Roll out the pastry thinly into a rectangle large enough to enclose the layered fillets and cut 5 narrow strips off one narrow end. Lay the spinach down the centre of the pastry, spread with the cottage cheese and season well with salt, pepper, allspice and garlic.

5 Remove the string or skewers from the fillets and lay on the cheese and spinach. Wrap up in the pastry, dampening the pastry edges to secure. Stand on a greased baking sheet and glaze with beaten egg or milk. Lay the strips of pastry over the roll and glaze it again.

6 Bake in a preheated oven at 200°C/400°F/Gas Mark 6 for 30 minutes until beginning to brown. Reduce the temperature to 180°C/ 350°F/Gas Mark 4 and bake for a further 20 minutes. Remove from the oven and leave to cool, then chill thoroughly. Serve in slices garnished with sage and cucumber.

RAISED TURKEY PIE

SERVES 6

FILLING:
350 g/12 oz raw turkey fillets, chopped
125 g/4 oz/ ½ cup lean raw pork, minced
125 g/4 oz/ ½ cup cooked ham, minced
coarsely or chopped finely
1 small onion, minced
60 g/2 oz/ ⅔ cup button mushrooms,
chopped roughly
1 tbsp chopped fresh parsley
good pinch of ground coriander
6 pickled walnuts, well drained
beaten egg or milk to glaze
1 tsp powdered gelatine
150 ml/ ¼ pint/ ⅔ cup chicken stock
salt and pepper

PASTRY:
350 g/12 oz/3 cups plain flour
1 tsp salt
90 g/3 oz/ ⅓ cup lard or white shortening
6 tbsp water
3 tbsp milk

1 Mix the turkey fillets with the pork, ham, onion, mushrooms, parsley and coriander, and season.

2 Sift the flour and salt into a bowl. Melt the fat with the water and milk, then bring to the boil. Pour on to the flour and mix to a dough. Roll out three-quarters of the dough and use to line a greased raised pie mould or loaf tin.

3 Put half the turkey mixture into the lined tin and arrange the walnuts over it. Cover with the remaining mixture. Roll out the reserved pastry, dampen the edges and position as a lid. Trim and crimp the edge. Make a steam hole in the centre, decorate with pastry leaves and glaze with beaten egg.

4 Bake on a baking sheet in a preheated oven at 200°C/400°F/ Gas Mark 6 for 30 minutes. Reduce the temperature to 180°C/350°F/Gas Mark 4, glaze again and bake for a further hour. When browned, cover with a sheet of greaseproof paper (baking parchment).

5 Dissolve the gelatine in the stock, bring to the boil, and season. Pour as much stock as possible into the cooled pie. Unmould when cold.

NUTBURGERS WITH CHEESE

MAKES 12

1 onion, finely chopped
1 garlic clove, crushed
1 tbsp olive oil
30 g/1 oz/ ¼ cup plain (all-purpose) flour
120 ml/4 fl oz/ ½ cup vegetable stock or
    milk
250 g/8 oz/2 cups chopped mixed nuts
    (including cashews, almonds, hazelnuts
    and walnuts)
60 g/2 oz/1 cup fresh breadcrumbs
2 carrots, coarsely grated
1 tbsp chopped fresh parsley
1 tbsp dried thyme
2 tbsp grated Parmesan cheese
1 tbsp lemon juice
1 tsp vegetable extract
1 egg, beaten
dried breadcrumbs
oil for deep-frying (optional)
mixed salad leaves (greens) to serve
salt and pepper

1 Fry the onion and garlic gently in
the oil until soft. Stir in the flour and
cook for 1–2 minutes. Add the stock or
milk gradually and bring to the boil.

2 Remove from the heat and stir in the
nuts, breadcrumbs, carrots, herbs,
Parmesan cheese, lemon juice, vegetable
extract and seasoning. Leave until cold.

3 Divide the mixture into 12 and roll
into even-sized balls.

4 Dip each piece first in beaten egg
and then coat in breadcrumbs.

5 Place on a well greased baking sheet
and bake in a preheated oven at
180°C/350°F/Gas Mark 4 for about
20 minutes, or until lightly browned and
crisp. Alternatively, deep-fry in oil heated
to 180°C/350°F for 3–4 minutes until
golden brown. The oil is at the correct
temperature for deep-frying when a cube
of bread browns in it in 30 seconds.

6 Drain on crumpled paper towels
and, when cold, arrange on a bed of
salad leaves (greens). Cover with clingfilm
(plastic wrap) or foil to transport.

PROVENÇAL TOMATO & BASIL SALAD

SERVES 6–8

500 g/1 lb tiny new or salad potatoes,
    scrubbed
4–5 extra-large tomatoes
2 kiwi fruit
1 onion, sliced very thinly
2 tbsp roughly chopped fresh basil leaves
fresh basil leaves to garnish

DRESSING:
4 tbsp virgin olive oil
2 tbsp balsamic vinegar
1 garlic clove, crushed
2 tbsp mayonnaise or soured cream
salt and pepper

1 Cook the potatoes in their skins in
salted water until just tender – about
10–15 minutes – then drain thoroughly.

2 To make the dressing, whisk
together the oil, vinegar, garlic and
seasoning until completely emulsified.
Transfer half of the dressing to another
bowl and whisk in the mayonnaise or
soured cream.

3 Add the creamy dressing to the
warm potatoes and toss thoroughly,
then leave until cold.

4 Wipe the tomatoes and slice thinly.
Peel the kiwi fruit and cut into thin
slices. Layer the tomatoes with the kiwi
fruit, slices of onion and chopped basil in
a fairly shallow dish, leaving a space in
the centre for the potatoes.

5 Spoon the potatoes in their dressing
into the centre of the tomato salad.

6 Drizzle a little of the plain dressing
over the tomatoes, or serve
separately in a bowl or jug. Garnish the
salad with fresh basil leaves. Cover the
dish with clingfilm (plastic wrap) and chill
until ready to transport.

TOMATOES

Ordinary tomatoes can be used for this
salad, but make sure they are firm and
bright red. You will need 8–10 tomatoes.

CHEESE, HERB & ONION ROLLS

MAKES 10–12

250 g/8 oz/2 cups strong white flour
1½ tsp salt
1 tsp dried mustard powder
good pinch of pepper
250 g/8 oz/2 cups granary or malted
* wheat flour*
2 tbsp chopped fresh mixed herbs
2 tbsp finely chopped spring onions
* (scallions)*
125–175 g/4–6 oz/1–1½ cups mature
* (sharp) Cheddar cheese, finely grated*
15 g/ ½ oz/ ½ cake fresh (compressed)
* yeast; or 1½ tsp dried yeast plus 1 tsp*
* caster (superfine) sugar; or 1 sachet*
* easy-blend yeast plus 1 tbsp oil*
300 ml/ ½ pint/1¼ cups warm water

1 Sift the white flour with the salt, mustard and pepper into a bowl. Mix in the granary flour, herbs, spring onions (scallions) and most of the cheese.

2 Blend the fresh yeast with the warm water or, if using dried yeast, dissolve the sugar in the water, sprinkle the yeast on top and leave in a warm place for about 10 minutes until frothy.

3 Add the yeast liquid (or the easy-blend yeast, oil and water) to the dry ingredients and mix to form a firm dough, adding more flour if necessary, to leave the sides of the bowl clean.

4 Knead until smooth and elastic – about 10 minutes by hand or 3–4 minutes in a food processor with a dough hook. Cover with an oiled polythene bag and leave in a warm place to rise for 1 hour or until doubled in size.

5 Knock back (punch down) and knead the dough until smooth. Divide into 10–12 pieces and shape as you prefer – into round or long rolls, coils, knots or other shape of your choice.

6 Alternatively, make one large plaited loaf. Divide the dough into 3 even pieces and roll each into a long thin sausage. Beginning in the centre, plait to the end and secure. Turn the plait round and complete the other half.

7 Place on greased baking sheets, cover with an oiled sheet of polythene and leave to rise until doubled in size. Remove the polythene.

8 Sprinkle with the rest of the cheese. Bake in a preheated oven at 200°C/ 400°F/Gas Mark 6 for 15–20 minutes for rolls, or 30–40 minutes for the loaf.

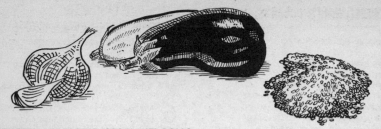

STUFFED AUBERGINE (EGGPLANT) ROLLS

SERVES 8

*3 aubergines (eggplants) (total weight
  about 750 g /1½ lb)*
*60 g/2 oz/ ⅓ cup mixed long-grain and
  wild rice*
*4 spring onions (scallions), trimmed and
  thinly sliced*
*3 tbsp chopped cashew nuts or toasted
  chopped hazelnuts*
2 tbsp capers
1 garlic clove, crushed
2 tbsp grated Parmesan cheese
1 egg, beaten
1 tbsp olive oil
1 tbsp balsamic vinegar
2 tbsp tomato purée (paste)
150 ml/ ¼ pint/ ⅔ cup water
150 ml/ ¼ pint/ ⅔ cup white wine
salt and pepper
coriander (cilantro) sprigs to garnish

1 Cut off the stem end of each
   aubergine (eggplant), then cut off
and discard a strip of skin from alternate
sides of each aubergine (eggplant).
Cut each aubergine (eggplant) into
thin slices to give a total of 16 slices.

2 Blanch the aubergine (eggplant)
   slices in boiling water for 5 minutes,
then drain on paper towels.

3 Cook the rice in boiling salted water
   for about 12 minutes or until just
tender. Drain and place in a bowl. Add
the spring onions (scallions), nuts, capers,
garlic, cheese, egg, salt and pepper, and
mix well.

4 Spread a thin layer of rice mixture
   over each slice of aubergine
(eggplant) and roll up carefully, securing
with a wooden cocktail stick (toothpick).
Place the rolls in a greased ovenproof dish
and brush each one with the olive oil.

5 Combine the vinegar, tomato purée
   (paste) and water, and pour over the
aubergine (eggplant) rolls. Cook in a preheated oven at 180°C/350°F/Gas Mark 4
for about 40 minutes until tender and
most of the liquid has been absorbed.
Transfer the rolls to a serving dish.

6 Add the wine to the pan juices and
   heat gently until the sediment
loosens and then simmer gently for
2–3 minutes. Adjust the seasoning and
strain over the aubergine (eggplant) rolls.
Leave until cold and then chill thoroughly.
Garnish with sprigs of coriander (cilantro)
and cover with clingfilm (plastic wrap)
and foil to transport.

SPANISH OMELETTE SQUARES

MAKES ABOUT 36 SQUARES

2 tbsp olive oil
1 onion, thinly sliced
1 garlic clove, crushed
1 courgette (zucchini), trimmed and
   grated coarsely
1 red, green or orange (bell) pepper,
   halved, cored and deseeded
175 g/6 oz/1 cup cooked potato, diced
90 g/3 oz/⅔ cup cooked peas
2 tomatoes, peeled, deseeded and cut into
   strips
2 tsp chopped fresh mixed herbs or 1 tsp
   dried mixed herbs
6 eggs
60 g/2 oz/½ cup Parmesan cheese, grated
salt and pepper

1 Heat the oil in a large frying pan and
   fry the onion and garlic until soft,
but not coloured. Add the courgette
(zucchini) and fry for 1–2 minutes. Turn
into a bowl.

2 Grill the (bell) pepper skin-side
   upwards under a preheated
moderate heat until the skin is charred.
Leave to cool slightly, then peel and slice
the flesh. Add to the onion mixture, with
the potato, peas, tomatoes and herbs.

3 Beat the eggs with 1–2 tablespoons
   water and seasoning, then mix into
the vegetables.

4 Line a shallow 20–23 cm/8–9 in
   square cake tin (pan) with non-stick
baking parchment. Do not cut into the
corners, just fold the parchment. Pour in
the egg mixture, making sure the
vegetables are fairly evenly distributed.

5 Cook in a preheated oven at
   180°C/350°F/Gas Mark 4 for about
15 minutes or until almost set.

6 Sprinkle with the cheese and either
   return to the oven for 5–10 minutes
or place under a preheated moderate grill
(broiler) until evenly browned. Leave to
cool. Remove from the tin (pan) and
transport still wrapped in the baking
parchment in an airtight plastic container,
or cut into 2.5–4 cm/1–1½ in squares and
stack up in a plastic container.

ROSTI POTATO CAKE WITH COURGETTES (ZUCCHINI) & CARROTS

SERVES 6

2 tbsp vegetable oil
1 large onion, sliced thinly
1 garlic clove, crushed (optional)
1 kg/2 lb potatoes
175 g/6 oz courgettes (zucchini), trimmed
125 g/4 oz carrots
½ tsp ground coriander
60 g/2 oz/½ cup mature (sharp) Gouda or
   Cheddar cheese, grated (optional)
salt and pepper

1 Heat 1 tablespoon of the oil in a
   large frying pan (skillet), add the
onion and garlic, if using, and fry gently
until soft, but only barely coloured –
about 5 minutes.

2 Grate the potatoes coarsely into a
   bowl. Grate the courgettes (zucchini)
and carrots, and mix into the potatoes
with the coriander and seasoning until
evenly mixed, then add the fried onions.

3 Heat the remaining oil in the frying
   pan (skillet), add the potato mixture
and cook gently, stirring occasionally, for
about 5 minutes. Flatten down into a cake
and cook gently until browned
underneath and almost cooked through –
about 6–8 minutes.

4 Sprinkle the top of the potato cake
   with the grated cheese, if using, and
place under a preheated moderate grill
(broiler) for about 5 minutes or until
lightly browned and cooked through.

5 Loosen the potato cake with a large
   palette knife (spatula) and slip it
carefully on to a plate. Leave until cold,
then cover with clingfilm (plastic wrap) or
foil and chill until required. Cut into
wedges and serve.

ALTERNATIVES

This also makes a delicious vegetable
accompaniment to any main course
dish. Other vegetables can be used –
parsnips, celeriac, leeks and fennel,
for example.

SEAFOOD PASTA

••

SERVES 6-8

175 g/6 oz/1½ cups dried pasta shapes
1 tbsp oil
4 tbsp French dressing
2 garlic cloves, crushed
6 tbsp white wine
125 g/4 oz baby button mushrooms,
  trimmed
3 carrots, sliced thinly
600 ml/1 pint/2½ cups fresh mussels in
  shells
125-175 g/4-6 oz frozen squid or octopus
  rings, thawed
175 g/6 oz/1 cup peeled tiger prawns
  (shrimp), thawed if frozen
6 sun-dried tomatoes, drained and sliced
3 tbsp chives, cut into 2.5 cm/1 in pieces
salt and pepper

TO GARNISH:
24 mangetout (snow peas), trimmed
12 baby corn
12 prawns (shrimp) in shells

1 Cook the pasta in boiling salted
  water with the oil added until just
tender – about 12 minutes. Drain.

2 Combine the dressing, the garlic and
  2 tablespoons of wine. Mix in the
mushrooms and leave to marinate.

3 Blanch the carrots for 3-4 minutes,
  drain and add to the mushrooms.

4 Scrub the mussels, discarding any
  that are open or do not close when
sharply tapped. Put into a saucepan with
150 ml/ ¼ pint/ ⅔ cup water and the
remaining wine. Bring to the boil, cover
and simmer for 3-4 minutes until they
open. Drain, discarding any that are still
closed. Reserve 12 mussels for garnish.
Shell the others and add to the mushroom
mixture with the squid and prawns
(shrimp).

5 Add the sun-dried tomatoes to the
  salad with the pasta and chives. Toss
well and turn on to a large platter. Blanch
the mangetout (snow peas) for 1 minute
and baby corn for 3 minutes, rinse under
cold water and drain. Arrange around the
edge of the salad with the mussels and
prawns (shrimp). Cover and chill until
ready to transport.

POACHER'S PLAIT

••

SERVES 4-6

PASTRY:
250 g/8 oz/2 cups plain (all-purpose) flour
pinch of salt
60 g/2 oz/ ¼ cup lard or white shortening
60 g/2 oz/ ¼ cup butter or block margarine
cold water to mix
beaten egg or top of the milk to glaze
350 g/12 oz puff pastry

FILLING:
500 g/1 lb pork sausage meat
175 g/6 oz/ ¾ cup lean bacon, derinded
  and chopped
1 onion, chopped finely
1 garlic clove, crushed
90 g/3 oz/1 cup mushrooms, chopped
1 tsp chopped fresh sage or ½ tsp dried
  sage
salt and pepper

1 To make the pastry, sift the flour and
  salt into a bowl and rub in the fat
until the mixture resembles fine
breadcrumbs. Add sufficient water to mix
to a pliable dough. Knead lightly, then
wrap in foil and chill.

2 To make the filling, combine the
  sausage meat, bacon, onion, garlic,
mushrooms, sage, a little salt and plenty
of pepper until evenly mixed.

3 Roll out the pastry on a lightly
  floured surface to a 30 cm/12 in
square and place the sausage meat
mixture in a block evenly down the
centre, leaving a 2.5 cm/1 in margin at the
top and base. Make cuts at 2.5 cm/1 in
intervals down both sides of the pastry to
within 4 cm/1½ in of the filling.

4 Fold up the top and bottom ends
  and then cover the filling with
alternate strips of pastry to make a plait.
Transfer carefully to a lightly greased
baking sheet and glaze with beaten egg
or milk.

5 Bake in a preheated oven at
  220°C/425°F/Gas Mark 7 for
20 minutes, then reduce the temperature
to 180°C/350°F/Gas Mark 4 and bake for
a further 30-40 minutes until golden
brown and crisp. Leave to cool, then
wrap in foil and chill.

CHICKEN SATAY KEBABS

MAKES 8

8 wooden skewers, soaked in warm water
*   for 30 minutes.*
1 tbsp sherry
1 tbsp light soy sauce
1 tbsp sesame oil
finely grated rind of ½ lemon
1 tbsp lemon or lime juice
2 tsp sesame seeds
500 g/1 lb chicken breast meat, skinned
90 g/3 oz Double Gloucester (red) or
*   Gouda cheese*
16 cherry tomatoes
crisp lettuce leaves, such as Little Gem
salt and pepper

PEANUT DIP:
30 g/1 oz/ ⅓ cup desiccated (shredded)
*   coconut*
150 ml/ ¼ pint/ ⅔ cup boiling water
125 g/4 oz/ ½ cup crunchy peanut butter
good pinch of chilli powder
1 tsp brown sugar
1 tbsp light soy sauce
2 spring onions (scallions), trimmed and
*   chopped*

1 Combine the sherry, soy sauce, sesame oil, lemon rind, lemon or lime juice, sesame seeds and seasoning in a bowl.

2 Cut the chicken into 2.5 cm/1 in cubes. Add to the marinade and mix well. Cover and leave for 3–6 hours, preferably in the refrigerator.

3 To make the dip, put the coconut into a saucepan with the water and bring back to the boil; leave until cold. Add the peanut butter, chilli powder, sugar and soy sauce and bring slowly to the boil. Simmer very gently, stirring all the time, for 2–3 minutes until thickened; then cool. When cold, stir in the spring onions (scallions), turn into a small bowl and cover with clingfilm (plastic wrap) and then foil to transport.

4 Thread the chicken on to 8 wooden skewers, keeping the chicken in the centre of each skewer. Cook under a moderate grill (broiler) for about 5 minutes on each side until cooked through. Leave until cold.

5 Cut the cheese into 16 cubes and then add one of these and a cherry tomato to each end of the skewers.

6 Stand each kebab on a crisp lettuce leaf, wrap in clingfilm (plastic wrap) or foil, or place in a plastic container. Serve with the peanut dip.

GARDEN SALAD

••

SERVES 6-8

500 g/1 lb tiny new or salad potatoes
4 tbsp French dressing made with olive oil
2 tbsp chopped fresh mint
6 tbsp soured cream
3 tbsp thick mayonnaise
2 tsp balsamic vinegar
1½ tsp coarse-grain mustard
½ tsp creamed horseradish
good pinch of brown sugar
225 g/8 oz broccoli florets
125 g/4 oz sugar snap peas or mangetout
2 large carrots
4 celery sticks
1 yellow or orange (bell) pepper, halved,
*   cored and deseeded*
1 bunch spring onions (scallions),
*   trimmed (optional)*
1 head chicory (endive)
salt and pepper

1 Cook the potatoes in boiling salted water until just tender. While they cook, combine the French dressing and mint. Drain the potatoes thoroughly, add to the dressing while hot, toss well and leave until cold, giving an occasional stir.

2 To make the dip, combine the soured cream, mayonnaise, vinegar, mustard, horseradish, sugar and seasoning. Put into a bowl and cover with clingfilm (plastic wrap) and then foil.

3 Cut the broccoli into bite-sized florets and blanch for 2 minutes in boiling water. Drain and toss immediately in cold water; when cold, drain thoroughly.

4 Blanch the sugar snap peas or mangetout (snow peas) in the same way but only for 1 minute. Drain, rinse in cold water and drain again.

5 Cut the carrots and celery into sticks about 6 x 1 cm/21/2 x ½ in; and slice the (bell) pepper or cut into cubes. Cut off some of the green part of the spring onions (scallions), if using, and separate the chicory (endive) leaves.

6 Arrange the vegetables in a shallow bowl with the potatoes piled up in the centre. Cover with clingfilm (plastic wrap), and transport the dip separately.

WALDORF SLAW

••

SERVES 4-6

4 celery sticks, preferably green
¼ white cabbage (about 250 g/8 oz)
60 g/2 oz/ ⅓ cup raisins
60 g/2 oz/ ½ cup walnut pieces
4-6 spring onions (scallions), trimmed
*   and cut into thin slanting slices*
2 green-skinned dessert (eating) apples
2 tbsp lemon or lime juice
4 tbsp thick mayonnaise
2 tbsp natural yogurt or natural fromage
*   frais*
2 tbsp French dressing
salt and pepper
2 carrots, trimmed, to garnish

1 Cut the celery into narrow slanting slices. Remove the core from the cabbage and shred finely.

2 Put the celery, cabbage, raisins, walnut pieces and spring onions (scallions) into a bowl and mix together.

3 Quarter and core the apples and slice thinly, or cut into dice. Put into a bowl with the lemon or lime juice and toss until completely coated. Drain and add to the other salad ingredients.

4 Whisk together the mayonnaise, yogurt or fromage frais and French dressing, and season well. Add to the salad and toss evenly through it. Turn into a serving bowl.

5 To make the garnish, cut the carrots into very narrow julienne strips about 5 cm/2 in in length and arrange around the edge of the salad.

6 Cover with clingfilm (plastic wrap) and chill until ready to transport. Alternatively, put the salad into a plastic food container with a secure lid.

VARIATION

This salad can be made using red cabbage for a change, and firm pears can be used in place of the apples.

VERONICA SALAD

....

SERVES 6

4 boneless chicken breasts, trimmed
2 tbsp olive oil
1 tbsp sunflower or vegetable oil
1–2 garlic cloves, crushed
1 onion, chopped finely
2 tbsp chopped fresh mint
4 celery sticks, sliced diagonally
175 g/6 oz/1½ cups black grapes,
*   preferably seedless*
125 g/4 oz/1 cup large white (green)
*   seedless grapes*
30 g/1 oz/2 tbsp butter or margarine
1 tbsp plain (all-purpose) flour
½ tsp curry powder
3 tbsp white wine or stock
5 tbsp milk
2 tbsp natural fromage frais
2 tbsp mayonnaise
1 head chicory (endive)
2 hard-boiled (hard-cooked) eggs
salt and pepper

1 Cut the chicken into narrow strips. Heat the oils in a frying pan (skillet), add the garlic and chicken and fry gently until well sealed. Add the onion and fry until tender.

2 Stir in the mint and plenty of seasoning. Drain off the oil and any juices immediately and put the chicken mixture into a bowl. Leave until cold. Add the celery to the chicken.

3 Reserve a few whole black grapes for garnish. If they are large or contain pips (seeds), cut the rest in half, remove any pips (seeds) and then add to the salad with the white (green) grapes.

4 Melt the fat in a pan, stir in the flour and curry powder and cook for 1–2 minutes. Add the wine and milk and bring to the boil, simmering until thick. Remove from the heat, season well, and stir in the fromage frais. Cover with cling-film (plastic wrap) and leave until cold.

5 Add the mayonnaise to the sauce and add to the chicken mixture, tossing evenly. Turn into a serving dish. Cut the chicory (endive) into lengths of 5 cm/2 in and arrange around the salad with the reserved grapes and eggs, sliced into quarters. Cover and chill.

DESSERTS

ORCHARD FRUITS BRISTOL

....

SERVES 6–8

4 oranges
175 g/6 oz/¾ cup granulated sugar
4 tbsp water
150 ml/¼ pint/⅔ cup white wine
4 firm pears
4 dessert (eating) apples
125 g/4 oz/¾ cup strawberries

1 Pare the rind thinly from 1 orange and cut into narrow strips. Cook in the minimum of boiling water for 3–4 minutes until tender. Drain and reserve the liquor. Squeeze the juice from this and 1 other orange.

2 Lay a sheet of non-stick baking parchment on a baking sheet or board. Heat the sugar gently in a pan until it melts, then continue without stirring until it turns a pale golden brown. Pour half the caramel quickly on to the parchment and leave to set.

3 Add the water and squeezed orange juice immediately to the caramel left in the pan with 150 ml/¼ pint/⅔ cup orange rind liquor. Heat until it melts, then add the wine and remove from the heat.

4 Peel, core and slice the pears and apples thickly (you can leave the apple skins on, if you prefer), and add to the caramel syrup. Bring gently to the boil and simmer for 3–4 minutes until just beginning to soften – they should still be firm in the centre. Transfer the fruits to a serving bowl.

5 Cut away the peel and pith from the remaining oranges and either ease out the segments or cut into slices, discarding any pips (seeds). Add to the other fruits. Hull the strawberries and halve, quarter or slice thickly depending on the size and add to the other fruits.

6 Add the orange strands to the syrup and bring back to the boil for 1 minute, then pour over the fruits. Leave until cold, then break up the caramel and sprinkle over the fruit. Cover and chill.

DOUBLE CHOCOLATE TERRINE

SERVES 6-8

WHITE MOUSSE:
250 g/8 oz/8 squares white chocolate
1½ tsp powdered gelatine plus 2 tbsp water
2 tbsp caster (superfine) sugar
2 egg yolks
150 ml/ ¼ pint/ ⅔ cup soured cream
150 ml/ ¼ pint/ ⅔ cup double (heavy) cream, whipped until thick

DARK MOUSSE:
175 g/6 oz/6 squares dark chocolate
2 tbsp black coffee (not too strong)
2 tsp powdered gelatine plus 1 tbsp water
2 tbsp rum
60 g/2 oz/ ¼ cup butter, softened
2 egg yolks
300 ml/ ½ pint/1¼ cups double (heavy) cream, whipped

RASPBERRY COULIS:
175 g/6 oz/1 cup fresh or frozen raspberries
about 1 tbsp icing (confectioners') sugar

TO DECORATE:
fresh raspberries
whipped cream

1   Line a 23 x 12 cm/9 x 5 in loaf tin with food wrap (plastic wrap), leaving plenty of overhang.

2   To make the white mousse, break up the chocolate and melt in a bowl, either in a microwave oven on Medium Power for 2 minutes or over a pan of gently simmering water. Remove from the heat and stir until smooth.

3   Dissolve the gelatine in the water in a bowl over simmering water. Leave to cool slightly, then beat into the chocolate with the sugar and egg yolks, and then the soured cream. Fold in the double (heavy) cream. Pour into the tin and chill until set.

4   To make the dark mousse, melt the chocolate with the coffee, and dissolve the gelatine in the rum with the water, as above. Stir the dissolved gelatine into the melted chocolate, followed by the butter. Stir until dissolved then beat in the egg yolks. Fold the cream through the mousse. Pour over the white mousse and chill until set.

5   For the coulis, sieve (strain) the raspberries and sweeten to taste with the sugar. Turn the terrine out, peel off the clingfilm (plastic wrap) and decorate the top with the raspberries and whipped cream. Spoon the coulis around the base to serve.

ORANGE PECAN PIE

SERVES 6-8

PASTRY:
175 g/6 oz/1½ cups plain (all-purpose)
  flour
pinch of salt
90 g/3 oz/ ⅓ cup butter
1 tbsp finely chopped pecan nuts
4–5 tbsp iced water to mix

FILLING:
150 g/5 oz/1¼ cups pecan nuts, halved
2 eggs
175 g/6 oz/1 cup light soft brown sugar
175 g/6 oz/generous ½ cup golden (light
  corn) syrup
grated rind of 1 large orange
1 tsp vanilla flavouring (extract)
icing (confectioners') sugar to decorate

1 To make the pastry, sift the flour and
salt into a bowl, then rub in the
butter until the mixture resembles fine
breadcrumbs. Stir in the pecan nuts
evenly, then add sufficient of the iced
water to mix to a firm but pliable dough.
Knead lightly until smooth.

2 Roll out the pastry and use to line
a 20 cm/8 in fluted flan ring, tin
(pan) or dish.

3 Arrange the pecan halves evenly
over the base of the pastry.

4 To make the filling, beat the eggs
with the sugar, golden (light corn)
syrup, orange rind and vanilla flavouring
(extract). When evenly blended, pour or
spoon over the pecans.

5 Stand the flan ring, tin (pan) or dish
on a baking sheet and bake in a
preheated oven at 190°C/375°F/Gas Mark
5 for about 40 minutes, or until the pastry
is crisp and the filling firm to the touch.

6 Leave the pie to cool completely and
then dredge lightly with sifted icing
(confectioners') sugar. Cover first with
clingfilm (plastic wrap) then with foil for
transporting. Serve the pie cut into
wedges.

WHITE CHOCOLATE BROWNIES

MAKES 8-12

60 g/2 oz/2 squares white chocolate
60 g/2 oz/¼ cup butter or margarine
175 g/6 oz/1 cup light soft brown sugar
½ tsp vanilla flavouring (extract)
2 eggs
75 g/2½ oz/ ⅔ cup self-raising flour, sifted
30 g/1 oz/ ¼ cup walnuts or other nuts,
  finely chopped
45 g/1½ oz/ ⅓ cup raisins

TOPPING:
60 g/2 oz/2 squares dark chocolate,
  melted
30 g/1 oz/1 square white chocolate, melted
icing (confectioners') sugar for dredging

1 Line a shallow 20 cm/8 in square tin
(pan) with non-stick baking
parchment or greased greaseproof paper.

2 Break up the chocolate and place in
a heatproof bowl with the fat. Melt
in a microwave oven on Medium Power
for 2 minutes, or over a pan of gently
simmering water. Remove from the heat
and beat in the sugar and vanilla
flavouring (extract) until smooth.

3 Beat in the eggs, one at a time, until
smooth, then fold in the flour. Add
the nuts and raisins and stir until evenly
mixed.

4 Pour the mixture into the prepared
tin (pan) and bake in a preheated
oven at 180°C/350°F/Gas Mark 4 for
35–45 minutes, or until the mixture is well
risen, firm to the touch and beginning to
shrink away from the sides of the tin
(pan). Leave to cool in the tin (pan), then
remove carefully and peel off the paper.

5 Melt the chocolates separately for the
topping. First spread the dark
chocolate over the top of the brownies.
As it begins to set, trickle the white
chocolate over it and, taking a fork or
skewer, swirl the chocolates together to
give a marbled effect. Leave to set.
Dredge with icing (confectioners') sugar.

6 Serve the brownies cut into squares
or fingers and transport in an airtight
container.

FLORENTINE TWISTS

MAKES ABOUT 20

90 g/3 oz/ ⅓ cup butter
125 g/4 oz/ ½ cup caster (superfine) sugar
60 g/2 oz/ ½ cup blanched or flaked
  (slivered) almonds, chopped roughly
30 g/1 oz/3 tbsp raisins, chopped
45 g/1½ oz/ ¼ cup chopped mixed peel
45 g/1½ oz/scant ¼ cup glacé (candied)
  cherries, chopped
30 g/1 oz/3 tbsp dried apricots, chopped
  finely
finely grated rind of ½ lemon
about 125 g/4 oz/ dark chocolate

1 Line 2–3 baking sheets with non-stick baking parchment; and grease 4–6 cream horn tins (moulds) or a fairly thin rolling pin, or wooden spoon handles.

2 Melt the butter and sugar gently in a saucepan and then bring to the boil for 1 minute. Remove from the heat and stir in the remaining ingredients, except the chocolate. Leave to cool.

3 Put heaped teaspoonfuls of the mixture on to the baking sheets, keeping them well apart, only 3–4 per sheet, and flatten slightly.

4 Bake in a preheated oven at 180°C/350°F/Gas Mark 4 for 10–12 minutes, or until golden brown. Leave to cool until they begin to firm up. As they cool, press the edges back to form a neat shape. Remove each one carefully with a palette knife (spatula) and wrap quickly around a cream horn tin (mould), or lay over the rolling pin or spoon handles. If they become too firm to bend, return to the oven briefly to soften again.

5 Leave until cold and crisp and then slip carefully off the horn tins (moulds) or remove from the rolling pin or spoons.

6 Melt the chocolate in a heatproof bowl over a saucepan of hot water, and stir until smooth. Either dip the end of each Florentine twist into the chocolate or, using a pastry brush, paint chocolate to come about halfway up the twist. Allow the chocolate to set.

BANANA PICNIC LOAF

MAKES 12 SLICES

175 g/6 oz/1 cup light soft brown sugar
125 g/4 oz/½ cup butter or margarine
2 eggs
250 g/8 oz peeled ripe bananas
  (2–3 bananas)
grated rind of 1 lemon
2 tsp lemon juice
250 g/8 oz/2 cups self-raising flour
½ tsp ground cinnamon
¼ tsp bicarbonate of soda (baking soda)
90 g/3 oz/ ½ cup no-need-to-soak dried
  apricots or prunes, chopped
60 g/2 oz/ ½ cup walnut pieces, roughly
  chopped
sifted icing (confectioners') sugar for
  dredging

1 Grease and line a 23 x 12 cm/ 9 x 5 in loaf tin (pan) with greased greaseproof paper or non-stick baking parchment.

2 Cream the sugar and fat together until light and fluffy and pale in colour. Beat in the eggs, one at a time.

3 Mash the bananas with the lemon rind and juice, and beat into the cake mixture.

4 Sift the flour, cinnamon and bicarbonate of soda (baking soda) together and fold evenly into the cake mixture, followed by the chopped apricots or prunes and walnuts.

5 Turn into the tin (pan), level the top and bake in a preheated oven at 180°C/350°F/Gas Mark 4 for about 50 minutes or until firm to the touch and a skewer inserted in the loaf comes out clean. Leave to cool in the tin (pan) for 10 minutes, then turn out on to a wire rack and leave to cool completely.

6 Before transporting, remove the paper from around the cake, sprinkle the top with sifted icing (confectioners') sugar and wrap in foil to carry. Serve cut into slices or wedges.

DINNER PARTIES – INTRODUCTION

Dip into these recipes for inspiration at any time of year. From elegant summery meals of Gazpacho (page 627) and Glazed Salmon (page 633) to wintry Creamed Pheasant Soup (page 626) and Venison with Plums (page 635), there are plenty of ideas. Vegetarians are catered for too: Mushroom Vol-au-Vent (page 629) or Ricotta and Spinach Parcels are sure to delight (page 631). And to end with a flourish, serve Baked Alaska (page 637) or Pavlova (page 639).

STARTERS

ARTICHOKE MOUSSE

SERVES 6

1 x 425 g/15 oz can artichoke hearts
150 ml/ ¼ pint/ ⅔ cup condensed
    consommé
juice of ½ orange
large pinch of grated nutmeg
4 tbsp warm water
1 sachet gelatine
2 egg whites, whisked
300 ml/ ½ pint/1¼ cups Greek-style yogurt
salt and pepper

SALAD:
3 large (bell) peppers, various colours
3 tbsp olive oil
juice of ½ orange
2 tbsp natural yogurt
2 tbsp chopped parsley

1 Drain the artichoke hearts, and reserve the liquid. Process with 3 tablespoons of liquid, the consommé, orange juice and nutmeg until finely chopped but not puréed. Season, pour into a large bowl and set aside.

2 Pour the water into a small bowl and sprinkle on the gelatine. Place the bowl in a pan of simmering water and stir until the crystals have dissolved, then remove and set aside to cool.

3 When the gelatine is syrupy and on the point of setting, blend well into the artichoke mixture. Stir in the yogurt, using an up-and-over movement, until thoroughly blended. Fold in the egg whites, using a metal spoon. Pour into a wetted ring mould or 6 individual moulds, cover and chill for at least 3 hours or until set.

4 Heat the grill (broiler) to high and sear the (bell) peppers close to the heat until evenly blackened all round. Plunge into cold water and as soon as they are cool enough to handle peel off the skins. Core and seed, cut into thick strips and leave to cool.

5 Beat together the olive oil, orange juice and yogurt and season. Pour over the (bell) peppers and stir in the chopped parsley.

6 Run a knife around the inside of the moulds and invert on to serving plates, shaking the mould to release it. Pile the salad into the centre of the mould and serve chilled, with crispy bread rolls or black rye bread.

CREAMED PHEASANT SOUP

••

SERVES 4-6

1 raw or cooked pheasant carcass or
    1 small oven-ready pheasant
1 onion, studded with 6 cloves
1.5 litres/2½ pints/6¼ cups water
60 g/2 oz/ ¼ cup butter or margarine
1 onion, chopped finely
45 g/1½ oz/ ⅓ cup plain (all-purpose) flour
½ tsp celery salt
¼ tsp ground coriander
30 g/1 oz/2 tbsp long-grain rice
125 g/4 oz/2 cups mushrooms, finely
    chopped
150 ml/ ¼ pint/ ⅔ cup single (light) or
    double (heavy) cream
2 tbsp chopped fresh parsley
salt and pepper
fried croûtons (see page 10) to serve

1 Put the pheasant carcass or the
whole bird, the clove-studded onion
and the water into a saucepan. Bring to
the boil, cover and simmer for about 1½
hours. Drain off and reserve 1.25 litres/
2¼ pints/5 cups of the stock. Remove
about 90 g/3 oz/ ½ cup of meat from the
carcass or from the leg or wing of the
whole bird. Chop finely.

2 Melt the butter or margarine in a
saucepan and fry the chopped onion
gently for about 3 minutes until soft but
not coloured.

3 Stir in the flour and cook for a
minute or so, then gradually stir in
the reserved stock and bring to the boil.

4 Add the seasoning, celery salt,
coriander, rice and mushrooms,
cover and simmer for about 20 minutes,
stirring occasionally.

5 Add the reserved pheasant meat and
the cream, adjust the seasoning and
bring back just to the boil.

6 Just before serving stir in the parsley
or, if preferred, stir in half the
parsley and use the remainder to sprinkle
over each serving. Serve with fried
croûtons.

CONSOMMÉ

••

SERVES 4-6

1.25 litres/2¼ pints/5 cups strong Beef
    Stock (see page 9)
250 g/8 oz/1 cup extra lean minced
    (ground) beef
2 tomatoes, skinned, seeded and chopped
2 large carrots, chopped
1 large onion, chopped
2 celery sticks, chopped
1 turnip, chopped (optional)
1 Bouquet Garni (see page 9)
2–3 egg whites
shells of 2–4 eggs, crushed
1–2 tbsp sherry (optional)
salt and pepper
Melba Toast (see page 54) to serve

TO GARNISH:
julienne strips of raw carrot, turnip, celery
    or celeriac (celery root) or a one-egg
    omelette, cut into julienne strips

1 Put the stock and minced (ground)
beef in a saucepan and leave to
stand for 1 hour.

2 Add the tomatoes, carrots, onion,
celery, turnip, if using, bouquet
garni, 2 of the egg whites, the crushed
shells of 2 of the eggs and seasoning.
Bring to almost boiling point, whisking
hard all the time.

3 Cover and simmer for 1 hour, taking
care not to allow the layer of froth
on top of the soup to break.

4 Pour through a jelly bag or scalded
fine cloth, keeping the froth back
until the last, then pour again through the
ingredients in the cloth into a clean pan.
The resulting liquid should be clear.

5 If the soup is not quite clear, return
it to the pan with another egg white
and the crushed shells of 2 more eggs.
Repeat the whisking process as before
and then boil for 10 minutes; strain again.

6 Add the sherry to the soup and
reheat gently. Place the garnish in
the base of warmed soup bowls and
carefully pour in the soup. Serve with
Melba Toast.

GAZPACHO WATER ICE

SERVES 4

500 g/1 lb/4 tomatoes
about 600 ml/1 pint/2½ cups boiling water
4 spring onions (scallions), chopped
2 celery sticks, chopped
1 small red (bell) pepper, chopped
1 garlic clove, crushed
1 tbsp tomato purée (paste)
1 tbsp chopped fresh parsley
salt and pepper
fresh parsley sprigs to garnish

TO SERVE:
shredded iceberg lettuce
bread sticks

1 Prick the skin of the tomatoes with a fork at the stalk end and place in a large heatproof bowl. Pour over enough boiling water to cover them. Leave for 5–10 minutes. After this time, the skin should start peeling away from the flesh. Leave for longer if necessary.

2 Skewer the tomatoes with a fork and peel away the skin. Slice the tomatoes in half, scoop out the seeds and discard. Chop the flesh.

3 Place the chopped tomatoes, spring onions (scallions), celery, (bell) pepper, garlic and tomato purée (paste) in a food processor or blender. Blend for a few seconds until smooth. Alternatively, finely chop or mince the vegetables then mix with the tomato purée (paste). Pour into a freezerproof container and freeze.

4 Remove from the freezer and leave at room temperature for 30 minutes. Break up with a fork and place in a blender or food processor. Blend for a few seconds to break up the ice crystals and form a smooth mixture. Alternatively, break up with a fork and beat with a wooden spoon until smooth.

5 Transfer to a mixing bowl and stir in the parsley and seasoning. Return to the freezer container and freeze for a further 30 minutes.

6 Fork up again. Serve with shredded iceberg lettuce and bread sticks, and garnish with parsley.

BAKED AUBERGINE (EGGPLANT), BASIL & MOZZARELLA ROLLS

SERVES 4

2 aubergines (eggplant), sliced thinly
    lengthways
5 tbsp olive oil
1 garlic clove, crushed
4 tbsp pesto sauce
175 g/6 oz/1½ cups Mozzarella cheese,
    grated
a few basil leaves, torn into pieces
salt and pepper
fresh basil leaves to garnish

1 Spread out the slices of aubergine (eggplant) on a work surface (counter). Sprinkle liberally with salt and leave for 10–15 minutes to extract the bitter juices. Turn the slices over and repeat. Rinse well with cold water and drain on paper towels.

2 Heat the olive oil in a large frying pan (skillet) and add the garlic. Fry the aubergine (eggplant) slices lightly on both sides, a few at a time. Drain them on paper towels.

3 Spread the pesto sauce on to one side of the aubergine (eggplant) slices. Top with the grated Mozzarella cheese and sprinkle with the torn basil leaves. Season with a little salt and pepper. Roll up the slices and secure with wooden cocktail sticks (toothpicks).

4 Arrange the aubergine (eggplant) rolls in a greased ovenproof baking dish. Place in a preheated oven at 180°C/350°F/Gas Mark 4 and bake for 8–10 minutes.

5 Transfer the rolls to a warmed serving plate. Scatter with fresh basil leaves and serve at once.

GRATED CHEESE

If you wish, buy ready-grated cheese from your supermarket or delicatessen, as it can be quite tricky to grate it yourself. Otherwise, you may find it easier to slice the Mozzarella thinly.

MINT & CANNELLINI BEAN DIP

SERVES 6

175 g/6 oz dried cannellini beans
1 small garlic clove, crushed
1 bunch spring onions (scallions),
*   chopped roughly*
a handful of fresh mint leaves
2 tbsp tahini (sesame seed paste)
2 tbsp olive oil
1 tsp ground cumin
1 tsp ground coriander
lemon juice
salt and pepper
sprigs of fresh mint to garnish
fresh vegetable crudités, such as
*   cauliflower florets, carrots, cucumber,*
*   radishes and (bell) peppers*

1 Soak the cannellini beans overnight in plenty of cold water.

2 Rinse and drain the beans, put them into a large saucepan and cover them with cold water. Bring to the boil and boil rapidly for 10 minutes. Reduce the heat, cover and simmer for 1½ –2 hours until tender.

3 Drain the beans and transfer them to a bowl or food processor. Add the garlic, spring onions (scallions), mint, tahini and olive oil.

4 Blend the mixture for about 15 seconds, or mash well by hand, until smooth.

5 Transfer the mixture to a bowl and season with ground cumin, ground coriander, lemon juice, salt and pepper, according to taste. Mix well, cover and leave in a cool place for 30 minutes to allow the flavours to develop.

6 Spoon the dip into serving bowls, garnish with sprigs of fresh mint and surround with the vegetable crudités.

CANNED BEANS

If using canned cannellini beans, use 2 x 425g/14 oz cans. Drain and rinse well. Add to the bowl or food processor at step 3. Chick-peas (garbanzo beans) may be used as an alternative.

AVOCADO CREAM TERRINE

SERVES 6

4 tbsp cold water
2 tsp vegetarian gelatine
1 tbsp lemon juice
4 tbsp mayonnaise
150 ml/ ¼ pint/ ⅔ cup thick creamy
*   natural yogurt*
150 ml/ ¼ pint/ ⅔ cup single (light) cream
2 ripe avocados, peeled and pitted
salt and pepper
mixed salad leaves (greens) to serve

TO GARNISH:
cucumber slices
nasturtium flowers

1 Place the water, gelatine, lemon juice, mayonnaise, yogurt, cream and avocado in a blender or food processor, or a large bowl. Process for about 10–15 seconds, or beat by hand, until smooth.

2 Transfer the mixture to a small saucepan and heat gently, stirring constantly, until just boiling.

3 Pour the mixture into a 900 ml/1½ pint/3½ cup plastic food storage box or terrine. Allow to cool and set, and then refrigerate until chilled – about 1½ –2 hours.

4 Turn the mixture out of its container and cut into neat slices. Arrange a bed of salad leaves (greens) on 6 serving plates. Place a slice of avocado terrine on top and garnish with cucumber slices and nasturtium flowers.

AVOCADOS

Avocados soon turn brown, so it is important to mix them with the lemon juice as soon as they are peeled and mashed to prevent this from happening.

CANTONESE BUTTERFLY PRAWNS (SHRIMP)

SERVES 4

12 raw tiger prawns (shrimp) in their shells
2 tbsp light soy sauce
1 tbsp Chinese rice wine or dry sherry
1 tbsp cornflour (cornstarch)
2 eggs, lightly beaten
8-10 tbsp breadcrumbs
vegetable oil, for deep-frying
salt and pepper
shredded lettuce leaves, to serve
chopped spring onions (scallions), to garnish

1 Shell and devein the prawns (shrimp) but leave the tails on. Split them in half from the underbelly about halfway along, leaving the tails attached.

2 Mix together the salt, pepper, soy sauce, wine and cornflour (cornstarch) in a bowl, add the prawns (shrimp) and turn to coat. Leave to marinate for 10-15 minutes.

3 Heat the oil in a preheated wok. Pick up each prawn (shrimp) by the tail, dip it in the beaten egg then roll it in the breadcrumbs to coat well.

4 Deep-fry the prawns (shrimp) in batches until golden brown. Remove them with a slotted spoon and drain on paper towels.

5 To serve, arrange the prawns (shrimp) neatly on a bed of lettuce leaves and garnish with spring onions (scallions), either raw or soaked for about 30 seconds in hot oil.

VARIATIONS

Butterfly prawns (shrimp) may also be served on a bed of crispy seaweed. This classic Chinese accompaniment provides the perfect foil for the luscious prawns (shrimp). Dried seaweed can be bought from Oriental stores and supermarkets. Follow the instructions on the packet to prepare it.

MAIN DISHES

CREAMY MUSHROOM VOL-AU-VENT

SERVES 4

500 g/1 lb puff pastry, thawed if frozen
1 egg, beaten, for glazing

FILLING:
30 g/1 oz/2 tbsp butter or margarine
750 g/1½ lb mixed mushrooms such as open cup, field, button, chestnut, shiitake, pied de mouton, sliced
90 ml/3½ fl oz/6 tbsp dry white wine
4 tbsp double (heavy) cream
2 tbsp chopped fresh chervil
salt and pepper
sprigs of fresh chervil to garnish

1 Roll out the pastry on a lightly floured surface to a 20 cm/8 in square. Using a sharp knife, mark a square 2.5 cm/1 in from the pastry edge, cutting halfway through the pastry.

2 Score the top in a diagonal pattern. Knock up the edges with a kitchen knife and put on a baking sheet. Brush the top with beaten egg, taking care not to let the egg run into the cut. Bake in a preheated oven at 220°C/ 425°F/Gas Mark 7 for 35 minutes.

3 Cut out the central square. Discard the soft pastry inside the case, leaving the base intact. Return to the oven, with the square, for 10 minutes.

4 Meanwhile, make the filling. Melt the butter or margarine in a frying pan (skillet) and stir-fry the mushrooms over a high heat for 3 minutes.

5 Add the wine and cook for 10 minutes, stirring occasionally, until the mushrooms have softened. Stir in the cream, chervil and seasoning. Pile into the pastry case. Top with the pastry square, garnish and serve.

ALMOND & SESAME NUT ROAST

••

SERVES 4

2 tbsp sesame or olive oil
1 small onion, chopped finely
60 g/2 oz/scant ¼ cup risotto rice
300 ml/ ½ pint/1¼ cups vegetable stock
1 large carrot, grated
1 large leek, trimmed and chopped finely
2 tsp sesame seeds, toasted
90 g/3 oz/ ¾ cup chopped almonds,
*   toasted*
60 g/2 oz/ ½ cup ground almonds
90 g/3 oz/ ¾ cup mature (sharp) Cheddar
*   cheese, grated*
2 eggs, beaten
1 tsp dried mixed herbs
salt and pepper
sprigs of flat-leaf (Italian) parsley to
*   garnish*
fresh vegetables to serve

SAUCE:
30 g/1 oz/2 tbsp butter
1 small onion, chopped finely
125 g/4 oz/1¼ cup mushrooms, chopped
*   finely*
30 g/1 oz/ ¼ cup plain (all-purpose) flour
300 ml/½ pint/1¼ cups vegetable stock

1 Heat the oil in a large frying pan (skillet) and fry the onion gently for 2–3 minutes. Add the rice and cook gently for 5–6 minutes, stirring frequently.

2 Add the vegetable stock, bring to the boil and then simmer for about 15 minutes, or until the rice is tender. Add a little extra water if necessary. Remove from the heat and transfer to a large mixing bowl.

3 Add the carrot, leek, sesame seeds, almonds, cheese, beaten eggs and herbs to the mixture. Mix well and season with salt and pepper. Transfer the mixture to a greased 500 g/1 lb loaf tin, levelling the surface. Bake in a preheated oven at 180°C/350°F/Gas Mark 4 for about 1 hour, until set and firm. Leave in the tin for 10 minutes.

4 To make the sauce, melt the butter in a small saucepan and fry the onion until dark golden brown. Add the mushrooms and cook for a further 2 minutes. Stir in the flour, cook gently for 1 minute and then gradually add the stock. Bring to the boil, stirring constantly, until thickened and blended. Season to taste.

5 Turn out the nut roast, slice and serve on warmed plates with fresh vegetables, accompanied by the sauce. Garnish the roast with sprigs of flat-leaf (Italian) parsley.

RICOTTA & SPINACH PARCELS

••

SERVES 4

*350 g/12 oz/3 cups spinach, trimmed and
    washed thoroughly*
30 g/1 oz/2 tbsp butter
1 small onion, chopped finely
1 tsp green peppercorns
500 g/1 lb puff pastry
250 g/8 oz/1 cup Ricotta cheese
1 egg, beaten
salt
sprigs of fresh herbs to garnish
fresh vegetables to serve

1 Pack the spinach into a large
    saucepan. Add a little salt and a very
small amount of water and cook until
wilted. Drain well, cool and then squeeze
out any excess moisture with the back of
a spoon. Chop roughly.

2 Melt the butter in a small saucepan
    and fry the onion gently until
softened, but not browned. Add the green
peppercorns and cook for 2 more minutes.
Remove from the heat, add the spinach
and mix together.

3 Roll out the puff pastry thinly on a
    lightly floured work surface and cut
into 4 squares, each 18 cm/7 in across.
Place a quarter of the spinach mixture in
the centre of each square and top with a
quarter of the cheese.

4 Brush a little beaten egg around
    the edges of the pastry squares
and bring the corners together to form
parcels. Press the edges together firmly to
seal. Lift the parcels on to a greased
baking sheet, brush with beaten egg and
bake in a preheated oven at 200°C/400°F/
Gas Mark 6 for 20–25 minutes, until risen
and golden brown.

5 Serve hot, garnished with sprigs of
    fresh herbs and accompanied by
fresh vegetables.

MUSHROOM & PINE KERNEL TARTS

••

SERVES 4

500 g/1 lb frozen filo pastry, thawed
125 g/4 oz/ ½ cup butter, melted
1 tbsp hazelnut oil
30 g/1 oz pine kernels
*350 g/12 oz mixed mushrooms, such as
    buttons, chestnut, oyster and shiitake*
2 tsp chopped fresh parsley
250 g/8 oz soft goat's cheese
salt and pepper
sprigs of parsley to garnish
*lettuce, tomatoes, cucumber and spring
    onions (scallions) to serve*

1 Cut the sheets of filo pastry into
    pieces about 10 cm/4 in square and
use them to line 4 individual tart tins,
brushing each layer of pastry with melted
butter. Line the tins with foil or baking
parchment and baking beans. Bake in a
preheated oven at 200°C/ 400°F/Gas Mark
6 for about 6–8 minutes, or until light
golden brown. Remove the tarts from the
oven and take out the foil or parchment
and beans carefully. Reduce the oven
temperature to 180°C/350°F/Gas Mark 4.

2 Put any remaining butter into a large
    saucepan with the hazelnut oil and
fry the pine kernels (nuts) gently until
golden brown. Lift them out with a
perforated spoon and drain them on
paper towels.

3 Add the mushrooms to the saucepan
    and cook them gently, stirring
frequently, for about 4–5 minutes. Add
the chopped parsley and season to taste
with salt and pepper.

4 Spoon an equal amount of goat's
    cheese into the base of each cooked
filo tart. Divide the mushrooms between
them and scatter the pine kernels over the
top.

5 Return the tarts to the oven for
    5 minutes to heat through, and then
serve them, garnished with sprigs of
parsley. Serve with lettuce, tomatoes,
cucumber and spring onions (scallions).

INDIAN CURRY FEAST

●●

SERVES 4

1 tbsp vegetable oil
2 garlic cloves, crushed
1 onion, chopped
3 celery sticks, sliced
1 apple, chopped
1 tbsp medium-strength curry powder
1 tsp ground ginger
125 g/4 oz dwarf (thin) green beans,
*   sliced*
250 g/8 oz cauliflower, broken into florets
250 g/8 oz potatoes, cut into cubes
175 g/6 oz/2 cups mushrooms, wiped and
*   sliced*
400 g/13 oz can chick-peas (garbanzo
*   beans), drained*
600 ml/1 pint/2½ cups vegetable stock
1 tbsp tomato purée (paste)
30 g/1 oz sultanas (golden raisins)
175 g/6 oz basmati rice
1 tbsp garam masala

SALAD:
4 tomatoes, chopped
1 green chilli, deseeded and finely
*   chopped*
7 cm/3 in piece of cucumber, chopped
1 tbsp fresh coriander (cilantro)
4 spring onions (scallions), trimmed and
*   chopped*

MINT RAITA:
150 ml/ ¼ pint/ ⅔ cup natural
*   yogurt*
1 tbsp chopped fresh
*   mint*
sprigs of fresh
*   mint to garnish*

1 Heat the oil in a large saucepan and fry the garlic, onion, celery and apple gently for 3–4 minutes. Add the curry powder and ginger, and cook gently for 1 more minute.

2 Add the remaining ingredients except the rice and garam masala. Bring to the boil, then reduce the heat. Cover and simmer for 35–40 minutes.

3 To make the salad, combine all the ingredients. Cover and chill.

4 To make the raita, mix the yogurt and mint together. Transfer to a serving dish, then cover and chill.

5 Cook the rice in boiling, lightly salted water until just tender, according to the instructions on the packet. Drain thoroughly.

6 Just before serving, stir the garam masala into the curry. Divide between 4 warmed serving plates, and serve with the salad, mint raita and rice. Garnish the raita with fresh mint.

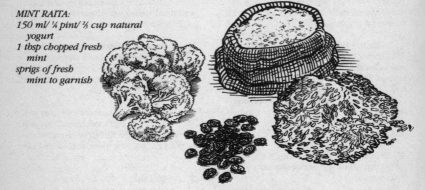

FILLED SOLE & SMOKED SALMON ROLLS

••••••••••••••••••••••••••••••••••••••

SERVES 4

60 g/2 oz/1 cup fresh wholemeal (whole
    wheat) breadcrumbs
½ tsp grated lime rind
1 tbsp lime juice
60 g/2 oz/ ¼ cup low-fat soft cheese
4 x 125 g/4 oz sole fillets
60 g/2 oz smoked salmon
150 ml/ ¼ pint/ ⅔ cup Fresh Fish Stock (see
    page 9)
150 ml/ ¼ pint/ ⅔ cup low-fat natural
    yogurt
1 tbsp chopped fresh chervil
salt and pepper
fresh chervil to garnish

TO SERVE:
selection of freshly steamed vegetables
lime wedges

1 In a mixing bowl, combine the
   breadcrumbs, lime rind and juice,
soft cheese and seasoning, to form a soft
stuffing mixture.

2 Skin the sole fillets by inserting a
   sharp knife in between the skin and
flesh at the tail end. Holding the skin in
your fingers and keeping it taut, strip the
flesh away from the skin.

3 Halve the sole fillets lengthwise.
   Place strips of smoked salmon over
the skinned side of each fillet, trimming
the salmon as necessary.

4 Spoon one-eighth of the stuffing on
   to each fish fillet and press down
along the fish with the back of a spoon.
Carefully roll up from the head to the tail
end. Place, seam-side down, in an
ovenproof dish and pour in the stock.
Bake in a preheated oven at 190°C/
375°F/Gas Mark 5 for 15 minutes.

5 Using a fish slice, transfer the fish to
   a warm serving plate, cover and
keep warm. Pour the cooking juices into
a saucepan and add the yogurt and
chopped chervil. Season to taste and heat
gently without boiling. Garnish the fish
rolls with chervil and serve with the
yogurt sauce, and the steamed vegetables
and lime wedges.

GLAZED SALMON

••••••••••••••••••••••••••••••••••••••

SERVES 8–12

2–3 kg/4–6 lb whole salmon, cleaned, with
    head left on
3–4 bay leaves
300 ml/ ½ pint/1¼ cups white wine vinegar
1½ tsp black peppercorns
4 cloves
1–2 onions, sliced thinly
1 lemon, sliced thinly

TO GARNISH:
about 450 ml/ ¾ pint/2 cups liquid aspic
    jelly
cucumber slices
stuffed green olives
mixed salad leaves
cherry tomatoes or tomato wedges
lime or lemon slices or wedges

1 Wipe the fish inside and out and, if
   liked, put 2 bay leaves in the cavity.
Half fill a fish kettle with water. Add the
vinegar, bay leaves, peppercorns and
cloves and bring slowly to the boil.

2 Lay the salmon on the metal rack
   with the onions and lemon slices
and carefully lower it into the fish kettle.

3 Bring slowly back to the boil, cover
   and then simmer very gently – the
water must not boil – allowing 5 minutes
per 500 g/1 lb.

4 Remove the kettle from the heat and
   leave the fish to cool in the water in
a cold place. When quite cold, remove
the fish carefully, drain and chill. Carefully
strip the skin off the fish.

5 Make up the aspic jelly following the
   directions on the packet. Leave to
cool, then chill half of it. When it begins
to thicken, brush a layer over the whole
fish, including the head. Add a second
and possibly a third layer of aspic to give
an even coating.

6 When set, transfer the fish to a
   serving dish. Garnish with thin slices
of cucumber and sliced stuffed olives
dipped in aspic so that they stick. Add a
final layer of aspic jelly to the whole fish
and chill until set. Garnish with salad
leaves, tomatoes and lime or lemon slices
or twists.

ORIENTAL MONKFISH TAIL WITH SWEET & SOUR VEGETABLES

SERVES 6

750 g/1½ lb monkfish tail
175 g/6 oz peeled prawns (shrimp),
defrosted if frozen
4 spring onions (scallions), chopped
1 fresh red chilli, seeded and finely
chopped
2 tbsp oyster sauce
175 g/6 oz/6 slices lean rindless back
bacon

SWEET & SOUR VEGETABLES:
250 g/8 oz/2 courgettes (zucchini),
trimmed
250 g/8 oz/2–3 carrots, peeled
1 red (bell) pepper, deseeded
125 g/4 oz/1⅓ cups mangetout (snow
peas), prepared
½ tsp grated lemon rind

SAUCE:
300 ml/ ½ pint/1¼ cups Fresh Fish Stock
(see page 9)
4 tbsp white wine vinegar
1 tbsp caster (superfine) sugar
2 tbsp tomato purée (paste)
2 tbsp light soy sauce
2 tsp cornflour (cornstarch) mixed with
4 tsp cold water

1 Strip away the skin and membrane from the monkfish. Slice in half by cutting along the sides of the bone.

2 Lay the fish between 2 layers of baking parchment and flatten to 1 cm/½ in thick with a rolling pin. Mix the remaining ingredients, except the bacon, to form a stuffing.

3 Press stuffing on to one half of the fish and top with the other piece. Lay 5 slices of bacon on baking parchment and place the fish on top. Fold the bacon over the fish and cover with the remaining bacon slice. Secure with string. Place the fish into 1 compartment of a large steamer. Bring a wok of water to the boil and put the steamer on top. Cover and steam for 20 minutes.

4 Meanwhile slice the vegetables except the mangetout. Place in the second steaming compartment with the mangetout and lemon rind. Turn the fish over and place the vegetable compartment on top. Steam for 10 minutes.

5 To make sauce, put the ingredients into a pan. Bring to the boil, stirring, and simmer for 5 minutes. Slice fish and serve with vegetables and sauce.

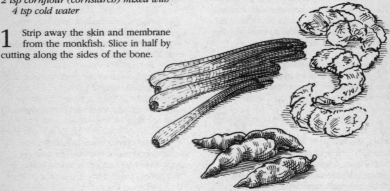

VENISON WITH PLUMS

SERVES 4

500 g/1 lb venison fillet (tenderloin)
2 tbsp olive oil
4 plums, halved, pitted and sliced
1 tsp chopped fresh sage
6 spring onions (scallions), white and
*   green parts, cut into 2.5 cm/1 in lengths*
1 tbsp cornflour (cornstarch)
2 tbsp orange juice
150 ml/ ¼ pint/ ⅔ cup stock
4 tbsp port
1 tbsp redcurrant jelly
1 tbsp brandy
salt and pepper
fresh purple sage sprigs to garnish
creamed potatoes to serve

1 Cut the venison into 1 cm/ ½ in strips. Heat the oil in a heavy-based frying pan (skillet) and fry the venison over a high heat for about 2 minutes until browned. Remove from the pan with a perforated spoon.

2 Add the plums, sage and spring onions (scallions) to the pan and cook for 2 minutes, stirring occasionally.

3 Mix the cornflour (cornstarch) with the orange juice and add to the pan. Add the stock, port and redcurrant jelly and heat, stirring, until thickened.

4 Return the venison to the pan, season to taste and pour in the brandy. Heat gently to warm through. Garnish with purple sage and serve with creamed potatoes.

VENISON

Venison is a fine-textured, dark red meat with very little fat, which makes it a healthy option. If venison is eaten young it is very tender, and better cuts such as saddle or loin can be roasted, but do not overcook them – they should still be fairly pink inside.

ROAST PHEASANT WITH TANGY CRANBERRY SAUCE

SERVES 4–6

1 brace oven-ready pheasants
1 lemon, quartered
4 tbsp melted dripping or butter, or
*   vegetable oil*
8 slices streaky bacon, derinded
salt and pepper
watercress to garnish

TANGY CRANBERRY SAUCE:
1 tbsp plain (all-purpose) flour
150 ml/ ¼ pint/ ⅔ cup stock
150 ml/ ¼ pint/ ⅔ cup red wine
finely pared rind and juice of 1 orange
4 tbsp cranberry sauce
125 g/4 oz shelled chestnuts, roasted and
*   boiled, or canned chestnuts (optional)*

1 Wipe the pheasants inside and out and place in a roasting tin (pan). Put half the butter and 2 slices of lemon in each cavity. Tie the legs together.

2 Brush 2 tablespoons of melted dripping or butter, or oil over each bird and season lightly. Lay the bacon slices over the breasts.

3 Roast in a preheated oven at 220°C/425°F/Gas Mark 7 for ¾–1¼ hours depending on the size of the birds, basting regularly until just cooked through and tender. Do not overcook or the flesh will become tough. Transfer to a serving dish and keep warm.

4 To make the tangy cranberry sauce, discard all but 2 tablespoons of the juices from the roasting tin (pan). Add the flour to the tin (pan) and cook, stirring, for a minute or so. Gradually stir in the stock and wine and bring to the boil, stirring until thickened.

5 Strain into a saucepan and add the orange rind and juice, the cranberry sauce and chestnuts, if using. Simmer for 3–4 minutes and adjust the seasoning. Garnish the pheasants with watercress and serve with the sauce.

DESSERTS

CRÈME BRULÉE

SERVES 4

4 egg yolks
600 ml/1 pint/2½ cups double (heavy)
cream
90 g/3 oz/ ⅓ cup light brown sugar

1 Beat the egg yolks until pale. Put the cream into a saucepan and set over a medium heat. Bring it to boiling point for about 30 seconds. Pour the cream on to the egg yolks, whisking all the time.

2 Return the cream and yolks to the saucepan, set over a gentle heat and stir until thickened, about 5 minutes.

3 Pour into individual ramekins or a large serving dish. Chill for 4 hours or overnight.

4 Sprinkle the brûlée with the light brown sugar to a thickness of about 5 mm/ ¼ in.

5 Place under a preheated very hot grill (broiler), until the sugar has caramelized to a golden brown. This takes about 3 minutes, depending on the heat of the grill (broiler), how far away from the grill (broiler) the brûlée is, and how thick the sugar is. Leave to cool before serving.

HANDY HINT

You may have seen a lozenge-shaped piece of iron on the end of a long handle in cook shops. This is a brûlée iron. It is usually about 7 cm/3 in round and designed to be held flat over the brûlée, after being heated to a very high temperature over a flame or electric ring. The thickness of the iron means that it stays hot for a few minutes, long enough to caramelize the sugar.

CHOCOLATE MARQUIS

SERVES 6-8

500 g/1 lb dark chocolate
125 g/4 oz/ ½ cup unsalted butter
30 g/1 oz/2 tbsp caster (superfine) sugar
4 whole eggs
1 tbsp plain (all-purpose) flour

1 Line a 20 cm/8 in springform tin (pan) with baking parchment.

2 Melt the chocolate, half of the butter and half of the sugar together in a heatproof bowl set over a saucepan of barely simmering water.

3 Beat the eggs and remaining sugar together until pale. Fold in the flour

4 Pour the chocolate mixture on to the batter and stir in gently with a wooden spoon,

5 Fold together with a whisk, lightly, but until well combined.

6 Pour the mixture into the lined tin (pan) and bake in a preheated oven at 230°C/450°F/Gas Mark 8 for 12 minutes only. It should still be slightly wobbly in the centre.

7 Run a knife between the edge of the dessert and the tin (pan), and then release the tin (pan). Tighten the tin (pan) again, and leave the marquis in the tin (pan) to cool. Freeze for at least 2 hours or until required.

8 Remove from the freezer at least an hour before serving to allow the dessert to come to room temperature. Cut into small slices to serve.

BAKED ALASKA

SERVES 4–6

125 g/4 oz/ ½ cup butter, softened
125 g/4 oz/ ½ cup caster (superfine) sugar
2 eggs, lightly beaten
125 g/4 oz/1 cup self-raising flour
2 tbsp brandy or sherry
2 tbsp raspberry jam
900 ml/1½ pints/3½ cups vanilla or
* raspberry ripple ice cream – do not use*
* 'soft scoop' ice cream*

MERINGUE:
4 egg whites
90 g/3 oz/ ⅓ cup caster (superfine) sugar

1 Grease and flour a 20 cm/8 in sandwich cake tin (layer pan).

2 Beat the butter and sugar together, until pale and fluffy. Beat in the eggs gradually. If the mixture starts to separate while you are doing this, add a little flour and continue.

3 Fold in the flour carefully, and pour the mixture into the greased tin (pan). Bake in a pre-heated oven at 190°C/375°F/Gas Mark 5 for 40 minutes. Transfer to a wire rack to cool.

4 About 30 minutes before serving, transfer the sponge to an ovenproof serving dish, trimming to fit if necessary. Sprinkle with brandy and spread with the jam. Freeze for 20 minutes.

5 If the ice cream block is not round, transfer it to a plate and re-form it to the shape of your dish, using foil or greaseproof paper (baking parchment),

6 Remove the sponge from the freezer and put the ice cream on top. Re-freeze until 10 minutes before serving.

7 To make the meringue, whisk the egg whites until stiff. Add the caster (superfine) sugar gradually and continue whisking until stiff and glossy.

8 Take the sponge and ice cream from the freezer and cover the ice cream completely with the meringue mixture. Use the back of a spoon to form peaks all over. Work quickly so that the ice cream does not melt.

9 Bake in a preheated oven at 230°C/450°F/Gas Mark 8 for 5 minutes only. Keep an eye on it, as the meringue burns easily. Remove and serve immediately before the ice cream melts.

ZUCCOTTO

SERVES 6-8

400 g/14 oz can of stoned (pitted) black
cherries, drained, or 500 g/1 lb fresh
black cherries, stoned (pitted)
2 tbsp maraschino
2 tbsp water
250 g/8 oz/6½ in Madeira (pound) cake,
thinly sliced, or 20 sponge fingers
3 tbsp orange-flavoured liqueur
600 ml/1 pint/2½ cups double (heavy)
cream
90 g/3 oz/ ⅛ cup caster (superfine) sugar
¼ tsp vanilla flavouring (extract)
45 g/1½ oz/ ⅓ cup mixed (candied) peel
2 tbsp ground almonds
90 g/3 oz/3 squares dark chocolate,
melted
2 tbsp rum
60 g/2 oz/ ½ cup hazelnuts, chopped

1 Put the cherries into a saucepan with the maraschino and water. Bring to the boil, remove from heat and leave to steep for 10 minutes.

2 Line the sides of a round 1.5 litre/ 2¾ pint/3 cup bowl with the sliced cake or sponge fingers. Drain the cherries and use the juice to moisten the sponge. Sprinkle the liqueur over the sponge. Put into the freezer.

3 Whip one third of the cream until stiff and stir in half of the sugar, the vanilla flavouring (extract), mixed (candied) peel and ground almonds. Spread this mixture in a layer over the sponge base and up the sides. Return to the freezer for 40 minutes until firm.

4 Whip one third of the cream until softly stiff, and fold in the cooled melted chocolate, the rum and hazelnuts. Spread this in a layer over the cream layer and return to the freezer.

5 Purée the cherries in a food processor, or mash well by hand, and stir in the rest of the sugar. Whip the remaining cream until stiff and fold in the cherries. Fill the centre of the bowl with this. Return to the freezer for 1 hour, or until ready to serve. If it is kept for longer than 2 hours in the freezer, remove 1 hour before serving. If you do not have a freezer, add a little powdered gelatine to the zuccotto. Dissolve 2 tablespoons or 2 sachets (envelopes) in 120 ml/4 fl oz/ ½ cup of hot water in a bowl set over a saucepan of simmering water. Stir a third of this into each layer.

6 To serve, unmould on to a chilled dish and decorate as you wish.

HOT MOCHA SOUFFLÉ

SERVES 6

butter for greasing
2 tbsp caster (superfine) sugar
2 egg yolks
3 tsp icing (confectioners') sugar
2 tsp plain (all-purpose) flour
150 g/5 oz/5 squares dark chocolate,
*   melted*
2 tsp instant coffee powder, dissolved in
*   1 tbsp hot water*
4 egg whites
icing (confectioners') sugar, to decorate

SAUCE:
60 g/2 oz/¼ cup granulated sugar
50 ml/2 fl oz/¼ cup water
100 g/3½ oz/3½ squares dark chocolate
1 tbsp instant coffee powder
75 ml/3 fl oz/⅓ cup whipping cream

1 Butter a 900 ml/1½ pint/3½ cup
soufflé dish. Dust with the caster
(superfine) sugar and tap out any excess.
Wrap a piece of baking parchment around
the soufflé dish, to twice the depth of the
dish. Secure with string or an elastic band.

2 Beat the egg yolks until pale and sift
in the icing (confectioners') sugar.
Stir in the flour, melted chocolate and
dissolved coffee.

3 Whisk the egg whites until just stiff
and fold into the soufflé mixture.

4 Pour the mixture into the soufflé
dish right up to the rim. Run the tip
of a knife quickly between the soufflé
and the edge of the dish. Bake in a
preheated oven at 180°C/350°F/Gas Mark
4 for 45 minutes. Do not open the oven.

5 Make the sauce. Put the sugar and
water into a saucepan. Simmer until
dissolved, then add the chocolate, instant
coffee powder and cream. Keep warm
until ready to serve.

6 Working quickly, remove the
parchment from the soufflé dish,
dust with the icing (confectioners') sugar
and take to the table before it sinks. Make
a hole in the top of the soufflé by
stabbing it with a knife, and pour in
the sauce.

PAVLOVA

SERVES 8

6 egg whites
½ tsp cream of tartar
250 g/8 oz/1 cup caster (superfine) sugar
1 tsp vanilla flavouring (extract)
300 ml/ ½ pint/1¼ cups whipping cream
400 g/13 oz/2½ cups strawberries, hulled
*   and halved*
3 tbsp orange-flavoured liqueur
fruit of your choice, to decorate

1 Line a baking (cookie) sheet with
baking parchment and mark out a
circle to fit your serving plate. The recipe
makes enough meringue for a 30 cm/
12 in circle.

2 Whisk the egg whites and cream of
tartar together until stiff. Gradually
beat in the caster (superfine) sugar and
vanilla flavouring (extract). Whisk well
until glossy and stiff.

3 Either spoon or pipe the meringue
mixture into the marked circle, in an
even layer, slightly raised at the edges, to
form a dip in the centre.

4 Baking the meringue depends on
your preference. If you like a soft
chewy meringue, bake at 140°C/275°F/
Gas Mark 4 for about 1½ hours until dry
but slightly soft in the centre. If you
prefer a dry meringue, bake in the oven
at 110°C/225°F/Gas Mark ¼ for 3 hours
until dry.

5 When you are ready to serve, whip
the cream to a piping consistency,
and either spoon or pipe on to the
meringue base, leaving a border of
meringue all around the edge.

6 Stir the strawberries and liqueur
together and spoon on to the cream.
Decorate with fruit of your choice, such
as slices of mango, apple or pineapple.
Serve immediately.

CHILDREN'S PARTIES

When your children demand something 'different' for their party, these recipes will come up with an answer. Make individual Funny Face pizzas (right) or Eggs Ahoy! sailboat rolls (below) to delight the guests. There are ideas a-plenty for cakes too, whatever the current enthusiasm: football, racing cars, cricket or swimming. For very young children, Tommy Tortoise (page 650) or Clarence the Clown (page 648) would be ideal.

EGGS AHOY!

MAKES 12

12 small or miniature bread rolls
3 hard-boiled eggs, shelled
1½ tbsp mayonnaise
50 g/2 oz/¼ cup butter or margarine
3 medium tomatoes
12 slices cucumber

1 Cut the tops off the bread rolls (forming a lid that will be used later) and scoop out some of the bread. Set the lids aside for the finishing touch.

2 Make breadcrumbs from the scooped-out bread by rubbing it along a coarse grater, or by using a food processor (a brief burst on high speed should be sufficient).

3 Chop the hard-boiled eggs and mix with about half of the prepared crumbs (use the remainder for another dish). Stir in the mayonnaise to bind the mixture together.

4 Butter the rolls then fill with the egg mixture and replace the tops.

5 Cut the tomatoes into quarters and remove the seeds. Place a slice of cucumber inside each tomato quarter.

6 Push a cocktail stick (toothpick) through each tomato quarter and cucumber slice, and use to represent a sail on each egg 'boat'. Serve as soon as possible to prevent the rolls going soggy. If ripe tomatoes prove hard to obtain, sails can also be made using a triangle of processed cheese.

PARTY CATERING

This is the perfect sandwich idea and the ideal opportunity to introduce mild herbs to children's food. Add 1-2 tsp chopped fresh parsley, chives or coriander to the egg mixture to introduce new flavours in a familiar format. Under-six-year-olds may be overwhelmed by the sheer excitement of a party so that their appetites disappear. Older children, however, will eat an astonishing amount – at least as much as adults. Be sure to have enough food on hand!

GAMEBOARD PIZZA SLICE

SERVES 1

1 thick slice of bread
1 tbsp pizza sauce, tomato purée or
*   tomato paste*
25 g/1 oz/ ¼ cup Cheddar cheese, grated
1 slice boiled or cooked ham
1 small tomato
½ green pepper, cored

1   Lightly toast the bread on both sides
    until it is just lightly golden brown.
(Overcooked bread will be too dry and
won't 'take' the flavours as well.)

2   Spread the slice of bread with the
    pizza sauce, tomato purée or tomato
paste. Sprinkle the cheese on top to cover
the slice evenly.

3   Cut the ham into long thin strips
    about 0.5 cm/ ½ inch wide and
arrange on top of the cheese in a criss-
cross pattern to look like a noughts and
crosses (tic tac toe) grid.

4   Slice the tomatoes to look like the
    noughts (zeros) in a game, and slice
the green pepper into thin strips so that
two can be placed over each other to
make crosses. Arrange a few noughts
(zeros) and crosses over the cheesy grid
(with perhaps a winning sequence!).

5   Cook under a preheated hot grill
    (broiler) until hot and bubbly, about
3–4 minutes. Serve on a heated plate.

EASY PIZZA SAUCE

The supermarket is a ready source of
pizza sauces, but if you are so inclined,
a fresh sauce can be quickly created
using the microwave. Drain and chop a
can of tomatoes, then place in a bowl
with a little garlic, oregano and salt and
pepper. Cook on high for 2½ minutes,
stirring once. The sauce will keep
sealed in the refrigerator for a few days.

FUNNY FACES

SERVES 4

1 quantity Bread Dough Base (see page
*   208)*
30 g/1 oz spaghetti or egg noodles
1 quantity Tomato Sauce (see page 209)
8 slices pepperoni-style sausage
8 thin slices celery
4 slices button mushrooms
4 slices yellow (bell) pepper
4 slices Mozzarella cheese
4 slices courgette (zucchini)
olive oil for drizzling
8 peas

1   Divide the dough into 4. Roll each
    piece out into a 12 cm/5 in diameter
circle and place on greased baking sheets.
Cover and leave to rise slightly in a warm
place for about 10 minutes.

2   Cook the spaghetti or egg noodles
    according to the packet instructions.

3   Divide the tomato sauce evenly
    between each pizza base and spread
out almost to the edge.

4   To make the faces, use pepperoni
    slices for the main part of the eyes,
celery for the eyebrows, mushrooms for
the noses and (bell) pepper slices for the
mouths.

5   Cut the Mozzarella cheese and
    courgette (zucchini) slices in half.
Use the cheese for the cheeks and the
courgettes (zucchini) for the ears.

6   Drizzle a little olive oil over each
    pizza and bake in a preheated
oven at 200°C/400°F/Gas Mark 6 for
12–15 minutes until the edges are crisp
and golden.

7   Transfer the pizzas to serving plates
    and place the peas in the centre of
the eyes. Drain the spaghetti or noodles
and arrange around the tops of the pizzas
for hair. Serve immediately.

INITIAL ANSWERS

....

MAKES 4

4 slices Cheddar cheese
100 g/4 oz canned sardines or mackerel,
drained
5-cm/2-inch piece cucumber, very finely
chopped
¼ small red pepper, cored, seeded and
finely chopped, or 1 firm tomato,
chopped
1 tbsp mayonnaise or natural yoghurt
salt and pepper
4 small slices of white or brown bread

1 Using initial cutters or a sharp knife,
cut 4 initials from the cheese slices
to represent the first letter of the name of
each of the diners. Gather together any
cheese trimmings and chop them finely.

2 In a small bowl, flake the sardines or
mackerel and mix with the
cucumber, red pepper or tomato,
mayonnaise or yoghurt, and salt and
pepper to taste, mixing well. Add the
reserved cheese trimmings and mix well.
Toast the bread on both sides until light
golden brown.

3 Spread the slices of toast with the
prepared sardine mixture, spreading
evenly to the edges of the bread.

4 Top each slice of bread with a
cheese initial. Serve as soon as
possible, ideally with a knife and fork.

INITIAL VARIATIONS

The initial idea can applied to other
recipes, too. If you are cooking for
non-fish eaters (particularly children),
use cheese initials to top ham, tomato
or pizza-style fillings.

The sandwich filling and cheesy
topping described above also make a
splendid topping for a pizza. For speed
and convenience use a ready-prepared
pizza base (about 23 cm/9 in in
diameter). Top with 4-6 tbsp tomato
sauce, spread with the prepared fish
mixture, top with the cheese initials
and bake in a hot oven for 12-15
minutes, until hot and bubbly.

CAKES

FOOTBALL

....

4-egg Madeira (Pound) Cake mixture (see
pages 568 and 571)
1 quantity butter cream (see page 541)
4 tbsp jam, strained
1 kg/2 lb/8 cups sugarpaste (see page 571)
black, blue and deep red liquid or paste
food colouring

1 Grease the 2 separate halves of a
spherical Christmas pudding mould,
about 12.5 cm/5 in in diameter, or
2 basins of 900 ml/1½ pints/3¾ cups
capacity. Place pieces of baking
parchment in the bottom of each and
dredge lightly with flour. Place the
containers on baking sheets, holding in
place with foil.

2 Divide the cake mixture between the
containers, filling no more than
three-quarters full and levelling the tops.
Bake in a preheated oven at 160°C/325°F/
Gas Mark 3 for about 1–1½ hours until
firm to the touch. Invert on a wire rack
and leave to set for 12–24 hours.

3 Trim the cakes evenly and sandwich
together with most of the butter
cream. Cut off a slice from the base so
that the ball will stand upright, and attach
to a cake board with butter cream. Brush
all over with jam.

4 Roll out about 625 g/1¼ lb/5 cups
sugarpaste and use to cover the ball,
moulding carefully to fit. Colour half the
remaining sugarpaste black, roll out and
cut into hexagons, 5 cm/2 in across.

5 Attach the hexagons evenly all over
the football, by dampening slightly,
so they stick and just touch. Leave to set.

6 Colour most of the remaining
sugarpaste deep maroon and the rest
pale blue. Roll out the maroon sugarpaste
to make a scarf, then roll out the pale
blue and add for a fringe and stripes.
Lay the scarf around the football. Use the
remaining butter cream to write 'Happy
Birthday' either on the board or the cake.
Leave to set.

RACING CAR

2 x 3-egg Quick Mix Cake or Madeira (Pound) Cake mixture, any flavour (see pages 568, 570 and 571)
6 tbsp apricot jam, strained
1 kg/2 lb/8 cups sugarpaste (see page 571)
blue and black liquid or paste food colourings
250 g/8 oz/2 cups royal icing (see page 542)
4 wooden cocktail sticks (toothpicks) or plastic skewers

1 Grease 2 roasting tins (pans) 28 x 18 x 4 cm/11 x 7 x 1½ in, and line with baking parchment. Spread the cake mixture evenly in the tins (pans). Bake in a preheated oven at 160°C/ 325°F/Gas Mark 3 for about 45–50 minutes until firm. Invert on wire racks and leave the cakes to set for 12–24 hours.

2 Trim the cakes to a width of 11 cm/ 4½ in wide, reserving the trimmings. Sandwich the cakes together with jam. Slightly taper one end of the cake and round the other end for the back of the car. About 10 cm/4 in from the back of the car cut out a wedge through the top layer of cake for the seat. Use a piece of the cake trimmings to build up the car behind the seat. Add a small elongated triangular piece of cake to the top of the bonnet (hood), attaching all with jam.

3 From the other trimmings, cut out 2 wheels of 5 cm/2 in and 2 of 6 cm/2½ in. The larger back wheels should be wider than the front ones. Brush the car and tyres with jam.

4 Colour 625 g/1¼ lb/5 cups of the sugarpaste bright blue. Roll out and use to cover the entire car, moulding to fit all the undulations, but cutting out a piece for the seat so it does not split.

5 Colour 250 g/8 oz/2 cups of the sugarpaste black. Roll out and use a piece to fit inside the seat area of the car, and to cover the tyres. Mark treads on the tyres with a sharp knife, then attach with cocktail sticks (toothpicks) and a dab of royal icing. Also mould a steering wheel, an anti-roll bar to put behind the seat, and 2 wing mirrors, and attach.

6 Colour the remaining sugarpaste grey, and use for a seat in the car, a front radiator, and trims to the wheels. Colour the royal icing grey and using a No 2 writing nozzle (tip), pipe spokes on the tyres and a radiator grille on the car. Pipe the age of the child for the car number and, if liked, a name or message on the car or board. Leave to set.

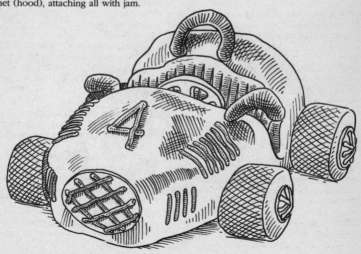

HOT AIR BALLOON

4-egg Victoria Sandwich (Sponge Layer Cake), Quick Mix Cake or Madeira (Pound) Cake mixture (see pages 568, 570 and 571)
6 tbsp apricot jam, sieved (strained)
1 kg/2 lb/8 cups sugarpaste or marzipan (see page 540 or 571)
yellow, orange, green and mauve liquid or paste food colourings
1 quantity butter cream (see page 541)
4 wooden skewers

1 Grease a 23 cm/9 inch bowl (about 2.25 litres/4 pints/2½ quart capacity) thoroughly. Spoon the cake mixture into the bowl, making sure it is evenly distributed, and level the top. Bake in a preheated oven at 160°C/325°F/Gas Mark 3 for about 1¼–1½ hours until firm to the touch and a skewer inserted in the centre comes out clean. Invert on a wire rack and let set for 24 hours.

2 Place the cake upside-down on a rectangular cake board and brush all over with the jam. Take about 125 g/4 oz/1 cup of the sugarpaste or marzipan and mould a piece to put at the base of the balloon to make it elongated.

3 Colour about 175 g/6 oz/1½ cups of the sugarpaste or marzipan mauve, then divide the remainder into 3 pieces and colour them yellow, orange and green respectively. Roll out about three-quarters of each of the 3 large pieces of sugarpaste or marzipan and use each to form a wide stripe around the balloon, so it is completely covered.

4 Shape 125 g/4 oz/1 cup of the mauve sugarpaste or marzipan into a small rectangle for the basket. Cut out various shapes in the different colours of sugarpaste or marzipan with a cutter or a sharp knife and attach them in even bands to the balloon to make it as pretty and vibrant as possible.

5 Attach the rectangular piece of sugarpaste or marzipan for the basket at the base of the balloon and stick the skewers into the basket and the base of the balloon to represent the ropes.

6 Colour half the butter cream green and the remainder orange. Put into piping bags fitted with small star nozzles (tips) and use to decorate both the basket and the balloon. Use a spare piece of green sugarpaste to make a banner and pipe on a message with the buttercream, if liked. Leave to set.

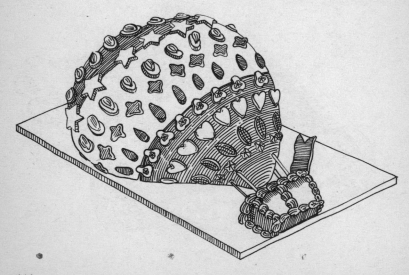

CROSSWORD PUZZLE

4-egg Victoria Sandwich (Sponge Layer
  Cake), Quick Mix Cake or Madeira
  (Pound) Cake mixture (see pages 568,
  570 and 571)
6 tbsp apricot jam, sieved (strained)
875 g/1¾ lb/7 cups sugarpaste (see page
  571)
blue, green and orange liquid or paste
  food colourings
250 g/8 oz/2 cups royal icing (see page
  542)

1 Grease and line a 23 cm/9 inch deep
  square cake tin (pan). Spread the
cake mixture evenly in it. Bake in a preheated oven at 160°C/325°F/Gas Mark 3
for 50–60 minutes (1–1¼ hours for Quick
Mix and Madeira (Pound) Cake). Invert
on a wire rack and leave to set for 12–24
hours. Stand the cake upside-down on a
30 cm/12 inch cake board. Brush all over
carefully with the apricot jam. Colour 500 g/
1 lb/4 cups of the sugarpaste mid blue.
Colour 300 g/10 oz/2½ cups of the
sugarpaste deep green and leave the
remainder white.

2 Roll out three-quarters of the blue
  sugarpaste and use to cover the top
of the cake. Mark the sugarpaste into a
crossword design of 12 lines each way
but leaving a margin of about 1 cm/ ½ inch
all round the edge. This should give
12 squares down and across.

3 Cut a piece of string long enough to
  reach round the outside of the cake,
then cut the string in half. Roll out the
deep green sugarpaste to the depth of the
cake plus about 1 cm/ ½ inch. Cut out
2 strips the length of each piece of string.
Place around the sides of the cake,
bending the overlap over the top edge of
the cake to reach the crossword, trimming
the corners as necessary.

4 Roll out the remaining blue
  sugarpaste. Cut into 4 cm/1½ inch
circles, flute the edges and then cut each
of these in half. Attach around the base of
the cake with a dab of apricot jam.

5 Roll out the white sugarpaste and
  cut into strips the width of the
squares on the crossword. Position to
make your message look like words in a
crossword, then mark each with a knife.

6 Colour the royal icing orange and
  put a little into a piping bag fitted
with a No. 2 writing nozzle (tip). Use to
fill in the letters. Put the remaining royal
icing in a piping bag fitted with a star
nozzle (tip) and pipe a star decoration
around the base. Complete the decoration
with stars and dots of royal icing.

CRICKET BAT

5-egg *Victoria Sandwich (Sponge Layer Cake), any flavour (see page 568 and 570)*
2 quantities butter cream (see page 541)
5 tbsp apricot jam, sieved (strained)
1 kg/2 lb/8 cups sugarpaste (see page 571)
brown, red, yellow, black and green liquid or paste food colourings

1 Grease and line a roasting pan about 30 x 25 cm/12 x 10 in. Spread the cake mixture in the tin (pan), making sure there is plenty of mixture in the corners. Bake in a preheated oven at 160°C/325°F/Gas Mark 3 for about 50 minutes (1–1¼ hours for Madeira (Pound) Cake) until well risen and firm to the touch. Invert on a wire rack and leave to set for 12–24 hours.

2 Cut a 2.5 cm/1 inch slice off one narrow end, halve this and sandwich together with butter cream for the handle. Cut the rest of the cake in half lengthways and sandwich together with butter cream. Round one end and cut away a slightly slanting slice towards the center of the cake on the long sides.

3 Brush the cake all over with the jam. Colour 625 g/1¼ lb/5 cups sugarpaste light brown. Roll out and use to cover the cricket bat, trimming around the base.

4 Colour the remaining sugarpaste deep red. Use some of it to cover the 'handle' of the bat after brushing with jam and position at the top of the bat. Roll out a tiny piece for a deep triangle to place at the top of the bat where it meets the handle.

5 Roll the remaining red sugarpaste into a cricket ball and mark the seams with the back of a knife, as in the photograph. Place beside the bat. Using some butter cream in a piping bag fitted with a fine writing nozzle (tip), pipe small lines around the ball for the markings.

6 Write the name of the child down the length of the bat. Colour the remaining butter cream green and put into a piping bag fitted with a star nozzle (tip). Pipe green stars all over the board to represent grass. Leave to set.

SNAKES & LADDERS CAKE

5-egg *quantity Victoria Sandwich (Sponge Layer Cake) or Madeira (Pound) Cake mixture, any flavour (see pages 568, 570 and 571)*
5 tbsp apricot jam, sieved (strained)
1 kg/2 lb/8 cups sugarpaste (see page 571)
green, blue, yellow, red, orange and black liquid or paste food colourings
1 quantity royal icing (see page 542)

1 Grease and line a 25 cm/10 inch square cake tin (pan). Spread the cake mixture evenly in it. Bake in a preheated oven at 160°C/325°F/Gas Mark 3 for about 1–1¼ hours, or until firm to the touch. Invert on a wire rack and leave to set for 12–24 hours.

2 Trim the cake and place upside-down on a cake board. Brush all over with jam.

3 Colour about 750 g/1½ lb/6 cups of the sugarpaste green and use to cover the whole cake, trimming off evenly around the base. Using the back of a knife, mark the top of the cake into 2 cm/ ¾ inch squares. Leave to set.

4 Colour about 60 g/2 oz/ ½ cup each of the sugarpaste red, blue and yellow, and shape these into snakes of various lengths. Place them on the board as in the photograph. Also shape 4 round counters about 1 cm/ ½ inch across, and colour each one a different colour, either red, blue, yellow or white.

5 Colour about half the royal icing pale green, put into a piping bag fitted with a writing nozzle (tip) and pipe numbers on all the squares; then, using a star nozzle (tip), pipe a decoration around the base of the cake with alternate stars and elongated stars. Add loops from star to star with the writing nozzle (tip).

6 Colour the remaining royal icing orange and put into a piping bag fitted with a fairly thick writing nozzle (tip). Pipe ladders on the cake as in the photograph. Finally, use the remaining sugarpaste to make into square dice; add tiny dots of black food colouring to complete the dice.

SWIMMING POOL

5-egg and 2-egg Victoria Sandwich
  (Sponge Layer Cake) mixture (see pages
  568 and 570)
1 quantity butter cream (see page 541)
6 tbsp apricot jam, sieved (strained)
1 kg/2 lb/8 cups sugarpaste (see page 571)
blue, green, pink, brown and orange
  liquid or paste food colourings

1 Grease and line a roasting pan about
  30 x 25 cm/12 x 10 in and another
of 28 x 18 x 4 cm/11 x 7 x 1½ in. Spread
the 5-egg mixture in the larger tin (pan)
and the 2-egg one in the smaller tin
(pan). Bake in a preheated oven at
180°C/350°F/Gas Mark 4 until firm to the
touch: about 50 minutes for the larger
cake and 25 minutes for the smaller.
Invert on wire racks and let set for 12–24
hours.

2 Place the large cake on a cake
  board. Trim the other cake and
attach on top of the larger cake at the
back with butter cream. Brush the whole
cake with jam.

3 Colour 175 g/6 oz/1½ cups sugarpaste
  blue. Roll out and cover the top of
the raised part of the cake. Colour 500
g/1 lb/4 cups sugarpaste green. Roll out
some of it and use to cover the rest of the
cake and up the sides of the pool just
overlapping the blue sugarpaste. Trim off
around the base.

4 Roll out 90 g/3 oz/ ¾ cup of white
  sugarpaste and cut into 2 cm/ ¾ inch
wide strips. Dampen and attach around
the top edge of the pool, Mark at intervals
to represent paving stones.

5 Colour 125 g/4 oz/1 cup of
  sugarpaste pale pink and use to
make the top half of 3 bodies, and a body
to sit on the side of the pool. Using a fine
paintbrush and food colouring, paint on
hair and other details. Leave to dry and
position in the pool. Colour the rest of
the sugarpaste in bright colours and shape
into 2 or 3 towels, to throw on the grass.

6 Shape the remaining green
  sugarpaste into trees and place
around the pool. Colour a tiny amount of
butter cream pink and put into a piping
bag fitted with a star nozzle (tip). Colour
the remaining butter cream green and put
into a piping bag fitted with a star or
thick writing nozzle (tip). Pipe grass
around the sides of the cake, working up
from the board; and pipe patches of grass
on the cake and around the edge of the
pool. Add flowers by piping pink stars of
icing (frosting) here and there.

CLARENCE THE CLOWN

6-egg Madeira (Pound) Cake mixture (see
pages 568 and 571)
6 tbsp apricot jam, sieved (strained)
1.25 kg/2½ lb/10 cups sugarpaste (see
page 571)
red, orange, black, yellow and blue liquid
or paste food colourings
500 g/1 lb/4 cups royal icing (see page
542) or 1½ quantities butter cream (see
page 541)

1 Grease and line a 30 x 25 cm/12 x 10
inch roasting tin (pan). Spread the
cake mixture evenly in it. Bake in a
preheated oven at 160°C/325°F/Gas Mark
3 for 1–1¼ hours. Invert on a wire rack
and leave to set for 12–24 hours.

2 Make a template for the clown and
cut out the shape carefully. Cut out
the arms and hat from the trimmings.
Place the cake upside down on a cake
board and brush all over with jam.

3 Colour 175 g/6 oz/1½ cups of the
sugarpaste flesh pink. Roll out and
use some of it to cover the head of the
clown. Mould the remainder into 2 ears
and attach to the head. Colour 125 g/
4 oz/ 1 cup of the sugarpaste black.
Reserve a scrap for the eyes and mould
the remainder into 2 feet.

4 Colour 625 g/1¼ lb/5 cups of the
sugarpaste orange. Roll out and use
to cover the clown's body, arms and hat.
Dampen the arms and attach to the body.
Use about 90 g/3 oz/ ¾ cup white
sugarpaste to mould into hands and
attach to the arms. Colour 90 g/3 oz/ ¾
cup of the sugarpaste blue and cut out
shapes to stick all over the body and hat.

5 Colour 60 g/2 oz/ ½ cup sugarpaste
bright yellow. Roll out and make
into a large bow tie. Roll out most of the
rest of the white sugarpaste and cut ovals
for eyes and mouth, and circles for spots
on face. Dampen and attach. Use the rest
of the black sugarpaste for the centres of
the eyes. Colour the remaining scraps of
white sugarpaste red and use for a nose,
mouth and eyebrows.

6 Colour two-thirds of the royal icing
or butter cream bright blue and the
remainder yellow. Put into piping bags,
the blue fitted with a star nozzle (tip) and
the yellow with a thick writing nozzle
(tip). Pipe a heavy blue ruff around the
neck, cuffs and feet of the clown. Pipe
yellow strands of hair at the back of the
head. Attach the feet, bow tie and hat,
and leave to set.

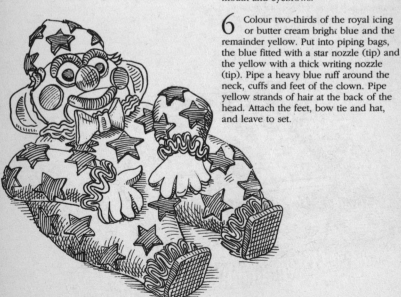

OPEN BOOK

6-egg *Victoria Sandwich (Sponge Layer Cake), Quick Mix Cake* or *Madeira (Pound) Cake* mixture (see pages 568, 570 and 571)

5 tbsp apricot jam, sieved (strained)

1.25 kg/2½ lb/10 cups sugarpaste (see page 571)

yellow, red, pink, green and orange liquid or paste food colourings

250 g/8 oz/2 cups royal icing (see page 542) or 1 quantity butter cream (see page 541)

about 50 cm/20 in 2.5 cm/1 inch wide satin ribbon

moulded and piped bells and shells (see page 569)

1 Grease and line a roasting tin (pan) about 30 x 25 cm/12 x 10 in. Spread the cake mixture evenly in it. Bake in a preheated oven at 160°C/ 325°F/Gas Mark 3 for 50–60 minutes. Invert on a wire rack and leave to set for 12–24 hours.

2 Place the cake upside-down on a cake board. Cut out a rounded strip down the centre of the cake, turn it upside-down and place on the right-hand page. Brush all over with jam.

3 Colour about 625 g/1¼ lb/5 cups of the sugarpaste with yellow colouring to turn it cream. Roll out most of it and use to cover the cake so it looks like a book. Trim off around the base. Using a sharp knife, make cuts into the sides of the cake so they look like pages.

4 Roll out the remaining cream sugarpaste to a 'page' half the size of the cake. Attach down the centre and fold it so the edge is slightly ruffled up.

5 Colour the remaining sugarpaste red. Roll out, cut into narrow strips and place around the base of the cake to represent the book's cover. Leave to set.

6 Colour the royal icing or butter cream deep pink and put into a piping bag fitted with a writing nozzle (tip). On the left-hand page print 'Mary, Mary, Quite Contrary', keeping it to the top of the page. On the other page write some of the rhyme.

7 Using the remaining sugarpaste and royal icing or butter cream, mould and pipe some tiny bells and shells in various colours and arrange along the bottom of the page for a garden, together with green royal icing or butter cream stems and leaves, and a sugarpaste watering can. Place the ribbon down the centre of the pages as a bookmark.

TOMMY TORTOISE

*4-egg Victoria Sandwich (Sponge Layer
Cake) or Quick Mix Cake (see pages
568 and 570)*
4 tbsp apricot jam, sieved (strained)
*500 g/1 lb/4 cups sugarpaste (see page
571)*
green, blue and brown food colouring
1 quantity butter cream (see page 541)
few sugarpaste flowers (see page 567)

1 Grease a 1.5 litre/3 pint/6 cup bowl
(about 23 cm/9 in in diameter)
thoroughly and put a disc of baking
parchment in the base. Add the cake
mixture and bake in a preheated oven at
160°C/325°F/Gas Mark 3 for 1¼–1½ hours
until well risen and firm. Cool briefly in
the bowl. Invert on a wire rack and leave
to set for 12–24 hours.

2 Place the cake upside-down on a
cake board and trim 2.5 cm/1 in
from each side to make the tortoise oval.
Cut a small V from the front for the head
and 2 Vs on each side for the feet, then
brush the cake all over with jam.

3 Colour 125 g/4 oz/1 cup sugar-paste
greenish brown. Use one-third of it
to mould into a head with a thick neck
and press into the head cavity. Mark 2
deep eyes, nostrils and a mouth with a

skewer. Divide the remaining sugarpaste
into 4 and shape into feet. Position and
then mark 4 toes on each foot with the
back of a knife.

4 Colour the remaining sugarpaste
green. Roll out to an oval that is
large enough to cover the cake. Lift
carefully and position over the cake.
Make cuts over the feet and around the
head, then trim so it just overlaps on to
the board. Carefully mould the edge of
the shell so it becomes thinner and also
turn it up slightly. Place a strip of rolled
paper towel under it, so it cannot fall
back again. Leave until quite set.

5 Using a fairly blunt skewer, mark
uneven circles, squares and other
shapes all over the shell so they all touch
and make a pattern as on a real tortoise.
Colour about a quarter of the butter
cream greenish brown and put into a
piping bag fitted with a No. 2 or 3 writing
nozzle (tip). Pipe a spiral inside each of
the marked shapes on the tortoise.

6 Colour the remaining butter cream
pale green and put into a piping bag
fitted with a star nozzle (tip). Pipe stars all
over the board to represent grass. Add the
sugarpaste flowers. Leave to set.

CHRISTMAS COOKING – INTRODUCTION

THE RUN-UP TO CHRISTMAS

Each year, Christmas seems to come around earlier and earlier. By late September the shops begin to get their stocks of Christmas goods, sending us into a state of mild panic. The actual break itself seems to get longer too, with many people taking up to two weeks off work. Which all adds extra pressure on those doing the preparations, knowing that the catering arrangements for family and friends have extended.

Relax! This step-by-step guide to cooking for Christmas will lead you through the days running up to the festivities and will give you an invaluable source of recipe ideas and information. Whether you've cooked countless Christmas lunches or this is your first time, this book will prove to be a handy reference source, giving you the know-how that's needed to help you survive until the New Year.

TURKEY TIPS

You will probably enjoy the flavour of a fresh turkey more than a frozen bird, but remember to order it in plenty of time from your butcher. Supermarkets also stock a vast number of fresh turkeys during the run up to Christmas, but if you don't have much space in your refrigerator, nor a cold larder or room to keep the bird in, you may have to wait until Christmas Eve to buy it, so make sure that you get to the shops early.

With a frozen bird, you shouldn't have any problems with availability, but you must remember to allow plenty of time for the bird to defrost thoroughly. Check the thawing times on the packaging, and allow up to 2 days for the turkey to thaw properly if it's a large bird. The turkey must defrost completely, otherwise the temperature of the bird in the middle does not get hot enough while it cooks, posing a potential health risk.

As soon as you can, remove the giblets from the inside of a frozen bird as it thaws. That way the air can circulate a little more easily and defrosting will be quicker. Refrigerate the giblets and use them for making gravy (see page 53).

COOKING TIMES FOR THE TURKEY

For cooking times, allow the following for different sized birds:

3.5–5 kg/7–10 lb:
30 minutes at 220°C/425°F/Gas Mark 7
3–3½ hours at 180°C/350°F/Gas Mark 4

5–7 kg/10–14 lb:
30 minutes at 220°C/425°F/Gas Mark 7
3½–4 hours at 180°C/350°F/Gas Mark 4

7–10 kg/14–20 lb:
40 minutes at 220°C/425°F/Gas Mark 7
4–5 hours at 180°C/350°F/Gas Mark 7

Do remember that if you have a fan-assisted oven, cooking times will be shortened. You may also wish to reduce the temperature by 10°C/25°F to avoid overcooking.

The best way to test whether the turkey is thoroughly cooked is to pierce the thickest part of the flesh with a skewer. If the juices run clear, then the bird is cooked, but if there is any trace of pink, return it to the oven to cook for longer.

Once the bird is cooked, allow it to rest for about 20 minutes to make carving easier. Keep it wrapped in foil to retain the heat.

COOKING THE GOOSE

If you've decided to have goose for Christmas for a change, make sure

INTRODUCTION

that you order well in advance to make sure that one is reserved for you.

Geese range in size from about 3 to 6 kg/6 to 12 lb, but as they do not have quite the same quantity of meat per pound compared to turkey, you may have to order a larger bird. Estimate 350 g/12 oz per person when choosing the weight of the bird.

Cook in the same way as for turkey, but do not butter the bird because it already has a very fatty skin, which eliminates the need. Allow 20 minutes per 500 g/1 lb plus 20 minutes at 190°C/375°F/Gas Mark 5.

Apple sauce is a traditional accompaniment to roast goose, as the sharpness of the fruit complements the flavour of the meat. Apricots also taste good, so add 60–90 g/2–3 oz of chopped dried apricots to one of the stuffing mixtures on page 50 if you are serving goose for Christmas dinner.

CHRISTMAS CAKES AND PUDDINGS
These are the two essentials when it comes to Christmas cooking, so it's very important to get the right recipes to produce the best results. You may have some family favourites that have been passed down from one generation to another, but if not, the two in this book will live up to everyone's expectations.

In both recipes, the dried fruit is soaked for several hours to plump it up and make it full of flavour. This has the added benefit of giving both cake and pudding a more mature taste. If you wish, you can soak the fruit for a much longer period than specified – up to 2 weeks – to give the cake or pudding a truly drunken flavour!

For the alcohol content of the cake, you can use brandy, rum or sherry. And after the cake has cooled completely in the tin, remove it and transfer to a large cake tin, without removing the lining paper. Pierce the top of the Christmas cake several times with a fine skewer and pour two or three tablespoonfuls of brandy, rum or sherry (the same as you used in the cake mixture) slowly over the top. This will help the cake to keep well – and it gives it a bit more oomph! Seal the tin and store the cake for up to 3 months.

The cake can be finished with maarzipan and sugarpaste icing (see pages 540 and 571) or follow the recipe on page 542 for royal icing instead.

Serving Christmas cake
Remember that Christmas cake tastes delicious served with a piece of cheese. Choose from white Stilton or the slightly honey-flavoured Wensleydale – both complement the rich fruity cake perfectly.

The Rich Christmas Puddings (see page 659) have a combination of brandy and stout to give them a deliciously dark and moist texture. Serve them with a couple of spoonfuls of fromage frais for a lighter finish, or make a quantity of Rum Butter or Brandy Butter. The recipes are given on page 654 – both taste superb.

USING LEFTOVERS
The golden rule for keeping leftovers of any description is to cool them quickly and then cover and refrigerate them. Never leave them in a warm kitchen for any length of time – that is a recipe for disaster. Food poisoning micro-organisms can multiply very quickly, making the

INTRODUCTION

food unsafe to eat. It won't necessarily taste 'off', but you could soon start to feel unwell. So don't spoil the festivities by being careless with the leftovers.

Never put warm foods into the refrigerator – you must allow them to cool properly first. The reason is that they raise the temperature of the inside of the refrigerator, and could possibly bring it up to the range where the growth of food spoilage bacteria is not inhibited. And don't forget to take good care of all foods, not just the turkey. Wrap them well and refrigerate, or freeze if appropriate, as soon as possible.

You may prefer to freeze some of the leftover turkey, wrapped well in foil, as it's easy to become bored with it. It's amazing how much more appetizing it can be in the middle of January, transformed into a lively stir-fry with lots of fresh vegetables and spices, or a satisfying turkey and ham pie, or even a curry!

PREPARATION AND PLANNING

Whatever you decide to do with the turkey leftovers, this step-by-step guide to Christmas cooking will turn the whole job of catering for your family and friends over the festive season into a pleasure, not a chore.

If you are well-prepared for the Christmas lunch, there is no need to worry. It is just like making a large Sunday roast, except you are probably catering for more people. Turn that to your advantage – remember, a job shared is a job halved (forget the one about too many cooks)! And with any luck, you might be able to put your feet up and enjoy a glass of sherry, knowing that everything is under control. The most important thing is to enjoy yourselves!

CHRISTMAS CHECKLIST

To get a grasp of Christmas preparations, it's an excellent idea to write a checklist of things you must buy and do, with a deadline date for certain requirements. It's very easy to forget something, so it makes sense to write things down on a piece of paper and cross them off as you go along. That way you can clear some space in your mind to think of other things. Use the checklist outlined here to give you the basics, and then add your own notes to make sure you have remembered everything.

Early October–late November
• Make the Christmas Cake.
• Prepare the Rum & Raisin Mincemeat.
• Make the mince pies and freeze them.

Late November–early December
• Decorate the Christmas Cake.
• Make the stuffings for the turkey or goose and freeze them.
• Prepare the Rich Christmas Puddings.
• Make the bottled accompaniments to the Christmas dinner – Cumberland Sauce, Cranberry & Red Onion Relish, etc.
• Make food gifts for presents or bazaars.

Early–mid December
• Do any prepare-ahead cooking for parties and buffets, to freeze or store – make the meringue base for the Satsuma & Pecan Pavlova; prepare the Frozen Citrus Soufflés; make the puff pastry horns for the savoury Chestnut & Mushroom Cornets and freeze them.
• Order the turkey if you are buying a fresh one.
• Buy the turkey if frozen.

INTRODUCTION

• Order extra milk, cream, etc. from the milkman for Christmas.
• Buy the wines, spirits, mixers, etc.
• Shop for all non-perishable foods.

One week before
• Make a list of all the fresh food you need.
• Jot down some reminder notes for things you might forget. (Like the turkey!)

23rd December
• Shop for your fruit and vegetables.
• If cooking a frozen turkey, remove it from the freezer and leave to defrost completely in a cool room.

Christmas Eve
• If cooking a fresh turkey collect it, and any meat that you need, from your butcher.
• Peel the potatoes and put them into water.
• Remove any frozen stuffings and the puff pastry cornets for the vegetarian dish from the freezer. Get some mince pies and brandy butter out too.
• Have a good night's sleep and get up early!

USEFUL RECIPES

ROYAL ICING
This recipe for royal icing can be used in place of the sugaarpaste icing given on page 571. Royal icing gives a hard consistency.

4 egg whites
1 kg/2 lb icing sugar

1. Sift the icing sugar using a non-metallic sieve.

2. Beat the egg whites lightly in a large bowl and add half the sugar, beating until smooth and glossy. Add the remaining sugar gradually.

3. Spread the icing smoothly over the cake, using a palette knife.

RUM OR BRANDY BUTTER
This recipe for traditional Brandy Butter uses soft brown sugar in place of the more usual white sugar. The brown sugar gives the Brandy Butter a delicious toffee-like taste and texture that is a real treat at Christmas.

90 g/3 oz light soft brown sugar
90 g/3 oz butter
3 tbsp rum or brandy

1. Beat the sugar and butter together until light and creamy, and then add the rum or brandy, beating well to mix.

2. Transfer to a dish, cover and chill until required. Keep for up to 3 weeks.

3. Alternatively, wrap well in freezer film or foil and freeze until Christmas, allowing a few hours to thaw before use.

ROAST TURKEY WITH BACON ROLLS

SERVES 8–10

5–7 kg/10–14 lb turkey, thoroughly defrosted if frozen
1 quantity of stuffing (see right)
125 g/4 oz butter
8 rashers streaky bacon

1 Remove the turkey giblets and use them for making the gravy (see page 656). Wipe the bird with paper towels, and then stuff the neck cavity of the bird loosely with the chosen stuffing. Do not pack it in too tightly, as it expands during cooking. Secure with string or skewers.

2 Place the turkey in a large roasting tin. Rub the butter all over it and cover loosely with foil. Roast in a pre-heated oven at 220°C/425°F/Gas Mark 7 for 40 minutes; then reduce the oven temperature to 180°C/350°F/Gas Mark 4 and roast for a further 2½–3 hours.

3 To make the bacon rolls, stretch the rashers with the back of a knife and cut in half. Roll up tightly.

4 Remove the turkey from the oven and discard the foil. Baste well. Tuck the bacon rolls around the bird and roast for a further 20–30 minutes, until the turkey is well-browned. Test that the turkey is thoroughly cooked by piercing the thickest part of the flesh with a skewer – the juices should run clear without any trace of pink. Cook for longer, if necessary.

5 Remove the turkey from the oven and allow it to rest for 15–20 minutes before carving. Serve with the bacon rolls.

DEFROSTING TURKEY

Make sure that a frozen turkey is completely defrosted before it is cooked – this is very important. The best way to defrost it is to put it in the refrigerator 2–3 days before Christmas Day, to allow it to defrost slowly.

Check the thawing times recommended on the packaging for the size of bird that you have bought.

STUFFINGS

ALMOND & LEMON MEATBALLS

MAKES ABOUT 20

30 g/1 oz butter
1 small onion, chopped finely
1 tsp finely grated lemon rind
1 tbsp chopped fresh parsley
1 egg
175 g/6 oz pork sausagemeat
175 g/6 oz fresh white breadcrumbs
125 g/4 oz nibbed almonds
salt and pepper

1 Melt the butter in a small saucepan and fry the onion gently until softened, about 5–8 minutes. Transfer the onion and butter to a blender or food processor and add the lemon rind, parsley, egg, sausagemeat and breadcrumbs. Season with salt and pepper, and blend for a few seconds to combine. Alternatively, mix all the ingredients together in a large bowl until thoroughly combined.

2 Form the mixture into about 20 small balls. Roll in the nibbed almonds and place around the turkey for the last 30 minutes of cooking time, or roast separately in a small baking dish with 2 tbsp vegetable oil.

SAGE & ONION STUFFING

MAKES ABOUT 500 G/1 LB

60 g/2 oz butter
2 large onions, chopped roughly
175 g/6 oz wholemeal breadcrumbs
1 tbsp crumbled dried sage leaves
1 tsp dried thyme
1 egg, beaten
salt and pepper

1 Melt the butter in a saucepan and fry the onions gently until softened, about 5–8 minutes.

2 Add the breadcrumbs, crumbled sage leaves and thyme. Season well with salt and pepper and mix in the beaten egg. Either use to stuff the turkey before cooking (see left) or transfer to a baking dish and bake with the turkey for the last 20 minutes of cooking time.

BREAD SAUCE & TURKEY GRAVY

BREAD SAUCE

SERVES 8-10

1 onion
5-6 cloves
450 ml/ ¾ pint milk
1 small bay leaf
90 g/3 oz fresh white breadcrumbs
15 g/ ½ oz butter
salt and pepper

1 Stud the onion with the cloves and put into a saucepan with the milk, salt and bay leaf. Heat until almost boiling and then remove from the heat. Allow to infuse for about 20–30 minutes and then remove the bay leaf.

2 Add the breadcrumbs and butter to the saucepan, stirring to mix. Cook gently for 10–15 minutes, stirring occasionally, and then remove the onion and cloves. Season with pepper.

TURKEY GRAVY

MAKES ABOUT 600 ML/1 PINT

turkey giblets, rinsed thoroughly
600 ml/1 pint vegetable stock
2–3 tsp cornflour, blended with a little cold water
2–3 drops of gravy browning (optional)
salt and pepper

1 Put the turkey giblets into a roasting tin and roast in a preheated oven at 220°C/ 425°F/ Gas Mark 7 for about 30 minutes, until well-browned. Remove from the oven.

2 Remove and discard the giblets. Add the vegetable stock to the roasting tin and cook on the hob, boiling steadily to produce a rich brown colour.

3 Add the blended cornflour to the gravy and cook, stirring constantly, until blended and thickened. Season to taste, adding a few drops of gravy browning, if necessary.

CRANBERRY & RED ONION RELISH

MAKES ABOUT 3 x 350 G/12 OZ JARS

30 g/1 oz butter
2 red onions
grated rind and juice of 1 large orange
500 g/1 lb fresh or frozen cranberries
125 g/4 oz sugar
4 tbsp red wine vinegar
4 tbsp red wine
½ tsp ground allspice
pinch of ground cinnamon

1 Slice the red onions thinly. Melt the butter in a medium saucepan and fry the onions gently until softened, about 8–10 minutes.

2 Add the orange rind and juice, and cook gently for 5 minutes.

3 Add the cranberries to the saucepan with the sugar, wine vinegar, red wine and spices. Heat until just boiling and then reduce the heat. Simmer until syrupy, about 15 minutes.

4 Pot the relish in sterilized small glass jars. Place a circle of greaseproof paper over the surface of each one, and then seal and label the jars. Decorate the lids with fabric or butter muslin and tie with string or ribbon.

ALLSPICE

Allspice is a single spice with the combined flavours of nutmeg, cinnamon and cloves, and it shouldn't be confused with mixed spice.

STORING

Make this relish 2–3 weeks before Christmas if you like. Remember to store it in the refrigerator after opening and use within 2 weeks.

GLAZED BAKED HAM

SERVES 12–16

3 kg/6 lb unsmoked gammon joint
about 36 cloves
3 tbsp clear honey
60 g/2 oz demerara sugar
finely grated rind and juice of 1 orange

TO GARNISH:
orange slices
bay leaves

1 Put the gammon joint in a large bowl and cover it with cold water. Leave it to soak overnight.

2 Drain the water from the gammon and discard it. Place the gammon in a large saucepan and cover it with cold water. Bring to the boil. Reduce the heat and cover the pan. Simmer gently for 3½ hours (30 minutes per 500 g/1 lb plus 30 minutes).

3 Drain off the cooking water and lift the ham on to a large board. Leave to cool for about 20 minutes, and then peel off the skin, leaving a good layer of fat around the ham.

4 Using a sharp knife, score the fat into a diamond pattern and stud with the cloves. Transfer the joint to a large roasting tin.

5 Heat the honey, sugar, and orange rind and juice gently in a small saucepan until the sugar has dissolved.

6 Brush the honey and sugar mixture liberally over the scored joint.

7 Bake in a preheated oven at 200°C/ 400°F/Gas Mark 4 for 20–30 minutes, until golden brown.

8 Serve cold, garnished with orange slices and bay leaves, accompanied by a dish of Cranberry Relish (see left) or Cumberland Sauce (see page 659).

CHESTNUT & MUSHROOM CORNETS WITH SHERRY SAUCE

SERVES 4

500 g/1 lb frozen puff pastry, thawed
1 small egg, beaten
60 g/2 oz butter
2 garlic cloves, crushed
125 g/4 oz shallots, chopped
350 g/12 oz chestnut mushrooms, sliced
125 g/4 oz canned chestnuts, chopped
180 ml/6 fl oz medium sherry
1 tbsp chopped fresh parsley
salt and pepper

1 Roll out the pastry thinly on a lightly floured work surface and cut into narrow strips. Moisten the edges of the pastry with a little water and use the strips to wind around 8 well-greased cream horn tins. Place them on a greased baking sheet, seam-side underneath. Brush with beaten egg, to glaze.

2 Bake in a preheated oven at 200°C/ 400°F/ Gas Mark 6, until golden brown, about 10–15 minutes.

3 Melt the butter in a large saucepan and add the garlic and shallots. Cook over a low heat for 15 minutes, until the shallots are very tender.

4 Add the mushrooms and chestnuts to the saucepan and cook over a medium heat for 3–4 minutes. Pour in the sherry and add the parsley. Simmer over a very low heat for 15–20 minutes.

5 Remove the cornets carefully from the tins. Spoon the mushroom mixture into them and arrange on warmed serving plates, allowing 2 per serving. Pour sherry sauce around them and serve with fresh vegetables.

VARIATION

Instead of making individual cornets, the puff pastry can be rolled into a large rectangle. Spoon the filling into the middle, dampen the edges of the pastry, fold over and seal. Bake in the oven at 200°C/400°F/Gas Mark 6 for 25–30 minutes, until risen and golden.

SEASONAL VEGETABLES

••

CRISPY ROAST POTATOES

SERVES 6-8

2 kg/4 lb potatoes
vegetable oil for roasting
salt

1 Peel the potatoes and cut them into large, even-sized chunks. Put them into a large saucepan of cold water with ½ tsp salt. Bring to the boil, and then reduce the heat. Cover and simmer for 8–10 minutes. Drain thoroughly.

2 Heat about 150 ml/ ¼ pint vegetable oil in a large roasting tin until very hot. Add the potatoes, basting thoroughly. Roast in a preheated oven at 200°C/400°F/Gas Mark 6 for about 1 hour, basting occasionally, until crisp and golden brown.

HONEY-GLAZED CARROTS

SERVES 6-8

1 kg/2 lb carrots
1 tbsp clear honey
30 g/1 oz butter
2 tsp sesame seeds, toasted

1 Put the carrots into a saucepan and barely cover with water. Add the honey and butter. Cook, uncovered, for about 15 minutes, until the liquid has just evaporated and the carrots are glazed. Serve, sprinkled with sesame seeds.

SPICED WINTER CABBAGE

SERVES 6-8

1 hard white cabbage
2 dessert (eating) apples, peeled, cored
    and chopped
few drops of lemon juice
30 g/1 oz butter
freshly grated nutmeg
salt

1 Shred the cabbage. Add the apples and lemon juice, and cook in a small amount of water in a covered saucepan for about 6 minutes. Drain thoroughly and season. Add the butter, tossing to melt. Transfer to a hot tureen and sprinkle with freshly grated nutmeg.

RUM & RAISIN MINCEMEAT

••

MAKES ABOUT 1.5 KG/3 LB

500 g/1 lb raisins
250 g/8 oz sultanas
250 g/8 oz currants
125 g/4 oz glacé cherries, halved
150 ml/ ¼ pint dark rum, brandy or sherry
2 medium dessert (eating) apples, peeled,
    cored and chopped finely
2 tsp mixed spice
½ tsp freshly grated nutmeg
125 g/4 oz chopped roast hazelnuts
250 g/8 oz dark muscovado sugar
4 tbsp hot water
60 g/2 oz butter

1 Put the raisins, sultanas, currants, glacé cherries and rum, brandy or sherry into a large bowl. Mix together thoroughly, then cover and leave in a cool place, stirring occasionally, for 12–24 hours.

2 Blanch the chopped apple in boiling water for 2 minutes, and then drain thoroughly.

3 Add the chopped apple to the soaked dried fruit mixture with the mixed spice, nutmeg and hazelnuts, stirring thoroughly.

4 Put the dark muscovado sugar, hot water and butter into a saucepan. Heat very gently, stirring frequently, until the sugar has melted. Add to the fruit mixture and stir well to combine.

5 Pack into sterilized jars, seal and label. Decorate the lids with scraps of colourful fabric, butter muslin or greaseproof paper and tie with string.

STERILIZING JARS

To sterilize jars, wash them thoroughly in hot, soapy water, rinse well with hot water and place on a baking sheet. Warm in a preheated oven at 110°C/225°F/Gas Mark ¼ for 10–15 minutes.

CUMBERLAND SAUCE

MAKES ABOUT 4 x 250 G/8 OZ JARS

500 g/1 lb redcurrant jelly
450 ml/ ¾ pint port
1 orange
1 lemon
2 tbsp Worcestershire sauce
pinch of cayenne pepper

1 Put the redcurrant jelly into a saucepan and heat gently, stirring to melt it.

2 Add the port to the jelly and heat gently, stirring frequently, until just boiling. Reduce the heat and simmer gently for about 15–20 minutes, or until the sauce has reduced by about one-third. It should be syrupy and quite runny. Leave the sauce to cool.

3 Pare the rind from the orange and lemon, and cut it into fine strips.

4 Squeeze the juice from the fruit. Add to the jelly mixture with the fine strips of rind, the Worcestershire sauce and the cayenne pepper.

5 Pot the sauce in sterilized small glass jars. When cooled, decorate the lids with scraps of bright fabric, butter muslin or greaseproof paper. Tie on with ribbon or string and label the jars.

PARING RIND

The best way to pare the rind thinly from citrus fruit is to use a potato peeler.

HOMEMADE PRESENTS

You can make this sauce at the beginning of December. Once opened, it will keep in the refrigerator for 10–14 days.

Cumberland Sauce makes a tasty gift for anyone who loves good food, so try making plenty of pots to add a homemade touch to your Christmas presents.

RICH CHRISTMAS PUDDINGS

MAKES 8

125 g/4 oz dark muscovado or molasses
* sugar*
250 g/8 oz seedless raisins
250 g/8 oz currants
125 g/4 oz fresh wholemeal breadcrumbs
125 g/4 oz carrots, finely grated
60 g/2 oz ground almonds
grated rind of ½ lemon
2 tbsp lemon juice
½ tsp ground cinnamon
½ tsp ground nutmeg
½ tsp mixed spice
4 tbsp sherry
150 ml/ ¼ pint stout
2 eggs
1 tbsp butter

1 Put the sugar, raisins, currants, breadcrumbs, carrots, almonds, lemon rind and juice, spices, sherry and stout into large bowl. Mix thoroughly, then cover and leave in a cool place for 6–8 hours, or overnight, if preferred.

2 Beat the eggs and add to the mixture, stirring well to combine.

3 Butter 8 150 ml/ ¼ pint dariole moulds, small pudding basins or teacups. Spoon in the pudding mixture, top each one with a circle of greaseproof paper and then cover tightly with foil.

4 Steam over simmering water for 3 hours, topping up with boiling water as necessary. Remove from the heat and leave to cool.

5 When completely cool, turn out the puddings and wrap tightly in greaseproof paper or foil. Wrap in butter muslin and tie with string.

6 Steam the puddings for 1½–2 hours on Christmas Day. Serve with Brandy Butter (see page 654).

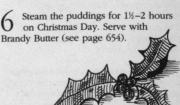

FROZEN CITRUS SOUFFLÉS

••

SERVES 4

1 tbsp powdered gelatine
6 tbsp very hot water
3 eggs, separated
90 g/3 oz caster sugar
finely grated rind and juice of 1 lemon,
    ½ lime and ½ orange
150 ml/ ¼ pint double (thick) cream
125 g/4 oz plain fromage frais
thin lemon, lime and orange slices to
    decorate

1   Tie greaseproof paper collars around
    4 individual soufflé or ramekin
dishes or around 1 large (15cm/6in
diameter) soufflé dish.

2   Sprinkle the powdered gelatine into
    the very hot (not boiling) water,
stirring well to disperse. Leave to stand
for 2–3 minutes, stirring occasionally, to
give a completely clear liquid. Leave to
cool for 10–15 minutes.

3   Meanwhile, whisk the egg yolks and
    sugar, using a hand-held electric
mixer or wire whisk until very pale and
light in texture. Add the rind and juice
from the fruits, mixing well. Stir in the
cooled gelatine liquid, making sure that it
is thoroughly incorporated.

4   Whip the cream in a large chilled
    bowl until it holds its shape. Stir the
fromage frais, and then add it to the
cream, mixing it in gently. Fold the cream
mixture through the citrus mixture, using
a large metal spoon. Using a clean whisk,
beat the egg whites in a clean bowl until
stiff, and then fold them through the other
ingredients.

5   Pour the mixture into the prepared
    dishes, almost to the top of their
collars. Allow some room for the mixture
to expand on freezing. Transfer the dishes
to the freezer and open-freeze for about
2 hours, until frozen.

6   Remove from the freezer 10 minutes
    before serving. Peel away the paper
collars carefully and decorate with the
slices of lemon, lime and orange.

TRADITIONAL CHRISTMAS CAKE

••

MAKES ONE 18 CM/7 IN SQUARE OR 20
CM/8 IN ROUND CAKE

finely grated rind of 1 orange
2 tbsp orange juice
500 g/1 lb seedless raisins
250 g/8 oz sultanas
250 g/8 oz currants
60 g/2 oz dates, stoned and chopped
175 g/6 oz glacé cherries, halved
150 ml/ ¼ pint dark rum
250 g/8 oz molasses sugar
250 g/8 oz butter
4 eggs, beaten
250 g/8 oz plain flour
pinch of salt
1 tsp ground mixed spice
1 tsp ground cinnamon
½ tsp ground nutmeg
60 g/2 oz ground hazelnuts or almonds
30 g/1 oz chopped hazelnuts or almonds

TO DECORATE:
3 tbsp apricot jam
glacé fruits
whole, shelled nuts

1   Put the orange rind and juice, raisins,
    sultanas, currants, dates, glacé
cherries and rum into a large bowl. Stir
well, then cover and leave in a cool place
for 1–2 days, stirring occasionally.

2   Line an 18 cm/7 in square or
    20 cm/8 in round cake tin with
double-thickness greaseproof paper.

3   Cream the sugar and butter together
    until fluffy, and then beat in the eggs
gradually. Sift the flour, salt and spices
together and fold into the mixture. Add
the ground and chopped nuts and the
fruit mixture. Stir gently, and then transfer
to the prepared tin, levelling the surface.

4   Bake in a preheated oven at 150°C/
    300°F/Gas Mark 2 for 2–2½ hours, or
until a fine skewer inserted into the centre
comes out clean. Cover the top with a
piece of brown paper after 1½ hours.
Leave to cool completely in the tin.

5   To decorate, warm the apricot jam
    and brush over the surface of the
cake. Arrange the glacé fruits and nuts
over the top in an attractive pattern.
Brush with apricot jam to glaze.

FESTIVE MINCE PIES

MAKES ABOUT 20

350 g/12 oz plain flour
pinch of salt
175 g/6 oz butter, chilled
45 g/1½ oz caster sugar
3 egg yolks, beaten
1–2 tbsp chilled water
500 g/1 lb Rum & Raisin Mincemeat (see
    page 658)
lightly beaten egg white
icing sugar for dredging

1 Sift the flour and salt into a large
bowl. Cut the butter into pieces and
then add to the flour. Rub in the butter
using your fingertips, until the mixture
resembles fine breadcrumbs.

2 Add the caster sugar to the flour
mixture. Mix the egg yolks with
1 tbsp of the chilled water. Make a well
in the centre of the flour mixture and add
the egg yolks, stirring with a round-
bladed knife to make a soft dough. Add
a little extra chilled water if the dough is
too dry.

3 Knead the dough lightly until
smooth, and then roll out two-thirds
of it thinly on a lightly floured surface.
Using a 7.5 cm/3 in biscuit cutter, stamp
out rounds and use to line patty tins.

4 Spoon the mincemeat into the patty
tins, to come about half-way up the
sides. Roll out the remaining pastry and
use Christmas biscuit cutters to cut out
shapes, such as stars, bells and trees.
Position on top of the mince pies and
brush with lightly beaten egg white.

5 Bake in a preheated oven at 220°C/
425°F/Gas Mark 7 for 15–20 minutes,
or until light golden brown. Leave to cool
slightly, and then remove from the tins.
Transfer to a wire rack and leave to cool
until they are not too hot to handle
comfortably. Serve while still warm,
sprinkled with icing sugar.

SATSUMA & PECAN PAVLOVA

SERVES 6–8

4 egg whites
250 g/8 oz light muscovado sugar
300 ml/ ½ pint double (thick) or whipping
    cream
60 g/2 oz pecan nuts
4 satsumas, peeled
1 passion fruit or pomegranate

1 Line 2 baking sheets with non-stick
baking parchment or greaseproof
paper. Draw a 23 cm/9 in circle on to one
of them.

2 Whip the egg whites in a large
grease-free bowl until stiff. Add the
sugar gradually, continuing to beat until
the mixture is very glossy.

3 Pipe or spoon a layer of meringue
mixture on to the circle marked on
the baking parchment; then pipe large
rosettes or place spoonfuls on top of the
meringue's outer edge. Pipe any
remaining meringue mixture in tiny
rosettes on the second baking sheet.

4 Bake in a preheated oven at 140°C/
275°F/Gas Mark 1 for 2–3 hours,
making sure that the oven is well-ventilated
by using a folded tea towel to keep the
door slightly open. Remove from the oven
and leave to cool completely. When cold,
peel off the baking parchment carefully.

5 Whip the double (thick) or whipping
cream in a large chilled bowl until
thick. Spoon about one-third into a piping
bag, fitted with a star tube. Reserve a few
pecan nuts and 1 satsuma for decoration.
Chop the remaining nuts and fruit, and
fold through the remaining cream gently.

6 Pile on top of the meringue base
and decorate with the tiny meringue
rosettes, piped cream, segments of
satsuma and pecan nuts. Scoop the seeds
from the passion fruit or pomegranate
with a teaspoon and sprinkle them on top.

STOLLEN

MAKES 2

60 g/2 oz glacé cherries
60 g/2 oz sultanas
60 g/2 oz seedless raisins
30 g/1 oz angelica, chopped
30 g/1 oz candied peel, chopped finely
6 tbsp rum
1 kg/2 lb plain flour
½ tsp salt
1 sachet (8 g) easy-blend yeast
125 g/ 4 oz caster sugar
½ tsp ground mace
1 tsp finely grated lemon rind
300 ml/ ½ pint milk
2 eggs, beaten
125 g/4 oz butter, melted
60 g/2 oz flaked almonds
350 g/12 oz Marzipan (see page 540)
icing sugar for dredging

1 Put the glacé cherries, sultanas, raisins, angelica and candied peel into a bowl. Add the rum and leave to soak overnight.

2 Sift the flour and salt into a large bowl and stir in the easy-blend yeast. Stir in the sugar, mace and lemon rind. Heat the milk until it is lukewarm, and then add to the beaten eggs with the melted butter, stirring well. Make a well in the centre of the flour and add the milk mixture, stirring to combine.

3 Gather the dough together and knead on a floured work surface until smooth and elastic, about 10–15 minutes. Drain the soaked fruit well and pat dry with paper towels. Press into the dough with the flaked almonds and knead lightly to incorporate it, but avoid overhandling or the dough could become discoloured. Keep your hands lightly floured to make it more manageable. Place in a large greased bowl, cover and leave to rise in a warm place until doubled in size, about 2 hours.

4 Knock back the dough and knead lightly until smooth. Divide into 2 equal parts. Roll each piece into a strip about 30 x 20 cm/12 x 8 in. Divide the marzipan into 2 pieces and roll into sausage shapes about 25 cm/10 in long. Lay on the dough, fold over and seal. Transfer to greased baking sheets and leave to rise until doubled in size.

5 Bake the loaves in a preheated oven at 190°C/375°F/Gas Mark 5 for about 30–35 minutes, until golden brown. Leave to cool on a wire rack and then dredge with plenty of icing sugar.

MULLED WINE

SERVES ABOUT 12

600 ml/1 pint orange juice
300 ml/ ½ pint water
3 cinnamon sticks
6 cloves
60 g/2 oz dark muscovado sugar
1 orange
1 lemon
1 litre/1¾ pints red wine
300 ml/ ½ pint brandy

1 Put the orange juice, water and spices into a large saucepan. Heat gently until almost boiling.

2 Add the sugar and stir until it has all dissolved.

3 Using a potato peeler, pare the rind from the orange and lemon. Add it to the saucepan. Slice the orange and lemon thinly and keep covered for using as decoration.

4 Pour in the red wine and brandy, heating very gently until the liquid is very hot, but not boiling. Remove from the heat.

5 Strain the mulled wine and discard the cloves and citrus rind. Keep the cinnamon sticks. Ladle into warmed glasses and serve hot, decorated with the orange and lemon slices and the reserved cinnamon sticks.

SERVING SUGGESTION

Mulled wine makes the perfect drink to serve with warm mince pies and brandy butter.

ALTERNATIVES

There is no need to use expensive wine in this recipe, so it can be quite economical to make. You could even try making a white wine version, substituting a 1 litre/1¾ pint bottle of medium-dry white wine for the red, and using ordinary granulated sugar instead of the muscovado.

WINTER FRUIT PUNCH

SERVES ABOUT 12

1 lime
1 kiwi fruit
few maraschino cherries
few mint sprigs
600 ml/1 pint English apple juice
600 ml/1 pint orange or pineapple juice
1 litre/1¾ pints lemonade

TO DECORATE:
1 apple, thinly sliced
1 kiwi fruit, thinly sliced
1 lime, thinly sliced
1 orange, thinly sliced
extra mint sprigs

1 Slice the lime thinly and cut the slices into quarters. Peel the kiwi fruit and cut into small chunks.

2 Put the pieces of lime and kiwi fruit, the maraschino cherries and mint sprigs into ice-cube trays and top up with water. Transfer to the freezer until frozen to use for decoration later.

3 Mix the apple juice, orange juice or pineapple juice and lemonade in a large glass jug or punch bowl.

4 Decorate the fruit punch with apple, kiwi fruit, lime and orange slices and extra mint sprigs. Ladle into tall glasses and top up with the ice cubes.

VARIATIONS

Make your own variations to this delicious drink by varying the types of fruit juice that you use. Substitute peach juice for the apple juice, for instance. Try tonic water instead of lemonade for a less sweet version and remember that if you are trying to watch your weight, you can buy low-calorie lemonade or tonic water to use in the recipe.

APPLE & MINCEMEAT SQUARES

MAKES ABOUT 12 SQUARES

250 g/8 oz butter
250 g/8 oz light muscovado sugar
500 g/1 lb self-raising flour
pinch of salt
1 large (size 1) or 2 small (size 3) eggs
500 g/1 lb cooking apples
finely grated rind of 1 lemon
2 tbsp lemon juice
4 tbsp mincemeat
60 g/2 oz demerara sugar
1 tsp ground cinnamon
30 g/1 oz coarse porridge oats
icing sugar for dredging

1 Put the butter into a saucepan and heat gently until melted. Add the muscovado sugar, stir thoroughly and leave to cool slightly.

2 Sift the flour and salt into a large bowl and make a well in the centre. Add the melted butter mixture. Beat the eggs and add to the mixture, stirring well to combine thoroughly.

3 Transfer two–thirds of the mixture to a greased and lined 30 x 25 cm/ 12 x 10 in shallow cake tin, pressing down well.

4 Peel and slice the apples thinly, and place in a bowl with the lemon rind and juice. (The juice helps to prevent the apples from turning brown.) Add the mincemeat, demerara sugar and cinnamon, stirring well to mix. Spoon over the prepared base in an even layer.

5 Mix the porridge oats into the reserved cake mixture and scatter evenly over the fruit.

6 Bake in a preheated oven at 190°C/ 375°F/Gas Mark 5 for about 35–40 minutes.

7 When cool, cut into squares and remove from the cake tin. Dredge with icing sugar before serving.

CHRISTMAS SHORTBREAD

MAKES ABOUT 24

125 g/4 oz caster sugar
250 g/8 oz butter
350 g/12 oz plain flour, sifted
pinch of salt

TO DECORATE:
60 g/2 oz icing sugar
silver balls
glacé cherries
angelica

1 Beat the sugar and butter together in a large bowl until combined (thorough creaming is not necessary).

2 Sift in the flour and salt and work together to form a stiff dough. Turn out on to a lightly floured surface. Knead lightly for a few moments until smooth, but avoid overhandling. Chill for 10–15 minutes.

3 Roll out the dough on a lightly floured work surface and cut into shapes with Christmas cutters. Place on greased baking sheets.

4 Bake the biscuits in a preheated oven at 180°C/ 350°F/ Gas Mark 4 for 10–15 minutes until pale golden brown. Leave on the baking sheets to cool for 10 minutes, then transfer to a wire rack to cool completely.

5 Mix the icing sugar with a little water to make a glacé icing, and use to ice the biscuits. Decorate with silver balls, tiny pieces of glacé cherries and angelica. Store in an airtight tin.

READY FOR THE TREE

If you want to use these biscuits to decorate the Christmas tree, wrap them in cellophane and tie them with narrow ribbon or coloured string. If you prefer, make larger biscuits, wrap in cellophane and tie with tartan ribbon.

CHOCOLATE YULE LOG

Makes one 23 cm/9 in log

few drops of vegetable oil
125 g/4 oz caster sugar, plus extra 2 tsp
4 eggs
60 g/2 oz plain flour
30 g/1 oz cocoa powder

FILLING:
90 ml/3 fl oz double (thick) cream
60 g/2 oz sweetened chestnut purée
2 tbsp brandy

CHOCOLATE BUTTER CREAM:
90 g/3 oz caster sugar
4 tbsp water
2 egg yolks
125 g/4 oz unsalted butter, softened
125 g/4 oz icing sugar, sifted
60 g/ 2 oz plain (dark) chocolate, melted

1 Grease and line a 33 x 23 cm/13 x 9 in Swiss (jelly) roll tin with a little oil and non-stick greaseproof paper. Cut a second piece of greaseproof paper a little larger than the tin and sprinkle with 2 tsp sugar. Set aside.

2 Whisk the sugar and eggs in a large bowl until very pale and light, using a hand-held electric mixer or wire whisk.

3 Sift the flour and cocoa powder together. Fold into the egg mixture gently. Pour into the prepared tin, level the surface and bake in a preheated oven at 220°C/ 425°F/Gas Mark 7 for 7–9 minutes until firm, yet springy to the touch. Turn out on to the sugared paper. Peel away the lining paper and trim the edges. Cover with a damp tea towel and leave to cool completely.

4 To make the filling, whip the cream until thick and stir in the chestnut purée. Sprinkle the brandy over the cake. Spread the cream mixture over the sponge and roll up from one long edge.

5 To make the chocolate butter cream, heat the sugar and water gently until the sugar dissolves, then boil rapidly until syrupy. Whisk the egg yolks, adding the sugar syrup in a steady stream, until the mixture becomes thick and pale. Add the butter and the cooled, melted chocolate. Beat in the icing sugar.

6 Cut a 7.5 cm/3 in slice from the chocolate roll and cut in half diagonally. Attach to the sides of the roll with some butter cream. Cover the log with the remaining butter cream and use a skewer or fork to make a bark pattern.

APRICOT BRANDY TRUFFLES

175 g/6 oz plain (dark) chocolate
60 g/2 oz dark muscovado sugar
30 g/1 oz butter
2 egg yolks
1 tbsp apricot brandy
1 tbsp milk
30 g/1 oz dried apricots, chopped finely
30 g/1 oz cake or biscuit crumbs
60 g/2 oz chocolate vermicelli or 30 g/1 oz
  cocoa powder

1 Melt the chocolate in a medium
  bowl placed over a pan of gently
simmering water. Add the sugar and
butter, stirring until melted.

2 Stir in the egg yolks, apricot brandy
  and milk. Heat gently, stirring
constantly, for 2 minutes.

3 Add the apricots and then mix in the
  cake or biscuit crumbs. Beat the
mixture thoroughly and leave to cool.
Then chill until firm enough to handle.

4 Form the mixture into about 20 balls
  and roll in chocolate vermicelli or
cocoa powder. Place in sweet cases and
store in a cool place.

5 To pack, wrap the truffles separately
  in cellophane, gather into a pouch
and tie with ribbon. Pack them in
attractive gift boxes.

6 Keep the truffles refrigerated and eat
  within 2 weeks.

HANDY TIP

Dusting your hands with a little cocoa
powder will help to prevent the
mixture from becoming too sticky
when forming it into balls.

SUBSTITUTES

Substitute rum or brandy for the
apricot brandy and use raisins instead
of dried apricots. Drinking chocolate
can be used instead of cocoa powder.

OLD ENGLISH TRIFLE

6 trifle sponges
3 tbsp raspberry jam
150 ml/ ¼ pint sweet sherry
125 g/4 oz seedless white grapes
125 g/4 oz black grapes, halved and
  deseeded
2 peaches, peeled, stoned and chopped
2 bananas
2 tbsp lemon juice
45 g/1½ oz cornflour
600 ml/1 pint milk
1 tsp vanilla flavouring
3 egg yolks
45 g/1½ oz sugar
300 ml/ ½ pint double (thick) cream

TO DECORATE:
glacé cherries
angelica
toasted flaked almonds

1 Split the trifle sponges in 2 and
  spread with the jam. Arrange in
the base of an attractive 2 litre/3½ pint
serving dish.

2 Sprinkle the sherry over the trifle
  sponges and spoon in the grapes
and peaches. Slice the banana and mix
with the lemon juice. Add to the trifle.

3 Blend the cornflour in a large jug
  with 4 tbsp of the milk. Heat the
remaining milk with the vanilla flavouring
until warm, and then pour on to the
blended cornflour, whisking well. Beat the
egg yolks and whisk them into the
mixture. Return to the saucepan and heat
gently until the mixture is thickened and
blended. Remove from the heat and add
the sugar. Pour over the fruit and leave to
cool completely.

4 Whip the cream until it holds its
  shape, and then spoon about one-
third of it into a piping bag fitted with a
star tube. Spread the remaining cream
over the custard. Pipe a border of cream
around the outside and decorate with
glacé cherries, angelica and toasted
almonds. Chill until ready to serve.

SPICED FRUIT GARLAND

SERVES 12

425 g/ 14 oz strong plain (bread) flour
½ tsp salt
60 g/2 oz butter
60 g/2 oz caster sugar
1 sachet (8 g) easy-blend yeast
180 ml/6 fl oz warm milk
1 egg, beaten

FILLING:
150 g/5 oz mixed dried fruit
30 g/1 oz glacé cherries, chopped
60 g/2 oz ground almonds
60 g/2 oz light muscovado sugar
1 tsp ground cinnamon
½ tsp ground nutmeg
30 g/1 oz butter, melted

TO DECORATE:
60 g/2 oz icing sugar
glacé cherries
chopped nuts
angelica

1 Sift the flour and salt together in a large bowl. Rub in the butter and then stir in the sugar and easy-blend yeast. Make a well in the centre and add the warm milk and beaten egg. Draw the flour into the egg and milk gradually, mixing well to make a smooth dough.

2 Knead the dough on a lightly floured work surface for 8–10 minutes. Place in a lightly oiled bowl and cover with a cloth. Stand in a warm place and leave to rise until doubled in size.

3 Knead lightly for 1 minute, and then roll out into a 40 x 23 cm/16 x 9 in rectangle. Mix together all the filling ingredients and spread over the rectangle, leaving a 2 cm/ ¾ in border around the edge. From the long edge, roll the rectangle into a cylinder, pressing the edge to seal it. Form the roll into a circle, sealing the ends together.

4 Lift the ring on to a greased baking sheet and then cut it into 12 slices at about 5 cm/2 in intervals, without cutting right through, keeping the circular shape. Twist each slice so that a cut surface lies uppermost. Leave in a warm place for 30–40 minutes to rise.

5 Bake in a preheated oven at 200°C/ 400°F/Gas Mark 6 for 25–30 minutes until risen and golden brown. Cool on a wire rack. Mix the icing sugar with a little water to make a thin glacé icing and drizzle over. Arrange the glacé cherries on top, and sprinkle with the chopped nuts and angelica.

CHRISTMAS TREE CLUSTERS

MAKES ABOUT 16

1 tbsp vegetable oil
30 g/1 oz popcorn kernels (unpopped
   corn)
30 g/1 oz butter
60 g/2 oz soft light brown sugar
4 tbsp golden syrup
30 g/1 oz glacé cherries, chopped
60 g/2 oz sultanas or raisins
30 g/1 oz ground almonds
15 g/½ oz nibbed almonds
½ tsp ground mixed spice

1 To pop the corn, heat the oil in a
   large saucepan that has a lid, or in a
special popcorn pan. The oil is hot
enough when a kernel spins around in
the pan. Add the popcorn kernels, put on
the lid and pop the corn over a medium-
high heat, shaking the pan frequently.

2 Remove the pan from the heat and
   wait until the popping sound
subsides.

3 Put the butter, sugar and golden
   syrup into a large saucepan and heat
gently, stirring frequently, to dissolve the
sugar. Do not allow the mixture to boil.
Remove from the heat once the sugar is
dissolved.

4 Add the popped corn, glacé cherries,
   sultanas or raisins, ground and
nibbed almonds, and mixed spice to the
syrup mixture, stirring well. Leave to cool
for a few minutes.

5 Shape the mixture into small balls.
   Leave to cool completely, then wrap
in cellophane and tie with ribbon.

POPPING CORN

Children will enjoy making some
Christmas Tree Clusters. Take care
when popping corn – the oil in the pan
is very hot and can burn.

BRANDY SNAP BOATS & BASKETS

MAKES ABOUT 30

125 g/4 oz butter
125 g/4 oz caster sugar
4 tbsp golden syrup
125 g/4 oz plain flour
pinch of salt
½ tsp ground ginger
1 tsp brandy

TO DECORATE:
300 ml/½ pt double (thick) cream
fresh fruit, such as cape gooseberries, kiwi
   fruit, grapes and nectarines

1 Grease and line 2 baking sheets with
   non-stick baking parchment. Butter a
rolling pin, to be used for shaping the
brandy snap boats. Butter the undersides
of 3 or 4 clean eggcups, to be used for
shaping the baskets.

2 Heat the butter, sugar and syrup
   gently in a small heavy-based saucepan, until the sugar has melted. (Do not
allow the mixture to boil.) Remove from
the heat.

3 Sift the flour, salt and ground ginger
   together, and add to the saucepan
with the brandy. Mix well until smooth.
Leave to cool slightly.

4 Drop teaspoonfuls of the mixture on
   to the baking sheets, allowing space
for the mixture to spread. Bake in a
preheated oven at 180°C/350°F/Gas Mark
4 for 7–10 minutes, until the mixture is
golden brown and bubbly.

5 Quickly place some of the cooked
   biscuits over the rolling pin. Arrange
some of the biscuits over the eggcups and
flute them to form baskets. Leave to cool
completely, then ease them off gently.

6 When ready to serve, whip the
   cream and fill the brandy snap boats
and baskets. Decorate with fresh fruit.
Serve soon, so that the biscuits do not
become soggy. (Unfilled boats and
baskets can be kept in an airtight tin for
7–10 days.)

MR SNOWMAN CAKE

6-egg Victoria Sandwich (Sponge Layer
    Cake), Quick Mix Cake or Madeira
    (Pound) Cake mixture, any flavour (see
    pages 568 and 571)
6 tbsp apricot jam, sieved (strained)
1.25 kg/2½ lb/10 cups sugarpaste (see
    page 571)
black, orange, yellow and green liquid or
    paste food colourings
250 g/8 oz/2 cups royal icing (see page
    654) or 1 quantity butter cream (see
    page 541)
desiccated (shredded) or flaked coconut

1 Grease and line a roasting tin (pan)
   about 30 × 25 cm/12 × 10 inches.
Spread the cake mixture evenly in it.
Bake in a preheated oven at 160°C/
325°F/Gas Mark 3 for about 50–60
minutes (1–1¼ hours for Quick Mix and
Madeira (Pound) Cake), or until firm to
the touch. Invert on a wire rack and leave
to set for 12–24 hours.

2 Draw a template of a snowman, cut
   out and place on the cake. Cut
around the template carefully and then
cut out the arms and a hat from the cake
trimmings. Place the body on a cake
board and brush all over with jam. Brush
the hat and arms with jam too.

3 Roll out about 750 g/1½ lb/6 cups
   of the white sugarpaste
and use to cover the body
and head.

4 Use the trimmings and another 125
   g/4 oz/1 cup of the white sugarpaste
to cover the arms of the snowman.
Dampen the arms and attach them to the
body.

5 Colour 45 g/1½ oz/⅓ cup of the
   sugarpaste black and use to make
3–4 round buttons, 2 eyes and a smiling
mouth; dampen and attach. Colour 30 g/
1 oz/¼ cup of the sugarpaste orange,
shape into a carrot, dampen and attach
for a nose.

6 Colour the remaining sugarpaste
   bright yellow and use to cover the
hat and make a brim for it, and also to
make a scarf. Attach to the snowman.
Colour the royal icing or butter cream
green and use to decorate the hat and
scarf, using a small star nozzle (tip). Leave
to set.

7 Sprinkle the coconut around the
   snowman to represent snow.

SANTA'S SLEIGH CAKE

• •

5-egg Victoria Sandwich (Sponge Layer
    Cake) or Madeira (Pound) Cake
    mixture, any flavour (see pages
    568, 570 and 571)
6 tbsp apricot jam, sieved (strained)
875 g/1¾ lb/7 cups sugarpaste (see page
    571)
red, brown, green, yellow and blue liquid
    or paste food colourings
1 quantity butter cream (see page 541)
few coloured sweets (candies)
2 long chocolate matchsticks
parcels (see page 569)
teddy bears (see page 569)
chocolate money and candy stick or rings
    (optional)

1 Grease and line a 23 cm/9 in square
cake tin (pan). Spread the cake
mixture evenly in it. Bake in a preheated
oven at 160°C/325°F/Gas Mark 3 for
about 1–1¼ hours (1¼–1½ hours for
Madeira (Pound) Cake) until well risen
and firm. Turn out and leave on a wire
rack for 12–24 hours to set.

2 Trim the cake and cut a 13 cm/
6 in slice off one side. Cut the slice
to the same width as the sleigh, then cut
in half diagonally and place one piece on
each end, as in the photograph. Place the
cake on a board. Trim the remaining
piece to make a sack.

3 Brush the cake all over with jam.
Colour about 500 g/1 lb/4 cups of
the sugarpaste red. Roll out and use to
cover the cake. Colour 175 g/6 oz/1½
cups of the sugarpaste brown; use 90 g/
3 oz/ ¾ cup to make 2 rolls about 28 cm/
11 in long and place along the base of
the sleigh each side for runners. Tilt each
end up slightly and put paper towels
underneath to hold them in place.

4 Colour the butter cream deep cream
and place in a piping bag fitted with
a star nozzle (tip). Pipe decorations
around the sides of the sleigh. Use the
sweets (candies) to decorate the sides of
the sleigh and attach a long chocolate
matchstick on each side with butter cream
for the shafts.

5 Roll out the remaining brown
sugarpaste and use to cover the
other piece of cake for a sack, and place
in the sleigh. Colour the remaining
sugarpaste blue, yellow and green. Form
the green and blue into small parcels, and
mould the yellow into teddy bears.

6 Arrange the parcels, chocolate
money, teddy bears and candy stick
or rings in the sleigh, and attach with
butter cream. Leave to set.

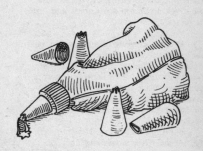

CHRISTMAS STOCKING CAKE

6-egg quantity Victoria Sandwich (Sponge
Layer Cake), Quick Mix Cake or
Madeira (Pound) Cake mixture, any
flavour (see pages 568, 570 and 571)
6 tbsp apricot jam, sieved (strained)
750 g/1½ lb/6 cups sugarpaste (see page
571)
red, green, yellow and blue liquid or paste
food colourings
holly leaves and berries (see page 567)
500 g/1 lb/4 cups royal icing (see page
542)
narrow Christmas ribbons
chocolate money

1 Grease and line a 30 x 25 cm/12 x 10
in roasting tin (pan). Spread the cake
mixture evenly in it. Bake in a preheated
oven at 160°C/325°F/Gas Mark 3 for
50–60 minutes (1–1¼ hours for Quick Mix
and Madeira (Pound) Cake) until well
risen and firm to the touch. Invert on a
wire rack and leave to set for 12–24
hours.

2 Draw a stocking shape on a sheet of
card the same size as the cake and
draw 3 or 4 shapes to use for parcels. Cut
out, place on the cake and cut around the
templates. Place the stocking on a cake
board and brush all over with jam. Brush
all over the pieces of cake for the parcels
as well.

3 Colour three-quarters of the
sugarpaste red. Roll out and use to
cover the stocking. Trim off around the
base. Also make about 6 holly berries.

4 Colour 90 g/3 oz/ ¾ cup of the
sugarpaste green. Roll it out and cut
out 18 holly leaves. Use the rest to cover
one of the parcels.

5 Colour half the remaining sugarpaste
blue and the rest yellow. Roll out the
yellow sugarpaste and cut 2 strips about 2
cm/ ¾ in wide and some small stars. Place
the strips across the stocking. Use the
remainder to cover another of the parcels.
Do the same with the blue sugarpaste.
Place the stars and holly leaves in
position.

6 Put some of the royal icing into a
piping bag fitted with a star nozzle
(tip) and the rest into a bag with a writing
nozzle (tip). Use the star nozzle (tip) to
pipe a decorative cuff around the top of
the stocking. Use the writing nozzle (tip)
to write 'Happy Christmas' and attach the
holly leaves and berries in bunches. Tie
ribbons around the parcels and position at
the top of the stocking together with the
chocolate money. Leave to set.

INDEX

G

H

W

Y

Z